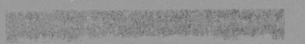

Contemporary
Literary Criticism

Guide to Gale Literary Criticism Series

When you need to review criticism of literary works, these are the Gale series to use:

If the author's death date is: | **You should turn to:**

After Dec. 31, 1959
(or author is still living)

CONTEMPORARY LITERARY CRITICISM

for example: Jorge Luis Borges, Anthony Burgess,
William Faulkner, Mary Gordon,
Ernest Hemingway, Iris Murdoch

1900 through 1959

TWENTIETH-CENTURY LITERARY CRITICISM

for example: Willa Cather, F. Scott Fitzgerald,
Henry James, Mark Twain, Virginia Woolf

1800 through 1899

NINETEENTH-CENTURY LITERATURE CRITICISM

for example: Fedor Dostoevski, George Sand,
Gerard Manley Hopkins, Emily Dickinson

1400 through 1799

LITERATURE CRITICISM FROM 1400 TO 1800
(excluding Shakespeare)

for example: Anne Bradstreet, Pierre Corneille,
Daniel Defoe, Alexander Pope,
Jonathan Swift, Phillis Wheatley

SHAKESPEAREAN CRITICISM

Shakespeare's plays and poetry

Gale also publishes related criticism series:

CONTEMPORARY ISSUES CRITICISM

Presents criticism on contemporary authors writing
on current issues. Topics covered include the social
sciences, philosophy, economics, natural science, law,
and related areas.

CHILDREN'S LITERATURE REVIEW

Covers authors of all eras. Presents criticism on
authors and author/illustrators who write for the
preschool to junior-high audience.

ISSN 0091-3421

Volume 30

Contemporary Literary Criticism

Excerpts from Criticism of the
Works of Today's Novelists, Poets,
Playwrights, Short Story Writers, Scriptwriters,
and Other Creative Writers

Jean C. Stine
Daniel G. Marowski
EDITORS

Gale Research Company
Book Tower
Detroit, Michigan 48226

STAFF

Jean C. Stine, Daniel G. Marowski, *Editors*

Roger Matuz, Jane E. Neidhardt, Robyn V. Young, *Senior Assistant Editors*

John G. Kuhnlein, Jeffrey T. Rogg, Lisa M. Rost, Jane C. Thacker,
Marjorie Wachtel, Debra A. Wells, *Assistant Editors*

Sharon R. Gunton, Thomas Ligotti, Phyllis Carmel Mendelson, *Contributing Editors*

Lizbeth A. Purdy, *Production Supervisor*
Denise Michlewicz, *Assistant Production Coordinator*
Eric Berger, Paula J. DiSante, Amy Marcaccio, *Editorial Assistants*

Linda M. Pugliese, *Manuscript Coordinator*
Donna Craft, *Assistant Manuscript Coordinator*
Colleen M. Crane, Maureen A. Puhl, Rosetta Irene Simms, *Manuscript Assistants*

Karen Rae Forsyth, *Research Coordinator*
Jeannine Schiffman Davidson, *Assistant Research Coordinator*
Kevin John Campbell, Victoria Cariappa, Rebecca Nicholaides,
Kyle Schell, Valerie Webster, *Research Assistants*

L. Elizabeth Hardin, *Permissions Supervisor*
Janice M. Mach, *Permissions Coordinator*
Filomena Sgambati, *Permissions Associate*
Patricia A. Seefelt, *Assistant Permissions Coordinator, Illustrations*
Mary M. Matuz, Susan D. Nobles, *Senior Permissions Assistants*
Margaret A. Chamberlain, Sandra C. Davis, Josephine M. Keene, *Permissions Assistants*
H. Diane Cooper, Dorothy J. Fowler, Kathy Grell,
Yolanda Parker, Diana M. Platzke, Mabel E. Schoening, *Permissions Clerks*

Frederick G. Ruffner, *Publisher*
James M. Ethridge, *Executive Vice President/Editorial*
Dedria Bryfonski, *Editorial Director*
Christine Nasso, *Director, Literature Division*
Laurie Lanzen Harris, *Senior Editor, Literary Criticism Series*

Copyright © 1984 by Gale Research Company

Library of Congress Catalog Card Number 76-38938
ISBN 0-8103-4404-1
ISSN 0091-3421

Contents

5

Preface

The last thirty years have brought about a type of literature which is directed specifically to a young adult audience. These works recognize the uniqueness of young adult readers while preparing them for the subjects, styles, and emotional levels of adult literature. Much of this writing has also had a definite appeal for adult readers and a discernible influence on their literature. Because of the importance of this subject matter and its audience, *Contemporary Literary Criticism (CLC)* devotes periodic volumes to writers whose work is directed to or appreciated by young adults. Until now, a collection of opinion has not existed which has centered on writers for the junior high to junior college age group. These special volumes of *CLC*, therefore, are meant to acknowledge this genre and its criticism as an important and serious part of recent literature.

In these special volumes we have broadened the definition of young adult literature to include not only writers who fit into the classic young adult mode, such as S.E. Hinton and Katherine Paterson, but also authors such as Ernest Hemingway and T.H. White, whose works are received enthusiastically by the young even though they were not originally the intended audience. In the latter category are writers whose works have such relevance for the young adult sensibility that they have achieved mass appeal. A distinctive feature of these special volumes is the inclusion of criticism on writers whose work is not restricted to book form. The works of many lyricists, for instance those of Neil Diamond and Stephen Sondheim, have been critically analyzed and accepted as serious literary creations. Since young people look to television and the theater to expand their knowledge and reflect their world view, the young adult volumes also feature criticism on scriptwriters and dramatists who appeal to the young, including Jacques Cousteau, Rod Serling, and Tennessee Williams in the present volume. Humorists such as Steve Martin, whom young people look to for both social comment and entertainment, are also included.

Each periodic special volume on young adult literature is designed to complement other volumes of *CLC* and follows the same format with some slight variations. The list of authors treated is international in scope and, as in the other *CLC* volumes, includes creative writers who are living now or have died after December 31, 1959. Since this volume of *CLC* is intended to provide a definitive overview of the careers of the authors covered, the editors have included approximately forty-five writers (compared to sixty-five authors in the standard *CLC*) in order to devote more attention to each writer.

Criticism has been selected with the reading level and interests of the young adult in mind. Many young adult authors have also written for younger children. Criticism on these works has been included when it is felt the works may be of interest to the young adult.

Format of the Book

Altogether there are about 900 individual excerpts in each volume—with an average of about 20 excerpts per author—taken from hundreds of literary reviews, general magazines, scholarly journals, and monographs. Contemporary criticism is loosely defined as that which is relevant to the evaluation of the author under discussion; this includes criticism written at the beginning of an author's career as well as current commentary. Emphasis has been placed on expanding the sources for criticism by including an increasing number of scholarly and specialized periodicals. Students, teachers, librarians, and researchers frequently find that the generous excerpts and supplementary material provided by the editors supply them with all the information that they need to write a term paper, analyze a poem, or lead a book discussion group. However, complete bibliographical citations facilitate the location of the original source as well as provide all of the information necessary for a term paper footnote or bibliography.

A *CLC* author entry consists of the following elements:

   • The **author heading** cites the author's full name, followed by birth date, and death date when applicable. The portion of the name outside the parentheses denotes the form under which the author has most commonly published. If an author has written consistently under a pseudonym, the pseudonym will be listed in the author heading and the real name given on the first line of the biocritical introduction. Also located at the beginning of the biocritical introduction are any important name variations under which an author has written. Uncertainty as to a birth or death date is indicated by a question mark.

- A **portrait** of the author is included when available.

- A brief **biocritical introduction** to the author and his or her work precedes the excerpted criticism. However, *CLC* is not intended to be a definitive biographical source. Therefore, *cross-references* have been included to direct the reader to other useful sources published by the Gale Research Company: *Contemporary Authors* now includes detailed biographical and bibliographical sketches on more than 77,000 authors; *Children's Literature Review* presents excerpted criticism on the works of authors of children's books; *Something about the Author* contains heavily illustrated biographical sketches on writers and illustrators who create books for children and young adults; *Contemporary Issues Criticism* presents excerpted commentary on the nonfiction works of authors who influence contemporary thought; and *Dictionary of Literary Biography* provides original evaluations of authors important to literary history. Previous volumes of *CLC* in which the author has been featured are also listed in the biocritical introduction.

- The **excerpted criticism** represents various kinds of critical writing—a particular essay may be normative, descriptive, interpretive, textual, appreciative, comparative, or generic. It may range in form from the brief review to the scholarly monograph. Essays are selected by the editors to reflect the spectrum of opinion about a specific work or about an author's writing in general. The excerpts are presented chronologically, adding a useful perspective to the entry. All titles by the author featured in the entry are printed in boldface type, which enables the reader to easily identify the works being discussed.

- A complete **bibliographical citation** designed to help the user find the original essay or book follows each excerpt. An asterisk (*) at the end of a citation indicates the essay is on more than one author.

Other Features

- A list of **Authors Forthcoming in *CLC*** previews the authors to be researched for future volumes.

- An **Appendix** lists the sources from which material in the volume has been reprinted. Many other sources have also been consulted during the preparation of the volume.

- A **Cumulative Index to Authors** lists all the authors who have appeared in *Contemporary Literary Criticism, Twentieth-Century Literary Criticism, Nineteenth-Century Literature Criticism,* and *Literature Criticism from 1400 to 1800,* along with cross-references to other Gale series: *Children's Literature Review, Authors in the News, Contemporary Authors, Contemporary Authors Autobiography Series, Dictionary of Literary Biography, Something about the Author,* and *Yesterday's Authors of Books for Children.* Users will welcome this cumulated author index as a useful tool for locating an author within the various series. The index, which lists birth and death dates when available, will be particularly valuable for those authors who are identified with a certain period but whose death date causes them to be placed in another, or for those authors whose careers span two periods. For example, F. Scott Fitzgerald is found in *Twentieth-Century Literary Criticism,* yet a writer often associated with him, Ernest Hemingway, is found in *Contemporary Literary Criticism.*

- A **Cumulative Index to Critics** lists the critics and the author entries in which the critics' essays appear.

Acknowledgments

The editors wish to thank the copyright holders of the excerpted articles included in this volume for permission to use the material and the photographers and individuals who provided photographs for us. We are grateful to the staffs of the following libraries for making their resources available to us: Detroit Public Library and the libraries of Wayne State University, the University of Michigan, and the University of Detroit. We also wish to thank Jeri Yaryan for her assistance with copyright research.

Suggestions Are Welcome

The editors welcome the comments and suggestions of readers to expand the coverage and enhance the usefulness of the series.

Authors Forthcoming in *CLC*

To Be Included in Volume 31

Marvin Bell (American poet, editor, and essayist)—Bell has enhanced his reputation as an important and influential contemporary poet with the publication of *Stars Which See, Stars Which Do Not See* and *These Green-Going-to-Yellow.*

Howard Brenton (English dramatist)—A significant innovator in the late 1960s English "fringe theater," Brenton often combines violent sexual imagery with radical theatrical techniques to reveal his socialist predilection.

J. V. Cunningham (American poet, critic, and editor)—Cunningham's terse, epigrammatic verse and his important literary theories have earned him the respect of major poets and critics.

Hilda Doolittle (H. D.) (American poet and novelist)—Her work and life as one of the leading Imagist poets is commanding new attention with the posthumous publication of *End to Torment* and *HERmione.*

Michel Foucault (French literary critic and philosopher)—Widely regarded as one of the most original thinkers of the twentieth century, Foucault examines in his writings the psychological origins of the human sciences.

Charles R. Larson (American novelist, short story writer, essayist, critic, and editor)—A renowned scholar of African, Indian, and other third world literatures, Larson recently published his third novel, *Arthur Dimmesdale.*

J. M. G. Le Clézio (French novelist, short story writer, essayist, and critic)—Loosely linked with such writers of the *nouveau roman* as Alain Robbe-Grillet and Nathalie Sarraute, Le Clézio rose to the forefront of the French literary scene in 1963 with his first novel, the plotless, darkly philosophical *Le Procès-Verbal.*

Bernard Mac Laverty (Irish novelist, short story writer, and scriptwriter)—Mac Laverty has earned critical acclaim for *Cal,* his recent novel about strife-torn Northern Ireland.

Czesław Miłosz (Polish poet and essayist)—The recent publication of *Visions from San Francisco Bay,* a collection of essays, and *The Separate Notebooks,* a volume of poetry, has provided further insight into the thought and literary development of this Nobel laureate.

Philip Roth (American novelist and short story writer)—Roth's work has been the subject of much critical attention following the publication of the final volume in the Zuckerman trilogy, *The Anatomy Lesson,* which deals with a middle-aged author suffering from writer's block.

D. M. Thomas (English poet, novelist, translator, editor, and critic)—Following his critically acclaimed novel *The White Hotel,* the recent publication of *Selected Poems* and the novels *Ararat* and *Swallow* has reinforced Thomas's reputation as a significant contemporary stylist.

Mario Vargas Llosa (Peruvian novelist, short story writer, and critic)—His latest novel, *Aunt Julia and the Scriptwriter,* has received virtually unanimous critical approval and has confirmed Vargas Llosa's place in the "Boom," a movement of outstanding literary creativity in Latin America.

To Be Included in Volume 32

Pat Barker (English novelist)—*Union Street,* a novel of working-class England told from the perspective of seven women, marks Barker's auspicious literary debut.

Malcolm Bradbury (English novelist, critic, and biographer)—A university professor, Bradbury offers a satirical view of academic life in his fiction, most recently in *Rates of Exchange.*

Philip Caputo (American novelist and memoirist)—Hailed for his moving Vietnam War memoir, *A Rumor of War,* journalist Caputo has subsequently published two well-received novels, *Horn of Africa* and *DelCorso's Gallery.*

Amy Clampitt (American poet)—Considered an important new poetic voice, Clampitt received high praise for *The Kingfisher,* her first volume of poetry.

Richard Hugo (American poet and essayist)—
A critically acclaimed poet who frequently
writes of the Pacific Northwest, Hugo is
most often praised for his compressed style
and highly rhythmic lines.

Joyce Carol Oates (American novelist, short
story writer, poet, dramatist, and critic)—
Recent additions to the canon of this
versatile and prolific author include *A
Bloodsmoor Romance, The Profane Art,
Mysteries of Winterthurn,* and *Angel of
Light.*

Tom Pickard (English poet, novelist, and scriptwriter)—Known for their fresh, unpretentious style, Pickard's prose and poetry
combine social issues with personal experiences.

Julian Symons (English novelist, critic, and
poet)—A prominent crime writer, Symons
has reaffirmed his stature with several
recent mystery publications, including *The
Name of Annabel Lee* and *The Tigers of
Subtopia.*

Wendy Wasserstein (American dramatist)—
Wasserstein's *Isn't It Romantic?,* a comedy
about two single women during the 1980s,
was a recent off-Broadway success.

Yvor Winters (American critic, poet, short
story writer, and editor)—One of the most
prominent literary critics of the twentieth
century, Winter is recognized for his innovative technique for analyzing poetry.

Max Frisch (Swiss-born German novelist and
dramatist)—With the recent publication of
his novels *Blue Beard* and *Gantenbein,*
Frisch has again been lauded for his insight
into human nature.

Günter Grass (German novelist, poet, and
dramatist)—Grass, whose work centers on
contemporary Germany, won international acclaim for his novel *The Tin Drum.*
Criticism in the forthcoming volume will
focus on his poetry and his recent novel,
Headbirths.

Thom Gunn (English poet, critic, and editor)—
Gunn is noted for combining traditional
verse forms with pop culture motifs. He
has recently published a volume of new
poems, *The Passages of Joy,* and a collection of autobiographical and critical
essays, *The Occasions of Poetry.*

A. R. Gurney, Jr. (American dramatist and
novelist)—Praised in both America and
England, Gurney's plays often utilize song,
music, and offstage characters to examine
white middle-class attitudes.

Ronald Harwood (South African novelist,
dramatist, and scriptwriter)—After writing plays and novels for twenty years,
Harwood achieved international fame
with his play *The Dresser,* which has also
been adapted for the screen.

Charles (Samuel) Addams

1912-

American cartoonist.

Addams specializes in the macabre. His use of black humor, a literary device in which humor is grounded in morbid situations, often through the juxtaposition of the familiar and the unexpected, is a significant aspect of Addams's cartoons. Despite the grotesque satire in much of his work, Addams's themes are relatively conventional; he examines family relationships and ordinary aspects of everyday life. As John B. Breslin notes, Addams's world "is only a slightly distorted mirror vision of the world we read about in our daily papers." Addams's work has appeared regularly in *The New Yorker* magazine since the 1930s and continues to be immensely popular.

The first Addams cartoon appeared in *The New Yorker* in 1933. By 1936, every second or third issue of the magazine carried one of his drawings. Although Addams's early work dealt with rather mundane subjects, by 1938 he had begun to depict his "family" of ghoulish characters: the emaciated, stylish young vampire-woman; her bug-eyed, demented lover (Addams said he could not bear to think of them as married); the old hag; the bald, flabby old man; the Boris Karloff-like butler; and the two satanic children. When, beginning in 1964, a television series aired starring this gruesome household, they reached an even wider audience. Addams was reluctant to allow his characters to be adapted for television, and he insisted on personally approving the names selected for them. The characters of "The Addams Family" show became: Morticia Addams, Gomez Addams (obviously the censors decided that the two had better be married), Grandmama, Uncle Fester, Lurch, Pugsley, and Wednesday. Soon after the show began, however, Addams complained that the characters were too nice, the situations too cute. The show was quite popular, nevertheless, and ran as a prime-time situation comedy for two seasons.

Because of the nature of his work, Addams has always been the source of much curiosity. Stories of his brushes with insanity abound. But Addams is, as Saul Steinberg defined him, "aggressively normal." He has said: "I attribute my success with the macabre to children. I guess my cartooning is sort of in a state of arrested intellectual development." Addams's depiction of wicked, antisocial behavior has long been favored by the monstrous child in young adults and adults. Addams has won the distinction of having his work exhibited in several important museums, including the Metropolitan Museum of Art in New York City and the Rhode Island School of Design Museum. He also won the 1954 Yale Humor Award and a special award from the Mystery Writers of America in 1961.

(See also *Contemporary Authors*, Vols. 61-64.)

© Nancy Crampton

BORIS KARLOFF

Why a collection of the drawings of Charles Addams [such as *Drawn and Quartered*] should need any written introduction at all is as far beyond me as the writing of one! Addams seems to me to be the one comedic artist today whose drawings need no letterpress at all. Supremely he has achieved the primary and essential purpose of any drawing serious or comic, which is to tell a story graphically in one blinding flash without a single written word of explanation. . . . [Few] men have realized and practised the earliest and most eloquent of all forms of story-telling as has Addams. When he does weaken and use an explanatory subtitle, it is nearly always an attempt to bolster up a story which is on the thin side. But that rarely happens. And even when the written comment does add a little spice, the drawing really does not need it. (p. i)

Perhaps Mr. Addams is happiest in his dealing with the macabre. His preoccupation with hangman's nooses and lethal doses is always innocent and gay. He has the extraordinary faculty of making the normal appear idiotic when confronted by the abnormal, as in his scenes of cannibals, skiers and skaters. Somehow one never dreams of questioning his premise, but only the rather childish alarm of the onlookers. (pp. i-ii)

Boris Karloff, in an introduction to Drawn and Quartered *by Charles Addams, The World Publishing Company, 1942, pp. i-ii.*

TIME

Readers of The New Yorker . . . know Artist Charles Addams as a tireless illustrator of the now commonplace question: Is the world going insane? . . . He cares not who makes a civilization's laws so long as he can draw its neuroses. Last week Artist Addams' screwy drawings were collected for the first time in book form (**Drawn and Quartered** . . .).

"The Art of Lunacy," in Time, *Vol. XL, No. 19, November 9, 1942, p. 48.*

IRIS BARRY

Naturally, an album of drawings ["**Drawn and Quartered**"] that comes prefaced by words from Boris Karloff [see excerpt above] would, in the normal course of events, turn out to be slightly macabre. As a matter of fact, the character that Karloff enacts on the motion picture screen lives, in between movies, inside Charles Addams's drawings. Here it feels thoroughly at home with the sinister sirens, pots of poison, reams of hangman's rope which are also often found therein.

There is considerable variety in Mr. Addams's cartoons—as witness the very unlike drawings of the taxidermist eying his fellow worker with professional interest, the stylish stout lady trying on a bullet-proof corset, and the elderly hag attempting to make a deposit in a mid-town bank—the deposit being a lumpy mattress no doubt hiding miser's pelf of some value. All of them make mock of quite every-day happenings and phrases which have been examined with a sharp beady eye and had a little salt thrown on their tails.

Yet what could be more deliciously pretty than a cartoon of the suburban lady who finds a besmocked yokel on her lawn with his woolly flock? "Crop thy lawn, lady?" he asks. This makes the present reviewer laugh immediately, for some reason. One or two of the others, however, are somewhat baffling. I think this may be because one fears to understand them.

Iris Barry, "Anyway, You Chuckle," in New York Herald Tribune Books, *December 13, 1942, p. 6.**

WOLCOTT GIBBS

New Yorker cartoons can be roughly divided into two classifications, which, back in the days when I was the most insanely miscast of an almost endless procession of art editors, were conveniently designated as "straight" and "nutty." (p. 5)

[The latter type], rather menacingly displayed in the pages of this book, [**Addams and Evil**] is harder to define, since it is less a criticism of any local system than a total and melodramatic re-arrangement of all life. Unlike the reportorial artist, whose scenes and personnel are ready-made, the man who draws pictures like those assembled here is obliged to create a nightmare landscape of his own and to people it with men, beasts, and even machines whose appearance and behavior are terribly at variance with the observable universe. He is, generally speaking, successful to the precise extent to which his creations seem peculiar, disturbing, and even outrageous to the normal, balanced mind. In my opinion, the subject of these notes—a man named Charles Addams—is one of the most outrageous artists in America in the sense that his work is essentially a denial of all spiritual and physical evolution in the human race. Some of this book is merely disconcerting— if, of course, it is no more than disconcerting for a couple in a hotel room to watch the sprouting of a pattern of knife points in the wall, unmistakably outlining a shrinking female form— but most of it is frankly devoted to man's crazy, triumphant return to the mud from which he came. The monsters in Ad-

dams' world are still in the minority . . . , but it is only too clear that actually these are the dominant strain, that somehow, as if God had shrugged His shoulders and given up the world, natural selection has reversed itself and presently our civilization will once again belong to the misshapen, the moonstruck, and the damned. (pp. 5-6)

Wolcott Gibbs, in an introduction to Addams and Evil *by Charles Addams, Simon & Schuster, 1947, pp. 5-7.*

WILLIAM GERMAIN DOOLEY

["**Addams and Evil**"] is the latest collection of irrationally sinister cartoons by Charles Addams from The New Yorker, a macabre mixture from the lower levels of Havelock Ellis case histories, centered upon a family group bound together in feline complicity and a murderous but happy neurosis. They have scalding cauldrons for Christmas carolers, their children's school activities include counterfeiting and coffin building, the nursery is decorated with octopi and a platypus. . . . Yet somehow it is all outrageously funny, probably because no matter how bad things are with you, they were never like this. It is the triumph of a family well adjusted to its environment.

This Addams version of the Jukes family, however, is by no means the whole book, merely a cohesive unit in a collection of linear comments on midgets, predatory plant-life, morticians, golfers, witch-doctors and murderous mates, all on a psycho-neurotic binge.

William Germain Dooley, "Bats in the Birdhouse," in The New York Times Book Review, *October 5, 1947, p. 16.*

THE TIMES LITERARY SUPPLEMENT

Mr. Charles Addams, in a very high and broad album of drawings [**Addams and Evil**], supplies . . . [an] element native to *The New Yorker,* an element constantly and ferociously at variance with the observable universe. Some of the cartoons in the magazine are, as Mr. Gibbs in his introduction to Mr. Addams's book points out [see excerpt above], social criticism of the normal and orthodox variety; but others, and Mr. Addams's are among them, are "less a criticism of any local system than a total and melodramatic rearrangement of all life." Gothic has gone to the artist's head, and a rash of drawings of a haunted castle inhabited by a sinister half-breed, a ruined and haggard beauty, a child with six toes and a shambling gorilla-giant of a servant is the result. Mr. Addams is strongly attracted to witch-doctors and witch brews prepared on midnight heaths under a gibbous moon, and he can disturbingly convey the impression that, lunatic and monstrous as everything undoubtedly is, it is yet close to twentieth-century earth, and that Nightmare Lane leads directly into Fifth Avenue.

"The New Yorker Spirit," in The Times Literary Supplement, *No. 2389, November 15, 1947, p. 592.**

LISLE BELL

If there is social significance in "**Addams and Evil**," the only thing to do is shudder and laugh it off. This can be done simultaneously. In a superb gallery of contented cretins, Charles Addams has gone about as far as imagination and wit can travel artistically in this direction—hovers diabolically on the macabre brink. What haunts us is not that these toads, vultures and vampires in subhuman form never have been bright since they were spawned out of the woodwork, but that they are so manifestly happy in a creepy sort of way. . . .

[We] salute the artist who has a uniquely sardonic way of saying: People are fungi.

> *Lisle Bell, "Autumn Outburst of Cartoons," in* New York Herald Tribune Weekly Book Review, *December 7, 1947, p. 7.**

CHARLES POORE

The quality of Chas Addams is not strained—it is a pictorial explosion of the demonic instincts in civilized man. As you look at his gruesome masterpieces week by week in The New Yorker you are somehow chillingly cheered to find that his satanic little children have survived their past ventures in walling each other up behind their basement's bricks, blowing the household to bits with thriftily home-made bombs, serving arsenic at their lemonade stands, and so on—and are still merrily working at simple problems in murder. . . .

Mr. Addams gets away—a very long way, indeed, too—with murder. What is the widespread appeal of his beautifully drawn examples of distinguished depravity? For, as John O'Hara points out in his foreword [to **"Chas Addams's Monster Rally"**], "anyone who ever saw an Addams drawing is an Addams fan." Isn't it the same urge that makes the killed-with-a-blunt-instrument-of-strange-oriental-design mystery story so popular in such decorous quarters? Well, to make a long review short, it is. And that's that. Addams is to horror stories as television is to radio.

> *Charles Poore, "Arsenic and Lemonade," in* The New York Times Book Review, *October 15, 1950, p. 7.**

JOHN MASON BROWN

[*The following essay first appeared in* The Saturday Review, *November 11, 1950.*]

[Mr. Addams's] hilarious derangements can now be relished in a collection of his cartoons inspirationally entitled *Chas Addams's MONSTER RALLY*.

Monsters, young or old, four-legged or two-headed, prehistoric or contemporary, simpering or nonchalant, are very much Mr. Addams's affair. His is a hobgoblin world of bats, spiders, broomsticks, snakes, cobwebs, and bloodletting morons in which every day is Hallowe'en. If his creatures hold life lightly and play with death as if it were a toy, it is because they are, each witch's or mother's son or daughter among them, jubilant nihilists.

They are as unburdened with consciences as they are with causes. Murder for them, regardless of their years, is something which exercises their ingenuity as planners without involving their emotions as people. They are Mr. Hydes untroubled by Dr. Jekylls. A teacher is no more appalled by erasing a sentence from the blackboard than they are by doing away with a husband, a wife, themselves, or the little girl next door. They do not kill to liberate anything except their own perversity or to express their disregard for the human race to which, in its average manifestations, they plainly do not belong. (p. 46)

William Shakespeare was a fellow who shared Mr. Addams's interest in violence, gore, ghosts, and murder. He, too, had a pretty taste for witches, knew the terrors of the midnight hour, and was on speaking terms with death. But the man from Stratford, though a genius, was run-of-the-mill enough to take a serious thing seriously. . . .

Mr. Addams, however, may I quickly add, is as different from Shakespeare as he is from Edgar Allan Poe. Nothing shocks him and no one is shocked by him. The more sinister his concepts are, the louder is our laughter and the greater our enjoyment. Clearly Mr. Addams invites us to enter a world which has nothing to do with the one in which we live except that, in the most glorious, undeviating, and giddy fashion, it turns all of its values topsy-turvy. (p. 47)

Elia's famous contention was that what made the artificial comedies of the Restoration and post-Restoration years acceptable was that they managed to get out of Christendom into a universe of their own. They were, therefore, safely beyond morality and police-court judgments. What Lamb would have made of Mr. Addams's work, I cannot guess. I do know that for those of us who dote on Mr. Addams's work, the point, the triumph, the delight of his drawings is that in their own uproarious and demented way they turn Elia's fantasy into a fact.

Mr. Addams's sense of the absurd is inexhaustible. It is not limited to his family of witches who live in their spooky and tattered ruin of an American Victorian home with their wayward offspring and those two unforgettable men, the leering defective with the Dewey mustache and the creature who out-Karloffs Boris Karloff.

Consider, for instance, the nurse who calmly pushes a pram in which some dear little monster is sleeping behind stout iron bars. Or the bride who heats a branding-iron in the living room on her wedding night while her groom unpacks in the next room. . . . Or the sick-looking cannibal who, sitting empty-handed at suppertime by a steaming caldron while his tribesmen are gobbling up their food, says plaintively, "Oh, I like missionary all right but missionary doesn't like me." (pp. 48-9)

Beyond dispute the age in which we live abounds in its monstrous aspects. No less surely Mr. Addams's is the paradoxical distinction of having reduced the horrors of the present by having added to them. If only the other horrors were as laughable as the ones with which he delights us! (p. 50)

> *John Mason Brown, "Welcome Monsters," in his* As They Appear, *McGraw-Hill Book Company, Inc., 1952, pp. 45-50.*

LISLE BELL

At this date, there is little need to dwell upon Mr. Addams's eerie magic and sinister charm as artist and master of the macabre. [In *Monster Rally*] he has preserved the family group of fiends we have cherished since we first met them. They are wonderful people, miraculously evoked from the woodwork and cobwebs in which they live, and the essence of their appeal—it seems to me—lies in their manifest domestic harmony rather than in their methodic diablerie. If the average American home reflected this fireside felicity, courts would be less clogged with cases of juvenile delinquency, marital discord and similar manifestations of family friction.

Study the record and you will agree. Between the subnormal husband and his wan, willowy witch wife there is never a cross word. The closest he comes to nagging is when he sees his mate arranging cut flowers (probably stolen off a casket) and remarks: "You're in a strange mood today, I must say."

They are obviously doting, yet understanding, parents. When mother says to the imp of Satan they have begotten: "Now kick Daddy good night and run along to bed," the scene is almost touching. Think of the tantrums and vocal violence attendant on bedtime in homes where the rumpus room is not given over to brewing poisons or decapitating playmates.

> Lisle Bell, "A Well Seasoned Banquet of Tasty Humor," in New York Herald Tribune Book Review, December 3, 1950, p. 10.*

DWIGHT MacDONALD

There must be a special reason why Americans find Addams's stuff refreshing. Perhaps it is because the cartoons, which deal largely with family life, provide a healthy antidote to the saccharine treatment of the same subject in our advertisements and other forms of mass culture. After the depressingly cheerful families of the beer ads, the pious celebrations of marital bliss on the radio, the sentimental gushing over the kiddies everywhere except in the home, it is wonderfully relaxing to see these themes treated with a reverse twist, a bend sinister. Addams works this profitable vein with great diligence.

He also, of course, exploits the American public's peculiar, and in some ways rather frightening, fascination with violence. Just as the detective story, once an exercise in rational deduction, has become a pretext for the intimate description of extreme violence, just as the so-called comic books have more and more gone in for the gruesome and the sadistic, so there is a certain significance in the rise of Addams as the most popular and distinctive of the cartoonists whose work appears regularly in the *New Yorker*. (p. 37)

Callousness is not funny, but it becomes so when carried to the pitch of the matron in flowered bathing suit running along the beach and shouting up at her husband, who, as the shadow on the sand all too clearly reveals, is being carried off by a huge bird of prey: "George! George! Drop the keys!" Even an auto-da-fé becomes comic when we see a stolid householder reflectively puffing on his pipe as he rakes the autumn leaves on his lawn into a neat pile around the feet of his plump and indignant spouse, bound firmly to a tree. The contrast between the homely, familiar *form* of the situations—autumnal leaf burning, loss of the bathhouse keys, a marital spat—and their ghastly *content* removes them from the range of our experience and leaves us free to laugh.

Addams has, furthermore, a deadly eye for the less attractive aspects of the middle-aged American male and female, and they themselves express emotions appropriate to the banal form of the situations but not to the gruesome content. The placid, ruminative expression of the portly householder raking the leaves to burn up his wife, and her own matronly figure and expression of malignant, impotent indignation—these make the scene funny instead of horrible.

There are ordinary people doing sinister things in an ordinary way. But Addams has a reverse formula, and it is the one for which he is best known: sinister people doing ordinary things in a sinister way. His Weird Family, his Bad Boy, and his flabby, fungous Moral Monster pursue their evil ends with

wholehearted earnestness; they have their code of morality, which happens to be just the reverse of ours.

Living in domestic affection in their cobwebby Victorian haunted house, the gruesome Family happily watch the installation of a picture window with a superb view of a cemetery, put a sign on their gatepost: BEWARE OF THE THING, send over to the neighbors to borrow a cup of cyanide, and entertain the kiddies at bedtime with shadow pictures of a vampire bat. . . . Fair is foul and foul is fair as Addams's people hover through the fog and filthy air.

There is one other distinctive Addams formula: the juxtaposition of the remote, archaic past and the brisk, cellophaned present. Hansel and Gretel read a neat inscription on the witch's gingerbread cottage: CONTAINS GLUCOSE, DRY SKIMMED MILK, OIL OF PEPPERMINT. . . . One witch says to another as she empties a box labeled WITCH'S BREW into a kettle teeming with writhing horrors, "It's marvelous! All you do is add water!" The Colonial bellman makes his nightly round: "Ten o'clock and all's well. Yes, sir, and all's well, too with toothsome, savory, mild Royal George Snuff, made from the finest Old Dominion tobacco leaf."

Addams generally brings a sinister quality even to his use of the familiar cartoonist's device of taking a cliché and giving it a twist, a procedure known in the trade as The Switch. "Oh, I like missionary all right," one cannibal explains to another, "but missionary doesn't like me." (pp. 37-8)

The most popular single cartoon Addams ever produced is not a "horror" cartoon at all. It appeared early in 1940 and shows one skier looking with amazement at another who has just passed a tree leaving tracks that separate to go on each side of the tree.

There are at least two sizable groups of people who don't see anything funny in the ski cartoon. A psychiatrist at an Illinois home for the feeble-minded asked her charges whether they saw anything absurd about the picture. Those with a mental age of ten or more saw that the tracks could not in fact have been made by the skier, while those under that level saw nothing wrong. No inmate, of any age level, saw anything funny.

Neither did the logical Germans when *Heute*, a German-language magazine put out by the Americans in the first year of the occupation, reprinted the cartoon. Hundreds of readers wrote letters like: "I don't see how this is possible. Please print the answer to this puzzle." Others supplied answers: two one-legged skiers; the skier went down on one ski on one side of the tree, returned and went down on the other ski on the other side; the skier slipped a foot out of one ski's harness just before reaching the tree; etcetera. There was, it must be said, a reader in Nuremberg who advanced the hypothesis that it was some sort of joke and went on to develop a general theory of humor.

Small wonder the Germans missed the point, since the ski cartoon, like much of Addams's work, is very much in the American grain, a lineal descendant of the tall tales of the frontier told by deadpan liars. Exaggeration seems to flourish in the American climate, and the impossible appeals to us as the essence of the comic.

In this sense, Addams's depiction of the prosaic in bizarre terms and of the bizarre in prosaic terms is in the line of the Paul Bunyan stories. Perhaps only an American humorist, with an American's knack for shifting gears between the real and the fantastic, could so consistently extract comedy from the macabre. (p. 40)

Dwight Macdonald, "Charles Addams, His Family, and His Fiends," in The Reporter, *Vol. 9, No. 2, July 21, 1953, pp. 37-41.*

BEST SELLERS

The genially fiendish imagination of "Chas" Addams is bountifully explored [in *The Groaning Board*] in more than a hundred cartoons and drawings, including eight in full color, which later *(nisi fallimur)* graced covers of *The New Yorker.* . . . Not all by any means feature the "Addams Family." In fact some of the best are not gruesome at all, just delightfully outlandish.

A review of "The Groaning Board," in Best Sellers, *Vol. 24, No. 15, November 1, 1964, p. 306.*

RUSSELL LYNES

The clanking of Addams' chains has become as seasonal as sleigh bells. If you have seen the TV show that is based on the characters he invented and have not been so revolted that you can never look in Addams' direction again, you will find his *The Groaning Board* . . . the standard Addams product with its reliable and perhaps soon to become tiresome quality of morbidity and expert drawing. (p. 142)

Russell Lynes, "Funny, Ha, Ha!" in Harper's Magazine, *Vol. 229, No. 1375, December, 1964, pp. 141-43.**

JOHN GRUEN

[*The following essay first appeared in 1967.*]

[Charles Addams is] still tops when it comes to projecting the nervous side of life. Thirty years on *The New Yorker* has not diminished his sting—nor, for that matter, his style, which is as unmistakable as a gabled and turreted Victorian house, an architectural vintage he seems, in effect, to have invented.

But for all his dipping into the well of black humor, Addams, the man, emerges an aristocrat. He's a gentleman of enormous charm—and talking with him is, unfortunately, not even a little bit painful. He comes on smooth and easy—and funny. (p. 161)

[Ask] him about black humor, and the answers get a little vague. Like, "It's been going on for centuries." Or, "People are generally discouraged about the state of the world." Prod him a little about his own work and he'll say, "It's really all based on real life. What didn't seem quite so macabre years ago, has suddenly become more so, today."

What about the chaos, the violence, the fear, the anxiety in all of our lives? Has it not been the fodder for today's black humor? Addams's reply is a tentative, finally unconvincing yes.

He seems not to want to go further. Either he can't, or he won't. Certainly, he's not verbal about it. And yet, he should be, since Charles Addams' cartoons, rooted, as they are, in the black-humor syndromes, continue to exert their influence. Eight books and countless drawings have wielded their black magic for years. . . . (pp. 161-62)

Indeed, it is ironic that, having been around for thirty years, the Addams cartoon has served today's black humorists almost as a vast collective unconscious, while Addams, himself, seems not quite aware of the implications inherent in his dark comic output.

Be that as it may, Charles Addams betrays none of the characteristics of a man tortured by society's evil ways. No terrifying traumas seem to have ignited or propelled his need to record man's darkest side—to record it humorously in the way, say, Tomi Ungerer has done it. While this is not to put down Addams as an innocent about the world he lives in, there seems to be little exterior, or, indeed, published, evidence to suggest a man driven by inner agonies or bitter recollections.

The Addams cartoon, singular, hilarious, and distinctly personal as it is, reflects a society that's only mildly off its rocker—at least by today's lunatic standards. It really doesn't claim to be anything more. The Addams cartoon engenders laughter by means of an outrageous juxtapositioning of several realities—none truly frightening or truly threatening.

Its social comment doesn't really shake one up. It sticks to the lunatic fringe of human activity, and it sticks to it with something close to genius. Addams is not involved with violence—certainly not with butchery. The blood seldom flows in an Addams cartoon. Man is never put through a meat grinder, and man's follies have more to do with the rising of the moon than with the rising of that famous cloud.

As for the Addams "family"—Morticia, Gomez, their children, Wednesday and Pugsley, Granny, Uncle Fester, and Lurch, the butler—they don't pose any immediate threat. Their black humor is quite safe. Almost cozy, you might say. They behave like eccentric relatives living in their own bizarre dreams, harming no one. One is amused, but not alarmed. (p. 162)

John Gruen, "Charles Addams, Tomi Ungerer," in his Close-Up, *The Viking Press, 1968, pp. 160-65.**

GEORGE A. WOODS

The rhymes are true Mother Goose, but the illustrations are pure Charles Addams which means you'd better start the very young on a more traditionally illustrated collection than **"The Chas. Addams Mother Goose"**. . . . Unless, of course, you want wee ones to know that the farmer's wife cut off the tails of those blind mice with an *electric* carving knife or to see the size of the ghoulish thing that upset Miss Muffet or what Jack Sprat and the Mrs. subsisted on. Better not let them see Wee Willie Winkie peering through the glass; they'll never go to bed. Come 7 or 11 you won't be able to keep them away from the book; meanwhile enjoy it yourself.

George A. Woods "A Gaggle of Goose and Grimm," in The New York Times Book Review, *October 29, 1967, p. 42.**

DELLA THOMAS

It isn't even necessary to open [*The Chas Addams Mother Goose*] to recognize the unique Addams brand of humor—the Mother Goose on the cover, aloft over a Neo-Gothic landscape, is the ubiquitous Little Old Lady in Tennis Shoes! Of course, there will be those who will object to such macabre interpretations as that of "Pease Porridge Hot" (in a witch's cauldron), "Dr. Fell" (a fiendish doctor turning on a Rube Goldbergish array of switches while a strapped-down patient looks on in alarm) or "Boys and Girls Come Out to Play" (in a cemetery).

The rhymes are untouched, but the illustrations are good gruesome fun for adults and young sophisticates. The publisher's "all ages" designation, however, might well exclude the traditional Mother Goose audience of kindergarten to third grade as it is doubtful that they would appreciate the visual incongruities that are the basis for this novelty approach to the nursery rhyme.

> *Della Thomas, in a review of "The Chas Addams Mother Goose," in* School Library Journal, *an appendix to* Library Journal, *December, 1967, p. 73.*

ZENA SUTHERLAND

Some element of the usual Addams style seems lacking [in *The Chas. Addams Mother Goose*], perhaps a spontaneity due to working with a prescribed text, so that the macabre touch seems, in some of the illustrations, superimposed and the pictures just aren't funny. There are a few pages that have high humor, a few that are grotesque, and the rest are simply a mite dull. Here and there, a picture demands the background not all children have: for example, the farmer's wife (and the farmer) in "Three Blind Mice" are adapted from "American Gothic." Older children who usually enjoy Addams may be put off by the nursery rhymes; not all children find this humor appealing, but those who do are a special group of readers who have early become devoted Addams fans.

> *Zena Sutherland, in a review of "The Chas. Addams Mother Goose," in* Bulletin of the Center for Children's Books, *Vol. 21, No. 6, February, 1968, p. 89.*

REGINA MINUDRI

Some [of the cartoons in *My Crowd*] are old favorites and some are new, but all are delightful cartoons in the inimitable, macabre, Addams' style. An archaeologist looking at cave drawings sees $E = MC^2$; a respectable-appearing devil asks Avis if they'd like to be No. 1; Santa Claus suggests to his elves that perhaps this year they ought to charge a little something; a family smilingly views the vista through their new picture window—a graveyard. As cartoons and monster movies are usually popular with YA's, this ought to do quite well.

> *Regina Minudri, in a review of "My Crowd," in* School Library Journal, *an appendix to* Library Journal, *Vol. 17, No. 4, December, 1970, p. 84.*

JOHN B. BRESLIN

[We] must not let go unnoticed a new collection of Charles Addams cartoons, *Favorite Haunts* . . . , especially when it represents one of the bargains of the season. It's been a dozen years since the last and those readers who open their *New Yorker* every week wondering whether the master has struck again can sate their appetites on this book. What a bizarre mind he has! And yet, after turning these pages you have to admit that the world he creates is only a slightly distorted mirror vision of the world we read about in our daily papers. Luckily for me, his art defies verbal description, so I can leave you to your own memories of favorite cartoons. (p. 426)

> *John B. Breslin, "The Triumph of the Photographer," in* America, *Vol. 135, No. 19, December 11, 1976, pp. 425-26.**

A. J. ANDERSON

As almost everyone knows, Addams has been drawing cartoons for *The New Yorker* for many years. This latest collection [*Creature Comforts*] represents sketches he has done for the magazine since 1976. It is no small praise to say that he is second to none as a master of the insidious effect. His nightmare vision leads him to construct designs of a ludicrous nature, in which the qualities and employments of the persons depicted are incongruous or incompatible. What you respond to is what is intended—a subtle haunting mystery that slowly engulfs you, like washed-out figments of a dream. His creatures, all of which wear that patented Addams expression, are horrifyingly funny, and his images exquisitely witty.

> *A. J. Anderson, in a review of "Creature Comforts," in* Library Journal, *Vol. 107, No. 2, January 15, 1982, p. 178.*

Fran Arrick

(Pseudonym of unidentified author) American novelist.

Arrick writes "problem novels" that focus on issues of particular concern to young adults. Arrick's protagonists are often faced with pressure from family and peers as they seek to establish their own identity. Their responses to these pressures reflect some of the more extreme measures undertaken by today's youth. For example, in *Steffie Can't Come Out to Play* (1978), Steffie runs away from her small-town family life in order to become a model in New York. She is victimized by a smooth-talking, well-dressed pimp who takes advantage of her naiveté and her desire for expensive clothes and leads her into prostitution. *Tunnel Vision* (1980) is the story of a young person's suicide. *Chernowitz!* (1981) depicts a Jewish boy who is harassed because of his ethnic background. In *God's Radar* (1983), Arrick portrays a fundamentalist Christian community in which pressure to conform to moral standards serves to control personality. Most critics agree that Arrick's books can promote discussion of difficult subjects that are relevant to young adults.

C. NORDHIELM WOOLDRIDGE

[Stephanie Rudd, the protagonist of *Steffie Can't Come Out to Play*, runs away] from Clairton, Pennsylvania to pursue a modelling career in New York City. She can hardly believe it when the man of her dreams appears at the train station and slips a protective arm around her shoulder. "Favor" is young, handsome, rich, and one of the slickest pimps in the Big Apple. . . . While for the most part resisting the temptation to sensationalize, Arrick unfortunately resorts to a superman-type rescue for her protagonist: one of two cops (whose third-person account of the street scene is interspersed with Stephanie's first-person narrative) suddenly shakes off 19 years of remaining uninvolved and breaks Favor's leg in the process of convincing him to let Stephanie go. It works. Stephanie finds herself inexplicably shut out by her "daddy" and "sisters," turns to a shelter which takes in young girls in her situation, and finally goes home. Neither plot, characterization, nor writing style emerge as distinctive in any way and the message to young teens weighs a bit heavy. All told, this is a just-adequate foray into some scantily explored and decidedly rough subject territory.

> *C. Nordhielm Wooldridge, in a review of "Steffie Can't Come Out to Play," in* School Library Journal, *Vol. 25, No. 3, November, 1978, p. 72.*

PATTY CAMPBELL

[*Steffie Can't Come Out to Play* is the type of book] that makes evil sound like fun, not by explicit sexual detail, but by its omission.

The book's subject is that classic cliché of the country girl seduced into prostitution. The story follows the stereotype point by point. . . .

[Fran Arrick] has tried so hard for "good taste" that she has made prostitution seem like a pleasanter way to earn a living than bagging burgers at MacDonald's. There is not one description of a sexual encounter. The weirdest behavior Steffie has to cope with is from a man who asks her to stand in front of an open window, and from another who gets his jollies from slipping her a dose of LSD. Granted, Steffie's very first experience is embarrassing because she has to approach the man; but her discomfort seems no worse than the sufferings of less sophisticated teenagers at the senior prom. On the other hand, there is lots of explicit talk of exactly how much money Steffie earns (it beats MacDonald's $2.65 an hour) and loving descriptions of the pretty clothes—silver boots, French jeans— her pimp buys her. Here is a book that would have been less problematic if it had had more sordid detail.

> *Patty Campbell, "Explicit Omissions," in* Wilson Library Bulletin, *Vol. 53, No. 4, December, 1978, p. 341.*

KIRKUS REVIEWS

In this unsensationalized story of teenage prostitution, ingenuous, small-town Stephanie arrives in New York with modeling aspirations, slips inevitably into The Life, and returns home after several months, appropriately wised up and apprehensive about her future. Author Arrick has used restraint and judgment in treating such a knotty subject, but [*Steffie Can't Come Out to Play*] seems plotted by intent rather than by inspiration. Steffie goes through the paces, enjoying a glittery new wardrobe and A-one attention from her glamorous pimp Favor, but her movements seem curiously mechanical, her experiences too carefully orchestrated. . . . Youngsters who look beyond the provocative jacket—Steffie, in low-cut gown and fur, leaning against an adult book store—will find a skewed but unmoralizing story with a much manipulated central figure.

> *A review of "Steffie Can't Come Out to Play," in* Kirkus Reviews, *Vol. XLVI, No. 24, December 15, 1978, p. 1361.*

ZENA SUTHERLAND

[For the most part, *Steffie Can't Come Out to Play*] is an explicit exposé of a life of prostitution; interspersed with the episodes about Steffie are episodes about two policemen who patrol the district she's in and who—suspecting that the new girl is younger than she looks—try to find a way to help her. Fortunately for Steffie (who tells the story, save for the material about the police), she's sent to a halfway house after her pimp is hospitalized, and her parents take her home. She's still fourteen, but she's old. Candid, frightening, and poignant, the story demands credulity in Steffie's naiveté, but if the reader accepts that, her plight is believable, since the characterization and motivation are consistent.

> *Zena Sutherland, in a review of "Steffie Can't Come Out to Play," in* Bulletin of the Center for Children's Books, *Vol. 32, No. 7, March, 1979, p. 110.*

LAURA GERINGER

[In *Tunnel Vision,*] Anthony, a 15-year-old "A" student, star of his high school swim team, respected by his teachers, idolized by his friends, favored by his parents, and nicknamed Mr. Perfect by his more rebellious sister, hangs himself with his father's neckties, leaving no note. Shocked and guilty, his nearest and dearest condemn themselves for not sensing that the boy's terminal depression of several months duration was more than teenage angst. But readers will be at as much of a loss as to why this particular kid wanted to end it all. . . . A nice, neighborhood cop, commenting upon the statistical frequency of juvenile suicide attempts in the American small town he inhabits, attributes the phenomenon to *Tunnel Vision:* "It's like each of them was caught inside a tunnel and they couldn't see any end to it or anything at all outside." Not much of an explanation but it's refreshing to find a realistic problem novel that doesn't read like psychological case study. The small, linked group of people who must come to terms with the tragedy described here are likable and ordinary. They are not particularly marked for disaster. It visits them almost casually. Arrick's spare, understated handling of their struggle to come to terms with the decision of a child they all loved to leave them and life behind rings true, and should prompt some heated discussions. (pp. 119-20)

Laura Geringer, in a review of "Tunnel Vision," in
School Library Journal, *Vol. 26, No. 8, April, 1980,
pp. 119-20.*

BOOKLIST

It's all here [in *Tunnel Vision*]—the shock, the bewilderment, the guilt, and the anger that are the classic symptoms of the aftermath of suicide. . . . While the motive for Anthony's death may be obvious to readers, Arrick leaves it credibly speculative for her characters and tackles the emotionally charged subject with intensity that approaches the sensational only once—in her handling of the tangential episode of [Anthony's girlfriend] Jana's rape. Noteworthy as well is Arrick's avoidance of a completely downbeat ending—she ensures that at least some of her characters emerge from the tragedy with broadened insight and newfound inner strength. Purposeful, but skillfully and successfully so. (pp. 1355-56)

A review of "Tunnel Vision," in Booklist, *Vol. 76,
No. 18, May 15, 1980, pp. 1355-56.*

KIRKUS REVIEWS

[*Tunnel Vision* is an] inoffensive but uninspired attempt to deal with teenage suicide via the reactions and memories of the parents, sister, cousins, friend, and sort-of girlfriend of a 15-year-old boy who has just hung himself. . . . His mother blames herself for accepting her husband's reassurances and not getting the kid to a psychiatrist. The girl blames her physical distance. (A rape victim, she's in bad shape herself.) And his sister blames their father who is preoccupied with business. Despite all their flashbacks, we never do get close to Anthony, his motives, or his personality. . . . Of the survivors, Arrick leaves the school-skipping, pot-smoking, burnout sister on the way to self-rehabilitation and the girlfriend able to touch the others in shared grief. None of this is lurid, but it isn't very affecting either.

A review of "Tunnel Vision," in Kirkus Reviews,
Vol. XLVIII, No. 15, August 1, 1980, p. 983.

GAIL TANSILL LAMBERT

Anthony Hamil, aged fifteen, hung himself with his father's neckties. The end of his life is the beginning of [*Tunnel Vision*]. Fran Arrick lets us in on the relentless horror, bewilderment, and grief suffered by members of his family and friends. The story is non-stop reading accompanied by an ache in the throat and misty eyes. (pp. 207-08)

[The] survivors are drawn together, and slowly and agonizingly share their anger and guilt along with their shock. Utterly vulnerable, they begin to see in each other and in themselves strengths and weaknesses they never looked for before.

Fran Arrick writes as if she knows her subject and characters well, and the subject matter is of particular interest these days, suicide being the second leading cause of death in American young people.

This book is recommended for parents of any age child. But for kids I worry that the ending could be construed as possibly encouraging or condoning suicide; also because the problem of guilt is dispensed with on the book jacket—"All felt to blame and none was." Blame is perhaps too harsh a word to use, but in every human relationship there are elements of imperfection that need examining and forgiveness. (p. 208)

Gail Tansill Lambert, in a review of "Tunnel Vision," in Best Sellers, *Vol. 40, No. 6, September, 1980, pp. 207-08.*

DOROTHY M. BRODERICK

When at 10 p.m. you say, I'll just read a few pages to get started and next you look up and it's midnight, it is hard to be critical of a book, and even harder to explain how so engrossing a read leaves one annoyed, frustrated and stomping around the house. The plot of *Chernowitz!* is the first person narration of Bobby Cherno's harassment by bully Emmett Sundback solely because Bobby is Jewish. There are name callings, a fiery cross (albeit it very small) tossed on the Cherno lawn, a swastika painted on a family car, and isolation from the other boys in the class. All because this bunch of suburban boy sheep follow blindly the leadership of an adolescent victim of child abuse by his divorced, drinking father. When Sundback injures Bobby's cat by swiping him with his motorcycle, Bobby vows revenge and sets Sundback up as a thief. True to the adolescent code, Bobby shares none of his harassment with anyone until his sense of guilt forces him to confide in his parents. The antisemitism being experienced is a personal problem and he will cope with it.

And therein lies the problem and weakness of the book. A book on such a serious problem must offer some insight into motivation, both of the victim and the victimizer. Antisemitism is not in the same category as harassment because one is too fat or too tall or too short. It is NOT a personal problem of the victim but a social problem and to treat it as less is to deny reality. Bobby is a reasonably okay kid: he plays soccer, skates, has a sailboat, is smart in school and has one reasonably good friend, although he is not a mad socializer. What escapes the reader is why Sundback singles Bobby out for harassment when in the community being portrayed there must be many Jews. As for bully Sundback, why does he choose antisemitism as his cause? Is being a battered child enough to make an antisemite? Why, being successful in his harassment does he not expand his harassment to other Jews?

A book that raises that many questions must be bought and discussed. It should be in the hands of history teachers and those dealing with values education and human relations. What the individual reader will gain from it is anyone's guess. . . . Both Sundback and Bobby are exactly the same at the end and while I know in my gut there are people who learn absolutely nothing from experience, I resent books with that message, particularly when I suspect the message received was not the message the author thought she was sending.

> *Dorothy M. Broderick, in a review of "Chernowitz!"* in Voice of Youth Advocates, *Vol. 4, No. 3, August, 1981, p. 23.*

KIRKUS REVIEWS

[*Chernowitz!* is a] one-issue but lifelike and involving novel about what happens when a sadistic school bully launches a campaign against a Jewish classmate. . . . Sundback involves the other ninth-grade boys, so that Bobby is ostracized by all of them, and even Brian Denny greets him on the school bus with "Move over, Jew bastard, you take up too much room." This from a former best friend, and the fact that Bobby hasn't one defender, is a little hard to accept—it might be more believable if we knew something about Brian and had a glimpse of Sundback at work on the others. However, Brian's overall behavior—avoiding or taunting Bobby when with the gang, calling him as if nothing had happened when Sundback is out of town—is all too recognizable, and Arrick's general picture of mass adolescent cruelty expressed in anti-Semitism is similarly convincing. . . . Arrick doesn't provide much insight into the psychology or dynamics of anti-Semitic behavior, but she makes the occurrence seem appallingly possible, and she effectively fastens kids' identification on its victimized but not defeated target.

> *A review of "Chernowitz!" in* Kirkus Reviews, *Vol. XLIX, No. 22, November 15, 1981, p. 1413.*

DICK ABRAHAMSON

[In *Chernowitz!*] Fran Arrick has written a powerful novel about prejudice. . . . Arrick does a fine job of describing the tiny snowball of prejudice picking up momentum and size and careening down the mountain. Bob's friends ostracize him partially out of fear that they might be Emmett's next victim.

Eventually Bob cannot stand the tormenting. He retaliates by concocting an elaborate scheme that frames the bully and gets him suspended. But such a victory is too shallow and Bob confesses to the frame-up and lets his parents and the principal know about his two years of harassment.

Upset at what's happened in her school, the principal calls an assembly. Movies of the holocaust are shown. Students are stunned by the horror, appalled at what human beings are capable of doing to one another. Bob is sickened by the films and leaves the auditorium for a drink of water. When he turns

around, there stands Emmett. "Did you and your daddy set that all up for me?" he asks. . . .

Instead of taking the easy way out and having Emmett repent, Arrick creates a far more powerful and realistic ending by leaving him unchanged. Bob realizes that there will always be Emmetts in the world, and that's worth discussing. (p. 80)

> *Dick Abrahamson, "New Novels That Go from Delight to Wisdom," in* English Journal, *Vol. 71, No. 4, April, 1982, pp. 80-3.**

STEPHANIE ZVIRIN

[In *God's Radar,* moving] from Syracuse to a small southern town is somewhat of a culture shock for the [Cable family]—especially for 15-year-old Roxie—but it isn't long before their neighbors, the Pregers, make them feel welcome by introducing them to the Stafford Hill Baptist Church community. . . . While her parents seem satisfied with Stafford Hill, Roxie isn't sure how she feels, and her struggle to sort out her confusion forms the crux of the story. Some readers will undoubtedly view the book as a judgment of fundamentalism, but the author does attempt to balance her portrait of the church. While she draws Stafford Hill members as unashamed proselytizers who lard everyday conversations with Bible verses (this includes young people as well as adults), she also emphasizes their sincerity and good works. Individual characterizations are not so evenhanded. Most supporting characters have been deliberately fashioned to express specific points of view about the church. Yet despite this lack of subtlety, Arrick has put together a compelling story, and what comes across with particular force is the frightening vulnerability of teenagers and the effect peer pressure has on their intellectual freedom.

> *Stephanie Zvirin, in a review of "God's Radar," in* Booklist, *Vol. 79, No. 20, June 15, 1983, p. 1333.*

C. NORDHIELM WOOLDRIDGE

The main attraction in Roxie's new small southern town is the mammoth Stafford Hill Baptist Church, which boasts attendance of up to 4000 at prayer meetings. . . . [In the course of *God's Radar* Roxie] develops a warm relationship with Jarrell (a Stafford Hill boy labeled "wild" by the rest of the school) but she finally succumbs to the pressure and, in a trance-like state, allows herself to be spirited away to prayer meeting while Jarrell waits on a street corner. This is a scathing and highly oversimplified indictment of fundamentalist Christianity carried to a legalistic extreme. Since Arrick has already passed judgment on the issue (even at their nicest, the Baptists wear the black hats), the tension is only plot deep and fails to truly challenge readers on a moral level.

> *C. Nordhielm Wooldridge, in a review of "God's Radar," in* School Library Journal, *Vol. 29, No. 10, August, 1983, p. 72.*

Judy (Sussman Kitchens) Blume

1938-

American novelist.

Blume is one of the most popular and controversial authors writing for young adults. She is known for her frank portrayal of the physical and emotional maturation of adolescents. Some adults consider her novels inappropriate for young readers. They object to Blume's treatment of such topics as menstruation, masturbation, and teenage sexuality. A number of critics have faulted her novels for lacking depth, and some have accused her of trivializing the problems and even the lives of teenagers. On the other hand, many critics praise Blume's ability to recreate the colloquial speech of young adults and commend her portrayal of adolescents who come to terms with their changing lives.

Blume first gained recognition with *Are You There God? It's Me, Margaret* (1970). This novel has two themes: Margaret's preoccupation with the physical signs of puberty, and her search for religious identity. Blume won acclaim for her warmly humorous treatment of female concerns, although several critics considered her depiction of Margaret's bodily changes overly graphic. *Forever . . .* (1976), with its detailed description of a first sexual encounter, was even more controversial. While some readers and critics have complained about the sexual content of Blume's novels, others praise her emphasis on individual responsibility in sexual matters.

Tiger Eyes (1981) is in some ways atypical of Blume's young adult novels. Sexual themes, which often preoccupy her protagonists, are deemphasized in this book in favor of examining the effects of death and senseless violence. Some critics consider this novel her most accomplished work. As with Blume's other young adult novels, *Tiger Eyes* has been praised for its effective blending of sophisticated themes and maturing characters.

Blume has remarked that she vividly remembers her own questions and emotions as a young person and she attempts to show readers that they are not alone in their fears and confusion. Her books are often set in suburbia, reflecting her own East Coast, middle-class background. Part of Blume's appeal, according to some critics, stems from her refusal to moralize as she emphasizes the need for individual and social responsibility. Several of her works have received regional book awards.

(See also *CLC*, Vol. 12; *Children's Literature Review*, Vol. 2; *Contemporary Authors*, Vols. 29-32, rev. ed.; and *Something about the Author*, Vols. 2, 31.)

NAOMI DECTER [LATER NAOMI MUNSON]

Miss Blume's works offer a child's-eye view of the trials and tribulations of life, and cover just about every social and emotional problem her readers are likely to encounter. *It's Not the End of the World*, for example, concerns a girl whose parents are getting divorced. The heroine of *Deenie* is a thirteen-year-old with curvature of the spine. *Tales of a Fourth Grade Nothing* is about sibling rivalry. *Are You There God? It's Me, Margaret*

is the story of a girl with a Jewish father and a Christian mother, trying to choose her own religion.

Miss Blume also writes about death, timidity, mob cruelty, and racial prejudice. But most of her books are in one way or another about sex. Her characters discuss their own sex lives or their parents'; they masturbate and menstruate; they worry about the size of their breasts and about kissing; they have wet dreams and they even have intercourse.

Given the sophistication of Miss Blume's material, her style is surprisingly simple. She writes for the most part in the first person: her vocabulary, grammar, and syntax are colloquial; her tone, consciously or perhaps not, evokes the awkwardness of a fifth-grader's diary. . . .

If the prose often seems at odds with the subject, however, it is perfectly suited to Miss Blume's imagination and characterization. Plot in the Blume books follows a rather strict pattern. There is, first of all, a "problem"—social or emotional; then, a hero or heroine to define, and other children to participate in, the problem; parents to pay the bills, drive the cars, and occasionally give a word of advice; the odd troublesome sibling or doting grandparent. The problem is resolved through the child's own experience, and the book ends.

Miss Blume's stock melodramas are staffed by stock characters—the Right People (from the author's point of view) and

the Wrong People. The Right People do and think the Right Thing, the Wrong People the Wrong Thing. One Right Person is virtually indistinguishable from another, and Wrong Persons bear a striking resemblance to other Wrong Persons. (p. 65)

These books are a perfect, if pint-sized, literary embodiment of contemporary enlightenment. They preach all the modern pieties and strike all the fashionable poses. They do so, moreover, with the rigidity of vision—and the social snobbery—that is the hallmark of their creed. There is in them no room for complexity of character, for conflicting emotions, or even for moral regeneration. Miss Blume's heroes never have an unacceptable thought; her villains, having once deviated from orthodoxy, are condemned absolutely to their villainy. And underlying everything is the sense that—whatever the issue—villainy is just the tiniest bit tacky.

All this, and sex to boot: Miss Blume has obviously found a winning combination. Her books not only cater to and reinforce the prejudices of her audience, they also answer a need peculiar to that community. For, quite apart from arousing and satisfying her young readers' prurient interest, the Blume books offer an ideal solution to the liberated parent who wonders how best to fulfill the uncomfortable duty of teaching his child sexual freedom. Judy Blume can safely be trusted to explain that *everyone* masturbates, and that it's the healthiest thing in the world—fun, too; that restrictions on youthful sexuality (especially female) are unhealthy relics of a repressed past; and that sexual intercourse is simply pleasurable and without consequence—as long as one is on the Pill.

The Blume ethic does not stop at erotic casualness. Miss Blume is as much a creature of her times and class spiritually as she is sexually. The consistent and overriding message of her books—for which, predictably enough, she has received the greatest acclaim—is that the proper focus of one's curiosity and concern is oneself. Everywhere Miss Blume garners high praise for her "respectful," "realistic," and "accurate" depiction of children's preoccupation with themselves.

Realistic, respectful, and accurate she is—with a vengeance. So respectful is she that not a childish thought or feeling is too pedestrian to merit her attention; so realistic that not a detail of a child's life—from breakfast menu to sleepwear fashions—is too tedious to go unrecorded; so accurate that an afternoon with Katherine, Deenie, or Jill must seem to her readers like a few hours alone in front of the bathroom mirror.

That a few more hours in front of the mirror is the last thing a young girl needs is a thought that does not seem to have occurred to Miss Blume or her army of fans. Yet the happiest magic of children's literature has always resided in its ability to burst the narcissistic bubble. One can, and does, learn any number of things from the March family, from Tom Sawyer, and even from Nancy Drew—for all their retrograde sociology. One learns to recognize and respect courage and honor; one learns the value of humor; at the very least, one learns to appreciate and emulate the spirit of adventure. Above all, one learns that life is full of things one has never seen; one learns the habit and the rewards of lifting one's eyes from one's own navel to look out upon the world.

Miss Blume finds the navel a much more worthy object of contemplation than the world—which is clearly why, in a narcissistic age, her limiting and narrowing vision should be heralded for its honesty and praised for its realism. (pp. 66-7)

Naomi Decter [later Naomi Munson], "Judy Blume's Children," in Commentary, *Vol. 59, No. 3, March, 1980, pp. 65-7.*

DAVID REES

What sort of picture would a being from another planet form of teenage and pre-teenage America were he able to read *Are You There, God? It's Me, Margaret* and *Forever*? He would imagine that youth was obsessed with bras, period pains, deodorants, orgasms, and family planning; that life was a great race to see who was first to get laid or to use a Tampax; that childhood and adolescence were unpleasant obstacles on the road to adulthood—periods (sorry!) of life to be raced through as quickly as possible, to be discarded as casually as Michael in *Forever* throws away his used contraceptive. He would discover that the young have almost no intellect and very few feelings; that falling in love is not a matter of complex emotions that seem at the time to change one's perception of people—indeed the whole world—out of all recognition; but that it is simply a question of should one go on the pill or not, swapping partners quite heartlessly, and whether one is doing it right in bed. He'd realize, with some surprise, that sex isn't even very erotic: that it's just clinical.

Adolescents do of course have period pains and worry about the size of their breasts or penises; they fall in love and some of them sleep together. There should obviously be a place for all these concerns in teenage novels; but to write about them, as Judy Blume does, to the exclusion of everything else is doing youth a great disservice. She succeeds quite magnificently in trivializing everything, particularly young people themselves. She would appear not to know that they do find time, whatever their emotional and sexual preoccupations may be, to be interested in and participate in a very wide spectrum of human existence. To serve them up the kind of stuff of which *Forever* consists is to underestimate totally their ability to think and to feel, not only about themselves but about the whole complexity of living that goes on around them.

Nor is that Judy Blume's only major fault. *Forever* has a bad taste, a want of sensibility, a heavy-handed clumsiness that is breath-taking. The reader's reaction is laughter—anything from an embarrassed snigger to falling out of a chair with hilarity—when he ought to feel moved or excited or enthralled. (pp. 173-74)

Consider the artless banality of this: "I came right before Michael and as I did I made noises, just like my mother." It's the same sort of language as "I went into the kitchen and fixed myself a cup of coffee." Most writers are aware that human activity is enormously rich and varied, and to give value to that variety, what is linguistically apt for one thing is inappropriate to another. But not so Judy Blume. She has no sense of the incongruous, not even a sense of humor. (p. 175)

One could go on with other examples, but it hardly seems worth it. It's enough to say that the triviality of her thinking is matched by the sheer shoddiness of her English. She employs the usual sub-Salingerese American first-person narration, but so unmemorably that it makes Paul Zindel's use of the technique look like startling originality. There is absolutely nothing in Judy Blume's style that defines it as specifically hers. . . . Judy Blume's novels are the ultimate in the read-it-and-throw-it-away kind of book. They seem to be saying that when you've read the text you'll be equipped to do the real thing and you won't have to bother with the tedious business of coming back to a story to find out what it's like. In other words, they are not only short-changing the young; they are short-changing literature. (pp. 175-76)

[*Are you There, God? It's Me, Margaret* is] as throwaway as *Forever*. The young reader learns about how to wear a bra and what it's like to have a period, and nothing else is offered that could induce her (a boy is unlikely to find anything in the story of any interest) to return to it and re-open its pages. (p. 176)

The trouble stems primarily from thinking that issues—such as how to get laid or what to do when you have your first period—are starting points for creative writing. They are not, and never can be. *Otherwise Known as Sheila the Great* is a marginally better book than *Forever* or *Are You There, God? It's Me, Margaret* because the issues—Sheila Tubman's various phobias about water and dogs—are made secondary considerations to the story, thin though the narrative is. . . . *It's Not the End of the World* is . . . about divorce, which is certainly a more interesting subject than menstruation. Clash of personalities, disruption of lives, emotional crises, are implicit in the material. It's probably her best book, though what I really mean is that it isn't as bad as the others. Certainly the reactions of the central character, Karen, to the break-up of her parents' marriage seem to ring true. Her sad attempts to bring the adults together again, and her facility for blaming herself when what happens isn't her fault at all, are characteristic of young children who have to suffer in such situations. Authentic, too, is her misunderstanding of trivial actions: she misinterprets them as being of great significance—imagining, for instance, that because her mother has gone to see the same lawyer twice she must be going to marry him. The inability of even the most well-meaning adults to explain what is going on when a marriage collapses, in terms that a child can comprehend, is also well done. But this is not sufficient. The narrator (it's yet another first-person story) sounds as if she is exactly the same person as the narrators in all Judy Blume's books. . . . There's an astonishing incapacity to show that people are different from one another in the way they think and feel and talk: it isn't good enough to suggest that they only differ in their actions. And there is the same entirely forgettable, drab, flat prose. . . . [This] kind of English, pared of all adornment, of anything that is colorful or stimulating or imaginative, sounds like someone trying to explain the most simple things of life to a non-English-speaking foreigner, and is about as exciting to read as the prose of a shopping list.

Then Again, Maybe I Won't is yet another non-novel, the problem this time being what happens if your father suddenly becomes very rich and the whole family moves out of a friendly close-knit lower-middle-class environment to an exceedingly well-to-do suburb, with different rituals, mores, and customs. It isn't a problem that many children are likely to face, but maybe the intention here is to say that life in the smart, private swimming-pool set is so awful in the way it corrupts Mum and Dad that would-be readers will stop hoping their fathers will suddenly find endless riches at their disposal. Whatever the intention is, and it isn't very clear, existence in the upper income bracket really isn't much like this. The *nouveaux riches'* treatment of Grandma, for example, is so callous as to be quite unbelievable, especially when the family background is Italian and Italians are noted for their close-knit family life style. The next-door neighbors are a pretty unattractive crowd, and are so obviously unpalatable to both the reader and the narrator, that it is not easy to see why Vic's mother should wish to imitate them so slavishly. Vic, as one comes to expect in a

Judy Blume novel, talks in the usual shopping-list English. . . . (pp. 176-79)

[Another] "problem" in *Then Again, Maybe I Won't* is twelve-year-old Vic's developing sexuality; he's worried that he doesn't have wet dreams and the other fellows do—presumably what Judy Blume feels is the masculine equivalent of having one's first period. Vic's feelings about wet dreams and Margaret's feelings about periods in *Are You There, God? It's Me, Margaret* are more or less identical, but these two bodily functions are profoundly different, psychologically, and Judy Blume is mistaken in leaving the reader with the impression that they are similar. That, and other elementary considerations—that writing about such topics so obsessively may cause hangups in the child reader where none existed previously—seem to escape the notice of her advocates.

In talking about the sexual development of young people Judy Blume is at her most insensitive, which is why *Forever* is easily her worst book. She has little idea, it seems, of what really occurs, emotionally, in adolescent sexual relationships, either in real life or in the teenage novel. (pp. 179-80)

> David Rees, "Not Even for a One Night Stand: Judy Blume," in his The Marble in the Water: Essays on Contemporary Writers of Fiction for Children and Young Adults, The Horn Book, Inc., 1980, pp. 173-84.

MARGARET MASON

"Newspapers are very big on facts, I think," muses Davis (Davey) Wexler, the 15-year-old daughter left behind after her father was shot in the chest [in *Tiger Eyes*]. "But not on feelings. Nobody writes about how it *feels* when your father is murdered."

Judy Blume does. And even if your father hasn't been murdered, even if you're no longer 15, and even if you'd rather think about something else, she puts you inside that girl: a luminous-eyed (thus the title) brownette, built like a swimmer, at once achingly vulnerable, funny and tough. In the proper cadence of grief—paralysis, anger, catharsis, gradual acceptance—you know how it feels, slowly, excruciatingly, over a school year's time. And maybe that's why kids like Blume's writing so much. You can cry with a friend, and then when you can't stand any more, she'll poke you in the ribs with a joke. Blume's often cynical, staccato style works splendidly as the voice of a child, who does not yet know enough to round out—and even forgive—adult idiocies.

Because Davey . . . er, Blume . . . talks to us in such a taut and dreamlike way, giving us images bit by bit, you'll keep reading to piece together the facts. . . .

Davey's real thoughts come to the surface—as if from a very savvy teen-ager's diary—in the midst of some terrible ironies. The most overt is that Davey, her mother and 7-year-old brother are struggling to come to grips with a decimating, anonymous violence while seeking security in Los Alamos (The Atomic City). (p. 9)

In Los Alamos the people with whom Davey, white and part Jewish, finds the most comfort are a well-educated and sensitive Hispanic boy named Wolf—assumed by Aunt Bitsy to be a maintenance man—and his father, who although dying was "full of life and full of love."

Blume . . . touches lightly on most teen-age issues: misunderstandings with adults, drinking, drugs, dating, a girl's crushes and conflicts about depending on a boyfriend. As for sex, there's only, parents might be relieved to know, some heavy necking (if kids still call it that).

What parents might find more disturbing is the realization that it's the little, special things about themselves that their children will remember and that will carry them through the toughest adversity. Davey's father had a warm and homey ritual—which I won't give away here—but her reenactment of it is one of the most poignant and healing scenes in the book. (pp. 9-10)

There's no hit-them-in-the-head moralizing in *Tiger Eyes* . . . , probably another reason why kids like Blume. Davey does, however, remind them subtly of their own good sense and remarkable resiliency. "Each of us must confront our own fears, must come face to face with them," she says. "How we handle our fears will determine where we go with the rest of our lives." (p. 10)

> Margaret Mason, "Judy Blume: Growing Up with Grief," in Book World—The Washington Post, September 13, 1981, pp. 9-10.

JEAN FRITZ

How does a girl feel when her father is shot? When he bleeds to death in her arms? Beginning with the father's funeral, Judy Blume [in "*Tiger Eyes*"] follows her 15-year-old heroine, Davey, step by step. . . . The love interest that is a frequent feature in Judy Blume's work is muted. Davey's friend Wolf, a college student (wise for his years and also wounded in spirit), helps her deal with her problems, even though the two have met only in brief encounters; still he is a central influence in helping her through.

This is a masterly novel, not to be dismissed as simply another treatment of death and violence. The reader empathizes not only with the heroine but with all the other characters. Each has his own story, and each lights up some aspect of the American scene. Take Uncle Walter, for instance, who spends his days making atom bombs yet misses the irony in his overprotection of Davey; he's so sensitive to danger that he won't let her take Driver's Ed. Surely "*Tiger Eyes*" belongs at the top of Judy Blume's list. (p. 58)

> Jean Fritz "The Heroine Finds a Way," in The New York Times Book Review, November 15, 1981, pp. 56, 58.*

ROBERT LIPSYTE

[Blume's] *Tiger Eyes,* should slip past the censors. There is no explicit sex and there are no objectionable words. It is her finest book—ambitious, absorbing, smoothly written, emotionally engaging and subtly political. It is also a lesson on how the conventions of a genre can best be put to use.

The plot of *Tiger Eyes* is a staple of juvenile novels. A family member dies and the survivors must reconstitute themselves. Standard props are used: A lovable cat and a comical younger brother pop up from time to time to loosen the tension. Textbook suspense is created early: A mysterious paper bag and a romantic young stranger are left unexplained for many pages.

Thus the reader . . . is comfortable in TV sitcom territory. Even the opening chapter, in which a 15-year-old girl is searching for shoes to wear to the funeral of her father, shot during the robbery of his 7-Eleven store, is out of Eyewitness News.

But the story deepens, takes turns. Davey Wexler, her mother and her 7-year-old brother flee Atlantic City for the Los Alamos, New Mexico, home of the dead man's older sister, a rigid, domineering clubwoman, and her husband, a fearful, insular weapons scientist. In the oppressive atmosphere of Bomb City, the childless couple attempt to take control of the lives of the three visitors. (p. 551)

Tiger Eyes never falters, never slides into melodrama or preachment. Blume is a crisp and often funny stylist with a gift for defining character through snappy dialogue. She is unafraid of emotion. And she offers no final answers. No one in *Tiger Eyes* changes forever, or emerges sadder but wiser, or even learns her lesson well. Rather, a girl and her mother weather a crisis, often helped and hindered by the same well-meaning, mean-spirited people, and now must go forward with their lives. (p. 552)

> Robert Lipsyte, "A Bridge of Words," in The Nation, Vol. 233, No. 17, November 21, 1981, pp. 551-53.

LYNNE HAMILTON

[Throughout] Blume's novels the age-old image of the female, a dependent, ineffectual creature whose importance can only be derived from a man, remains drooped over its pedestal. Conservative watchdogs accuse Blume of iconoclasm; but in fact her portrayal of young women helps perpetuate both the female stereotype and the status quo. Her adolescents may sprout breasts, but in a more fundamental sense they do not develop. Bland, passive, and unfocused, they are locked in Neverland where the future is a dirty word.

The static quality of Blume's heroines is particularly striking in novels about twelve- to eighteen-year-olds. More than any other stage of life except infancy, adolescence is characterized by change. The word *means* 'growing towards adulthood'. (p. 88)

[In] literature it is typically heroes and not heroines who, after trial and testing, emerge the wiser for their experience. . . . Still the female *Bildungsroman* is not absent from our literary heritage, *Emma* [by Jane Austen] and *Jane Eyre* [by Charlotte Brontë] being examples of novels that do grant girls the right to passage. (pp. 88-9)

In the four novels I want to consider—*Are You There God? It's Me, Margaret, Deenie, Tiger Eyes,* and *Forever . . .*—Blume herself sets up the *Bildungsroman* expectation. Each of her heroines confronts a potentially transforming experience: a religious quest, a physical affliction, the loss of a parent, or sexual emergence. For psychologists like Erik Erikson, such crises are 'turning points' or 'moments of decision' that are essential for growth. . . . In her adolescent novels, however, Blume demystifies the purported 'crises'. Pain, religion, death, and sex, she says in effect, are 'no big deal'. Her young heroines are given the answers before they have had a chance to grapple with the questions. By reducing, dismissing, or denying the crises, Blume prevens them from occasioning passage. Her heroines adjust and cope; they do not suffer and change.

Although hardly of Augustinean or Dantean dimensions, Margaret's crisis is religious: she can't decide whether to join the Jewish Community Centre or the Y. She visits a church and a synagogue by finally postpones her decision indefinitely. . . . With religion out of the way, Margaret finds the long-awaited bloodstains on her underpants. A biological event substitutes for spiritual choice. Her prayer to be 'like everyone else' has been answered. Although she is no further along in her quest than she was in chapter one, Margaret pronounces herself now 'almost a woman.'. . . . (p. 89)

Deenie's crisis is physical. Near the beginning of the novel, the thirteen-year-old heroine is diagnosed as having adolescent scoliosis—curvature of the spine. For the next four years, night and day, she will have to wear a Milwaukee brace. Her secret dream of being on the cheerleading squad will never be realized. Once again Blume sets up the reader's *Bildungsroman* expectations, spelling out the medical details of the malformation and documenting the treatment as if these had metaphorical significance. But what might have been life-altering for Deenie turns out to be merely inconvenient. . . .

In Blume's most recent novel, *Tiger Eyes,* the heroine does appear to make progress of a sort. Ridden with fear, fifteen-year-old Davey Wexler, whose father was shot to death in his 7-11 store in Atlantic City, takes refuge with her mother and younger brother at an uncle's house in Los Alamos, New Mexico. Through time, therapy, and of course a boyfriend, Davey confronts the memories of the fateful night and seems to accept her loss. At the end of the novel, she returns, apparently mended, to resume her life in Atlantic City.

While Blume's treatment of religion and physical affliction with the younger heroines is primarily reductive, her handling of death and loss seems dishonest. Davey never fully experiences what it means to be without a father. Wolf, the boyfriend who plays the key role in Davey's recovery, is in many ways a father surrogate. (p. 90)

Wolf differs markedly from the stock 'cute boy' in the adolescent roster. At twenty he is much older than Davey: a Caltech student, he is also much smarter. In spite of an erotic pull, their physical contact is, for a Blume novel, curiously minimal. Instead, Wolf plays mentor to Davey, teaching her how to hike New Mexico's steep canyons and giving her a book to read about the area. Like her young father, Wolf leaves Davey, but she is certain she will see him again. . . . [Rather] than allowing Davey to confront death fully, Blume has in effect mitigated its finality. Yet neither the heroine nor the author seems aware of the deception. Davey claims to have changed 'deep down inside'. But once again, what might have been a linear progression or a spiral ascent turns out to be merely circular after all.

As in *Tiger Eyes,* human beings in *Forever* . . . also fill functional slots; but this time the heroine substitutes lovers rather than father figures for one another. At seventeen, Katherine Danziger is old enough to wonder whether she even *is* still an adolescent. The novel is a do-it-yourself account of her sexual emergence, complete with gynaecological examination and choice of contraceptive. Sex for Blume is too wholesome and uncomplicated to trigger crises, however. Katherine experiences none of the horrors that usually accompany teenage sex in fiction. . . . The only small cloud in this novel's otherwise unrelievedly clear sky appears when Katherine falls for another boy while counselling at a summer camp. Michael is angry; Katherine is depressed. She decides she's not ready for 'forever' after all. But her recovery is swift and complete. She switches from Michael to Theo, and her life goes on as before.

Like religion, physical affliction, and death, first love is no big deal.

Besides reducing the crises which might have promoted the adolescent heroines to adult life, Blume also avoids another related agent of change: the generational showdown. In literature, alienation from a parent or parent figure often accompanies adolescent crises. . . . [By] defying their parents, whether in literature or in life, adolescents are often defining themselves. In Blume's novels, parent-child friction abounds; but only rarely does confrontation occur. (pp. 90-2)

If Blume prevents the crises and conflicts which might prod adolescents out of childhood, she also fails to provide examples of adult women who might entice the heroines into growing up. The unappealing role of women in teenage fiction has been amply documented: adults generally play negative or indifferent roles, and mothers in particular are nagging, weak, and manipulative. While it is perhaps unreasonable to expect adolescent novels to portray dynamic, fun-loving, interesting parents—especially mothers—Blume's mothers are an unusually dreary lot. They are if anything even more unformed than their daughters. As a rule they have neither jobs nor skills nor interests. And they all depend on men. . . . [These] women are too vaguely sketched to contradict the covert message that the majority of Blume's women convey: to be an adult woman means not being anyone at all. (p. 93)

Lacking both present adversity and a prospect of future fulfilment—the carrot and the stick—to propel them towards adulthood, Blume's adolescents seem doomed to inhabit an intellectual, moral, and emotional limbo. Theirs is a world that offers neither mystery, power, belief, or values. Such a world might seem merely humdrum—Dorothy's Oz without the magic or Nancy Drew's River Heights without the sleuthing—if only Blume's characters like [L. Frank] Baum's and Carolyn Keene's were immortal. But for Blume's heroines the clock is ticking. In three of the four novels, the heroine marks her birthday. There is no question of anyone staying twelve or fifteen or eighteen forever. They are approaching the future even as they set their faces against it. (p. 94)

As an adult, Judy Blume once remarked that she found her life to be 'more exciting, more rewarding, and more full of adventure' at twelve than it was later on. Given the roles to which women have been relegated for thousands of years, Blume's assessment is perhaps understandable. At the same time, an author with this perspective can hardly be expected to depict the growing-up process in positive terms. In recent years, the opportunities for women to lead exciting, rewarding, adventure-filled lives have increased. It seems quite possible that the new generation of writers will contain more members who find their lives to be more satisfying as adults than as adolescents. We await their novels, some of which, we hope, will celebrate the female rite of passage. (p. 95)

Lynne Hamilton, "Blume's Adolescents: Coming of Age in Limbo," in Signal, *No. 41, May, 1983, pp. 88-96.*

FAITH McNULTY

On my first exposure to Blume, a few years ago, I turned out to be immune to Blume fever. Her realism struck me as shallow, and I was put off by her knack for observing unpleasant details. Recently, I read her again, determined to find her magic formula, and I am now ready to amend my views. In a Judy

Blume book, realism is everything. True, it has no great depth, but it is extraordinarily convincing. True, she includes unpleasant details—things we all notice but usually don't mention—yet they increase the credibility that is the source of her magnetic power. Blume's technique might be compared to *cinéma vérité*. She writes as though filming the landscape of childhood from the eye level of a child. She focusses on nearby objects and immediate events with a child's intense gaze, picking out details that evoke instant recognition. As in a play, dialogue carries the story along. It is colloquial, often funny, and always revealing. Blume doesn't waste words. Her stories are told in the first person—sustained soliloquies that are prodigies of total recall. Each book begins on a note of candor. We have the feeling of reading a secret diary—something the writer intended only for himself. Thus, it seems natural when usually private matters are included. Often, they are things that have to do with the dawning of sex, and though most are quite innocuous it is a shock to see them suddenly exposed in print. The effect is a mesmerizing intimacy, which convinces Blume's readers that she writes the whole truth about what kids think and feel. (pp. 193-94)

No report on Blume is complete without a look at **"Forever,"** the book for which some critics have not forgiven her. **"Forever"** is the case history of a teen-ager's affair, in which Katherine, seventeen, deludes herself that she is truly in love and sleeps with Michael, also seventeen. Blume's description of what Katherine and Michael do in bed, and what Katherine feels, is a carefully worded answer to questions hygiene manuals fail to address. The affair ends when Katherine falls out of love and realizes emotions can be unreliable. I found the encounter one of the dullest on record, but it is easy to see that a naïve reader must find it fascinatingly revealing. It is equally obvious that such a book could kick up quite a storm.

Without the revelations of **"Forever"** and the small, stunning shocks that Blume sprinkles through her other books like nuts in a brownie, she might not have lured so many millions of readers, but she has also won her audience through honest work, superior craftsmanship, and a talent for recreating an evanescent period of life—the years from nine to thirteen. She writes about the loneliness of being young; about youthful secrets—fear, anxiety, longing, guilt. It is rough being a kid, she often says. Her kids are swept along by capricious currents. They struggle to keep their sense of humor, and to keep their heads above water. At the end of the story, they find their feet for a moment of equilibrium as they contemplate the next stage of life. . . . I find much in Blume to be thankful for. She isn't scary or sick. She writes clean, swift, unadorned prose. She has convinced millions of young people that truth can be found in a book and that reading is fun. At a time that many believe may be the twilight of the written word, those are things to be grateful for. (pp. 198, 201)

Faith McNulty, "Children's Books for Christmas," in The New Yorker, *Vol. LIX, No. 42, December 5, 1983, pp. 191-95, 198, 201-02, 204-08.**

Marion Zimmer Bradley

1930-

American novelist, short story writer, editor, and critic.

Bradley is a prolific science fiction and fantasy writer who is best known for her series of novels tracing the evolution of the planet Darkover. While the *Darkover* novels comprise a diversity of plots and time periods, they share a common setting and similar thematic concerns. Although all Darkovans are descendants of explorers from Earth, two different cultures have evolved. The Terrans rely on communal support and advanced technology, while the Darkovans are self-reliant and antitechnological. Bradley does not openly favor either one; her work often explores the conflicts that arise from opposing forces, and the *Darkover* novels, like her other works, usually end in reconciliation. Lester del Rey calls Darkover "one of the most fully realized of the worlds of science fiction," and critics in general praise Bradley's literate writing, intricate characterizations, and logical plots.

Among the serious issues addressed in the *Darkover* novels are the importance and the problems of communication between individuals. The first *Darkover* novel, *The Sword of Aldones* (1962), centers on Lew Alton and his acute sense of isolation which stems from both his physical deformities and his dual heritage—Darkovan and Terran. In *The Forbidden Tower* (1977), however, Bradley employs the Darkovans' telepathic powers in order to explore the extreme emotional and physical closeness of the four protagonists.

An undercurrent of feminism runs throughout the *Darkover* series. Bradley frequently examines sex roles and the limitations they place on the individual. One of the most notable examples of this idea occurs in *The Shattered Chain* (1976). Revolving around the struggles of three women for independence and self-realization, this novel explores both the necessity of choice and the inevitable pain and hardship that result from the freedom to choose. Critics have praised Bradley's ability to incorporate feminist and utopian ideals into the harsh realism of Darkover without diminishing the credibility of the characters or their society.

Bradley's feminist interests are also evident in her recent non-*Darkover* novel, *The Mists of Avalon* (1982). This novel, which retells the Arthurian legend from the viewpoint of the women involved, has received considerable critical attention. Critics on the whole are impressed with Bradley's accurate and detailed evocation of the times and consider *The Mists of Avalon* an important addition to the chronicles of Arthur. Aside from these novels, Bradley has also written numerous other works ranging from science fiction to science fantasy. Although most of her works are favorably received by critics, it is largely Bradley's *Darkover* series which gave rise to her popular appeal.

(See also *Contemporary Authors*, Vols. 57-60; *Contemporary Authors New Revision Series*, Vol. 7; and *Dictionary of Literary Biography*, Vol. 8.)

Photograph by Modern Art. Courtesy of Marion Zimmer Bradley

. . . is both literate and exciting, with much of that searching "fable" quality that made "Lord of the Flies" so provocative. (p. 16)

Theodore Sturgeon, "If . . .?" in The New York Times Book Review, April 22, 1973, pp. 14, 16.*

DAN MILLER

Bradley's tales of fantasy and adventure on the planet Darkover have quietly and deservedly gained a considerable following. This latest installment [*The Shattered Chain*] explores an important and heretofore neglected aspect of that feudalistic culture—the role of women. . . . Although filled with characteristic epic sweep, the present novel is more cerebral, and the Amazons emerge with far more dignity and heroism than their pejorative name implies. As with the others in the series, no knowledge of the previous books is required for enjoyment.

Dan Miller, in a review of "The Shattered Chain: A Darkover Novel," in Booklist, Vol. 73, No. 1, September 1, 1976, p. 22.

LESTER DEL REY

[The first two books in Bradley's *Darkover* series, written in 1962, have been reissued.] *The Planet Savers* . . . was origi-

THEODORE STURGEON

A writer of absolute competence is Marion Zimmer Bradley, who should be more widely read. Her **"Darkover Landfall"**

26

nally little more than a long novelette; it's followed here by a new Darkover short story, a curious piece for Bradley, but quite good.

The Sword of Aldones . . . is a full novel, and the one that really began the *Darkover* cult. It's a complicated story of *Comyn* intrigue and dark matrix magic, foreshadowing the later *Heritage of Hastur*. It also presents a somewhat different Darkover than we find in later novels. Bradley refused to be bound by consistency—wisely, I think, since Darkover has evolved and improved. But even the early stories have the wonderful allure of this strange world.

Lester del Rey, in a review of "The Sword of Aldones," in Analog Science Fiction/Science Fact, *Vol. XCVII, No. 3, March, 1977, p. 169.*

LESTER DEL REY

Marion Zimmer Bradley is rapidly becoming one of the best writers in our field. Book by book . . . she has been increasing her command of the craft and art of writing. The [deepening] of her characterization and the widening of her grasp of background, along with the increasing honesty and inventiveness of her plotting, are all joyous developments to behold.

Her **"Darkover"** stories are her best known ones, of course. And they depend on psi-effects to a major extent—a subject which I don't normally enjoy very much. Frankly, while I found the early Darkover novels fairly good reading, I wasn't much impressed. Now I look forward to each one with the keenest anticipation.

The latest is *The Forbidden Tower*. . . . And it lived up to my anticipation in every way, despite the fact that much of the story involves a sort of love relationship among a group of people—something that becomes unendurably treacly in the hands of a lesser writer.

This is a direct sequel to *The Winds of Darkover*. In that, the Terran Andrew Carr was drawn into a crisis between Darkovian people and another race that had learned to control the psi-crystals that are the source of Darkovian power. He rescued a Keeper (a sort of virgin priestess), and at the end was riding off with her toward his new home on Darkover.

This book picks up immediately with their intended marriage. (pp. 170-71)

Somehow, the characters—even many of the lesser ones—become very real. And the background of Darkover—by this time a most fascinating world—is deepened. Psi, which is too often just a magic gimmick, becomes more and more a believable alternate body of science; each book recently has developed more and more of the understructure of this; as Bradley uses it, it no longer bothers me, but becomes a truly fascinating alternate.

I found it splendid, and can't recommend it too highly. (p. 171)

Lester del Rey, in a review of "The Forbidden Tower," in Analog Science Fiction/Science Fact, *Vol. XCVII, No. 11, November, 1977, pp. 170-71.*

PAUL McGUIRE III

The Forbidden Tower is a sequel to *The Spell Sword.* Although one need not have read the earlier book to understand and enjoy this one, it does concern the same characters and picks up the action exactly where the other left off. Yet, aside from that, and background, the two novels have nothing in common. *Forbidden Tower* is the most psychological and sexual novel of the series while *Spell Sword* is the most straight action adventure. . . .

Ms. Bradley's ability to create intricate characters economically and then reveal them through interaction with events and each other is awesome. Her people are a product of their world. Just as Huckleberry Finn could only exist on Mark Twain's Mississippi, the men and women in this novel are by and of Darkover. Well, all but one. Carr is a Terran and his confusion and cultural shock to the reader that identifies with him are at times actually painful. The characters do not serve to reveal Darkover to the reader but vice versa. In fact to some extent the real revelation made to the reader is of himself.

Isolation in one form or other is almost constantly present. . . .

In [*The Forbidden Tower*], the most confined of Ms. Bradley's novels, the isolation ultimately is that of a person within himself, separate in mind and body from others. Ms. Bradley explores this in a way thorough and entertaining, impossible anywhere but SF. All her characters are telepathic and at times they have minds linked to briefly become what is nearly a single entity. Yet even their relationships are filled with hurt feelings, misunderstandings, anger, important things left unsaid or telethought, and insecurity. One begins to wonder if *any* two people can have true personal communication and understanding at all, on any basis. Using SF to make metaphor real, Ms. Bradley also implies that attempting to do so is dangerous, and that to succeed one must first gain, face and accept self-knowledge.

If I have implied all this suddenly appeared out of the blue without precedent in the series I have misled you. It is just so very much more startlingly apparent and important in this book. Also don't think that this is all some dry cerebral novel. One cares about her passionate characters and there is plenty of sense of wonder mixed with the drama, and yes, derring-do is done.

Paul McGuire III, in a review of "The Forbidden Tower," in Science Fiction Review, *Vol. 7, No. 1, February, 1978, p. 43.*

LESTER DEL REY

[*Stormqueen!* is] another story of Darkover—by now one of the most fully realized of the worlds of science fiction. This time, however, it isn't about the period when Darkover has been discovered by the men of Earth, with the conflict placed between the natives and the Terran Empire.

Instead, Bradley has gone back long before the coming of the terrans. . . .

As has been the case for all her recent novels, this is a complicated story with many threads and subplots. But the key to it all is Dorylis, a young girl whose *laran*, or psychic power, is such that she can control the storms and direct lightning to strike where she wills. She's still a child, however—a rather badly spoiled child. And unless she can discipline herself to master her talent, it must master and destroy her—and those about her. . . .

I'm not entirely happy about one small section near the end where Dorylis suddenly seems to have a change of heart that isn't justified as well as I'd expect from Bradley; she seems suddenly too mature and too altruistic. But that's a small point in an excellent story, in all other ways.

I enjoyed the novel, and hope now that Bradley will go on to cover a lot more of the history of Darkover, hitherto only revealed in tantalizing hints.

> *Lester del Rey, in a review of "Stormqueen," in* Analog Science Fiction/Science Fact, *Vol. XCVIII, No. 8, August, 1978, p. 173.*

IAN WATSON

I'm an admirer of Darkover. This remote, chilly world under a blood-red sun . . . is a marvellous creation—and though the same characters, or their parents or children, wind in and out of the books and though there is a prevalent stock theme (the collision of Darkovan and Terran, the latter discovering strange affinities) yet the various books of the cycle aren't formulaic or mere lead-ons from one to the others; all exist solidly and independently, some for better, some for worse. (p. 92)

[*Darkover Landfall* and *The Spell Sword* are], in the chronology of Darkover, the first two novels—though, since Bradley dips into the Darkovan mythos when and where she pleases, not the first two to be written by any means. The cover calls them "science fantasy", with suggestions of Sword & Sorcery, and for a long time I confess I was put off entering Darkover by the aura of mighty-thewed barbarians hefting cutlasses, priestesses in negligée, eldritch forces and warring fiefs that emanated from the Ace and DAW paperbacks. . . . Not a bit of it, though. Good solid sf, this. A real culture is here, as well-realized as Le Guin's Gethen, not a wish-fulfilment one. The paranormal is intelligently handled. The swordplay and "primitivism" is all appropriate, necessary, and vital.

Yet is this the place to start in on Darkover? I don't really think so. These two novels are comparatively minor ones in the cycle—by far the better of the two, *The Spell Sword*, paling beside its mature successor *The Forbidden Tower*. . . . The events that happen after *Spell Sword* are much more harrowing and gripping—and the way Bradley organises her book there's no need to read the predecessor first to appreciate the successor to the full. And *Darkover Landfall*—the only work set before the Terrans arrived on Darkover in force, two millennia earlier when a human starship of colonists crashed, is entirely disconnected from the rest of the cycle—a prelude, and almost an unnecessary one. . . . [If] you start here, in a minor key, be assured that there are major keys already played elsewhere. (pp. 92-3)

> *Ian Watson, in a review of "Darkover Landfall" and "The Spell Sword," in* Foundation, *No. 14, September, 1978, pp. 92-3.*

DAVID A. TRUESDALE

The closing chapters [of *Stormqueen!*] are tremendous; emotionally draining as well as mentally stimulating as Bradley takes us on an out-of-the-body mind journey to the very borders of the Otherworld. This makes up quite nicely for all the breast-beating and continual detailed maneuvering of plot and characters, although the detailing of the basics of matrix mechanics was welcomed indeed.

The prose is quite clear, crisp and powerful, and Bradley's arguments are logical and reasonable. She deals with the contemporary issues of genetic engineering, abortion, men and women as sex objects, what understanding, compassion and a call to reason can accomplish—all against a backdrop of feudal intrigue and inheritance by a people who are struggling and groping to understand and control their powers of telepathy, telekinesis and other psi powers.

A very well done is to be given this thoughtful and detailed wonderment. (p. 34)

> *David A. Truesdale, in a review of "Stormqueen!" in* Science Fiction Review, *Vol. 7, No. 4, September, 1978, pp. 33-4.*

CHERRY WILDER

[*The Forbidden Tower*] continues from *The Spell Sword;* the alien Catmen have been vanquished, though at heavy cost. Damon Ridenow and Andrew Carr marry the twin sisters Callista and Ellemir of the house of Alton. Both men are displaced persons. Andrew has given up all his ties to Earth and is feeling his way in a new culture. Damon has been denied his vocation as a Keeper, one of the highly trained telepaths who work in the Towers. The ancient science of the Comyn lords of Darkover centres rigidly upon the training and discipline received in these towers and is hedged with prohibitions.

The force of these taboos falls most heavily on Callista, who renounces her vows as a Keeper, trained in the Tower of Arilinn, to marry Andrew, the man who saved her psychically and physically from the aliens. . . . Keepers, through their psychic power and their link with a sentient matrix jewel, are literally untouchable: the attempted violation of a Keeper, for instance, would result in the death of the rapist. This power is exercised unconsciously, like a reflex; Callista, who loves Andrew deeply and whose defences were lowered somewhat during her rescue, must wait until she loosens up again.

This appears at first a rather titillating problem, a private difficulty impinging on the bustling public life of the great Alton house at Armida. But those readers who anticipate a cheerful defloration about the middle of the book have underestimated Marion Zimmer Bradley. Callista's cruelly imposed frigidity is at the very centre of the book and it is examined with increasing depth and widening implications until the final pages. . . .

The way in which the threads are gathered up: the need for a wider use of telepathic healing, the superstitious narrowness of the taboos, the painful and unnecessary discipline imposed on the immature female adepts . . . , even the dynastic implications of Callista's marriage, this interweaving is skilfully done.

The mechanism of Darkover's psychic world with its paraphernalia of screens, monitoring, matrices and trips to the astral plane or overworld, is described with firm authority. The background of Darkover is beloved and familiar territory for the author. We have the feeling that she no longer invents Darkover, she simply goes there. The culture is nicely balanced between a harsh environment, a feudal society complicated by the presence of telepaths and a high degree of sexual liberty and closeness. (p. 106)

It is fair to ask just how well the characterisation stands up in a book where the four main characters Damon and Ellemir and Andrew and Callista end up closer than the average husband and wife. Are the twin sisters Ellemir and Callista simply another example of fairy-tale splitting of the Frodo/Sam or

closer still, the Lethonee/Sorayina type? The verdict is "not proven"; there is more to both girls than a simple warm/cold duality. Damon is the best developed character and Andrew, we notice, becomes more sympathetic as he is drawn into the culture of Darkover. The Keeper, Leonie, hovering on the verge of myth, and the old lord, Dom Esteban, wholly human, are well-drawn supporting characters.

All this is done in a loping, down-to-earth style; we have a sense not so much of padding but of purposeful backing and filling. The writing is not pretty but it is not inflated; the author rises to the occasion many times. The episodes in the over-world, where Damon has built a small shelter and must later expand it into the Forbidden Tower of an independent Keeper, are well done. The adventure in time is appealing and perhaps there exists already in the mind of the author or in an earlier book, the same scene from the point of view of Damon's ancestor, Varzil, confronted by a descendant from the future. It is a measure of the seriousness of the work that this episode stands out almost as light relief; the total impression of the book is one of cumulative psychic power. . . . (pp. 106-07)

The personality of the author, tough-minded, practical, spiritual, hums in the background of this novel like a matrix jewel. Marion Zimmer Bradley writes with a moral purpose of Victorian intensity, but it is liberal and liberating. (p. 107)

> *Cherry Wilder, in a review of "The Forbidden Tower," in* Foundation, *No. 15, January, 1979, pp. 105-07.*

JEAN LORRAH

[*The Bloody Sun* is] a telepathic wish-fulfillment fantasy written by a skilled and talented author who can make it all come alive. This is a rewritten version of an earlier book in the well known *Darkover* series, but it retains the same intriguing story of Jeff Kerwin, who must find and then fight for his heritage on the planet Darkover. . . . Jeff's self-discovery is the same journey young people must always make, yet it is told in a romantic context of secret societies, unknown ancestry, and, of course, young love. The only serious flaw to a reader's enjoyment comes toward the end of the book, where Bradley has inserted a great deal of material to link this book with *The Forbidden Tower*; those who have not read the other novel may get bogged down in myriad references to people they don't know. If they skip that, though, there is an action packed and satisfying ending. . . .

> *Jean Lorrah, in a review of "The Bloody Sun," in* Voice of Youth Advocates, *Vol. 2, No. 5, December, 1979, p. 52.*

PUBLISHERS WEEKLY

[In "**Two to Conquer**"] Bard di Asturien is a brutal, insensitive man, a misogynist who believes all women wish to be mauled by him. . . . One day Bard murders a childhood friend and is exiled by the king. But with the death of the king Bard returns, and (in a particularly unconvincing bit of hocus-pocus) conjures up his double, Paul Harrell. . . . Paul and Bard eventually marry their true loves and actually live happily ever after. This installment in Bradley's popular *Darkover* series is mechanical, hokey and talky. Further burdened by a soap opera sensibility, the book only occasionally ascends to the level of pure and simple storytelling.

> *A review of "Two to Conquer," in* Publishers Weekly, *Vol. 217, No. 16, April 25, 1980, p. 78.*

DIANE C. YATES

Fans of Bradley's *Darkover* series will welcome [*Two to Conquer*], set "toward the end of the Ages of Chaos, during . . . the Time of the Hundred Kingdoms." It is the story of Bard de Asturien, the Kilghard Wolf; ambitious, a mighty warrior, but tragically flawed even as the greatest of Shakespeare's heroes: he is unable to love. . . . Although set on the fantastic world of Darkover, the story is about the most realistic human emotions. Beautifully written and profoundly moving, it demonstrates that the power of friendship and love between human beings can transcend the usual stereotypes of man/woman relationships.

> *Diane C. Yates, in a review of "Two to Conquer," in* Voice of Youth Advocates, *Vol. 3, No. 6, February, 1981, p. 37.*

ROLAND GREEN

[*Sharra's Exile*] is a direct sequel to *The Heritage of Hastur* and not entirely intelligible to readers unfamiliar with the earlier book. . . . Darkover is becoming such a complex world that the "mature" Darkover novels (beginning with *Heritage*) are likely to be heavy going for the reader unfamiliar with the series. For loyal Darkover readers, however, this latest work will be a feast, displaying as it does all of Bradley's great gifts for characterization, world building, and sheer storytelling.

> *Roland Green, in a review of "Sharra's Exile," in* Booklist, *Vol. 78, No. 7, December 1, 1981, p. 483.*

DEBBIE NOTKEN

Darkover is rather a controversial taste—like certain foods, very few people are neutral on the subject. I confess to having been hooked long ago and to reading each new Darkover book with anticipation and interest. The current offering, *Sharra's Exile,* is actually a major reworking of the very weak *The Sword of Aldones,* one of the two earliest Darkover books. . . .

Sharra's Exile is a worthy sequel to *The Heritage of Hastur,* which is probably the single most popular Darkover novel. It is written in the same form, alternating between the viewpoint of Regis Hastur and that of Lew Alton. Bradley is remarkably successful at combining the bones of her old story with the meat she has added in the intervening twenty years and those who liked *The Heritage of Hastur* will be perfectly satisfied with its companion volume. . . .

[This] should not be missed. Bradley does tend to over-write, and her situations border on the implausible, but that is part of the stuff of which Darkover is made, and it works.

> *Debbie Notken, in a review of "Sharra's Exile," in* Rigel Science Fiction, *No. 3, Winter, 1982, p. 41.*

ROLAND GREEN

The Darkover saga is now beyond question one of the most notable feats of storytelling in the history of sf, not to mention one of the most popular. [*Hawkmistress!*], laid in the time of the Hundred Kingdoms, when Darkover was torn by petty wars, is the story of Romilly MacAran, who possesses a special form of telepathy that allows her to communicate with hawks and horses. . . . A very fine coming-of-age story, with excellent characterization and pacing and powerful handling of Romilly's telepathic links to animals; it would deserve high praise even if it didn't have a ready-made audience. Highly recommended . . . for introducing new readers to Darkover.

Roland Green, in a review of "Hawkmistress!" in
Booklist, Vol. 79, No. 4, October 15, 1982, p. 294.

SUSAN M. SHWARTZ

"You cannot take hawks without climbing cliffs."

The ironic realism of this proverb underlies Marion Zimmer Bradley's Darkover novels. For every gain, there is a risk; choice involves a testing of will and courage. Darkover—a stark world of inbred telepaths, forest fires, blizzards, and a precariously balanced ecostructure—is not one of the bliss-filled utopias that fill books of speculative fiction. Unlike such places, in which, it seems, consensus and good intentions promote social well-being, on Darkover any attempt at change or progress carries with it the need for pain-filled choice. From the very settlement of Darkover, after an accident that caused colonists to crash onto an unknown world, people accepted the necessity of deliberate choice. (p. 73)

Starting from **Darkover Landfall,** in which the colony director explains how women, since their fertility is affected by forced adaptation to a new planet, must be sheltered, Bradley traces the decline of women's status from people who must be protected from hard manual labor because they are so valuable and continues (in **Stormqueen** and **Two to Conquer**) to reveal the consequences of this choice: protectiveness becomes oppression. By the time of the Ages of Chaos, women have essentially two options: to provide laran heirs or to opt out—with all the penalties that implies in a rigidly patriarchal culture—into membership in one of the sisterhoods. Underlying Bradley's work and her main theme of choice is specific emphasis on the roles of women on Darkover and the choices open to them. Since their roles are restricted, their choices are correspondingly restricted. Any choices outside the time-honored ones are laden with risk and made only with great pain and sacrifice.

The pain of choice for Darkovan women is especially apparent in **The Shattered Chain,** Bradley's novel about the Free Amazons, or, as they are more properly called, the Order of Renunciates. . . . [In] **The Shattered Chain,** the Amazons (or Renunciates) became a metaphor for female and human conditions on Darkover and elsewhere of being bound by old choices, refusing to remain so, and—through enduring the pain of choice—arriving at new solutions and restored integrity. (p. 74)

The Shattered Chain opens with a series of conflicts that directly concern women. Years after the capture of a Comyn noblewoman and the death by torture of kinsmen who tried to rescue her, she reaches out telepathically to touch Rohana Ardais, Lady of that Domain and a skilled telepath who left her work in a tower when her clan married her off. Defying her lord's ban on interference in Dry-Town affairs, Lady Rohana recruits Kindra n'ha Mhari's band of Amazons to rescue her kinswoman Melora. Because Rohana is the only one capable of telepathic communication with her, she must accompany the Amazons. So she cuts her hair, dons Amazon clothing, and attempts to adapt to Amazon ways. These actions are radical enough for a Lady of the Comyn. But she discovers that life among the

Amazons is not merely a matter of wearing trousers and persevering in the face of fear. It is, as she learns, life in the face of one dramatic renunciation. And it requires a total reevaluation of all of Rohana's attitudes. (p. 76)

The chains that must be shattered in this story take many forms. There are indeed those chains that the Dry-Town women wear, signs of ownership, luxurious uselessness (a chained woman is one fewer person for the work force), and subjugation. But there are more subtle psychic chains as well. For example, the reason why Melora dared contact Lady Rohana was that she saw her adolescent daughter Jaelle "playing grown-up" by binding her own wrists with ribbons. Most important of all, the chains in the book are the enslaving attitudes of men and women. . . .

The shattering of intellectual and spiritual chains is most pronounced in Lady Rohana. Although she has hired Amazons out of desperation, she shares many of the Domains' preconceptions about them. . . . She is surprised to learn that they do not seduce young girls, that they do not neuter women on a regular basis, and that they are kind, even motherly. Once freed of these attitudes, Rohana extends her mental liberation from the Amazons and examines her own world. . . . (p. 77)

Rohana's freedom takes the form of intellectual independence. In this new liberation, she questions most of the customs that have previously bound her. (p. 78)

At this point, Rohana faces the consequence of her intellectual freedom. If she decides that, yes, she *is* only an instrument to give Gabriel Ardais sons, she may either continue to live with him—no better than chattel herself—or she may free herself and accept the consequences of social outlawry. And if she is *not* merely an instrument to bear sons, she must decide what she is to her husband and whether her value to him is worth the having.

She has learned that even intellectual freedom—before taking any action—carries its consequences of pain and doubt. (p. 79)

Here Bradley demonstrates her understanding of human nature by allowing Rohana's reflections to run contrary to the preachments of those popular and critical writers who paint liberation only in the rosiest terms. For every woman who "ups and leaves" her responsibilities, there remain burdens that other people must shoulder. (pp. 79-80)

Experienced, mature, saddened by her own hardships, Rohana expresses Bradley's philosophy of choice to Jaelle: "Every woman must choose what risks she will bear." (pp. 84-5)

Rohana's mental image of "a great door swinging wide, both ways, an opened door between locked away worlds" is transmitted to [others, including her daughter Jaelle,] as the book ends. This door is a choice, taken in pain and renunciation, that enables people to go on to other choices that may produce joy. Opening such a door is a risk, but only through risk can true joy come. (p. 85)

Perhaps the most personal of Bradley's examinations of choice is her work with Lew Alton and Regis Hastur in **Heritage of Hastur.** If the Amazons represent her statement on women making choices, the characters Lew and Regis are choice makers who are important, personally, to Bradley's development as a writer. Both appeared in her fiction from the time when Darkover was a series of unpublished manuscripts about a place called Al-Merdin, a pleasant amalgam of Henry Kuttner, A. Merritt, and J.R.R. Tolkien. In the Al-Merdin stories, Regis is a youth out to vindicate a friend, while Lew Alton developed into what Bradley . . . calls her animus, her private voice in her fiction.

In *Heritage of Hastur,* Regis and Lew are portrayed as interrelated as their bloodlines and the choices each must make. Structurally and emotionally they are foils to one another.

Regis begins as a prince, accepted, but not gifted with laran. Therefore, he regards himself as an outcast, a feeling intensified by his lack of parents and close friends. Lew, on the other hand, is a superb telepath and has experienced the closeness of a Tower circle and of a loving family, but he too feels himself an outcast because the Comyn Council has refused to regard him as more than a legitimatized heir. Neither Regis nor Lew feel as if they fit in. And they both reach the same conclusion: their lives would be simpler if they could opt out: Lew to a Tower or to his renegade kindred at Aldaran; Regis—audaciously enough—into the service of the Terran Empire.

Neither wants any part of the Comyn, which attempted to arrange their lives, marriages, careers, even their thoughts. But where Regis rebels overtly against Comyn control after his friend Danilo is disgraced, Lew rebels against his father because of a cruel misunderstanding. Their reasons for making choices thus become important because they control the choices available. Regis realizes that "he, who had once sworn to renounce the Comyn, now had to reform it from inside out, single-handedly, before he could enjoy his own freedom." His choice is to rebuild. (pp. 85-6)

Regis takes on the burden of responsibility he does not want. And like the women in *The Shattered Chain,* he accepts the fact that on Darkover, choice consists not so much of shattering chains but of choosing what chains will bind him. Choice compels him to shoulder increasingly arduous burdens. And, like Rohana before him, Regis sees how these duties may produce satisfaction. (p. 87)

At the end of *The Sword of Aldones,* [Lew] is depicted as an exile. Regis becomes, essentially, the savior of Darkover by participating (*The World-Wreckers*) in an alliance with Terran telepaths and science. Neither is completely satisfied. Each has lost too much for that. But as Rohana Ardais, wisest of all of Marion Zimmer Bradley's characters, says, "I did not say I had no regrets . . . only that everything in this world has its price, even such serenity as I have found after so many years of suffering." Like Regis, Rohana has everything she wants but her freedom. That would have cost too much. Nevertheless, what they both make of what they have is Darkover's salvation and a tribute to Bradley's realistic understanding and exposition of human psychology. (pp. 87-8)

> *Susan M. Shwartz, "Marion Zimmer Bradley's Ethic of Freedom," in* The Feminine Eye: Science Fiction and the Women Who Write It, *edited by Tom Staicar, Frederick Ungar Publishing Co., 1982, pp. 73-88.*

MAUREEN QUILLIGAN

Of the various great matters of Western literature—the story of Troy, the legend of Charlemagne, the tales of Araby—none has more profoundly captured the imagination of English civilization than the saga of its own imperial dream, the romance of King Arthur and the Round Table. . . .

The story of Arthur traditionally begins as the story of male lust. . . .

In "The Mists of Avalon," Marion Zimmer Bradley's monumental reimagining of the Arthurian legends, the story begins differently, in the slow stages of female desire and of moral, even mythic, choice. Stepping into this world through the Avalon mists, we see the saga from an entirely untraditional perspective: not Arthur's, not Lancelot's, not Merlin's. We see the creation of Camelot from the vantage point of its principal women—Viviane, Gwenhwyfar, Morgaine and Igraine. This, the untold Arthurian story, is no less tragic, but it has gained a mythic coherence; reading it is a deeply moving and at times uncanny experience.

In Mrs. Bradley's novel Viviane is the Lady of the Lake, High Priestess of Avalon and sister of the Lady Igraine. In a vision granted by the Great Goddess, Viviane has foreseen a Britain united in peace under a high king who will remain true to Avalon and the old religion of pagan Goddess worship while tolerating the new religion of the male Christ that is now winning its way across the land. Viviane accordingly chooses her sister, Igraine, to give birth to this future king, Arthur. She also chooses and trains Morgaine, Igraine's daughter and therefore Arthur's half-sister, to succeed her as priestess of the mysteries of Avalon. However, Viviane's plan to insure a doubly royal heir for Arthur goes awry: She selects Morgaine as the priestess-virgin to be deflowered in the primitive ritual Arthur must carry out to become king. Horrified to learn that this incestuous union with her half-brother has made her pregnant, Morgaine leaves Avalon, abandoning her duty as High Priestess and sowing the seed of future tragedy. Thus Mrs. Bradley gives us a plot behind the plot of the Arthurian story as we have known it. (p. 11)

The more traditional story too is all here in . . . "The Mists of Avalon": all the jousts, tourneys and battles. And all the familiar romance and sexual desire is here, with some new additions. . . .

What [Mrs. Bradley] has done here is reinvent the underlying mythology of the Arthurian legends. It is an impressive achievement. Greek, Egyptian, Roman, Celtic and Orphic stories are all swirled into a massive narrative that is rich in events placed in landscapes no less real for often being magical. Nor is it a surprise to find at this time a rewriting of the "matter of Britain" from the female perspective. . . . Looking at the Arthurian legend from the other side, as in one of Morgaine's magic weavings, we see all the interconnecting threads, not merely the artful pattern. . . .

In Mrs. Bradley's version, Morgaine finally learns that she is herself the Goddess, herself the Fairy Queen. In this recognition, "The Mists of Avalon" harks back to the 14-century "Sir Gawain and the Green Knight," one of the first and perhaps the most perfect Arthurian poem in English; only at its end do we discover that the scheme to test Gawain's chastity and temper the pride of Arthur's court, which is the central story of the poem, has been Morgan's. Suddenly to bring in Morgan has often seemed to scholars a cheat in an otherwise flawless poem. "The Mists of Avalon" rewrites Arthur's story so that we realize it has always also been the story of his sister, the Fairy Queen. (p. 30)

> *Maureen Quilligan, "Arthur's Sister's Story," in* The New York Times Book Review, *January 30, 1983, pp. 11, 30.*

LAWRENCE M. CAYLOR

With *The Mists of Avalon* the reader enjoys a new perspective: that of the women [in the Arthurian legends]. . . . Furthermore, the development of the novel depends not on a contest between good and evil, Christianity and paganism, nor on the characters themselves so much as it does on the tension that frowns as a new culture overshadows and obliterates an older one. Thus Marion Zimmer Bradley has written of a present urgency in a mythical setting, and written magnificently at that! (p. 2)

Perhaps the most beautiful and wonderful image in the story is that of Avalon/Glastonbury, separated by a magical veil of mist, two worlds sharing a single island, one tradition on different planes. The passage from the real world to the mystical will linger in the reader's mind long after battles, pageants and Pellinore's dragon have faded from memory; the question, too, of which world was the more real will remain.

Marion Zimmer Bradley deserves high praise for her work since this great and sweeping book successfully ties together legend and lore. Slightly archaic usages and references to ancient events as recent or current establish the period without identifying it, thereby adding to the mythical setting. My only complaint is in the use of "karma" and "firewater," both of which evoke decidedly non-Arthurian images; but these are mere motes in a brilliant panorama.

Read *The Mists of Avalon* . . . and revel in the wonder of it. (p. 3)

> *Lawrence M. Caylor, in a review of "Mists of Avalon," in* Best Sellers, *Vol. 43, No. 1, April, 1983, pp. 2-3.*

BEVERLY DEWEESE

Most readers know the story of King Arthur; however, Marion Zimmer Bradley, in *Mists of Avalon* has written an especially vivid, unorthodox version of this romantic tale. Bradley's narrator is Morgaine, a Druid priestess, and her England is populated by those who worship the Lady (the Earth Mother) and those few who are turning to the harsher, more intolerant Christianity—a religion which equates chastity with good and sex with evil.

The story centers on the struggle between the two religions and the efforts of each to bring peace to England—by controlling King Arthur. (pp. 20-1)

Bradley's many realistic, complex characters involve the reader; however, the most fascinating aspect of this novel is the depiction of the long struggle between Druidism and Christianity. There is little doubt that Bradley sympathizes with the Druids, whose religion, according to her, encouraged sensitivity, tolerance and respect for females. The most lyrical passages are those describing the priestesses and their shrine, a lovely island called Avalon, located just on the other side of this dimension. There is the feeling that the world lost much of value when Avalon slipped—or was hidden—from us.

In short, Bradley's Arthurian world is intriguingly different. Undoubtedly, the brisk pace, the careful research and the pro-

vocative concept will attract and please many readers. Her strong female characters are a delight, though a few readers may be annoyed by her many references to mothering. But this is a minor objection in an impressive book. Overall, *Mists of Avalon* is one of the best and most ambitious of the Arthurian novels. . . . (p. 21)

> *Beverly Deweese, in a review of "Mists of Avalon," in* Science Fiction Review, *Vol. 12, No. 2, May, 1983, pp. 20-1.*

SUSAN L. NICKERSON

[In *Thendara House*] Bradley has pulled together characters and plot elements from four or five previous stories and has turned out another intricate and richly detailed investigation of the roles of women and men on Darkover. . . . With none of the heavy-handedness of Bradley's "feminist" novel *The Ruins of Isis*, this is thought-provoking, dramatic, and engrossing.

> *Susan L. Nickerson, in a review of "Thendara House," in* Library Journal, *Vol. 108, No. 16, September 15, 1983, p. 1811.*

ROLAND GREEN

The latest entry in the enormously and deservedly popular Darkover saga [*Thendara House*] is a direct sequel to *The Shattered Chain*. . . . This book is more uneven than the last Darkover novel, *Hawkmistress!* . . . , and hence is less than ideal as a starting point for the saga. However, Bradley's prose is up to its usual high standard, many scenes have raw power, and enormously serious questions are addressed.

> *Roland Green, in a review of "Thendara House," in* Booklist, *Vol. 80, No. 3, October 1, 1983, p. 222.*

KLIATT YOUNG ADULT PAPERBACK BOOK GUIDE

The name of Marion Zimmer Bradley is a guarantee of excellence. Creative imagination, strong, fleshed-out characters, compelling style, an uncanny ability to make all totally credible combine to involve readers from the first page, never releasing them until long after the last page. [*Thendara House*], another in the famed *Darkover* series, deals with conflicts—conflicts between loyalties, between personal relationships (hetero- and homosexual) between cultures, between short and long views, between personal desires and planetary needs, between sexes, and so on. The question is, Can conflicts change from "against" to "with"? . . . It is a long book worth careful reading, especially by anyone interested in the role of women in any culture or time.

> *S.A.L., in a review of "Thendara House," in* Kliatt Young Adult Paperback Book Guide, *Vol. XVII, No. 8, November, 1983, p. 1.*

Claude Brown

1937-

Black American nonfiction writer.

Brown has used his writing to help promote a greater aware-ness of the adversities confronting the youth of black ghettos. Brown grew up in a Harlem environment ruled by violence, crime, and drugs, where he developed skills as a fighter and thief at a very early age. In his widely read autobiography, *Manchild in the Promised Land* (1965), Brown relates his ex-periences "roaming the streets with junkies, whores, pimps, hustlers, the 'mean cats' and the numbers runners" and how he survived and eventually overcame this way of life. Many critics and readers found *Manchild* to be horrifyingly realistic and deeply moving. Brown's depiction of the degrading effects of ghetto life impressed readers, and he was praised for powerfully expressing his anger without outrage, rhetoric, or sermonizing. In a 1965 interview, Brown stated his reason for writing *Manchild:* "I'm trying to show more than anything else the humanity of the Negro. Somebody has to stop prob-lemizing and start humanizing the Negro."

Brown's second work, *The Children of Ham* (1976), depicts a group of young adults in Harlem who help each other rise above the squalor of their environment. This book was not as widely praised as his first. However, many agreed that Brown again achieved a sensitive and brutally realistic portrait of people who struggle against the corrupting influence of their environment and the indifference of society as a whole.

(See also *Contemporary Authors*, Vols. 73-76.)

© *Bruce Davidson/Magnum Photos, Inc.*

ELIOT FREMONT-SMITH

The scene [in **"Manchild in the Promised Land"**] is Harlem, the street, the trap, and the first word of Mr. Brown's narrative is the imperative, "Run!" But at the moment he could not run. He was 13 years old, a veteran of the street, and he had just been shot in the stomach while trying to steal some bed-sheets off a clothesline. (Later, much later, after he had moved downtown, he would twice be nearly killed again, by police-men who could not believe a Negro was merely living in a white man's building, not robbing it or raping someone or shooting dope.)

Run! But first he fought, which is how a boy grows up in Harlem: he talks tough about "the Man," the whites, and fights other Negroes. When he was nine, Claude Brown was a mem-ber of the élite thieving section of the Harlem Buccaneers, a notorious bopping gang. At 11 he was sent to the Wiltwyck School for "emotionally disturbed" boys, for a two-year stay. Back on the street, he turned to pushing marijuana and cocaine. At 14 he was sent to the Warwick Reform School for the first of three stays. Again he returned to Harlem, and always to the street, the place of growing up.

And then, eventually, he did run; he escaped the street. He went to school; he learned to play the piano; he graduated from Howard University; he wrote this book; he is now studying for a law degree.

What was different about Claude Brown? How did he escape? Most of his generation, most of the "cats" he knew, did not. Instead, they died, in spirit if not in body. They died, he reports—and no doubt are dying still—from dope and jail and prostitution, from never having found a sense of person or of purpose, from hopelessness, from being the garbage of the street and knowing it, from growing up in Harlem.

Mr. Brown offers a few clues to his survival, and gives credit to a few individuals who cared enough to help at certain crucial moments. More important, however, as this book testifies, he somehow found, or perhaps was born with, the right combi-nation of inner resources to survive; early courage and tenacity were somehow tempered with intelligence and insight. He is now able to write, with immense control, about the debasement and self-abasement and destruction of his friends. He can re-cord their (and his own) bitter, piteous and doomed attempts to escape the street through further loss of self-esteem—through pointless challenge and violence, through the masquerade of hipness and exotic argot that substitutes for the sense of mas-culinity denied to Negro men (his younger brother's name is Pimp), through cult-religions, through turning homosexual, through symbolic weapons and irrelevant, useless goals (to own a Cadillac), through drugs. All this he can write about in detail, and without the anger or resentment that he shows is justified, but blinding all the same.

Somewhere near the middle of his book, this report from hell, Claude Brown tells of running into a girl he once knew and loved and yearned for. Now, no longer beautiful, she wanted to borrow money, would pay him back by "turning a trick or two." He declined the offer, but gave her the money, and watched as she got the heroin to take her to her private "promised land." The passage sums up the quiet terror of this book, and the fate of a generation of Negroes who came of age in Harlem.

Eliot Fremont-Smith, "Coming of Age in Harlem: A Report from Hell," in The New York Times, August 14, 1965, p. 21.

NAT HENTOFF

There are strengths in *Manchild in the Promised Land,* and for some there will be more basic discoveries than the guided tour of violence, junk, hookers and "correctional" waystops. . . .

The mobile, vivid portraits in *Manchild* range through all kinds of cats, beautiful and lost. Mostly lost. Friends die of an overdose or take up residence in jail; girls Brown went to school with turn tricks on street corners to feed the habit; his younger brother becomes a junkie and then goes up on an armed robbery conviction (though he does get his high school diploma in jail).

As a chronicler of those years of violence and then of "the plague" (heroin), Brown is expert if often repetitious. (A hundred less pages would have made for a much tauter book.) As an analyzer of himself, he is less penetrating. He tells us of his decision at 17 to leave Harlem for a time and return to school. He tells us of his realization that he didn't have to go to jail, that he could be free of the quicksand. But the process by which that recognition was won is glossed over. In that respect, what should have been the core of his resurrection is hardly explored at all.

Brown, furthermore, hits at only the surface of those social forces that maintain the ghetto. When a judge gives him another chance, he tells him, "Man, you not givin' us another chance. You givin' us the same chance we had before." . . .

Yet none of these fragmentary indictments nor the rising motif in *Manchild* of a growing collective pride in being black brings Brown to a recognition of the need for counter-power in the ghetto if the beautiful cats who make it are not to continue to be small in number—especially as cybernation accelerates. . . .

True, impotent anger finally turns inside. And Brown was able to transmute his rage into a sense of his own worth. He created his own self-fulfilling prophecy. And that's why his story will reassure at the same time as it disturbs the other, white America. If Claude Brown could do it, others can. Through Operation Head Start. Through "quality, integrated education" some day. Through that "War on Poverty" with its wooden bullets. But where are enough jobs to come from for those in today's Harlems? And radically rehabilitated housing—not just one block—let alone integrated neighborhoods? Without counter-power, political counter-power, the promised land will continue to be a desert for most of the poor. And for the black poor, it will be a desert with fewer and fewer mirages.

Claude Brown broke free, but for many black teenagers in today's under-class, the decision to stop running on a treadmill is getting harder and harder to reach. With political and economic power where it is, the odds are too high for more and more of them. And the odds are getting higher.

Nat Hentoff, "Sprung from the Alley, a Rare Cat," in Book Week—The Sunday Herald Tribune, August 22, 1965, p. 5.

ROMULUS LINNEY

Claude Brown's **"Manchild in the Promised Land"** is the autobiography of a young man who grew up in Harlem. It is a Pilgrim's Progress through the deadly realities of the 28-year-old author's childhood and youth during the 1940's and 1950's. It brings to sharp focus and vivid life the desolations and survivals of his contemporaries during that dark night of the Negro soul.

It is written with brutal and unvarnished honesty in the plain talk of the people, in language that is fierce, uproarious, obscene and tender, but always sensible and direct. And to its enormous credit, this youthful autobiography gives us its devastating portrait of life without one cry of self-pity, outrage or malice, with no caustic sermons or searing rhetoric. Claude Brown speaks for himself—and the Harlem people to whom his life is bound—with open dignity, and the effect is both shattering and deeply satisfying.

He tells the story of a generation as well as an individual. In his youth, Claude Brown was a violent hoodlum, a thief, a bully, a hustler, who had to look upon himself as an aristocrat of petty crime in order to justify his being. But his mind grew doubtful even as his fists and schemes were furious. As we follow him in and about his life, from a point where he lies bleeding from a gunshot wound at the age of 13, we meet head-on the desperate life of his people. We follow him along the streets that frighten and fascinate him, into the homes, bars, churches, brothels, alleys, crap games, riots, gangs, murders and reform schools that he describes with straightforward and skillful knowledge.

We know the dogged persistence of his parents in their failure to comprehend their own situation, who must defend their own abject existence against the rebellious rages of their children, and we shudder at the resulting mixture of brutality and devotion. We follow the reasoning of children who must fight savagely, often to kill, and their logic is horrible and exact. We learn the methods of thieves, whores, pimps, pushers, junkies, faggots and cold-blooded killers; their desires and thoughts are so perfectly natural that we know very well that in their place we would do the same.

The great plague of dope traffic that struck in the fifties, raged unchecked and changed the fabric of Harlem life, is dealt with openly, for the author had his part in it. Yet its victims are among the most moving and sympathetic people that we meet. When an older Claude Brown returns to Harlem and looks around for the friends of his youth, we feel the weight of his destiny at the fate of so many of his generation—those who are dead, or those waiting for him to join them in prison, to meet again in the close, incorrigible fraternity of children's centers, reform schools and jails. Scene after absorbing scene joins us to Harlem life, but we always face it through the thought and feeling of the people themselves and never by the pretense of a false objectivity or through self-righteous judgments.

His story is not all savagery, however. Very often it is told with humor. There are moments of delight: the description of

Vassar girls romping about at the reform school with the little colored boys who peek up their dresses and smash up their bicycles; the author bravely pretending old-fashioned salvation, rolling on the floor in his $150 suit and screaming for Jesus, all to get the preacher's daughter into bed. And careful notice is taken of those who somehow grew up intact—like Turk, a prize fighter, and Danny, a conscientious father—who were able to face their harsh lives with realistic but determined hope.

But the final strength of this autobiography rests in the survival of the author himself. How did it come about? What miracle was passed, that an almost murderous hoodlum whose personality was dissolving in the fears of his youth could achieve not only self-control, but a judgment so balanced and a compassion so undeceived? Brown dedicates his book to Eleanor Roosevelt and to the Wiltwyck School she founded, where he first became aware, if only dimly, that human virtue did exist, that the unerring eye of the bullied child for the monstrous hypocrisy of adults does not see everything. He pays understanding tribute to Ernst Papanek, a director of the school. He dramatizes the cold incorruptibility of Judge Jane M. Bolin, who sent him there, and the concern of the Rev. William M. James, who helped try to save the author's young brother from drug addiction. In many places he acknowledges the help he received, but help alone did not save him.

Claude Brown presents us no piercing visions or great miracles that must sweep all problems from the path of the urban American Negro. His book recognizes that no human life is so composed. And while he approves the energy and impact of the Muslims, he will not hold the flag for them or any movement that draws sharp battlelines, any more than he would burden the utterly defeated with futile dreams. He knows that something else must happen to his ravaged, delinquent friends. . . . (p. 1)

Claude Brown recently graduated from Howard University, and will attend law school next year. Again, the question: how did he survive? What did he come to understand and where did his understanding come from?

More than anything else, his book reveals that his personal regeneration came not only from dedicated individuals and institutions, not only from his own toughness and clarity of mind, but from the agonies of the defeated friends he so deeply respected and loved, who have been destroyed. He owes his understanding to the damned of Harlem; upon their fallen lives he erects his own future and his truest guidance is here recorded in their hopeless struggles and brave despairs. The book is written for them, and they possess it most completely. Through it their anonymous lives reach our own and shake us, while Claude Brown's allegiance to them, to himself, and to the children of his generation grows quiet and sturdy, until finally it is solid as granite.

"Manchild in the Promised Land" is a mature autobiography of the coming of age of one hidden human being, whose experience and generation are absolutely crucial to any future history of the American people. (p. 14)

> *Romulus Linney, "Growing Up the Hard Way," in*
> The New York Times Book Review, *August 22, 1965,*
> *pp. 1, 14.*

MARTIN TUCKER

The man who would understand miracles is as dull as the general who drafts answers to an army of rhetorical questions.

Yet in literature at least, miracles have to seem natural—that is, as belonging to the nature of things an author is creating.

Claude Brown's miracle is that from a childhood spent amidst crime, poverty, dope, promiscuity, violence and perversion, he managed to wrest himself into a belief that life could be different and better than that. The streets, as he says in his autobiography [*Manchild in the Promised Land*], were his home, though never his house; his house was a place with which he never made peace till he moved from it, while the streets were what gave him his sense of individuality. Brown begins his book when, at thirteen, he is struck by a bullet when trying to steal bedsheets and linen from a clothesline. He ends it in the present, as a student in his late twenties ready to graduate from a good university. During the course of the book Brown reminisces about his first experiences in "catting" (spending the night away from home); his bebopping jousts with the Buccaneer gang; his numerous visits to Children's Court; and his two years at Wiltwyck School for Boys. (p. 700)

Brown's response to life, both in the liturgical immediacy and in his lyrical retelling, provides an affirmation of Harlem's problems and its hopes for a change. His search is for a meaningful father. He has a real one, whose activity consists of work five days a week, alcohol and spirituals on Saturday night and Sunday morning, and whipping of his sons on any day; but, like all the other boys in the book, Brown does not have a father he can either talk to or respect. The dominant figure in the Brown family is Claude's mother, who, through her excessive worry over her sons, often drives them out into the street. Mrs. Brown's anguish is even soothed by the arrest of her youngest son for armed robbery, because she can at least know where he will be at night, and know that he may have a chance at rehabilitation. (p. 701)

Yet Brown's miraculous autobiography suffers from a canker: the miracle of his salvation is presented brilliantly, but the causes for it remain vague. Brown himself seems evasive when he discusses the spiritual and psychological changes that separated him from his gang and made possible his new life. It is possible that Brown has obeyed too well the maxim of the professional story-teller: dramatize but do not tell; show but do not explain. Whatever the reason, Brown's book fascinates by its immediate power of honest statement and unadulterated speech, but disappoints as an intellectual expression. The disappointment is certainly minor compared to the success Brown has accomplished in his vignettes of Harlem life, but it is a flaw that stands out among his achievements.

The book has the gaiety of adventure, even though the events it describes are grim. The reader is admitted into a wonderfully recreated world: Claude's wings and flutterings, his jail "cottage," his romance with a Jewish girl who tries to seduce him and with whom he falls in love, his friends' descent into heroin addiction, and his own rebirth. What is missing is the sense of how it came about. The achievement of Claude Brown is spectacular, but the wonder and the drama of the miracle that made it possible is dwarfed by the writer's failure to enter profoundly into that other country beside Harlem—the hero's mind and spirit. (pp. 701-02)

> *Martin Tucker, "The Miracle of a Redeemed Harlem*
> *Childhood," in* Commonweal, *Vol. LXXXII, No. 22,*
> *September 24, 1965, pp. 700-02.*

WILLIAM MATHES

The book came to me along with the summer's meager trickle of new offerings, at a time when publishers seem to be lying low, waiting to spring their really important fall lists on the world: *Manchild in the Promised Land,* by Claude Brown. Though it came with a benediction by Irving Howe, I put it aside, thinking it was just another book by an angry young Negro.

There is no doubt that Negroes have much to be angry about, and I am all for anger, righteous or otherwise. Not hate, but anger. There is room for dialogue in that emotion. It gets things moving; someone answers with shock; someone applauds; something happens. Nevertheless, I am growing more than a little tired of the persistent and somewhat high-pitched anger of James Baldwin and his imitators (my ears are ringing), even of the too restrained and too fraught-with-love anger of James Farmer and Roy Wilkins. In such anger there is limited communication. What is needed now is not more of such blatancy, such shrill response to hurt and deprivation, but words that convey hurt and deprivation themselves, words that can permit many people—especially white people—to identify with the Negro. So far we have lacked words that impart the feelings of what it is like to be a Negro in this country at this time.

Claude Brown answers this need. (p. 456)

I began *Manchild* reluctantly and came to weep and laugh over it, finishing with mounting excitement. Although this much enthusiasm over a book is foreign to me—and I know I must sound like a dustjacket copy writer—I was profoundly moved. Although I cannot know with certainty, I think I know now what it feels like to be a Negro growing up in Harlem. There is an honesty here, an ingenuousness, that will insinuate its story under the toughest hides. More than any book I have read in years, *Manchild* probes past the fabric of order and conventional response and finds that place in all of us that knows about pain and terror and the slim hope of being born by chance and dead for sure.

This is a book that insists on an affective response; it appeals to a reader's emotional abilities, rather than his intellectual. Still feeling the effect of it, I want to try to explore some of the reasons this book seems to me to herald a new—and more widely acceptable—Negro talent. I use "Negro" here advisedly. Brown appeals to us in his first work as a Negro, not as a writer or student or chronicler of society. He is a man who is a Negro; this fact motivates his story. This fact is the personal condition of adversity upon which he is forging a viable personality, and upon which he nearly failed to stay alive: between these poles is an identity, a personality, a man. The Negro, transcending his birthright, becomes Prometheus; he becomes a uniquely eloquent, modern Everyman. And it is precisely this quality that is an antidote to and an extension of Farmer's restrained fury and Baldwin's cries of impotence.

No, I am not a Negro and all I know directly about Harlem is a feeling of sadness—and revulsion—from having passed through it in a cab. I cannot say for sure whether or not Mr. Brown's account of being a Negro in Harlem is accurate, or that he is, as I believe he is, an accurate spokesman for that *Zeitgeist.* This is the same kind of question as whether or not Samuel Pepys was a valid chronicler of his slice of Restoration England. The consensus is that he was, and for the same reason that Brown conveys within his book verification of his chronicle.

Certainly, we can check Brown and Pepys against history. Others have written about London in the 1660's; you could walk across Harlem on the heads of sociologists and demographers. But Pepys and Brown convey—and this is why they are read—the feeling of being alive in their respective milieus. Their commitments to their times and lives are their verification. What communicates is their involvement and their lives. Neither is read for his writing ability—Pepys' diary has to be severely edited to be rendered readable; Brown makes all the mistakes one can make in his autobiography, including mixing the language and jargon of his new academic self with the slang of Harlem. But they are read for other reasons, more important reasons than their accuracy and their talent. The force of their experience and their desire to understand what they experience find common ground in all human beings. Whether we write a book or not, all of us are overwhelmed by our lives and are continually trying to forge meaning from the mass of our everydays.

One difference between Pepys and Brown (among many) is important: Restoration England is safely past; we may experience it and we may share it through Pepys. But Brown's story is a tragedy, contemporary tragedy. His has the seed of a greater tragedy, if only a few of us are able to share it, share the feeling of being a Negro in America today. By the time Brown's book is a classic, the issues he documents will have destroyed or transformed our nation and the world, for that matter.

Another difference is that Brown, unlike Pepys but like Robert Graves in *Goodbye To All That,* is recapitulating. He is looking back as he moves on, passing from one world into another with trepidation, regret, and triumph. Pepys wrote within the frame of his everyday, letting it design his narrative. Pepys did not write for publication, so far as we know. Perhaps Brown did not either when he began *Manchild,* but he had the choice to publish or not, and Pepys did not.

In some ways Pepys' method might have been better for Brown. Toward the end of his book, especially, Brown wanders and stumbles between his old life and his new, between the words and ideas of Harlem and the jargon and conceptions of a college graduate with psychological predilections. In some ways Brown's method would have suited Pepys. In it he would have been able to elaborate and extend many of the events of his life, giving substance and depth to them. One way gives the advantage of spontaneity and a lack of artifice, while the other permits reconsideration and gentle perusal.

But these are ancillary issues. The impact of each writer is in his personal life and his individual responses—through a kind of "True Confessions" technique that has been working well since the first shaman gathered an audience around a fire and began telling them what had happened to him in the forest. The pitfalls of this method are repetition and sentimentality, which Brown—Pepys less often—avoids well. If anything, Brown is not sentimental. . . . (pp. 456-58)

Writers like Pepys and Brown are read for a variety of reasons, as recorders of a way of life, a place, a time, as curious participants in a contained and fascinating world, because their personalities are compelling and vital. But their lasting quality seems to be in their literary innocence, their candor, their ability to convey in words something of their experience. This could be said of any writer of merit, as well as the fact that there is in them a compulsion, if you like, which forces them to get at and describe the truth as they know it, to get it all down, the way it was, the way it felt. They know that their experience is important and they communicate this feeling of importance to the reader. In spite of—some would argue because of—their lack of studied professionalism and their literary innocence, they create emotions in their readers, rather than word-tricks on paper. Pepys and Brown elicit different emotions, surely, but still it is the emotional quality of their writing that secures them readers.

But Pepys never wrote for public consumption; his journals were discovered and published in 1825. Claude Brown is off to law school, having shared with us his farewell to Harlem. *Manchild* is such a good book, it makes one hope that Brown would think twice before giving up writing. The civil rights movement could certainly use a non-pious, non-furious spokesman. And, perhaps more important, American letters could use a writer with Brown's instinctive sense of psychological drama, his apparently natural ability to communicate complex and highly evocative patterns of contemporary life. (pp. 459-60)

William Mathes, "A Negro Pepys," in The Antioch Review, Vol. XXV, No. 3, Fall, 1965, pp. 456-62.

GEORGE DENNISON

Claude Brown's story of growing up in Harlem deals at great length with juvenile crime, the life in the streets, poverty, the curtailment of schooling, changes in the attitudes of Negroes toward themselves and toward whites, the role of the Black Muslims among the poor, and so forth. These are all issues of public concern, and this fact has been reflected in the way [*Manchild in the Promised Land*] has been praised and criticized. It has been called "a major American autobiography," "a Pilgrim's Progress," and "the voice of a generation and a people." From a more radical point of view, it has been criticized for its serious political and cultural omissions. In view of all this, it may be well to begin with a few simple and personal words about the experience of reading it.

I found the early pages interesting and sometimes delightful. Before I reached the middle I was rather bored—or not bored exactly, for the book was still interesting, but unsatisfied, annoyed, detained. Toward the end I felt that I was being conned. Within a few days I had forgotten the book—which is to say that it had not touched me deeply in heart or mind. Several weeks later I read it again and found that I still admired its energy and sense of detail, but cared even less for its self-conceit and for the personal cunning which makes Brown hurry on from event to event, bypassing everything that interferes with his movement. And so the question came up of how I should review it. Should I try to account for its ambiguities: that it is vigorous, yet basically passive; that it seems to be confessional and frank, yet in the end is reticent and terribly politic? Would it make sense to analyze the peculiar reactions to it: that, for instance, Brown's accession to a conventional career should be called a "Pilgrim's Progress," as if life in the middle class were the equivalent of the Celestial City? And where did these questions come from, anyway? Why put so much pressure on a lively and unpretentious autobiography?

But the facts of the case are the other way around: the pressures came first. They *are* the public squabble, with all its agonies and conflicts, and Brown has tailor-made his book so as to wedge it firmly into the familiar structure. This is no mean feat, but it is not a serious one. By serious I mean disinterested, willing to serve the truth.

The nub of the matter can be seen in Brown's frequent praise of himself as an "operator." He is so confident of his ability that one imagines he would be surprised to hear his book described that way—as the work of an operator. But that is

what it is—no would-be, either: the real McCoy. And to be an operator takes talent, energy, and daring.

Brown's attitude, in the first half of the book, is the objective, amiably ruthless stance of tough little ten-year-olds who really size things up well and are always shouting out the unpleasant truth their elders are avoiding—and who burst into tears when they find an adult who does not avoid it. The style shifts, in the second half—perhaps with an inevitable progression—to that of the shrewd, good-natured politician who does well enough and never stunningly by the people, the state, and himself, handing all three undeniable goods and buying all three off. The limitations of this stance are obvious. It cannot afford either the whole truth or the whole feeling. Most important of all, it is incapable of re-structuring experience, since it was engaged from the beginning in an act of manipulation. Thus Brown's tale of life does not add up to the picture of a life. Yet it is admirably gregarious, and for my own part I would rather read an operator like Brown than any number of *littérateurs* (James Baldwin, for instance, in his novels). At the same time, however, I get much more from an artist like Richard Wright than I get from Brown. (p. 82)

[*Manchild in the Promised Land*] is not a tale of deprivation. In the early, swiftly-moving vignettes of life in Harlem, Brown is attracted by energy, resourcefulness, pride, style, toughness, the lore and the traits of the hipsters who make it to the top in Harlem. This is largely what he talks about. The boy he shows us is proud of the amount of trouble he can get into, and is well aware that most adults have sadly withdrawn from life. He is not so concerned with hardship, then, as with the resources of youthful pride and vitality in the face of it. If public school is stultifying and pointless, you get out. If you are hungry and cannot find a job, you steal. And so on. One effect of this free-booting spirit is that a great many odds and ends of Harlem life are brought together vividly. One senses a community that has preserved many of the face-to-face customs of an earlier time, and that, because of the hardships and dangers of the Negro's lot, puts a high value on two virtues which have all but vanished from the white middle class: courage and mother-wit. Another effect comes about through contrast. The lives of Brown's street-gang friends lie outside the mores not only of the white majority but of the Harlem majority as well. We are familiar with the studies which tell us, for instance, that sexual repression and delay are injurious, but we have not many pictures of twelve-year-olds in bed together. We are familiar, similarly, with the loss of liberty and self-esteem occasioned by the multiplicity and the ignorant enforcement of our laws, but we are not familiar with the day-to-day existence of the young men who break the laws. Brown's testimony on all these points is interesting. Perhaps it is valuable, though my own feeling is that he has not looked into his own circumstances very deeply.

It is the second of these two effects which provokes such confusion in the liberal press. For who has not been stultified in school or suffered sexual frustration in early youth? Brown's young friends seem to be exceptions. But they end badly; and Brown himself "straightens out." Perhaps there is a sigh of relief in such enthusiastic phrases as "Pilgrim's Progress." In any event there is a curious resting in the status quo, though it was the status quo which gave us all those studies of the ills of modern life. (pp. 83-4)

If Brown gives us more—a great deal more—than tourists ordinarily get, he nevertheless will not let us be more than tourists. He will not expose himself. While reading this book

I thought of the somber pride of Richard Wright in *Black Boy*, and of the strong, sweet spirit of Ralph Ellison in *Invisible Man*. There are no such qualities in *Manchild in the Promised Land*. There is no voice. Brown is trapped in the secondary environment of issues and opinions, the world of commerce and the newspapers, and the need to *make it*. He keeps telling us that there is really human life behind these things—and so there is, but it is only too evident that Brown himself is not much concerned with it. (p. 84)

> George Dennison, "Cooling It," in Commentary, *Vol. 41, No. 1, January, 1966, pp. 82-4.*

DANIEL AARON

Brown lived through the ordeal of early adolescence because he was tough, intelligent and lucky. He cut loose from his parents, came of age in the school prisons where he was fortunate enough to find a few white supervisors who could give him a reason for living. At 17 he had passed the crisis. The move from his home, he says, 'was a move away from fear, toward challenges, towards the positive anger that I think every young man should have'.

[In *Manchild in the Promised Land*] Brown tells his story in the guise of the delinquent who simply reports in the scatological argot of the slums what he said and saw and did. Occasionally, the voice of the mature Brown interpolates. The narrative is meandering and repetitive, its course matching that of the wild boys and girls whose misadventures finally blur into common disaster. Inviting comparison with the work of James Baldwin and Ralph Ellison, this isn't the 'magnificent' and 'tremendous' book it has been declared to be by some American reviewers. Neither can it be dismissed, in the phrase of an irritated Negro critic, as a piece of 'social science fiction' that dramatises the stereotypes of urban sociology. Brown may have touched up the colours of his Harlem nightmare, but like the anti-pastoral autobiographies of Richard Wright and Edward Dahlberg, it sounds authentic and may stand as an honest record of one American life.

> Daniel Aaron, "Out of the Closet," in New States-man, *Vol. 72, No. 1847, August 5, 1966, p. 204.*

ANN ALLEN SHOCKLEY

Two very pointed autobiographies heavily instilled with that very elusive but provocative term called *soul* are Claude Brown's *Manchild in the Promised Land* . . . and Piri Thomas' *Down These Mean Streets*. . . . These two books—widely sprinkled with similarities in experiences, rebelliousness, and search for identity—are suffused with the outpourings of word soul as gripping and heartrending as the blues of Aretha Franklin's soul songs.

Claude Brown, a Negro imprisoned in the festering Harlem ghetto, and Piri Thomas, a dark-skinned Puerto Rican hemmed in El Barrio of Spanish Harlem, relate with deep-felt honesty their rebellion against society and eventual determination to survive during the forties and fifties. Both books in tough, raw, nitty-gritty language tell how two youths are victimized by the inequities of being born poor in a society of plenty, and of having dark skins. Their courage and will to subsist when thrown by family breakdown into the streets is the heart of these personal narratives.

The books, in Ray Charles' blues cry, do not make you "feel all right" after reading. The violence and savagery unmasked in trying to live with and up to the code of the streets do not make for "nice" reading. But for those youths who live along these streets, fight the same battles, brave the sickness of poverty and inadequate schools, the books are excellent for proving that men as defiant against society as Claude Brown and Piri Thomas *did* finally have the sanity to try to steer themselves in a more meaningful direction. (p. 396)

The revealing lives of these two men are written without rancor and apology. The books make excellent therapeutic books for mature, disadvantaged ones who feel there is no way out. By reading true histories of those who have lived, shared, and experienced stifling poverty amidst the brutality of the streets, but managed to escape through self-determination, the books should prove to be elevating and rewarding.

The language of both books is earthy and realistic, but certainly not without words heard or seen before. The narratives are easy to read although somewhat different in style. Claude Brown's book reads like fiction with slices of humor and objectiveness. Piri's book is hip, cool, and swinging with a glossary of the Spanish words used throughout in the back. Even those disadvantaged youths who dislike reading and consider it "for the birds" would find these nonfictional accounts interest holding.

There is no doubt the books are filled with soul. The soul of hardship, misery, rootlessness, defiance, but tempered by the will for survival. Above all, they possess the soul *knowledge* that there *can* be a promised land down those mean streets. (p. 398)

> Ann Allen Shockley, "Two Books with Soul: For Defiant Ones," in English Journal, *Vol. 58, No. 3, March, 1969, pp. 396-98.**

ISHMAEL REED

In case you haven't heard, scag is another name for heroin. Substitute the word devil for scag and *The Children of Ham*, Claude Brown's first book since *Manchild in the Promised Land*, becomes a medieval mystery in which scag has supernatural power over people. They come under its influence because of bad homes, society, and one fellow says he became addicted because he was from the country instead of the city. . . .

The children of Ham don't use [scag] any more and hold views about junkies which lend credibility to a recent New York Times article reporting a shift in attitudes among blacks regarding black criminals. . . .

When I met Claude Brown at Notre Dame, I expected to meet Mr. Ghetto coming at me like a swaggering ostrich handing out all kinds of jive, you dig? Instead, I found someone who talked like the host for Masterpiece Theatre, and who ordered in French. The author of *Manchild in the Promised Land* had gone to etiquette school. "You're the first black Wasp, Claude," I remarked.

Occasionally, the black Wasp comes through. Even Claude Brown can't breathe life into an image like "the rats were as big as cats." Claude has returned to his old stomping grounds, only this time he's the tourist. His predictable glossary, "cops . . . blow . . . dudes," is from an old rock record which provided background music at a suburban barbecue. From time to time the tourist abandons his subjects and addresses the liberal audience this book is intended for: "The common tragedy among these youngsters is that by the time they reach the age of nineteen or twenty they are thoroughly and irreversibly demoralized."

I wanted to say, "they know that already, Claude." They've been told that for 20 years through reports, fiction, nonfiction, poetry, motion pictures, documentaries, etc. Through every conceivable medium and from every point of view, yet the heroin problem is worse, claiming 400,000 victims. There are more white addicts than black and the addict population of Los Angeles exceeds that of New York. (p. E1)

Claude Brown means well. His conclusion is that if you care for each other as the children of Ham care for each other you won't need heroin. *All you need is love!* I wonder what the mothers and fathers of those suburban junkies who've received more care and love than any generation in history with the exception, perhaps, of some child emperors, would say about that. All you need is love. Claude means it.

In the midst of his eloquent, futile pleas, and interesting, often poetical, testimony from his subjects concerning politics (colorful), and their values (flashy cars and clothes), there's a considerable amount of homosexual rape, lesbianism, thievery, murder, and whoring. Mr. Brown meant for his book to be an earnest illustrated sermon directed at arousing the American conscience, but the book will be read as a peepshow. . . .

The author of *The Children of Ham* meant his book to be about some extraordinary people of ambivalent morality who transcended the situation in which they were thrust. But the book will become popular because of the Bowery parts.

Claude Brown has the best intentions, and some of the children of Ham might be touched by the magic wand of publicity and rescued from their plight. But for every bright and ambitious Hamite there are thousands who won't be rescued. Claude Brown is best at writing about himself in the first person. That book, when he writes it, will be a classic, and it will be post-Harlem.

You can't go home again. (p. E2)

> *Ishmael Reed, "The First Black Wasp," in* Book World—The Washington Post, *April 11, 1976, pp. E1-E2.*

ANATOLE BROYARD

["The Children of Ham" concerns] a group of young black people ranging in age from 14 to 22, who live as a "family" in a condemned tenement in upper Harlem, a shell of a building owned, we are told, by the City of New York. They heat the building with gas that has never been turned off and need never be paid for. Their electricity is tapped from the still-functioning hall lights. Its use is never questioned either. Water still runs, just as mysteriously, in the house. There are rats in the halls "as big as cats," and "some of the apartments have garbage piled up in them five feet high, and that makes opening the door a very difficult task for those whose nasal passages are sufficiently insensitive to permit entry."

The children furnished the place by stealing: And then we stole some sheets, boosted some blankets, grabbed a chair from in front of a store and so on. They support themselves by begging, stealing, whoring and similar odd jobs. This keeps them in clothes, wine, marijuana and other creature comforts. Most of them have left home, they say, because one or both parents are junkies. A few have parents whom they describe as alcoholics.

As we all know, Claude Brown published a best seller in 1965 called **"Man-Child in the Promised Land."** In that book, Mr. Brown described himself as the "baddest" boy on the block, and there were some critics, both black and white, who doubted the "facts" of his autobiography. **"The Children of Ham"** presents itself as a group biography, and here is one critic, at least, who doubts its authenticity as well.

If the book were well written, perhaps it would not matter whether it was true or not. Most good fiction is "true" in a sense. But Mr. Brown cannot write at all. "We keep hoping that one day somebody will devise a solution to this affliction in Harlem. The common tragedy among these youngsters is that by the time they reach the age of 19 or 20 they are thoroughly and irreversibly demoralized." These are examples of the author's prose style. If "people became aware of her sensitivity, she would be defenselessly exposed to a ruthless world." "Sheryl has committed so many urbane deeds . . ." ". . . she has both capability and the proclivity for inflicting mayhem." . . .

It is a toss-up who is more boring—Mr. Brown, in his sententious social worker's jargon, or the "children" themselves. . . .

In each chapter of **"The Children of Ham,"** we hear the 13 members of the "family" telling their stories in their own words. We learn that Salt-Noody has a compulsion to spray his name all over Harlem; that Dee Dee believes in astrology; that Snooky is wild about cars and guns; that Connie regards Harlem as a prison; Nita wants to become a lawyer because she "likes to lie"; Lee "would like to get a job," and more of the same.

We discover how various members of the "family" feel about various drugs, about whites, about sex, about religion, about politics. We are told of a drug dealer who has shopping bags full of paper money littering her apartment. White cops "are some of the foulest forms of life." Hebro wants to play football; somebody else wants to play basketball.

All this is told to us in a largely arbitrary and colorless slang. "Scag" is heroin; a "jones" is a drug habit; a man is a "dude"; clever is "swift"; getting along with someone is being "tight"; a hick or square is a "gator"; New York City is the "Apple." These "translations" do nothing to disguise the banality and puerility of what is being said. They suggest, rather, that it may be time for these particular blacks to consider closing the gap between themselves and white society by speaking English. If it is "understanding" they want, this would be one of the ways of approaching it. **"The Children of Ham"** suffers from a monotony of negatives and oversimplifications, and these do not sound any better when they are ungrammatically phrased. A case can be made out for slang, but the insistence of the children on deliberately evading grammar is not so much the expression of a personal style as it is a pointless and uninteresting nonconformity.

Talented black writers like Ralph Ellison, Leon Forrest, John Wideman and Albert Murray can make music out of black speech, but Claude Brown cannot. Nor can **"The Children of Ham,"** no matter how much they ham it up.

> *Anatole Broyard, "A Monotony of Negatives," in* The New York Times, *April 16, 1976, p. 25.*

ARNOLD RAMPERSAD

Harlem is once again on Claude Brown's mind, and it should be on ours. With *Manchild in the Promised Land* and now *The Children of Ham,* he has established himself as the true epic poet of modern Harlem. *Manchild* chronicled his escape from disaster there; *Children of Ham* is his testimony that no such escape is totally possible, that one *must* go home again or live and die a traitor. Brown brings the survivor's guilt to his reportage; this is the story of other menchildren and women-children left behind in his escape though born after his time. The manic humor of *Manchild* is gone. Harlem is an apocalypse and the story is revelation itself. Though the autobiographer of *Manchild* was part Poor Richard, part Horatio Alger hero, and part con man, with the work itself his most sophisticated and lucrative hustle, Brown's best instincts are toward the rational, the moral and the prophetic, and between the first book and the second he has had much time to think of his fate and that of his people. . . .

His literary method is simple. Armed with a tape-recorder and, perhaps, some means of inducing his subjects to relax, he allows them to tell their stories, transcribing their remarks verbatim, filling in the empty spots with impressions, explanation and facts. Of the 13 stories, four focus on the women of the group; one is about its youngest member, 14-year-old Snooky; another is about Stretch, who is close to 50 and a friendly outsider. In essence, though, they tell one tale.

The religion of this community is survival. The armor of their creed is unity and compassion for one another. Each child has been abandoned, more or less, by his or her family. . . . The Devil in their creed is "scag," "the white boy"—heroin; the devil's angels are the junkies, who must be terrorized to keep their distance, unless, as in the case of Lee, the group decides to make an exception. The prime force of these children's lives is fear—fear of becoming a worshiper, fear of becoming a wino (lower in status than a junkie in Harlem), fear of being overtaken by the Harlem fate. The greatest compliment is to be called "swift"—a "swift dude" or a "swift chick"; speed is of the essence, and flight the better part of valor.

In the most harrowing section of that book, the narrator of *Manchild in the Promised Land* related how heroin destroyed his brother Pimp. In *The Children of Ham,* all lives have been warped by its power. . . .

If it has any impact at all, this work should ice, once and for all, the myth of Harlem propagated so assiduously since Harlem's brassy age in the early '20s, during the years when, as Langston Hughes put it, "the Negro was in vogue." The grotesque irony of Harlem as Promised Land in the title of Brown's first book is attenuated, then reversed in *The Children of Ham.* The myth of Canaan persists for these youths, but the promised land is now anywhere but Harlem. (p. 25)

Ancient as a ruin, these cave dwellers are as childlike as their most recent fantasy, illusion or dream. Their urge to rational intellection is constant and intense, if predictably inchoate, and their desire for learning heartbreaking in its misdirection. Dee Dee writes poetry, and Hebro the muscle man, seeing Nita turning in the sunlight by a window, thinks of eternal beauty, but visions and ideals live fitfully in this foul air. Snooky wants a gun and a Cadillac; Mumps, a gifted thief, wants a legitimate cover for his hustle and intends to go to college to find it; Jill dreams of being an actress. Lee, with a BA in sociology, wants to go home to Florida, but a fix keeps getting in the way. Hebro, the athlete, intends to lift himself up into the world of

high salaried ballplayers. They do not see the white world as now more sympathetic or understanding, only as more vulnerable to black force.

A familiar term at the end of the last century among certain liberal reformers concerned the "unconscious moral heroism" of the poor. Perhaps it is fatuous to apply such a term to juvenile delinquents, but if self-preservation is a moral duty, then these are moral heroes of the first order. Though the book is about youth and death, its human subjects are short on self-pity. Indeed, the only pathetic character in the book is its narrator. I do not mean Claude Brown, but his persona, who visits the scene of disaster with an open notebook and a closed mouth. He exemplifies the predicament not of the author but of the reader, the person of education and means from whom the accusations of neglect and abuse in the book demand response. The book itself, of course, is the supreme act of intervention in the tragedy of these lives, but that is to Claude Brown's credit, not to ours. Nor, paradoxically, to his narrator's. Intending to be distant and scientific, an empirical sociologist gathering facts, he tries in vain to conceal his insecurities within a laconic style. But occasional pious moralizings, hip expressions, ripples of self-conscious, nervous humor and crass judgments flesh out a picture of a human being that every sensitive reader should recognize at once. Consciously or unconsciously, Brown reveals his deep discomfort in dealing with his material; this is a glaringly honest book.

The Children of Ham invites comparison with the most successful of those books that record, fictionally or factually, the crusades of children against the world of their fathers and mothers. From this perspective and in the context of the rise of the American city, it is alike in its power, if not in its art, to Stephen Crane's first novel, *Maggie, A Girl of the Streets;* as a book about those young people whose primary gift is a determination to live, it reminds one of the diary of another tenement prisoner struggling for the right of survival, Anne Frank. In any event, *The Children of Ham* is among the more important books published in recent years. (pp. 25-6)

> *Arnold Rampersad, in a review of "The Children of Ham," in* The New Republic, *Vol. 174, No. 19, May 8, 1976, pp. 25-6.*

GEORGE DAVIS

If you lived on a block in Harlem where nearly every family had been destroyed by heroin, these might be a few of the reasons you would find a deteriorating tenement a more inviting place to live than home. "**The Children of Ham**" is Claude Brown's account of about a dozen teen-agers who banded together to fend for themselves and provide a place of relative security in these garbage-strewn fire traps—a place that their families failed to provide, a place to belong, a space to live in and interact free of the "monster" heroin that dominated their homes and the narrow Harlem side street out front. . . .

The youths transformed several apartments into habitable places they called "spots," where they could *be* when there was no other place to be. Here, as Claude Brown tells it, they encouraged each other to stay clean and stay in school, or to develop whatever latent talents each might have. We are not told how much time Brown spent with them but it is apparent that he knows them well. They are a remarkable set of young people, for they have learned how to survive in an environment as harsh as the desert.

In it, they move like nomads maintaining little connection to anything except each other. Unfortunately Brown does not let the reader get close enough to them to see the intricate psychological conditioning that makes survival possible. At too many times we view the youths from too great a distance with Brown simply telling us about them instead of allowing us to get a fuller picture by watching them interact.

"The Children of Ham" is a report, a chronicle of completed action that fails to come alive as we read it. Yet, in some ways, it proves that **"Manchild in the Promised Land,"** Brown's best-selling autobiography of more than a decade ago was no fluke. Brown has a good eye for detail and for the language of this environment. **"Manchild"** remains one of the great personal, nonideological views of life in the rawest parts of Harlem. **"The Children of Ham"** scans a neighborhood that 10 years of neglect has rubbed even more raw, and in it Brown was obviously aiming for the same impact.

But it was Brown's ear for language and the sense of personal involvement conveyed that made reading **"Manchild"** an unforgettable experience. Without this language and the feel of particularity, the author forfeits his great advantage—the authenticity, the storyteller's gift and the remarkable ability to see with humor and humanity what others only partially see through clouds of outrage and cant.

Claude Brown is one of the few reporters on this beat who knows enough to write about it as an insider without sentimentality or false pride. The proof is here that he did the reconnaissance. Unfortunately, he or his editors did not make the best use of the data.

> *George Davis, "How to Survive in Harlem," in* The New York Times Book Review, *August 15, 1976, p. 24.*

CHRIS SMITH

Eleven years ago Claude Brown published an autobiographical masterpiece, *Manchild in the Promised Land.* It poignantly told white America what it meant to grow up in the slums of Harlem. [*The Children of Ham*] is Brown's second book, and it should also have a startling impact.

It is the true story of a group of young, abandoned black Americans ranging in age from fourteen to twenty-two who live in the shell of a condemned and deserted city apartment building in upper Harlem. The whole area resembles a bombed-out city and is ghostly in its abandonment. . . . This is part of urban America through which millions of white Americans commute. The book also concerns "the stuff that history won't even wanna talk about."

In this building and in this urban jungle live the children of Ham. Claude Brown unforgettably sketches chapters on each young person. He clearly records the personalities, the hopes and dreams of such characters as Salt-Nobody, Big Brother Hebro, Mumps Shaft, Snooky, Jill, Dee Dee, and other "Hamites." A family, a tribe of the human race is described—including a "mother," Jill, a former prostitute, graduate of reform school and jail, and at eighteen a stable influence on the family.

The most amazing thing, to me, were the strengths of the family. The children protect each other. Most of them have resisted or overcome the heroin epidemic in the area. They loathe the "heroin worshippers" that nod away their lives on the street corners. The children support each other's dreams of future education, of being a sports hero, of being a farmer, and of running a clothing store. They survive in a most hostile world.

Brown as a writer has once again magnificently portrayed the poetry of human existence. The reader laughs, weeps, and lives with the children of Ham. Highly recommended.

> *Chris Smith, in a review of "The Children of Ham," in* Best Sellers, *Vol. 36, No. 6, September, 1976, p. 207.*

The Clash

(Nicky) Topper Headon 1956?-

Mick Jones 1956?-

Paul Simonon (also Simenon) 1956?-

Joe Strummer (born John Mellor) 1953?-

English songwriters.

The Clash are one of the most important rock groups to have emerged from the English New Wave and Punk movements of the late 1970s. Their songs, which one reviewer has described as "raw and angry," reflect the disillusionment of British urban youth in what they believe to be a repressive, ineffectually governed society. The Clash's musical style mixes funk, reggae, rhythm and blues, rockabilly, and traditional rock with lyrics that stress the importance of social awareness and activism.

The Clash's debut album, *The Clash*, was released in England in 1977. Two of the album's most popular songs, "White Riot" and "White Man in Hammersmith Palais," are overtly political statements against authoritarianism. Although the album generated much critical attention as a significant New Wave album, it was considered "too crude" for release in the United States. Upon its release in an altered form in America, *The*

Clash became a best-selling album. On their second album, *Give 'Em Enough Rope* (1979), the Clash continued to express their political ideals in such songs as "English Civil War," a commentary on the erosion of the English social structure. In the lyrics on the album, Joe Strummer and Mick Jones, the primary writers, "capture the moods of the urban England of the 1970s better than just about anybody else," according to Richard Riegel. *London Calling* (1980) is considered by most critics to be the Clash's best recording. In its experimentation with blues, urban soul, gospel, and rockabilly, the album exhibits the influence of American music on the overall sound of the group. Many reviewers praised its diversity and compared *London Calling* to the Rolling Stones' *Exile on Main Street* and the Beatles' *White Album*.

The Clash's next full-length recording, *Sandinista!* (1980), was not as well received. While the songs on the album are similar to the Clash's earlier material in their emphasis on the power of political action among the working class, some critics suggested that the group had lost their originality, while others contended that the album was too long and covered too many topics. *Combat Rock* (1982), the Clash's most commercially successful recording, furthered their reputation as an issue-oriented group with such songs as "Rock the Casbah," a critique of the censure of Western pop music in Iran.

In 1983, Mick Jones and Topper Headon left the group and were replaced by Nick Sheppard and Vince White. Despite the departures of Jones and Headon, who were very popular with their fans, the Clash remain among the most influential major New Wave bands. Their popularity among both critics and listeners derives from a sincere commitment to social change, their energetic music, and their charismatic live performances.

TOBY GOLDSTEIN

The Clash began their career in 1976 as an opening act for the Sex Pistols in Britain's punk cellars. At the time they were raw, directed, and angry. Since then they have become a lot more polished, but their aim at selected targets is still arrow straight, and they're angrier than ever.

Their first LP, **"The Clash,"** . . . sounded like it had been recorded in a laundry room with a buzz saw as the featured instrument. Through the garbled production emerged such songs as . . . *London's Burning* and *I'm So Bored with the U.S.A.*— just the sort of pleasantries that corporate ears love to hear. The album became a U.K. best-seller and an import favorite. . . .

[They] remained true to the uncompromising nature of both their music and politics, issuing such singles as *Complete Control, Clash City Rockers,* and *Capitol Radio.* . . .

All of these are powerful songs you should know by heart, but you've probably never heard them since the Clash have been anonymous in the U.S. until now. Not that CBS's meager debut campaign for **"Give 'Em Enough Rope"** should improve matters much. A music trade has called the LP an important New Wave product, but only in small print way in the back pages. . . . [The] Clash will not have an easy time of it in the U.S. There is no media charmer like the Pistols' Johnny Rotten in this group, and Mick Jones, Joe Strummer, Paul Simenon, and Nicky "Topper" Headon don't extend themselves to the press. Currently split from their manager, their direction lies in their own hands. . . .

The Clash are not above using a riff from, for instance, the Who's *I Can't Explain* and turning it into the foundation of *Guns on the Roof*—a documentation of several group members' arrest for shooting pigeons. Their delivery is as ugly as the reality they depict. The rhythm section of Simenon and Headon is relentless and over it Strummer's voice is as gravelly as the city dump. As if to reinforce their own goal of straight-forwardness, they changed the title of the album's conclusion from *That's No Way to Spend Your Youth* to *All the Young Punks (New Boots and Contracts)*, acknowledging in one line Mott the Hoople, Ian Dury, and their breakup with management. In the Hoople's case, "all the young dudes carry the news." But on **"Give 'Em Enough Rope,"** all the young punks make the news—even if they hang themselves in the process.

> Toby Goldstein, *"The Clash: The Quietest Debut in Corporate History,"* in High Fidelity, *Vol. 29, No. 2, February, 1979, p. 114.*

STEVE SIMELS

The thing you have to understand about the Clash is that, good as they are, you must take them with a grain of salt. God knows, we need bands that have more on their minds than a fat royalty statement, but I'm old enough to remember the revolutionary rhetoric of a lot the Sixties musicians, and while

I doubt that the Clash will wind up their career singing million-selling love songs *à la* the Jefferson Starship, that prospect does help put things in perspective somewhat. So the Clash's political commitment, however well intentioned, does not impress me particularly.

Actually, given that most of their concerns are not terribly relevant to an American audience . . . , the Clash are already being presented here not as an especially political band, but rather as keepers of the rock-and-roll flame, sort of like Bruce Springsteen, and on that level I find them quite exciting. Oh, they have a lot of growing to do; their lack of polish in the great, early Who/Kinks tradition seems less an act of homage and more like simple inexperience. . . . They've got real melodies . . . , which already puts them head and shoulders above the American heavy-metal brigade. In short, anyone who remembers with affection a neat little working-class combo of a few years ago called Mott the Hoople will have little trouble liking ["**Give 'Em Enough Rope"**]. (pp. 107-08)

> Steve Simels, in a review of, *"Give 'Em Enough Rope,"* in Stereo Review, *Vol. 42, No. 2, February, 1979, pp. 107-08.*

RICHARD RIEGEL

After a few weeks of reverent listening, I still can't say for certain what [*Give 'Em Enough Rope*] is really "about", though I know that I like it a helluva lot, and I know that just as with the first set, I can never seem to listen to it often enough; new facets lunge out at me each time I give it another spin.

Complicating the analytical procedure are a couple of thorny facts: there's no libretto enclosed, again this time (the Clash have always insisted that people not understand them too quickly); and some of the anger-chocked vocals . . . remain absolutely unintelligible to this Yank (what *is* that mysterious singsong chorus to **"All the Young Punks"**?). Mind you, I'm not complaining, nor am I forgetting that the Rolling Stones never went broke overestimating the aural acuity of their fans.

Apparently, the Clash have given me just enough lyrical rope to make me *think* (their stated aim in all their interviews), just enough to solve the concept of the album in my own time, or to hang myself up trying. I've got a long way to go with this album, but that's the kind of depth I've sought in my music and art all along. . . .

Joe Strummer and Mick Jones capture the moods of the urban England of the 1970's better than just about anybody else tackling this present moment. . . .

[Here] are some stabs at a preliminary textual analysis: **"English Civil War"** is "about" the political apocalypse imminent in the continuing decay of England's socioeconomic structure; the Clash are even now casting their lot with the antiwar side to come. **"Safe European Home"** is both an appreciation and a satire of the Clash's U.K. vantage point, where revolution appears both more urgent and less frightening than it could be in the ol' rocked 'n' rolled U.S.A.

"Drug-Stabbing Time" and **"Julie's on the Drug Squad"** are similarly black-humored accounts of (justifiable) paranoia among the denizens of the London drug scene. . . . **"Stay Free"** is popper in sound than you ever dreamed the Clash could be, and celebrates the intellectual independence this band has forged for themselves since they kissed formal education good-bye.

"**Last Gang in Town**" and "**All The Young Punks**" (the latter tune erroneously, prophetically listed as "**That's No Way To Spend Your Youth**" on the jacket) alternately regret and applaud the inevitable passing of punk, due any day now. "**Tommy Gun**" is a self-explanatory, per Nicky Headon's rata-tat-tat drumming. "**Cheapskate**" is odd, but could very well concern a modern miser(?) derived from English literary archetypes popularized by everyone from [Charles] Dickens to [John] Entwhistle.

"**Guns on the Roof**" lines up the Clash squarely against totalitarianism, a stance you might well expect from such an apolitical band of politicians. "**Guns on the Roof**" also happens to contain my favorite Clash couplets of the season: "I'd like to be in the U.S.S.R. / Making sure that these things come / I'd like to be in the U.S.A. / Pretending that the war's all done!"

Almost exactly. The war (take your pick) is far from all done, and the crafty social engineers in the Clash are playing their best to bring the future home to all of us, before we get lost in the past for good.

> *Richard Riegel, "Future Shock Now (If You Want It)," in* Creem, *Vol. 10, No. 10, March, 1979, p. 52.*

CHRIS BRAZIER

The Clash's first album is at last being released in the States. If you can legitimately refer to it as their first album, that is. Despite the identical cover . . . ["**The Clash**"] is a very different album from the one released over here in the summer of '77 as punk took hold and the rebellion seemed real.

Their debut was, as far as I'm concerned, *the* punk album—a classic, even if it's more dated (because it was so relevant at the time) than other contemporaneous classics such as, say, [Bruce Springsteen's] "Born To Run". It emerged at a time when everyone (well, everyone with some wit) was trying to understand what punk was saying, and when some of us, already excited by the youth and the music, were fervently hoping that the rebellion would turn out to have direction and meaning beyond the mere replacement of wrinkled superstars with acned ones.

"**The Clash**", then, was not only magnificent for its encapsulation of punk-as-rock (far rawer and faster than the Pistols' first records had been, angrier but less cynical, and thus a more accurate reflection of the initial spirit), but also for its determination to show the social background of the "insurrection". Here the rage is righteous and not just the inarticulate flailing mass of undirected masculine aggression that people read it as, that punk all too soon became.

This anger had clear origins and clear targets. "**The Clash**" was the response of the young victim to the callous failure of capitalism to create a fair, caring society.

In "**Career Opportunities**" the kid is offered the filthiest jobs with no other alternatives but the armed forces or crime (unless you include rock 'n' roll, the Clash's actual escape-route); in "**Janie Jones**" the boredom of the office job is deadly and the message "let them (i.e. employers, the Establishment) know exactly how you feel"; in "**Remote Control**" the singer is conditioned into accepting his lot, his own humanity discarded, and the source of this "repression" is isolated.

Okay, so these aren't mature political responses, developed and articulate—that wasn't the point. But as a response to an unjust world it certainly penetrated deeper than the "Money. Fun. Boilers." reactionary hedonism that rock always slips into so easily.

Besides, its claim to come from a deprived street level, so unfashionable now, made it all the more moving at the time. The picture conjured up in "**London's Burning**" of the kid running through the concrete wasteland of the housing estate, with cars racing around him and televisions mesmerising the tower blocks above him, was unforgettable—if punk had a visual backdrop, this alienating urban scene was it. . . .

All of these are included on the American album, together with . . . "**What's My Name**", "**Hate And War**", and "**I'm So Bored With The USA**" (the last being another illustration of the Clash's great value—the rant at TV cop culture is predictable, but no one else at the time would have used such a song to attack America's support for the world's right-wing dictators).

But they are jumbled around to accommodate four of the group's singles since 1977, so that the first side begins with "**Clash City Rockers**" and travels via "**Complete Control**" and "**White Man In Hammersmith Palais**" to arrive at "**I Fought The Law**".

The wisdom of all this is dubious, since the original album was punk's quintessential document, and the few Americans who want to understand what it meant will hardly be aided by this infusion into it of later Clash themes and attitudes. . . .

[The] middle of the reconstituted first side is nothing short of devastating, containing as it does The Clash's two greatest individual achievements, the magnificent "**Complete Control**" (ironically juxtaposed with "**Remote Control**", to great effect) and "**White Man**", as well as "**White Riot**" and "**London's Burning**".

Powerful stuff, and I'm glad of my copy of that, yet the end of the side undermines the whole album. The closer is Sonny Curtis's "I Fought The Law", which is attractive enough musically but is nothing more really than a piece of outlaw chic.

"**The Clash**" was fond of dwelling on the battle with the law, but in its honesty it transcended the level of mere chic. The inclusion of "I Fought The Law" on this pseudo-debut mars it seriously at the same time as it asks the Clash an uncomfortable question: Did they get lost in the myths about rock 'n' roll heroes that pervade the self-congratulatory "**Clash City Rockers**" and "**Jail Guitar Doors**," . . . or will they come out the other side still fighting? I'm still hoping.

> *Chris Brazier, "Second Bite at the Apple," in* Melody Maker, *September 1, 1979, p. 13.*

TOM CARSON

As a documentary of rock & roll teenagers battling first for good times and then for survival in a blasted urban landscape, the Clash's debut album [*The Clash*], released in England in 1977 but never made available here, had an astonishing immediacy. You got the feeling that it was recorded virtually in the street, while the National Front marched and the threat of riots flickered all around. And yet the story the LP told—with rage and humor—was as complex, as varied and finally as universal as the American tale of the eternal outsider that critic Greil Marcus found in the music of the Band. Perhaps more than any album ever made, *The Clash* dramatized rock & roll as a last, defiantly cheerful grab for life, something scrawled on the run on subway walls. Here was a record that defined rock's risk and its pleasures, and told us, once again, that this music was worth fighting for. (p. 76)

By patching together tracks from the first LP along with the later, obsessively self-referential singles made before last year's *Give 'Em Enough Rope,* the American version of *The Clash* tries to tell two stories at once: a gritty journalistic account of one nameless punk's 1977 journey through England side by side with the tale of the not-so-nameless, self-consciously embattled punk stars the Clash later became. It doesn't quite work. Because the Clash is a band that redefines itself with each new release, hearing the songs out of chronological order is maddeningly disconcerting—especially to American audiences unfamiliar with the original context.

Though the tunes omitted here were the lesser ones on the British edition of *The Clash,* they added a lot to that record's vivid sense of wholeness, to the feeling of a single dramatic moment caught in all its shifting facets. The new version, by contrast, is scattershot and marooned—full of worthwhile nuggets but lacking a center. Its double focus is confusing in more ways than one: you hear the band wrestling with its legend without ever quite being allowed to hear the music that created the legend in the first place.

And yet, after all that, what we are left with is still extraordinary. This music has a barbed urgency that no one else has ever matched: sparse, coarse, lunging and extreme, it's always—barely, almost desperately—held under control. The later material grafted onto the U.S. *Clash* is richer and fuller, exchanging the flinty, humorous lower-depths eye of the earlier numbers for a flailing melodrama that's layered with doubt and ambiguity. . . . There's absolutely no loss of tension, however. In the chilling **"White Man in Hammersmith Palais,"** the corruption of rock & roll mirrors the disintegration of a whole society—destruction accumulates by bits and pieces, voices shout and whisper distress signals in the background. Then the horror crystallizes and hits you full in the face: "If Adolf Hitler flew in today," Joe Strummer accuses, his voice a corrosive welt of rage and terror, "they'd send a limousine anyway."

If the centerpiece of the original album was **"Janie Jones"** . . . , the thematic core of the new edition is the Clash's cover version of . . . "I Fought the Law." Though its lyrics admit defeat, this song's greatness has always been that it explodes with a triumphant, transcendent pride. . . . Strummers digs into the vainglorious words with a meaty gusto that makes it sound as if he wouldn't have it any other way. "I Fought the Law" is flamboyantly self-aggrandizing in a manner that the group's older material would never have allowed. And yet the performance is terrific, savagely exuberant in the face of doom.

"Complete Control" goes even further. Like so many Clash tunes, it escalates a minor incident into a full-scale war: a protest against the Clash's record company becomes a life-or-death battle for rock & roll itself. . . . Joe Strummer's singing roars up from the depths with a message of no surrender even as the music threatens to flatten him for good. **"Complete Control"** may be the most desperately heroic call to arms ever put to vinyl.

Like Francis Coppola's camera journeying upriver in *Apocalypse Now,* this LP roves over scenes of a struggle that seems as endless as it is brutal. At times, the Clash's melodramatic impulse, their incessant need to fling themselves into the center of every storm and turn their experience into epic allegory,

plays them wrong. Too many songs rehash the same ground: **"Gates of the West,"** an account of the band's tour of America . . . sounds condescending, in marked contrast to the bitterly truthful working-class resentment of **"I'm So Bored with the U.S.A."** But that same instinct allows the Clash to ram home lessons that no one else has put so directly before—as in the album's autobiographical closer, **"Garageland,"** where Strummer flings down what might be the group's credo. "The truth," he sings, "is only known by guttersnipes."

The Clash's militant politics struggle in a void: sometimes they're less the product of an actual battle than an attempt to get people to go out and fight on their own. In **"White Riot"** . . . which is not about a riot but about wanting one Strummer makes his plea as plain as possible:

> All the power is in the hands
> Of people rich enough to buy it
> While we walk the street
> Too chicken to even try it.

　　　　　　　　　　　　　　　　　　　　　(pp. 77-8)

This music takes chances as a matter of course—it never deals in anything but ultimates. But the rhetoric is always charged and pointed with incisive, specific details. The hero of these tunes, whether he's Joe Strummer or just a punk, never becomes a liberal Everyman. Whether he's mocking the welfare state in **"Career Opportunities,"** reaching out for solidarity in "Police & Thieves" (the Clash's tribute to reggae as punk politics) only to abandon all hope of it in the Hammersmith Palais, or finding his old mates all dead or in jail in the ringing **"Jail Guitar Doors,"** the hero's anger, his rough, deflating wit and his defiant spirit remain uniquely his own. The force of character and the sense of the epic in the band's songs, for all their topical urgency, have a grandeur that's almost Shakespearean.

The British edition of *The Clash* was, triumphantly, about staying alive in a wasteland. The American version of *The Clash*—less certain, less fulfilled than its predecessor—is about chaos. The new packaging reveals the contradictions: the grainy photograph of a London riot that adorned the 1977 LP like a newspaper headline is now balanced by glossy liner photos and a helpful (though oddly incomplete) lyric sheet. It's an attempt to make the Clash look more like everyone else. But they aren't like anyone else. Despite the trimming and the compromises, their music remains a crackling live wire that can't be silenced. What it has to say is part of our currency, too. And anyone in America who still cares about rock & roll must listen. (p. 78)

Tom Carson, "The Clash: Street-Fighting Men," in Rolling Stone, *Issue 302, October 18, 1979, pp. 76-8.*

JOHN PICCARELLA

The persistent paradox of the Clash has been that their punk standards demand defiance of the requirements and rewards of the music business, while their artistic standards demand that they work that neighborhood. The persistent wonder of the Clash is how every release is a fresh attack on the complications, compromises and frustrations of their impossible project, how they charge into rock mythology with their integrity intact. . . .

On the picture sleeve of the **"London Calling"** single, two teenagers sit in front of a phonograph with six records on the floor—Elvis [Presley], the Beatles, the Stones, [Bob] Dylan, the Sex Pistols, and *The Clash.* In other words, this band considers itself one of the greatest. By all the evidence, except sales, that is where they belong. Not only did their debut album speak for a movement and sum up a period of rock and roll history, but it made the most powerful and coherent political statement in popular music since folk Dylan—that is, since such a statement became possible in LP form.

What happened after that was amazing. . . . The best English punk band became the best rock and roll band in the world in three quick strides as we waited for something/anything to be etched in American vinyl. *Give 'Em Enough Rope* held their ground, venturing further stylistically and turning their street politics into world-Clash analysis. But the labored-over layers of production embodied a hard-won ambivalence rather than an easy triumph. The Clash had lost their innocence, the stakes were higher, and, especially in the singles released after the album, the result was inconclusive.

Claiming roots of all kinds—[Phil] Spector, Beatles, r&b, rockabilly, urban soul, and especially reggae—*London Calling* is an expansive gamble on greatness. Double albums are like that, either plagued by filler ("Could-have-been-a-great-single-album") or genuinely monumental. *London Calling* is a great one. With its almost-live, thrown-against-the-wall production, it doesn't fuss over that extra level of sonic brilliance that was *Give 'Em Enough Rope*'s aim, but that's good—in *Rope*'s tighter context, one or two weak songs out of 10 were a lot more crucial than three or four out of 19 are here. Mythic straws are grasped and held at every turn. . . .

From the slow bluesy shuffle of the fugitive **"Jimmy Jazz"** to the bright strutting confidence of **"Rudie Can't Fail,"** with comments on both upper-class (**"Koka Kola"**) and lower-class (**"Hateful"**) drug abuse, and from the working-class injustice of **"Clampdown"** to the justice-among-thieves of **"Wrong 'Em Boyo"** and **"The Card Cheat"** to the revolutionary call-to-arms of Paul Simonon's **"Guns of Brixton,"** the Clash translate experience and myth into street-life morality. This commitment is extended into previously unexplored personal realms, particularly the mixed message of sexual equality in **"Lover's Rock."** The history-as-fiction world view that *Give 'Em Enough Rope* developed in songs like **"English Civil War," "Guns on the Roof,"** and **"Last Gang in Town"** is combined with personal experience in **"Spanish Bombs"** to create a past-present historical romance that is unique in rock and roll for its combination of observation and book-learned facts. But I think the deflation of naive ideas about other cultures that occurred in **"White Man (In Hammersmith Palais)"** and **"Safe European Home"** were even more sophisticated and are unmatched by anything on this album.

As in the past, the most personal songs are the ones sung by Mick Jones. The album's uncredited final cut, apparently called **"Train in Vain,"** is a desperate pop-soul romance, and **"Lost in the Supermarket,"** whose bored-homebody lyrics sound like they were written by Jones's mother and could have been, has a similar sentimental feeling. But the most autobiographical song, reminiscent of *Give 'Em Enough Rope*'s **"Stay Free,"** is **"I'm Not Down,"** upon whose street-tough declaration of having been there the self-mythologizing **"Four Horsemen"** is built.

Self-righteous as the Clash have always been, their combination of anger, frustration, street-wise experience and world-class idealism combine here with a complexity that achieves important ideological resolutions. The heroism of Clash rebellion

not only requires the outlaw courage of **"The Guns of Brixton"** and the pride of **"I'm Not Down"** and **"Four Horsemen."** Even as they cry "We're gonna fight brother / We're gonna raise hell" in **"Death or Glory,"** they point to the tragedy and potential brutality of glory underachieved. It is this tension between desperation and blind ambition that gives the Clash's bravado its urgency. And nothing defines this tension so much as the on- and offstage relationship of Strummer and Jones. Their interdependence is an amplification of the [John] Lennon/[Paul] McCartney relationship: Strummer's raw, angry, thick-headed energy and Jones's control and craft. And *London Calling,* by virtue of its variety if nothing else, is the album that establishes their scope. With anthemic force to match early Dylan and the Stones' confidence in their own ability to appropriate and redefine the music's history, the Clash are the great rock and roll band of our time.

> John Piccarella, "The Clash on Main Street," in
> The Village Voice, Vol. XXV, No. 5, February 4,
> 1980, p. 61.

SAM SUTHERLAND

Until now, the Clash has been lionized as much for its potential as for the quality of its recorded work. To a rock intelligentsia frustrated by the genre's commercialism and subsequent loss of urgency, the awkward angles and rough edges of the band's early singles and albums were proof of its authenticity. (p. 120)

Yet this recklessly honest British quartet has been as limited as it has been liberated by the very passion so central to its critical esteem. It has been the galvanic live show that fleshed out the earnest rapport the band sought with its audience, on record, too often the narrow stylistic range and intensity of performance obscured the humor and humanism that emerged so vividly on stage.

"London Calling" transcends that paradox, achieving a quantum leap in the breadth and clarity of the Clash's music. As such, it marks a triumphant turning point for the band, and possibly for the new rock movement with which it is associated. This is openhanded, openhearted rock modeled on classic sources and requiring little additional explanation beyond the songs themselves. . . .

The band's thematic concerns remain as provocative as before, based on the populist ideals it sees threatened by the repressive realities of Ireland, Jamaica, and its native England. If the Clash's targets are the same, its aim is more careful. **"London Calling"** thus achieves a stirring balance of psychological detail and moral force, similar to Elvis Costello's **"Armed Forces"** in its indictment of Western decadence.

Such weighty themes still lead Joe Strummer and Mick Jones to chew their lyrics with angry relish, braying as much as singing them in rheumy, full-throated abandon. But the added shadings here more convincingly convey pathos, humor, and even joy—not just anger. . . . [**"London Calling"**] is far more consistent and coherent than either of its single-disc predecessors. (p. 122)

> Sam Sutherland, in a review of "London Calling,"
> in High Fidelity, Vol. 30, No. 4, April, 1980, pp.
> 120, 122.

MICHAEL GOLDBERG

[With *London Calling,* the] Clash have created a classic rock album which, literally, defines the state of rock and roll and against which the very best rock of this decade will have to be judged. (p. 32)

On this new album, the Clash explore the terrain of American music, even as they reshape it to fit their own purposes. **Brand New Cadillac** may be an out and out rockabilly song that Carl Perkins could appreciate, but the lyrics are as contemporary as, well, women's lib. . . .

Wrong 'Em Boyo updates the folk song *Stagger Lee* with a ska beat and the punch of Stax Records style horns. **Jimmy Jazz** finds the group working in a near blues idiom, while **Revolution Rock** comments wryly on the "punk rock revolution," as the Clash dive into a rock-steady reggae groove.

Lyrically, the Clash remain the outstanding social conscience of rock and roll, railing against materialism, sexism, stardom, capitalism, nuclear power and more. Not only do they make their smorgasbord of subjects and styles fit in a loosely conceptual way, but they stamp all the songs indelibly with their own identity. Probably, it is Joe Strummer's unforgettable voice that gives the Clash their unique sound. On previous tracks, Strummer's singing style was memorable as a raging howl. Now, though he still carries the authenticity of London street fights in his voice, he shows a mellower, more controlled side when he offers a Tom Waits-like approach on **The Right Profile**, a loving, slightly silly tribute to Montgomery Clift that sounds as though it was recorded in a London pub.

The killer, however, is the title track, **London Calling**. Set to a military beat, Strummer sings of impending world crisis. . . . Guitars come crashing down with relentless fury. This is rock and roll to start a revolution; powerful stuff that exhales the intense fire that has been the mark of classic rock and roll: songs like *My Generation* by the Who, *Money* by the Beatles and *Gimme Shelter* by the Rolling Stones.

Certainly the socially conscious lyrics, breadth of musical styles, sense of humor and strong group identity are reasons why I value this disc so highly, as well as the way the Clash weave fact and fiction, seriousness and fun into an immensely playable album that you can think about or just dance to.

This is, simply, the best rock and roll album since the Rolling Stones early '70s masterpiece, *Exile on Main St.* (p. 35)

> Michael Goldberg, "The Clash," in down beat, *Vol. 47, No. 5, May, 1980, pp. 32, 35.*

JOHN MORTHLAND

From the raw rage of their epochal first album to the fiery precision of this third one, the evolution of the Clash has been one of the most engrossing spectacles in recent pop music. All along they have been voraciously absorbing old styles and techniques and appropriating new ones. Although nothing on "London Calling" quite comes up to the three British singles (particularly **Complete Control**) the group released between their first two albums, it would take a real nit-picker to find much wrong with this two-disc set. (p. 90)

The Clash draws on nearly everything that has come before them, but without really aping anything. Reggae, which they have always worked with so knowingly, is represented here by **Rudie Can't Fail, Lover's Rock**, and **Revolution Rock**. But, on both **Jimmy Jazz** and **Wrong 'Em Boyo**, they also dig back into the r-&-b that helped shape reggae. **Boyo** is a classy piece of rock phrasemaking as good as the title song. . . . **Brand New Cadillac** is updated rockabilly, and the music (though not

the lyrics) of **I'm Not Down** sounds like it could have been written by Jimi Hendrix. On **The Card Cheat** the group takes a few tips from Phil Spector. Yet, despite all these easily traceable influences, the Clash still sounds like no one else.

Thematically the new songs are also more expansive, in this respect continuing the progress the Clash's second album made over their first. The lyrics are much less specifically British, more international, with almost as many references to nuclear meltdowns as to war. They manage to draw morals (as in **Wrong 'Em Boyo** and **Death or Glory**) without being overly moralistic; they condemn drug consumption among the upper crust (**Koka Kola**) without ignoring its devastating presence among their own former peers (**Hateful**). And though **Four Horsemen** may ascribe a presumptuous mythic status to the Clash, **Spanish Bombs** provocatively juxtaposes the luxury they enjoy as rock stars with a less attractive imagery: that of the civil war in Spain and the urban guerrilla warfare in Northern Ireland today. And in **Train in Vain** . . . they tackle relationships between men and women with the same guts and intelligence they apply to other subjects.

Call it "punk" if you must, or just call it "contemporary rock." . . . [The Clash have] built convincingly on their original premises and have managed to reach their [audience] without compromising. (pp. 90-1)

> John Morthland, "Ramones/The Clash," in Stereo Review, *Vol. 44, No. 6, June, 1980, pp. 90-1.**

PATRICK HUMPHRIES

Critics of the Clash will welcome **"Sandinista"** with fangs open, as it confirms just *why* they dislike the band so much.

The title alone reeks of the political "awareness" which many find so glibly unattractive. . . .

Fans, however, will find in the **"Sandinista"** package a confirmation that the Clash do still *care*. In hard terms, they go one better than their last Christmas present of **"London Calling"**, and put their mouths where their money is. . . .

For me, the strength of **"London Calling"** was its diversity, the absorption of the various influences—rock 'n' roll, rockabilly and reggae—into the Clash mainstream, vinyl proof that they had progressed, without forsaking their original power and passion by broadening their overall sound and horizons. Testified by the gloriously epic **"The Card Cheat"**, which blew away any lingering doubts that the Clash were forever condemned to songs never far removed from the arterial Westway.

Since then, even the reggae **"Bankrobber"** and **"Call Up"** singles demonstrated that the Clash were still in control, harnessing the reggae rhythms while maintaining their energy as a rock band, while being the Clash.

Yet **"Sandinista"** is a floundering, mutant of an album. The odd highlights are lost in a welter of reggae/dub overkill.

The Clash espouse reggae with the zeal of new converts, like the blinkered socialists who returned from [Joseph] Stalin's Russia with: "I have seen the future—And it works!" on their lips, oblivious to any faults.

Sadly, **"Sandinista"** does not build upon the foundations which were laid during their last majestic outing.

What makes the package such a disappointment is that it represents an emasculation of the raw, urgent energy of the Clash, and suggests—in its bewildering aimlessness—that the band are floundering, uncertain of their direction.

The quantity of the material suddenly made available does not compensate for its manifold deficiencies.

Lyrically, it's as interesting as ever: the anti-conscription testament of **"The Call Up"**, the Profumo type affairs on **"The Leader"**, chronicled through the scavenging eyes of the Sunday papers.

"Something About England" is a telling encapsulation of English life, effective in its stark imagery. Or the scathing **"Washington Bullets"**, with its harsh criticism of American imperialism.

But it's that track, and the romantic **"Rebel Waltz"**, which call into question (again) Strummer's chic rebel obsessions. The rebel fantasies (as on **"Bankrobber"**—thief as rebel, or **"Rebel Waltz"**, its lines about "A song of the battle, that was born on the flames, and the rebels were waltzing on air").

It's the black and white way which the band equate rebels with all the right causes. On the biting indictment of tower block life—**"Up In Heaven (Not Only Here)"**—The Clash tack on a Phil Ochs song at the end.

Strangely enough, I was reading a biography of Ochs—"The Death Of A Rebel"—and had just reached the point where Ochs switched his allegiance from Elvis Presley to Fidel Castro, recognising them both as media manipulators. I wonder if Joe Strummer's read "The Death Of A Rebel"? . . .

I believe that the Clash do still care, and remain a radical, committed band. Their espousal of reggae is seen by some as a superficial, white dalliance with an indigenous black music form. But then, the argument against that is that by championing reggae, they are doing more to stop the insidious growth of racism by simply being *white* guys playing *black* music.

But here, their adoption of reggae, in all its essentially similar forms, is simply too much, the similarity palls over six sides. In the process, it also threatens to diminish the raw, raucous sound of the band who—at their best—were, the best! . . .

The Clash are a band who have suffered a great deal of critical flak, virtually from their inception. I, for one, do not doubt their sincerity; the songs come from the heart, and not the one worn on any convenient sleeve.

Despite their conviction, slogans carry much more power if you can dance to them, but if skanking the night away carries you through, then this is/are the album(s) for you.

"Sandinista" strikes me as a sporadic, unwieldy work. A sprawling statement which comes as a disappointment after the consistent excellence of last year's offering. That aside, I can't wait for the next Clash album.

> Patrick Humphries, "Rebel Chic," in Melody Maker, December 13, 1980, p. 19.

VAN GOSSE

Confronting the Clash's epic monstrosity *Sandinista!* is like being a teacher . . . and having one of your favorite little buggers show up one day and say, "Gee, Mr. Gosse, you know that story we were s'posed to hand in today?" "Yeah kid I know your dog ate it." "No sir, I did this instead." And he hands you a three-volume memoir, in crayon. Thanks a lot, you say, resisting the urge to dismember. Tell them it's fab fingerpainting and next week they want to redo [Pablo Picasso's] *Guernica*. . . .

The limitations of this immense product (36 tracks, they're not all songs) are the limitations of [Joe Strummer] talent, and when *Sandinista!* hits full stride, which is quite often, it's usually because Joe has blundered up the right tree and found a niche that suits him, instead of a Jamaican crooner's soapbox or the pulpit of a sixth-form poetry mag.

Joe's getting on a bit now. He started out busking in the London subways, but now he's reading Marx and displaying all the geopolitical profundity of a bag lady. What a shame. When he was young and dumb he was sharp as a whip writing about what he knew firsthand. Back underground, Joe! Now his teen-dream imagination gets all misty-eyed, and as it's unfortunately more cinematic than literary, turns out crap like **"Rebel Waltz"** with campfires, gallant defeats, and "rebels waltzing on air." Much worse is the *Porgy and Bess* style condescension of **"The Equaliser,"** which starts out with "No! Gangboss No! We Don't Want The Whip!" (I kid you not) and rises to "Geneva, Wall St., who makes them so fat?" Who indeed, Joe? The height of this idiocy is the subtle anti-imperialist ballad **"Washington Bullets,"** wherein Joe, after throwing Afghanis and Tibetans into his righteous stew, ends by invoking the happy Nicaraguans once more and then actually breaks into Mexican bandit yells, oles, general fake latino noisemaking. Fiesta time, amigos: eat the loco gringo.

Despite many such egregious violations of the First Law of Lyrics, which is that they not be too embarrassing to sing along with, the big problem is more strictly musical. A great song stylist can get away with singing "baby I love you oo-whoo baby" 300 times in a row. Not Joe. Unlike the rest of the Clash, he is still, will probably always be, an amateur. In fact, the further they depart from his natural propensity for full-voiced anthemic fervor, the more trouble Joe seems to have. He's been able to stretch in some genres, and when inspired to write lines that scan (music has a beat, so must the words), compose identifiable tunes, and control himself at the mike, it's our Joe of old, better than ever. Otherwise you get sing-song declamation, disconnected melodramatic narratives, and a lot of whooping, wheezing, and hollering. One entire side—number six—is worthless, except for an old Clashsong sung by the two little sons of the keyboard player Blockhead Mickey Gallagher. . . .

[There] are at least as many instances where Joe triumphs, precisely because he is in his milieu: snarly voodooey clashabilly (**"Midnight Log"**); hilarious gospel (**"Sound of the Sinners"** . . .); snappy disco parody (**"Ivan Meets G.I. Joe,"** a thermonuclear mano a mano at Studio 54); even a brilliant, impromptu bit of Tom Waitsish babble, funk, and acoustic guitar (**"Junkie Slip"**). And there is **"London Calling"**'s sadder, grimmer child, **"The Call Up,"** with that patented Clash-march beat, eloquent anti-militarist message, and simple, haunting words that only Joe Strummer could phrase so well—"There is a rose that I want to live for, though God knows I may not have met her."

All this rational discourse does not hint at how strange *Sandinista!* is. . . .

What's the verdict, Captain Hack? Well brother workers, I can only say this is surely value for money. It contains a wealth of new favorites, along with a few a mite peculiar, and a bit of plain dreck too. It seems less complete, more diffuse than *London Calling,* but is in fact a better record—more fire in the belly, tougher playing. Much as I deplore the current moronic fashion of comparing pop bands and movie directors, when the Clash do a (mediocre) song called **"Charlie Don't Surf,"** the analogy is too blatant to ignore. Consider *Sandinista!* the *Apocalypse Now* of pop music: occasionally silly, awkward, and pretentious, but essentially powerful, a labor of love, of grandeur. Whoo-ee. See, in your mind's eye, fat Marlon [Brando] lisping T. S. Eliot amid the corpses, then hear, in your mind's ear, earnest Joe screaming "No! Gangboss No!"

> Van Gosse, "The Clash's Red Elephant," in The Village Voice, *Vol. XXVI, No. 3, January 14-20, 1981, p. 87.*

JOHN PICCARELLA

Nothing could have helped get me through the unreal mass depression—the mourning ten years too late for the death of the Sixties and the Beatles that grew out of the grief over John Lennon's murder—than the release of the Clash's *Sandinista!* a few days later. Its three records—thirty-six tracks to get lost in—ask and answer some of the right questions about violence and nonviolence, history and the future, crime and the law, revolution and fascism, worldwide *angst* and hope.

If the Clash, by insisting on their own heroism, continue their willingness to gamble it all away and still keep winning, they may yet inspire a viable rock-culture politics. Last year's standard-setting—and standard-bearing—*London Calling* was a bold show of strength that doubled the stakes in bravado. . . . *Sandinista!* is an everywhere-you-turn guerrilla raid of vision and virtuosity. . . . [The] new LP is a sprawling, scattered smoke screen of styles, with an expanded range that's at once encyclopedic and supplemental. . . . (pp. 57-8)

In the initial critical confusion over their postpunk leap of faith, the Clash embraced both reggae-dub and mainstream moves for a combination of rhythmic immediacy (which they already had) and studio sophistication (which they didn't). *London Calling* achieved the champion status its grand gestures aimed at by Clash-ifying the extremes of white-black, popular-obscure rock history and bringing them to a common higher ground. Without *London Calling*'s machismo, *Sandinista!* tries harder and goes further. While *London Calling* was a flexing of muscle that claimed Clash style could pull off anything, *Sandinista!* says to hell with Clash style, there's a world out there. By featuring odd instrumentation (violins, steel drums, bagpipes), different production values in different studios, and guest musicians, *Sandinista!* gives the unsettling impression that this isn't necessarily the band you expected to hear when you bought the album. . . .

Sandinista! is the first LP since some of the psychedelic productions of the Sixties that keeps growing by virtue of density and bulk alone, slowly revealing its constantly changing layers of substance over several listenings. Sequencing and structure definitely work to its advantage. The set builds its collection of styles through sides one and two, finally arriving at a real Clash rocker about the time most discs are drawing to a close. *Sandinista!* peaks with sides three and four (the most solid) and winds down with side five. Side six acts as a kind of unnecessary coda. Throughout, there are great segues—not just great songs but combinations that contrast and amplify each other (side two is a perfect example). Catch the shifts from the calypso-like **"Let's Go Crazy"** to the cocktail jazz of **"If Music**

Could Talk" to **"The Sound of the Sinners"** gospel romp that ends side three. Or the heart of the album, the complementary political statements of **"The Equaliser," "The Call Up"** and **"Washington Bullets."** Just when you've begun to settle in, there are some surprise vocals at the finish of side four and the start of side five.

London Calling was the Clash's *Exile on Main Street,* and *Sandinista!* is their *White Album.* Both *Sandinista!* and *The White Album* share a deliberate, diverse, postmasterpiece fragmentation, plus the fusion of whimsy and urgency that going-for-broke aesthetics create. And, like *The White Album, Sandinista!*'s forward- and backward-gazing experiments could signal the end of group solidarity. The street-chant vocal unison of Clash choruses that generally provides the political metaphors (as well as most of the hooks) is essential to the band's strength. . . .

If the ambition of *London Calling* was to recast the whole of (largely American) rock & roll history, then *Sandinista!* wants a place in the cultural traditions of the world. Its lyrics—and its melodies and rhythms—make reference not only to the U.S. and the U.K. but to the U.S.S.R. and places in Europe, Asia, Africa, Central and South America and the Caribbean. And the inclusion of lead vocals by women, children, friends and taped voices, as well as by every member of the band (the songs are now credited to the Clash, not Strummer-Jones), all reinforce the global reach. . . . [We're] offered music and dance as antidote—not only as release but as positive community spirit.

This counterculture rallying goes beyond the already established reggae connections to include other cultural identifications. There are a variety of exploited-class anthems with styles to match, and many of the LP's seeming throwaways—the raps, the jazz, the blues and rockabilly and gospel ditties—serve to broaden *Sandinista!*'s cross-cultural base. The album's title comes from the calypsolike **"Washington Bullets,"** a tune about American support of fascist Third World regimes and how the Somozas' Nicaraguan government finally fell to the Sandinistas without it. The future of such revolutionary movements with [Ronald] Reagan as president, given his secretary-of-state appointment and stated intentions to reform the diplomatic corps, looks grim. The Clash's attempted marriage of grass-roots American and Third World musics becomes almost visionary politics in this light. And that's why the Clash are vital. They exemplify an awareness that offers hope to their fans. Like the Beatles (largely by accident), the Clash (largely by intent) have the potential to organize a rock & roll audience into an optimistic political body, or at least to provide the right information.

But before we get carried away, it must be said that rock culture might be a pretty naive place to galvanize consciousness—and that being the greatest rock & roll band of our time is something like being the greatest serious composer or the greatest baseball player, with the same limited political impact on the real world. Though I don't anticipate Clashmania any more than I expect youth culture to riot over Pierre Boulez' latest score or Reggie Jackson's batting average, I do think that having little kids sing **"Career Opportunities"** on side six is more than a cute joke. If this is the Clash offering one of their old hits as a future childhood favorite, it's also putting an anthem about economic deprivation into the mouths it was meant to help feed.

We can still use that stubborn Sixties morality, and we would do well to remember the missed opportunity of punk—the revolution that wasn't—without the simple postures of either of those under-achieved countercultures. But we also need these postmovement, postideological, private and public "count me out—and in" complications of identification and distance, of participation in and respite from the varieties of violence in the world and the inequalities that cause them. If I were younger, I'd write something on a bathroom wall. It'd be a lot shorter and more to the point. Maybe LENNON LIVES, CLASH RULE and ROCK AGAINST REAGAN. And I wouldn't worry about the improbabilities. (p. 58)

> John Piccarella, "Red-Hot Rock & Roll, a Joyful
> Noise and Politics That Live," in Rolling Stone,
> Issue 338, March 5, 1981, pp. 57-8.

ADAM SWEETING

"Combat Rock" is a fairly logical successor to "Sandinista!" . . . , but it's leaner and more concentrated—still eclectic, not very electric. Lots of layers.

Because of their sloppiness, The Clash frequently manage to persuade the listener that they can't write tunes any more and don't give a toss. This isn't true—the music here is varied and mostly works. Their attitude and subject matter remains ambiguous, though, often delivering attractive *imagery* but leaving you with doubts about its motivation. . . .

The Clash wish they'd been born ten years earlier. They're steeped in a Sixties "radical" sensibility, preoccupied with Vietnam veterans, street poetry, guerilla struggles, death-as-film noir.

So, you have Allen Ginsberg delivering a few lines about urban angst as a preface to "Ghetto Defendant" a song which could easily have been written in Chicago in 1968. . . .

It's strange that the blood and broken heads and napalmed children can seem so romantic now. There's a darkness here, yes, but it's distanced, a zoom shot from a low-flying helicopter. Like editors of old documentary film, The Clash reprocess imagery through the shifting lenses of their music—reggae, some funk, hints of salsa, jungle-line scene painting, a bit of rock.

But is voyeurism valid? You could argue that "Guns Of Brixton" was prophetic, but you didn't even have to go there to know that. It's all on TV, innit? Similarly, "Red Angel Dragnet" here finds Paul Simenon changing the scenario but singing the same song, this time about New York's Guardian Angel vigilante subway patrols. . . .

[This song is] intercut with quotes from Paul Schrader's script for "Taxi Driver"—"Thank God for the rain to wash the trash off the sidewalk". The subject is serious, but the inspiration is someone else's. The song isn't *really* about the people's fight against street violence, it's about a Martin Scorsese movie.

With "Sean Flynn", same again. It's ostensibly inspired by the Vietnam journalist and son of [actor Errol Flynn], but doubtless The Clash have nicked the idea from Michael Herr's "Dispatches" or "Apocalypse Now". . . .

Seen this way, "Combat Rock" is merely showbiz, a demonstration of the boundaries rock 'n' roll (or whatever it is) can never cross. But it's a record, not a book, and the music is increasingly effective the more you listen to it. The Clash have always been able to throw in a few surprises to keep you

guessing, though here the hard, dry mix means you have to work at it.

But anyway, the tough, ragged dance beat of "Overpowered By Funk" is swiftly effective. "Car Jamming" has a persuasive jerking motion fired up with hard rhythm guitar, and "Rock The Casbah" is a seductive Latin shuffle driven by chunky piano chords. "Straight To Hell" is plaintive, quietly desperate. . . .

Result: I like the record, hate the title. I have doubts about the more exploitative aspects of The Clash and the way they milk death and repression until they become meaningless, but I'll be listening to "Combat Rock" for a while yet.

> Adam Sweeting, "Celluloid Heroes," in Melody
> Maker, May 15, 1982, p. 17.

TOM CARSON

Combat Rock—a misnomer; it ought to be *Combat Fatigue*, or maybe *Burn Ward*—really is every bit as chilling a portrait of the artist's failure in the midst of cultural hara-kiri as [Sly and the Family Stone's] *There's a Riot Going On,* with the difference that no one involved seems to have realized it. Maybe not just punk but everything it spawned has turned into a lurchingly ugly sick joke where the party favor everybody sits down on itsn't a fart-cushion but a junk needle; and maybe they themselves are so horror-gripped by the futility this engenders that one of their members has already been dragged down by it, and the rest are in a heartsick daze; but are they gonna admit any of that? Fuck no, they're the rockin' socialists—the agit-prop must go on. So the album's formal content remains public gestures toward rebellion, let the good times roll, and educate-the-masses, while death seeps into the songs privately and uninvited—in the sad weariness of much of Joe Strummer's singing, in the weirdly figurative and near-incomprehensible imagery holding sway over supposedly straightforward protests songs, in the ceaseless junk requiems inserted appropriately or no, and in a continuously attenuating musical swansong that the sprightly production works to conceal—before becoming overt only as a wistful P.S. (p. 83)

The final word for this record, though, is "sentimental"—the source of its not-infrequent affecting moments, as well as its ultimate shambles. *Sandinista!* expanded from (not on) rock and roll just as *London Calling* expanded from punk, but both albums were also symbolic retrenchments: the band quit playing punk because it couldn't be pure anymore, and they were looking for something undefiled—first delving into bohemia's romantic past and then scattering forward into folk internationalism, and thereby falling into the pathetic fallacy that all other cultures were more innocent than theirs even as they tried to graft Clash-consciousness onto same. *Combat Rock,* with its forced funk and well-meant but weak third worldisms turned willy-nilly into the soundtrack for irreducibly Anglo-Saxon attitudes, is where the collage falls apart: one of the most touchingly fucked-up cuts here is "Sean Flynn," which uses Vietnamese folk music to eulogize—not the Irish political prisoner the unwary title-reader might guess, but Errol Flynn's son, who with all due respect got his ass shot off in a war he went to for the glory hunting.

I thought he sounded pretty cool, too. But the truth is the Clash's romanticism isn't tenable anymore, not least because it's running out of real-life objects it can project itself on (the one value that punk still makes necessary). Disbelief can't be suspended over an abyss . . . . But if the Clash are still like the us they helped to create they find it very painful to face head-on a world where punk romanticism can't exist even as a possibility. Instead of doing anything about it, their current take on the grimmest subjects only turns peculiarly escapist, wishful even in its melancholy. I find **"Ghetto Defendant's"** heroin lament moving, but I'd find it more so if I didn't suspect that all the generalized rhetoric is there as much to salve the wound as lay it bare—if it didn't substitute a ghetto for an individual, maybe. **"Straight to Hell"** is the other ploy, the protest singer solving the problem that human nature makes him repeat himself by finding ever-less-known injustices—another reason this album feels like such a grab-bag. (pp. 83-4)

Tom Carson, "The Clash: Cowabunga!," in The Village Voice, *Vol. XXVII, No. 24, June 15, 1982, pp. 83-4.*

DAVID FRICKE

[The] message of *Combat Rock*—the Clash's fifth album and a snarling, enraged, yet still musically ambitious collection of twelve tight tracks on a single disc—is pop hits and press accolades be damned. This record is a declaration of real-life emergency, a provocative, demanding document of classic punk anger, reflective questioning and nerve-wracking frustration. It is written in songwriter-guitarists Joe Strummer and Mick Jones' now-familiar rock Esperanto, ranging from the loco-motive disco steam of **"Overpowered by Funk"** and the frisky Bo Diddley strut of **"Car Jamming"** to the mutant-cabaret sway of the LP's chilling coda, **"Death Is the Star."** And like every Clash record from 1977's **"White Riot"** on, it carries the magnum force of the group's convictions in the bold rhythmic punch of bassist Paul Simonon and drummer Topper Headon and the guitar-army bash of Strummer and Jones. Yet *Combat Rock*'s overwhelming sense of impending doom suggests the Clash still have no pat answer to the age-old musical question: after sounding the alarm, what more can a rock & roll band do?

That crisis of confidence only spurs the band on. A desperate spirit rings loud and clear in Strummer's asthmatic coyote howl, "This is a public service announcement . . . with guita-a-h!," which detonates the album's opening salvo, **"Know Your Rights."** . . . Strummer tries satiric outrage on for size. "You have the right," he spits, "to free speech / As long as you're not dumb enough to actually try it." The joke gets a little lighter in **"Rock the Casbah,"** a smart-alecky, funk-inflected romp complete with snappy hook and spry party piano, about the banning of pop music by Moslem fundamentalists in Iran. But the meaning is clear. Having rights and exercising them are two different things. And replacing one oppressor with another does not a revolution make.

It's not surprising, then, that the Clash are so taken with outlaw ethics, marked here by **"Sean Flynn"** and **"Red Angel Dragnet."** . . . The Clash see in the [Guardian] Angels a mirror image, bucking the system in order to improve it.

For the most part, *Combat Rock* is short on practical solutions and long on the horror of the problems. **"Straight to Hell"** contrasts a bouncy neocalypso beat and an almost pastoral synthesizer whine with a bitter Strummer indictment of the raw deal handed the boat people and other human fallout from the Indo-Chinese wars. (pp. 42-3)

At the same time, *Combat Rock* is stirring, inspirational rock & roll, arranged with god pop sense and shot through in concentrated doses with the imagination and vigor that were spread throughout *Sandinista!* If the words don't carry you, then the manic dance fever of **"Overpowered by Funk"** . . . and Mick Jones' strident punch-up, **"Should I Stay or Should I Go?"** . . . certainly will. Because above all else, *Combat Rock* is an album of fight songs. Whereas most of the false prophets and nonstop complainers washed up by the New Wave await a brave new world, the Clash are battling tooth, nail and guitar to salvage the one we've got, in the only way they know. *Combat Rock* may not have the answers, but it may be our last warning: sign up or shut up. (p. 43)

David Fricke, "The Clash Bash Back," in Rolling Stone, *Issue 372, June 24, 1982, pp. 39, 42-3.*

IRA ROBBINS

From the start, the Clash has made a religion out of being non-conformists—either by rarely doing what would appear to be in thier best interests, or by refusing to fulfill people's expectations of them. The secret to all this, of course, is that they themselves don't know what's next on the agenda; their unpredictability isn't so much a smokescreen as a blank screen. As a result, a lot of speculative writing constantly dogs them. Every new record runs into the same futile argument: Are they true musical revolutionaries, discarding any style that has become uncomfortable, or are they merely dilettantes, easily bored and petulantly moving on to new toys? . . .

London Calling, all four sides of it, took in so much more musical territory than its predecessor, the hard-rocking, love-it-or-leave-it *Give 'Em Enough Rope,* that it left some listeners ummoved and uncertain about the Clash's new direction. Yet there were enough comforting noises to satisfy most fans who were able to hear the Clash building on and expanding, not denying their prior work.

Sandinista! was decidedly more troublesome, No matter how much you loved the Clash there was no way to wholeheartedly endorse the whole thing. They had failed to edit themselves, and the great moments were diluted by the chaff, to a varying degree depending on who was listening. No one could convincingly deny its excellence or relevance but, again, a lot of people had trouble reconciling this new version of the Clash with their prior understanding of the group.

In the great tradition of David Bowie and (now) Elvis Costello, the Clash had become chameleons, shedding some of their past each time they entered the studio. They have always been defiantly unconcerned about losing old fans on new terrain—and some fans found that no amount of slavish loyalty could make the music meaningful any longer. For many, I gather, *Sandinista!* did the trick. Hardier Clash followers will find *Combat Rock* presenting them with a whole new set of challenges.

For a group once so down-to-earth that even their concessions had integrity, the notion of an "arty" Clash album was unthinkable. regardless of an artistic ethos that embraced reggae, rockabilly, blues and more, the notion of Allen Ginsberg reciting poetry on a Clash album would have been too ridiculous. That collaboration, "Ghetto Defendant," works to good effect, but the relationship between this record and the unpretentious Clash of yore is tenuous. If you like **"I'm So Bored with the**

USA" or "**Train in Vain**," *Combat Rock* might just as well be by the Osmond family for all its guarantees of Clashitude.

Before all this gets totally misread, I want to clarify two points. First, this is an almost great album. Second, the Clash has every right to make whatever kind of music it wants, but the band's audience has an equal right not to follow them on their adventures. At this stage, every Clash record must be considered by itself. Comparisons to the previous work of a band with the same name hardly matter anymore.

Okay, so here's the album. It's called *Combat Rock* and it's by a group called the Clash. I understand that the drummer who played on the record has left the band for political reasons. That means this must be pretty serious stuff. And from the first song on the first side, "**Know Your Rights**," it is. This street-corner polemic, powered by a one-note rhythm track, is intellectually interesting but hardly a song. Thus the first challenge: a song that is actually a speech ("public service announcement," Strummer calls it) with guitar. No pretense here, but not really what you expect on an album either. "**Car Jamming**" is a rap-influenced song. . . . An emphasis on percussive sounds . . . make it rather tedious.

Although the Clash has never been obsessed with scoring hit singles, their prior attempts in that direction have been pretty amusing. "**Should I Stay or Should I Go?**," probably the simplest thing they've ever recorded, may be raw and raucous but it sounds like a chart-topper. . . . For a group that tries so damn hard to be serious, this reveals an almost exuberant sense of fun. . . .

"**Rock the Casbah**" moves and grooves, proving that style changes can't suppress the Clash's unique noise. "**Red Angel Dragnet**" throws in a weird counterpoint between *Taxi Driver's* protagonist, Travis Bickle, and Paul Simonon's spoken vocals. The band's perennial fixation with American cinema and the urban nightmare—blended perfectly in the movie that's now taking the rap for John Hinckley—are brought together for a powerful number. "**Straight to Hell**" shows that the Clash

hasn't lost its ability to sound tender and sensitive. It's one of the album's most beautiful tracks. . . .

If *Combat Rock* had stopped there, with one side of excellence, it would have been half a great album. Side two is where all the confusing stuff starts. "**Overpowered by Funk**" includes spoken graffiti propaganda from Futura 2000 and a repetitive, "I wanna be black" riff sound. . . . [Sticking] one track that can be played on what is euphemistically called "urban" radio in the midst of an album not likely to appeal otherwise to that audience seems more of a calculated move than if they covered [Kim Carnes's] "Bette Davis Eyes." Should the Clash try a little opera and some country/western as well?

My "rockist" prejudice considers the non-rock of "**Sean Flynn**" a flop. . . . [This] track (ostensibly about Errol's son) makes neither sense nor a clear impression, even after numerous playings. "**Ghetto Defendant**," the most pretentious item here, creates a great dark mood, even if Ginsberg's words make no sense and sound quite foolish. "**Innoculated City**" trods some traditional ground but even Mick Jones's multi-tracked vocal can't improve a basically tepid song, and the montage with a TV commercial for toilet bowl cleaner is so clichéd and obvious that it's embarrassing. The final track is a Strummer campfire tale ("**Death Is a Star**") set to a waltz-like shuffle with Tymon Dogg's cocktail lounge piano and Topper Headon's brushes(!). It's attractive and almost likable, but naggingly pretentious all the same.

The Clash has built a career on innovation and activism. Their fight for acceptance has been hard but successful. The challenge of consistently battling consistency has made their job much harder than it might have been had they been willing to settle for the easy way out. No one can fault them for their sincerity or musical integrity, but no one has to like their records either. *Combat Rock* is a near-great album, but the budding artsiness it evidences suggests that the old Clash is gone and nearly forgotten.

Ira Robbins, "Entering the Combat Zone," in Trouser Press, *Vol. 9, No. 7, September, 1982, p. 32.*

(Leroy) Eldridge Cleaver

1935-

Black American essayist and editor.

Cleaver was one of the most significant figures of the black protest movement during the 1960s. He is best known as the author of *Soul on Ice* (1968), a collection of autobiographical vignettes, historical and political commentaries, and sketches of popular culture which at the time of its publication was described by one critic as a "disturbing report on what a black man, reacting to a society he detests . . . finally becomes."

Cleaver was born in Wabbaseka, Arkansas, and later moved with his family to Watts, an all-black district of Los Angeles. While in his teens, Cleaver spent time in various juvenile reformatories for petty thefts and narcotics sales. In 1954, he was convicted for possession of marijuana and sentenced to two and a half years at the California State Prison at Soledad. He completed his high school education in prison and studied the works of such social and political thinkers as W.E.B. DuBois, Karl Marx, Thomas Paine, and François Voltaire. Later, in one of his essays in *Soul on Ice,* Cleaver stated that in 1954, the year the United States Supreme Court outlawed segregation, he began to form "a concept of what it meant to be black in white America." Shortly after his release from Soledad, Cleaver was convicted of rape and assault with intent to commit murder and was sentenced to a prison term of two to fourteen years. He served the bulk of his sentence at Folsom Prison, where he became a member of the Black Muslims, a religious sect composed of black separatists. Malcolm X, who was at the time an influential leader of the Black Muslims, became a role model for Cleaver. In 1965, while still in prison, Cleaver began writing the essays that were later collected in *Soul on Ice,* and with the aid of his attorney smuggled several of them to the editor of the leftist magazine *Ramparts.* In June, 1966 *Ramparts* published "Notes on a Native Son," Cleaver's now-famous literary attack on James Baldwin. Later in that year—with the support of the editorial board of *Ramparts,* Norman Mailer, and other prominent literary figures—Cleaver was granted a parole. He took a position on the writing staff of *Ramparts* and eventually became the magazine's senior editor. While living in Oakland, California in 1967, Cleaver met Bobby Seale and Huey P. Newton, the co-founders of the Black Panther Party for Self-Defense. The Black Panther party was originally formed to protect black citizens against police brutality and harassment in the San Francisco Bay area. Impressed with the party's militant ideology and politics, Cleaver joined the Black Panthers and began touring America as their Minister of Information.

Cleaver gained national attention in 1968 with the publication of *Soul on Ice.* Initial critical reaction to the book was varied. While the skillful prose and bitter frankness of Cleaver's essays were widely praised, a number of critics contended that his perception of American race relations was extremely narrow and as destructive as that of the system he condemned. Some found offensive Cleaver's use of profanity and blasphemy in *Soul on Ice,* and many were dismayed by the essay "Notes on a Native Son," in which Cleaver viciously assails the prevalence of homosexuality as a theme in James Baldwin's works and attacks Baldwin personally for his sexual preferences and

alleged hatred of black people. Gertrude Samuels accused Cleaver of finding "a sexual reason for hating virtually all social and political aspects of American life." However, many critics lauded Cleaver for his passionate insight into the state of American race relations and hailed him as a promising and powerful writer.

In April, 1968, two days after Martin Luther King's assassination, Cleaver was charged with parole violation following a shoot-out between Black Panther members and the San Francisco police. He spent two months in jail before a California Superior State judge ruled that he was being held as a political prisoner. After his release, Cleaver was nominated as the Peace and Freedom Party candidate for president, but in November he was ordered to return to jail when a higher court reversed the earlier decision. Rather than return to jail, he fled the country and lived at various times in Cuba, Algeria, and Paris. *Post-Prison Writings and Speeches* (1969), published while Cleaver was a fugitive, offers a detailed presentation of the Black Panthers' political ideology and attempts to eradicate public conceptions of the Panthers as a violent hate-group. Although some critics appreciated Cleaver's candor, most charged that the book contained too many revolutionary clichés and that Cleaver had adapted his language to political fashion. Shane Stevens dismissed *Post-Prison Writings and Speeches* as "mere propaganda" and charged Cleaver with sacrificing the Panthers' cause for his own self-interests.

In 1975 Cleaver became a born-again Christian and returned to the United States, where he faced a variety of criminal charges. Four years later, in 1979, Cleaver published *Soul on Fire*, a retrospective work about his involvement and eventual disillusionment with the Black Panthers, his years in prison, and his spiritual and political regeneration. Critics were generally disappointed with the book, noting the absence of the fiery rhetoric and analytical skill associated with Cleaver's earlier writings. However, some welcomed this new position and praised the work as a mature compromise with the forces of authority Cleaver had categorically damned in his previous works. *Soul on Fire* is often considered a companion work to *Soul on Ice*, and Cleaver commented that the word "Fire" in the title represents his conversion from a hostile, racist ex-convict to a compassionate, patriotic Christian. Some ex-Panther members denounced Cleaver's new political stance and accused him of acting as an FBI informant in exchange for leniency in the courts. He was sentenced to serve 2,000 hours of community service. Upon completion of his sentence in 1983, Cleaver began touring the country as a public speaker and evangelist.

(See also *Contemporary Authors*, Vols. 21-24, rev. ed.)

MAXWELL GEISMAR

[*Soul on Ice*] is one of the discoveries of the 1960s. In a literary epoch marked by a prevailing mediocrity of expression, a lack of substantial new talent, a kind of spiritual slough after the great wave of American writing from the 1920s to the 1940s, Eldridge Cleaver's is one of the distinctive new literary voices to be heard. It reminds me of the great days of the past. It has echoes of Richard Wright's *Native Son*, just as its true moral affinity is with one of the few other fine books of our period, the *Autobiography of Malcolm X*, and as it represents in American terms the only comparable approach to the writings of Frantz Fanon.

In a curious way Cleaver's book has definite parallels with Fanon's *Black Skin White Masks*. In both books the central problem is of *identification* as a black soul which has been "colonized"—more subtly perhaps in the United States for some three hundred years, but perhaps even more pervasively—by an oppressive white society that projects its brief, narrow vision of life as eternal truth. (p. xi)

Cleaver is simply one of the best cultural critics now writing, and I include in this statement both the formal sociologists and those contemporary fictionists who have mainly abandoned this province of literature for the cultivation of the cult of sensibility. (I am aware also of what may be considered excessive praise in this introduction; in that case I can only beg the reader to stop reading me and start directly with Cleaver.) As in Malcolm X's case, here is an "outside" critic who takes pleasure in dissecting the deepest and most cherished notions of our personal and social behavior; and it takes a certain amount of courage and a "willed objectivity" to read him. He rakes our favorite prejudices with the savage claws of his prose until our wounds are bare, our psyche is exposed, and we must either fight back or laugh with him for the service he has done us. For the "souls of black folk," in W.E.B. Du Bois' phrase, are the best mirror in which to see the white American self in mid-twentieth century.

It takes a certain boldness on Cleaver's part, also, to open this collection of essays with the section not merely on rape but on the whole profound relationship of black men and white women. There is a secret kind of sexual mysticism in this writer which adds depth and tone to his social commentary; this is a highly literary and imaginative mind surveying the salient aspects of our common life. There follow the Four Vignettes—on Watts, on the Muslims, on Catholicism and Thomas Merton, and on the heroic prison teacher called [Chris] Lovdjieff. Here we begin to feel the reach and depth of Eldridge Cleaver's mind on emotional and philosophical issues as well as historical and social ones—and yes, "heroic," a note barely sounded in contemporary fiction, is not inappropriate for certain parts of this deeply revolutionary collection of essays. (pp. xii-xiii)

But it is the part of the book called "Blood of the Beast," and such pieces as "The White Race and Its Heroes," that I find of primary importance, and of the greatest literary value. Describing himself as an "Ofay Watcher," Cleaver describes this historical period and this American culture in terms of the most astringent accuracy, the most ruthless irony, and the most insistent truthfulness. He reminds us of all the simple verities that decades of Cold War distortion and hypocrisy have almost wiped from our historical record—our historical consciousness.

The book is a handsome account of those years in the early sixties when the Civil Rights campaign stirred up a national psyche that had been unnaturally comatose, slothful, and evasive since the McCarthyite trauma. There is an atmosphere of turbulence in these essays, moving from the advent of the Beats and Jack Kerouac's *On The Road* to LeRoi Jones' revolutionary verses and then back to the Abolitionists (so scorned and despised by the Southern revisionist historians of the modern epoch), to Harriet Beecher Stowe and to that famous Fourth of July peroration for the slave race by Frederick Douglass in 1852.

In the concluding part of this book it seems that Eldridge Cleaver has reached his own spiritual convalescence, his healed spirit (no longer racist or narrowly nationalist), and his mature power as a writer—and how those pages do sparkle! . . . **"Notes on a Native Son"** is the best analysis of James Baldwin's literary career I have read; and while Cleaver calmly says things that no white critic could really dare to say, there is not a trace of petty artistic jealousy or self-vanity in his discussion—such as that, for example, which marked Baldwin's own repudiation of his former mentor, Richard Wright. The essay called "Rallying Round the Flag" gives us the plain, hard, truthful Afro-American view of the Vietnam war which Martin Luther King, just lately, has corroborated—it is in fact the world view of our aberrant national behavior in southeast Asia. But just as this volume opens on the theme of love, just as Eldridge Cleaver never misses the sexual core of every social (or racial) phenomenon, so it closes on it. (pp. xiii-xv)

I had forgotten to mention the wonderfully ironic descriptions of the Twist as the social symptom of the new age of dawning racial equality. Here, as with the Beatles and Rock n' Roll, when Eldridge Cleaver moves into the area of mass entertainment in the United States, he is as close as he ever comes to an open laughter at the white man's antics; just as in the concluding apostrophe from the Black Eunuch to the Black Queen—to the fertile black womb of all history—he reminds us how civilization has always mocked human gaiety. (p. xv)

Maxwell Geismar, in an introduction to Soul on Ice *by Eldridge Cleaver, Delta, 1968, pp. xi-xv.*

RICHARD GILMAN

[The following essay was first published in The New Republic, *March 9, 1968.]*

There is a growing body of black writing which is not to be thought of simply as writing by blacks. It is not something susceptible of being democratized and assimilated in the same way that writing by Jews has been. The movement there was, very roughly, from Jewish writing to Jewish-American writing to writing by authors "who happen to be Jews." But the new black writing I am talking about isn't the work of authors who *happen* to be black; it doesn't make up the kind of movement within a broader culture by which minorities, such as the Jews or the Southerners in our own society, contribute from their special cast of mind and imagination and their particular historical and psychic backgrounds something "universal," increments to the literary or intellectual traditions.

These black writers I am speaking of take their blackness not as a starting point for literature or thought and not as a marshaling ground for a position in the parade of national images and forms, but as absolute theme and necessity. They make philosophies and fantasias out of their color, use it as weapon and seat of judgment, as strategy and outcry, source of possible rebirth, data for a future existence and agency of revolutionary change. For such men and women, to write is an almost literal means of survival and attack, a means—more radically than we have known it—to *be,* and their writing owes more, consciously at least, to the embattled historical moment in which black Americans find themselves than to what is ordinarily thought of as literary expression or the ongoing elaboration of ideas. (pp. 3-4)

The black man doesn't feel the way whites do, nor does he think as whites do—at the point, that is, when feeling and thought have moved beyond pure physical sensation or problems in mathematics. "Prick me and I bleed," Shylock rightly said, but the difference begins when the attitude to the blood is in question: black suffering is not of the same kind as ours. Under the great flawless arc of the Greco-Roman and Judeo-Christian traditions we have implicitly believed that all men experience essentially the same things, that birth, love, pain, self, death, are universals; they are in fact what we mean by universal values in literature and consciousness. But the black man has found it almost impossible in America to experience the universal as such; this power, after all, is conferred upon the individual, or rather confirmed for him, by his membership in the community of men. Imagine how it must be to know that you have not the right to feel that your birth, your pain, your joy or your death are proper, natural elements of the human universe, but are, as it were, interlopers, unsanctioned realities, to be experienced on sufferance and without communal acknowledgment.

"We shall have our manhood. We shall have it or the earth will be leveled by our attempts to gain it." So writes Eldridge Cleaver in his book, *Soul on Ice,* a collection of letters, essays, reflections and reports from his life which go to make up a spiritual and intellectual autobiography that stands at the exact resonant center of the new black writing I have been referring to. Cleaver's book is in the tradition—that just-formed current—of Malcolm X's, and the latter is its mentor in the fullest sense. Unsparing, unaccommodating, tough and lyrical by turns, foolish at times, unconvincing in many of its specific ideas but extraordinarily convincing in the energy and hard morale of its thinking, painful, aggressive and undaunted, *Soul on Ice* is a book for which we have to make room, but not on the shelves we have already built. (pp. 5-6)

[Cleaver] has his eye on a hundred manifestations of American ugliness or depravity or dishonesty, but he is not a social critic for *our* sake: his is a Negro perspective, sight issuing from the "furious psychic stance of the Negro today," and in its victories of understanding, its blindness and incompletions, its clean or inchoate energies, its internal motives and justifications, his writing remains in some profound sense not subject to correction or emendation or, most centrally, approval or rejection by those of us who are not black.

I know this is likely to be misunderstood. We have all considered the chief thing we should be working toward is that state of disinterestedness, of "higher" truth and independent valuation, which would allow us, white and black, to see each other's minds and bodies free of the distortions of race, to recognize each other's gifts and deficiencies as gifts and deficiencies, to be able to quarrel as the members of an (ideal) family do and not as embattled tribes. We want to be able to say without self-consciousness or inverted snobbery that such and such a Negro is a bastard or a lousy writer.

But we are nowhere near that stage and in some ways we are moving farther from it as polarization increases. And my point has been that it would be better for all of us if we recognized that in the present phase of interracial existence in America moral and intellectual "truths" have not the same reality for blacks and whites, and that even to write is, for many blacks, a particular act within the fact of their Negritude, not the independent universal "luxury" work we at least partly and ideally conceive it to be. (p. 9)

Cleaver's book devotes a great deal of space to his elaboration of a structure of thought, a legend really, about the nature of sexuality in America today. Some of it is grand, old-fashioned Lawrentian and Maileresque mythmaking. . . . Some of it is a Marxist-oriented analysis which ends by creating certain large controlling figures with which to account for experience. These are the white man, the Omnipotent Adminstrator, the white woman, the Ultrafeminine, the black man, the Supermasculine Menial; and the black woman, the Subfeminine Amazon. Sexually each has been forced into a role, as a result of his or her position in the society, and this frozen typology is what we have to battle against.

I find it unsatisfying intellectually, schematic and unsubtle most of the time. I don't want to hear again that the white man has been cut off from his body or that the black male has been forced back into his, that the black penis is more alive or the white woman's sexuality is artificial and contrived. Yet I don't want to condemn it, and I am not sure I know how to acknowledge it without seeming patronizing. For Cleaver has composed a myth to try to account for certain realities, black realities more than white ones: the fascination of black men with white standards of female beauty, the painfulness of having one's sexuality imprisoned within class or racial lines, the refusal of the society to credit the black man with a mind, the split between black men and women.

He knows what he is talking *from,* if not fully what he is talking *about,* and it is not my right to compare his thinking with other "classic" ways of grappling with sexual experience and drama; it isn't my right to draw him into the Western academy and subject his findings to the scrutiny of the tradition. A myth, moreover, is not really analyzable and certainly not something which one can call untrue.

But Cleaver gets me off the hook, I think, by providing me with a very beautiful section to quote, a letter **"To All Black Women, From All Black Men,"** in which ideas are subordinated to intense feeling and in which the myth's unassailable usefulness is there to see. In it he addresses the black woman as "Queen-Mother-Daughter of Africa, Sister of My Soul, Black Bride of My Passion, My Eternal Love," and begs forgiveness for having abandoned her and allowed her to lose her sense of womanness. The last lines of the letter, and the book, make up an enormously impressive fusion of Cleaver's various revolutionary strands, his assertion of a black reality, his hunger for sexual fullness and the reintegration of the self, his political critique and program and sense of a devastated society in need of resurrection. . . . The passage is not addressed to me, and though I have called it beautiful and impressive and so on, that is out of the habit of the judge-critic, and I don't wish to continue in this strange and very contemporary form of injustice, that of sanctioning black thought from the standpoint of white criteria. I will go on judging and elucidating novels and plays and poetry by blacks according to what general powers I possess, but the kind of *black writing* I have been talking about, the act of creation of the self in the face of that self's historic denial by our society, seems to me to be at this point beyond my right to intrude on. (pp. 10-12)

Richard Gilman, "White Standards and Black Writing," in his The Confusion of Realms, *Random House, 1969, pp. 3-12.**

DAVID EVANIER

The style throughout [*Soul on Ice*] is pop Leftism, a mixture of sex and revolution characteristic of the New Left around the world. . . . Horst Krueger describes this combination as it appears in West Germany: "the era of Sex and Socialism. Eros is on the Left and beautiful is our youthful rebellion. Make love and carry the banner of the Vietcong high." Cleaver adds to this a brashly violent note and a sure literary talent. . . .

A Black Muslim who renounced Elijah Muhammed's teachings to join Malcolm X, Cleaver pronounces the white world doomed. Differentiating good white people from bad, however, he sees young white radicals joining Negroes in building a Socialism in the United States that is similar to "third world" Marxism.

More interesting is Cleaver's obsession with white women: "It intensified my frustrations to know that I was indoctrinated to see the white woman as more beautiful and desirable than my own black woman." About the white woman who caused Emmett Till's murder by accusing him of flirting with her, he writes: "I looked at her picture again and again, and in spite of everything and against my will and the hate I felt for the woman and all that she represented, she appealed to me." (p. 23)

The subject recurs, but Cleaver never really deals with it in depth, although sexual love for whites is the basis on which he condemns James Baldwin [in his essay **"Notes on a Native Son"**]. He considers Baldwin a prisoner of his lust for white men, and compares him unfavorably with Richard Wright. Addressing him as "Sugar," he says that Baldwin's character in *Another Country*, Rufus Scott, "the weak craven-hearted ghost," is to Bigger Thomas in *Native Son*, "the black rebel of the ghetto and a man," what Baldwin is to "the fallen giant," Wright. For Baldwin, "the only way out . . . psychologically is to embrace Africa, the land of his fathers, which he refuses to do." Richard Wright "reigns supreme for his

profound political, economic and social reference"; Baldwin's "characters all seem to be fucking and sucking in a vacuum."

At the close of this essay on Baldwin, Cleaver points to the prophets: "'Will the machine gunners please step forward,' said Leroi Jones in a poem. 'The machine gun on the corner,' wrote Richard Wright, 'is the symbol of the 20th century.'" And, of course, [Norman] Mailer: "There's a shit-storm coming."

In an essay in *Notes of a Native Son*, James Baldwin observed, "the reality of man as a social being is not his only reality and that artist is strangled who is forced to deal with human beings solely in social terms." Cleaver restricts his own potential, confining his writing to a series of machine-gun blasts that capture the mood of the black militants. He reveals an innate gift for language at every turn, but he makes it the servant of the fashions of a political movement. When the movement assumes new directions (one assumes that the trend toward nihilism and self-destruction ultimately will change), hopefully Cleaver will find that his stylish Leftism was a small achievement measured against the talent he could develop if he tries. (pp. 23-4)

[By] forcing all his experiences into a social mold, he too often excludes complexity, ambiguity, the variety of human beings. His people are millions of black cardboard figures getting into revolutionary formation. Not one distinguishable human being, not one unique personality, appears in these pages. Not even Cleaver himself. (p. 24)

David Evanier, "Painting Black Cardboard Figures," in The New Leader, *Vol. LI, No. 7, March 25, 1968, pp. 23-4.**

SHANE STEVENS

Soul on Ice is a collection of essays straight out of Dante's *Inferno*. The hell is there, and its name is America. Cleaver takes the reader on a journey down into the bowels of the nation, stopping to explore many of the levels of suffering. What he has to say about the black man in America, about the mystique of the white woman, about black heroes and villains, about Vietnam, and about the whole insane racial fabric of this country is said with freshness and insight and a power of conviction that will frighten those who like their truths diluted. As with Malcolm X, Cleaver's book is a spiritual autobiography. An odyssey of a soul in search of itself, groping toward a personal humanism which will give meaning to life.

Because this quest for individual dignity is at the core of the central dilemma of our times, this book is important. Because Cleaver has the consummate skill to express the inexpressible— to give shape to the time-bomb ticking in the black man's skull—this book is extraordinary. I welcome Eldridge Cleaver as a soul brother in despair. I welcome him also as an individual who is attempting in his writing to carve out a life style of his own.

Let those who would deny the book's essential truth deny it. Let those who would question the book's horrific vision question it. But let the white man no longer ask what the black man wants and why.

Where does Cleaver go from here? What happens to Cleaver, the black writer, depends on what happens to Cleaver, the black man. For those of us who believe that the writer must grapple with the moral issues of his day, that he must view himself in the context of events and not just from his own personal needs, these are dangerous times. The urge to be a full-time revolutionary in a country so desperately ill is overwhelming. Yet the writer must always retain a certain part of himself on the periphery of events if he is to be most effective. At last, one can only support the other, much as a rope supports a hanged man. Many of us are hanging in this year of fire, 1968. And America is hanging with us. Make no mistake about it. Barring unimaginable change, by summer this country will be a riot of color. And I am not speaking about the tulip beds along the Potomac. And neither is Eldridge Cleaver when he says that ''no Slave should die a natural death. There is a point where Caution ends and Cowardice begins.''

That is the point of no return. And for the American black man that point is right here and now. (pp. 44-5)

Shane Stevens, ''Quest for Dignity,'' in The Progressive, Vol. 32, No. 5, May, 1968, pp. 44-5.

JULIAN MAYFIELD

There used to be a lot of nonsense written about black writers being outside the mainstream of American literature. This was because, for the most part, their work followed the protest tradition, and resisted the fads which sought to obscure the realities of history, economics, and the distribution of political power. Black writers, with varying degrees of success, clung stubbornly to the conviction that the black experience in America was worth exploiting. Now we know that it is worth more than most of us imagined, that it is integral to the American experience, not a marginal back street, and that the nation's survival may depend on how quickly it understands this and changes accordingly.

These thoughts are prompted by a remarkable book, *Soul On Ice*. . . . [Cleaver is] no stranger to violence, but neither are any of us any more. I feel more like a war correspondent as I sit down to review this book, for there are riots and fires raging in more than 100 of our cities and towns in the wake of the Memphis assassination. So I am only vaguely shocked when a friend telephones to say that Eldridge Cleaver has just been shot, and a fellow Black Panther member killed while attempting to surrender to the Oakland police. If that doesn't put our young writer into the American mainstream, which is violence, I don't know what will.

First it must be said that *Soul On Ice* is beautifully written by a man with a formidably analytical mind. His talent might have gone undiscovered and undeveloped had he not been busted by The Man at an early age and thrust into prison society, which really is just American society in microcosm, stripped naked. (p. 638)

Eldridge Cleaver, like all engaged artists (LeRoi Jones, the early [Jack] Kerouac, the early [Norman] Mailer, the early [James] Baldwin) makes you twist and flinch because he is no damned gentleman. He throws light on the dark areas that we wish he would leave alone. He is definitely not for everybody, and as much as I go for *Soul On Ice*, I realize that not all of him is for me. For example, I think that altogether too much space and soul-searching is devoted to the black male-white female hangup, a subject on which he can be maddening, but, I am sorry to say, terribly accurate. I doubt if many of his readers will care that he fell in love with his lawyer (happily a woman and presumably white), and they will wonder why in heaven's name he wants us to read their love letters. I didn't. . . .

This brilliant book is only the first by Eldridge Cleaver. If he somehow survives the California cops for another year or two, God only knows what he will come up with next. Whatever it is, it won't put anybody to sleep. (p. 640)

Julian Mayfield, ''The New Mainstream,'' in The Nation, Vol. 206, No. 20, May 13, 1968, pp. 638, 640.

ROBERT COLES

All the essays [in *Soul on Ice*] deal with racial hurt, racial struggle, and racial pride. Mr. Cleaver is a black man, and he is not going to let either himself or anyone else forget that fact—in case it is possible for an American of either race to do so. Ralph Ellison and even James Baldwin want above all to be writers, and Cleaver says no, that is impossible, that is foolish, and certainly that is wrong.

I am with Ellison and Baldwin all the way, but the author of a book with the stark, unrelenting title *Soul on Ice* would expect that of me, a reasonably unharassed white middle-class professional man who, really, in many ways had it made from birth. I don't at all like the nasty, spiteful way Mr. Cleaver writes off *Invisible Man* or *Another Country*. I don't like the arrogant and cruel way he talks about Baldwin's life and his personality. I don't like the way he lumps white men, all of them, indiscriminately together, and I'm sick and tired of a rhetoric that takes three hundred years of complicated, tortured American history and throws it in the face of every single white man alive today. Mr. Cleaver rightly wants to be seen for the particular man *he* is, and I don't see why he should by the same token confuse the twentieth-century traveling salesman with the seventeenth-century slave trader. If he wants us to understand American history, and in fact see its economic and political continuities, all well and good; but it is really stupid to tell today's white people that they caused what in fact gradually and terribly happened. What can anyone do with that kind of historical burden, ''do'' with it in the sense of coming to any personal or psychological resolution?

I suppose one thing that can be done is what Maxwell Geismar does in his short and thoroughly unsurprising introduction [see excerpt above]. Mr. Geismar has abandoned himself without qualification to Mr. Cleaver's scorn and outrage. The black man cries out, and the white man says yes, yes, no matter what. Eldridge Cleaver is a promising and powerful writer, an intelligent and turbulent and passionate and eloquent man. But Geismar ironically treats him with the ultimate condescension of exaggerated praise, and even worse the cruelty that goes with using a man as an irrelevant foil. (pp. 106-07)

[If] I were Eldridge Cleaver I'd watch out. Praise is like power; there is nothing as corrupting (and yes, insulting) as absolute praise, particularly when one's very humanity is denied. (Which writer is without a ''trace'' of ''self-vanity''?)

Nevertheless, apart from the introduction to this book, and apart from its black nationalism, there are some really lovely and tender and even exquisite moments to be found—when the author becomes a writer, not a pamphleteer and not a propagandist and not a devious, cruel literary critic, but a man who wants to struggle with words and ideas and tame them. There are ostensibly four parts to the relatively slim volume, but actually it is split in two. ''Letters from Prison'' and ''Prelude to Love—Three Letters'' show how one inmate of a jail becomes something much more, a literate, sensitive, and intelligent human being. There are white millionaires who have failed where Cleaver has succeeded.

How did he succeed? *Why?* We ought to ask such questions, even as we do with Malcolm X, Cleaver's great hero. People like me can tear Cleaver and Malcolm to shreds. We can discover the bad "background" they come from. We can find pathology everywhere—mental illness, physical disorder, social chaos, cultural disintegration. . . .

Yet at times he writes vivid, compelling prose. He has a sense of humor. He knows how to be astringent one minute, ironic the next. He can be tolerant and compassionate, far more so in my opinion than the man who wrote the introduction to this book. He is full of Christian care, Christian grief and disappointment, Christian resignation, Christian messianic toughness, and hope. He loves his lawyer, a white woman, and pours out his love to her in three beautiful, incredibly subtle and blunt and unsparing and unforgettable letters. How did he do it—learn to write, learn the really impressive theological subtleties that are addressed to his lawyer? . . .

Of course he also learned the other things, the handy political and sociological clichés that have blinded black and white men everywhere in every century. But above all we must notice what he has done: begun (and only begun) to master the writer's craft. For that achievement Eldridge Cleaver deserves our unashamed awe, our admiration, and our insistence that like every other writer he work harder, rid himself of unnecessary baggage, and put to word the startling ironies that he knows from real life but sees and comprehends out of his mind's life. He ought to spare us nothing, but he ought to spare himself very little either. Inside a developing writer there is, there has to be, a kind of ice that somehow uses but also transcends the weather, the scene, the hot and cold of the outside world. (p. 107)

> *Robert Coles, "Black Anger," in* The Atlantic
> Monthly, *Vol. 221, No. 6, June, 1968, pp. 106-07.*

MICHAEL COOKE

The movement of Americans of African ancestry to fulfill the vision of a necessary, if unpromised, land boasts its ranks of orators, defenders spiritual and real, legal philosophers and paralegal militants, prophets, and martyrs. So much is to be expected. But is it not strange that this movement has produced no satirist, no one to do for black and white what [Jonathan] Swift did for Ireland and England? . . . Why is there nobody but the Smothers brothers to whip out the moral dilapidation at the base of what, with choice neutrality, we call "political behaviors and socioeconomic conditions"? (p. 102)

[One] suspects that more than social style now inhibits satire; *that* might as readily invite it. And so one wonders if the hard reckless laughter, the irreverent wit, the brooding condensed to explosiveness, the sense of outrage and conscience and love—all of which mark Eldridge Cleaver's voice in the urgent claim of so many Americans to live themselves America's vision of itself—really mark Cleaver as a satirist *in potentia* or a satirist *manqué*. The author of *Soul on Ice* has the satirist's mood but not his mission, some of his perceptions without his sense of design. The working design, meantime, may appear less than obvious. (pp. 102-03)

Not strictly satire or autobiography, *Soul on Ice* strikes one as a *satura* tentatively placed on an autobiographical stand, a mixed dish of letters, dramatic vignettes, politics, history or historiography, journal, character sketch, psychology, reportage, and sacred address. What sustains it, along the way, is its clear sense that formal circumstances differ from substantive conditions, a sense of freedom and candor that continually promises, and delivers, the "creative moment."

Something heroic, if also blithely romantic, appears in the following distinction between accident and reality: "I'm in prison . . . a Negro . . . [have] been a rapist, and . . . have a Higher Uneducation. . . . But what matters is that I have fallen in love with my lawyer [Beverly Axelrod].'' . . . And some may relish the realism and wit of Cleaver's idea that venturing to attend a WASP (White Anglo-Saxon Protestant) church would have caused him to be cut down and martyred: "St. Eldridge the Stupe."

The book also sustains itself by a kind of patterned unpredictability. One repeatedly finds that what at first seems a mere record of experience revolves into a recreation of the spirit and power of experience. Cleaver almost appears to be aware of this, and in control of it; at least, in one of the letters, he hesitates to make a statement because it may be "predictable and trite," but makes it of course, and it comes out all the more real and lively for his moment of reticence. In this vein sensible but not distinguished reflections on pre-1968 politics suddenly turn inspired with the anticipation that America might come out against Lyndon B. Johnson; the description of the "Jewish stud out of New York" livens and leavens a somewhat routine account of prison experience; a catechism on "Domestic Law and International Order" curves and soars into poetry and drama. . . . (pp. 103-04)

Another kind of planned unpredictability arises from Cleaver's unsettling definition of the audience. The "Letters from Prison" (neo- or pseudo-Pauline) are neither addressed nor open, and the reader is more vitally exposed than the writer to the difficulties of defining the literary relationship—the writer's life style is in the line, not on it. Of course the letter as an artistic genre tends to threaten the reader with embarrassment, since he may find himself willy-nilly playing intruder, or snoop, or even censor (as in the case of Cleaver's love letters, where the reader as outsider implicitly hinders the private writer's freedom of utterance). But Cleaver goes further, asking the reader who avoids such pitfalls to make of himself a tacit, and fit, correspondent. More explicitly challenging, Cleaver will bring off abrupt changes of address: now he is speaking about people, analytically, then of a sudden is speaking to *us*, accusingly. (p. 105)

For the individual sections, the essay on Baldwin stands out as a piece of writing and of scandal. Its principle of criticism, to search out the man in the work, is reminiscent of D. H. Lawrence; its form is beautifully modulated from hero-worship to misgiving to disaffection to pity and repudiation. The charge against Baldwin, that he hates Negroes and is substantially irrelevant, may or may not be sound (perhaps the question should be in what sense he has a funky soul), but it is ingeniously and eloquently made.

The letter "On Becoming" also strikes home, as a Mailerish, idiosyncratic version of a politico-historical event, the 1954 Supreme Court decision on school desegregation. Cleaver the instant outlaw of freedom might seem to bring to very life the argument from prudence against that decision and all like it;

but do we blame the banker for being agitated when he learns that massive embezzlement has been going on in his bank? A corollary point, since Cleaver obviously had not known what he was missing, is that theft counts as a wrong when committed, though action against it must wait upon discovery.

Another piece, "The Allegory of the Black Eunuchs," is something of a tour de force of sex and psycho-social drama, too densely packed with experience and too fiercely direct not to be a little blinding and obscure. By contrast, the final address **"To All Black Women, from All Black Men"** has an aura of the holy, with its humble resolution and grave affection making it, in the original sense, an act of atonement and of adoration.

But it is unjust to ourselves as well as to Eldridge Cleaver to put down *Soul on Ice* as a *de facto* anthology. The tendency of his own mind is to seek a discriminating synthesis, which can see a turning away from rebellion in Malcolm X and a turning toward rebellion in white youth of America as hopeful signs of the same redeemed future, or see that prison, however brutal, can be a man's path beyond "the usual multiplicity of [artificial] social relations" and into "the total impact of another individual upon himself" in a "beautiful relationship."

From the outset, in the "Letters from Prison" and especially in the title piece, **"Soul on Ice,"** Cleaver makes it clear that he is concerned with the varieties and vicissitudes of human relationship. And it is this concern which ultimately, and naturally, sustains and unifies the work. The rhythm of *Soul on Ice* carries from a negation of relationship in the opening piece, to a tentative contact in the next, and thereafter a tortuous course of forward flashes, sidelong sweeps, and backward swings, until the final piece, the culminating statement of relationship, **"To All Black Women, from All Black Men."** Within this rhythmic pattern Cleaver makes precise and very telling use of letters. For the letters, which announce the necessity and ideal of a beautiful relationship, at first speak at large, to no one in particular, but reappearing are addressed to one person, Beverly Axelrod, who answers and so makes personal and real what has been but general and tentative. Now Cleaver, having successfully spoken as one man to one woman, can and does undertake to speak for men in a class to women in a class.

It may be too much to say that a Platonic expansion and elevation of feeling is taking place. On the other hand, a real expansion and elevation of feeling, with Platonic overtones, does take place. For if *Soul on Ice* is what [Ernest] Hemingway might have called a true book, a book true to experience, the experience has paradox or plurality in it. Here is not only experience, but the soul of experience, and that soul, already ambiguously on ice, is also on fire and in one sense expanding. (pp. 105-07)

> *Michael Cooke, "Eldridge Cleaver: Humanist and Felon," in* The Yale Review, *Vol. LVIII, No. 1, October, 1968, pp. 102-07.*

NAT HENTOFF

[The following excerpt was taken from an interview with Cleaver conducted by Hentoff for Playboy Magazine.*]*

PLAYBOY: You have written [in *Soul on Ice*] that "a new black leadership with its own distinct style and philosophy will now come into its own, to center stage. Nothing can stop this leadership from taking over, because it is based on charisma, has the allegiance and support of the black masses, is conscious of its self and its position and is prepared to shoot its way to

power if the need arises." As one who is increasingly regarded as among the pivotal figures in this new black leadership, how do you distinguish the new breed from those—such as Roy Wilkins [of the NAACP] and Whitney Young [of the Urban League]—most Americans consider the established Negro spokesman?

CLEAVER: The so-called leaders you name have been willing to work within the framework of the rules laid down by the white establishment. They have tried to bring change within the system as it now is—without violence. Although Martin Luther King was the leader-spokesman for the nonviolent theme, all the rest condemn violence, too. Furthermore, all are careful to remind everybody that they're Americans as well as "Negroes," that the prestige of this country is as important to them as it is to whites. By contrast, the new black leadership identifies first and foremost with the best interests of the masses of *black* people, and we don't care about preserving the dignity of a country that has no regard for ours. We don't give a damn about any embarrassments we may cause the United States on an international level. And remember, I said the *masses* of black people. That's why we oppose [New York Congressman] Adam Clayton Powell. He's not militant enough and he represents only the black middle class, not the masses.

PLAYBOY: Since you consider yourself one of these new leaders representng the masses, what are your specific goals?

CLEAVER: Our basic demand is for proportionate participation in the real power that runs this country. This means that black people must have part of the decision-making power concerning all legislation, all appropriations of money, foreign policy—every area of life. We cannot accept anything less than that black people, like white people, have the best lives technology is able to offer at the present time. Black people know what's going on. They're aware of this country's productivity and they want in on the good life.

PLAYBOY: So far—apart from your willingness to resort to violence in achieving that goal—you haven't proposed anything specific or different from the aims of the traditional Negro leadership.

CLEAVER: OK, the best way to be specific is to list the ten points of the Black Panther Party. They make clear that we are not willing to accept the rules of the white establishment. One: We want freedom; we want power to determine the destiny of our black communities. Two: We want full employment for our people. Three: We want housing fit for the shelter of human beings. Four: We want all black men to be exempt from military service. Five: We want decent education for black people—education that teaches us the true nature of this decadent, racist society and that teaches young black brothers and sisters their rightful place in society; for if they don't know their place in society and the world, they can't relate to anything else. Six: We want an end to the robbery of black people in their own community by white-racist businessmen. Seven: We want an immediate end to police brutality and murder of black people. Eight: We want all black men held in city, county, state and Federal jails to be released, because they haven't had fair trials; they've been tried by all white juries, and that's like being a Jew tried in Nazi Germany. Nine: We want black people accused of crimes to be tried by members of their peer group— a peer being one who comes from the same economic, social, religious, historical and racial community. Black people, in other words, would have to compose the jury in any trial of a black person. And ten: We want land, we want money, we want housing, we want clothing, we want education, we want justice, we want peace.

PLAYBOY: Peace? But you've written that "the genie of black revolutionary violence is here."

CLEAVER: Yes, but put that into context. I've said that war will come only if these basic demands are not met. Not just a race war; which in itself would destroy this country, but a guerrilla resistance movement that will amount to a second Civil War, with thousands of white John Browns fighting on the side of the blacks, plunging America into the depths of its most desperate nightmare on the way to realizing the American Dream.

PLAYBOY: How much time is there for these demands to be met before this takes place?

CLEAVER: What will happen—and when—will depend on the dynamics of the revolutionary struggle in the black and white communities; people are going to do what they feel they have to do as the movement takes shape and gathers strength. But how long do you expect black people, who are already fed up, to endure the continued indifference of the Federal Government to their needs? How long will they endure the continued escalation of police force and brutality? I can't give you an exact answer, but surely they will not wait indefinitely if their demands are not met—particularly since we think that the United States has already decided where its next campaign is going to be after the war in Vietnam is over. We think the Government has already picked this new target area, and it's black America. A lot of black people are very up tight about what they see in terms of preparations for the suppression of the black liberation struggle in this country. We don't work on a timetable, but we do say that the situation is deteriorating rapidly. There have been more and more armed clashes and violent encounters with the police departments that occupy black communities. Who can tell at which point any one of the dozens of incidents that take place every day will just boil over and break out into an irrevocable war? Let me make myself clear. I don't dig violence. Guns are ugly. People are what's beautiful; and when you use a gun to kill someone, you're doing something ugly. But there are two forms of violence: violence directed at you to keep you in your place and violence to defend yourself against that suppression and to win your freedom. If our demands are not met, we will sooner or later have to make a choice between continuing to be victims or deciding to seize our freedom. (pp. 90-1)

PLAYBOY: Have you considered the possibility that you could be wrong about the chances of waging a successful guerrilla war? Don't you run the risk that all your efforts toward that end—even if they don't escalate beyond rhetoric—could invite a massive wave of repression that would result in a black bloodbath and turn the country's ghettos into concentration camps?

CLEAVER: It seems to me a strange assumption that black people could just be killed or cooped up into concentration camps and that would be the end of it. This isn't the 1930s. We're not going to play Jews. The whole world is different now from what it was then. Not only would black people resist, with the help of white people, but we would also have the help of those around the world who are just waiting for some kind of extreme crisis within this country so that they can move for their own liberation from American repression abroad. This Government does not have unlimited forces of repression; it can't hold the whole world down—not at home *and* abroad.

Eventually, it will be able to control the racial situation here only by ignoring its military "commitments" overseas. That might stop *our* movement for a while, but think what would be happening in Latin America, Asia, and Africa. In that event, there would be a net gain for freedom in the world. We see our struggle as inextricably bound up with the struggle of all oppressed peoples, and there is no telling what sacrifices we in this country may have to make before that struggle is won.

PLAYBOY: Do you think you have any real chance of winning that struggle—even without Government repression—as long as the majority of white Americans, who outnumber blacks ten to one remain hostile or indifferent to black aspirations? According to the indications of recent public-opinion surveys, they deplore even *nonviolent* demonstrations on behalf of civil rights.

CLEAVER: At the present stage, the majority of white people are indifferent and complacent simply because their own lives have remained more or less intact and as remote from the lives of most blacks as the old French aristocracy was from "the great unwashed." It's disturbing to them to hear about Hough burning, Watts burning, the black community in Newark burning. But they don't really understand why it's happening, and they don't really care, as long as *their* homes and *their* places of work—or the schools to which they send their children—aren't burning, too. So for most whites, what's happened up to now has been something like a spectator sport. There may be a lot more of them than there are of us, but they're not really involved; and there are millions and millions of black people in this country who *are*—more than the census shows. Maybe 30,000,000, maybe more. A lot of black people never get counted in the Census. It's not going to be easy to deal with that large a number, and it won't be possible to indefinitely limit the burning to black neighborhoods—even with all the tanks, tear gas, riot guns, paddy wagons and fire trucks in this country. But if it does come to massive repression of blacks, I don't think the majority of whites are going to either approve it or remain silent. If a situation breaks out in which soldiers are hunting down and killing black people obviously and openly, we don't think the majority will accept that for long. It could go on for a while, but at some point, we think large numbers of whites would become so revolted that leaders would arise in the white community and offer other solutions. So we don't accept the analysis that we're doomed because we're in a minority. We don't believe that the majority in this country would permit concentration camps and genocide. (p. 94)

PLAYBOY: Suppose you're right in claiming that most whites, for whatever reason, would not support massive repression of blacks in this country. These same whites, however, don't want black violence, either—but as you point out, most don't fully grasp the dimensions of the injustices against which that violence is a rebellion, nor do they understand why it continues in the wake of several milestone civil rights laws and Supreme Court decisions. The familiar question is: "What more do they want?" How would you answer it?

CLEAVER: I can only answer with what Malcolm X said. If you've had a knife in my back for 400 years, am I supposed to thank you for pulling it out? Because that's all those laws and decisions have accomplished. The very least of your responsibility now is to compensate me, however inadequately, for centuries of degradation and disenfranchisement by granting peacefully—before I take them forcefully—the same rights and opportunities for a decent life that you've taken for granted as an American birthright. This isn't a request but a *demand*, and the ten points of that demand are set down with crystal clarity in the Black Panther Party platform.

PLAYBOY: Many would doubt that you're serious about some of them. Point four for instance: "We want all black men to be exempt from military service."

CLEAVER: We couldn't be *more* serious about that point. As a colonized people, we consider it absurd to fight the wars of the mother country against other colonized peoples, as in Vietnam right now. The conviction that no black man should be forced to fight for the system that's suppressing him is growing among more and more black people, outside the Black Panther Party as well as in it. And as we can organize masses of black people behind that demand for exemption, it will have to be taken seriously.

PLAYBOY: Are you equally serious about point eight, which demands that all black prisoners held in city, county, state and Federal jails be released because they haven't had fair trials; and about point nine, which demands that black defendants be tried by all-black juries?

CLEAVER: We think the day will come when these demands, too, will receive serious attention, because they deserve it. Take point eight. All the social sciences—criminology, sociology, psychology, economics—point out that if you subject people to deprivation and inhuman living conditions, you can predict that they will rebel against those conditions. What we have in this country is a system organized against black people in such a way that many are forced to rebel and turn to forms of behavior that are called criminal, in order to get the things they need to survive. Consider the basic contradiction here. You subject people to conditions that make rebellion inevitable and then you punish them for rebelling. Now, under those circumstances, does the black convict owe a debt to society or does society owe a debt to the black convict? Since the social, economic and political system is so rigged against black people, we feel the burden of the indictment should rest on the system and not on us. Therefore, black people should not be confined in jails and prisons for rebelling against that system—even though the rebellion might express itself in some unfortunate ways. And this idea can be taken further, to apply also to those white people who have been subjected to a disgusting system for so long that they resort to disgusting forms of behavior. This is part of our fundamental critique of the way this society, under its present system of organization, molds the character of its second-class citizens.

PLAYBOY: Have you considered the consequences to society of opening the prisons and setting all the inmates free? Their behavior may in one sense be society's fault, but they're still criminals.

CLEAVER: We don't feel that there's any black man or any white man in any prison in this country who could be compared in terms of criminality with Lyndon Johnson. No mass murderer in America or in any other country comes anywhere close to the thousands and thousands of deaths for which Johnson is responsible.

PLAYBOY: Do you think that analogy is valid? After all, Johnson has been waging a war, however misguidedly, in the belief that his cause is just.

CLEAVER: Many murderers feel exactly the same way about *their* crimes. But let me give you another example: Compare the thieves in our prisons with the big businessmen of this country, who are in control of a system that is depriving millions of people of a decent life. These people—the men who run the Government and the corporations—are much more dangerous than the guy who walks into a store with a pistol and robs somebody of a few dollars. The men in control are robbing the entire world of billions and billions of dollars.

PLAYBOY: *All* the men in control?

CLEAVER: That's what I said, and they're not only stealing money, they're robbing people of life itself. When you talk about criminals, you have to recognize the vastly different degrees of criminality.

PLAYBOY: Surely no criminality proved in a court of law should go unpunished.

CLEAVER: As you know, the poor and the black in this country don't seem to make out as well as the rich and the white in our courts of "justice." I wonder why.

PLAYBOY: You still haven't answered our question about the social consequences of releasing all those now behind bars.

CLEAVER: Those who are not in prison could be put through a process of real rehabilitation before their release—not caged like animals, as they are now, thus guaranteeing that they'll be hardened criminals when they get out if they weren't when they went in. By rehabilitation I mean they would be trained for jobs that would not be an insult to their dignity, that would give them some sense of security, that would allow them to achieve some brotherly connection with their fellow man. But for this kind of rehabilitation to happen on a large scale would entail the complete reorganization of society, not to mention the prison system. It would call for the teaching of a new set of ethics based on the principle of cooperation, as opposed to the presently dominating principle of competition. It would require the transformation of the entire moral fabric of this country into a way of being that would make these former criminals feel more obligated to their fellow man than they do now. The way things are today, however, what reasons do these victims of society have for feeling an obligation to their fellow man? I look with respect on a guy who has walked the streets because he's been unable to find a job in a system that's rigged against him, but doesn't go around begging and instead walks into a store and says, "Stick 'em up, motherfucker!" I prefer that man to the Uncle Tom who does nothing but just shrink into himself and accept any shit that's thrown into his face. (p. 95)

PLAYBOY: One of the passages in *Soul on Ice* had particular impact on many young white people who felt they had been drummed out of "the movement." You wrote: "There is in America today a generation of white youth that is truly worthy of a black man's respect, and this is a rare event in the foul annals of American history." Having since worked in collaboration with the Peace and Freedom Party, do you still think as highly of the new generation of white youth?

CLEAVER: I'm even more convinced it's true than when I wrote those lines. We work with these young people all the time, and we've had nothing but encouraging experiences with them. These young white people aren't hung up battling to maintain the *status quo* like some of the older people who think they'll become extinct if the system changes. They're adventurous: they're willing to experiment with new forms; they're willing to confront life. And I don't mean only those on college campuses. A lot who aren't in college share with their college counterparts an ability to welcome and work for change.

PLAYBOY: Do you agree with those who feel that this generation of youth is going to "sell out" to the *status quo* as it moves into middle age?

CLEAVER: I expect all of us will become somewhat less resilient as we get into our 40s and 50s—if we live that long—and I'm sure that those who come after us will look back on us as being conservative. Even us Panthers. (p. 100)

Nat Hentoff, *"Playboy Interview: Eldridge Cleaver,"* in Playboy, *Vol. 15, No. 12, December, 1968, pp. 89-108, 238.*

JACK RICHARDSON

The madness takes its toll, but it should be clear, before all critical connection between the black and white sensibility breaks down, that, for the Negro writer, madness comes not in hating the white world but in hating it without style. A lucid rage can be an effective cultural weapon; literary delirium tremens can only bog down everyone's anger. This frenzy to set up an official literary barricade, to uncover symbols and tales which will promote some sort of atavistic tribal unity, can lead very quickly to a crippled art that threatens nothing. In the rush to do away with the racial double consciousness, it cannot be forgotten that art produces its own version of this division and that it has its own standards of manhood. What Eldridge Cleaver, for example, does to the white consciousness in *Soul on Ice* is shattering precisely because he appreciates and meets those standards, and so can pick apart with angry humor all the ripe details of that anger's object.

This collection of letters, essays, and dramatic monologues does what good books have always done: it presents a new stirring of experience that causes hidden sediment to rise where we can all clearly see it. Cleaver does not simply cry monster; he carefully strips away the lunatic raiment of both blacks and whites, sometimes affecting an ingenuous amazement at what he finds beneath, sometimes becoming a lyric moralist fired to rage over what he sees as dangerous threats to life. (p. 12)

From personal outrage, to revolutionary enthusiasm, and then into self-irony with a profession of love that scales things back to human size—Cleaver's style can cover a great deal of ground without stinting on its subject, for beyond having a rare honesty, it has a dramatic temper that makes it a point gently to remind us of who is speaking and from where.

If there is a major theme in *Soul on Ice,* it is Cleaver's use of the old Mind-Body difficulty, which he changes from an epistemological problem into a social and psychological one. When he looks at American society he sees it primarily as a function of this dualism, split into such categories as "The Omnipotent Administrator" and "The Supermasculine Menial." The Administrator has permitted The Menial certain rights: in physical areas—with, of course, the exception of sex—he may excel, but any aspiration to administrative prerogatives—e.g. the attributes of mind—is taboo. Thus Cassius Clay went too far when he became Muhammad Ali, for this was evidence that some intellectual process had taken place, and, what was worse, The Menial, The Body, did not hesitate to articulate just what that process was.

With a rueful anger, Cleaver uses this image in an intuitive rather than a sociological way to discuss some of the more interesting events of recent years. The transition from the Eisenhower to the Kennedy era, for example, he considers the beginning in the long-needed merger of the mind and body

polarities, and he is devastating when he describes the white psyche thawing out as it tried to put on a little flesh by taking up the new—for the blacks, old—rock sound and the dances that went with it. Anyone who remembers Society's invasion of The Peppermint Lounge in the early Sixties knows the appositeness of Cleaver's description:

> They were swinging and gyrating and shaking their dead little asses like petrified zombies trying to regain the warmth of life, rekindle the dead limbs, the cold ass, the stone heart, the stiff, mechanical disused joints with the spark of life.

That Cleaver sees this as a small, comical hope for the country does not mean his judgment of the white world is any the less exacting than that of LeRoi Jones; it is simply delivered in a human voice that convinces because of the heavy dues it must have paid in experience in order to write so well. . . . He does not have to set down "Blackness" as a subject, because every twist of intelligence, every turn of phrase make this identity a self-sufficient fact that needs no invective nor analogy to jazz to come into sharp relief; and as old categories of thought break apart, minds like Cleaver's are sorely needed, minds that can fashion a literature which does not flaunt its culture but creates it. (pp. 12-13)

Jack Richardson, *"The Black Arts,"* in The New York Review of Books, *Vol. XI, No. 11, December 19, 1968, pp. 10-13.**

LINDSAY PATTERSON

In **"Soul on Ice,"** Eldridge Cleaver's reflections on the plight of American society somehow sounded like those of a prodigiously intelligent man describing a tree though never having seen one. Reading those prison essays, however, you knew that he had read and digested every manual on the subject. The result was, up to a point, brilliant and revealing. Beyond that point, lurked some empty although eloquent abstractions, patently incorrect in their assumptions, judgments and conclusions. . . .

[In his astonishing collection **"Post-Prison Writings and Speeches"**] Cleaver in freedom has visualized clearly and precisely the trees, as well as the forest.

"The Decline of the Black Muslims" and "The Death of Martin Luther King: Requiem for Nonviolence," are essays on two approaches to the racial problem that Cleaver asserts are "played out." "Open Letter to Ronald Reagan," written in May, 1968, after Cleaver was arrested for violation of parole, denies the charges brought against him and asserts that he was, in fact, a "political prisoner." The black revolutionary theme is discussed in "Psychology: The Black Bible," an evaluation of Frantz Fanon's "The Wretched of the Earth," and in "The Land Question and Black Liberation," an essay on black-power activism vs. the land-acquisition policy of Marcus Garvey and the Black Muslims.

After reading this urgently important book, no one should fail to realize how accurately Cleaver pinpoints the American malaise and its relationship to current world affairs—or just how remarkable a man he is, or how valuable. . . .

The Panthers, according to Cleaver (despite what many ill-informed whites think), never advocated "people going around inventing hostilities and burning down schools." Rather, as Cleaver says, they urged that hostilities in the black community be "focused on specific targets." The police, of course, a prime one. (p. 6)

Unlike some militants who have no plan or design other than to level society and kill off whites (and then what, another Biafra?), Cleaver realizes that a coalition of responsible persons is needed: ". . . we need sane people in this country; we need sane black people, and we need sane white people. Because we recognize that the Black Panther party can't do it by itself, black people can't do it by themselves. It's going to take white people who recognize the situation that exists in this world today to stand up, yes, to unite with their black brothers and sisters." But he warns: "If the white mother country is to have victory over the black colony, it is the duty of the black revolutionaries to insure that the Imperialists receive no more than a Pyrrhic victory, written in the blood of what America might have become."

Our history fairly bulges with the names of the right men at the right time who rescued America from the brink of disaster. Lately, however, we seem bent on destroying these saviors before they can accomplish their mission. Few men can equal the intellectual and moral growth achieved by Robert Kennedy (about whom Cleaver has some harsh things to say), Malcolm X or Cleaver in such a short span of time. Kennedy and Malcolm X are silenced forever; Cleaver, for his own survival, has been forced into exile. Time has run out. America can no longer afford to treat her would-be deliverers capriciously. Perhaps there is no future for America, and what we have been witnessing is the ugly portent.

Intellectually, I refuse to accept that. But reality is here and now, and the white man must stop playing games with the black man. One of the many games is window dressing—the illusion of substantive change by "tokenism"—which the white man considers his most skillful game. Cleaver assesses the growing disgust of black America correctly when he says, "There is a large and deepening layer of black people in this country who cannot be tricked anymore by having a few black faces put up front."

The horror of it all is that even after the millions of words of protest, the peaceful demonstrations and the violence, white America listens still with only a half-cocked ear. Is human dignity too much to ask? "We start with the basic principle," says Cleaver, "that every man, woman and child on the face of the earth deserves the very highest standard of living that human knowledge and technology is capable of providing. Period. No more than that, no less than that." (pp. 6, 38)

> *Lindsay Patterson, "A Call for Black and White Sanity," in* The New York Times Book Review, *April 27, 1969, pp. 6, 38.*

HAROLD CRUSE

Reviewing Eldridge Cleaver's second book, *Post-Prison Speeches and Writings,* demands a critical license like that of reviewing the aspects of a man's life which consigned him to purgatory. Moreover, the review itself can offer little promise of comfort and less in the way of advice to the man in question, whose likely response would be: "If I could live life all over again, I'd do the same thing." There is, then, but one legitimate line of investigation, since we already know why the man lived the way he did. This approach would ask two questions, "Why must he do it again in that way, if he could?" and "Is there really no other way?"

But even this tack is not very promising, because it offers no easy answers to these questions which would even begin to satisfy those who adhere to any of today's "revolutionary" trends in America. For if there is anyone among them who has demonstrated the full measure of his devotion to "putting one's head on the line," it is Eldridge Cleaver. What more can one demand after that? What is there more to be said about Eldridge Cleaver, the writer-activist-revolutionary, that is legitimate critically and politically apt?

In the first place, [*Post-Prison Speeches and Writings*] presents a peculiar problem because of the nature of its content and style. . . . [We] must deal here not with Cleaver, the literary essayist, but with Cleaver, the activist, the revolutionary, the political ideologist. Also with Cleaver, the Black Panther Party's Minister of Information and associate editor of *Ramparts* Magazine. One must deal in part with all of these facets of Eldridge Cleaver because the man defies facile classification. He did not emerge from what was considered, during periods like the 1930s, the proper path to conventional revolutionary politics. His political personality is as unprecedented as the situation of racial confrontation in which he and his ideas became famous. . . .

Out of prison, Cleaver faced a very complex world, in a tense and agitated human mosaic in black and white tones. For Cleaver, as he said in prison, real history, black history, "began with Malcolm X." But Malcolm X's organization, the OAAU [Organization of Afro-American Unity], had died with him, and Cleaver hoped and tried to revive it. His search for an organization reminiscent of Malcolm X's movement ended when he encountered the Black Panther Party. As the Panther's Minister of Information, he started a new political career. "Without the Panthers," [as Robert Scheer says in his introduction to *Post-Prison Speeches and Writings*], "Cleaver would undoubtedly have developed a much more personal career-oriented, literary way of life. With the Panthers, he became a disciplined political revolutionary as well as a literary polemicist, although there was hardly any time for writing."

But Cleaver never sought a "literary way of life"; in fact he deliberately did otherwise: he searched for political involvement because he held a "belief in the necessity of black political revolution . . ." In this self-assumed role, Cleaver experienced in his unique way what several other black writers discovered before him: revolutionary political activity and literary creation simply do not mix. This is why "there was hardly any time for writing."

Perhaps it is safe to assume that this was the way Cleaver wanted it. For a serious writer in prison, particularly a philosophical one, there is hardly a better place to pursue the writer's lonely commitment to literature than in isolation, free from external infringements such as the need to "earn a living." The outside world is hard on the would-be writer, especially if he is black. After enduring the arduous course of literary commitment and exile, the black writer then runs the hazards of literary success: he is then induced, if not commanded, to become a black spokesman. Then he is asked: what are his political commitments? If he is willing, he succumbs and becomes, like Cleaver, a "literary polemicist," and, ultimately, a political revolutionary. (p. 13)

Cleaver, like many others, was first legitimized by the very mass media whose social role most of us attack as the corrupting propaganda agency of the "power structure." In this fashion are writers, revolutionary or otherwise, trapped by the system in ways many of us do not like to admit. But in viewing Cleaver's essential ideas, one is led to ask, What did the Black Panthers and the Peace and Freedom Party really think about Cleaver's political ideas which the mass media ignored?

This question may not appear legitimate on first sight, but it is. It is ironic that in our society the propagandist of unpopular political ideas cannot depend on his allies to propagate his views. Neither the Old Left nor the New Left could or would publish Eldridge Cleaver widely—they have neither the resources nor the disseminating range to equal the visibility given Cleaver by the mass media. It was one sector of the "power structure" that jailed him, controlled him, negated him, and finally hounded him into exile. But it was another sector of the "power structure" that facilitated and sustained his literary and political celebrity.

We must admit that Frantz Fanon was right, for the United States is structurally unlike those societies in the Third World that spawn revolutionary anti-colonialist movements in Algeria, Kenya, Angola, and heroes like Mao Tse-tung and Che Guevara. The wish to emulate these Third World movements in the United States is understandable, but the revolutionary leaders in the Third World would find Cleaver's access to publishing houses and television studios incomprehensible. It is with the social and political reality of the United States in mind, as well as the nature of his alliances, that we must consider Cleaver's views.

We know fairly well the ideas of the Black Panther Party's self-defense program *before* the arrival of Cleaver: land, bread, housing, education, justice, peace, the end of police brutality, freedom for black prisoners, peer jury trials, exemption of blacks from military service, to name the most important. But the appearance of Cleaver in the Black Panther ranks as a major spokesman and ideologist brought to the fore again that touchy question of the possibility and the necessity of a black nationalist-white leftist political alliance. For one thing, the jailing of one Panther leader, Huey Newton, made such an alliance a necessity if Newton was to be saved. Funds and legal aid were needed. Cleaver, however, recurrently voices the theme of black and white unity as a fundamental political necessity for the Panther movement which, as he explained to Nat Hentoff in the *Playboy* Interview [see excerpt above], . . . was intended by him to become "*the* black national movement" of America. . . . (pp. 13-14)

This is the way Cleaver more than anyone else personifies the Malcolm X legacy. Malcolm came to disavow "black racism," as it is called. So Cleaver found a way to reconcile "political nationalism" to a black and white coalition. (p. 14)

Cleaver differs not at all from other committed American militants, for, like them, he is basically American, with the same radical hang-ups and contradictions. It is the quality of his rhetoric that is unique but, as Nat Hentoff pointed out in his interview, Cleaver is just as much a prisoner of the reformist bind and the agony of its unfulfilled promises as anyone else who, under inexorable and excruciating pressures, must resort to revolutionary slogans and threats. . . . (p. 15)

Robert Scheer states that Cleaver "thrives in chaos" and is "very much the impulsive, lusty, bohemian writer." The variety of his perceptions reveal this—they roll out of his mind and on to paper or tapes chaotically, in an avalanche which he is hard put to constrain or keep within a political frame. Inevitably, then, after giving full play to his political imagination,

wherein everything, including sex, is given a political configuration, Cleaver falls back on Karl Marx:

> Let's pay our respects to Brother Karl Marx's gigantic brain, using the fruits of his wisdom, applying them to this crumbling system, and have some socialism, moving on to the classless society.

So it all comes down to that, which is where many of us came in. Before Cleaver mentions Marx, he points out that "The basic problem in this country is political confusion." True, but does the injection of Marxian ideas into this situation help to clear up this confusion? If Cleaver thinks so, then we are entitled to ask, what does he think the American Marxists have been about all the years before Cleaver appeared? Have they been adding clarity to confusion? The answer is: not much. In addition to attaching himself to the agony of his (and our) legacy of present-day political confusion, Cleaver innocently and in desperation has attached himself to the agony of the American white Left. We know that misery loves company, this was always so; but our experience in the American morass tells us that *the will to make a revolution is not the same thing as having the means to make it.*

It is a good thing that some black nationalists have arrived at that level of political maturity which allows them to dispense with enough "black racism" to understand that "Whitey," too, is caught in a tight bind in America, right along with his "black colonial subjects." But history has at last handed the black brother a torch to light up the path out of this darkness. Although certain young diehards are using the torch for incendiary purposes, the more sophisticated are called upon to understand *their* own condition in the interests of a heightened black social awareness. Questions arise: Shall the black nationalist militants accept poverty grants in the ghettos, before or after applying the torch, or shall they opt for the revolutionary millennium, during which time someone else will take advantage of the government's grants anyway! Here is one economic source of political confusion, or vice versa. It is very, very real, and what answer can Marx or Mao give to this black political and economic dilemma? (pp. 15-16)

[Behind] the "political confusion" which Cleaver sees as the American malaise lies a vast, ignoble legacy, a grossly distorted interpretation of the political, economic, cultural, racial, and ethnic ingredients that comprise the national development. In short, the American "political confusion" is a reflection of the confusion over "national purpose." Americans generally have no agreement on who they are, what they are, or how they got to be what they are. They do not respond to their situation out of any real sense of historical determination, because their "history," when they are aware of it, gives them no guidelines to the resolution of present difficulties.

Thus the black search for "identity" (or Fanon's "cultural matrix") only underscores the fact that *all* Americans are involved in an identity crisis. Since whites and blacks do not identify with each other, it only means that neither blacks nor whites are really identifying with the realities of the American experience which bound them together so fatefully in what is supposed to be the "cultural matrix" of a nation. Thus the implied threat of the division of the nation into "two nations black and white" is another way of saying that the American experiment in nationhood has been a historical failure of the first magnitude.

Simplistically and biologically, the black and white confrontation is called a "racial" conflict, a carry-over from black slavery. But deep down, historically and psychologically, it is a *cultural conflict* over the seeming incompatibility of "group values" and aspirations which manifest themselves in our political, economic, and cultural institutions. The implied premises of these institutions are, ultimately, the perpetuation of Anglo-Saxon Protestant supremacy, which is the white-skinned side of cultural nationalism.

For this important reason Cleaver's attack on what he perceives as black "cultural nationalism," its meaning and social role, is not only superficial, but also reveals a narrow-minded and antihistorical point of view. There are some black nationalists for whom, as Cleaver charges, "posturing, dress, or reviving African cultural roots" is the be-all and end-all of "cultural nationalism." It becomes *their* form of psychological "liberation" from the values of white culture especially when it culminates in dropping "slave names." Call it romanticism, but every movement has its share of romantics. People have called [Marcus] Garvey's "Back to Africa" nationalism "Political Nationalism," but it was also scoffed at as being "highly romantic" and "utopian."

Cleaver posits the necessity for political revolution in opposition to the search for identity implicit in black "cultural nationalism," as if to say that in America blacks and whites can collaborate in making revolution without a program that will deal with the problem of black cultural identity or cultural nationalism. The Marxists have long maintained this position, but this reviewer, while understanding the logic of this position, will continue to maintain that it is erroneous. (pp. 16-17)

The problem with Eldridge Cleaver and those of his generation who opt for "political revolution" is that a new set of social and philosophical concepts are needed to substantiate political activism toward more and specified goals. To say that America is a racist society is not enough—there is more to it than that. If American racism created the institutions, it is now the institutions themselves which legitimize the racist behavior of those who are the products of the institutions. The problem, then, is how to deal *structurally* with these institutions—how to alter them, eradicate them, or build new and better ones? What is the method of social change to follow the demonstrations, the oratory and polemics, the jailings, the agony, and the exiles? (p. 18)

> *Harold Cruse, "The Fire This Time?" in* The New York Review of Books, *Vol. XII, No. 9, May 8, 1969, pp. 13-18.*

JAMES FOREST

[*Post-Prison Writings and Speeches*] is hard reading, not because [Cleaver] has lost his gift for words, but because the cross and nails are so real, as is the unknowing assent to their use by the rest of us. The chase is real, the cruelty is inquisitional, the casualties and deaths paralyze the tongue.

The book is no sequel, in any usual sense, to *Soul on Ice*. It emerges from a crowded life. The language straddles street and hermitage. The meditations and outrage that Eldridge shares come from immediate crises in which he is always a participant, no matter how hard he attempted to exempt himself beforehand in his apprehension of the Adult Authority and his appetite for some degree of normalcy and calm.

The book is unkind. As is put by a Harlem proverb, "It's hard to love the landlord when the plumbing doesn't work." For Cleaver the plumbing of society stopped working before he was born. In fact his floor had never been served by it in the first place, at least not on this continent. Love of the landlord was incomprehensible from the beginning. Nor is there any evidence that Cleaver ever experienced "the Man" other than as an armed enemy preferring his death to societal renovation. . . .

What is the wonder with Eldridge, what is the wonder and miracle and perhaps ultimate strength of the poor, is the ability to transcend these horrors, to remain sane, to hope that even still the earth will become a communal inheritance—to believe that the Lazarus of starving men and banquet tables will at last either rejoin humanity or leave it. All such hope and sanity has survived in Cleaver, despite the anger, and with it a certain holy doubt and humor about himself. . . . (p. 85)

If a grocer shoots to kill when his store is threatened with robbery, no protest is raised in the white community. The dogma is in the air we breathe, though best left unsaid: property is more sacred than life. If a black man declares, Let us defend ourselves, or if he determines that he no longer wishes to live in that burning house we call a way of life, the cries are heard: *Violence!* (as if pacifism were the American way); *Reverse racism!* (though it is not skin color but white passivity that black radicals cry out against); and, not least, *You don't have to use that kind of language!* (while those of angelic tongue go about the patriotic work of tolerating, even underwriting, the burning of black-haired people).

Cleaver is tough medicine. His book is grating. But it is generous in its honesty and even inspiring in its implied belief that communication is still worth attempting, that even we cushioned white people may at last discover that we too are being used and damaged and that revolution will not occur until more of us live out the revolution. (pp. 85-6)

> *James Forest, "The Funk of Life," in* The Critic, *Vol. 27, No. 6, June-July, 1969, pp. 82-6.*

SHANE STEVENS

[Cleaver's] volume of "post-prison" writings and speeches (a phrase stamped on the book jacket and used as part of the title on the title page, no doubt to squeeze out every last drop of sensationalism) . . . is sheer polemics. Even worse, it is mere propaganda. Manifestoes, diatribes, threats, exhortations—the whole bag of propagandist tricks is here. Ostensibly to fill a political need. In actuality, to fulfill a simple economic greed: money. No, I'm not blaming Cleaver, although there is much that he can, and will, be blamed for. He apparently did not have much to do with it, now that he is [living in exile in Algiers]. Those who should be blamed know who they are. . . .

During the past year I have talked with Cleaver, sitting with him one night into the small hours of the morning in the offices of *Ramparts* magazine. I was a sponsor of the International Committee to Defend Eldridge Cleaver. In my review of *Soul on Ice* in the May, 1968, issue of *The Progressive* [see excerpt above], I wrote that "this book is important . . . this book is extraordinary." I asked America to give the book a hearing because it had freshness and insight and a power of conviction. I believed it then, and I believe it now. Eldridge Cleaver is a soul brother, and I don't like what has been happening to him.

Sadly, it must be said, **Post-Prison Writings** does no one any service, least of all Cleaver. Many of the writings have appeared elsehwere, mainly in the pages of *Ramparts*. For the most part they should have remained there, for in this last year of his American life Cleaver was devoting himself exclusively to the political situation. In many respects it was akin to the last year of [comedian and social satirist] Lenny Bruce's life, wherein he addressed himself solely to his legal efforts. A pattern of paranoia emerged that was to hamper Bruce in his work and in his ability to view the world. As the shouting increases, conviction lessens. And when this is applied to writing, the power disappears.

The articles in Cleaver's new book are flabby; some are mere exercises. To pick several at random: "The Decline of the Black Muslims," "My Father and Stokely Carmichael," and "The Land Question and Black Liberation." All heat, no light. All polemical, none convincing. All the power gone. Perhaps only in "Shoot-out in Oakland" are there traces of the writer using words to convey real feeling rationally arrived at. As for the speeches, well, speeches are always best being spoken. And Cleaver is a good speaker, very good indeed. Perhaps, as is recognized now with James Baldwin—that he is a fine essayist and not a novelist—Cleaver will be seen to be a better speaker than writer. (p. 28)

So much for the book. I cannot find words strong enough to condemn the cheapness of this sordid affair. If Cleaver were just another self-styled revolutionist out for a little personal power, I would say nothing. Let them publish anything for a fast buck, and be damned. But Cleaver is more than that. Unfortunately, because of the notoriety, the book will have wide circulation. His reputation as a writer deserves better than that.

What went wrong? Where did Cleaver fail, and where did America fail him—even beyond the fact that it bore him into a racist society as a second-class citizen and made him never forget it? Toward the end of my review of *Soul on Ice* in *The Progressive* I asked the question: "Where does Cleaver go from here?" And I answered it by suggesting that what happens to him as a writer depends on what happens to him as a man: "The urge to be a full-time revolutionary in a country so desperately ill is overwhelming. Yet the writer must always retain a certain part of himself on the periphery of events if he is to be most effective."

Unfortunately, tragically, Cleaver became that full-time revolutionary; at least in his own mind. He devoted all his energies to his cause and thereby lost the very existence without which a writer can not function. He became a purveyor of propaganda, a writer of tracts, a maker of speeches. All his thoughts were channeled to one end, and the true writer that perhaps existed within slowly smothered and died. There is a world of difference between a propagandist and a writer of conviction. A world as wide as the difference between *Soul on Ice* and the present collection.

But even beyond that, Cleaver failed himself because of his total commitment to the Black Panthers. At the outset, the Black Panther Party had some semblance of revolutionary zeal in that it subscribed to the traditional revolutionary doctrine of alliances among all oppressed groups. The Black Panthers saw, or pretended to see, their role as leaders in a class struggle. (pp. 28-9)

Now, however, with each passing day the Black Panthers are veering more and more toward a racist-based ideology of a black liberation struggle. Whites will still be "used," but only in subordinate roles. And then, only when needed. Racism is in the saddle, regardless of the honeyed words being spoken. Cleaver, for all his spoken and written protestations as a people-lover, cannot be excused from sharing in this guilt.

Further, Cleaver has allowed himself to become a focal point of a "cult of personality" syndrome, which is death to any revolutionary attitude. He, among the Black Panther leadership, is not alone in this, yet he has done nothing to negate this tendency. His—and the Black Panthers'—adoration of Che Guevara labels the present attitude for what it is: sheer romanticism. . . .

The Black Panthers have scuttled their claim to any revolutionary fervor that could amount to anything, and they are being co-opted and nullified into just another hostile group that will be handled militarily. For this, Cleaver is as guilty as anyone else.

Finally, where did White America fail Cleaver? I mean beyond the harassment, the injustices, the debilitating hatred from known enemies. I am talking about the white liberals who bought and paid for Eldridge Cleaver—C.O.D. Almost from the time he left prison they looked upon him as Jesus Christ returned. They gave him the heady wine of instant fame: He was good copy. They gave him golden robes of green paper: He then shared in their guilt at amassing their wealth. And they crucified him on the altar of politics: resurrecting him as long as he wrote what they wanted to read. They put him up for President in the cruelest joke since the Hunchback of Notre Dame was jeered as king.

From a writer who wrote what he wanted to say to a publicist who wrote what they wanted to hear. All in one easy stage. Harry Golden had it right: It could happen only in America.

There are 200 million stories in this sick country. This has been one of the sickest of them. (p. 29)

Shane Stevens, "Eldridge Cleaver: 'A Soul Brother' Gone Wrong," in The Progressive, *Vol. 33, No. 7, July, 1969, pp. 28-9.*

MEDIA & METHODS

To: English Chairman
From: Principal
Re: "Soul of Ice"

Will you kindly respond to the following questions relative to the book "Soul of Ice" which is currently being used by Mr. _____.

1. Was this book approved by the chairman?

2. Were students requested to purchase this book from personal funds?

3. Did Mr. _____ consider other books on "black power" before this particular book was selected?

4. Do you personally feel that the objectionable parts destroy the literary value of the book?

The utilization of this book has caused a great amount of concern among many parents. I must have your answers to the above questions as I feel quite sure that this matter will probably go to the Board of Education. Thank you.

—The Principal

To: Principal
From: English Chmn. HS
Re: "Soul of Ice" (sic)

In response to your letter of April 17:

1. We are not teaching "Soul of Ice" in Mr. _____'s class. The book he is using is called **"Soul *on* Ice."** I approved the use of that book in a discussion with Mr. _____.

2. If you recall, we were at the point of discovering that a large sum of money ticketed, or rather, budgeted, for books for the English Dept. was not available. . . . I told Mr. _____that the sum was no longer available. He then said that he thought that students would be willing to purchase the book from personal funds. I consented to this arrangement.

3. Yes, there was discussion about other books on "black power," but because the book has been hailed by many sources, because Cleaver has been and is in the news, we decided on **"Soul on Ice."** However, it is absolutely unfair to label this a black power book. You will understand this after you read it.

4. The psychiatrist Robert Coles wrote in "Atlantic Monthly," "He [Cleaver] is full of Christian care, Christian grief and disappointment, Christian resignation, Christian messianic toughness, and hope" [see excerpt above].

In some ways, **"Soul on Ice"** reminds me of a book of confessions; in particular, sections of it recall to my mind "The Confessions of Saint Augustine."

No, the objectionable parts do not destroy the literary value of the book, in my opinion. If you read the book, you will find much, much more that is objectionable that has nothing to do with sex. **"Soul on Ice"** is a book full of pain, Cleaver's pain— and it is that pain that is objectionable. Taken all together, this book is a black man's spiritual odyssey away from hate and crime towards understanding, and 'convalescence,' Cleaver's own term. . . .

All in all, a dramatic and troubled book, written by a tormented black man in search of sanity.

> *"Aux Armes!"* in Media & Methods, *Vol. 6, No. 1, September, 1969, p. 38.*

BAYARD RUSTIN

The political transformation of Eldridge Cleaver is one of the most profoundly interesting human dramas of our era. However, tracing his evolution is less my concern than the content and clarity of his thinking. Cleaver is saying many things that badly need saying and that are either not being said or not being said so well.

Cleaver's message is to remind us just how revolutionary the democratic idea really is. His emphasis on the importance of democracy may seem commonplace, but his views are powerful because they are the result of both theory and experience. His passionately felt beliefs have caused him to perceive the importance of turning the clichés of democracy back into ideals.

Cleaver, who once denounced the United States as "evil," "criminal," and "crazy," now describes himself as a patriot. He is certainly that, but at the same time he is both more and less. Unlike some previous refugees from totalitarian ideologies, Cleaver has not gone over to an opposite and equally extreme doctrine. Instead he is a radical democrat, who sees in the United States the best embodiment of the democratic ideal. (p. 20)

To those who would attempt to stereotype Cleaver as a right-wing superpatriot, he has himself provided the best answer: "The greatest mistake we have made as a nation is to allow our shining principles to lapse so far into disuse that we misname them clichés." Thus, Cleaver's patriotism is not narrow chauvinism but a sophisticated attempt to merge national pride with the fuller implementation of the American principles of democracy, equality, and justice. Cleaver's analysis is remarkably reminiscent of that of George Orwell, perhaps the most astute political observer of the twentieth century. Orwell criticized the British left for denigrating nationalism as necessarily reactionary and provincial. It was the patriotism of the British working class, he argued, that saved Britain from defeat at the hands of [Adolf] Hitler. In a letter to the *Los Angeles Times* Cleaver advanced the concept of a progressive and democratic patriotism that recognizes that "admitting our weaknesses does not negate our strengths. And glorifying in our strengths, as we rightly should, does not necessitate covering up our weaknesses."

Cleaver has not abandoned his belief in the necessity of fundamental social and economic transformations. He now insists that the method to achieve change is through democratic processes and not by violent revolution. Unlike some American radicals who have recently made a purely tactical endorsement of democracy because revolution is not likely to succeed in the United States, Cleaver has a profound appreciation of the human significance of democracy. Cleaver judges that political democracy is more important than economic democracy. It is easier, he contends, to add economic democracy to political democracy than to add political democracy to the sham economic democracy of the Communist states or the third-world dictatorships.

In the process of altering his views about democracy, Cleaver's feelings about the black struggle in America have also changed. From his experiences abroad he has concluded that the United States is far ahead of the rest of the world in solving its racial problems. In a recent interview, Cleaver outlined his perspective on black progress in the United States thusly: "Black people need to realize very fundamentally that they are full and equal citizens of the U.S. We can no longer afford to 'fence straddle' about where we are going. We can no longer afford to ask: Are we going to stay here and be integrated, or are we going to go back to Africa, as we have been saying since slavery? Are we going to separate into five states like the black Muslims used to talk about? . . . We are as much a part of the United States as any Rockefeller, and we can no longer afford to ask such questions." Not surprisingly, Cleaver has grown much closer to those mainstream black leaders he used to denounce. He has said, "I want particularly to apologize to Martin Luther King on some points. I now appreciate his awareness that the basic relationship between communities of people has to be one of love."

Cleaver's defense of democracy is all the more persuasive because he has not only lived in totalitarian countries and third-world dictatorships, but he was also once an adherent of those regimes. Indeed, Cleaver's most valuable function may be to dispel the myths about these societies. His idea of proletarian internationalism was but a concentrated version of the still persistent romanticism about the third world and a too common naïveté about the nature of Communism. Having lived in the third world, Cleaver is uniquely qualified to communicate the truths that the third world is "an empty phrase," that there are "incredible differences" in the third-world countries, and that many third-world countries are tyrannies.

The analysis that Cleaver makes of Communism is penetrating and insightful. He observes that "communists strap onto people the most oppressive regimes in the history of the world. Regimes that are dictatorships, dictatorships in the name of the proletariat, not by the proletariat." Cleaver criticizes détente for propping up the Soviet regimes and concludes that if the United States is truly to be a force for democracy in the world "we have an obligation to help in the disintegration of the Soviet regime." That is a harsh judgment, to be sure, but it flows naturally from Cleaver's commitment to democracy. (pp. 20-1)

I do not know how many on the left will listen to Cleaver. Certainly they will make every effort to avoid confronting his challenge to their uncritical acceptance of political myths. Sympathizers with the radical currents of the past decade cannot help but be made uncomfortable by Cleaver's proposition that it is time to sum up the questioning process, to abandon mistaken notions, and to come to some conclusions. I suspect that, nonetheless, the intensity and intelligence of Cleaver's views will force the confrontation whether or not it is desired.

Cleaver, I am convinced, is capable of speaking to a far larger audience than his former followers and sympathizers. He may well have to endure a long apprenticeship to redeem himself in the eyes of those who still suspect him or cannot yet forgive his past. Cleaver recognizes that it may be a long time before many people will agree with him.

The return of Eldridge Cleaver to the United States is a summing up of the decade of the sixties and a sign of new possibilities. In the sixties Cleaver became an almost mythical figure for thousands of young blacks and whites; but today, I believe, he is an authentic hero. . . .

Even in Cleaver's early writings there was a strongly humanistic strain. Unfortunately, his desire for a better world was so strong and consuming that he condemned a system that was unable to immediately meet his stringent demands for perfection and justice and embraced an ideology that was destructive of human values. It is to Cleaver's credit that he had the strength and intelligence to reevaluate his beliefs and to avoid the temptations of despair and cynicism. His change is best reflected in his comment: "Somehow, man is less grand than I would have thought. He's still OK, but he's less grand." This attitude of realism, responsible optimism, and genuine humanism undergirds Cleaver's political views. (p. 21)

Bayard Rustin, "Eldridge Cleaver and the Democratic Idea," in The Humanist, Vol. 36, No. 5, September-October, 1976, pp. 20-1.

RICHARD GILMAN

A little over 10 years ago I reviewed Eldridge Cleaver's *Soul on Ice* [see excerpt above]. . . . I said then (and on rereading the book still think) that Cleaver was a gifted writer but one whose particular qualities of rage, resentment and quasimystical aspiration in a context of racial struggle put him outside many of our literary canons. The review led to an agitated discussion . . . in which I tried to refine and clarify the distinctions I had drawn in the first piece.

The chief one was between what I called writing of a more or less traditional kind that happened to be by blacks (or "Negroes" at the time; that usage still held sway) and writing of a political and ideological cast that was intended mainly as a source of morale for blacks. My point was that the former could and ought to be judged the way we judge any sort of writing, but the latter, a provisional, tactical sort of thing, resisted—legitimately, I thought—our cultivated, humanistic, "white" standards.

Whatever the virtues or defects of this argument, it's been rendered academic, in Cleaver's case at least, by his new book. *Soul on Fire* has none of the sense of urgency of its predecessor, none of its intelligent participation in crucial issues of the mind and of politics. A slipshod, ill-written, spiritless piece of work from any point of view, its only virtue is that it provides some information, for those who might feel the need of it, on Cleaver's years in exile, after fleeing the United States while under indictment, in Cuba, Algeria and finally Paris. (p. 29)

In any case, his rationale for being in political exile eroded, his hopes for a solution to his problems with the law raised by the advent of a new admininistration in Washington, Cleaver negotiated for his return and in the late fall of 1975 left Paris for the States. He had gone into exile as a dramatic and even charismatic figure and returned as a footnote to the history of his times.

Along with his growing patriotism, he tells us, he had experienced while abroad a rising impulse toward religion, which culminated, shortly before his departure from France, in an abrupt and unconditional surrender. Thus the change in the titles of his books from "Ice" to "Fire," reflects, as he says, his movement from the status of a prison inmate to that of a born-again Christian. When it was revealed a year or so after his return that he had become heavily engaged in evangelical activity the general reaction was, understandably, skepticism, while that of his former associates was compounded of fury and contempt. These things being so, [*Soul on Fire*] is in large part an effort to establish his sincerity.

Well, such matters aren't properly subject to judgment, except perhaps from a long perspective in which a life may be seen in relation to a credo, and I for one am disposed to grant Cleaver what he asks. He's sincere, then, but the trouble is that he's become entirely uninteresting.

What's most surprising about Cleaver's change of heart and mind is the complete loss of eloquence it seems to have brought about. *Soul on Ice* was streaked with bad writing, but that stemmed I think from impatience or an excess of vitality and was more than atoned for by the many passages of sharp, accurate, often lyrical description and observation. . . . (pp. 30-1)

Soul on Fire has none of this fineness and originality. The account of his Paul-like conversion, for example, is doubtless honest but it makes for bad literature and probably bad theology too. He is sitting in his vacation apartment near Cannes gazing out on a beautiful night sky. He is depressed, thinking about committing suicide. Suddenly he sees an image of himself, a profile that had been used on Black Panther posters, in a shadow on the moon, and starts trembling. "As I stared at this image it changed, and I saw my former heroes paraded before my eyes. Here were Fidel Castro, Mao Tse-tung, Karl Marx, Friedrich Engels, passing in review—each one appearing for a moment of time, and then dropping out of sight, like fallen heroes. Finally, at the end of the procession, in dazzling, shimmering light, the image of Jesus Christ appeared . . . I fell to my knees.''

The book is filled with clichés and platitudes, as well as with an astonishing naiveté about what educated readers might or might not be expected to know. When Cleaver talks about going to bed as a child he thinks it necessary to print the entire prayer that begins ''Now I lay me. . . .'' He says that ''it must have rained for forty days and forty nights'' and that ''American violence is homemade like apple pie.'' . . .

When his writing isn't obvious and simpleminded it's gnarled and pretentious. . . . (p. 31)

It is all very sad. Whether or not Cleaver had the capacity to sustain an intellectual career of any kind at the center of political or cultural issues is debatable, but what's beyond dispute are the losses implicit in this book. The question isn't one of religion in itself but of the peculiar likelihood in America that if one gains faith one has to relinquish thought. Perhaps Cleaver's erratic and wayward talnet thrived on a transient conjunction with the pressures and dramas of the period; but at least he was connected to it and was able to see and judge.

Now he rejoices in meetings with Billy Graham, and is happy to have [Watergate conspirator and born-again Christian] Charles Colson as his ''brother'' and the admiration of one Art DeMoss, president of the National Liberty Corporation of Valley Forge, who describes ''Eldridge . . . and the Lord'' as ''a great combination.'' These people too are of our time, but at the cocksure, self-righteous edge of it where there is no space to turn, to ''maneuver'' the way Cleaver once so brilliantly did. (pp. 31-2)

> *Richard Gilman, in a review of "Soul on Fire," in* The New Republic, *Vol. 180, No. 3, January 20, 1979, pp. 29-32.*

JACQUES G. SQUILLACE

[*Soul on Fire*] projects back to the sixties, when men and women, educators and policy-makers, blacks and whites were caught in a moral bind, demonstrating for human dignity and equal rights. And who better to articulate that era than a notorious black militant revolutionary?

By and by, the book contains all the ''whats'' the reader may want to know about Eldridge Cleaver. It is a collection of the events of his life that shaped him into the man he was to become. . . . There is retrospection on the Panther cause, its principles, terminology, possibilities and programs, and the public misconceptions of the Panther organization. There is reflection on the doctrine of Marxism, which Cleaver came to disavow because of its short-sighted materialism, and its lack of the historical tradition of respect for the individual and his rights, there are descriptions of his exile in Algiers and Paris, and his travels within North Korea, North Vietnam, China, Russia, Cuba and the Third World and his final disenchantment with their systems of government.

But more significantly, indeed more impressively, *Soul on Fire* is maybe the final chapter to Cleaver's becoming. I view his earlier book, *Soul On Ice* and this book as a unity, complementing each other as the two communicate Cleaver's personal, spiritual odyssey from provocative essayist to ''born again'' Christian. The two works read in conjunction give the whole story and complete insight into the man.

He is not simply a zealot or reactionary, but an individual who has experienced pain, injustice, and asks the philosophic question, ''what is being?'' He moves through *Soul on Ice* with a hunger to reaffirm his existence, sometimes in anger, sometimes with abundant pride, but the need is there to speak out, to comment, to seek truth. For Cleaver, that truth is finally found and realized through Christ. . . .

Soul on Fire is Cleaver's proclamation of faith, and his exhortation for Christ. Cleaver is alive and well, again working within and for humanity, with a new identity and a new cause. He is a dynamic and remarkable individual with a lucid masculine style, though at moments the tone can be cynically bitter specifically when he looks back on the misrepresentation of the Panther cause or the killings of his black brothers. But Cleaver has not forsaken or forgotten the original passion for human dignity which inflamed him to reach out in his writings.

> *Jacques G. Squillace, in a review of "Soul on Fire," in* Best Sellers, *Vol. 38, No. 11, February, 1979, p. 351.*

Christopher Collier

1930-

James L(incoln) Collier

1928-

Photograph by Curtis K. Salonick 766 East Northampton Street, Wilkes-Barre, PA 18702. Reprinted by permission of Scholastic Inc.

American novelists and nonfiction writers.

The Collier brothers have collaborated on several historical novels for young adults. Christopher, an American history scholar, provides the historical framework, while James, an established fiction writer, creates characters who represent various responses to historical events. The Colliers attempt to show that history can be interpreted in many ways, unlike the often static recounting of incidents presented in many textbooks. The Colliers often set their stories in colonial America and depict common people who undertake heroic struggles. They examine such topics as racism, sexism, freedom, and war in a historical context, suggesting that the past can provide a useful guide for modern social behavior.

The Colliers have been praised for presenting contrasting perspectives of historical events. In *My Brother Sam Is Dead* (1974), for instance, they depict the Revolutionary War as an internal war fought between those Americans who were loyal and those hostile to British rule. They show that many people opposed rebellion and they present the effects of war on both individuals and families. This novel won wide acclaim for its portrayal of a family divided because of the war. Many of the Colliers' protagonists struggle for social justice. In *War Comes to Willy Freeman* (1983), a young black female attempts to overcome racial and sexual prejudice in pre-Revolutionary America.

The Colliers' work has been generally well received by critics. Many find their blend of historical facts and fictional characters both entertaining and informative.

(See also *Children's Literature Review*, Vol. 3; *Contemporary Authors*, Vols. 9-12, rev. ed.; *Contemporary Authors New Re-*

vision Series, Vol. 4; and *Something about the Author*, Vols. 8, 16.)

JOYCE ALPERN

[*My Brother Sam Is Dead*] in many ways fits the traditional mold of period adventure. Like Esther Forbes's Newbery winning *Johnny Tremain*, its hero, Tim Meeker, is a boy caught up in the events of the American Revolution, who rubs elbows with historical luminaries and grows to manhood under the war's demands. The startling difference here is that Tim Meeker goes through the war totally immune to the Spirit of '76. In fact the only ardent Patriot to play a major part in this novel is Tim's older brother Sam, an idealistic, sometimes rather sophomoric youth who catches the war fever from his Yale classmates.

To modern readers Tim's lack of partisanship seems rather surprising. After all the Revolution remains one of the few really popular wars in our history. . . . Certainly it provides one occasion when juvenile authors can comfortably take sides, presenting the rebels simply as "our side" and exploiting patriotic sentiment in the service of adventure or pedagogy.

Now the Colliers . . . have the nerve to ask us whether, had we been around in '76, we might not have thrown in our lot with the Tories. It's a presumptuous, downright cheeky question. But Tim's experiences really are enough to make us wonder what we'd have done in his place.

From the book's first moment, when brother Sam shows up at the family's door dressed in his new Continental uniform . . . , Tim is caught between his hero worship of Sam and his father Eliphalet's stern disapproval of this rebellion over "a few pence in taxes." . . .

Tim sees his share of action all right, and during these violent confrontations (sometimes graphically but never callously described) Tim is forced to take sides. Yet despite his shifting loyalties—he sometimes considers himself a Tory, sometimes a Patriot—Tim is clearly intended to represent the third side of the war, the uncommitted citizen who must pay the price for the bloody passions of others. For the most part, this works very well. Tim himself is believably confused. Too young to have developed any firm convictions, he is soon left with the responsibility of caring for his mother and the family business, a burden which soon becomes his own private war. Worst of all, in the end brother Sam is arrested on a trumped-up charge of stealing cattle and hanged by the very Continental army he had served so loyally.

This final twist, abrupt and unlikely as it seems, is actually logical because the Colliers have shown so realistically the disorganized state of the Continental army at this time. . . .

My Brother Sam is obviously, at times very unsubtly, an antiwar novel. . . . But young readers, who will find the story very easy going indeed, will probably be most surprised to learn how many average people actually opposed the Revolution. Even for more sophisticated students, it is still surprising to see Tories presented as other than rich, cranky old traitors. Yet while the Meeker family's story might spice up some otherwise dull history lessons, it is unlikely to convince anyone that the Revolution was a mistake.

Joyce Alpern, "Not a Bad Tory," in Book World— The Washington Post, *January 12, 1975, p. 4.*

OLIVIA COOLIDGE

The Bloody Country is an exciting and well-written novel concerning a little-known episode in American history, namely the conflict between Pennsylvania and Connecticut for the ownership of the Wyoming Valley, which was awarded to Pennsylvania by Congress in 1782.

Ben Buck, his parents, his sister Annie and her husband, together with the family slave Joe Mountain, half Indian and half Black, form part of a group of Connecticut settlers which Pennsylvanians now try to dispossess. . . . The Bucks, who have worked desperately to build their flour mill on the banks of the Susquehanna near Wilkes Barre, soon find that their sacrifice and toil count for nothing. If they are driven back to Connecticut with the loss of all they own, Ben sees no future save work as another man's servant, never getting a chance to raise a family or have a place of his own. This grim prospect gradually forces him to reflect on the position of Joe Mountain. . . . Ben's struggles to see Joe as a person rather than a chattel give depth to the plot and serve to develop his character and those of family members.

The action is consistently exciting, starting with the Indian raid which kills Ben's mother, going on to the mounting tension caused by acts of violence against the Connecticut settlers, and climaxed by a tremendous flood of the Susquehanna, which devastates the valley and wipes out the mill. . . . But nothing can keep the Buck family down. Ben and his father rebuild the mill, while "the government" finds it too expensive to continue supporting with troops those speculators who have been trying to take over. Thus all comes right in the end, even for Joe Mountain, while Ben achieves a solid maturity.

The government does not come well out of this story, though it is evident that there are lawyers fighting about the case, even if the Bucks know little about them. But since Ben and his father are indestructible, they wear the government down at least as successfully as do the legal men in Philadelphia. *The Bloody Country* is a dramatic, well-constructed, thoughtful book which gives a vivid picture of the hard work and persistence so often needed by the successful pioneer.

Olivia Coolidge, "The Founding Fighters," in Book World—The Washington Post, *May 2, 1976, p. L3.**

ZENA SUTHERLAND

As they did in their other story of the American Revolution, *My Brother Sam Is Dead,* the Colliers [in *The Bloody Country*] focus on a small geographical area and use it to explore the conflicting loyalties and abrasions between groups of colonists. Here the setting is a Pennsylvania valley community whose residents, emigrants from Connecticut, are persecuted by the Pennamites, older residents who claim the land and who use the help of the British and of a local Indian tribe to drive the newcomers away. . . . Most of the book is based on fact; the community is Wilkes-Barre. The story is dramatic and convincing, the characters drawn with depth and vigor, and the book especially valuable for its exploration of issues and philosophy in a way that enhances the narrative impact of a fine example of historical fiction.

Zena Sutherland, in a review of "The Bloody Country," in Bulletin of the Center for Children's Books, *Vol. 30, No. 4, December, 1976, p. 55.*

HUGHES MOIR

In *My Brother Sam Is Dead,* the first book created by Jim and Kit Collier, the complexity of issues about the Revolutionary War and war in general is explored in ways perhaps unique in children's literature. The story, set in Connecticut, shows a family torn between divided partisanship toward the war: the Loyalist dimension (Mr. Meeker's concern with maintaining his business and protecting his family) versus the Patriot dimension (young Sam Meeker's decision to join the rebel forces). Sam's younger brother, Tim, remains at home and is left with the ultimately unresolved conflict of torn personal loyalties. In the end both his father and brother are killed, providing the reader with biting ironies. His father is killed by the British when he attempts to deliver his cattle to the British troops; Sam is executed by his Patriot regiment after falsely being accused of stealing cattle that belonged to his family. In the end neither Tim nor the reader can make any clear-cut commitment to either side of the conflict. The theme of this book—sharply defined by the events of the story and useful as a "guide to contemporary behavior"—is explained by Kit Collier:

> In a complex way it deals with why Americans did and did not become involved in the war. We wanted to show also that war unleashes forces that one does not know what the outcome may be. Hence, the usefulness of history to explain our present, for example, Lebanon and Viet Nam.

As a work conceived to present concepts related to the issues of war, *My Brother Sam Is Dead* portrays the Revolutionary War not as the good guys versus the bad guys, but rather as a *civil war* where families and communities were divided in public opinion. It was not an easy war to fight or to make decisions about. (p. 377)

Since at the time of the American Revolution all people living in America were British subjects, the war was not fought between the Americans and the British, but rather between groups of Americans whose loyalties were different. If the war is viewed as between the Patriots and the British government, then it was indeed a war of revolution. However, those who fought against each other were indeed Americans whose loyalties were split and, therefore, were the central characters in a civil war. . . . Any oversimplification of the issues involved denies historical realities and is, therefore, not useful to understanding contemporary events and issues.

In their second book, *The Bloody Country,* the Colliers have attempted to confront the reader with more complex issues. The family leaves their colonial home in Connecticut and moves to the frontier of the Susquehanna Valley in what is now Pennsylvania. The treachery and greed that the family encounters while trying to carve out a place to live are presented with a realism that may be found shocking. Kit Collier defends the book in this way:

> In *Bloody Country* there is a deliberate effort to present bloodiness and gore in an effort to combat the deadened feeling about war and violence which is a result of television. We are attempting to combat the absence of feeling about violence and a skewed view of human life.

The relative balance between property values and the value of human lives is the pivotal conflict around which the story evolved. As such, it fairly portrays issues related to the American frontier at any time in our history and in any historical setting. This history of the dominant white culture in relation to minority ethnic groups—particularly black Americans, American Indians, Asian Americans, and Mexican Americans—has, as its central theme, the conflict of these two values. While the presentation of this conflict in *Bloody Country* is scaled down in locale and historical events, the reader is forced to deal with the contradictions in greater depth in this story.

The historical moods of James and Christopher Collier are, then, more than just a good "read." They delve into our history with an eye for truth—truth that may result in contradiction and uncertainties. The stories are at the same time readable and challenging to our conception of the reality of human events and the need for faith in human values. . . . [The] combined talents [of the Colliers] offer young readers not only a story worth reading, but an opportunity, through their books, to deal with fundamental human issues in a way not possible in most literature. (pp. 377-78)

> Hughes Moir, "Profile: James and Christopher Collier—More Than Just a Good Read," in Language Arts, Vol. 55, No. 3, March, 1978, pp. 373-78.

KIRKUS REVIEWS

[In *The Winter Hero,* the American Revolution] is over, but in western Massachusetts there's new unrest: laws passed way off in Boston—where it seemed too costly to send representatives —are making the poor farmer poorer, and aggrandizing the rich. When hot-tempered Peter McColloch's oxen are taken to satisfy a debt, he hies himself to Daniel Shays—and the Colliers launch us into the story of Shays' dubiously-named "Rebellion," as seen by 14-year-old Justin Conkey. . . . There's precious little glory, insistent-volunteer Justin finds, as Shays' Regulators are outmaneuvered, outmanned, outgunned and, time after time, run away. . . . This is truly history talked out and walked out. Less effective is Justin's injection into the house of Peter's lordly creditor as servant and spy . . . and Justin's relations with everyone, including his worried but resolute sister, carry more intellectual than emotional conviction. Still, with Peter's fate hanging in the balance till the last—will he be executed or pardoned?—pages keep turning. And as a dramatized argument, the book is more than respectable. For, of course, the defeated rebels elect their own to the next legislature, with encouraging results; had they done so before, the whole uprising might have been avoided.

> A review of "The Winter Hero," in Kirkus Reviews, Vol. XLVI, No. 21, November 1, 1978, p. 1192.

ZENA SUTHERLAND

Like the other historical novels by the Collier brothers, [*The Winter Hero*] is fiction skilfully based on fact, and an appended note makes clear which is which. . . . As is true of the earlier books, the story has a dramatic plot and good style, historical information nicely integrated into the plot and the dialogue, and that final element that marks the best in historical fiction: it gives the reader an understanding of the personal conflicts, the practical needs, the ideological principles, and the background that contributed to an event. The political oppression and financial burdens suffered by Massachusetts citizens in 1787, seen through Justin's eyes, are as vivid as his descriptions of confrontations between farmers and government troops.

*Zena Sutherland, in a review of "The Winter Hero,"
in* Bulletin of the Center for Children's Books, *Vol.
32, No. 6, February, 1979, p. 97.*

PAUL HEINS

Although Shays' Rebellion might seem to be an unpromising
subject for a historical novel for young readers, the authors of
My Brother Sam Is Dead . . . have courageously but not always
successfully made the most of it [in *The Winter Hero*]. Seen
from the point of view of Justin Conkey, who was fourteen at
the time, the events of the story transcend the urgent question
of taxation in America and emphasize the boy's desire to prove
himself a hero. . . . The language is plain and full of understatement; the events and the unusual situations historically
verifiable; but the last two-thirds of the novel gives the impression of a briefly developed chronicle and fails to sustain the
dramatic interest, the suspense, and the vivid characterization
of the opening. (pp. 67-8)

Paul Heins, in a review of "The Winter Hero," in
The Horn Book Magazine, *Vol. LV, No. 1, February,
1979, pp. 67-8.*

ZENA SUTHERLAND

[*Jump Ship to Freedom* is] told by young Dan Arabus, whose
father had fought in the patriots' army and had become a free
man, while Dan and his mother still belonged to Captain Ivers.
In an adventurous tale of danger and pursuit, Dan runs away
after a frightening sea voyage and is taken under the wing of
an elderly Quaker who is en route to the Constitutional Convention in Philadelphia. . . . The notes that follow the story
draw a careful distinction between fact and fiction, and explain
the authors' decision to shape the dialogue and terminology to
preserve accuracy and convey a period flavor. The dramatic
story is solidly constructed, well-paced save for a rather lengthy
description of a storm at sea, and sensitive to the changes in
Dan as he begins to understand that a man can be proud,
intelligent, and compassionate whether he is rich or poor, black
or white; it is, however, inconsistent in the use of plural and
singular in "plain talk," the Quaker speech patterns.

*Zena Sutherland, in a review of "Jump Ship to Free-
dom," in* Bulletin of the Center for Children's Books,
Vol. 35, No. 2, October, 1981, p. 26.

STEPHEN KRENSKY

[The] past is not always a dusty place with mold growing in
the corners, a fact born out by **"Jump Ship to Freedom,"** a
fast-paced narrative about a black slave in 1787.

Daniel Arabus is the slave, a bright but somewhat cowed teenager owned by Captain Ivers of Stratford, Conn. Daniel has
been told that feeling lowly and stupid is an inherent condition
in "negroes," but his natural intelligence says otherwise.
Through his eyes the Colliers have subtly documented the ironic
idiocy of regarding men and women as property when they are
so demonstrably human beings. Daniel's one source of pride
is the memory of his recently drowned father. Jack Arabus had
fought bravely in the Revolution, serving in his master's place
in exchange for his freedom. When Captain Ivers tried to renege
on this promise, Jack sued him and won. The facts of the actual
case are the basis for the Colliers' story. . . .

The Colliers have done an excellent job of re-creating the flavor
of the Colonial period without overwhelming the story with it.
The description of a working clipper ship is rough and taut,
not just the romanticized account of so many yarns. . . .

Throughout his journeys, Daniel measures himself and his earlier perception against the people he encounters. His growing
self-esteem is not starkly determined, however. Not every black
character he meets is good, not all the white ones bad. As
Daniel shakes off the doctrines of inferiority instilled in him
from birth, he learns that each person must earn respect on his
own merits.

When Daniel gains the freedom to do that, he is a slave no
longer.

Stephen Krensky, "An Escape from Slavery," in The
Christian Science Monitor, *October 14, 1981, p. B10.*

CYNTHIA KING

Daniel Arabus is a 14-year-old runaway slave from Stratford,
Conn., who overhears certain arguments that preceded the North-
South compromise on slavery. How he ends up carrying the
crucial message to the Constitutional Convention in Philadelphia in 1787, while posters are being circulated for his capture,
is the story the Collier brothers tell.

Though **"Jump Ship to Freedom"** is patterned like their other
novels . . . , it is not as strong. Once again a young boy is
thrust into a pivotal moment in Revolutionary history. But Dan
Arabus is not as convincing as the authors' other heroes. . . .

Dan is almost miraculously perceptive, analytical, brave, resourceful and just plain lucky. But his experience, credible or
not, illuminates a historical time and place in fine detail, even
as it dramatizes a black youth's struggle to understand how
political events shape his life.

*Cynthia King, in a review of "Jump Ship to Free-
dom," in* The New York Times Book Review, *February 14, 1982, p. 28.*

JOEL TAXEL

This important novel [*Jump Ship to Freedom*] touches on an
issue all-too-rarely treated in historical fiction for young people; namely the fiercely debated question of how the new Constitution would deal with the issue of black slavery. . . .

Another noteworthy aspect of this exciting novel is the dramatic
change we see in Daniel's self-esteem. At the outset, we see
a boy who has internalized the myths about black inferiority
used to justify their enslavement. His adventures and contacts
with more enlightened attitudes lead to a growing understanding that he too is a person of dignity and worth.

*Joel Taxel, in a review of "Jump Ship to Freedom,"
in* The ALAN Review, *Vol. 9, No. 3, Spring, 1982,
p. 25.*

DONNARAE MacCANN

[*My Brother Sam Is Dead*] appears to have been inspired by
the anti-war movement of the 70s, although the book is about
the American Revolution. Young Timothy cannot decide whether
to be a "Patriot" like his beloved brother or a Tory like his
beloved father. In the climactic incident, Timothy's brother,
Sam, a dedicated member of the Continental army, is suddenly

executed by his own commanding general because of an alleged theft. Authors Christopher and James Lincoln Collier seem to be trying to stun the reader with a triple-layered irony: Sam's arrest for a crime he didn't commit, his indictment for literally stealing from himself and his death at the hands of his compatriots. The unrealistic plot complications reduce credibility, and the book comes close to what Albert Guérard has defined as propaganda: A book that "tries to snatch an intellectual decision by means of a sentimental appeal." (p. 20)

> *Donnarae MacCann, "Militarism in Juvenile Fiction," in* Interracial Books for Children Bulletin, *Vol. 13, Nos. 6 & 7, 1982, pp. 18-20.**

JOEL TAXEL

Rather than suggesting Americans shared a consensus about the correctness of the rebellion against the king, *My Brother Sam Is Dead* (1974) contains a picture of a family and community bitterly divided on this very issue. . . .

Caught in the middle of this dispute is Tim, Sam's younger brother and the novel's protagonist. The tragedy of war is evident in the conclusion of the novel which finds Sam executed by his own army for a crime he did not commit, while his father dies after languishing aboard a disease-ridden British prison ship after being incarcerated for no apparent reason. Tim, finding hypocrisy and duplicity on both sides, chooses not to fight and instead sits out the war in the tavern with his mother. (p. 34)

[*My Brother Sam Is Dead* was] written at the height of the Vietnam War, a conflict that spurred large numbers of Americans to engage in active, often vociferous dissent against their government's foreign policy. That the anti-war movement was on the mind of the Colliers seems clear, for *My Brother Sam Is Dead* is, above all, an anti-war novel; a bitter denunciation of the folly and futility of war as a mode of social action. . . .

Much of the discussion surrounding *My Brother Sam Is Dead* stemmed from a belief that it had "something new" to say about the Revolution. Co-author Christopher Collier disputes this claim, pointing out instead that what made the book different was its incorporation of the Progressive interpretation of the Revolution rather than the Whig/Consensus viewpoint. Unlike the Whig and Consensus historians who . . . focus on the role played by political and ideological matters in precipitating the rupture between king and colonies, Progressive historians, and their "New-Left" descendents, were concerned with the nature of the government to be established *after* home-rule was secured. This Progressive/New-Left interest in "who should rule at home" caused these historians to emphasize the part played by economics and class conflict in generating the Revolution. Although *My Brother Sam Is Dead* does show the divisions within at least one New England Community, it offers little insight into the issues behind these divisions. While an historical novel can hardly be expected to contain the detail of an historical monograph, the lack of at least some detail makes *Sam* somewhat disappointing. This is not, however, to diminish the novel's significance. *Sam,* as an anti-war novel, has much to say to young readers, not only about the Revolution, but (indirectly) about the way history and fiction are informed by present day concerns. (p. 35)

> *Joel Taxel, "Historical Fiction and Historical Interpretation," in* The ALAN Review, *Vol. 10, No. 2, Winter, 1983, pp. 32-6.**

JOEL TAXEL

[*Jump Ship to Freedom*] details a young black's involvement in the constitutional compromise that left intact the brutal slave system. *War Comes to Willy Freeman* details the events that preceded those depicted in that work.

Willy Freeman is a free, thirteen-year-old black girl living in Revolutionary War Connecticut. After witnessing the brutal slaying of her father by the British, she returns home to find that her mother has disappeared. Her search for her mother takes place against a backdrop of the war's final months and the efforts of Captain Ivers to re-enslave her. This novel is one of a precious few which discuss the plight of blacks during the Revolution: Do they believe the promises of freedom tended by both the British and the Americans? Unfortunately, while we *are* privy to Willy's thoughts about this momentous issue, we never really get involved in her drama. A disappointing novel about an important and ignored aspect of American history.

> *Joel Taxel, in a review of "War Comes to Willy Freeman," in* The ALAN Review, *Vol. 10, No. 3, Spring, 1983, p. 25.*

HOLLY SANHUBER

Once again the Colliers deal with the impact of war on humanity. The nature of [*War Comes to Willy Freeman*], a fast-paced adventure, precludes extensive character development. Willy is an endearing creature, though, and her exploits and daring ensure exciting reading. The Colliers certainly have a gift for using dialect realistically without it becoming obtrusive, although the sometimes use of the word "nigger" by both blacks and whites . . . may offend modern sensibilities. More disturbing to some readers may be the fact that although Willy bemoans woman's lot as unequal and unfair—the authors acknowledge she may sound too modern—she twice uses the fact of her gender to save her life.

> *Holly Sanhuber, in a review of "War Comes to Willy Freeman," in* School Library Journal, *Vol. 29, No. 8, April, 1983, p. 121.*

RICHARD SLOTKIN

The Colliers' *War Comes to Willy Freeman,* set during the American Revolution, has as its protagonist a black girl whose father dies in the British attack on New London, Connecticut (1781). . . . The inner life of Willy Freeman is the real matter of this story, which deals with the primary early-teen issues of individuation and separation from parents and parental authority. The issues implicitly correspond to the themes of the War of Independence, which gives the history an emotional resonance. The sexual role-playing Willy engages in also raises questions of sexual identity that are so critical during puberty, and do so in a way that readers concerned with overcoming sexual stereotypes will find interesting. Likewise, Willy's blackness gives her (and the reader) a unique and provocative perspective on the ideological issues of the Revolution—liberty, equality and independence.

The historical settings are recognizable, but not so familiar as to smack of the textbook. The issues are historically valid, but they have relevance for the lives of the book's modern audience. This is a novel that is as much about character as it is about history; and that balance of elements is just right not only for historical fiction, but for novels of any kind. (p. 18)

Richard Slotkin, "Tales of Two Cities," in Book World—The Washington Post, *May 8, 1983, pp. 15, 18.**

MARILYN KAYE

Once again, as in **"My Brother Sam Is Dead"** and **"Jump Ship to Freedom,"** the brothers James Lincoln Collier and Christopher Collier place an ordinary fictional character smack in the center of an extraordinary historical event. [In **"War Comes to Willy Freeman"**] they weave a compelling drama that allows readers to experience the plight of blacks during the Revolutionary War. . . .

"War Comes to Willy Freeman" makes the historical setting seem remarkably immediate. An afterword called "How Much of This Story Is True?" places the tale in a historical perspective that confirms its credibility. The facts are all here, and the authors' fictional interpretation is evocative and believable.

Marilyn Kaye, in a review of "War Comes to Willy Freeman," in The New York Times Book Review, *May 8, 1983, p. 37.*

Pat Conroy
1945-

American novelist and nonfiction writer.

Conroy is the author of *The Water Is Wide* (1972), a factual account of his teaching experience with disadvantaged black children, and of two autobiographical novels, *The Great Santini* (1976) and *The Lords of Discipline* (1980). The latter novels are strongly influenced by Conroy's Southern upbringing and his close association with military life. All three of Conroy's works have been made into films.

Conroy wrote *The Water Is Wide* to expose the injustice of his dismissal from his teaching position on Daufuskie Island, off the coast of South Carolina, where he felt he was making significant improvements in the lives of his students despite opposition to his untraditional methods. Although the book is laden with the cynicism which resulted from his clash with school administrators, Conroy also accepts blame for his self-righteous attitude and for losing his chance to oversee the development of young people. It has been suggested that the book is an indictment of those members of Conroy's generation who rigidly followed their ideals at the expense of achieving their goals. *The Water Is Wide* was the basis for the 1974 film *Conrack.*

The Great Santini is the story of a Marine fighter pilot and his family and revolves around his relationship with his eldest son. The father, who called himself "The Great Santini" after his war exploits, makes no distinction between military life and family life, and he dominates his wife and children. As in his first book, Conroy wrote *The Great Santini* partly to purge himself of negative emotions, in this case those concerning his father. Conroy discovered the love between his father and himself which had been overshadowed by hatred since Conroy's childhood. The tension between these two emotions is at the center of *The Great Santini.*

The Lords of Discipline takes place during a cadet's senior year at a military college. The setting is based on The Citadel, a prestigious Southern military school which Conroy attended. Conroy again explores the power struggles and viciousness which can make military life brutal, even during times of peace. Critics found *The Lords of Discipline* realistic and effective in its emotional impact.

(See also *Contemporary Authors,* Vols. 85-88 and *Dictionary of Literary Biography,* Vol. 6.)

ANATOLE BROYARD

He's not much of a stylist and his sense of humor needs work, but Pat Conroy has a nice, wry perspective and a wholehearted commitment to his job. It's a hell of a job and **"The Water Is Wide"** is a hell of a good story. . . .

Why did Pat Conroy want to go to Yamacraw [Island]? Because he was young and ambitious and he loved teaching. Even more important, he was a do-gooder, enveloped in a "roseate, dawn-like and nauseating glow" at the masochistic prospect of accepting a job in which the odds were all against him. A former

© Jerry Bauer

redneck and self-proclaimed racist, he brought to Yamacraw the supererogatory fervor of the recently converted. . . .

Mr. Conroy's first job was to prove to his pupils that learning could, and should, be fun. His theory of pedagogy held "that the teacher must always maintain an air of insanity, or of eccentricity out of control, if he is to catch and hold the attention of his students." He believed in "teacher dramatics, gross posturings and frenzied excesses to get a rise out of deadhead, thought-killed students. . . ." Two things he did not realize were that his students would take his antics literally and that they could hardly understand a word he said. Nor could he understand them at first, because they spoke a local version of the Gullah dialect. . . .

Mr. Conroy's modesty will not allow him to claim much for his year at Yamacraw, but he did get his pupils to listen to Beethoven and Brahms by alternating them with James Brown. He also opened their minds to an outer world they had never even conceived of. And, most memorable of all, he taught them to trust a white man and to believe that he cared about them.

After his first year, Mr. Conroy "desperately" wanted to return to Yamacraw, but he was fired on the grounds of insubordination, failure to respect the chain of command and lateness when his boat got lost in the fog or buffeted in heavy water.

The real reason was never in doubt: He had tried to do too much too soon. If he had been more diplomatic, if he could have conquered his ego, the author says with commendable candor, he might have been allowed to continue.

He refuses to make a villain out of the school superintendent who fired him. Unlike many liberal do-gooders, Mr. Conroy does not see all conservatives, racists, reactionaries or rednecks as one-dimensional monsters. In his eyes, they are as much victims of their history—at least in their thinking—as the black people whose problems they haven't even begun to understand.

> *Anatole Broyard, "Supererogating Down South," in* The New York Times Book Review, *July 13, 1972, p. 33.*

JAMES J. BUCKLEY, JR.

Although the circumstances of [the teaching assignment portrayed in *The Water Is Wide*] were atypical, the lessons [Conroy] taught and the lessons he learned should be known by every novice teacher, for they have universal applicability. Of primary importance is Conroy's evaluation of his entire experience. Unlike those who have chronicled their confrontations with the establishment of urban schools, Conroy expresses the realization that he should have tried to fight the system by working through it, for although this method is less flamboyant and demands more than a modicum of perseverance, it allows the children, in whom a reformer professes to believe, to continue to receive his assistance and thus make demonstrable progress. And, after all, isn't the task of meeting the individual needs of each child under less than ideal circumstances the reason why such reformers should be in the teaching field?

With remarkable perceptiveness, the author describes the process of his maturation and that of his pupils, and thereby shows how a teacher may acquire the wings to fly over educational adversities, when "the water is wide."

> *James J. Buckley, Jr., "Education in Ferment: New Wine, Aging Skins," in* America, *Vol. 127, No. 7, September 16, 1972, p. 181.*

JIM HASKINS

"They gave me a boat, told me 'Good Luck,' and that was all they told me," Conroy recalls [in **"The Water Is Wide"**]. Apparently, however, he had a tape recorder in hand and photographers in tow. Conroy's brief sojourn into the life of Yamacraw Island seems to have been a planned "experience," one from which he was determined to garner a book.

This is not to negate the experiential value of Conroy's travels into the wilds of the Sea Islands, but it is to suggest that as educational literature **"The Water Is Wide"** offers nothing. Conroy does not provide any of the badly needed alternative suggestions for alleviating or controlling the stifling ignorance that is an ever-present part of the American education scene. Perhaps this was not his intent; if so, his writing style unfortunately belies it. . . .

When Conroy arrived at the little schoolhouse on Yamacraw, the average reading ability of the 17 students in grades five through eight was first grade level. We never really know if Conroy attempted to teach them to read as opposed to remembering information by rote, or if he tried to apply his call-answer technique to the teaching of information more fundamental to their Sea Islands existence.

Conroy's book is worth reading if only for the acknowledgments, which read like the Charleston and Columbia, South Carolina, social register. It is entertaining and very readable as a sympathetic view of the Sea Islands and as the story of a young white Southerner's awakening. It gives interesting insights and observations about the processes of black Southern rural education from a young white Southerner's point of view; but it would seem that while Conroy understood that the water is wide, he did not "keep the river on his right."

> *Jim Haskins, "Rural Education Sea Islands Style," in* The New York Times Book Review, *September 24, 1972, p. 10.*

JAMES N. HUTCHINS

In a novel which displays a keen insight into family life on a military base, author Pat Conroy appears to be writing his autobiography. Indeed, the dedication of [*The Great Santini*] in effect verifies this. As a result, the book is an unadulterated, realistic view of a military family ruled by an authoritarian father who has more faith in the military institution than he has in his own family. . . .

Pat Conroy not only depicts the general course of family life on a military base but also delves into the conflicts that are seemingly endemic to a "lifer's" family. Paramount is the omnipresent father-son conflict between Bull and Ben and its effects on the rest of the family which, at times, reduce the relationship between the members to a state of psychological warfare.

Perhaps the most interesting aspect of *The Great Santini* is the manner in which Conroy contrasts the social reality of the "outside" with the relative social isolation of the servicemen. Mr. Conroy suggests that one possible reason for family "fall-outs" is that the constant interaction on the part of the rest of the family with non-military affairs, as opposed to the officer who is internalized into and remains part of the military institution, blocks communication.

The Great Santini is a fine, sensitive novel that deserves to be read by all servicemen with families. Those not affiliated with the armed forces would find it enjoyable reading. . . .

> *James N. Hutchins, in a review of "The Great Santini," in* Best Sellers, *Vol. 36, No. 6, September, 1976, p. 180.*

THE VIRGINIA QUARTERLY REVIEW

The strength of [*The Great Santini*] . . . is its realism. The dialogue, anecdotes, and family atmosphere are pure Marine. . . . At the heart of the book is the search of the 18-year-old son to find himself while learning to understand and love his rigidly authoritarian Marine father, the "great Santini." A good novel and enjoyable reading, though the descriptive writing is somewhat juvenile. As usual, when one reads a first novel so heavily autobiographical, one wonders if the author has exhausted his experiences and if a second novel will be inferior.

> *A review of "The Great Santini," in* The Virginia Quarterly Review, *Vol. 52, No. 4 (Autumn, 1976), p. 134.*

ROBERT E. BURKHOLDER

Pat Conroy's first novel, *The Great Santini* (1976), is a curious blend of lurid reality and fantastic comedy, which deals with approximately one year in the life of Ben Meecham and his family. It is primarily a novel of initiation, but central to the concept of Ben's initiation into manhood and to the meaning of the whole novel is the idea that individual myths must be stripped away from Ben and the other major characters before Ben can approach reality with objectivity and maturity. In *The Great Santini* individual myths seem to consume the characters, functioning as ways of perceiving the world and as cushions against the reality that myths seem to ignore.

The title of the novel emphasizes the important role myths play, since "The Great Santini" is the identity Colonel Bull Meecham assumes when he wishes to assert his unquestionable authority as head of his household. The Great Santini, however, is merely one facet of the mythos which controls Bull Meecham's life. Colonel Meecham is a Marine Corps fighter pilot of more than twenty years service at the time of the action of the novel. . . . He sees the Marine Corps of the early 1960's as a perversion of the traditions he remembers from his early years in the Corps, immediately before and during World War II, but his awareness of change does not keep Bull from adopting his faulty memories as a way of life. . . . Because Bull is unwilling or unable to change his attitudes at will, he has endangered his relationship with his family; each member of the family recognizes that Bull might react to any family situation, from a backyard game of one-on-one basketball with his son, Ben, to arranging the house on moving day, with the same intensity and violence he would unleash in a dogfight.

That the Old Corps myth serves as both a cover and a crutch for the real Bull Meecham is evident in several revealing scenes. The first intimation that a far more sensitive man than we suspect lies beneath Bull's mask is his reaction to Zell Posey's confession of how he attempted to join the service during World War II. As Posey, who lost his leg as a child in a boating accident, speaks sincerely of his desires, Bull is described as "fidgeting as he always did when someone stripped away an outer layer of himself and revealed something intensely personal," as though he is made uncomfortable at the thought that all men are really two people: the public, mythic self and the real, private man. The nature of the private man who lurks inside the mythic, Old Corps Bull is seen only in glimpses, the most important of which is the revelation of Bull's overpowering fear of death: "Bull himself was obsessed by a carefully concealed fear that he would die in a plane, and he knew that death in flight could assume many shapes." . . . Clearly, Bull uses the myth of The Great Santini's invulnerability not only to conceal his fear from others but to blunt his realization that death was a real possibility each time he climbed behind the controls of a jet fighter.

Lillian, Bull's wife, also has a protective myth in which to believe when the stress of real situations becomes too great. Born and raised in a Southern Baptist family, Lillian became a convert to Catholicism before marrying Bull. The result of her conversion is a hybrid religion in which she focuses her Baptist zeal on the icons and rituals of Catholicism in much the same way as Bull focuses his energy on the trappings and traditions of the Marine Corps. Perhaps the chief symbol of the true nature of Lillian's variation of Catholicism is her "shrine," composed of a number of Catholic icons—statuettes of the Virgin Mary and the Archangel Michael, a crucifix, and a font of holy water—but placed within it incongruously is a

plastic model of an F-8 Crusader. The anachronistic presence of the fighter among Lillian's religious treasures suggests that those treasures, together with her beliefs, serve as the same sort of buffer from fear as Bull's myth of The Great Santini. (pp. 32-3)

Conroy makes clear that one of his novel's most important concerns is Ben's search for something in which to believe. Therefore, Ben "tries on" many beliefs of others and discards most of them because they do not suit him. Ben can, at times, be awed by the power of ritual and tradition related to the Catholic/Marine myth, as when Bull gives him a World-War-II-vintage flight jacket for his birthday. . . . But Ben is destined never to accept the Catholic/Marine concept of God as "the hellmaker, the firelover, the predatory creator," choosing rather to believe in the baby Jesus of Christmas who "would not send anyone to the flames." . . . However, Ben ultimately dismisses Catholicism and all formal religion because he cannot reconcile the contradictions of a system which is taught by the alcoholic Father Pinckney and the old shrew, Sister Loretta, with his perception of Catholicism as analogous to sex, in that both are life-giving.

Clearly, much of Ben's search for a private mythology is inextricably caught up in his vision of the ideal father. Just as Ben makes a conscious choice to believe, at least briefly, in God as the infant Jesus rather than God as the wrathful Old Testament Jehovah, he spends much of the novel contrasting all the father figures who happen into his life to Bull, who sees himself as a sort of latter-day Jehovah. From the family's past, we have memories of Major Finch, a better pilot than Bull despite his not having "to drink and brag and kick his kids around." . . . Vergil Hedgepath, Ben's godfather, also serves to illustrate that a man can command respect without cruelty. Toomer Smalls fulfills the role of surrogate father by teaching Ben all the secrets of Southern boyhood which Bull dismisses as meant only for girls. Finally, Dave Murphy, Coach Spinks, and Mr. Dacus all seem to embody, at one time or another, Ben's vision of the coach as ideal father.

No doubt we are to make a connection between sports and religion or, more properly, to see sports as a religion which not only creates happiness but supplies purpose. For example, basketball is seen more as a moral system than a game. . . . (pp. 33-4)

Ben's religious commitment, then, through a major part of *The Great Santini* is to the closed value system of sports, but much of the point of the novel involves Ben's initiation into manhood, during which sports must necessarily be supplanted by a more practical and realistic system of belief. Ben's ultimate realization about the religion of sports is that it is the best system in the world if it remains inviolate. If, however, the real world with all its chaos and misery imposes itself on this artificial "life reduced to a set of rules," then the codified life becomes more chaotic and miserable than the real world, as seen in the horrible lingering death of Coach Dave Murphy in a cancer ward and in Ben's breaking Peanut Abbott's arm during the biggest game of the year. (p. 35)

One of the things we realize about Ben's search for belief through most of the novel is that, despite his claims concerning his differences with Bull, it is completely conditioned by Bull's attitudes: Ben is a Catholic because Bull is, Ben is an athlete because Bull was, and all signs point to the possibility that, if Bull had not died, Ben would have attended a mediocre college, gone to flight school after graduation, and become a Marine pilot just like Bull. While Bull is alive, Ben not only lives in the shadow of the Santini myth but feels a need to compete with the myth. Bull's death changes all Ben's possibilities, as well as his way of viewing the Santini myth. If his search has been shielded by that myth through most of the novel, then we can also see Ben growing away from the protection that following in the shadow of The Great Santini affords. Ben's progression away from dependence upon his father begins long before Bull's death, an event which wrenches Ben from the security of his father's shadow to a more objective perspective.

The first hint we have of Ben's progress beyond Santini is his decision to disobey a direct order to help Toomer Smalls when Ben suspects he is in trouble. Earlier in the novel Ben's strategy for peaceful coexistence was to stay away from Bull and anger him as little as possible, but with friendship and loyalty on the line, Ben risks Bull's wrath, takes his punishment, and explains his action when Bull asks why he has disobeyed an order: "Because you'd have done it. Santini would have done it." . . . Paradoxically, by acting more like his father, Ben develops the independence of mind which will ultimately free him from Santini. (pp. 35-6)

Clearly, Ben loves his father, but we must not think that Ben has become another version of Bull simply because he, wearing Bull's flight jacket, assumes his father's role for the family's return to Atlanta [after Bull's death]. . . . His task now is to evaluate his position in what he describes as "a Santiniless world," . . . and his objective evaluation of his place in that world is the most convincing evidence for Ben's having reached a new level of maturity and independence. . . . [To] deny his father's overpowering identity, Ben twice insists: "I am not Santini" . . . ; in the first act of his newly realized freedom, he imagines a different sort of god, composed of the best qualities of all his family and friends. The god, pieced together from experience, has none of Bull's qualities and is the completely benevolent father Ben has searched for throughout the novel. Logically, Ben uses the new god to reinforce his earlier experience of independence—when he loathed his father's drunken brutality, but fought that brutality with love—by using him to translate all the hate he had felt for Santini into love. Such love is the result of Ben's independence and the perspective he has gained as a consequence of his passage into manhood, and his recognition that "the hatred would return" . . . only reinforces the idea that Ben has reconciled himself to the myth his father projected and, finally, can allow himself his true feelings toward the true Santini.

The story of Ben Meecham's initiation into the world of his fathers, therefore, is essentially a story of the experiences which deflate the protective myths that individuals build around themselves as buffers against day to day chaos and tragedy. In the end, that Ben reconciles himself to his father's death is not so important, because he has learned to use his experience to assess his father in human rather than mythic terms. Ben, with the reader, comes to realize that, tragically, when Bull Meecham goes down in flames, the most hidden, most human parts of him die, while the myth of The Great Santini lives on. (pp. 36-7)

Robert E. Burkholder, "The Uses of Myth in Pat Conroy's 'The Great Santini'," in Critique: Studies in Modern Fiction, *Vol. XXI, No. 1, 1979, pp. 31-7.*

FRANK ROSE

The Lords of Discipline is Conroy's rendering of life in an institution whose mission is the making of men—or rather, the making of men and the breaking, deliberate and absolute, of those boys who fail to measure up.

What Conroy has achieved is twofold; his book is at once a suspense-ridden duel between conflicting ideals of manhood and a paean to brother love that ends in betrayal and death. Out of the shards of broken friendship a blunted triumph emerges, and it is here, when the duel is won, that the reader finally comprehends the terrible price that any form of manhood can exact. Conroy's personal triumph is in conveying all this in a novel that virtually quivers with excitement and conviction.

The story centers on four senior cadets who have roomed together since their plebe year: Mark Santoro and Dante "Pig" Pignetti, physical specimens of Italian descent from up north; Tradd St. Croix, "the honey prince," effete young aristocrat from the cobwebs of old Charleston; and the narrator, Will McLean, awkward, self-conscious, rebellious, and sharp-tongued, a low-born Irish cracker too sensitive to play Southern military man with much enthusiasm. . . .

The Institute is about to get its first black cadet, and as the year begins the commandant gives Will the unofficial assignment of making sure he gets through his plebe year without being castrated, lynched, or worse. . . . Soon after the grotesque breaking-in period (known as cadre) gets underway he assumes responsibility for another plebe as well, a fat-faced Carolina boy named Poteete who has the misfortune to be perceived as a crybaby. It is Poteete's spectacular breakdown and almost anticlimactic suicide that set Will on his pursuit of the shadowy brotherhood known as the Ten.

The Ten is a secret mafia whose existence has long been rumored but never proven, a silent and malevolent force dedicated (or so it is said) to maintaining the purity of the Institute—racial purity included. For Will, they become the insubstantial embodiment of all evil, the ultimate perversion of power. But though they provide the impetus that propels the four roommates headlong into disaster, thematically they seem almost superfluous. For *The Lords of Discipline* is not simply about the abuse of power by a few; it is about the allure power holds for everyone, the weak most of all.

Will's clash with the Ten, though it makes for compelling reading, soon develops the unlikely thrill quotient of a Hardy Boys adventure, but his clash with the idea of discipline is recounted with gravity and passion and style. (p. 11)

Conroy does not neglect the perverse sexuality that the lust for mastery implies: "His lips touched against my ear in a malignant parody of a kiss," Will informs us after he's been anally threatened by a cadre officer's swagger stick during the induction known as Hell Night. . . .

As with the Spartans, however, the ritual violation of boys is not without purpose: Will goes on to cite the birth of "a malignant virility" in the hearts of plebes that night, a virility they would come to use against future boys on this same quadrangle. Conroy's dispute is with this idea of virility. His is a harsh judgment, stunningly rendered. But he does not reject all he has learned, for he is a Southerner and no Southerner can escape his upbringing entirely. A sense of brotherhood is implanted on the quadrangle as well, and it is not coincidental that his narrator's most terrible moments occur at the end, when Will takes on the Ten and the code of brotherhood is betrayed. Love your friends, Conroy warns; they are all that matters.

Will bears an uncommon resemblance to Ben Meecham, the Marine brat and high-school basketball star who bests his father and, in a moment of supreme Oedipal fulfillment, drives off with his mother and siblings in *The Great Santini,* Conroy's autobiographical first novel. There are times, in fact, when Will's tale sounds less like a work of fiction than like an anguished cry from the heart—except, of course, that it is so tightly bridled, Conroy having learned well the importance of order and mystery and control, those ideas which stand at the center of the military mystique. The problem with Conroy is that he has seen too well, learned too much. "A Southern man is incomplete without a tenure under military rule," Will tells us in the prologue. "I am not an incomplete Southern man. I am simply damaged goods, like all the rest of them." (p. 13)

> *Frank Rose, "The Martial Spirit and the Masculine Mystique," in* Book World—The Washington Post, *October 19, 1980, pp. 11, 13.*

HARRY CREWS

[With **"The Lords of Discipline"**], Mr. Conroy has found a great subject and has produced a book so superior to his other efforts that it might have been written by a different person. In fact, I read the first 200 pages thinking that this not only was a very good book but also one so memorable and well-executed that it would become the yardstick against which others of its kind would be measured. Alas, the next 300 pages proved this not so.

"The Lords of Discipline" deals with those beautiful, terrible years when a boy struggles toward manhood, when he must try to decide wherein honor lies, when he is faced with making the decision about what he wants and what he is willing to pay to get it. And he must, during this dreadfully uncertain time, bear the burden of what his parents want and expect of him, as well as the crushing pressure of his peers. Some fight their way through to their own truth; others bend or break during the ordeal.

Will McLean, the boy at the center of this story, makes the passage to manhood without breaking, but he is left with deep and permanent scars. . . .

In the second section of the book, the story that has been set into motion thus far stops and Will McLean relives his own nightmarish plebe year. This may seem an unlikely way for the novel to proceed, but to my mind it works and is natural and necessary. Here Pat Conroy lays open the barbaric nature of the human heart. Boys set upon other boys like packs of dogs. For the plebes, there is no recourse, no redress. They either bear it or break. Some break, and many who don't become sadists. (p. 12)

The story has more twists than a snake's back. There are reversals inside reversals. Mysteries sprout like mushrooms after a summer rain. The greatest plot reversal comes in the final 10 or so pages. But I was not surprised; I knew who the arch villain was long before he was revealed. Even if I had been surprised, I don't think I would have cared. It's that kind of book.

Simply put, after a very auspicious start, Pat Conroy's creative energies are sidetracked during the course of this book. Ultimately, he is more interested in posing and solving clever puzzles than in developing the character of the human beings inside those puzzles. Consequently, the reader remains unmoved . . . by the ultimate betrayal that ends the novel. (p. 43)

> *Harry Crews, "The Passage to Manhood," in* The New York Times, *December 7, 1980, pp. 12, 43.*

Robert (Edmund) Cormier

1925-

American novelist, short story writer, editor, and journalist.

Cormier writes of individuals in conflict with social and political forces. His protagonists often find themselves in situations which place them in direct opposition to powerful adversaries, both identified and unknown. These protagonists eventually come to realize, as does Adam in *I Am the Cheese* (1977), that in order to survive they must learn to stand alone. Without moralizing, Cormier's novels stress the importance of self-reliance and self-respect. His combination of realism, sensitivity, and originality has made him popular with both readers and critics and has moved him to the forefront of contemporary young adult novelists.

Many of Cormier's subjects stem from his experiences as a newspaper reporter and human interest columnist. For instance, the models for Gracie of *A Little Raw on Monday Mornings* (1963) and Tommy Battin of *Take Me Where the Good Times Are* (1965) were interviewed by Cormier while on assignment. Other themes are rooted in Cormier's personal life: his father's death from cancer was the stimulus for *Now and at the Hour* (1960), and his son's refusal to sell candy for his high school served as the background for *The Chocolate War* (1974). These novels are fast-moving and establish personality in short, quick strokes.

The Chocolate War was Cormier's first book for young adults and since its publication he has written exclusively for that audience, often facing controversy over the appropriateness of pessimistic themes for young adult readers. His novel *After the First Death* (1979), which portrays the capture by terrorists of a busload of children, has stimulated the same debate among critics as Cormier's earlier works. While some critics denounce his writing as bleak and fatalistic, others praise Cormier's honesty in dealing with evil. Critics have found a more optimistic tone in two other recent Cormier works. *Eight Plus One* (1980), a collection of short stories, concentrates on the intricacies of relationships, particularly between fathers and sons, while *The Bumblebee Flies Anyway* (1983) depicts a group of terminally ill adolescents who are able to assert some control over their destinies.

(See also *CLC*, Vol. 12; *Contemporary Authors*, Vols. 1-4, rev. ed.; *Contemporary Authors New Revision Series*, Vol. 5; and *Something about the Author*, Vol. 10.)

Photograph by Richard S. Finkle

son, Ben. . . . Most teen thrillers stop short of child killing, but before Cormier is through the death toll is swollen with Ben's suicide (after which pill-popping Dad goes mad); a likable little boy slain and another O.D.-ed on drugged candy. The graphic brutality and cynical inhumanity exhibited by both sides will not set well with some. But, bloody as it is, this taut teaser is perfectly controlled, marked by grim humor . . . and hard-hitting headline verité.

> Pamela D. Pollack, in a review of "After the First Death," in School Library Journal, *Vol. 25, No. 7, March, 1979, p. 146.*

PAMELA D. POLLACK

The Chocolate War (1974) and *I Am the Cheese* (1977) . . . didn't pull many punches, but Cormier's [*After the First Death*] is another class of calculated shocker. A bus with a girl driver and a load of six-year-old campers is hijacked by Palestinian-type terrorists, among whose demands is exposure of a military brainwashing project, Inner Delta. The tense, claustrophobic on-the-bus scenes are related by teen guerrilla Miro (protégé of political bomber Artkin) and Kate, the cute, coquettish bus driver with a weak bladder but strong nerves. These are intercut with the anguished outpourings of the guilt-ridden head of Inner Delta and the Brigadier General's terminally depressed preppie

STANLEY ELLIN

In two justly admired novels, **"The Chocolate War"** and **"I Am the Cheese,"** Robert Cormier has dealt with the betrayal of youth, creating landscapes familiar but unnervingly strange—as in a di Chirico painting—in which one sees a boy in mid-adolescence, exceptionally decent and sensitive, standing alone as invisible forces gather against him.

The betrayals themselves, perpetrated by the elders who were by nature designed to be the boy's strength and support, are breaches of trust that lead to the extinction of trust and the spirit it fires. Parents, teachers, mentors, Mr. Cormier makes plain, can each have their own self-serving need to manipulate the young people in their charge, and when they act on that need the consequences can be deadly.

Presented in narrow focus, never moralizing, written in a lean and graphic prose that creates great tension, the novels provided an experience that this reader cannot shake off. The images and ethical questions they raised are still fresh and troubling, and provided an emotional background for the reading of Mr. Cormier's new book, "**After the First Death.**"

Here, fixing on the same theme of betrayal, the author widens his focus. (pp. 30-1)

In this small epic of terrorism and counter-terrorism and their consequences, Mr. Cormier pulls no punches. The brutality is all there, the intimations of sexuality in the young, the sour judgments of values by their elders, whose values have been rotted by political cant—are all presented without sermonizing in a marvelously told story. "**After the First Death**" more than sustains the reputation its author has won with "**The Chocolate War**" and "**I Am the Cheese**"; it adds luster to it.

Putting all three books together, one disturbing aspect becomes clear: Their basic theme, no matter how brilliant the variations on it, suggests unrelieved despair. The world of Mr. Cormier's people is a Dantean Inferno without any hint of Purgatorio or Paradiso. This is, of course, an antidote to the mindless Happy Ending school of literature but, like most such medicine, it does leave a bitter taste in the mouth. (p. 31)

> Stanley Ellin, "You Can and Can't Go Home Again: 'After the First Death'," in The New York Times Book Review, April 29, 1979, pp. 30-1.

L. J. DAVIS

Time was, not so very long ago, when books for adolescent readers centered on such things as a pair of plucky youths and their adventures on an island. Islands were neat. For one thing, there were rarely parents on them, and if the plot dictated that our protagonists were to arrive there via shipwreck, the wrecked ship in question fairly bulged with keen survival gear. When there were villains, they inevitably possessed hearts as black as coal, and they were, even when not very bright, the most interesting people around.

I graduated to Horatio Hornblower and Sherlock Holmes, spent some time with [Joseph] Conrad and [André] Gide, and now seem to have come full circle with Rex Stout. . . . Nothing in my experience, therefore, prepared me for the jolt I received on reading Robert Cormier's *After the First Death*. It appears that things have changed in a certain quadrant of juvenile fiction. The trouble is, they haven't changed enough.

The plot, which is a little flooring for a while, revolves around the hijacking of a school bus full of tots by a band of ruthless foreign terrorists. . . . Now, there is no denying that Cormier writes fluently and well; although the book does contain one very large, cheap trick, its suspense and anguish are genuine and sustained, and it is an altogether serious undertaking. We are dealing, it would seem, with the real world.

That having been said, a few quibbles are in order. While I am the last person in the world to advocate parental censorship (anyway, it doesn't work) and while I am perfectly aware of all the worthy arguments that stress the need for relevance in juvenile fiction, I nevertheless find myself wondering first, why anybody would buy such a book for either his kid or

himself, and second, whether the kid would read it if he did. Cormier's craft is considerable—so considerable, in fact, that it takes a brief, unsettling while to realize that we're actually back on that island with those same plucky youths, except that the island is now a bus and one of the youths is helpless and the other is neurotic. The terrorists are drawn with some care, and it takes a similar while to grasp that they, too, haven't really changed. However, despite their contemporary rhetoric and Cormier's attempts at humanizing interior monologues, murdering infants is all they can think of to do when the chips are down. Meanwhile, the behavior of the general commanding the rescue, who also happens to be the father of the neurotic boy, is bizarre to the point of brain damage. (This is understandable, for he is one of the villains too.)

As for the book's attracting a teen readership, therefore, I think not; *The Hardy Boys Meet the Red Brigades and Get Killed and Go Nuts* is hardly anybody's cup of tea. Doubtless a few teenagers will read it, and a few of them may actually finish it, but Cormier is aiming at an audience that exhibits an almost biological craving for fantasy and role models; and he provides neither. This is not to imply, by the way, that fantasy and role models are hostile to the purposes of literature or that the same book cannot serve both youth and age. . . . Cormier's problem is that he has linked a commendable seriousness of purpose and a gripping and workable plot with an antique shallowness of execution. It is a mixture that can only make the adults uneasy and put the kids to sleep.

> L. J. Davis, "Hardy Boys Meet Red Brigade," in Book World—The Washington Post, May 13, 1979, p. K3.

BILL CRIDER

[*After the First Death*] is a strangely disturbing book. . . . There is nothing particularly new about [using terrorism as a plot], but the book is filled with enough suspense, violence, and sudden death to keep any reader turning the pages.

What makes this book different from others of the same sort? The people involved. Cormier is not really interested in violence *per se* but in how violence affects peoples' lives, especially the lives of innocent people. . . . How can two naive young people deal with a complete disregard for human life and suffering? How can they possibly understand the feelings that drive the hijackers? And what can happen to a father's mind when his plans go awry and his son is tortured and shot because of the father's miscalculation?

Cormier is not interested only in the innocent, however. He is even more detailed in his revelation of the character of Miro, the sixteen-year-old terrorist who is looking forward to killing his first man. What makes Miro what he is, and why does he fight for a homeland that he has never seen, will in all probability never see? Cormier tries to answer these questions with a vivid description of Miro's life in refugee camps, his training in terrorist tactics, and his devotion to his leader, the enigmatic Artkin. It is a tribute to the author's skill that he succeeds in making Miro a sympathetic monster. (pp. 115-16)

> Bill Crider, in a review of "After the First Death," in Best Sellers, Vol. 39, No. 4, July, 1979, pp. 115-16.

GERALDINE DeLUCA

Novels for young adults that deal with social issues of one sort or another have been around for quite awhile now. In fact, social relevance seems to be a primary feature of the genre, the attempt to catch the reader by surprise with unconventional characters and situations as much a part of the books' basic ingredients as the adolescent hero himself. Many of these novels, however, stop short of fully exploring the issues they introduce. It is enough, the sentiment seems to be, that the subjects are unveiled. . . . There have of course been exceptions, but the message of most of these novels, like that of the most traditional literature, is that, the appeals of passion and rebellion notwithstanding, the conventionally moral side of things must prevail.

Recently, however, young adult works have begun to take a truly more realistic, at times frightening, and occasionally defiantly happy turn. Conventionally moral endings are not always provided; ambiguous or complex situations are allowed to remain so; and themes are a little more daring. (p. 125)

[The] novels of Robert Cormier have consistently transcended the limitations of the genre. He has avoided the thin characterizations and glib language that are so familiar to us perhaps because he is faithful to his own vision, writing more truly for himself than many other writers for this audience. He is unafraid to bring a story to its aesthetically inevitable conclusion, and his lucid prose style, which is easily accessible to adolescents, seems natural rather than contrived to catch the interests of that audience.

His newest work, *After the First Death,* continues the exploration of issues presented in his first two novels for adolescents. His preoccupation with the child as victim and with mind control will be familiar to his readers. In *The Chocolate War,* an untrained adolescent's cool observations of people's vulnerabilities allow him to exploit and control them. In *I Am the Cheese,* the manipulators are the forces of government, empowered to change and ultimately destroy lives in the name of national security. This newest work combines both forms of control. Cormier explores both the very personalized form of brutality and intimidation employed by international terrorists and the behind-the-scenes government manipulations that may engender and result from such terrorism.

The book recounts the events that occur when four foreign terrorists—Cormier doesn't specify their nationality—hijack a busload of children in order to exact political demands from the generals at a nearby army base. The work's main characters are two of the terrorists: Artkin, the professional, whose pseudonym suggests that he has divested himself of his natural feelings and made his cause his life, and Miro Shantas, an orphan, whom Artkin plucked from the streets and trained; Kate Forrester, the seventeen year old bus driver; and Ben Marchand, the son of the general to whom the terrorists are directing their demands. Cormier makes the link between personal relationships and the machinations and power struggles of government by balancing the father-son relationships of Artkin and Miro, and Ben and the general against the larger events of the novel, showing how each father ultimately sacrifices his son for his cause.

Artkin has created in the desperate child Miro a person with no identity except that of the terrorist, a ''mirror'' perhaps of Artkin, or of some elusive ideal. Miro's relationship with Artkin and Artkin's approval rest on his performing well as a terrorist, on not allowing himself any of the vulnerabilities of

human feeling. As the young woman Kate discovers, Miro is a monster of innocence. . . . Cormier does not ask us to sympathize or forgive. In fact, he seems to have a special interest in the unforgivable. He is fascinated by the pathology. But, in this novel more than his earlier works, he explores the circumstances that nurture characters who stir our hatred and fear. He also forces us to consider the extent to which we are all manipulated by powers we seldom think about—powers invested in people like the well-meaning but misguided General Marchand, for example.

Marchand, the conscientious American psychologist turned general, is ultimately just as fanatical as Artkin. As a psychologist he has designed a process to monitor the behavior of the children in the local army school, and since his son attends, he knows the son's strengths and weaknesses well. When the moment of negotiation with the terrorists arrives, he is willing to use Ben as a go-between, knowing full well that the boy will crack when seized and tortured. He even gives the boy some incorrect information so that he will have something to confess. Once Ben's weakness and his father's dependence on it becomes apparent to him, he is irreparably damaged. He has lost his innocence in such a brutal way that there is no longer any help for him. As the Dylan Thomas epigraph to the book states, ''After the first death, there is no other,'' and Ben, having endured extreme psychic and physical pain, having been reduced and victimized, can only contemplate suicide. The book opens, after the hijacking is over, with his journal to his father. . . . Finding the journal after his son has killed himself, Marchand imagines a surreal conversation between himself and the dead boy. Haunted by the suicide, Marchand tries to justify himself, and with the same rationale used by the terrorists, he explains: ''I was serving my country. I am a patriot, Ben. I did it for my country. Not for myself.'' Ben answers with a colder clarity than he could achieve in life:

> *Is a country worth that much, Dad? How could I have gone through life knowing what I had done? Knowing that my cowardice had served my country? Where did that leave me, Dad?*
>
> I'm sorry, Ben. I was sorry as soon as I told you. As soon as I saw your face and realized what I had done. I thought: I'll make it up to you. If it takes months, years. I'll earn your forgiveness.
>
> *And then I died. . . .*

The ambiguity of the ''then'' seems purposeful. After the death of his spirit, there was nothing left in Ben's mind but suicide.

As the excerpt above suggests, the form of narration is somewhat experimental. The book opens with Ben's journal and, after fifteen pages, shifts to Miro's perspective. Events from that point on are narrated in the third person, but through the alternating eyes of Kate and Miro, with brief returns to Ben and to the dialogue. The parts are skillfully juxtaposed, and it is with the discovery of each character's point of view and personality that the issues of the story emerge, with Cormier demonstrating how well-meaning people go about destroying each other in futile attempts to control their world.

Though the political concerns are adequately explored, Cormier's primary focus is on the individuals. He develops them, elicits sympathy for them, and then as often as not destroys them. One minor example involves one of the children on the bus. He draws a brief sketch of the boy, gives us a touching detail about him—he is anxious about being late because he has often heard himself referred to as a "late baby"—and then we see him led off the bus and shot. The effect is horrifying, but we can see the honesty of Cormier's method. He seems to be saying they are all individuals with histories, feelings, families, and it is only by forgetting this, by becoming numbed by rhetoric or by too much brutality in one's past, that human beings become capable of destroying so casually. So while one could argue that Cormier is too pessimistic a writer for adolescents, the book stands finally not as a cynical but a loving work. Cormier's portraits are deeply compassionate. Kate, who was braver than she ever thought she could be; Miro who killed her in a moment of pain because he couldn't stand to hear what she revealed to him about himself; and Ben who killed himself to stifle his sense of shame—all three are innocents who tried to live up to some impossible ideal fostered upon them by dangerously misguided adults. (pp. 139-44)

> Geraldine DeLuca, "Taking True Risks: Controversial Issues in New Young Adult Novels," in The Lion and the Unicorn, Vol. 3, No. 2, Winter, 1979-80, pp. 125-48.*

NORMA BAGNALL

Recently we have seen a trend in literature for young people that some call realism, but in fact it is not realistic at all. Realism is an honest attempt to picture people and events as they really are. To portray things from the brutal or dark side only, as is being done in current literature, is no more realistic than presenting only those sweet and idealistic stories of an earlier age.

As an example, *The Chocolate War,* by Robert Cormier, is described as a realistic junior novel, and it meets some of the requirements for realism. Cormier has written honestly, I believe, what he thinks could happen at a private boys' school in the 1970s when one student decides to flout the system. Such honesty is basic to realism. He has also structured the novel masterfully; each incident builds up independently of the others, yet each contributes strength to the structure of the story, all with careful understatement. Cormier knows his craft; he has written a compelling novel.

But it is not realistic. In it there are no adults worth emulating; Jerry is the only decent kid, and he is victimized by his peers, with the cooperation of school officials. Only the ugly is presented through the novel's language, actions, and imagery; goodness and honor are never rewarded. Love and concern for other people is ignored, and hopelessness pervades the entire story. The presentation of people and events shows only the evil, the ugly, and the sordid. It is not appropriate for young people because it presents a distorted view of reality and because it lacks hope. (p. 214)

The language in the novel is ugly as well. It has become popular to "tell it like it is," and for some writers this means including the crude slang we know kids use. So Cormier uses much of it, but generally it is appropriate to its context and will probably not disturb the book's readers; kids can handle four-letter-words with greater ease than my generation can. However, I don't think it is necessary for a writer for young adults to feed back to them their own slang any more than it is necessary for a writer for five-year-olds to include the bathroom language he or she knows five-year-olds use and find titillating.

The actions of the characters are almost without exception ugly, exemplifying only the most sordid side of their natures. Our senses are assaulted by kinds cringing, sniveling, humiliating each other, stealing, and bullying. There are frequent references to masturbation and vomiting. Jerry, in particular, vomits a lot, an ugly picture but one that is perhaps in keeping with the one-sided view the book presents. The adults' actions are not as sordid, but they are as depressing. They nag, drink, sleep, watch television; they are trapped in dull jobs; they do dull things. None are involved in anything worthwhile with their children. People, we are told by Archie, "are two things: greedy and cruel." Cormier's people certainly are. (p. 215)

The Chocolate War has been compared to [John Knowles's] *A Separate Peace* and to [William Golding's] *Lord of the Flies,* which is expected. All deal with boys forming their own societal group complete with rules, taboos, value systems, and leaders—like any society.

But in *A Separate Peace* there are some sympathetic adults, adults to trust and to emulate. There is genuine, healthy rapport among the boys on the playing field. The book does not include tasteless language, and ugly incidents are limited to those essential to the story line. Finally, there are forgiveness and love to offset an otherwise harsh story.

Lord of the Flies tells an ugly story with cynical harshness, and it includes many ugly incidents and much ugly imagery, but it is set in a real jungle, on an island, with the boys completely cut off from adult intervention. *The Chocolate War* takes place in a large New England city, and involves more than eight hundred adults directly concerned with the society of boys. It goes beyond *Lord of the Flies* in that it suggests that adults are no more willing or capable of controlling their environment than are youngsters. It insinuates that it is possible that this many parents and teachers would be totally unconcerned about their own children or their students. It states not only that civilization can break down on an isolated island among a group of British school boys, but that it has broken down also for a large and diverse group of adults in a major American city.

This distorted view of humanity, this strange sense of what makes civilization work is hammered home by the conclusion of the story. Hints are given throughout that justice will finally triumph. Through foreshadowing we are led to believe that Jerry is going to win his battle, but this is just a trick of the author's. (p. 216)

[Jerry] does not win. He is brutally beaten and carried away broken and unconscious. The reader feels tricked. This completes Cormier's destruction of all that is good and honorable and becomes the most disturbing element in the book. Jerry, like us, is let down with a sickening thud.

So I struggle with *The Chocolate War*. I do not believe writers should be dictated to by librarians, by parents, by me, about what they should write. Yet I am disturbed by this book because, in spite of being brilliantly structured and skillfully written, it presents a distorted view of reality and a feeling of absolute hopelessness that is unhealthy. . . .

It is as inaccurate to present only the sordid and call it realistic as it has been in the past to present only the idealistic. It is probably even more damaging. *The Chocolate War* endorses and supports the thesis that one is better off not struggling for what is right because one cannot win and thus is, in effect, an object lesson in futility. (p. 217)

Norma Bagnall, "Realism: How Realistic Is It? A Look at 'The Chocolate War'," in Top of the News, *Vol. 36, No. 2, Winter, 1980, pp. 214-17.*

ALLEEN PACE NILSEN

The process of naming characters is a fascinating area of young adult literature. In some of the best books, characters' names have been chosen or devised so carefully that they qualify as poetry. Many of them are phonologically interesting, employing such poetic devices as rhyme, repetition, and rhythm. The communication is often on more than one level with different readers appreciating different connotations and different layers of symbolism. And also like poetry, they are semantically compact in that they communicate a great deal of information within a very few syllables. . . .

Once I began noticing interesting names, they seemed to appear in almost everything I read. But a nagging suspicion began to grow that perhaps I was reading more into the names of characters than their creators ever intended. . . . As a way of checking my suspicions, I decided to write to an author and ask specifically about the process of creating names. I chose to write to Robert Cormier because of the craftsmanship shown in his three books: [*The Chocolate War, I Am the Cheese,* and *After the First Death*]. . . . Cormier is one of a relatively small number of contemporary authors for young readers who makes use of the full range of techniques available to skilled literary artists. (p. 3)

[A] specific question that I put to him was whether he had named the evil gang in *The Chocolate War* the Vigils as an ironic reference to vigil lights which are the devotional candles placed before shrines or images. When I read the book, I was struck with an image of the boys in the gang standing like vigil lights before their leader, Archie, who basked in the glow of their admiration. If Cormier had intended this comparison, it would have been consistent with the many other religious references in the book which highlighted the irony of there being so much evil in a religious school. Cormier answered that he chose the name because it was a shortened form of *vigilante.* Nevertheless he agrees that the religious connotation is there and in looking back he realizes, "that the devotional aspect of vigils was also very much a part of my choice." (pp. 3-4)

Cormier says he loves contrasts, sharp ones, in both his characters' names and the names of his books, for example the sweet *Chocolate* and the devastating *War.* And when he is choosing names he will choose the harsh, hard sounds for the villains like Archie and softer sounds for someone like Jerry. When he named Brother Leon in *The Chocolate War,* he was looking for "a bland soft name to contrast with Archie because Leon was a bland-appearing man. And so is evil bland in its many disguises." In Cormier's latest book, *After the First Death,* he again relied on contrast for the name of General Mark Marchand, "the harsh *Mark* and the soft *Marchand,* the contrast I often seek because we are all made of shares of softnesses and hardnesses." . . .

When Cormier has a background character who is important not as a unique personality but more for the particular role played, then he will rely on a fairly obvious name as he did with Stroll in *After the First Death.* He chose the name because it suggested coolness and casualness even during difficult times. He wrote that in *I Am the Cheese* he very deliberately devised the name of Brint to suggest someone bloodless and cold, cf. *flint* and *glint.* . . .

Since authors live much longer with the characters than do readers, chances are that an author will think about names at a deeper symbolic level than will most readers. For example, Cormier says that as far fetched as it now seems, one of the images that occurred to him when he chose the name for *I Am the Cheese* was that of "Swiss cheese full of holes as Adam was full of psychological holes." This comparison probably occurred to very few readers, but when Cormier chose the name of Adam's girlfriend, Amy Hertz, he had in mind the double meaning, "hurts," because he knew when he introduced her that she would have the power to hurt Adam. She didn't, yet readers write in to him asking if she were part of the plot. They are suspicious because of the telephone call she made from her father's office. They want to know if the call was as innocent as she claimed it to be. How much of their suspicion was aroused by Amy's last name and how much by other factors in the book is impossible to know. (p. 4)

Alleen Pace Nilsen, "The Poetry of Naming in Young Adult Books," in The ALAN Review, *Vol. 7, No. 3, Spring, 1980, pp. 3-4, 31.**

BETTY CARTER AND KAREN HARRIS

In the winter 1980 issue of *Top of the News* Norma Bagnall describes **The Chocolate War** as a hopeless novel about the forced sale of candy in a boys' parochial high school [see excerpt above]. She considers it an unrealistic picture of adolescent life and unsuitable reading material for teenagers. We think her description is inaccurate and her criticism unwarranted.

Cormier's novel is only superficially about the fund-raising activities at a Catholic institution; its greater concerns are with the nature and functioning of tyranny. While it demonstrates the inability of a decent individual to survive unaided in a corrupt and oppressive society, it does not imply that such defeat is inevitable. To see the book as something "which could happen at a private boys' school in the 1970s when one student decides to flout the system" is to confuse setting with substance and plot device with purpose.

Cormier persistently uses figurative language as one device to remind the reader that the meaning of the book is not limited to the confines of the story line or the campus of Trinity High. After Archie decides that Jerry Renault's first assignment will be to refuse to sell chocolates, Obie notices that "the shadows of the goal posts definitely resembled a network of crosses, empty crucifixes." This reference to the central symbol of Christianity should certainly suggest that more is at issue than merely the selling of chocolates. When Jerry, defying the Vigils, announces he still will not accept the candy, the effect is cataclysmic: "Cities fell. Earth opened. Planets tilted. Stars plummeted." The author has clearly moved the action from the campus to the cosmos.

The metaphorical quality of the three power structures within the school is spelled out specifically and hinted at obliquely. The most obvious symbol is the athletic department, which provides for the testing of individuals, including each one's willingness and ability to withstand physical abuse. The football field is an arena where violence is ritualized, sanctioned, and even demanded. After the brutal fight in which Jerry is physically beaten and psychologically destroyed, he warns his friend to "play ball." This metaphor, taken from sports, is not restricted to the game but encapsulates the lesson Jerry has so painfully learned: he had better cooperate with the power structure or he will be crushed.

The most significant object in the story is the poster in Jerry's locker that asks: Do I Dare Disturb the Universe? When Cormier introduces it he describes it in detail, suggesting through Jerry's uncertainty that the caption may be subject to various interpretations. The question does not remain idle, tucked away in Jerry's locker, but is raised repeatedly when anyone—Jerry, his father, his classmates, his teachers—either challenges or bows to the demands of the establishment. Jerry ponders, expands, and twists the quote, and as his definition of the universe grows and changes, he realizes he is not just a single individual but a part of an interlocking social order. Following Jerry's ruminations, readers gain similar insight into the book's intent and theme. Cormier is clearly not writing about this existential question solely within the context of an isolated secondary school, but as it is applicable to the larger world.

Bagnall's criticism that *The Chocolate War* is not realistic is equally insupportable. She claims Cormier's work is distorted because "only the ugly is presented . . . goodness and honor are never rewarded."

Northrop Frye claims that "the world of literature is a world where there is no reality except that of the human imagination. . . . There are two halves to literary experience. Imagination gives us both a better and a worse world than the one we usually live with, and demands that we keep looking steadily at them both." If Cormier chooses to concentrate on the "worse world," he is exercising a literary privilege claimed by many major writers since Sophocles. Although this is not the only side of reality, it is certainly a significant one and remains a persisting concern of authors because it is a persisting component of human behavior.

It may be desirable for a library collection to encompass the full spectrum of human imagination, but such a comprehensive range cannot be reasonably required of every individual work. Condemning Cormier for ignoring the sunnier aspects of human behavior is as inappropriate as castigating [Helen] Cresswell for avoiding serious matters in *The Bagthorpe Saga*.

Literary realism is not journalistic reporting. . . . [Novelists] choose particular elements of the world—distill, concentrate, and juxtapose them in such a manner as to illuminate a particular facet of the human condition. This, it seems to us, is exactly what Robert Cormier accomplishes in his junior novels, remaining well within the tradition of literary realism.

In *The Chocolate War* he has chosen to focus on tyranny and evil—not as vague abstractions, but given flesh and substance in the persons of Brother Leon and Archie. Bagnall disapproves of Cormier's concentration on that which is displeasing and concludes that the book is inappropriate for youngsters because its language, actions, and imagery are ugly. The unpleasant should not be confused with the unsuitable. Cormier's responsibility to his craft requires him to present characters and images, not as one would like them to be, but as they must be in order to make the novel and its message credible. Consequently, the language and images are disturbing, but then, so is tyranny. To mask evil with delicate similes would only diminish its potency, and to introduce a noble adult to save the day would truly be unrealistic.

Bagnall contends "*The Chocolate War* endorses and supports the thesis that one is better off not struggling for what is right because one cannot win and thus is, in effect, an object lesson

in futility." Such a reading makes sense only if Jerry's destruction is inevitable. The reason Jerry was not saved was because he stood alone. But he need not have been alone, as Cormier states clearly and with consummate irony through the words of Brother Leon when he falsely accuses Bailey of cheating. The boys at Trinity could have come to Jerry's defense, if they had not lacked courage. Mr. Renault could have saved his son if he had not been so self-absorbed. The brothers could have checked Leon's ambitions if they had had the will. No one did. Jerry paid a terrible price for everyone else's inadequacies.

Robert Cormier does not leave his readers without hope, but he does deliver a warning: they may not plead innocence, ignorance, or prior commitments when the threat of tyranny confronts them. He does not imply that resistance is easy, but he insists it is mandatory. (pp. 283-85)

Betty Carter and Karen Harris, "Realism in Adolescent Fiction: In Defense of 'The Chocolate War'," in Top of the News, *Vol. 36, No. 3, Spring, 1980, pp. 283-85.*

MYRA L. KIBLER

Many books on the shelves for adolescent reading subscribe to the idea that by age sixteen or seventeen, a female's primary developmental task is to be able to attract the attentions of a worthy male. Certainly achieving a feminine social role is one of the adolescent's tasks, and many high school girls do equate that task with attracting a male and subordinate all other concerns to it. It would be too restrictive for teachers, critics, or publishers to specify any particular concept of female identity as proper for the young adult audience, and yet those who have a concern for young adolescent literature should be aware of the problem and should look at the way books present female identity. . . .

Known for flaunting formulas and writing honestly, Cormier produces works too strong for some adults who still try to offer youth a protected image of reality. But out of the same integrity that turns stomachs in *The Chocolate War* comes a beautiful portrait of a girl in the character of Kate Forrester in *After the First Death*. Cormier does not evade the sexual attraction issue. Kate and Miro develop an interest in each other that Cormier expected would become a love story. . . . But yielding to the forces at work in the novel, he wrote it differently. The point should be made clearly that sexual attraction or not is irrelevant; female identity, like male identity involves sexuality but is not to be reduced to sexuality.

In *After the First Death* the catalyst for self-awareness and identity-achievement is the crisis situation in which Kate must summon all her resources for her own survival and that of the children on the school bus. The problems she confronts—the conflict between her desire for personal survival and her feeling of responsibility for the children, her effort to penetrate the mental machinations of a terrorist and subvert them, her consciousness of the weakness of her own body—all suggest that her achievement can best be seen in full-fledged human terms, a concept of identity that goes beyond sexuality. (p. 25)

Myra L. Kibler, "Female Identity in the Young Adult Novel," in The ALAN Review, *Vol. 8, No. 1, Fall, 1980, pp. 25, 32.**

LEIGH DEAN

The short story is not my favorite form, but Robert Cormier is one of my favorite authors. Here, in this collection [*Eight Plus One*], a gentler, calmer, more vulnerable side of him is revealed. Sometimes, the narrator is an adolescent; more often he is an adult. He is always male, and addresses us in the first person. The stories are about relationships: about fathers, about sons, about fathers and sons, and fathers and daughters, and about husbands. . . . Each story is prefaced by a remarkable "introduction," with a life all its own. In these, Mr. Cormier shares his journey in the craft of writing. Although this collection succeeds on many levels, I don't think Robert Cormier's younger fans will enjoy this volume as much as his adult fans. Still, Mr. Cormier is a very special writer.

> *Leigh Dean, in a review of "Eight Plus One," in* Children's Book Review Service, *Vol. 9, No. 3, November, 1980, p. 26.*

KENNETH L. DONELSON AND ALLEEN PACE NILSEN

The book that we have chosen as an example of the best of modern realism for young adults is Robert Cormier's *The Chocolate War* (1974). It contains the kind of realism that many other books had been just leading up to. Its message about conformity and human manipulation is all the more powerful because the young protagonist is so vulnerable. (p. 186)

In selecting *The Chocolate War* as a touchstone example, we asked ourselves several questions about the book. These same or similar questions could be asked when evaluating almost any problem novel. First, does the book make a distinctive contribution? Does it say something new or does it convey something old in a new way? And if so, is it something of value?

Robert Cormier was praised by *The Kirkus Reviews* because he dared to "disturb the upbeat universe of juvenile books" with *The Chocolate War.* He did not compromise by providing a falsely hopeful conclusion, nor did he sidestep the issue by leaving it open for readers to imagine their own happy ending. Until Cormier, most writers for young readers had opted for one of these two approaches. (pp. 187-88)

The plot of a book must be examined to see how closely it grows out of the characters' actions and attitudes. Is it an idea that could easily have been dropped into another setting or onto other characters? With Cormier's book, there wouldn't have been a story without the unique but believable personalities of both Jerry and Archie, as well as of Brother Leon. The problem was not so bizarre or unusual that it overshadowed the characters, nor were the characters such unusual people that readers could not identify with them or imagine themselves having to deal with people like them. It is because the characters at first appear to be such ordinary people that readers are drawn into the story. The theme is similar to that in [William] Golding's *Lord of the Flies,* but because Golding's book is set on a deserted island in the midst of a war it could be dismissed as unrealistic. Cormier's book has an immediacy that is hard to deny. The problem is a real one that teenagers can identify with on the first or literal level, yet it has implications far beyond one beaten-up fourteen-year-old and 20,000 boxes of stale Mother's Day candy.

It's common in evaluating a book to question the role of the setting. Is it just there or does it contribute something to the mood or the action or to revealing characterization? In *The*

Chocolate War the story would not have been nearly so chilling without the religious setting. It provided contrast. In some ways the evil in Archie is less hideous than that in Brother Leon, the corrupt teacher who enlists Archie's help in making his unauthorized investment pay off. The brother hides behind his clerical collar and his role of teacher and assistant headmaster, whereas Archie only identifies himself as a nonbeliever in the so-called "Christian ethic." For example, when his stooge Obie asks him how he can do the things he does and still take communion, he responds, "When you march down to the rail, you're receiving the Body, man. Me, I'm just chewing a wafer they buy by the pound in Worcester."

Another question especially relevant in respect to books for young readers is the respect the author has for the intended audience. Cormier showed a great deal of respect for his readers: nowhere did he write down to them. The proof of his respect for them is in some of the subtle symbolization that he worked into the story and the care with which he developed his style. For example, the irony of the whole situation is exemplified in the gang's name, the *Vigils.* The word is cognate with *vigilant* and *vigorous,* which certainly Archie is, but its origin is in religious language where it meant the keeping of a watch on the night preceding a religious holiday. Today, vigil lights are candles placed devotionally before a shrine or image. This is comparable to the way that the members of the gang stand before Archie, who basks in the glow of their admiration. Another example of Cormier's subtlety is the fact that Archie's name has such meanings as "principal or chief" as in arch-villain, "cleverly sly and alert," and "at the extreme, that is, someone or something most fully embodying the qualities of its kind." (pp. 188-89)

> *Kenneth L. Donelson and Alleen Pace Nilsen, "The New Realism: Of Life and Other Sad Songs," in their* Literature for Today's Young Adults, *Scott, Foresman and Company, 1980, pp. 181-204.*

ZENA SUTHERLAND

While [*Eight Plus One*] should interest many young adult Cormier fans, it seems even more suitable for an adult audience, not because of the difficulty or sophistication of the writing but because of the subject matter; most of the stories are written from an adult's viewpoint. Many have autobiographical overtones, and while they are not as trenchant or exciting as the author's *The Chocolate War* and *I Am the Cheese,* they are adroitly crafted, perceptive, and often poignant vignettes about the complexities of human relationships. (pp. 67-8)

> *Zena Sutherland, in a review of "Eight Plus One: Stories," in* Bulletin of the Center for Children's Books, *Vol. 34, No. 4, December, 1980, pp. 67-8.*

ROBERT WILSON

[In the stories in *Eight Plus One*] Cormier writes mostly about the pains and dilemmas of teenagers, but often with the distance and nostalgia of a father. These are his most successful stories; others, told from the point of view of the teenager, work less well, because the language sometimes seems forced and artificial.

> *Robert Wilson, in a review of "Eight Plus One," in* Book World—The Washington Post, *January 11, 1981, p. 7.*

ANNE SCOTT MacLEOD

Robert Cormier is a conspicuous oddity in his chosen field. Writing for the adolescent reader, he has departed from standard models and broken some of the most fundamental taboos of that vocation. Each of his hard-edged novels for the young goes considerably beyond the standard limits of "contemporary realism" to describe a world of painful harshness, where choices are few and consequences desperate. Moreover, his novels are unequivocally downbeat; [*The Chocolate War, I Am the Cheese* and *After the First Death*] violate the unwritten rule that fiction for the young, however sternly realistic the narrative material, must offer some portion of hope, must end at least with some affirmative message. Affirmation is hard to find in Cormier's work, and conventional hopefulness is quite irrelevant to it.

But while these sharp breaks with accepted practice have been much noted by reviewers, and have furnished Cormier's reputation for bleakness, curiously little notice has been taken of another, and, to my mind, equally interesting departure from the norm in his novels. Quite aside from his attitudes and conclusions, Cormier is a maverick in the field of adolescent literature because he is writing what are, at bottom, political novels. George Orwell once claimed that there is no such thing as a "genuinely nonpolitical literature," but the dictum seems to me inapplicable to most writing for young adults. A consistent feature of almost the whole body of adolescent literature is its isolation from the political and societal, its nearly total preoccupation with personality. The typical adolescent novel is wrapped tightly around the individual and the personal; questions of psychological development and personal morality dominate the genre. In fact, most authors of adolescent literature seem to take for their model adolescents themselves, with their paramount interest in self, individual morality, interior change, and personality.

Cormier, on the other hand, is far more interested in the systems by which a society operates than he is in individuals. His novels center on the interplay between individuals and their context, between the needs and demands of the system and the needs and rights of individuals—in other words, on the political context in which his characters, like all of us, must live. He is, obviously, concerned with moral questions, but the morality involved is of a wholly different order from the purely personal moral concerns of most teen novels.

Cormier's political cast of mind explains the relative unimportance of characterization in his work. Inner character is less to him than situation. In *Chocolate War,* for example, the wellsprings of Archie's evil are never adequately explained, and Jerry's motivation for his lonely rebellion, while plausible enough, is not dwelt upon at any great length. Certainly it is not the centerpiece of the narrative, as it would be in most teen novels. Adam, of *I Am the Cheese,* is more a victim than a protagonist. If we care about what happens to him, it is not because of any crucial internal decision he must make, but precisely because he is the helpless victim of processes he cannot affect, let alone control, and because we recognize the circumstances of his tragedy as part of the world we actually live in. In *After the First Death,* characterization is again—as several critics have complained—clearly secondary to the situation set out in the novel, and to Cormier's view of the commitments and choices that have brought about that situation. (pp. 74-5)

The evil in *Chocolate War* is initiated by individuals, but not contained in them. Archie and Brother Leon are manipulators: Archie manipulates the Vigils, Brother Leon manipulates his students; together, during the chocolate sale, they manipulate the whole school. Yet neither could work his will without the cooperation of others. The acquiescence of the community is essential to their power, as the classroom scene makes clear. In an episode that is a virtual cliche in school stories, Brother Leon singles out a student for torment, accusing him of cheating, mocking and humiliating him, while the rest of the class laughs uncomfortably. If this were all, the scene would simply establish (without much originality) that Brother Leon is the kind of teacher who abuses the power of his position for some private satisfaction. But Cormier's interest here is not really Brother Leon, still less the reasons for his abuse of position. What he wants to demonstrate is the source of the power, which is, of course, the students themselves. The harassment goes on exactly as long as the class lets it; when at last one student speaks up in mild protest, the spell breaks. And it is Brother Leon himself who points the moral, asking contemptuously why no one had objected sooner, suggesting the parallel with Nazi Germany.

Still, the message of the novel as a whole is neither so simple nor so hopeful as the episode might imply. If it were, then Jerry's lone dissent would succeed, would break the combined power of Archie and Brother Leon—and would place the novel squarely in the long American tradition of the triumphant lonely hero tale. Instead, there is that final scene which laid the cornerstone of Cormier's reputation for bleakness: Jerry carried away on a stretcher, his face too battered to allow him to speak the message he wants to convey to Goober. . . . The lone dissent has not only failed, it is repudiated. The American Adam is brought low; Huck Finn turns Jim over to the slave-catchers, Gary Cooper lies in his own blood in the street at high noon—no wonder the reviewers gasped. In one brief, bitter paragraph, Cormier has abandoned an enduring American myth to confront his teenaged readers with life as it more often is—with the dangers of dissent, the ferocity of systems as they protect themselves, the power of the pressure to conform.

In his second novel, *I Am the Cheese,* Cormier dispenses with metaphor. This stark tale comments directly on the real world of government, organized crime, large-scale bureaucracy, the apparatus of control, secrecy, betrayal, and all the other commonplaces of contemporary political life. Its message is, if possible, even less ambiguous than *Chocolate War's.* The most optimistic reader will find it hard to locate an exit as the story moves to a conclusion. Adam is doomed, as his parents were; he will be "obliterated" one way or another because he is a threat to one or possibly to both of the systems with which his life is entangled. There is certainly some ambiguity about the role played in this tragedy by Mr. Grey, supposedly the family's government protector. Might he have been instead their betrayer? Which side did he really work for? As the narrative rolls coldly on, it occurs to the reader that it hardly matters. And this is clearly Cormier's point. The two systems are equally impersonal, and equally dangerous to the human being caught between them. What matters to the organization—*either* organization—is its own survival, not Adam's.

I Am the Cheese is the most Kafka-esque of Cormier's three novels. The narrative technique, combined with a nearly overwhelming sense of loneliness, helplessness, and hopelessness give the novel a surreal quality. When his parents are murdered, Adam is left in a world empty of human figures; he has only memories of those few he has loved and lost. It is as though he were alone in a computer room where every machine is programmed to cancel him out; he is like a mouse in a maze, searching for an opening, unaware that every exit has been blocked. The language of the "psychiatrist's" reports, bleached of emotional accuracy, underlines the impersonal, bureaucratic character of Adam's cold enemies. And when Adam's trip to Vermont is revealed for what it is, a bicycle ride within the fenced grounds of the institution where he is confined, the sense of nightmare recalls [Franz] Kafka's terrifying world.

After the First Death both reiterates and extends concepts found in the earlier books. The plot is built around an episode of political terrorism—the ultimate weapon of an outnumbered dissident group—directed against the technically superior, equally purposeful security apparatus of the established government. In the course of the story, Cormier explores the outer limits of patriotism and the inner perception of fanaticism. Here, as in the first two novels, Cormier shows privileged position and privileged information used to manipulate the weak and the unwary. Here, as in *I Am the Cheese,* the discussion of political evil is cast in fiercely contemporary terms, and the shadow of statism stretches long over the narrative.

One episode brings into sharp focus concepts central to this novel and also, I think, to Cormier's general outlook. The scene takes place between Miro, the young terrorist, and Kate, the girl who is to become Miro's "first death." The tentative human relationship created between them when Kate encourages Miro to talk about his past dissolves abruptly when Kate recognizes the depth and the terrible simplicity of Miro's dedication to his political purpose. For the sake of a country he has never seen, and never really expects to see, Miro has made himself into an instrument of guerrilla warfare. Save for his mentor, Artkin, he has no connection with the actual world of human life, nor does he expect any. He envisions no future for himself, takes no interest in his own qualities except as they make him an efficient weapon in a struggle whose political terms he cannot possibly know. He has no feeling for the innocent victims, past or potential, of the undeclared "war" he wages; indeed, he cannot even understand what it is Kate expects him to feel for them. In short, as Kate realizes with shock, he is "a monster." Not only monstrous, Miro is innocent as well:

> The greatest horror of all was that he did not know he was a monster. He had looked at her with innocent eyes as he told her of killing people. She'd always thought of innocence as something good, something to cherish. People mourned the death of innocence . . . But innocence, she saw now, could also be evil. Monstrous. . . .

The attitude toward innocence explicitly expressed in this passage seems to me to underlie all three of Cormier's books and goes far to explain his break with prevailing standards for adolescent novels. Like Kate, most literature for the young has assumed that innocence, particularly in the young, is desirable, and that its loss is a regrettable, if inevitable, part of the transition from childhood to adult life. The celebration of innocence is a romantic attitude, of course, and one that has been losing ground, even in children's literature, for many decades. But Cormier is forcing the pace considerably in his work and it is political, rather than personal innocence that he is talking about. He is saying that political innocence is a dangerous quality, that it can be a kind of collaboration with evil, that innocence is often acquiescence through moral neutrality in the abuse of power by the powerful, and in the sacrifice of the individual to the political organization.

In this novel, Miro's awful innocence has a parallel in the other "monster" of the story, Ben's father, General Marchand. Like the terrorists, the General has dedicated his life to the service of his country; like Artkin, he has extended his own commitment to his son's life, which becomes forfeit to the State's needs. (pp. 75-8)

When is it that such men as Artkin and Miro and Marchand become monsters? It is not when they murder or lie or torture, but earlier, at the point where they make the initial choice to surrender their moral will to the State. They disavow their humanity in the same moment that they seal their innocence by choosing never to question nor even to contemplate questioning. Cormier makes it abundantly clear that, in the political context they have accepted, the General's decisions and Artkin's are not only logical, they are correct. It is humanly that the choices are monstrous. Ben's suicide, Raymond's murder, and Kate's death are Cormier's comment on the human cost of political abstraction; in the end, he tells us, the price is often paid by those who have been given no choice in the matter.

Cormier's teen novels are not "great books"; I doubt that they will outlast their topical relevance. But they are important books just the same. Cormier writes of things few books for the young acknowledge at all. He has evoked a political world in which evil is neither an individual phenomenon nor a personality fault explainable by individual psychology, but a collaborative act between individuals and political systems which begins when the individual gives over to the system the moral responsibility that is part of being human. He suggests that innocence can be a moral defect, that evil is (as Hannah Arendt has said) banal, and, above all, that political bureaucracies are often—perhaps always—a potential danger to individual freedom because they are fundamentally committed to their own perpetuation, which is always threatened by individual dissent. (pp. 79-80)

Neither the issues Cormier poses nor the answers he implies belong to the same moral world as the themes of adjustment, acceptance, and understanding that undergird most adolescent fiction. Instead, his work opens again the complex questions of the function of literature and of whether that function varies with the age of the intended reader. Cormier's three adolescent novels answer for him. . . . (p. 80)

> Anne Scott MacLeod, "Robert Cormier and the Ad-
> olescent Novel," in Children's literature in educa-
> tion, Vol. 12, No. 2 (Summer), 1981, pp. 74-81.

ROGER SUTTON

Until very recently, simple romances were "out" in YA realism, replaced by novels about various social concerns: drug abuse, premarital sex, and so on. Instead of a character being the focus of the novel, a condition became the subject of examination. With individual books often described as "tough," "honest," and "hard-hitting," the genre became known as the "New Realism." Kenneth Donelson and Alleen Nilsen claim that not only had there been a shift in subject matter in the contemporary realistic novel for young adults, but that there had been a shift in fictional mode as well: from romantic to ironic, and sometimes tragic [see excerpt above].

Tragedy, cynicism, irony: certainly these were foreign to Betty Cavanna's Diane Graham or [Rosamond] du Jardin's Tobey Heydon. But are they that typical of the teen problem novel? How often, really, does the bad guy win out? . . .

It is self-deluding to call these novels tragic, and those critics who claim that the New Realism is characterized by a tragic or ironic mode engage in critical mythmaking. Though they may speak to such problems as runaways and prostitution, problem novels are usually about *solutions* to those problems, and about the integration of the wayward (or waylaid) protagonist into responsible, adult society. They are therefore more properly defined as belonging to the mode of low mimetic comedy, that of most popular fiction and certainly that of the teen novel of the 1950s. Taking these books too seriously is not a harmless endeavor; it deludes us into thinking that we are giving young adults truly substantial literature, rather than simply entertaining them. (p. 33)

"What about Robert Cormier?" is a question that must be raised here. Cormier has, to my mind, unreasonably become a symbol for all that is good and bad in adolescent literature. His books are certainly not typical of the New Realism, for two reasons. They have unhappy endings and, as Anne MacLeod has noted [see excerpt above], his books do not concern "the individual and the personal," do not concern themselves for the most part with "psychological development and personal morality," a major preoccupation of typical realistic novels for teens. Yet, Betsy Hearne cited *The Chocolate War* . . . as indicative of a "trend of didactic negativity." Donelson and Nilsen call the same novel a "touchstone example" of the problem novel [see excerpt above], and Rebecca Lukens, using Cormier as her example, claims that "the world-view in popular literature has flipped," to a view in which "the pervasive forces of the unseen and the sinister are in control."

Cormier's three novels for adolescents all tell compellingly of a universe where the good guys lose. But under the grim, no-win surface lies a very conventional, respectable morality: wrong may triumph over right, but the reader is certainly shown which is which.

Jerry, in *The Chocolate War,* refuses to sell candy for the parochial school fund drive. He is the only student who won't, and in the end he is brutally beaten in a rigged fight witnessed by the entire school. Jerry, the good guy, loses. He goes down fighting, though, and his defeat only shows more clearly the difference between him and the bad guys, who can triumph only through the use of physical force. This is a very simple book: Readers know who to root for all the way. What if, though, Jerry gave in and became the best chocolate salesman of them all? This kind of ironic sophistication, while commonplace in fiction for adults, is absent from Cormier's work and from adolescent literature in general.

When adolescent novels do trade in tragedy, they do so in a very safe way, encouraging readers to identify with an innocent protagonist. All of Cormier's protagonists are virtuous and brave and all of them—even the terrorist Miro in *After the First Death* . . .—are trying to do the right thing. They are not victims of their own mistakes or tragic flaws so much as they are victims of an evil beyond their control. . . . Even the most grim, most tragic novels for teenagers leave readers unchallenged and inviolate. They arouse passions of indignation at the evil actions of others, yet do not make the reader confront himself as anything less, or more, than innocent. *Things can go wrong,* these tragic novels say, *but it's not your fault.* (pp. 34-5)

Let us stop pretending that we are offering teenagers "hard-hitting," "shattering" realism and let us stop talking about "tragic" when we just mean sad. We don't often offer truly

challenging realism to young adults, but we have talked and written ourselves into believing it is so. (p. 35)

Roger Sutton, "The Critical Myth: Realistic YA Novels," in School Library Journal, *Vol. 29, No. 3, November, 1982, pp. 33-5.**

ZENA SUTHERLAND

In [*The Bumblebee Flies Anyway*], a story that is as trenchant as it is poignant, Cormier shows the courage and desperation of adolescents who know that their deaths are imminent. Barney, sixteen, is the only patient who is in the experimental hospital who is not in the group of the doomed but is there as a control: all of them are there voluntarily, some to contribute to research and some, like Mazzo, hoping for a quick death. . . . Barney thinks of a plan that will give Mazzo the quick, daring death he wants; secretly he reconstructs a life-size model of a car from the dump next door, pulls the plug on Mazzo's life-support system, and helps him to the roof where the car waits to be pushed off for one last glorious flight. The story, which has an element of twin telepathy, involves questions of medical ethics and freedom of choice, and ends with Barney, who in the course of his treatments and his conversation with his doctor, has learned that he too is going to die, remembering with persistent joy, despite his gray fog of pain, the beauty of the flight, his last achievement. This is, although it is tragic, a stunning book: Cormier creates convincingly the hospital world of the terminally ill, the pathos of Barney's love for Cassie [Mazzo's twin sister] and his struggles with the hallucinations induced by the treatments that are designed to block his knowledge and help him forget his true condition. It moves, with relentless inevitability, like an ancient Greek tragedy, with the compassion of the staff a contrapuntal note, to the requiem of hopeless despair that, for each patient, still holds some passion for an affirmative act of life. (pp. 3-4)

Zena Sutherland, in a review of "The Bumblebee Flies Anyway," in Bulletin of the Center for Children's Books, *Vol. 37, No. 1, September, 1983, pp. 3-4.*

HAZEL ROCHMAN

With the grimmest of subjects Cormier has written his most affirmative novel [*The Bumblebee Flies Anyway*]. . . . The book has some serious flaws, notably in the depiction of Cassie, who we are told is "vibrant and compelling," but who remains an abstraction. But this is a fine novel, even better on rereading, with a startling poetry in the simplest phrases. Young adults will be caught up in the terrifying thriller, the scientific facts about memory, the controversial issue of medical ethics. They will also be moved by the vision in the wasteland: Barney's power to define himself and reach out, through love and knowledge and arduous painful struggle.

Hazel Rochman, in a review of "The Bumblebee Flies Anyway," in School Library Journal, *Vol. 30, No. 1, September, 1983, p. 132.*

SALLY ESTES

Subtle foreshadowing and well-crafted metaphors and similes [in *The Bumblebee Flies Anyway*] enable readers to mentally visualize setting, action, and characters; and there is a rhythm to Cormier's writing that compels reader reaction much the way a musical score underlines emotion in films. The story's climactic blockbuster is marred only slightly by a double denouement—one weak, the other fitting. The depressing situation aside, the overall effect is one of a reaffirmation of the humanity of humankind that contrasts with the images projected by *The Chocolate War, I Am the Cheese,* and *After the First Death.* (p. 38)

> *Sally Estes, in a review of ''The Bumblebee Flies Anyway,'' in* Booklist, *Vol. 80, No. 1, September 1, 1983, pp. 37-8.*

W. GEIGER ELLIS

What's a person to say? He's done it again. Cormier is Cormier. [*The Bumblebee Flies Anyway*] is consistent with his other successes by focusing on the struggle between individuals and an institution. Institutions are dehumanizing, but humans do not succumb easily—or necessarily. While the larger theme is unchanged, he has forced us to think in yet another arena, for the battle we see here involves the medical establishment. Yet it would be a disservice to suggest that *Bumblebee* is an exposé of the world of medicos; it explores the boundaries of human spirit together with the possibilities within these boundaries.

> *W. Geiger Ellis, in a review of ''The Bumblebee Flies Anyway,'' in* The ALAN Review, *Vol. 11, No. 1, Fall, 1983, p. 23.*

NANCY C. HAMMOND

A master of taut, twisting plots and clear prose, [Cormier, an] inventive writer, creates sufficient mystery, deception, and irony [in *The Bumblebee Flies Anyway*] to rival the force of *I Am the Cheese.* . . . But because the narrative events are less ambiguous, the feelings less subtle, and the symbolism more obvious, the reader's discoveries are diminished. Although the Madonna-like Cassie and her parallel story are less convincing and some secondary characters are clichés, Barney and the others do come alive. And their ability to triumph in some measure over the depersonalizing situation represents a marked change from the author's previous work. (pp. 715-16)

> *Nancy C. Hammond, in a review of ''The Bumblebee Flies Anyway,'' in* The Horn Book Magazine, *Vol. LIX, No. 6, December, 1983, pp. 715-16.*

Thomas B(ertram) Costain

1885-1965

Canadian-born American novelist, nonfiction writer, biographer, and editor.

Costain's career as a novelist began with the publication of *For My Great Folly* (1942), a historically based fiction about John Ward, a seventeenth-century English pirate. He continued to produce popular and best-selling historical novels, among which were his best-known and critically acclaimed *The Black Rose* (1945) and *The Silver Chalice* (1952). In addition, he gained further popularity with his "Pageant of England" series, which includes four nonfiction volumes, covering the years 1066-1485, and narrates events which revolve around the British monarchy and other important figures.

Costain's first novel set the pattern for those that followed in its extensive background research, intrigue, colorful detail, fast-paced action, vast scope of scene, and other elements of epic adventures. The novels are often set in the Middle Ages and use many terms and details appropriate to the period. Costain believed that history should come alive for the reader and demonstrate how the past has contributed to the present. His recurring topics are social change, the rise of the common people, and the decline of chivalry. Costain's characters are courageous, skillful, hardy, and based on historical figures; he makes them realistic by adding appropriate personal details. His foremost skill is his narrative ability, which is enhanced by solid construction and interesting "period" miscellany.

Critics acknowledge the popularity and entertainment value of Costain's novels. They do, however, note certain stylistic weaknesses. His extensive use of obscure terms is viewed as an affectation; his colloquial language and the attitudes of many of his characters are thought to be too modern for the times in which they are supposed to have lived. Scholars claim that Costain's presentations of history, like his characters, are simplified to the point where they do little to enrich the reader's sense of an unfamiliar era. Nevertheless, Costain tried to do justice to his subjects by extensively consulting experts and imaginatively blending fiction with fact. Costain's books are still considered good examples of well-constructed historical fiction, and they demonstrate his intention to make history appealing to modern readers through an emphasis on its romantic and adventurous aspects.

(See also *Contemporary Authors*, Vols. 5-8, rev. ed., Vols. 25-28, rev. ed. [obituary] and *Dictionary of Literary Biography*, Vol. 9.)

The Granger Collection, New York

JANE SPENCE SOUTHRON

The historical side of ["**For My Great Folly**," an] immensely entertaining novel set in England and the Mediterranean must be dealt with first despite the author's disclaimer of a factual foundation for much of it. It was a critical time: the opening years of the reign of the Scottish King of England whose fatuous attempts to wrest freedom from his subjects led, afterward, to civil war and the establishment of a Commonwealth. If you were entirely ignorant of the history involved you could take the story as sheer fiction and enjoy it throughout on that different plane. It is not unleavened fiction. A very important slice of it, for which Mr. Costain gives himself no credit, is the vivid and substantially accurate picture of King James I's corrupt court painted here with neither bias nor exaggeration. But there are other historical matters that invite inquiry.

To begin with, the book is built up round Captain John Ward, pirate, whose dossier in the pirates' "Who's Who" tells us little more than that he was of lowly birth and settled, eventually, at Tunis. While vouching for his story of Ward's piratical exploits, which, he says, "follows the historical facts closely enough," Mr. Costain admits that the picture he has given of the man himself is "completely imaginary." Apart from Ward's use, at variance with the rest of his character, of the sinister "cant" slang of the London underworld, a very sound, romantic job has been made of his career and personality. But one would like to know more exactly what degree of authenticity can be assigned to the Mediterranean sea fights so splendidly depicted here. (pp. 6-7)

[Also,] Mr. Costain's own justification for his too-flattering portrait of pretty, fascinating but utterly unscrupulous and money-mad Ann Turner would seem to have slender basis in recorded fact.

That the writer's "most serious purpose" has been fulfilled is beyond a doubt. The early part of the seventeenth century is shown here, as he aimed at showing it, in a multiplicity of colorful detail. Dress, food, travel, housing, town and country living, court life, shipboard life, the life of London's criminal class (too-over-emphasized for complete fictional enjoyment) and, most interestingly of all, the merchant world of an England growing increasingly trade conscious, are woven into a gorgeous, rare tapestry as backcloth for a beguiling drama.

And here we are on uncriticizable ground. If Ward takes stage-center as pirate, he has to halve all the romantic and many of the fighting honors with young Roger Blease, the story's narrator and as appealing a hero as book ever had. Nor could you ask for a likelier—or more delightful—heroine than Katie Ladland. . . .

It is a very natural and a very lovely love story with as touching and heart-warming a climax as you will find anywhere in romantic literature. . . . Mr. Costain knows his business; and there will be no romantic-adventure lover left unsatisfied. (p. 7)

> *Jane Spence Southron, "Novels by Anita Pettibone, Dorothy Macardle and Others: The Pirate," in* The New York Times Book Review, *July 26, 1942, pp. 6-7.*

BEN RAY REDMAN

[The] main story-line of **"Ride with Me"** is the line of Frank's pursuit of Gabrielle through the corridors of history, with many fine shows along the way. It is a line that will be followed with pleasure by those who take their historical fiction by the pound, who demand only that heroines be beautiful and heroes dauntless. But the judicious will, I am sure, mark down **"Ride with Me"** as a brave but unsuccessful essay in the difficult field of the historical novel.

Evidences of Mr. Costain's industry are manifest on every page, and there is no doubt as to the genuineness of his interest in and enthusiasm for the Napoleonic period, in which his people have such being as he gives them. But industry and interest and enthusiasm are not enough when material is ineffectively organized, when trivial byproducts of research clutter pages, when characters are wooden, when the reader must plod instead of being pulled, when the author scants or shoots around scenes that might have been his biggest. That he has taken in a lot of territory and quite a chunk of history does not suffice, in view of the fact that his central historical figure is only a shadow, and the other figures from life no more than names. We are given glimpses of General Sir Robert Wilson ("Riding Bobby"), to the tale of whose exploits this book was originally dedicated . . . but it all adds up to very little, certainly not to the image of a man and a hero. (pp. 9-10)

> *Ben Ray Redman, "Francis Ellery's Crusade," in* The Saturday Review of Literature, *Vol. XXVII, No. 34, August 19, 1944, pp. 9-10.*

K. SHATTUCK MARVIN

The Literary Guild has bestowed its accolade upon **"The Black Rose,"** and its author, Thomas B. Costain, deserves another one for the research which went into its writing. Perhaps the relish which Mr. Costain obviously derived from his labors will serve as his reward.

Thirteenth century England and the same period in China, plus an interval spent on the medieval silk routes overland into China, are the great pictures in this book. As they are a new

milieu for historical romances, they are in themselves absorbing, but against them the characters move rather pallidly. Mr. Costain's aforementioned relish prevented him from giving us much more than a hazy picture of Walter, Tristram, Engaine and Maryam, for whose ilk the reader of numerous historical romances may have by now only a hazy interest, anyway. A neat job is done on medieval Oxford, Edward I, castle life in England, travel in a trans-Asiatic caravan, and China with the Mongols sweeping down on the Sung Kingdom to unify the nation. The "dreaming spirit" of the University and the Arthur Rackham-Maxfield Parrish vision of a castle perish in the reader's mind before a far more vivid and enjoyable white light of truth with details pleasant and unpleasant. Thirteenth century vocabulary abounds magnificently but enigmatically. . . .

The plot sprawls loosely against the vivid panorama. Walter, a student at Oxford, finds himself the recipient of a small fortune which he decides to increase by a journey to fabulous Cathay, under whose spell he has fallen during a lecture by Friar Roger Bacon. In the company of Tristram, a fellow student and fellow townsman, he sets forth for a land which few have seen. . . .

The route is that of Marco Polo; and the exotic excitements are those of the lines "In Xanadu did Kublai Khan. . . ." The arrival of the English pair in Hangchow coincides with the fall of the Sung Empire and the unification of China under one-man rule—that of Kublai Khan: scenes strangely prophetic of latter-day developements.

Cathay reached, fortunes made, Walter and Tristram return to England accompanied as ever with high adventures. A new modern England is emerging—another prophetic touch—as they return, for the power of the barons has been broken and the Norman-Saxon bitterness is disappearing under the wise kingship of Edward I. Mr. Costain has written a tale that hums along until the last sentence.

> *K. Shattuck Marvin, in a review of "The Black Rose," in* Commonweal, *Vol. XLII, No. 25, October 5, 1945, p. 602.*

WILLIAM DU BOIS

Readers of Mr. Costain's earlier novels. . . , will know that he has a special alchemy for every setting he chooses; those who flocked to **"The Black Rose"** by the hundred thousands will need no invitation to return for more. They will not be disappointed in **"The Moneyman."**

The author sets his stage brilliantly with his opening chapter. Moving with the great Jacques Coeur (the *argentier du roy,* or King's Moneyman) through the splendors and stenches of the Louvre, from the queen's card-table to the king's closet, form the perfumed presence of the king's mistress to the hard-backed benches where the king's captains cool their heels, we see the multi-colored tapestry of the Middle Ages in all its hectic splendor, breathe the rot of chivalry in its last, maudlin muddle. Mr. Costain makes it abundantly clear that this was indeed the dark hour before the dawn; seen through the eye of the Moneyman, a modern born centuries before his time, the ridiculous pomp of Charles VII's court takes on new meaning—and the Moneyman's part in the over-all pattern becomes a first-rate dramatic pivot. (p. 1)

Mr. Costain's plots and counter-plots, like Mr. Costain's genius for color, are his own patented secret: they will not even be sketched in this review. Suffice it to say that things end well enough for [two of his central characters, d'Arly and his lady], after the last breathless gallop, the last agonized turn of the rack. Coeur's end was something else again: like most great men who are born too soon, he was dismembered by his century. The author makes no attempt to underwrite the monstrous injustice of his last, long trial, the too-easy short cut of a sovereign deep in debt to his most faithful subject.

The book teems with sharp vignettes of the period: fictional characters are matched neatly with historical, and only the captious will find fault with the counter-pointing. Dunois stalks the corridors of the Louvre as the curtain rises—a great graying cynic who still remembers the Maid, and how they raised the siege of Orleans together. Jacques de Lalain, that final, noisome flower of knighthood, is there with his bombast—and Mr. Costain has a fine time puncturing his facade. . . . Chivalry's last weird contortions are here in full, from the precise protocol of a challenge to the proper sampling of a wine-cup: the chain-mail rattles, the jeweled breastplate creaks—and we see the man beneath, to his absurdly inflated heart.

As always in a Costain novel it is hard to recall where history leaves off and apocrypha begins: Coeur's defiance of his evil judges is no less real than d'Arly's invasion of Charles VII's hideout to rescue his loved one, in time's nick. Both fact and fancy are illumined with a wealth of detail. (pp. 1, 26)

But Mr. Costain's alchemy is his own, and no paraphrase can do it justice. Less nimble practitioners have ventured among the stacks to revive a dusty century—and choked their readers with the dust. It is this novelist's achievement that he can bring the faded colors to instant life that he can resurrect princes and popinjays again in all their gaudy, human splendor. **"The Moneyman"** makes the plight of Jacques Coeur as real and as important as the fall of a liberal in tomorrow's headlines. (p. 26)

> *William Du Bois, "Two Novels, Richly Caparisoned," in* The New York Times Book Review, *July 13, 1947, pp. 1, 26.**

THE ATLANTIC MONTHLY

What are the ingredients of a good historical novel? What is in an author's mind when he chooses a period in which to place his story? Is it to provide color and background to enrich with a romantic haze a story not quite strong enough to stand on its own legs? Does the author set out to "explain" history in a popular way? Or is he writing for the pot, knowing that any craftsmanlike cloak-and-dagger job will find a good market? These and other unanswerable questions bedevil this particular reader of *The Moneyman*. . . .

[Mr. Costain] is a consistent and successful producer of this sort of thing—as his three previous novels have shown. *The Moneyman* is a good enough story, well enough told. . . .

The author has made Jacques Coeur and the Sire d'Arlay into modern-minded men. The former foresees a state of things when wealth, wisely administered, and sound economics will replace outworn feudalism. The Sire d'Arlay has come to regard chivalry as an empty fraud. Things are pretty bad in fifteenth-century France but, given a few characters with modern American ideas, they will work out all right in the end and the world will be better in our next volume. In fact, the world will probably keep on getting better and better, which is a very nice, comfortable thought in 1947.

This is, therefore, a kind of "hindsight" historical novel. The present is always with us, looking down its nose at the past. We see fifteenth-century France as a brutal, colorful pageant of error and evil, of romance and misery, which we readers, as superior spectators, can regard in our wisdom. This happy position makes the book easy to understand; we like the swordplay and the action and the suspense, and we are pleasantly aware of our own superiority to the misguided creatures who caper and prance before our eyes.

Neither we nor the author is in or of the period described. The book is well enough documented as to manners and customs, the clothes and the armor, the food and the gallantry, but it is all objective. Nothing is taken for granted. It has to be explained. We have to see it through the eyes of Mr. Costain and his modern-minded characters. (p. 122)

This objective, hindsight historical novel writing has its obvious virtues and advantages, but it is hard to write from that standpoint and produce a work of art. One cannot re-create a period if one cannot speak and think and react in its rhythm and idiom. Mr. Costain can no more place himself inside the body and mind of a fifteenth-century Frenchman than Mark Twain's Yankee could creep into the soul of Sir Kay, the seneschal. . . . Only by hindsight could a lowborn moneyman like Jacques Coeur acquire stature. At the time, he was not the kind of person one wrote about.

Compare this kind of thing with the historical novels eminent Frenchmen of our day have written about their own countrymen. The suave and unexplained incarnations of their periods who appear in the novels of Anatole France and Henri de Régnier are creations as authentic in art as they are learned in documentation. Or take a novel placed in the sixteenth century, such as Maurice Maindron's *Le Tournoi de Vauplassans*. Here we are wholly and magically drawn into the idiom of an age that is past.

A *Moneyman* written in that idiom would probably not be appreciated by the Great American Public. But it would more nearly approach the standards of attempted artistry. (pp. 122-23)

> *A.W., "American Romance in the French Court," in* The Atlantic Monthly, *Vol. 180, No. 3, September, 1947, pp. 122-23.*

CHARLES LEE

Here is Thomas Costain at his best, in a well-constructed novel. . . . **"High Towers"** has something for all: historical solidity, biographical interest, glamour. It is rich with learning, alive with adventure.

Its larger enchantments deal with the fabulous Le Moyne family and the growth of the French Empire in North America during the early years of the eighteenth century. Within this framework Mr. Costain offers a satisfying quantity of love stories, excitations and intrigues. The gaudiness of certain of his effects does not depend on specious spectacle; the dazzle is inherent in the tale. He fictionalizes history; he does not fabricate hysteria. He writes of human beings, not of supermen and hussies.

It is true that he will now and again detour the reader to a footnote, making him unnecessarily conscious of the midnight oil. This is less true of his occasional parentheses . . . , and on the whole his researches are well-integrated with the text.

The result is a story swirling with incidents, comic, tragic, agitating, but always entertaining. . . .

"High Towers" is a skillfully wrought entertainment. Even its clichés, like that of the mother who cannot reveal herself to her daughter, are expertly managed. There are memorable scenes—Pierre battling the plague, Phillippe befuddling a group of scalp-minded Indians, Jean working with destiny amidst the mud and tents of New Orleans. There is matter, too, for the thoughtful, on love, duty, happiness, money, and even in connection with the more beneficent aspects of imperialism and conquest. But most readers will be grateful for Mr. Costain's double sorcery: he erases the headlines of the hour as he creates a spell of yesteryear.

> Charles Lee, "Empire-Builders in the Wilderness," in The New York Times Book Review, *January 2, 1949, p. 5.*

GEOFFREY BRUUN

"Historians' English," Philip Guedalla asserted, "is not a style; it is an occupational disease." To this verdict Thomas B. Costain would add a fervent Amen. The author of **"The Black Rose"** and **"The Moneyman"** has turned from his triumphs in historical fiction to write a popular history [**"The Conquerors"**]. "The picture that emerges," he submits in a pugnacious preface, "is, in my opinion, an honest and complete one." On this point some critics may have their reservations, but few will deny that the picture is detailed, diverting, and undeniably dramatic.

"The Conquerors" opens a series which will be known as **"The Pageant of England."** It covers, as the tedious textbook writers would say, the period from 1066 to 1216. . . .

Thomas Costain belongs to the school of Michelet in his conviction that history ought to be a resurrection of the flesh, and he is in the great tradition of Scott and Dumas in his ability to make it fascinating. Every descriptive passage in this unflagging pageant is a triumph of sensuous detail. . . .

A reviewer feels ungracious looking for flaws in such a brilliant and enjoyable performance. Yet professional historians, faithful to what Mr. Costain derides as their "sacred code," are certain to censure the latitude of some of his interpretations. For his own part, he goes out of his way to bait the academic brotherhood who would confine Clio to their airless seminars. They will retaliate no doubt by denouncing **"The Conquerors"** for errors of fact, with all the energy of experts hurling cannonballs at cobwebs. The quarrel is at best a profitless one. Mr. Costain could not have staged this lively pageant without drawing on the preliminary labor of innumerable scholars. If he omits footnotes and mocks at "old Ibid, that ubiquitous Man Friday of the historians" he assures us a moment later that he has authenticated all the scores of speeches which he quotes. His bibliography of almost two hundred secondary works shows how widely he ranged to garner the details on "currency, minting, monastic life, sheep raising, weaving, heraldry, architecture, archery" and other topics that form a background for his dialogue. If further evidence were needed, the neat and charming maps, the twenty-page index and the scrupulous proofreading are guaranties that this is no casual book although it may be aimed at "the casual reader."

Despite his raillery at "the traditions of the craft" and the plodding historians who bury the sublime in the meticulous, Mr. Costain is passionately devoted to Clio in his fashion.

What he forgets is that the more fluently that frail Muse speaks the dialects of the streets the more difficult she finds it to say no in any of them. This glowing book is the proper stuff of history, but not all of it as written is history proper, if Mr. Costain will permit the distinction.

> Geoffrey Bruun, "History's Drama and Color," in New York Herald Tribune Book Review, *November 20, 1949, p. 12.*

THEODORE MAYNARD

Mr. Costain comes to the point in his first sentence: "There is no need for another history of England unless it can be given popular appeal." The best-selling novelist openly declares for the same sort of thing in his new field as that which proved such a success in the old, and there can be little doubt that he will obtain it.

Nevertheless I have my reservations with regard to his performance, as I have also with regard to his novels, in whose dexterity I admit, as in the case of this initial excursion into history, I can find a good deal to praise. [**"The Conquerors"**] is orderly and has a fund of information of the kind that does not usually appear in works of this category. Color and vivacity are here, and I certainly do not consider them faults, for even historians are (or should be) writers, and writers are, almost by definition, people who hope to be read. As against the professional historians, who are sure to attack this book, I am willing to defend it, at any rate for its claim of a right to avoid the usual stuffy manner. I also commend it for a fairer treatment of Catholic issues—particularly as regards the quarrels between Henry II and Thomas à Becket and King John and Pope Innocent III—than is usual among the top-lofty professionals.

Having said as much, however, I must register a few animadversions of my own. . . . My objections are of two main sorts: one is that Mr. Costain's efforts to be interesting at all costs are a little too strained and obvious; the other is that those efforts are not always successful. It boils down to this: Mr. Costain, though he has great competence, does not always show good taste and judgment, and his literary style is far from equal to the task he has attempted. So liable is he to slip into such banalities as "putting no reliance in that possibility" and "an effort to effect a settlement" . . . that by counter action he deliberately sprinkles his pages with odd or obsolete words which oblige the conscientious to rush to the encyclopedia or the dictionary to dig out his meaning. (pp. 219-20)

This, like so much else, strikes me as affectation. . . . It astonishes me that a former editor of the *Saturday Evening Post* and the author of a series of eagerly devoured novels should throw such difficulties in his readers' way. Rather it would astonish me were I not sure that Mr. Costain knows better than I what his immense public likes, and that (as I suspect) he knows that he has to cover up his stylistic deficiencies by eccentric devices.

Some of the merits of the book I have mentioned, along with what are, I think, legitimate reasons for irritation. Whatever may be alleged against Mr. Costain—the stressing of detail, however insignificant, merely because it is picturesque, and a too selective treatment of his subject—it must be said that this man knows how to tell a good story. Something more is needed from a historian than that, but that also is needed and it is abundantly supplied here. (p. 220)

Theodore Maynard, in a review of "The Conquerors," in Commonweal, *Vol. LI, No. 7, November 25, 1949, pp. 219-20.*

CHARLES LEE

Thomas Costain has won a large and admiring public with novels of historical romance, most of which are set in the Middle Ages. In his new novel ["**Son of a Hundred Kings**"] he brings his readers back to more recent times—Canada in the Nineties—without disturbing the splashy colors which dominate his canvas. Substituting a vivid memory for the customary research—Mr. Costain grew up in Canada during the years he writes about—he tells the story of 6-year-old Ludar Prentice, who was shipped from England to his father in Canada, and enters upon various adventures, chiefly Victorian.

A spree of old-fashioned yarning, it is richly sub-plotted in the Dickensian manner with structural gingerbread and replete with disenchanting editorial intrusions by the author. Its three "books" are packed with curlicues of contrivance. . . .

Ludar grows up with William Christian, a benign and dreamy inventor, and his nagging wife, Tilly. He meets the feuding members, young and old, of the Craven clan, chooses sides, goes to school, falls in love with the daughter of the local newspaper publisher, and works his way through hard times and the terrible teens.

Then, at the very moment when he feels he may win milady's hand from his rival (a Craven enemy, of course), he becomes involved in a murder.

This is only the central matter in an exceedingly busy story. Yet it is not revealing anything to add that in the end the wicked get punished, the fallen reform, and the virtuous live happily ever after. The usual Costain period touch is manifested by frequent references to such paraphernalia as brass-toed shoes, Psyche knots, Crokinole boards, Fauntleroy suits, gaslight, Morris chairs, and horseless carriages. Much of the dialogue is unlifelike, the characterization superficial, and the narrative wooden. However, "**Son of a Hundred Kings**" . . . will doubtless appeal to the large audience searching only for what the author calls "Story—with a capital letter."

Charles Lee, "Victorian Adventures," in The New York Times Book Review, *October 22, 1950, p. 4.*

GEOFFREY BRUUN

Mr. Costain's name is known to millions who have enjoyed "**The Black Rose**" in print or technicolor. In 1949 he turned from historical romances to write history itself and revivified English annals from Hastings to Magna Carta. The venture demonstrated that he could stick fairly close to authentic sources and still invest his story with the glamor that characterized his fiction. His aim was to write the sort of history that has a strong popular appeal. "In succeeding volumes," he predicted, "which will deal with periods where the records are more full, it will be easier to accomplish the purpose which I have begun."

His second volume in this "**Pageant of England**" series ["**The Magnificent Century**"] has now appeared, carrying the narrative through the long reign of Henry III (1216-1272). Whether the somewhat fuller records of the thirteenth century made the task of writing easier he does not say and the result leaves the answer in doubt. He covers fifty-six years in slightly less space than he devoted to the preceeding century and a half, but there

is no appreciable gain in substance and structure. Make no mistake—this is still one of the most colorful and romantic histories of England yet written. The bright speed of the first volume is still there although the prose has become a little less exuberant. Fuller records, however, can make writing heavier rather than easier as Mr. Costain may come to realize. . . .

The central theme of a volume that opens a year after Magna Carta should be the struggle of the lords, lay and ecclesiastic, to limit the extravagance and favoritism of an irresponsible monarch. Mr. Costain tries to develop this theme but it remains incomplete. . . .

Mr. Costain has several passages in which he surveys European culture in the large, notably his chapter on Roger Bacon and on the Faith of the Century. But he is predominantly engrossed with the score of characters he has selected for discussion. Though some are historically significant and he reveals the forces and ideals of the age through them his real interest is focused on their individual stories because he thinks the stories worth retelling. They are.

It is impossible to project the spell of Mr. Costain's prose in a review. Part of the secret lies in his use of quaint and tantalizing words, as when he completes a royal menu with "dilligrout and karum pie." Part derives from his preference for the concrete and avoidance of the abstract. Introducing Peter des Roches, for instance, he admits that no picture or description of this wily schemer survives, and then affirms confidently, "The imagination may be allowed some latitude in picturing him." Peter appears life-size, down to his orphreys of modest black and the ring on his thumb. The stickler for historical accuracy may cavil at such liberties and doubtless will. But Mr. Costain rarely fails to indicate when a statement rests on reputable authority and when it is based on reasonable assumptions.

There are slips, of course—what scholar can entirely avoid them? Only an "author omniscient" could know his characters well enough to say (as Mr. Costain says of Hubert de Burgh) that he "undoubtedly had no knowledge whatever of the nature and use of poison." And a glance at the nearest encyclopedia should have persuaded him to strike out the suggestion that the flying buttress first "came into existence" in England. But Mr. Costain is writing for the public, not for the pedants. Readers who want to enjoy a book about the reign of Henry III that is crammed with human interest and popular appeal will find "**The Magnificent Century**" magnificent history.

Geoffrey Bruun, "Colorful and Romantic," in New York Herald Tribune Book Review, *September 23, 1951, p. 6.*

G. B. HARRISON

To Mr. Costain's vigorous narrative can legitimately be applied the overworked metaphor kaleidoscopic, for, like the images in that ancient toy, it abounds in simple bright colors, ever shifting their pattern. In this new volume of *The Pageant of England* [*The Magnificent Century*] he covers the reign of the regrettable John's son, Henry III, who ruled England for over fifty years, marked by incompetence, extravagance, petulance, broken promises, civil war, violence and magnificent buildings. The story, as befits a pageant, is reduced to simple terms and certain figures and events stand out clearly—William the Marshal, Hubert de Burgh, Simon de Montfort, the shifty king, and young Edward who becomes king. . . . (p. 204)

The Magnificent Century is a good specimen of popular historiography, but it illustrates the difficulty of writing colorfully about a period inadequately documented and poorly illustrated by its contemporaries. Mr. Costain has done his best, but the novelist and the student within his breast are at odds, and at times he suffers from creditable scruples. He itches to sketch a person or to describe a character, and the records elude him. He must therefore fall back on the imaginary peep into the past. . . . There are so many of these reconditioned worthies that the reader grows sceptical. . . . (pp. 204-05)

Indeed for an author who eschews footnotes and is more concerned with painting than with minute scholarship, it is better to omit the bibliography and the apologetics of "would," "doubtless," and—most deadly of all—"we may be sure." The professional student will not take *The Magnificent Century* seriously anyway; the common reader, for whom the book is intended, wants a good tale, and he does not trouble whether the portrait of Queen Eleanor is based on a dozen original sources or has been touched up by Mr. Costain's fervid pen. It should be added that those who like pageants of history will enjoy *The Magnificent Century* and learn much from it; and they will look forward to the next volume. (p. 205)

> *G. B. Harrison, in a review of "The Magnificent Century," in* Commonweal, *Vol. LV, No. 8, November 30, 1951, pp. 204-05.*

THOMAS CALDECOT CHUBB

In 1949 Thomas Costain temporarily turned aside from a successful series of historical novels to commence a long history of England in which it was his intention to apply his persuasive imagination to the sober realm of fact. It began well, and the first two volumes have won justified applause. **"The Conquerors,"** starting in 1066, and **"The Magnificent Century,"** which told the tale of Magna Charta John's artistic but unstable son, Henry III, are indeed the sort of books that convert chronicles of the dead past into summer reading. And they do this with at least reasonable respect for what really occurred.

Yet good as they are they are not Thomas Costain at his best, and I am sure this reviewer is not the only one who, reading them with pleasure, still thought nostalgically of **"The Black Rose"** and **"The Moneyman."** For Mr. Costain is, after all, not a historian but a novelist immersed in history. Historical fiction is the area of his most notable achievement. . . .

For that reason, it is good to see Mr. Costain back at the old stand again and with so excellent a book. **"The Silver Chalice"** . . . is an outstanding historical novel. Its theme alone marks it as different and original. Never a man of timid fancy, Mr. Costain has now dared to deal with one of Christianity's most hallowed legends. The "silver chalice" which gives the book its name is the frame for Joseph of Arimathea's most carefully guarded treasure, the modest "battered cup" of the Last Supper. Laid in Palestine and elsewhere when men still lived who had seen Jesus of Nazareth with mortal eyes, this novel is the story of the Holy Grail.

The plot of the book is not important. . . . What is important is the feeling and the background against which this love story is laid. In a sense, **"The Silver Chalice,"** ranging as it does from Jerusalem through Antioch to Rome, is a modern "Quo Vadis," and like [Henryk Sienkiewicz's] "Quo Vadis" it is at once reverent enough to be a Christian document and colorful enough to deserve the same kind of full Hollywood treatment.

That it is full of action and adventure goes without saying. We all know Thomas Costain. But it is also well stocked with well-drawn characters. . . .

The real characters are equally well done. St. Luke the physician, St. John of the Apocalypse, St. Paul, Joseph, St. Peter (disguised as the innkeeper's assistant, Cephas) and even the too-frequently done Nero [Emperor of Rome] all have the stamp of men who actually live and breathe.

It is not possible to demonstrate by quotation the skillful way in which Mr. Costain has accomplished this, for he does not do it by compact presentation but rather by a word here and another there as these characters are slowly introduced to us and then defined. Yet, the reader who has pursued this story . . . will have seen face to face the good (and in one case, the evil) geniuses of the early days of Christianity.

It was a difficult thing to do. The novelist who invents his own characters is restricted only by the limitations of his own imagination, but the one who re-creates an historical personage has to conform to what we know or believe that personage to have been. This is a test of creative ability which Mr. Costain passes with high honors.

"The Silver Chalice" is not without fault. Mr. Costain still cannot resist using too many obscure words and the moral might be better pointed up if its hero were not "a certain rich man" who did not see any necessity of "selling his cloak and giving to the poor." Even at that, it is Thomas Costain at better than his average. And that is more than good enough.

> *Thomas Caldecot Chubb, "Around a Modest, Battered Cup," in* The New York Times Book Review, *July 27, 1952, p. 4.*

RICHARD WINSTON

Over the past thirteen years Thomas B. Costain has been writing books whose sales are reckoned in the millions. His earlier novels are crowded with bold adventurers and desirable slave girls who meet one another in exotic places. Lately Mr. Costain has turned to non-fiction and he has been rendering the pageantry of English history with something of the dash and color that he puts into his novels. Now, back with fiction again, he has attempted to combine the two genres in a novel of family destinies in nineteenth century England, **"The Tontine,"** big in size and scope, jam-packed with characters, covering four generations and the better part of the nineteenth century. . . .

Mr. Costain's novel centers upon the participants in the Waterloo Tontine (a fictional one), founded by a gangster named Hark Chaffery for his own profit, but quickly taken out of his hands and placed on a legal, businesslike basis by Samuel Carboy, the financier who dominates the book. Staking his fortune on his faith in England and the Duke of Wellington, Sam Carboy strides into the London Stock Exchange on the day of the Battle of Waterloo and buys while everyone is selling. When word of Napoleon [Bonaparte's] defeat at last reaches London, prices rise again, and Carboy uses the profits of his day's speculation to build one of the greatest industrial empires in England. He expels his ornamental partner, George Grace, from the firm of Grace and Carboy and becomes a moving spirit of England's rapid economic expansion.

Mr. Costain traces the varied fates of the Graces and Carboys down to the formation of a new firm of Grace and Carboy by the great-grandsons of the original partners. In the meanwhile he has taken long looks at fashions in clothes throughout the Victorian period, the slang and manners of different decades, the movements for reform of the early abuses of industrialism, and the gradual improvement of social conditions. (p. 1)

Toward the end Mr. Costain plots some ingenious surprises for his readers. He introduces a weird set of villains, handles them with great adroitness and deadpan humor, and writes in his best vein in the long, slow but never dull dénouement of the book.

He is not at his best all through, however. The writing is often flat and flavorless. In his determination not to produce another adventure novel he deliberately blunts the points of action. Excitements are whipped up and come to nothing. Characters in whom the reader is just growing interested die off suddenly and implausibly, or vanish from the scene for twenty-five years. Many others are never seen; they are known only as shadowy references. Stylistically, the conscious or unconscious imitation of the manner of [Charles] Dickens never quite comes off. Coincidence—as Mr. Costain freely admits in some awkward asides to the reader—sometimes has its arm pulled nearly out of joint.

Nevertheless, Mr. Costain's very large following is not going to feel cheated. There is romance, history and color enough in this novel to satisfy a wide variety of tastes. (p. 11)

> *Richard Winston, "Mr. Costain's Double-Decker,"*
> in New York Herald Tribune Book Review, *September 25, 1955, pp. 1, 11.*

EARL W. FOELL

["**The Tontine**"] is not nearly so grim . . . as its title would suggest. In fact, the great Waterloo Tontine that was hatched by an unsavory criminal boss hard on the heels of Wellington's historic victory provides only the mere framework for this sprawling Dickensian romance. The meat that plumps out its two large volumes is a very palatable, lively picture of England during the industrial revolution. . . .

Mr. Costain is a good story teller. His action moves, however heavily loaded with detail. His characters are "characters," not unlike those of Dickens or, perhaps, Damon Runyon. His plot traces the lives of four generations of the above-mentioned families in alternating episodes (sometimes involving one family, sometimes all three) that raise almost more suspense in transit than at the final climax when the results of the tontine once more take the center of the stage.

And Mr. Costain knows his period setting down to the last finial on a duke's antique highboy, the most minute pungency in a Bermude garden. With no break in the speedy pace he sets for unraveling his many plots and subplots, historian Costain sketches in the details of a complete nineteenth century backdrop for his characters to play upon. And although none of these characters is explored very deeply, the sum total of the author's having developed such a gallery of distinctive, colorful individuals and such a turbulent, tactile setting is that he successfully presents the character of a whole age.

There are drawbacks, of course. Many of his actors seem to be almost entirely black or white, sweet or conniving. The love stories sometimes have a courtly, Victorian unnaturalness about them. And occasionally Mr. Costain's headlong pace is slowed to a zestless canter by his tendency to overdescribe furniture and furnishings.

But then it is really the author's antique-collector spirit which makes this venture into the lively not-too-distant past such a general success. To those who, like this reviewer, were brought up on family reading from Dickens (one adventure sequence per weekend), "**The Tontine**", should be a pleasing find.

> *Earl W. Foell, "Sprawling Dickensian Romance,"*
> in The Christian Science Monitor, *September 29, 1955, p. 11.*

GEOFFREY BRUUN

Readers who enjoyed "**The Black Rose**," "**The Silver Chalice**," and the half-dozen other historical novels Mr. Costain has written . . . , will find "**Below the Salt**" equally diverting. It has somewhat less zest and humor than its predecessors and somber overtones prevail throughout most of the story. But it combines all the popular ingredients of a medieval romance. . . .

The research Mr. Costain undertook . . . has given him an intimate understanding of English society in the age of the Angevin kings. His scenes, including the signing of the Magna Charta, have an authentic air, and so have the historical characters he introduces. . . .

Perhaps because his main plot has inherent limitations, being largely a narrative of frustrations and dreams before the dawn, Costain has framed it in a secondary plot with modern characters. The device whereby he links a thirteenth-century theme with its twentieth-century reprise strains credulity, but the overall effect is fanciful and entertaining reading.

> *Geoffrey Bruun, "Plantagenet Princess," in New York Herald Tribune Book Review, September 22, 1957, p. 10.*

CHARLES W. FERGUSON

The title of Thomas B. Costain's new volume ["**The Three Edwards**"] refers to the three Edwards who were successive kings of England during the turbulent and crucial era that began in 1272 and ended in 1377. . . .

Of such a vital and prophetic era, Mr. Costain has made excellent use in this new unit of his continuing "**Pageant of England**." For the most part his narrative moves with the pace of swiftly changing events. The eye runs through page after page with curiosity, recognition and delight. Occasionally generalizations and anachronistic comment make the reader blink, but the force of the story carries him steadily forward.

Only toward the end of the third Edward's reign does the book tend to run down rather than build up. It becomes too populous even for a pageant. The author seems bent on using up his material and upon seeing that full credit is given to the supporting cast. This desire in itself is a healthy one, and it accounts for much that is good in the narrative as a whole.

Mr. Costain has a sharp eye for significant detail. . . . He has time to note in an age torn by conflict that buttons were introduced—if only as an ornament, not for function. He can turn aside to observe small incidents, to salute subalterns who may in the long run affect human behavior as much as storied events.

This quick perception of the obscure may stay a narrative now and then, but it also deepens it. In the bulk of his book Mr. Costain combines pace and detail admirably. His account falters toward the end; at the very end it gathers strenth again:

the strength of suspense. And the way is prepared for another installment in the unfolding if uneven story of England's greatness.

Charles W. Ferguson, "Troubled Kings in Turbulent Times," in The New York Times Book Review, *October 19, 1958, p. 10.*

PAUL M. KENDALL

In **"The Three Edwards,"** Thomas B. Costain continues his history of England since the Norman Conquest (*The Pageant of England:* **"The Conquerors," "The Magnificent Century"**). The volume deals with a turbulent reach of human experience, stretching from the thirteenth century of iron-fisted Edward I, law-giver and conqueror, when French was still the language of law-court and great hall, to the restless unhappy close of the reign of Edward III. . . .

To a popular historian like Mr. Costain, the period offers a wonderful story and barbed personalities: the romantic struggles of Wallace and Robert the Bruce, the inept life and horrible death of Edward II, the victories of Crécy and Poitiers, the visitation of the Black Death; and, beneath this brave outward show, the tides of social and intellectual change.

With such material, which Mr. Costain develops with an eye to entertaining fact, **"The Three Edwards"** will doubtless please numerous readers.

This is not to say, however, that Mr. Costain lives up to his opportunities. The trouble with **"The Three Edwards"** is that it is not popular enough, if "popular history" is to be identified with good yarn-spinning, deft characterization, and a technicolored setting of the scene. Instead of trying to convey a sense of the times, Mr. Costain tends to write of medieval men and women as if they were playing out domestic scenes in a small American town. His over-neighborly style gossips away much of the genuine excitement of his subject. We are given a running commentary on his materials rather than an imaginative deployment of them.

Mr. Costain's language is at times flat or inept with verbal infelicities that are a by-product of a style that can be relentlessly cozy. . . .

But the main weakness of **"The Three Edwards"** is perhaps a symptom of the times rather than a fault of Mr. Costain. A reader who, under the spell of TV quiz programs, is avid for facts, will be delighted with this book. Mr. Costain is never so in the grip of his story that he will not turn aside from it to give the derivation of a word, mention a quaint custom, or summarize the marital histories of forgotten princesses. . . .

Furthermore, there seems to be no controlling purpose which determines the relative importance of these facts. Even the Black Death is little more than just another item, its vast and poignant consequences muffled in perfunctory comment. Instead of seeing a picture of the past unfolding before our eyes, we hear the snap of file cards as one by one they unload their burden of information. And the information is not always to be trusted.

In the introduction to **"The Conquerors,"** Mr. Costain writes ". . . there is no need for another history of England unless it can be given popular appeal." But history cannot be *given* popular appeal, certainly not by chopping it down to suburban size. On the contrary, the popular appeal of history must be vigorously elicited—and Mr. Costain would have been the man to do it, if only his imagination had been fired by his materials.

Paul M. Kendall, "Costain's Pageant Rolls On," in New York Herald Tribune Book Review, *January 4, 1959, p. 6.*

GEOFFREY BRUUN

As a novelist Mr. Costain has always been at his best when he gave his rollicking fancy a free rein. His favorite formula is to fling a handful of worthy and attractive people into the maelstrom of disastrous historical events and then bring them safely to harbor in the final pages. He surrounds these core characters with a picaresque train of supernumeraries and keeps the drama of their adventures moving at an exhilarating gallop. . . .

[In **"The Darkness and the Dawn"**] the historical setting is Europe in the middle of the chaotic fifth century when Attila the Hun assailed the dissolving Roman Empire. . . .

Nicolan and Ildico [are] the hero and heroine of **"The Darkness and the Dawn."**. . . They and a few loyal friends symbolize the decent people of this world, struggling with courage and dignity against the rising tide of barbarism. One gathers that the spread of their humane ideals will be the dawn that follows the darkness of Rome's eclipse. . .

It is excusable to reveal the outcome of a Costain novel because that outcome may be anticipated from the first. The magic of this tale does not depend on the plot but on the crisp colloquial dialogue, the tense succession of episodes, the kaleidoscopic changes of scene. Each new setting is flashed to life on the mind in a few compelling phrases. Each character springs to life in a purposeful attitude, his role announced by unequivocal speech or gesture. The economy with which the author achieves this impression of vibrant life, of constant movement and animation, largely explains his popular appeal. He is a born teller of tales, a master of the electrifying narrative.

Yet there are limitations to his method, less apparent but not less real. His fictional characters are seldom complex and never profound. They belong to our time or to no time as much as to their own. Like their historic background they are oversimplified. They do little to enlarge or enrich the reader's historical sense and understanding of an alien age. Mr. Costain has demonstrated in his **"Pageant of England"** series that he can reconstruct the historic past in patient detail when he chooses but he has not done so here. The mood, the image of the fifth century which he projects in **"The Darkness and the Dawn"** is a simulation, not an authentic recreation of that confused and tragic time.

Geoffrey Bruun, "The Days of Attila the Hun," in New York Herald Tribune Book Review, *October 11, 1959, p. 7.*

MILLICENT TAYLOR

When Thomas Costain's **"The Conquerors,"** came out more than a dozen years ago, and was followed two years later by his **"The Magnificent Century,"** they gave us a treatment of history refreshingly colorful and new. Here indeed was "The Pageant of England" as rich as events woven into medieval tapestries—stories of tournaments, battles, the storming of castles, arranging of international marriages, the plots and counterplots of family intrigues, and more dimly perhaps yet ominously persistent, the struggles of submerged peasants, the growing power of the guilds, the self-realization of citizens of London.

Perhaps it is just as well that Mr. Costain eventually decided to end his "Pageant" with the coming in of the Tudors. The extent of research for these histories—popular in style but sound in substance—seems a life work in itself. . . .

"The Last Plantagenets," picking up England's story where "The Three Edwards" leaves us, gives us six kings from Richard II and great Henry V and the events of his all-too-short reign, with the Battle of Agincourt and his winning of the French princess Katherine. Here, too, are John Ball and the tragic Peasants' Revolt, the devious intrigues of Margaret of Anjou, the political maneuverings of Warwick the King-maker—all as fascinating as any swift mystery story. It is history as made by people—people one comes to know well—and events so vividly presented as to seem personally experienced. Nor are the people all kings and queens and their conniving relatives. William Caxton is here, as is also John Wycliffe.

But among them all the most interesting character—because we may long have been unwittingly misled concerning him—is Richard III, the last Plantagenet. Was he really the cruel plotter, usurper, and murderer that Shakespeare's magnificent play and all the school history textbooks depict to us? Did he do away with the little princes in the Tower?

If this absorbing final volume of "The Pageant of England" series were significant for no other reason, it should have interest for this Apologia pro Richard III. Mr. Costain is a scholar: he leaves no stone unturned, no manuscript, letter, rumor, or event untested. And this author finds conclusive evidence that the story and character of Richard as handed down for posterity to swallow is entirely from Henry Tudor, the successor who defeated him and took his throne. . . .

One leaves the Plantagenets with a certain regret. Theirs was a colorful and lusty era. It is of course right that the pageantry and wrongs of feudalism, the extravagance and intrigues of kings and their plotting relatives were made to give place. Heartening were the brave efforts of commoners and peasants toward a recognition of human dignity—a glorious part of this story of England's march of freedom. This was a significant era of break-up, of emergence, of genuine progress. We return to the task of solving the problems of our own time with understanding enriched and courage strengthened for having lived so fully in those pregnant and dramatic days.

> Millicent Taylor, "The Last of the Line," in The Christian Science Monitor, *January 25, 1962, p. 7.*

MILLICENT TAYLOR

Thomas Costain's flair for bringing to life periods of history dominated by fascinating personalities takes us in ["The Last Love"] to St. Helena during Napoleon's final exile. It is mainly the story of a loyal and delightful friendship between the great Corsican—now a tragic and lonely figure—and the generous-hearted tomboy daughter of William Balcombe, a distinguished Englishman stationed there. . . .

The book is frankly a novel, not a history—yet the story of this friendship is fact, and most of the characters are actual persons. In some extensive flashbacks the author gives historical and biographical background material leading up to St. Helena.

The main events of the story itself are substantiated in diaries and other records turned up by Mr. Costain's sound and indefatigable research. These include among others the feud carried on between the proud ex-Emperor and the governor, the visits without permits that Betsy managed, and the loan of Napoleon's horse to Betsy for the Deadwood races. All of it reads like fact, however, although as in any historical novel some of the characters are of course fiction, and some of the events. The additions, Mr. Costain states, are "concerned chiefly with detail.". . .

But inevitably it is Napoleon who dominates for the reader this absorbing account. Costain's skill at giving intimate insights into a great historical character has never been better shown. . . .

It is the drama unfolding in vivid and convincing detail that fascinates the reader. An ex-Emperor shorn of position and power is seen here as a very human and attractive man, who in his final years of frustration and regret is enriched by and grateful for an unusual friendship with a young English girl—his "Betsee."

> Millicent Taylor, "Napoleon and His English 'Betsee'," in The Christian Science Monitor, *September 26, 1963, p. 13.*

Jacques-Yves Cousteau
1910-

French nonfiction writer, filmmaker, and oceanographer.

Cousteau is widely known to the general public for his films and books about his marine explorations. He has shared the beauty and wonder of the ocean world with millions of readers and viewers in many languages. He teaches that humans must be careful to respect and conserve that world. Cousteau is also known, especially to oceanographers, for his contributions to marine research. He has helped advance the development of diving and exploration techniques, underwater photography, and nautical archaeology. Scientists sometimes point out that in his films and books Cousteau presents generalizations rather than well-documented scientific evidence. Cousteau, however, claims that he calls himself an explorer, not a scientist. Cousteau's films have won four Academy Awards, eight Emmy Awards, and two Cannes Film Festival Awards.

Cousteau served as a captain in the French navy and worked with the French Resistance during World War II. He collaborated on the invention of the aqualung, a lightweight, self-contained breathing apparatus that allows divers to swim freely underwater for extended periods. *The Silent World* (1953), written with Frédéric Dumas, recounts the testing of the aqualung as well as the initial voyages of *Calypso*, Cousteau's well-equipped research vessel from which he and his crew of divers and photographers conduct their work. This book won immediate critical and popular acclaim. *The Living Sea* (1963), which Cousteau wrote with James Dugan, relates the subsequent expeditions of the *Calypso* crew, including a successful experiment in underwater human habitation. The photographs accompanying these texts, and the motion picture documentaries of the expeditions of *Calypso*, have provided the public with an unusual and imaginative vantage point from which to view the sea. With his popular television series *The Undersea World of Jacques Cousteau* (1968-1976) and his series of books grouped under the title *The Undersea Discoveries of Jacques Cousteau*, many of which were written with Philippe Diolé, Cousteau and his crew have introduced the world of whales, sharks, dolphins, and other sea animals to mass audiences. His organization, The Cousteau Society, has published a twenty-volume reference series which offers a wide range of information pertaining to the sea. For his pioneering efforts at increasing knowledge of the marine environment and for making the sea accessible through mass media, Cousteau has won honors and awards from many nations and organizations.

(See also *Contemporary Authors*, Vols. 65-68.)

RACHEL L. CARSON

"We have tried to find the entrance to the great hydrosphere because we feel that the sea age is soon to come."

So Captain Jacques-Yves Cousteau, a French navy gunnery officer, sums up his motives for devoting fifteen years to pioneering undersea explorations, in the course of which he has made more than 5,000 dives. Cousteau's work is an important

Claus Meyer/Black Star

milestone on the road of man's return to the sea. The era of the "menfish" began when he, along with Philippe Taillez, another naval officer, and Frédéric Dumas, an experienced civilian diver, made successful descents with the first aqualung a decade ago.

Aqualung equipment consists of one to three tanks of compressed air strapped on the diver's back, a face mask, and a mouth piece through which the diver inhales air from his tanks and exhales. He is completely self-contained. . . .

"The Silent World" is a fascinating book, the distillation of Cousteau's experience undersea. After the war he and his associates salvaged torpedoed vessels and the scuttled French fleet, swimming freely through the rigging encrusted with barnacles, weed-hung and ghostly; they swam down shadowy gangways, passing from deck to deck and exploring drowned cabins and engine rooms. Turned archaeologists, the aqualungers found the remains of an argosy presumably sunk about 80 B.C. while en route from Athens to Rome with loot that included Ionic columns, marble statuary, and bronze figures. The divers filmed fishermen's trawl nets as they lumbered along the ocean floor, sending up fishes like frightened rabbits. They followed a submarine laying mines and photographed men emerging from the escape hatch.

Captain Cousteau succeeds admirably in giving his readers a sense of personal participation in these explorations of a strange world. We feel that we know what a diver sees, feels, and thinks as he descends into the blue twilight of the sea.

Through the diver's mask, objects seem larger and nearer than they are. Tropical reefs are a fairyland riot of color down to perhaps twenty-five feet; below that level, colors rapidly fade into a twilight blue. At fifty feet, red becomes black and orange disappears. Down 120 feet, the blood of a man or a fish runs green. Deeper, only ultraviolet is left. But even in the "blue zone" the colors are there, if unseen. When the divers took down powerful electric lights, they were dazzled by a "harlequinade of color dominated by sensational reds and oranges, as opulent as a Matisse." . . .

For many years that veteran of countless helmet dives, William Beebe, has been telling us that the so-called "monsters of the deep" are monsters only in the imagination of writers who are over-imaginative and under-experienced. Capt. Cousteau convincingly seconds Dr. Beebe. The octopus, the manta ray, the moray eel—alarming as their appearance may be—are creatures who wish only be be allowed to go about their normal occupations, and these definitely do not include molesting human divers. Only on sharks does Capt. Cousteau reserve judgment, having found their behavior unpredictable. A twenty-five-foot "man-eater" fled in seeming alarm at the sight of divers. The quite different story of an encounter with a much smaller shark is too thrilling and full of suspense to spoil by telling it here.

One could go on indefinitely about the carnival behavior of fish during a rainstorm, about the eerie quality of the undersea world at night, about the octopus "city" where each of these extraordinary mollusks occupied a "house" roofed with a flat stone propped up, like a lean-to, with other stones. This is a book that leads us on, page by page, and when the end is reached we are very likely to begin again at Page 1.

And beyond its ability to stir our imaginations and hold us fascinated, this is an important book. As Capt. Cousteau points out, in the future we must look to the sea, more and more, for food, minerals, petroleum. The aqualung is one vital step in the development of means to explore and utilize the sea's resources.

> *Rachel L. Carson, "The Strange, Dramatic Sea-Depths Where Man Can Now Venture," in* New York Herald Tribune Book Review, *February 8, 1953, p. 3.*

GILBERT KLINGEL

If you are one of those imaginative people who in fancy or reality would like to enter another world where none of the ordinary rules apply, and where on every hand scenes new to the eye of man unfold in endless succession, then **"The Silent World"** is the book for you. It is the story of Capt. Jacques-Yves Cousteau of the French Navy and of his development of the "aqualung." . . . The book is profusely illustrated and the underwater shots, particularly those in full color, are extraordinary.

Captain Cousteau tells of exploring sunken ships, including a Roman galley filled with a cargo of wine jars, some of them still sealed and bearing the initials of ancient Greek wine merchants, and of retrieving antique marble and statuary looted from the Greeks by the conquering Romans and lost at sea centuries ago. With Captain Cousteau one enters drowned caverns into which the light of day has never penetrated; one of

these, the cave of the Fountain of Vaucluse, very nearly cost the author his life.

The book unfolds one fascinating undersea panorama after another. . . .

Captain Cousteau, unlike so many writers about the deep, has not marred his stories with supercharged prose. There are no hair-raising tales of encounter with sea denizens; instead he devotes an entire chapter to portraying many of these "monsters" as they really are. We learn that octopi cannot be induced to bite, and wish nothing more than to be let alone. Similarly, reputedly savage morays and conger eels are shown to be veritable "home bodies" showing resentment only when their dens are deliberately invaded. . . .

Only sharks are treated with concern, and one of the most interesting chapters in the book deals with an encounter with a shark of unknown species which cornered Captain Cousteau and his friend Frederic Dumas (the civilian diver who helped test the aqualung) near the body of a dead whale. It is as good a shark story as any I have read.

By far the better part of the book is the latter half, in which Captain Cousteau describes in detail the appearance of his undersea world and its inhabitants. One wishes he had devoted even more space to this and less to the development of his equipment. In sum, however, he has made a worth-while contribution to deep-sea exploration methods and has placed the thrill of ocean investigation within the reach of nearly everyone.

> *Gilbert Klingel, "A World of Lost Ships and Shy Octopi," in* The New York Times Book Review, *February 8, 1953, p. 3.*

ROBERT C. COWEN

Reading Jacques-Yves Cousteau's captivating new book [**"The Living Sea"**], I had a strong impulse to hand in this review and immediately take off to find *Calypso*. From this, his ocean-going research ship, the famed French undersea explorer has helped to open a fascinating and challenging underwater world.

Some academic oceanographers have found it fashionable to discount his exploits. But the years of effort that have been compressed into the pages of this book speak for themselves of the great contribution Captain Cousteau has made to oceanographic science.

He would himself lay no claim to being a scientific expert. Yet from the aqualung to his most recent innovation of the diving saucer, a jet propelled submarine, which will carry two men comfortably to depths of 1,000 feet, he has done as much if not more than any other contemporary marine explorer to open the way to a new opportunity for undersea research.

In **"The Living Sea,"** as in his earlier best seller **"The Silent World,"** Captain Cousteau conveys the sense of adventure and the vision that continue to inspire his work. Perhaps the most striking comparison between the two books is that the enthusiasm has not flagged at all while the vision has greatly matured.

Captain Cousteau has always seen his work as an advancement of men's capabilities as well as a personal adventure. He has never been content to rest at one level of achievement, such as perfecting aqualung diving. Instead he has moved steadily to enlarge men's undersea explorational capabilities in imaginative yet practical ways.

His latest effort, the one with which the book ends, is his now-famous experiment in undersea living. In this, two of his men lived in a watertight "hut" on the continental shelf for several days, when not working with aqualung. It is the forerunner of what may one day be submarine research communities in which men can live at the pressure of the water in which they explore without having to return to the surface every few hours as in ordinary diving.

In short, Captain Cousteau sees mankind entering an era in which the sea will become for it a new environment to be understood, worked with, and beneficially exploited.

At the same time, he sees great need for men to re-orient their viewpoint to this new perspective. The time has come to stop thinking of the sea merely as a dumping ground and hunting preserve or a highway for ships. . . .

Readers of the National Geographic magazine, to which Captain Cousteau contributes regularly, will recognize many familiar episodes in his book. . . . Yet for them, and for new reader acquaintances, he has presented an exciting and thought-provoking new statement of his work.

> *Robert C. Cowen, "The Sea As a Dwelling Place: Cousteau's Wet World," in* The Christian Science Monitor, *April 25, 1963, p. 11.*

DESMOND YOUNG

Recently, as the exploration of the oceans and the sea-bed has become less commercial and more scientific in purpose, books about diving have won a wide readership. All of us are entranced by the new knowledge brought up from this secret world.

No man has done so much to open the door to this world and to reveal its mysteries as Capt. Jacques-Yves Cousteau. Certainly no other man is so uniquely fitted for the self-imposed task. A seaman, qualified to command any vessel in the French fleet, superb navigator, highly skilled diver, gunner, aerial observer, inventor of the Aqua-Lung, he is also a scientist, with a gift for explaining scientific problems.

Captain Cousteau's previous book, **"The Silent World,"** was translated into 22 languages and sold more than three million copies in English alone. It will be surprising if **"The Living Sea"**—which he has written with freelance writer James Dugan—does not surpass that record. Whether Captain Cousteau is describing the recovery of artifacts from a Greek galley sunk more than two centuries before Christ, or his battle to prevent the dumping of radioactive waste into the Mediterranean, he is unfailingly interesting.

His descriptions gracefully combine literary style and scientific nomenclature. . . .

The mobile base for the explorations reported in this book was the oceanographic ship Calypso, well-equipped with depth-probing devices and a professional diving team. The log unfolded in these pages records episodes ranging over the Atlantic, the Mediterranean and the Red Sea. Included are trips to discover ocean-bed oil deposits and to help lay electrical cables in the Gulf of Lion off the south coast of France. There is a strange journey to "hunt water underwater"—that is, a fresh water supply for the sea town of Cassis east of Marseille.

There is something along the way for all tastes. Oddities abound for curiosity-seekers. Cousteau reports seeing a number of creatures never reported before, including "a fish twenty inches long and shaped exactly like a draftsman's triangle. It was the shade and thinness of aluminum foil with a ridiculous little tail." He records also, on his underwater writing pad, a squid that squirts white ink; a shark observed at 13,000 feet, where no shark has any right to live; and a wall of breakers in the Red Sea that resolved itself into thousands of dolphins prancing 15 feet into the air to breathe.

Perhaps most astonishing is an undersea avalanche set off by Cousteau and his partner Houot with their bathyscaph off Toulon. A wall gave way on the edge of a huge trench, muddying the sea for miles and almost burying the bathyscaph. Later, Cousteau remarked to a scientist he knew: "Remember that canyon off Toulon that you charted so carefully? You'll have to do it again. Houot and I have just wrecked it."

For the scientifically minded interested in the progress and possibilities of submarine exploration, there are chapters on the revolutionary *"soucoupe plongeante,"* or "Diving Saucer". This is an underwater vehicle designed to allow its occupants to examine in safety and comfort the continental shelf which comprises 8 per cent of the oceanic surface of the globe—an area equal to that of Asia. (p. 1)

The DS-2, as Cousteau called his saucer, is no Jules Verne pipedream. Apart from some initial trouble with batteries, it has been completely successful in more than 60 scientific missions and the tape-recorded underwater logs have yielded a mass of information on life in the sea. The other devices used include the Deepsea Camera Sled, which travels miles below the surface photographing phenomena never before seen by man; submarine self-propelled "scooters" for use with the Aqua-Lung and nylon anchor-cables six miles long to which a vessel can ride.

The historically minded may prefer to read about the salvage of tools, fittings, pottery and 7,000 wine amphorae—earthware containers that were "the jerry cans of antiquity"—from the sunken wreck off Marseille. There is something strangely intriguing to Cousteau in the notion of sipping wine that was bottled and shipped commercially more than two thousand years ago—and finding that it has the resinous flavor of Greek wines of today.

No less intriguing is the notion of producing a *Homo Aquaticus,* a new man free to roam below the surface as his cousins do above. In an experiment which is the climax of the book, two men, under Captain Cousteau's supervision, lived and worked under water continuously for a week, in a chamber with a hatch open always to the sea and kept down by internal air pressure. Through this liquid door they passed in and out: inside they lived and read and slept and watched television. The experiment, which produced some strange psychological effects—the men became detached about worldly concerns, such as modesty, for example—may be of great importance. It is characteristic of Captain Cousteau that he does not forget that Sir Robert Davis, the great British expert on diving, now aged 93 and still active, devised just such an underwater dwelling more than 30 years ago. (pp. 1, 36)

[The] author does a service by pointing out that for the Aqua-Lung enthusiast, the sea is still a dangerous place—not only because of sharks. Though Cousteau exceeds it himself, 140 feet is still the normal limit of safety for even the skilled skin-diver. Below that lies depth-drunkenness, "the zone of rapture," where a man loses all sense of risk.

The amateur would be wise to limit himself, not to 140 feet, but to half that depth at the outside. . . . Most of us must, then, be content to see all these submarine marvels vicariously. Thanks to Captain Cousteau, we can do so, with immense pleasure, in this entrancing book. (p. 36)

Desmond Young, "Beneath the Waves a Secret World," in The New York Times Book Review, April 28, 1963, pp. 1, 36.

THE TIMES LITERARY SUPPLEMENT

Although the trumpetings of jacket blurbs should not be taken too seriously there is one phrase that never fails to arouse the reviewer's suspicions: scientific accuracy. Rarely is this claim made for a scientifically accurate book and it is disappointing to find that *The Shark* is no exception. First in a series of studies on underwater life by Jacques Cousteau and his son [Philippe Cousteau], it is said by the publishers to set "an incredibly high standard for those that will follow", not least in its "scientific accuracy" and "whole mood of scientific enquiry".

What the reader actually receives is a series of anecdotes of a type now standard in shark books, and a series of quite preposterous "scientific" statements for which the term *codswallop* is the mildest warning that can be given to an unsuspecting public. Sharks are said to possess, *inter alia*, an "obscure millenary instinct", "a superior reproduction organism", "sensorial canals" of the "lateral system" that contain "finely lidded nerve cells" which release "a nervous influx . . . instantly communicated to the brain" but they lack a "swimming bladder". It is quite wrong to press such garbled language upon the layman but these absurdities are interspersed with statements that are either misleading or quite incorrect. . . .

Throughout, there is a tendency to attribute qualities to *the* shark, an unspecified and evidently highly resourceful representative of its two hundred and fifty fellow species.

It may seem unfair, in view of the deserved success of the Cousteau formula in underwater films, to belabour what is clearly a popular account of an adventure voyage. The object of the voyage was to produce twelve films for television, of which that on sharks was to be the first, and it is in this sphere that the Cousteaus can continue to make a valuable contribution (provided that the commentary rises to some degree of scientific accuracy).

A great part of the failure of the book lies with the inadequacy of the translation which appears to have been done by the authors themselves. They ignore the fact that neither scientific terminology nor French lyrical descriptions can be merely transcribed.

"Submarine but Superficial," in The Times Literary Supplement, No. 3584, November 6, 1970, p. 1308.

THE NEW YORKER

[Jacques and Philippe Cousteau] recently (1967-68) spent about a year studying sharks at point-blank range in the Red Sea and in the western Indian Ocean, and it is probable that they (and their colleagues) now know more about that almost ubiquitous marine predator than anybody else in the world. This magnif-

icently illustrated book ["**The Shark: Splendid Savage of the Sea**"] (a hundred and twenty-four eerie, deep-sea color photographs and many drawings, diagrams, and maps) is a stirring narrative account of their highly specialized education. The authors, who speak to us in turn, acknowledge that the shark is still very largely a mystery, and their observations, though interesting, are few. . . . For the most part, the Cousteaus simply show us what they saw and let us conclude as we wish. It is a fascinating experience. (pp. 182, 184)

A review of "The Shark: Splendid Savage of the Sea," in The New Yorker, Vol. XLVI, No. 38, November 7, 1970, pp. 182, 184.

JOSEPH T. EVANS

[*The Shark*] consists of a series of fascinating narrations by the world famous underwater explorer Jacques-Yves Cousteau and his son Philippe. It concerns their preparation and voyage on the *Calypso* to seek, study, research, and photograph the activities and habitual movements of sharks. There are vivid, exciting narratives of encounters with sharks—sharks of different species and size, from the large whale shark to the hammerhead and dogfish. Experiences with the beautiful, agile, graceful vultures of the sea are told in a very special way proper only to one who has encountered them face to face or has watched them from within the protective cages that were used to study these "killers of the deep." . . .

Included with this narration are many magnificent colored photographs of beautiful underwater sights. In addition to these, photos depicting various activities of sharks from simple curiosities to extreme aggression are also included. Some of these photographs were taken with a wide angle lens about four feet from the shark.

This is a very interesting book for anyone desiring knowledge about this ancient, beautiful, graceful yet dangerous, savage creature which rules the sea and is feared by all men.

Joseph T. Evans, in a review of "The Shark," in Best Sellers, Vol. 30, No. 16, November 15, 1970, p. 345.

THE TIMES LITERARY SUPPLEMENT

Although good intentions are no substitute for quality, one cannot resist some sympathy for the author [of *Life and Death in a Coral Sea*] whose *Silent World* opened a new realm for millions, whose aqualung pioneered rewarding fields for both research and enjoyment, and whose books, films and other activities are seriously dedicated to underwater exploration. There are few men like Jacques-Yves Cousteau, but they have an important role to play in the development of science, chiefly because they provide that imaginative energy so necessary if research projects are to reach beyond the resources of any one institute. . . .

In 1967 [he] began his voyage in the Calypso, once a minesweeper but now fully equipped for underwater research. M Cousteau dubbed this voyage a "permanent expedition", although the immediate aim was to gather material for twelve television films and six books to defray costs. The first book, . . . [*The Shark*] was not satisfactory, chiefly because of its scientific inaccuracy, inept translation and lack of elementary editorial polish. The present book, on coral reefs, pretends to much less and is an interesting, uncomplicated account of the standard underwater adventures that may be expected by those who have not yet donned mask and flippers. Fortunately, science has been relegated to four appendixes and a glossary (presumably by Philippe Diolé), leaving the text free from those errors that marred the shark volume. . . .

[It is] unfortunate that accounts of territoriality among reef fishes, or of the interesting relationship between clownfishes and anemones, are not given the benefit of recent studies. More than one hundred colour plates, some excellent, some a trifle blurred, redeem the text and set the reader firmly in that world that M Cousteau has done so much to explore. Together with such men as George Bond and Edwin Link, he will be remembered as one of the great underwater pioneers; and while his books and films may lack biological precision they will always be regarded as an integral part of his total achievement.

> *"In Seas Beneath," in* The Times Literary Supplement, *No. 3625, August 20, 1971, p. 1007.*

E. F. BARTLEY

There is no question about the fact that Jacques Cousteau is an interesting showman as well as a competent researcher of the ocean depths. That he writes well is attested to by [*Life and Death in a Coral Sea*]. . . . Credit also must be given to the technical writing assistance of Philippe Diolé and the capable translation by J. F. Bernard. . . .

In addition to giving the reader many new insights into the world of the sea, Cousteau provides an account of the exploration processes themselves. Historical aspects of sea exploration are woven into the text in order that one can get some feeling for the advances that have been made. The description of Cousteau's new diving saucers, called fleas, gives a look into how far advanced the art of diving has become. The design and construction of this equipment must have been a most complicated project in its own way.

Space limits the inclusion of each of the items that the reviewer found intriguing and felt worthy of mention; suffice it to say that there is an abundance of informative and interesting material. Mention must be made of the numerous times that Cousteau warns of the dangers to the existence of sea life that pollution is causing. He gives detailed proof of the deterioration that has taken place and adds his voice to the many that have been raised in warning that action must be taken to protect the environment.

> *E. F. Bartley, in a review of "Life and Death in a Coral Sea," in* Best Sellers, *Vol. 31, No. 17, December 1, 1971, p. 397.*

NELSON BRYANT

["**Life and Death in a Coral Sea**" is] the absorbing story of the Cousteau teams' investigation of coral reefs in the Indian Ocean and the Red Sea. Cousteau is undoubtedly the best-known marine explorer in the world today, having been introduced to millions through his magnificently photographed television shows, and this book maintains his tradition of excellence. The style of the book is easy and lively and much of it reads like a diary. (p. 62)

> *Nelson Bryant, "A Natural Beauty," in* The New York Times Book Review, *December 5, 1971, pp. 58, 60, 62.**

THE TIMES LITERARY SUPPLEMENT

Diving for Sunken Treasure is a popular account of M Cousteau's expedition to the site of what he believes to be the Silver Bank, near Puerto Rico, in search of the remains of the wreck of the Nuestra Señora de la Concepción, the treasure galleon salvaged by William Phipps in 1687. Working from the research vessel Calypso, he found a wreck which he believed might be the treasure galleon. The book tells the story of the "excavation" of the wreck, and the subsequent discovery that the wreck concerned actually dates from 1756. This slim narrative is skilfully bulked out by masses of information obtained from the usual sources on Spanish treasure fleets of the seventeenth century, and photographs of existing museum treasures.

The story is told in the present tense, and the translation from the French is rather curious, Cousteau having been left at the literary mercy of his fellow-countrymen since the death of his American collaborator, James Dugan. Indeed, the book seems less a book than a television script expanded to book length— which is in fact what it is. The expedition was financed by American television as one of a series of wonderful television films. The book is less wonderful. It is attractive but has little nourishment. There are numerous misspellings and misused technical terms. One wonders whom the glossary was meant for. Ship terms are often either elementary or wrong.

It is a pity that the authors could not have taken a little more trouble both with the excavation and with the book.

> *"Up from the Bottom," in* The Times Literary Supplement, *No. 3653, March 3, 1972, p. 241.**

H. J. CARGAS

The Ocean World of Jacques Cousteau promises to be an epic. Having seen [*Oasis in Space, The Act of Life,* and *Quest for Food*], the first three volumes of the 20 book set, I am impressed by what quality work can be published at such a reasonable price. . . .

The texts, expectedly, are excellent. Whether they were ghost written or translated from French we are not told, but they have the same clarity and adventuresomeness that Cousteau's television specials have. The introduction to the first volume, *Oasis in Space,* may surprise with its pessimistic message. The oceans are in danger of dying and thus the threat to mankind is enormous. But the situation is remedial and Captain Cousteau tells what the approach will be in this set. ". . . we want to explore the themes of the ocean's existence—how it moves and breathes, how it experiences dramas and seasons, how it nourishes its host of living things, how it harmonizes the physical and biological rhythms of the whole earth, what hurts it and what feeds it—not least of all, what are its stories."

Cousteau is clearly not only a scientist but a poet as well. He embodies the humanistic vision through an artistic sensibility which is rooted in the knowledge and skills of his science. He is a unique contributor to man's progress.

The photographs in all three volumes are, in many cases, dazzling —in all cases helpful. (p. 395)

Oasis in Space discusses the mysteries of the ocean and water as the essence of life. The ocean is described as the cradle of life, behavior patterns—protective and destructive—are indicated, the interdependence of ocean life is beautifully rendered, and the dangers to the sea are pointed out. Only the conclusion of this volume seems somewhat facile, possibly too poetic. We read that "Man takes off for the conquest of space, only to find that the solar system is a dustbin of dead celestial bodies. The truth is that man is alone—a lonely, pulsating, thinking creature—in the universe." That kind of position seems rather premature, today, given the hypotheses of other scientists and theologians as well.

"Dying for Survival" is the title of the Introduction to *The Act of Life,* the second book of the set. Evolution, adaptability, is the key to this one. The balance of nature, survival of the fittest, reproduction, parental care, these are the topics covered. The last chapter is actually a poem bearing the title of this volume. We can't help admiring Cousteau's continued enthusiasm for and wonder of his life's work.

Quest for Food discusses the various types of feeders, fishing methods, mariculture (sea farming) and the now recognized important subject of the balance of nature. Man will find that "by destroying the fertility of the sea he has condemned his own civilization."

While this set is about the sea, Cousteau never forgets to relate everything to Man and this is perhaps the greatest value of this undertaking. How things relate, how the environment is totally interdependent is something we are just beginning to take seriously. *The Ocean World of Jacques Cousteau* is a wonderful contribution in that direction. (pp. 395-96)

> *H. J. Cargas, "Professionally Speaking," in* Catholic Library World, *Vol. 45, No. 8, March, 1974, pp. 395-96.*

SCIENCE BOOKS

[*Three Adventures: Galápagos, Titicaca, The Blue Holes*] is the account of three unrelated trips by Cousteau and his film crew to the Galápagos, the Andes and British Honduras. . . . The account is interesting, but the quality of the writing varies greatly; many sections are sadly prosaic. Sometimes the translation limps; for example, in a description of the habits of a crab (which, like most crabs, is a scavenger) found in the Galápagos. . . . Overall, the information presented in the book is scanty and superficial, and the general quality of writing is unimaginative. Each time the author seems just on the verge of describing or explaining some natural event in detail, he veers off to another scene. . . . The spectacular photography will be enjoyed by junior high and older students, the text may be enjoyed as a travelogue, but the book provides no more than minimal information about the natural history of the areas visited. (pp. 32-3)

> *A review of "Three Adventures: Galápagos, Titicaca, The Blue Holes," in* Science Books, *Vol. X, No. 1, May, 1974, pp. 32-3.*

BETTY MINEMIER

The 20-volume set, *The Ocean World of Jacques Cousteau,* is Grolier's answer to increasing demands for authoritative, attractive, accessible materials on the newest "big science" — oceanography.

Oceanography, or Cousteau's preference, marine science, is not new, but recent interests and efforts by governments and industries equate it with the space and atomic sciences.

Ocean World popularizes marine information, stresses causes and concerns about pollution, could affect every curricular area, and should stimulate students' interests in marine-related careers. . . .

A remarkable reference achievement, *The Ocean World of Jacques Cousteau* should prove both valuable and very popular in libraries, classrooms, and science centers.

> *Betty Minemier, in a review of "The Ocean World of Jacques Cousteau," in* Instructor, *Vol. LXXXIV, No. 7, March, 1975, p. 125.*

PHILIP MORRISON AND PHYLIS MORRISON

The bulk of the beautifully illustrated volume [*Dolphins*] recounts the dolphin experiences of Cousteau and the others over nearly 30 years: following, admiring, luring, capturing, feeding, training and swimming with dolphins of varied species in the several seas. The posthuman intelligence attributed by some to the dolphins gets little support here. Most original are accounts of human whistle speech, unfortunately only a few pages and photographs, and a long and detailed record of a visit with fisherfolk on the desert coast of Mauritania who have for a very long time regarded the local dolphins as their special allies. The dolphins in their season press great schools of mullet close to the shore, where the men can take them abundantly in their nets. It is probable that this is not the dolphins' purpose, but it would be "very difficult to convince the Imragen" that their sacred dolphins are not benevolent. The book is so wide in its attention that it is more diffuse than one would like, but it remains a remarkable treatment all the same. A glossary, art reproductions, a species summary and a list of where one can encounter trained dolphins worldwide are valuable accessories to the narrative. (p. 128)

> *Philip Morrison and Phylis Morrison, in a review of "Dolphins," in* Scientific American, *Vol. 233, No. 6, December, 1975, pp. 127-28.*

DOROTHY NEEDHAM

Countless secrets of the sea are revealed in ["**The Ocean World of Jacques Cousteau**," a] thrilling multidimensional study of the ocean's wonders, dangers, demands, riches, challenges, beauty, problems, creatures and visitors.

Although a reference work, comprehensively indexed in volume 20, each book reads like a suspenseful adventure story with thousands of characters relating to each other in a single setting. All the major branches of oceanography are included— marine physics, chemistry, biology, geology and engineering—but unfamiliar scientific terms are scrupulously avoided. Breathtaking color photographs used lavishly throughout the set tell marvelous tales of their own to nonreaders and casual browsers.

> *Dorothy Needham, "Science Reviews: Eureka!" in* Teacher, *Vol. 94, No. 3, November, 1976, pp. 130-33.**

BOOKLIST

The Ocean World of Jacques Cousteau (hereafter *Ocean World*) is a 20-volume set concerned with the oceans generally and, more specifically, with marine life and exploration. This is a revised edition of *The Ocean World of Jacques Cousteau* produced in 1974. According to the publisher, the 1975 edition resulted from revisions made by Captain Cousteau after thorough reassessment of the original edition. (p. 742)

Ocean World is, according to its publisher, intended for student use through senior high school and for home use by both children and adults. This review will assess the set's appropriateness for this broad spectrum of readers. . . .

The broad thematic organization of *Ocean World* distinguishes it generally from a more systematic and tradition approach which might have emphasized the academic disciplines such as geography, geology, marine biology, and their appropriate subdivisions. For example, *marine life* or *biology* could have been subdivided by such topics as "ecology," "plant life," "animal life," etc. Further subdivisions could have been taxonomic characteristics, organismic systems, and the like. Cousteau's "horizontal" or thematic arrangement is the more holistic and permits greater attention to interrelationships. Its attendant drawback is a greater dispersion of related material. And since broad themes tend toward indistinct definition, greater reliance must be placed on the thoroughness and precision of the set's indexes. The problem is somewhat exacerbated by the selection of . . . titles for some volumes which make it difficult to know the theme, and indeed the themes of some volumes remain vague even after an examination of the contents. (p. 743)

It should also be noted that occasionally material is included in a volume that seems to have little in common with the theme. For example, in the volume entitled *Instinct and Intelligence,* a section of one chapter deals with the interrelationship between food and sex. No mention is made of instinct or intelligence, and the material might more logically have been placed in the *Act of Life,* which deals with sexual matters, or in the one covering the quest for food.

In general, the first ten volumes treat biological themes, while the last ten concentrate on geography and exploration. No strict separation is made. Volume 13, *A Sea of Legends,* deals with the sea in legend, myth, and art; volume 19, *The Sea in Danger,* looks at pollution and conservation. The volumes concerned with exploration and geography seem generally to be more authoritatively handled than those dealing with biological topics. This may be due to the fact that knowledge in the former areas tends to be strictly cumulative, rather than qualifying, in nature—as is frequently the case in the biological sciences. Inattention to some minute thread within the expanding tapestry of scientific findings can often totally invalidate a statement about the life sciences.

Ocean World also differs from most traditional reference works in its frank espousal of respect for the delicacy of natural relationships and its encouragement of conservational attitudes. The set includes frequent references to Cousteau's own work, as well as the explorations and the historical and contemporary researches of others. Nearly every volume contains references to Cousteau's famous research ship *Calypso.* These personal notes add a dimension of interest commonly lacking in encyclopedic sets.

The material is reasonably accurate, but there are some errors, especially in discussions of biological subjects. Occasionally the errors seem to be the result of oversimplification which can perhaps be defended as inevitable if the material is to be comprehended by children. Were all the exceptions, reservations, and other complexities dealt with, the work would quickly be elevated to a level comprehensible only to specialists. Less

defensible are confused presentations or misleading statements, such as the assertion that an average cubic foot of sea water has as many as 20,000 microscopic plants. If by "plants" is meant species of plants, it has not been possible to substantiate this undocumented statement. If individual organisms are meant, this figure conflicts with a subsequent statement that this same volume of water may hold 12 million plant cells or diatoms. But the greatest objection to the assertion is its implication that there is a "typical" volume of sea water and that meaningful statements can be made about it. In fact, the sea is composed of a number of zones—littoral, pelagic, etc.—the populations of which vary greatly. Even in well-defined areas such as the Sargasso Sea, the plants and associated animals tend to cluster so that comparatively lush patches are set off by areas with dilute concentrations of life. And there are other complicating facts such as "rips"—those foamy areas where two ocean currents converge—which tend toward high and diverse populations.

Again, with respect to coverage, there seems to be a bias towards dramatic aspects of marine life. But this is understandable in that unusual behavioral patterns and spectacular creatures are precisely where much interest resides, especially for the younger person or one with more elementary knowledge of marine biology.

The illustrative material which makes up a substantial part of the *Ocean World* is composed largely of photographic plates with occasional maps, charts, and colored drawings. . . . According to the publishers, the set contains more than 2,600 color pictures, 103 black-and-white pictures, and 197 maps, charts, drawings, and tables. In general the illustrative material is well chosen and helpful, although a serious lack in some photographs is scale or size information. A number of illustrations with little reference value, such as a photograph of a city street crowded with vehicular traffic, have been included. These add pictorial substantiation to a chapter on air pollution and frequently enliven and reinforce points made in the text. The charts and diagrams included are generally useful and accurate. (pp. 743-44)

In summary, *The Ocean World of Jacques Cousteau* is a popularly written encyclopedia of marine life, oceanography, exploration, and conservation with somewhat better treatment of the latter three areas than of marine life. The work's content is adequate for young people and adult slow learners, but its treatment of biological topics tends to make it less suitable for secondary schools and adults capable of addressing more difficult materials. As a reference resource the set has deficiencies in organization and adequacy of access, but since a comparable better work is not available, *The Ocean World of Jacques Cousteau* can be recommended for homes and libraries serving children. (p. 744)

A review of "The Ocean World of Jacques Cousteau," in Reference and Subscription Books Reviews, *a separate publication within* Booklist, *Vol. 73, No. 10, January 15, 1977, pp. 742-44.*

MICHAEL ALLABY

Jacques-Yves Cousteau is that cliché, the "living legend". Strangers walk up to shake him by the hand and accept his autograph signed on any scrap of paper they can find. His superstar status might well be the envy of many an aspiring entertainer.

Each of his television films is seen by something like 120 million people; in Britain alone his audience can exceed 10 million. He has made 65 films for the cinema and television, he has written more than 30 books, and his articles appear in mass circulation magazines. His success gives him authority: the man who has mastered the media is obeyed. His films are edited only under his personal supervision, although he does permit the original commentary, written for the US market, to be rewritten for Britain. All the same, it is his story that is told, and in his way.

The films are pure entertainment, of course, and this accounts for their popular appeal. Yet they are more. They aim to inform and they advance Cousteau's personal view of the world. They are, unashamedly, conservationist propaganda. Cousteau's vision of the natural world and the threats to it is simple, and it is expressed simply and powerfully, mainly to viewers who lack the information or the scientific training to evaluate it.

The formula is dangerous, but it is difficult to picture Cousteau himself as the power-crazed demagogue his skills might enable him to become. He is quiet, gentle, witty, relaxed, highly intelligent and very well informed. (p. 172)

It is [Cousteau's] concentration on entertainment that has attracted considerable criticism, for films that are undoubtedly attractive may sometimes appear to possess a scientific content that is not there. His capture of two fur seals, "Pepito" and "Cristobal", for example, in order to see whether marine mammals can be tamed, like dogs or horses, made splendid popular television, but whether it had any scientific value at all is, to say the least, doubtful. Film of his divers catching hold of the fin of a fin whale to be towed along is charming, but, entertainment apart, what is the purpose? Even his almost magical film of the mating "orgy" of small squid left many questions unanswered and even more unasked. The Calypso left when shooting was completed, and she did not return. If there should be a conflict of interest between science and entertainment, entertainment wins.

Cousteau is not a marine biologist, but describes himself as a manager of scientists. Depending on the purpose of the expedition, a specialist accompanies the Calypso on each of her voyages as an adviser, but even so the contribution Cousteau has made to marine biology is minimal. Other popular marine writers and film makers—such as Hans Hass and Thor Heyerdahl—have managed to combine their entertaining with serious research the results of which have been published. Hass has published 135 scientific papers, Cousteau none.

This is due only partly to the exigencies of working for television. It suits Cousteau's own temperament. "We are explorers," he says, "and explorers are not settlers". He sees himself as a pioneer, opening the way for others to follow. As soon as he has skimmed off the cream, he is content to move on.

At the same time, his record of technical innovation is impressive. From his development of the aqualung to his work with experimental dwellings to test the physiological effects of prolonged periods spent living and working on the sea bed, he has sought and found—or caused to be found—solutions to problem after problem.

Each year, Calypso sails with a new silhouette, her equipment changed, modified, augmented. Many of the techniques developed by his team, and much of the equipment he has helped to develop or has tested, is in commercial use.

It is significant that while he takes only one academic scientist on each trip, he is able to attract and hold a team of divers whose training, skill and experience would bring them highly paid work anywhere.

Ironically, this very success exposes him to further criticism. He estimates that there are now something like five million people in the world using aqualungs, and some of them dive frequently. The invasion of the sea bed by divers is approaching the scale of a full tourist invasion, and it is producing rather similar local environmental damage. Cousteau shrugs. It is, he says rather disingenuously, the fate of new inventions. He has profited from the manufacture and sale of diving equipment, but even if he had no commercial interest in its sale, he could hardly help but popularise it with the films by which he earns his living. At least he has persuaded the company—not without a long struggle—to stop marketing weapons for spear fishing or to advertise other equipment as being essential to the spear fisher. They concentrate now on promoting underwater photography as a preferable activity.

Cousteau has speared fish, but only for food during the war to feed his family and friends. That kind of dire need is the only justification for spear fishing that he will accept.

Indeed, he is emphatic in his condemnation of fishing of all kinds. "It is as hopeless to count on fish as it would be to count on tiger meat to feed the world." Sea fish are usually high on food chains, so in a sense he is right, although it might be fairer to compare fish with all terrestrial carnivores rather than with just one species! (pp. 173-74)

Sweeping statements of this kind are characteristic of him, and they are worrying to those who devote their time to trying to avert the very dangers that concern him. He denies having ever said that the seas are dead, but his opinion that they are severely threatened by pollution is combined with the view that international agreements almost invariably fail. Sometimes he can contradict himself. He fears that despite international treaties forbidding it, parts of Antarctica may be developed for mineral extraction.

At the same time he admits that it may prove difficult to persuade coal miners to work through the Antarctic winter!

Recently he has been involved in underwater archaeology, and this has brought home to him the vulnerability of civilisations to natural calamities and so reinforces his fear and opposition to nuclear power. He points out that all our civilisations have flourished, and most of them died, during 6000 years, which is equivalent to 100 human lifespans. Nuclear wastes must be stored for much longer periods than this, and he finds the risk unacceptable. Even here, though, he is careless: it is the long-term storage of plutonium that he fears. It is mistakes of this kind that provide the levers by which otherwise sensible arguments can be toppled. . . .

By now he will be at sea again, in search of new adventures, new material that he will use with consummate skill to advance his very personal view of conservation. Many film stars have become conservationists. Cousteau may be the first conservationist to become a film star. The phenomenon is unique, fascinating, and at times more than a little disturbing. (p. 174)

Michael Allaby, "In Person: Technological Merman," in New Scientist, *Vol. 75, No. 1061, July 21, 1977, pp. 172-74.*

BOOK BAIT: DETAILED NOTES ON ADULT BOOKS POPULAR WITH YOUNG PEOPLE

Although Cousteau's newer books are fascinating to read, they do not strike immediate fire as [*The Silent World*] does. The beginning paragraph, when the author and his friends unpack the first aqualung, captures the reader's attention at once, and the interest never wanes. Here is all the excitement of science fiction along with the reality of the here and now. Here is a high-spirited, adventure-packed, personal narrative of undersea salvage, scientific research, and exploration in the Mediterranean. With the aqualungs (of which Cousteau was co-inventor) he and his men dived nearly naked into pressures that have crushed submarines. Cousteau describes what it is like to be a "manfish" swimming with sharks, mantas, and octopuses. The dives made by the Undersea Research Group to locate and explore wrecks (some had sunk during World War II and one went down about 80 B.C.) taught them a lot about work at great depths. The Group also hunted unexploded mines after World War II. One of the most exciting chapters is "Cave Diving" in which Cousteau tells how they nearly lost their lives in penetrating the Fountain of Vaucluse. Another contains the accounts of Cousteau's audacious 50-fathom dive into the zone of rapture, where divers become like drunken gods because of the pressure, and of the 396-foot dive which took a brave companion's life. What began as curiosity about the unknown beneath the sea developed into serious oceanographic study, of which his later books are a result.

Young people who like sea stories or who have had some experience with snorkels and fins are intrigued with the descriptions of the underwater forms of life. Underwater exploration calls for close camaraderie among the divers, constant vigilance, physical fitness, and high courage. (pp. 33-4)

> *"Book Bait: 'The Silent World',"* in Book Bait: Detailed Notes on Adult Books Popular with Young People, *edited by Elinor Walker, third edition, American Library Association, 1979, pp. 33-5.*

JAMES P. STERBA

It is difficult to criticize anything with Jacques Cousteau's name on it, especially a book as beautiful to look at as [**"The Ocean World"**]. Captain Cousteau has done more than anyone else to educate people about their "water planet." He has been a buoyant, indefatigable scout of the saltwater world, and through his films of his underwater adventures he has invited us to come along with him. (p. 12)

For the past several years, Captain Cousteau has been dashing about the globe, ringing the tocsin. In **"The Ocean World"** he sounds the alarm yet again: "Now the crisis is at hand. This is not the raving of a placard-carrying doomsayer, but the observation of thousands of learned and concerned individuals. I am 100 percent pessimistic when I predict some sort of a disaster, for it will surely come."

Since he cannot accept the resignation that such pessimism implies, however, he quickly adds: "But it is in our power to reduce dramatically its seriousness and its consequences. Yet I am also 100 percent optimistic for recovery after the disaster. After the deluge, the sun will shine, and men will hope again that the golden age will come."

This eight-pound volume is a welcome addition to the coffee table or bookshelf because of its 385 photographs, most of them striking color shots of the undersea world. Only a few of them, however, were taken by Cousteau's band aboard the Calypso; most were chosen from the collections of such talented underwater photographers as Carl Roessler, Paul Tzimoulis and Eda Rogers. And simply as a book of photographs, **"The Ocean World"** does not stand up to Mr. Roessler's own collection, "Underwater Wilderness," or the several volumes of Douglas Faulkner.

Furthermore, the text is laborious, winding through 48 encyclopedic chapters on history, biology and the adventures of the Calypso. Based on a 20-volume series that Captain Cousteau published between 1972 and 1974, the book reads like the narration of so many of his films—which is what it started out as. It seems much too general for either armchair scientists or fellow divers. (pp. 12, 36)

Though it is somewhat carelessly recycled, **"The Ocean World"** is nonetheless well packaged and better on the whole than popular volumes published recently on the sea and what man is doing to it—and, ultimately, to himself. Since Captain Cousteau is a pioneer and an adventurer, not a scientist, we can forgive his tendency toward clichés, generalities and self-promotion. He found a way to earn a living doing what he loved to do most, exploring the oceans, and we are all the richer because he took us with him. (p. 36)

> *James P. Sterba, "The Fragile Beauties of the Deep,"* in The New York Times Book Review, *January 13, 1980, pp. 12, 36.*

Neil (Leslie) Diamond
1941-

American songwriter.

Diamond rose to fame in the 1960s with the recordings of his compositions "Cherry, Cherry" (1966) and "Sweet Caroline" (1969). Since then he has consistently secured top positions on the record charts with numerous hit singles, albums, and the motion picture soundtracks for *Jonathan Livingston Seagull* (1973) and *The Jazz Singer* (1980). Diamond's songs are in a wide range of styles, including ballad, pop and country rock, folk, and gospel, as well as rhythms from African and Caribbean music. Because of his diversity, Diamond attracts a variety of audiences. His exploration of universal themes, such as the search for identity in "I Am, I Said" (1971) and "Be" (1973) and the elusiveness of love in "You Don't Bring Me Flowers" (1978) and "Love on the Rocks" (1980), has also contributed to his popularity.

Diamond's songs often reflect his personal experiences. His album *Beautiful Noise* (1976) was inspired by his years as a Tin Pan Alley lyricist. Similarly, the story of *The Jazz Singer*, a movie remake in which Diamond starred as an actor and for which he wrote the lyrics, parallels Diamond's break with his traditional Jewish family in his pursuit of a career in music.

With a Grammy, a Golden Globe award, and an Oscar nomination, all for *Jonathan Livingston Seagull*, and more than twenty gold and platinum records, Diamond's popular and financial success is indisputable. Yet critical response has not always been favorable: some reviewers consider Diamond's lyrics sentimental, pretentious, and clichéd. Critics generally agree, though, that Diamond's engaging melodies and powerful performances make him one of the most appealing entertainers in contemporary music.

(See also *Contemporary Authors*, Vol. 108.)

© *Images Press*

WILLIAM BENDER

In the past three years, Diamond has turned out enough hit songs (among them: *Kentucky Woman* and *Sweet Caroline*) to keep the current champion, Burt Bacharach, watchful and busy. But where Bacharach plods as a performer, Diamond dances.

In person, Diamond has a naturalness and relaxed cool that are fine foils for rhythms as infectious as a Mardi Gras parade. His voice still has a touch of the crooner, but it can turn soulful. His songs delve ingeniously into hard and soft rock, blues, gospel, even country rock—a range of styles that Bacharach does not even try to match. (p. 46)

[His album *Tap Root Manuscript*] is ample proof of Diamond's versatility. Side 1 contains *Cracklin' Rosie* (a reference to the joys of loosening up with a sparkling pink wine), a Top Ten single for two months last fall, as well as [his remake of Bob Russell's and Bobby Scott's] *He Ain't Heavy . . . He's My Brother*, currently the No. 22 single.

Side 2 is devoted entirely to *The African Trilogy*, which grew out of Diamond's interest in gospel music and his desire to explore its rhythmic roots. Using African beats—more so-

phisticated than African melodies—Diamond grandly started out to depict the three principal stages in a man's life: birth, maturity, death. Though the trilogy finally grew to six parts, Diamond liked the original title and kept it.

Trilogy or six-pack, it is a stunning example of pop crossbreeding: *Soolaimon*, for example, is a pulsating toe-tapper that Diamond terraces forcefully with one climax after another. In contrast are [the] . . . tender lines from a children's chorus called *Childsong* that opens the work. . . . (p. 47)

> *William Bender, "Tin Pan Tailor," in* Time, *Vol. 97, No. 2, January 11, 1971, pp. 46-7.*

MELODY MAKER

Besides "**Cracklin' Rosie**," [Neil Diamond's] hit single, "**Tap Root Manuscript**" contains what is presumably his *magnum opus* to date, a seven-part work called (somewhat paradoxically) "**The African Trilogy**," subtitled "A Folk Ballet." Diamond's note on the sleeve explains that this is his homage to African music, and it's obviously a very heartfelt thing. Fortunately he does it from his point of view, rather than throwing in a load of pseudo-Africanisms, and if the result isn't terribly profound, at least it's entertaining (what?). Particularly enjoyable are the groovy "**Soolaimon**" and a track called "**Miisa**," which calls to mind the "Missa Luba" by the Choir of King Baudoin. . . . On the other side there's Neil's smooth rendering of "He Ain't Heavy," which made the American charts as a single, and a beautiful song called **"Coldwater Morning,"** with a fine arrangement by Lee Holdridge. A very worthy album, then, but I hope that **"The African Trilogy"** doesn't presage a venture into heaviness and pretension. I'd be happy if he just kept writing things like **"Cherry Cherry"** and **"Sweet Caroline."**

> *R.W., "Diamond in Darkest Africa," in* Melody
> Maker, *February 27, 1971, p. 15.*

ALEC DUBRO

Diamond's latest album, *Tap Root Manuscript*, is a half step at being Artistic.

Side One is the usual—a couple of dynamite singles and a couple of not-so-hot singles. **"Cracklin Rosie,"** which made it to number one nationally, is excellent Neil Diamond. Named after the wine of the same name . . . Rosie's a good chick. Diamond isn't afraid to throw in a little early-Sixties schmaltz. He has thoroughly bypassed, or ignored "rock"—progressive or otherwise. He's chosen to go ahead with straight pop. But, two things set him apart from, say, Bobby Vee. One is that he has a really knockout voice—once it might have been called a "strong baritone." And two, he's deeply involved with the music he writes.

"He Ain't Heavy . . . He's My Brother," one of the only songs Diamond has recorded that he didn't write, is a good example of the straight-out-soul that Neil Diamond can sing. **"Free Life"** is another good cut, although it hasn't made it on Top-40. **"Done Too Soon"** is one of the duds. Reminiscent of Paul Simon's "A Simple Desultory Phillipic," it's just a rhyming list of famous, groovy people who were ahead of their time—done too soon.

Side Two is the Artistry, open to question. This is *The African Trilogy* (a folk ballet). It's a varied and ambitious work. . . .

[The music is] certainly far less pretentious than its introduction. The worst of it has been identified as: "wimoweh" off-key, the "Missa Luba" by Doc Severinsen, or the sound track to *Elephant Walk*. In its better parts, though, it's quite charming—children's chorus, interpretations of African music and the like. The only trouble is, I haven't any idea who would want to listen to it. Certainly not the audience he has. No one interested in African ballet. Freaks leave the room when it's on. . . .

Neil Diamond *Gold*, on the other hand, is probably his best album. . . . [This] record is all his best songs, from early and late, with something added. *Gold* is recorded live and he comes across much better on this record than he does on his singles. . . .

The version of **"Kentucky Woman"** he does is the best one I've ever heard. In fact, all his get-it-on songs, **"Thank the Lord For the Nightime," "Sweet Caroline," "Brother Love's Traveling Salvation Show"** sound better for being reduced to a kind of whoop and holler presentation. It's not the kind of record you'd want to play all the time. Neil Diamond is not a singer of great depth, nor is his music many-faceted. But, frequently it just hits the spot.

The slow stuff on *Gold* is very pretty: **"And the Singer Sings His Songs"** and **"Solitary Man"** have the straightforward ap-

proach of country music. It's unabashed sentiment and you have to be willing to meet the singer halfway. Sometimes, his excesses are too much. **"Cherry Cherry"** is unconvincing emotion and he murders **"Both Sides Now."** But, those are exceptions. . . .

Neil Diamond is a talented song writer and an excellent singer, but he is limited. I can understand his wanting to go past Top-40 writing, but, by overreaching himself, as he does on *African Trilogy*, he'll keep himself in Top-40. Whatever his moves, I hope he keeps writing singles. They're among the best there are.

> *Alec Dubro, in a review of "Gold" and "Tap Root Manuscript," in* Rolling Stone, *Issue 79, April 1, 1971, p. 47.*

ROY HOLLINGWORTH

[Neil Diamond's songs during a 1972 concert on Broadway] are pretty, and poppy, and in the way he delivers them—melancholic, and ultra-romantic. . . . And yet, they are as see-through and substantial as a Woolworth's nylon nightie in the rain.

Their chording is simplistic, and oft to be the same—and his voice is want to drone on, and on, and on. It creaks like an oldish door, and is seldom delivered from higher than the Adam's apple. It is a rather shaky attempt at drama. It can make you utter the expression "ugh!" and "ahhh," but seldom "wow."

They are the sort of songs that if you think only a little, you'll be able to guess as near as dammit what the next line will be. To be truthful, they lack imagination to an awful extent.

His rhyming is dead easy. Examples: Dove rhymes with love, heart rhymes with part, and willow rhymes with pillow etc. It would be far more interesting if he rhymed dove with shove, or heart with tart, on occasion, and attempted to write something a little different. As it stands Neil Diamond is heart rhyming with part, and dat's dat. (pp. 10-11)

> *Roy Hollingworth, "Diamond Jubilee," in* Melody
> Maker, *October 21, 1972, pp. 10-11.*

PAUL KRESH

The best thing about [the movie *Jonathan Livingston Seagull*] . . . is Neil Diamond's score, and the Columbia recording of the original soundtrack . . . is thus a lot easier to take than the movie for which it was prepared.

Mr. Diamond, who recently has delved into soft rock, blues, gospel, country music, and soul since his emergence as a rock superstar a few years ago, supplies a kind of contemporary tone poem that captures the serenity of the scene from the earliest chords, and manages to blend an up-to-date idiom with an impressionistic feeling for the moods of weather and rock seascapes, summoning a suggestive power that enables this music to stand on its own. There are also a number of songs like *Be* and *Skybird* and *Lonely Looking Sky* that attempt to translate the ideas of the story into folk-musical terms and do succeed in conveying a wide-sky, windswept mood despite lyrics that seem to draw their inspiration more from Hallmark than from nature. In addition, there is a frankly religious "anthem" with lyrics consisting entirely of such words as "*sanctus*" and "*kyrie*" and "*gloria*." The anthem's controlled exaltation speaks well for Diamond's taste and inventiveness: I have never heard a children's chorus intoning popular music less objectionably.

> *Paul Kresh, "Jonathan Livingston Popstar," in* Stereo Review, *Vol. 32, No. 2, February, 1974, p. 94.**

TOM NOLAN

"I've seen the light," the first song [on *Serenade*] begins, and Neil Diamond reads his line with the slovenly confidence of an illuminated saloon singer, a cosmic Sinatra hinting at some grand message to come. But all that Diamond has to offer are bland musings adrift on an empty sea of strings, a handful of spiritual cliches ("Plainly it is all a circle") pegged to a gallery of culture heroes—from Picasso to Longfellow to Christ—and sung in a variety of dialects either embarrassing or aggravating, depending on whether sympathy is placed with the singer or the listener.

> *Tom Nolan, in a review of "Serenade," in* Rolling Stone, *Issue 184, April 10, 1975, p. 68.*

BOB KIRSCH

["**Beautiful Noise**"] is one of the most satisfying and commercially viable albums Diamond has come up with in years, an energetic "up" set that showcases more of the Diamond versatility as a singer and songwriter than both of his past Columbia efforts combined. . . .

[The album] opens with two uptempo, goodtime songs. "**Beautiful Noise**," as well as being the title cut, is an uptempo expression of some of the joys of the city, especially the era of the late '50s and early '60s in New York when Diamond was first beginning to make noise as a songwriter. The LP, incidentally, is loosely based around the personal feelings of Diamond in that period. . . .

"**Stargazer**," also probably autobiographical, is another uptempo cut with an almost dixieland clarinet and trumpet break, a song that could easily be adaptable for a Broadway show. One must assume the "Stargazer" is Diamond, or at least someone he knows or knew, a song full of warnings that are happily disregarded.

"**Street Life**" is another tune that could easily become part of a show, a song that sounds almost as if it could have been included in "West Side Story" and a song that again offers the joys of the city when most in the business are exalting the joys of the country.

Diamond, of course, has not abandoned his mastery of the ballad. "**If You Know What I Mean**" and "**Dry Your Eyes**" (co-written with [Robbie] Robertson) are probably the most effective in this format, with the themes of love and the ballad style combined well—a combination Diamond perfected some time ago. One other ballad, "**Lady-Oh**," is noteworthy especially for the jazzy Tom Scott tenor sax solo.

"**Don't Think . . . Feel**," and "**Surviving The Life**" are the kind of up, optimistic cuts one does not generally associate with Diamond. The first cut is a good natured Caribbean sounding song while the latter is a call to join in, do the best you can and things will probably turn out for the best.

There are other good cuts, like "**Jungletime**" and "**Signs**." But the best part of this set are not the individual songs. The best is the variety in writing and singing styles Diamond has come up with and the variety in arrangements he, Robertson, [Nick] DeCaro and [Bob] James have conceived. The music cannot be categorized. Whatever has brought about the various changes, it's Diamond's best in years.

> *Bob Kirsch, in a review of "Beautiful Noise," in* Billboard, *Vol. 88, No. 28, July 4, 1976, p. 66.*

STEPHEN HOLDEN

In *Beautiful Noise,* Neil Diamond recollects his days as a scuffling young Tin Pan Alley writer. Though the songs are better crafted than those on *Serenade*, there remains an enormous disparity between Diamond's sentimental three-chord songs and their portentous interpretations. . . . If "**Beautiful Noise**," "**Jungletime**," and especially "**Street Life**" and "**Surviving the Life**" begin to evoke New York clamor and hustle, none conjures the feelings Diamond wants nearly as well as the classic score for *West Side Story* did. Still, these songs contain the seeds for a possible Broadway revue. . .

Diamond's ballads "**Lady Oh**," "**If You Know What I Mean**," "**Signs**" and "**Home Is a Wounded Heart**," repeat the formulas of the earlier hits "**Holly, Holly**," "**I Am, I Said**," and "**Longfellow Serenade**." Here, Diamond's flowery clichés and stentorian declarations are underscored with lavish orchestration in an attempt to create pop record equivalents of turn-of-the-century concert chestnuts. . . . Though Diamond's redundant musical ideas make those songs far less substantial than most of the standard concert song repertoire, it is a tribute to his oratorical skill that they work as dramatic, if corny, pop ballads.

> *Stephen Holden, in a review of "Beautiful Noise," in* Rolling Stone, *Issue 219, August 12, 1976, p. 64.*

JOE GOLDBERG

Both in conception and delivery, Diamond tends toward melodrama. The spiritual progenitor of some of his most effective numbers, like "**I Am . . . I Said**," is the "Soliloquy" from [Richard Rodgers's and Oscar Hammerstein's] *Carousel.* On a bad day, he can slip over into the sentimentality of a Rod McKuen or the bathos of a Vegas lounge act singing "My Way" after dedicating it to The Chairman of the Board [Frank Sinatra], but he usually manages to keep his head above water. And this time, he's come up with a remarkable record [*Beautiful Noise*]. . . .

This is by no means a perfect record. Despite the variety of subject and musical approach, the songs have a certain sameness when heard all at once. Some of them are reminiscent of other music, some of Diamond's own work.

I can see that most of what I've written here extends praise with one hand and snatches it away with the other. That's not quite what I mean. Diamond is an artist somewhat like Leonard Bernstein: prodigiously gifted, trying to surpass himself and the form he's working in, and so commercial and so much a street boy that there's a slight taint to the best things he does. Sometimes, you don't like yourself for liking him.

But he's accomplished one very important thing with this album. Unlike Broadway shows, albums are to be experienced many times. . . . *Beautiful Noise* doesn't diminish with repeated playings. It grows. The more you listen, the more you hear.

Joe Goldberg, in a review of "Beautiful Noise," in Creem, *Vol. 8, No. 5, October, 1976, p. 69.*

MELODY MAKER

["**Love at the Greek**"] is "**Hot August Nights**" part two (or to be more accurate, parts three and four, for this is another live double). The formula is much the same: Diamond performs note-perfect versions of hits old and new, adding only a few grossly sexual "oooohs" and "aaaahs"; predictably, a thousand women go wild in the background. The difference, though, between him and a dozen other middle-of-the-road singers in the same field is that Diamond can write excellent songs, and no matter how unhip the circumstances it's impossible to ignore them. They're strong on melody, usually interesting lyrically (particularly those from "**Beautiful Noise**", which is, naturally, heavily featured), and, above all, sound modern. Even the oldies here, like "**Kentucky Woman**" . . . and "**Sweet Caroline**," are jazzed up and given a fresh coating of syrup. On the debits, there's almost a complete side devoted to the mediocre "**Jonathan Livingston Seagull**," but to set against it is a fabulous treatment of "**The Last Picasso**", the highlight of "**Serenade**". A beautiful noise, indeed.

M.O., in a review of "Love at the Greek," in Melody Maker, *March 19, 1977, p. 31.*

PETER REILLY

Here's Neil Diamond, the Bard of the American middle class (the "feeling" part, that is), throwing his considerable box-office weight around in another garish album [*Love at the Greek*], this one recorded before a packed audience at the Greek Theatre in Los Angeles. The warmth of the appreciation from Diamond's pin-drop-quiet audience as he slobbered his way through something like his five-song tone poem *Jonathan Livingston Seagull* was probably enough to melt a box of opera creme chocolates on that historic night. . . . Diamond also runs through such of his other lollipops as *Stargazer* and *The Last Picasso* to the uproarious delight and deep-deep feeling of his audience. Just think, they've banned saccharin and let Neil Diamond go absolutely free! There is *no* justice.

Peter Reilly, in a review of "Love at the Greek," in Stereo Review, *Vol. 38, No. 6, June, 1977, p. 96.*

RAY COLEMAN

In the good old showbiz tradition of razzamatazz and "Give-us-a-song, Neil" atmosphere invoked by the theme and material of [the movie "The Jazz Singer", in which Diamond stars,] Diamond has risen to the bait with his customary and admirable lack of humility. In fairness, some of the songs are so strong as to stand up completely outside the film; "**America**" is a majestic piece of heart-pounding nationalism, with tune and lyrics by Neil, sung with all the tub-thumping passion of his early hits, and with a similar beat to "**Cracklin' Rosie**", which we all know was magnificent.

"**Love On The Rocks**", co-written by Diamond and Gilbert Becaud, is as simple and as good a song as the throwaway title indicates, and "**Hello Again**" enables Diamond to inject that passionate intimacy into a straight ballad that has won him millions of middle-class hearts.

Ray Coleman, in a review of "The Jazz Singer," in Melody Maker *November 29, 1980, p. 18.*

VICKI PIPKIN

[The movie "The Jazz Singer"] allows Diamond's strength in music to be used extensively, and that helps the sometimes corny musical drama. . . .

[The] interpersonal conflict between [father and son] . . . provides the best emotional moments of the EMI film in both dialog and music. For example, when his father rents his clothing to mourn the son's "death," a Jewish custom signifying that he has been disowned, Diamond heads for parts unknown, dirty, scuffy, and poignantly delivers "**Hello Again**" and "**Amazed and Confused.**"

"**Love on the Rocks**," a powerful ballad in true Diamond style, is done at a studio session where a famous rock singer was to make it uptempo instead. . . .

Diamond wrote and performs the music on Capitol Records and collaborated on selected compositions with Gilbert Becaud, Richard Bennett, Alan Lindgren and Doug Rhone.

He gets in a few country licks complete with fiddle on "You Are My Sunshine," and movingly delivers "**Songs Of Life.**" Even the traditional Jewish songs, done in Hebrew offer a special sensitivity.

And the predictable conclusion to "The Jazz Singer" cannot remove the thunder from Diamond's up-tempo and style in "**America.**"

But the movie is titled "The Jazz Singer" although it does not contain one jazz or jazz-fusion number. This will, no doubt, bring frowns from jazz purists and fusionists alike.

Vicki Pipkin, "No Jazz Heard in 'Jazz Singer' Film," in Billboard, *Vol. 92, No. 51, December 20, 1980, p. 20.*

JAY COCKS

[Neil Diamond] has written and sung some of the smoothest and best contemporary pop, yet he remains a performer in search of a tradition, a megabucks pilgrim looking for roots he never had and a place in which to settle. Rock really is not his neighborhood; his fur-lined melodies and forthright sentimentality make him stand out among rockers like a Coupe de Ville at a demolition derby. Diamond has been a smash act in Las Vegas, but he is neither as smooth as Sinatra, as cloying as Wayne Newton nor as annoying as Steve Lawrence.

All this difficulty about categorization and definition sometimes gives even Diamond pause. "I fell between two musical generations," he admits. "I love Sinatra and Eddie Fisher. Yet I really loved the Beatles." The only folks who don't seem at all confused—or at least don't care if they are—are the millions of fans. . . . Diamond loyalists right now are making their boy's latest efforts two of the year's hottest records. *Love on the Rocks,* a typically canny Diamond ballad, is currently No. 2 on the charts, while the album it comes from, *The Jazz Singer,* is fifth among the top LPs. . . .

The low drama and high sentiments of [the movie *The Jazz Singer,* in which Diamond stars,] may be only a glossy reflection of Diamond's life and sometimes troubled times. But the movie does pull off at least one tricky proposition: it finally and snugly tucks Neil Diamond inside a tradition. He is revealed as a rouser, a showman, a kind of bandmaster of the American mainstream. Like [Al] Jolson's, even Diamond's slickest movements seem sincere. The stuff may be corny, but it's never prefab. Neil leans into the *Kol Nidre* as if it were a sacred version of his sound-track anthem for *Jonathan Livingston Seagull*. One may question his taste, but not his enthusiasm or his exuberance. *America,* his up-tempo celebration of the immigrant glories of American life that opens and closes *The Jazz Singer,* is equal parts Emma Lazarus and Irving Berlin, and none the worse for it. It is too close to Diamond's heart to be purely sappy. It is a showman's show-stopper, and it is not a bad little tune for a pilgrim, either.

Jay Cocks, "Bandmaster of the Mainstream," in Time, Vol. 117, No. 4, January 26, 1981, p. 71.

STEPHEN HOLDEN

Neil Diamond's quasi-classical melodies and oratorical vocals evoke a Hollywood Moses gesticulating wildly toward the heavens. This hasn't always been the case. In the late Sixties and early Seventies, Diamond was content to churn out cheerful pop-country hits (**"Sweet Caroline," "Cracklin' Rosie"**) that had no artistic pretensions. But with *Jonathan Livingston Seagull,* his music became curdled with intellectual self-importance.

On the Way to the Sky is a typically overblown collection of tuneful trifles that aren't nearly as strong as last year's score for *The Jazz Singer*. . . .

Though Diamond is unfailingly melodic and his booming bass-baritone smolders with emotion, the arrangements and lyrics here are pure Las Vegas kitsch.

Stephen Holden, in a review of "On the Way to the Sky," in Rolling Stone, Issue 365, March 18, 1982, p. 67.

NOEL COPPAGE

There's an interesting contrast [in *Heartlight*] between how seriously Neil Diamond takes himself and how seriously the songs take anything. Collaborating mostly with Burt Bacharach and Carole Bayer Sager, Diamond has finally managed to re-create the spirit of Tin Pan Alley—in other words, he's recycling the mainstream pop music of 1953.

Ironically, although he has been trying to move uptown for years, Diamond still sings with the real-person earnestness of his Brooklyn roots. Combine that with the too-sophisticated-to-be-sincere nature of the songs, the 1953-style orchestral settings . . . , and you can imagine my various and not quite compatible reactions. Some of the stuff here is attractive enough in its own way; it just doesn't respond to Diamond's attempts to breathe life into it.

Noel Coppage, in a review of "Heartlight," in Stereo Review, Vol. 48, No. 2, February, 1983, p. 73.

Philip K(indred) Dick

1928-1982

American novelist and short story writer.

Dick has been one of the most acclaimed science fiction writers of the past thirty years and his work is praised for encouraging confrontation with the problems and enigmas of human existence rather than escape into outer space adventure. His work is also noted for its inventive treatment of the complex relationships between illusion and reality. For example, one of Dick's techniques for emphasizing the elusive nature of reality is to explore in his stories the idea that consciousness may be manipulated through drugs or the influence of an outside force. Barry N. Malzberg has called Dick's works "strange, rending, off-center visions which probed at the borders of reality and finally ruptured reality itself." Another characteristic of Dick's fiction is his projection of a near future in which machines acquire human traits, while many humans lose those traits—kindness, empathy, warmth—that differentiate them from machines. Dick's characters are antiheroic; at best they survive in this environment by caring about each other.

In the first three years of his career, Dick wrote the majority of his numerous short stories; in 1955, with the publication of *Solar Lottery,* he shifted to writing novels almost exclusively. His early novels, including *Eye in the Sky* (1957) and *Time out of Joint* (1959), establish his long-standing question: "What is reality?" and its corollary "Who, or what, controls it?" A second and very creative period of Dick's career began with his Hugo Award-winning novel, *The Man in the High Castle* (1962). Critics consider this work the best example of Dick's use of parallel worlds. By considering two possible realities—that the United States either won or lost World War II—Dick compares the insight of one character with the belief of the masses. Dick's second major concern is exemplified in *Do Androids Dream of Electric Sheep?* (1968). This work features very humanlike androids and a protagonist who kills them by profession. When the lines become blurred between human and android, the hero questions the morality of his occupation. In 1982 the novel was adapted to film as *Blade Runner. Valis* (1981) initiated an experimental stage in Dick's writing in which he delves further into metaphysics in search of reality and a higher being. *Valis, The Divine Invasion* (1981), and *The Transmigration of Timothy Archer* (1982) are considered a trilogy, for the works, though unrelated in any obvious way by setting, character, or incident, are bound thematically.

Critics find Dick's work diffcult to evaluate. While they admire his unique, often startling visions, they lament his careless, unsystematic style. His complex narrative structures are difficult to decipher, though some critics maintain that this difficulty is indicative of his profundity. It has been said that Dick can take the most trite elements of science fiction and make them significant, humorous, and, at times, even poetic. He is sometimes accused of losing control of his work, becoming sidetracked in his narrative or trapped without a plausible resolution. Despite this, Dick is credited with displaying sympathy for his characters, thus giving his work an admirably humanistic quality.

LOCUS/Paul Nelson

(See also *CLC*, Vol. 10; *Contemporary Authors*, Vols. 49-52, Vol. 106 [obituary]; *Contemporary Authors New Revision Series*, Vol. 2; and *Dictionary of Literary Biography*, Vol. 8.)

GEORGE TURNER

[*The following excerpt was first published as "Back to the Cactus" in* SF Commentary, *November, 1970.*]

I have always enjoyed Dick's work on the superficial level of entertainment and yet have been aware of dissatisfaction on deeper levels. After a year without him, *Ubik* crystallises the dissatisfaction; my day as a Dick fan is nearly over.

Here is the book of a man who shudders between the real and the unreal, who sees alternatives as realities and realities as a transient phase among alternatives. Alternatives and realities co-exist, and even influence each other (*Ubik, Now Wait For Last Year, Three Stigmata of Palmer Eldritch*) and through this incredibly complex universe Dick tries to trace a path. It can't be done. The human brain cannot reduce an infinite number of possibilities to a story pattern simply by selecting what appeals, particularly when one realises that effects can initiate their own causes, as in *Counter-Clock World.*

Many years ago Dick announced his theme in *Eye in the Sky*, but the depth of his involvement was not observable in that lighthearted piece of fun. Perhaps the tales featuring the Perky Pat game were the first real step into the confusion. These predicated a search for alternative reality on the part of the players; later *The World Jones Made* and *Time Out of Joint* suggested that perhaps it was the author who searched.

In *Martian Time-Slip* the sense of all possible reality vanished, became a shifting thing. Later books have tended to become extended metaphors of this idea, and have become increasingly disfigured by unresolvable complexities which only tend to show that the idea itself is invalid and/or cannot be expressed in the prose of an apparently material universe. (pp. 47-8)

In *Ubik* we are given the living and the half-living; the half-living are actually dead but existing in another version of reality until their vestigial remainders of consciousness finally drain away. Their "reality" is subject to manipulation by a strong personality among the half-living, which piles complexity on complexity until inconsistencies begin to stand out like protest banners. The plotting is neat but cannot override the paradoxes. The metaphor fails because it cannot stand against the weight of reality as we know it.

This is plainly an obsession with Dick. He is too intelligent not to know that his plots are snow jobs, so one can only assume that he is being defiant, shouting, "I know it is so, and some day I'll find a way to demonstrate it." My bet is that he won't. (p. 48)

> *George Turner, "Philip K. Dick Saying It All Over Again," in* Philip K Dick: Electric Shepherd, *edited by Bruce Gillespie, Norstrilia Press, 1975, pp. 47-8.*

BRIAN W. ALDISS

[*The following excerpt was published in a special issue of* Science-Fiction Studies *devoted to the work of Philip K. Dick.*]

The setting [of *Martian Time-Slip*] is Mars, which is now partly colonised. (p. 42)

This web of civilization is stretched thin over utter desolation. There is no guaranteeing that it can be maintained. Its stability is threatened by the Great Powers back on Earth. For years they have neglected Mars, concentrating dollars and man-hours on further exploration elsewhere in the system; now they may interfere actively with the balance of the colony.

Behind this web exists another, even more tenuous: the web of human relationships. Men and women, children, old men, bleekmen (the autochthonous but non-indigenous natives of Mars) all depend, however reluctantly, on one another. (pp. 42-3)

Behind these two webs lies a third, revealed only indirectly. This is the web connecting all the good and bad things in the universe. The despised Bleekmen, who tremble on the edge of greater knowledge than humanity, are acutely aware of this web and occasionally succeed in twitching a strand here and there, to their advantage; but they are as much in its toils as anyone else.

These three webs integrate at various coordinate points, the most remarkable point being AM-WEB, a complex structure which the UN may build some time in the future. . . . [That structure's] function in the novel is to provide a symbol for the aspirations and failures of mankind. The structure will be a considerable achievement when completed; which is not to say that it is not ultimately doomed; and part of that doom may be decreed by the miserable political and financial maneuverings which form one of the minor themes of this intricately designed novel. . . .

One of the attractions of Dick's novels is that they all have points at which they inter-relate, although Dick never introduces characters from previous books. The relationship is more subtle—more web-like—than that. (p. 43)

Dick's kaleidoscope is always being shaken, new sinister colours and patterns continually emerge. The power in the Dickian universe resides in these [building] blocks, rather than in his characters; even when one of the characters has a special power (like Jones's ability to foresee the future in *The World Jones Made*), it rarely does him any good.

If we look at two of the most important of these building blocks and observe how they depend on each other for greatest effect, we come close to understanding one aspect of Dickian thought. These blocks are the Concern-With-Reality and the Involvement-with-the-Past.

Most of the characteristic themes of SF are materialist ones; only the concern-with-reality theme involves a quasi-metaphysical speculation, and this theme Dick has made peculiarly his own. . . . [In his later books], Dickian characters . . . [frequently] find themselves trapped in hallucinations or fake worlds of various kinds, often without knowing it or, if knowing it, without being able to do anything about it. (pp. 43-4)

And it is not only worlds that are fake. Objects, animals, people, may also be unreal in various ways. Dick's novels are littered with fakes. . . . Things are always talking back to humans. Doors argue, medicine bags patronize, the cab at the end of *Now Wait for Last Year* advises Dr. Eric Sweetscent to stay with his ailing wife. All sorts of drugs are available which lead to entirely imaginary universes, like the evil Can-D and Chew-Z used by the colonists on Mars in *Palmer Eldritch*. . . .

Of course, there are many ways of falling into the pit, one of which is to have too much involvement-with-the-past. (p. 44)

Trouble comes when the interest with the past and all its artifacts builds into an obsession. . . .

And this is indeed where Dick parts company . . . with many another writer, in or out of SF. If he sees little safety in the future, the past is even more insidiously corrupting. . . . The past is seen as regressive; one of the most striking Dickian concepts is the "regression of forms" which takes place in *Ubik,* that magnificent but flawed novel in which the characters try to make headway through a world becoming ever more primitive, so that the airliner devolves into a Ford trimotor into a Curtis biplane, while Joe's multiplex FM tuner will regress into a cylinder phonograph playing a shouted recitation of the Lord's Prayer. (p. 45)

With the past so corrupting, the present so uncertain, and the future so threatening, we might wonder if there can be any escape. The secret of survival in Dick's universe is not to attempt escape into any alternate version of reality but to see things through as best you can; in that way, you may succeed if not actually triumphing. The favoured character in *Martian Time-Slip* is Jack Bohlen. . . . His voice is business-like, competent, and patient; these are high-ranking virtues in the Dickian anthropology. It is significant that Jack is a *repairman* . . .—a survival-rich job, since it helps maintain the status quo. Similar survivors in other novels are pot-healers, traders, doctors, musical instrument makers, and android-shooters (since androids threaten the status quo).

The characters who survive are generally aided by some system of knowledge involving faith. The system is rarely a scientific one; it is more likely to be ancient. In *Martian Time-Slip,* it is the never-formulated paranormal understanding of the Bleek-men; Bohlen respects this vague eschatological faith without comprehending it. . . . The *I Ching,* or *Book of Changes,* the four-thousand-year-old Chinese work of divination, performs a similar function in *The Man in the High Castle,* whilst in *Counter-Clock World* Lotta Hermes randomly consults the Bi-ble, which predicts the future with an alarming accuracy. In both Dick's two early masterpieces, *Time-Slip* and *High Castle,* this religious element—presented as something crumbling, un-reliable, to be figured out with pain—is well-integrated into the texture of the novel.

Dick's next great book, *The Three Stigmata of Palmer Eldritch,* was written very soon after *Martian Time-Slip,* and the two are closely related. . . . To my view, *Eldritch* is a flawed work, over-complicated, and finally disappearing into a cloud of quasi-theology; whereas *Martian Time-Slip* has a calm and lucidity about it. But in *Eldritch* we also find an ancient and unreliable meta-structure of faith, in this case embodied in the ferocious alien entity which fuses with Eldritch's being. (pp. 45-6)

[In *Martian Time-Slip*] Jack Bohlen desperately needs a tran-scendental act of fusion; he is estranged from his wife, sold by his first employer, threatened by his second, invaded by the schizophrenia of the boy he befriends. He sees in this mental illness, so frighteningly depicted in the book, the ultimate en-emy. From this ultimate enemy come the time-slip of the title and that startling paragraph which seems to condense much of the feeling of the book—and, indeed, of Dick's work in gen-eral, when Bohlen works out what Manfred's mental illness means:

> It is the stopping of time. The end of experi-ence, of anything new. Once the person be-comes psychotic, nothing ever happens to him again.

This is the maledictory circle within which Dick's beings move and from which they have to escape: although almost any change is for the worse, stasis means death, spiritual if not actual.

Any discussion of Dick's work makes it sound a grim and appalling world. So, on the surface, it may be; yet it must also be said that Dick is amazingly funny. The terror and the humor are fused. It is this rare quality which marks Dick out. This is why critics, in seeking to convey his essential flavour, bring forth the names of [Charles] Dickens and [Franz] Kafka, earlier masters of ghastly comedy. . . .

Dick, like Dickens, enjoys a multi-plotted novel. As the legal metaphor is to *Bleak House,* the world-as-prison to *Little Dor-rit,* the dust heap to *Our Mutual Friend,* the tainted wealth to *Great Expectations,* so is Mars to *Martian Time-Slip.* It is exactly and vividly drawn; this is Mars used in elegant and expert fashion as metaphor of spiritual poverty. In functioning as a dreamscape, it has much in common with the semi-alle-gorical, semi-surrealist locations used by Kafka. . . . (p. 46)

Dick's alliance, if one may call it that, with writers such as Dickens and Kafka makes him immediately congenial to En-glish and European readers. It may be this quality which has brought him reputation and respect on this side of the Atlantic before his virtues are fully recognized in his own country. (pp. 46-7)

Brian W. Aldiss, "Dick's Maledictory Web: About and Around 'Martian Time-Slip'," in Science-Fic-tion Studies, *Vol. 2, No. 5, March, 1975, pp. 42-7.*

STANISLAW LEM

[*The following essay was published in a special issue of* Science-Fiction Studies *devoted to Philip K. Dick's works.*]

In SF there is little room left for creative work that would aspire to deal with problems of our time without mystification, oversimplification, or facile entertainment: e.g., for work which would reflect on the place that Reason can occupy in the Uni-verse, on the outer limits of concepts formed on Earth as in-struments of cognition, or on such consequences of contacts with extraterrestrial life as find no place in the desperately primitive repertoire of SF devices (bounded by the alternative "we win"/"they win"). . . . Whoever brings up the heavy artillery of comparative ethnology, cultural anthropology and sociology against such devices is told that he is using a cannon to shoot sparrows, since it is merely a matter of entertainment; once he falls silent, the voices of the apologists for the culture-shaping, anticipative, predictive and mythopoeic role of SF are raised anew. (pp. 56-7)

Is creative work without mystification possible in such an en-vironment? An answer to this question is given by the stories of Philip K. Dick. While these stand out from the background against which they have originated, it is not easy to capture the ways in which they do, since Dick employs the same ma-terials and theatrical props as other American writers. From the warehouse which has long since become their common property, he takes the whole threadbare lot of telepaths, cosmic wars, parallel worlds, and time travel. In his stories terrible catastrophes happen, but this too is no exception to the rule, for lengthening the list of sophisticated ways in which the world can end is among the standard preoccupations of SF. But where other SF writers explicitly name and delimit the source of the disaster, whether social (terrestrial or cosmic war) or natural (elemental forces of nature), the world of Dick's stories suffers dire changes for reasons which remain unascertainable to the end. People perish not because a nova or a war has erupted, not because of flood, famine, plague, draught, or sterility, nor because the Martians have landed on our doorstep; rather, there is some inscrutable factor at work which is visible in its man-ifestations but not at its source, and the world behaves as if it has fallen prey to a malignant cancer which through metastases attacks one area of life after another. (p. 57)

The forces which bring about world debacle in Dick's books are fantastic, but they are not merely invented *ad hoc* to shock the readers. We shall show this on the example of *Ubik,* a work which, by the way, can also be regarded as a fantastic grotesque, a "macabresque" with obscure allegorical subtexts, decked out in the guise of ordinary SF.

If, however, it is viewed as a work of SF proper the contents of *Ubik* can be most simply summarized as follows:

Telepathic phenomena, having been mastered in the context of capitalistic society, have undergone commercialization like every other technological innovation. So businessmen hire te-lepaths to steal trade secrets from their competitors, and the latter for their part defend themselves against this "extrasensory industrial espionage'' with the aid of ''inertials,'' people whose psyches nullify the ''psi field'' that makes it possible to receive others' thoughts. By way of specialization, firms have sprung up which rent out telepaths and ''inertials'' by the hour, and the ''strong man'' Glen Runciter is the proprietor of such a firm. The medical profession has learned how to arrest the agony of victims of mortal ailments, but still has no means of curing them. Such people are therefore kept in a state of ''half-life'' in special institutions, ''moratoriums'' (a kind of ''places of postponement''—of death, obviously). If they merely rested there unconscious in their icy caskets, that would be small comfort for their surviving kin. So a technique has been developed for maintaining the mental life of such people in ''cold-pac.'' The world which they experience is not part of reality, but a fiction created by appropriate methods. None the less, normal people can make contact with the frozen ones, for the cold-sleep apparatus has means to this end built into it, something on the order of a telephone. (pp. 57-8)

Numerous dilemmas arise here: should the ''half-lifer'' be informed of his condition? is it right to keep him under the illusion that he is leading a normal life?

According to *Ubik,* people who, like Runciter's wife, have spent years in cold sleep are well aware of the fact. It is another matter with those who, like Joe Chip, have come close to meeting with a violent end and have regained consciousness imagining that they have escaped death, whereas in fact they are resting in a moratorium. In the book, it must be admitted, this is an unclear point, which is however masked by another dilemma: for, if the world of the frozen person's experiences is a purely subjective one, then any intervention in that world from outside must be for him a phenomenon which upsets the normal course of things. So if someone communicates with the frozen one, as Runciter does with Chip, this contact is accompanied in Chip's experiences by uncanny and startling phenomena—for it is as if waking reality were breaking into the midst of a dream ''only from one side,'' without thereby causing extinction of the dream and wakening of the sleeper (who, after all, cannot wake up like a normal man because he is not a normal man). But, to go a step further, is not contact also possible between two frozen individuals? Might not one of these people dream that he is alive and well and that from his accustomed world he is communicating with the other one—that only the other person succumbed to the unfortunate mishap? This too is possible. And, finally, is it possible to imagine a wholly infallible technology? There can be no such thing. Hence certain perturbations may affect the subjective world of the frozen sleeper, to whom it will then seem that his environment is going mad—perhaps that in it even *time* is falling to pieces! Interpreting the events presented in this fashion, we come to the conclusion that all the principal characters of the story were killed by the bomb on the Moon, and consequently all of them had to be placed in the moratorium and from this point on the book recounts only their visions and illusions. (p. 58)

If we approach the fictional world pedantically, no case can be made for it, for it is full of contradictions. But if we shelve such objections and inquire rather after the overall meaning of the work, we will discover that it is close to the meanings of other books by Dick, for all that they seem to differ from one another. Essentially it is always one and the same world which figures in them—a world of elementally unleashed entropy, of decay which not only, as in our reality, attacks the harmonious arrangement of matter, but which even consumes the order of

elapsing time. Dick has thus amplified, rendered monumental and at the same time monstrous certain fundamental properties of the actual world, giving them dramatic acceleration and impetus. All the technological innovations, the magnificent inventions and the newly mastered human capabilities (such as telepathy, which our author has provided with an uncommonly rich articulation into ''specialties'') ultimately come to nothing in the struggle against the inexorably rising floodwaters of Chaos. Dick's province is thus a ''world of pre-established disharmony,'' which is hidden at first and does not manifest itself in the opening scenes of the novel; these are presented unhurriedly and with calm matter-of-factness, just in order that the intrusion of the destructive factor should be all the more effective. . . . In a world smitten with insanity, in which even the chronology of events is subject to convulsions, it is only the people who preserve their normality. So Dick subjects them to the pressure of a terrible testing, and in his fantastic experiment only the psychology of the characters remains non-fantastic. They struggle bitterly and stoically to the end, like Joe Chip in the current instance, against the chaos pressing on them from all sides, the sources of which remain, actually, unfathomable, so that in this regard the reader is thrown back on his own conjectures.

The peculiarities of Dick's worlds arise especially from the fact that in them it is waking reality which undergoes profound dissociation and duplication. . . . The end-effect is always the same: distinguishing between waking reality and visions proves to be impossible. The technical aspect of this phenomenon is fairly inessential—it does not matter whether the splitting of reality is brought about by a new technology of chemical manipulation of the mind or, as in *Ubik,* by one of surgical operations. The essential point is that a world equipped with the means of splitting perceived reality into indistinguishable likenesses of itself creates practical dilemmas that are known only to the theoretical speculations of philosophy. (p. 59)

There is no question of using a meticulous factual bookkeeping to strike a rational balance for the novel, by virtue of which it would satisfy the demands of common sense. We are not only forced to but we ought to at a certain point leave off defending its ''science-fictional nature'' also for a *second reason* so far unmentioned. The first reason was dictated to us simply by necessity: given that the elements of the work lack a focal point, it *cannot* be rendered consistent. The second reason is more essential: the impossibility of imposing consistency on the text compels us to seek its global meanings not in the realm of events themselves, but in that of their constructive principle, the very thing that is responsible for lack of focus. If no such meaningful principle were discoverable, Dick's novels would have to be called mystifications, since any work must justify itself either on the level of what it presents literally or on the level of deeper semantic content, not so much overtly present in as summoned up by the text. Indeed, Dick's works teem with non sequiturs, and any sufficiently sensitive reader can without difficulty make up lists of incidents which flout logic and experience alike. But . . . what is inconsistency in literature? It is a symptom either of incompetence or else of repudiation of some values (such as credibility of incidents or their logical coherence) for the sake of other values.

Here we come to a ticklish point in our discussion, since the values alluded to cannot be objectively compared. There is no universally valid answer to the question whether it is permissible to sacrifice order for the sake of vision in a creative work—everything depends on what kind of order and what kind of vision are involved. (p. 60)

Dick is, so I instinctively judge, perfidious in that he does not give unambiguous answers to the questions provoked by reading him, in that he strikes no balances and explains nothing "scientifically," but rather just confounds things not only in the plot itself but with respect to a superordinated category: the literary *convention* within which the story unfolds. For all that *Galactic Pot-Healer* leans toward allegory, it does not adopt this position either unambiguously or definitively, and a like indeterminacy as to genre is also characteristic for other novels by Dick, perhaps to an even higher degree. We thus encounter here the same difficulty about genre placement of a work which we have met with in the writing of Kafka. (p. 61)

[The] convention of SF requires rational accounting for events that are quite improbable and even seemingly at odds with logic and experience. On the other hand, the evolution of literary genres is based precisely on violation of storytelling conventions which have already become static. So Dick's novels in some measure violate the convention of SF, which can be *accounted to him as* merit, because they thereby acquire broadened meanings having allegorical import. . . . His novels throw many readers accustomed to standard SF into abiding confusion, and give rise to complaints, as naive as they are wrathful, that Dick, instead of providing "precise explanations" by way of conclusion, instead of solving puzzles, sweeps things under the rug. (pp. 61-2)

A second characteristic trait of Dick's work, after its ambiguity as to genre, is its tawdriness which is not without a certain charm. . . . Dick has a rule taken over a rubble of building materials from the run-of-the-mill American professionals of SF, frequently adding a true gleam of originality to already worn-out concepts and, what is surely more important, erecting with such material constructions truly his own. The world gone mad, with a spasmodic flow of time and a network of causes and effects which wriggles as if nauseated, the world of frenzied physics, is unquestionably his invention, being an inversion of our familiar standard according to which only we, but never our environment, may fall victim to psychosis. Ordinarily, the heroes of SF are overtaken only by two kinds of calamities: the social, such as the "infernos of police-state tyranny," and the physical, such as catastrophes caused by Nature. Evil is thus inflicted on people either by other people (invaders from the stars are merely people in monstrous disguises), or by the blind forces of matter.

With Dick the very basis of such a clearcut articulation of the proposed diagnosis comes to grief. We can convince ourselves of this by putting to *Ubik* questions of the order just noted: who was responsible for the strange and terrible things which happened to Runciter's people? The bomb attack on the Moon was the doing of a competitor, but of course it was not in his power to bring about the collapse of time. An explanation appealing to the medical "cold-pac" technology is . . . likewise incapable of rationalizing everything. The gaps that separate the fragments of the plot cannot be eliminated, and they lead one to suspect the existence of some higher-order necessity which constitutes the destiny of Dick's world. Whether this destiny resides in the temporal sphere or beyond it is impossible to say. When one considers to what an extent our faith in the infallible beneficence of technical progress has already waned, the fusion which Dick envisages between culture and nature, between the instrument and its basis, by virtue of which it acquires the aggressive character of a malignant neoplasm, no longer seems merely sheer fantasy. This is not to say that Dick is predicting any concrete future. The disintegrating worlds of

his stories, as it were inversions of Genesis, order returning to Chaos—this is not so much the future foreseen as it is future shock, not straightforwardly expressed but embodied in fictional reality, it is an objectivized projection of the fears and fascinations proper to the human individual in our times.

It has been customary to identify the downfall of civilization falsely and narrowly with regression to some past stage of history. . . . Such an evasion is often employed in SF, since inadequacy of imagination takes refuge in oversimplified pessimism. Then we are shown the remotest *future* as a lingering state of feudal, tribal or slave-holding society, inasmuch as atomic war or invasion from the stars is supposed to have hurled humanity backward. . . . [But works using this resort] merely reveal an insufficiency of sociological imagination, for which the atomic war or the interstellar invasion is only a convenient pretext for spinning out interminable sagas of primordial tribal life under the pretense of portraying the farthest future. (pp. 62-3)

Such expedients are foreign to Dick. For him, the development of civilization continues, but is as it were crushed by itself, becoming monstrous at the heights of its achievement. . . .

Alarm at the impetus of civilization finds expression nowadays in the slogans of a "return to Nature" after smashing and discarding everything "artificial," i.e. science and technology. These pipe dreams turn up also in SF. Happily, they are absent in Dick. The action of his novels takes place in a time when there can no longer be any talk of return to nature or of turning away from the "artificial," since the fusion of the "natural" with the "artificial" has long since become an accomplished fact.

At this point it may be worthwhile to point out the dilemma encountered by futuristically oriented SF. According to an opinion quite generally held by readers, SF ought to depict the world of the fictional future no less explicitly and intelligibly than a writer such as [Honore dé] Balzac depicted the world of his own time in *The Human Comedy*. Whoever asserts this fails to take into account the fact that there exists no world beyond or above history and common to all eras or all cultural formations of mankind. That which, as the world of *The Human Comedy*, strikes us as completely clear and intelligible, is not an altogether objective reality, but is only a particular interpretation . . . of a world classified, understood and experienced in a concrete fashion. The familiarity of Balzac's world thus signifies nothing more than the simple fact that we have grown perfectly accustomed to this account of reality and that consequently the language of Balzac's characters, their culture, their habits and ways of satisfying spiritual and bodily needs, and also their attitude toward nature and transcendence seem to us transparent. (p. 63)

[The] image of the future world cannot be limited to adding a certain number of technical innovations, and meaningful prediction does not lie in serving up the present larded with startling improvements or revelations in lieu of the future. . . .

Situations and concepts can be understood only through relating them to ones already known, but when too great a time interval separates people living in different eras there is a loss of the basis for understanding in common life experiences which we unreflectingly and automatically imagine to be invariant. It follows that an author who truly succeeded in delineating an image of the far future would not achieve literary success, since he would assuredly not be understood. Consequently, in Dick's stories a truth-value can be ascribed only to their generalized basis, which can be summed up more or less as follows: when people become ants in the labyrinths of the technosphere which they themselves have built, the idea of a return to Nature not only becomes utopian but cannot even be meaningfully articulated, because no such thing as a Nature that has not been artificially transformed has existed for ages. . . .

The impossibility of civilization's returning to Nature, which is simply equivalent to the irreversibility of history, leads Dick to the pessimistic conclusion that looking far into the future becomes such a fulfilment of dreams of power over matter as converts the idea of progress into a monstrous caricature. This conclusion does not inevitably follow from the author's assumptions, but it constitutes an eventuality which ought *also* to be taken into account. By the way, in putting things thus we are no longer summarizing Dick's work, but are giving rein to reflections about it, for the author himself seems so caught up in his vision that he is unconcerned about either its literal plausibility or its non-literal message. . . . Dick has presented us not so much with finished *accomplishments* as with fascinating *promises*. (p. 64)

The writings of Philip Dick have deserved at least a better fate than that to which they were destined by their birthplace. If they are neither of uniform quality nor fully realized, still it is only by brute force that they can be jammed into that pulp of materials, destitute of intellectual value and original structure, which makes up SF. Its fans are attracted by the worst in Dick— the typical dash of American SF, reaching to the stars, and the headlong pace of action moving from one surprise to the next— but they hold it against him that, instead of unraveling puzzles, he leaves the reader at the end on the battlefield, enveloped in the aura of a mystery as grotesque as it is strange. Yet his bizarre blendings of hallucinogenic and palingenetic techniques have not won him many admirers outside the ghetto walls [of science fiction], since there readers are repelled by the shoddiness of the props he has adopted from the inventory of SF. Indeed, these writings sometimes fumble their attempts; but I remain after all under their spell, as it often happens at the sight of a lone imagination's efforts to cope with a shattering superabundance of opportunities—efforts in which even a partial defeat can resemble a victory. (pp. 66-7)

Stanislaw Lem, "Philip K. Dick: A Visionary among the Charlatans," translated by Robert Abernathy, in Science-Fiction Studies, *Vol. 2, No. 5, March, 1975, pp. 54-67.*

ROGER ZELAZNY

Brian Aldiss has called [Philip Dick] "one of the masters of present-day discontents", a thing readily apparent in much of his work. But one of the great fascinations his work holds for me is the effects achieved when he dumps these discontents into that special machine in his head and turns on the current. It is not simply that I consider it a form of aesthetic cheating to compare one writer with another, but I cannot think of another writer with whom to compare Philip Dick. Aldiss suggests [Luigi] Pirandello, which is not bad for the one small aspect of reality shuffling. But Pirandello's was basically a destructive machine. It was a triumph of technique over convention, possessed of but one basic message no matter what was fed into the chopper. Philip Dick's is a far more complicated program. His management of a story takes you from here to there in a God-knows-how, seemingly haphazard fashion, which, upon reflection, follows a logical line of development—

but only on reflection. While you are trapped within the spell of its telling, you are in no better position than one of its invariably overwhelmed characters when it comes to seeing what will happen next.

The characters are often victims, prisoners, manipulated men and women. It is generally doubtful whether they will leave the world with less evil in it than they found there. But you never know. They try. (p. 3)

The worlds through which Philip Dick's characters move are subject to cancellation or revision without notice. Reality is approximately as dependable as a politician's promise. Whether it is a drug, a time-warp, a machine or an alien entity responsible for the bewildering shifting of situations about his people, the result is the same: Reality, of the capital "R" variety, has become as relative a thing as the dryness of our respective Martinis. Yet the struggle goes on, the fight continues. Against what? Ultimately, Powers, Principalities, Thrones, and Dominations, often contained in hosts who are themselves victims, prisoners, manipulated men and women.

All of which sounds like grimly serious fare. Wrong. Strike the "grimly", add a comma and the following: but one of the marks of Philip Dick's mastery lies in the tone of his work. He is possessed of a sense of humour for which I am unable to locate an appropriate adjective. Wry, grotesque, slapstick, satirical, ironic . . . None of them quite fits to the point of generality, though all may be found without looking too far. His characters take pratfalls at the most serious moments; pathetic irony may invade the most comic scene. It is a rare and estimable quality to direct such a show successfully. (pp. 3-4)

I have read almost all of Philip Dick's stories and I have never put down a single one with that feeling all readers know at some time or other, that a writer has cheated, has taken an easy way out, rather than addressing himself with his full abilities to the issues he has invoked. Philip Dick is an honest writer in this respect—or, if I am wrong and he does ever handle something in the other fashion, then it is a tribute to his artistry that he succeeds so well in concealing it.

Inventiveness. Wit. Artistic integrity. Three very good things to have. To say them, however, is perhaps to talk more about the mind behind the words than the ends to which they are addressed. For to say them in all good-intentioned honesty about a story results mainly in a heaping of abstractions.

A story is a series of effects. I owned at the beginning that Philip Dick's effects fascinate me even more than the social discontents pulsing through the neon tube in front of the wrinkled mirror suspended by the piano wire from the windmill of his mind. He is a writer's writer, rich enough in fancy that he can afford to throw away in a paragraph ideas another writer might build a book upon. I cannot detail these effects. But then, I could not have written the label for the Ubik can either. It is the variety and near-surreal aptness of his juxtapositions which defends this matter, too, against facile categorisation. The subjective response, however, when a Philip Dick book has been finished and put aside is that, upon reflection, it does not seem so much that one holds the memory of a story; rather, it is the after effects of a poem rich in metaphor that seem to remain.

This I value, partly because it does defy a full mapping, but mainly because that which is left of a Philip Dick story when the details have been forgotten is a thing which comes to me at odd times and offers me a feeling or a thought; therefore, a thing which leaves me richer for having known it. (p. 4)

Roger Zelazny, in an introduction to Philip K Dick: Electric Shepherd, *edited by Bruce Gillespie, Norstrilia Press, 1975, pp. 3-4.*

BRUCE GILLESPIE

[The following essay was written in 1967 and first published in a shortened form in SF Commentary, *January, 1969.]*

Nobody has ever accused Dick of being stupid, unoriginal, or dull, but no reviewer I've ever seen has been able to put his finger on the ways in which Dick is intelligent, original, and fascinating. One can but try.

Part of the problem is that Philip Dick's novels have several characteristics which divide him from other sf writers, and tend to sever communication with the average sf reader. As one can point out so easily, long passages in his books, although seldom whole books, are badly written by any standards. (p. 10)

Dick also shows some of the sentimentality we generally associate with the *other* sf writers, but his direction usually heads away from this approach. When sentimentality does appear in full soporific splendour (Barney Mayerson and Emily Hnatt in *The Three Stigmata of Palmer Eldritch,* for example), usually it is so undermined by the framework of the novel that it becomes necessary rather than repellent.

These complaints are quibbles, at best, but they are factors that prevent Dick from writing with the bland smoothness of a John Wyndham or an Arthur Clarke. I am not saying that other types of sf writers are masters of language or are not subject to sentimentality. However, I do think that the faults of the older professionals do not disturb and annoy the reader in quite the way Dick's faults do. His best writing stands in glaring contrast with his worst.

Other features of his writing cut him adrift far more noticeably from both his fellow writers and from sf readers. Most disturbing are the illogicalities of plot and character with which he tends to undermine what might otherwise be regarded as "perfect" stories in the best of American sf traditions. In many of his novels (although he tows the line in his short stories) he appears to set himself and the reader a multi-obstacle race which both writer and reader have only a fair chance of completing. The reader drops out first, and nurses a bruised and weary sensibility to the end of the race. Afterwards he files a strong internal protest, and either refuses to take up the challenge again or approaches the next Dick book with great trepidation. (pp. 10-11)

The sheer weight of "ideas", symbols, plot factors, or whatever can be suffocating. They are introduced at surprising intervals, and are juggled around in dismaying succession. At first sight, the whole book might seem alien to even the most hard-boiled sf reader.

Dick's noticeable inability (shared by nearly all other sf writers) in the field of "characterisation" has its own drawbacks. In each of Dick's novels, all the action is seen through the mind's eye of one or other of his characters. Dick's use of the "viewpoint character" has its own special brilliance. However, such an obviously managed character elicits about as much sympathy from the reader as his favourite television camera. Therefore the centre of identification should fall back on the shoulders of the author, as in [Henry] Fielding's *Tom Jones.* However,

all we are ever likely to see of Dick's face in his own novels is a mocking smile. This technique leaves even his best work oddly centreless. Other sf authors solve this problem by using only one character as the viewpoint of the novel. This reinforces the suspense element of the story, and gains sympathy for the protagonist. But Dick's novels are jigsaw patterns of identifications. In few of his novels does Dick bother to complete the picture. (p. 11)

Between the reviewers and myself, it is extremely difficult to locate exactly the source of Dick's fascination to readers and his undoubted importance to students of sf. The traditional approach . . . (criticism in terms of Plot-Character-Description) raises more problems than it solves. It is only in novels such as *The Three Stigmata of Palmer Eldritch,* in which Dick punches his way out of his self-made paperbag, that we find a clue to his real power.

In this novel Dick finds a central symbol that is adequate to the whole book—the figure of Palmer Eldritch himself. However, this central idea is not so much important for what it shows about Dick's use of Plot or Characters, or because it is such a good "idea". To approach Eldritch or the novel itself in this way, is to see the flame and the cloud, feel the blast and wind, and not to notice the exploding atomic bomb. (p. 13)

[During the course of the book], Dick traces the conversion of the whole of existence into the playground of Eldritch's mind. The figure that was merely mythic at the beginning of the novel has become Godlike by the end. We are faced with a world where the mere idea of a benevolent, or even omnipotent God, seems ludicrous. Humanity is completely cut off from these resources of both objective and spiritual reality that usually give us the self-assurance to keep living.

How does Dick do it? How does he prevent the book from becoming as mad as the world pictured?

Most obviously, because of his own intelligence and toughmindedness which can evaluate chaos without falling into it or indulging himself in it. No author, however great, could create this book and survive, if he really extended his own resources and conducted a completely radical inquiry into the nature of people under such stress. After all, what is left of people after they are subjected to such pressure? Dick cannot create characters (rather than "viewpoints") who are strong enough to be called representatives of humanity. Dick's own attitude is still too abstract and limited to appreciate the full implications of the world of *Palmer Eldritch.* But Dick does not conduct his novel like a [Fëdor Mikhailovich] Dostoyevsky. Dick's prose is its own excellent "melodrama", the compact, brilliantly (rather than extensively) imaginative prose of a [Victor] Hugo, of a [Charles] Dickens at his best, and of a very small number of other science fiction writers. From this point of view, *The Three Stigmata of Palmer Eldritch* is one of the few masterpieces of recent science fiction.

Although it is a touchstone, *The Three Stigmata of Palmer Eldritch* is only one of many Philip Dick books, and is certainly not representative of his usual methods. It is a summit, so the vegetation on the slopes can have quite a different hue.

Possibly the best book to discuss in contrast with *Palmer Eldritch* is the over-rated Hugo winner, *The Man in the High Castle.* . . . Although the reviewers unanimously call this Dick's best book, and despite the Hugo Award itself, I can still admire the book only partially, and scratch my head, wondering what the fanfare was about.

To some extent, *The Man in the High Castle* is a textbook demonstration of Dick's best qualities. The prose is never less than incisive and the *average* effect is probably as good as in *The Three Stigmata of Palmer Eldritch*. For instance, the first paragraphs of the novel catch a mood of sharply observed normality that, at the same time, warns the reader that much information has been withheld. (p. 15)

Apologists for *The Man in the High Castle* have paid special attention to the kinds of writing in the novel that are new for Dick, and probably unique within his work. In Chapter 14, Dick comes closest in any of his writing to a genuine exploration of the emotions and intellectual standing of one of his characters. Mr Nobusuku Tagomi, the Trade Mission official and expert in the *I Ching,* finds his world crumbling under the pressure of the events of the novel. Dick's writing is as powerfully abstract as ever but, for once, Dick is more concerned with his character as a victim than as a mere viewpoint. One need only compare Barney Mayerson (whose personal suffering is never a point of issue) and Tagomi to see the difference. Dick's wider perceptions within this novel go to waste. As in all of his novels, Dick is not content to explore the viewpoint of one particular character. The variety of characters and the alternation between them is far more dismaying in *The Man in the High Castle* than it was in *The Three Stigmata of Palmer Eldritch*. (pp. 15-16)

The problem is that each of these characters has equal status in the plot, or the reasons are left unclear why some characters are emphasised more than others. If Dick adopts this highly patterned structure to keep readers interested, then he fails. Because each character is interesting in his or her own right, the reader hopes for long sequences which might develop the possibilities of the main characters. This hope is disappointed; Dick constructs a jigsaw in which no character completes the pattern.

If Dick adopts this structure in order to present a composite picture of a fully imagined world (in which Japan and Germany won the Second World War and together occupy America) then I would say that he fails completely. No character has interests and a viewpoint wide enough to see the whole picture. We know little more about the society of this alternate America at the end of the novel than we did at the beginning. Dick has shown many times that he is no political scientist, and I can only regret his failure to illustrate how such a political system would affect the lives of those who live under it. Compared with *The Three Stigmata of Palmer Eldritch,* whose world is fully developed, but credible only within the novel, *The Man in the High Castle,* more than any other novel that Dick has written, is of the "What if . . .?" variety. However, Dick seems incapable of extrapolating the complete possible effects of fascism on American (unbelievably mild, for most of the characters), or of constructing his *own* bizarre type of novel, in which the reader does not bother to ask if it could "really happen".

The Man in the High Castle seems like a very different book from *The Three Stigmata of Palmer Eldritch*. The problem is that Dick depends on the same sort of manoeuvre as in *Palmer Eldritch* in order to unify and order his book. Dick needs a meaningful central symbol as the axle of his world. However, he tries to turn the book on two central ideas (*I Ching* and Hawthorne Abendsen, the "man in the high castle") and fails to make either of them give movement to the whole book. *I Ching* has the kind of mythic importance that lends suspense and flavour to the novel's proceedings. However, the evocation of the Japanese life-style and the dependence upon a precognitive procedure is ultimately a static device: it *aids* the plot but *is* not the plot; its use does not polarise conflicts and settle issues.

Hawthorne and his book *The Grasshopper Lies Heavy* (a science fiction jaunt in which America and the Allies won the War) are initially even more fascinating to the reader than is *I Ching*. Dick wants Abendsen (who remains vague and mythical to the end of the novel, instead of acquiring the reality of a character) to be the crux of the action. But the last chapter, centring on Abendsen, is a disappointing end to the novel.

The two main symbols, as well as the other fascinating notions that festoon the narrative, and could have been invented only by Philip Dick, eventually have little meaning for the reader. They remain static within the novel. They do not change shape and illuminate the reader's view of the newly created world, but remain merely a part of it. Because Dick is a skilled storyteller, the emptiness of the book does not become apparent until the end, however. *The Man in the High Castle* is like a car full of perfectly working machinery, none of whose pieces connect with each other. The vehicle just does not go. (p. 16)

Bruce Gillespie, "Mad, Mad Worlds: Seven Novels of Philip K Dick," *in* Philip K Dick: Electric Shepherd, *edited by Bruce Gillespie, Norstrilia Press, 1975, pp. 9-21.*

ANGUS TAYLOR

Although it is often noted that Philip K. Dick is concerned with "the nature of reality," the assumption is usually that he is merely playing parlor tricks, that he is a clever sleight-of-hand artist whose entertainments are conjured out of thin air and exhibit little philosophy other than a fashionable nihilism or despair in the face of a universe thought too large and unregulated for comprehension. Yet Dick is far from being the unrelenting pessimist he is often considered. Rather, through his often dark vision he assumes a critical stance against the world-view that informs modern society; beyond this he presents a vision of a brighter world not beyond the reach of those informed of its possibility. But between unexamined reality and affirmed possibility lies an arduous journey: from the destruction of one world of knowledge to the creation of another. Dick's fiction is the story of this journey. (pp. 9-10)

In fiction, and increasingly in the public mind, the gods and demons of yesterday have become the aliens of today. Aliens are symbols of the intrusion of the unknown into the realm of the human—meteorites of mystery and unease buried in the collective human psyche. If the image of the alien plays so large a role in the fiction of Philip K. Dick it is because he deals always with man's fallen state; and it is the realization, often sudden and unexpected, of his condition that initiates the frightful but necessary struggle toward a new reality. (p. 11)

Beyond the well-charted territory of normal human experience, then, is the undiscovered country that puzzles the will. If the alien presence is often the manifestation of a higher order, then the higher order, that reality which lies beyond satisfactory human comprehension, is not necessarily hospitable to the human traveller. (p. 14)

[In *The Three Stigmata of Palmer Eldritch* the] fear of being used, of being a pawn under the control of some greater entity, is . . . apparent in the relation of Barney Mayerson and Leo Bulero to Palmer Eldritch, and raises the question of Dick's preoccupation with forms of schizophrenia. Writing on the subject, R. D. Laing has noted that "if one experiences the other as a free agent, one is open to the possibility of experiencing oneself as an *object* of his experience and thereby of feeling one's own subjectivity drained away. One is threatened with the possibility of becoming no more than a thing in the world of the other, without any life for oneself, without any being for oneself." Palmer Eldritch, the higher entity, possessed intrinsically of greater freedom of action, threatens to turn those of lesser possibility into objects in its *scheme of things*. What Dick is doing is carrying the concept of alienness beyond the societal level, into the region of personal subjectivity. The concept of the alien, which makes its initial appearance in outer space, is carried to its logical conclusion in inner space, where it reappears as *alienation*. It is Dick's compelling fusion of inner and outer space which lends his work much of its power. (p. 15)

Laing writes: "If there is anything the schizoid individual is likely to believe in, it is his own destructiveness. He is unable to believe that he can fill his own emptiness without reducing what is there to nothing. He regards his own love and that of others as being as destructive as hatred . . . He descends into a vortex of non-being in order to avoid being, but also to preserve being from himself." *We Can Build You* provides another illustration of this; it is a novel concerned very consciously with the descent into schizophrenia and with love "as destructive as hatred." Schizophrenia is also a central theme in *Clans of the Alphane Moon,* in which Dick constructs a whole society divided among groups exhibiting various forms of mental illness, in *Martian Time-Slip* and, on a metaphoric level, in *Do Androids Dream of Electric Sheep?*

This recurrent use of the schizophrenia theme illustrates Dick's concern with the mechanistic reduction of human relations to states of being that are unable to maintain themselves against the destructive forces of nature. For Dick, the natural tendency of a universe stripped of creative human meaning is entropic regression toward a state of chaos and anomie, and he sees the tendency everywhere, even in the steady accumulation of "kipple," or useless objects, like junk mail or empty match folders, in an apartment. (pp. 16-17)

Jason Taverner, famous television personality in *Flow My Tears, the Policeman Said,* awakes one morning to find that no one else remembers who he is, that he has no secure legal status in society, and must live by his wits from moment to moment. The bottom has dropped out of the world he always accepted as reality and took for granted. Into his life has come the unknown, the unexplained, the primal chaos and isolation that underlies the *Augenblick* of stability that man has imposed on nature. Throughout Dick's work there is this continual opening of the abyss, which recalls the intention of the Surrealist movement, announced in its "Declaration of 27 January 1925," to prove to human beings "how fragile their thoughts are, and on what unstable foundations, over what cellars they have erected their unsteady houses."

The presence of the abyss reveals Dick's position as fundamentally existential. [Jean-Paul] Sartre's dictum that man is "condemned to be free" neatly sums up Dick's view of man's place in the universe. This is the position from which Dick begins, the starting point for his fictional explorations. The social order is not predetermined, fixed, or constant; the elemental, impersonal forces of the cosmos itself militate against the maintenance of any secure human reality. All roads in his fiction lead to this apocalyptic revelation (though they do not

end there). When "objective" social reality breaks down, the individual is starkly confronted with the problem of dealing anew with the world beyond himself, of coming to terms with the non-self. The individual divided from his social and physical surroundings is likely to become increasingly divided against himself. Alienation implies a lack of integration with an environment perceived as unrelated to oneself and beyond control. "It is a splitting apart of the two worlds, inner and outer, so that neither registers on the other." . . . More specifically, this lack of interaction is at the level of personal experience or the animate; the exchange between inner and outer space has been reduced to the simply mechanical. (pp. 17-19)

Unlike many other writers, Philip K. Dick has not hesitated to inject his science fiction with a liberal infection of chaos. The return of *alienated* Thors Provoni or Palmer Eldritch from the interstellar void shatters the statistical regularities of the familiar solar system; the alien presence announces the intrusion into human affairs of a different order of existence, manifesting itself as fate or divine will. In a literature that has prided itself on rational extrapolation and shunned the chaos implicit in more outright forms of fantasy, such a quantum leap into the unexpected strikes a note very close to heresy. This is not to say that flights of fantasy, manifestations of the divine, auguries of new universes have been absent from science fiction, but that their relevance to the field has tended to be downgraded as technicians have set about carefully graphing themselves into the future or churning out entertaining re-runs of plots signifying little.

Dick is not the first to understand the importance of the improbable as a method of casting light on the possible. [H. G.] Wells understood implicitly that the real purpose of science fiction, apart from its value as entertainment, was to describe the evolving potentials of man-in-society, and that technology stood at the nexus between man and his continually changing relationship with the world around him. (pp. 21-2)

Yet even Wells maintained that the kind of fantasy he wrote should be based on a *single* fantastic premise; apart from this the author should strive to make the details of his story as realistic as possible. It was only by keeping the rest of the story as close to everyday reality as possible that the fantastic aspect gained credibility. Otherwise, the story would inevitably degenerate into senseless contrivance. Science fiction, which has tended to look upon itself as the kind of "realistic" literature referred to by [Robert A.] Heinlein, has generally been loath to stray far from the path prescribed by Wells.

Not so Philip Dick. Dick everywhere violates Wells' prescription of a single fantastic premise. And if there are sf writers not bound by the old principle, few, if any, are willing to go as far as Dick in denying the necessity of anchoring one's fiction in a reality the reader can believe. In fact, Dick generally goes out of his way to *prevent* the reader from accepting the fictional world before him as "normal," "ordinary," or believable in any everyday sense. For Dick, the details of everyday reality are fantastic. Everyday reality does not remain constant, either subjectively or objectively, and therefore it is not the implications of a single trend or occurrence he is investigating, but the implications of complex trends or multiple occurrences. Dick is a pioneer of the "post-Wellsian system" of multiple-premise "fantastic realism" anticipated by Julius Kagarlitski. (p. 22)

[A] dreamlike quality is accentuated by the interchangeability and mutability of Dick's landscapes. Places are seldom described in detail—or at least not in any characteristic detail that might lend them an air of uniqueness. Zurich, Switzerland, is indistinguishable from Marin County, California, in Dick's techno-dreamworld of the future. Or, to look at it another way, it might be said that the transient mass-production artificial environment of California has swallowed up the entire world in most of his stories. It is a lack of permanence, of rootedness—a lack of *solidity*—that marks the settings of these stories. The material world is almost wholly man-made and is locked in a dialectic with the human consciousness. Here, where fiction exists in a dialectical relationship with reality, the outrageous can be commonplace. In *Counter-Clock World* Dick does not hesitate to conceive a world in which metabolic processes run backward, so that persons greet each other with "good-bye" and bodies rise from the grave, revitalized, to grow younger. The merging of the literal and the symbolic infuses the world with new meaning, so that inner experience is writ large upon the face of outer environment. Dick's work is characterized by what John Brunner has called "an almost hallucinatory sharpness of detail"—but it is a sharpness of detail that extends beyond mere enumerative naturalism to the very quality of objects themselves: a magic realism in which things are seen double, simultaneously familiar and unexpected. (p. 24)

Talking doors, suitcases that act as psychiatrists, newspapers that publish themselves, "creditor jet-balloons" with articulation circuits, rats clutching crude weapons—it is a world subjectively anthropomorphized and at the same time *not* anthropomorphized, but merely displaying its objective dialectical response to the human. If Dick's stories are filled with objects and machines that mimic life, and life forms that more specifically imitate human forms, this is neither more nor less than the imaginatively logical extension to the world at large of the common robot figure in the literature.

The robot in science fiction is not simply a mechanism, nor is it, simply, a human being in disguise. It is both and neither. In addition to its morphological and functional relatedness to its organic analogues, it assumes a symbolic role in the literature. . . . Dick has simply infused his entire panoply of fictional props with intimations of . . . larger significance. Thus, like the robot, other objects, natural or artificial, may participate with human beings in a single universe. (pp. 25-6)

His characters move through intensely *manufactured* landscapes, built primarily upon human interaction, and devoid of solid external furniture. In their fantastic secondary worlds, without matrices of the commonplace, they are constantly blundering, appalled, against the ragged edges of nothingness. Jory's incomplete half-life stage-front world in *Ubik* can be taken as a paradigm of Dick's fictional constructions. (p. 26)

Dick's language, besides being usually quite colloquial, also contains some delightful quirks, such as exhibited when his characters occasionally correct each other's grammar or assist each other in recalling literary quotations.

Lack of scenery promotes detachment from even a fictional "objective" reality and enhances the argument for the subjective. Even the objectivity implied in viewing events consistently from the standpoint of a single character falls by the wayside in many of Dick's stories, as he shifts the focus among his several protagonists—and this is made a deliberate narrative ploy in *A Maze of Death*. . . . Style reinforces vision at this point, and what may appear as serious defects in style from

one critical vantage become logical moves from another, given this particular writer's will to his particular vision.

In degrading the solidity of his scenery Dick waves a red flag in the reader's face. He undermines the illusion that sf can be entirely divorced from fantasy, that it is futurology, extrapolation, or prediction. He undermines the plot in its superficial aspect by throwing roadblocks in the way of the smooth succession of events, and asks us to divert our attention, to search out and accept the poetic core of the work; he tries to focus our attention on the plot as a "net" for catching something strange and otherworldly. The difficulty many readers have in accepting Dick's fiction may thus spring from their extrapolative bias, and their lack of interest in sf as a form of poetry. Where other authors may clothe their poetic themes in relatively "realistic" or futurological plots—perhaps bowing, however unconsciously, in the direction of the naturalistic standards that have dominated literature until recently—Dick is more unashamedly aware of sf's intimate association with fantasy.

Dick's style is inextricably tied to his world-view, his conception of a universe laced with a good dash of existential absurdity. . . . Dick's fictions, while they may delight some and baffle others, are characterized by a wonderful inventiveness, unencumbered by convention, and limited only by the demands of internal logic. The range of invention in his stories, his extravagant style, his outrageous humor—all attest to a developed sense of play. Bruce Gillespie has aptly referred to *Dr. Bloodmoney* as one of Dick's "circuses" [see excerpt above] and it is truly a three-ring atmosphere of marvels that is conjured up in many of his stories.

If the world is worth examining, then it is worth examining with a slightly jaundiced eye. For Dick, a sense of the ridiculous is inseparable from a true vision of the startling, everyday world. Admittedly, there may be a tendency to get carried away sometimes. . . . But in general Dick's madcap antics work, for he has a deft sense for the absurd amid the commonplace of life. His straight-faced wackiness may seem incongruous in the context of the issues he tackles, but then he has always worked through juxtaposing seemingly incongruous elements and making of them multifaceted wholes. (pp. 27-8)

In Dick's universe the "normal" orderly reality of the human world exists only precariously; this delicately constructed negentropic reality exists only through the systemic configurations of human society. Persons who allow themselves to become separated from the society of their fellows are in that much more danger of having their individual realities undermined. (p. 34)

The failure of an individual to integrate himself with reality as defined through learned cultural values results in the breakdown of his perception of that reality. (pp. 34-5)

Human perception of the world is a function of social interaction. And here we approach the heart of Dick's work; in his fiction he presents an unsystematic series of explorations into the sociology of knowledge.

The need of humans for the company of their fellows is not only perceptual, but spiritual as well. The detachment and introversion of the schizophrenic reduces his ability to experience the presence of others in a meaningful way. The authentic human experience—"man's specific humanity"—is identified by Dick with the capacity for *empathy*. Thus human society is seen not only as the basis of secure reality, but also as the vehicle for the expression of man's authentic nature. (pp. 35-6)

The struggle between form and chaos rages through all of Dick's work. Life is a function of organization; the vital, creative force is negentropic, in opposition to the entropic tendencies of the universe at large. (p. 39)

And though the struggle is never over in this world, there are always glimmerings of new worlds waiting, and prophets like Wilbur Mercer of *Do Androids Dream of Electric Sheep?* to point the way, however ambiguously—if not in the direction of salvation, then at least toward a kind of self-acceptance and the hope of a new start, in this life or the next. For though corruption touches all the works of humankind, and the body itself must disintegrate, perhaps the *idea* underlying the outward form is permanent, and we can all be reborn. . . . (pp. 39-40)

Empathy or love, the ability of human beings to interact in a meaningful manner, is the foundation on which the ideal world can be constructed. (p. 42)

It should be noted, then, that the ideal, or Platonic, realm in Dick's sense is not given in the meaning of having been imposed from on high; rather, it exists as a goal consciously set by mankind for itself. Out of the ground of human association arise over time new cultural configurations, and today Dick sees us on the verge of another transformation. . . . The world uninformed with a vision of divine animation is reduced to the level of the "merely" mechanical, but, when informed, exhibits life and meaning at all levels, the mechanical included.

The concept of God is not to be confused with that of a transcendental deity; it denotes instead the realization of the human potential through the creation of a better world—a dialectical movement whereby man remakes himself and his environment in the process of becoming reconciled to that environment. Dick's position remains fundamentally existential, but not despairing. . . . (pp. 43-4)

His heroes are relatively ordinary folk, regardless of whether they can divine the future or possess telepathic ability. The characters that populate Dick's fantasies are everyday men and women, together, adrift in an uncommon universe. How they survive, and what they make of their lives, depends to a very large degree on how they relate to each other. (p. 45)

> *Angus Taylor, in his* Philip K. Dick & the Umbrella of Light, *T-K Graphics, 1975, 52 p.*

URSULA K. LeGUIN

Philip K. Dick comes on without fanfare. All his novels are published as science fiction, which limits their "packaging" to purple-monster jackets, ensures but restricts their sales, and, above all, prevents their being noticed by most serious critics or reviewers. His prose is austere, sometimes hasty, always straightforward, with no Nabokovian fiddlefaddle. His characters are ordinary—extraordinarily ordinary—the inept small-businessman, the ambitious organization girl, the minor craftsman or repairman, etc. That some of them have odd talents such as precognition makes no difference, since they inhabit a world where precognition is common; they're just ordinary neurotic precognitive slobs. His humor is dry and zany. . . . Finally, his inventive, intricate plots move on so easily and entertainingly that the reader, guided without effort through the maze, may put the book down believing that he's read a clever sci-fi thriller and nothing more. The fact that what Dick is entertaining us about is reality and madness, time and death, sin and salvation—this has escaped most readers and critics. Nobody notices; nobody notices that we have our own home-grown [Jorge Luis] Borges, and have had him for 30 years.

I think I'm the first to bring up Borges, but Dick has once or twice been compared with Kafka. One cannot take that very far, for Dick is not an absurdist. His moral vocabulary is Christian, though never explicitly so. The last word is not despair. Well as he knows the world of the schizophrenic, the paranoid, even the autistic, his work is not (as Kafka's was) autistic, because there are other people in it; and other people are not (as they are to [Jean-Paul] Sartre) Hell, but salvation. (p. 33)

There are no heroics in Dick's books, but there are heroes. One is reminded of Dickens: what counts is the honesty, constancy, kindness and patience of ordinary people. The flashier qualities such as courage are merely contributory to that dull solid goodness in which—alone—lies the hope of deliverance from evil. . . .

[Dick], like Dickens, keeps a direct line open to the unconscious, it is the powerful personal psychic imprint that dominates in retrospect. Further, his novels are linked by obsessively recurring motifs and details, each of which is itself a key or cue to the nature of reality in the Dick Universe. A disc-jockey circling a planet in a satellite, bringing reassurance to distressed folk on the surface; the android, the person who is (or is schizophrenically perceived to be) a maze of circuitry; the Wonder Drug or process which alters reality, usually toward a shift or overlap of time-planes; precognition; entropy, decay, the tomb-world; the subworld (often a Barbie Doll-type toy): all these themes, and others, interconnect, one or another dominating each book, each implying the others. In the earlier and some recent books, the compulsiveness of the themes is evident, threatening the artist's control. The earlier books, of which *Maze of Death* and *Time Out of Joint* are good examples, suffer somewhat from the tension of overcontrol; and from *Ubik* through *Flow My Tears* a gap has been growing between the expression of rational opinion or belief and the intractable, overwhelming witness of the irrational psyche. When in full control of his dangerous material, Dick has written at least five books which walk the high wire with grace from end to end: *The Man in the High Castle, Dr. Bloodmoney, Martian Time-Slip, Clans of the Alphane Moon* and the extremely funny *Galactic Pot-Healer.*

The task of a writer who writes about madness from within is an appalling one. . . . The price paid is a price no artist, nobody, can be expected to pay; the prize won is invaluable. These are genuine reports from the other side, controlled by the intelligence and skill of an experienced novelist, and illuminated by compassion. . . . And therefore Dick can compress all the shock and splendor of salvation into a few characteristically offhand sentences, and three plain words:

> One of the Bleekman females shyly offered him
> a cigarette from those she carried. Thanking
> her, he accepted it. They continued on.
>
> And as they moved along, Manfred Steiner felt
> something strange happening inside him. He
> was changing.

The shy offer of a cigarette is a thoroughly Dickian gesture of salvation. Nobody ever saves the Galactic Empire from the Tentacled Andromedans. Something has indeed been saved, but only a human soul. We are about as far from the panoply of space opera as we can get. And yet Dick is a science fiction writer—not borrowing the trappings to deck out old nonsense with shiny chromium fittings, but using the new metaphors *because he needs them;* using them with power and beauty, because they are the language appropriate to what he wants to say, to us, about ourselves. Dick is no escapist, and no "futurist." He is a prophet, yes, but in the I Ching sense, in the sense in which poets are prophets: not because he plays foretelling games with [Ayn] Rand, or extrapolates the next technological gimmick, but because his moral vision is desperately clear, and because his art is adequate to express that vision. (p. 34)

> *Ursula K. LeGuin, "Science Fiction As Prophesy,"* in The New Republic, *Vol. 175, No. 18, October 30, 1976, pp. 33-4.*

PHILIP STRICK

Dick does not make easy reading. He lacks the informality of [Arthur C.] Clarke, the vocabulary of [Anthony] Burgess, the pointillism of [John] Fowles. His phrasing is often clumsy, bathetic, despairing, a tangle of moods and impressions hurled like warnings of imminent catastrophe. His characters tumble angrily past as if their appearance in the narrative were an unwelcome distraction. The first paragraphs of a Dick novel habitually plunge us into an environment so intact with images, purposes and objectives as to incline us to reconsider the accuracy of our own perceptions. The typical Dick hero is similarly in a state of confusion, seeing himself as an insignificant component in an elaborate social mechanism requiring effort, conformity and commitment for no very clear reward. The rules of the game may change at any moment, nothing is permanent, and a malignant, vaguely godlike presence monitors his every move in the expectation of failure. Dick's is the science fiction of the average citizen attempting an unremarkable survival in an environment that considers him uninteresting and expendable. Far from the bright, muscular heroic myths of *Star Wars* or *Superman,* it lurks in the dark labyrinths of paranoia.

What renders his work so absorbing is its inventiveness and its humour, dizzyingly based on a lunatic logic. Both are combined in the premise of *Do Androids Dream of Electric Sheep?,* the 1968 novel on which [the film] *Blade Runner* is based. The near eradication of Earth's animal life other than man has resulted in the measurement of wealth by ownership of livestock, and in accordance with a catalogue that gives current values as if for antiques or second-hand cars, people acquire goats, sheep and cows as status symbols. If they can't afford genuine animals, they settle for working models. One of the most valuable creatures listed is the toad, said to have been extinct for years; when, near the end of the book, one is discovered in the desert, hopes of a fabulous reward are high until it proves to have a tiny control panel in its abdomen. Against this bizarre background of pervasive fakery, the erosion of authentic humanity by undetectable android imitations has all the plausibility of a new and lethal plague whereby evolution would become substitution and nobody would notice the difference. The notion is rich with political and metaphysical implications, but Dick pins it firmly on the obvious target of technology through which, should man wish to lift a finger, future prosthetics will do it for him. And in his view, defeat is already in sight. (pp. 169-70)

> *Philip Strick, "The Age of the Replicant," in* Sight and Sound, *Vol. 51, No. 3, Summer, 1982, pp. 168-72.**

PATRICIA S. WARRICK

What is the authentically human? What is the nature of the alien elements that are threatening and vitiating living, intelligent human beings? These questions are deeply rooted in Philip K. Dick's work, and to them he has provided a bizarre variety of answers, answers that are constantly being pushed aside and replaced by new possibilities. Finding an answer to the question of what is truly human and what only masquerades as human is, for Dick, the most important difficulty facing us. Some of Dick's richest metaphors stem from the profusion of electronic devices which populate his near-future wasteland landscapes—electronic constructs that in his early fiction menace the few humans surviving a nuclear holocaust; constructs that, evolving over the years toward ever more human forms, become instructors to man in the search for authenticity and wholeness.

The setting of Dick's near-future fiction is often a twilight world shrouded in smog and dust, decaying into rusty bits and useless debris. "Kipple" accumulates as the process of entropy advances. The wasteland may be a battlefield smouldering in radioactive ash, a vast "junkyard" containing the rotting remnants of West Coast suburbia, or a Martian landscape, virtually lifeless except for the Earth colonists whose electronic constructs assist in nearly fruitless gardening attempts. . . . How is man to survive and remain human in this desert of decay?

Dick's visionary landscape is dark, but not devoid of hope. He shares the arid wasteland view of contemporary culture held by other dystopian writers, but he struggles against capitulation to despair. He throws torches of possibility into the darkness of the future as he sees it. These torches reveal that survival can be achieved not by returning simplistically to an earlier pastoral world view, nor by a destructive repudiation of technology. Instead, technology must be transformed, and in turn man will be transformed. The future—if we survive—will be new, radical, unexpected. It will be a world where, as man and his electronic technology seed each other with possibilities, new forms will begin to appear. (pp. 189-90)

[This essay] will trace the process of Dick's artificial constructs from their first appearances in his short stories of the 1950s, through the mid-1960s, and finally, through the last period, the late 1960s and 70s, when he becomes increasingly obsessed with metaphorical androids—humans who have lost their humanness and become mere mechanical constructs unable to respond with creativity and feeling. This journey through his fiction is indeed a process and not a progression. Dick's world is a world in motion where destinations are never reached, where utopia is never achieved. (p. 190)

To follow the evolution of his electronic constructs through the maze of his large body of fiction is no easy journey. We often become confused, lost, or disoriented. For every path we select, we uneasily suspect that we have neglected another, more fruitful route. But occasionally he lifts us out of the labyrinth, and from this broader perspective we are given fleeting glimpses of hidden patterns and possible meanings.

One such pattern is the evolving reciprocal relationship between man and the artificial constructs (machines) which he builds. From the earliest to the most recent of Dick's fiction, his presentation of machines undergoes a series of transformations. At first he presents electronic constructs as merely automatons; then they become will-less robot-agents of enemy or alien forces, while masquerading as humans. Next, robots become increasingly more like humans, with a sense of personal identity and a concomitant will to survive; and finally robots actually become superior to humans. At the same time, humans follow a reverse process of devolution. They first fight automated machines; next they become more vitalized and machinelike themselves; then they withdraw into schizophrenia as they reject exploitation by economic and political machinery; and finally schizoid humans become like androids, with mechanical programmed personalities.

Electronic devices animate the devastated settings of almost all of Dick's novels. Typically, few animals have survived the radiation fallout, but objects have become animated. (pp. 191-92)

In a number of works, the electronic constructs shift from the background setting to the foreground and become major participants, central characters, in the narrative. The fiction of Dick's first period, the 1950s, is primarily short fiction; its tone is dystopian as it explores the horrors of paranoid militarism, totalitarianism, and the manipulation of people through the mass media. Robots and electronic constructs threaten or actually annihilate humanity in a number of these stories. (p. 192)

[A] major work of interest to our study in Dick's first period is *Vulcan's Hammer* (1960). This novel is preparatory exercise for Dick's subsequent works exploring the theme of totalitarian control, the most notable of which is *The Man in the High Castle* (1962). In *Vulcan's Hammer* a sophisticated computer, Vulcan 3, is used to help run the world government after a devastating war. The totalitarian rule of this machine provokes the hostility of the population, especially that of a fanatical group called The Healers. . . . Vulcan 3 does seemingly paranoid or irrational things. Everyone surrounding the computer is regarded as an enemy to be destroyed. North American Director William Barris, the primary narrator of the novel, wonders whether we have merely anthropomorphized the mechanical construct or whether it really possesses the characteristics of intelligent life. (p. 194)

The military machine, the political machine, the economic machine: these are important concerns for Dick. *Vulcan's Hammer* is his first lengthy study of humans who have become so tightly locked into a rigid structure that their roles as members of the organization form the totality of their lives. He suggests the irrational darkness of the mechanical drive to dominate by killing in his description of Vulcan 3, as "buried at the bottom level of the hidden underground fortress. But it was its voice they were hearing." . . . (p. 195)

In this quotation the computer functions simultaneously and equally on a literal and metaphorical level. The unique richness and depth of Dick's writing may be attributed to the way he fuses the literal and metaphorical so tightly that his images and concepts reverberate in our minds in an almost "stereoscopic" manner. His technique, best described as a complementary process, is to create a fictional world where metaphors from our mundane or everyday world become real: "Computers seem like intelligent beings" becomes "Computers *are* humans." A shift of mental perspective is required to go beneath the surface of the plot and catch the meaning. The fictional image is consciously and deliberately a literal metaphor. Beyond that, in reversal it tells us: Men, driven by unrecognized impulses deeply hidden in the substrata of their minds, become machines who kill.

Dick's next novel, *The Man in the High Castle,* deals further with the theme of the totalitarian state as a machine of domination and destruction. Vulcan 3 now becomes the Nazis, whose paranoid suspicions lead them to plot a sneak nuclear attack on their Japanese allies, whose world view is in many ways the polar opposite of that of the Nazis. This juxtaposition of opposing viewpoints is at this point the essence of the Dickian creative process. Reality is for him a bipolar construction; the closest we can come to grasping it is to mirror in fiction the polarities. (pp. 195-96)

At this early stage in his creative development, Dick looks at one world view from the perspective of its opposite, and then in a separate work reverses the process. Thus *Vulcan's Hammer* is a metaphor for machines as destructive humans; *The Man in the High Castle* is a metaphor for humans become destructive machines. In the novels that follow—for example, *The Penultimate Truth* and *Do Androids Dream of Electric Sheep?*—both views are present in a single work. The skilled reader who has become used to these contradictions "sees" from opposite directions simultaneously. He is rewarded with a fleeting epiphany—Dick's vision of reality as process. (p. 196)

In his prodigiously productive middle period, Dick published a half dozen very-good-to-excellent novels, three of which—*Martian Time-Slip* (1964), *The Three Stigmata of Palmer Eldritch* (1964), and *Dr. Bloodmoney* (1965)—are generally considered his finest works to date. Two of the other novels, *The Penultimate Truth* and *The Simulacra* (both 1964), are competent but unexceptional novels of interest because automata figure significantly in their plots. In this middle period, Dick's attention shifts from the military, his primary subject in the 1950s, to economic and political matters. His use of point of view also alters, as does his view of reality. He no longer uses a third person point of view, but rather multiple narrative foci. . . . The relatively fixed reality of his earlier works now begins to distort and oscillate in uncertain hallucinations, suggesting that our illusions of stable appearances are very fragile fictions. (pp. 196-97)

Dick's early robots were machines sent by alien enemy forces to attack man. In his middle period, the actual man-made robot or simulacrum became the paradigm for the capitalist-fascist-bureaucratic structures locking the individual in a prisonhouse of false illusions created through electronic constructs. The technologist became a demonic artificer serving the devil of economic greed. In the fiction of the late 1960s, another shift in the evolution of Dick's imagination occurs, as evidenced by a shift in emphasis from the outer space of the social realm to the inner world of the mind. The robot no longer walks wasteland streets or peers from vidscreens via electronic images; rather he haunts the human consciousness and stares out through a mask of flesh. Dick has become aware, he tells us now, that "the greatest pain does not come down from a distant planet, but up from the depth of the human heart." His attention moves to the human as a machine or android. (pp. 204-05)

In his recent fiction exploring the mechanical, his earlier view of androids as artificial constructs masquerading as humans gives way to a view of androids as humans who have become machines. Now robots and men have reversed roles. *Do Androids Dream of Electric Sheep?* (1968) creates a metaphor for this process. In *We Can Build You* (serialized in magazine form in 1969), automata assume the compassion and concern of the authentic human: the Abraham Lincoln simulacrum, although a schizophrenic character, is superior in his insight and humanity to the humans in the novel.

Read as a dramatization of inner space, *Do Androids Dream?* merits recognition as one of Dick's finest novels, a view contrary to most of the current critical judgment. Stanislaw Lem in "Science Fiction: A Hopeless Case—With Exceptions" [see excerpt above] recognizes the novel as "not important," but then dismisses it as disappointing because it does not offer unequivocal answers to the questions of internal logic that it raises. But the point is, Dick is picturing an inner world that is *without* the logical consistency Lem demands. For Dick, the clear line between hallucination and reality has itself become a kind of hallucination. (p. 205)

The novel sets up a series of opposing ideas: people—things; subject—object; animate—inanimate; loving—killing; intuition—logic; human—machine. Double character sets abound; Rick Deckard and Phil Resch; Rachael Rosen and Pris Stratton, John Isidore and Wilbur Mercer. We can only know the penultimate truth; we are always one reflection away from reality, and we see it as in a mirror. Thus the sets of characters mirror truths to each other. For Dick this encounter—not an encounter of truth, but only a reflection of the truth—is caught best in an image used by Saint Paul, who speaks of our seeing "as if the reflection on the bottom of a polished metal pan."

The complexity of structure and ideas in this rich novel point up the evolutionary process of the Dickian imagination in the fifteen years since those first short stories about robot warfare. But the question for which Dick invents his array of answers is the same as it was then: What happens when man builds machines programmed to kill? The answer Dick fears, is that man will become the machines that kill. This is what Rick Deckard learns about himself: in pursuing the enemy android with a view to kill or be killed, he takes on the characteristics of the enemy and becomes himself an android. In one of the most powerful chapters of the novel (Chapter 12), Rick encounters his double, the android bounty hunter, Phil Resch, who enjoys killing. This mirror episode provides Rick with the insight that he has been transformed into an android-killing machine. (pp. 206-07)

The secondary plot of the novel records the encounter of John Isidore, a subnormal "chickenhead," with the androids. Contrary to Rick, who hunts androids to kill them, John empathizes with them. He is a follower of Mercerism and is easily able to identify with every other living thing. Wilbur Mercer is a mysterious old man whose image on the black empathy box serves as a focus for the theological and moral system called Mercerism. Its followers unite through empathy, the energy capable of transporting the human mind through the mirror so that it unites with the opposite and sees from the reverse direction. Mercer, in a gentle test of endurance which transcends suffering as he endlessly toils up a barren hill, is reminiscent of Albert Camus' Sisyphus. John Isidore, grasping the handles of the black empathy box, undergoes a "crossing-over," a physical merging with others accompanied by mental and spiritual identification. . . . (p. 207)

Reversals and negations like Rick's in loving and killing, are compounded throughout the novel. Mercer, the mystic, turns out to be a fake—not a religious leader but an alcoholic has-been actor. The allegedly real toad Rick discovers on his desert journey and cherishes as an omen of spiritual rebirth turns out to be an electric one. What does it all mean? Rick's final insight answers the question: "Everything is true, everything anybody has ever thought." . . . He could just as well have said that everything is false. It all depends on the perspective from which you view "reality." (p. 208)

How does one survive in this universe of uncertainty where everything is both true and false? Like John Isidore, one em-

pathizes with and responds to the needs of all forms, blinding one's eyes to the inauthentic division between the living and nonliving, between the machine and man. Like the shadowy Wilbur Mercer, one endlessly climbs up, suffering the wounds of rocks mysteriously thrown, but never reaching a destination. Mercer's hill mirrors Sisyphus' fate, his rocks the stones of martyred Stephen, his empathy the forgiving, uniting love of Christ.

Only when the divisions Dick has mirrored in the novel are healed by an inner unity growing from an acceptance of all things will artificiality be replaced by authentic existence. If you hold the nineteenth-century view of yourself as a unique, concrete thing, says Dick, you can never merge with the noosphere. The left-hemisphere brain, the isolating android intellect, must merge with the right-hemisphere brain, the collective intuition that we all share. These dream images, if we will listen, partake of the creative power that can transform us from mere machines into authentic humans.

We Can Build You cannot be ignored in a study of Dick's androids because it proposes new pathways in the labyrinthian possibilities of machine intelligence: but it cannot be applauded because it creeps along in a dramatic near-paralysis uncommon to Dick's fiction. The failure is twofold. First, the novel relies on exposition, not metaphor, to make many of its statements. Additionally, it concerns itself with two themes which are not closely related. When, as he can, Dick yokes the unlikely in grotesque marriage, he is brilliant. In this novel, however, the two themes fail to resonate; we are left with a sense of dispassionate incongruity. The first theme concerns the creation of simulacra whose intelligence has all the attributes of human intelligence. How are such forms to be regarded—ethically, legally, and philosophically? What are the implications of destroying such high-level intelligence? Is there a difference between killing an intelligent being and an equally intelligent machine? A writer as different from Dick as Isaac Asimov has successfully dramatized these issues in what is unquestionably his greatest story, "The Bicentennial Man" (1976). Dick plays with the possibilities of this theme in desultory probings, but he actually seems to be more concerned with the second theme: the transformation of the protagonist, Louis Rosen, into an android. This theme makes use of an idea which apparently remained in Dick's mind after he finished the superb *Do Androids Dream?* It can be summarized as: What are we to make of the human who glorifies reason, logic, individual prudence, and self-concern while at the same time he suppresses emotional responses—love, fear, and passion? The answer Dick gives is that we can no longer regard him as human; he has become a logic machine, an android, a schizoid personality. (pp. 208-10)

Is reality only a fiction; or must man make up fictions because reality is unknowable? Are space and time uncertain in their order because man has not yet learned to understand them; or does the universe of space and time eternally move with the mystery beyond human probing? Is the authentic human mind with its high intelligence unique and irreplaceable; or will machines become more intelligent than man? Can they explore new worlds from which man is barred? Dick in his fiction is a seeker who searches not for definitive answers to these puzzles, but for possibilities. His early short stories are straightforward metaphors, simple mirrors, presenting to us the bizarre possibilities his imagination sees. His later metaphors move into realms of increasing complexity and his mirroring device becomes a doubly ironic metaphor composed of opposites facing each other. In order to comprehend this type of metaphor, we have to see in several directions at the same time, to let our awareness slip simultaneously in both directions through the mirror, viewing the polarities of possibility from each direction in the same instant. Thus, for Dick, the enlightened human consciousness is not a *state* of being but an *event* or process of eternal passage between contraries.

We cease our labyrinthian journey through Dick's phantasmagoric worlds of evolving intelligence, human and artificial. It brings us to no conclusion, but perhaps to a peaceful, exhilarating delight at being lost in the metaphorical maze of his and our own imagination. We reach no goal, but share our guide's awareness that nothing can be preserved, either by machines or man. (pp. 213-14)

What future will unfold for artificial intelligence? Will it increasingly assume and perhaps eventually subsume human intelligence? What of the human brain's capacity to dream, to throw up fireworks of possibility lying outside mundane reality? Will machine intelligence achieve that gift, too? What is the answer to the question Dick's title asks: *Do* androids dream of electric sheep? We know that Dick, according to his own philosophy, would want us to accept only the answer we discover as we look in the mirror of his fiction and see our own awareness reflected back to us. But we can also be certain of his answer. Yes, as each form contains within itself the shadow-image of the potential forms that seed its inevitable transformation, so do androids also dream. (p. 214)

Patricia S. Warrick, "The Labyrinthian Process of the Artificial: Philip K. Dick's Androids and Mechanical Constructs," in Philip K. Dick, *edited by Joseph D. Olander and Martin Harry Greenberg, Taplinger Publishing Company, 1983, pp. 189-214.*

Ian (Lancaster) Fleming

1908-1964

English novelist, short story writer, essayist, scriptwriter, and journalist.

Fleming's secret agent James Bond is one of the most widely known characters in popular fiction. The fourteen books in the series—including *Casino Royale* (1953), *From Russia, with Love* (1957), *Doctor No* (1958), and *Goldfinger* (1959)—have sold millions of copies and all of them have been made into successful films. Bond's immense popularity has been attributed to his appearance at a time when readers were especially receptive to a glamorous and heroic character with whom they could identify. In addition, the Bond books have three elements basic to their appeal: beautiful women, grotesque villains, and extravagant plots. Fleming intended Bond himself to be a "dull, uninteresting man to whom things happened"; thus Fleming gave him no extraordinary characteristics or achievements. However, their exotic backgrounds, elegant surroundings, and Bond's dangerous exploits made the novels an effective focus for readers' wish-fulfillment. Critics also attribute the success of the series to Fleming's ability to blend convincingly realistic details into the preposterous elements of his stories.

From 1939 to 1945, Fleming was personal assistant to the director of British naval intelligence and he sometimes used his own wartime experiences as the basis of Bond's escapades. Fleming once attempted to take the money of some German agents in a card game just as Bond did with Le Chiffre in *Casino Royale;* however, where Fleming failed, Bond succeeded. Critics have been tempted to see Bond as the personification of his creator. They do have certain interests in common, such as gambling, sports, and cars, but Fleming maintained that Bond is simply the incarnation of his own adolescent fantasies.

Critical response to Fleming's books has varied. Some reviewers have commended Fleming's ability to build suspense and his sense of place and atmosphere; others have castigated him as a purveyor of bad fiction and an offensive code of moral principles. In a 1958 attack on Fleming's work, Bernard Bergonzi criticized the Bond adventures as morally destructive. Paul Johnson focused this attack when he called *Doctor No* the "nastiest book" he had ever read, and then went on to denounce Bond and his creator for excessive displays of "sex, sadism, and snobbery." Kingsley Amis's book *The James Bond Dossier* is an extended defense of Fleming and a laudatory examination of his works. The Bond books have also been analyzed as modern treatments of ancient myths and legends. Despite this attention from critics, Fleming insisted that his intent was not to write "literature," but to keep the reader turning the page.

(See also *CLC*, Vol. 3; *Contemporary Authors*, Vols. 5-8, rev. ed.; and *Something about the Author*, Vol. 9.)

Photograph by Harrods of London. Courtesy of Glidrose Publications Ltd

R. D. CHARQUES

Casino Royale. An alternative title, I suggest, having never quite known how baccarat is played, would be *The Gambler's Vade-Mecum*. A Secret Service thriller, lively, most ingenious in detail, on the surface as tough as they are made and charmingly well-bred beneath, nicely written and—except for a too ingeniously sadistic bout of brutality—very entertaining reading. Bond, a bold and all but heartless British secret agent, *versus* Le Chiffre, an enigma of a Soviet agent wrapped in M.V.D. mystery. The scene is a rakish small gambling resort near Dieppe, where, with really terrific *aplomb* on Mr. Fleming's part, the first desperate round is fought at the baccarat table. Enter—or, more exactly, exit—at this point the stunning Vesper, blue-eyed and sensual-lipped, Bond's No. 2 chosen by headquarters. It is, as it happens, the cue for (the prettily imagined) Smersh, the pinnacle of the Soviet secret police structure, a name derived from two words meaning—not "roughly," by the way, but quite literally—"Death to Spies." There are spills and thrills, stratagems and surprises still to come, and at any rate for Bond, by now not quite so heartless, there is a shattering and awful eye-opened at the very last. The public schoolboy in him, I suspect, would be inclined to murmur, "Well done, Smersh!" In its kind, *Casino Royale* is equally well done.

> *R. D. Charques, in a review of "Casino Royale,"* in The Spectator, *Vol. 190, No. 6512, April 17, 1953, p. 494.*

THE TIMES LITERARY SUPPLEMENT

Mr. Ian Fleming's first novel [*Casino Royale*] is an extremely engaging affair, dealing with espionage in the [L.] Sapper manner but with a hero who, although taking a great many cold showers and never letting sex interfere with work, is somewhat more sophisticated. At any rate he takes very great care over his food and drink, and sees women's clothes with an expertness of which Bulldog Drummond would have been ashamed. . . . [The] especial charm of Mr. Fleming's book is the high poetry with which he invests the green baize lagoons of the casino tables. The setting in a French resort somewhere near Le Touquet is given great local atmosphere and while the plot itself has a shade too many improbabilities the Secret Service details are convincing. Altogether Mr. Fleming has produced a book that is both exciting and extremely civilized.

> *"Spices and Charlatans,"* in The Times Literary Supplement, *No. 2672, April 17, 1953, p. 249.**

ANTHONY HARTLEY

Mr. Ian Fleming's latest thriller [*From Russia With Love*] will be another shot in the arm for addicts, and it would be unfair to him and them to reveal the plot beyond saying that its author has undoubtedly studied Sherlock Holmes and that a lot of it takes place in Istanbul. These new surroundings, however, bring with them no slackening of tension. Perhaps we could have done without the conducted tour of the Russian Secret Service which Mr. Fleming provides in his early chapters, but guns and knives are used freely later on, and there are plenty of those little touches, so revelatory of character, which Bond's fans have learned to look for. . . .

For, after all, the strength of these thrillers lies in the man Bond. Mr. Fleming's plots have deteriorated a good deal since *Casino Royale*. He now no longer even tries to obtain from his readers that willing suspension of disbelief which we accord so readily to Eric Ambler. In the Amberland south of the Danube and east of the Adriatic his local colour stands up particularly badly to the comparison. I never feel that Mr. Fleming really knows what it is like to beard a Macedonian Komitadji in his den, and the political background of his novels is not so much shaky as non-existent. . . .

In style Mr. Fleming could do with some transatlantic lessons. Raymond Chandler's descriptions of furniture or clothing invariably help the plot along by establishing either character or atmosphere. Mr. Fleming, on the other hand, uses his mastery of advertising patter purely for its own sake. His account of Bond's London breakfast rises to lyrical heights of self-parody and will probably be quoted in future as one of the great purple passages of English twentieth-century prose, quite equal to [Walter] Pater on the Mona Lisa or Newman on himself. I personally take pleasure in these stylistic triumphs, but there is no doubt that they come rather within the category of divine digressions than of aids to narration. . . .

And here we are back at the hero of our time. Back at the things that make Bond attractive: the sex, the sadism, the vulgarity of money for its own sake, the cult of power, the lack of standards. How very sinister that this should be our modern [Richard] Hannay, the successor to a long line of Empire-savers! How deplorable that he should actually appear to like kicking people in the stomach! You could do [a George] Orwell on Bond for hundreds of pages, and you would be right. And yet. . . . And yet. . . . *'J'aime les anthropophages,'* said a French missionary. *'Ils sont si francement carnivores.'* At least neither Mr. Fleming nor his hero shares the twentieth-century characteristic vice of cant. They are both carnivorous to the

back-teeth and like their meat well hung. This, coming in the age of the murderous vegetarian, is rather pleasant than otherwise. For myself I am inclined to wish Bond many years and quick promotion in the order of St. Michael and St. George. I feel quite sure Mr. Fleming is too.

> *Anthony Hartley, "A Hero of Our Time,"* in The Spectator, *Vol. 198, No. 6720, April 12, 1957, p. 493.*

DAN JACOBSON

The substance of Mr. Fleming's book [*The Diamond Smugglers*] is a series of reminiscences by a pseudonymous 'John Blaize,' describing his experiences as an official of the International Diamond Security Organisation. . . . The trade in illicit diamonds is described as 'the greatest smuggling racket in the world'; and it is clear there are many people and a great deal of money involved in the business.

When we get down to cases, however, the difficulty is—as Mr. Fleming himself admits—that realistic writing about such matters is likely to be 'full of loose ends, and drabness and despair'; and the reader who goes to the book in search of high adventure may find that the malefactions of 'Sammy Silberstein' and 'Henry Orford' and the rest are no more necessarily thrilling to read about than a place like Kimberley, say, is to visit. On the other hand, Mr. Fleming has not given himself nearly enough space to individualise—and thus make interesting, for another reason—the very drabness and shabbiness of the people and the operations he describes. The author does try hard to generate the thriller atmosphere, with many significant asides, and even more significant reticences; but the material he has gathered together is recalcitrant. (pp. 844-45)

The most interesting section of the book is that dealing with the situation in Sierra Leone. Apparently there are hundreds of square miles of bush in that country being cheerfully worked by gangs of illicit African diggers. . . . [There] was nothing that the Diamond Corporation could do but to surrender some of its rights, legalise the squatters—and then buy the diamonds from them, as it was already doing with those diamonds smuggled by the squatters across the border into Liberia. This is the stuff for a large-scale farce . . . or for some serious political reflection; but Mr. Fleming's book seems to indicate that there really isn't much in it for a writer of thrillers. (p. 845)

> *Dan Jacobson, "Not So Sparkling,"* in The Spectator, *Vol. 199, No. 6755, December 13, 1957, pp. 844-45.*

BERNARD BERGONZI

A reviewer in *The Listener* described *Casino Royale* as 'Supersonic John Buchan', and a comparison between the two authors is extremely revealing. Fleming's hero, James Bond, like Buchan's Richard Hannay, is a Secret Service agent, continually either chasing or being chased by enemy spies, often at the point of death but always saved by some improbable turn of events. Hannay's adversaries, before and during World War I, were the somewhat casual and heavy-handed emissaries of Imperial Germany: in the Bond stories, which are set against the background of the Cold War, the enemy is the far more efficient and deadly Soviet counter-espionage organization called S M E R S H (except in *Diamonds are Forever,* where Bond takes time off to deal with a team of American gangsters and diamond-smugglers). . . . [Bond] is a thoroughgoing professional, and at the top of his class; he is one of the three double 'O' numbers in the British Secret Service, which means he has liberty to kill when necessary; he is an expert pistol shot, boxer, and knife thrower, is always armed and sometimes wears steel-capped shoes (one can't imagine Hannay doing *that*). (pp. 220-21)

The professionalism of Mr Fleming's hero is reflected in the far greater slickness and pace of the writing; one is well aware that [Ernest] Hemingway and the American thriller have intervened since Buchan, who often seems, in comparison, wordy and excessively leisurely. Yet it would be a mistake to assume that Fleming is the better *writer*—he certainly isn't. Buchan could write very well, whereas Fleming rarely rises above the glossy prose of the advertising copywriter.

Anyone who has performed the somewhat thankless task of reading a thriller analytically will know that in even the most fast-moving and tautly-written specimens there is plenty of matter not strictly relevant to the plot: it is there partly to keep the reader's interest in the characters and the world they inhabit; no work can be pure action and nothing else. Often—and the Sherlock Holmes stories are a famous example—it is this 'affective superstructure', as one may call it, which stays in the mind rather than the plots themselves. With Buchan one remembers the loving descriptions of the moors and high places of Scotland. . . . There is, too, in Buchan a pronounced ethical element, for he was the immediate heir of a period of self-congratulatory Imperialist morality which had manifested itself in such varying forms as the Boy Scout movement and [Rudyard] Kipling's *If*. One of the major ideas to emerge from Buchan's novels is that if the heroes are not necessarily cleverer than the Germans (or other opponents like Medina) they are certainly more virtuous, so that they *deserve* their ultimate victory. Much of this patriotic ethic now seems impossibly priggish and even hysterical; nevertheless, it *was* an ethic, and did uphold such traditional Western and Christian virtues as respect for one's enemies and chivalry towards women. (pp. 221-22)

Mr Fleming's affective superstructure, apart from some graphic accounts of underwater swimming in *Live and Let Die,* is mainly concerned with gambling, potent fantasies of 'High-Life', and, of course, sex and violence—separately or in various combinations. I pass over the gambling scenes—baccarat in *Casino Royale,* bridge in *Moonraker,* racing in *Diamonds are Forever*— since I don't understand them, though they seem immensely plausible, and one must respect Mr Fleming's detailed knowledge of these topics. And of many other topics, one might add: the inner workings of Soviet bureaucracy, Harlem night life, vintage sports cars, small arms, helicopters, how to make a vodka martini, early American locomotives, the habits of tropical fish: he has an encyclopaedic range. Yet, if Mr Fleming's facts are interesting, his fantasies are vastly more so, at least in a symptomatic way. His fantasies of upper class life can only be a desire to compensate for the rigours of existence in a welfare state: they have an air of vulgarity and display which contrast strongly with those subdued images of the perfectly self-assured gentlemanly life that we find in Buchan or even Sapper. . . . (pp. 222-23)

If there were no more to Mr Fleming's fantasies than [the] harmless and moderately funny visions of Gracious Living, there would be nothing to object to. But they form a comparatively minor part of the affective superstructure of the novels: sex is far more dominant, and the erotic fantasies in which

Bond is continually involved are decidedly sinister. Here the contrast with Buchan could not be greater. (p. 224)

In Fleming one is rarely far from the pornographic, as in Bond's first sight of Tiffany Case, the heroine of *Diamonds are Forever;* she is sitting half-naked astride a chair, looking at herself in a mirror across the back of it. . . . It would, I suppose, be absurd to point out that as far as the *plot* goes there is no reason why Miss Case should not have been fully dressed when Bond called. And so throughout the books. (p. 225)

Where the relations between the sexes are concerned, Mr Fleming's characteristic mode of fantasy seems to be that of a dirty-minded schoolboy.

Not that this is all. There is also a strongly marked streak of voyeurism and sado-masochism in his books. Bond, sitting in a Harlem night club, watches a strip-tease act which is described with the utmost enthusiasm by Mr Fleming. . . . And in the last book [*From Russia, With Love*] there is a thoroughly nauseous episode in which Bond, in Istanbul, is allowed as a special privilege to watch a fight to the death between two Macedonian gypsy girls who are contending for the same man. . . . I must emphasize that this little incident has nothing whatever to do with the plot: it merely serves as a divertissement before the shooting starts. . . . Mr Fleming describes scenes of violence with uncommon relish, and it is these that really bring his books down to the horror-comic level. The sado-masochistic note is unmistakable throughout. In *Casino Royale,* for instance, Bond is captured by a Communist agent from whom he has previously won forty million francs at the gaming tables. In an endeavour to make him confess where the money is hidden, Bond is stripped naked and tied to a chair from which the seat has been removed; he is then systematically beaten on the genitals with a carpet-beater for about an hour. It is interesting to recall that the *New Statesman* described this book as 'a thriller for an intelligent audience' and that a reviewer in *The Times Literary Supplement* [see excerpt above] found it 'both exciting and *extremely* civilized' (my italics: one would like to know what this gentleman considers even moderately barbarous). (pp. 225-26)

What, briefly, emerges from Fleming's novels—in the completest possible contrast to Buchan's—is the total lack of any ethical frame of reference. It is all a question of *sensations,* more or less *fortes.* When Bond succeeds it is not because Right is on his side, but simply because he is rather quicker on the draw, a little more handy with the throwing knife, just that much faster at lashing out with the steel-capped shoe. Occasionally he engages in some brief and moody reflections which are presumably meant to place him in the kind of moral dimension genuinely occupied by, say, Raymond Chandler's Phillip Marlowe, or some of Eric Ambler's heroes. But these are patently bogus—and even dishonest. For instance, on page 172 of *From Russia, With Love* we are told that Bond has never killed in cold blood: yet in *Casino Royale* he gives a detailed account of the way in which he killed a Japanese cipher expert in New York and a Norwegian double agent in Stockholm (for which he was given his double 'O' number in the Service).

No, most of the time it is quite simply Bond fighting it out with no holds barred, and no irrelevant speculations about the ideological struggle between Communism and the West allowed to intrude. And when S M E R S H are succeeding— as throughout the last book, for instance—I have a strong suspicion that Mr Fleming, on the imaginative plane, at least, admires them for it; for they succeed because they are *really* tough, more powerful than anyone else, more ready to get in and shoot first, more brilliantly ingenious in their methods. And, of course, quite unhampered by outworn ethical considerations.

It may be objected that I have taken a far too serious view of works which are intended to be pure 'entertainment' and no more: but, as I have suggested, Buchan was an 'entertainer' working in basically the same *genre,* and his books are almost wholly free from Mr Fleming's radical defects. It is the difference between them that is significant. George Orwell, and, more recently, Mr Hoggart, have shown us how works of entertainment may have an enormous symptomatic importance, and we are entitled to profit by their lessons. Mr Hilary Corke, reviewing **Live and Let Die** in *Encounter* in 1954, described it as 'a work that appeals, I think, to a baser human instinct than the smudgy postcards hawked at the more central London tube-stations', and the three subsequent novels have powerfully reinforced this opinion. Mr Fleming, I imagine, knows just what he is doing: but the fact that his books are published by a very reputable firm, and are regularly reviewed—and highly praised— in our self-respecting intellectual weeklies, surely says more about the present state of our culture than a whole volume of abstract denunciations. (pp. 227-28)

> Bernard Bergonzi, ''The Case of Mr Fleming,'' in The Twentieth Century, Vol. 163, No. 973, March, 1958, pp. 220-28.

MARTIN DODSWORTH

Mr Bergonzi's extremely interesting essay . . . 'The Case of Mr Fleming' [see excerpt above] raises two important points about the examination of popular culture. The first is the necessity of getting close to the audience for the particular form under study. We often speak of the literature of wish-fulfilment, without considering how seriously the public takes this sort of thing. I think that Mr Bergonzi is guilty of this fault in castigating the *New Statesman* public for its approval of Mr Fleming's books, which, he claims, rely for their appeal on sex, snobbery and violence.

How *could* the *New Statesman* call **Casino Royale** 'a thriller for an intelligent audience', Mr Bergonzi asks in amaze. I want to attempt an answer: what these books offer besides sex, violence, etc. First of all, there is the literal excitement of the story (what will happen next?); but equally important is the extravagant absurdity of the situations. Although, as Mr Bergonzi noted, irony is quite lacking in the narration, there is an irony of situations; the comedy lies in telling a story of glaring implausibility with an absolutely straight face. For example, when we learn that the Secret Service branch in Istanbul is entirely staffed by the children of its polyphiloprogenitive director Darko Kerim, we cannot help laughing—but it would be fatal if Mr Fleming laughed too. Similarly, the vulgar parody of 'gracious living' is *meant* to seem absurd.

This is not to deny that there is a very marked streak of sadistic violence in these books—but it *exceeds* the limits of paperback brutality.

The scene in **Casino Royale,** where Bond's genitals are beaten with a carpet-beater, is not titillating but actively repellent. It is interesting in this connection to remark that Bond on the whole suffers more than his enemies; and it is tempting to suggest a motivation deeper than the commercial instinct behind the violence in these books. Class, as Mr Bergonzi noted,

plays a large part in them—Bond is a representative of the upper-income bracket. It is for this that he suffers; he expiates the sins of his class by suffering for the greater good. By his suffering, the forces of SMERSH are rendered powerless to the community; the price he pays is the loss of his own integrity—he becomes the 'cold', 'mean', 'cruel' Secret Service agent. James Bond is a sacrificial victim and a modern version of the king killed in the Sacred Wood.

Bond's identification with a superior 'upper' class produces a double response—the audience sees him as funny ('vulgarity and display') but also as obliged to justify himself. This attitude to class is distinctly twentieth century and is certainly that of many *New Statesman* readers. My suggested reading is of course, a sophisticated version of what goes on in these novels; but it is a reading to be taken into account. (p. 478)

The trouble is, of course, that Mr Bergonzi distrusts any public that approves of the popular novel, despite his attempts at impartiality. Mrs Leavis has been before and made all clear— hence the strong moral bias of the criticism, my second point of objection. For Bond's morals must be seen in the context of the scheme suggested above. He is a good man who allows himself to be subject to corruption for the good of society as a whole. Doubtless, the books sell on the appeal of the vicious side of Bond's character; and it is easy by selective quotation to make this seem the only possible aspect to consider. But it is worth mentioning that despite Bond's 'meanness', etc., he falls desperately and romantically in love with the heroines of at least three of the novels. . . .

To sum up—immorality is certainly the greater part of Mr Fleming's subject-matter, but his attitude to it as expressed by Bond is quite equivocal and forms the basis for a sharp ironic technique of story-telling that puts him in a class far apart from John Buchan. After all, to be capable of doubts about the absolute nature of your moral system is better than to be utterly ignorant of the possibility of such doubts. (p. 479)

> Martin Dodsworth, in a letter to an unidentified recipient on March 19, 1958, in The Twentieth Century, Vol. 163, No. 975, May, 1958, pp. 478-79.

SIMON RAVEN

I have just been reading a long complaint, in the monthly *The Twentieth Century,* about the unsatisfactory tone of Ian Fleming's novels. The author of this complaint, Bernard Bergonzi [see excerpt above], having remarked that these novels are similar to John Buchan's in subject (spies and pursuits), then goes on to say that, whereas Buchan's books are fundamentally decent and do depend on an ethic of sorts, Commander Fleming's tales are without any ethical frame of reference and have an 'affective superstructure' of a perverted and anti-social nature. . . .

Now this is a quiet and well-argued article, but it does appear to reach a most naive conclusion. I mention it here because this type of complaint, about Commander Fleming and others, is increasingly in evidence and has always seemed to me to be entirely beside the point. Since when has it been remarkable in a work of entertainment that it should lack a specific 'ethical frame of reference'? I don't suggest that any of Fleming's books, least of all the latest one, **Dr. No,** should be left around in the nursery any more than [John Vanbrugh's] *The Relapse* or [Ovid's] *Ars Amatoria.* What I do suggest is that Commander Fleming, by reason of his cool and analytical intelligence, his informed use of technical facts, his plausibility, sense of pace, brilliant descriptive powers and superb imagination, provides sheer entertainment such as I, who must read many novels, am seldom lucky enough to find. It may well be, as Mr. Bergonzi suggests, that Fleming's conscious reaction to the dowdiness of the Welfare State has induced him to create fictitious pleasure-domes so splendiferous as to be merely vulgar: the menus in *Dr. No* are a joy to read for all that. It may be that James Bond, hero of *Dr. No* and all Fleming's novels, is indeed the super-colossal father-figure of every juvenile delinquent that ever there was: he certainly 'sends' me. I venture to suppose that, whether you approve of him or not, whether you are a banker, a lawyer, a soldier or a turf accountant, he will 'send' you too.

Simon Raven, "Gilt-Edged Bond," in The Spectator, Vol. 200, No. 6771, April 4, 1958, p. 438.*

PAUL JOHNSON

I have just finished what is, without doubt, the nastiest book I have ever read. It is a new novel entitled *Dr No* and the author is Mr Ian Fleming. . . . By the time I was a third of the way through, I had to suppress a strong impulse to throw the thing away, and only continued reading because I realised that here was a social phenomenon of some importance.

There are three basic ingredients in *Dr No,* all unhealthy, all thoroughly English: the sadism of a schoolboy bully, the mechanical, two-dimensional sex-longings of a frustrated adolescent, and the crude, snob-cravings of a suburban adult. Mr Fleming has no literary skill, the construction of the book is chaotic, and entire incidents and situations are inserted, and then forgotten, in a haphazard manner. But the three ingredients are manufactured and blended with deliberate, professional precision; Mr Fleming dishes up his recipe with all the calculated accountancy of a Lyons Corner House. . . .

Fleming deliberately and systematically excites, and then satisfies the very worst instincts of his readers. This seems to me far more dangerous than straight pornography. In 1944, George Orwell took issue with a book which in some ways resembles Fleming's novels—*No Orchids for Miss Blandish.* He saw the success of *No Orchids,* published in 1940, as part of a discernible psychological climate, whose other products were Fascism, the Gestapo, mass-bombing and war. But in condemning *No Orchids,* Orwell made two reservations. First, he conceded that it was brilliantly written, and that the acts of cruelty it described sprang from a subtle and integrated, though perverse, view of human nature. Secondly, in contrasting *No Orchids* with *Raffles*—which he judged a healthy and harmless book— he pointed out that *No Orchids* was evil precisely because it lacked the restraint of conventional upper-class values; and this led him to the astonishing but intelligible conclusion that perhaps, after all, snobbery, like hypocrisy, was occasionally useful to society.

What, I wonder, would he have said of *Dr No*? For this novel is badly written to the point of incoherence and none of the 500,000 people who, I am told, are expected to buy it, could conceivably be giving Cape 13s. 6d. to savour its literary merits. Moreover, both its hero and its author are unquestionably members of the Establishment. (p. 430)

Orwell, in fact, was wrong. Snobbery is no protection: on the contrary, the social appeal of the dual Bond-Fleming personality has added an additional flavour to his brew of sex and sadism. Fleming's novels are not only successful, like *No Orchids;* they are also smart. . . . Our curious post-war society, with its obsessive interest in debutantes, its cult of U and non-U, its working-class graduates educated into snobbery by the welfare state, is a soft market for Mr Fleming's poison. Bond's warmest admirers are among the Top People. . . . It has become easier than it was in Orwell's day to make cruelty attractive. We have gone just that much farther down the slope. Recently I read Henri Alleg's horrifying account of his tortures in an Algiers prison; and I have on my desk a documented study of how we treat our prisoners in Cyprus. I am no longer astonished that these things can happen. Indeed, after reflecting on the Fleming phenomenon, they seem to me almost inevitable. (p. 432)

Paul Johnson, "Sex, Snobbery and Sadism," in New Statesman, Vol. LV, No. 1412, April 5, 1958, pp. 430, 432.

ROBERT HATCH

Fleming's tradition is sub-literary. Since 1954 he has written novels at the rate of one-and-a-half a year; you can read them without undue strain at the rate of one-and-a-half a night. His field is the secret service thriller—a well-recognized, well-paid, almost routine English trade. Why then should his books have sold more than a million copies, why should the responsible English critics be in a state of outrage; why, for example, should Paul Johnson devote a leading article in *The New Statesman* [see excerpt above] to an attack of boisterous passion against this entertainer? (pp. 566-67)

[Americans] are not going to be so taken by surprise. We have had Mickey Spillane and Raymond Chandler and one gets hardened to such things. Though it must be admitted that Mr. Fleming is a concentrated example of published nastiness. His stock in trade contains, first, the snobbish accoutrements that one expects in diplomatic thrillers. His hero, James Bond, eats, smokes, drinks, drives and sleeps with only the fanciest products of our civilization. He is, in a word, a god-awful false gentleman, but so are most British sleuths.

But they are not usually pathological killers and sexual oddities. Bond enjoys hurting people and he enjoys being hurt. He also fattens on horror, crawling horror, for the most part, with many legs. In *Doctor No,* the newest book, Fleming indulges him in this taste by letting a centipede explore his body for three pages.

As for sex proper, the author has said that perhaps Bond's "blatant heterosexuality is a subconscious protest against the current fashion for sexual confusion." Bond is blatant, all right, but if he is unconfused he is also arrested. He likes girls who have been raped into frigidity, but who converse about sex with the air of offhand availability that keeps imaginative schoolboys awake nights. . . .

I'm more interested in the situations Mr. Fleming himself thinks erotic. He has a way of combining sex and fear, sex and pain that bodes ill for the suggestible. . . .

Fleming knows his trade in the more usual ways. He has a flair for outlandish information—the economics of guano, high strategy of cards and chess, the culture of tropical fish, voodoo, old coins, and of course small arms ballistics—all tossed off with an easy authority calculated to bedazzle the non-expert. He also has keen eyes and ears; when he describes the landing of a plane, the layout of a Harlem nightclub, the bed of a tropical sea or the routine of a Saratoga mud bath, it is done

with the precise and telling words that distinguish a good reporter. Fleming's detail is what really carries his stories—the
plots are not very ingenious and the details are ludicrous. Stripped
of their surface plausibility, they would scarcely hold a comic
book reader. . . .

No one should take such stuff seriously—it is for trains and
sleepless nights. Why then the turmoil in the British journals?
The answer, I think, is that Fleming seduces the English and,
as they are decent people, they resent it. He seduces them with
the rare liquors, bath salts, racing cars and fine leather that are
not part of the Welfare State. More seriously, he dangles before
them the dream of Empire. Bond is perhaps the last world
policeman the English will ever know. He hunts the enemy in
New York, Haiti, Turkey, South Africa, France, Belgrade.
Wherever peace and the superiority of the Anglo-Saxon people
is threatened, the arm of British justice reaches out and Bond
is its fist. One book (**Moonraker**) is concerned with a new super
missile which, overnight, will restore to England her former
omnipotence. It turns out that the builder is a mad Nazi who
intends to destroy London, and this is perhaps the cruelest twist
to British illusions that Fleming has perpetrated. But the bait
is in every book—Bond is [Sir Francis Drake, Cecil Rhodes,
and the Duke of Wellington], combined in a twentieth-century,
post-concentration camp type of vigilante and he's a powerful
chimera.

For us this is less seductive, but Fleming has a false lure for
Americans as well (he is a very calculating man). The enemy
in his books is Russia, more specifically a super-secret terror
organization called "SMERSH." All the mad villains, all the
heartless plots, all the bestial tortures are inspired by the world-
hungry Russians. And they are everywhere. This vision of the
world is an FBI nightmare. As in everything he does, Fleming
seems to document his case against the Kremlin and its subhuman supermen. It would be a pity if we fell again under the
paralyzing dream of the omnipresent beast. Bond doesn't even
work for us, and there is obviously no one else. (p. 567)

> Robert Hatch, "Excitement from England," in The
> Nation, *Vol. 186, No. 25, June 21, 1958, pp. 566-
> 67.*

NEWSWEEK

The cruelly sophisticated yet boyishly winsome mask of British
intelligence agent James Bond (007) conceals the identical mask
of Commander Ian Fleming, RNVR. In this collection of frivolous travel articles about thirteen cities around the world
["**Thrilling Cities**"] . . . , the fictitious mask is off, but the
inner one remains impenetrable. Fleming really tells very little
about the essence of his experiences abroad while ostensibly
telling all. Nevertheless, for the countless people who enjoy
the squeaky-clean, anxiety-free hazards and the smear-proof
Playboy sex of the Bond novels, here is a sizable package of
raw materials for do-it-yourself escapism. . . .

Ian Fleming's thrilling clichés invoke a feeling of Anglo-Saxon
superiority to Abroad and the lesser breeds who live there.
Unlike Kipling, however, Fleming condescends without
preaching—not, it seems, because of any new-fangled recognition of international moral equality. It is simply that he has
nothing to suggest, except that might is still right, make-believe
might is better than nothing, and, whatever you do, shake,
don't stir, the Martinis. . . . When he travels, Fleming's attention is focused, he says, "on the bizarre and perhaps the
shadier side of life." A melancholy confession.

Although the articles are not new, at the end of each of them
a reasonably up-to-date practical guide is appended, listing
hotels, restaurants, and other amenities recommended by London Sunday Times correspondents. Some of the expertise seems
rather obvious . . . , but Fleming's sieve is a fine one and he
has panned some bright little nuggets of esoterica. . . .

> "Bond's Baedeker," in Newsweek, *Vol. LXIII, No.
> 24, June 15, 1964, p. 103*.

O. F. SNELLING

The Spy Who Loved Me . . . is the most unusual [James Bond
book] of all. It marked a new departure for Ian Fleming. Hitherto, he had played the part of God, so to speak, looking down
upon his remarkable creation and describing Bond's thoughts
and actions in the third person. He did it well, better than any
of his contemporaries, in my submission. I think there is little
doubt that he could have gone on for many years doing much
the same sort of thing. . . . (pp. 94-5)

I admire Ian Fleming for attempting what he did attempt. But
when I first read the book I did not. Conditioned to expecting
narratives written to something of a formula, as far as the broad
plot is concerned, this book had a disturbing effect on me as
well as on a great many others. For a start, James Bond does
not make an appearance in it until more than halfway through
it. . . . Then again, when Bond does show up, we get little of
that engaging character-drawing we have come to expect, hokum
though it may be. No cocktails, 'shaken, not stirred', no new
information about Bond's fads and prejudices, and not a sign
of M and the old crowd at Universal Export. This time we get
a yarn purportedly written by the girl in the case, and so every
observation, every description of her adventures is set down
as it is seen by her. (p. 95)

It has been suggested that in this book Ian Fleming had dried
up, that he had no ideas for a lengthy James Bond adventure
in the usual tradition, and that he foisted on to a gullible public
a well-padded novelette liberally sprinkled with sexy interludes, finally chucking Bond into the spree as something of a
sop. Certainly, the pattern of the book is so different from the
others that at first glance it does look as if this criticism might
be partly true. But Fleming wasn't the first popular author to
deviate from a well-tried formula. . . . Sapper adopted the first
person narrative style in *The Final Count*, the fourth and last
of Bulldog Drummond's rounds with Carl Peterson. It wasn't
absolutely necessary to the story. I feel that Sapper did it
primarily to give us a new slant on his hero: Drummond at
work as seen from the point of view of a complete outsider,
an ordinary little man drawn by circumstances into a fantastic
adventure with this hulking, imperious character.

I believe that Fleming had much the same idea in mind. He
had already created a living being with whom we had thrilled
and rollicked closely through some eight lengthy escapades.
We had watched Bond's exploits, his hazards and his amours
with a perennial, all-seeing eye, benign observers aware of his
history, of his everyday habits and even of his thoughts. But
how would he appear to a frightened and bewildered girl caught
up in a nightmarish ordeal with no-one to turn to for help?
How would he look through the eyes of this somewhat silly
and romantic chit when he suddenly and quite accidentally
walked in out of the stormy night to save her?

And Vivienne Michel *is* a silly, romantic chit. Fleming spends
the first third of the book developing her, and that fact is fully

established as far as I am concerned. My main criticism of *The Spy Who Loved Me* is that too much time is spent on the maudlin reminiscences of her past life before she eventually got into the fix she did, and yet I am obliged to admit that this is the way such a girl *would* relate a narrative. The impact of James Bond on her life at this crucial moment is so great that in the later telling of it all it is necessary for her to inform us in detail of the other men she had known, for comparison's sake. (pp. 96-7)

Circumstances eventually find her all alone and temporarily in charge of [an] empty motel on a dark and stormy night, with the wind howling through the pines and Vivienne, not unnaturally, a trifle apprehensive. The whole thing is a little bit nightmarish, even before two strange and sinister men turn up out of the wild night. The situation takes on the aspect of a very, very bad dream indeed when it becomes apparent that her two visitors are psychopathic thugs, obviously with some specific underhand job to do on this very spot. The idea of having a pretty girl with them there, too, is quite pleasant, particularly to one of them. Vivienne is in a perilous position, to put it mildly, with criminal assault just about the best thing she has to look forward to, when who should turn up, of all people?

The whole narrative, to this point, has been a build-up for the entrance of James Bond. If the tale seems an off-beat one for Ian Fleming, I can't agree with those who think this experiment failed. If I were an attractive young girl, confused, unhappy and terrified out of my wits, I think I know how I would feel towards a dark, mysterious and handsome stranger who unexpectedly walked in out of the storm to save me. I would feel much the same as Vivienne, I'm sure.

Bond rescues her from death, and also from that fate worse than death, although they do both get knocked about a bit in the process. What with a fire in the motel and a few cuts and bruises, they feel quite grimy and in need of a bath. Relaxing a little later, they take a shower—together! It's amazing what danger can do to make sexually exciting girls discard their inhibitions and the shackles of convention when Bond is around. (pp. 100-01)

There now follows a love scene so ardent and shameless that any reader who might earlier have entertained doubts as to whether he was reading a Bond book soon has them quickly dispelled. And Vivienne Michel, only a short while previously trembling at the inevitability of being roughly violated, now has very different views about the matter. 'All women love semi-rape. They love to be taken. It was his sweet brutality against my bruised body that had made his act of love so piercingly wonderful.'

Obviously, it all depends on the man who is raping you. (p. 101)

[On] re-reading all of [the Bond books], it is apparent that Ian Fleming was merely serving an apprenticeship with [*Casino Royale*], that initial essay into sensational fiction. . . . [His second book, *Live and Let Die*,] is far superior in characterization, in pace and in excitement. Some of its descriptions I find enthralling. While I have never thought that Fleming was at his best when writing about America and Americans, I believe that his Harlem chapters in this book are some of his finest. 'Nigger Heaven' and 'Table Z', while not entirely necessary to the narrative, are absolutely essential to the atmosphere, and his handling of urban negro dialect is, to me, completely convincing. (p. 120)

James Bond hasn't—or at least he didn't have—a very great respect for American gangsters. 'They're not Americans. Mostly a lot of Italian bums with monogrammed shirts who spend the day eating spaghetti and meat-balls and squirting scent over themselves.'

He passes this opinion to the Chief of Staff early on in *Diamonds are Forever*. . . .

But—'That's what you think,' says the Chief of Staff. He proceeds, in a single paragraph, to give Bond a brief summary of organized American crime in a manner so succinct and knowledgeable as to suggest that the night before he had been reading [Burton Turkus's] *Murder Inc.*, or one of the similar factual books that followed in its wake. He finishes: 'You're going to take those gangs on. And you'll be by yourself. Satisfied?' (p. 127)

> Bond's face relaxed. 'Come on, Bill,' he said. 'If that's all there is to it, I'll buy you lunch. It's my turn and I feel like celebrating . . . I'll take you to Scotts' and we'll have some of their dressed crab and a pint of black velvet. You've taken a load off my mind. I thought there might be some ghastly snag about this job.'

Cocky, complacent, over-confident? Is he riding for a fall? The tone of these early pages certainly suggest that James Bond is tending to underrate the diamond smugglers he has been briefed by M to foil, and that he is in for a nasty jolt. It follows, I think, that Ian Fleming holds pretty high cards. The implications are that Bond is going to have no cake-walk during this particular exploit. Now Fleming knows more than a bit about the subject of this book . . . and it is quite obvious that he is familiar with locales like the Jamaica race-track, in upper state New York, and with the casinos of Las Vegas, where much of the action takes place. He also knows that American gangsters are not spaghetti-eating Italians and very little more. I think that it was his intention to show the Spangled Mob as an extremely powerful underworld organization and its leaders as ruthless and frightening criminals, and with James Bond finally aware of a healthy respect for these top-notch hoodlums of the new world.

I don't think Ian Fleming has ever failed to give us an enthralling and exciting story, but in my opinion he came nearer to failing in this objective in *Diamonds are Forever* than in almost any other of his books. With the best will in the world I can't take Jack Spang and his brother, Seraffimo Spang, very seriously. They are extremely tough guys indeed, admittedly, but little more than that. Compared with most of the other villains there seems to me to be little about them that is frightening, dreadful or sinister. (pp. 128-29)

Among James Bond's many adversaries, we remember this one for his frightening looks, that one for his excessive sadism, and the other because he's so smooth and unflappable. They are *all* pretty calm and unruffled, I suppose, each one has a nice line in torture and rather enjoys putting it into practice, and not a man jack among them is exactly what you would call prepossessing in appearance. All in all, they are a very unpleasant bunch. Of the lot, I think that Col. Rosa Klebb is the most unpleasant of all—whichever way you take her. Or should I say *it*? Strictly speaking, I suppose Col. Klebb is female, and should be designated by the appropriate gender. But any resemblance she bears to femininity or femineity is purely accidental.

Rosa appears in *From Russia, With Love*. She is the Head of Otdyel II, the department of SMERSH in charge of Operations and Executions, and Ian Fleming surpasses himself with the character he draws for this nastiest of all nasty females. (p. 130)

[Of] all these deliciously absurd books, *From Russia, With Love* is the one that I like the best. Not only does it have my favourite heroine, Tatiana, it also has Rosa Klebb, the woman I love to hate. It has the best plot, in my opinion, and the best writing. . . . I think the book has much to commend it. Its atmosphere is wonderful: its pace—leisurely at first—compelling and *crescendo*. It positively overflows with delightful characters: herein May makes her bow. Then there's Darko Kerim—(what a throwaway!)—Tania herself, and the memorable Rosa. (p. 133)

[The title character of *Goldfinger*, Auric Goldfinger,] looks ludicrous, he thinks like a paranoiac, and he plans a scheme which, at first glance, is utterly farfetched. All this *should* add up to one of the most laughably ridiculous books ever published. I have no doubt that there are a few people who think it is. Millions of others don't: they read it absorbingly and recommend it strongly to those who haven't. It is one of Fleming's more popular efforts among a near dozen, not one of which has proved to be exactly unpopular. This is despite its many extravagancies of invention and imagination.

Ian Fleming walked an extremely shaky tight-rope across a pond of very thin ice when he wrote *Goldfinger*. It is only that the mixing of my metaphors might become *too* maladroit that I hesitate to say outright that he eventually came down firmly on both feet. But you know what I mean, I'm sure. (pp. 139-40)

Difficult to accept though Auric Goldfinger and his ambitions and activities may be, the book in which he figures is one of the most entertaining pieces of hokum ever penned. Fleming, who had earlier held us spellbound with a lengthy game of baccarat, a nine-page meal and then eighteen pages of bridge, here surpasses himself. He devotes no less than two chapters— thirty-three pages—to a game of golf between Goldfinger and Bond. I, for one, would not have had this particular game shortened by a single line, although I do not play golf and have never understood the compulsive hold it has on so many people. . . . I can only humbly conclude that I am under the spell of a master when I become absorbed by passages dealing with pastimes and occupations with which I would normally have not the slightest concern. (pp. 140-41)

What with its characters and its situations, *Goldfinger* is perhaps the most bizarre example in a generally somewhat extraordinary output. But it is also, I submit, at the same time one of the best. (p. 142)

> *O. F. Snelling, in his* Double O Seven James Bond: A Report, *Neville Spearman—Holland Press, 1964, 160 p.*

KINGSLEY AMIS

[*The Man with the Golden Gun* is] a sadly empty tale, empty of the interests and effects that for better or worse, Ian Fleming had made his own. Violence is at a minimum. Sex too. . . . And there's no gambling, no gadgets or machinery to speak of, no undersea stuff, none of those lavish and complicated eats and drinks, hardly even a brand-name apart from Bond's Hoffritz safety razor and the odd bottle of Walker's de luxe Bourbon. The main plot, in the sense of the scheme proposed

by the villains, is likewise thin. Smuggling marijuana and getting protection-money out of oil companies disappoint expectation aroused by what some of these people's predecessors planned: a nuclear attack on Miami, the dissemination throughout Britain of crop and livestock pests, the burgling of Fort Knox. The rank-and-file villains, too, have been reduced in scale.

In most of the Bond books it was the central villain on whom interest in character was fixed. . . . Scaramanga is just a dandy with a special (and ineffective) gun, a stock of outdated American slang and a third nipple on his left breast. We hear a lot about him early on in the 10-page dossier M consults, including mentions of homosexuality and pistol-fetishism, but these aren't followed up anywhere. Why not?

It may be relevant to consider at this point an outstandingly clumsy turn in the narrative. Bond has always been good at ingratiating himself with his enemies, notably with Goldfinger, who took him on as his personal assistant for the Fort Knox project. Goldfinger, however, had fairly good reason to believe Bond to be a clever and experienced operator on the wrong side of the law. Scaramanga hires him after a few minutes' conversation in the bar of a brothel. . . . Bond wonders what Scaramanga wants with him: 'it was odd, to say the least of it . . . the strong smell of a trap.' This hefty hint of a concealed motive on Scaramanga's part is never taken up. Why not?

I strongly suspect—on deduction alone, let it be said—that these unanswered questions represent traces of an earlier draft, perhaps never committed to paper, wherein Scaramanga hires Bond because he's sexually interested in him. A supposition of this kind would also take care of other difficulties or deficiencies in the book as it stands, the insubstantiality of the character of Scaramanga, just referred to, and the feeling of suppressed emotion, or at any rate the build-up to and the space for some kind of climax of emotion, in the final confrontation of the two men. But of course Ian Fleming wouldn't have dared complete the story along those lines. Imagine what the critics would have said!

To read some of their extant efforts, one would think that Bond's creator was a sort of psychological Ernst Stavro Blofeld, bent on poisoning British morality. An article in this journal in 1958 [see Paul Johnson's excerpt above] helped to initiate a whole series of attacks on the supposed 'sex, snobbery and sadism' of the books, as if sex were bad *per se*, and as if snobbery resided in a few glossy-magazine descriptions of Blades and references to Aston-Martin cars and Pinaud shampoos and what-not, and as if sadism could be attributed to a character who never wantonly inflicts pain. . . .

These are matters that can't be argued through in this review. But it seems clear that Ian Fleming took such charges seriously. Violent and bloody action, the infliction of pain in general, was very much scaled down in what he wrote after 1958. Many will regard this as a negative gain, though others may feel that a secret-agent story without violence would be like, say, a naval story without battles. As regards 'sex' and 'snobbery' and the memorable meals and the high-level gambling, these, however unedifying, were part of the unique Fleming world, and the denaturing of that world in the present novel and parts of its immediate forerunners is a loss. Nobody can write at his best with part of his attention on puritanical readers over his shoulder.

Ian Fleming was a good writer, occasionally a brilliant one, as the gypsy-encampment scene in *From Russia, With Love* (however sadistic) and the bridge-game in *Moonraker* (however snobbish) will suggest. His gifts for sustaining and varying action, and for holding down the wildest fantasies with cleverly synthesised pseudo-facts, give him a place beside long-defunct entertainer-virtuosos like Jules Verne and Conan Doyle, though he was more fully master of his material than either of these. When shall we see another? (pp. 540-41)

> *Kingsley Amis, ''M for Murder,'' in* New Statesman, *Vol. LXIX, No. 1777, April 2, 1965, pp. 540-41.*

GENE SMITH

I do not care for Mr. Bond. I do not care for him at all. In this I am at variance with Mr. Amis, who in *The James Bond Dossier* convicts me and all like me of being perishing little snivelers [see excerpt below], nearsighted 20th-century weaklings whose sexual inadequacies lead us, twisted little devils that we are, to condemn a fully committed man who does things his way and only his way. Priggish Puritan prude snipes at never-bend stout English oak. Red glare gleams in eye—Mr. Amis points out that all Bond-villains have a red glare in their eyes—as cheapmake Everyman says bad things about keen hero.

With the lines drawn, and with only a wistful thought about the jokes that could be made concerning Mr. Amis' first name, let us look at *The Man With The Golden Gun,* the last book to come from Mr. Fleming's typewriter before his death a year ago. The book begins where *You Only Live Twice* has left off. In that opus, it will be recalled, Bond's memory has been driven away by a conk on the head. He has forgotten who he is and what he is. . . . [He] has forgotten that you can recognize a Jew by his ear lobes (*Casino Royale*) and that you can't hurt a Negro by hitting him in the head (*Live and Let Die*). . . . With the opening of *The Man With the Golden Gun,* we learn that Bond has somehow gone off to Russia, where he's been brainwashed. Now he is back in London giving his Chief, old M, a glazed-eye look along with some Russian propaganda. . . . But he is dragged away, re-brainwashed, and shipped off to give the business to The Man With The Golden Gun, the hottest killer in the world. From there the book goes downhill. Felix Leiter, the old CIA man—who, like most likable Yanks, comes from Texas (*Casino Royale*)—turns up, and there is a bang-up train ride and international crooks and dancing girls and what-not. Not a great work.

Which brings us to why I don't like Bond and, by implication, his creator. I don't like them because, unlike many people, I don't think for one minute that Ian Fleming is spoofing us in these books with their seemingly learned allusions to exotica in food, flora, customs, history. I simply will not accept the view that it was all a big gag on Fleming's part. . . . Where the Bond movies are loaded with gags and the audience often roars with laughter, there is not an iota of humor in the books. Because some of my best friends have absolutely anonymous ear lobes, and because Joe Louis was twice knocked out by blows to the head, I feel I can say that these Fleming-truisms are *not* truisms. And because I have now read his books carefully, I feel that I can say that to him they *were* truisms. He is not putting us on. It is not a spoof.

One finds this unspoofifying to be offensive. . . . [Where] Fleming bombs away at our sensibilities with hunchbacks, with giant-headed, eyebrowless and eyelashless Negroes, with exclamation point-shaped men, with wrinkleless polished skulls, with three-nippled gunmen, one gets the feeling that these worthies are not meant to serve as caricatures. It really seems that Fleming seriously says to his readers that funny-looking people want a little watching; that they are more than likely up to some funny business. Well, you will say, didn't Jonathan Swift write about these guys bigger than the Pan-Am building, almost, and about teeny-weenies smaller than the figures on a five-inch transistor television set? Yes, but it wasn't the same thing. Swift effectively showed us that beneath the facade of normal-seeming people were things grotesque, misshapen, strange. One might appear quite normal to one's fellows, but to an outsider, differently placed and structured, one may appear tiny and insect-like, or immense, or wild, or evil-smelling—especially evil-smelling. Fleming says, Would you buy a used car from a guy who limps or has bug-eyes? And Fleming answers, Nah. (pp. 1, 17)

I believe Mr. Fleming is guilty of giving the three of us, you, me, Mr. Amis, a 13-volume snow job. The question is, did Fleming know it was a snow job? There is nothing wrong with pulling off a snow job, particularly if you sell about sixty zillion books and have a piece of 007 films, chewing gum, raincoats, toiletries, etc.; but it is not so good if you snow yourself in the process. And when you get Mr. Amis and an entire horde of other people caught up in your drifts, it is even less good. I think Mr. Fleming got lost in the flakes drifting down all around him, and got to taking it seriously, and ended up as a true believer in James Bond's elegance, relevance, and significance. Mr. Amis is also slogging away, galoshes filling up and muffler coated with frost, and you, also, may be out there frolicking about without sled. But I'm not. I'm home in front of the fireplace.

I have nothing against Mr. Fleming. . . . One of his bridge partners was W. Somerset Maugham, who, like Fleming, was once in the employ of British Intelligence and who once wrote a book called *Ashenden or the British Agent*. . . . *Ashenden* caught Europe during 1914-18 with its sculptured patterns and tortured loyalties; *Ashenden* saw the conflicts and the shiftings; *Ashenden* made us catch our breath and ended by teaching us even while it entertained us at the bidding of its author, who always said he was just a storyteller. But Bond? And Fleming? Fleming said his only desire was to make sure the reader kept turning the page. Well, he did that. But once turned, the page was forgotten. Now there will be no more. So long, 007. (p. 17)

> *Gene Smith, '' 'Goldigger'; or, Did 007's Creator Perpetrate a Remarkable Snow-Job?'' in* Book Week—The Sunday Herald Tribune, *August 29, 1965, pp. 1, 17.*

ANTHONY LEJEUNE

''ENDIT'': this single cablese word, prophetic and appropriate, is the title of the last chapter of the last James Bond novel, *The Man with the Golden Gun*. From the hospital bed where he lies recovering from bullet wounds, Bond cables M, refusing the knighthood which a grateful government has offered him.

In *You Only Live Twice* we left Bond, bemused from the holocaust which closed his duel with Blofeld, heading blindly for Vladivostok. We now learn what happened to him there, and in what strange condition he returned to London. This opening sequence is the most interesting part of the book. Afterwards, Bond is perfunctorily de-brainwashed and sent, good as new, to hunt down ''Pistols'' Scaramanga, the deadliest gunman in the Caribbean. . . .

The plot, as in several of Fleming's later books, contains little more than would make a respectable short story, and both its setting and some of its incidents are reminiscent of previous adventures. *The Man with the Golden Gun* is undeniably slight, but like everything Fleming wrote, intensely readable.

I saw him last a few weeks before he died. He seemed very tired. The effort of invention had become increasingly difficult. He found it particularly hard, he said, to think of new villains; and indeed Scaramanga is scarcely in the same league as Mister Big or Sir Hugo Drax or Rosa Klebb. Outrageous devices no longer bubbled up in his mind; it had been a long time since he contrived anything as gasp-provoking as Dr. No's death by guano or Goldfinger's purchase of a Corporal missile with which to assault Fort Knox.

In a sense, Fleming's job was finished. He had irrevocably transformed the *genre* in which he worked: and, unlike so many intellectuals who toy with the thriller, he had done so from exactly the right point of view. He enjoyed and respected the work of his predecessors, John Buchan, Sapper, Leslie Charteris, and had no wish to rebel against them, merely to bring their formula up to date. Anti-heroes, disillusionment, the seamy side, never attracted him. Deliberately, he produced fairy stories for worldly adults, and he made them as glossy and sensually appealing as he could. He was a sophisticated man who knew how things worked. The effect he aimed at, and splendidly achieved, was one of glamorized realism.

It subtly flattered the reader, and brought Fleming success on a scale which nobody could have predicted. . . .

[With] the appearance of *Moonraker* James Bond really left the launching-pad (as Fleming put it). And, from that moment, the highbrow critics, who had praised *Casino Royale,* and the amateur sociologists, leftists to a man, turned and rent him.

"Sex, sadism and snobbery" were the charges they brought. *The Man with the Golden Gun* contains no sex beyond a chaste kiss; no sadism in the proper sense, though inevitably some bloodshed; and certainly no trace of snobbery. These never were, in fact, characteristics of Fleming's work. Cruder sex and harsher cruelty are to be found in almost any of the sordid, "outspoken" and ostensibly realistic modern novels which highbrow critics delight to honor. But there is, admittedly, a difference. In highbrow novels sex and violence are treated gloomily: in Fleming's stories they are presented cheerfully and with frank enjoyment. This is what leftists hate, just as they hate fox-hunting not because it gives pain to foxes but because it gives pleasure to humans.

A similar jealous puritanism underlies the charge of snobbery. The critics who brought it cannot have meant that Bond was a social snob. Bond is virtually classless: he has very little money of his own, and doesn't even possess a tail-coat: M, not he, is a member of Blades'. But he appreciates quality, in food, in drink, in all the apparatus of living. Originally, Fleming introduced brand names and gastronomic details as part of the streamlining and glamorizing process: they contributed realism and they were pleasant for the reader to imagine. Later he amused himself by giving an unsolicited advertisement to commodities and craftsmanship of which he approved.

But leftists are galled by the contemplation of material luxury and standards beyond those of the masses; so they disapproved of Fleming's approval, and even more of his presumption in stating it without a blush. They called Bond vulgar, a curious word on leftist lips: and they accused him of fascism, ignoring

his confessed admiration for President Kennedy. . . . (pp. 776-77)

Fleming shrugged all these criticisms off; but he paid, I think, more attention to them than he cared to admit. Consciously or unconsciously, he subdued the flavor of his narrative, which was a mistake. It weakened the books without appeasing his enemies.

The character of James Bond had, in any event, changed and developed since its original conception. Bond was to have been a mere "blunt instrument in the hands of government," as featureless as his name. But he soon acquired flesh and blood and personality, a heart as well as a mind, idiosyncrasies and hopes and fears; and his name, which Fleming picked for its ordinariness, has now become a romantic symbol all over the world.

The humanizing of Bond went perhaps too far. In *The Spy Who Loved Me* Fleming tried, foolhardily and with disastrous results, to see him through the eyes of a girl. In the next book, Fleming, slightly chastened, returned more or less to the proper formula; but Bond, like Sherlock Holmes after the Reichenbach Falls, was never quite the same man again. . . .

The Man with the Golden Gun is by no means [Fleming's] worst. Bond makes a decent last bow.

But "ENDIT" cannot really be the final word. Fleming has gone, having given more pleasure to mankind than most of us can ever hope to do; but Bond survives, with a life of his own, Bond and pseudo-Bond merging into a single epic figure. With his Walther PPK nestling in its Berns Martin Triple-draw holster, and a full-throated roar from twin exhausts of his supercharged Bentley, James Bond has passed triumphantly into the Valhalla of immortal heroes. (p. 777)

> Anthony Lejeune, "To Valhalla with Twin Exhausts," in *National Review, Vol. XVII, No. 36, September 7, 1965, pp. 776-77.*

KINGSLEY AMIS

What Bond is, obviously enough, is a *secret agent.* He sees himself in these terms, rather self-consciously, at a climactic point in *Moonraker.* Bearers of this designation, which no doubt belongs more to fiction and imagination than to life, have flourished at least since the turn of the century. It's a nebulous calling, ranging from the almost completely freelance status of a Bulldog Drummond to the straight Foreign Office employment of William le Queux's Duckworth Drew, one of the earliest practitioners. This breadth of scope makes the idea more evocative, so much so that it probably focuses more daydreaming and fantasy-spinning than any other semi-mythical occupation. (p. 2)

Bond's professionalism is one of the best things about him, both as a moral quality and as a relief from that now defunct and always irritating personage, the gifted amateur who is called or just happens to wander in when MI5 is baffled and the Cabinet in despair. However, Bond is given to lapses of judgment so appalling and so rich in dire results that he needs every particle of our esteem for his forethought on other occasions, and every ounce of Mr. Fleming's talent for camouflaging such blunders by pace and mystification, in order to avoid forfeiting our respect forever. (p. 10)

[In *Dr. No*] Bond, with all his experience, always up to things like putting hairs in the locks of his suitcases so that he can tell whether or not people are searching his luggage, lets his attention wander and is deservedly taken prisoner. (p. 11)

Three of Mr. Fleming's favorite situations are about to come up one after the other. Bond is to be wined and dined, lectured on the aesthetics of power, and finally tortured by his chief enemy.

The last of these three has inevitably attracted more attention than the first two. These days any book in which one character inflicts physical pain on another risks being given the *sadism* label, just as any scene in which two unmarried persons embrace courts that of *compensation-fantasy*. . . .

Bond's tendency to find himself tied to a chair under scientific torment is an important feature of his total character. *Sadism*, even so, comes in here oddly, I feel, since it's Bond and not any of his opponents whom the reader is invited to identify with, and Bond suffers pain, never wantonly inflicts it. *Masochism* is a more appropriate label at first sight, but is impaired by the difficulty that the masochist enjoys being knocked about. Bond gives no sign of pleasure when, for instance, he gets his little finger broken by Mr. Big's lieutenant. But I suppose he might really be enjoying himself all the time, almost without knowing it. (p. 12)

All talk about a sexual component in Bond's sufferings mistakes the author's intention and misrepresents the reader's response. When Le Chiffre goes to work on Bond's testicles with a carpet beater, to take the most conspicuous case, a very well-established and basic element of the thriller story is at work. The incident has two closely related effects. It makes us feel admiration and sympathy for the hero and fear and hatred for the villain. All these feelings are heightened by the particularly dreadful and cruel method of torture used by Le Chiffre. To have pulled Bond's hair and given him a lot of lip would have been ineffective, upon both Bond and the reader. (p. 13)

The effect of [the] ground base of violence [in the Bond books] is partly to entertain the reader by showing him glimpses of a semi-fantasy world he might like to inhabit, but dare not. In addition, however, he is also the more likely to admire Bond as one who not only inhabits such a world by choice, but survives the worst it can do to him and comes out on top. Further, against a background so variously lethal, Bond can be seen as relatively responsible—never killing wantonly; never, or hardly ever, in cold blood. . . . Now and then he even struggles with his conscience over the morality of the whole thing. (p. 14)

[Bond] started life about 1818 as Childe Harold in the later cantos of [Lord] Byron's poem, reappeared in the novels of the Brontë sisters, and was around until fairly recently in such guises as that of Maxim de Winter in Miss Daphne du Maurier's *Rebecca*. . . . [The] Byronic hero is lonely, melancholy, of fine natural physique, which has become in some way ravaged, of similarly fine but ravaged countenance, dark and brooding in expression, of a cold or cynical veneer, above all *enigmatic*, in possession of a sinister secret. . . .

[Bond functions] as a latter-day Byron, at once more dilapidated and more *soigné*. He has never quite gotten around to the traditional facial antic of *curling his lip* at all the works of man, but he wouldn't surprise us if he did. Mr. Fleming has brought off the unlikely feat of enclosing this wildly romantic, almost narcissistic, and (one would have thought) hopelessly out-of-date persona inside the shellac of a secret agent, so making it plausible, mentally actable, and, to all appearance, contemporary. (p. 26)

Keeping Bond and the women away from one another is a difficult task. . . . The first thing to grasp here is that Bond is *attractive to women*. To notice that this is true of some real men as well as of many fictional men, and that most real men are perfectly acceptable to some women, seems beyond the power of the average book reviewer. One need not be misshapen or sexually panic-stricken or a voyeur to get vicarious enjoyment out of a fictional man's amours, though to hear the critics talk one would never believe it. (p. 34)

[There are limits to Bond's sexual activities], even if critics can't remember them. Bond collects almost exactly one girl per excursion abroad, which average he exceeds only once, by one. This is surely not at all in advance of what any reasonably personable, reasonably well-off bachelor would reckon to acquire on a foreign holiday or trip for his firm. Critical horror at Bond's sexual victories, I feel, can have its own element of "compensation." (p. 36)

Bond's success with women is totally explicable within the terms of the novels. Women take to him because he likes them and knows how to be kind to them. He has, of course, further advantages. Other things being equal, women prefer handsome men to ugly and brave men to cowardly. There seems nothing to be done about that. Any number of us, however, could afford to take a couple of leaves out of Bond's book. Unlike many heroes of more ambitious fiction, Bond is good-tempered and not moody. Women appreciate that in a man. (p. 42)

[Fleming] evolved something approaching a formula for the presentation of Bond's fair quarry. Its most noticeable feature is that, so to speak, the given girl appears in the first place. After reading a couple of Bonds we know that at some stage in any one of them, as ally or as confederate of the enemy (but never as public librarian or best-friend-in-the-Navy's-little-sister—always as novel and as isolated a figure as possible), wandering about on a Caribbean beach or heralded on the road by the sexy boom of twin exhausts, *she* is going to turn up. (p. 43)

Physically, [the] Bond-girl varies little from book to book. (p. 44)

Bond-girl has athletic and other abilities, can swim and dive, wields a rifle or a bow and arrow, sets about rescuing herself from danger without waiting for Bond's help, a couple of times (in the persons of Tiffany Case and Kissy Suzuki) gets him away to safety when he's in no state to move unaided. If this is a dream-girl, she deserves more respect than harem types or gossip-column international-set types. . . .

Nor is Bond-girl what the popular critical view says she is, "an animated pin-up, conceived purely as a sexual object" (James Price on *The Spy Who Loved Me* in the *London Magazine*). (p. 46)

A pinup can't have difficulties or fears or suspicions or hopes, personal or emotional baggage of any kind. Bond-girl . . . always has these, and they're of one basic kind. Under a wide variety of covers—worldliness (Tiffany Case, Pussy Galore), outdoor-girl self-sufficiency (Honey), international-set glossiness (Tracy), belief in the organization (Tatiana)—Bond-girl is a defenseless child of nature, a wanderer in a hostile world, an orphan, a waif.

She's an orphan in the most literal sense. Almost without exception she has no family at all, and if there are any remnants—Domino's brother, Tilly's sister—they soon disappear. Such contacts as she may have are bad: a brutal husband, a gangster lover, a ruthless political machine she longs to escape from. . . . Bond's part is not to break down Bond-girl's defenses, but to induce her to lower them voluntarily. The general moral paraphrases out eventually as something like: "Even the toughest and/or most beautiful women are likely to be warm and gentle at heart and will respond to warmth and gentleness." This ought to be a truism, but it isn't. (pp. 48-9)

The moral content of Mr. Fleming's work, the values expressed or implied, whether through Bond or directly by the author, have been denounced all over the place. (p. 73)

I should have thought that a fairly orthodox moral system, vague perhaps but none the less recognizable through accumulation, pervades all Bond's adventures. Some things are regarded as good: loyalty, fortitude, a sense of responsibility, a readiness to regard one's safety, even one's life, as less important than the major interests of one's organization and one's country. Other things are regarded as bad: tyranny, readiness to inflict pain on the weak or helpless, the unscrupulous pursuit of money or power. These distinctions aren't excitingly novel, but they are important, and as humanist and/or Christian as the average reader would want. They constitute quite enough in the way of an ethical frame of reference, assuming anybody needs or looks for or ought to have one in adventure fiction at all.

What (if anything) holds this elementary moral system together is belief in England, or at any rate a series of ideas about her. (p. 74)

Throughout Bond's adventures no Englishman does anything bad. . . .

To use foreigners as villains is a convention older than our literature. It's not in itself a symptom of intolerance about foreigners. (p. 75)

Where Mr. Fleming scores is in having made national prejudices *knowledgeable*. . . . Thus it's not the Turks as a whole who are no good, but the Turks of the plains. . . . If the French are to be looked down on, it's not for having produced Laval, General Salan, and the rest, but because all, repeat *all*, French people suffer from liver complaints. The East is admittedly suspect *en bloc:* you never get a warm, dry handshake there, only a banana-skin effect. . . . Any fool can dislike the Chinese or the Japanese; the smart man's best-hated Asian is the Korean. . . .

I find all this enjoyable, a clever extension of the general *au fait*-ness that Mr. Fleming has made such a corner in. (p. 76)

The villains of British cloak-and-dagger fiction have always tended to be motivated by a dislike of England on top of a general commitment to knavery. This dislike may be irrational in that England will not have done them and theirs any tangible harm, but rational in that they construe the mere existence of England as a threat to everything they value. . . . The anti-England machination gets a good outing in Mr. Fleming's works. (pp. 81-2)

The attitudes about England that underlie all this are mostly dramatized, put into plot or character rather than openly avowed; there are some things one doesn't have to talk about. However,

Bond does open up enough to warn Goldfinger against underestimating the British. . . . (p. 82)

Bond's side, M's side, England's side, is the side to be on, the right side as well as the winning side or the side we happen to be reading about.

I accept this. What keeps Bond at it may be just desire to do his job, devotion to M and trust in M's judgment, personal obstinacy, plus the vaguest patriotism, but the combination is credible. I also find a belief, however unreflecting, in the rightness of one's cause more sympathetic than the anguished cynicism and the torpid cynicism respectively of Messrs [John] le Carré and [Len] Deighton. More useful in an adventure story anyway, and more powerful. . . . (p. 83)

Not much mind is needed to notice that Bond's adventures have been getting more fantastic all the time and some critics have actually done it. With the striking exception of Hugo Drax's plot to obliterate London, the operations of the earlier villains were comparatively modest in scope. . . . (p. 98)

[The] fantastic element in the various conspiracies is always played down; the methods used are described in apparently exhaustive detail, with a constant emphasis on logic and forethought, and the utmost use is made of realistic background material. Thus we know perfectly well that even if there are international criminal cartels like SPECTRE, they couldn't hijack a NATO bomber with a couple of nuclear bombs on board and wouldn't try. But *if* there were and they could and would, then they'd use someone exactly like Petacchi to do the job for them. . . . We don't notice how thin SPECTRE's ultimate chances of delivering the bombs may be while we're running our mental fingers over the solidity of the ship that is to do the delivering. (pp. 98-9)

This might be called the imaginative use of information, whereby the pervading fantastic nature of Bond's world, as well as the temporary, local, fantastic elements in the story, are bolted down to some sort of reality, or at least counter-balanced. In addition, it provides motives and explanations for action; and the information itself is valuable, not simply *as* information, but in the relish and physical quality it lends to the narrative. . . .

The imaginative use of information and so on is rather a mouthful, and it's so highly characteristic of these books, so much their very essence, that I don't see why it shouldn't be called the Fleming effect. (p. 100)

When a writer is attacked more or less purely as a writer, rather than as a social or psychological scourge, what takes the first shock of the assault is likely to be his style. On the fundamental level of literacy, the matter of getting the words into something like order and the commas in roughly the right place, Mr. Fleming survives scrutiny. He leaves out a question mark occasionally, but in general he knows how to punctuate; it's this, perhaps, that gives the run of his sentences a slightly old-fashioned air. Grammar is another disappearing craft he has mastered, though he produces one of the finest displaced nominatives of the century when Bond examines his intentions toward Vesper: "As a woman, he wanted to sleep with her, but only when the job had been done." The same carelessness makes him write, for instance, that a skier's knees are his Achilles heel.

These minor slips are less daunting than the sudden lurches into the idiom of the novelette which turn up every few chapters.

The trains on the other lines were engineless and unattended—waiting for tomorrow. Only Track No. 3, and its platform, throbbed with the tragic poetry of departure. (*From Russia, with Love* . . .)

And at the station one could hear the heartbeat of the town. The night sounds of the trains were full of its tragedy and romance. (*Goldfinger* . . .)

It is an intoxicating moment in a love affair when, for the first time a man puts his hand under the table at a restaurant and lays it on a girl's thigh and she slips her own hand over his and presses it against her. The two gestures say everything that need be said. All is agreed. All the pacts are signed. And there is a long minute of silence during which the blood sings. (*Diamonds Are Forever* . . .)

(pp. 123-24)

It's often maintained that style as such doesn't exist. Passages like these get us down not because they sin against some abstract criterion of how something may or may not be expressed, but, so the argument would run, because they show the writer failing to grasp, and ultimately failing to want to grasp, the emotions of travel in the first two cases and the nature of sexual attraction (let's say) in the [third]. . . . Anybody, again, who had been really moved by these would have made up his own way of talking about them. . . . (p. 124)

There's a certain truth in this. Mr. Fleming's accounts of sexual relationships never seem to get much further than physical attraction, Bond's kindness and the girl's response to it, and some sentiment on both sides expressed usually in direct general statements: "all the pacts are signed" and so on. I find none of this offensive, but it is limited, largely because Bond, who is first and foremost the hero of an action story, isn't suitable as a participant in the kind of carefully explored mutual involvement the novel of the last hundred years has gotten us used to. Human relations at large get a poor showing in the Bond books. Many people in them, from Honeychile Rider to Hugo Drax, make a vivid impression on our mind's eye and ear, but the way they connect up with Bond, and with one another, is obscure, or thin, or just not there.

A look at the context of the quotations about trains, however, will show how fallacious it can be to contend that periodic laziness of expression means lack of real feeling or interest. The sense of energy and movement in the Orient Express chapters of *From Russia, with Love*, of a peculiar excitement about the physical ambience of the train and the feel of the places it goes through—all this is unmistakable, and characteristic. With any kind of journey in prospect or progress, added drive comes into the writing, making us share Bond's—and the author's—delight in trains, cars, aircraft, ships, boats. (p. 125)

Mechanized travel is so deeply built into our day-to-day habits that to swing the reader into participation every time testifies to a certain power and freshness. The same talent works the other way round, pointing up the tangible, prosaic elements in remote or exotic places and activities. The contemporary becomes romantic, if you like, the merely romantic solidly contemporary. The books are full of set pieces in which this fusion takes place. . . . (pp. 125-26)

These are not mere backgrounds to action, or interludes; they promote and express action. Any adventure writer can be expected to keep things moving in general, to throw in chases and fights and to handle these adequately: Mr. Fleming's chases are never just matters of speed and danger, and his fights aren't just slugging matches. More than this, the action of any given book never moves, so to speak, in a single straight line; it isn't a simple matter of a steady, or jerky, closing-in by Bond on his quarry. There are diversions that embody a lot of action in themselves as well as bearing on the main quest, sometimes surpassing it in originality and compactness. (p. 126)

[The] huge virtue of never stooping to pretentiousness, of never going in for any kind of arty or symbolical flannel, cost Mr. Fleming a formidable amount of critical acclaim, but it did as much as anything to bring him readers. Whatever the rights and wrongs of using literature as an escape from life, there's a lot to be said for using one kind of literature as an escape from others. Nobody—or hardly anybody—denies the value of writing that reflects the complexity of life, however inadequately it does so even at its best. In proportion as we value it, perhaps, we have time for participating in the excitement of single-heartedly pursuing simple goals and of fighting clearly defined external enemies. And if Mr. Fleming has got to have a moral justification found for him, like everyone else, then I suggest that it wasn't valueless to help you and me to see our troubles in perspective by showing us a not especially intelligent or sensitive man triumphing over far worse obstacles than any we're likely to have to face.

Mr. Fleming did himself a double injustice by professing merely to keep us turning his pages, an underrated feat anyway. He asked for cavalier treatment by so doing and he also diverted attention from what he offered besides straightforward action. He regularly put this first out of conscientiousness, thereby tending to conceal the emotional conviction he brought to so many of the milieus in which his action takes place. But, at a second look, it's hard to miss his feeling for climate and times of day, for beaches and the sea, for trees, shrubs, birds, fishes, for Royale-les-Eaux, Crab Key, Piz Gloria, Echo Lake, and the rest as places in their own right. (p. 130)

Most of the above had already been written when Ian Fleming died. I hope I've sufficiently conveyed my admiration for what I think he did best. When a few Easters have gone by without a new Bond adventure, regret at the passing of his creator may well help to bring about an assessment of his proper place in literature. This, as I see it, is with those demi-giants of an earlier day: Jules Verne, Rider Haggard, Conan Doyle. Ian Fleming has set his stamp on the story of action and intrigue, bringing to it a sense of our time, a power and a flair that will win him readers when all the protests about his supposed deficiencies have been forgotten. He leaves no heirs. (p. 132)

Kingsley Amis, in his The James Bond Dossier, *The New American Library, 1965, 142 p.*

ALEX CAMPBELL

[In *Octopussy*] Commander James Bond, British Secret Service Agent 007, shows himself to be the dove some of us had long suspected. Dispatched by his frosty-eyed chief, "M," to Checkpoint Charlie in Berlin to kill a Soviet sniper, Bond disobeys for sentimental reasons. . . .

Without further question, Bond now joins the knightly company of story-book heroes. All of them are athletic, daring and handsomely virile, but their chief mark of distinction is that their patron saint is George and they chivalrously spend much of their time saving pretty girls from dragons of one kind or another. That, in essence, is what Bond does in his last adventure, at Checkpoint Charlie.

Probably there should never have been any doubts about Bond being a true-blue hero. . . . Nevertheless, Fleming, presumably deliberately, caused many readers to confuse Bond with the currently more prevalent anti-hero. Fleming did this by two devices. He supplied Bond with a different girl in every story, instead of a steady; and he had Bond treat her more like a whore than a heroine. In *On Her Majesty's Secret Service* the heroine actually gets bumped off, and in *Live And Let Die* she commits suicide. More than once Bond disgustedly describes his Secret Service missions as dirty as well as dangerous.

Fleming was keen to be "in." He wanted to be the best-seller he became, and he knew the vogue was for tough anti-heroes who would sooner bash a girl's face in than go to bed with her. But Bond, though he is a tough dove, is never a tough. He is quick on the draw, drives fast cars, kills villains, but all the stories imply what the last one spells out: Shooting girls just isn't his style. . . .

Bond may be as well-known as Tarzan. This is encouraging to those of us who've never accepted the anti-hero, with his lousy manners and false hair on his chest. Does anybody *really* admire Mike Hammer? What's good about a Tarzan who tosses the girl to the cheetah instead of saving her from it? But a problem arises. Who will take Bond's place? There are disconcertingly few other story-book heroes around any more, and some of the best are getting pretty long in the tooth. . . .

Does this mean the stage will soon be empty of heroes and dominated by hawks, who at the word of command will eagerly proceed to Berlin or any other checkpoint, to bump off any number of girls and the prettier the better? Or is there, somewhere, a new Bond getting ready to jump out of somebody's typewriter, to thwart the villains and save the heroine? If there is, may his adventures match the courage of the late Ian Fleming. . . .

Alex Campbell, "The Very Last of 007," in The New
Republic, *Vol. 155, No. 1, July 2, 1966, p. 29.*

BERNICE LARSON WEBB

The legendary Teutonic superman Beowulf would seem to have a counterpart today in the teenagers' culture hero James Bond, secret agent 007. . . . [An] essential similarity exists both in general framework of the narrative and in plot details of the two bodies of work.

Elements common to traditional hero-romances are present, of course, in both the Beowulf epic and the Bond novels: improbable adventures, heroic ideal of brave leader and loyal followers, concept of the hero as representative of good, pagan culture with overlay of Christianity, and absence of romantic love. But in addition to these general correspondences, interesting similarities in detail strengthen the strange parallelism found in the careers of these two supermen. Fleming's last novel, *The Man with the Golden Gun,* provides a particularly startling set of comparisons with *Beowulf* and should, perhaps, be scrutinized at this time despite the possibility of Anglo-Saxon scholars' accusations of irreverence and irrelevance. (p. 1)

Mythological and supernatural connotations, appropriate to the legends of heroes, appear in both *Beowulf* and *The Man with the Golden Gun.* The villains of *Beowulf*—Grendel, Grendel's mother, and the dragon—who represent threats to the security of the lands they inhabit, are markedly difficult to combat because they exist outside the normal order of life. The Danish monsters become so great a menace, in fact, that an outsider—Beowulf in the role of savior from afar—must come to fight them. In *The Man with the Golden Gun,* too, the villain exists outside the normal order of life. This ruthless assassin, as Fleming points out, has become "something of a local myth" in the Caribbean area because of the widespread killings and maimings he has accomplished without effective reprisal by law enforcement officers or other bystanders. . . . Furthermore, his association with gangsters from the United States and Europe in communistic political and war activities has begun to carry his reputation across national borders, a fact which gives justification for Bond's entering the scene.

The supernatural elements of these villains extend beyond their personalities to the tools or weapons they wield. In the monsters' cave in Denmark is kept an ancient sword which possesses a magic quality: it is the only sword which can be used effectively against Grendel's mother. In addition to conventional weapons, the blood of these creatures is supernaturally potent. The blood of the Geatish dragon fatally poisons its victims, and perhaps even more powerful than the dragon's blood is that of the Danish monsters. Even though in Beowulf's hands the giant sword is capable of killing Grendel's mother, its blade melts like an icicle when exposed to the hot blood of the creature it has wounded. Scaramanga's use of a golden gun with golden bullets fits into a mythological frame of reference, and he strengthens the mythological connotation by making the special features of his favorite weapon functional as well as decorative. For his gold-plated Colt .45 he provides special bullets with a heavy, soft gold core jacketed with silver and cross-cut at the tip, designed for a dum-dum type of wounding effect.

In mythological character, destructive qualities, and international notoriety, then, Scaramanga is analogous, in composite, to the dragon and the monsters which ravage the lands of the Danes and the Geats. These villains are formidable opponents for Bond and Beowulf. (pp. 2-3)

In the beginning of the story each of the two protagonists must undergo interrogation before being admitted into the presence of the man in command of mead hall or office. . . . After due questioning about lineage, homeland, and motives, Beowulf identifies himself and his family to King Hrothgar's satisfaction and pleasure. . . . Only one person close to the king, Unferth ("who sat at the feet of the lord"), remains suspicious and jealous of Beowulf. Unferth, however, is later the one who lends Beowulf an excellent sword for use on the expedition against Grendel's mother.

Because James Bond's death in Japan has been erroneously reported at the headquarters office in London, he has some difficulty in establishing his identity when he returns home. . . . His fingerprints are checked, the fabric of his raincoat is identified and dust from the pockets is examined, and his knowledge of relevant names and facts is verified. These tests establish that Bond is no impostor, and an interview is set up with M., although the Chief of Staff, second in command to M., remains for some time as wary of Bond's motivation as Unferth was of Beowulf's.

The unfounded report of Bond's death, of course, has a stronger parallel in *Beowulf* in its correspondence to the premature mourning for the hero during his visit to the underwater cave of the monsters. In the Anglo-Saxon epic the waiting warriors, seeing blood rise to the surface of the lake nine hours after Beowulf has descended into the water, believe that he has been killed. . . . In *The Man with the Golden Gun* Secret Service headquarters at London accept without adequate proof the Japanese explanation of Bond's disappearance. British officials admit that there's "something odd about 007's death. No body. No solid evidence"—but, nonetheless, they announce his demise to the press.

Beowulf and Bond both have moments of gloom concerning the fulfilment of their respective missions and the preservation of their respective lives. A sense of impending doom being one of the characteristics of Anglo-Saxon poetry, Beowulf demonstrates this attribute in appropriate degree. Likewise, Bond, as a product of the twentieth century, reflects the cynicism and despair often found in today's prose and poetry. (pp. 3-4)

Omens often occur in adventure stories. By a strange quirk, a prophecy is made for Bond in the early part of his first evening in Jamaica which applies without change to either Bond or Beowulf at this point in their adventures. In fact, Beowulf in the eighth century fulfils in completely literal manner a prophecy which Bond twelve centuries later carries out figuratively. While waiting, depressed, in Kingston International Airport, Bond reads his daily horoscope in the local newspaper: "CHEER UP!" the prognostication states. "Today will bring a pleasant surprise and the fulfilment of a dear wish. But you must earn your good fortune by watching closely for the golden opportunity when it presents itself and then seizing it with both hands." As it happens, Beowulf on his first night in Heorot seizes Grendel with both hands and fulfils his "dear wish" by pulling the monster's arm out of its socket. Bond, for his part, acts figuratively in seizing his opportunity, but with similarly profitable results. Discovering a clue to Scaramanga's whereabouts, Bond during his first night in Jamaica attaches himself to his antagonist and, eventually, permanently disarms the gunman.

Each of the two heroes is housed in luxurious surroundings during his stay in the murderer's realm, and the incidents which occur there, allowing for the changes necessitated by a difference in time of twelve centuries, are bizarrely similar. Beowulf is a guest in the gold-plated mead hall Heorot, built by Hrothgar twelve years before. Lofty and high-gabled, the building has become renowned throughout nations for its size, strength, and beauty. . . . But Heorot remains uninhabited beyond the daylight hours because the murderous night raids of the monster Grendel keep away even the bravest of the king's warriors after sundown. No one dares to stay in the hall overnight until Beowulf comes to defend it. Bond, not to be outdone by the earlier folk hero, stays at the luxurious new Thunderbird Hotel. . . . Despite the inducement of private beach and swimming, deep-sea fishing, and private railway, however, the hotel has remained unused, for the Cuban war scare has frightened off the tourist trade. The Thunderbird is being opened now for the first time, for special guests, with Bond hired for a few days as a security guard.

Throughout their stay Beowulf and Bond perform surprisingly similar actions. Even more worthy of note is the fact that the biographer of each man has selected similarly minute details to set down. An innocent bedroom scene, which takes place soon after arrival, may be used to illustrate this point. In the room assigned to him, each man is described in the process of undressing. Beowulf "took off from himself the iron corselet, and the helmet from his head, and gave his figured sword, choicest of weapons, to the retainer who waited on him, and bade him guard the war-harness!" Bond likewise "took off his clothes, put his gun and holster under a pillow, rang for the valet, and had his suit taken away to be pressed."

In Beowulfian and Bondian circles, favorite diversions are fighting (sword or bare hands for Beowulf and gun for Bond), drinking (ale, mead, beer for Beowulf and bourbon for Bond), and feasting. The two heroes are, therefore, exposed to royal entertainment as well as violence in their respective lodging places. (pp. 5-7)

A further correspondence in the two plots is that two murders apiece are carried out by the enemy (or, in one case, murder has been committed very recently and is discovered at this time) during the short period spent by the protagonists in Heorot and the Thunderbird Hotel. The Beowulfian monsters and the Bond villain each kill one minor personage: Grendel seizes and eats a sleeping warrior in Heorot; Scaramanga kills a visiting Las Vegas hotel man in the Thunderbird Hotel. But carrying more repercussions in their respective circles, and providing more pertinent correspondence for the purposes of the present analysis, are the murders of relatively more important persons. In Denmark, the monster mother of Grendel comes into Heorot to kill Eschere, King Hrothgar's dearest counselor, and carries his body off to the swamp. There she eats what she wants and throws the remainder of her human feast into the lake at the edge of the wood. In the Caribbean, Scaramanga murders Commander Ross, a valuable official in the High Commissioner's office in Kingston. Scaramanga's casual report of the murder echoes the cannibalistic qualities of the Danish monster and suggests as well a similar location for the remains of the victim: "I eat one of their famous secret agents for breakfast from time to time," he tells one of his henchmen. "Only ten days ago, I disposed of one of them. . . . His body is now very slowly sinking to the bottom of a pitch lake in Eastern Trinidad. . . ."

Gory details in the two narratives are, indeed, almost eerily similar. (pp. 7-8)

In the latter part of *The Man with the Golden Gun* elements from Beowulf's three adventures—the fight with Grendel, the fight with Grendel's mother, and the fight with the dragon—are combined in the battle between Bond and his powerful adversary Scaramanga. As the wounded Grendel does, the wounded Scaramanga drags himself across the swamp, infested with ancient reptilian water-monsters or twentieth-century snakes, as the circumstance may be. Soon thereafter, just as the hero Beowulf travels across the swamp to search out the last monster left alive for him to fight, Grendel's mother, so the hero Bond travels across the swamp to find the criminal Scaramanga after all the latter's henchmen have been killed in the collapse of the sabotaged Orange River railway bridge. Only after a deliberate search by each of these two heroes does he find the enemy and enter into mortal combat with him. Finally in the sequence of events, Beowulf's fatal treatment by the dragon is echoed . . . closely by Scaramanga's near-fatal injuries to Bond. . . . (pp. 8-9)

In the praise rendered by their contemporaries to Beowulf and Bond, it is interesting to note the significance given to virtue, each hero being considered a representative of good. At the end of the Anglo-Saxon epic the final words of eulogy for the deceased Beowulf place emphasis on the saintlier of his virtues: "the people of the Geats . . . said that he had been of earthly kings the mildest and the gentlest of men, the kindest to his people. . . ." Near the end of *The Man with the Golden Gun*, when Felix Leiter sends the police to Bond's aid in the final encounter with Scaramanga, he outlines the situation in black-and-white terms. "He . . . said that a good man was after a bad man in the swamp. . . ."

The reward for heroic accomplishment, however, is much more than kind words. For all the mighty efforts and all the painful encounters in the lands of the Teutons and the Jamaicans, formal recompense must be offered to Beowulf and to Bond, for generous bounty given by the overlord to his worthy warriors is one of the characteristics of the heroic ideal. Both Beowulf and Bond (Beowulf serving Hygelac and Hrothgar, Bond carrying out M.'s orders) risk their lives and receive appropriate rewards. At the court of King Hrothgar, Beowulf gains both adulation and gifts after eliminating the two marsh monsters. . . . In addition to expensive gifts and extravagant praise, King Hygelac bestows the rank of chief on the hero, and eventually, highest reward of all, the realm is bequeathed to Beowulf as king. (p. 10)

Bond has the privilege of having the representatives of two overseas nations bring their homage to him after he has accomplished his mission. For him, chiefs of the people come from far and near along the airways. Recovering from his wounds in a hospital bed, he is honored by delegates from three countries, assembled under instructions from the Prime Minister of Britain. . . . Then, to climax all awards, a secret coded dispatch arrives from M. announcing that, in view of the nature of services performed, Queen Elizabeth expects to confer a knighthood on Commander Bond.

Only at this point do the actions of Bond digress markedly from those of Beowulf. Whereas Beowulf graciously accepts all honors and the obligations thereby incurred—including a lively fifty-year reign as king—Bond breaks out in a nervous sweat at the thought of becoming a knight. . . . Bond has many admirable qualities: he is brave and resourceful; he is morally strong enough to refuse any monetary bribe; he is honorable enough to scruple against killing an opponent in cold blood. But the thought of the responsibilities inherent in a knighthood is too much for him. Weakly, he orders his secretary to send a cable declining the honor.

And this one digression from the well-marked Anglo-Saxon path laid out by Beowulf reveals a difference which becomes more significant than the mass of similarities pointed out between the two British culture heroes. It is true that Bond frequently achieves his goal through the intervention of coincidence, accomplices, and luck. These interventions are, however, beyond his control. Actually, perhaps through a certain sense of inferiority, he tries harder to prove his independence than Beowulf does. Beowulf, although he rarely allows an assistant to participate in any climactic encounter, always has a small group of faithful warriors in the background to lend moral support. Thus, although Bond's stature as heroic figure is necessarily weakened to some degree because of fortuitous outside help, his heroic character remains unblemished. But by the single act of declining a British knighthood James Bond and his bard destroy the image that they have tried through several thousand pages of labored writing to maintain. Bond shows, in short, that he can never really be the man Beowulf is. Despite

evidence to the contrary, he can never satisfactorily be fitted into the heroic Anglo-Saxon mold.

But one cannot blame him and his bard for trying. Ian Fleming recognized a hero when he saw one and did his best to duplicate. He resurrected an Old English success story with a golden formula and played that formula for all it was worth. (pp. 11-12)

> Bernice Larson Webb, "James Bond As Literary Descendant of Beowulf," in South Atlantic Quarterly, *Vol. LXVII, No. 1, Winter, 1968, pp. 1-12.*

ANN S. BOYD

Don't try to read any of the Bond adventures seriously! To read Bond as a scholastic exercise surely would smack of what's been termed "comic incommensurability." Bond was meant for fun, for escape, and legitimately requires the "willing suspension of disbelief"! Just like the fairy tale of the princess and the pea, real literary critics can't sleep very well when they try to read Fleming just like they'd read James Joyce. If Fleming was interested in what Kierkegaard termed "indirect communication," the least we can do is to read him the way he intended! The only real value in rereading Fleming is to discover that there is more to his series of thriller adventures than one originally might suspect. (p. 26)

[The] series of Bond novels is directly relevant to "adolescents" searching for values and a hero figure, one who would defend justice and humanity. (p. 27)

[A] careful analysis of the completed work reveals it as the saga of a modern knight of faith whose adventures involve a gallery of modern demons which have been attacking contemporary mankind just as diabolically as Medusa and all the other legendary demons and dragons attacked mankind in ages past. Rather than casting pearls before swine, Fleming's genius has cast swine as the personifications of the devil before a hero who is willing to sacrifice all for the great pearl of life and faith.

Individually the Bond adventures parody the form of the detective thrillers: secret agent 007 proceeds to seek out and destroy various adversaries, each of which surpasses its predecessor in the manner of diabolic test or ordeal he presents for Bond to endure. . . . The pattern bears close analogy to the adventures of the mythological hero which Joseph Campbell discusses definitively in *The Hero with a Thousand Faces*. The processes are identical but the metaphors have been changed—a .25 Beretta instead of a sword, a flamethrowing marsh buggy instead of a real live dragon. (pp. 28-9)

[Beginning with the first novel, Bond is involved] in a "humanization" process. Initially, we read, he has never been made to suffer "by cards or by women," knowing that when that happened he too would be branded with the "deadly question-mark" which he had recognized so often in others, "the promise to pay before you have lost; the acceptance of fallibility." In *Casino Royale* both cards and a woman go wrong for him: by the eleventh chapter ("The Moment of Truth") he had been beaten and cleaned out at cards, and it is only because of Felix Leiter's contribution that he is able to continue and win all of Le Chiffre's money; and at the end of the book the integrity of his love for Vesper Lynd disintegrates with her suicide and the realization that she had been a double agent.

The losses which Bond suffers in this book—at cards, in love, and by physical torture (a diabolical "spanking")—set the pattern for each of the following books, in which he gradually becomes less machine-like and more human, until finally he is the bumbling operative whom the critics josh and suggest should be renumbered "006½." At the conclusion of *Casino Royale* Bond realizes that in his previous career he has merely been playing at the child's game of Red Indians, and so he resolves to leave the business of espionage to the "white-collar boys" who can "spy and catch the spies," while he himself will "go after the threat behind the spies, the threat that made them spy."

In the pursuit of Bond's pledge Fleming leads the readers of his subsequent adventures down a Möbius-strip primrose path into a surrealistic world in which things are seldom what they seem to be. Evidences of this verbal surrealism are to be found in Fleming's hyper-attention to minuscule details, his disregard for really probable plots, the poetic "fancies" of the names he gives his characters, and the description of surrealistic scenes in which he comments upon the strange unreality of a particular situation. (pp. 31-2)

Fleming reserves his primary surrealistic effect, however, for secret agent 007's encounters with the grotesque caricatures who serve as the various personifications of evil in the twentieth-century world. (p. 33)

If Fleming had pitted his secret agent 007 only against the realistic enemies in the "normal" spy routine, one would not have been able to perceive so clearly his basic intention. In *Goldfinger,* however, he provides his own clue: "Goldfinger said, 'Mr. Bond, they have a saying in Chicago: "One is happenstance, twice is coincidence, the third time it's enemy action."'" To continue the metaphor, by the time Bond has tilted with his fourth adversary we may be sure that the series is concerned with armed warfare against Satan's contemporary minions.

Fortunately our hypothesis does not have to rest upon the evidence presented in this surrealistic questioning of values in the Bond series alone. For in instigating the original idea for, and publication of, *The Seven Deadly Sins,* Fleming provided left-handed direct evidence for what his right hand had been doing indirectly all along. In this collection of essays by seven distinguished authors on the seven ancient deadly sins (Envy, Pride, Covetousness, Gluttony, Sloth, Lust, Anger), Fleming admits his own "dreadful conclusion that in fact all these ancient sins, compared with the sins of today, are in fact very close to virtues." (pp. 33-4)

The archdemon of Fleming's original roster of sins is the spirit of accidie (or accidia or acedia), which may be translated as indifference, carelessness, or apathy. (p. 34)

In addition, even though he recognizes that the great authors could not have written their masterpieces without the depiction of the seven sins and their consequences, Fleming suggests a list of "seven deadlier sins": Avarice, Cruelty, Snobbery, Hypocrisy, Self-Righteousness, Moral Cowardice, and Malice. . . . [He] concludes: "As a man in the street, I can only express my belief that being possessed of the ancient seven deadly sins one can still go to heaven, whereas to be afflicted by the modern variations can only be a passport to hell." . . .

Critics have viewed the Bond adventures from various angles: yet one clue which they have overlooked is Fleming's own suggestion that we have been looking for sin in the wrong places, that we must go "after the threat behind the spies, the threat that made them spy" and the source behind the obvious source—not automation or the bomb but man's inhumanity and apathy regarding his fellowman. (pp. 34-5)

The simple little eight-word plot which Fleming apparently utilized as the basic matrix within which he manipulated all of his plots was just this: "St. George slays evil dragon, rescues forlorn princess." Fleming's use and transformation of this plot reflects his own real genius, for this theme is the ideal vehicle for him to employ as an "objective correlative" in parallel with his questioning the seven deadly sins of the twentieth century. This theme is part of an ancient legend which most people are acquainted with only superficially as a cultural relic or cliché, but it has played an important role in the traditional symbolism of the Christian faith because it represents the continuing encounter between good and evil. (pp. 43-4)

As Christina Hole points out, the symbol of St. George represents "an enduring symbol of high courage, loyalty, and self-devotion to the cause of the weak and endangered." Although Fleming has represented this image within the métier of the secret agent, he is merely following the precedents of the visual artists, who continually have represented the traditional image within contemporary milieu. . . . (pp. 46-7)

Images are essential . . . for the communication between individuals which makes possible a positive sense of community. For, as [Herbert Read states in *Icon and Idea*]:

> We establish love by communication, and over against the unconscious group soul, we must create a conscious group soul, a community of integrated and interrelated personalities. The means towards this end are always active.

It is in this context, then, that we may review the various attributes of the image of the secret agent. The appeal of this image is immediate, linking cold-war tension of the present with the archetypal qualities of the hero figure of classical mythology, and representing the past in the idiom of the present, not under the banner of great literature but rather through the penetrating gift of the popular storyteller to capture the spirit of the times. (p. 55)

[The] one thing which Bond has which completely overshadows all [other spies and secret agents in contemporary fiction] is his repertory of villains—his honest-to-goodness, larger-than-life villains which he must encounter and destroy! These are extraordinary villains indeed—far from the campy extremes of television's Batman series, for on one hand they are the twentieth-century dragons lying in wait for a twentieth-century St. George, and on the other hand, in the poetic fancies of our subconscious, they are the modern personifications of the devil in new clothes.

By establishing this repertory of villains, with one bold stroke Fleming jumped obliquely across the chessboard of contemporary literature with his twentieth-century knight and commenced the hero quest of this age. With blithe indifference to literary styles and a sincere recognition of the limits of his own literary capabilities, he carried out his peculiar ploy right under the averted noses of critics and commentators who have been longing for such a hero figure. With daring presumption he ignored the fashionable posture of the existentialists who bemoan the loss of meaning in our age of ambiguity. Instead of a man dangling by the puppet strings of contemporary malaise a la Herzog, he has presented a professional capable of mission and responsibility. From a shoddy "world full of grey," Fleming leaped into a technicolor world with a new palette of vivid sins for portraying our times. One by one he carefully set up the false gods of our society just like ducks in a carnival shooting-gallery and then proceeded to knock them down.

Take away the girls and the guns in almost every other secret agent story and there's nothing left but an empty balloon from a neatly configured scheme of intrigue. Take away the girls and the guns from Fleming's saga, tighten up the gaps between the thirteen adventures, and you have a series of hero deeds comparable to those of the Red Cross Knight in Edmund Spenser's *Faerie Queene* or of [John] Bunyan's Christian in *Pilgrim's Progress*. (p. 75)

One of the first suspicions we might have regarding Fleming's modern repertory of demons is that possibly they could reflect his revised perspective concerning the nature of the seven deadly sins. . . . His revised list of what he termed the seven deadlier sins . . . had included Avarice, Cruelty, Snobbery, Hypocrisy, Self-Righteousness, Moral Cowardice, and Malice. In addition, on the side he also included Sloth in its extreme form of accidie, as the only one of the original seven which would have his own wholehearted condemnation. (p. 82)

That accidie continued to be Fleming's prime concern is evident as we examine the entire series. In doing so, we see that the specter of accidie is constantly revealing its face to the reader in a variety of forms. In a mild version it is present in two of the minor villains, Emilio Largo, who made a "fetish of inertia," and Rosa Klebb, whose besetting vice was a laziness combined with a psychological and physiological neutrality which was able to relieve her of "so many human emotions and sentiments and desires."

However, the face of accidie is presented with greatest force in the descriptions and confessions of Fleming's three major villains: Mister Big, Doctor No, and Blofeld. As the first of this demonic trio, Mister Big represents the aesthete, who states that he is suffering from "boredom or accidie," because he is able to take pleasure only in artistry, in polish and finesse. . . .

The second, on the other hand, is the technician, as represented by Doctor No, who is characterized by a "supreme indifference" and a mania for power. . . . (p. 86)

The most imposing personification of accidie, however, is the one presented in the third and most demonic version by the figure of Blofeld, specifically in his last characterization as "Shatterhand" in *You Only Live Twice*. In his final encounter scene with Bond at his Castle of Death, he appears as a modern version of Giant Despair, dressed in a "magnificent black silk kimono across which a golden dragon sprawled" and proceeds to deliver the ultimate apologia for Sloth. . . .

Bond is able to destroy this version of Giant Despair and blow up his Doubting Castle. And at this point, many themes begin to converge. Not only does James Bond represent a modern St. George, but the primary dragon or devil which he must battle is that of the capital sin of our generation, the sin of sloth, the accidie which is a refusal of life and joy, the utter indifference, carelessness, and inertia. . . . (p. 87)

In each of many artistic attempts to depict the legend of St. George we can see how it was brought up-to-date within contemporary situations. As various artists projected their own conditions into the story we can find St. George depicted in different ways: as a noble Roman youth with classical beauty and strength, or as a valiant knight clad in an amazing assortment of clothes and armor and with the faces of different patrons who had commissioned specific works. By perceiving Fleming's representation of secret agent 007 as a contemporaneous St. George, we can accept his premise as far as bringing the image up-to-date. The most important factors are the dynamics of the action involved, not the clothes or the gadgets. (p. 106)

By investigating the dynamics involved in images, we can begin to appreciate why it is inadequate to present an image of St. George alone. An image in itself can have great power. It can evoke action on both conscious and unconscious levels. Men may seek to imitate a hero figure by the unconscious mimicry of some ideal model, or they may deliberately undertake to act out a role. A little girl playing with her dolls illustrates the former, Don Quixote the latter. Neither way in itself is adequate, for the image then becomes either an icon or an idol. The factor of insight is missing, that fusing together of conscious understanding with emotional involvement, which produces commitment, will, courage, and action growing out of integrity. Fleming reflected some understanding of these dynamics, when he referred to Bond's "playing Red Indians" in the beginning of *Casino Royale* and when he stated at the conclusion of *Diamonds Are Forever*, "It reads better than it lives."

James Bond therefore in the role of secret agent 007 is not adequate to represent the image of St. George, not only because the movie version of his adventures has drifted so far away from Fleming's material, but also because these stories as fiction remain within the realm of myth or fantasy. In Marshall McLuhan's terms, Bond is a "hot image" and we need a "cool" one which is able to indicate commitment and complete involvement in depth. What we need is not the James Bond who was Fleming's original hero figure—a St. George in secret agent's clothing, nor the second James Bond who captured the attention of the mass audience, but a real-life figure in whom we might trace out the underlying dynamics of the image of St. George within an authentic situation in history. (pp. 106-07)

> *Ann S. Boyd, in her* The Devil with James Bond, *Greenwood Press, Publishers, 1975, 123 p.*

LeROY L. PANEK

The perspective given by eighty-odd years of spy novels shows Ian Fleming to be a minor writer who, himself, did little to advance the form. Fleming possessed only meager talents as a maker of plots, and he fails absolutely when compared with the men who are popularly assumed to have been his teachers—Buchan and Sapper. He fails to render more than cartoon reality in his characters, either major or minor. With setting Fleming does do a bit better, as he needs to create settings to cover the lacunae in these other areas and to pad out his books in order to make them novels, and short novels at that. Finally, he has little to say in the way of theme: his conservatism is inarticulate and muzzy-headed when compared to, say, Buchan's or even Cheyney's. (p. 201)

More than anything, Fleming as a writer brings to mind [Graham Greene's] *Our Man in Havana* . . . , where an author's fantasies, sometimes innocent, sometimes playful, grow out of the writer's grasp and become reshaped by the world. Fleming's creations certainly live lives of their own and plenty of people believe in them, but Fleming himself was hard-pressed to continue creating them out of Edwardian materials, padding from his travels, and from half-serious, half-fake fragments from his own fantasy life.

There are any number of traps for anyone trying to deal with Fleming's novels as novels. He eggs us on to play along with his psychological foolery; he encourages us to slip on the biographical fallacy; he pushes us to wind ourselves up in highlighted detail so that we will overlook the paucity of his books. (pp. 201-02)

[According to John Pearson in *The Life of Ian Fleming*] Fleming found the spur to thriller writing in his contact with the tradition (albeit adulterated) of the American hard-boiled detective. . . . The link with the hard-boiled detective is as good a place as any to begin an assessment of Fleming's spy novels, for not only Pearson ties him to this tradition, but other writers put him in line with Peter Cheyney—the English agent of the Hammett-Chandler school.

Going back to Cheyney and his importation of tough-guy fiction, the hard-boiled story has a number of characteristics which separate it from other kinds of crime writing: 1) it deals with sordid crime and slimy people; 2) it elevates the detective/agent above both criminals and ordinary citizens; 3) it portrays violence, but this writers often minimize through choreography or stylization; 4) it stresses the work ethic, personal integrity, and other romantic motives; 5) it deals with sexuality but again in a less than real convention; 6) it stresses action over thought; 7) it employs a hero notable for his stamina, courage and persistence; 8) it uses dialogue compounded from colorful slang and witty retorts; 9) it communicates through a terse, understated style; 10) it stresses stoic resignation toward events and people. (p. 202)

Fleming fits some of these criteria, but not all of them. His books all deal with disagreeable people—although after *From Russia, With Love* he colors his villains a bit more with the tradition of the ''gentleman crook'' which comes from the English thriller—but Fleming does not show us very much of them beyond mouthing a psychological label. Likewise, moving out of the manicured detective story, Fleming may narrate us to the edge of some sordid events (rape and castration usually) but they, too, belong to the game of quack psychiatry which he plays rather than a realistic urge. The big crimes in Fleming's books do not belong to the hard-boiled tradition of grubbiness, but rather to the international morality of the spy novel. Fleming does, though, raise his hero not only above criminals but also above ordinary citizens. . . . Other than establishing certain, playful frameworks for characterization, . . . , and demonstrating that Bond is exuberantly heterosexual, much of Fleming's use of sexuality draws on the love-romance rather than the hard-boiled tradition. In terms of action, almost all of Fleming's novels suffer from comparison with the hard-boiled story: they do not stress action but use it as a cap for a series of placement scenes of big gulps of padding. . . . Bond, like Sam Spade or Mike Hammer, certainly has courage, stamina and persistence, but, once more, this draws on the schoolboy story (as seen at the end of *The Man with the Golden Gun* where Bond cannot finish off Scaramanga unless it is a fair fight) as well as Fleming's half-hearted attempt to probe how far the physical and psychic fiber of a man can be strained. . . . Finally, in terms of style, Fleming learned little from hard-boiled writers. His pseudo-shocking openings and short sentences come from journalism as Vivienne's remarks on style in *The Spy Who Loved Me* make clear. Neither is Bond's dialogue particularly witty or tart. If people believe that, they have been duped by the American-

made and American-rewritten Bond films which give the hero non-canonical utterances. . . . (pp. 203-04)

On the whole, Fleming qualifies as a hard-boiled writer, but only by a slim margin. Some of his similarities can be found in much mid-century crime fiction—the increase in sex and violence for instance. Some of his similarities to hard-boiled writers merge with native traditions like the schoolboy story. Fleming learned little about narration or action from the hard-boiled tradition, and the source of his morality lies elsewhere. Perhaps most importantly, Fleming drew a few details and one of his continuing obsessions from American tough-guy fiction. The most apparent of these details, of course, are Bond's secretaries. . . . Another superficial detail from the hard-boiled story is the attention paid to guns in the Bond books. This is particularly Spillanesque: Bond absolutely feels that his pistol is an extension of himself. The gun lore with its details of calibre, stopping power, etc. is only one facet. Spillane gleefully uses the gun as the penis figure and Fleming follows along, making this explicit in the materials about Scaramanga's fascination with his golden gun. (pp. 204-05)

Guns, ultimately, form only part of that section of the hard-boiled tradition which holds most importance in shaping Fleming's world. The gangster is that section which holds Fleming's fascination. . . . Three of the novels (*Live and Let Die, Diamonds are Forever* and *The Man with the Golden Gun*) deal almost exclusively with gangsters as antagonists. Indeed, in almost all the novels the villains are more gangster than political antagonist. (p. 205)

Nonetheless, Fleming's novels are not gangster stories in the hard-boiled mode where Spade or Marlowe share some of the filth of their environment. Bond has nothing in common with Drax or Scaramanga or any of the others. (p. 206)

[The] love romance also plays a large role in the Bond books. Here again we return to the world of Oppenheim and LeQueux, for these inventors of the spy novel not only wrote love romances but also, invariably, mixed elements of the love romance into their spy plots. . . .

Most often in the twenties and thirties we get a breezy and subordinate boy-meets-girl, girl-gets-kidnapped action in with the spy adventure. But this is not what I mean in regard to the love romance in Fleming. I am talking about the *cliched* but immensely popular kind of love story: stories like [E. M. Hull's] *The Sheik* . . . or those by Barbara Cartland, which have their own sets of conventions of plot and character paying careful attention to defining love. Among these conventions we find motifs like the woman with the secret, defrosting the standoffish man or woman, the initiation to love, and examining the ''exciting'' relationship between violence and sex. (p. 209)

Fleming fills Bond's sexual fantasies and some of his actions with a combination of moderate violence and sexual fulfillment. He holds up his hero as the ice man, cold, hard and unyielding toward women. This stance, however, as in the romance, is only a veneer. Bond, underneath, is really a sentimental softie, melting and vulnerable once the first violent onslaught of love expires. He, like the romance hero, constantly carries a torch for lost love; and he constantly loses love once he finds it. . . . Fleming's hero is no flower-hopping bumblebee, but, in the terms of the love romance, a tragically unlucky lover thwarted most often by circumstances but occasionally, as in *You Only Live Twice,* by the iron demands instilled into him by his career. (p. 211)

Fleming also puts a tiny bit of the detective in Bond: in the early books Bond combines the logical and the intuitive detective as shown in Fleming's repeated use of "he reflected" and "he felt"—especially in *Casino Royale*. Bond, though, is no detective: he does not solve problems with his head or his inspiration. Neither is any of Fleming's novels a detective plot in any meaningful way. Most readers can guess what Drax is up to in *Moonraker* long before the operatives in the book do. Fleming, though, used some detective structure in his early books because he knew of no other ways to unify his plots. He left it as quickly as he could find another way of doing things.

Structurally Fleming essentially worked with the episode. He makes *Casino Royale,* for instance, out of three separate incidents (the card game, the kidnapping and the love story), and though he tries to unify them with character and crumbs of detective structure, the episodes fall apart, making the last third of the novel a detachable love romance short story. Throughout Fleming's novels, in fact, we find that the chief unifying elements, the threats provided by the villains, rest on the nonsensical premises like the Soviet blue movie in *From Russia, With Love* and Dr. Shatterhand's suicide park in *You Only Live Twice*. His imagination almost always works in episodes. Thus he repeats his favorite episode, the card game, in *Casino Royale, Moonraker* and *Goldfinger*. Here Fleming is at the height of his powers. He sees gambling as the symbol (albeit hackneyed) of risk and . . . he also uses it to represent the high life. Additionally, for the thriller writer, these card games provide a long series of capture and escape involving luck and skill and they compact these things into a limited capsule of space and time. Fleming handles these episodes with some facility. With other kinds of episodes he is less sure. At his worst Fleming builds up a few episodes into a short novel (and all his novels are quite short) by adding padding. Sometimes this padding, like the fight of the two gypsy women in *From Russia, With Love,* adds a spot of sensationalism and lightly brushes on character. At its worst, though, Fleming's padding degenerates into incompetent travelogue. . . . (p. 212)

Finding that detective structure had no place in Bond's world, Fleming came up with a new way of tying disparate episodes together in *Diamonds are Forever*. He binds up this pointless episodic novel with a framing story about diamond smugglers on the South African veldt. He used the same device with more elaboration and success in *From Russia, With Love*. . . . Although after this novel Fleming dropped the articulated frame story, he did in *Thunderball* evolve it into split narration which switches from the bad guys to the good guys. In leaving this technique, though, he lost his most effective method of binding incidents together and stumbled into structural messes like *You Only Live Twice*.

With *Dr. No* Fleming focused some of his earlier material by returning to the pattern established in *Live and Let Die* and learned from the thriller writers of early in the century. All his early books, save *Diamonds are Forever,* depend on large, grotesque villains. Returning for inspiration to Fu Manchu, however, moves Fleming toward the villain who is not only enormously powerful and grotesque, but who is also part intellectual and part "gentleman crook." . . . This tradition fuels *Goldfinger* and all the Blofeld books (*Thunderball, On Her Majesty's Secret Service* and *You Only Live Twice*), but it runs out of steam, especially in the Blofeld books, after Fleming has exhausted the original exploration of the gentleman crook. . . . (p. 213)

In lots of ways Bond is a bungler. . . . [In] *Moonraker* Bond's only plan is to light a cigarette on the launch pad until Gala suggests resetting the rocket's gyros; in *Diamonds are Forever* he watches a jockey being tortured and then needs to be saved, in turn, by Tiffany and Felix. It goes on and on. . . . But why does Fleming do this? One of his motives lies in his desire to make Bond a realistic figure instead of a cartoon.

If, indeed, Bond's general ineffectiveness in the worlds of action and love comes from Fleming's desire to draw a realistic picture, we can be absolutely sure that this is the motive in his delineation of another side of Bond's character. Strung throughout the novels we find Fleming introducing passages which reflect Bond's revulsion with his role as spy and assassin. (pp. 214-15)

Much of this, though, is baloney. Bond does, after all, act as an assassin. (p. 215)

Part of Bond undeniably goes back to the traditions of the adventure hero. Plenty of adventure heroes, Hannay for example, begin their experiences starting from the bog of ennui. Fleming follows right along. At the start of many of the novels he consciously sinks Bond into the torpor of routine life. . . . Bond needs to be out doing things; he needs adventure. . . . Hence Bond the gambler presides in Fleming's card games, Bond the race car driver presides in Fleming's car chases, and Bond the killer presides over the final clashes with the villains. Here is no super-conscious intellectual who winnows motive and meaning. Bond really likes the killer's life. Fleming says so in *Dr. No:* "The license to kill for the Secret Service, the double-O prefix, was a great honour. It had been earned hardly. It brought Bond the only assignments he enjoyed, the dangerous ones." (pp. 215-16)

What gives here? How can Fleming tell us about Bond's victims and then deny them four books later? How can he give Bond a sensitive conscience and then show him intent on adventure? Is he trying to show us a schizoid hero? Of course not: Bond is no schizophrenic. Fleming, if confronted with Bond's irregularities, would probably give us the "foolish consistency" answer which many readers take. We can always concentrate on the manic regularities of the externals of dress and ritual (which exist, perhaps, to give focus to an otherwise shifting character) and forget about personalities. Or we can say that Fleming was a lazy and inexperienced maker of characters. Even after reading all twelve of the Bond novels we know very little of Fleming's hero aside from the externals. In *From Russia, With Love* Fleming may try a bit harder and give us a few glimpses into Bond's inner world (during his flight to Turkey, for example), but we see very little of this elsewhere. Perhaps the main reason for this, aside from general unconcern, is Fleming's narrative manner. First person narration is the staple of action spy fiction. . . . But Fleming, conceivably because of his ties to Oppenheim, opts for third person narration and because of this choice coupled with limited talent, he gives us a picture of the world which occasionally approaches vividness—but he also gives us a muddled picture of his characters.

But, ultimately, it is not the narrative. Manning Coles as well as other writers can do perfectly consistent spy stories in the third person. It is Fleming. Give him a continuing character and, chances are, he will blur it and muddle it up by shifting his sources and aims. (pp. 216-17)

[Fleming] has little interest in people *qua* people; he uses the characters as psychological counters in a game of simplified psychology. . . . Fleming even includes a physio-psychological level to Bond which Adam Hall would later take up in the Quiller books. In a number of novels he talks about just how much physical and psychic stress a man can endure with Bond as the subject of the experiment and with M. and the staff psychiatrist as observers. This gloss of psychology, of course, gives a modern motive to the knight-dragon fairy tale upon which Fleming builds his novels. But lurking underneath is the suggestion of spoof. This peeps through in *The Man with the Golden Gun* where Fleming paints with broad strokes Scaramanga's background as an elephant boy and an account of the pistol-penis symbolism. This could be Fleming's psychological primer for pre-adolescents, but I think it is spoof. Fleming enjoyed constructing vignettes of abnormal psychology for his villains and put them into the books as a lark. Dr. No shows this best of all. How can we take seriously a man who makes his pseudonym, Julius No, out of a conscious rejection of his father so that it reads No Julius?

Indeed, rather than being exercises in craftsmanship, Fleming's novels are exercises in self-indulgence. Bond's habits are Flem-ing's habits, the filler in the books comes from material picked up on journalistic jaunts . . . , and the villains emerge from fiddling with popular psychology. With these Fleming raked together material from the love romance and the Victorian spy story, and added a modicum of construction learned from Buchan or Sapper. Occasionally he worked on structuring a novel, like *From Russia, With Love, Dr. No,* or *Thunderball,* and these are his best efforts. Nevertheless, his best are poor stuff when compared to his predecessors or successors in the spy novel. No publisher today would even consider printing *Casino Royale,* and if it were not for the films, James Bond would mean as little to the contemporary consciousness as, say, Okewood of the Secret Service. It is, then, historical accident which has made a public figure of a muddled hero created by a third-rate hack. (pp. 218-19)

LeRoy L. Panek, "Ian Fleming," in his The Special Branch: The British Spy Novel, 1890-1980, *Bowling Green University Popular Press, 1981, pp. 201-19.*

John (Edmund) Gardner

1926-

English novelist, short story writer, and autobiographer.

Gardner is perhaps best known as the writer who resurrected Ian Fleming's secret agent 007, James Bond. Prior to the continuation of the Bond series, however, Gardner created several notable characters of his own. The first of these, Boysie Oakes, was deliberately planned as an amusing contrast to 007. Oakes is an inept, blundering coward who barely makes it to the end of each episode. He first appeared in *The Liquidator* (1964) and was the protagonist in at least eight novels published between 1964 and 1975. These works were generally well received by critics.

Gardner also invented other heroes who differ from the usual protagonists in spy fiction. These include Derek Torry, whose hatred of criminals and doubts about religion often lead him to confused, violent action in the name of duty, and Big Herbie Kruger, who views his own life and work as a failure. In *The Return of Moriarty* (1974) and *The Revenge of Moriarty* (1975), Gardner delves into the past to recreate Sherlock Holmes's enemy within the framework of the Victorian underworld. Although Gardner was praised for his vivid depiction of the time period in which he set these books, many Holmes fans were disappointed in Gardner's efforts to revive the series.

On the whole, Gardner's characters are considered successful creations. Critical reception was not enthusiastic, however, when Gardner revived James Bond in *Licence Renewed* (1981), *For Special Services* (1982), and *Icebreaker* (1983). In these works, Gardner attempted to capture the haughty, charming, invincible secret agent of Fleming's novels. However, Gardner's Bond is older, somewhat subdued, and, according to most critics, much less charismatic. Perhaps, as Reginald Hill suggests, Fleming's works were too much a product of the 1950s and 1960s to be translated to the 1980s, despite Gardner's efforts to update the technical aspects of espionage. Nonetheless, Gardner's Bond novels have been very popular; many readers, as well as some critics, find the books first-rate entertainment.

(See also *Contemporary Authors*, Vol. 103.)

© Jerry Bauer

FRANCIS HOPE

[In John Gardner's *The Liquidator*], 'L', the secret service killer who never kills and is terrified by flying in aeroplanes, is a sort of Ferdinand the Bull of the spy world; but there is enough real ingenuity in the plot to save him from the cloying cosiness of protracted parody. A few jokes about brand-names, and Sapperish smirks . . . fail to come off, but the whole achieves the cheerful mixture of self-indulgence and self-parody that marks the Bond films.

> Francis Hope, "Olden Times," in New Statesman, Vol. LXIV, No. 1745, August 21, 1964, p. 253.*

ANTHONY BOUCHER

["The Liquidator"] starts off as a deliberate (and skillful) parody of James Bond, presenting in Boysie Oakes, of the Department of Special Security, a professional killer with all of Bond's surface qualities and a quite unexpected inner deficiency. It then goes on to involve this amusingly conceived character with an elaborate espionage-and-assassination plot, developed with neatness and finesse. In other words, Mr. Gardner succeeds in having it both ways: he has written a clever parody which is also a genuinely satisfactory thriller.

> Anthony Boucher, in a review of "The Liquidator," in The New York Times Book Review, October 18, 1964, p. 46.

ELIZABETH J. HOWARD

Mr. Gardner's *Understrike* is his second novel about the British Security Agent Boysie Oakes, and this time he is involved in the test firing of a lethal missile from an American submarine, with the Russians the baddies. Boysie Oakes, as before, is depicted as lovably human—i.e., keen on girls, frightened of pain and death, neurotically forgetful, careless and even stupid, but somehow winning through. I find this portrait too sophisticated to be gripping: the indulgent smile which I think the author means one to wear about Boysie to the point of faceache, prevents me from gasping or stretching my eyes, which is all I want to do when I read this kind of book. It is all rather an indoor romp—like playing cowboys in the squash court. (p. 727)

Elizabeth J. Howard, "The Strange Adventure," in The Spectator, *No. 7145, June 4, 1965, pp. 727-28.*

ANTHONY BOUCHER

John Gardner's cowardly and inept secret agent, [Boysie Oakes] is sent to San Diego to witness a hush-hush submarine trial, in **"Understrike"** . . . ; and the Russians send along a carefully trained duplicate to take over his place. This seems, naturally, less fresh and ice-breaking than Boysie's first case; but Gardner still brings off the trick of eating his cake and having it, presenting a neat parody and a genuine sex-and-violence thriller in the same story.

Anthony Boucher, in a review of "Understrike," in The New York Times Book Review, *August 1, 1965, p. 24.*

DOROTHY B. HUGHES

No matter how wearied you may be of the run of spies, the exploits of Boysie, England's less than adroit agent, must be excepted. He is as uninhibited . . . [in **Understrike**] as he was in his debut, **The Liquidator.** How he travels to San Diego to observe a weapons test, and what logically ensues from Boysie on the scene, is more hackle-raising and infinitely more entertaining than any adventure of Bond, Solo, Drake, or whatever your favorite. John Gardner is here to stay.

Dorothy B. Hughes, "Delivering Us from Bondage," in Book Week—The Washington Post, *August 8, 1965, p. 19.**

THE TIMES LITERARY SUPPLEMENT

The first part of this latest adventure of cowardly killer Boysie Oakes [**Madrigal**] is charming, with pretty send-ups of Len Deighton plus a touch of Bond, yet missing the usual fault of send-ups—insufficient plot. But by the second half Boysie has found manhood and we are in another kind of thriller. Both are above par, but they don't quite jell. And where does newly bold Boysie go from here?

"Criminiscule," in The Times Literary Supplement, *No. 3420, September 14, 1967, p. 824.**

REGINALD HERRING

The time has been when detection was one thing and sex was another. . . .

Today the rules have changed. Our heroes go to it with a mechanical alacrity which almost suggests that they are operated by an unusually large wheel. Where their predecessors were content to wait for the final paragraph before settling euphemistically into the heroine's embrace, they possess her in the most specific manner, often as early as Chapter 2: et seq. Possession, in fact, is nine-tenths of the narrative. Only time will tell whether this is merely a new convention—superseding, as it may be, the homicidal butler—or whether, as seems increasingly likely, thrillers are becoming a branch of erotic literature.

Founder Member suggests that they are. Its author, Mr. John Gardner, hit some time ago on the sound idea that, since most James Bond imitations were bound to be trash, his should make a virtue of necessity and be trash on purpose. His anti-hero,

Boysie Oakes, is compounded by nature of lethargy and lechery. Totally unsuited to secret service work, recruited into it only through some ghastly blunder, he tolerates his employment for the sake of its by-products. His readers follow suit.

They are less surprised than he is when, early in **Founder Member,** he resumes his acquaintance with a Miss Chicory Triplethrust. That acquaintance, which is intimate, Mr. Gardner describes in terms which are alternately bald and meaningless. Quite soon we are told that Miss Triplethrust's breasts are 'perfect orbs.' Topologically, this is impossible. Metaphorically, it is unhelpful to a degree. If the contours of Miss Triplethrust are relevant to the action—and they are certainly involved in it—Mr. Gardner owes us either precision or evocation. Grapefruit? Soccer balls? Poached eggs? He does not say. Instead he leaves the reader to do the work—perfectly possible, indeed, but possible without the expense of buying Mr. Gardner's book.

(Note that Mr. Gardner's subject was instructively treated, some years ago, in Mr. Robert Robinson's *Landscape with Dead Dons*, whose heroine, Miss Balboa Tomlin, is partly of Latin-American extraction. Mr. Robinson's chosen likeness was two coffee ice-creams with cherries on top.)

Founder Member contains two girls to supplement Miss Triplethrust (*imponere Pelio Ossa*) and a plot of no consequence whatever. (p. 446)

Reginald Herring, "Lie Back in Anger," in The Spectator, *Vol. 222, No. 7345, April 4, 1969, pp. 446-47.**

ALLEN J. HUBIN

Inspector Derek Torry of Scotland Yard, in John Gardner's **"A Complete State of Death"** . . . is at once an engaging and troubled cop, a character sketched in much greater depth than we are accustomed from the usually lighter-hearted Mr. Gardner. Torry . . . has become emotionally overinvolved in his mission, his hatred of criminals impairing his judgment and jeopardizing his career. And now, when a crucial investigation of a widespread criminal operation draws him into repeated critical situations, the Catholicism he thought he'd shed rises to confront his sexual involvements and add to his burden of guilt. This is a "message" novel, only slightly pretentious, relevant but underpaced.

Allen J. Hubin, in a review of "A Complete State of Death," in The New York Times Book Review, *October 5, 1969, p. 36.*

THE NEW YORKER

["**A Complete State of Death**" is a] superior crime story with a superior hero. The story has to do with a masterminded transatlantic syndicate that operates a finishing school for talented would-be criminals on a big estate near London, and with a looming graduation-day caper. The hero, whose destiny it is to uncover this technological triumph, is a Scotland Yard inspector who stands well apart from his fellows. . . . He is brilliant at his job, impatient of regulations, and so loathes crime that his interrogations often end in blows and bruises. Mr. Gardner shows us this complicated man from every aspect, and he emerges, in the old-fashioned sense, as a character—credible, understandable, and commanding.

A review of "A Complete State of Death," in The New Yorker, *Vol. XLV, No. 34, October 11, 1969, p. 204.*

THE CRITIC

[In *A Complete State of Death*] John Gardner has crafted a moderately suspenseful tale about an English subsidiary of the Crime Syndicate, presided over by a very U type who trains his recruits and plans their activities as did the commando officers on the late TV shows. . . . The diverting and occasionally exciting plot is hindered by Gardner's Scotland Yard man, one Detective Inspector Derek Torry (nee Torrini) who is a pre-Vatican II Catholic, beseiged by doubt, guilt and adolescent sexual fantasies about women's underwear. One Graham Greene a century is probably enough.

A review of "A Complete State of Death," in The Critic, *Vol. 28, No. 2, November-December, 1969, p. 107.*

BEST SELLERS

Although John Gardner's new Boysie Oakes novel, **"Air Apparent"** . . . , climaxes with gun-running and an attempt to overthrow a government, everything leading up to the principal event is either banal or confused or both. Oakes, a former special agent, scarcely gives any evidence of professional qualification. A dummy air-agency is set up to help Boysie with his work—naturally it has three glamorous secretaries who double as hostesses. But Boysie falls for a beautiful model who works for a mysterious group which may be either for or against Boysie. Confused? So is the story—hardly worth the price.

A review of "Air Apparent," in Best Sellers, *Vol. 30, No. 23, March 1, 1971, p. 530.*

THE TIMES LITERARY SUPPLEMENT

After a number of books on the "comedy-suspense" formula, John Gardner has attempted a "straight" novel of some size and complexity [*Every Night's a Bullfight,* published in the United States as *Every Night's a Festival*]. It is certainly a workmanlike job, and while it convinces, entertains and sometimes surprises, it lacks depth: everything about it smacks of professionalism and competence; but it doesn't make us think, it has no significance.

Douglas Silver is a well-known director of stage plays. He is appointed director of the tired, established Shireston Festival, set in a sleepy town and noted for its dullness. Silver perks it up. His season of four Shakespeare plays . . . all startle in some way or another. . . .

[There are many] characters, clashes of temperament, enmities—so many, in fact, that the novel impresses as much through quantity as quality.

What detracts from the book is that Douglas Silver—the "rock hard activator with the quick tongue, yet quite approachable"—appears from Mr. Gardner's unqualified account as an out and out [jerk]. It's hard to decide whether his clichés are the verbal rot of his register of society and profession, or Mr. Gardner's. There is a chi-chi lack of stringency, or satire, in a setting begging for it. Mr. Gardner celebrates Theatre, eulogizes "professionalism", and especially his own conceptions

of the four plays the Shireston company put on. The real hero is Shakespeare, who somehow survives Douglas Silver and his enthusiasms—and Mr. Gardner.

"Behind the Scenes," in The Times Literary Supplement, *No. 3639, November 26, 1971, p. 1469.*

VINCENT J. COLIMORE

["Every Night's A Festival"] does nothing to dispel the idea that theatrical people spend much of their time in bed with one another. . . . The author gives explicit descriptions of the sexual act, both normal and otherwise. Evidently, this is the formula for a successful novel, a little plot and plenty of sex, with a variation of black-and-white sex thrown in to make everything more attractive. . . .

One thing **"Every Night's A Festival"** does do—it helps the reader to make the distinction between the product of the artist and the artist's life. In this case, most of the actors involved, and their director too, are so sexually oriented that sex life comes very close to interfering with dramatic production. . . .

As an insight into the lives of theatrical people, **"Every Night's A Festival"** is interesting reading.

Vincent J. Colimore, in a review of "Every Night's a Festival," in Best Sellers, *Vol. 32, No. 20, January 15, 1973, p. 478.*

THE TIMES LITERARY SUPPLEMENT

Like many others of his colleagues John Gardner, best known for his funny thrillers about Boysie Oakes, has turned to Victorian England [in *The Return of Moriarty*], with Moriarty, back from the Reichenbach Falls, picking up the threads of his vast criminal empire in London. So far as convincingness goes, this Moriarty, at Gardner's chosen level of period melodrama, is perfectly adequate, and Gardner sensibly never lets the surely unmanageable Holmes appear in person. There are many felicities but the fantasy is overloaded, and never gets off the ground, just plods remorselessly, overcrowdedly, at last boringly on.

A review of "The Return of Moriarty," in The Times Literary Supplement, *No. 3798, December 20, 1974, p. 1437.*

CHARLES NICOL

[According to John Gardner in *The Return of Moriarty*], nobody disappeared into the boiling pool at the base of the Reichenbach Fall; instead, Holmes and Moriarty agreed on a truce. Neither was to return to London for three years, and after that they would keep out of each other's way. Preposterous! Holmes would never have agreed.

Gardner's Moriarty is a young fratricide who often disguises himself as his deceased elder brother, the mathematics professor—apparently the disguise had fooled Holmes. He does indeed control most of the crime in London, but his modus operandi is clearly borrowed from *The Godfather*. . . .

Gardner's reluctance to present Holmes himself is something of a mystery; after his unlikely explanation that Holmes refuses to deal further with Moriarty, he invents an Inspector Crow to take on the role of detective in hot pursuit. Incidentally, no fewer than four love interests are developed here, three for the criminals and one for the inspector. Incidentally again, Gardner has a certain limited ability to dig up and use odd facts (such as the five or six convincing but unnecessary period menus listed in the novel). He could probably write a sloppy best-seller in the tradition of *Airport, Hotel, Supermarket, Laundromat,* and *Parking Lot.* Instead, he hopes to write a sequel to this Moriarty junk. He shouldn't. (p. 114)

> *Charles Nicol, "Some Baker Street Irregulars," in* Harper's Magazine, *Vol. 250, No. 1497, February, 1975, pp. 112-14, 116.**

MARGUERITE YOUNG

"The Return of Moriarty," by John Gardner, [is] based on the concept that Moriarty and Sherlock Holmes did not perish in the Alps and that Moriarty resurfaced in the London underworld. . . . Something of the vitality of the old Dickens London of crime, which also inspired Doyle, may be found in these highly researched tales.

From these tales American readers may learn that a "dolly-mop" is a whore, that a "drum" is a building, house or lodging, that a "dipper" is a pickpocket, and a "duffer" is a seller of stolen goods. We learn that a "lackin" is a wife, that a "macer" is a cheat, a "magsman" is an inferior cheat, that a "monkery" is the country, and "palmers" are shoplifters. Not surprisingly, the mastermind of crime, when last seen, is heading for America, a new world for the establishment of his dark empire. (pp. 24, 26)

> *Marguerite Young, "The Great Detective," in* The New York Times Book Review, *February 2, 1975, pp. 21, 24, 26.**

MARGHANITA LASKI

John Gardner's Boysie Oakes, the lily-livered government liquidator, used always to provide some mildly enjoyable fun, but Gardner, too, has also been drawn into Holmes-mania, and will be, his blurb indicates, for two more books after last year's **Return of Moriarty.** Of Boysie he now seems weary, opening his tale of assassins' revenge in an atmosphere of seedy incapacity and ending with more or less the old set-up renewed, though Mostyn, Boysie's horrid master, has bought it. Boysie's inconsistency was always tricky—now a lily-liver, now a male Touchfeather—but it used to come off. In *A Killer for a Song,* it does not.

> *Marghanita Laski, "Deaths for the Idle," in* The Listener, *Vol. 93, No. 2398, March 20, 1975, p. 380.**

KIRKUS REVIEWS

There's no particular reason to assume that Holmes' followers or even faddists will be drawn to this second in the series [*The Revenge of Moriarty*]. . . . The Napoleon of Crime has become a charismatic don; Holmes is attempting to withdraw from cocaine; and Moriarty's plots and coups are less dumfounding than dumb. This tale is primarily concerned with Moriarty's attempts to bring his international colleagues into line—the German crime lord is humiliated by a jewel robbery; the Frenchman by an elaborate hoax involving the Mona Lisa; the Italian by his own lust; the Spaniard is dead. Inspector Crow is presumably immobilized by adultery (there's a good deal of un-Doylean sex). It's no surprise when this heavyhanded ex-

ercise is climaxed by an encounter on the stairs of Holmes and Moriarty disguised as one another. To Holmes' fiddle, add the faddle.

> *A review of "The Revenge of Moriarty," in* Kirkus Reviews, *Vol. XLIII, No. 21, November 1, 1975, p. 1251.*

JONI BODART

YA's who enjoyed **The Return of Moriarty** . . . will also like this latest appearance of the "Napoleon of Crime" [in **The Revenge of Moriarty**]. . . . Fast-paced, readers will have fun following Moriarty's adventures, crimes, disguises, plots, and counter-schemes. (pp. 57-8)

> *Joni Bodart, in a review of "Revenge of Moriarty," in* School Library Journal, *Vol. 22, No. 5, January, 1976, pp. 57-8.*

CHARLES G. BLEWITT

Believe it or not, [*The Revenge of Moriarty*] is agonizingly slow and uninteresting reading. Neither the theft of the Mona Lisa nor the "bawdy" sexual matters add anything like life to this work. One feels as though he is reading an arithmetic equation—Moriarty will systematically bring all betrayers in line with his Alliance, by doing A, B, and C. Yet, there are a number of bright spots along the way. Certainly, some of the descriptions of the fogged-in London underworld of the Victorian era, with its "lurkers," "toolers," and "cracksmen," create the desired eeriness. It's also heartening to see that some honest-to-God human beings emerge, like the concupiscent Inspector Crow. But, all things considered, $8.95 is a lot of capital for a novel which is so elementary.

> *Charles G. Blewitt, in a review of "The Revenge of Moriarty," in* Best Sellers, *Vol. 36, No. 1, April, 1976, p. 3.*

NEWGATE CALLENDAR

"The Cornermen" brings the American Mafia to London, and blood runs in the streets. Scotland Yard eventually brings things under control. There is plenty of action in "The Cornermen," but the writing is clumsy and the construction awkward. There are no believable characters here—Gardner's heroes and villains are all cardboard figures. But at least they create a sizable racket.

> *Newgate Callendar, in a review of "The Cornermen," in* The New York Times Book Review, *September 26, 1976, p. 36.*

MARGHANITA LASKI

The terrifying power of the Nazis over writers' imaginations is undiminished, despite the difficulty that now its men are old or dead. John Gardner, in **The Werewolf Trace,** has found a new device with which to re-evoke the horror now and in England; but his recall of the unspeakable last days of Hitler and the Goebbels family is more powerful than the fictional modern threat—apart from the threat of The Trade, prepared to act almost as unspeakably to safeguard what are seen as British interests. This is Gardner's best so far—what a versatile creature he is! (p. 459)

Marghanita Laski, ''Fresh Spring Crimes,'' in The Listener, *Vol. 97, No. 2503, April 7, 1977, pp. 458-59.**

GENE LYONS

John Gardner knows that the Nazis still sell books but seems a bit uneasy about it—a dilemma he resolves by contriving to have it three ways at once. **"The Werewolf Trace"** . . . is simultaneously laden with detailed lore about the final days in Hitler's bunker, debunking of the excesses of an intelligence service obsessed with the eradication of nonexistent evil, and a ghost story as well. Even more astonishing, at least to the point where one turns the pages to see how on earth he is going to bring it all off, the book actually works.

''Werewolf'' is the British code designation for a 9-year-old boy who may, or may not, have survived the last hours of the Third Reich and who just might be primed to become ''Werewolf, the inheritor of the Reich, the next in line within the Nazi Apostolic succession.'' But even if that were true, which agent Vincent Cooling doubts, what conceivable damage could such a person—now a naturalized British citizen and furniture importer living a quiet suburban life with his wife and 3-year-old daughter—cause? . . .

Lacking Gardner's narrative facility, I am unable in this space to do more than add that the house in which the putative Führer lives is quite incidentally haunted by the ghosts of an earlier tragedy involving a child killed by a hawk, and is situated across the street from Cooling's mother's apartment as well. All of which enables our man to pose as a researcher into the ''paranormal'' and helps bring matters to a head. Gardner's prose style is an adequate vehicle for this sort of thing, no more, no less—just about right for a screen treatment, which in a sense is what this is. (p. 14)

Gene Lyons, ''Intriguing Intrigue,'' in The New York Times Book Review, *May 15, 1977, pp. 14, 22.**

FRANCIS GAVIN

[*The Werewolf Trace*] continues to puzzle me after having thought about it for several hours. Often it is quite satisfying and genuinely mature, but at times it is very predictable and even slick in a very juvenile way. (p. 106)

[A plot] summary may suggest yet another standard mystery novel, but Gardner clearly intends to do more than entertain. The real themes are the dangers of certain obsessions, the problems produced by the abuse of power and the insensitive use of technology, and the importance of a basic respect for another's privacy. The way in which Gardner rather cleverly reverses our expectations about the outcome calls attention to serious concerns while poking fun at the usual tidy moralistic conclusions of many such novels.

The novel suffers when Gardner seems to be imitating Ian Fleming at his worst. In addition, he relies a bit too much on stock characters. (pp. 106-07)

Despite reservations, I would think readers particularly keen about mystery novels will find much of interest here. (p. 107)

Francis Gavin, in a review of ''The Werewolf Trace,'' in Best Sellers, *Vol. 37, No. 4, July, 1977, pp. 106-07.*

THOMAS BEDELL

[Should they read **"The Nostradamus Traitor"** admirers of Gardner know he] will take an implausible—if not preposterous—premise, weave in enough characters, adventures, mysteries, and twists that, once begun, one has little choice but to continue on to the conclusion to see if the author can possibly unravel it all. Gardner can, and does in a wow finish; after all, he used to be a magician. . . .

Red herrings abound. Soon it is not only things that don't seem to be as they should. People don't seem to be who they're supposed to be. Someone—maybe everyone—is lying. . . .

Rust Hills, Esquire's fiction editor, has written: ''The more successful a story based on mystery is in the middle, the more likely it is to fail in the end. The interest, ultimately, is not in the characters and the actions they take, but in the mystery and how it will be solved.''

One could say the same about **"The Nostradamus Traitor"** though ''fail'' is an unnecessarily harsh word to apply. While short on the richer character development or graceful prose one might expect in a work by [John] le Carré or [Len] Deighton, the book remains a marvel of plotting. If its long-range satisfactions are scant, it is, within its own limited genre, an involving and pleasurable read. No more, but no less either.

Thomas Bedell, ''Digging Around in Old Plots,'' in The Christian Science Monitor, *June 27, 1979, p. 19.*

NEWGATE CALLENDAR

An unusual idea, based somewhat on historical fact, is the centerpiece of John Gardner's [**"The Nostradamus Traitor."**]. . . . It is well known that Hitler and some of his high command took astrology and other occultism rather seriously. And anybody who takes occultism seriously is going to take Nostradamus seriously. To this day there are those who believe that the prophecies of the 16th-century astrologer-physician are uncanny anticipations of the future; that everything he predicted has come true.

Anyway, Mr. Gardner has written a book on two levels of time. **"The Nostradamus Traitor,"** an espionage novel in the le Carre or Deighton pattern, takes place mostly in the France and Germany of 1941, in flashbacks, and also in the London of the late 1970's. But most of the book has to do with the exploits of the first British agent to penetrate occupied France. Nostradamus, as the title indicates, plays a prominent part in the action. The action of 1941 bears heavily on the action of 1978; everything interlocks.

It was le Carre who established the formula of spies and their masters, and **"The Nostradamus Traitor"** is a skillful exemplar of the species. The masters, always suspicious, taking nothing for granted, brilliant eccentrics all, construct a mosaic, working on intuition as much as on fact. The reader knows in advance that one of the good guys is going to turn out to be a very sour apple indeed: but which one? That is part of the fun, and Mr. Gardner knows how to lead the reader down false trails. **"The Nostradamus Traitor"** is a much tauter, better-written book than the last few Gardner novels that have crossed this desk, and it is guaranteed to keep any reader, no matter how sophisticated, on edge as the duplicity unfolds.

Newgate Callendar, in a review of "The Nostrada-mus Traitor," in The New York Times Book Review, *July 15, 1979, p. 26.*

KIRKUS REVIEWS

[*The Last Trump* is set in] the mid-1990s, and Russia has conquered Europe, with Britain (rotted with leftists from within) surrendering to a Soviet "peace-keeping force" and the US "neutralized" by having its intelligence apparatus totally sabotaged. There's only one hope to avoid nuclear holocaust (China's ready to decimate the whole western world): Operation Golgotha, a plan created back in the 1970s that involves missiles already secreted throughout Europe (aimed at the USSR), with details of the plan divided up and hypnotically implanted in the minds of assorted undercover British agents (a novelist, a theater director, etc.). So the US Prez (Ted Kennedy, apparently) activates Golgotha by sneaking US-based British agent Paul Fadden back into England, complete with the code-sentence that will unlock the Golgotha info from these hypnotized agents, whom he must identify and track down one by one. . . . Nonsensical pseudo-Buchanesque folderol, of course—not helped much by cutesy 1990s touches (Bernstein's Eighth Symphony is played, Dame V. Redgrave hobbles by on a cane) or lots of lazy, clichéd prose. But Gardner . . . is always an agreeably straightforward storyteller, confident and professional enough to squeak by with even so foolish a concoction as this one.

A review of "The Last Trump," in Kirkus Reviews, *Vol. XLVIII, No. 17, September 1, 1980, p. 1176.*

JESSICA MANN

[John Gardner] is not so successful in *The Garden of Weapons* as he was in his previous books. The world of secret services is by definition intangible and hard to comprehend, but Gardner has sometimes managed to expose it to outsiders more clearly. This one follows Herbie Kruger, the spymaster in an earlier Gardner book, as he retraces his steps during the years since he left the rubble of post-war Berlin, both physically and in memory. It's ingenious and eventful, but not interesting enough for the concentration required.

Jessica Mann, in a review of "The Garden of Weapons," in British Book News, *January, 1981, p. 10.*

HENRY McDONALD

[John Gardner] has sometimes been compared to Ian Fleming, but in fact the hero of this new spy thriller [*The Garden of Weapons*]—a German-born, British intelligence officer named Herbie Kruger—bears little resemblance to James Bond. Herbie . . . is fat, sexually impotent, passionately devoted to the music of Gustav Mahler . . . and tends to regard himself, in both his life and work, as a failure—a view which the events of *The Garden of Weapons* do much to support.

All of which, it might seem, not only distinguishes Gardner's hero from that of Fleming's but provides little in the way of character or plot which could serve as a basis for a spy thriller. In fact, however, Herbie and his troubles serve beautifully. *The Garden of Weapons* is a skillfully crafted novel which sustains a high level of suspense from start to finish.

Herbie's troubles begin when he learns that a spy network he set up in East Berlin to warn against Russian nuclear attack

had been infiltrated by a double agent at its inception 15 years ago. . . . [The] double agent turns out to be—in a sense—Herbie himself.

It is such ingeniousness, however, which lies at the source of the only major flaw of *The Garden of Weapons;* toward the end Gardner gets so carried away with the intricacies of his plot that he almost lets his story line run away with him. The reader may as a result feel left behind; that Gardner's imaginative feats will bore him, however, I very much doubt.

Henry McDonald, in a review of "The Garden of Weapons," in Book World—The Washington Post, *April 5, 1981, p. 10.*

EDWARD CLINE

John Gardner attempts to revive James Bond in **"License Renewed"** . . . , an earnest simulation of an original story as it might have been written by the late Ian Fleming. . . .

To his credit, Mr. Gardner has not aimed for a laugh rating, as others have. One can see the meticulousness of his craft as he tries to recreate the atmosphere of understated electricity and suspense that is the hallmark of Fleming's novels; in the thought processes, nuances of speech and descriptions of its characters; in the breaks in the narrative and the deft switching of scenes; in the climax; in the footnote-like quality of the final chapter.

Bond's enemy this time is Anton Murik, an outcast nuclear scientist. . . . Mr. Gardner's villain is a true altruist; he really doesn't want the $50 billion ransom for himself; he really wants to make a contribution to mankind's well-being, even if he must eliminate mankind to do it. Mr. Fleming's villains were more plausible and more interesting than this. . . . Murik the villain, even for the vast scope of his plan, is too sincere, and, like most genuine altruists, too boring for words. He is not worthy enough an opponent for James Bond.

Furthermore, the attention to detail for the sake of plausibility that Mr. Fleming was noted for comes off in **"License Renewed"** as so much pedantry; and the Bond discrimination for the better things in life, as handled by Mr. Gardner, has the crude ring of name-dropping. The dialog does not quite work, and neither does the narrative. In the end, it leaves one with the impression of a grayish, half-finished sketch of something that might have been interesting.

"License Renewed" points up the futility of faithful imitation. No matter how well a writer—or any artist, for that matter—manages to capture the style or content of an original idea or work of art, something will always be missing: originality.

Edward Cline, "A New James Bond Novel by Fleming's Successor," in The Wall Street Journal, *June 4, 1981, p. 26.*

JESSICA MANN

Ian Fleming's James Bond books were never as crass as *Licence Renewed.* Writing for himself, Gardner is intelligent and original. In this Fleming rip-off, he reproduces Fleming's faults without their saving charms, except that he has cut down on the sex and sadism. Fleming's plots were always preposterous, but they carried a crazy, unifying conviction. Gardner's is just illogical. And how the mighty Bond is fallen; he has become a dull, dim—too many knocks on the head in the past, perhaps?—middle-aged man who chooses the wrong trade-names to advertise.

*Jessica Mann, in a review of "Licence Renewed,"
in* British Book News, *July, 1981, p. 391.*

PAUL STUEWE

[In *Licence Renewed* the] licence is the immortal James Bond's, but the failure to renew the spirit of Ian Fleming's classic thrillers rests with author Gardner. Bond has been amusingly updated for the conservation-conscious 80s. . . . But these innovations do not begin to atone for a dreadfully static plot and a decidedly tame collection of villains. Gardner has a good grasp of Bond's character and may well make better use of it in the future, but his first attempt at reviving the 007 legend is a crashing bore.

Paul Stuewe, "Talk of the Devil . . . Musical Memoirs . . . A Duo on Dance," in Quill and Quire, *Vol. 47, No. 8, August, 1981, p. 31.**

STANLEY ELLIN

["**For Special Services**"] is a James Bond story—Mr. Gardner's second try at rattling those moldering bones—and, as the author's foreword suggests, it was inspired not by any of the nine Muses but rather by a consortium of 007's copyright holders and publishers, along with the Saab motor car company of Sweden, which now provides Bond with his transportation.

At this point I will say that, after considering the extraliterary alliance associated with the venture, I don't believe any writer could have done better with this curious project than John Gardner, but it is simply a defeating project to start with. Ian Fleming was a dreadful writer, a creator of books for grown-up boys, a practitioner of tin-eared prose. As evidenced by his writings, he was also by nature a ferocious and humorless snob, a political primitive, a chauvinist in every possible area whose ideas about sexuality apparently were implanted by fevered readings of "Lady Chatterly's Lover."

John Gardner, creator of the inimitable and delightful Boysie Oakes among other characters, is the antithesis to all this, a writer of style and wit with a sharp-eyed, acidulous and yet appreciative view of humanity and its foibles. Fleming's shoes are simply too tight and misshapen for Mr. Gardner to wear comfortably. Fleming, however, did offer the reader one thing no imitator can possibly duplicate: total identification with and commitment to his hero and his works as the products of an uninhibited wish fulfillment.

When, on film, Bond was transmuted into the charismatic and sardonic Sean Connery, we were getting a different 007 altogether; it is this cinematic Bond that Mr. Gardner, his risibilities not always in control, presents to us off and on. How else to explain a 30-foot python that is not only capable of ingesting a full-grown man but also of carefully removing the victim's indigestible shoes before doing so? Or the fact that ice cream, no special flavor noted, is the device by which the villains, having dosed gallons of it with the ultimate tranquilizer, will seize control of the American forces guarding NORAD and, consequently, the killer satellite it operates? Yes, I did say ice cream. . . .

There are some good things among the zany proceedings: an automobile road race described to nerve-racking effect; the amusing relationship between the aging Bond and the youthful

Cedar Leiter; a climax where Bond is drugged into imagining he is the woolly-headed Gen. James A. Banker, U.S.A.—all pure John Gardner at his Boysie Oakes best. This still doesn't compensate for the awkwardness of the whole project. The reader will do better to head for anything by Mr. Gardner that isn't imitation Fleming. As pure Gardner, he is quite a writer.

Stanley Ellin, "Was the Ice Cream Doped or Dopey?" in The New York Times Book Review, *May 30, 1982, p. 19.**

ROBIN W. WINKS

James Bond is dead, and John Gardner's second effort to remove the nails from that coffin, though not so dreary nor so silly as the first, is nonetheless very thin gruel. *For Special Services* . . . is exceptionally bad when read, as I have just done, back-to-back with Ian Fleming's "From a View to a Kill," a story embedded in *For Your Eyes Only*. . . . The aging Bond is now teamed with Cedar Leiter, daughter of his old friend, and he goes up against a reincarnation (son? daughter? who knows?) of Blofeld in an appalling and sexist, though highly cinematic, confrontation with the usual mix of sadistic cheats in Amarillo and like romantic places. The book is full of one sentence paragraphs—did Fleming ever really write this way?—and obligatory "who'll sleep in the one bedroom, who on the couch" scenes once calculated to titillate fourteen-year-olds. The whole is marked by an appalling cynicism toward the reader; one wonders why Gardner, who has written some perfectly acceptable books of his own, largely modest parodies of the genre, did not study the formulas well enough to understand them. (pp. 38-9)

Robin W. Winks, in a review of "For Special Services," in The New Republic, *Vol. 186, No. 25, June 23, 1982, pp. 38-9.*

JOHN A. BARNES

License Renewed is a return to the "classic" Bond story that Ian Fleming himself eventually grew weary of, his weariness resulting in aberrations such as *The Spy Who Loved Me*. Anton Murik, international nuclear physicist and Laird of Murcaldy, is the brilliant and extremely unattractive villain. . . . Mary Jane Mashkin, Murik's female sidekick, is no Rosa Klebb or Irma Bunt, but she is serviceable. The heroine, Lavender Peacock (a name I am sure Ian Fleming would have been proud of), is a conventional Bond heroine, not one of the semi-equals that have been showing up in the films of late. . . . [Bond] does not seem to be so witty or quite so charming as he used to be. But, needless to say, Bond escapes from a good many impossible situations on his way toward foiling the bogus Laird of Murcaldy's plan to seize six of the world's nuclear power plants. *License Renewed* is a good solid thriller, guaranteed to entertain, and it bodes well for James Bond's return to active duty.

John A. Barnes, in a review of "License Renewed," in National Review, *Vol. XXXIV, No. 14, July 23, 1982, p. 913.*

REGINALD HILL

I was not pre-inclined to like John Gardner's second James Bond adventure *For Special Services* . . . , and I didn't. I missed Mr. Gardner's first conjuration of 007 but I believe it enjoyed considerable success, and I've little doubt that this one will too. Mr. Gardner is far too good a writer not to make a fair stab at the job. No mere arranger of other men's flowers, he is of course a thriller writer of the first water, author of many novels in many veins, and creator of that splendidly reluctant agent, Boysie Oakes. In *For Special Services* he resurrects SPECTRE and chucks in a mad millionaire, a plot to rule the world with the help of drugged ice-cream, killer ants, giant pythons and a no-holds-barred car-race. The glamour is supplied, significantly, by the daughters of old acquaintances. . . .

All this is done with technical skill and some panache, but in the end Bond belongs so much to the 50s and early 60s . . . that to translate him to the 80s without making him grow up is an almost impossible task. Mr. Gardner effects a decent enough compromise, smudging over the passage of time by updating the technology but sticking firmly with the old style of plot, and modernizing Bond's externals in small ways while hardly touching his character. The result is very fair escapist stuff, but time and again I found myself asking the, I hope, not impertinent question, if this man wasn't called James Bond, how good a thriller would this be? And the answer, I'm afraid, is, not half as good as what Mr. Gardner is capable of giving us when he follows his own creative bent. Bring back Boysie Oakes!

> *Reginald Hill, "Espionage and Kidnapping," in* Books and Bookmen, *No. 326, November, 1982, p. 24.**

ROGER MANVELL

[*For Special Services* is] John Gardner's second venture into Bond territory. . . . Gardner's Bond is to some significant extent reshaped, probably influenced by the extraordinarily successful series of films freely adapted from Fleming's work which has lightened the original Bond image, adding not only humour and tongue-in-cheek burlesque but also charm and even sympathy to the somewhat unpleasant, sadistic slant in the original characterization of this twentieth-century man of action. These highly entertaining fantasies require a particular skill to invent, a skill with which John Gardner seems well endowed, especially the capacity to blend sufficient genuine technological knowledge with a vivid imagination that makes the impossible sound feasible. . . . In *For Special Services* Bond is once again pitted against the Gothic threats devised by SPECTRE. . . . Bond having in the past slain the original SPECTRE leader, Blofeld, a successor emerges in protean shape, and Bond, aided by every kind of technical device, engages in splendid single combat on our behalf with civilization's arch-enemies.

> *Roger Manvell, in a review of "For Special Services," in* British Book News, *February, 1983, p. 120.*

KIRKUS REVIEWS

[In *Icebreaker* James Bond is] in Finland and Russia—for more of the same, just colder. This time Gardner's neo-Bond (who's less vividly characterized with every book) is sent by M to join three other agents—a CIA man, a KGB man, and beauteous Rivke of Israel's Mossad—in an action against the NSAA, a neo-Nazi group that has been responsible for heaps of recent terrorism. The plan? To catch the NSAA in the act of getting arms supplies . . . which are coming from Russia, of all places,

near the Finno-Russian/Arctic-Circle border. But Bond suspects that the operation is not quite what it seems to be. . . . So it goes, with the requisite bursts of techno-violence . . . , kidnaps, grenades, mild smirks of sex, double-crosses, triple-crosses (can Bond even trust M himself), and a final dollop of missile warfare. And though the formula is tired beyond belief, the scenery's nice, the pacing is competent—and the readership has proven to be uncommonly loyal.

> *A review of "Icebreaker," in* Kirkus Reviews, *Vol. LI, No. 3, February 1, 1983, p. 146.*

ANATOLE BROYARD

[John Gardner's **"Icebreaker"**] strikes me as deficient in many of the basic requirements. I see now why Mr. Fleming is so hard to imitate: though his books were not brilliantly written, they were, like Bond himself, very smooth. What made them so easy to read was an almost complete absence of awkwardness. The illusion of unseriousness was seriously maintained.

Mr. Gardner, however, is all awkwardness. Every time I try to enter into his latest conspiracy we bump heads. It's one thing to accept an improbable plot and quite another to accept an improbable style. I'm willing to suspend my disbelief, but not my affection for the English language. I don't see why, when Mr. Gardner can learn all about the various weapons, machines and intelligence procedures he describes, he can't do a bit of basic research in ordinary narrative technique. . . .

In conversation, Bond "gives" or "signifies an affirmative," instead of saying yes. In a tense moment, he "dripped acid from each word." People, including Bond's chief, the magisterially impassive M, "snarl" and "snap." M even coughs, "playing for time," while talking to Bond. Since he has sent for Bond in order to brief him, it's not clear why he should be playing for time, unless Mr. Gardner feels that everybody in a suspense novel has to engage, under all circumstances, in strategic delay. . . .

The figures of speech in **"Icebreaker"** remind me of the intelligent suggestion some critic made that all figures of speech be removed from language, on the ground that they inevitably debase it. . . .

Even Bond is deteriorating. In his hotel, he is forever "sweeping" the room for listening devices, even though he knows that the switchboard too is tapped. Again, Mr. Gardner shows an indiscriminating use of a standard thriller device: Always sweep your room. At the moment of truth, Bond's pistol becomes stuck in the waistband of his trousers. The plot of **"Icebreaker"** is a muddle about a neo-Nazi party. Mr. Gardner has taken too seriously the stories about the duplicity of secret agents, and as a consequence people in the book keep changing sides. It's his favorite, almost his only plot device.

> *Anatole Broyard, "James Bond Revised," in* The New York Times, *April 9, 1983, p. 17.*

MEL WATKINS

"Icebreaker" is John Gardner's third James Bond novel, and this British author . . . has begun to influence the rather stock presentation of the 007 series. In Fleming's hands Bond tended toward a kind of macho cartoonishness. . . . Mr. Gardner, in this latest novel, has added a touch of the plot subtlety of less insistently action-oriented thrillers. . . .

The most intriguing aspect of this Bond caper, however, is determining who among the Icebreaker team is a double agent. The final scenes are as surprising as they are exciting.

Although Mr. Gardner's Bond is less raffishly macho and arrogant than previously depicted, the spirit of the 007 series remains intact, and few Fleming admirers are likely to object. There is, in fact, something appealing about a James Bond who can react to women with some sympathy and admit to confusion at a crucial moment.

> *Mel Watkins, in a review of "Icebreaker," in* The New York Times Book Review, *April 24, 1983, p. 16.*

Joanne (Goldenberg) Greenberg

1932-

(Has also written under pseudonym of Hannah Green) American novelist and short story writer.

Greenberg is best known for her autobiographical novel *I Never Promised You a Rose Garden* (1964). One of the first books about mental illness that is told from the viewpoint of the patient rather than the analyst, *Rose Garden* charts the course of Deborah Blau, a young schizophrenic caught between the real world and her own secret world, the kingdom of Yr. When *Rose Garden* was first released, it received little notice either from critics or the general public. Gradually, however, it started gaining popularity and today it is widely considered one of the most sensitive and revealing portraits in contemporary literature of a struggle against severe mental disorder.

Rose Garden is based on Greenberg's own experience with schizophrenia; she wrote it under the pseudonym Hannah Green in order to protect her young children from the knowledge that she had been institutionalized as a teenager. Most early reviewers rightly guessed that the book is nonfictional and considered *Rose Garden* more valuable as an honest account of mental illness and life in a mental institution than as a literary work of art. As Brigid Brophy noted: "Should it turn out to be a work of fiction, its value would vanish overnight." Critics generally attribute this to the inconsistency of Greenberg's approach and her sketchy characterizations. They feel that she focuses too much on Deborah's illness and the course of her therapy and does not adequately develop Deborah or her doctor as personalities in their own right. However, other critics praise her ability to describe Deborah's mental state so thoroughly that her madness becomes comprehensible and her escape into Yr appealing. Even those critics who dispute *Rose Garden*'s literary merits generally feel that Greenberg's writing is competent enough to maintain the emotional power and the realism on which the success of the book ultimately depends. Young adult readers readily identify with Deborah's longing to escape reality and her feelings of alienation from the world.

Greenberg's other novels and short story collections have not attained such widespread popularity, but they have been well-received by critics. Although her works differ markedly from each other in terms of setting and plot, a common theme found in many of them is the alienation that results from lack of communication. Whether the result of a physical handicap, as in *In This Sign* (1968), or rigid adherence to religious or familial creeds, as in *The King's Persons* (1963) and *Founder's Praise* (1976), respectively, Greenberg skillfully and realistically captures the sources of alienation. Critics often praise her accurate portrayal of the diverse settings, times, and occupations which provide the background for her fiction.

(See also *CLC*, Vol. 7; *Contemporary Authors*, Vols. 5-8, rev. ed.; and *Something about the Author*, Vol. 25.)

GEORGE E. GRAVEL

[*The King's Persons*] re-creates a little-known aspect of English history with an attention to the nuances of commonplace life

usually lost amid the panoply of historical romances that are preoccupied with large and glamorous movements. It is centered on the massacre of the Jews of York in 1190, which came as a climax to the anti-semitism aroused during a decade of Jewish immigration resulting from similar atrocities in Paris. . . .

This background is studied by Mrs. Greenberg through a reporting of day-to-day events . . . in three areas. Most prominent is the Jewish section of York, where the reader meets Rabbi Elias, the chief spokesman; Baruch, one of the wealthiest men in England; Abram and Rana, Baruch's son and wife respectively; Josce, Baruch's former partner; and Bett, attractive Christian servant-girl. A second part of the action is set at the nearby monastery and, through Brothers Lewis and Simon, it explores the diocesan decay and strife within the Church. Finally, the role of the nobility is shown chiefly through Baron Malabestia and his squire, Richard de Kuckney. A subordinate theme is the love between Abram and Bett, frustrated by their environment.

In quiet, unspectacular fashion the bulk of the book depicts the ordinary, daily relationships among these three elements of medieval society. Ultimately they build into a bloody massacre led by Malabestia that ruthlessly and treacherously slaughters the leaders of the Jews and disperses the whole Jewish community. Abram escapes but is separated from Bett and he flees finally to solitude in southern England.

The picture is sympathetic to the Jewish viewpoint, as well it might be. Yet without denying the blot on Christian history that these events constitute, one does wish that the Church were a bit more robustly counterbalanced by some representatives who practice rather than merely speak Christ's teaching. . . . This [novel] is a good antidote for the selfrighteously inclined; but one that also calls for adult discernment.

> *George E. Gravel, in a review of "The King's Persons," in* Best Sellers, *Vol. 22, No. 23, March 1, 1963, p. 442.*

TIME

[In *The King's Persons,* Greenberg has] written a bad novel and a good book. Her plot reads like a combination of Abram's Irish Rose and a study of that tedious 20th century malaise, Lack of Communication. But if her fiction is wanting, her historiography is not. With painstaking care, she has woven each of the skeins of medieval life into a vivid tapestry that shows the loutishness and insensitivity of the baronial landholders, the obtuseness of the peasantry, the twisted fervor of churchmen who found virtue in the wholesale slaughter of heretics, and the disturbing contrast between the warmth of Jewish communal life and the demeaning nature of usury. (p. M24)

> *"Pogrom in Yorkshire," in* Time, *Vol. LXXXI, No. 13, March 29, 1963, pp. M23-M24.*

THE TIMES LITERARY SUPPLEMENT

This penetrating novel [*The King's Persons*] is set in the Jewry of York, long established and reasonably secure. . . . Then in 1182, when the book opens, [the Jews] accept a large group of refugees driven from France by young King Philip. . . . [As] the number of local Jews is suddenly increased Gentiles feel disturbed.

Good men, both Christian and Jewish, explore the common ground of both their faiths, and try to bridge the remaining gap by personal friendship. But tension mounts, until a pogrom at the coronation of King Richard increases the flow of refugees. . . .

Until she describes with great power the final massacre Miss Greenberg proceeds largely by recounting discussions between her leading characters. Although she is skilful in presenting the public opinion of the twelfth century these discussions sometimes ignore verisimilitude. In a new and ardent monastery a novice may sit on a fence by the hour, chatting with his Jewish friend; we happen to know that Ailred of Rievaulx never spoke a world of idle conversation to anyone during his whole novitiate. But these opportunities for busy men to pass hours in friendly chat are a minor flaw in a thrilling, intelligent and disturbing book.

> *"Fire and Sword," in* The Times Literary Supplement, *No. 3201, July 5, 1963, p. 497.*

R. V. CASSILL

Deborah Blau's psychosis—the focus of [**"I Never Promised You a Rose Garden"**]—is the flowering, in the second American-born generation, of her family's social and domestic pathology. The illness is, at the same time, an expedient, for survival amid the contradictions with which her inherited world is furnished, and an irrationally cunning search for the mental health which would be a fit culmination of a flight from the Old World to the New. . . .

In mid-adolescence, the other world, which [Deborah] calls Yr, is ready to receive her. She has no language left to protest her half-chosen abduction into this glamorous and tormenting world except an attempt at suicide. The present drama of the novel begins when her parents are forced to interpret this bloody appeal correctly and take her to a mental hospital.

In the hospital, Deborah's symptoms get spectacularly worse. . . . When standard therapies are of no avail, she is transferred to a "locked ward" reserved for the most disturbed patients. Only the stalwart and wise Dr. Fried refuses to concede that her symptoms are a true index of the progress of the disease. The doctor discerns a will to survive still actively frustrating Deborah's attempts at mental and physical self-destruction. And from this tap root of hidden strength the hard work of doctor and patient at last induces a growth that desperately seeks the living weather of reality.

Hannah Green (a pseudonym . . .) has done a marvelous job of dramatizing the internal warfare in a young psychotic. She has anatomized, in full detail, the relationship between a whole, sick human being and the clinical situation—including doctors, other patients and the abstract forces of institutional life. With a courage that is sometimes breathtaking in its concessions — in its serene acceptance of risks—the author makes a faultless series of discriminations between the justifications for living in an evil and complex reality and the justifications for retreating into the security of madness. One surrenders to the authority of Miss Green's thematic statement because she has foreseen, admitted and passed beyond all the major objections that might be made to it.

Yet, convincing and emotionally gripping as this novel is, it falls a little short of being fictionally convincing. Our attention is fixed on the roles played by the characters rather than on their essential humanity. We are made to care whether the doctor will succeed as doctor, whether the patient will successfully overcome her illness, while the real fictional question of the cost and value of such successes is ultimately slighted. It is as if some wholly admirable, and yet specialized, nonfictional discipline has been dressed in the garments and mask of fiction. The reader is certainly not cheated by this imposition— nor is he truly satisfied.

> *R. V. Cassill, "A Locked Ward, a Desperate Search for Reality," in* The New York Times Book Review, *May 3, 1964, p. 36.*

HASKEL FRANKEL

It is difficult to appraise *I Never Promised You a Rose Garden* as a work of fiction, which is what Hannah Green . . . chooses to call it. As a novel it is flawed; as nonfiction it is a painfully memorable case history told with great honesty. . . .

Mrs. Green never attempts to shock the reader or to sensationalize for large sales. When Deborah is driven to inflict burns upon herself with stolen cigarettes, the author relates the incident from so deep a vantage point within the patient's mind that one sees the logical illogicality which is the ever-present truth in the behavior of the disturbed.

In Dr. Fried she has conveyed a true portrait of the analyst at work—serving as a warm wall against which Deborah can throw herself mentally, always to bounce back against herself with gradually decreasing intensity. Mrs. Green's picture of the patients, their lives among themselves and in relation to the hospital staff, is also revealingly fresh.

However, the two-steps-forward, one-step-backward progression of Deborah's surfacing to life lacks that tightness which fiction requires. The chapters devoted to Deborah's family seem not so much subplot as stage waits while a Greek chorus wrings its hands. There is nothing the family can add to Deborah's history that Deborah and her analyst do not more powerfully disclose.

Nevertheless, be it fiction or non-, *I Never Promised You a Rose Garden* is absorbing, powerful, and moving.

> Haskel Frankel, *"Alone in the Kingdom of Yr,"* in Saturday Review, *Vol. XLVII, No. 29, July 18, 1964, p. 40.*

THE TIMES LITERARY SUPPLEMENT

Case-records of psychoanalysis (without the repetitions) can be fascinating. Miss Green . . . gives us more than that [in *I Never Promised You a Rose Garden*]; she tries to create the whole world of the mental hospital as the schizophrenic sees it, as the doctor sees it, as the nurses see it, and as the parents, terrified and ignorant, see it from outside.

The book is seldom naive, seldom humorous, sometimes ironical. . . .

There is a contrast between the responsible morality expected of the staff, and the freedom of the insane, who often take advantage of it. . . . Miss Green is excellent when conveying relief and delight at the freedom from the propriety, freedom from lies, and most of all the freedom to call mad mad, crazy crazy. She is excellent too on the inventiveness of the insane.

But she has her failures. The parents are unconvincing; the sympathetic German woman doctor is sometimes trite and sentimental as well as sometimes profound. There are the rather predictable gradual unearthing of truths, the weakness of the father, the anti-semitism of the summer camp, [and] the jealousy and guilt towards the younger sister. . . . [The] author does her best to convince us of the excitement and difficulty that Deborah experiences in making friends and adjusting herself generally to the real world. But although the doctor keeps saying that she must show Deborah how exciting the real world can be (at the same time without promising her "a rose garden"), the author never quite succeeds in making it so. In fact, Miss Green is rather better at describing the terror and imaginativeness of the schizophrenic than she is at the return to normality: her normality is perilously close to dullness.

> *"Calling Mad Mad,"* in The Times Literary Supplement, *No. 3259, August 13, 1964, p. 721.*

BRIGID BROPHY

Hannah Green is—almost literally—a naturalist, in that she analyses neither by the creative method of the artist nor in the anatomist's or evolutionist's sense. Hers is a purely descriptive, and to that extent external, account of a natural phenomenon, even though the phenomenon itself is a subjective feeling—what it feels like to be insane. . . .

[*I Never Promised You a Rose Garden*] makes the impression of being only nominally a novel; should it turn out to be a

work of fiction, its value would vanish overnight. In this context, it is almost a mark of the author's honesty that the short passages where the narrative leaves Deborah—usually to follow the parents home and enter into their misgivings—are only just adequate, the work less of imagination than of conscientiously fair-minded reconstruction. In the record of Deborah's own experiences, conscientiousness is intensified into a positive and no doubt painful passion to tell the whole truth and nothing but the truth—about the encroachment on Deborah's mind of Yr, the kingdom of her systematic delusions; the wasteful, uncreative over-intellectualism of schizophrenia (there is a whole Yri language) and its bitter, compulsive puns—truly sick jokes, which presently explode into the violence which gets Deborah removed to the dreaded Ward D; the *camaraderie* between patients, their ganging up against certain attendants, the delicacy whereby patient does not mention to patient their common knowledge that mental illness is partly a refuge from reality.

That knowledge is virtually the limit of both patients' and doctors' insight. Therapy goes hardly beyond a patient's being put into—or herself requesting—an ice-packed bed. Deborah reveres her European refugee doctor; that she adopts the doctor as an alternative mother is obvious: but it is never made explicit. Doctor and patient do not analyse or even acknowledge the adoption. The doctor's name, Dr Fried, reads like a schizophrenic pun itself, on *peace, freed* and *Freud;* if it is one, it is pretty well the only allusion to Freud in the book. The sessions are conducted in terms of pre-Freudian, of positively Euripidean, psychology, with the doctor sending messages, via Deborah, to the Yri powers, to the effect that they do not really exist. If the doctor is remarkable, it is for her moral honesty, of which the patient's own exceptional honesty can take advantage. The eventual cure is spontaneous. A naturalist indeed, the author leaves one gaping at 'the wonders of nature'—the sheer force of the life force in a girl of 16. (p. 221)

> Brigid Brophy, *"An Yri Story,"* in New Statesman, *Vol. LXVIII, No. 1744, August 14, 1964, pp. 221-22.**

JOYCE CAROL OATES

This group of twelve excellent short stories [*Rites of Passage*] is all the more remarkable for its being not only artistically "beautiful" but morally and spiritually beautiful as well. Though Miss Greenberg hardly writes of people with happy problems—her characters include the deaf, the wives and mothers of the deaf, the epileptic, isolated farmers who have eased into insanity, young women hemmed in by banal, crushing circumstances, aging men impatient to die and get it accomplished—she is able through her almost miraculous sense of the complexities of the human predicament to make each person, hopeful or hopeless, demonstrate for us a way of surviving.

And yet that sounds grim—"surviving"—and doesn't do justice to the surprising range of energies and inventiveness Miss Greenberg's people possess. In one of the finest stories, **"And Sarah Laughed,"** the wife of a totally deaf man begins to realize, as the years pass, the need in her to express the "said-unsaid" nuances of love. . . . Some of the stunning subtlety of Miss Greenberg's novel about the deaf, *In This Sign,* is evoked by a few swift revelations here—and we, the "normal," we who take so for granted the incredible miracle of human language, are made to realize what the universe might be without words, without the effortless pitting of "inflection against meaning."

If only "the need to communicate" hadn't become such a cliché—if only so much of our deepest human mystery hadn't been trivialized—the worth of Miss Greenberg's fiction could be more easily appreciated. Her stories are, in fact, about the need to communicate; and, in story after story, she sets forth characters populating entirely believable, dense, frightening worlds (or visions of worlds—because her people suffer in their isolation), sometimes establishing contact with another person, sometimes reaching out but falling, sometimes falling back, selfishly, content in failure.

"The problem is deception," says the nightmare-plagued wife of **"To the Members of the D.A.R.,"** itself a nightmarish story about the quite normal sanity-insanity of family life. But the problem is also self-deception, almost a greedy desire to fall back into isolation, ignorance, insanity; and so the paranoid farmer of the collection's title story betrays the boy he has lured into sharing his madness with him, casting him out, making him again an "object" and denying his humanity. Do we risk making others human?—do we risk ourselves, the invulnerability of our closed linguistic systems? Miss Greenberg's people struggle with this question, do not take it lightly, flippantly; it is the very question of their lives. And yet, being human, they fall continually into other states of perception.

> *Joyce Carol Oates, "The Need to Communicate,"* in Book World—The Washington Post, *March 19, 1972, p. 3.*

ROGER SALE

[All but one of the stories in **"Rites of Passage"**] are just stories, instances where the energy and trust have gone into seeing how the story can best be told and not into the characters and events themselves. The exception is the title story, about a boy who feels he has been denied the opportunity to become a man because he has been raised by maiden relatives and who leaps at a chance to prove himself by going to work on a farm. The farmer turns out to be old, broken down, paranoiac about other farmers he is sure are out to destroy him and take his land, especially about his neighbor, Koven, who he imagines to be spying on him, poisoning his stream, digging potholes in his road etc. . . .

[Greenberg] knows how important it is for her boy hero to gain a father. . . . As a result, she never tries to explain or justify the boy's eagerness to earn the trust of the old farmer or to entangle himself in the other's follies. When the boy agrees to kill the neighbor farmer, it is only his way of becoming the old man's son, and we are asked to see it only as that, to let the other or larger moral and emotional issues emanate from that, if at all.

It is, of course, only after he has committed the murder that the boy begins to realize how fearfully wrong the farmer's fantasies are. He sees first that their farm has not benefited at all from Koven's death, then that Koven could never have spied on them from his house because they live on higher land, then that the stream was polluted by the incompetence of the old farmer, and the pieces fall into a far different place from the one in which he had excitedly first put them. . . .

At the very end of the story Joanne Greenberg resorts to a cheap, short story writer's touch, but the rest is fine, a subject worth trusting and writing such trust demands. The boy's desire

not to be a loser embraces the man's insistence that they cannot win; characters and author are thus both possessed in a powerful way. **"Rites of Passage"** may not be a story for the ages, but I hope someone gives it a prize. (p. 4)

> *Roger Sale, "Whom Can You Trust?"* in The New York Review of Books, *Vol. XVIII, No. 8, May 4, 1972, pp. 3-4, 6.*

VICTOR HOWES

Joanne Greenberg's stories concern special cases, strangers in a crowd, people cut off by loneliness and misunderstanding from the abrasive but corrective contacts of their fellows. . . .

Sometimes Mrs. Greenberg's stories veer toward tragedy, sometimes toward the comic. Happy endings are not outside her purview, though her best and longest story, the title story, **"Rites of Passage"** starts happily and takes a sudden sinister bend. It is a powerful tale, involving a "Macbeth"-like *folie a deux,* demonstrating yet once more the principle of division of responsibility, where one partner wills the illicit act, and the other performs it.

Mrs. Greenberg's locales are mainly rural, her backgrounds frequently ethnic. When her stories have John Cheever in their sights, they falter. When they favor Willa Cather, they gain in strength. . . .

Joanne Greenberg is not afraid to risk sentimentality. Occasionally she achieves it. But more often she comes through as an authoritative voice claiming human status and human understanding for neglected pockets of experience, buried lives, half-forgotten isolates who live, too often, on the fringes of our inattention.

> *Victor Howes, "Fiction: Speaking for the Stranger,"* in The Christian Science Monitor, *August 9, 1972, p. 9.*

KARY K. WOLFE AND GARY K. WOLFE

While [*I Never Promised You a Rose Garden*] was generally received well critically as a didactic work concerning mental illness, many reviewers had reservations about its value as fiction. . . . It soon became publicly known that the novel is *not* entirely fiction, of course, and in the years following these initial reviews, as the book phenomenally grew in popularity, relatively little attention was paid to it as anything other than a highly readable case history. And yet there is much evidence, both from the novel itself and from Greenberg's other works, that the book is an attempt at a coherent novel and not merely fictionalized autobiography.

In *Rose Garden,* Greenberg has tried to portray the often chaotic imagery of schizophrenia and the often uneven process of therapy, and to impose upon these realities of her own experience the order and structure of a unified narrative. This is not to suggest that she has deliberately misrepresented either her illness or her therapy for the sake of novelistic expediency; rather it is to suggest that the aesthetic elements of the book exist on two principle levels. For example, the imagery of mountains, which serves a number of complex functions in the context of Deborah's own schizophrenic world, is introduced into the narrative late enough so that it can also function in aesthetic terms as an image of the struggle toward sanity, toward resolution of conflict: "All Deborah heard were the sounds of her own gasps of exhaustion as she climbed an Everest that was to everyone else an easy and a level plain.'' . . . Similarly, the imagery of the underworld (''the Pit''), which seems to appear more or less at random within the context of the illness, is for the sake of the narrative organized into the more familiar aesthetic pattern of the underworld journey: descent, chaos, and purifying ascent. The danger of this kind of dual use of imagery, of course, is that it tends to lead the reader to confuse the structure of the novel with the structure of therapy, and the pattern of aesthetic imagery with the pattern of schizophrenia. Such confusion is furthered by the commonplace belief that there is some sort of *de facto* relationship between insanity and art, and one must wonder if in fact such works as *Rose Garden* are popularly read as novels *about* schizophrenia, or as vicarious schizophrenic experiences. . . . But this question is merely another way of asking the reason for the popularity of these books, and perhaps it can be in part answered by looking at the four key aspects of *Rose Garden* itself: characterization, structure, style and imagery, and rhetoric.

The central element in characterization . . . is the nature of the protagonist herself. The protagonist in *Rose Garden* is 16-year-old Deborah Blau, a plain but highly intelligent and witty girl whose psychosis involves an elaborately imagined, almost Blakean universe called Yr, with its own pantheon of gods, its own language, and its own landscapes. During the course of the novel, Deborah moves in both the real world and this world of her own creating. But the ''real world'' in this novel is the world of the mental hospital and its surroundings, a world that is in its own way as artificial as the one Deborah has created. The arbitrary and sometimes hostile nature of this reality is what provides the book's title; in warning Deborah that reality is not necessarily more rewarding than the world of Yr, and in arguing that Deborah's choice must be based on deeper criteria than mere comfort, the therapist Dr. Fried says, ''I never promised you a rose garden. I never promised you perfect justice.'' . . . And in making this statement, Dr. Fried herself is reminded of her days in Nazi Germany, as if to underline to the reader the point that ''reality'' is not necessarily morally superior to the world of the psychotic. In fact, it is this real world, the ''our-side,'' represented initially in the novel by the almost mythic figure of Doris Rivera, a patient who has apparently successfully ''gone outside,'' this is the mystery. The artificial worlds of the hospital and the psychosis itself are clearly delineated; the world outside is presented only slightly near the end of the novel.

Deborah must somehow learn to function in all three worlds: her own mind, the hospital, and finally the outside. Each world has a different landscape, a different set of rules, even a different language, and in each world the character of Deborah is developed along certain lines congruent with the fictional reality of that world. And in each world, she must pass from a stage of passivity to one of self-determination and control. Put another way, Deborah must undergo a process of education on three levels: first mastering the workings of her own mind, then mastering the fairly simple rules of life with the other patients in the hospital, and finally mastering the more complex rules of life on the outside. This multifaceted educational process, together with Deborah's adolescence and her relative innocence in each situation, suggests the kind of education undergone by the adolescent protagonists of the *bildungsroman*. It is also, of course, a stylized version of the process of socialization in the development of any personality, and it may be for this reason that it is easy to identify with Deborah's problems, stated as they are in such bizarre terms.

Deborah is also appealing because she is essentially an heroic figure, and her Kingdom of Yr is an heroic, even mythopoeic, world. In that world, she initially seems to identify with Anterrabae, ''the falling god,'' who is later revealed to be her own version of Milton's Satan . . . , with all its associations of heroic defiance, eternal punishment, and the underworld. . . . [She] must declare her self-mastery by renouncing all her gods and the Kingdom of Yr itself—an act which dramatically parallels the myth which gave rise to Anterrabae in the first place, and which in itself represents a kind of Promethean defiance. Deborah renounces her own security in favor of knowledge of the world and freedom; such an ideal is not uncommon in Romantic poetry and fiction.

Another reason for Deborah's success as a popular heroine is her appeal to our own fantasies of irresponsibility. Almost anything she does is excusable in the context of the fiction, and as such she represents, however perversely, a kind of absolute behavioral freedom. She doesn't necessarily get away with all her actions, but she isn't entirely responsible for them either, and it is likely that this freedom is, on a rather basic level, an example of the sort of wish-fulfillment that characterizes much popular literature. The freedom has its limits, however, and these limits seem at least in part defined by the necessity of maintaining reader sympathy. None of the violence on Deborah's part is directed at anyone other than herself, and the general absence of sexual motives and experience from her story—even though it seems likely that such experiences would comprise a significant element of her psyche—give her the aspect of the ''innocent.'' Not even her most repulsive actions, such as her continued self-mutilation, are sufficient to remove our sympathies from her, and in this respect she is not unlike many other adolescent heroines in popular fiction.

The structure of the novel also may be a contributing factor to its popularity, for despite all its images of doom and confusion, *Rose Garden* is essentially comedic. There is from the outset a feeling of imminent resolution and hope; like the traditional fairy tale, elements of horror may be introduced as long as there is no overall feeling of despair. Part of this may be due to the journey motif; the suggestion of a journey naturally implies that the journey will have an end, and in the case of Deborah, this end is relative sanity (the alternative end, death, is only suggested slightly in the novel in brief references to her earlier suicide attempt). *Rose Garden* begins literally with a journey—the trip to the mental hospital—and continues with Deborah's movement from ward to ward and finally back out into the world. This movement, though not effortless, seems inevitable, and its inevitability is reinforced by the time sequence of the book. Deborah is in the hospital for three years, and in each of these years, springtime represents a progression towards sanity. The first spring arrives when Deborah first secures her relationship with Dr. Fried by learning that she is of value to the doctor: '''If I can teach you something, it may mean that I can count at least somewhere'.'' . . . The second spring is characterized by Deborah and her friend and co-patient Carla declaring their friendship and running away from the hospital in a show of self-assertion and fun, prompting the doctor in charge to comment, '''I'm kind of proud of you'.'' . . . The third spring, coming at the conclusion of the book, includes Deborah's successful passing of the high school equivalency exams—an act which symbolically certifies both her maturity and her sanity. The three episodes taken together constitute Deborah's learning about the value of her person to others, then asserting that value, and finally proving it with the socially accepted measure of the high school exams. She finally emerges from her private world and prepares to leave the hospital in springtime, just as she had entered it, three years earlier, in the autumn. The three years become metaphorically compressed into one cycle of the seasons, and the inevitability of this cycle—the inevitability of spring—lends to the novel an overall tone of hope.

Yet another source of popularity may be the book's imagery. The idea of the "secret garden"—the private respite from the world that is known only to the child—has long been popular in children's and adolescent literature, and it is not unlikely that Deborah's Kingdom of Yr is just such a garden to many readers. Though on a more intense level, it is not unlike Frances Hodgson Burnett's secret garden in her book of that title, or C. S. Lewis's Narnia. Its landscape is a wildly romantic, exciting one of fire and ice, and its language bears resemblance, though on a much more complex level, to the "secret codes" popular among children. In other words, Yr, though the myth of a psychotic mind, is still a myth, and as such bears strong attraction for the imagination. Thus, as we have mentioned earlier, some of the attraction that readers feel for the novel may be akin to the attractions of Blake, or Lewis, or Tolkien.

Finally, and probably most importantly to the novel's professional audience, there is the didactic element. *Rose Garden* has been used as a supplementary text in many university psychology courses because of its accurate dramatization of facts about psychosis and therapy. . . . It appears, then, that the book is widely read as an object lesson in mental illness, and that for many its value as fiction is secondary to its value as case history. And it seems likely that a didactic motive was one of the major reasons the book was written in the first place; a number of novelistic decisions seem to be made on didactic (i.e., what will teach most effectively) rather than aesthetic (i.e., what will work best as fiction) grounds. We learn a great deal more about Deborah's psychosis than we do about her actual personality, for example. Such didacticism may occasionally weaken the novel as fiction, but it probably adds to its popularity.

Rose Garden, then, brings together in a single book many of the elements that have gone into the making of a popular narrative genre. And in terms of the popular audience, it is the book most responsible for the present ascendance of that genre. Part autobiography, part fiction, part educational tract, it is in many ways one of the most significant popular books of the last twenty years. (pp. 902-06)

> *Kary K. Wolfe and Gary K. Wolfe, "Metaphors of Madness: Popular Psychological Narratives," in* Journal of Popular Culture, *Vol. IX, No. 4, Spring, 1976, pp. 895-907.*

JAMES R. FRAKES

Few experiences are more calculated to shrivel a reviewer's heart than to read a publisher's blurb describing a new novel as "an American saga. . . ." So it's a pleasure to discover that ["**Founder's Praise**"] triumphs over the epithet.

Of course, there's still the problem of the "three generations," but Joanne Greenberg . . . keeps the lines clear and the relationships functional throughout. And the historical sweep never calls exhausting attention to itself, World War I passing in a single paragraph. But the Dust-Bowl years are dwelt on obsessively, mote by relentless mote. And rightly so, for out of the death of the land in this southeastern Colorado farming

community blossoms the "vision of the Presence" granted to Edgar Bisset and transforming him from a silent withdrawn man to an eloquent and joyful giver of life and hope. The transformation is rendered with the kind of open-eyed respect and tenderness with which Sherwood Anderson approached his simpler characters, but Edgar is not allowed to become a "grotesque"—at least not while he's alive. (p. 28)

When Edgar dies, the inevitable happens: the dancing edges toward ritual, the dancers become The Apostles of the Spirit of the Lord, "Praises" proliferate, and schisms emerge. Edgar Bisset, fallible and human in life, is turned into an icon known as "The Founder." The man who had no answers except celebration of the Presence becomes, once safely dead, the font of eternal wisdom and patristic authority.

The bulk of this darkly beautiful and disturbing novel is devoted to the rise and dissolution of this new religion [derived from Edgar's vision] and particularly to its mixed effects on those lucky and unlucky enough to be kin of The Founder. . . . Edgar's grandnephew decides that the mistake of the Apostles (and, one supposes, that of America) was to cherish innocence. Tough issues, but they're dealt with dramatically and persuasively in this gnarled book, which never indulges in cheap mockery or cynical patronizing of the religious impulse.

Joanne Greenberg brings unclouded vision and sureness to bear on almost everything she touches—landscapes, drought, insects, small-town insularity, family love and jealousy, the paradoxical vitality of the life-draining demands of farming. In unorthodox but refreshing fashion, minor figures are often given the sharpest insights. Charlie Dace, for example, an ex-con hired-hand, a man with "a face that left no memory," almost imperceptibly moves from the fringes to the center of the novel. Much more than just a chorus-chanter or wry commentator, Charlie grows into what Wright Morris calls a "witness." . . . It seems eminently right that, when **"Founder's Praise"** whirls to conclusion, not with the melodramatic obliteration of the Apostles but with one crippled survivor clinging to "the possibility of God" and "the wonder," we should tune out on the last page listening to Charlie reminiscing about Edgar Bisset—the complex man, not the monolithic Founder. (pp. 28, 30)

> *James R. Frakes, in a review of "Founder's Praise," in* The New York Times Book Review, *October 31, 1976, pp. 28, 30.*

PAUL GRAY

In [*High Crimes and Misdemeanors,* a] collection of ten short stories, Joanne Greenberg seems eager to make things go bump in the daytime. Take the case of Aunt Bessie, a nice Jewish woman who one day stops believing in God. Watched by a cautiously admiring niece, Bessie goes on to renounce faith in banks, germs and electricity, although her unplugged television set somehow still carries whatever programs she wants to watch. Only when Bessie decides that all natural laws, including gravity, are myths does she receive her alarmingly literal comeuppance. Her niece finds her floating like a balloon about the house, being hectored and scolded by mysteriously televised rabbis. She pleads her disbelief, to no avail. "Foolish woman," a rabbi replies, "a soul goes in and out of belief a hundred times a day. Belief is too fragile to weigh a minute on. You stopped running after Him, looking for Him, struggling with Him. Even His Laws you turned from!"

Although the whimsy in this story is nicely done, Bessie's punishment strikes a censorious note that is less happily picked up throughout the book. Greenberg draws a number of characters only so that she can quarter them. . . .

Greenberg displays little of the sympathy she expended on the mentally ill in *I Never Promised You a Rose Garden* (1964) and on the deaf in *In This Sign* (1972). People in these stories are self-maimed, and get treated accordingly. The artistic regimen is ascetic. "Talmudic Law," one of her characters explains, "forbids the overdecorated letter, a letter for art's sake and not for the formation of legible words." Nothing is overdecorated here; Greenberg spends little time telling where her characters live or what they look like. In one story, a parent complains about a wayward son, but it is impossible to tell whether the speaker is mother or father.

What remains clearly legible throughout is Greenberg's complaint against contemporary society and what one character calls the "weekend-guest view of life." Aunt Bessie bobbing helplessly across her ceiling is a comic parable of the effects of freethinking, except that the author is not laughing. Her stony integrity often redeems these stories from irritating knuckle-rapping. They engage the mind, unsettle it and survive as disputatious reminders of first principles and last things.

> *Paul Gray, "Stony Parables," in* Time, *Vol. 115, No. 3, January 21, 1980, p. 89.*

HILMA WOLITZER

The stories in *High Crimes and Misdemeanors* have a strong connecting theme—spiritual questing and questioning. Men and women consider not only the existence of a deity, but their own existential purpose, their own capacities for good and evil. Greenberg pursues this theme with startling invention and with an effective blend of mischief and melancholy. . . .

In **"Flight Pattern,"** a temporarily earthbound *malakh* (angel) longs for the "appetites and surprises" in the life of his human companion, Ben. "'Don't envy us,'" Ben advises. "'We are usually very lonely.'" And adds later, "'Don't you know that we can't shut our ears to sound or our minds to a constant bombardment of thoughts and wishes, good and bad, fantasies, old songs, bad jokes? How can you want that? It isn't free will, it's free *whim*!'" Eventually the *malakh* spreads his wings and escapes such mortal misery.

Characters in other stories work their magic, too, against the limits of their condition. Friends try to buy extra time from the CIA for a dying rabbi, and a woman adds mystical ingredients to a cake so that her frail, elderly aunts will be fortified against neighborhood crime. The rabbi appears to get better, and the aunts' terror is reduced to fear and then blooms into a fearless power. The stories bloom, too, in Joanne Greenberg's capable hands. As in all good fiction, there are no easy resolutions and no moralizing. But the reader's own beliefs and imagination are vigorously stirred.

> *Hilma Wolitzer, "Fables of Identity, Parables of Passion," in* Book World—The Washington Post, *March 2, 1980, p. 14.**

GERRY McBROOM

Although Joanne Greenberg wrote a novel which was popular with young adult readers (*I Never Promised You a Rose Garden*), [*High Crimes and Misdemeanors*] is not for most ado-

lescent readers. The plots and characters have little with which these readers will relate. . . .

As the title states, Greenberg's short stories deal with crimes and misdemeanors. . . . Whether realistic or fantastic, the stories all comment on contemporary life with an emphasis on Modern American Jewish life.

One does not have to be Jewish, however, to enjoy the writing style and the delightful characters Greenberg has created. She skillfully uses both first and third person narration, strong dialog, realistic settings, some autobiographical material, and excellent character development in these stories. Throughout, she is able to create humor and credibility, never stretching the fantasy to the unbelieveable or impossible. Mature readers will enjoy Greenberg's well-written stories and subtle comments on contemporary life.

> *Gerry McBroom, in a review of "High Crimes and Misdemeanors," in* The ALAN Review, *Vol. 7, No. 3, Spring, 1980, p. 19.*

SANFORD PINSKER

The ten stories of *High Crimes and Misdemeanors* often dazzle and always delight. They are worthy companions to the stories in Miss Greenberg's earlier collection, *Rites of Passage* (1972), full of the moral concern and magical twists we have come to associate with Greenberg's best work.

At least half of these most recent stories are intriguing additions to that slippery category known as American-Jewish fiction. In her stories, Jewishness is less a cultural condition than it is an unacknowledged spiritual realm. In short, she takes Jewish ideas—and more important, the Jewish God—seriously. **"Certain Distant Suns"** begins on a note that one would never find in a story by, say, Philip Roth: "In the end we found out that Aunt Bessie, in the fifty-sixth year of her life and three weeks before the Seder, had stopped believing in God." Rather than satirizing Aunt Bessie, by listing the contents of her refrigerator or the weave in her wall-to-wall carpeting, Greenberg lets the premise generate a condition that quickly wrenches it from the rational, the mundane, the commonsensical. Aunt Bessie's abrupt decision affects an entire family, because it was *her* turn to host the Passover Seder. . . . (pp. 511-12)

At times one suspects that too much has been sacrificed for endings that would have made crackjack installments on the old "Twilight Zone" T.V. show. **"Like a Banner"** is such a tale, with its composite of James Thurber's Walter Mitty (in this case, an ambulance driver who fantasizes himself as the dashing, glamorous Dr. Life) and Nathanael West's ersatz-savior, Miss Lonelyhearts, and its predictable lesson. **"Flight Pattern"** is another, in which a bumbling dope smuggler is hounded by a very persistent angel.

Also: One suspects there is a self-conscious, bookish character to much of Greenberg's dabbling in the supernatural, the cabalistic, the Judaically occult. On the other hand, a less encumbered story like **"Merging Traffic"** (a tale of separate reunions, of lives that did not touch in a high school that divided the Beautiful and the Lucky from those made of unheroic stuff, and lives that will not touch even years later) is more immediate, more powerful and much more poetic.

Nonetheless, *High Crimes and Misdemeanors* is worth reading and, more important, it warrants re-reading. Its stories have the rare ability to first surprise and then convince. That sort of high praise is usually restricted to very good poems. Greenberg's collection makes an impressive case that it is also appropriate to the short story. (pp. 512-13)

Sanford Pinsker, in a review of "High Crimes and Misdemeanors," in Studies in Short Fiction, *Vol. 17, No. 4, Fall, 1980, pp. 511-13.*

RUTH R. WISSE

[A] convincing study of an American Jewish family in transition . . . is Joanne Greenberg's *A Season of Delight*. . . . [Mrs. Greenberg] has often written on Jewish subjects, and this latest work is satisfyingly mature.

Grace Dowben, its heroine, has lived for years in the Pennsylvania town of Gilboa. . . . Though she has other satisfactions and other worries, her own sense of responsibility for the perpetuation of [the Jewish] people runs as the unbroken theme of her life—and of this book. Even her flare-up of love for a young man in town is bound up with the desire to reawaken him as a Jew.

It should be said that the best parts of the book have nothing to do with the Jewish theme. Joanne Greenberg, who is herself a member of a fire-fighting and emergency-rescue team in the Colorado town where she lives, has included in this novel some wonderful descriptions of such a squad, of its members, its functions, and the way it works. Gilboa Fire and Rescue serves both heroine and novel as an ideal emblem of civic responsibility and creative personal activity.

On the emergency squad Grace can bring immediate relief to victims of disaster. Securing the welfare of the Jews is not so easy, especially since in this area Grace has no firm remedy to offer. Her own love of Jewish ritual and her informed appreciation of its ceremonies and teachings is not based on faith, because, as Grace admits, "Belief is a gift with us," and not one that is transferable to one's children, either. She herself is haunted by several ghosts of the murdered Jews of Europe who fight among themselves about just what sort of legacy they would have her inherit from them, but who become collectively her fiercest reason for Jewish survival. Fortunately, the author understands all the pitfalls of such an argument, and tries to parry the unspoken objections, but she still seems to need it for its emotional power. In an elaborate metaphor (for which she apologizes in advance: "Don't laugh") she compares the Jews to a hemorrhaging body, in deep and possibly irreversible shock if no immediate transfusion is forthcoming.

The book leaves no doubt about the author's or the heroine's disciplined response to this state of emergency, only about their ability to make it meaningful to others. In the book itself, Grace's influence on the younger generation is left an open question. . . . [The] prose is at its weakest when it tries to be most persuasive. In a work where so much else succeeds, this is particularly regrettable. (p. 86)

Ruth R. Wisse, "Rediscovering Judaism," in Commentary, *Vol. 73, No. 5, May, 1982, pp. 84-7.**

NORMA B. WILLIAMSON

In *A Season of Delight* Mrs. Greenberg takes a woman who could fit about half a dozen popular stereotypes and exposes the unique human being beneath. Grace Dowben is a middle-aged Jewish housewife, attempting to deal with the pain and sense of loss engendered by the finality of her children's leaving home. . . . Her delight in her Jewish heritage is sharpened when a young man of Jewish parentage, but agnostic upbringing, joins the unit, and Grace teaches Ben the traditions rejected by her son and daughter. In time, however, Grace discovers that Ben is much more to her than a substitute for her lost son. . . . Mrs. Greenberg clearly believes in traditional values, along with such old-fashioned themes as good and evil, but there is humor and compassion in her treatment of both, making her always a joy to read.

Norma B. Williamson, in a review of "A Season of Delight," in National Review, *Vol. XXXIV, No. 20, October 15, 1982, p. 1297.*

MEG ELLIOTT GARBER

A middle-aged woman, Grace, marriage secure and happy, nest empty. A young man, Ben, 20 years younger, single, a thoughtful stranger. These are the characters who meet as paramedics on a small town ambulance, are drawn to each other, and finally grow to love each other during *A Season of Delight*. Joanne Greenberg has masterfully created these real people along with a host of secondary characters to play out this complicated portrayal of emotions. *A Season of Delight* is neither a garish, contrived plot of illicit love nor a simplistic, unrealistic romance. It is a thoughtful narrative of a woman given to self reflection. . . .

The book is excellent, but I cannot imagine a teenager having much in it to personally identify with. Its possible value on an adolescent's reading list might be the insight it could provide into the emotions and experiences of one's mother.

Meg Elliott Garber, in a review of "A Season of Delight," in The ALAN Review, *Vol. 10, No. 2, Winter, 1983, p. 27.*

ROBERT C. SMALL

When Eric, a handsome, shallow, charming man in his early twenties causes a terrible automobile accident, he is changed by the event and by his shock at the easy sentence he receives. Drunk and stoned, he kills all of the Gerson family, including three children, except the mother Helen. Later during his probation, he encounters Helen and despite the tragedy that he has caused, they fall in love and marry. . . . [Years later,] Helen and the . . . [children of this second marriage] are killed in a car wreck. After his grief has lifted a bit, Eric begins to wonder whether or not Helen may have arranged their first encounter, their marriage, and the second accident in order to satisfy her fierce sense of justice. . . .

[*The Far Side of Victory* is] a strange and moving book that is about guilt and penitence, at least at first, but becomes a portrait of Helen, not Eric, and of the adult life that her childhood has condemned her to. It is a book that, I suspect, readers will either admire greatly or despise. I admired it greatly.

Robert C. Small, in a review of "The Far Side of Victory," in The ALAN Review, *Vol. 11, No. 1, Fall, 1983, p. 31.*

SUSAN DOOLEY

What Greenberg is writing about in her gentle and perceptive book [*The Far Side of Victory*] is how hard it is to know the people you love—and how that knowledge, once gained, must be tenderly held. . . .

[*The Far Side of Victory*] is Eric's book as he probes the mind and life of the woman he has come to love, a woman as closed as he is open. Shut into darkness by the poverty and ugliness of her childhood, she teaches him that, ''There was, there must be even now, a secret race, a whole foreign race of children who yearn for school because it isn't home, whose vacations are dreaded and who watch the warming days of May creep over the desk tops with sinking hearts, made lonelier still, more bereft, because all the others count the days to summer and swarm out of the schoolhouse with joy at the end of the last day, free.''

Joanne Greenberg . . . once more reaches to the hearts of her readers.

> *Susan Dooley, in a review of ''The Far Side of Victory,'' in* Book World—The Washington Post, *October 2, 1983, p. 6.*

GREGORY MAGUIRE

[*The Far Side of Victory* is dramatic] and engaging from the start. . . . [The] writing is clear and worth savoring. The development of a strange but powerful romance between Eric and Helen, the eventual break with their former lives, and their professional establishment in a community small enough to need them and large enough to give them room to heal are all described with patience and restraint. . . . Mysterious and suspenseful but rewarding in its characterization and its analysis of small-town politics and society, the book provides a subtle and complex treatment of love and growth. (p. 740)

> *Gregory Maguire, in a review of ''The Far Side of Victory,'' in* The Horn Book Magazine, *Vol. LIX, No. 6, December, 1983, pp. 739-41.*

Bette Greene

1934-

American novelist, nonfiction writer, and scriptwriter.

Greene's upbringing in a small Arkansas town provides the background for her three novels for young adults. The isolation which Greene experienced as a member of one of the few Jewish families in that town is strongly conveyed in her first novel, *Summer of My German Soldier* (1973), and in its sequel, *Morning Is a Long Time Coming* (1978). The first book takes place during World War II and concerns Patty Bergen, a Jewish youngster who befriends a German prisoner of war. The sequel follows Patty on a quest to Germany in search of the soldier's family. Some critics consider Greene's characters oversimplified, but it is generally agreed that in both books Greene effectively portrays Patty's growing awareness of the town's anti-Semitism.

Another concern in these works is Patty's need for independence from her repressive parents. This theme is further developed in Greene's novel *Them That Glitter and Them That Don't* (1981). Like Patty, the teenage protagonist of this work realizes that in order to live by her own standards she must leave home. Critics praise the novel for its realistic depiction of the tensions between adolescents and their families.

Greene has also written two novels for children: *Philip Hall Likes Me. I Reckon Maybe* (1978), and *Get On Out of Here, Philip Hall* (1981).

(See also *Children's Literature Review*, Vol. 2; *Contemporary Authors*, Vols. 53-56; *Contemporary Authors New Revision Series*, Vol. 4; and *Something about the Author*, Vol. 8.)

© Nancy Crampton

PETER SOURIAN

["**The Summer of My German Soldier**"] is an exceptionally fine novel about a young girl whose mediocre parents don't like her, precisely because she is an inconveniently exceptional human being. 12-year-old Patty Bergen begins to learn to her genuine surprise that she is a lovable person, "a person of value," from a German P.O.W. escapee in Arkansas during World War II.

The prisoner, son of a professor at the University of Göettingen, is an anti-Nazi, while Patty's Jewish father is very much a Nazi, really, and part of Patty's trouble is that she keeps on being able to tell who is the real Nazi in spite of herself. Life would be so much easier if she could stop up her ears, dim her eyes and accept convenient, stereotype versions of reality without question.

But she is exceptional and, because she is, she gets it with both barrels. The townspeople of Jenkinsville (with certain notable exceptions—a decent sheriff, a black maid), mixing up their stereotypes in a confused effort to deal with a rather unique situation, end up calling her a "Jew Nazi-lover," and she ends up in the Arkansas Reformatory for Girls because she fed and hid her P.O.W. without telling anyone.

In some ways Bette Greene's material is not promising. Her characters could easily have come out of an ordinary movie melodrama. Along with the loving black maid, there's a nasty minister's wife, a hard-boiled girl reporter, a bigoted business man, a town gossip, a spoiled-brat little sister and a chicken-soup grandma. The incidents, the kind of suspense and the tears evoked, all skirt cliché as well; and the author's moral values might too; yet the writing is fresh. . . .

The reason for the book's freshness . . . is its fineness, in the literal sense. The stuff of it is fine, like the texture of Patty herself. The detail is too meaningfully specific, too highly selective to be trite. Armed with earned moral insight, Mrs. Greene sneaks past our conditioned reflexes satisfyingly often.

> *Peter Sourian, in a review of "The Summer of My German Soldier," in* The New York Times Book Review, *November 4, 1973, p. 29.*

AUDREY LASKI

[*Summer of My German Soldier* seems to me likely] to disturb a reader as young as its 12-year-old heroine, because of the domestic violence and bitterness it records. And though sex does not happen in it, the heroine's vicious father is convinced that it must since his daughter has done the unthinkable for a Jewish girl and helped a German soldier to escape.

Audrey Laski, "Partridge in a Pear Tree," in The Times Educational Supplement, *No. 3261, December 9, 1977, p. 21.**

MYRA POLLACK SADKER AND DAVID MILLER SADKER

Some of the finest books about World War II devastate . . . simplistic conceptions and emphasize that no life may be held cheaply and that there must be regard for the enemy. These books portray acts of compassion that do not recognize enemy lines and that unite human beings despite the inhumanity of war.

One book, exceptional for its portrayal of this theme as well as for its sensitively developed characterizations, is Bette Greene's *Summer of My German Soldier*. . . . To some, the story of a Jewish girl harboring a Nazi casts aspersions on the loyalty of all Jews and uncovers barely concealed feelings of anti-Semitism. For others, however, the story of an act of compassion between a Jewish girl and a German boy becomes symbolic of the love that is possible even amidst the callous atrocities of war. (pp. 310-11)

Myra Pollack Sadker and David Miller Sadker, "War and Peace," in their Now Upon a Time: A Contemporary View of Children's Literature, *Harper & Row, Publishers, 1977, pp. 286-317.**

JACK FORMAN

[*Morning Is a Long Time Coming,* an] autobiographical novel set four years after the author's *The Summer of My German Soldier* . . . , opens in the same small Arkansas town. Still alienated from her father, mother, and grandparents, Patty Bergen graduates from high school, then sets out for Europe instead of going to college. In France, Patty has her first love affair with a young teacher, Roger, but feels torn between him and her need to find the parents of the German POW she once unsuccessfully hid (recorded in Greene's first novel). Wracked by a bleeding ulcer brought on by the tensions with her family and her lover, she finally leaves Roger to go to Göttingen, Germany in search of the POW's family. . . . Having come to terms with her anxieties, she returns to France for a rapprochement with Roger. Green's portrayal of a Southern Jewish family in the 1940s is strong and honest, but the depiction of Patty's relationship with Roger is strangely forced and detached. Despite this central flaw, however, the novel will attract teens because of its sensitive treatment of the loosening of familial bonds.

Jack Forman, in a review of "Morning Is a Long Time Coming," in School Library Journal, *Vol. 24, No. 8, April, 1978, p. 93.*

PETER SOURIAN

["**Morning Is a Long Time Coming**"] is the sequel to "**Summer of My German Soldier.**" . . . In that exceptionally fine novel, Bette Greene delineated the way in which an exceptional young girl could end up being called a "Jew Nazi-lover" precisely on account of the finest aspects of her nature.

In "**Morning Is a Long Time Coming,**" thematic concerns involving fineness or individuality in contention with coarseness and conformity are further considered. Patty, now 18, graduates from high school with an obsession to travel to Goettingen to visit her dead P.O.W.'s mother. . . .

Bette Greene excels at depicting the process by which Patty arrives at each moral insight along the way of her literal and figurative journey, first to Paris and then to Germany.

It is not necessary to have read the earlier novel to read this one. In fact, some of Patty's current realizations seem to me repetitious of the insights she had earned earlier; along with convincing scenes of growth and development in Patty's continuing story, there are occasional traces of petulance and a nagging sense of superiority in Patty that made me dangerously sympathize with her awful mother a few times.

There is in Patty a kind of self-contradictory trait that often accompanies the fine strengths of exceptional individuals, and more might have been made of that sort of complexity.

Also, while Patty is annoyingly quick to doubt herself when she should not, she is often slow with any perspective on her real foibles. It's no doubt to be expected, especially in a young person, but Patty's creator, too, sometimes seems a little slow in this respect.

Nevertheless, this is a very worthwhile book, with wider scope than the modesty of its design might indicate. There is freshness in Bette Greene's treatment of young romance, and Patty's affair with a French boy is just right. But what makes it transcend the standard romantic intrigue is how the ethnic and cultural identities of such different people are integrated with their individualities, and yet kept distinct, and how these people relate to one another and then grow from the common experience. All of this is delicately understood and handled, as is the psychologically acute, bittersweet denouement that takes place in Germany.

Peter Sourian, "The Nazi Legacy, Undoing History: 'Morning Is a Long Time Coming'," in The New York Times Book Review, *April 30, 1978, p. 30.*

GEOFF FOX

[In *Morning Is a Long Time Coming*], Patty Bergen's awakening sexuality is realized in her love for Roger, a Parisian. With him, she finally sloughs off the inhibitions of her upbring in Jenkinsville, Arkansas (population 1,170). She is 18, and the independence which prompted her defiance in Bette Greene's earlier (and excellent) *Summer of my German Soldier* is still feared and resented six years later by the community and her mean-spirited parents. Patty's journey from red-necked America to Paris and Roger allows the recognition that the ugly duckling she has always been told she is has become a particularly articulate and perceptive swan. Since Patty is the narrator, the journey is charted with wit and energy.

The lessons she learns reflect concerns—and idioms—of contemporary America: to accept yourself for who you are, to be owned by no-one and yet to learn to receive as well as to give, to deal with the Problem of one's need for a mother. The action of this novel lies within Patty, and she is characterised with subtlety and even tenderness.

Geoff Fox, "Parents and Lovers," in The Times Educational Supplement, *No. 3308, November 24, 1978, p. 48.**

KEVIN WILSON

The story [in *Morning Is a Long Time Coming*] is predictable enough and so is the heroine's situation, but the novel is saved from banality by the effectiveness of the narrator's technique. By telling the story in the first person the novelist succeeds admirably. The story could have become over-burdened with the bitterness and the adolescent preoccupations of a very unhappy young woman. It does not.

The author also succeeds in mimicking the speech of a nineteen year old. As a result the story is quite realistic and not overly melodramatic. The reader cannot help but empathize with the alienation of the heroine.

> *Kevin Wilson, in a review of "Morning Is a Long Time Coming," in* Best Sellers, *Vol. 38, No. 9, December, 1978, p. 291.*

JUDY MITCHELL

No one would accuse *The Summer of My German Soldier* of being an upbeat story. It seems, first of all, to operate on the principle of reversing some standard elements of holocaust literature: the American child is a Jew, but she offers safety to a fugitive German prisoner-of-war.

Her father and mother are terrible people, and Patty's isolation from everyone else in Jenkinsville, Arkansas, is so palpable that some of the children who suffered through the war in Europe seem fortunate by contrast. Patty loved Anton, gave him what help she could, and mourned his death when that help was not enough. For this she is repudiated by her family and persecuted by the townspeople. Her Jewishness is an embarrassment to other Jews. . . . *Summer of My German Soldier* catches the despair of the holocaust and its aftermath by indicating that one sensitive, loving little girl and one gentle German boy are no match for the times in which they live. They make a symbolic commitment to reaching out, and because of this they swell the list of victims. (pp. 16-17)

> *Judy Mitchell, "Children of the Holocaust," in* English Journal, *Vol. 69, No. 7, October, 1980, pp. 14-18.* *

SUSAN F. MARCUS

[In *Them That Glitter and Them That Don't* Greene] once again places her young heroine in a family too occupied with their own lives to love or care about her. But this time, unlike Patty Bergen [the central character of *Summer of My German Soldier*], the girl manages to emerge not unscathed by circumstances, but strengthened by facing up to them. Because everyone in Bainesville, Arkansas, distrusts her conniving Gypsy mother and disdains her drinking father, Carol Ann Delaney must endure her own lonely life. When she is unexpectedly called upon to sing before her high school class, her classmates finally begin to pay attention to her and to appreciate the talent that she has always dreamed would take her to Nashville and

to fame. But her high school graduation day brings to Carol Ann the realization that most of her so-called friends and, more cruelly, Mama have abandoned her after all and that she must in turn leave her little brother and sister now if she is ever to improve any of their lives. As she leaves Bainesville for Nashville, Carol Ann calls upon those same Gypsy instincts which she has resented in her Mama to help her survive. . . . [Carol Ann] will keep her readers turning the page (pulling for her) as she honestly faces, and overcomes, her painful situation. (pp. 122-23)

> *Susan F. Marcus, in a review of "Them That Glitter and Them That Don't," in* School Library Journal, *Vol. 29, No. 8, April, 1983, pp. 122-23.*

MICHELE SLUNG

[In *Them That Glitter and Them That Don't,* Greene] shouts through her characters' conversation, bringing a sophisticated, wise-cracking tone and a cosmopolitan awareness that doesn't match up with the folk of Dexter County, Arkansas. Carol Ann Delaney, not surprisingly, wants to flee her surroundings and better herself, and the way she envisions doing it is by becoming a country singer, "all aglitter in a gown of sequins and feathers," lavishly praised by "the country and western music critic for *The New York Times*." Or, singing some of her favorite songs, Carol Ann thinks of herself as "there inside those batty Beatles' world within a world. Their zany, joyful world of 'The Yellow Submarine.'" None of this thought or language rings true. Bette Greene may have grown up in Arkansas, but she's East Coast now, through and through. And there are dozens of similar examples scattered around the book: it's like dress-up in reverse, with a grown woman hunched down, trying to fit her shoulders into a child-sized jacket.

> *Michele Slung, "Adolescent Heroines," in* Book World—The Washington Post, *May 8, 1983, p. 14.* *

MARY M. BURNS

Skillfully constructed, [*Them That Glitter and Them That Don't*] is persuasively real. And while Carol Ann as narrator is undoubtedly the central character, the personality of her mother—half child, half con artist—is a brilliant creation, demonstrating that the parents' uncaring attitude toward their daughter should be understood as dependence rather than malice. Humor rising naturally from the circumstances transforms the grim details of Carol Ann's life into an optimistic chronicle. As she proudly tells her music teacher, she is, like most Gypsies, a survivor—and her argument is convincing.

> *Mary M. Burns, in a review of "Them That Glitter and Them That Don't," in* The Horn Book Magazine, *Vol. LIX, No. 4, August, 1983, p. 453.*

Judith (Ann) Guest

1936-

American novelist.

Guest's first novel, *Ordinary People* (1976), propelled her to fame as a best-selling author and was adapted into an award-winning film. *Second Heaven* (1982), her second published novel, had been started several years before *Ordinary People* was written. Both books are set in contemporary middle-class suburbia, both have a troubled adolescent male as a central figure, and both portray characters grappling with such problems as suicide, depression, divorce, and child abuse. There are strong thematic similarities between the two works as well, as Guest herself notes: "Communication is a preoccupation of mine; so is domination. How people dominate other people and why they do it. How you get out from under that if you want to, and whether you really want to." Thus, although Guest places her characters in unusually harsh circumstances, her works concern issues which most young adults face.

Ordinary People was the first unsolicited manuscript which Viking Press had accepted for publication in twenty-seven years. The novel relates the story of a young man reentering high school and family life after spending time in a mental institution. Guest describes Conrad's struggle with insanity and depression and the ways in which pain can both bring a family closer together and tear it apart. Critics praised Guest's realistic and sensitive portrayal of Conrad and found it superior to her characterization of the adults in the novel. Despite the opinion of some critics that the events of *Ordinary People* are too neatly orchestrated and potentially maudlin, the book is elevated above the level of formulaic pulp fiction by Guest's ear for dialogue, especially where young people are concerned.

While most critics thought Guest avoided melodrama in *Ordinary People*, many suggest that she was less successful in *Second Heaven*, in which she tells of three lonely, troubled people who try to help one another. Cat and Mike, both divorced, offer sixteen-year-old Gale the emotional and legal help he needs to escape the clutches of his abusive father and in the process assuage some of their own loneliness. In this novel, Guest sets up a clear conflict between good and evil; she allows good to triumph in a courtroom conclusion which many critics considered too idealistic. Like *Ordinary People*, *Second Heaven* is very tightly organized; some critics expressed a desire to see Guest relinquish some of the control with which she writes. However, critics did not suggest that *Ordinary People* was a fluke; nearly all found much to praise in *Second Heaven*.

(See also *CLC*, Vol. 8 and *Contemporary Authors*, Vols. 77-80.)

© *Thomas Victor 1984*

a sense of guilt he couldn't shake and still can't, even after trying to commit suicide, hospitalization, and now his return home. Home being the place where you keep your distance—from an indifferent, inaccessible mother and perhaps a too protective father who have to come to terms with other difficulties. This finds Conrad attempting to deal with everyone's unease, particularly his own. . . . This has none of the sentimental over-indulgence of [Hannah Green's *I Never Promised You a Rose Garden*], the obligatory referral and potential market (young people will also like this). Where it does succeed, and succeed it does, is in communicating a sense of life both felt and experienced without ever trespassing beyond actuality. *Ordinary People* is an exceptionally real book.

A review of "Ordinary People," in Kirkus Reviews, Vol. XLIV, No. 5, March 1, 1976, p. 271.

KIRKUS REVIEWS

Ordinary people on any street where you live, people you might know, people you'll know better at the end of this straight, unassuming, encroaching first novel [*Ordinary People*]. A family, or what's left of it—the Jarretts, after the circumstantial whim which took the life of their eldest boy in a boating accident and left Conrad, less "perfect," but much nicer with

MELVIN MADDOCKS

Ordinary People is a quite good but thoroughly conventional novel that reads, in fact, like the old-pro product of an intelligent, thoroughly practiced veteran. Ms. Guest's hardly unorthodox subject is a middle-class American family from the Middle West. Make that upper-middle-class. . . .

Picking up the story after Conrad returns home [from a mental hospital], Ms. Guest deals with love and hate, forgiveness and the lack of it, madness and death—the themes appropriate to Greek tragedy. But she must deal with them in the terms of the well-made suburban novel. Panic equals the rattle of father's ice cube in one-too-many martinis. Despair equals the hundred small ways a Christmas Day falls apart, even when the keys to a new Le Mans for Conrad lie under the tree. Loneliness gets spelled out in the instructions on a frozen TV dinner.

The author writes almost too unerringly clever dialogue. Everything is buried under the ubiquitous wisecrack—the ironic putdowns and self-putdowns by which Americans play tag with their terror of failure. For failure is finally what *Ordinary People* is about. It may be Guest's ultimate irony that the older brother's drowning and Conrad's attempted suicide are only symbols for spiritual death—for a thousand subtle methods of neglect and undernourishment by means of which loved ones kill and are killed within the family circle.

What is this emotional malaise for which domesticated Americans pay the day-to-day price? Here again Guest is conventional. Too much self-control, she implies, too little trust of one's feelings. Thus the nearest to a savior the novel boasts is a flip-hip psychiatrist who eats doughnuts, drinks awful instant coffee and shares the floor with his patients because he can't afford a couch. His message to Conrad comes perilously close to the slogan of the '60s: LET IT ALL HANG OUT. Guest's alternate solution: the love of a good woman. Jeannine, who sings soprano in the choir to Conrad's tenor, almost backs into the '50s.

The form, the style of the novel dictate an ending more smooth than convincing. As a novelist who warns against the passion for safety and order that is no passion at all, Guest illustrates as well as describes the problem. She is neat and ordered, even at explaining that life is not neat and ordered. Thus the suburban novel takes on the manicured-lawn aspects of its subject; and in its well-lighted game rooms the characters seem like padded billiard balls, they carom so discreetly.

Give the author credit though. She has written a truly haunted story in which agony gives gloss a run for the money. The Furies in her suburb are real, even if she seems to banish them with a spray of Airwick. (p. 68)

> *Melvin Maddocks, "Suburban Furies," in* Time, *Vol. 108, No. 3, July 19, 1976, pp. 68, 70.*

DOROTHEA D. BRAGINSKY

In *Ordinary People,* Judith Guest portrays the emotional demise of a family with depth, subtlety, feeling and intelligence. . . .

The book opens with young Conrad's return from a mental hospital where he spent several months following a dramatic, bloody suicide attempt. The story that unfolds is his and his parents' efforts to become ordinary people again. The unexpected disorder of their well-ordered lives, however, makes it impossible for them to continue as before. The further tragedy of their lives is that they know no other way to be. . . .

Somewhat surprisingly, the story is told through the eyes of Conrad and his father. The mother's point of view, even though she is foremost in the men's lives, is barely articulated. We come to know her only in dialogues with her husband and son, and through their portrayals of her. For some reason Guest has

given her no voice, no platform for expression. We never discover what conflicts, fears and aspirations exist behind her cool, controlled facade.

Nonetheless, the Jarretts' inner struggles, their attempts to communicate, and their reactions are exquisitely though painfully detailed. Guest understands and articulates the human frailties that lead to conflict, hurt feelings, withdrawal, and isolation. Although it would have been easy for her to resort to psychiatric clichès, the author maintains the integrity of her novel and of her characters by using strictly human terms to describe their predicament; the language of grief, anger, guilt, and hope.

> *Dorothea D. Braginsky, in a review of "Ordinary People," in* Psychology Today, *Vol. 10, No. 3, August, 1976, p. 84.*

PADDY KITCHEN

[In *Ordinary People*] Judith Guest takes an 'ordinary' . . . family in which the son, 17-year-old Conrad Jarrett, has just returned home from a mental hospital, eight months after a suicide attempt. Her technique is to reveal information about Conrad and his parents, Calvin and Beth, in a colloquial, present-tense, piecemeal way—a method more often found in thrillers or adventure stories. She uses the technique extremely skilfully, with twists and turns that come like the proverbial unexpected buckets of cold water. There is nothing sentimental in the way she presents her characters. . . .

Psychologically, the book might have been even more probing if the problem rested between these three characters. But it has been detonated by the death of a fourth—Conrad's drowned elder brother. This tragedy has stripped away the normality which fuelled the parents' daily life, and has revealed their inadequacies. . . .

Sentimentality comes in with the psychologist, Dr Berger, whose kindly, nonconformist ways help Conrad to accept himself. Berger seems so percipient and humane that one questions the likelihood of such a perfectly balanced doctor-patient relationship. That understanding and love are needed to restore the members of the Jarrett family to 'normal' functioning is acceptable; but the epilogue where Conrad terminates his meetings with Berger . . . , and feels strong enough to renew a relationship with his old schoolfriend . . . , *and* manages to feel accepting towards his absent mother . . . , seems a little too warm and rosy. The book has been compared to *Catcher in the Rye,* which I also found sentimental, and young readers of the Seventies may empathise with Conrad Jarrett just as those in the Fifties did with Holden Caulfield.

> *Paddy Kitchen, "Sentimental Americans," in* The Listener, *Vol. 97, No. 2494, February 3, 1977, p. 158.**

JANET G. STROUD

Probably the best . . . of the books that depict the emotionally disturbed [is] *Ordinary People.* . . . *Ordinary People,* as so many have observed, is not an ordinary book. It is a very skillfully constructed, extremely sensitive book. . . .

The characterizations in *Ordinary People* are excellent; it is a very thorough examination of the ways other people react to a person who has had a nervous breakdown. Conrad's mother is only concerned about the mess he made in the bathroom when he tried to commit suicide and considers his suicide attempt in some way a personal affront to her. Father is overprotective and excessive in his concern for Conrad; he constantly watches for signs of another breakdown. The parents' widely differing perceptions of Conrad and his illness constitute a source of strife for them and quite literally tear them apart.

Other people's reactions to him also vary: some are openly hostile, some are overly solicitous, and some are simply embarrassed by the whole situation. Above all, everyone is intensely interested in him, and ever watchful to see if he'll try it again. (p. 291)

> Janet G. Stroud, *"Characterization of the Emotionally Disturbed in Current Adolescent Fiction,"* in Top of the News, *Vol. 37, No. 3, Spring, 1981, pp. 290-95.**

MICHELE M. LEBER

Guest's first novel, *Ordinary People* . . . , was such a publishing/media event that her second is bound to be closely scrutinized and compared. *Second Heaven* may disappoint; its subject of child abuse and its juvenile detention center setting are farther from the mainstream, and its structure (alternate sections from the viewpoint of three main characters) is less tight. But what Guest does well—getting into the heart, soul, and mind of a troubled teenager—she does marvelously well. . . . More pain and less polish than *Ordinary People,* but the same strong core of sensitivity and insight.

> Michele M. Leber, *in a review of Second Heaven,* in Library Journal, *Vol. 107, No. 13, July, 1982, p. 1344.*

KIRKUS REVIEWS

Ordinary People was no fluke: [Guest's second novel *Second Heaven*] again expertly catches middle-class loners in the first crackles of seismic rebellion against closet miseries—and again zooms in close on adolescent terror. The principal grownups this time [Catherine "Cat" Holzman and lawyer Michael Atwood] are two insular people, both recovering (with each other's eventual help) from divorce. . . . Cat and Michael still remain only mildly, distantly connected . . . until one night 16-year-old Gale Murray, fainting and seriously burned, arrives at Cat's door: abused since infancy by a maniacal, religious-fanatic father . . . , Gale has been irrevocably alone. . . . Understandably, then, both Cat and Michael are drawn into Gale's strangulated life—as Cat gives him a temporary home and Michael becomes his lawyer. (Placed in a juvenile detention center, Gale awaits trial for "incorrigibility.") And after more anguish and savagery for poor, uncommunicative Gale, all three isolated, ordinary people will be liberated, will open up and reach out, finding new havens/heavens in one another. Despite the slightly unconvincing melodrama of Gale and his predicament: a totally involving triptych of hurt, healing souls—. . . [*Second Heaven* has] the same direct, plainly mesmerizing impact that was the hallmark of Guest's near-legendary debut.

> A review of *"Second Heaven,"* in Kirkus Reviews, *Vol. L, No. 16, August 15, 1982, p. 942.*

JONATHAN YARDLEY

To get right to the question at hand, the answer is *Yes* Judith Guest *has* done it again. The hundreds of thousands of readers who were touched and amused by her lovely first novel, **"Ordinary People,"** are going to find themselves touched and amused by her second, **"Second Heaven."** If from time to time Guest seems to be straining in the effort to demonstrate that she is no one-shot phenomenon, who's to complain? The virtues of **"Second Heaven"** are manifold, and far more consequential than its few flaws. (p. B1)

[**"Second Heaven"**] strikes a number of universal chords. Set in Detroit, it involves three people who decide—slowly, painfully, with fear and trepidation—to take the risk of engaging themselves in the lives of the others. The narrative moves from one point of view to another: Mike Atwood, a lawyer who was divorced a few years ago . . . ; Catherine (Cat) Holzman, more recently divorced, now trying to find a place in life for herself; Gale Murray, a physically and psychologically battered 16-year-old boy whom she has taken into her house.

Gale's father, a tight-lipped religious fanatic, has tracked him down to Cat's residence and demanded that the law return him to the home he has fled. The boy is put in a juvenile detention center pending disposition of his case. Mike regards the entire situation as ridiculous and hopeless, but agrees to represent the boy as a favor to Cat; he is strongly drawn to her, and indeed is falling in love with her. At first the relationship between the lawyer and his young, frightened client is hostile and fruitless, but as the lawyer comes to understand the desperation of the boy's circumstances, and as the boy begins to realize that he can trust the lawyer, they find ways to work together. The obstacles to a satisfactory resolution are very large, but this trio of unlikely and initially unwilling allies finds ways to overcome them.

Certainly this tale is, by comparison with that of **"Ordinary People,"** a bit contrived and artificial, and certainly the parallels between the two books need no elaboration—the troubled teen-aged boy, the clumsy adult efforts to help him, the slow development of mutual trust, the discovery that it is better to be together than alone. But neither contrivance nor familiarity can disguise the skill and most particularly the sensitivity with which Guest tells her story. She is an extraordinarily perceptive observer of the minutiae of domestic life, and she writes about them with humor and affection.

[Guest] understands the nuances of people's feelings about the most intimate and mysterious aspects of their lives, and she knows how to describe those feelings accurately and honestly. Yes, she has a sentimental streak; it is just about impossible to imagine her writing a book with an unhappy ending, even though the world she otherwise so faithfully depicts does not, in fact, have many happy ones to offer. But she is an intelligent writer, and a witty one, and the courage she demonstrates in risking failure after her first great success is wholly admirable. So, in every respect that really matters, is **"Second Heaven."** (p. B15)

> Jonathan Yardley, *"Heaven & Earth: Judith Guest's Encore to 'Ordinary People',"* in Book World—The Washington Post, *September 22, 1982, pp. B1, B15.*

NORMA ROSEN

[In] **"Second Heaven,"** Judith Guest brings her own passionate moral concerns to a fine, old-style, high-drama confrontation with evil. (p. 12)

As in **"Ordinary People,"** the teen-age boy in **"Second Heaven"** is evoked with great tenderness and insight. When Miss Guest curves her writing arm about the shoulders of a troubled boy he must sooner or later yield up his heart and mind to her, no matter how hard he tries to hold back.

The book's suspenseful climax is the custody hearing. . . . The result is a rousing three-cheers-for-love dénouement. Yet this reader must withhold one of those cheers. For one thing, "love—that most passionate of religions" is called upon to redress so much that it hardly seems fair—or plausible. Gale has deep emotional problems. He has been abused for years and has repressed all feeling. He cannot bear to be touched. He communicates in some ways with Cat but with almost no one else. No therapist is called in to help him. A hopeful sign at the end of the book is that he is able to cry. Some readers may believe that is evidence enough of his having been healed. Others may secretly hope that Dr. Berger will step across from his office in **"Ordinary People"** to do for Gale what he did for the suicidal boy in Miss Guest's first book.

In **"Second Heaven"** we are in a kind of Manichaean Midwestern world. On the one hand there are the clear evils of control, rules, order. They are associated with inability to love, fanaticism, brutality. Clutter and lack of organization are good— they can let in love. Yet in the context of the author's anti-neatness and anticontrol themes, the technique of the novel itself appears at times to be almost a subversion: the quick-march pace, the click-shot scenes, the sensible, serviceable inner monologues unvaried in their rhythms.

Here and there are puzzling contrapuntal hints. Protectiveness is sometimes equated with bullying, as in the case of Cat's ex-husband. Yet when Cat sees unsupervised children in a playground she wonders if they are loved. Michael's law partner speaks of the way middle-class children bully and abuse their parents. These undeveloped variations make one wonder if Miss Guest has failed to provide enough handholds for her imagination. Beneath the surface of **"Second Heaven"** we can just make out another novelist, wrestling with subtler relationships of good and evil. Though her heroine scorns religion, Miss Guest's interest as a novelist is clearly with the perfecting of the human spirit in a way that comes close to religious concern. One hopes that in her next work she will let deftness go for a while and allow the creative clutter of her thinking to win the day. (pp. 12, 18)

> *Norma Rosen, "The Wounded Healing the Wounded,"*
> *in* The New York Times Book Review, *October 3,*
> *1982, pp. 12, 18.*

PETER S. PRESCOTT

One of the things that popular fiction can do well is to work up in its readers a little awe at the horrors that life makes available to us all and then conclude in a way that leaves us feeling rather good: life does work, doesn't it? Judith Guest is a master of just such performances. Admirers of her immensely likable first novel, **"Ordinary People,"** will feel cozily at home with her second [**"Second Heaven"**]. Again, a damaged adolescent boy stands at the center of her story; again, the extent of his wounds will not be immediately apparent. Again, two adults with problems of their own attempt to save the boy from cooperating in his own destruction. . . .

Guest is not just a popular novelist; she means to bring some art to what she writes, and does. She scrambles her narrative, dividing it among the points of view of her three principals

and introducing important information through a complicated sequence of flashbacks. It's an ambitious procedure and on the whole works well, though occasionally Guest's prose turns flaccid and she delays too long telling us just where we are in time. More effectively, she suggests some neat parallels between Cat's and Michael's situations and Gale's. The problems they face in choosing between marriage and divorce, for instance, can be extended to Gale's divorce from his family: "It was not bondage versus freedom but bondage versus aloneness, the total absence of personal ties." Cat's dependence on her former husband mirrors Gale's dependence on the father who so savagely abuses him.

Some more good things: in the scenes between Michael and his former wife, Guest gives us one of fiction's few portrayals of a really civilized divorce. Nor is child abuse a theme frequently visited by responsible novelists, but Guest has done her homework and got the legal aspects of the problem right. More important, she understands precisely the victim's psychology: the child's dread need to be beaten as well as his prayer for relief. Her characters, Gale's parents excepted, are all complex and sympathetic people, and her story gets more interesting as it goes along. Few novels manage to do that.

> *Peter S. Prescott, "Unsweet Sixteen," in* News-
> week, *Vol. C, No. 14, October 4, 1982, p. 73.*

CHRISTOPHER LEHMANN-HAUPT

I can't complain that I wasn't moved by Judith Guest's **"Second Heaven."** . . . I was moved, I really was. I felt tense and worried in all the right places and sighed with relief when I ought to have and cheered when the heroine, Catherine (Cat) Holzman, snaps at her psychiatrist: "I think you make a fetish out of refusing to give advice. It's not natural. You should see someone about it." (Lo and behold, he then gives advice!)

I even cried in the one or two places I was supposed to, which is no more or less than the author, with her apparently exquisite sense of control, would have wanted. . . .

Certainly, **"Second Heaven"** can't really be accused of being clichéd. The prose may be a little bland (and riddled with split infinitives). And some passages may sound like watered-down William Faulkner. . . .

All the same, Mrs. Guest has a way of waking us up to the fine details of behavior and feeling—for instance, the way a snowy day can make somebody feel good. . . . Or the way the pain of being newly divorced can sneak up and hit a person at unpredictable and embarrassing moments. Or the subtle little tensions that can sabotage the best of intentions when broken families are trying to be civilized. What I'm saying in a roundabout way is that Mrs. Guest's characters almost always seem alive.

Why am I being peevish then, and damning her altogether-competent novel by praising it left-handedly? It's just that everything in the book is so neat and polished, so precisely timed and calibrated: the way the newly divorced people dovetail, conveniently providing a surrogate mother and fatherly counselor for battered Gale Murray. The way the offspring of the various broken families mirror one another, and the too-neat irony that the worst-off children in the story are the products of intact marriages.

The way that Gale overcomes his terror and inarticulateness in the nick of time at his custody hearing, like the cavalry galloping over the hill to save the fort at the 11th hour. The way that important memories crop up in such a way as to intensify the scenes that succeed their recollection. The reader continually gets the feeling that Mrs. Guest is working with plumb line and level and trowel to build her airtight perpendicular walls of plot development. Or rather—since every good novelist must work with such tools—there is a feeling of actually being able to see Mrs. Guest at work with them.

Perhaps all I'm saying is that I wish **"Second Heaven"** had some sort of mark of inimitable individuality to distinguish it—some crazy, inexplicable development or some peculiar flight of prose—an ugly mark, as it were, to distract the observer's eye from its too-symmetrical features. What it comes down to is that **"Second Heaven"** . . . is a lot better than slick, but far short of being inspired. I guess I long for a story as carefully crafted as this to take off and soar a little.

> *Christopher Lehmann-Haupt, in a review of "Second Heaven," in* The New York Times Book Review, *October 25, 1982, p. C25.*

TIME

In her second work of fiction [*Second Heaven*], Best-selling Author Judith Guest . . . has rearranged the furniture, repapered the bathroom and polished the silver. Unfortunately, these are the only alterations she has made in prose style or personnel. . . .

The members of the trio play discords and harmony based upon Guest's familiar melodies: "As for love . . . what did anyone ever really know about it? You did what you had to do." The effect is relieved only when the author writes about what is further from her own experience. Gale's sojourn in a county facility for problem children moves with a poignant freshness and a depth of emotion, proving that, in Guest's case, talent advances with the imagination. Away from the shaded streets of suburbia, her gift appears anything but ordinary.

> *A review of "Second Heaven," in* Time, *Vol. 120, No. 17, October 25, 1982, p. 82.*

JUDITH CHETTLE

In Victorian times the high middle ground of literature may have been overcrowded. In recent years it has been almost deserted, as writers of literary ambition fled in terror lest they be tainted by its association with some need for moral force and good sense. But Judith Guest, who enjoyed considerable success with her first novel, **"Ordinary People,"** has with **"Second Heaven"** again deservedly claimed this middle ground for her own.

Guest is a writer whose particular talent is to articulate the concerns and interests of, well, ordinary people. She describes with sympathy those who, for the most part, live or aspire to live on that high middle ground where good and evil do struggle, where happiness is not expected to come easily, and love is a giving, not a taking.

The main characters are a trio of two adults and an adolescent, whose lives resemble three lines narrowing until they meet, rather than three points of a triangle destined always to be separate. . . .

Gale Murray, a teen-age boy almost irreparably harmed by the savagery of his fanatically religious father, represents the third line. His sudden appearance and subsequent stay in Cat's home is the ultimate cause of the three lines converging in an ending we know will be happy, though Guest is suddenly in too much of a hurry to dispel a few nagging doubts about Gale's easy recovery. . . .

Judith Guest's acute perceptions of how most of us feel and think makes **"Second Heaven"** especially noteworthy. She eschews the sensational, knowing that restrained reporting of the unpleasant is more effective. In describing the journey of these three people to a satisfactory equilibrium, she has given us a book that is neither pop schlock nor great literature but a work of humanity and good sense to which we can respond with pleasure.

> *Judith Chettle, "Fine Novel of Ordinary Lives," in* The Christian Science Monitor, *November 6, 1982, p. B5.*

PRISCILLA JOHNSON

Judith Guest, whose first novel, *Ordinary People* . . . , was both a popular and a critical success, has written another dramatic and moving story [*Second Heaven*]. This time the focus is not on an "ordinary" nuclear family, but on three lonely people who feel rejected by their families and whose lives come together by chance. . . . The touching final chapter gives promise of a new "family" to be formed by these three, who fill real needs in each other's lives. This ending is happier, though less realistic, than the bittersweet conclusion to *Ordinary People*. Guest again takes us into the hearts and minds of real and likable people. She writes of post-divorce problems and troubled teenagers with great insight and sensitivity. This heartwarming story will not disappoint her many fans.

> *Priscilla Johnson, in a review of "Second Heaven," in* School Library Journal, *Vol. 29, No. 4, December, 1982, p. 87.*

KLIATT YOUNG ADULT PAPERBACK BOOK GUIDE

In *Ordinary People,* Guest told us about one failed family and the pain of an adolescent boy suffering from a mother's coldness and guilt over a brother's death. In *Second Heaven,* Guest writes about three failed families, from the viewpoint of one member of each. . . .

Most YA readers will be drawn to Gale's character, his strength in surviving, his confusion, fear, shame, and angry rebellion against authority. Guest tells poignantly how abuse hurts the spirit as well as the body of a child and, though she ends the story in a positive way, the reader knows clearly that Gale will always suffer in some way from his father's beatings. The loneliness, aimlessness, depression, worry over children and other concerns of the adult characters, Michael and Cat, will be less understandable to YA readers, many of whom might find it difficult to begin the novel starting with Michael's point of view. . . .

Guest, once again, involves us in the lives of others, giving us characters we care about, who teach us about ourselves and about life in middle-class families in our times.

> *A review of "Second Heaven," in* Kliatt Young Adult Paperback Book Guide, *Vol. XLIII, No. 1, January, 1984, p. 10.*

Ernest (Miller) Hemingway

1899-1961

American short story writer, novelist, nonfiction writer, journalist, poet, and dramatist.

Hemingway is regarded by many as one of the greatest writers of the twentieth century. Considered master of the understated prose style which became his trademark, Hemingway was awarded the 1954 Nobel Prize in literature. Both his novels and short stories have evoked an enormous amount of critical commentary; although his literary stature is secure, he remains a highly controversial writer. His narrow range of characters and his thematic focus on violence and machismo, as well as his terse, objective prose, have led some critics to regard his fiction as shallow and insensitive. Others claim that beneath the deceptively limited surface lies a complex and fully realized fictional world. His supporters note the supreme importance of the things left unsaid. As Hemingway commented in *Death in the Afternoon* (1932), the "dignity of movement of an iceberg is due to only one-eighth of it being above water." Despite the fact that his style is variously applauded and denounced, Hemingway is one of the most widely imitated writers of contemporary literature.

Critical assessment of Hemingway's writing frequently focuses on the connections between his life and his work. Born and raised in affluent, suburban Oak Park, Illinois, Hemingway spent the greater part of his life trying to escape the repressive code of behavior set by his strict, disciplinarian parents and their society. His first break from home came in 1918 when he volunteered for service in World War I. Hemingway was stationed in Italy for only a few weeks before he was wounded and forced to return to Oak Park. Scarred physically and emotionally from the war and stifled by his home environment, Hemingway, according to some critics, began a quest for psychological and artistic freedom that was to lead him first to the secluded woods of northern Michigan, where he had spent his most pleasant childhood moments, and then to Europe, where his literary talents began to take shape.

Although Hemingway's most significant works include such renowned novels as *The Sun Also Rises* (1926), *A Farewell to Arms* (1929), and *For Whom the Bell Tolls* (1940), as well as his Pulitzer Prize-winning novella, *The Old Man and the Sea* (1952), critical response to his longer fiction has been less uniformly favorable than to that of his short stories. The short stories in his first major publication, *In Our Time* (1925), are increasingly considered to be some of his most successful works and are seen to embody the predominant stylistic and thematic concerns which mark all of his later fiction. The majority of these stories focus on Nick Adams, a protagonist often discussed as the quintessential Hemingway hero and the first in the line of Hemingway's "fictional selves."

Nick Adams stories are scattered throughout Hemingway's collections, including *In Our Time, Men without Women* (1927), *Winner Take Nothing* (1933), and *The Fifth Column and the First Forty-Nine Stories* (1938). Although the Nick Adams stories were not initially identified as a unified sequence, Philip Young, a noted Hemingway scholar, edited a volume in 1972 which collects these stories and places them roughly in chro-

nological order based on Nick's maturation. Young has been influential in directing critical attention to connections between Hemingway's work and his early life.

Like Hemingway, Nick Adams spent much of his early youth in the Michigan woods, went overseas to fight in the war, was wounded, and returned. The early stories set in Michigan, such as "Indian Camp," "The End of Something," "The Three-Day Blow," and "The Doctor and the Doctor's Wife," introduce Nick as a vulnerable adolescent attempting to understand a brutal, violent, and confusing world. On the surface, Nick, like Jake Barnes in *The Sun Also Rises,* Robert Jordan in *For Whom the Bell Tolls,* and, in fact, all of Hemingway's protagonists, appears tough and insensitive. However, critical exploration has resulted in a widespread conclusion that the toughness stems not from insensitivity but from a strict moral code which functions as the characters' sole defense against the overwhelming chaos of the world. Cleanth Brooks, Jr. and Robert Penn Warren, in their influential exposition of the short story "The Killers," noted that "it is the tough man, . . . the disciplined man, who actually is aware of pathos or tragedy." Though he seems to lack spontaneous human emotion, the hero "sheathes (his sensibility) in the code of toughness" because "he has learned that the only way to hold on to 'honor,' to individuality, to, even, the human order . . . is to live by his code."

One of the most popular and provocative of the Nick Adams stories is "Big Two-Hearted River." For many years its ambiguities puzzled critics and other readers. On the surface it simply recounts Nick's solitary fishing expedition along the Big Two-Hearted River in northern Michigan. However, there is an air of unsettling calm underlying the uneventful plot. As is characteristic of Hemingway's fiction, the terse, almost journalistic prose, the compressed action, and the subdued yet suggestive symbolism point to a deeper meaning than appears on the surface. In the late 1930s Edmund Wilson introduced the idea that the "thing left out" of "Big Two-Hearted River" is its entire social context. He proposed that Nick has recently returned from war and that the "touch of panic" which surrounds him is in fact his shock and withdrawal from the brutal nature of life. Nick's escape along the Big Two-Hearted River, like Huck Finn's along the Mississippi, can be seen in a wider context as a rejection of society as a whole. In 1952 Philip Young, expanding on Wilson's theory, suggested that all of Hemingway's fiction revolves around the psychologically wounded hero, which in turn reflects Hemingway's own relentless struggle to face the world with "grace under pressure." Earl Rovit notes that "in a sense, (Nick Adams) is a released devil of our innocence. . . . He suffers our accidents and defeats before they happen to us. . . . On this level, then, the Nick Adams projection is a vital defensive weapon in Hemingway's combat with the universe." Wilson's and Young's theories, though controversial, have been widely accepted and form the basis of critical interpretation of Hemingway's fiction.

Like William Faulkner, Hemingway began his literary career by publishing poetry; he also wrote a play, *The Fifth Column* (1937). But these works are considered less significant contributions to his overall literary achievement. In 1961, at the age of 61, Hemingway committed suicide, thus ending the life of one of the most influential prose stylists of the twentieth century.

(See also *CLC*, Vols. 1, 3, 6, 8, 10, 13, 19; *Contemporary Authors*, Vols. 77-80; *Dictionary of Literary Biography*, Vols. 4, 9; *Dictionary of Literary Biography Yearbook: 1981;* and *Dictionary of Literary Biography Documentary Series*, Vol. 1.)

In this volume commentary on Ernest Hemingway is focused on the Nick Adams stories.

EDMUND WILSON

Ernest Hemingway's *In Our Time* was an odd and original book. It had the appearance of a miscellany of stories and fragments; but actually the parts hung together and produced a definite effect. There were two distinct series of pieces which alternated with one another: one a set of brief and brutal sketches of police shootings, bullfight crises, hangings of criminals, and incidents of the war; and the other a set of short stories dealing in its principal sequence with the growing-up of an American boy against a landscape of idyllic Michigan, but interspersed also with glimpses of American soldiers returning home. It seems to have been Hemingway's intention—*'In Our Time'*— that the war should set the key for the whole. The cold-bloodedness of the battles and executions strikes a discord with the sensitiveness and candor of the boy at home in the States; and

presently the boy turns up in Europe in one of the intermediate vignettes as a soldier in the Italian army, hit in the spine by machinegun fire and trying to talk to a dying Italian: 'Senta, Rinaldi. *Senta,*' he says, 'you and me, we've made a separate peace.'

But there is a more fundamental relationship between the pieces of the two series. The shooting of Nick in the war does not really connect two different worlds: has he not found in the butchery abroad the same world that he knew back in Michigan? Was not life in the Michigan woods equally destructive and cruel? He had gone once with his father, the doctor, when he had performed a Caesarean operation on an Indian squaw with a jackknife and no anaesthetic and had sewed her up with fishing leaders, while the Indian hadn't been able to bear it and had cut his throat in his bunk. . . . Even fishing in Big Two-Hearted River—away and free in the woods—he had been conscious in a curious way of the cruelty inflicted on the fish, even of the silent agonies endured by the live bait, the grasshoppers kicking on the hook.

Not that life isn't enjoyable. Talking and drinking with one's friends is great fun; fishing in Big Two-Hearted River is a tranquil exhilaration. But the brutality of life is always there, and it is somehow bound up with the enjoyment. Bullfights are especially enjoyable. It is even exhilarating to build a simply priceless barricade and pot the enemy as they are trying to get over it. The condition of life is pain; and the joys of the most innocent surface are somehow tied to its stifled pangs.

The resolution of this dissonance in art made the beauty of Hemingway's stories. He had in the process tuned a marvelous prose. Out of the colloquial American speech, with its simple declarative sentences and its strings of Nordic monosyllables, he got effects of the utmost sublety. F. M. Ford has found the perfect simile for the impression produced by this writing: 'Hemingway's words strike you, each one, as if they were pebbles fetched fresh from a brook. They live and shine, each in its place. So one of his pages has the effect of a brook-bottom into which you look down through the flowing water. The words form a tesellation, each in order beside the other.'

Looking back, we can see how this style was already being refined and developed at a time—fifty years before—when it was regarded in most literary quarters as hopelessly non-literary and vulgar. Had there not been the nineteenth chapter of *Huckleberry Finn*?—'Two or three nights went by; I reckon I might say they swum by; they slid along so quick and smooth and lovely. Here is the way we put in the time. It was a monstrous big river down there—sometimes a mile and a half wide,' and so forth. These pages, when we happen to meet them in Carl Van Doren's anthology of world literature, stand up in a striking way beside a passage of description from [Ivan] Turgenev; and the pages which Hemingway was later to write about American wood and water are equivalents to the transcriptions by Turgenev—the *Sportsman's Notebook* is much admired by Hemingway—of Russian forests and fields. Each has brought to an immense and wild country the freshness of a new speech and a sensibility not yet conventionalized by literary associations. Yet it *is* the European sensibility which has come to Big Two-Hearted River, where the Indians are now obsolescent; in those solitudes it feels for the first time the cold current, the hot morning sun, sees the pine stumps, smells the sweet fern. And along with the mottled trout, with its 'clear water-over-gravel color,' the boy from the American Middle West fishes up a nice little masterpiece.

In the meantime there had been also Ring Lardner, Sherwood Anderson, Gertrude Stein, using this American language for irony, lyric poetry or psychological insight. Hemingway seems to have learned from them all. But he is now able to charge this naïve accent with a new complexity of emotion, a new shade of emotion: a malaise. The wholesale shattering of human beings in which he has taken part has given the boy a touch of panic. (pp. 174-76)

Going back over Hemingway's books today, we can see clearly what an error of the politicos it was to accuse him of an indifference to society. His whole work is a criticism of society: he has responded to every pressure of the moral atmosphere of the time, as it is felt at the roots of human relations, with a sensitivity almost unrivaled. Even his preoccupation with licking the gang in the next block and being known as the best basketball player in high school has its meaning in the present epoch. After all, whatever is done in the world, political as well as athletic, depends on personal courage and strength. With Hemingway, courage and strength are always thought of in physical terms, so that he tends to give the impression that the bullfighter who can take it and dish it out is more of a man than any other kind of man, and that the sole duty of the revolutionary socialist is to get the counter-revolutionary gang before they get him.

But ideas, however correct, will never prevail by themselves: there must be people who are prepared to stand or fall with them, and the ability to act on principle is still subject to the same competitive laws which operate in sporting contests and sexual relations. Hemingway has expressed with genius the terrors of the modern man at the danger of losing control of his world, and he has also, within his scope, provided his own kind of antidote. This antidote, paradoxically, is almost entirely moral. Despite Hemingway's preoccupation with physical contests, his heroes are almost always defeated physically, nervously, practically: their victories are moral ones. (pp. 195-96)

> Edmund Wilson, *"Hemingway: Gauge of Morale,"* in his The Wound and the Bow: Seven Studies in Literature, *1941. Reprint by Farrar Straus Giroux, 1978, pp. 174-97.*

CLEANTH BROOKS, JR. AND ROBERT PENN WARREN

[This essay was originally published in 1943.]

[In addition to the structure of **"The Killers,"** as it concerns the relations among incidents and with regard to the attitudes of the characters,] there remain as important questions such items as the following: What is Hemingway's attitude toward his material? How does this attitude find its expression?

Perhaps the simplest approach to these questions may be through a consideration of the situations and characters which interest Hemingway. These situations are usually violent ones: the hard-drinking and sexually promiscuous world of *The Sun Also Rises*; the chaotic and brutal world of war as in *A Farewell to Arms, For Whom the Bell Tolls,* or **"A Way You'll Never Be"**; the dangerous and exciting world of the bull ring or the prize ring as in *The Sun Also Rises, Death in the Afternoon,* **"The Undefeated," "Fifty Grand"**; the world of crime, as in **"The Killers,"** *To Have and Have Not,* or **"The Gambler, the Nun, and the Radio."** Hemingway's typical characters are usually tough men, experienced in the hard worlds they inhabit, and apparently insensitive: Lieutenant Henry in *A Farewell to Arms,*

the big-game hunter in **"The Snows of Kilimanjaro,"** Robert Jordan in *For Whom the Bell Tolls,* or even Ole Andreson. They are, also, usually defeated men. Out of their practical defeat, however, they have managed to salvage something. And here we come upon Hemingway's basic interest in such situations and such characters. They are not defeated except upon their own terms; some of them have even courted defeat; certainly, they have maintained, even in the practical defeat, an ideal of themselves, formulated or unformulated, by which they have lived. Hemingway's attitude is, in a sense, like that of Robert Louis Stevenson. . . . (pp. 319-20)

For Stevenson, the world . . . is, objectively considered, a violent and meaningless world—"our rotary island loaded with predatory life and more drenched with blood . . . than ever mutinied ship, scuds through space." This is Hemingway's world, too. But its characters, at least those whose story Hemingway cares to tell, make one gallant effort to redeem the incoherence and meaninglessness of this world: they attempt to impose some form upon the disorder of their lives, the technique of the bullfighter or sportsman, the discipline of the soldier, the code of the gangster, which, even though brutal and dehumanizing, has its own ethic. . . . The form is never quite adequate to subdue the world, but the fidelity to it is part of the gallantry of defeat.

It has been said above that the typical Hemingway character is tough and, apparently, insensitive. But only apparently, for the fidelity to a code, to a discipline, may be an index to a sensitivity which allows the characters to see, at moments, their true plight. At times, and usually at times of stress, it is the tough man, for Hemingway, the disciplined man, who actually is aware of pathos or tragedy. The individual toughness (which may be taken to be the private discipline demanded by the world), may find itself in conflict with some more natural and spontaneous human emotion; in contrast with this the discipline may, even, seem to be inhuman; but the Hemingway hero, though he is aware of the claims of this spontaneous human emotion, is afraid to yield to those claims because he has learned that the only way to hold on to "honor," to individuality, to, even, the human order as against the brute chaos of the world, is to live by his code. This is the irony of the situation in which the hero finds himself. Hemingway's heroes are aristocrats in the sense that they are the initiate, and practice a lonely virtue.

Hemingway's heroes utter themselves, not in rant and bombast, but in terms of ironic understatement. This understatement, stemming from the contrast between the toughness and the sensitivity, the violence and the sensitivity, is a constant aspect of Hemingway's method. . . . Just as there is a margin of victory in the defeat of the Hemingway characters, so there is a little margin of sensibility in their brutal and violent world. The revelation arises from the most unpromising circumstances and from the most unpromising people—the little streak of poetry or pathos in **"The Pursuit Race," "The Undefeated," "My Old Man,"** and, let us say, **"The Killers."** (pp. 321-22)

[Ole Andreson of **"The Killers"**] fits into this pattern. Andreson won't whimper. He takes his medicine quietly. But Ole Andreson's story is buried in the larger story, which is focused on Nick. How does Nick Adams fit into the pattern? Hemingway, as a matter of fact, is accustomed to treat his basic situation at one or the other of two levels. There is the story of the person who is already initiated, who already has adopted his appropriate code, or discipline, in the world which otherwise he cannot cope with. . . . There is also the story of the process of the initiation, the discovery of evil and disorder, and the first step toward the mastery of the discipline. This is Nick's story. (But the same basic situation occurs in many other stories by Hemingway, for example, **"Up In Michigan,"** **"Indian Camp,"** and **"The Three-Day Blow."**)

It has been observed that the typical Hemingway character is tough and apparently insensitive. Usually, too, that character is simple. The impulse which has led Hemingway to the simple character is akin to that which led a Romantic poet like [William] Wordsworth to the same choice. Wordsworth felt that his unsophisticated peasants or children, who are the characters of so many of his poems, were more honest in their responses than the cultivated man, and therefore more poetic. Instead of Wordsworth's typical peasant we find in Hemingway's work the bullfighter, the soldier, the revolutionist, the sportsman, and the gangster; instead of Wordsworth's children, we find the young men like Nick. There are, of course, differences between the approach of Wordsworth and that of Hemingway, but there is little difference on the point of marginal sensibility.

The main difference between the two writers depends on the difference in their two worlds. Hemingway's world is a more disordered world, and more violent, than the simple and innocent world of Wordsworth. Therefore, the sensibility of Hemingway's characters is in sharper contrast to the nature of his world. This creates an irony which is not found in the work of Wordsworth. Hemingway plays down the sensibility as such, and sheathes it in the code of toughness. . . . The typical character is sensitive, but his sensitivity is never insisted upon; he may be worthy of pity, but he never demands it. The underlying attitude in Hemingway's work may be stated like this: pity is only valid when it is wrung from a man who has been seasoned by experience, and is only earned by a man who never demands it, a man who takes his chances. Therefore, a premium is placed upon the fact of violent experience. (pp. 322-23)

> *Cleanth Brooks, Jr. and Robert Penn Warren, "'The Killers', Ernest Hemingway: Interpretation," in* Understanding Fiction, *edited by Cleanth Brooks, Jr. and Robert Penn Warren, Appleton-Century-Crofts, Inc., 1959, pp. 306-25.*

CARLOS BAKER

[Hemingway's] first forty-five stories may be conveniently taken as a kind of unit, since they were all written within ten years, and since they represent what Hemingway thought worthy of including in his first three collections: *In Our Time* (1925), *Men Without Women* (1927), and *Winner Take Nothing* (1933). Taken together or separately, they are among the great short stories of modern literature.

Their range of symbolic effects is even greater than the variety of subjects and themes employed. The subjects and themes, in turn, are far more various than has been commonly supposed. Like any writer with a passion for craftsmanship, Hemingway not only accepts but also sets himself the most difficult experimental problems. Few writers of the past fifty years, and no American writers of the same period except [Henry] James and [William] Faulkner, have grappled so manfully with extremely difficult problems in communication. One cannot be aware of the real extent of this experimentation (much of it highly successful, though there are some lapses) until he has read through the first three collections attempting to watch both the surfaces and the real inward content. (p. 119)

If we read ["**Big Two-Hearted River**"] singly, looking merely at what it says, there is probably no more effective account of euphoria in the language. . . . It tells with great simplicity of a lone fisherman's expedition after trout. He gets a sandwich and coffee in the railway station at St. Ignace, Michigan, and then rides the train northwest to the town of Seney, which has been destroyed by fire. From there he hikes under a heavy pack over the burned ground until he reaches a rolling pine-plain. After a nap in a grove of trees, he moves on to his campsite near the Two-Hearted River. There he makes camp, eats, and sleeps. Finally, as sum and crown of the expedition, there is the detailed story of a morning's fishing downstream from the camp. At the surface of the story one finds an absolute and very satisfying reportorial accuracy.

During one of the colloquies of Dean Gauss, [F. Scott] Fitzgerald, and Hemingway in the summer of 1925, **"Big Two-Hearted River"** came up for consideration. Both of Hemingway's friends had read it in the spring number of Ernest Walsh's little magazine, *This Quarter*. Half in fun, half in seriousness, they now accused him of "having written a story in which nothing happened," with the result that it was "lacking in human interest." Hemingway, Dean Gauss continued, "countered by insisting that we were just ordinary book reviewers and hadn't even taken the trouble to find out what he had been trying to do." This anecdote is a typical instance of the unfortunately widespread assumption that Hemingway's hand can be read at a glance. (pp. 125-26)

For here, as elsewhere in Hemingway, something is going on down under. . . . Malcolm Cowley, one of the few genuinely sympathetic critics of Hemingway, has suggested that "the whole fishing expedition . . . might be regarded as an incantation, a spell to banish evil spirits" [see *CLC*, Vol. 13]. The story is full of rituals. There is, for example, the long hike across the country—a ritual of endurance, for Nick does not stop to eat until he has made camp and can feel that he has earned the right to supper. There is the ritual of homemaking, the raising-up of a wall against the dark; the ritual of food-preparation and thoughtful, grateful eating; of bedmaking and deep untroubled sleep. Next morning comes the ritual of bait-catching, intelligently done and timed rightly before the sun has warmed and dried the grasshoppers. When Nick threads one on his hook, the grasshopper holds the hook with his front feet and spits tobacco-juice on it—as if for fisherman's luck. "The grasshopper," as Mr. Cowley says, "is playing its own part in a ritual." The whole of the fishing is conducted according to the ritualistic codes of fair play. When Nick catches a trout too small to keep, he carefully wets his hands before touching the fish so as not to disturb the mucous coating on the scales and thus destroy the fish he is trying to save. Down under, in short, the close reader finds a carefully determined order of virtue and simplicity which goes far towards explaining from below the oddly satisfying effect of the surface story.

Still, there is more to the symbolism of the story than a ritual of self-disciplined moral conduct. Two very carefully prepared atmospheric symbols begin and end the account. One is the burned ground near the town of Seney. The other is the swamp which lies farther down the Big Two-Hearted River than Nick yet wishes to go. Both are somehow sinister. One probably legitimate guess on the background of the first is that Nick, who is said to have been away for a long time, is in fact a returned war-veteran, going fishing both for fun and for therapeutic purposes. In some special way, the destroyed town of Seney and the scorched earth around it carry the hint of war—

the area of destruction Nick must pass through in order to reach the high rolling pine plain where the exorcism is to take place. In much the same way, the swamp symbolizes an area of the sinister which Nick wishes to avoid, at least for the time being.

The pine plain, the quiet grove where he naps, the security of the camp, the pleasures of the open river are, all together, Nick's "clean, well-lighted place." In the afternoon grove, carefully described as an "island" of pine trees, Nick does not have to turn on any light or exert any vigilance while he peacefully slumbers. The same kind of feeling returns that night at the camp after he has rigged his shelter-half and crawled inside. "It smelled pleasantly of canvas. Already there was something mysterious and home-like. . . . He was settled. Nothing could touch him. . . . He was there, in the good place. He was in his home where he had made it." Back in the low country around Seney, even the grasshoppers had turned dark from living in the burned-over ground. Up ahead in the swamp "the big cedars came together overhead, the sun did not come through, except in patches; in the fast deep water, in the half light, the fishing would be tragic. . . . Nick did not want it." For now, on his island between sinister and sinister, Nick wants to keep his fishing tender and if possible comic.

"Big Two-Hearted River" was based on an expedition which Hemingway once made to Michigan's northern peninsula. His determination to write only those aspects of experience with which he was personally acquainted gave a number of the first forty-five stories the flavor of fictionalized personal history. He was always prepared to invent people and circumstances, to choose backgrounds which would throw his people into three-dimensional relief, and to employ as symbols those elements of the physical setting which could be psychologically justified by the time and place he was writing about. But during the decade when the first forty-five stories were written, he was unwilling to stray very far from the life he knew by direct personal contact, or to do any more guessing than was absolutely necessary.

The recurrent figure of Nicholas Adams is not of course Hemingway, though the places Nick goes and the events he watches are ordinarily places Hemingway had visited or events about which he had heard on good authority and could assimilate to his own experience of comparable ones. Future biographers will have to proceed warily to separate autobiographical elements from the nexus of invented circumstances in which they may be lodged. For present purposes it is enough to notice that well over half of the first forty-five stories center on Nick Adams, or other young men who could easily be mistaken for him.

They might be arranged under some such title as "The Education of Nicholas Adams." It could even be said that when placed end to end they do for the twentieth century roughly what Henry Adams did for the nineteenth, though with obvious differences in formality of approach. The education of Henry Adams in Boston, Quincy, Berlin, London, and Washington presented an informative contrast with the education of Nicholas Adams in Chicago, northern Michigan, Italy, and Switzerland. Nick's life in the twentieth century was on the whole considerably more spectacular than Henry's in the nineteenth; it was franker, less polite, less diplomatic. Chicago, where Nick was born just before the turn of the century, was a rougher climate than Henry's mid-Victorian Boston, just as Nick's Ojibway Indians were far more primitive than Henry's Boston Irish. Partly because of the times he lived in and partly, no doubt, because he was of a more adventurous temperament,

Nick came more easily on examples of barbarism than Henry was to know until his visit to the South Seas. In place of the Great Exposition of 1900 which so stimulated Henry's imagination, Nick was involved in the World's Fair of 1914-1918. But in retrospect one parallelism stood out momentously: both Henry and Nicholas had occasion to marvel bitterly at how badly their respective worlds were governed.

Nick's father, Dr. Henry Adams, played a notable part in Nick's early education. . . . Though they gradually grew apart, they were the best of companions during Nick's boyhood. In middle life Dr. Adams died by his own hand for reasons that Nick sorrowfully hints at but does not reveal.

Ten of the stories record Nick's growing-up. He recalls the move from one house to another and the accidental burning of Dr. Adams's collection of Indian arrowheads and preserved snakes. One Fourth of July, he remembers (and it is one of the century's best stories of the growing-up of puppy-love) there was a ride in a neighbor's wagon back from town past nine drunken Indians, while bad news of his girl, Indian number ten in the story called **"Ten Indians,"** was relayed to him by his father on his return home. . . . It was part of his informal education to be manhandled by two gangsters in a Chicago lunchroom, and to share supper with two tramps, one of them a dangerously punch-drunk ex-prizefighter, in the woods near Mancelona, Michigan.

Like Hemingway, Nick Adams went to war. The earliest glimpses of his career as soldier come in the sixth and seventh miniatures of *In Our Time*. One shows Nick fiercely praying while Austrian artillery pounds the Italian trenches near Fossalta di Piave. In the other, he has been hit in the spine by an Austrian bullet and is leaning back with paralyzed legs against the wall of an Italian church. (pp. 126-30)

There are no Nick Adams stories of the homecoming, the process which Henry Adams found so instructive after his service abroad. The fate of the male character in **"A Very Short Story"** might, however, be thought of as one episode in the postwar adventures of Nick Adams. In a base-hospital at Padua, he falls in love with a nurse named Luz—an idea much expanded and altered in *A Farewell to Arms*. But when the young man returns to Chicago to get a good job so that he can marry Luz, he soon receives a letter saying that she has fallen in love with a major in the Arditi. The protagonist in **"Soldier's Home"** is called Harold Krebs, and he is a native of Oklahoma rather than Illinois. But once again the story might have had Nick Adams as its central character. Like Nick's mother, Mrs. Krebs is a sentimental woman who shows an indisposition to face reality and is unable to understand what has happened to her boy in the war.

Nick Adams returned to Europe not long after the armistice. **"Cross-Country Snow"** reveals that he is married to a girl named Helen who is expecting a baby. **"Out of Season"** and **"Alpine Idyll"** could easily be associated with Nick's life on the continent, while the very moving **"Fathers and Sons,"** which stands as the concluding story in Hemingway's collected short fiction, shows Nick on one of his return trips to the United States, driving his own son through familiar country and thinking back to the life and the too early death of the boy's grandfather, Dr. Henry Adams.

The story of Nick's education, so far as we have it, differs in no essential way from that of almost any middleclass American male who started life at the beginning of the present century or even with the generation of 1920. After the comparatively happy boyhood and the experimental adolescence, the young males went off to war; and after the war, in a time of parlous peace, they set out to marry and build themselves families and get their work done. The story of Adams is a presented vision of our time. There is every reason why it should arouse in us, to use the phrase of Conrad, "that feeling of unavoidable solidarity" which "binds men to each other and all mankind to the visible world."

Future biographers, able to examine the Nick Adams stories against the full and detailed background of Hemingway's life from his birth on July 21, 1899, until, say, his thirty-first birthday in 1930, should uncover some valuable data on the methods by which he refashioned reality into the shape of a short story. What they may fail to see—and what a contemporary evaluator is justified in pointing out—is that Hemingway's aim in the Nick Adams stories is always the aim of an artist. He is deeply interested in the communication of an effect, or several effects together, in such a way as to evoke the deep response of shared human experience. To record for posterity another chapter in his own fictional autobiography does not interest him at all. (pp. 130-31)

> Carlos Baker, in his Hemingway: The Writer As Artist, 1952. Fourth edition reprint by Princeton University Press, 1972, 438 p.

EARL ROVIT

There are, as criticism has come slowly to recognize, not one but two Hemingway heroes; or, to use Philip Young's designations, the "Nick-Adams-hero" and the "code-hero." The generic Nick Adams character, who lives through the course of Hemingway's fiction, appears first as the shocked invisible "voice" of the miniatures of *in our time*; he grows up through Hemingway's three volumes of short stories and at least four of his novels, sometimes changing his name to Jake Barnes, Frederick Henry, Mr. Frazer, Macomber, Harry, Robert Jordan, Richard Cantwell; and he makes his final appearances (appropriately un-named as when he first entered the fictional stage) in Hemingway's last two published stories in 1957. The code-hero also figures in Hemingway's earliest fiction. He dies of a *cogida* as Maera in *in our time,* and he is resurrected in a considerable variety of shapes, forms, and accents (usually non-American) through the bulk of Hemingway's creative output. His manifestations would include the Belmonte of *The Sun Also Rises*; Manuel in **"The Undefeated"**; the Major of **"In Another Country."** . . . (p. 55)

For convenience sake I will refer to the Nick Adams hero as the *tyro* and to the "code-hero" as the *tutor;* for it is basically an educational relationship, albeit a very one-sided one, which binds them together. The tyro, faced with the overwhelming confusion and hurt (*nada*) inherent in an attempt to live an active sensual life, admires the deliberate self-containment of the tutor (a much "simpler man") who is seemingly not beset with inner uncertainties. Accordingly, the tyro tries to model his behavior on the pattern he discerns. However, the tyro is *not* a simple man; being in fact a very near projection of Hemingway himself, he is never able to attain the state of serene unself-consciousness—what [Henry] James once called nastily "the deep intellectual repose"—that seems to come naturally to the tutor. What he can learn, however, is the *appearance* of that self-containment. He can laboriously train himself in the conventions of the appearance which is "the code"; and he can so severely practice those external restraints as to be

provided with a pragmatic defense against the horrors that never cease to assault him.

It may be salutary to digress slightly to what we can call "The Education of Nick Adams" because there is some inevitable confusion surrounding it. In one sense the education is thoroughly abortive; Nick at the end of his multi-chequered career is as terrified and lost as he was, for example, in his encounter with the stark, machined horror of the Chicago gangsters in **"The Killers."** In the following quotation is the tyro, aged somewhere in his mid-fifties, trying to cope with the loss of his eyesight (**"Get a Seeing-Eyed Dog"**): "Because I am not doing too well at this. That I can promise you. But what else can you do? Nothing, he thought. There's nothing you can do. But maybe, as you go along, you will get good at it." The tyro, with his unfair inheritance from Hemingway of a particularly fecund and hyperactive imagination of disaster, has lost nothing of his capacities to be afraid—in spite of his long indoctrination in the craft of courage. In fact, he has rather increased his capacities, for his accumulated experience of horror has taught him many more things of which to be afraid. Measured pragmatically, however—and the defense never pretends to be more than a pragmatic one—Nick *does* survive for an astonishingly long time. He does, as Hemingway puts it, get pretty good at it as he goes along.

If we sketch briefly Nick's biography, we will be able to judge somewhat better the values of his education and to note also the varying ways that Hemingway employed him as shock absorber and seismographer of emotional stress. Nick is born, roughly at the turn of the twentieth century, somewhere in the Midwest. His father, a physician, is fond of hunting and shooting, and is concerned to teach Nick the proper ways of handling a rod and a gun. Dr. Adams has incredibly sharp eyesight and is a better wing-shot than Nick will ever be. He is also intimidated by his wife—a suspiciously indistinct character who is a blur of polite nagging and vague religious sentiments—and, on one occasion, Nick is shocked to see his father back down from a fight. The pattern of cowardice and intimidation, never actually explained, comes to a disgusting (to Nick) finale when his father commits suicide in the 1920's with Nick's grandfather's gun. (pp. 55-6)

As a boy, Nick's adventures are an extreme distillation of the excitements, perplexities, and terrors that are classically supposed to accompany adolescence. . . . His characteristic response to the situations in which he finds himself is open-eyed shock; he registers the events as though he were a slow-motion camera, but rarely if ever does he actively participate in these events. He never really gets into a fight; he does not argue; he does not retreat to protect his sensibilities. Like the camera, he has a curious masochistic quality of total acceptance and receptivity. At about this point we begin to suspect that the adventures of Nick Adams are approximately as realistic as "The Adventures of Tom Swift," although any individual episode in the serial is gratifyingly convincing. We begin to suspect that Hemingway's tyro figure is a projection into the nightmare possibilities of confusion, pain, and immolation; that his adventures are mythic fantasies, guided by the rhythms of intense fear and alienation. That, in short, Nick Adams is a sacrificial victim, bound time and time again to the slaughtering-table to be *almost* slaughtered in order that his creator and readers may be free of fear. (pp. 56-7)

Such is Nick Adams, surely *not*, as one critic explains, "[the story of a man's life which] differs in no essential way from that of almost any middleclass American male who started life at the beginning of the present century or even with the generation of 1920'' [see excerpt above by Carlos Baker]. There is very little that is realistically representative in the career of Nicholas Adams, nor, I would submit, is there meant to be. In a sense—which his name suggests—he is a released devil of our innocence, an enfleshment of our conscious and unconscious fears dispatched to do battle with the frightening possibilities that an always uncertain future holds over our heads. He is the whipping-boy of our fearful awareness, the pragmatic probability extrapolated into a possible tomorrow to serve as a propitiary buffer against the evils which tomorrow may or may not bring. He suffers our accidents and defeats before they happen to us. . . . Hemingway plays him as the sacrificial card in his hand which will finesse the ruthless king; he is the defeated victim, but in experiencing his defeat, Hemingway (and we) can ring ourselves in invisible armor so that we will be undefeated if and when the catastrophes of our imagination do actually occur. On this level, then, the Nick Adams projection is a vital defensive weapon in Hemingway's combat with the universe. (p. 59)

[The] tyro and the tutor figures . . . were central to the typical Hemingway fiction. . . . (p. 78)

There are, I suppose, three characteristic Hemingway stories: those in which the tyro appears more or less alone; those in which the tutor dominates the space of the fiction; and those in which the tutor-tyro axis regulates the revolution of the story. . . . [The] tyro story is an exposition of severe emotional reaction, with the tension of the story dependent on the contrast between the accumulated momentum of the emotion demanding to be released and the resisting forces within the style and content which attempt to restrain that release. The tyro story thus tends to resemble an unexploded bomb in imminent danger of explosion. The tutor story has a greater degree of narrative distance and therefore depends less for its effect on the creation of an immediate emotional impact. It is a form of exemplary story with the developed tensions released along the channels of pathos. Its direction will move inevitably toward the genre of the fable and the parable. And the tutor-tyro story follows the structure of the educational romance or, as it has been called, the "epistemological story," that characteristically American variation on the *Bildungsroman* (which is too loosely termed an "initiation" or "rites of passage" story). Its direction tends to lead to a revelation of "truth," generally in the form of self-discovery or self-realization. These three forms are, of course, not that distinct and arbitary in Hemingway's work, and there is a constant infiltration of one form into the other.

The tyro stories, in their purest form, are those Nick Adams stories in which there are no other significant characters except Nick. These would include **"Big Two-Hearted River: Parts I and II," "Now I Lay Me,"** and **"A Way You'll Never Be."** **"Now I Lay Me"** is a straight first-person narration, while the other two are presented from an impersonal third-person viewpoint so closely focused on the tyro character as to make the narrative device very similar to James's use of a "lucid reflector." In terms of Nick's biography, **"Now I Lay Me"** (1927) comes first; a direct recounting of his convalescence in Milan after the Fossalta wound, it deals largely with his almost Proustian inability to go to sleep and with the various ways he diverts his mind from dangerous preoccupations that might carry him over the thin edge. The last full third of the story records the banal dialogue between Nick and a wounded fellow soldier, John. . . . The story doesn't quite work, however,

although the straight interior memory passages are excellent; for the two sections of the story never quite engage each other. The first section is narrated with an interest that diverts the reader's attention from the state of Nick's mind to his memories themselves; and the second section has perhaps too flatted a key to provide the necessary contrast. We are meant to feel, I think, that Nick is in a far other country than the more prosaic, less sensitive John; this is one of Hemingway's recurrent themes, but I do not find it successfully dramatized within the texture of the prose.

"A Way You'll Never Be" (1933), second in the Nick chronology, deals with his shell-shocked return to his outfit after his release from the hospital. His nerves are shattered and his mind has a tendency to jump around and off, as though its flywheel were disconnected. There is some experimentation with stream-of-consciousness exposition, valuable for what it tells us about Nick; but these sections are not so selectively controlled as those in **"The Snows of Kilimanjaro"** and in *For Whom the Bell Tolls*. In spite of the tone of the story—and there is more obvious hysteria in it than anywhere else in Hemingway's fiction—it fails to create a meaningful tension. There just simply isn't any real conflict in the plot, the structure, or the style to make this a potential bomb. The best part of the story—a part which does develop a real tension—is the description of Nick's ride over the war-pocked road to his meeting with Captain Paravicini.

"Big Two-Hearted River: Parts I and II" (1925), third in the sequence of Nick's adventures, describes approximately twenty-four hours of activity from the time Nick gets off a train in desolated Upper Michigan to hike to a suitable campsite until he calls the fishing over for the day on the following afternoon. Although the story has no plot of any significance, and nothing happens that is in any way untoward in such a fishing trip, it builds up an almost unbelievable tension and has justly been considered one of Hemingway's finest fictions. It is really a *tour de force* of style, since it is almost exclusively the style which persuades the reader that Nick is in a most precarious state of nervous tension which he is desperately holding under clenched control. From having read other Nick stories, the reader may be prepared to fill in the antecedent background to this innocuous fishing trip; but even without that background the dramatic situation of the story seems obvious. (pp. 78-80)

The story operates . . . on two levels. On the first it describes the self-administered therapy of a badly shocked young man, deliberately slowing down his emotional metabolism in order to allow scar tissue to form over the wounds of his past experience. On another level it represents the commencement of the journey into self. But this journey is highly cautious: "He did not want to rush his sensations any." He makes sure that he has a good safe place from which to operate. He fishes first in the brightly lit part of his stream of consciousness. And even there he acts with slow, controlled care; precipitate action may frighten away the quarry he seeks, or it may even frighten off the seeker. He knows that the big fish are in the almost dark places, in the frightening mist-hung swamps of his awareness; he knows also that, if he is to find himself, it is there that he ultimately must look. Meanwhile he gathers his courage together and takes the first measured steps of exploration into the undiscovered country of his mind. There will be plenty of time to fish the swamp.

"Big Two-Hearted River" can be seen, then, as a tyro story which generates its power not from what it actually says, but from what it does not say. It is the latter, the unspoken volumes which shriek from beneath the pressure of the taut prose exposition, that expresses the emotional communication to the reader. This technique, which we may call "the irony of the unsaid," is one of Hemingway's favorite tricks and one of his most powerful ways of transmitting the shock of emotion in prose. This common device of the miniatures of *in our time* (his earliest tyro stories) Hemingway uses to great advantage in those tyro stories which confront Nick with situations of severe violence with which he is unable to cope. Thus, in **"The Killers,"** in **"The Battler,"** and in **"An Alpine Idyll,"** situations are developed of such moral outrage as to demand a comment or an indication of appropriate reaction. The situations themselves are reported impersonally and even laconically; the presentation, as in **"Big Two-Hearted River,"** emphasizes the disparity between what has happened and what ought to be the reaction. Hemingway's artful refusal to give an overt outlet to these reactions in the events or the style of the fictions brings the crescendo of tension to a breaking point. Hemingway . . . holds his pressure on the line until he has exacted the maximum degree of strain; if he slackens it, the reader may get away; if he pulls it too tight, the line may break (as it does in **"An Alpine Idyll"**) and the reader will be free. But when it is just right, as in **"Big Two-Hearted River,"** the reader is caught and forced into response. (pp. 82-3)

[The] third typical Hemingway structure . . . [is] the tutor-tyro story. In such a story—**"The Short Happy Life of Francis Macomber"** and **"In Another Country"** are good examples—the protagonist is placed in a learning relationship to one or more characters and events which will teach him something about the nature of life; how best to live it; and also, more important, something about himself. These then tend to be stories of *growth,* and many critics have somewhat inaccurately dubbed them "initiation" stories or chronicles of the "rites of passage." (p. 94)

In Hemingway's stories of this type, the protagonist is always the tyro. Sometimes, as in **"In Another Country,"** this is difficult to see; but it is always the tyro figure who encloses and structures the story. These stories are usually narrated in the first person; but, when narrated from an impersonal viewpoint, they achieve the same effect through a variation of the Jamesian device of the "reflecting consciousness." Also, since the tyro is generally in a state of stress or imbalance, this tutor-tyro story frequently merges with the straight tyro stories or "unexploded bomb" stories. **"The Killers"** or **"The Battler,"** for example, might be included in this type. The distinctive feature of the epistemological story, it seems to me, is the emphasized presence within the story of a tutor figure who serves as a model of instruction for the tyro. Such a tutor must have created for himself a specific *modus vivendi* which is pertinent to the tyro's immediate emotional needs. The tyro . . . cannot become as adept as the tutor. But he can learn some partial lessons, and he can, in processive pragmatic fashion, learn who and what he is at the specific time of the learning. He can also lay plans for the immediate future. These last two points should be borne in mind because they help to explain why absolute systems are incompatible with Hemingway's vision of himself and the world. Hemingway's view of man . . . accepts and even demands the possibility of change. Thus his epistemological stories are "growth" stories in which the new shapes of growth are unpredictable beforehand. (p. 95)

"In Another Country" seems at first to be more of a sketch than a story. Narrated in first person by Nick Adams, it describes in seemingly random fashion his experiences undergoing rehabilitation treatment for his knee wound in Milan. He, along with other wounded, reports to the hospital every afternoon to work on the therapeutic machines. He becomes friendly with three wounded officers, all of them deservedly decorated for valor in combat. . . . It is clear that the experiences of battle and of being wounded have set the four of them off "in another country" from the people who jostle them on the streets. Similarly, the hospital is separated from the main part of the city by a network of canals; and, from whatever direction it is approached, it can only be entered by crossing a bridge. However, Nick's three friends, "the hunting hawks" who have proved their bravery, read the papers on his decorations and realize that he is not really one of them; his decorations have been given him because he is an American. He is not friendly with them after that because they have already crossed a bridge that is at the moment beyond his approach. Nick does stay friendly with a boy who was wounded on his first day at the front, because he also is not a "hawk."

It is at this point that Nick meets the Major . . . and from this point on in the story, Nick appears to become merely a spectator-recorder of the Major's travail. But to read the story in this way is to miss Hemingway's careful construction of background in the first section. Nick knows that he would not have performed as bravely as the "hunting hawks," and he worries about his real or potential lack of bravery. Set apart by an unrecrossable bridge from the people who have not suffered the immediate violence of war, he is also set apart from those who have fought bravely and without fear: "I was very much afraid to die, and often lay in bed at night by myself, afraid to die and wondering how I would be when I went back to the front again." The Major's agony and his heroic hold on dignity under the burden of his wife's sudden death—a dignity which does not place itself above showing emotion in basic physical ways—become an object lesson to Nick which is directly relevant to his concern with bravery. The "hunting hawks" believe in bravery; it is because they do that they can reject Nick. The Major "did not believe in bravery"; he also had no confidence in the machines that were to restore his hand. He does believe in grammar, in punctuality, in courtesy, and in following the line of duty. And in the story he becomes an exemplar of courage and of dignified resolution in meeting disaster. His actions point out to Nick that a man should find things he cannot lose; that is, a man should slice away from his thoughts and convictions all the illusions that he can live without. And to Nick's immediate concern, he demonstrates that bravery is merely another illusion. He teaches Nick that there is "another country" he can enter which is open to him even with his fear. And this is a country in which unillusioned courage is a more valuable human quality than bravery.

One of Hemingway's masterful achievements in modern short-story technique is exhibited in the structure of this story. His device of "the irony of the unsaid" takes on another employment in his handling of the educational climax of Nick's studies. Nowhere does he indicate that Nick learned anything from the Major's example. Reading the story swiftly, it appears that Nick is not even present at the denouement. But from the first magnificent paragraph describing the cold autumn in Milan to the last description of the Major looking emptily out the window, the selection of every detail is controlled by Nick's mind and by his urgent concern with his fear. The power of the Major's resolution is communicated because it makes a powerful impression on Nick. Nick does not state its impression on him, probably because he has not yet synthesized his impressions into a conceptual form. But they have been synthesized in the narrative structure through juxtaposition and a repetition of the bravery theme. Hemingway once wrote proudly that he chose not to put a "Wow" at the ends of his stories: he preferred to let them end and hang fire, as it were. In a story like **"In Another Country,"** we can see the device handled with consummate artistry. The reader is forced into a participative position; he dots the "i's" and crosses the "t's" and learns Nick's lesson simultaneously with him. At times Hemingway's use of this structure becomes so over subtle as to be entirely lost to a reader, and the story drifts away into vignette or sketch (**"The Light of the World," "Wine of Wyoming"**); less frequently, the lesson is too well learned and overly articulated at the end, and the story becomes the text for a moralizing sermon (**"The Gambler, The Nun, and the Radio"**). But in those cases where the "wow" is deliberately withheld to create a cogent meaningful ambiguity at the end, the tutor-tyro stories can be extremely effective. (pp. 96-8)

> *Earl Rovit, in his* Ernest Hemingway, *Twayne Publishers, Inc., 1963, 192 p.*

JOSEPH DeFALCO

In the attempt to get at the "truth" of real-life experience and to attain the ideal of writing a "classic" that he initially posed for himself, Hemingway began in his early volumes of short stories to describe the adventures of a boy on the threshold of manhood. As Philip Young and Carlos Baker have pointed out in their studies, half of the stories of *In Our Time* (1925), the first short story collection, are devoted to the development of Nick Adams. They are arranged chronologically, moving from Nick's boyhood to his young manhood, and all of these stories are thematically related. Several more stories about the same character appear in the next two collections, *Men Without Women* (1927) and *Winner Take Nothing* (1933). Of importance to the whole of Hemingway's fiction is this early focus on a young hero, for if Philip Young is correct, this hero is to become the prototype "Hemingway Hero" who later will have essentially the same background that Nick has had through his childhood, adolescence, and young manhood. More important than a mere similarity of background in the successive protagonists is the resemblance they bear to each other psychologically. All experience the same needs in meeting the struggle and frustration of twentieth-century man, and even of all men of all times. Some become involved in war, suffer wounds, and are forced to reconcile the psychological disturbances created by these hurts. Others are forced to come to terms with the reality of the traumata created by the pressures of a hostile environment. (pp. 13-14)

In his fiction Hemingway examines the effect upon the inner being of the traumata that modern man has experienced in the world. This attempt to get beyond surface manifestations and deal with more basic, primal contexts led Hemingway to apply certain distinct, psychologically symbolic techniques in his fiction. When these work for him, the entire tone and texture of his prose comes to a close approximation of the "classic" he always tried to write.

At the outset, Hemingway gives Nick Adams and the other protagonists a responsive sensibility. This technique is not a simple device of characterization intended solely to illuminate the character's inner feelings. More expansive, it parallels the questioning attitude that heroes have exhibited in literature since Homer shaped the epic form. Homer forged into two epic works the whole of Greek thought and culture. Just as his heroes

in their victories and defeats represented the needs and drives and experiences of that culture, so Hemingway has for the twentieth century attempted to expand the significance of the experiences of his protagonists into a range far exceeding local and subjective considerations of ordinary fictional conflict. In short, he has tried to write "classics" by capturing the tone and tensions of his own culture.

As his organizing principle, Hemingway chose to depict a series of heroes who become progressively older and experience both literally and psychologically what all men of the twentieth century have experienced over a period of almost fifty years. When these heroes seem unusually introspective and the themes seem too narrow and local, Hemingway may have failed as a craftsman, but he has not lost sight of his ideals. Even in those works where he has been criticized most for organizational failures, one step further in his overall plan has been developed. This plan to view man's relationship to his culture, to the other men in that culture, and ultimately to the cosmos, he carefully develops throughout his short stories. An investigation of this pattern in them reveals the substance of an underlying organization which is the core of his artistry.

In the short stories focusing on Nick Adams and in the other short stories of the three collections, inner attitudes are externalized by means of symbolic reflection. These symbolizations manifest themselves in a variety of conventional ways, but they also appear in unique and quite unexpected combinations. Sometimes characters represent particular attitudes, or episodes point up conflicts, or a sequence of images is repeated a sufficient number of times to create symbolic formations; many times there is a major, controlling symbol from which all of the details take their meaning. One of the most important symbolizations takes the form of a ritualization of a familiar activity, thereby objectifying the intense struggle of the characters in their attempt to find a solution to their inner turmoil. In this way Hemingway maintains a studied control over his material, and this careful control forms a contrast to the content. Ordered artistry is always juxtaposed to the chaos in which most of the central characters find themselves.

In the development of Nick Adams as the leading protagonist in the early short stories, Hemingway utilizes one of his most significant symbolic devices to project his themes. This is the journey artifice. In one sense, all of Hemingway's works employ some aspect of this motif. (pp. 14-16)

[At] least two broad areas of interpretation and movement in all works of art may be recognized: the surface level, or outward movement, with the literal development of plot; and the psychological level, or inner movement, incorporating imagery and symbol as the primary means of expression. In Hemingway's works the employment of the journey artifice provides an outstanding example of these two movements. In his use of the artifice one can discern the employment of a surface narrative technique as his simple, mechanical method of furthering plot development, but one can just as surely discover that the content of his novels and stories, the more meaningful revelation, is far below the surface and lies in the realm of symbolic allusion. In part, the high artistry of Hemingway's fiction is derived from his ability to utilize these levels of meaning in such a way as to fuse the content of a work with its form. (p. 21)

When Hemingway gave the hero of so many of his early stories the name of "Nick Adams," he was doing more than designating a simple appellation to stand for a character. Rather, he intentionally used a symbolic name as a conscious device to illustrate what the character himself would reveal throughout every story in which he appeared. (p. 25)

The surname is particularly appropriate inasmuch as Nick Adams is in a very real sense a second Adam. He is not in any literal sense the progenitor of a whole race, but he does typify a whole race of contemporary men who have encountered irrational elements in their environment and have been forced to deal with them. In the stories in which Nick is depicted as a young boy, he is the innocent, akin to the first Adam before the Fall. But as in the biblical story, the state of innocence is short-lived, and the serpent here too enters the "garden." In this case, however, the entry is not a blatant caricature of the forces of evil; it is the subtle growing of awareness of the incalculable events that disturb the natural order of things, of the caprice in that disturbance, and, what is more important, it is a growing of awareness of the irrational forces that operate within the self.

Hemingway directly reinforces the implications of the name "Adam" as incorporating the forces of evil and the chthonic by giving his hero a first name that might easily be associated with "Old Nick" or Satan, the archetype of evil. Having thus named his character, Hemingway in one stroke characterizes the inherited tendencies of all men. The tension created by the implications of the association of these names is in itself archetypal in its suggestion of the eternal struggle between the forces of good and evil. But the hero in the Hemingway stories encounters evil in many guises, and it goes by many names, be it a wound—literal or psychological—terror in the night, death, or anything else. Always, however, evil is inescapable and unpredictable. In many ways what the Hemingway hero must learn throughout the stories is the nature of evil, and the tension created by the struggle of opposing forces within himself provides the underlying dynamics for the learning process.

Experience itself may be one of the guises of contingent evil. Just as surely as eating the fruit of the tree of knowledge precipitated Adam's fall, so for the innocent the initial encounter with elements foreign to the womb-like existence of home and mother is the first stage of a long and dangerous journey. To the individual involved, retreat from the implications of this first encounter might seem possible, but once exposed, his own nature automatically commits him to the entire journey. If he denies the validity of the commitment, he merely postpones the inevitable or damns himself eternally to the regions of infantile fantasy.

In the short story **"Indian Camp,"** the first of the "Nick" stories of *In Our Time,* Hemingway illustrates the compelling tendency to revert to the state of naïve innocence once the first contact with forces outside the protected environment has been made. Nick as a young boy accompanies his father, a doctor, to an Indian village where an Indian woman is to have a baby. . . . Certain revelations concerning the doctor's character emerge because of the method of delivery, for he has failed to bring along the proper equipment. The operation must be performed with a jack-knife and without benefit of an anesthetic. As a result of the woman's screams during the operation, her husband, who has been lying all the while in the overhead bunk with a severe ax wound, commits suicide by cutting his own throat.

Although the surface plot is of some consequence in itself, the major focus of the story is Nick's reaction to these events. This emphasis clarifies in light of the initiatory motif around which

the story is constructed, and a seemingly slight interlude with a bizarre ending is revealed as having more than situational import. In this story Hemingway establishes a controlling symbol, the Indian camp itself. As in other stories, the camp is suggestive of the primitive and dark side of life. It is a manifestation of the intrusive and irrational elements that impose upon the secure and rational faculties where order and light prevail. For Nick, whose own home is across the lake, the night journey to the camp has all the possibilities of a learning experience. But he must be prepared to accept the knowledge it can give him. As it turns out, Nick is incapable of accepting the events he has witnessed, and the initial preview of the realities of the world is abortive. (pp. 26-8)

Nick's denial of the learning experience begins when he addresses his father as "Daddy" instead of "Dad," as he had at the beginning. But the most telling revelation of the abortive nature of the learning situation comes when he asks, " 'Is dying hard, Daddy?' " Having witnessed the bizarre events at the camp, the question reflects his inability to grasp the significance of his exposure to pain and death. . . .

Nick's refusal to accept the terrors of pain and death and the father's inability to cope with them are revealed in an ironic light in the conclusion: "In the early morning on the lake sitting in the stern of the boat with his father rowing, he [Nick] felt quite sure that he would never die." . . . But Nick has been exposed to some of the primal terrors of human experience, and his "feeling" is depicted as illusory and child-like because it is a romantic reaction to the experience he has undergone. (p. 32)

[The] early stories preface to a considerable extent many of the activities in which the hero of the later ones will engage. Whether he is in the guise of Nick Adams—the new Adam— or under some other apellation, the hero must learn to adjust to contingencies, reconcile himself to them, and eventually create for himself a new moral center in harmony with his own innermost drives. . . . [The] tremendous task of self-discovery requires the loss of all former attachments that indicate infantile dependence. As the hero divests himself of all former ideals, the creation of a new self must follow. (p. 39)

In **"Indian Camp"** and in **"The Doctor and the Doctor's Wife,"** Nick is depicted as a young boy on the threshold of adolescence. His actions and responses are unemotive and childlike. . . . This is typical of the young innocent about to begin the greater journey, but that journey is one that requires a positive commitment to an essentially moral purpose.

In the third story of the Nick sequence the title serves as a rubric to the surface plot as well as to the underlying psychological level of the story. **"The End of Something"** as a title indicates that this is to be a story of termination; it also poses a question as to the nature of the "Something."

The plot concerns Nick and a girl friend, Marjorie, and relates the events of a night fishing trip the two have taken. Nick has apparently planned in advance that this is to be the finale of their romantic interlude, for after preparing for the night's fishing and making the camp he tells Marjorie that "it isn't fun anymore." . . . The story closes with a touch of irony, for Nick is unhappy with the outcome of the episode. (p. 40)

In the final portion of this story a definite progression has been accomplished in the development of Nick Adams from child to adolescent, for with the exhibition of his inner feelings he has at the same time revealed his sensibility. No longer is he girded in the armor of protective infantile illusion and detachment; he takes a positive course of action, and he alone must bear the brunt of its consequences. The "Something" that has come to an end is his belief in the efficacy of romantic illusion. (p. 41)

"**The Three-Day Blow**" is the fourth in the sequence, and it expands the characterization of Nick. In this story Hemingway depicts a boastful, adolescent central character. His actions and attitudes, however, re-enforce the importance of the initiation into life encountered in "**Indian Camp**," the destruction of the father figure in "**The Doctor and the Doctor's Wife**," and the insight gained into the cycle of existence in "**The End of Something**." The story may be said to be a story of recapitulation.

The subject matter directly complements "**The End of Something**." The events take place not long after those depicted in the earlier story and illustrate Nick's reactions. Essentially an adjustment story, it relates Nick's coming to Bill's cabin and talking of baseball, literature, and his affair with Marjorie. At the conclusion, having first decided to get drunk, then having decided not to get drunk, they go out to find Bill's father and to hunt. The surface line of action is obviously scant, but that is of little significance. What is important is the revelation of Nick's attitudes toward his experiences and toward life in general.

At the psychological level something quite different is expressed from what at first glance seems obvious at the literal level. Nick here engages in a fantasy of infantile regression and escape within that regression. This tendency is not unusual in any journey toward discovery of the self; for the implications of experience with the forces beyond the control of the individual are terrifying. No one would choose to destroy himself— an act which is what the discovery of the self implies—unless under the severest provocation. Thus it is that all heroes who set out on this journey have at some point faltered on the way. Nick Adams is no exception. (pp. 44-5)

[At] the end of the story he is poised at the peak of his infantile optimism: "None of it was important now. The wind blew it out of his head. Still he could always go into town Saturday night. It was a good thing to have in reserve." . . .

Hemingway apparently was keenly aware of and much interested in the inability of youth to accept the reality of a given situation. In all of these early stories, even though an external narrator relates the events, it is the youthful Nick's sensibility that is always the central focus. . . . The hero's exposure to the variety of forces which operate in the world and over which he has no control point to Hemingway's concern with the relationship of all men to an external world not of their making. The fact that many of the stories are complementary to each other, as in the Nick sequence, illustrates not so much Hemingway's concern with one generic hero as his intense desire to explore the various psychological implications of the first, almost primal experiences with life. (p. 49)

[Both] war and bullfighting have always been recognized as the major metaphorical bases for much of Hemingway's fiction. Since both emphasize the importance of adjustment to death, this common denominator provides a view of the interworkings of Hemingway's artistry when it concerns itself with either bullfighting or war.

Philip Young, in his full-length study, attaches a personal significance to Hemingway's concern with the death theme. Young suggests in Freudian terms that Hemingway suffered from a traumatic neurosis incurred by a severe wound in the First World War. As a means of adjusting to the neurosis, Hemingway acts under a "repetition-compulsion," which is the need to repeat an experience over and over. Hemingway's fiction, Young suggests, may be like Freud's war patients' dreams, in which the dreamers obeyed the repetition-compulsion, contrary to Freud's own notion of wish-fulfillment and the pleasure principle. (pp. 102-03)

In another and more recent full-length study, John Killinger, though repeating Carlos Baker and Philip Young on Hemingway's concern with death, refers to the Hemingway hero as one who has the existentialist pose. (p. 103)

These and other commentaries indicate the importance of Hemingway's concern with death and violence. Whether his hero emerges with a healthy or sick mind, or whether he reflects an extreme individualism, can be judged only by examining the particular story in which he appears. What seems certain, however, is that Hemingway chose to focus upon these motifs as part of his attempt to explore the reactions of man under the pressures of the extreme in psychological and physical environment. (p. 104)

In the two stories entitled "**Now I Lay Me**" and "**A Way You'll Never Be**," Hemingway treats a young protagonist in the war. In the first the narrative identifies the character as "Nick," presumably Nick Adams. In the second he is identified as "Nick Adams," and most commentators consider that the same person is meant. (pp. 104-05)

In a somewhat different manner than in "**Now I Lay Me**," Hemingway in "**A Way You'll Never Be**" treats the compulsive tendencies of an obviously "sick" hero. Although the two stories employ as protagonists characters who have been wounded in war and suffer deep underlying traumata, and although both "dream" while awake, the major similarity exists in Hemingway's treatment of the motif of adjustment to death and the ramifications of that theme. The whole of the dramatic action in "**Now I Lay Me**" takes place while the central character lies in his bed afraid of losing his soul in sleep, and the ensuing account is one of a waking-dream state. In "**A Way You'll Never Be**" the dramatic action follows a literal journey through a land that is suggestive of the trauma the protagonist has suffered. What is more, the narrative method differs in that "**Now I Lay Me**" is told in the first person, with the narrator relating in a self-analytic fashion his journey through certain major life experiences; in the other, "**A Way You'll Never Be**," the point of view is a central intelligence which objectifies the experience in the description of external realities away from the "sick" mind of the hero. This use of point of view is extremely important to the thematic emphasis of the story, for the tale is of an individual who is poised on the borderline of sanity and insanity, reality and unreality, and, ultimately, life and death. The point of view thus supports the central emphasis of the story by depicting both the inner thoughts of the character and the real world about him.

The framework of the conflict evolves from Hemingway's execution of the form of the story and his employment of at least the surface outline of the conventional journey motif. When Nick Adams is introduced at the beginning of the story, he arrives upon a scene of death and desolation caused by the war. The central intelligence describes in a matter-of-fact fashion the horrors depicted in the aftermath of a battle scene. The long descriptions and the cataloguing of the dead soldiers' paraphernalia is similar to the extended portrait of a battlefield in **"A Natural History of the Dead,"** but here the scene serves to establish an important detail of setting which becomes the substructure of the whole story. The world to which Nick Adams has returned is the world of the dead. What follows the initial description of the land of the dead is a picture of a reality that is just as grotesque as this initial scene.

The central focus of the plot concerns Nick's visit to a battalion encamped along the bank of a river. The commander is an old acquaintance with whom Nick has endured many bitterly difficult war experiences. Nick has apparently just been released from a hospital after suffering a head-wound which has left him, as he puts it, "nutty." (pp. 114-16)

As he becomes further involved in the action, it becomes evident that this is a journey of return for him. The places he passes, the landmarks he observes, and the meeting with his former soldier-comrade are all part of a world Nick has formerly been a part of in an intimate fashion. That he no longer belongs is apparent for many reasons, and his friend, Para, directly tells him to go back. In his response, Nick reveals his need to re-establish contact with the familiar in order to regain his former identity. (p. 116)

Nick's periods of mental disorientation alternate with periods of complete rationality. When he has less lucid moments the innerworkings of his mind and his need to reconcile past trauma become evident, for his lapses function as an unconscious desire to create order out of his chaotic experiences. . . .

[**"A Way You'll Never Be"**] is directly associated with Nick's need to reconcile the hurts suffered in his war experiences with his personal plight in the present. Hemingway graphically illustrates the extent to which the character has approached complete and final disorientation by the use of a triadic image [of a house, a stable, and a river in a dream]. . . . (p. 117)

Nick's journey back into the recesses of his mind as a result of wounds suffered in the war is directed toward a clarification of the processes of life and death and the role the individual must play. In many ways he is a kind of Lazarus who has returned. What marks him as different from the biblical character is that in his journey Nick has lost rather than gained reconciliation. Death, insanity, and complete dissociation are still close at hand, as evidenced in his "dream" of the house, stable, and canal. Both house and stable are given a yellow color in the shifting emphasis of the repeated image, and the river runs "stiller" and "wider," depending upon how close he is to a state of utter detachment from reality. These are comforting and alluring manifestations of the death state conjured up by Nick's unconscious, and they suggest the pull toward total irrationality. For him they are directly ambivalent in their connotations. He recognizes they are "what he needed," and still they frighten him. At one point they frighten him "especially when the boat lay there quietly in the willows on the canal." . . . This fear signals a very close proximity to total regression into the death-state, and the classical association with the river Styx and the boat provided for passage into the realm of death is evident.

Hemingway capsules the meaning of the images in a final dream sequence when the one-for-one relationship of the trauma Nick has sublimated into the triadic image is revealed: "He shut his eyes, and in place of the man with the beard who looked at him over the sights of the rifle, quite calmly before squeezing off, the white flash and the clublike impact, on his knees, hot-sweet choking, coughing it onto the rock while they

went past him, he saw a long, yellow house with a low stable and the river much wider than it was and stiller." . . . The direct identification of the recurring image with death as the result of a particular wound brings the thematic emphasis of the story into direct focus. Having made the journey of return to the scenes of his initial trauma, Nick can now make the association demanded by the dreams. Thus fortified, he is equipped to leave this symbolic realm of death and return to other pursuits. . . . He has no function or purpose there any longer, for, literally, it is "a way he'll never be" again. He has reconciled himself to the knowledge of death, and any further return would be a useless repetition. He directly states his own positive step toward reconcilement to the Captain before he leaves: "'You don't need to worry,' Nick said. 'I'm all right now for quite a while. I had one then but it was easy. They're getting much better. I can tell when I'm going to have one because I talk so much'." . . . (pp. 118-20)

As Nick goes back, the central intelligence projects his thoughts, and all the images are peaceful and pleasant. The canal image is again mentioned, but in this context the victory over the forces it represents is apparent: "In the afternoon the road would be shady once he had passed the canal." . . . It also becomes evident at the conclusion that this is a new Nick, in the sense that he not only has overcome the possibility of slipping completely into the realm of regressive insanity but also that he has progressed beyond the stage of romantic notions concerning war. Passing a certain road in his projection of the return trip, he recalls: "It was on that stretch that, marching, they had once passed the Terza Savoia cavalry regiment riding in the snow with their lances. The horses' breath made plumes in the cold air. No, that was somewhere else. Where was that? 'I'd better get to that damned bicycle,' Nick said to himself. 'I don't want to lose the way to Fornaci'." . . . The emphatic rejection of the romantic in war concretely illustrates the change in Nick's personality. Although he still drifts from rationality, he does have control. He has essentially reconciled himself to his trauma by this return journey. (p. 120)

War suggests in all these stories a process of dehumanization. The mode of survival, the real hope for man, always emanates from within individuals, and the response to be valid must be individual. A man's "road of trials" which he must travel throughout life is thus symbolized by the war-metaphor. Whether or not the particular protagonist is cognizant of the implications of his own isolated situation always depends upon his own strength of character. Few men are able to restore or find their own humanity under such stress. Hemingway does not aim to reveal man's continual victory over the forces represented by war, and neither does he aim to show man's continual defeat. These stories are portraits of man as an individual in conflict with overwhelming forces, and the reactions are those of man as a human being, not as a romantic caricature. (pp. 136-37)

Joseph DeFalco, in his The Hero in Hemingway's Short Stories, *University of Pittsburgh Press, 1963, 226 p.*

CLINTON S. BURHANS, JR.

In Our Time incorporates [the Nick Adams stories in a broad] . . . unity of form and theme and in a complexity of structure well worth exploring. Reading the book for these qualities yields unexpected and exciting dividends, for it reveals that *In Our Time* is indeed a consciously unified work built on a noble model and containing the careful artistry and the central vision of the world and the human condition which characterize Hemingway's writing from beginning to end. As such, *In Our Time* is not only the first of Hemingway's major works but also the best introduction to his thought and art in the rest.

When it was published on October 5, 1925, *In Our Time* was the culmination of a long development and a combination of previously published and new work. Several of the sixteen inter-story vignettes had originated as newspaper dispatches . . . and all, as well as two of the stories which began as vignettes, were published together in Paris as *in our time* in January, 1924. Of the fourteen stories, ten had been published earlier. For the 1925 *In Our Time,* Hemingway took the vignettes of the Paris *in our time,* made two of them into the stories **"A Very Short Story"** and **"The Revolutionist,"** changed the order of the rest and used them as interchapters between the stories, and added four new stories, **"The End of Something," "The Three-Day Blow," "The Battler,"** and **"Cat in the Rain."** And finally, for the 1930 edition of the book, he added the introductory sketch now entitled **"On the Quai at Smyrna."** Clearly, in all this maneuvering, Hemingway was getting at something more coherent and significant than a simple anthology of loosely related stories and sketches.

The title points in the same direction by suggesting that a common theme unifies the individual pieces which comprise the book. Several critics have implied such a theme by identifying the title as an ironic echo from the Book of Common Prayer: "Give peace in our time, O Lord"; and certainly *In Our Time* defines a world and a human condition in which there is very little peace of any kind. Moreover, in the Paris edition of the vignettes in 1924, the title *in our time* is printed on a cover format composed of newspaper clippings—designed, apparently, to suggest to potential readers that the book reflects the events and qualities of contemporary life. And by keeping for the expanded *In Our Time* of 1925 this title under which the vignettes had appeared as a separate and unified work, Hemingway subtly implies that they are not subordinate introductions to the stories but the essential context in which the stories must be read and understood. (pp. 313-14)

If the structure of the vignettes and of the stories and the intimate relationship between the two point to a central theme unifying *In Our Time* at its deepest levels, their content argues the same thematic unity even more forcefully. Here, Hemingway is saying, here are the world and the human condition with the masks off, with all the fraudulent illusions stripped away. It's not a pretty world and certainly not a very safe or comfortable one for men to live in; but, taken as it really is, it's a world men can live in with meaning and value if they look in the right places for them.

"To give the picture of the whole between examining it in detail"—Hemingway in his letter to [Edmund] Wilson defines unequivocally his thematic purpose in both the vignettes and the stories. Centering on war, bullfighting, and crime, the vignettes are significantly related in substance as well as in structure. War, of course, concerns the chaos and violence of conflict between and within nations; crime is the lesser chaos and violence within social groups; and bullfighting, in Hemingway's view a spectacle combining real rather than merely acted violence and tragedy controlled by esthetic forms and rules, symbolizes a way to face a world and a human condition characterized by war and crime. In these impressionistic sketches, then, Hemingway outlines the world and the human condition as he sees them and suggests what man must be and do in such

a world; and the stories derive their unifying significance as detailed explorations of the premises posed in the vignettes.

In this context, the vignettes can be grouped not only by general content but also by common theme. Six focus on events and characters reflecting primarily the qualities which to Hemingway identify the world as it really is "in our time." . . . These six vignettes . . . reflect in general the world which Nick, the soldier in **"A Very Short Story,"** and Krebs in **"Soldier's Home"** experience in detail.

A second group of five vignettes, while continuing to reflect the nature and the qualities of the world, centers even more specifically on various ways in which men immediately threatened by such a human condition respond to it. . . . Together, these vignettes show men responding to harsh experience with fear, drunkenness, disillusion, hypocritical prayer, and dissociation. None of these responses, however understandable, is either admirable or very practical; and the sketches reflecting them . . . occur at the beginning, in the middle, and at the end of the book as constant reminders that natural and uncontrolled responses to the world as it really is "in our time" are simply not enough.

The remaining vignettes, the six on bullfighting, complete the thematic "picture of the whole" by dramatizing the attitudes and qualities through which man can face the human condition and make it meaningful. In *Death in the Afternoon,* Hemingway defines the aspect of the bullfight which most interests him. . . . [It] contains life's basic realities—violence, suffering, inevitable death; and it imposes human meaning and order on these realities by containing them within the forms and rules of esthetic ritual and by requiring that the bullfighter stake his life against the bull's with courage and grace. Written some eight years before *Death in the Afternoon,* these vignettes reflect in outline and in subtle shading the same view of the bullfight which Hemingway details in the later work. (pp. 316-18)

As a group, these vignettes recapitulate the implications of the other two thematic groupings. . . . But the bullfight vignettes go further to show the qualities men must and can have to live as men in such a world and human condition: courage, responsibility, determination, skill, and grace. The world, Hemingway implies, is for most men in one way or another only a bullring in disguise; and these positive qualities enable men not to escape its inevitable realities but to impose on them a human dignity and value. Stressing this thematic projection of the "picture of the whole," the bullfight sketches . . . dominate the last half of the vignettes. And in this position they occur between and provide background for stories most of which deal not with the initiation themes of the first six or seven stories but rather with the problems of living in the world as it really is.

For if the vignettes are masterfully organized in structure and theme to reveal the "picture of the whole," the stories are no less impressively arranged to examine "it in detail." If they do not have the unity of central character and event and the consistent development of a novel, they have nevertheless a complexly interwoven thematic unity in themselves and in their relationship to the vignettes which seems too often overlooked. For the stories explore and develop in a variety of characters and events the two themes working centrally in the vignettes: the problem of recognizing and accepting the world and the human condition as they really are; and the consequent problem of trying to live with meaning and value in such a world and human condition.

The first five stories reflect both problems; but, inevitably in view of Nick's age, they focus primarily on the first, on his initiation into actuality. In a series of crucial experiences involving the most fundamental human realities and relationships—pain and suffering, birth and death, conflict and violence, love and loss, topsy-turvy disorder—Nick is forced to recognize that the world and his place in it are neither comfortable nor orderly and that few human stories have a conventional happy ending. In **"Indian Camp,"** he discovers that nature is not always beautiful and orderly in her processes nor concerned at all with human suffering. (pp. 318-19)

Birth and death, Nick discovers, are alike commingled with violence and suffering; and in between, man lives on the knife-edge of paradox. Going home across the lake, with the sun rising above the hills and fish jumping in the warm water, Nick feels sure he will never die. But this feeling clearly rises from its own denial: like Hemingway in *Death in the Afternoon*, Nick knows now that "all stories, if continued far enough, end in death, and he is no true-story teller who would keep that from you."

Of all the Nick Adams stories in the book, **"The Doctor and the Doctor's Wife"** is the only one not obviously centered on Nick and on what he learns from experience in the world of actuality. Here, his father backs down from a senseless fight with a man who wants to avoid working out a debt he owes the doctor, and Nick's mother refuses to believe that anyone could really behave so. Nick doesn't appear in the story until the last few lines, when his father finds him reading beneath a tree and tells him his mother wants to see him. Without hesitation, Nick replies that he wants to go with his father, and does.

Whether or not Nick saw his father's quarrel and retreat is uncertain, but there is at least some indication that he did. Such is the implication of the story's position amid other accounts of Nick's deepening understanding and insight; in this direction, too, point his immediate desire to go with his father and his consequent rejection of his mother's appeal. But the issue is not essential; the story serves the same thematic function in either event. Extending into society **"Indian Camp"**'s focus on nature's disorder, violence, and indifference to human suffering, **"The Doctor and the Doctor's Wife"** contrasts three ways of looking at man and his interrelationships. At one extreme is Dick Boulton, primitive, violent, and amoral, willing to beat up the doctor to avoid paying what he owes him. At the other is the doctor's wife, romantic, sentimental, and religious, unwilling to believe that anyone could be so motivated. In between is the doctor, rational, non-violent, and civilized, recognizing Dick for what he is but too intelligent to take a meaningless beating for some quixotic concept of bravery. This, then, is the real world which Nick must learn to live in, both in nature and in society. And whether or not he saw the quarrel, Nick's immediate choice to go with his father into the woods implies an acceptance of the doctor's position in denial of the two extremes which challenge it.

In the next two stories, Nick's education in actuality deepens. Apparently simple and artless but complexly woven and brilliantly evocative, **"The End of Something"** and **"The Three-Day Blow"** are as much two episodes in a single story as are the two parts of **"The Big Two-Hearted River."** In **"The End of Something,"** Nick falls out of love and learns thereby that violence, suffering, and death are inner as well as outer realities. There is no reason for his falling out of love, no explanation for it; like falling *in* love, it just happens. (pp. 320-21)

In **"The Three-Day Blow,"** Nick and his friend Bill talk and drink while an early autumn storm blows around the cottage. They discuss the peat flavor of Irish whiskey, but neither has ever seen peat . . .; baseball, but conclude that "'there's always more to it than we know about'" . . . ; and novels of impractical romance and thwarted love. . . . Against this background of ignorance and obscurity, they talk about the equally mysterious end of Nick's love for Marjorie. "'All of a sudden everything was over,' Nick said. 'I don't know why it was. I couldn't help it. Just like when the three-day blows come now and rip all the leaves off the trees'." . . . Bill warns him that he might get involved with Marjorie again, and Nick is surprised into new joy. If falling in love is not absolute, neither is falling out of love, and perhaps he *will* love Marjorie again. "There was not anything that was irrevocable. . . . Nothing was finished. Nothing was ever lost." . . . In any event, Nick now looks at love in perspective: outdoors, "the Marge business was no longer so tragic. It was not even very important. The wind blew everything like that away." . . . (p. 321)

"The Battler" takes Nick away from his family and friends and involves him in a world in which everything is topsy-turvy. . . . [He learns that] the world is a confused and treacherous place, but not without love and compassion.

As these stories present Nick with the actualities of the world and the human condition, the next two stories deepen this initiation theme into disillusion. Neither protagonist is named Nick Adams; but both, without any substantial or significant change, could be young Nick a few years later. **"A Very Short Story"** was originally a vignette in the 1924 *in our time,* but Hemingway prints it here as a story, apparently to make use of its disillusion theme. Moreover, the vignette which precedes it practically forces the reader to associate the protagonist of **"A Very Short Story"** with Nick Adams. In this vignette—the only one which links two stories so directly—Nick moves from his boyhood Michigan world to the greater world of his young manhood, and he finds their actualities much the same. Wounded in the general slaughter of World War I, he decides to make "a separate peace." Similarly, the protagonist of **"A Very Short Story"** is a wounded American soldier. He falls in love with his nurse, and they decide to marry, but she insists on their waiting until he returns home and is settled in a good job. While he is gone, she falls in love with an Italian major and dismisses her earlier affair as puppy love. Later, the disillusioned American gets gonorrhea making love in a taxi. As Nick Adams learned that love can come and go like an autumn storm and as he found that war is ultimately stupid butchery, so the protagonist of **"A Very Short Story"** discovers that love, no matter how deep and true, can be betrayed and lost—and even for the best reasons.

In the second of these disillusion stories, **"Soldier's Home,"** a Marine—again, similar in background and experience to Nick Adams—returns from fighting in most of the major American battles to the Midwestern world in which he had grown up and finds himself isolated and a stranger. Krebs had been a good soldier; whatever else the war had been for him, he had found being a soldier simple and honest, and he had been proud of doing his job well. . . . [When he comes home] he finds the relationships of civilian life based on politics, intrigue, sentimentality, and still more lies. . . . Ironically, Krebs is disillusioned less by the war than by the normal peacetime world which the war has made him see too clearly to accept.

For Nick Adams and others like him, then, the world "in our time" turns out to be exactly what the vignettes suggest it is—

a puzzling and disillusioning place in which beauty and wonder, love and compassion, are strangely mixed with cruelty, violence, suffering, loss, alienation, and death. But the vignettes also imply that recognizing the world for what it is forms only one dimension of the human problem: equally vital is the consequent dimension of imposing a human order and meaning on such a world. And in the next two stories, Hemingway turns from the actuality of disillusion to the problem of man's idealism confronted by it.

In **"The Revolutionist,"** the narrator describes a sensitive and idealistic young Hungarian communist whom he obviously likes and admires, not for the young man's beliefs but for the way he holds them. . . . Within experienced and tested idealism, he has in full measure that courage which Hemingway defines as grace under pressure. Like Villalta and Maera in the bullfight vignettes, the young revolutionist personifies the way a man can face the violent and disillusioning actualities of the world and give his life order and meaning and value.

This realistically positive significance in **"The Revolutionist"** and the story's central place in the book help to explain why Hemingway changed it to a story from its original form as a vignette in the 1924 *in our time.* For the hard-earned idealism of the young revolutionist contrasts directly with the childish romanticism of **"Mr. and Mrs. Elliot"** in the following story. (pp. 321-23)

Unlike the young revolutionist, [the Elliots'] ideals are abstract, untested, and unearned, without roots in experience and knowledge. Consequently, Mr. and Mrs. Elliot are totally unprepared for the disillusioning actualities of life and of real human relationships, and they are bitterly disappointed. Worse, they respond to this disappointment by seeking escape in further romanticism. . . .

At the center of *In Our Time,* then, these two stories focus on idealism and romanticism in conflict with disillusioning actuality and on two contrasting responses to this conflict. . . .

From a focus on initiation into life as it really is "in our time," on some of the characteristic disillusions of that life, and on the problems of giving it a human meaning and value, Hemingway in the next three stories [**"Cat in the Rain," "Out of Season,"** and **"Cross-Country Snow"**] explores in further detail the paradoxical and topsy-turvy nature of the human condition and the difficulties of living in it. Here, the characters are neither young innocents in their first contacts with actuality nor mature people shaken by profound disillusion nor contrasting idealists; instead, they are ordinary people in ordinary situations which have developed unaccountably contrary to what the people involved have expected or desired. (p. 324)

The world as it actually is "in our time" set against man's expectations and hopes; and his consequent problems and difficulties in trying to live in it with meaning and order—these, then, are the central themes which Hemingway explores "in detail" in the stories as he had made them "the picture of the whole" in the vignettes. Completing this pattern, the final two stories function as a coda, each restating and focussing sharply on one of these two unifying themes. Indeed, this function helps to explain the otherwise puzzling position of **"My Old Man"**: on the surface, the story seems to belong both chronologically and thematically with the early Nick Adams stories. But in its young narrator's complete initiation and total disillusion, particularly as expressed in the last line, **"My Old Man"** makes a stark restatement of one major theme [initiation into an amoral universe] and a perfect bridge to the compelling

restatement of the second [the fundamental problem of living in this kind of world] in **"Big Two-Hearted River."** (p. 326)

Many writers on Hemingway have pointed out that **"My Old Man,"** one of his earliest stories, reflects the influence of Sherwood Anderson and that *The Torrents of Spring* (1926) is at least partly a lampooning declaration of full independence from Anderson. Between these extremes, however, *In Our Time* testifies to the deep and continuing influence of the older writer. In 1925, the year in which *In Our Time* was published, "Hemingway told Scott Fitzgerald that his first pattern had been Anderson's *Winesburg, Ohio*"; and in its complex unity, in Hemingway's avowed intention "to give the picture of the whole between examining it in detail," *In Our Time* turns the clear light of an ironic and contradictory actuality on the world of the first quarter of the twentieth century as *Winesburg, Ohio* had shone it on midwestern America.

Like its model, then, *In Our Time* is neither anthology nor novel but a new form, a literary hybrid, with something of the variety of the anthology combined with something of the unity of the novel. Moreover, in its view of the world and of man's efforts to live in it with meaning and order, in its conscious and intricate structure, in its ironic and symbolic method, and in its lean, intensified style, Hemingway's first book reflects the central intellectual and esthetic concerns which dominated his life and writing from beginning to end. Grow and develop, broaden and deepen, these concerns may, but change essentially they seldom do; and the later harvest is implicit in these, its first shoots. Better than any other single work, more than any one or few of its stories and vignettes, the unified whole of *In Our Time* introduces Hemingway's world and the art in which he creates it. (p. 328)

> Clinton S. Burhans, Jr., "The Complex Unity of 'In Our Time'," in Modern Fiction Studies, *Vol. XIV, No. 3, Autumn, 1968, pp. 313-28.*

CHAMAN NAHAL

It is now accepted by almost every critic of Hemingway that the hero in his work deserves special attention. Philip Young sees the Hemingway protagonist as a sick man, wounded physically and psychically [see *CLC*, Vol 13]. Carlos Baker reads in him symbolic meanings, expressive of the contemporary emotional tensions [see excerpt above], Leo Gurko has written a full-length book on the subject, for to him Hemingway's novels are essentially portrayals of the hero as the "individual man" [see *CLC*, Vol. 6]. Thus, it is almost generally agreed that one of the important expressions of the Hemingway literary aesthetics is his hero. As it happens, his shorter fiction, now to be considered, offers as wide a scope as his novels for describing the Hemingway hero. (p. 80)

It is a mistake to imagine that Hemingway wrote all [his] stories and sketches merely to promote or develop only one character—that is, Nick Adams. This is a miscalculation made by most critics of Hemingway; they have all tried to concentrate on Nick Adams. Superficially the stories give that impression, for you meet Nick in them at different age levels and his aging follows a chronological sequence. But artistically each story is complete in itself, a major aesthetic consideration when we try to see whether or not there is a link between the stories. The link between them is only the general association that always runs through the entire body of a writer's work; in no way is one story dependent on the other for the completion of its meaning. Thus, it would be more helpful to see each story separately and to think of Nick Adams in the plural rather than in the singular. There are many Nick Adamses in the stories, and the name does not necessarily identify the same character.

It would be more useful to imagine that Hemingway in these stories was concerned with a question of choice, of priorities. He seems to have put the stories, or the writing of them, to the same use as Shakespeare put his history plays; he thought out his ideas and his technique in them, and used them as a kind of workshop. If the Shakespearean hero—to continue the analogy—was initially worked out by Shakespeare in the Henry V trilogy, the Hemingway hero took shape for Hemingway in *In Our Time, Men Without Women,* and *Winner Take Nothing.* (p. 81)

[Hemingway] had Nick Adams in mind from the beginning, for the simple reason that he knew this character rather intimately, based as it was on his own life. But he had a s well several other types of humans before him. The preoccupation of the artist in these stories is therefore not so much with the development of a mythical figure based on one character as with the exploration and establishment of his preferences.

Philip Young, in *Ernest Hemingway,* seems to assume that each story was written to complete the development of Nick Adams, as if with each separate sketch something new were added on to Hemingway's presentation of that character. This is true insofar as physical details vary from story to story to accommodate the new age level at which Nick appears in them. But it does not appear that Hemingway consciously used a method of accretion in these tales. The conclusion Young reaches in his chapter on the Hemingway hero is: "He has seen a great deal of unpleasantness, not only in the war but . . . in Michigan as well; and he has been wounded by these experiences in a physical way, and—since the spine blow is both fact and symbol—also in a psychical way." Beginning with the first story in *In Our Time,* and continuing through the stories in the order in which they appear in the book, he tells us each time: "This is Nick's initiation to pain" (**"Indian Camp"**); this teaches Nick "about the solidarity of the male sex" (**"The Doctor and the Doctor's Wife"**); this teaches about "a somewhat peculiar attitude toward women" (**"The End of Something"**), and so on. He adds confidently, "Nick is learning things," meaning thereby that the principal concern of Hemingway is Nick Adams and his complete identification with his hero.

But in the very next chapter of his book, Young offers the theory of what he calls the "code hero" in Hemingway. The code hero is what Hemingway's ideal concept of man is, his concept of honor and courage. To quote Young: "This code is very important because the 'code hero,' as he is . . . called, presents a solution to the problems of Nick Adams, of the true 'Hemingway hero,' and for Hemingway it was about the only solution." This surely is confusing. Is Young for the code hero or the true hero, then? Who was Hemingway for?—for the code hero or the true hero? According to Young, Hemingway obviously was for the code hero, as the code gave Hemingway "about the only solution" he could think of for Nick Adams, his true hero. So who in the opinion of Young was the real Hemingway hero, the code hero or the true hero? If it was the code hero that really mattered to him, why should Hemingway have devoted all his stories to the development of a non-code hero, Nick Adams? And if the true hero, Nick Adams, is the real hero, what is the code hero doing here?

The simple explanation is that Hemingway in these stories is undertaking an enormous experiment. In addition to Nick, there

are many characters in the stories who are substantially different individuals from Nick. To give a brief list, they are Doctor Adams, the He of **"A Very Short Story"**; Krebs of **"Soldier's Home"**; the I of **"Now I Lay Me"**; the I of **"After the Storm"**; the Old Waiter in **"A Clean, Well-lighted Place"**; the I of **"The Light of the World"**; Mr. Johnson and Mr. Harris in **"Homage to Switzerland"** [and others]. . . . (pp. 82-4)

If we like, we may say that some of these characters are like Nick and that they supplement his image. But that would be oversimplifying the aesthetic issue involved. For Hemingway these characters are what they are; they represent no one but themselves. In the stories in which they appear, they are the center of attraction and Hemingway sees them as such. To give one example, the story **"The Doctor and the Doctor's Wife,"** is about Doctor Adams, or perhaps it is about the doctor's wife or about the Indian, Dick Boulton, who picks the quarrel with the doctor. These are the main characters of the story, and none of them is identical with Nick.

Again, as far as plot goes, this story has nothing whatsoever to do with Nick, and it is difficult to see how Young reads the story as primarily about Nick. Nick has not watched the quarrel between his father and Dick Boulton, he has not heard the remarks of his mother addressed to his father; he is nowhere near the scene. And yet in Young's words, what has happened has revealed to Nick the companionship he can form with his father as a male and how unhappy and dissatisfied he is with his mother. Later still, Young adds that Nick cannot bear his mother's inability to admit evil or come face to face with it. One fails to understand how any of these observations is justifiable.

Hemingway's heroes are not "sick," nor are they particularly "heroic." The key word for understanding the Hemingway hero, according to my reading, is spontaneity. The Hemingway hero is a man immensely alive to everything, and in his spontaneity he has the vital capacity to react to life in innumerable and unpredictable ways.

That is the true Hemingway hero: a genuinely spontaneous individual. This kind of spontaneity is impossible to acquire unless one has learned the art of quieting the ego. Ultimately, therefore, the spontaneity gets tied up with creative passivity. The desire in his heroes is to feel everything *fully*—and therefore slowly, egolessly. "He did not want to rush his sensations any," says Hemingway about Nick in **"Big Two-Hearted River,"** and the expression is typical. The life of the trout, of the mink, and of the mosquitoes and the grasshoppers that is painted in the story comes rushing to Nick because of his extreme spontaneity, his extreme sensitivity to what is going on around him. In spite of what is commonly believed about his characters, Hemingway's heroes are not in the least egotistical. For egoism and sensitivity in an individual cannot go together. It is possible to have one or the other—not both. His hero thus acts from dark sources within his own self and is perennially in touch with the unknown of existence. (pp. 84-5)

[In] almost all the stories we can discover two distinct modes of action: systolic [or active] action and diastolic [or passive] action. In the latter, which is the more important mode of the two, the systolic action comes to a standstill. These are moments when the entire systolic action that has preceded is in a way relived and consolidated, and the individual made ready for the next systolic move in the light of his experiences of the diastolic period. The moments of diastolic action are moments of return to one's deepest self; they are moments of mystical revelation. They are *not* moments of analysis, of self-analysis, or of "conscience," as Hemingway once cynically put it. These are moments when the individual recognizes, without the shadow of a doubt, that the rhythm of all life is much greater than that of his own individual self.

In the short stories, the diastolic action is introduced in two ways. Either the entire story is divided into two halves, not necessarily equal, where the first offers the systolic action and the second the diastolic. Or the diastolic action and the moments of pause are interspersed in the main movement of the story. (pp. 86-7)

Since the second kind requires greater craftsmanship, the stories where the diastolic action is interspersed are superior and structurally more complex. (p. 87)

[In **"Big Two-Hearted River"**] the systolic and the diastolic states alternate from the beginning and they come and go all the time. There is the physical countryside around Nick and his fishing in it that represent the systolic action. And then there is what the country does to him. That is the diastolic action. (p. 105)

In Part II, we read of Nick's camp as a "good" camp. Is that atmosphere, or Nick's reaction symptomatic of the paranoid? Nick has simply come to revisit his "old man" river. He was not less happy than most other men, from what we read in the story. He had not come here looking for a refuge, or an escape. It is just a visit. But as soon as he gets here, the greater life of the countryside overwhelms him, and he becomes aware of the greater mystery of life, the greater holiness of it.

An important passage in the story is when Nick, having pitched his tent, crawls into it:

> Inside the tent the light came through the brown canvas. It smelled pleasantly of canvas. Already there was something mysterious and homelike. Nick was happy as he crawled inside the tent. He had not been unhappy all day. This was different though. Now things were done. There had been this to do. Now it was done. It had been a hard trip. He was very tired. That was done. He had made his camp. He was settled. Nothing could touch him. It was a good place to camp. He was there, in the good place. He was in his home where he had made it. Now he was hungry.

The passive, the creatively passive, surrender of the individual to the cosmos is extremely well conveyed. Nick has now re-established his contact with the unknown. It is very much like the Zen concept of an individual's relatedness to the life around him. The life of the individual has a meaning only in the corporate life of the total universe.

The actual fishing is done in Part II of **"Big Two-Hearted River."** With meticulous care, and with much delight, Hemingway gives us every single detail of the machinery and mechanism of fishing: from the point where the bait is prepared to the pulling in of the trout, we are told that Nick is "excited" or "happy" or is having a "good feeling." The pulse of the cosmos beats mysteriously around him and he is an integral part of that cosmos. The systolic and diastolic pattern is also maintained in Part II. Frequently the forward movement of the story comes to a halt, and we see Nick reveling in his present sensation: "He did not want to rush his sensations any." At

the moment, the sensation is one of disappointment because he has just lost a good trout. But . . . [there is also tranquility]. (pp. 106-07)

[The story] finally closes with the promise of many more happy days for Nick. For the river of life is truly "big" and "two-hearted," and it has spells enough to hold him for a lifetime. (p. 107)

The Hemingway hero that emerges in [**"Big Two-Hearted River"** and other] stories is a highly sensitive individual, who derives his sensitivity from his ability to be in tune with the spirit of the universe. He is a highly passive human, by choice, as this enables him to respond to the cosmic rhythm more effectively. He values moments of action, but moments of creative resignation he values even more. He is not a particularly serene individual, but then, cultivated serenity is as much a pose as deliberate self-assertion, and he wants to be free of poses. He, however, has the capacity of true religious awareness of life. This awareness keeps him disturbed most of the time—that restlessness or disturbance being a part of the very design of living—but now and then he lapses into an unusual calm. The calm is not of his own making; it comes to him from the outside. At such moments he is more like a mystic than a man of action. (pp. 118-19)

> *Chaman Nahal, in his* The Narrative Pattern in Ernest Hemingway's Fiction, *Fairleigh Dickinson University Press, 1971, 245 p.*

PHILIP YOUNG

[Until the publication of *The Nick Adams Stories*], the stories involving Nick have always appeared so many to a book, in jumbled sequence. As a result the coherence of his adventures has been obscured, and their impact fragmented. (p. 5)

Arranged in chronological sequence, the events of Nick's life make up a meaningful narrative in which a memorable character grows from child to adolescent to soldier, veteran, writer, and parent—a sequence closely paralleling the events of Hemingway's own life. In this arrangement Nick Adams, who for a long time was not widely recognized as a consistent character at all, emerges clearly as the first in a long line of Hemingway's fictional selves. Later versions, from Jake Barnes and Frederic Henry to Richard Cantwell and Thomas Hudson, were all to have behind them part of Nick's history and, correspondingly, part of Hemingway's.

As is true for many writers of fiction, the relationship between Hemingway's work and the events of his own life is an immediate and intricate one. In some stories he appears to report details of actual experience as faithfully as he might have entered them in a diary. In others the play of his imagination has transformed experience into a new and different reality. (pp. 5-6)

The first Nick Adams fiction appeared almost a half-century ago, the last in 1933, and over the years a great deal has been written about it. Among the unpublished manuscripts Hemingway left behind him, however, eight new contributions to the over-all narrative were discovered. Presented here [in *The Nick Adams Stories*] for the first time, inserted in the places in time where the events fall, they are varied in length and apparent purpose. Three accounts—of how the Indians left the country of Nick's boyhood, of his first sight of the Mississippi, and of what happened just before and after his wedding—are quite brief. If the author had larger plans for any of them, such are unknown; they might be read simply as sketches in an artist's notebook. In two other cases his plans are self-evident, for here we have the beginnings of works that were never completed. Nick on board the *Chicago,* bound for France during World War I, was the start of a novel called *Along with Youth* that was abandoned long ago. Similarly, though much later, the plot of **"The Last Good Country"** was left in mid-air, and many pages would have been required to resolve it. Two other pieces are known to have originated in Nick stories already published. **"Three Shots"** tells how the young boy became frightened while on a camping trip. It once preceded the story called **"Indian Camp."** And Nick's "stream of consciousness" reflections on his writing career once (anachronistically) concluded **"Big Two-Hearted River."** Of these new works only **"Summer People,"** very likely the first fiction Hemingway wrote about Nick Adams, can be regarded as a full-length, completed story. (pp. 6-7)

[These] pieces throw new light on the work and personality of one of our foremost writers and genuinely increase our understanding of him. (p. 7)

> *Philip Young, in a preface to* The Nick Adams Stories
> *by Ernest Hemingway, Charles Scribner's Sons, 1972,*
> *pp. 5-7.*

PHILIP YOUNG

[Philip Young, a noted Hemingway scholar, originally wrote the essay excerpted below as an introduction to The Nick Adams Stories *(1972).]*

[As we follow Nick in *The Nick Adams Stories*] across the span of a generation in time we have got a story worth following. As it turns out, Hemingway arranged it (consciously or otherwise) in five distinct stages—that is, the original fifteen stories occur in five segments of Nick's life, three stories to each part. "The Northern Woods," as the first section is called, deals with heredity and environment, parents and Michigan Indians. "On His Own" is all away from home, or on the road, and instead of Indians, prizefighters. "War" is exactly that, or as the author put it later on, "hit properly and for good." Then "A Soldier Home": Michigan revisited, hail and farewell. And fifth, "Company of Two": marriage, Europe revisited, and finally looking backward, a sort of coda.

Maybe it will also appear now and at long last that in Nick Hemingway gave us the most important single character in all his work—the first in a long line of fictional self-projections, the start of everything. Later protagonists from Jake Barnes and Frederic Henry to Richard Cantwell and Thomas Hudson were shaped by Nick, were all to have (if only tacitly) his history behind them. So had Hemingway. Not that everything that happens to Nick had happened to him. Indeed the author remarks right here, in the fragment called **"On Writing,"** that "Nick in the stories was never himself. He made them up." To an extent that is of course true; the autobiography is transmuted. But it is bemusing that at the very moment when the writer is categorically disassociating himself from his persona he makes him interchangeable with himself, as the "he," the consciousness of the piece, shifts from Nick to Hemingway back to Nick again. . . . But the real point is that this extended and disciplined self-portrait became a significant story in its own right: the story of an American born with the century, complicated in boyhood and badly hurt in a war, who came to terms with what happened and turned it to lasting fiction. (p. 6)

"It's the account of a boy on a fishing trip," . . . [wrote] Scott Fitzgerald . . . about **"Big Two-Hearted River."** "Nothing more—but I read it with the most breathless unwilling interest I have experienced since Conrad first bent my reluctant eyes upon the sea." In 1926 Hemingway was happy to settle for such published praise. But Fitzgerald might have asked himself why nothing more than a fishing trip should have galvanized his attention. If he had done so he might have discovered that he was responding perfectly to what Hemingway called in those days "my new theory that you could omit anything if you knew that you omitted . . . and make people feel something more than they understood." The things he had left out before were never really crucial, but this time an omission made all the difference. As he pointed out years later, "The story was about coming back from the war but there was no mention of the war in it."

There is no doubt, however, that the perilous state of Nick's nervous system, unmentioned in the story, accounts for the intensity of the writing, which is what arrested Fitzgerald. Here is the quintessential Hemingway style: simplicity, forged under great pressure, out of complexity. The trout, "keeping themselves steady in the current with wavering fins," reflect Nick as in a mirror. . . . Acting, and not thinking, his trip proves a remarkable success. He will carry his scars, but will never be badly shaken again. Fishing is better therapy than Milan's; for Nick the war in Italy ended in Michigan. (pp. 13-14)

[In **"Fathers and Sons"**] Nick looks backward to his boyhood and rounds it off. Nick is now thirty-eight and a writer; [his] son is about the age of Nick when he first appeared in **"Indian Camp."** The action has covered a generation. The doctor who discussed suicide with his boy in the first story has now committed it, though we are told only that he is dead—another important omission. And as Nick remembers how useless his father was on the subject of sex, which he learned about from Trudy instead, so now he cannot talk to his boy about the doctor's death, though he knows that sooner or later they will have to visit "the tomb of my grandfather" (the boy has been raised abroad). A son is now father to the son, things have come full circle, and in his collected *First Forty-Nine Stories* Hemingway put this one forty-ninth.

The tale is told, but if Nick's history seems in retrospect to amount to slightly more than the sum of its chapters it may be because his progress through the first third of our century is at once representative, distinctive, and personal. Representative as a national passage from the innocence of a shaky pre-war security through the disillusionment of a European ordeal-by-fire, and the rejection of much that a previous age had stood for, to "normalcy." Distinctive for memories of specific experiences the exact like of which we never had. And personal as the recreated autobiography of a culture hero of his time. But if anyone still feels more than he can account for in remembering Nick, he might ask what if anything Hemingway omitted from the story as a whole. The answer is so obvious that it might never dawn on us. The Nick Adams fiction is about leaving Oak Park, but there is no mention of Oak Park in it.

The text may be taken from [his sister] Marcelline. When Ernest was flopping loose in their suburban house on his return from the war he spoke to her one day about "all the other things in life that aren't here. . . . There's a whole big world out there. . . ." What he omitted is what he escaped from. What he escaped to, for the rest of his life and all of his career, moves against a background he expunged. Oak Park was rejected for Michigan, and when that became a small world it was in turn put behind for a greater one. All that is simple to understand. But it is hard to realize today how great was the *need* for rebellion—how preposterous were things *At the Hemingways,* the name of Marcelline's affectionate book. (pp. 17-18)

What Hemingway called "Mr. Young's trauma theory of literature" is not retracted: the wounds in Italy are still climactic and central in the lives of Hemingway and all his personal protagonists. Nor is there any reason to withdraw the notion, which the author also objected to, that he wrote chiefly about himself; he was not lacking in imagination, but to live his life as he wished, then to write about it, was the way he basically operated. Neither is there any reason to abandon the idea that the adventures of Nick Adams were foreshadowed by *The Adventures of Huckleberry Finn.*

But a different emphasis can be put on this combination. Huck's rebellion was of course from Aunt Sally—and St. Petersburg, which Twain did not omit. Nick's rebellion is a given—omitted but as basic as the wound, and prior to it. Almost nothing Hemingway ever wrote could be set in Oak Park; it is extremely doubtful that he could have written a "wonderful novel" about the place. What he could write about happens "out there"—an exact equivalent for what, departing "sivilization" for the last time, Huck called "the territory." In the overall adventure, life becomes an escape to reality. No reward whatever is promised, and the cost in comfort and security is high. Out there can kill you, and nearly did. But it beats "home," which is a meaner death, as Ernest tried to tell Marcelline. (pp. 18-29)

> *Philip Young, "'Big World Out There': 'The Nick Adams Stories'," in* Novel: A Forum on Fiction, *Vol. 6, No. 1, Fall, 1972, pp. 5-19.*

T. G. VAIDYANATHAN

A proper consideration of the Nick Adams stories has been seriously bedevilled by the current critical orthodoxy surrounding the notion of 'initiation'. The desire to 'initiate' or 'educate' Nick is more apparent in the critics than in his creator who, for the most part, is content to let Nick fool around, in and around Michigan, before lighting out for the territory ahead—Europe. The reason for this pedagogical obsession is to be sought in the desire of the critics to relate the Nick stories to the early novels, especially *The Sun Also Rises* and *A Farewell to Arms,* and see in Nick dim adumbrations of the sensitive but impotent Jake Barnes and the equally sensitive but potent Frederick Henry. A new departure with the same end in view (viz. Nick's 'initiation') has been to see the 'complex unity' of *In Our Time* by the simple manoeuvre of converting even non-Nick stories into crypto-Nick stories, thus giving Nick more chances for education [see excerpt above by Clinton S. Burhans, Jr.]. Meanwhile, manful efforts are being made through the columns of *Studies in Short Fiction* to establish the splendid autonomy of the stories and even pieces like **'The End of Something'** and **'The Three-Day Blow'** which tell the same story, are allowed, like Himalayan peaks, to exist in splendid isolation. But even here the old siren song of initiation is heard with all the sweetness of heard melodies. We must remain thankful that the two parts of **'Big Two-Hearted River'** are still seen as parts of the same whole. It is to be hoped that critical ingenuity will not introduce a rift at least here.

'Initiation' was first employed by Philip Young in his early study in 1952 to describe the character of the Nick Adams

stories in *In Our Time,* although Edmund Wilson, in his still useful 1939 essay [see excerpt above] had already laid the foundations. 'A typical Nick Adams Story,' writes Young, 'is of an intiation.' And later, more definitively, he observes: 'The pattern of Nick Adams' development . . . is of a boy who, while with his father up in Michigan, and without him on his own as a hobo or with friends, *has been learning some lessons about life*' (italics mine). This definition seems to have had a hypnotic influence on Hemingway criticism, for, with minor exceptions, many later writers on Hemingway have been under its spell. . . . Joseph De Falco's *The Hero in Hemingway's Short Stories* [see excerpt above] is written directly under the protective shadow of Young and although he is patently annoyed when the stories don't fit the master's categories, he consistently toes the line. And so does Earl Rovit in his 1963 study: 'For convenience' sake I will refer to the Nick Adams hero as the *tyro* and to the code-hero as the tutor: for it is basically an *educational relationship,* albeit a very one-sided one, which binds them together [see excerpt above].

In the face of this formidable array of Hemingway criticism it may seem a little presumptuous to ask whether the notion of 'initiation' is at all useful to an understanding of Hemingway's short fiction. Yet so pervasive has been its influence on criticim and so limiting its results when applied to the stories that it looks as if it is time to take stock again and ask some fundamental questions. To start with: What is initiation? . . . [We may] define an 'initiation' story as one which shows a significant change in its protagonist, either in his knowledge of the world or of himself or which shows a moral change directly in him or both and this/these change(s) must point to or lead him towards an acceptance of the world.

Obviously many so-called 'initiation' stories do not satisfy any of the above conditions. Most of Hemingway's early stories, for instance, merely bring their protagonist, Nick Adams, to the threshold of maturity without actually making him cross it. (pp. 203-05)

To take the [favourite of Cleanth Brooks and Robert Penn Warren]: **'The Killers'.** The authors concluded, in their now famous reading, that the story is 'a discovery of evil' by Nick the protagonist [see excerpt above]. Recent criticism . . . has cast doubts even on this foundational assumption and has put forward Ole Andreson as the real protagonist of the story. But we need not go so far. Assuming Nick to be the protagonist, can we say that at the end he gains in self-knowledge or knowledge of the world or that he is a thoroughly changed man, morally speaking? What we find in the story is that at the end he merely expresses an *intention* to leave the town. As to self-knowledge, he merely states: 'I can't bear to think about him waiting in the room and knowing he's going to get it. It's too damned awful.' This is perhaps what any young man of his youth and inexperience would have felt. It hardly deserves the ennobling label of self-knowledge. And in what sense can we say with Brooks and Warren that it is 'a discovery of evil'? What evil? The evil of gangsterdom? Or the evil of indifference in Sam, the cook? Or the evil of apathy in Ole Andreson himself? All we know is that Nick can't bear to think about it. Yet [Adrian H. Jaffe and Virgil Scott], blind to the facts of the story, can confidently assert [in their *Studies in the Short Stories*] that the story shows 'a person who suddenly discovers the basic nature of existence'. Such is the power of the myth.

'The Killers' is an excellent short story but, unfortunately, it does not meet the requirements of either a *weak* or a *strong* initiation story. We cannot even confidently assert that its protagonist has been brought to the threshold of maturity because the 'episodic' nature of the story, which has been completely overlooked by the critics, does not permit of any such facile inferences. The plot is static and the feeling generated at the end is one of horror at the plight of Ole Andreson who is taking his imminent murder with a disquieting apathy. The focus is too little on Nick for us to expect any change in him. A careful examination of many of the early stories will similarly reveal Nick not at the centre of the experience described, but very likely at the periphery. He is mostly a spectator of the action and only occasionally moves to the centre. And even when he does so it is often (with important exceptions) not clear what kind of experience he has had and whether this will leave any permanent marks on him.

A good example of the latter kind of story is **'The Battler'**. Here, certainly, there can be no doubt that Nick is at the centre of the experience described. To start with, he is 'busted' by the brakeman on the freight train and gets a black eye. This is our introduction to the naive Nick who has certainly left home and has nowhere in particular to go. He meets another ex-champ in this story (as in **'The Killers'**), Ad Francis, and the two get on famously till Ad's Negro assistant, Bugs, appears on the scene. Unexpectedly, tensions erupt to the surface and Nick's refusal of a knife to Ad—this at the instance of Bugs—brings things to a boil. The ex-champ suddenly turns belligerent and invites Nick to a fight which is forestalled by Bugs knocking his friend out cold with a blackjack. Nick is curious to know how the champion got 'crazy' and Bugs obliges Nick and the reader with a detailed biographical sketch. And yet at the end of the story there is no indication at all how all this has affected Nick. The reader is certainly the wiser at the end but the spare, taut third person narration tells us nothing of Nick's state of mind. Here Nick is at the centre of the story but passively, transparently, letting the main action flow through him; there is little indication that it has done anything to him. (pp. 205-07)

Nor is this an isolated instance. Of the early stories, **'The End of Something'** and **'The Three-Day Blow'** certainly have Nick at the centre of the action. To begin with, even the title of the first story could be a warning against reading anything specific into the 'something' that has ended. A recent reading of the story has rightly drawn attention to the opening paragraph where the history of Hortons Bay has been described in ways which prefigure the decline of the Nick-Marjorie relationship. This would imply that the course that Nick's love for Marjorie has taken is a natural one and is as remorseless as it is inevitable. Nick of course feels a certain amount of remorse for the break-up: 'I feel as though everything has gone to hell inside of me. I don't know, Marge. I don't know what to say.' But any assurance we may draw that Nick has 'learnt' anything from this break-up is quickly shattered by the next story which is a continuation of the same theme. Nick goes to his friend Bill's home and after rambling around several topics (chiefly literary) the friends return to the subject of Nick's break-up. Bill speaks in a misogynic vein but evokes little response from Nick. But when he casually remarks that by thinking about it too much one might 'get back into it' again, Nick feels extraordinarily bucked up: 'He felt happy now. There was not anything that was irrevocable . . . Nothing was finished. Nothing was ever lost.' This piece of childish regression has of course been quietly ignored by initiation-obsessed critics. Not only do we get the impression from this story that Nick, at this stage, is incapable of any growth but we also feel that he has been all along like this. (pp. 207-08)

It is time to take stock of Nick as his picture emerges from the early stories. In doing this it will be helpful . . . [to look at] the closing remarks concerning Nick in the so-called 'initiation' stories. (p. 210)

[It is undeniable that with the possible exception of **"The Battler"**] Nick has consistently resolved an unfamiliar situation either though (*a*) wish fulfilment (**'Indian Camp'** and **'The Three-Day Blow'**) where the meaning of the experience gone through (death, a broken love affair) is denied through a wish that makes the opposite kind of experience (immortality, resumption of the love affair) possible, or (*b*) refusal to think (**'The End of Something,' 'The Doctor and the Doctor's Wife'** and **'The Killers'**) by which the strain of the experience undergone (disappointment in love, disillusion with a parent, horror at human apathy) is nullified, or (*c*) flight (**'The Killers'** and, perhaps, even **'The Battler'**). (p. 211)

[In the crucial interchapter which reports on the wounding of Nick in the war, we] are not surprised to read that Nick has made 'a separate peace.' This is of a piece with his behaviour in all the stories concerning his boyhood. He has always run away from problems. He has been an escapist all along and now he will not face up to the consequences of enlisting. We learn in **'Now I Lay Me'** that he joined the war because 'he wanted to' and presumably he wants to quit now because he simply wants to. This is not to deny that Nick ever learns from experience but only that the experience he learns from is not of a piece with his experiences as a boy. In other words, what is denied is that there is a *continuum of cumulative experiences,* strung in a convenient linear order, all of which contribute to Nick's education. But this is precisely what the initiation critics claim. Here is Edmund Wilson [see excerpt above]:

> The shooting of Nick in the war does not really
> connect two different worlds: has he not found
> in the butchery abroad the same world that he
> knew back in Michigan?
>
> (p. 212)

And a final quotation from Clinton S. Burhans, Jr., the most recent spokesman of the 'initiation' school [see excerpt above].

> In this vignette [**'A Very Short Story'**]—the
> only one which links two stories so directly—
> Nick moves from his boyhood Michigan world
> to the greater world of his young manhood, *and
> he finds their actualities much the same.*

Are the 'actualities' of war in Europe and peace in Michigan really the same for Nick? They can be the same only in the interests of a theory that demands that they be the same. . . . That Hemingway saw life 'steadily and saw it whole' (in the Arnoldian sense) is not in dispute here for there is a sense in which the cruelties of life are equally reflected in war and peace. We are not concerned with this philosophical (if, somewhat, Darwinian) truth. We are solely concerned with Nick and asking if these widely separated experiences were the same to him. His spiritual agonies as the result of his war experiences are given in stories like **'In Another Country'**, **'Now I Lay Me'** and **'A Way You'll Never Be'** and we can certainly say that he *suffered* during this period and it seems reasonable to assume that he *learnt* from his suffering. There is evidence, for instance, in **'A Way You'll Never Be'** (presumably a Nick Adams story) that he returns to the actual scene of his injury to find out why he wakes up each night 'soaking wet, more frightened than he had ever been in a bombardment, because of a house and a long stable and a canal.' That he does find out to the extent of regaining his mental health we know from stories like **'Big Two-Hearted River'** and **'Cross-Country Snow'** to which [we] should turn for signs of the matured Nick. But simply to equate the mythical wounds of his boyhood with the very complex and real wounds of his manhood—both physical and mental—is to obscure the meaning of what Nick really learnt from life. His suffering and learning due to war merely throw into relief his young boyhood innocence, his ignorance and vulnerability, an ignorance so marked that it led him to volunteer for the Italian army in World War I, because, as he explains to his orderly John in **'Now I Lay Me'**, 'I don't know, John. I wanted to, then.' That is indeed, as John rightly observes, 'a hell of a reason'.

'A Way You'll Never Be', then, is the embryonic Nick Adams initiation story. De Falco, however, makes much larger claims for it:

> It . . . becomes evident at the conclusion that this is a new Nick, in the sense that he not only has overcome the possibility of slipping completely into the realm of regressive insanity but also that he has progressed beyond the stage of romantic notions concerning war.

The evidence for all this is rather slender and by no means unequivocal in its implications. Nick's uncertain memory at the end as to when exactly, 'marching, they had once passed the Terza Savoia cavalry regiment riding in the snow with their lances' and his immediately ensuing panic: 'Where was that? I'd better get to that damned bicycle . . . I don't want to lose the way to Fornaci' is enough to warn us that all is not still well with him.

But all is *very nearly well* with the Nick of **'Big Two-Hearted River'** and, finally, we do meet a very poised Nick in **'Cross-Country Snow.'** . . . Both these stories have *completed* actions and *reversals* which signify the points at which the learning has taken place. The first story shows Nick back from the war fishing in Michigan. It richly deserves the enormous critical reputation it has enjoyed since Malcolm Cowley drew attention, in his introduction to the **Portable Hemingway** in 1944 [see *CLC*, Vol. 13], to 'the shadows in the background', to the fact that parts of the story take place in an inner world. Its studied division into two parts, its subdued utterance hinting always at a faint menace, its quiet rendering of the precariously maintained equilibrium of Nick, all go to make it a fulcrum on which the gradually emerging maturity of Nick swings into focus for the first time. . . . (pp. 213-15)

[Furthermore, there] can be no mistake that Nick is a very different person in [**'Cross-Country Snow'**] from the boy we knew from the early stories. He has indeed grown up. There is neither fantasy nor wish-fulfilment about his thinking now, nor a refusal to think and face up to actualities, nor any panicky flight from reality. The Nick of **'Cross-Country Snow'** leads in a straight line to the Nick of **'Fathers and Sons'** (the last of the first forty-nine stories), where Nick Adams is telling his young son how it all was in our time and in his time. The Hemingway wheel has come full circle. (p. 217)

T. G. Vaidyanathan, " 'The Nick Adams Stories' and the Myth of Initiation,' in Indian Studies in American Fiction, *M. K. Naik, S. K. Desai, S. Mokashi-Punekar, eds., Macmillan, India, 1974, pp. 203-18.*

STUART L. BURNS

In his preface to **The Nick Adams Stories** [see excerpt above], Philip Young quite correctly notes that the eight hitherto un-

published sketches and fragments add new dimension to our understanding of one of Hemingway's earliest fictional protagonists. Indeed, by bringing all the fiction involving Nick Adams together into a single volume, Professor Young has performed a needed and important service for Hemingway scholarship. If one was uncertain before, one can be certain now that Hemingway must have, at one time, planned a story cycle or novel featuring Nick as the central character—something similar to Sherwood Anderson's *Winesburg, Ohio* or William Faulkner's *The Unvanquished*.

It is equally certain that **The Nick Adams Stories** does not have the esthetic continuity achieved in the aforementioned works; nor is Nick Adams as consistently characterized or developed as are George Willard and Bayard Sartoris. Indeed, one may further assert that, valuable as the material is in other contexts, it does not add to the "coherence of his adventures," as Young has intimated. That it does not is partly Young's fault, but primarily due to the unmanageability of the material itself. For the fact is that in his statement regarding the arrangement of the stories, Young has seriously oversimplified matters. . . . (p. 133)

Young makes three assertions . . . worthy of note: 1) That the *Stories* presents Nick's adventures in chronological order; 2) That Nick's experiences parallel Hemingway's own; 3) That in the present arrangement of the stories, Nick emerges as a consistent character. Young's first and third premises are demonstrably incorrect. The placement of **"The End of Something"** and **"The Three-Day Blow"** as postwar experiences violates the internal evidence within those stories. But even if one were to put them where they belong—at the beginning of the section entitled "On His Own"—that would only partially solve the problem. To include the fragmentary material is to render a logical chronology impossible. On the other hand, Young's second premise is valid; yet this premise appears to have led to his erroneous misplacement of the two stories mentioned above.

One rather obvious example will illustrate my point. Hemingway obviously *was* relying on his own postwar experiences for some of the material he puts into **"The End of Something"** and **"The Three-Day Blow."** . . . But while the incidents providing the source for the fiction are certainly postwar, the fictional time-setting just as certainly is not. Nick Adams's breakup with Marjorie occurs before he enters the war, in the fall of 1916. First of all Nick's "method" of getting rid of Marjorie is essentially adolescent, as is his naïve conversation about drinking, in the companion story. More to the point is Nick and Bill's discussion of baseball in **"The Three-Day Blow."** When Nick mentions that he'd "like to see the World Series," Bill responds, "They're always in New York or Philadelphia now." . . . During the same conversation, the two boys discuss John McGraw's (manager of the New York Giants) recent purchase of "Heinie Zim." . . . They are clearly referring to Heinie Zimmerman, Giant third baseman from midsummer 1916 through 1921. Assuming that the boys' conversation occurs in the fall of 1916, then Bill's statement about the World Series always being in New York or Philadelphia also makes general sense. Between the years 1911 and 1916, Boston was the only site of a World Series in addition to the cities he mentions.

Of course, one could argue that Hemingway had a poor memory or was indifferent to actual facts when inserting baseball lore into his stories. But there would seem to be too much evidence to the contrary. For example, in **"Crossing the Mississippi,"**

Hemingway's details about the 1917 series between the White Sox and the Giants are precise even to the point of his reference to Giant outfielder Happy Felsch's first-game home run off White Sox pitcher Slim Solee.

Viewed as the experiences of a veteran of the war, these two stories shake the reader's faith in Nick's development or maturity. That a person who has suffered the traumas of war should, after his return, be "impressed" by the philosophy that "opening bottles is what makes drunkards" . . . is simply incredible. So, for that matter, is Nick's naïve comment regarding a love scene in a book he has recently read. Says Nick:

> It's a swell book. What I couldn't ever understand was what good the sword would do. It would have to stay edge up all the time because if it went over flat you could roll right over it and it wouldn't make any trouble. . . .

Perhaps Candide or Don Quixote could have retained this kind of innocence; but not Hemingway *or* his fictional self. In short, the Nick Adams who appears in **"The End of Something"** is at best a callow youth, unforgivably boorish if we must perforce view him as a returned veteran. The fact is, however, that we need not so view him. Whether Hemingway, as a returned veteran, actually indulged in such adolescent antics as he details in **"The End of Something,"** or whether he took a real experience and modified it so it would express the adolescent character of his protagonist, is beside the point here. The important thing is that Hemingway clearly intended the events to happen to, and to be typical of, a seventeen-year-old youth, not a twenty-year-old, war-scarred veteran. (pp. 134-36)

[At] some point Hemingway clearly abandoned his plan to shape the stories about Nick Adams into a volume which would have the form of a novel like *The Unvanquished* or even an ordering protagonist like George Willard. Inasmuch as the unpublished sketches contain sequential contradiction, it is fruitless to speculate on what the correct chronology would have been or *should be*. A more valid approach might be to arrange them in an order that would clarify and enhance a thematic progression, if it is possible to do so.

I believe it is possible. (p. 138)

[The] consistency of Nick's character is not so much evidenced by his developing maturity as by his continuing and frustrated efforts to return to "the good country," that Edenic time and place before his fall from innocence—a time represented by the presence of trout streams, Indians, and uncomplicated sexual encounters.

A major theme in *The Nick Adams Stories* is that of loss. In relation to this theme it appears that **"The Last Good Country"** may have occupied a strategic position in Hemingway's plan for the work. In that story Adams doubly alienates himself from Eden: by violating nature through his poaching activities and by involving himself in some complicated love affair from which no pure relationship with his kid sister can redeem him. (pp. 139-40)

One can see why Hemingway at one time appended the section **"On Writing"** to **"Big Two-Hearted River."** For the Nick Adams of that story is not just trying to recover his equilibrium after the shock of the war, as Young suggests. Certainly that is part of it; but essentially Nick is trying, ineffectually, to recover his lost innocence or, failing in that as he must, to find a *method* to protect himself against the psychologically unsettling awareness of the realities of sex and death he has acquired.

One need not argue whether Hemingway's ultimate choice of fishing over writing as a metaphor for ordering existence against the crippling realities of war and women was a better or a poorer choice. One might note, however, that by discarding the section **"On Writing,"** he passed up the opportunity to use *both* writing and fishing as metaphoric defenses against the ravages of growing up. In doing so he varied once more, in his fiction, from the pattern he set for his life. (p. 140)

Stuart L. Burns, "Scrambling the Unscrambleable: 'The Nick Adams Stories'," in Arizona Quarterly, *Vol. 33, No. 2, Summer, 1977, pp. 133-40.*

LINDA W. WAGNER

When F. Scott Fitzgerald commented to Hemingway that Catherine Barkley in *A Farewell to Arms* is less successful than some of the women from his early short stories, he showed again his acute literary judgment. As Fitzgerald phrases it, "in the stories you were really listening to women—here you're only listening to yourself." Whatever the reason for the distancing that was to mar Hemingway's portrayal of women characters from 1929 on (except for Pilar, Maria, and Marie Morgan), there is little question that Hemingway was at his most sympathetic and skillful in drawing the female leads of the short stories of *In Our Time* and *Men Without Women* and of *The Sun Also Rises*. (p. 239)

One of the most striking characteristics of Hemingway's women in his early fiction is their resemblance to the later, mature Hemingway hero. . . . [In] Hemingway's earlier stories—**"Up in Michigan," "Indian Camp," "The End of Something," "The Three-Day Blow,"** and **"Cross-Country Snow"**—the women have already reached that plateau of semi-stoic self awareness which Hemingway's men have, usually, yet to attain.

When Marjorie understands her rejection in **"The End of Something,"** she behaves so admirably that Nick feels the impact of his loss doubly, and continues to mourn it throughout **"The Three-Day Blow."** "'I'm taking the boat,'" she called to him as she moved away, out of reach of both touch and sound. What the expected female behavior was is indicated a few lines later as Bill appears on the scene:

> "Did she go all right?" Bill said.
>
> "Yes," Nick said, lying, his face on the blanket.
>
> "Have a scene?"
>
> "No, there wasn't any scene."
>
> "How do you feel?"
>
> "Oh, go away, Bill! Go away for a while."

If Hemingway/Nick were to choose at that moment, he would surely prefer Marjorie's pride and grace to Bill's insensitive smirking.

"The End of Something" is one of the earliest of Hemingway's well-made, well-imaged stories. In these, much characterization is accomplished through the attribution of the insightful perception. Marjorie, here, sees the old mill as both an emblem of their relationship ("There's our old ruin, Nick") and something magical ("It seems more like a castle"). In response to each suggestion, "Nick said nothing." An early version of the dialogue gives us Nick as a sharp-tongued anti-romantic:

'What's that ruin, Nick?'

'It's Stroud's old mill.'

'It looks like a castle.'

'Not much.'

An inability to see clearly, perceptively, is Robert Cohn's flaw by the time of *The Sun Also Rises*; finding these early male protagonists—Nick, Bill, Harold Krebs—marked by the same insensitivity provides interesting parallels. Truly stories of male initiation, the short stories of *In Our Time* and *Men Without Women* tend to give us male characters who *need* that initiation. They learn from Hemingway's women. Or, tragically, they fail to learn. (pp. 239-40)

It can certainly be said that fascination with women characters, if not the characters themselves, dominates *In Our Time*. . . . Although the interspersed vignettes might suggest more externally oriented themes of war and bullfighting, of the stories included in the collection, only five or six have a focus other than a woman character or a relationship. And even within the vignettes, a character's humanity is gauged by his or her sympathy toward the life processes—birth as well as death. (p. 242)

For Hemingway, the prototype of marriage was that tragic relationship between his parents. Their marriage appeared early in his fiction with **"The Doctor and the Doctor's Wife"** (a story virtually untouched from manuscript to publication), **"Indian Camp,"** and in the magnificent house-cleaning scene of **"Fathers and Sons."** (p. 243)

Marriage for Hemingway—at least fictionally—was never an ideal state. Rather, his ideal seemed to be caught most effectively in the companionship of man/woman, boy/girl, brother/sister—a relationship bound by caring and sacrifice but not by obligation and power. . . . A story of peril and macho bravado, **"The Last Good Country"** conveys the tender rapport between brother and hero-worshiping little sister. It is also a story of Nick as initiator rather than initiated. "We're partners," Littless says, as she accepts her brother as guide and protector. Yet when Nick longs to kill the boy who turned him in, he realizes that Littless's greater moral consciousness will protect him, will keep him from harming anyone. . . . (p. 244)

"The Last Good Country," though unfinished and hence never published until the Nick Adams stories were collected, also moves through images, and one passage in particular gives the sense of Nick's love for Littless, his affinity with nature, and his admiration for personal qualities like pride and grace:

> They went along down the creek. Nick was studying the banks. He had seen a mink's track and shown it to his sister and they had seen tiny ruby-crowned kinglets that were hunting insects and let the boy and girl come close as they moved sharply and delicately in the cedars. They had seen cedar waxwings so calm and gentle and distinguished moving in their lovely elegance with the magic wax touches on their wing coverts and their tails, and Littless had said, 'They're the most beautiful, Nickie. There couldn't be more simply beautiful birds.'
>
> 'They're built like your face,' he said.
>
> 'No, Nickie, Don't make fun. Cedar waxwings make me so proud and happy that I cry.'

'When they wheel and light and then move so proud and friendly and gently . . .'

It also works to create that image of Utopia that Hemingway will repeat throughout his work—the undiscovered, untouched country (or sea); the place free from corruption, malaise, personal dishonesty; the place clean and well lighted; the place—whether geographical or anatomical—found through initiative (travel, exploration, sexual discovery); the country that gives answers instead of only dilemmas.

The pervasive imagery begins here, in one of the few pieces of Hemingway's fiction which include a gentle and loving male and female relationship. But that there are few Hemingway stories in which male-female love is idyllic, that his second story collection was titled **Men Without Women,** lies less in his attitudes toward his women characters (at least in his early fiction) than in his characterization of male characters as adolescent, selfish, misdirected. There is evidence of much sympathy on Hemingway's part of the women he portrays in this early fiction, and his focus is not to narrow—to concentrate almost obsessively on the reflexive self—until after *A Farewell to Arms*. It is as if the young Hemingway believed in the romantic, mystic ideal of a genuine love, of a man's finding ultimate completion with a woman, until the catastrophe of his father's death. (pp. 244-45)

Marred, saddened, mistrustful of marriage because of his childhood experiences, Hemingway gave up most attempts to draw sympathetic women characters after he wrote the vehicle for expressing his own deep bereavement. *A Farewell to Arms* is not a romantic novel; it is instead a novel about loss. And the loss is that of his father, not of Catherine or a child. . . . Unable to trust that better experiences would be his, Hemingway transferred that emotion into some of the most powerful of his fiction—the loss of Santiago, of Robert Jordan, and particularly of Thomas Hudson in *Islands in the Stream*. It is Hudson who relinquishes all relationship with women, reaching humanity through his love for his sons—the male tie again reinforced. (pp. 245-46)

Truer than he may have known, Fitzgerald's words of analysis, that Hemingway had stopped listening to his women characters. In his early fiction, Hemingway's attention was on women as themselves. In the later novels and stories, because his attention had been usurped by the deaths of his father and other men, women characters exist primarily to give the Hemingway character another dimension. The angle of vision is skewed, oblique; it still reflects, but less accurately. And Robert Lowell's theory—that any good poet creates for us *his* world—is once again borne out: the last Hemingway world was utopian, full of seas and energy and words, but strangely devoid of women. (p. 246)

Linda W. Wagner, "'Proud and Friendly and Gently': Women in Hemingway's Early Fiction," in College Literature, *Vol. VII, No. 3, Fall, 1980, pp. 239-47.*

KENNETH S. LYNN

In the summer of 1924, Ernest Hemingway wrote to Gertrude Stein and Alice B. Toklas to report on the progress he was making with a long short story in which he was "trying to do the country like [Paul] Cézanne and having a hell of a time and sometimes getting it a little bit. It is about 100 pages long and nothing happens and the country is swell, I made it all up, so I see it all and part of it comes out the way it ought to, it is swell about the fish, but isn't writing a hard job though?"

The story in question was **"Big Two-Hearted River,"** which in addition to being swell about the fish and as visually powerful as a Cézanne landscape, turned out to be a nice little masterpiece of psychological indeterminacy. . . .

[The] story abounds in details of how splendid the fishing is and what a good time Nick is having. Yet some sort of problem is lurking on the margins of his mind. . . .

For a decade and a half after its appearance as the concluding episode of *In Our Time* (1925), **"Big Two-Hearted River"** was admired by literary critics for its ambiguities. Then in the late 1930's this situation changed, when Edmund Wilson took it upon himself to improve the story by making it more explicit. The experience that has given Nick Adams "a touch of panic," Wilson asserted in 1939, is "the wholesale shattering of human beings in which he has taken part" [see excerpt above]. The statement had no basis in fact. For World War I is not mentioned in **"Big Two-Hearted River,"** and there is no reference in the story to feelings of panic.

That Wilson nevertheless described Hemingway's hero as the psychological victim of a brutal war was a measure of the extent to which his literary sensibility was ruled by political nausea. In the early 30's, Wilson's nausea had led him to the Marxist faith, because Marxism called for the total rejection of the entire existing society. With visions of destruction dancing in his head, Wilson had dedicated himself to writing an ambitious book on European radical thought. *To the Finland Station* was completed in 1939, but by that time the author had come to the realization that the Marxist cure for social disease was no solution. (p. 24)

Turning away from the study of radical political thought, he reread Hemingway—and promptly found in **"Big Two-Hearted River"** the vision of a sensitive writer whose suffering has been caused not by mistakes he himself has made, but by the belligerency of great powers. The commentators have been wrong in accusing Hemingway of an indifference to society, Wilson proclaimed at the end of his essay, for in fact "his whole work is a criticism of society."

When, in 1940, Malcolm Cowley finally ceased apologizing for Stalinism, he, too, began to cast about for non-Marxist modes of continuing his assault on the moral credentials of capitalist society. America's entrance into the war against Hitler made this problem particularly difficult for him, but Wilson's overinterpretation of Hemingway seems to have showed him how to solve it. In addition to shoveling much more warvictim material into **"Big Two-Hearted River"** than Wilson had done, Cowley's introduction to the *Viking Portable Hemingway* (1944) [see *CLC*, Vol. 13] went on to insist that a haunted, hypnagogic quality characterizes all of Hemingway's work. His stories are told against the background of the countries he has seen, Cowley said, but

> these countries are presented in a strangely mortuary light. In no other writer of our time can you find such a profusion of corpses: dead women in the rain; dead soldiers bloated in their uniforms and surrounded by torn papers; sunken liners full of bodies that float past the closed portholes. In no other writer can you find so many suffering animals: mules with their forelegs broken drowning in shallow water off the quay at Smyrna; gored horses in the bull ring; wounded hyenas first snapping at their own entrails and then eating them with relish.

In a strangely mortuary light. To a critic who had argued all through the 1930's that the difference between the Soviet Union and other countries was the difference between life and death, it must have felt like vindication to write those words, and to append to them that long list of fearsome illustrations. For while history had revealed that the critic might have been a bit incautious in his praise of the Soviet Union, Hemingway's stories certainly seemed to confirm Cowley's judgment of the rest of the world.

Was it really accurate, though, to say that Hemingway had presented France, Spain, Switzerland, the United States, and the other countries he knew as a series of hypnagogic visions? Convincing proof of this bold proposition would have required a great many demonstrations across the whole range of his work. The *Viking Portable*'s editor, however, stuck to a strikingly limited number of stories; indeed, there was one story he kept coming back to again and again. In the end, all the credibility of his "nightmares at noonday" interpretation was invested in his comments on **"Big Two-Hearted River."**

Cowley's Nick Adams is in far worse psychological shape than Edmund Wilson's. The evidence of his condition is not to be found in the story, to be sure, but that was nothing to worry about because "Hemingway's stories are most of them continued," and in a somewhat later book that *In Our Time* there is a story called **"Now I Lay Me"** that "casts a retrospective light" on **"Big Two-Hearted River."** The later story is concerned with "an American volunteer in the Italian army who isn't named but who might easily be Nick Adams." (The critic is in error. The volunteer is named, and his name is Nick.) As a result of being wounded in action, the young man is afraid to go to sleep at night. "I had been living for a long time," he confesses, "with the knowledge that if I ever shut my eyes in the dark and let myself go, my soul would go out of my body." This confession, we are assured, enables us to appreciate the psychological fragility of the man who is fishing the Big Two-Hearted River.

Among the things Cowley neglects to tell us about **"Now I Lay Me"** is that the frightened American soldier is lying in a room a scant seven kilometers behind the lines. Moreover, the soldier knows that, as surely as autumn follows summer, he will have to return to the fighting—and in fact at the end of the story we learn of his later participation in the "October offensive." The story, in short, is very much like another Hemingway story called **"In Another Country,"** in which a recuperating American soldier lies in bed at night in Milan, "afraid to die and wondering how I would be when I went back to the front again."

In **"Big Two-Hearted River,"** we are in a very different world. Nick is a civilian, safely back in the United States. Now that he no longer has any worries about coming under fire again, has his psyche healed as rapidly as his body has, or is he still afraid to close his eyes at night, lest his soul take flight? Hemingway's answer is clear. "Nick lay down . . . under the blankets. He turned on his side and shut his eyes. He was sleepy. He felt sleep coming. He curled up under the blanket and went to sleep." So much for the retrospective light cast by **"Now I Lay Me."**

Cowley's essay on Hemingway is not a work that can bear careful scrutiny; it does not even give the correct year of Hemingway's birth. Yet no sooner was the essay published than it began to influence critics everywhere. A young man named Philip Young, for instance, "ported a *Portable Hemingway* . . .

half way across Europe during World War II," and after the war he wrote a book that carried Cowley's critical extravagances to further heights of absurdity. The wound Hemingway suffered in World War I, Young contended, had so deeply traumatized him that he spent his entire life as a writer composing variations on the story of the psychically crippled "sick man" who fishes the Big Two-Hearted River [see *CLC*, Vol. 13]. Alas, Young never thought to ask himself whether reading the *Viking Portable Hemingway* against the dramatic backdrop of World War II had not made it all too easy for him to believe in the obsessive importance to Hemingway of World War I. Nor did Young ever suspect that Cowley's conversion of a sun-drenched, Cézannesque picture of a predominantly happy fishing trip into a tale as spooky as any of [Edgar Allan] Poe's or [Nathaniel] Hawthorne's was governed by an ideological purpose, which was to bathe American life in a strangely mortuary light.

Intellectual naiveté, however, was not the only reason Cowley's introduction slew the minds of so many critics. In the wake of the triumph of American power in World War II, the anti-American prejudice of intellectuals who automatically identified themselves with powerlessness became more virulent than ever before, and anti-American interpretations of American literature sprang up like poisonous weeds. In *Huckleberry Finn*, for instance, Huck's decision at the end of the book to cross over into the Oklahoma Territory for a few weeks of howling adventures with Tom Sawyer and Nigger Jim before returning to his home town in Missouri was transformed by post-World War II critics into a decision to secede forever from American society, because American society sickened the boy.

It was the critics, however, who were sickened by American society, not Huck Finn, and their endorsement of a war-wound interpretation of the life and work of Hemingway was a further reflection of their bias. Thus the late Mark Schorer, in an essay published in 1962, projected upon the author of **"Big Two-Hearted River"** his own sense of social victimization. Only July 8, 1918, while on service with the Red Cross on the Italian front, Schorer wrote, Hemingway "was severely wounded by the explosion of a mortar shell and the next three months he spent in a hsopital in Milan. Nothing more important than this wounding was ever to happen to him. A wound was to become the central symbol of nearly everything he was to write, and the consequences of a wound his persistent thematic preoccupation."

Carlos Baker had a golden opportunity to overturn the prevailing clichés when he undertook to write his massive *Ernest Hemingway: A Life Story* (1969). But the weight of thirty years of accumulated critical authority was too much for Baker, and the opportunity was lost. (pp. 24-6)

[As can be seen in the recently published *Ernest Hemingway: Selected Letters, 1917-1961*, between] the time he arrived at his parents' home in Oak Park, Illinois, in January 1919, and his reembarkation for Europe in the late fall of 1921, the returned war veteran wrote many letters to many people. In none of them is there either an explicit or implicit indication of the sort of psychic malaise that literary criticism would subsequently assign to the autobiographical hero who fishes the Big Two-Hearted River. An emotion of startling intensity does surge to the surface of the correspondence in the middle of these postwar years, but the name of that emotion is not panic, or hypnagogic horror, or anything like. It is anger, an all-consuming anger, of the sort he manifested when he was jilted by the nurse. And

what would trigger it would be a contest of wills with his mother. (p. 27)

Right from the start of his career as a creative writer, Hemingway . . . sought to pursue his war with his mother by fictional means. From the vantage point of Paris's Left Bank in 1924, he looked back upon Oak Park in anger, as he worked upon the stories that became the book called *In Our Time*. **"The Doctor and the Doctor's Wife,"** the second of the stories in the book, presents a sanctimonious wife, her hen-pecked husband, and their little boy. Instead of obeying his mother's request that he come up to the bedroom where she is lying with the blinds drawn and a Bible beside her, the boy goes off for a walk in the woods with his father. In **"Soldier's Home,"** the seventh story, we meet a mother who willingly cooks breakfast for her war-veteran son, but who doesn't allow him to "muss up" the morning newspaper—it is the Kansas City *Star*, we learn—which he wants to read while eating. She then completes the young man's annoyance by asking him if he loves her, to which he replies, "I don't love anybody," and by urging him to kneel and pray with her, to which he replies, "I can't." In both of these stories, the need to comply with a mother's demands is defied by a rebellious son. The final story in *In Our Time,* as we have seen, centers on a fisherman who feels, as he enters the woods, that he has left everything behind, "the need for thinking, the need to write, other needs." Whether the "other needs" he has escaped include the need to please his mother is never made clear.

Yet if the fisherman's dark thoughts in **"Big Two-Hearted River"** are choked off before they reach the level of consciousness, Grace Hall Hemingway was surely on the story-teller's mind. The satisfaction Nick takes in referring to his tent as his home, for instance, derives from the author's inability either to forget or to forgive his mother's banishment of him four years before from their home in Michigan. As Nick sets up the tent, he is defiantly establishing a counter-domicile—and as he proceeds to hang his pack from a nail that he has "gently" driven into a pine tree, to prepare a delicious meal of beans and spaghetti, to brew his coffee by a carefully described method, and to clean up after himself with scrupulous thoroughness, he is defining a counter-domesticity. Hemingway may have rebelled against the values of his mother and father, but he was also marked by them; in the woods, Nick Adams apes the cooking skills and the careful housekeeping habits that Hemingway had observed in his father on fishing and hunting trips and in his mother at home.

Happiness for the hero of **"Big Two-Hearted River"** is an inordinate concern with small details. On the one hand, his obsessiveness keeps dark thoughts at bay; on the other hand, it demonstrates how responsible he is. Before reaching down into the stream to touch a trout resting on the bottom, Nick conscientiously wets his hand, "so that he would not disturb the delicate mucus that covered him. If a trout was touched with a dry hand, a white fungus attacked the unprotected spot." The author who would cry out to his mother that his work was nothing to be ashamed of, and that the day would come when she would be proud of him, could not have continued writing if he had not believed himself to be, in his own way, a moralist. He had incorporated into himself too much of her personality to have embraced the nihilism with which his interpreters have been so eager to associate him.

The question of why the author elected not to specify the nature of the malaise that underlies Nick's happiness in **"Big Two-Hearted River"** can never be answered with certainty. But the most plausible answer is that, unlike **"The Doctor and the Doctor's Wife"** and **"Soldier's Home,"** in which sons are clearly unhappy in the homes of their mothers, **"Big Two-Hearted River"** takes place in the woods. If Nick Adams had been revealed as a man so angry at his mother that he could not even forget her when he was off on a fishing trip, readers might simply have concluded that Nick was an emotional adolescent. The only way to avoid such a judgment would have been to show Nick using his time in the woods to sort out his feelings about his mother and come to an understanding of the tension between them. Writing that kind of story, however, would have required of Hemingway a degree of self-understanding that he would never achieve.

"I had a wonderful novel to write about Oak Park," he told the literary critic Charles Fenton in 1952, but "would never do it because I did not want to hurt liveing [*sic*] people." The excuse rings false. Neither as a man nor as a writer had Hemingway ever hesitated to hurt living people, and furthermore both of his parents were dead when he wrote to Fenton. If pangs of conscience had previously stayed his hand, why did he not write the Oak Park novel at some point during the ten years of life that remained to him after his mother's death in 1951? Clearly, it was not a concern for protecting his parents that forever prevented him from writing the book, but rather his own failure to master its materials. A novel-length exploration of the experience of growing up in Oak Park would have led Hemingway into a swamp filled with deep water and overgrown with trees, in which big trout might be hooked but not landed. (pp. 28-9)

Across the entire length of his adult life, Hemingway kept a double record of his feelings by writing stories and by writing letters. In contrast to the appalling frankness of the letters, the stories suppress information, conflate memories, play tricks with time-frames, speak in symbols. But with the help of the letters, they can be decoded and, at long last, properly understood. In the light of this understanding, the interpretation of Hemingway's fiction that originated forty years ago in Edmund Wilson's misreading of **"Big Two-Hearted River,"** and that was then magnified by Malcolm Cowley into a misreading of the entire *oeuvre,* can also be recognized for what it really is: the exploitation of an author's work for ideological purposes.

Taken together, the letters and the stories show that what happened to Hemingway on July 8, 1918, did not give him nightmares for the rest of his life. If World War I played hob with his future, it was not because of a wound but because it suddenly propelled a rebellious youth who was barely out of high school into a very much bigger and more exciting world than the one he was slowly getting to know as a newspaperman in Kansas City.

Perhaps his separation from his mother and the values she stood for could never have been accomplished in the spirit of mutual understanding and love that Sherwood Anderson describes so delicately in his account of the relationship between young George Willard and his mother in *Winesburg, Ohio.* Perhaps, like figures in [a Eugene] O'Neill tragedy, Hemingway and his mother were doomed to claw and slash at one another, no matter what. The high-gear acceleration in his development that resulted from the war, however, certainly did not enhance the chances of establishing peace on the home front. Hemingway came back to Oak Park in 1919 spoiling for a fight, and his mother was waiting for him. (p. 33)

Kenneth S. Lynn, "Hemingway's Private War," in Commentary, *Vol. 72, No. 1, July, 1981, pp. 24-33.*

S(usan) E(loise) Hinton

1950-

American novelist.

Hinton helped to change the tone of young adult fiction with the publication at age seventeen of *The Outsiders* (1967). Dissatisfied with the pristine portrayals of teenagers in traditional adolescent novels, Hinton drew on experiences in her hometown of Tulsa, Oklahoma, to create this popular story of class conflict and gang rivalry. Critics were impressed with Hinton's unpretentious narrative style and her skillful development of plot and character. Unlike formulaic teenage novels, *The Outsiders* and Hinton's subsequent works, *That Was Then, This Is Now* (1971), *Rumble Fish* (1975), and *Tex* (1979), deal with such topics as violence, poverty, alcoholism, and drug addiction.

Hinton's works revolve around lower-class teenage male protagonists who are unhappy with their lives and hostile toward others. Each of the young men experiences a conflict between his inner feelings and his reputation among his peers. In *The Outsiders*, Ponyboy Curtis realizes that the upper-class teenagers he is expected to hate have many of the values that are important to him; Bryon Douglas, in *That Was Then, This Is Now*, is disturbed because his best friend is a drug dealer; and Rusty-James in *Rumble Fish* and Tex in *Tex* both recognize the futility of pretending to be invulnerable.

Some critics fault Hinton for sexism in her portrayals of machismo protagonists and suggest that her female characters are inadequately developed. However, Hinton has been praised for the complexity of her protagonists and for the sensitivity she reveals beneath their tough surfaces. The popularity of Hinton's novels among young adults has been further enhanced by film adaptations of *The Outsiders*, *Rumble Fish*, and *Tex*.

(See also *Children's Literature Review*, Vol. 3; *Contemporary Authors*, Vols. 81-84; and *Something about the Author*, Vol. 19.)

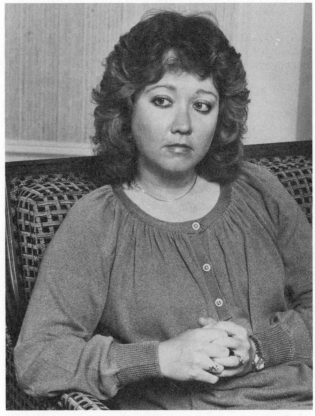

© Thomas Victor 1984

and saying more with greater storytelling ability than many an older hand. (pp. 64-5)

Lillian N. Gerhardt, in a review of "The Outsiders," in School Library Journal, *an appendix to* Library Journal, *Vol. 13, No. 9, May, 1967, pp. 64-5.*

LILLIAN N. GERHARDT

It is rare-to-unique among juvenile books . . . to find a novel confronting the class hostilities which have intensified since the Depression. The setting of [*The Outsiders*] is a small Oklahoma city, which underscores the national scope of a current problem and by-passes the subliminal reactions that attach to major cities. The boys in this book are neither unimaginable urban sophisticates nor unassimilated Puerto Ricans or Negroes running berserk; they are the pioneer-stock legatees of Huckleberry Finn. Ponyboy, the 14-year-old narrator, tells how it looks and feels from the wrong side of the tracks and of guerrilla raids into his territory by the traditional, well-heeled enemy from the residential district, and the beating that led to a murder charge and two deaths. The story is exciting and those difficult-to-serve kids at the culturally detached bottom of society can respond to this book, with its revelations of the latent decency of the urban slum characters, who are nearly but not yet hopeless. . . . The jacket says the author is a teenager. A writer not yet practiced in restraint perhaps, but nevertheless seeing

THOMAS FLEMING

Can sincerity overcome clichés? In ["**The Outsiders**"], by a now 17-year-old author, it almost does the trick. By almost any standard, Miss Hinton's performance is impressive. At an age when most youngsters are still writing 300-word compositions, she has produced a book alive with the fresh dialogue of her contemporaries, and has wound around it a story that captures, in vivid patches at least, a rather unnerving slice of teen-age America.

"**The Outsiders**" is told in the first person by 14-year-old Ponyboy Curtis—a "greaser" or lower class kid who slicks his hair and slouches around in T-shirts and jeans. Arch rivals of the Greasers are the Socs—short for Socials, kids with Madras shirts and Mustangs. Apparently in Tulsa, where Miss Hinton sets her story, the poor guys don't beat up the rich guys. It works the other way around—and she uses this switch to build up quite a head of self-pitying steam for her hero and his friends. (pp. 10, 12)

Hinton's fire-engine pace does not give the reader much time to manufacture doubts. And the final confrontation between Ponyboy and the Socs, in which he realizes they too are pretty mixed-up kids, is a comforting if not quite believable ending. (p. 12)

> *Thomas Fleming, in a review of "The Outsiders," in* The New York Times Book Review, *Part II, May 7, 1967, pp. 10, 12.*

WILLIAM JAY JACOBS

Like Salinger's Holden Caulfield, Ponyboy [in *The Outsiders*] is a romantic. He watches sunsets and looks at the stars and aches for something better. He muses that the moon he sees from his back steps is the same one that a Soc girl he admires can see from her patio on the other side of town. But as much as the sensitive, thoughtful Ponyboy resembles Holden, his milieu is irrevocably different. All around him are hostility and fear, along with distrust for the "system." As the story ends he sees a buddy shot down by the police under a street light. It was too late for him, but was it too late to tell other boys who are mean and tough and hate the world that there is still good in it—and would they believe you? (p. 201)

Admittedly, this is not on all counts a remarkable book. The dialogue sometimes rings false, and the message may be a shade too profound to be mouthed by teen-aged "hoods." Still there is little of the pretentiousness here, the whining tone, that characterizes the first statements of youthful authors. (p. 202)

> *William Jay Jacobs, "Reaching the Unreached," in* The Record, *Vol. 69, No. 2, November, 1967, pp. 201-02.**

A. CHAMBERS

The only major flaw [in *The Outsiders*] is that the book is written with self-indulgence, and could profitably have been cut. Apart from this, even the over-didacticism of its first person narrative—it is as didactic as modern pop songs—comes off the page with such absorbed conviction, such persuasive truth and emotional power that one accepts it. The story has humour, passion, tenderness, intelligence, action a-plenty and, best of all, compassion.

> *A. Chambers, in a review of "The Outsiders," in* Children's Book News, *Vol. 5, No. 6, November-December, 1970, p. 280.*

SHERYL B. ANDREWS

Using the background and a sprinkling of the characters from her first book, *The Outsiders*, [in *That Was Then, This Is Now* S. E. Hinton] tensely builds up an atmosphere of violence, catalyzed constantly by the vicious cycle of justice which demanded that every score be personally settled by some means of retribution. . . . The scenes portrayed are sometimes ugly; the decisions forced on the characters are often motivated by basic survival needs, emotional as well as physical; and Bryon's final commitment to himself and to his future is harshly and realistically underlined in an ending that offers no pat promises. This is a disturbing book and perhaps in some senses a too contemporaneous one, but it will speak directly to a large number of teenagers and does have a place in the understanding of today's cultural problems. (p. 389)

> *Sheryl B. Andrews, in a review of "That Was Then, This Is Now," in* The Horn Book Magazine, *Vol. XLVII, No. 4, August, 1971, pp. 388-89.*

MICHAEL CART

There are many similarities between this second book by S. E. Hinton ["That Was Then, This Is Now"] and her first, "The Outsiders." Both are powerful, realistic stories about being young and poor in a large Oklahoma city. But instead of a gang of rich kids spoiling for a fight, the antagonist in this more ambitious novel is time.

"That Was Then, This Is Now" attempts to show how time changes 16-year-old Bryon Douglas and his relationships with those he loves. . . .

The phrase "if only" is perhaps the most bittersweet in the language, and Miss Hinton uses it skillfully to underline her theme: growth can be a dangerous process. As Bryon moves toward maturity he faces the dangers of the emotional vacuum that waits to be filled after loss of innocence. But "if only" is also a tricky device, encouraging an easy descent from pathos to bathos, and if there is fault to be found with "That Was Then, This Is Now" it is that at its end, when love and hate have run their course, all that is left to Bryon is not honest and believable grief but life-denying self-pity. Despite Bryon's difficult education in maturity, his central decisions . . . are made not intellectually but emotionally. It is unfortunate that Miss Hinton has indulged herself in this way, for otherwise she has written a mature, disciplined novel, which excites a response in the reader. Whatever its faults, her book will be hard to forget.

> *Michael Cart, in a review of "That Was Then, This Is Now," in* The New York Times Book Review, *August 8, 1971, p. 8.*

THE TIMES LITERARY SUPPLEMENT

S. E. Hinton's *That was Then, This is Now* is a searing and terrible account of what life can be like for east-side youths in an American town—on the look out for easy money, for chicks, for drink, for the fast car to hot-wire and, sometimes, for hard drugs. This is a book which is both violent and tender, a book in which the hero, Bryon, grows from being a kid, when he "had all the answers", into a young manhood beset by questions. After a long search, he and his girl friend find her young brother high on LSD in a hippy house. . . . When Bryon gets home sickened by the realization that this child may never fully recover, he reaches under his buddy's mattress for a packet of fags—and finds phials of drugs instead. Should he betray his best friend who is quite obviously a pusher? In deciding painfully to call the police, Bryon gains, and loses, all. A starkly realistic book, a punch from the shoulder which leaves the reader considerably shaken.

> *"Punching from the Shoulder," in* The Times Literary Supplement, *No. 3634, October 22, 1971, p. 1318.**

JOHN ROWE TOWNSEND

[S. E. Hinton] was in her teens when she wrote *The Outsiders* . . . , a novel of violence and feuding between greasers and socialites. The book is technically remarkable for so young a writer; its background appears authentic; but true feeling is hopelessly entangled with false, bad-film sentimentality, and the plot is creakingly unbelievable. It may be noted that, just as slum children in novels by middle-class writers can easily be nice middle-class children under the skin, so the greasers in this book by 'a seventeen-year-old whose best friends are greasers' sometimes look like sheep in wolves' clothing. (p. 295)

> *John Rowe Townsend, "How Young Is an Adult?" in his* Written for Children: An Outline of English-Language Children's Literature, *revised edition, J. B. Lippincott, Publishers, 1974, pp. 291-300.**

JANE ABRAMSON

As gut-wrenching as the "sneaky pete" her hero guzzles down, S. E. Hinton's latest novel [*Rumble Fish*] won't sit well with book selectors who demand that children's fiction end hopefully, if not happily. No hard-nosed punk, young Rusty-James rapidly loses everything meaningful to him—his girl, his "rep" as number one tough guy, and, most important, his idolized older brother. . . . Stylistically superb (the purposely flat, colorless narrative exactly describes Rusty-James' turf of pool halls, porno movie houses, and seedy hang-outs), this packs a punch that will leave readers of any age reeling.

> *Jane Abramson, in a review of "Rumble Fish," in* School Library Journal, *Vol. 22, No. 2, October, 1975, p. 106.*

ANITA SILVEY

The dialogue and [Rusty-James's] monologue [in *Rumble Fish*] are vibrant and authentic, and the narrative moves quickly and dramatically from one event to another. But essentially the material of the book remains undeveloped, and the commentary glib and superficial. . . . By her third book, the outcome for S. E. Hinton appears to be unpromising; her writing has the same style and the same perception as it had when she was seventeen. Instead of becoming a vehicle for growth and development, the book, unfortunately, simply echoes what came before. She is no longer a teenager writing about teenagers today, and the book raises the question whether, as an adult, she will ever have much of importance to say to young readers. (pp. 601-02)

> *Anita Silvey, in a review of "Rumble Fish," in* The Horn Book Magazine, *Vol. LI, No. 6, December, 1975, pp. 601-02.*

ROBERT BERKVIST

[In **"Rumble Fish"**] Rusty-James longs to live up to the reputation of his older brother, referred to only as the Motorcycle Boy. Rusty-James is on a macho trip at his junior high school, where he wants to be the toughest cat around since his brother was expelled. Rusty's father drinks, his mother has disappeared, his best friend is decent enough but too weak to exert any influence. When the Motorcycle Boy comes back to town, Rusty follows his idol one step too far. The fall is shattering for them both.

"Rumble Fish" . . . makes its bleak points tellingly enough, despite a curiously remote quality. Much of the latter, I think, stems from that Motorcycle Boy, who clanks through the story like a symbol never quite made flesh.

> *Robert Berkvist, in a review of "Rumble Fish," in* The New York Times Book Review, *December 14, 1975, p. 8.*

DOROTHY NIMMO

Rumble Fish belongs, essentially, to one of the established forms of children's books, the animal story, in which the child is given the opportunity of living in the skin of the grizzly bear or the wild horse. The experiences of the animal are felt by the child, though in a different way from that in which the animal feels them. So in *Rumble Fish* the boy's emulation of his older brother, his alienation from his father, his rejection of school and authority—the things many children feel—are projected onto the terrible dangerous animals who live in the concrete jungle. They are sufficiently distanced for the child to identify with them without being overwhelmed. This is a story about an alien way of life, just as the animal stories are, and like most of them it falls into the trap of sentimentalising its subject. But it is an improvement on S. E. Hinton's earlier books, better constructed and more restrained. I think it is an Action Man; a dolly, in spite of its combat gear and fierce armoury of weapons.

> *Dorothy Nimmo, in a review of "Rumble Fish," in* The School Librarian, *Vol. 24, No. 4, December, 1976, p. 335.*

THE COUNCIL ON INTERRACIAL BOOKS FOR CHILDREN

[In *Rumblefish,* Hinton's] portrayal of men and women is decidedly sexist. The machismo creed is heavily reinforced by Rusty James' refusal to cry, his need to keep up a tough-hood front, his faith that his strong hands are more valuable than a good mind. Girlfriend Patty is jealous and manipulative, turning her tears on and off at will. Girls are classified as "good," cheapies to mess around with, pretty possessions, housewives or runaway mothers.

Behind a colorful and action-packed facade, Ms. Hinton promotes negative images and values. (pp. 215-16)

> *"Rumble Fish," in* Human—And Anti-Human—Values in Children's Books: A Content Rating Instrument for Educators and Concerned Parents, *edited by the Council on Interracial Books for Children, Inc., Racism and Sexism Resource Center for Educators, 1976, pp. 215-16.*

PAXTON DAVIS

"Tex" is a tale of coping with and surviving the trials and uncertainties of adolescence. Tex himself faces odds, to be sure: His father is a rodeo cowboy who's rarely around, and Tex and his older brother Mason must make do for themselves; he's got troubles at school and scuffles with his friends. Worse, though, he and Mason have problems that won't go away: In Tex's view, Mason is bossy and mean; moreover, he's sold their horses, in order to keep them going and the animals from starving.

Problems abound, in other words, and those aren't the only ones the author places on Tex's shoulders. He and Mason are held up and kidnapped by a hitchhiker (though clever Tex extricates them from the predicament); girl friend Jamie alternately asks for and rejects sex; there's a question about Tex's true parentage; at the end, Tex has a shoot-out with a drug pusher.

There's too much going on here. Even by the standards of today's fiction, S. E. Hinton's vision of contemporary teen-age life is riper than warrants belief.

Nevertheless, there are good things. The scene, the American Southwest, is rendered keenly. Mason, the older brother, is more than he seems to Tex, and Miss Hinton permits us to see it. The bewilderments of adolescence are often painfully caught. Yet "Tex" smacks, somehow, of Snoopy's "It Was a Dark and Stormy Night," busier and more melodramatic than the real life it purports to show. Perhaps it's like this these days, but "Tex" makes the case unconvincingly.

> *Paxton Davis, in a review of "Tex," in* The New York Times Book Review, *December 16, 1979, p. 23.*

MARGERY FISHER

Susan Hinton's attention has always been directed towards the crucial, changing relationships of adolescence but in the thirteen years since the first publication of *The Outsiders,* when the young author was writing to some extent from her own experience, she has taken a larger canvas on which to group more varied characters. *Tex* has a wider spread than her earlier books, first and most obviously in the geographical sense, because her setting here is Californian farmland rather than city streets. This is something more than just an extended background. The tensions between Tex McCormick, who is fifteen, and his protective older brother Mason, are no less urgent and claustrophobic than those operating in the urban gangs of the earlier books, but they have an added force because of the isolation of the brothers in the dusty roads and paddocks where Tex rides his horse and his motor-bike, where the two of them wait for their restless father to return. . . . [Frustration] and anxiety drive [Mason] to illness, and in practical terms to the desperate measure of selling the horses, an action which brings to a head Tex's growing need to assert himself, to deny Mason's anxious control and claim his own identity.

Tex is a true survivor. Accepting insecurity and domestic hardship, this rough, explosive boy has an unexpected contentment which the author has brilliantly conveyed through his reactions to the important and the minor crises of his fifteenth summer and autumn. (p. 3686)

Susan Hinton has shown in this book that first-person narrative can work. Tex's manner—blunt, colloquial, exploratory and openly egotistical—suits the setting and builds up the boy's character so that his view of his peers and of the adults who affect his life seems natural and inevitable. . . . In soliloquy, in reported dialogue, in the plain account of day after day, Tex has opened his character to the reader together with a view of a landscape, a house, a city and a group of friends, neighbours, associates. Phrases and sentences seemingly casual and unstudied have been carefully devised to carry clues to personality and event in a totally natural way. . . . In this new book Susan Hinton has achieved that illusion of reality which any fiction writer aspires to and which few ever completely achieve. (pp. 3686-87)

> *Margery Fisher, in a review of "Tex," in her* Growing Point, *Vol. 19, No. 1, May, 1980, pp. 3686-87.*

LANCE SALWAY

[S. E. Hinton], it seems to me, gets right to the heart of how and why people behave towards one another, in this case two teenage brothers in rural Oklahoma. . . . *Tex* is the first of her books that I've read, but it certainly won't be the last. . . . [It's] a brilliant study of a fraternal relationship: moving, powerful, funny, and entirely convincing. It's odd, really, that the novel works so well when so many of the elements in the story are highly theatrical. The young narrator-hero, among other things, is kidnapped by a deranged gunman, is shot by a desperate junkie, and discovers that he isn't really his father's son. Each of these events would have sufficed for a novel on its own and it takes some courage to pack them all into one book. But a writer as good as Hinton can carry it off effortlessly; one believes implicitly in the characters and cares what happens to them.

> *Lance Salway, in an extract from "Book Post," in* Signal, *No. 32, May, 1980, p. 121.*

SUSAN THOMPSON

Some writers—Susan Hinton for example—have turned the [peer] group . . . , its interactions and meanings, into the subject matter of a novel. Hinton's teenage groups grow up too fast, leading grim lives on the wrong side of the law; they carry knives and guns and are no strangers to violence or murder. . . . [In *The Outsiders* toughness] is exaggerated and the beauties of friendship and kinship are sentimentalized by frequent repetition. There are also rather heavily delivered messages about young people, particularly the poor ones, being helplessly drawn into the inner-city whirlpool of violence and crime and missing the opportunity to discover the worthwhile things in life.

Theorists have acknowledged the role of social class in determining young people's behaviour and identity: adolescence is not merely a psychological or biological event, nor do all adolescents, as we once assumed, belong to a single subculture characterized chiefly by its opposition to adults and the status quo. There are differences among young people themselves, often as a direct result of their class origins. Hinton's novel does recognize such distinctions, but without examining them in any depth, using the stereotypes of working and middle class simply as justification for the hostility between the two gangs. In fact she proceeds to overthrow the significance of the class barrier by pointing to the futility of gang warfare and exposing the myths behind the stereotypes. The greasers, for example, imagine that the working class has a monopoly of life's problems, but Ponyboy is made to see that, while the socs have the edge financially, they experience their troubles too. The gang ideal itself begins to ring hollow: teenagers who break allegiance to their own gang in order to speak on equal terms with a member of the opposing force are shown to be the most admirable and mature. Ponyboy finds himself more flattered to be known by his own name than 'grease', the call name of the gang. Although appearance, dress and habits of speech, as well as emotional support and physical protection derive from the gang, family and closest friends are probably more important. (pp. 114-15)

> *Susan Thompson, "Images of Adolescence: Part II," in* Signal, *No. 35, May, 1981, pp. 108-25.**

Zora Neale Hurston

1901?-1960

Black American novelist, folklorist, essayist, short story writer, dramatist, anthropologist, and autobiographer.

Hurston is recognized as an important writer of the Harlem Renaissance, an era of unprecedented excellence in black American art and literature during the 1920s and 1930s. She is now considered among the foremost authors of that period—having published four novels, three nonfiction works, and numerous short stories and essays—and she is also acknowledged as the first black American to collect and publish Afro-American folklore. Hurston has only recently gained substantial critical attention. Her fiction, which deals with the common black folk of her native southern Florida, was considered obsolete with the advent of the "protest novel" as presented by such writers as Richard Wright and James Baldwin during the 1940s and 1950s. In recent years, however, Hurston's work, particularly her novel *Their Eyes Were Watching God* (1937), has undergone substantial critical revaluation.

Hurston was born in Eatonville, Florida, the first incorporated black township in the United States and the setting for most of her novels. At fourteen, she left Eatonville to work as a maid with a traveling Gilbert and Sullivan theatrical troupe. In 1923 Hurston entered Howard University. Her first short story was published in *Stylus*, the university literary magazine. She won a scholarship to Barnard College in New York City in 1925, where she studied anthropology under Franz Boas, one of the most renowned anthropologists of the era. After her graduation in 1928 Hurston continued her graduate studies with Boas at Columbia University. While in New York, Hurston became involved in the Harlem Renaissance, publishing short stories and establishing friendships with many important black authors. Along with Langston Hughes and other black writers, Hurston founded *Fire!*, a literary magazine devoted to black culture, in 1927. However, the magazine folded after its first issue due to financial difficulties and a destructive fire. fire.

With the assistance of fellowships and a private grant from a New York socialite interested in "primitive Negro art," Hurston returned to her hometown to collect folklore. *Mules and Men* (1935) is the result of Hurston's anthropological field work and academic studies. The book includes many folktales, which the tellers call "lies." These "lies," which contain hidden social and philosophical messages, were an important part of the culture of that region. Hurston also provides descriptions of voodoo practices and beliefs. Critics of the time praised *Mules and Men* for its information on folklore practices. However, some black critics, especially Sterling Brown, charged that Hurston ignored racial oppression and exploitation in the South. These accusations recurred throughout Hurston's literary career.

In her first novel, *Jonah's Gourd Vine* (1934), Hurston combined her knowledge of folklore with biblical themes. Loosely based on the lives of her parents, *Jonah's Gourd Vine* centers on John Pearson, a respected minister and town leader, and the life and death of his first wife, Lucy Potts. Written in the southern black dialect that Hurston used throughout her fic-

Courtesy of Clifford J. Hurston, Jr.

tion, *Jonah's Gourd Vine* received critical attention for her "notable talents as a story teller." In *Moses, Man of the Mountain* (1939) Hurston successfully utilized data obtained from her studies in folklore and voodoo. Basing her story on the premise that most black Americans view their heritage as similar to that of the Hebrews in ancient Egypt, Hurston wrote *Moses* as an allegorical novel of American slavery. Moses is portrayed not as a prophet but as a powerful magician and voodoo practitioner. Critics praised Hurston's imaginative depiction of Moses, and some considered her use of black dialect important to the development of the narrative.

Most critics maintain that *Their Eyes Were Watching God* is Hurston's best work. The novel, now considered by some a classic in feminist literature, tells the story of a woman's quest for fulfillment and liberation in a society where women are objects to be used for physical burden and pleasure. Upon publication, critical opinion of the novel varied. Otis Ferguson contended that the book "is absolutely free of Uncle Toms," while Richard Wright accused Hurston of manipulating white stereotypes of black people to attract white readers. Other black critics at the time attacked Hurston for her lack of racial awareness. Contemporary critics, among them Alice Walker and June Jordan, have refuted these charges, asserting that Hurston was acutely aware of the racial climate of the time and describing the novel as an affirmation of black culture.

Critics generally agree that Hurston's last published novel, *Seraph on the Suwanee* (1948), is her most ambitious but least successful work of fiction. The novel is thematically similar to *Jonah's Gourd Vine* and *Their Eyes Were Watching God. Seraph on the Suwanee* is the story of a neurotic woman's search for self-esteem and her attempt to return the love of her husband. In this book, Hurston's major characters are poor whites instead of the black inhabitants of Eatonville of her previous novels. This radical change prompted some black critics to label Hurston an assimilationist. The absence of the colorful prose that was associated with Hurston's earlier work has also been noted.

In her autobiography, *Dust Tracks on a Road* (1942), Hurston revealed her stance on race relations in America. She maintained that black artists should celebrate the positive aspects of black American life instead of indulging in what she termed "the sobbing school of Negrohood." Some critics attribute Hurston's early years in Eatonville as the major source for that position, for Eatonville was the first organized effort by blacks at self-government. However, Hurston did acknowledge racial prejudice, and she published essays on the problem in several journals and magazines. Hurston's early play *Color Struck!* (1925) addresses bigotry within the black community, which favors light-skinned over dark-skinned blacks. Recent critical discussion indicates that the original manuscript of *Dust Tracks on a Road* included severe criticism of American racial and foreign policy, but these sections were omitted because Hurston's editors felt that some readers might interpret her views as an attack on America's role in World War II.

Many critical studies of Hurston have focused on her private life. Early in her career she depended on white patronage for support and financial assistance. Langston Hughes wrote that Hurston was "simply paid just to sit around and represent the Negro race." Other writers who knew Hurston during the 1920s and 1930s contend that she intentionally portrayed the role of a childlike primitive in order to advance her career. Hurston was caught between the emphasis on the "exotic" aspects of the Harlem Renaissance and the angry voice of black literature during the 1940s and 1950s. Although some people have questioned Hurston's integrity, her work is valued for its knowledgeable depiction of black culture and for its insight into the human condition.

(See also *CLC*, Vol. 7 and *Contemporary Authors*, Vols. 85-88.)

FANNIE HURST

[*Hurst, a popular novelist in the 1920s and 1930s, employed Hurston as a secretary-companion during Hurston's first years in New York City.*]

Here in ["Jonah's Gourd Vine"] there springs, with validity and vitality a fresh note which, to this commentator, is unique.

Here is negro folk-lore interpreted at its authentic best in fiction form of a high order.

A brilliantly facile spade has turned over rich new earth. Worms lift up, the hottish smells of soil rise, negro toes dredge into that soil, smells of racial fecundity are about.

As a matter of fact, not even excepting Langston Hughes, it is doubtful if there is any literary precedent for the particular type of accomplishment that characterizes "Jonah's Gourd Vine."

Miss Hurston has penetrated into the complicated lore and mythology of her people with an authority and an unselfconsciousness that has not its equal in similar annals. Even through what might easily be dialectic mists, her negroes emerge on the authenticity of her story-telling. (p. 7)

The author's treatment of whites is as natural and without change of key as it would need to be if she is to succeed in keeping universality the dominant note of her book.

Humor, heartache, ambition, frustration, superstition, fear, cussedness, fidelity and infidelity flow naturally behind white and black pores.

Point of departure between races leaps from the springboard of the teeth rather than from the deeper recesses of the heart, and whatever racial issues are raised are borne out of the grandly natural sources of the power of the author's story-telling.

John and Lucy Pearson, and every inhabitant of the narrative, move against a background embroidered in folk-lore and symbolism, yet themselves so real and so human and so true, that rising above the complicated machinery of color differentiations, they bring the reader to fresh realization that races, regardless of pigmentation, behave like human beings. (p. 8)

> *Fannie Hurst, in an introduction to* Jonah's Gourd Vine *by Zora Neale Hurston, J. B. Lippincott Company, 1934, pp. 7-8.*

JOSEPHINE PINCKNEY

["**Jonah's Gourd Vine**"] is the product of a fortunate combination of circumstances. [Hurston] writes as a Negro understanding her people and having opportunities that could come to no white person, however sympathetic, of seeing them when they are utterly themselves. But she writes as a Negro whose intelligence is firmly in the saddle, who recognizes the value of an objective style in writing, and who is able to use the wealth of material available to her with detachment and with a full grasp of its dramatic qualities. Considering her especial temptations, her sustaining of the objective viewpoint is remarkable. She writes of her people with honesty, with sympathy, without extenuation. The white man is portrayed but little and then without bitterness. This is a novel about Negroes and she is not to be deflected by controversy from her preoccupation with her characters as the stuff of art....

Miss Hurston makes effective use of biblical rhythms in the passages that describe mass emotions quickening and becoming richer as they mount to a climax. John Buddy, the central figure of "**Jonah's Gourd Vine**," becomes later the Rev. Pearson, and his sermons are poems in Old Testament style, exemplifying that affinity of the Negro for the strong rhythms of Hebrew poetry....

There is some uncertainty in the handling of the narrative. Quarrels, trial proceedings, conflicts occur which are never resolved but merely slip out of the story as though the author had conceived them as links in a progression but had forgotten her intention.... When all is told this background is what lingers most vividly in the mind—a group composed of many deftly-drawn personalities, childlike, shrewd, violent, gay; and all the colors drawn together by the strong ingredient of Negro humor.

> *Josephine Pinckney, "A Pungent, Poetic Novel about Negroes," in* New York Herald Tribune Books, *May 6, 1934, p. 7.*

MARGARET WALLACE

"**Jonah's Gourd Vine**" can be called without fear of exaggeration the most vital and original novel about the American Negro that has yet been written by a member of the Negro race. Miss Hurston . . . has made the study of Negro folklore her special province. This may very well account for the brilliantly authentic flavor of her novel and for her excellent rendition of Negro dialect. Unlike the dialect in most novels about the American Negro, this does not seem to be merely the speech of white men with the spelling distorted. Its essence lies rather in the rhythm and balance of the sentences, in the warm artlessness of the phrasing.

No amount of special knowledge of her subject, however, could have made "**Jonah's Gourd Vine**" other than a mediocre novel if it were not for Miss Hurston's notable talents as a storyteller. In John, the big yellow Negro preacher, and in Lucy Potts, his tiny brown wife, she has created two characters who are intensely real and human and whose outlines will remain in the reader's memory long after the book has been laid aside. They are part and parcel of the tradition of their race, which is as different from ours as night from day; yet Miss Hurston has delineated them with such warmth and sympathy that they appeal to us first of all as human beings, confronting a complex of human problems with whatever grace and humor, intelligence and steadfastness they can muster. (pp. 6-7)

Not the least charm of the book . . . is its language—rich, expressive and lacking in self-conscious artifice. From the rolling and dignified rhythms of John's last sermon to the humorous aptness of such a word as ''shickalacked,'' to express the noise and motion of a locomotive, there will be much in it to delight the reader. It is to be hoped that Miss Hurston will give us other novels in the same colorful idiom. (p. 7)

Margaret Wallace, ''Real Negro People,'' in The New York Times Book Review, *May 6, 1934, pp. 6-7.*

H. I. BROCK

[Here, in "**Mules and Men**,"] is the high color of Color as a racial element in the American scene. And it comes neither from Catfish Row nor from a Harlem with a jazz tempo affected by the rhythm of Broadway to which contribute so many exotic strains newer to that scene than the African. In this book . . . [Hurston] has invited the outside world to listen in while her own people are being as natural as they can never be when white folks are literally present. This in an environment in the deep South to which the Negro is as native as he can be anywhere on this Western Continent. . . .

[Hurston] has gone back to her native Florida village—a Negro settlement—with her native racial quality entirely unspoiled by her Northern college education. She has plunged into the social pleasures of the black community and made a record of what is said and done when Negroes are having a good gregarious time, dancing, singing, fishing, and above all, and incessantly, talking.

The talk (as those fragmentary memories of long ago come back to remind us) runs on such occasions generally to competition in telling what are unashamedly labeled ''lies.'' These ''lies'' are woven out of the folklore of the black race in the South—with its deeper African background dimmed by years and distance. It is the same folklore, of course, out of which have been rescued for our nurseries the milder elements—the tales of Br'er Rabbit, Br'er Fox and the rest of the talking animals that children reared in the South had listened to long before Uncle Remus made them classic for the whole country.

But as the feast is spread here it is not always nursery fare. Not by any means. Some of it is strong meat for those who take life lustily—with accompaniment of flashes of razor blades and great gusts of Negro laughter.

The book is packed with tall tales rich with flavor and alive with characteristic turns of speech. Those of us who have known the Southern Negro from our youth find him here speaking the language of his tribe as familiarly as if it came straight out of his own mouth and had not been translated into type and transmitted through the eye to the ear. Which is to say that a very tricky dialect has been rendered with rare simplicity and fidelity into symbols so little adequate to convey its true values that the achievement is remarkable.

At the end you have a very fair idea of how the other color enjoys life as well as an amazing roundup of that color's very best stories in its very best manner—which is a match for any story-telling there is in the two qualities of luxuriant imagination and vivid and expressive language.

H. I. Brock, ''The Full, True Flavor of Life in a Negro Community,'' in The New York Times Book Review, *November 10, 1935, p. 4.*

FRANZ BOAS

Ever since the time of Uncle Remus, Negro folk-lore has exerted a strong attraction upon the imagination of the American public. Negro tales, songs and sayings without end, as well as descriptions of Negro magic and voodoo, have appeared; but in all of them the intimate setting in the social life of the Negro has been given very inadequately.

It is the great merit of Miss Hurston's [*Mules and Men*] that she entered into the homely life of the southern Negro as one of them and was fully accepted as such by the companions of her childhood. Thus she has been able to penetrate through that affected demeanor by which the Negro excludes the White observer effectively from participating in his true inner life. Miss Hurston has been equally successful in gaining the confidence of the voodoo doctors and she gives us much that throws a new light upon the much discussed voodoo beliefs and practices. Added to all this is the charm of a loveable personality and of a revealing style which makes Miss Hurston's work an unusual contribution to our knowledge of the true inner life of the Negro.

To the student of cultural history the material presented is valuable not only by giving the Negro's reaction to everyday events, to his emotional life, his humor and passions, but it throws into relief also the peculiar amalgamation of African and European tradition which is so important for understanding historically the character of American Negro life, with its strong African background in the West Indies, the importance of which diminishes with increasing distance from the south.

Franz Boas, in a foreword to Mules and Men *by Zora Neale Hurston, Kegan Paul, Trench, Trubner & Co., Ltd., 1936, p. 5.*

THOMAS CALDECOT CHUBB

[If] "**Jonah's Gourd Vine**" is a story with a background of sociology, "**Mules and Men**" is a social study with gusto of a story. Indeed, it is hard to think of anybody interested in the negro whom this new book will not delight. The southern raconteur who justly prides himself upon his large store of stories about the colored man will here find himself beaten on his own ground, but having gained a new supply of tales to tell. The student of folk-lore will find a well-filled source-book. And he who loves the negro, or is amused by him, or burns for his wrongs, or thinks he ought to know his place, will find, each of them, as good a portrayal of the negro's character as he is ever likely to see.

Not, either, a one-sided portrayal. The gaiety, the poetry, the resourcefulness and the wit are set down, but so also are the impulsiveness, the shiftlessness, the living in the moment only. Short of associating with the negro daily, there is no way you can learn more about him. Indeed, from Miss Hurston you will find out many things that, even if you live surrounded by negroes for a long time, you might never know. For as she says, "the negro, in spite of his open-faced laughter, his seeming acquiescence, is particularly evasive." He tells the white man what he thinks the white man wants to know, or what he feels he ought to know.

The book is divided into two parts. The first part deals with "Folk Tales" and the second with "Hoodoo." I find the second part interesting, but dare not judge it. I am aware that hoodoo plays a great part in the lives of certain negroes, but I have the teasing conviction that it has always been, and always will be over-emphasized because of those who like its appeal to the romantically macabre. The first part, however, is magnificent. (pp. 181-82)

Quite expectedly, most of these stories are humorous, and a large part of what remain are fantastic; but there are a few grim, a few ghostly and a few sardonic. Of the humorous stories, the greater part deal with slaves who outwit "de ole marster," or with animals, representing the negro, who outwit animals representing the white man. For I am sure everybody must now realize that Brer Rabbit is "the brother in black," as is also Brer Gopher when he outwits rather than outruns Brer Deer. Such ugliness as there is, is mainly in the background. (p. 182)

Thomas Caldecot Chubb, in a review of "Mules and Men," in The North American Review, *Vol. 241, No. 1, March, 1936, pp. 181-83.*

THE TIMES LITERARY SUPPLEMENT

There is nothing in the title to indicate that ["**Mules and Men**"] is a picture of the negro mind revealed with commendable objectivity by a negro writer with a vivid pen. It is straining the term to call these stories folk-lore, since in themselves they are individual flights of fancy. Yet in sum they project, as it were, a composite image of the American negro's imagination with its whimsicality, its American love of exaggeration, and its under-dog's admiration of victorious cunning constantly pitted against the dominance of the white man. Two-thirds of the book consists of tales of varying degrees of tallness: there are tales of animals, parallel exploits to those of Brer Rabbit, tales telling why the porpoise has his tail on crossways, and how the possum lost the hair off his tail. . . .

The book therefore reads rather like a compilation of stories for after-dinner speakers, but actually it is scientific in intention and in method. This applies also to the chapters on Hoodoo—the magic ritual practised by the Southern negros. . . . [Here

the author] describes circumstantially the superstitious rites involving the slaughter of animals and the usual devices of sympathetic magic which are used to injure an enemy, compose a love dispute, or exert supernatural powers. Here was the scientific mind submitting itself to the most severe discipline in the study of superstition by becoming for the time being superstitious, but emerging with enough detachment to describe its position in a parable of the cat who washed its face and "used its manners" *after* it had eaten the rat.

A review of "Mules and Men," in The Times Literary Supplement, *No. 1779, March 7, 1936, p. 200.*

NICK AARON FORD

[*This essay was originally published in 1936.*]

[One] can readily see why Miss Hurston's first novel, **Jonah's Gourd Vine,** was received with small enthusiasm from certain quarters of the Negro race. With a grasp of her material that has seldom been equaled by a writer of her race, she had every opportunity of creating a masterpiece of the age. But she failed. She failed not from lack of skill but from lack of vision. The hero, John Buddy, who rose from an outcast bastard of an Alabama tenant farm to a man of wealth and influence, could have been another Ben Hur, bursting the unjust shackles that had bound him to a rotten social order and winning the applause even of his enemies. But unfortunately, his rise to religious prominence and financial ease is but a millstone about his neck. He is held back by some unseen cord which seems to be tethered to his racial heritage. Life crushes him almost to death, but he comes out of the mills with no greater insight into the deep mysteries which surround him. Such a phenomenon, although not intended by Miss Hurston as a type of all Negro manhood, is seized upon by thoughtless readers of other races as a happy confirmation of what they already faintly believe: namely, that the Negro is incapable of profiting by experience or of understanding the deeper mysteries of life. (pp. 99-100)

Nick Aaron Ford, in a postscript to his The Contemporary Negro Novel: A Study in Race Relations, *McGrath Publishing Company, 1968, pp. 94-102.*

SHEILA HIBBEN

[Zora Hurston] is an author who writes with her head as well as with her heart, and at a time when there seems to be some principle of physics set dead against the appearance of novelists who give out a cheerful warmth and at the same time write with intelligence. You have to be as tired as I am of writers who offer to do as much for folks as Atlas, Joan of Arc, Faith, Hope and Charity, Numerology, NBC and Q.E.D. to be as pleased as I am with Zora Hurston's ["**Their Eyes Were Watching God**"]. . . .

Readers of "**Jonah's Gourd Vine**" and "**Mules and Men**" are familiar with Miss Hurston's vibrant Negro lingo with its guitar twang of poetry, and its deep, vivid humor. If in "**Their Eyes Were Watching God**" the flowers of the sweet speech of black people are not quite so full blown and striking as in those earlier books, on the other hand, the sap flows more freely, and the roots touch deeper levels of human life. The author has definitely crossed over from the limbo of folklore into the realm of conventional narrative.

As a great many novelists—good and bad—ought to know by this time, it is awfully easy to write nonsense about Negroes.

That Miss Hurston can write of them with simple tenderness, so that her story is filled with the ache of her own people, is, I think, due to the fact that she is not too much preoccupied with the current fetish of the primitive. In a rich prose (which has, at the same time, a sort of nervous sensibility) she tells the tale of a girl who "wanted things sweet with mah marriage, lak when you sit under a pear tree and think."

If I tried to tell you the plot of **"Their Eyes Were Watching God"** (an inept enough title, to my mind) I would only make a mess of it, so dependent is the story upon Miss Hurston's warm, vibrant touch. There are homely, unforgettable phrases of colored people (you would know, all right, that a man wasn't fooling if he threatened to kill you cemetery daid); there is a gigantic and magnificent picture of a hurricane in the Everglades country of Florida; and there is a flashing, gleaming riot of black people, with a limitless exuberance of humor, and a wild, strange sadness. There is also death. . . . Mostly, though, there is life—a swarming, passionate life, and . . . there is a sense of triumph and glory when the tale is done.

> *Sheila Hibben, "Vibrant Book Full of Nature and Salt," in* New York Herald Tribune Books, *September 26, 1937, p. 2.*

RICHARD WRIGHT

Miss Hurston seems to have no desire whatever to move in the direction of serious fiction. (pp. 22, 25)

Miss Hurston can write; but her prose is cloaked in that facile sensuality that has dogged Negro expression since the days of Phillis Wheatley. Her dialogue [in *Their Eyes Were Watching God*] manages to catch the psychological movements of the Negro folk-mind in their pure simplicity, but that's as far as it goes.

Miss Hurston *voluntarily* continues in her novel the tradition which was *forced* upon the Negro in the theater, that is, the minstrel technique that makes the "white folks" laugh. Her characters eat and laugh and cry and work and kill; they swing like a pendulum eternally in that safe and narrow orbit in which America likes to see the Negro live: between laughter and tears. . . .

The sensory sweep of her novel carries no theme, no message, no thought. In the main, her novel is not addressed to the Negro, but to a white audience whose chauvinistic tastes she knows how to satisfy. She exploits that phase of Negro life which is "quaint," the phase which evokes a piteous smile on the lips of the "superior" race. (p. 25)

> *Richard Wright, "Between Laughter and Tears," in* New Masses, *Vol. XXV, No. 2, October 5, 1937, pp. 22, 25.**

OTIS FERGUSON

It isn't that [*Their Eyes Were Watching God*] is bad, but that it deserves to be better. In execution it is too complex and wordily pretty, even dull—yet its conception of these simple Florida Negroes is unaffected and really beautiful.

[There is] some very shrewd picturing of Negro life in its naturally creative and unself-conscious grace (the book is absolutely free of Uncle Toms, absolutely unlimbered of the clumsy formality, defiance and apology of a Minority Cause). And when Tea Cake [the central character's husband] swaggers

in with his banter and music and rolling bones and fierce tender loyalty, there is a lot more picturing of what we would never have known: Darktown and the work on the Everglades muck, the singing and boasting and play-acting, people living the good life but, in the absence of the sour and pretentious and proper, seeming to live it in a different world. It is the time of the Big Blow in Florida, and though Tea Cake and [the central character] Janie fought through it, the aftermath left the man with hydrophobia, and she had to kill him like a dog. Janie went back to her town after that, her late years to be mellowed with the knowledge of how wide life can be.

If this isn't as grand as it should be, the breakdown comes in the conflict between the true vision and its overliterary expression. Crises of feeling are rushed over too quickly for them to catch hold, and then presently we are in a tangle of lush exposition and overblown symbols; action is described and characters are talked about, and everything is more heard than seen. The speech is founded in observation and sometimes wonderfully so, a gold mine of traditional sayings. . . .

But although the spoken word is remembered, it is not passed on. Dialect is really sloppy, in fact. Suggestion of speech difference is a difficult art, and none should practise it who can't grasp its first rule—that the key to difference must be indicated by the signature of a different rhythm and by the delicate tampering with an occasional main word. To let the really important words stand as in Webster and then consistently misspell all the eternal particles that are no more than an aspiration in any tongue, is to set up a mood of Eddie Cantor in blackface. The reader's eye is caught by distortions of the inconsequential, until a sentence in the supposedly vernacular reads with about this emphasis: "Dat wuz uh might fine thing fuh you tuh do."

And so all this conflict between the real life we want to read about and the superwordy, flabby lyric discipline we are so sick of leaves a good story where it never should have been potentially: in the gray category of neuter gender, declension indefinite.

> *Otis Ferguson, "You Can't Hear Their Voices," in* The New Republic, *Vol. LXXXXII, No. 1193, October 13, 1937, p. 276.*

STERLING BROWN

[*The following essay was originally published in 1937.*]

[Zora Neale Hurston's] short stories **"Drenched With Light," "Spunk"** and **"The Gilded Six Bits"** showed a command of folklore and idiom excelled by no earlier Negro novelist. *Jonah's Gourd Vine* (1934) recounts the rise of handsome, stalwart John Buddy from plowboy to moderator of the Baptists of Florida. But his flair for preaching and praying is exceeded by his weakness for women. . . . Loosely constructed, the novel presents authentic scenes of timber camps, railroad gangs with the "hammer-muscling men, the liars, fighters, bluffers and lovers," and the all-colored towns of Florida. The folk-speech is richly, almost too consistently, poetic. The characters are less developed than the setting; and the life they live is self-contained and untroubled. Nevertheless, *Jonah's Gourd Vine* contains the stuff of life, well observed and rendered.

A trained anthropologist as well as a native of Florida, Zora Neale Hurston has made in *Mules and Men* (1935) the first substantial collection of folktales by a Negro scholar. Zestful towards her material, and completely unashamed of it, she ingratiated herself with the tellers of tall tales. . . . Miss Hurston's ''big old lies'' are a delight to read. . . . Unfortunately, *Mules and Men* does not uncover so much that white collectors have been unable to get. The tales ring genuine, but there seem to be omissions. The picture is too pastoral, with only a bit of grumbling about hard work, or a few slave anecdotes that turn the tables on old marster. The bitterness that E.C.L. Adams recorded in *Nigger to Nigger* is not to be found in *Mules and Men*.

Miss Hurston's second novel, *Their Eyes Were Watching God* (1937) is informed and sympathetic. . . . There are good sketches of the all-colored town where comic-serious debates and tall tales are told on the mayor's store porch. But the love story and the poetic folk-speech are the chief interests. The people, ''ugly from ignorance and broken from being poor,'' who swarm upon the ''muck'' for short-time jobs, do not get much attention. (pp. 159-61)

> Sterling Brown, ''Southern Realism,'' in his ''Negro Poetry and Drama'' and ''The Negro in American Fiction,'' *Atheneum, 1969, pp. 151-68.**

CARL CARMER

Folklore is a spontaneous product of vitality and imagination. It needs a careful interpreter whose reports have these same two qualities. Seldom has there been a happier combination than that of the vivid, fantastic folklore of the West Indies and interpreter Zora Neale Hurston. . . . [She is] one of the most delightfully alive personalities of our day. She knows what she is talking about and she talks with a zest and a humor and a genuineness that make her work the best that I know in the field of contemporary folklore.

The first part of **''Tell My Horse''** is a sort of practice walk-around in Jamaica. . . . Stopping off at that British island to hunt the wild hog, collect proverbs, observe marriage customs, hear the ''Night Song After Death'' served to let her get her hand in for the big job ahead.

It is when Zora Hurston begins writing about her life and observations among the denizens of the misty mountains of Haiti that she becomes incomparable. A few works on Haitian lore have been too dully sensational, a few have been dully academic. Miss Hurston's book is so filled with the spirit of her subject that the whole feeling of its spine-chilling supernatural grotesquerie encompasses the reader and he has a hard time convincing himself that he is reading the authentic work of an honest, painstaking scholar.

Perhaps because she is herself a Negro, Miss Hurston makes her readers conscious of the deep current of racial poetry that runs beneath the rituals of Haitian life. Her sympathies are so strong that she seems to identify herself with her subject. She is but another folk teller of the tales she has uncovered, even a better teller than those who have preceded her. . . .

Zora Hurston has come back from her visit to the two near islands with a harvest unbelievably rich. Her book is full of keen social comment relieved with constant humor, it is packed with good stories, accounts of folk religions, songs with both music and words as all songs should be reported. There are few more beautiful tellings of a folk tale than ''God and the Pintards,'' the last story in the volume.

> Carl Carmer, ''In Haiti and Jamaica,'' in New York Herald Tribune Books, *October 23, 1938, p. 2.*

PERCY HUTCHISON

[**''Moses: Man of the Mountain''**] is the story of Moses as the Negro sees and interprets [him]. . . . None the less reverent in conception than that of the white man, there is one aspect of the work of the great leader of the Israelites which holds particular fascination for the Negro, so that his view becomes especially interesting, and, again always in a reverent way, entertaining. All primitive peoples have an inordinate love of magic, or what appears to be magic, and the African most of all. His descendants in this country may hold that the magic of the radio is more awesome than such relics of voodoo prestidigitation as they may have witnessed or heard about. But even they have traditions that will not die, and one of them, according to Zora Neale Hurston, is that Moses was just about the greatest magician ever in the world. He led his followers out of bondage, because his was better ''medicine'' than that of Pharaoh's magicians. He talked to God face to face, but he had been singled out by God for this honor because Jehovah recognized the superlative magical power of Moses. Consequently there comes about almost a transposition of Moses and God in the Negro's point of view of their relationship, or so it would seem from Miss Hurston's pages. Moses seems almost to be greater than God. But this is not irreverence, for it is undoubtedly due to the fact that it was easier for a primitive mind to endow a human being with mystical powers than to grasp a purely rational concept of deity. The author's Man of the Mountain is a very living and very human person. . . .

For some reason not apparent the author reduces the dialect as she proceeds, and although a more closely knit narrative is the result, the book loses something in flavor. Moses, rescued by Pharaoh's daughter, is brought up as an Egyptian prince, as the leader of an army; not for a long time is he to be the Mountain Man. According to the Book of Exodus Moses was threescore years of age when he delivered the Children of Israel out of their bondage, but little is told of Moses during the intervening years. It is the legendary Moses whom the Negroes have built that Miss Hurston gives us in the first part of the book, a Moses painted in rich imagination. . . .

It is impossible to say to what extent Miss Hurston has woven many legends and interpretations into one and how often she is making verbatim use of given, but, presumably, only orally extant, tradition. But the narrative becomes one of great power. It is warm with friendly personality and pulsating with homely and profound eloquence and religious fervor. The author has done an exceptionally fine piece of work far off the beaten tracks of literature. Her homespun book is literature in every best sense of the word.

> Percy Hutchison, ''Led His People Free,'' in The New York Times Book Review, *November 19, 1939, p. 21.*

CARL CARMER

The story of Moses has roots deep in the Hebraic imagination and Jews are proud to call it their own. Their minds have been especially busy with it in the last few years as the old narrative of persecution and injustice has repeated itself.

Now [in **''Moses: Man of the Mountain''**] Zora Neale Hurston has told the story of the law-giver from the point of view of another race, also once enslaved and persecuted, and it has lent itself so aptly that it has become a fine Negro novel. Miss Hurston has made a prose tapestry that sparkles with characteristic Negro humor though it never loses dignity. With a cunning that never lessens her integrity she has laid a new emphasis here, assumed a different motivation there, and the tale has emerged as honest and as strong as ever—and wholly alien to its racial origin. Naturally a comparison with Roark Bradford's stories of Negro figures in Biblical tales suggests itself, but Miss Hurston's characters are less naive than those of "The Green Pastures." They have much the same humor, the same directness, but they are more sophisticated and more wise—as befits a serious novel. Moses and Aaron and Miriam and Zipporah are characters in whose changing relationships any novelist could well delight.

The most exciting thing about this exciting book is its serious use of Negro speech rhythms to tell the story. That Negro song is the most powerful influence on American music is a truism few deny. Readers have long admired the homely and poetic figures of speech which environment and temperament have inspired in American Negroes. But not many of us are aware of how much our native language has been enriched by the distinctive inflections and sharply defined rhythms of the talk of black Americans. The prose of Miss Hurston, who is an accomplished scholar as well as a sensitive artist, teaches us to realize the contribution her race is making to American expression.

Carl Carmer, "Biblical Story in Negro Rhythm," in New York Herald Tribune Books, *November 26, 1939, p. 5.*

PHILIP SLOMOVITZ

[It] is exceedingly interesting to read a new biography of the Hebrew prophet [Moses] written by an American Negro. Zora Neale Hurston has already acquired fame as a writer, and in *Moses: Man of the Mountain* she reveals marked ability as a student and interpreter of Negro folkways. It is a magnificent story, but it is weak in its interpretation of the ethical contributions of the prophet and in its treatment of the code of laws handed down by him. For to Jews, Moses is primarily the lawgiver, the great creator of the great code known as the Decalogue. But Miss Hurston presents Moses as a great "voodoo man," which is the position given him by the Negro. Her distinctive contribution is her brilliant study of the problem of emancipation, done as perhaps only a Negro could do it.

In the introduction, Miss Hurston explains that the reason Moses is revered as he is by her people is because he had the power to go up the mountain to bring down the laws and because he talked with God face to face. She describes the early life of the Hebrews in Egypt, and in the course of conversations she interprets their attitudes, fears, reactions and hopes. There is a discussion, for instance, between Amram and a comrade before the birth of Moses. They speak of Pharaoh and the lack of nerve on the part of the people to deal with him. Amram's comrade says that he hates himself for not trying violence against Pharaoh even if they kill him for it. Amram replies: "That's what I hate 'em for too, making me scared to die. It's a funny thing, the less people have to live for, the less nerve they have to risk losing—nothing." Throughout this study there is alternate defiance and determination. When bolstered up by a leader like Moses, the people gain courage. When their stomachs happen to be empty, they cry for slavery.

Miss Hurston portrays Moses as an Egyptian who had met with displeasure at Pharaoh's court. But aside from this deviation from accepted biblical fact, she adheres to the biblical story.

She is especially effective when she deals with Moses' miracle-producing powers and she ascribes to him extreme strength in his right arm as the producer of miraculous results.

Her Moses knows his people and understands what it means to deal with slaves. When Aaron suggests to him a shorter road than the wilderness of the Red Sea, Moses replies: "I know it, Aaron, but our people are leaving slavery. It takes free men for fighting. The Philistines might let us through without fighting, but it is too much of a risk. If these people saw an army right now they would turn right around and run right back into Goshen."

Equally significant is Miss Hurston's interpretation of Moses' reaction to the report of the spies sent to study the Promised Land. When he finds that they are still dominated by a slave psychology, he decides that the only way out of the difficulty is to keep the Hebrews in the wilderness for forty years until the generation of slaves has disappeared and Israel has become a people of free men.

Miss Hurston has written a splendid study of slave emancipation. From this point of view her biography of Moses is invaluable.

Philip Slomovitz, "The Negro's Moses," in The Christian Century, *Vol. LVI, No. 49, December 6, 1939, p. 1504.*

ARNA BONTEMPS

[Zora Neale Hurston's autobiography] **"Dust Tracks on a Road"** should not be read for its comments on the Negro as a whole. Miss Hurston feels that God made Negroes, as he made all other people, "duck by duck." She says, "That was the only way I could see them." She urges the powerful of the earth to "think kindly of those who walk in the dust." She suggests to the humble ones that they respect those who are not so humble. She invites all to be kissing-friends in the hope that we may breed, please God, hundreds of generations hence, a noble world. Meanwhile, she concludes, if we don't all meet in this world, we may "meet at a barbecue."

Miss Hurston deals very simply with the more serious aspects of Negro life in America—she ignores them. She has done right well by herself in the kind of world she found.

Arna Bontemps, "From Eatonville, Fla. to Harlem," in New York Herald Tribune Books, *November 22, 1942, p. 3.*

BEATRICE SHERMAN

["**Dust Tracks on a Road**"] is a thumping story, though it has none of the horrid earmarks of the [Horatio] Alger-type climb. Zora Neale Hurston has a considerable reputation as anthropologist and writer. When her autobiography begins she was one of eight children in a Negro family with small prospects of making a name for herself. Yet her story is forthright and without frills. Its emphasis lies on her fighting spirit in the struggle to achieve the education she felt she had to have. The uses to which it was put—good uses too—were the fruit of things that cropped up spontaneously, demanding to be done. . . .

Her whole story is live and vivid. Told in gusty language, it is full of the graphic metaphors and similes that color Negro speech at its richest, sometimes in direct quotations from folk stories—those lying sessions at the village store—and sometimes woven in with her own warm style. There is no "hush-mouth modesty" about the book, for Zora Neale Hurston would not "low-rate the human race" by undue expurgation of her story. . . .

[There] are philosophical chapters on books (the Hurston books), love, "My People!" and religion. Then impression simmers down to a feeling that the author regards the Negro race much as she regards any other race—as made up of some good, some bad and a lot of medium. The problems they face are those of any other race, with the disadvantage of being a younger lot. Anyway, her story is an encouraging and enjoyable one for any member of the human race. Any race might well be proud to have more members of the caliber and stamina of Zora Neale Hurston.

> Beatrice Sherman, "Zora Hurston's Story," in The
> New York Times Book Review, November 29, 1942,
> p. 44.

WORTH TUTTLE HEDDEN

Though **"Seraph on the Suwanee"** is the love story of a daughter of Florida Crackers and of a scion of plantation owners, it is no peasant-marries-the prince tale. Arvay Henson, true Cracker in breeding, is above her caste in temperament; James Kenneth Meserve is plain Jim who speaks the dialect and who has turned his back on family, with its static living in the past, to become foreman in a west Florida turpentine camp. Neither is it a romance of the boy-meets-girl school. Beginning conventionally enough with a seduction (a last minute one when Arvay is in her wedding dress), it ends twenty-odd years later when the protagonists are about to be grandparents. In this denouement the divergent lines of Miss Hurston's astonishing, bewildering talent meet to give us a reconciliation scene between a middle-aged man and a middle-aged woman that is erotically exciting and a description of the technique of shrimping that is meticulously exact. Emotional, expository; meandering, unified; naive, sophisticated; sympathetic, caustic; comic, tragic; lewd, chaste—one could go on indefinitely reiterating this novel's contradictions and still end helplessly with the adjective unique.

Incompatible strains in the novel mirror the complexity of the author. Miss Hurston shuttles between the sexes, the professions, and the races as if she were man and woman, scientist and creative writer, white and Negro. She is at her best as a man among men objectively portraying Jim and his work-a-day life with such verisimilitude that we never doubt "whatever God neglected, Jim Meserve took care of." A fight in a bar complete with appropriate obscenity, a struggle between a man and a diamondback, between a pilot and the sea, are her meat, and, in the speech of her characters, she do know how to cook it. . . .

With Arvay and domestic routine Miss Hurston is less successful, holding her guilt-ridden seraph too consistently in the cloudy sky of the emotions. She knows every intimate detail of Arvay's physical self and reveals it to the point of absurdity, but she has to construct a visible Freudian fretwork to give us understanding of her psychic self. On the other hand, only a woman could animate the adolescent and adult Arvay, now going her wishy-washy unhappy way, now facing facts and courageously burning her past when she burns her house. . . .

The generic life of the Florida Cracker from the cradle to the grave is so documentary in the dramatization of mores and language it seems incredible that one not born to the breed, even though a neighbor and an anthropologist, could be its biographer. Miss Hurston knows her Florida Negro as she knows her Florida white and characterizes them with the same acumen, but she gives them no more attention than the plot demands. In Jim's relation with the colored workmen whose know-how has helped him get rich, in Arvay's petulant jealousy of them, in her triumph over her past when she sits at the table with Titty-Nipple and Cup-Cake, the old southern adage that the aristocrat is the darky's best friend is symbolically italicized. . . .

Reading this astonishing novel, you wish that Miss Hurston had used the scissors and smoothed the seams. Having read it, you would like to be able to remember every extraneous incident and every picturesque metaphor.

> Worth Tuttle Hedden, "Turpentine and Moonshine,"
> in New York Herald Tribune Weekly Book Review,
> October 10, 1948, p. 2.

DARWIN T. TURNER

A study of Zora Neale Hurston, writer, properly begins with Zora Neale Hurston, wanderer. In her autobiography, *Dust Tracks on a Road*—in her artful candor and coy reticence, her contradictions and silences, her irrationalities and extravagant boasts which plead for the world to recognize and respect her—one perceives the matrix of her fiction, the seeds that sprouted and the cankers that destroyed.

Contradictions in the autobiography reveal that the content was prepared with concern for its appeal to readers, especially white readers. By reporting her father's frequent warnings that her impudence would cause her to forget to remain in the docile, subservient position to which Southern society assigns Afro-Americans, Miss Hurston created a self-image as a fearless and defiant fighter for her rights. In actuality, however, even white acquaintances were astonished by her apparent indifference to her own dignity or that of other blacks. (pp. 90-1)

In contrast to her affable reactions to the white people in her book are her violent rivalries and antagonisms toward other blacks. Obviously envious of her father's attention to her sister, she unnecessarily reminded readers that the sister did not become famous. She insisted that her brother used her as his wife's slave. She wrote vituperatively about a jealous, "old, fat, black" servant who caused her to be fired and about another "jealous hussy" who tried to kill her. With obvious relish she reported the details of a fight with her stepmother, whom she hated. . . . [Years afterward] she searched for her stepmother, hoping to resume the battle; but, after finding her, Miss Hurston pitied the aged woman's infirmity. It is psychologically impossible that any human being who would want to kill so many members of her own race should never have resented members of another race. Such a dichotomy of blacks and whites cannot exist except to myopic vision.

Two causes for the myopia suggest themselves. One, the desire to sell her book caused Miss Hurston to conceal her resentment of white Americans. Two, she genuinely enjoyed the paternalism of her white friends.

If the first hypothesis is true, Miss Hurston was a hypocrite; if the second is true, she was immature and insecure. Either hypothesis dissuades one from expecting any perceptive appraisal of the interrelationships of the races in her autobiography, and none is to be found. (pp. 93-4)

The Zora Neale Hurston who takes shape from her autobiography and from the accounts of those who knew her is an imaginative, somewhat shallow, quick-tempered woman, desperate for recognition and reassurance to assuage her feelings of inferiority; a blind follower of that social code which approves arrogance toward one's assumed peers and inferiors but requires total psychological commitment to a subservient posture before one's supposed superiors. It is in reference to this image that one must examine her novels, her folklore, and her view of the Southern scene.

Despite the psychological limitations which color her works, her novels deserve more recognition than they have received. While publishing more books than any Afro-American woman before her—four novels, two collections of folklore, and an autobiography—she was one of the few Southern-born Afro-American writers who have consistently mined literary materials from Southern soil. Gifted with an ear for dialect, an appreciation of the folktale, a lively imagination, and an understanding of feminine psychology, she interwove these materials in deceptively simple stories which exhibit increasing artistic consciousness and her awareness of the shifting tastes in the American literary market.

Her relative anonymity may be blamed on two causes. First, during her most productive period—the 1930s—widespread poverty limited the sale of books. Second, her tales of common people form a seemingly quiet meadow overshadowed by commanding, storm-swept hills on either side. To the rear, in the twenties, stands the exoticism of the Harlem Renaissance—Claude McKay's lurid depictions of Harlem, Wallace Thurman's satirical invective, Langston Hughes's jazz rhythms, and Countee Cullen's melodious chauvinism. On the other side, in the forties, stands the lusty violence of Richard Wright, Frank Yerby, Ann Petry, and Willard Motley. Most of Zora Neale Hurston's stories, in contrast, seem to be quiet quests for self-realization.

Ironic, psychologically perceptive stories first brought her to the attention of Charles S. Johnson and various other editors. **"Spunk"** and **"The Gilded Six-Bits"** typify this early work. (pp. 98-9)

Miss Hurston revealed the same talents in her novels. The simply narrated tales, the credible, likable characters, and the colorful dialogue evoke tenderness and amusement. But in the greater length of the novels, she showed weaknesses. She caricatured less important figures, exaggerated the language, and sacrificed structure for the sake of folktales.

Jonah's Gourd Vine (1934), her first novel, is based on the lives of her parents. Written after she had collected the folktales subsequently published in *Mules and Men* (1935), the novel exemplifies both her strengths and her weaknesses. (p. 100)

Although Miss Hurston delineated her protagonists credibly, she exaggerated minor figures. Because she hated her stepmother, Miss Hurston caricatured Hattie, John Buddy's second wife, as a vituperative, ignorant, immoral, vindictive monster. Miss Hurston designed a black girl, Mehaley, as a comic foil for Lucy. Whereas Lucy is intelligent, educated, affectionate, and relatively obedient to her mother's rigid morality, Mehaley is slothful, sensual, and amoral. The contrast reaches a farcical climax in the difference between Lucy's marriage and Mehaley's. Lucy marries John Buddy in a simple, decorous ritual performed with the reverence customary for a sacrament of the church. Mehaley's wedding is delayed first by the tardiness of the bridegroom. It is further delayed by her father, a self-appointed preacher, who refuses to permit an ordained minister to perform the ceremony. After the father prevails and after the bridegroom again imprisons his aching feet in his new shoes, the marriage vows are recited by the illiterate father, who pretends to read the words from a book which he believes to be the Bible but which is actually an almanac. That evening, the bride postpones consummating the marriage until she has satisfied her craving for snuff. (pp. 101-02)

Exploitation of the exotic weakens the dialogue, which constitutes both the major strength and the major weakness of the novel. Effectively, Miss Hurston created a dialect, or dialects, which, if not authentic, nevertheless suggest a particular level of speech without ridiculing the speaker. The language also exhibits the rural Southern blacks' imaginative, vivid use of metaphor, simile, and invective. . . . The verisimilitude of the language is intensified not merely by the dialect and idiom but even by words, such as "lies," "jook," "piney wood rooters," which require definition in the glossary.

But exploiting the appeal of this language, she piled up metaphorical invective to a height difficult for any mortal to attain. . . . (pp. 102-03)

In the novel, Miss Hurston experimented with symbols with varying degrees of success. The image of "Jonah's gourd vine" does not seem to represent John effectively because no Jonah exists. The fact that John Buddy is created by God and is smitten by God furnishes merely a strained analogy. Miss Hurston, however, used a railroad train more effectively. One of the first objects which John sees after he has crossed the creek, the railroad locomotive impresses him as the most powerful, potentially dangerous force he has ever known. More than a machine or even an agent for transportation, however, it symbolizes his sexual awareness. Coming into his consciousness when he first enters a world of heterosexual relationships, it dominates his thoughts and finally destroys him.

Their Eyes Were Watching God (1937) is artistically superior to *Jonah's Gourd Vine,* perhaps because it centers upon a protagonist with whom Miss Hurston could identify fully. (pp. 104-05)

Although Miss Hurston wrote *Their Eyes Were Watching God* in seven months, she demonstrated considerable improvement in her skill as a novelist. Feeling no compulsion to compensate her protagonist for suffering, she developed the story logically. Unfortunately she weakened the story by the highly melodramatic conclusion alleviated only by the romantic sentiment that Teacake still lives in Janie's memory.

Although the death of the protagonist, John Buddy, ends *Jonah's Gourd Vine* and the grief of the protagonist, Janie, concludes *Their Eyes Were Watching God,* neither novel overwhelms a reader with a sense of tragedy. A lighter mood develops, not so much from Miss Hurston's emphasis upon a philosophic acceptance of grief as from her frequent admixtures of comedy and her tendency to report dramatic incidents rather than to involve the reader with the emotions of the characters.

In her second novel Miss Hurston improved her characterization by caricaturing less frequently and by delineating minor characters more carefully. In fact, Nanny, Janie's grandmother, is one of Miss Hurston's most effectively drawn characters. Feeling that life cheated her by enslaving her, Nanny vows that her granddaughter will enjoy the happiness she herself has never known. But seeking to realize herself through her granddaughter, she fails to allow for Janie's personality and aspirations. (pp. 105-06)

Despite her general improvements, however, Miss Hurston continued to exhibit defects evidencing her inability to complete her transformation from a short-story writer into a novelist. She weakened the plot by a careless shift of point of view and by digressions. (p. 107)

Miss Hurston committed her most serious structural blunder in chapter six. In the first four chapters she developed the poignant relationship of Janie and Nanny, lyrically explored Janie's personality, and described the brief course of Janie's marriage. In chapter five Miss Hurston altered her tone by abandoning the serious, contemplative dialogue of the earlier chapters in order to imitate the impudent, jovial chatter of the Eatonville folk who spy upon the newcomers, Janie and Joe Starks. In chapter six, however, the longest in the book, Miss Hurston interrupted the narrative in order to include folktales and amusing sketches of local inhabitants. Digressive and unnecessary, the chapter merely suggests that Miss Hurston did not know how to integrate the folk material which she considered essential for local color. She weakly justified the inclusions as illustrations of the kinds of tales which Janie wishes to hear more often. Later in the story, Miss Hurston introduced similar materials more plausibly as a part of the banter between Teacake and Janie and as the evening or rainy day diversion of the workers with whom Janie and Teacake live.

Either personal insensitivity or an inability to recognize aesthetic inappropriatenesses caused Miss Hurston to besmirch *Their Eyes Were Watching God* with one of the crudest scenes which she ever wrote. While Joe Starks is dying, Janie deliberately provokes a quarrel so that, for the first time, she can tell him how he has destroyed her love. During the early years of their twenty-year relationship, Joe Starks jealously sheltered her excessively; during the later years he often abused her because he resented her remaining young and attractive while he aged rapidly. But in a quarrel or two Janie repaid him in good measure by puncturing his vanity before the fellow townsmen whose respect and envy he wished to command. Never was his conduct so cruel as to deserve the vindictive attack which Janie unleashes while he is dying. For Janie, the behavior seems grotesquely out of character. It is characteristic, however, of Miss Hurston's continual emphasis upon intraracial and intrafamilial hatred. Probably no other Afro-American fiction maker before Richard Wright so fully and frequently described violence within black families.

The thought of *Their Eyes Were Watching God* is more persuasive than that of *Jonah's Gourd Vine*. Through Nanny, Miss Hurston denounced slavery and the wives of slave owners; through Teacake she ridiculed the Southerners' habit of selecting certain blacks as their pets while abusing the others; and through Mrs. Turner she ridiculed Negroes who hate their race. She succeeded best, however, in delineating perceptively a woman whose simple desires mystify the men in her life. Janie merely wishes to live and to love, to laugh and to joke with people. But her husband and her first lover fail to understand that her happiness depends upon love. Because she does not love her first husband, she feels insulted because he wants her to prepare his breakfast, chop wood, and plow in the fields. As long as she loves Joe Starks, however, she is willing to clerk in his store. When she no longer loves him, she resents his wanting her to continue to work. Because she loves Teacake, she works beside him in the fields after he has confessed his loneliness without her. All Janie wants is to love,

to be loved, and to share the life of her man. But, like the witch in [Geoffrey Chaucer's] Wife of Bath's tale, she first must find a man wise enough to let her be whatever kind of woman she wants to be.

Miss Hurston's most accomplished achievement in fiction is *Moses, Man of the Mountain* (1939), which provided a format in which she could best utilize her talents for writing satire, irony, and dialect. (pp. 107-09)

If she had written nothing else, Miss Hurston would deserve recognition for this book. For once, her material and her talent fused perfectly. Her narrative deficiencies are insignificant, for the reader knows the story. Her ridicule, caricature, and farce are appropriate. The monstrous Hattie of *Jonah's Gourd Vine* and Mrs. Turner of *Their Eyes Were Watching God* reappear aptly in the jealous, accursed Miriam, who actually becomes a sympathetic figure after she has been cursed with leprosy. Finally, attuned to folk psychology, Miss Hurston gave the Hebrew slaves an authenticity that they lack in the solemn Biblical story. (pp. 109-10)

The chief art of the book is the abundant comedy. Humor emerges even from the mere contrast of the bombastic speech of the Egyptians, the realistic speech of the educated people, and the credible dialect of the slaves. But a good joke, at best, is merely a joke. Miss Hurston's joke entertains readers but does not comment significantly on life or people.

In her final novel, *Seraph on the Suwanee* (1948), Miss Hurston for the first time focused upon white protagonists, in a work so stylistically different from her earlier efforts that it reveals her conscious adjustment to the tastes of a new generation of readers. Although *Seraph* is Hurston's most ambitious novel and her most artistically competent, its prolonged somberness causes many readers to yearn for the alleviating farce and carefree gaiety of the earlier works. (p. 111)

Although *Seraph* is not a black story in white face, it significantly parallels the earlier novels in most respects. For instance, despite differences of dialect and ambition, the protagonists of *Seraph* have their prototypes in *Their Eyes Were Watching God*. Like Janie, Arvay Henson, a woman of the lower caste of Southern society, is searching for love. Like Teacake, Jim courts charmingly and boldly; like Joe Starks, he dedicates himself to providing comfort for his mate. Even the familiar vituperative caricatures recur—in Arvay's slovenly sister Larraine and her husband, Carl Middleton.

If the differences in race are ignored, *Seraph* is distinguished from the earlier novels chiefly by Miss Hurston's emphasis upon the protagonist's psychological dilemma, more specific and more realistic descriptions of locale, more lurid details in the accounts of sexual relationships, and the omission of farcical incidents and of folktales. Each of the first three heightens the dramatic or at least the melodramatic quality of the story; therefore, the absence of the exotic charm of the humor, the language, and the folklore seems the only possible basis for a complaint that this novel is less interesting than earlier ones.

To defend *Seraph* against the unwarranted objection, however, is not to imply that the novel is Miss Hurston's most successful. Even though Miss Hurston structured the novel more competently than any other, she betrayed her intention by her thought, and she betrayed her ability by her tone. A writer who proposes a psychological study must do more than describe a behavior pattern and report or dramatize neurosis; he must interpret the relationship of the two in such a way that a reader recognizes that the action is a manifestation or a result of the emotional state. In other words, the author must comprehend psychological complexity sufficiently that he not only supplies an objective correlative but also demonstrates that it actually is a correlative. Because Miss Hurston was herself impulsive rather than rational and because she approached people intuitively rather than analytically, she failed to control her materials. (pp. 113-15)

Furthermore, [Miss Hurston] betrayed her talent by adopting a new tone. To write a best seller for the forties, she added sex and sensation to her usual fare. In her earlier works, by restrained emotion and detachment, she had made the griefs pathetic but bearable; in *Seraph,* however, she plunged readers into the deep and bitter emotions of a sick world. Doubtlessly, she proved to be a competent guide to that world. But since many other writers can guide such tours, it is regrettable that Miss Hurston did not restrict her tours to the world of the healthy.

Although an examination of her novels is the chief focus of this study, no consideration of Zora Neale Hurston would be complete without an appraisal of her work as folklorist. *Mules and Men* (1935) and *Tell My Horse* (1938), as well as her autobiography, clearly evidence Zora Neale Hurston's talents as a reporter and her weaknesses as a scholar. (pp. 115-16)

Although *Mules and Men* is interesting, it is disappointingly superficial for the reader who desires more than entertainment. Miss Hurston repeatedly identified herself as an anthropologist, but there is no evidence of the scholarly procedures which would be expected from a formally trained anthropologist or researcher in folklore. Instead of classifying or analyzing tales, she merely reported them in the chronological order and the manner in which they had been told to her. Furthermore, she failed to ask or to answer essential questions. For instance, her internship as a witch doctor required her to prescribe charms and cures. Although a reader eagerly wishes to learn some results of her treatments, Miss Hurston dropped the matter after reciting the details of the prescriptions.

It cannot be said in her defense that Miss Hurston regarded the folklore with the eye of a novelist rather than a scholar. Although interested in the personalities of the storytellers, the idiom spoken by Afro-Americans, and the banter and the flirtation which accompany and encompass the storytelling sessions, she did not attempt to transform the folktale into art, as Joel Chandler Harris did with the Uncle Remus materials or as Charles Waddell Chesnutt did in "The Goophered Grapevine." Perhaps Miss Hurston neglected these matters because she was overly concerned with her major topic—Zora Neale Hurston. . . . Nevertheless, despite the superficiality which limits its scholarly importance, *Mules and Men* is an enjoyable work of competent journalism, which offers valuable insight into a class of people and a way of life.

Tell My Horse (1938) reflects even more disastrously Miss Hurston's regrettable inability to distinguish the important from the unimportant, the significant from the trivial. Although she had proposed a study of the voodoo of Haiti and the West Indies, she produced instead a travelogue of her experience, her reactions to the people, and her descriptions of the country. Such travelogues attain significance only if they have been prepared by political scientists or sociologists capable of evaluating their experiences. Miss Hurston not only lacked such training, but she also proved herself to be irritatingly naïve. (pp. 117-18)

Tell My Horse has value only in Miss Hurston's account of Jamaican and Haitian folktales and voodoo customs, which are more fascinating than those of *Mules and Men* because they are less familiar to American readers. Especially intriguing are the descriptions of the witch doctors and of Zombies (the living dead). Miss Hurston even included a photograph purported to be that of a Zombie. *Tell My Horse* reveals Miss Hurston's usual talent for gathering material, her skill in reporting it, and her characteristic inability to interpret it.

Because of her simple style, humor, and folklore, Zora Neale Hurston deserves more recognition than she ever earned. But, superficial and shallow in her artistic and social judgments, she became neither an impeccable raconteur nor a scholar. Always, she remained a wandering minstrel. It was eccentric but perhaps appropriate for her to return to Florida to take a job as a cook and maid for a white family and to die in poverty. She had not ended her days as she once had hoped—a farmer among the growing things she loved. Instead she had returned to the level of life which she proposed for her people. (pp. 119-20)

> *Darwin T. Turner, "Zora Neale Hurston: The Wandering Minstrel," in his* In a Minor Chord: Three Afro-American Writers and Their Search for Identity, *Southern Illinois University Press, 1971, pp. 89-120.*

ADDISON GAYLE, JR.

Despite structural and formal defects, *Jonah's Gourd Vine* is most important for its depiction of the character of the black woman. Lucy is far from being completely developed as a character. She does, however, contain elements seldom seen in fiction by men which feature black women. Moreover, Miss Hurston, in her portrayal of Lucy, has begun early to deal with the conflict between black men and women, which receives fuller explication in Chester Himes's *Lonely Crusade* and John Williams' *Sissie* later in the century. The conflict centers around two victims of the same oppressive society. Take John and Lucy as metaphors of black men and women. John, unlike his stepfather, the former slave, is set free in a world which denies him the normal route for the pursuit of manhood. According to Miss Hurston, therefore, he must prove his manhood by having sexual relationships with women other than his wife. He has discovered, in other words, that the black man's route to manhood lay in the exploitation of black women. For no other men in the Euro-American society is this true.

It is not too far wrong to suggest that despite Miss Hurston's fondness for John, in him she has substantiated the theses concerning the black man's overt sexuality; if not more sexually potent than other men, he is assuredly more promiscuous. Thus, John, the metaphor of black men, remains, for Miss Hurston, essentially a creature of appetite, insatiable even though offered such a delectable morsel as Lucy Pearson. Her loyalty, perseverance, and love border upon the messianic. What her husband lacks in courage, strength, and initiative, she more than compensates for. The conflicts, therefore, given such personalities can be resolved only when black men correct the defects in character. That this was the author's implicit commentary upon black men might be attributable to her distorted conception of them. The chances are, however, that she was less interested in John Pearson than in Lucy, less interested in the men of her novels than in the women, who receive more multidimensional treatment.

In *Jonah's Gourd Vine* and *Their Eyes Were Watching God*, she views them as modern women, patterned upon paradigms of the past, those of the courage and strength of Harriet Tubman and Sojourner Truth. Far from being the images of old, the willing copartners of white men in the castration of black men, her women are, instead, the foundations of a new order, the leavening rods of change, from whose loins will eventually come the new man. Past stereotypes aside, therefore, her women need only search for greater liberation, move even beyond the stoiclike devotion of a Lucy Pearson, move toward greater independence and freedom. Put another way, black liberation meant burying the old images and symbols that had circumscribed black women along with black men. (pp. 143-44).

Much of her second novel, *Their Eyes Were Watching God* (1937), centers around the theme of the liberated black woman. In *Jonah's Gourd Vine*, Lucy Pearson, though an improvement over women in previous black novels, is, nevertheless, still the picture of loyalty and devotion. She is a woman hovering always near rebellion and assertion of individuality, yet she lacks the determination or, perhaps, desire to break completely with past mores and folkways. Janie Starks, the central character of Miss Hurston's second novel, has no such problem. She is a more completely developed character, and like her male counterparts in the fiction of [Claude] McKay and [Rudolph] Fisher, capable of moving outside the definitions of both black and white imagists. (p. 144)

In rebelling against the definition of black women and moving to assert her own individuality, Janie must travel the route of tradition. The ending of *Their Eyes Were Watching God*, therefore, is in the beginning, and the novel, which gains its immediacy through first-person narration, merges past and present through use of flashbacks. In the opening pages of the novel, Janie, the outsider, returns to tell her own story. She left the town of Eatonville with Teacake, happy-go-lucky gambler and part-time worker who, said the townspeople, was "too young for her." For them, such an act constituted rebellion against old and accepted standards of conduct. For Janie, however, rebellion has brought about a dignity and stature unknown before, has transformed her from a dreamer to an activist, has enabled her to participate in experiences unusual for women of her time. (p. 145)

Their Eyes Were Watching God, a novel of intense power, evidences the strength and promise of African-American culture. Miss Hurston, like Fisher, [Jean] Toomer, [Langston] Hughes, and McKay, went to the proletariat to seek values, to create and recreate images and symbols that had been partially obliterated or distorted through years of white nationalist propaganda. Her characters were outsiders in America because they were the inheritors of a culture different from that of others. . . . They remain, however, oblivious as well to the gods of the Euro-Americans and are thus nomads in a world where identity for black people is founded upon the theology of such modern-day saints as Vachel Lindsay and Carl Van Vechten.

Yet the novel functions as an antithesis to [Van Vechten's] *Nigger Heaven*. For Miss Hurston's characters, sex, atavism, joy, and pleasure do not constitute the essence of a people who must continually wage warfare for their very existence. The Lasca Sartorises and the Scarlet Creepers are revealed not only as vicious stereotypes when measured against Teacake and Janie but as cruel figments of the white imagination, created in order to enslave men anew. In addition, the novel also repudiates the values and images bequeathed black literature

in the works of [James Weldon] Johnson and [Jessie] Fauset. Fidelity to Euro-American values, to prosperity and status, are equally as enslaving and debilitating. . . . (p. 147)

Janie Starks, however, is not the completion of the new paradigm, but only evidence of an important beginning. After returning to the town from which her search for freedom began, she remains an outsider and yet is not able to continue her rebellion beyond the immediate present. Like Teacake, she, too, is dead to the realities of the world in which she lives. For though the white world remains more symbol than actuality for her, it is in actuality that it is oppressive. Thus the questioning, restless spirit which led to rebellion against the tradition that circumscribes her, due to race and sex, must lead her to challenge the equally restrictive patterns that deny physical freedom. This was the task of writers more talented and more angry than Miss Hurston, and that Janie Starks does not measure up in this respect, detracts neither from her importance as a character nor from the importance of *Their Eyes Were Watching God*. (pp. 147-48)

> *Addison Gayle, Jr., "The Outsider," in his* The Way of the New World: The Black Novel in America, *Anchor Press/Doubleday, 1975, pp. 129-52.**

THERESA R. LOVE

[Miss Hurston's goal in her nonfiction] was not merely to collect folklore but to show the beauty and wealth of genuine Negro material. In doing so, she placed herself on the side of those who saw nothing self-defeating in writing about the black masses, who, she felt, are more imaginative than their middle-class counterparts. Consequently, few of the latter are included in her works. Often, her characters work and live in sawmill camps. Some are sharecroppers. Some work on railroads. Most are uneducated and provincial. A statement from her short story, **"John Redding Goes to Sea,"** sums up their way of life: "No one of their community had ever been farther than Jacksonville. Few, indeed had ever been there. Their own gardens, general store, and occasional trips to the county seat—seven miles away—sufficed for all their needs. Life was simple indeed with these folk." . . . To the anthropologist, their economic and cultural isolation made them the proper source for folk materials in their purest form. (pp. 425-26)

Her decision to write about the ways of the folk necessitated her use of their dialect as a means of achieving verisimilitude. Of course, the careful student of a writer must always remember that the writer's rendition of a dialect may or may not be authentic. Many writers are merely following a literary tradition—that of attributing certain speech patterns to a given social or ethnic group for artistic reasons. . . . [Most] of Miss Hurston's characters are represented as being speakers of Black Dialect, and . . . she herself abandons her use of the General Dialect when she pictures herself as a researcher among those who speak the variant dialect. . . . (p. 426)

[It] would seem that Miss Hurston's use of Black Dialect forms substantiates the theory that she is willing to sacrifice her interest in anthropology—which discipline would emphasize the need for photographic descriptive passages—for the sake of artistic expediency. Otherwise her works might now be facing the same fate as those of Joel Chandler Harris, whose Uncle Remus tales are seldom read because of the difficulty which the modern reader has with the heavy, nineteenth-century Black Dialect in which they are written.

A careful student of Zora Neale Hurston must also distinguish between her use of slang and her use of dialect. In the short story **"Story in Harlem Slang,"** there is Black Dialect, but there is also "black slang." . . . Interestingly enough, . . . [slang] terms almost never appear in her novels, in which she is discussing the inhabitants of Florida, or in her books of folklore, but they do appear in this story about two Harlem pimps, who would like to think that they are irresistible to women, especially since they depend on women for a livelihood. They would also like to think that they have become more urbane since they have come north. They are not the simple, naïve men who watch girls from the porch of Joe Clark's store, which is the setting of most of Miss Hurston's works. They are, in the common vernacular, "hip." The writer thus gives them an appropriate vocabulary and thereby shows how skillfully she can combine her learning and her artistic abilities. (pp. 427-28)

The frequent religious and moral flavor of the myths and legends of black people might be taken as an indication that religion plays a strong part in their lives, and, certainly, the works of Zora Neale Hurston would seem to suggest that she thought so herself. Any discussion of her attitude toward the religious practices of blacks must, however, take into account the fact that she makes a distinction between those who practice true Christianity and those who are hypocrites. . . .

In Miss Hurston's fiction, few examples of . . . devout love can be found among those characters who profess to be Christians, for she depicts many of them as being full of greed and malice. (p. 433)

[The] churchgoers in *Jonah's Gourd Vine* are additional examples of Miss Hurston's attack on the belief that all blacks are basically religious, for she draws a fine line between those who profess adherence to the principles of Christianity and those who practice them. . . . [The] deacons of Zion Hope, the Reverend John Pearson's church in *Jonah's Gourd Vine,* are conniving and treacherous. They are entirely without mercy as they gossip about their pastor's illicit relations with women. These middle-class churchgoers are as malicious as the spiteful Miriam and the other Israelites whom Moses leads to freedom in Miss Hurston's novel, *Moses, Man of the Mountain.* Thus the novelist shows that, while it is true that many blacks profess Christian leanings, they differ greatly in the quality of their religious practices.

Zora Neale Hurston is so well known as a folklorist that her work as a novelist and as an essayist is often overlooked. Yet it is necessary to go to her novels and to her essays to recognize that she is also a philosopher who believes that personal and social happiness depends upon the practice of the central Christian virtue, love. The treatment of the minister in *Jonah's Gourd Vine* is an example of the sorrow and hurt which result from one who is incapable of love. (p. 434)

[John Pearson] betrays a woman who loves him, as well as a spiritual flock that looks to him for guidance. In utter despair, he drives onto a railroad track and is killed by a train, an act symbolic of his destruction by the worm which has continued to nibble away at his honest desire to be a good preacher and a faithful husband and father. Thus Miss Hurston . . . pictures his fall as the result of his inability to love.

The belief that love is a necessary ingredient in personal and social happiness may be seen in other novels and stories written by Miss Hurston. In the short story **"The Gilded Six Bits"** Joe continues to love Missy May, his wife, although she has been unfaithful to him, just as Jamie, in **Their Eyes Were Watching God,** continues to love her husband, Tea Cake, even though he has stolen a rather large sum of money from her. Conversely, in **Seraph on the Suwanee,** Miss Hurston's only novel in which the main characters are white, Arvay, an uneducated woman, is incapable of returning the love of Jim Meserve because he comes from an antebellum Georgia family of wealth and status. Frustrated because he cannot convince her of his good intentions, he leaves her. Thus, whereas the marriages of the two black couples hold fast in the face of adversity because of their love for each other, that of the white couple disintegrates because of the lack of it.

In the novel, Arvay is symbolic of persons who harbor prejudices of one kind or another. . . . [It] is not until Arvay is able to love her fellow men, without consideration of social and racial differences, that she is able to experience personal love.

Finally, Zora Neale Hurston has a special message for her people. Acknowledging that they have suffered many injustices, she insists that they turn from bitterness to hope. In one of her essays, "High John De Conquer," she recounts the legend of the African spirit who was brought to America by African slaves. A good spirit, he was always near when they needed him. Thus, when mothers were bereft of their babies by greedy slave traders, when scalding salt was poured on their backs which were trenched by strong leather straps, and when neither they nor their parents nor their parents before them could remember the royal-blue African skies, they endured because John the Conqueror was always there to give them hope. Some of Miss Hurston's friends told her that he went back to Africa after emancipation, since his work was done. Other said that he fused himself into a root where he waits to help the downtrodden, the needy, and the lovelorn. All they have to do is to find his hiding place, carry it in their pockets, or bury it in their hair, and immediately he will begin working.

Zora Neale Hurston never believed that "High John De Conquer" has gone back to Africa. Nor did she believe that he resides in some kind of root. She believed that he lives in the hearts of black men and that all they have to do is to call upon him. He will then bring them hope. Soon thereafter, they will find that they have love, and laughter too. Then they will overcome, which is the sum of her hope and aspirations for her people. (pp. 435-37)

*Theresa R. Love, "Zora Neale Hurston's America,"
in* Papers on Language and Literature, *Vol. 12, No. 4, Fall, 1976, pp. 422-37*

ROBERT E. HEMENWAY

Folklore, Hurston said, is the art people create before they find out there is such as thing as art; it comes from a folk's "first wondering contact with natural law"—that is, laws of human nature as well as laws of natural process, the truths of a group's experience as well as the principles of physics. These interpretations of nature, called "unscientific" or "crude," often turn out to be wise and poetic explanations for the ways of the world. The parable of the hog under the oak tree—he eats and grunts but never looks up to see where the acorns are coming from—teaches less about the laws of gravity than about the importance of looking for the sources of good fortune. . . . The folklorist learns to respect these wondering beliefs as artistic expressions which teach one how to live, and Hurston had learned a good deal about both art and life. . . . (p. 159)

She was faced, however, with a scholarly problem: what was her responsibility in explaining the lore? What stance should she take in relation to the folk? How could she make others see this great cultural wealth? The final answers came in *Mules and Men.* Not published until 1935, the book was largely completed between March, 1930 . . . and September of 1932. . . . By the time readers shared in her discoveries, some of her ideas were six years old, and Hurston had gone on to a career as a novelist and dramatist. As she organized her field notes during 1930-32, she conceptualized black folklore, exploring the ways black history affected folk narratives, hypothesizing about racial characteristics in traditional communication. This mature conception of folklore changed only slightly over the years, and it antedates her best work as an artist. Even though her first novel was published prior to *Mules and Men,* it was written after she had completed the folklore research. In a sense, her career as a folklorist ended when she finished with her field notes, and after the fall of 1932 she usually conceived of herself as a creative writer—even when writing about folklore. (pp. 159-60)

The intimacy of *Mules and Men* is an obtained effect, an example of Hurston's narrative skill. She represented oral art functioning to affect behavior in the black community; to display this art in its natural setting she created a narrator who would not intrude on the folklore event. A semifictional Zora Neale Hurston is our guide to southern black folklore, a curiously retiring figure who is more art than life. The exuberant Zora Hurston who entertained the Harlem Renaissance is seldom in evidence in *Mules and Men.* In her place is a self-effacing reporter created by Hurston the folklorist to dramatize the process of collecting and make the reader feel part of the scene. (p. 164)

It is easy to overlook Hurston's craft as she mediates between self and material in this presentation; yet she shaped *Mules and Men* in somewhat the same manner in which Henry David Thoreau created a unified experience in *Walden.* His two years of residence at Walden Pond were condensed into a book structured around one year's seasonal cycle. Hurston condenses a two-and-a-half-year expedition into one year and nine months, with a one-year segment (Florida) and a nine-month segment (New Orleans). Her two return trips to Eatonville in 1927 and 1928 are telescoped into a single dramatic homecoming. (p. 165)

Hurston had to provide a frame for the adventures and insights of a complicated experience; she had to select from a multitude of situations and personalities. One way to unify could have been, like Thoreau, to stress the personal significance of the various encounters. Yet *Mules and Men* is ultimately a book very different from *Walden* precisely because Hurston did not choose the personal option. Her adventures go purposely without analysis. While Henry David Thoreau embarks on a voyage of spiritual discovery, Zora Neale Hurston always remains close to the shore, her description directed away from the inner self toward the words of her informants.

The scholarly folklorist of the thirties was expected to subordinate self to material in the interests of objectivity. The intent was to leave the emphasis on the folklore texts that were being added to the "body of knowledge." After describing the corpse, the folklorist could perform an autopsy in order to learn how the living organism functions. The cold text, isolated on the page for scientific study, implied the living folk, but the folk themselves were secondary to the artifact collected. . . . Much of *Mules and Men* is a simple reporting of texts. . . . Yet Hurston also breathed life into her narrative by presenting her-

self as a master of ceremonies, a transitional voice. Instead of observing a pathologist perform an autopsy, the reader keeps in sight a midwife participating in the birth of the body folklore. The effect is subtle and often overlooked. *Mules and Men* does not become an exercise in romantic egoism; it celebrates the art of the community. Where the reader of *Walden* comes away with visions of separating from society in order to gain spiritual renewal, the reader of *Mules and Men* learns a profound respect for men and women perpetuating an esthetic mode of communication; the impulse is not to isolate oneself, but to lose the self in the art and wisdom of the group.

From the very first pages Hurston creates a self-effacing persona inviting the reader to participate in collective rituals. She arrives in Eatonville knowing . . . [her college degree means] nothing to the loafers on the store porch, for they will define their community in their own terms, identify people according to kin. They are like African *griots* who preserve the genealogy of a tribe which has not developed a written language. Hurston portrays herself as a town prodigal returned to collect "them big old lies we tell when we're jus' sittin' around here on the porch doin' nothin'." She is an educated innocent whose memory of the village folklore has been diminished by her urban experience and academic study; she must renew community ties.

Yet Arna Bontemps testified that many of the *Mules and Men* tales were a vivid part of Hurston's storytelling repertoire when she arrived in New York, well before she ever studied or collected folklore. . . . The Zora Neale Hurston of *Mules and Men,* then, is deliberately underplaying her knowledge of Eatonville so that the reader will not feel alienated. Because she saw from a dual perspective, both from within the community and from without, Hurston the writer could select those experiences which would attract the reader and let the folk speak for themselves. Hurston the narrator admits only to a desire to hold a microphone up to nature. (pp. 165-67)

There is an ambivalence here that has sometimes been criticized. Is *Mules and Men* about Zora Hurston or about black folklore? If the former, the self-effacement makes the reader want to know more about what was going on in her mind, more about her reaction to the communities that embraced her. If the latter, there is a need for folklore analysis. Are hoodoo candles a form of fire worship comparable to the use of fire in Christian ritual? What is the cross-cultural structure of the folktale? These deficiencies are the price Hurston paid for her two-fold purpose. On the one hand, she was trying to represent the artistic content of the black folklore; on the other, she was trying to suggest the behavioral significance of folkloric events. Her efforts were intended to show rather than tell, the assumption being that both behavior and art will become self-evident as the tale texts and hoodoo rituals accrete during the reading.

Hurston presents the artistic content in the communication by stressing how "facile" is the "Negro imagination." The participants in a tale-telling session are all capable of verbal adornment. . . . A story-teller is someone who can "plough up some literary and lay-by some alphabets." The scholar never steps in to stress the ingenuity of a particular metaphor or the startling effectiveness of an image. She wants to reveal, in her words, "that which the soul lives by" in a rural black community; although there was a need for a transitional voice, only by stepping to the background could she allow unhampered expression. She did not want her readers reminded too often that a folklorist was there to take it all down. . . . [Hurston's technique] was to become one of the folk, a position which did not allow for the detachment of the analytical observer.

This deliberate lack of analysis places a special responsibility on the reader. The tales of *Mules and Men* are *not* quaint fictions created by a primitive people. They are profound expressions of a group's behavior. (pp. 167-68)

Mules and Men is not all folktales and hoodoo. It also contains many sayings, fragments of songs, rhymes, and legends. There is little explanation, however, of how all this folklore assumes any significance beyond the immediate entertainment. . . . Rhyme as a creative response to a prosaic world goes unanalyzed. Brer Rabbit is not discussed as an allegorical figure symbolizing black cunning. Hoodoo as an alternative science with a worldview as valid as any other goes unexplored. The universality of trickster figures like John goes unanalyzed. There is deliberately no cross-cultural reference, although many of the tales also appear in other cultures. There is no reference at all to the scholarship in the field.

These remarks are not necessarily criticisms, for Hurston makes *Mules and Men* a very readable folklore book. But the subordination of Hurston the scholar to Hurston the narrator can cause the reader to miss her attempts to provide the data for scholarly study. There is a consistent and subtle attempt, for example, to demonstrate how traditional tales are perpetuated. A small boy is encouraged to speak, then praised for the "over average lie" he contributes to the lying session. Presumably he will grow up a storyteller. When Joe Wiley asks if anyone has heard the story about "Big Talk," the reply is, "Yeah, we done heard it, Joe, but Ah kin hear it some 'gin." When a man says he will tell a tale for his wife, his listener responds, "Aw, g'wan tell de lie, Larkins if you want to. You know you ain't tellin no lie for yo' wife. No mo' than de rest of us. You lyin' cause you like it." There is psychic satisfaction in the repetition of narratives. (pp. 172-73)

[Hurston] had written earlier about the dramatic properties of black expression. She saw drama permeating "the Negro's entire self" and felt that "every phase of Negro life is highly dramatized. No matter how joyful or sad the case there is sufficient poise for drama. Everything is acted out." . . . (p. 174)

Mules and Men, for all her attempts to indicate a context for each tale and to hold together the disparate experience, left out much of the drama. The storyteller gestured, postured, winked, and laughed during the story; yet it was difficult to present these actions without distracting from the texts themselves. At the time, Hurston considered the presentation of texts her primary responsibility. (p. 175)

The immediate reception of *Mules and Men* was mixed. The nature of both the praise and the dissatisfaction came to characterize Hurston's public reputation for the next twenty years. Reviewers liked the book and recommended its lively stories. The *Saturday Review* called it "black magic and dark laughter," stressing the "entertainment" value. But Zora had not intended the book as light reading, and some reviewers accepted her invitation to a more serious interpretation. Written by a black author, about black people, it was assumed to reveal "what the Negro was really like," a subject of immense fascination to whites and of obvious vested interest to black readers. . . . Henry Lee Moon of the [National Association for the Advancement of Colored People] reviewing the book in the *New Republic,* urged a larger meaning. Zora had not presented the life of the race as he lived it in New York City, but he was willing to assert that "*Mules and Men* is more than a

collection of folklore. It is a valuable picture of the life of the unsophisticated Negro in small towns and backwoods of Florida."

Discussed on this basis for a few months, the book finally drew the public attention of Sterling Brown. (pp. 218-19)

Brown stressed Zora's academic training and praised her rendering of the tales. He disliked some of the "sensationalism" in the hoodoo section, but on the whole found it worthy. He was less certain than Moon about the book's value as a portrait of black life. It was authentically done as far as it went, but the portrait of the South was incomplete; missing were the exploitation, the terrorism, the misery. . . . He concluded, "*Mules and Men* should be more bitter; it would be nearer the total truth."

Many black intellectuals believed that books by black authors needed to tell the "total truth" to white America. Books about the race should aim to destroy the absurd beliefs and racist fantasies of the suppressing culture, and such books would necessarily at times be bitter. But even if Hurston had consciously tried to avoid bitterness, Brown's criticism was important. She had not been writing for pure entertainment—although publisher's demands may have veered *Mules and Men* in that direction—and she had offered a portrait of the race meant to be taken as a behavioral example. Her preface promised access to the interior of the black mind, a report on what blacks deliberately kept from whites. But if this was her purpose, why had she excised the sharper edges, the harsher tones, of her rural informants? (pp. 219-20)

Mules and Men has a disembodied quality about it, as if it came from a backwoods so far to the rear that American social history of the twentieth century had not touched its occupants. At a time when the Communist party was recruiting large numbers of black people, primarily because it was the only political party in America advocating an end to segregation, and when Richard Wright and Langston Hughes were creating a proletarian literature, Zora Hurston had deliberately chosen not to deal with the resentment of the black community. Why?

The reasons were strategic and philosophic, although she later admitted that publisher's restrictions also played a part. Hurston had a conception of the black image in the popular mind, and she felt that it derived largely from a mistaken notion of the black folk. The total truth was relative, making the class struggle seem less important than the need for an altered perception of black folklore. . . . She once complained about the "false picture" created by black writers dwelling on the race problem, producing writing "saturated with our sorrows." This picture was false because it distorted: "We talk about the race problem a great deal, but go on living and laughing and striving like everybody else." By leaving out "the problem," by emphasizing the art in the folkloric phenomenon, Hurston implicitly told whites: Contrary to your arrogant assumptions, you have not really affected us that much; we continue to practice our own culture, which as a matter of fact is more alive, more esthetically pleasing than your own; and it is not solely a product of defensive *re*actions to your actions. She felt that black culture manifested an independent esthetic system that could be discussed without constant reference to white oppression.

The price for this philosophy was an appearance of political naïveté and the absence of an immediate historical presence. . . . Zora's approach was oblique and open to misinterpretation. She chose to write of the positive effects of black experience because she did not believe that white injustice had created a pathology in black behavior. . . . (pp. 220-21)

Zora had begun collecting folklore in the twenties with the conscious intent of celebrating the black folk who had made a way out of no way, like their folk heroes. She liberated rural black folk from the prison of racial stereotypes and granted them dignity as cultural creators. A black social scientist trying to destroy racial stereotypes held by the majority culture, she simultaneously urged black people to be proud of the folk heritage. This may sound commonplace today, but it was unusual then, since a common tactic for destroying white stereotypes was to document black literacy, cite the number of black college graduates, and describe the general black movement into the middle class. (The other side of the coin was to document all the discriminatory practices that denied equal opportunity and kept the black middle class from growing larger.)

Zora was concerned less with the tactics of racial uplift than with the unexamined prejudice of American social science. She became a folklorist at a time when white sociologists were obsessed with what they though was pathology in black behavior, when white psychologists spoke of the deviance in black mental health, and when the discipline of anthropology used a research model that identified black people as suffering from cultural deprivation. Hurston's folklore collections refuted these stereotypes by celebrating the distinctiveness of traditional black culture, and her scholarship is now recognized by revisionist scientists questioning the racial assumptions of modern cultural theory. (pp. 329-30)

[Hurston's collections] defiantly affirmed the cultural practices manifest in the folkore of "the Negro farthest down." She provided, as [John] Szwed has suggested, an alternative view to the pathological theories, even before some of them were formulated. Because she was not a formal theorist, and because her books were meant for a popular audience, her theoretical assumptions about the distinctiveness of Afro-American culture were often masked, and did not receive the attention they deserved. Zora's method was presentational. She saw black Americans as cultural creators, and she documented the creation, not by amassing statistics for behavioral studies, but by presenting examples of oral tradition that expressed a behavioral system. Her attempt to distinguish black culture from white forecast the direction of much subsequent research; in the last thirty years the social sciences have begun to systematically collect the data that Zora Hurston indicated was there all along. We now have a body of "scientific" literature that provides evidence for the existence of a number of distinctive Afro-American cultural domains, including that domain of black esthetics which so interested her. (pp. 330-31)

> *Robert E. Hemenway, in his* Zora Neale Hurston: A Literary Biography, *University of Illinois Press, 1977, 371 p.*

SHERLEY ANNE WILLIAMS

Hurston's evocations of the lifestyles of rural blacks [in *Their Eyes Were Watching God*] have not been equaled; but to stress the ruralness of Hurston's settings or to characterize her diction solely in terms of exotic "dialect" spellings is to miss her deftness with language. In the speech of her characters, black voices—whether rural or urban, northern or southern—come alive. Her fidelity to diction, metaphor, and syntax—whether in direct quotations or in paraphrases of characters' thoughts—rings, even across forty years, with an aching familiarity that

is a testament to Hurston's skill and to the durability of black speech. Yet Zora's personality and actions were so controversial that for a long time she was remembered more as a *character* of the Renaissance than as one of the most serious and gifted artists to emerge during this period. She was a notable tale-teller, mimic, and wit, confident to the point of brashness (some might even say beyond), who refused to conform to conventional notions of ladylike behavior and middle-class decorum. To one of her contemporaries, she was the first black nationalist; to another, a handkerchief-head Uncle Tom. . . . [To] others of our generation, Zora was a woman bent on discovering and defining herself, a woman who spoke and wrote her own mind.

Something of the questing quality that characterized Zora's own life informs the character of Janie—without, of course, the forcefulness of Hurston's own personality. In this and other instances, the character is more conventional than the author, for despite obvious idealizations, Janie operates in a "real" world. Her actions, responses, and motivations are consistent with that reality and the growing assertiveness of her own self-definitions. Where Janie yearns, Zora was probably driven; where Janie submits, Zora would undoubtedly have rebelled. Author and character objectify their definitions of self in totally different ways. Zora was evidently unable to satisfactorily define herself in a continuing relationship with a man, whereas such definition is the essence of Janie's romantic vision and its ultimate fulfillment provides the plot of the novel. But in their desire and eventual insistence that their men accord them treatment due equals, they are one. (pp. ix-xi)

> *Sherley Anne Williams, in a foreword to* Their Eyes Were Watching God: A Novel *by Zora Neale Hurston, University of Illinois Press, 1978, pp. v-xv.*

ROGER SALE

[*Their Eyes Were Watching God*] is not a great novel, or anything like that, but it is one of those books about which it can be said that if it had not been written, there would be something that most of us would not know; it belongs on Randall Jarrell's wonderful list of books that are very good and unimportant. Its chief problem is a language problem, one easily illustrated by a passage like this:

> "'Taint no use in you cryin', Janie. Grandma done been long uh few roads herself. But folks is meant to cry 'bout something' or other. Better leave things de way dey is. Youse young yet. No tellin' whut mout happen befo' you die. Wait awhile, baby. Yo' mind will change."

Nanny sent Janie along with a stern mien, but she dwindled all the rest of the day as she worked.

The black talk itself takes some getting used to, since few black writers use it so unabashedly, so it sounds more like Joel Chandler Harris than Richard Wright. One not only gets used to it, though, but comes to love it as Hurston herself did, as its own kind of English. The real difficulty is the shift from "Youse young yet" to "stern mien," and Hurston's standard English never quite loses its literariness, even when it is being used to say something interesting or important. (p. 153)

The one standard English paragraph the book unquestionably needs is the second, on the first page: "Now, women forget all those things they don't want to remember, and remember everything they don't want to forget. The dream is the truth.

Then they act and do things accordingly.'' So Janie, the child of a rape, is told in the passage above by her grandmother that she'll be best off marrying a responsible older man with sixty acres; she does, but reluctantly, and the marriage never takes, and Janie soon runs off with Joe Starks, an ambitious young man who has heard of Eatonville and is going there to make his fortune. He succeeds, too, by opening the town's general store, then by getting himself elected mayor, but he also succeeds in drying up Janie's affection for him by insisting she become Miz Mayor, a pretty object, who can help with the business only by obeying his orders and who is to stay out of men folks' business. After almost twenty years together, Joe dies, leaving Janie reasonably well off, and then Tea Cake, a man in every respect as terrific as his terrific name, enters. Tea Cake is the perfect image of a shiftless nigger, a gambler and a migrant farm hand, but he wins Janie the night they meet by asking her to play checkers, and, when she says she doesn't know how because her husband would never let her learn, he teaches her, and insists they play by the rules. A feminist man, really, or at least the perfect lover. (pp. 153-54)

[Tea Cake is] marvelous, good on every page; no man written about by a woman, this side of [Jane Austen's Darcy in *Pride and Prejudice* and George Eliot's Lydgate in *Middlemarch*] maybe, seems to ring as true as he does. Alice Walker says there is no book more important to her than *Their Eyes Were Watching God* because of the ways it allows her to identify with Janie; not caring to do that, I can only conclude there is much here for anyone, and I hope lots of people find this novel. . . . [It shows] that Zora Hurston was that kind of person which my students claim almost anyone is—but which few truly are—unique. (p. 154)

> Roger Sale, "Zora," in The Hudson Review, *Vol. XXXII, No. 1, Spring, 1979, pp. 151-54.*

ALICE WALKER

A friend of mine . . . [told] me that she and another woman had been discussing Zora Neale Hurston and had decided they wouldn't have liked her. They wouldn't have liked the way—when her play *Color Struck!* won second prize in a literary contest at the beginning of her career—Hurston walked into a room full of her competitors, flung her scarf dramatically over her shoulder, and yelled "COLOR..R. R STRUCK..K. K!'' at the top of her voice.

Apparently it isn't easy to like a person who is not humbled by second place.

Zora Neale Hurston was outrageous—it appears by nature. She was quite capable of saying, writing, or doing things *different* from what one might have wished. Because she recognized the contradictions and complexity of her own personality, Robert Hemenway, her biographer, writes that Hurston came to "delight" in the chaos she sometimes left behind.

Yet for all her contrariness, her "chaos," her ability to stir up dislike that is as strong today as it was fifty years ago, many of us love Zora Neale Hurston. (p. 1)

We love Zora Neale Hurston for her work, first, and then again (as she and all Eatonville would say), we love her for herself. For the humor and courage with which she encountered a life she infrequently designed, for her absolute disinterest in becoming either white or bourgeois, and for her *devoted* appreciation of her own culture, which is an inspiration to us all.

Reading *Their Eyes Were Watching God* for perhaps the eleventh time, I am still amazed that Hurston wrote it in seven weeks; that it speaks to me as no novel, past or present, has ever done; and that the language of the characters, that "comical nigger 'dialect' '' that has been laughed at, denied, ignored, or "improved" so that white folks and educated black folks can understand it, is simply beautiful. There is enough self-love in that one book—love of community, culture, traditions—to restore a world. Or create a new one.

I do not presume to judge or defend Zora Neale Hurston. I have nothing of finality to say of Hurston the person. I believe any artist's true character is seen in the work she or he does, or it is not seen. In Hurston's work, what she was is revealed. (p. 2)

Is *Mules and Men* racist? Or does it reflect the flawed but nonetheless beautifully creative insights of an oppressed people's collective mythology? Is **"The Gilded Six-Bits"** so sexist it makes us cringe to think Zora Neale Hurston wrote it? Or does it make a true statement about deep love functioning in the only pattern that at the time of its action seemed correct? Did Zora Neale Hurston never question "America" or the status-quo, as some have accused, or was she questioning it profoundly when she wrote phrases like "the arse-and-all of Democracy"? Is Janie Crawford, the main character in *Their Eyes Were Watching God,* light-skinned and silken-haired because *Hurston* was a colorist, as a black male critic has claimed, or because Hurston was not blind and therefore saw that black men (and black women) have been, and are, colorist to an embarrassing degree?

Is Hurston the messenger who brings the bad news, or is she the bad news herself? Is Hurston a reflection of ourselves? And if so, is that not, perhaps, part of our "problem" with her?

I think we are better off if we think of Zora Neale Hurston as an artist, period—rather than as the artist/politician most black writers have been required to be. This frees us to appreciate the complexity and richness of her work in the same way we can appreciate Billie Holiday's glorious phrasing or Bessie Smith's perfect and raunchy lyrics, without the necessity of ridiculing the former's addiction to heroin or the latter's excessive love of gin.

Implicit in Hurston's determination to "make it" in a career was her need to express "the folk" and herself. Someone who knew her has said: "Zora would have been Zora even if she'd been an Eskimo." That is what it means to be yourself; it is surely what it means to be an artist. (pp. 2-3)

It has been pointed out that one of the reasons Zora Neale Hurston's work has suffered neglect is that her critics never considered her "sincere." Only after she died penniless, still laboring at her craft, still immersed in her work, still following *her* vision and *her* road, did it begin to seem to some that yes, perhaps this woman *was* a serious artist after all, since artists are known to live poor and die broke. But you're up against a hard game if you have to die to win it, and we must insist that dying in poverty is an unacceptable extreme.

We live in a society, as blacks, women, and artists, whose contests we do not design and with whose insistence on ranking us we are permanently at war. To know that second place, in such a society, has often required more work and innate genius than first, a longer, grimmer struggle over greater odds than first—and to be able to fling your scarf about dramatically while you demonstrate that you know—is to trust your own self-evaluation in the face of the Great White Western Commercial of white and male supremacy, which is virtually everything we see, outside and often inside our own homes. That Hurston held her own, literally, against the flood of whiteness and maleness that diluted so much other black art of the period in which she worked is a testimony to her genius and her faith. . . .

Zora Neale Hurston, who went forth into the world with one dress to her name, and who was permitted, at other times in her life, only a single pair of shoes, rescued and recreated a world which she labored to hand us whole, never underestimating the value of her gift, if at times doubting the good sense of its recipients. She appreciated us, in any case, *as we fashioned ourselves*. That is something. And of all the people in the world to be, she chose to be herself, *and more and more herself*. That, too is something. (p. 4)

> Alice Walker, *"Dedication: 'On Refusing to Be Humbled by Second Place in a Contest You Did Not Design: A Tradition by Now',"* in I Love Myself When I Am Laughing . . . And Then Again When I Am Looking Mean and Impressive *by Zora Neale Hurston, edited by Alice Walker, The Feminist Press, 1979, pp. 1-5.*

JOHN ROBERTS

It is appropriate that *Mules and Men* and *Their Eyes Were Watching God* should be reissued almost simultaneously. Both works can rightfully be considered classic studies of Afro-American culture. Zora Neale Hurston—novelist, folklorist, and essayist—wrote about Afro-American culture with an insight and perception shared by few black writers.

Throughout her varied career Hurston tended to combine her two passions, folklore and literature, in interesting and compelling ways. She has often been accused of making her folklore studies too literary and her literary works too folkloristic, a criticism which has some merit. *Mules and Men* stands as a testament to this inclination in Hurston's treatment of folklore materials. Although the narrative structure of *Mules and Men* was included because of publisher's objections to printing the straight folklore texts collected by Hurston, it provided her with a unique opportunity to present storytelling context. In the process, she demonstrated a folkloristic sophistication and sensitivity to folklore processes shared by few of her contemporaries. (pp. 463-64)

Although Hurston did not address herself to the theoretical and interpretative questions raised by her collection, there is still much about the volume that suggests caution in approaching it. Despite the generous amount of information included concerning her collecting experiences, Hurston tells us very little of how she was able to get the stories written down, especially during some of the tense moments she describes. There is no mention of either recording equipment or the use of pad and pencil during the sessions. This leads one to question the authenticity of the transcriptions. Did Hurston take the same liberties with the folklore texts that she took with the dialogue? There is good reason to suspect that she did exactly that in order to create the smooth narrative flow of *Mules and Men*. For some the lack of comparative notes on the tales and hoodoo practices will pose a problem.

Despite the problems this volume presents to the professional folklorist, it remains a worthwhile and extremely useful book in many ways. The experiences which Hurston describes are valuable to any potential collector. The variety of the material and the realistic settings of the storytelling events as well as the interaction between the participants invite comparisons with more recent field collecting experiences. Despite Hurston's inclination to be literary in her presentation of folklore, her understanding of Afro-American culture is impeccable. Also her descriptions of the "jooks" and the activities which occurred within them preserves an important and often overlooked aspect of Afro-American culture. Her ability to capture the rhythms not only of black speech but also of black life is unsurpassed.

Their Eyes Were Watching God is an often overlooked classic of Afro-American literature. Those interested in the use of folklore in literature will find it a rich source for study. It undoubtedly offers Hurston's most mature use of folklore in the novel. (pp. 464-65)

The drama of Janie's existence can be seen as a metaphor for oppression on a grander scale. Hurston's primary symbol for this situation in the novel becomes the mule. . . . In a stratified society, the black woman is of the lowest stratum. The literal and symbolic uses of the mule throughout the novel suggest not only its importance in the agrarian South of Hurston's time, but it also evokes the folktales which compare its plight to that of the black man. In Janie's case the use of the mule also suggests the tale in which the mule acts as a trickster, causing the black man to be punished for reporting the fact that he can talk. Like the mule, Janie is expected to work for Joe and act as an ornament for his store. Any indication of intelligence is stopped immediately.

That we are expected to compare Janie's plight with that of the mule is further illustrated in the episode with Matt Bonner's mule. Although Matt's mule is given personality traits, he remains a beast of burden, a possession to be used to satisfy Matt's needs in much the same way that she is used by Joe. This is the source of Janie's empathy for the mule. But human beings are not mules. Joe Stark can buy Matt's mule and set it free, but Janie must assert her own will if she is to be free to seek the kind of life she desires. (p. 465)

Teacake is Hurston's major folkloristic triumph in the novel. Through Teacake she translates the blues aesthetic into a character. His approach to life emanates from the blues tradition and the lifestyle associated with it. He is willing to take life as it comes and, most important to Janie, he is willing to allow her the same privilege. . . . With Teacake, Janie discovers that she does not have a defined role as such. She eases herself into life on the mucks—the card games, the carousing and, of course, the blues. (pp. 465-66)

It is the irony of the novel that Janie finally finds happiness and fulfillment as a woman and human being with Teacake, when happiness had been defined for her all along in terms of social respectability and material possessions. It is Teacake, the bluesman, and the life-style that he represents from which her grandmother and Joe Stark had tried so desperately to protect her. Just as the bluesman finds cathartic relief by immersing himself in the emotions of his songs, Janie finds relief by immersing herself in that aspect of black life that she had been sheltered from.

Mules and Men and *Their Eyes Were Watching God* demonstrate Hurston's ability to portray black life in its complexity and beauty. The problems of racial prejudice make themselves felt only incidentally in Hurston's works. She chose to focus on the internal black community attempting to discover the universal through the individual experiences of the members of the group. (p. 466)

John Roberts, in a review of "Mules and Men" and "Their Eyes Were Watching God," in Journal of American Folklore, *Vol. 93, No. 370, October-December, 1980, pp. 463-66.*

LILLIE P. HOWARD

There is no indication that Zora N. Hurston was ever well known—as a writer or as a person—among the masses during her lifetime. With an impressive group of people—the elitists—on the other hand, she enjoyed brief periods of notoriety. . . . While a few lampoon her for what they consider her lack of social consciousness, her tendency to transcend racism and prejudices by disallowing them a major role in her works, and for technical and narrative deficiences in her fiction, most praise her for her ability to tell a good story well, for her vivid and unforgettable figurative language, for her staunch individualism, and for the sense of "racial health" that permeates her fiction. (p. 170)

Hurston was undeniably before her time. . . . [She] was a black nationalist when black nationalists were being discredited and deported. What really made her premature, however, was all the beauty and struggle of *Their Eyes Were Watching God* where marriage is largely defined in sexual terms; where one mate must remain petal open and honest for the other; where mere sex may take place without consummation of the marriage since consummation only takes place when the right dust-bearing bee comes along; where the quality of one's life counts more than the quantity of it; where poetry is more essential than prose, love more essential than money, sharing paramount to dominating; where one's dream is the horizon and one must "go there to know there." All that and more made Hurston extraordinary; all that makes the beauty of *Their Eyes Were Watching God* almost unbearable today, makes one wonder if even today the world is ready for Zora Neale Hurston.

Her works are important because they affirm blackness (while not denying whiteness) in a black-denying society. They present characters who are not all lovable but who are undeniably and realistically human. They record the history, the life, of a place and time which are remarkably like other places and times, though perhaps a bit more honest in the rendering. They offer some light for those who "ain't ne'er seen de light at all."

In spite of, if not because of, the mystery which surrounds her, Zora Neale Hurston has become a star of late, steadily twinkling hither and yonder casting her folkloric beams to show her awed followers the way. . . . She walks brightly among us now. Her truth marches on. (pp. 174-75)

Lillie P. Howard, in her Zora Neale Hurston, *Twayne Publishers, 1980, 192 p.*

CHERYL A. WALL

The critical perspectives inspired by the black consciousness and feminist movements allow us to see Hurston's writings in a new way. They correct distorted views of her folklore as charming and quaint, set aside misperceptions of her characters as minstrels caught, in Richard Wright's phrase, "between laughter and tears" [see excerpt above]. These new perspectives inform this re-evaluation of Hurston's work. She asserted

that black people, while living in a racist society that denied their humanity, had created an alternative culture that validated their worth as human beings. Although that culture was in some respects sexist, black women, like black men, attained personal identity not by transcending the culture but by embracing it.

Hurston's respect for the cultural traditions of black people is the most important constant in her career. This respect threads through her entire oeuvre, linking the local-color short fiction of her youth, her ethnographic research in the rural South and the Caribbean . . . , her novels, and the essays she contributed to popular journals in her later years. . . . Because her focus was on black cultural traditions, she rarely explored interracial themes. The black/white conflict, which loomed paramount in the fiction of her black contemporaries, in Wright's novels especially, hardly surfaced in Hurston's. Poet and critic June Jordan has described how the absence of explicitly political protest caused Hurston's work to be devalued [see *CLC*, Vol. 7]. Affirmation, not protest, is Hurston's hallmark. . . . Hurston appreciated and approved the reluctance of blacks to reveal "that which the soul lives by" to the hostile and uncomprehending gaze of outsiders. But the interior reality was what she wished to probe. In that reality, blacks ceased to be "tongueless, earless, eyeless conveniences" whose labor whites exploited; they ceased to be mules and were men and women.

The survival of the spirit was proclaimed first and foremost through language. As a writer, Hurston was keenly sensitive to the richness of black verbal expression. Like Langston Hughes and Sterling Brown, she had no patience with theories of linguistic deficiency among blacks; she ignored racist assumptions that rural blacks spoke as they did because they were too stupid to learn standard English. Hurston, whose father was a Baptist preacher, was well acquainted with the tradition of verbal elegance among black people. From her father's example, she perceived how verbal agility conferred status within the community. His sermons had demonstrated as well the power of his language to convey the complexity of the lives of his parishioners. Early in her career, Hurston attempted to delineate "characteristics of Negro expression." She stressed the heightened sense of drama revealed in the preference for action words and the "will to adorn" reflected in the profusion of metaphor and simile, and in the use of double descriptives (*low-down*) and verbal nouns (*funeralize*). To her, the "will to adorn" bespoke a feeling "that there can never be enough of beauty, let alone too much." Zora Hurston shared that feeling, as the beautifully poetic prose of her novels attests. The collective folk expression was the soil that nourished the individual expression of her novels. After a lengthy dialogue with her homefolk, Hurston was prepared to change some words of her own. (pp. 372-73)

Mules and Men holds the distinction of being the first collection of Afro-American folklore published by an Afro-American. . . . Unlike many of its predecessors, it presents the lore not to patronize or demean but to affirm and celebrate. Written for a popular audience, it is highly readable; after nearly half a century, it has lost none of its capacity to delight. *Mules and Men* contains seventy folktales, but it is more than a transcription of individual texts. . . . By showing when a story is told, how, and to what purpose, Hurston attempts to restore the original meanings of the tales. Folktales, she understood, serve a function more significant than mere entertainment; "they are profound expressions of a group's behavior." They cannot be comprehended without reference to those whose values and beliefs they embody. Consequently, the tales in *Mules and Men* are not collected from faceless informants, but from real men and women whose lives readers are briefly invited to share. Sharing their lives more profoundly, Hurston was ultimately forced to confront the role of women in rural black life. Her response, necessarily personal and engaged, gave shape to her most successful fiction.

Hurston met the woman who most informed this response soon after she arrived in Polk County, Florida, in January 1928. The sawmill camp where Hurston settled was an even richer repository of the folktales, worksongs, blues and cries, proverbs, and sermons than Eatonville had been. And of the people who lived there, Big Sweet was the most memorable. Hurston devoted several pages of her autobiography, *Dust Tracks on a Road* (1942), to her friendship with this woman; the influence of Big Sweet is highly visible in characters in Hurston's novels. Although Hurston gives few details about her appearance, the woman's name, with its suggestions of physical power and sexual attractiveness, of strength and tenderness, aptly sums up her character. . . . Though fearsome, Big Sweet is not feared as much as she is respected, because the community draws a distinction between meanness and the defense of one's integrity. . . . Big Sweet becomes the author's guardian and guide. (pp. 374-75)

A crucial incident recounted in *Mules and Men* pits Big Sweet against her arch rival, Ella Wall. . . . Ella Wall enters the camp "jook" (a combination dance hall, gaming parlor and bawdy house) and sends a bold message to Big Sweet's man. The two women exchange verbal insults and then physical threats, until the conflict is halted by the arrival of the white quarters boss. While Ella Wall is disarmed and thrown off the job, Big Sweet stands up to the white man and refuses to yield her weapon. . . . Big Sweet's increased respect is not earned at the cost of her femininity. Her value as a woman is in fact enhanced by her fierce conduct. After the argument, her lover proudly escorts her home.

Zora Hurston knew that approval of Big Sweet was not shared by the world outside the lumber camp. The life of this hard-living, knife-toting woman was the stuff of myriad stereotypes. And Hurston seemed all too aware of this judgment when she wrote, "I thought of all I had to live for and turned cold at the thought of dying in a violent manner in a sordid sawmill camp.". . . Passages such as this have caused some critics to accuse Hurston of being condescending and self-serving in her presentation of the poor. She does seem to be playing to her audience here; *sordid* voices their opinion of the camp and its people. It does not express Hurston's view. Her problem was to legitimize Big Sweet's conduct without defending it or positing sociological explanations for it. (pp. 376-77)

The portrayal of Big Sweet anticipates the process of self-discovery Hurston's fictional heroines undergo. Like her, they must learn to manipulate language. The novels disclose Hurston's awareness that women, like children, are encouraged to be seen but not heard. . . . It was Big Sweet's talk though that first captured Hurston's attention. Her words were emblematic of her power, for they signaled her ownership of self. The ability to back up words with actions was a second indicator of an independent self. The care Hurston took to legitimize Big Sweet's behavior intimated the expected reaction to an assertive woman. Nevertheless, Hurston believed that individual black women could base their personal autonomy on communal traditions. In so doing, her characters achieved their status as heroines.

Lucy Potts Pearson is such a character. Although her husband John is its main protagonist, *Jonah's Gourd Vine* traces Lucy's coming of age as well as his. (pp. 378-79)

[John's] greatest fascination is with words. The verbal play of the plantation's children, the ribald ditties of youths, and the prayers and sermons of the elders spark John's imagination. To win Lucy's love, he must learn to speak for himself. Both lovers search for words that can express mutual affection and respect. (p. 379)

Recognizing that Lucy will not be swayed by the charms that capture other girls' affection, John yearns to master her language. Lucy assures him that he can learn recitations better than she, and he enrolls in school. Neither realizes that the needed words cannot be found in textbooks. They can only be learned from a deeper engagement with the folk culture. John achieves this when he spends a time in a work camp, where "next to showing muscle-power, [he] loved to tell stories." Upon his return, he is prepared to court Lucy in the traditional style. This time she is the one who must master a new tongue. (p. 380)

Although her book learning is commendable, Lucy is clearly not sufficiently conversant with the rituals of her own culture. This suggests an immaturity and lack of experience that would render her an unsuitable wife. The situation is saved only when Lucy helps John improvise a new ritual that can substitute for the old. The instrument is a handkerchief out of which John has crafted what Hurston calls "a love knot." The lovers hold opposite ends of it throughout the conversation, and when Lucy misses the riddle, she points John's attention to the knot. Regaining her ground, she asks John to state what is on his mind. Wary, he asks first for a kiss. . . . The kiss unlocks the poetic power that characterizes John's speech for the rest of the novel. . . . Their acting out of the courtship ritual predicts a marriage between two active partners, both of whom are able to manipulate language and negotiate respect between themselves and with others. It does not, however, foretell a marriage between equals. The prerogatives of maleness ultimately undo the balance.

Although he continues to profess and feel love and respect for Lucy, John Pearson does not remain faithful to her. . . . He struggles against his weakness, expresses remorse when he fails, yet lacks all insight into his behavior. A serious flaw in the novel is Hurston's failure to provide a compelling motivation for John's conduct. A reader may infer that John's irresponsibility is, at least in part, a legacy of slavery. (p. 381)

Lucy is, by contrast, a new black woman. Whenever John is irresponsible, Lucy is prepared to compensate. What he lacks in ambition and initiative, she is more than able to supply. She had defied her family to marry him and remains steadfast in her love and loyalty. She even looks with compassion on John's struggle to conquer the "brute beast" within, a struggle that intensifies after he is called to the ministry. John's spiritual call is genuine, but his acceptance of it also permits him to design a self-image independent of the white world. His move to Eatonville has further encouraged this possibility. There he can assume his rightful role as leader, his talents can be given free rein. The canker that galls is his recognition that Lucy deserves much of the credit for his success. . . .

[The] following passage . . . measures the damage the marriage suffers.

"Lucy, is you sorry you married me instid uh
some big nigger wid uh whole heap uh money
and titles hung on tuh him?"

"Whut make you ast me dat? If you tired uh
me, jus' leave me. Another man over de fence
waiting fuh yo' job." . . .

John's reaction to Lucy's verbal play is a violent threat; he
will kill her if she ever repeats that fanciful remark. He stakes
out claims of ownership, vowing to be Lucy's first and last
man. Calming himself, he asks why Lucy has said such a thing.
Her response is telling: "Aw, John, you know dat's jus' uh
by-word. Ah hears all de women say dat." Lucy is answering
John in terms sanctioned by the folk culture, terms that allow
for her autonomy. She is engaging in the same kind of verbal
sparring the courtship ritual required. The "by-word" would
permit Lucy to negotiate respect in this exchange too, but John
is no longer concerned with Lucy's ability to participate in
cultural traditions. He concedes that the expression is a common one, but forbids her to use it.

Lucy continues to be supportive of John's career. Through her
maneuvering, John becomes pastor of a large church, moderator of the State Baptist Association, and mayor of Eatonville. He can never accept her assistance as a complement to
his gifts. . . . John's real defense against what he perceives to
be Lucy's domination is other women. Of course, she cannot
retaliate in kind. Words are her only defense, righteous, chas-
tising words that strike fear in John's heart but fail to make
him change his ways. (p. 382)

[Lucy] has mastered the language and absorbed much of the
wisdom of her culture. In the end, she apprehends some of its
limitations. She hears the silence where the sayings affirming
female identity should be. She espies the untaught knowledge
that no one can live through someone else and begins to teach
it. Without her realizing it, the folk culture through her husband
had assigned Lucy Pearson a "place"; she warns her daughter
to be on guard against such a fate. Loving John too much, she
has acquiesced in her own suppression. At her death, she remains on the threshold of self-discovery. (p. 383)

Published before *Mules and Men* though written afterward,
[*Jonah's Gourd Vine*] was Hurston's first opportunity to share
at length the discoveries of her fieldwork. She incorporated so
much of her research that one reviewer objected to her characters being mere pegs on which she hung their dialect and
folkways. The objection is grossly overstated, but it does highlight a problem in the book. Too often the folklore overwhelms
the formal narrative. The novel is enriched nonetheless by its
numerous examples of the Negro's "will to adorn," many of
the expressions coming directly from Hurston's notes. She
believed resolutely that blacks aspired for and achieved beauty
in their verbal expression. With extraordinary care, she sought
to reproduce their speech exactly as it was spoken. Given these
concerns, John Pearson's was necessarily the key role. As
preacher, hence poet, he represented the verbal artistry of his
people at its height. . . . This profound engagement with his
culture causes John's struggle to reconcile his physical and
spiritual selves to take precedence over Lucy's effort to claim
her autonomy. In Hurston's second and most compelling novel,
the female quest is paramount. The heroine, through acquiring
an intimate knowledge of the folk culture, gains the self-knowledge necessary for true fulfillment.

With the publication of *Their Eyes Were Watching God,* it was
clear that Zora Neale Hurston was an artist in full command

of her talent. Here the folk material complements rather than
overwhelms the narrative. The sustained beauty of Hurston's
prose owes much to the body of folk expression she had recorded and studied, but much more to the maturity of her
individual voice. The language of this novel *sings.* Unlike
Lucy, Janie, the heroine of *Their Eyes,* is a fully realized
character. During the twenty-odd years spanned by the plot,
she grows from a diffident teenager to a woman in complete
possession of her self. Two recurring metaphors, the pear tree
and the horizon, help unify the narrative. The first symbolizes
organic union with another, the second, the individual experiences one must acquire to achieve selfhood. Early reviewers
thought of the novel as a love story, but recent commentators
designate Janie's search for identity as the novel's major theme.
Following the pattern we have observed, Janie's self-discovery
depends on her learning to manipulate language. Her success
is announced in the novel's prologue when, as a friend listens
in rapt attention, Janie begins to tell her own story.

The action of the novel proper begins when Janie is sixteen,
beautiful, and eager to struggle with life, but unable to articulate her wishes and dreams. Her consciousness awakens as
she watches bees fertilizing the blossoms of a pear tree. . . .
Janie's response to the scene and her acceptance of its implications for her own life are instructive: "Oh to be a pear tree—
any tree in bloom!" Janie acknowledges sexuality as a natural
part of life, a major aspect of her identity. Before she has the
chance to act on this belief, however, her grandmother inter-
poses a radically different viewpoint.

To Nanny, her granddaughter's nascent sexuality is alarming.
Having been unable to protect herself and her daughter from
sexual exploitation, Nanny determines to safeguard Janie. Janie
must repress her sexuality in order to avoid sexual abuse; the
only haven is marriage. Marriage had not been an option for
Nanny, who as a slave was impregnated by her master; her
mistress had forced her to flee with her newborn infant. Her
daughter was raped by a black schoolteacher, convincing Nanny
that male treachery knows no racial bounds. . . . She arranges
for Janie to marry Logan Killicks, an old man whose sixty
acres and a mule constitute his eligibility. "The vision of Logan
Killicks was desecrating the pear tree, but Janie didn't know
how to tell Nanny that." So she assents to her grandmother's
wish.

Joe Starks offers Janie an escape from her loveless marriage.
He arrives just after Logan Killicks, despairing of his efforts
to win his wife's affection by "pampering" her, has bought
a second mule and ordered Janie to plow alongside him. Perceiving that Killicks's command threatens to reduce her to the
status her grandmother abhorred, Janie decides to escape with
Joe. Their marriage fulfills Nanny's dreams. Eventually it causes
Janie to understand that the old woman's dreams are not her
own. Initially though, Joe Starks cuts a fine figure. Stylishly
dressed and citified, he is a man of great ambition and drive. . . .
Tempering her reservations that "he did not represent sun-up
and pollen and blooming trees," Janie resolves, "he spoke for
far horizon. He spoke for change and chance." . . . (pp. 383-
85)

It quickly becomes apparent that, like Nanny, Joe has borrowed
his criteria for success from the white world. He takes Janie
to Eatonville because there, he believes, he can be a "big ruler
of things." His ambition is soon realized. He buys property
and opens a store which becomes the town's meeting place.
He decrees that roads be dug, a post office established, a street
lamp installed, and town incorporation papers drawn. Already

landlord, storekeeper, and postmaster, Joe runs for mayor to consolidate his power. After his election, he builds a large white house that is a travesty of a plantation mansion, and then furnishes it in the grand manner right down to brass spittoons. (pp. 385-86)

Joe assigns [Janie] the role of "Mrs. Mayor Starks." She must hold herself apart form the townspeople, conduct herself according to the requirements of his position. Under no circumstances must she speak in public. Starks first imposes this rule during a ceremony marking the opening of the store. The ceremony has occasioned much speechmaking, and toward the end, Janie is invited to say a few words. Before she can respond, her husband takes the floor to announce:

> Thank yuh fuh yo' compliments, but mah wife don't know nothin' 'bout no speech-makin'. Ah never married her for nothin' lak dat. She's uh woman and her place is in de home. . . .

Joe's announcement takes Janie by surprise. Unsure that she even wants to speak, she strongly resents being denied the right to decide for herself. . . . Being forbidden to speak is a severe penalty in an oral culture. It short-circuits Janie's attempt to claim an identity of her own, robs her of the opportunity to negotiate respect from her peers. Barred from speaking to anyone but Joe, she loses the desire to say anything at all. (p. 386)

After seven years of marriage, Janie recognizes that Joe requires her total submission. She yields. As she does so however, she retains a clear perception of herself and her situation, a perception that becomes her salvation in the end. . . . Facing the truth about Joe allows Janie to divorce him emotionally. She accepts her share of responsibility for the failure of the marriage, knowing now that if Joe has used her for his purposes, she has used him for hers. Yet she understands that her dreams have not impinged on Joe's selfhood; they have been naive but not destructive. By creating inside and outside selves, she hopes to insulate the core of her being from the destructive consequences of Joe's dreams. She cannot claim her autonomy, because she is not yet capable of imagining herself except in relationship to a man. Still, she is no longer willing to jeopardize her inner being for the sake of any such relationship.

Janie remains content to practice a kind of passive resistance against Joe's tyranny until he pushes her to the point when she must "talk smart" to salvage her self-respect. . . . So unaccustomed is Joe to hearing his wife "specify" that he imputes nefarious motives to her words. Ill and suspicious, he hires a hoodoo doctor to counteract the curse he believes Janie is putting on him. No curse exists, of course, but Starks is dying of kidney disease and of mortal wounds to his vanity. As he lies on his deathbed, Janie confronts him with more painful truths. (pp. 386-87)

The attack on her dying husband is not an act of gratuitous cruelty; it is an essential step toward self-reclamation. Moreover, in terms of the narrative, the deathbed episode posits a dramatic break with Janie's past. She is henceforth a different woman. Independent for the first time in her life, she exults in the "freedom feeling." Reflecting on her past, she realizes that her grandmother, though acting out of love, has wronged her deeply. At base, Nanny's sermon had been about things, when Janie wanted to journey to the horizons in search of people. Janie is able at last to reject her grandmother's way and resume her original quest. That quest culminates in her marriage to Tea Cake Woods with whom she builds a relationship totally unlike the others she has had. (pp. 387-88)

[With Tea Cake], Hurston explores an alternative definition of manhood, one that does not rely on external manifestations of power, money, and position. Tea Cake has none of these. He is so thoroughly immune to the influence of white American society that he does not even desire them. Tea Cake is at ease being who and what he is. Consequently, he fosters the growth of Janie's self-acceptance. Together they achieve the ideal sought by most characters in Hurston's fiction. They trust emotion over intellect, value the spiritual over the material, preserve a sense of humor and are comfortable with their sensuality. Tea Cake confirms Janie's right to self-expression and invites her to share equally in their adventures. . . .

[Although Tea Cake is a strongly idealized character, he] has had difficulty accepting Janie's full participation in their life together. Zora Hurston knew that Tea Cake, a son of the folk culture, would have inherited its negative attitudes toward women. She knew besides that female autonomy cannot be granted by men, it must be demanded by women. Janie gains her autonomy only when she insists upon it. Under pressure, Tea Cake occasionally falls back on the prerogatives of his sex. His one act of physical cruelty toward Janie results from his need to show someone else who is boss in his home. In the main though, Tea Cake transcends the chauvinistic attitudes of the group. (p. 388)

The marriage of Janie and Tea Cake ends in the wake of a fierce hurricane that is vividly evoked in the novel. In the process of saving Janie's life, Tea Cake is bitten by a rabid dog. Deranged, he tries to kill Janie, and she shoots him in self-defense. Despite these events, the conclusion of *Their Eyes Were Watching God* is not tragic. For, with Tea Cake as her guide, Janie has explored the soul of her culture and learned how to value herself. . . . Having been to the horizon and back, as she puts it, she is eager to teach the crucial lesson she has learned in her travels. Everybody must do two things for themselves: "They got tuh go tuh God, and they got tuh find out about livin' fuh theyselves." . . . This is Janie's text; the sermon she preaches is the novel itself. She has claimed the right to change her own words.

Hurston was never to duplicate the triumph of *Their Eyes Were Watching God*. In her subsequent novels, she changed the direction of her work dramatically. *Moses: Man of the Mountain* (1939) is a seriocomic novel which attempts to fuse Biblical narrative and folk myth. *Seraph on the Suwanee* (1948) is a psychological novel whose principal characters are upwardly mobile white Floridians. Although Hurston's willingness to experiment is admirable, the results are disappointing. Neither of her new settings is as compelling as the Eatonville milieu. Though the impact of black folk expression is always discernible, it is diminished and so is the power of Hurston's own voice. In these novels, the question of female autonomy recedes in importance, and when it is posed in *Seraph*, the answer is decidedly reactionary. (pp. 388-89)

[In *Seraph on the Suwanee* Hurston] restates the major themes of *Their Eyes Were Watching God*, perhaps in a misguided attempt to universalize them. Here the protagonist is Arvay Henson Meserve, who like Janie searches for self-identity. She is hindered in her quest by the deep-rooted inferiority she feels about her poor cracker background. For the wrong reason, she has come to the right conclusion. As Hurston depicts her, she is inferior to her husband Jim and the only identity she can attain is through accepting her subordinate role as his wife. . . . Early in the novel, Arvay reflects that if she married Jim, "her whole duty as a wife was to just love him good, be nice and kind around the house and have children for him. She could do that and be more than happy and satisfied, but it looked too simple.'' The novel demonstrates that it is much too simple, but at the conclusion the happiness Arvay supposedly realizes is achieved on exactly these terms. The problem is Hurston's inability to grant her protagonist the resources that would permit her to claim autonomy. Although Arvay ''mounts the pulpit'' at the end of the novel, she has no words of her own to speak.

Ultimately, Arvay's weakness may be less a personal problem than a cultural one. Though black characters play minor roles in the novel, black cultural traditions permeate the narrative. They influence everyone's speech, so much so that at times the whites sound suspiciously like the storytellers in Eatonville. Jim relishes the company of his black employees, whom he treats in a disgustingly condescending manner; and one of his sons, after being tutored by a black neighbor, leaves home to join a jazz band. Unlike the earlier protagonists, Arvay cannot attain her identity through a profound engagement with the folk culture, because she has no culture to engage. The culture of the people Arvay despises has supplanted her own. Seen from this perspective, *Seraph on the Suwanee* is not as anomalous or as reactionary a work as it otherwise appears.

From any vantage point, however, it represents an artistic decline. Hurston was at her best when she drew her material directly from black folk culture; it was the source of her creative power. Throughout her career, she endeavored to negotiate respect for it, talking smart then sweet in her folklore and fiction, proclaiming its richness and complexity to all who would hear. Her most memorable characters are born of this tradition. In portraying them, she was always cognizant of the difficulties in reconciling the demands of community and the requirements of self, difficulties that were especially intense for women. The tension could not be resolved by rejecting the community or negating the self. Hurston challenged black people to dig deep into their culture to unearth the values on which it was built. Those values could restore the balance. They could give men and women words to speak. They could set their spirits free. (pp. 391-92)

> *Cheryl A. Wall, "Zora Neale Hurston: Changing Her Own Words," in* American Novelists Revisited: Essays in Feminist Criticism, *edited by Fritz Fleischmann, G. K. Hall & Co., 1982, pp. 371-93.*

Roger Kahn

1927-

American nonfiction writer, journalist, novelist, and editor.

Best known as a sports journalist, Kahn has written for *Esquire, Sports Illustrated, Time,* and for the *New York Herald Tribune,* where his coverage of the Brooklyn Dodgers appeared regularly during the early 1950s. Kahn's prose style is described by many critics as straightforward yet sentimental, and he is commended for his success in recapturing the romantic essence of professional baseball in an era when the sport is considered by many to be a corporate enterprise.

Kahn's first book-length study of baseball, *Inside Big League Baseball* (1962), was written primarily for young adult readers. It is recommended by critics for its concise history of the sport and for Kahn's descriptions of many former major league ballplayers. Kahn's most critically acclaimed work, *The Boys of Summer* (1972), is a nostalgic book about the Brooklyn Dodgers of the 1950s. He fuses reminiscences of the past with present-day profiles of the players, and also includes a complete history of the Dodger organization. As one critic said, Kahn puts the reader "back in touch with our heroes without either cosmetizing or demeaning them." Some critics found especially informative the section on former Dodger owner Branch Rickey and his role in recruiting and signing Jackie Robinson, the first black player in the major leagues. *A Season in the Sun* (1977) is another retrospective work on baseball, but Kahn also focuses on the contemporary profit-making aspects of the game. Although the book's format is similar to that of *The Boys of Summer,* critical reception was generally less favorable, with some reviewers describing its content as loose and rambling.

Kahn has also published two novels for adult readers. *But Not to Keep* (1979) is about a journalist's attempt to cope both with fame and personal problems. *The Seventh Game* (1982) is a baseball story about an aging pitcher during the World Series. Kahn is also the author of *The Passionate People: What It Means to Be a Jew in America* (1968) and *The Battle of Morningside Heights: Why Students Rebel* (1970).

(See also *Contemporary Authors,* Vols. 25-28, rev. ed.)

VIRGINIA KIRKUS' SERVICE

More than any other sport, baseball has fascinated Americans since possibly the first formal game was played on the Elysian Fields of New York back in 1846. Though Roger Kahn speculates as to why this is so, he is largely concerned with the ballplayers themselves as they work their way from the minors to the majors, as they go through spring training and enter the race for the pennant, as they undergo the hectic, exhilarating ordeal of the World Series. By observing the techniques of pros like Early Wynn, Stan Musial and Mickey Mantle, the reader [of *Inside Big League Baseball*] can begin to comprehend the enormous energies, both mental and physical, expended in the game. He also learns the difference between inspired and routine management through anecdotes about managers like [Leo] Durocher. . . . Mr. Kahn has written a diamond-studded chronology of American baseball which probes its glitter and glory to reveal its demands and rigors.

> *A review of "Inside Big League Baseball," in* Virginia Kirkus' Service, *Vol. XXX, No. 1, January 1, 1962, p. 11.*

IRVING T. MARSH

["**Inside Big League Baseball**"] is one of the simplest and clearest descriptions of the fascinations of big-time baseball that has come across this desk. It's addressed to pre-teenagers, but it has enough inside information to make it fascinating reading for any follower of the game no matter what his (or her) age, and it is authoritatively written by a man who covered major league baseball for many years and still is covering it.

> *Irving T. Marsh, in a review of "Inside Big League Baseball," in* Books, *May 13, 1962, p. 32.*

HEYWOOD HALE BROUN

The world of which Roger Kahn writes in *The Boys of Summer* ended less than a quarter-century ago, and its continuity, statistically and intellectually apparent, is an illusion of symbolic logic in which baseball seems to be the same old game because the measurements of the diamond have not changed.

In truth, the Brooklyn Dodger team which was Kahn's to cover for the *Herald Tribune* was the last leap of the flame of romance in baseball, as the *Tribune* was the last fiercely individualist newspaper. Measurements in sport and journalism are now so changed that comparisons are not only odious but meaningless.

The Dodger Corporation, by the legal thinking which decrees that a corporation is a person, is technically alive and operates on the west coast. No logic can give life to the *Tribune,* and yet Kahn, carrying the material object of a baseball glove which he got old Dodgers to sign as he traveled among them recently, has assembled and organized memories so keen that those . . . who are old enough can weep, and those who are young can marvel at a world where baseball teams were the center of a love beyond the reach of intellect, and where baseball players were worshiped or hated with a fervor that made bubbles in our blood. . . .

Brooklyn seemed a fine place in which to grow up to the young Roger Kahn, whose own Proustian material object is perhaps a baseball, the one he threw with his father, the one he didn't catch at Camp Al-Gon-Kwit, the ones he watched the Dodgers throw and catch and hit when at last he realized that his dugout would be the press box.

Pivoting like a good second baseman he takes us out of his own Brooklyn world to the Brooklyn world of the Dodgers, and at last after mega-boxes of baseballs have gone their different ways, he takes a *Carnet de Bal* trip around the country to visit old Dodgers, and finds tragedy but not unhappiness, disaster but not defeat, and some notable victories of the human spirit.

In a sports world whose executives seem to come from the pages of Molière, its publicists and apologists from [Georges] Feydeau, and whose ideal image seems that of [Charles Dickens's character] Uriah Heep, it is refreshing and heartbreaking to see, in Kahn's pages, the passion, devotion, and anger he carried to the Dodger Vero Beach training camp 20 years ago, and to perceive as the book ends that in 20 years he has not left an ounce of them behind.

As a small boy Roger Kahn read and reread his father's copy of *Pitching in a Pinch,* a volume put together in 1912 by [New York Giant pitcher] Christy Mathewson and a ghost-writer. In a Pilgrim's Progress through sport which might have shaken John Bunyan, Kahn seems to have clung to the high ideals of the "greatest pitcher ever to toe the mound."

He has done this without ever being taken in by the Pecksniffian pomposities which politicians and press agents have tried to palm off as the high purpose of sport. He has not seen sport as the handmaiden of the establishment, the puffer of patriotism, or the serpentine servant of office holders who associate themselves with victory without sharing the agony of its achievement. . . .

Some may find all this unrealistic and sentimental but it doesn't seem so to a once-young man who walked out of Yankee Stadium on a terrible April day long ago, when a stranger ran out to right field wearing Babe Ruth's number on his back.

It's nice to know that though the medicine show moguls of baseball can, with a wave of a ledger, take our teams away, a thousand accountants with a thousand erasers cannot obliterate the memories Roger Kahn has saved here for us.

Heywood Hale Broun, ''Brooks, Bums, Dodgers, Men,'' in Bookworld, *Chicago Tribune, February 27, 1972, p. 4.*

GRACE LICHTENSTEIN

Any baseball book that begins with a quotation from Dylan Thomas can't be all good. But then, [**''The Boys of Summer''**] is about a team so extraordinary that Marianne Moore wrote poems to it, so perhaps Roger Kahn's pretentiousness is not entirely out of place. The ''boys of summer'' were named [Pee Wee Reese, Jackie Robinson, Gil Hodges, Roy Campanella, Duke Snider, Andy Pafko, Billy Cox and Carl ''Skoonj'' Furillo]. They were the starting lineup of the best team the majors ever saw—the Brooklyn Dodgers of the early 1950's.

As Kahn makes clear, they were remarkable both for the depths of their personalities and for the range of their skills. Gil Hodges, Roy Campanella and Duke Snider took turns hitting 40 home runs a season. Hodges, Billy Cox and Carl Furillo were acknowledged as the finest glove men of their day. Jackie Robinson taught a new generation how to steal bases. Two, Robinson and Campanella, made the Hall of Fame.

Given the assignment of breaking baseball's color line in 1947, the Dodgers, captained by Pee Wee Reese of Kentucky, made it look easy and won the pennant too. Yet in the clutch games (against the Phillies in 1950, the Giants in 1951, the Yankees in 1952 and 1953) they inevitably choked. ''Wait 'til next year,'' was more than a slogan; it was a way of life. . . .

As a young sportswriter for The Herald Tribune, Kahn covered the Dodgers for two of their most heroic, frustrating seasons in 1952 and 1953. The first half of the book is both an autobiography and a history of the team, with emphasis on those years.

Kahn is at his best describing how the Dodgers were able to achieve a feeling of racial harmony in a time before the Supreme Court had made integration an acceptable American idea. Robinson, he relates, broke down many of the initial barriers simply through the force of his intelligence and his overpowering gifts as an athlete. . . . Forced to sleep in black hotels throughout the South, Robinson nevertheless instructed the other black players to mix with whites at team dinners. Baited with racial epithets by Eddie Stanky, Robinson made sure the press got the story.

Not that the team itself didn't have its own racial tensions. According to Kahn, when Junior Gilliam was about to become the starting second baseman Billy Cox and others openly bad-mouthed the ''nigger'' who would make the Dodgers the first team to have more than four blacks on the field at one time.

Kahn notes, too, that newspapers (then as now) shied away from telling the truth about racial conflicts in their sports columns. ''Write baseball, not race relations. Story killed,'' wired an editor after Kahn filed a piece on the Robinson-Stanky feud.

Unfortunately Kahn . . . gives us in this first section far too much of the Kahn family and the Tribune city room, and too little of the Dodgers themselves. Also, since he stopped reporting the team after 1953, his review of its last four seasons in Brooklyn is skimpy. One could take serious issue with his judgment that the 1955 Dodgers, who brought Brooklyn its first World Series crown after 75 years, were ''past their prime.'' Maybe that victory was an anticlimax for a writer who had gone on to other things.

The second half of the book consists of interviews Kahn conducted with 13 of the fifties Dodgers, "the boys of summer in their ruin." Here the old memories take on a new dimension, because there is a sad irony in many of the portraits. . . .

Not every portrait is successful—Robinson in particular remains a two-dimensional symbol—and there are gaps. Where is Don Newcombe, that hulking brawler? Where is Billy Loes, the only pitcher dumb enough to lose a bunt in the sun? What about Cal Abrams, Brooklyn's one sorry excuse for a Jewish star in the pre-Koufax years?

Never mind. What counts is that Roger Kahn has composed a very stylish piece of fifties nostalgia that puts us back in touch with our heroes without either cosmetizing or demeaning them. Those were simpler times, before baseball was toppled from its throne as the national pastime, and the intervening years have not been kind to the sport or its players . . . . **"The Boys of Summer"** is a measure of the distance between then and now.

> Grace Lichtenstein, *"The Last Days of the Daffy Brooklyn Dodgers,"* in The New York Times Book Review, *March 5, 1972, p. 32.*

PETER S. PRESCOTT

There are many ways to waste one's youth; I wasted mine rooting for the Yankees and the Republicans. They were my teams, not because they won but because they were near: Yankee Stadium was an hour's drive from my home; the Democrats, a little farther. Brooklyn was *terra incognita*—no one I knew had ventured there—though when my radio wandered off-course I could hear Red Barber speaking a nearly familiar language from a place called Ebbets Field. Not everyone, I knew, worshiped [Tommy] Henrich and [Charles "King Kong"] Keller, though it would take time for me to learn the inevitablity, the necessity, of defeat, the kind of defeat that makes men endure. My Yankees would presently exhibit it; Kahn's book about the Brooklyn Dodgers investigates and celebrates it. . . .

"The Boys of Summer" invites us to remember what we once knew of these men—breaking curves, fast moves to the right, balls rising into the upper deck—and to recognize that our memories are not of men, but of figures in a landscape. The men come through in this book, not as fallen angels—the perspective on ballplayers that Jim Bouton adopted in "Ball Four"—but as whole men, seen in the totality of their lives so far. Kahn not only shows us what they are, he looks at how they began. A sense of awe, picked up as a child, persists as he reports on their present condition.

Kahn's book is knowledgeable, leisurely and anecdotal, as good informal baseball writing must be. But it is more: Kahn never forgets that he is writing about men in relation to a certain discipline, a certain level of achievement, a certain process of decline, and as such his book acquires a cumulative power. It is not just another book about baseball or a boy growing up to like baseball, but a book about pain and defeat and endurance, about how men, anywhere, must live. I fear that people who are bored by baseball will not read it, which would be as bright a decision as for those bored by military history to overlook [Leo Tolstoy's] "War and Peace."

> Peter S. Prescott, *"The Glory of Their Times,"* in Newsweek, *Vol. LXXIX, No. 11, March 13, 1972, p. 94.*

MURRAY POLNER

Judged on its own nostalgic terms, *The Boys of Summer* is a glorious recollection, recalling for us the spurious perfection of Brooklyn in the 1940s and early 1950s, its Brooklyn *Eagle*, which screamed joyously in a six-column spread in 1941, "WE WIN!" after the team won its first pennant in twenty-one years. Brown v. Topeka was far away in some state that couldn't even field a major league team; Joe McCarthy's extravaganzas had little impact on our schoolboy parochialism. What had it all to do with the collective fellowship we belonged to, with identifying with the "national game?" I suppose our instinct for survival encouraged those voyeuristic fantasies; but, at the same time, love of baseball, really the Dodgers, mattered very much.

I remember my friend Chick who, while his mother wept in terror after he had received his induction notice in 1951, was too frantic about the Giants catching up to worry about himself. Chick died in Korea and the Dodgers lost the pennant that year and the year after. I know how upset he would have been.

Does anyone understand? Van Lingle Mungo, flawless and certain as a right-handed fastballer, was my personal hero. When the *Mirror* reported that he had been chased nude through a Havana hotel with his lady of the moment, her husband in pursuit, my friends and I bristled at such irresponsibility: how dare some Cuban upset our Opening Day pitcher? Durocher was suspended for associating with hoods at the race track. We shook and we cursed. Who would manage *us?* When Dixie Walker, Alabama-born and the "People's Cherce" in Brooklyn, threatened to lead a player strike against the admission of blacks into baseball, he nonetheless remained popular—as did the newly-admitted black athletes. Tortuous dialectics and factionalism did not get you into the World Series. Adulated, celebrated, venerated, the players as men were the only impeccable people I had ever known. (pp. 387-88)

[However,] we all grow up sooner or later, and our fancies are punctured. For baseball, many have commented, is Jeffersonian, a rural game born of a gentler age, far from the venality of cities. Even that is a myth, for the cities have turned out plenty of athletes. But *The Boys of Summer* came from more pastoral settings—from Viola, Anderson, Woonsocket, Plainfield and Reading. Unlike professional football, with its chorus of super-patriotism and practiced violence, baseball remains what is has always been—a refuge and a pacifier, a glorification of "a past," wrote someone, "which may have never been ours, but which we believe was, and certainly that is enough." (pp. 388-89)

> Murray Polner, in a review of *"The Boys of Summer,"* in Commonweal, *Vol. XCVI, No. 16, July 14, 1972, pp. 387-89.*

DONALD HALL

Baseball is too often confused with the Major Leagues, or even with Joe Garagiola and the Game of the Week. But baseball is also college and Little League, high school and vacant lot and American Legion and Class A. **"A Season in the Sun"** takes its form from Roger Kahn's notion of baseball's scope. To make this book, Kahn spent last summer touching down at the four corners of the baseball world. . . .

From the affluence of Chavez Ravine, Kahn's **"Season"** slopes downward to Houston and the hapless Astros, who are more than $30 million in debt; then to Paul Patrick McKernan in

Pittsfield, Mass.; then to Artie Wilson, car salesman who starred in his heyday for the Negro leagues, coming up to the Majors only at the end of his career; then to Early Wynn, that intelligent and aggressive gentlemen who pitched during four decades in the Major Leagues and won 300 games; to the island of Puerto Rico, where the population is baseball crazy; to Bill Veeck, baseball-crazy genius and owner of the Chicago White Sox; finally to the bright sun of autumn, the Apollo of the 1976 World Series, the great John Bench.

There are places Kahn doesn't travel. I would have wished an encounter with a rookie, where Methodist boys from Oklahoma meet stars of Brooklyn streets hipper than Mick Jagger; where ex-cane-cutters from the Dominican Republic meet Arizona State communications majors. I would have wished a visit to the ball players of Triple A, who wait nightly for the message to see the manager. My only complaint against **"A Season in the Sun"** is its length—there isn't enough of it.

Admirers of **"The Boys of Summer,"** Kahn's great reminiscence of the old Brooklyn Dodgers, may find **"A Season in the Sun"** too slim, but they will find it thick with the old virtues. Kahn began as a newspaperman, turned into a magazine journalist; he is superb as an interviewer, masterful at retelling anecdotes. In the lineup of baseball's prose-writer superstars, each writer plays his own position with his own special skill. Roger Angell describes the game from bleachers and box seats, better than anyone else—reasoning, rendering, responding to the game in prose as graceful as a pitcher's motion. Pat Jordan enters the player's feelings, remembering his own experience as he watches Bruce Kison. Tom Clark describes the antic eccentrics of the national pastime with a straightforward, surrealistic sobriety; he could do a play-by-play of a Mel Brooks movie. But for baseball's characteristic stories—anecdotes and lore the game is rich with—Roger Kahn is best of all, with his sweet ear for the cadence of baseball talk. . . .

When a game is rained out this summer, or next winter when a blizzard has delayed delivery of The Sporting News, take Roger Kahn's **"A Season in the Sun"** down from the bookshelf to hear the soft baseball voices repeating old games in your ear, stories for summer nights or for long winters away from the diamond and the green. (p. 5)

> Donald Hall, "Mother Could Hit a Curve Ball," in The New York Times Book Review, *July 3, 1977, pp. 5, 17.**

HOWARD MEANS

"Baseball's inherent rhythm, minutes and minutes of passivity erupting into seconds of frenzied action, matches an attribute of the American character," Kahn writes in *A Season in the Sun.*

A better book—such as his earlier *The Boys of Summer,* a nostalgic, moving account of the diaspora of the Brooklyn Dodgers of the mid-1950s—might lend greater weight to his thesis, if only because it showed how that rhythm worked its way into the lives of men who played the game. But *A Season in the Sun,* however engaging, is too loose and rambling, too much a rework of a series of articles Kahn executed for Sports Illustrated, too overladen with his own wives and family to be that book.

What sticks from Kahn's book is what sticks from nearly all baseball accounts—the anecdotes: Early Wynn throwing a beanball at his own son, Minnie Minoso lining a single at age 53

for Bill Veeck's White Sox, Veeck describing Dodger owner Walter O'Malley as having a face "that even Dale Carnegie would want to punch."

Not that this is an unimportant contribution, for that richly anecdotal baseball lore—the quirks of character and action of the men, many from small towns and largely uneducated, who have played the game—is what separates baseball from the other, more fast-paced and rigidly controlled, more automatous national sports.

"Baseball," Kahn quotes Bill Veeck, "is a wonderful arena for jugglers, clowns, and hustlers." But the sum total of baseball is more than the accretion of all the cranks and eccentrics who have played it. Baseball is more than the national dowager, more than the national pulse or pastime; it is the national product. Its story—its movement south and westward, out of the cities and into the suburbs, out of the minors and into television, out of baggy pants and into tailored uniforms, from autocratic owners to syndicate men and collective bargaining—is the story of its customers; and that is a story that bears telling. (p. E8)

> Howard Means, "Diamonds Are Forever," in Book World—The Washington Post, *July 31, 1977, pp. E7-E8.**

KIRKUS REVIEWS

Kahn's sentimentality works well enough in his boys-of-summer-ish nonfiction—but here, in his whiny first novel [*But Not to Keep*], it glops over everything uncontrollably. David Priest (in Hebrew, Priest = Kahn) is a journalist and ghost writer with a bad case of the itchies; first annoyance to be got rid of is his wife Joyce, gone to fat and martinis. He remarries—to years-younger Caroline—only to find that 14-year-old son Joel is now agonized into choosing which parent he cares to live with. A messy, rending custody case is the upshot. As such, the book could have been palatable. . . . [But] Kahn, embarrassingly, interrupts his narrative early to announce: "Aside from genius and politics, talent and venality, you always rooted for the artist over the reviewer, provided only that the artist did his honest best. Bardic best. Symphonic best. Bad best. Best, any best, deserved decency. It was frightening to stand naked out there, naked and vulnerable and stained by hope." Kahn stuffs the novel with this kind of anxious, self-dramatizing filler; there's so much of it that the reader turns perverse, starts rooting for the slings and arrows that hail down upon the hero. The last 40 pages work—the custody fight—but the rest is self-indulgent and strictly "bad best."

> A review of "But Not to Keep," in Kirkus Reviews, *Vol. XLVII, No. 6, March 15, 1979, p. 346.*

MICHAEL J. BANDLER

The subject of veteran journalist-sports essayist Roger Kahn's first novel [**"But Not to Keep"**] is the interrelationship between two evolving institutions, one threatened, the other on the advance. The institution seemingly on the verge of collapse—or at least somewhat battered—is marriage. The one that appears to be holding its own is fatherhood, especially the single-parent variety.

Writing from an autobiographical perspective—if one takes as fact the personal details in the author's last book, **"A Season in the Sun"**—Kahn has fashioned a sober glimpse of contemporary society that is at once an indictment and a benediction. It sharply criticizes those forces—primarily the legal community and the courts—that compound the anguish inherent in a divorce and resultant custody proceedings. And yet, it blesses the supposed victims, the survivors—the sundered couple and the offspring—without casting stones at one parent or the other. . . .

Kahn has never been known, in his previous writings, to hew to a narrow theme, and his first venture into fiction is faithful to that broad pattern. He confronts other beleaguered institutions, such as religion and race, and vents himself on the hypocrisy and bigotry that incessantly pollute the rarefied air of "Society." He offers caustic impressions of intellectual snobbery, and—in a brief but telling broadside—bites the hand that feeds him by spoofing publishers' quests for the surefire best-seller.

"But Not to Keep" is a novel about traditions. Clear away the prejudice, bitterness, and violence that Mr. Kahn uncovers and what remains is another tradition—marriage—wrecked on seemingly inconsequential shoals. The consequences, though, loom largest for the young survivor of that split. He needs to be understood. In this sensitive, occasionally frustrating, yet honest and credible first novel, Roger Kahn obliges.

> *Michael J. Bandler, "Tradition under Judgement," in* The Christian Science Monitor, *July 18, 1979, p. 19.*

WES LUKOWSKY

[In Kahn's second novel, *The Seventh Game*,] he once again turns to baseball. John Longboat, a 41-year-old pitcher, prepares himself for the seventh game of the World Series—and the last of an illustrious career—by reminiscing about his on-and-off-the-field exploits. The reader is reluctantly herded through a tour of Longboat's poor Oklahoma childhood, his minor-league scramblings, and his major-league success. . . . It doesn't take nearly that long, however, to realize that Kahn is way off his form here. Like a made-for-TV movie, the novel offers just enough to grab your interest but barely enough to hold it. The author's reputation will ensure initial demand, but expect some disappointed readers. Even a veteran like Kahn can be caught looking at strike three every once in a while.

> *Wes Lukowsky, in a review of "The Seventh Game," in* Booklist, *Vol. 78, No. 16, April 15, 1982, p. 1041.*

DANIEL OKRENT

"The Seventh Game" is a novel about an aging pitcher on the mound for the last game of a world series (probably the last

game of his career), and of the life he has lived up until this particular October afternoon. Mr. Kahn commits enough writerly sins to send himself back to the minors. The book is littered with borrowings, from his own work (he tosses compliments at friends he encountered and evokes the places he visited on his summer's research for **"A Season in the Sun"**), from other baseball books (most notably, and regrettably, those by hacks of the 40's and 50's) and even from Tom Wolfe. . . . (pp. 11, 21)

But worse than the attributable borrowings are the clichés so firmly grounded in bad baseball literature that they are beyond tracing. He gives us predictably venal owners, dishonest agents, subliterate players (save, of course, for the [Nathaniel] Hawthorne-reading, [Claude] Monet-appreciating protagonist), a World War II bombercrew lineup (players and coaches named Dubcek, O'Hara, Levin, Domingo—I *think* it's Domingo; sometimes it appears as "Santo Domingo"—and Roosevelt Delano Dale). The hero is a fine man, happily married to a loyal peach of a girl, yet he's having an affair with the well-bred sister-in-law of the baseball commissioner. All major-league teams mentioned in the book go by their own names, except for the two meeting in the series—the New York Mohawks and the Los Angeles Mastodons (Mastodons? For a baseball club? Roger Kahn is the last writer I'd expect to display a tin ear).

That Roger Kahn should write such a book just doesn't make sense. He brings his special gift to bear on only a few episodes, mostly near the book's end. The hero's relationship (every ballplayer's relationship?) with his wife—or, rather, hers with him—is captured in a brief and unerring speech. . . .

And [Kahn's] portrait of the particularly hypocritical, snobbish and horny baseball commissioner is a gem.

But these exceptions are rare. **"The Seventh Game"** is flat, sloppy and pointless: Needlessly displaying his erudition, Kahn places the Medici in Venice and sets the duration of a law-school education at four years; losing track of his own characters, at the close of the book he grafts a trait onto one character that he had earlier ascribed to another. Yet the book provides a cautionary lesson. There are intelligent, observant, acute nonfiction writers who simply should confront fiction as a smart hitter confronts a low slider on the outside corner: They should let it go and wait for the pitch they can hit. (p. 21)

> *Daniel Okrent, "Imaginary Baseball," in* The New York Times Book Review, *July 25, 1982, pp. 10-11, 21.**

Norma Klein

1938-

American novelist, short story writer, and poet.

An author of fiction for all ages, Klein is best known for her socially realistic novels for pre-teens and teenagers. These differ from traditional young adult novels in their frank and sympathetic treatment of unconventional subjects, their implicitly feminist viewpoint, and their candid depiction of alternative lifestyles. For example, *Mom, the Wolf Man and Me* (1972), Klein's first and most commercially and critically successful novel, is narrated by a well-adjusted eleven-year-old girl whose mother has never been married. The story involves the girl's relationship with her mother and her mother's boyfriend, the "Wolf Man."

Nearly all of Klein's works deal with love and family conflicts and feature female protagonists. Klein considers herself a feminist and writes for "girls who are active intellectually, who are strong, interesting people." Thus, *Love Is One of the Choices* (1979) tells of two high school friends who experience their first love affairs and the conflicts the affairs cause with their personal and professional goals. Like this novel, many of Klein's works involve the sexual initiation of her protagonists. Although abortion is treated in some of her stories, as are other problem subjects such as lesbianism and divorce, Klein does not present pregnancy and emotional scarring as the inevitable result of teenage sex.

Critical reaction to both the subject matter and the literary value of Klein's work has been divided. Some critics question the appropriateness of the language she uses and the situations she portrays; they often object to the explicit sex scenes and her depiction of parents who condone premarital sex. Other critics feel that Klein's work has filled a need for novels which treat changing contemporary values in a frank and accepting manner. Many critics, however, even those who approve of her treatment of controversial issues, find her characters underdeveloped and her plots simplistic. They contend that her overly optimistic view of life leads her to understate the pain and conflict inherent in many of her situations. For instance, one critic has noted that in *It's Not What You Expect* (1973), Klein treats abortion as a purely financial problem. However, critics often praise the realism of her dialogue, her sensible, humorous tone, and her portrayal of parents as people with problems and weaknesses of their own. They cite these, as well as her compassion and frankness, as the source of Klein's popularity among young adults.

In Klein's adult works, which include short story collections as well as novels, the protagonists are older but the thematic concerns are similar to those in her young adult fiction. For example, *Give Me One Good Reason* (1974), like *Wolf Man*, involves a woman who decides to have a child even though there is no man in her life. Klein's short stories are generally considered her most successful works of adult fiction; her recent collection, *Sextet in A Minor* (1983), contains the short story "The Wrong Man," which received an O. Henry award in 1983.

(See also *Children's Literature Review*, Vol. 2; *Contemporary Authors*, Vols. 41-44, rev. ed.; and *Something about the Author*, Vol. 7.)

© Thomas Victor 1984

KIRKUS REVIEWS

Except for the raffish effrontery of the closing **"Apocalypse at the Plaza,"** the opener [of *Love and Other Euphemisms*], a short novel really, is both the smartest and the sharpest in this collection of reasonably sophisticated see-through stories. The novella is **"Pratfalls"** in which Rachel is the rather imperturbable casualty of the contemporary scene . . . and it is all quite funny. In between, the episodes deal with more susceptible young women, uncertain to unstable to unhappy, and only one of them (**"The Boy in the Green Hat"**) relies on a somewhat trickier device for its double-take denouement. . . . The stories are glossy (in fact two of them appeared in *Mademoiselle* and *Cosmopolitan*), alert and easily entertaining.

A review of "Love and Other Euphemisms," in Kirkus Reviews, *Vol. XL, No. 9, May 1, 1972, p. 552.*

LETTY COTTIN POGREBIN

Motherhood is sacred. But only when it happens to married women.

Children are precious. But only when they're born after the wedding. Mothers and children who fail to satisfy the above qualifications are somehow rendered less sacred and less precious. Society has a name for such unfortunate deviates from the American norm. We call them "unwed mothers" and "illegitimate children"—two categories which just happen to coincide with the Library of Congress catalog listings assigned to Norma Klein's novel, **"Mom, the Wolf Man and Me."** . . .

[If we were to steer] clear of a book bearing such socially tragic labels, [we] would miss meeting an extraordinary, dear, funny bunch of almost ordinary people: 11-year-old Brett, who worries that her mother will get married and turn normal; kooky, competent Mom—photographer, peace-marcher, iconoclast in blue jeans who treats her daughter as a full-fledged person; Grandma, who never quite comes to terms with *her* daughter's way of life; Grandpa, as enviable a father-figure as any girl could wish—a sensitive, compassionate psychoanalyst who keeps an imaginary alligator in his tub; Theo (whom Brett dubs The Wolf Man), a bearded bear of a man who teaches the mentally retarded, bakes bread and talks "in this very regular way, as though he didn't know you were a child and he wasn't"; and all the other friends with their very human problems familiar to children's lives though not often to their literature.

"They have to have been married" says a school friend struggling to comprehend Brett's status. "You couldn't have been born otherwise."

Confusing morality with sexuality has burdened our children with all sorts of misinformation (not to mention a stunted view of their erotic potential). But Brett has no trouble setting her friend straight. She's a matter-of-fact, unselfconscious child who refuses to consider herself pitiable. In truth, Brett feels kind of sorry for everyone else—for her friends who have regular parents, her neighbor whose divorced mother spends hours on make-up and men problems, or any child who must endure a set bedtime, an organized meal or a patronizing attitude. . . .

Brett likes her life just as it is. And through her eye of perception, we share the tension of the novel: will Mom and Theo go the way of all flesh—from love to marriage to a baby carriage? Our conditioned reflex demands a happy ending. Our socialized expectation decrees that a happy ending means getting married. But in this daffy, daring novel the syllogism is no longer automatic—and so we care terribly about Brett's feelings and Mom's decision.

Adult readers (and there should be many) need this book for revivification and a glimpse of what they're calling alternate life styles. Our children need this book to bridge the credibility gap in their sex education. The Library of Congress needs a severe chastisement for their myopic system of classification. And Norma Klein deserves our thanks for a story that replaces moral labels with real human beings.

> *Letty Cottin Pogrebin, "A Young Indian and a New Father: 'Mom, the Wolf Man and Me',"* in The New York Times Book Review, *September 24, 1972, p. 8.*

C.D.B. BRYAN

There is an unmistakable flatness to ["**Love and Other Euphemisms**"] . . . . The euphemisms she writes about are "marriage," "divorce," "separation," "affairs," "engagements," but none of the characters seem convincingly alienated or bitter or agonized or angry enough to want to refer to "love" euphemistically. They are all too polite.

Her collection contains one novella, **"Pratfalls,"** and five short stories, three of which to all intents and purposes are about the same sort of Jewish girl as Rachel Ovcharov Wittiker, the heroine of the novella, who wants to be interesting, wants to have people talk about her, but who instead of making things happen waits for things to happen. (p. 31)

Her strengths as a writer lie in her obviously good eye for detail but her weakness is her characters. In **"Magic"** the girl spends the weekend with her prospective in-laws, a brother-in-law who has had a nervous breakdown and not thoroughly recovered, and the tensions that one is to believe are created by the banality of her anticipated surroundings are enough to make the girl want out. But who says she deserves any better? In **"An American Marriage"** a couple decide to consult separate analysts before calling an end to their marriage. And the girl, while at her analyst's office, says, "God, make me a more interesting neurotic." Amen. In **"Apocalypse at the Plaza"** a wife calls her ex-husband and invites him to lunch with her now-husband. It is potentially a good scene, the crazed dropout artist's ex versus the conventional, up-tight businessman, and when they meet the two men begin discussing clothes and down deep you realize they really are discussing clothes. So-o-o-o what?

It's only in **"The Boy in the Green Hat,"** that the author begins to realize her potential. The wife is the sort whose postnatal depression is dangerously severe with symptoms of paranoia thrown in. The wife has come back from the park with the small child and says she has been followed by a boy in a green hat. The husband must find out if she really was followed or whether this is a recycling paranoia and depression. The wife finds out he is checking up on her and her reaction, of course, is that he doesn't trust her, which compounds her paranoia and despair. It is, by far, the best story in this collection.

I think Norma Klein's problem might be lack of confidence. She needs to take charge of her characters more firmly. There is a little too much of people just going through their paces; she is a little too-well-mannered, as though she had someone whose opinion she valued too highly or whose feelings she didn't want hurt looking over her shoulder. She will learn, I hope, to write her next book for *herself*. And for that one she should take off the kid gloves and not sit up quite so straight at her typing table. (pp. 32-3)

> *C.D.B. Bryan, in a review of "Love and Other Euphemisms," in* The New York Times Book Review, *October 15, 1972, pp. 31-3.*

MARILYN R. SINGER

Norma Klein has a fund of right ideas on life and is giving them to just the right age group. Pre-teens are concerned about how they will shape their lives, but they rarely find any clues in the fiction written for them. [In *Mom, the Wolf Man and Me*] they are treated to a commendably honest view of the way some people choose to live. Though the 11-year-old narrator Brett and her friends are always in the foreground, the grown-ups actually dominate the story. This won't offer any identification problems for young readers, however, because for once the adults are as human as the children (Brett's mother in particular); they are still growing, changing, having problems, trying solutions. . . . [Brett] loves her mother and their free style of life, prefers it to the more conventional homes of her friends, and is only occasionally hassled by society's reactions to it. If anything, the author makes Brett almost too matter of fact, but it's a good antidote to the controversial issues: if the 11-year-old narrator can be so casual about her mother not being married and having intercourse then there's no reason for readers and librarians to get upset. The only other fault that might be found here is the relative lack of action. . . . Rich characters and dynamic interactions, much humor and warmth are the book's justification. Best of all, the author makes readers aware that their lives will be shaped by the values they have. And it's all done without preaching! (pp. 60-1)

> Marilyn R. Singer, in a review of "Mom, the Wolf Man and Me," in School Library Journal, an appendix to Library Journal, Vol. 19, No. 4, December, 1972, pp. 60-1.

LOIS E. SAVAGE

["It's Not What You Expect"] can be consumed in one delicious, non-stop gulp. It is a smooth witty tale which makes one laugh out loud. The action revolves around Oliver and Carla, fourteen-year-old twins, who master-mind a scheme for opening a gourmet restaurant during summer vacation.

Upon leaning back to let the story settle into place, one becomes aware that this book is a very slick statement about the diversity of moral codes prevalent in the America of 1973. The twins react differently to the separation of their parents, their father's affair, and the abortion performed on the girl friend of an older brother in the family.

Carla clearly is upset. . . . Oliver, on the other hand, has the last word. He equates maturity with acceptance of such things as a natural, normal part of life. Only a naive romantic would lose sleep over them.

The question is, which attitude do you wish to present to young adult readers?

> Lois E. Savage, in a review of "It's Not What You Expect," in Best Sellers, Vol. 33, No. 4, May 15, 1973, p. 98.

CAROLYN BALDUCCI

If there were a single word to describe "It's Not What You Expect," it might be "modest." But "modest" only in the very best sense of that word: restrained, unpretentious, calm, clear, unconfused. In the young adult genre, this is a rare set of attributes. Norma Klein, author of "Mom, the Wolf Man and Me," is not only singularly adept at delineating fine female characters but knows she shouldn't impose Categorical Imperatives on her young readers. Indeed her novels reveal that life is a mystery and a pretty good one, at that. (p. 8)

To salvage what portends to be an emotionally tense summer, Carla and her twin brother Oliver (a food maven) and her 18-year-old brother Ralph and several other young friends start a restaurant, and their project succeeds. Moreover, through some trip-mechanism of fate, in mentioning Ralph's girlfriend's abortion to her mother, Carla discovers that her mother had not only had a love affair (and abortion) prior to meeting Carla's father, but that the young man's tragic death had left deep—unspeakably deep—scars. This revelation, coming from a woman at a time when things seem to have hit rock-bottom, makes Carla feel grown-up, priviledged to be female and closer to the woman whom she'd previously regarded as a maternal anomaly. When the marital crisis is over, Carla sees her parents as individuals with experiences and problems unconnected to the family. With her father's return, things aren't quite the same. However, as Oliver sagaciously observes, "They never were that way to begin with."

Through a natural ("modest") blend of comedy and mellowed irony, the story comes across without much fuss. If Carla and Oliver with all their classical music and Gourmet magazine hang-ups seem a bit middle-aged, well, that's the way kids are at 14. What many writers (not Norma Klein!) have forgotten is that while kids at this age may be quite knowledgeable in a factual sense, their sympathies are misered for themselves. It's only years of experience—vicarious and direct—that weld one's emotional response to the details of another person's life. In the words of Bob Dylan, "Ah, but I was so much older then, I'm younger than that now." (pp. 8, 10)

> Carolyn Balducci, "Children and Adults, Trouble and Fun: 'It's Not What You Expect'," in The New York Times Book Review, June 3, 1973, pp. 8, 10.

EILEEN KENNEDY

Why shouldn't an intelligent and independent thirty-two-year-old woman have a baby by her lover whom she doesn't want to marry? One good reason why is that if she's snappish, surly, and selfish as this female narrator, no child needs her. This very slight novel [Give Me One Good Reason], told from the point of view of a heroine with the impossible name of Gabrielle Van de Poel, recounts the impact Gabrielle's decision has on her liberated, arty parents, her earth-mother sister who makes raising two children seem a herculean task, and her sister-in-law who hates children. Because nobody in this novel suffers from any moral strictures—among the various characters there is an unbelievable number of abortions and extramarital affairs—I kept wondering what Gabrielle was making such a fuss about. (pp. 376-77)

I found the characters cold, unconvincing, and endlessly manipulative of other people, especially the metallic Gabrielle. On the other hand, the writing is sparse and clean, with crisp dialogue and an insistence on concrete details that gives the book a certain immediacy. Let's say if the reader's idea of the good life is found among the values portrayed in New York Magazine, that reader might find this book meaningful, significant, and oh, so real. I didn't. (p. 377)

> Eileen Kennedy, in a review of "Give Me One Good Reason," in Best Sellers, Vol. 33, No. 16, November 15, 1973, pp. 376-77.

LUCY ROSENTHAL

What a winning novel Norma Klein has written—for young people of all ages and for free spirits everywhere. Reading Give Me One Good Reason—her first full-length adult novel—is like spending time in the company of an open-minded, tactful, decent, and generous friend. . . .

Her output is an example of reciprocity between children's and adult literature. In Klein's children's books, her respect for her young readers is marked by her inclusion, in a fashion totally integral to the story, of preoccupations and materials which used to be the exclusive preserve of so-called adult novels: illegitimacy . . . , divorce or separation . . . , sexual intercourse between unmarried adults. . . . In Give Me One Good Reason, Klein shows her adult readers, in turn, an affection along with an ability to beguile and convert the mood by employing those story-facilitating devices—things happen constantly and for the most part end happily—that are the traditional hallmarks of children's literature.

In this newest novel she touches such adult preoccupations as affection between the sexes, relations between parents (wed and unwed) and children (small and grown), relations between sisters and sisters-in-law and brothers, adults and children *not* their own, and—as they say—love and work. Given her technique, it's hardly surprising that the novel has something of the character of an adult fairy tale. Things frequently work out for the beleaguered heroine so much more happily or conveniently than they often do in life: a day-care center for Gabrielle Van de Poel, the young unwed and pregnant heroine of the story, is just around the corner from the scientific laboratory where she will continue to work at her good job; money is no object and the lack of it no handicap; Rudolf Biedermyer, the kind cabdriver who stops for Gabrielle and her two Great Danes on a terribly rainy New York day is really a doctor taking time off to mull over vocational options (would he rather be an artist?) and later to court Gabrielle; Gabrielle, in the absence of a husband or a helping man, has parents and other relatives who can backstop her as baby-sitters and in other ways once her child is born; and so on. Klein is not offering here fairy-tale anodynes or whitewash of adult misery. Her purpose is partly instructive: she is saying, one suspects, that this is how society, with a few changes, could work, in some instances *ought* to work, and in some already does. . . .

Pregnancy, outside of marriage or in ambiguous marital circumstances, is a recurrent motif of Klein's writing. Far from being obsessional, it seems to serve the purpose of exploring the problem of a woman's free exercise of options in a changing society, of a questioning by her women characters of the institution of marriage, or at least of having the women in these stories bring out into the open a reluctance to marry or an ambivalence about marriage women may have always felt but until recently did not feel free to express. The motif of pregnancy here also is perhaps a metaphor for creativity: how do we live life's possibilities to the full, whether literally pregnant or not? Pregnancy, the impending birth of a baby, makes the drama of these stories impend also. . . .

In *Give Me One Good Reason,* Gabrielle has no qualms about her relation to her work. She is an established and talented biochemist. And she has no qualms about her pregnancy. "This must be one of the most planned born-out-of-wedlock babies in the history of man." What she *has* qualms about is marriage. (p. 36)

[This book sees] the virtues of different life-possibilities and lifestyles, of the kinds of social extensions human beings, free and not-so-free, are making and can make in a changing society. The life-possibility toward which Gabrielle moves is the one of full and deep commitment to a loving man. . . .

Give Me One Good Reason is a happy book and a humane one. Its humanity offsets a certain lack of prose distinction, though the prose is more than serviceable. Klein's novel is more life-like than literary, a storyteller's book, not a poet's, the work of a writer engaged more with life and its possibilities than with language and its resources for language's own sake. Certainly a women's literature has room for both or all kinds of writers, and one is grateful for Norma Klein.

"I hate happy endings," Gabrielle laments at book's end. I love them, and in this instance believe in them—and in this book. (p. 37)

Lucy Rosenthal, "A Singular Parent," in Ms., *Vol. II, No. 7, January, 1974, pp. 36-7.*

THE BOOKLIST

[In "**Taking Sides,**" the] author has probed another unusual family situation with her customary frankness and stylistic flair that just avoids glibness. Twelve-year-old Nell is getting used to her parents' second divorce. . . . She copes with New York sophistication and a superdeveloped sense of responsibility until her father has a heart attack. . . . One wonders if in revealing the human frailties of parents, the author might be creating a breed of over-mature children; in spite of this, her story is readable and speaks openly to the concerns of many preadolescents.

A *review of "Taking Sides," in* The Booklist, *Vol. 70, No. 22, July 15, 1974, p. 1254.*

ALICE BACH

After their second marriage and divorce (to each other) Nell's parents arrange that Nell and her younger brother Hugo will live in New York with Dad, who writes science books at home, while Mom will live in the country with her friend Greta and commute to her New York job. . . .

The ups and downs of living with Dad . . . are related to us by Nell in a meandering fashion. ["**Taking Sides**"] drags along, evoking in the reader a sense of having been trapped by a self-important bore, the you'll-never-guess-what-happened-to-me person who grabs your arm at a party and tries to implant meaning to an inconsequential tale with frenetic hand motions and overemphasized phrases.

The musings of lackluster Nell create a novel that is sitcom slick but prose poor. . . .

All Nell hands over to us is information—snippy remarks about helpless Arden [her father's girlfriend], admiring words for outdoorsy loner Greta, predictable bickerings with Hugo, amazement at a woman "being so fat and being married." But the subtle shadings of feelings and wonderings that lie beneath the surface of real people are never revealed or examined.

Although she tells us she's the smartest one in her class, Nell can't differentiate in intensity between asking her grandma for a Tampax and trying to extract a vital promise from her father after his heart attack. "Do you promise to live until I'm grown up with my own family?" "I promise."

In not exploring this remarkable promise from father to daughter, Norma Klein has packaged a piece of meretricious reassurance, the lying about life, that has signaled the sloppiest of children's fiction since Nancy Drew solved every case just in the nick of time. . . . The pain of sickness, the tensions of separation, the fear of death are as deeply felt here as the steamroller that momentarily flattens a cartoon character. Like that feckless creature, Nell skitters away, unaffected, unhurt and seemingly incapable of any residual caring, thought, or emotion.

Since Norma Klein has chosen to act as faithful scribe to trendy teen-age dialogue and scattered teen-age thoughts, she has avoided the writer's essential task—to reflect upon and shape the material of the novel with a special perspective, a vision unique to each writer's imagination. By blunting the writer's sharpest tool, the imaginative use of language, she has denied the reader a sense of place of orientation in the world that the novel purports to create.

Alice Bach, in a review of "Taking Sides," in The New York Times Book Review, *September 29, 1974, p. 8.*

MARGERY FISHER

[A book like *Mom, the Wolf Man and Me*] can easily suffer from the wrong kind of comment. The picture of an unmarried mother who makes a virtue out of her situation could offend those who believe that books of this kind should always classify and computerize good and bad. It would be a pity if such a shrewd, perceptive study of individuals were outlawed or, conversely, if it were praised for a courageous stand against convention. In fact this is an expert example of first-person narrative, in which every detail and every conversation, reported or direct, is properly related to Brett, the speaker throughout. From her comments we can deduce a great deal about the smugly conventional Evelyn, who gets her ideas from *A Child's Guide to Divorce* and is so disastrously unprepared for life; about Grandma, who deplores her daughter's way of life, and Grandpa, who believes in freedom and courage; above all, we can guess at what Brett partly understands, her mother's approach to life. It is a relief to read a book written in a mood so far from the usual lugubrious, sickly or melodramatic tone of novels for the 'teens. Norma Klein's crisp, witty, intelligent style indicates that she is primarily interested in character—in the fascinating differences between one human being and another, the surprising effect they can have on one another. To do this through the words of a girl of eleven—brash, abrupt, unintrospective, sometimes naïve—is a real achievement.

Margery Fisher, "Who's Who in Children's Books: 'Mom, the Wolf Man and Me,'" in her Who's Who in Children's Books: A Treasury of the Familiar Characters of Childhood, *Holt, Rinehart and Winston, 1975, Wiedenfeld and Nicolson, 1975, p. 54.*

MARGARET STRICKLAND

[*The Sunshine Years*, a sequel to *Sunshine*,] is composed of nine sequential episodes based on the TV series. Sam, a young leader of a struggling singing group, married Jill's mother, Kate, just before she died of cancer at 20. Raising a young daughter by himself, Sam suffers from typical mother-hen-type fears and doubts. . . . Though it's contemporary and fast reading, the use of profanity is questionable, as is the inconsistency of Sam's sexual code when he has affairs with sexually liberated Nora and ambitious Montana Smith (a girl) while Jill is asleep upstairs yet stutters with embarrassment when Jill matter-of-factly and innocently tells it like it is between him and Montana using terms Sam has obviously employed to explain sex to her.

Margaret Strickland, in a review of "The Sunshine Years," in School Library Journal, *Vol. 22, No. 8, April, 1976, p. 90.*

KATHA POLLITT

As readers frequently eluded by lovely apartments, interesting work and pleasant affairs may suspect, Norma Klein's approach to life is as resolutely cheerful as a suburban breakfast nook. . . . [In **"Girls Turn Wives,"** nothing] seems to stop—or even momentarily waylay—her characters from growing, learning, fulfilling themselves. Even the disruption of Jess's marriage by her husband's infatuation with a wraithlike woman poet eventually serves to straighten out her marital difficulties and make her a better wife. It's nice that someone is telling women they can have both children and a career, that best of all possible worlds. . . . But Jess and Hannah's problems are solved so smoothly one can't help wondering if they ever really existed.

Katha Pollitt, in a review of "Girls Turn Wives," in The New York Times Book Review, *April 25, 1976, p. 49.*

ALLEEN PACE NILSEN, KAREN B[EYARD-] TYLER, AND LINDA KOZAREK

If in their reading, reluctant readers are looking for an emotional experience, then they want the highs and the lows to be packed tight against each other. They haven't much patience with the long drawn out in-betweens. They want struggles where the odds are great and everything is super-sized.

One such struggle, with which most teenagers are now familiar, is the story of Jacquelyn M. Helton, the young mother who learns at eighteen that she has fatal bone cancer. Norma Klein's novel *Sunshine* is based on the television movie suggested by Helton's journals. Readers, reluctant and enthusiastic, who wept over the movie and watched the resulting TV special, will want to read this touching and unavoidably moving novel. The first person narrative is written in the honest and occasionally introspective style which permits identification with the brave young woman as she struggles to keep alive her hopes and dreams. (p. 93)

Alleen Pace Nilsen, Karen B[eyard-] Tyler, and Linda Kozarek, "Reluctantly Yours, Books to Tempt the Hesitant," in English Journal, *Vol. 65, No. 5, May, 1976, pp. 90-3.**

MARGARET BURNS FERRARI

I read Norma Klein's story for adolescents, **Mom, the Wolf Man and Me,** with delight, and so I was anxious to read and review her new novel, *Girls Turn Wives*. I was disappointed. The freshness she brought to a story about a girl, her divorced mother and her mother's new boyfriend, has deteriorated into empty trendiness in *Girls Turn Wives*. In telling the story of two 37-year-old Barnard alumnae who are still friends, one a lean, frigid, career-oriented intellectual and the other a frumpy, unaccomplished but happy mother of three, Klein uses every cliché imaginable and almost no irony at all.

Right now, there is so much fiction and drama about women discovering themselves that the subject is becoming trite. . . . Without fresh insights, there is little to recommend another novel on the theme, and Norma Klein does not bring any.

Her writing leaves out the real complexities of living. . . . Problems are easily solved, death is quickly sidestepped, affairs are gracefully ended with no one hurt, husbands and wives are charmingly reunited after separations, no one is lonely for long and kids say the cutest things. Klein writes like a Walt Disney staff writer, which is irritating in a novel that clearly wishes to represent social reality. . . .

What is most annoying about Klein's book is that it might have been quite good. Instead, it suffers from the superficiality of Judith Rossner's *Looking for Mr. Goodbar*, without achieving that novel's sheen. . . . The book has its moments, but . . . it will only seem emotionally satisfying to addicts of happy endings.

Margaret Burns Ferrari, in a review of "Girls Turn Wives," in America, *Vol. 135, No. 1, July 10, 1976, p. 18.*

ANN A. FLOWERS

[*Hiding*] is well-titled, for hiding is the central idea in the plot and the key to the character of the heroine. Eighteen-year-old Krii Halliday has been an introvert all her life. She chooses to attend—instead of an American college—a ballet school in London, hoping to cover her self-consciousness by a costume and by what she assumes will be considered her foreign peculiarities. . . . Krii becomes involved almost unwillingly in a rather dreary love affair with Jonathan, a young English choreographer, and when he suddenly marries another girl because he is enraged at Krii's inability to express her feelings, she becomes even more secretive. . . . Realizing that she is too small to become a first-class ballet dancer and depressed by Jonathan's marriage, she returns home and impulsively hides for a week in the attic of her parents' house. Somewhat unconvincingly, the author uses this brief respite to give her the courage to return to the world, enter college, and fight her constant impulse to hide herself away. Her quiet, introspective personality, her cool observation, and her secretiveness seem real; and although her struggles to escape from herself are rather touching, they can be almost as irritating to the reader as they were to Jonathan. (pp. 629-30)

Ann A. Flowers, in a review of "Hiding," in The Horn Book Magazine, *Vol. LII, No. 6, December, 1976, pp. 629-30.*

MARILYN WILLISON

A simple little novel that deserves popularity is Norma Klein's *Hiding*. . . . This short book is about an eighteen-year-old girl who is spending a year in London studying ballet. She stumbles into a love affair that forces her to re-evaluate her life goals, her personality, and her family. She has a very fecund sister, an aloof and sometimes sarcastic brother, and parents who have a most unconventional relationship. How our little ballerina changes—and what changes she initiates—are intriguing. *Hiding* documents far more than the life-changing week she spends in her parents' attic. Both the dialogue and characters are plausible and while this book is primarily directed at young readers, I think that it has tremendous appeal to readers of any age. I relished every page.

Marilyn Willison, "Feminist Front," in West Coast Review of Books, *Vol. 3, No. 2, March, 1977, p. 58.**

CAROL SCHENE

[In *It's OK If You Don't Love Me*] 17-year-old Jody enjoys sex and takes informed precautions to avoid pregnancy. . . . Jody spends a lot of time analyzing her actions in an annoyingly flip way, a trait she comes by naturally since her twice-divorced mother discusses having her tubes tied as if she were deciding to have her shoes shined. Conversations between characters are very frank, often including a smattering of four-letter words, but Klein is disappointingly blasé in dealing with the real decisions young high school age women must make about the opposite sex.

Carol Schene, in a review of "It's OK If You Don't Love Me," in School Library Journal, *Vol. 23, No. 9, May, 1977, p. 83.*

DAN WAKEFIELD

Norma Klein has a nice sense of what teen-agers today might be feeling about themselves, each other, their bodies and minds, their friends and parents. . . . [**"It's O.K. If You Don't Love Me"**] is low-key, credible, frank and gutsy. . . .

[The] author manages to write in an open, intelligent manner about such potentially ticklish subjects as contraception, pregnancy, racial, religious and regional prejudice [and] mother-daughter jealousy. . . . Despite all this, you never have the sense that you are getting an informational handbook dressed up as a novel.

Best of all, Norma Klein avoids the darkest and most dangerous pitfall of an adult writing a dramatic story about adolescents: She is never condescending. One ends the book liking not only the teen-age characters but also the author who had the empathy, understanding and talent to create them.

Dan Wakefield, "Firepersons and Other Characters," in The New York Times Book Review, *May 1, 1977, p. 10.**

KLIATT YOUNG ADULT PAPERBACK BOOK GUIDE

Told in the first-person, *Hiding* is painfully introspective. So much is crammed into its pages however, that no event or character (except its narrator's) is explored in any depth. The reader is left unsure whether to sympathize with its supersensitive heroine, or to find her ridiculous. Still, readers who can ignore the strain on their credulity will find a certain appeal in the story, especially if they also at time have felt like retreating from the rat race—and who has not?

C.B.J., in a review of "Hiding," in Kliatt Young Adult Paperback Book Guide, *Vol. XII, No. 1, Winter, 1978, p. 9.*

JOYCE SMOTHERS

With minimal plot and maximal dialogue, the author brings [the two protagonists of *Love Is One of the Choices*] through their respective sexual awakenings and to new realization of their inner—and outer—selves. Klein's characters are reactions against stereotypes: a father who cooks and a mother who doesn't, a boy who loves *Alice in Wonderland*, and lots of people over forty who admit to having and enjoying sex. The book moves right along, with many very funny conversations. But the world she has created is a rarefied one, in which everyone is brilliant and/or sophisticated, and there is always time to talk. It's fun to visit, but does anyone really live there?

Joyce Smothers, in a review of "Love Is One of the Choices," in Library Journal, *Vol. 103, No. 20, November 15, 1978, p. 2351.*

NORA JOHNSON

[In **"Love Is One of the Choices,"**] Caroline and Maggie, seniors at a Manhattan private school, both children of divorced parents, have simultaneous love affairs—Caroline with Justin, the 28-year-old married (but separated) science teacher for whom she baby-sits, and Maggie with Todd, a boy from another school, whom she meets during a debating contest. Maggie, a raging feminist, fights the pull toward committed love that draws Caroline so dangerously.

The writing is pleasant enough but irritatingly simplistic. . . . What happens to the young people is moderately interesting, but I really wanted to know more about the briefly-dealt-with parents who have chosen to bring up teenagers in the city and must decide about things such as sex in the apartment, for themselves and their children. . . . But if I were 18 and at Brearley again, I think I'd like this book. The issues that once preoccupied 21-year-olds have moved back four years and are described here openly and rather engagingly, and the adult world doesn't seem too forbidding.

> *Nora Johnson, "Love and Madness," in* The New York Times Book Review, *March 25, 1979, p. 28.**

PATTY CAMPBELL

A pleasant surprise from an author whose recent work has been disappointing is *Love Is One of the Choices,* by Norma Klein. Ever since *Mom, the Wolfman, and Me,* we have been hoping for another book from her that takes a look at modern manners with compassion and wit. *Love Is One of the Choices* is that book—but much, much more. No junior novel, this, but a fully articulated and insightful double love story. The contrast between fiercely independent Maggie and artistic and dreamy Caroline is accentuated by the men they choose for first lovers. Brilliant Maggie meets her match in pleasant, determined Todd, and Caroline's fantasy love for Justin, her high school science teacher, becomes reality when his neurotic wife leaves him. Both young women struggle, but in different ways, to keep their own identities in the face of the temptation to surrender to emotional security.

A source of tension for the reader is that each appears to have chosen the man that would be right for the other. In the end the characters explore this perception and then set it aside. The story has a wealth of funny or poignant moments that hang in the memory: the friendly intellectual sparring between Maggie and her psychiatrist father, fragile Caroline's terror at a quarrel with Julian, Maggie and Todd's cheerful and matter-of-fact first bedding. Here is a love story that we can give to YA's without apology.

> *Patty Campbell, in a review of "Love Is One of the Choices," in* Wilson Library Bulletin, *Vol. 53, No. 8, April, 1979, p. 579.*

JOYCE SMOTHERS

Similar to Judy Blume's *Forever* in style and appeal, this slick screenplay novelization [*French Postcards*] will be popular with teenage readers. Three nice American college kids arrive in Paris for their junior year abroad, and each embarks on his/her own sexual odyssey. . . . The protagonists spend a disproportionately small amount of time worrying about academics. Most of the local color seems to be straight from Fodor or Fielding. Sexual encounters, while casual and very frequent, are not explicitly described. (pp. 2236-37)

> *Joyce Smothers, in a review of "French Postcards," in* Library Journal, *Vol. 104, No. 18, October 15, 1979, pp. 2236-37.*

PAULA J. TODISCO

[*French Postcards*] purports to chronicle the activities of four young American students during a year of study in Paris, but the backdrop might as well be Hoboken, or the moon, for all the attention given to developing a sense of locale. The so-called students carry adolescent self-absorption to a ludicrous extreme, concerning themselves solely with not missing any opportunity to "do it" with some of the natives (they also do not have to worry about birth control, pregnancy, or VD). The characters, both American and European, are unencumbered by personalities, depth, or much in the way of feelings (with the exception of sexual desire). Unfortunately, the forthcoming movie and Klein's name on the cover of the paperback are sure to bring demands for this very poorly written title filled with vulgar language. (p. 97)

> *Paula J. Todisco, in a review of "French Postcards: A Screenplay Novelization," in* School Library Journal, *Vol. 26, No. 3, November, 1979, pp. 96-7.*

BOOKLIST

The sexual fantasies and emotional realities of late adolescence are depicted [in *French Postcards*] with Klein's customary skill and stylistic shorthand as the initial risks of entering the world of adult relationships set up the characters for an often bewildering speed course in psychological maturation.

> *A review of "French Postcards: A Novel," in* Booklist, *Vol. 76, No. 8, December 15, 1979, p. 595.*

C. NORDHIELM WOOLDRIDGE

The summer 15-year-old Alison Rose [of *Breaking Up*] spends in California with her father and his wife throws several wrenches into her normally easy-going life. A sudden attraction for best friend Gretchen's older brother Ethan creates problems in the girls' relationship; and then there are the ugly things Daddy starts saying about Mom and close friend Peggy. In the end, Ali concludes that "there are different ways of loving people." . . . Executed in the facile, first-person style of an author not writing but merely recording what her protagonist is thinking, this is no literary gem. The plot is slow getting started and the juxtaposition of the mother's healthy, loving lesbian relationship with the father's insecure traditional marriage is too carefully orchestrated.

> *C. Nordhielm Wooldridge, in a review of "Breaking Up," in* School Library Journal, *Vol. 27, No. 2, October, 1980, p. 156.*

NORMA BAGNALL

Ali is into sex, masturbation, and reading *Playgirl,* and she is concerned with all of life that centers on her own narrow world. Conversation (and [*Breaking Up*] is mainly conversation) is about bodily development, lifestyles, going braless, and making out. The book suffers from lack of story, from stereotyped characters, and from uninteresting (or no) plot —what we call meaningless writing. It is too bad that the writer of *Mom, the Wolf Man and Me* would foist this on us.

Very young adolescents may read this because of their interest in sex and development, but *Breaking Up* will never make C. S. Lewis' qualification that a good book for young people must also have meaning for adults; my seventeen year old and I both found it insipid.

Norma Bagnall, in a review of "Breaking Up," in The ALAN Review, *Vol. 8, No. 3, Spring, 1981, p. 13.*

JAY MERYL

An assertive, healthy lesbian parent is featured in . . . [*Breaking Up*], one of the few books for teenagers which presents homosexuality as an acceptable alternative lifestyle.

On a summer visit to her re-married father in California, fifteen-year-old, middle-class Ali develops a gradual awareness, understanding and eventual acceptance of her mother Cynthia's relationship with Peggy. . . .

Throughout the novel, Ali becomes clearer about her own sexuality as well. . . . Such issues as jealousy, sexual relationships, divorce, pregnancy, abortion and love are explored realistically and matter-of-factly.

I have several criticisms of the book. Although the usual stereotypes of lesbians (masculine, man-hating, unsatisfied women) are contradicted, not enough information is provided about Cynthia and Peggy's relationship. Ali and her mother have a moving discussion about Cynthia's lifestyle, but it does not tell the reader much about her mother's daily life, personality or beliefs.

In addition, the negative comments about the lesbian lifestyle from Ali's father are left uncontradicted, even when Ali decides to return to New York. Readers could conclude that Harold's biased opinions are valid.

Furthermore, homosexuality is not presented as an option for teenagers in this book, though there is clearly a character (Ali's best friend Gretchen) who does not fit into heterosexual roles. Gretchen is very attached to Ali and does not have an interest in boys, yet the reader is left with the impression that she will grow up lonely and unfulfilled.

Characterization is occasionally stilted. . . .

Despite my reservations, it is enlightening to see a novel which deals with lesbianism in a positive way and credits teenagers with the ability to make decisions for themselves and to feel deeply for each other.

Jay Meryl, in a review of "Breaking Up," in Interracial Books for Children Bulletin, *Vol. 12, No. 3, 1981, p. 19.*

DEBORAH HOLLANDER

The greatest frustration in reading [*Domestic Arrangements*] is the seeming lack of concrete values toward sexuality and life in general presented by the parents of two teenage daughters, Tatiana and Cordelia. The sophistication level of the mother, Samantha, is indistinguishable from that of her daughters. For example, when 14 year old Tatiana asks if her boyfriend can sleep overnight with her, Mom replies, "sure, for how long?" with little concern. The daughters model Samantha's tendency to flirt, cajole, and manipulate Neil, the father. Neil is a noncommittal character. When Tatiana asks her father for a diaphragm for a Christmas present (her 16 year old sister had received one the year before) Dad's response is, "I don't feel comfortable with the idea, you're fourteen sweetheart. That's

still extremely young." As a reader this was quite disturbing; after all Dad has been very much aware of Tatiana's intimate relationship with her boyfriend for several months.

We question the audience Norma Klein directed this book toward. The messages and values presented throughout make us feel this book is inappropriate for school library consideration.

Deborah Hollander, in a review of "Domestic Arrangement," in Voice of Youth Advocates, *Vol. 4, No. 4, October, 1981, p. 34.*

MARILYN LOCKHART

As the plot [of *Wives and Other Women*] flashes between 1970 and today, Klein relates the story of three warm, sympathetic characters who point out the author's central themes—that women see each other as either wives or mistresses and that this can be a repeating pattern of their lives. . . . Full of insights, realistic dialogue, and warm and human interactions, this is engrossing and lively recommended reading.

Marilyn Lockhart, in a review of "Wives and Other Women," in Library Journal, *Vol. 107, No. 11, June 1, 1982, p. 1112.*

STEPHANIE ZVIRIN

Hit harder than her brother or sister by their parents' separation, 14-year-old Robin [narrator of *The Queen of the What Ifs,*] is even more disturbed by her father's affair with another woman. . . . Personal concerns about sex and romance surface to complicate her life further, but they take a clear second place to worries about her family. The portrait of the liberal, slightly offbeat Jewish family . . . , almost a hallmark of Klein's writing, is once again evoked, and the author demonstrates a sure feel for natural, realistic dialogue. But her fans will miss the force and energy of some of her previous books and find her characters, though quite likable, curiously insubstantial.

Stephanie Zvirin, in a review of "The Queen of the What Ifs," in Booklist, *Vol. 78, No. 20, June 15, 1982, p. 1364.*

EVE SIMSON

Much of [*Wives and Other Women*], which spans the years 1970-81, centers on conversations about the sexploits of several middle-aged characters. The message seems to be: Don't trust your spouse. She/he is cheating on you, most likely with someone she/he works with. So you might as well have your one-night stands too. . . .

None of the characters is admirable. Even though they have interesting careers, they remain dull people who in futile attempts seek through sex an escape from the dullness of their lives.

Eve Simson, in a review of "Wives and Other Women," in Best Sellers, *Vol. 42, No. 6, September, 1982, p. 218.*

PUBLISHERS WEEKLY

[*Sextet in A Minor*] provides a wonderfully varied look at the way we live now in the novella, the title story, which contrasts the voices of two couples, the Tomlinsons (and their son Jimmy) whose marriage is disintegrating, and newlyweds who are just beginning. The sixth voice is Mr. Carlisle, a bachelor, another guest at the pensione in the Alps where they all stay on their brief holiday. Klein's counterpointing of contrasting voices is as amusing as it is moving. . . . Klein seems in complete control of her material, manages to capture speech patterns beautifully, and to probe carefully the emotions and sensibilities of those she describes. (pp. 47-8)

> *A review of "Sextet in A Minor: A Novella and Thirteen Stories," in* Publishers Weekly, *Vol. 222, No. 25, December 24, 1982, pp. 47-8.*

WILLIAM BRADLEY HOOPER

Sexual attraction is the theme binding together [the stories in *Sextet in A Minor*]. . . . Dialogue—the major element in character/plot realization—is of central importance in each story. Klein has a fine ear for the word usage, rhythms, and hesitations found in both casual and impassioned speech. She places her characters in situations that are not deeply complicated; all the stories are easy to follow, yet not predictable, and all have one thread or another relevant to the common problems and resolutions that arise in daily life.

> *William Bradley Hooper, in a review of "Sextet in A Minor: A Novella and 13 Short Stories," in* Booklist, *Vol. 79, No. 15, February 15, 1983, p. 763.*

MARSHA HARTOS

Near the end [of *The Queen of the What Ifs*] Mom talks about the value of love in terms other than sexual, but one statement cannot erase the opposite message developed throughout the book. Klein does not present a realistic picture of life. Instead she exploits teenage girls' natural interest in sex. There are careless mistakes: Mom is said to have attended two different colleges; Robin says she gives two cello lessons a week but describes three pupils; her friend Terry tours France but returns instead from Rome. Klein's fans may have no objections to *The Queen* . . . , but librarians may prefer more thoughtful and careful writing.

> *Marsha Hartos, in a review of "The Queen of the What Ifs," in* School Library Journal, *Vol. 29, No. 8, April, 1983, p. 125.*

BARBARA KOENIG QUART

Norma Klein's collection of stories, *Sextet in A Minor,* opens with the title novella, set at a Swiss lake resort. The choreography among its six characters . . . sounds the note of marital discontent and sexual musical chairs that continues through almost all the stories that follow. Most of these have New York City settings . . . vaguely Jewish, certainly wealthy and rather jaded and cynical. Written in prose that is lively, quick and sure, these tales of the mismarried, of stolen but unenthusiastic adulteries, of marriages that frame shock treatments and suicide confirm yet again that if marriage and men are still remarkably much on women writers' minds, it is mostly as disordered thoughts and bad dreams. (p. 741)

> *Barbara Koenig Quart, "First, the Bad News," in* The Nation, *Vol. 236, No. 23, June 11, 1983, pp. 738-41.**

DENISE P. DONAVIN

An unlikely encounter between a used-car dealer and an expectant, unsettled, and distressed teenage couple sets off a chain of not-unforeseeable events. Klein's treatment of these troubled, searching individuals [in *The Swap*] is direct, poignant, and effective. . . . While the focus is on the dilemma of the teens, Klein's development of her adult characters—especially the car dealer, Misha Edelman, who is in a quandary over the recent death of his wife, son, and grandson—gives an extra dimension to the story of a too-young mother trapped in an unworkable marriage.

> *Denise P. Donavin, in a review of "The Swap," in* Booklist, *Vol. 79, No. 22, August, 1983, p. 1448.*

LOIS A. STRELL

Beginner's Love is hardly for beginners. And yet, what adult would bother reading a slow moving book about two 17 year olds just for a little sex? On the other hand, some teens would read a poorly written book, with shallow characters, minimal plot and insipid dialogue, just for a little sex. But in this case, they'd probably skim "for the good parts." Shy Joel has trouble meeting G-I-R-L-S. . . . Joel tells the story in first person "stream of ramble." The dialogue is written in Valley Girl talk ("Like, you know . . . ," followed by some long-winded and tiresome thought). Every other sentence alludes to sex whether it's necessary or not. . . . The depth of dialogue, feeling and emotion is embarrassingly shallow. This makes [Judy Blume's] *Forever* seem like Pulitzer Prize material.

> *Lois A. Strell, in a review of "Beginner's Love," in* School Library Journal, *Vol. 30, No. 2, October, 1983, p. 180.*

KEVIN KENNY

Never one to shy away from the topic of sex . . . , Norma Klein's latest work addresses the intricacies of initial romantic and sexual rumblings. *Beginners' Love* chronicles several tumultuous months in the life of a shy and somewhat insecure 17-year-old. (p. 203)

Klein's novel is both explicit and thought-provoking. Joel's musings on sex and the relationship in general ring true, and the book contains a number of interesting minor characters. Only Leda's characterization is questionable, with her analogy between forgetting to brush her teeth sometimes and forgetting to insert her diaphragm sometimes being particularly inane for a supposedly intelligent young woman. Klein's explicitness and the somewhat casual abortion should insure controversy in some areas. Subject matter and readability, however, should insure popularity. . . . (pp. 203-04)

> *Kevin Kenny, in a review of "Beginners' Love," in* Voice of Youth Advocates, *Vol. 6, No. 4, October, 1983, pp. 203-04.*

DENISE M. WILMS

Bizou is a French child born of a black American woman, Tranquility, who went to model in Paris and married a well-known photographer. After his death she stayed because the French, according to Tranquility, are much more tolerant on racial matters. Bizou, then, is quite cosmopolitan as she embarks on an American vacation with her mother. But then her mother disappears, leaving Bizou in the charge of Nicholas, a just-met fellow traveler who is about to start med school. . . . [*Bizou*] moves easily, and Bizou's dilemma is one that holds interest. Klein's development is a bit pat: Nicholas is a little too good to be true. Also, there is the occasional obscenity and almost obligatory portrayal of unconventional lifestyles that one expects from Klein. However, she is a practiced hand at keeping readers afloat. Never deep and sometimes irritating, this is nevertheless very readable and full of popular appeal.

> *Denise M. Wilms, in a review of "Bizou," in* Booklist, *Vol. 80, No. 4, October 15, 1983, p. 360.*

ANNE CONNOR

Klein's popular fast pace will attract readers unconcerned with her bland style, shallow characterization and an astoundingly unrealistic plot. She uses the problems of racism and child abandonment to make [*Bizou*] relevant, but fails to deal with them in any significant manner.

> *Anne Connor, in a review of "Bizou," in* School Library Journal, *Vol. 30, No. 3, November, 1983, p. 94.*

Steve Martin

1945?-

American comedian, scriptwriter, fiction writer, and actor.

Martin's fame rests on his reputation as a stand-up comedian. His comic approach, which one critic calls "inspired lunacy," is characterized by nonsensical, off-the-wall zaniness. Martin believes that comedy is more a matter of an entire character than of specific jokes or stunts; accordingly, he has created a strong stage personality to tie together his "flights of nonsense." Martin's humor depends on the unlikely combination of a respectable, "normal" person with wild, uninhibited behavior. For instance, Martin will walk onto the stage looking like a composed professional, tell a joke with a ridiculous or nonexistent punch line, and then laugh like an idiot. Martin notes that this contrast is the primary source of his success: "There's got to be order for my comedy to work, because chaos in the midst of chaos isn't funny, but chaos in the midst of order is."

Martin wanted to become involved in show business at an early age. When he was ten years old he began working as a vendor at Disneyland; in the next eight years he found ample opportunities there to develop the skills he gradually incorporated into short routines: banjo playing, magic, and comedy. In 1964 Martin detoured from his career ambitions to enroll in Long Beach State College as a philosophy major. He studied for three years until, as he has said, "everything became pure semantics, nothing had meaning. It was like losing your mind." Martin then enrolled in a television writing course at the University of California at Los Angeles in pursuit of an entertainment career. His first break came in 1968, when he was hired as a comedy writer for the highly controversial and popular television show "The Smothers Brothers Comedy Hour." Difficulties with network censors caused the show to be cancelled during the 1968-69 season, but in 1969 Martin and the show's ten other writers received Emmy awards for their work. As a result of this success, Martin was in great demand, and he wrote for Glen Campbell, Pat Paulsen, Sonny and Cher, and other television performers. However, he quickly tired of writing formulaic material for others, and he quit television writing in 1971 to become a stand-up comedian.

During his first few years as a performer, Martin often appeared as the opening act at rock concerts, but audiences generally were unreceptive. In an attempt to gain wider recognition, Martin tried to create an image based on wild clothing, long hair, and beads. Although he met with some success, including his first guest appearance on "The Tonight Show" in 1973, Martin began to attract greater attention when he significantly altered his approach in 1975. The short hair and white, three-piece, tailored suit he adopted contrasted sharply with his favorite props: bunny ears, fake arrows-through-the-head, and balloon animals. As Martin's dress became more conventional, his act became more outrageous and his popularity quickly grew. He appeared on television more frequently and in 1976 guest-hosted the popular "Saturday Night Live" show for the first time. Seemingly overnight, Martin's appeal became widespread; he performed at large arenas usually reserved for rock concerts, and audiences showed their enthusiasm by wearing fake arrows and bunny ears to his shows.

Lynn Goldsmith/L.G.I. © 1978

In addition to his live performances and television appearances, Martin has also recorded several albums. His first record, *Let's Get Small* (1977), won a Grammy award, as did his next, *A Wild and Crazy Guy* (1978). However, Martin's book of humorous sketches, *Cruel Shoes* (1977), was less successful. Most critics consider the stories and short pieces in this book to be slight and suggest that Martin's brand of humor is nearly impossible to translate into book form. More recently, Martin has been involved in films as an actor and scriptwriter. His first film success, *The Absent-Minded Waiter* (1977), is a short piece based on a skit Martin originally wrote for "The Smothers Brothers Comedy Hour." The film, in which Martin portrays a hilariously inept waiter, received an Academy Award for best short comedy film. Martin appeared in and cowrote the screenplays for several full-length motion pictures, including *The Jerk* (1979), *Dead Men Don't Wear Plaid* (1982), and *The Man with Two Brains* (1983), and also starred in the films *Pennies from Heaven* (1981) and *The Lonely Guy* (1983). Although critical reception to these works has been mixed, with one critic lauding Martin's ability to convert "expertise into the highest form of imbecility" and others finding the films just silly, they have been very popular with the general public.

Although critics find it difficult to define Martin's distinctive style, his deliberately goofy behavior and sometimes childish jokes elicit frenzied enthusiasm from his audience. His routines are frequently taken directly from the slapstick skits of early comic movies, but he makes these routines new by parodying them. Pauline Kael notes that Martin "gets us laughing at the fact that we're laughing at such dumb jokes. . . . He does the routine straight, yet he's totally facetious." Despite mixed reaction to this "dadaesque philosopher turned goofball," as one critic defined him, Martin is among the most popular comedians in America.

(See also *Contemporary Authors,* Vols. 97-100.)

SUSAN PETERSON

The nature of Steve Martin's humor defies pat definition. He wanders from downright silly sight gags such as repeated bumbling with the microphones to ironic quips about every subject imaginable (car seats to solar energy heat), to quirky musical excursions on the banjo somewhat reminiscent of the early Smothers Brothers.

All is executed from a rather mock-humble stance, with Martin himself professing to be uncertain as to why he makes people laugh. It could be, he claims, the pieces of bologna he puts in his shoes before going on stage.

The audience is led to attribute its appreciation of this madness to not only the humorist's, but also its own loony sense of humor. It is Martin's endearing gift to have succeeded in confirming that sense of fun in those present. (pp. 35, 37)

> Susan Peterson, "Steve Martin, Liberty," in Billboard, *Vol. 89, No. 7, February 19, 1977, pp. 35, 37.*

DAVE MARSH

Steve Martin has become the comedic rage by the usual means: introducing a couple of readily imitable phrases into the vernacular (excuse me if I don't repeat them). More than that, his characterizations have made being an asshole fashionable again; all he lacks is a lampshade. For this, he deserves a humanitarian award. Now, when you do stupid things people think you're being paid for it.

Unfortunately, the least deliberately absurd thing Martin has done was committing his act to vinyl. The problem with *Let's Get Small* isn't that the routines are the same old stuff we've seen on the *Tonight Show* and *Saturday Night;* they are, but that's not the issue. The issue is that this isn't a funny record, mostly because Martin doesn't sound like Martin. (This has something to do with the recording quality.) Because so many of Martin's bits involve ridiculous voices, a purely aural presentation of his humor seemed to have possibilities; it turns out that seeing him do all that dumb shit is as important as hearing him. (p. 94)

> Dave Marsh, in a review of "Let's Get Small," in Rolling Stone, *Issue 252, November 17, 1977, pp. 94, 96.*

BRUCE MALAMUT

Jokers like David Steinberg and George Carlin are just that—jokers and no more, whereas [Steve Martin and Randy Newman] (even sounds like a comedy team, eh?) are great U.S. humorists in the ironic and equivocal tradition of Mark Twain,

Robert Benchley and the Marx Bros. You never quite know when they're being serious. They are both depraved and blasphemous—queers, nigguhs, bilinguals, schmucks who listen to this stuff ("who actually pay for it," as Martin puts it)—nothing is sacred. . . .

Not to mention both of their attitudes toward the racial question. Both would be happy to A-bomb Rhodesia off the face of the map—after all, it'd be far more efficient than those stupid Geneva talks. Thank God both are apolitical (but look out Barry Goldwater if they weren't). . . .

Both of these Orange County sons share an ambiguous love for Americana which is more realistic and cynical than modern or idealistic. . . .

The major difference between them is that where Newman has a heart (& a big one, judging by the likes of his most beautiful love songs), Martin shows no pity—he is supercilious to the point of psychopathology. But both Newman and Martin react to the same America, from Newman's brilliant Kurt Weill-like short-stories and lovable deviates, to the wide-eyed gruesomeness of Martin's most brutal skits. "Comedy is *not* pretty," he lectured a New York audience between two bits called **"Happy Feet"** and the mortifying **"Cruel Shoes"** concerning a masochistic foot fetishist's customized toe gear. The effect of this inspired juxtaposition was like grokking a perfectly sculptured bronze of the bilevel masks of tragicomedy. The only competition between these two faces of Dr. Sardonicus is to see who can be more rank and smile the widest simultaneously.

> Bruce Malamut, "Evil Minds, Dirty Habits," in Crawdaddy, *December, 1977, p. 82.*

DAVID FELTON

[Steve Martin's] jokes are funny—not just funny but, you know, *different*, weird, "out there." Like his description of all the world's religions: "And the fourteen invisible people came down from the sky with the magic rings that only Biff could read."

Sometimes they're shocking: "Not too many people smoking out there tonight, that's pretty good; it doesn't bother me when I'm in a sleazy nightclub like this, 'cause I'm used to it, but if I'm in a restaurant, and somebody says (*low moron voice, sort of like* [Red] *Skelton's Clem Kadiddlehopper*), 'Hey, mind if I smoke?' I'll say (*righteous but cool, like a salesman*), 'Uh, no, do you mind if I fart?'" . . .

Sometimes they seem to con the audience, with a little sting at the end. . . .

Sometimes they're highly structured, like a whole routine that parodies a common theme by substituting one word. . . .

Sometimes they're totally spontaneous, like the way he handled a heckler last year at the Boarding House; "You're not the Zebra Killer, are you? 'Cause if you're not, I'd like you to meet him."

And sometimes they're just really dumb. . . .

And sometimes they're not jokes at all: "Here's something you don't see every day. (*Steve leaps into the air several times, stretches his mouth open with both hands and roars like a raving lunatic.*) Aarrrgh!"

But jokes or not, traditional or far-out, these foolish bits and pieces have two things in common: one, they are utterly without redeeming social importance; they're like little pills you swallow that make you laugh—no message, no ulterior motive or purpose. And two, Steve doesn't really need them to be funny. It's true, I've seen it happen many times—Steve walks onstage and in thirty seconds, without telling one joke, reduces his audience to a state of helpless giddiness that lasts for the rest of the show. Sometimes they start laughing even before he comes out because he has this habit, as the club announcer is introducing him, of clowning around in the wings just enough to make the first few rows go nuts. Then he walks on with a superconfident air about him—Las Vegas Professional—wearing maybe a handsome white suit or a handsome dark one, an expensive-looking banjo strapped to his ever-so-nonchalant body, and with a voice as corny and mellow as Mel Torme's he says something like this:

"Well, welcome to the show, ladies and gentlemen. My name's Steve Martin, I'll be out here in just a minute, and uh . . . let's get goin', we're gonna have some fun tonight, huh? (*Laughs like an imbecile*) How much was it to get in? Four dollars? (*Laughs arrogantly, like the joke's on you*) Okay, you paid the money, you're expecting to see a professional show, so let's not waste any more time, here we go with Professional Show Business, let's go, hey! (*Steve steps back and starts tuning his banjo; he is consumed by the process, pawing at the pegs, fretting over the frets. Finally he looks up at the audience, beams, strides forward and bangs his head into the mike.*) Okay, we're movin' now, eh folks? Yes, these are the good times and we're having them, ah ha ha ha.''

I mean, what *is* this shit? Here's one of the hottest comedians in the business, certainly one of the best looking, best dressed, quickest witted, most poised, most imaginative and most accomplished in such varied arts as magic, juggling, banjo playing and fun balloon animals—and he's standing up there acting like a *jerk*, an *idiot*, a fucking *asshole*! And that's the whole point. It's like . . . Steve Martin basically has one joke and he's it. And it drives the crowd wild, not just during the show but long afterward. (pp. 61-2)

Well, that's really not quite true, because the whole point about Steve Martin, what makes Steve Martin so special . . . is that eventually, maybe a day or two after the show, his audience stops laughing . . . and they start acting . . . really . . . weird. They start acting like Steve Martin; they start talking like him, moving like him, wearing some of his corny trickshop props. Some writers, you may have already guessed, start writing like him. They simply can't help it, and quite frankly, I'm not sure they'll ever be able to stop. . . .

It's like . . . Steve plays with his audience, he makes them part of the joke; he sets them up and slaps them down, and by acting like an asshole, he lets them do the same to him. This isn't comedy; it's campfire recreation for the bent at heart. It's a laughalong for loonies. Disneyland on acid. (p. 62)

But he does have this higher insight. He breaks down barriers. He allows us to see the comedian in all of us. And I believe that really *is* important in today's world. In his own way, Steve Martin *is* a light, a source, an inspiration and a leader.

It's just that . . . well . . . you'd be an asshole to follow him. (p. 63)

David Felton, "King of Hearts Come Down and Dance," in Rolling Stone, *Issue 253, December 1, 1977, pp. 58-67.*

TONY SCHWARTZ

Martin's style is a pie in the faces of Lenny Bruce, Dick Gregory, Mort Sahl and all the iconoclastic comics who dominated the stand-up scene in the '60s and whose legacy has been passed down to most of today's best comedians. Now, the prevailing style is less political, but it retains an ethnic edge and an outsider's perspective. Woody Allen mines a mother lode of anxiety and insecurity, pleading the case for the little guy. Lily Tomlin urges that attention be paid to society's outcasts. Richard Pryor spins complex tales of survival in the ghetto.

All Steve Martin asks is that everyone have a good time. His approach is a throwback to vaudeville, slapstick and the comedy of his childhood idols, Red Skelton and Jerry Lewis, but it is flecked with a '70s penchant for self-parody. Along with Chevy Chase and Martin Mull . . . , Martin is part of a counter-revolution in American comedy: white and middle-class in appearance, mock arrogant in posture and unthreatening in its message. His act, which he writes himself, speaks to an audience raised on television and sophisticated about show-business affectations. Martin shapes his parodies with the gentle affection one might expect from a comedian who got his start at Disneyland. He has a sharp eye for human foibles, but he turns his insights into comic bits so absurd that only a fool would take offense. . . .

Even when Steve Martin makes jokes at his own expense, he lets you know that *he* knows it's all part of the act. He makes a contorted effort to play a chord on his banjo, then breaks into a riff that reveals how well he can really play. He picks up a handful of oranges, announces that it's time for juggling, drops them on the floor, then picks them up again and begins juggling as though it were the easiest thing in the world. He performs a magic trick with a candle—first making it vanish, then revealing its hiding place by leaving his arm ostentatiously outstretched. No sooner does the audience break up than he folds his arm at the elbow and proves that the trick worked after all. What makes you laugh so hard is the sight of this reasonable man so shamelessly shedding his inhibitions, this boy who should know better gleefully acting naughty—and getting away with it. (p. 61)

Tony Schwartz, "Comedy's New Face," in Newsweek, *Vol. XCI, No. 14, April 3, 1978, pp. 60-2, 64, 69-71.*

TOM CARSON

[Outside] of (maybe) Woody Allen or Lily Tomlin, I don't think the Seventies have provided a single comic genius. . . . Steve Martin has yet to prove he's a great, funny man.

Martin isn't a talent anymore, he's a commodity. His first album, *Let's Get Small,* went platinum, winning a Grammy and several important cover stories in the process. The new LP, *A Wild and Crazy Guy,* promises to do a lot better. Yet it's a slovenly piece of work, slackly performed and miserably edited. The routines don't build—they're not even routines, in any real sense of the word. Instead, the comedian simply meanders from one random one-liner to the next, and he's not in a terrific hurry to get there either. . . . But from the sales and audience response, it's clear that his fans don't care. To them, Steve Martin can do no wrong, and they're buying whatever's offered just to hear their hero mouth the title line.

All the set pieces are already familiar: **"A Wild and Crazy Guy"** (has anyone ever traveled so far on *one* routine?) from *Saturday Night Live*, **"King Tut"** from the single of the same name. Though the latter is basically a one-shot joke, it's probably the best thing Martin's ever done. The song's point may be obvious, but at least there is one. And next to almost everything else on the album, **"King Tut"** gleams like gold.

Most of the new material sounds puerile and secondhand. Martin gags his way through a chorus of "I'm in the Mood for Love" and announces: "Some people have a way with words; other people, uh. . . ." (This jape, with slight variations, is repeated throughout the LP. It does not age well.) What's truly ironic is that Steve Martin, apart from a handful of brilliant catch phrases, really doesn't have much feel for language. With his distinguished / silly white hair and dapper / sappy white suit, he's a mod Everyman gone wrong in a singles bar—i.e., funnier to look at or think about than to listen to. . . . [He's] hopelessly incapable of the kind of pointed, speed-freak rapping that, say, Robin Williams excels at. At its worst, Martin's is a desperation humor so obvious and threadbare he even has to resort to dirty-word punch lines (à la Mel Brooks) to rescue some of his hoariest chestnuts from the fire.

Hailed as a throwback to the "clean" comedians of the Fifties, Martin has very little in common with great subversives like [Sid] Caesar and [Ernie] Kovacs (though his funny-voices bits are quite derivative of both men—especially of Caesar's comic Germans). Clean, apolitical comedy is one thing, while cartoonish mediocrity that wholeheartedly supports a decade's social clichés instead of deflating them is another. Childishness can be charming, but when you calculate it as closely as Martin does, it simply becomes hard to take.

The Fifties joker that Martin does remind me of is Milton Berle. Indeed, the former's aren't-I-funny balloons and the arrows through his head are a perfect Seventies equivalent of the latter's pink tutus. There's a smug, emasculated quality—a rancid, showbiz condescension—in Martin's humor that's very reminiscent of Uncle Miltie's pushy, anything-for-a-laugh excess. And, like Berle, Martin owes his vast popularity to the fact that you can laugh at him without feeling at all threatened. He's hip in an era when being hip means being safe. Liking Steve Martin is now blue-chip security in every high-school clique in America. (pp. 87-8)

> Tom Carson, "Peeling the Top Bananas," in Rolling Stone, *Issue 285, February 22, 1979, pp. 87-9.*

PUBLISHERS WEEKLY

Rising comic star Steve Martin apparently has wide appeal, but ["Cruel Shoes," a] collection of 50 of his short routines, finds us reacting with irritation rather than chuckles. Short to the point of terseness (and sometimes pointlessness) the pieces are snide commentaries on what Martin sees as the pretentiousness of certain segments of society. The titles of **"The Diarrhea Gardens of El Camino Real"** and **"Turds"** convey the bathroom level of much of his humor. . . . It's difficult to find the source of Martin's popularity in these trivial offerings. . . . Perhaps it takes the tube to transmit his macho wit.

> A review of "Cruel Shoes," in Publishers Weekly, *Vol. 215, No. 18, April 30, 1979, p. 105.*

ROY BLOUNT, JR.

As a monologist, Martin is no Richard Pryor or Lily Tomlin (to name the two great stand-up comedians since W. C. Fields) or Lenny Bruce or Randy Newman or Bob or Ray. The best thing about his TV special last season was *The New York Times*'s preview of it. To read in the newspaper of record that a man was to deliver on prime time network television a long sketch about turtle wrangling was gratifying; the sketch itself, one felt, was long. On his big-selling live album [*A Wild and Crazy Guy*], Martin performs worn material rather perfunctorily for an audience that seems intent on getting hysterical without grounds. His appeal to the young borders on the bubble gummy.

But Martin has done wonderful things: the original *Saturday Night* version of his **"King Tut"** song and dance (though if "Born in Arizona,/Moved to Babylonia" were the other way around, it would sound just as silly and yet have a point), his swinging-immigrant-guy character (though Dan Aykroyd is even more impressive as the brother), and various transcendent appearances on the [Johnny] Carson show. . . .

Prose, on the evidence of *Cruel Shoes*, is not Martin's element: "I decided to secretly follow this dog. I laid about a hundred yards back and watched him. . . . As I approached, I could hear the sounds of other dogs moving lightly. . . . I remember throwing them bones now and then, and I could recall several of the dogs seemingly analyze it before accepting it." The syntax is not that bad throughout, but only one bit (**"The Nervous Father"**) in *Cruel Shoes* has what could be called happy feet. (p. 20)

Writing is something many a book has done without. *Cruel Shoes*, however, lacks not only style but also character. Fields, Groucho Marx, and Fred Allen all spoke with decidedly less timbre and snap in print than orally, but each of them produced a readable book or two that at least evoke—if they fail quite to render—the author's voice. Precious little from Martin's slim volume would be funny, let alone original, even if fleshed out by Martin's bunny-ear apparatus and fine awful smile.

One chapter is called **"Dogs in My Nose."** It is three paragraphs long and seems to go on and on and on. Further nasal whimsy appears under the heading **"Comedy Events You Can Do"**: "Put an atom bomb in your nose, go to a party and take out your handkerchief. Then pretend to blow your nose, simultaneously triggering the bomb." The reader who does not know five fourth graders with better nose jokes than that is not traveling in a fast enough crowd.

Now, drolleries that do not quite come off may yet be estimable; sometimes not quite coming off is the better part of coming off. But some of these brief sketches suggest Richard Brautigan on a particularly languid day. There are several apparently straight, though furtive (but not furtive enough), poems. There are jibes at leaden philosophers that—although or because Martin was once a serious student of philosophy himself—are leaden (though thin). **"Cows in Trouble"** and **"The Day the Buffalo Danced"** are topics worth developing, but what Martin gives us is surely not the *way* discontented cows would act and definitely not how buffalo would dance.

An item about a nationality called Turds approaches risible flatness, but why "Turdsmania" for the country's name? Turdsey, perhaps. Turdwana. There is something to be said for this sentence from **"Poodles . . . Great Eating!"**: "The dog-eating experience began in Arkansas, August, 1959, when Earl Tauntree, looking for something to do said, 'Let's cook the dog.'" But "experience" is not quite the word, the town in Arkansas should be given, there ought to be a comma after "do," and "Tauntree" is not a funny name.

In this reviewer's estimation. Which is not to deny that one would perhaps give up all one's estimation for the abililty to tie a balloon buffalo. And make it dance. *Like a buffalo.* (pp. 20,22)

Roy Blount, Jr., "Martin's Talking Feet," in Es- quire, Vol. 92, No. 2, August, 1979, pp. 20, 22.

ROGER ANGELL

Watching **"The Jerk,"** a comedy starring Steve Martin, is like spending an afternoon on the rickety rides of some sleazo travelling carnival . . . : now and then, an involuntary laugh is bumped out of us by an unexpected lurch or spin of the Whip, but most of the attractions are so slow and noisy and uncomfortable that even while we continue to smile (we're here for *fun,* aren't we?) we are mostly aware of the encompassing smells and dirt, and of the dimness of effort that has gone into the whole feeble entertainment. Steve Martin, of course, has been a star turn on television's "Saturday Night Live," but **"The Jerk,"** of which he is co-author, owes much more to Mel Brooks. I am not a perfectly uncritical Brooks fan, but compared to this movie his "Blazing Saddles" and "High Anxiety" are super-rides, from which we emerge with a gasping "Wow!" and a little weak-kneed stagger as we rejoin our friends on the ground. Steve Martin plays a back-country innocent (a white boy somehow raised by a black family in Mississippi: a laugh right there, see?) who goes out into the world and accidentally makes and then loses a fortune. The Poor Sap is an ancient and useful comedy device, but Mr. Martin's Navin Johnson doesn't know *anything* (when it comes time to kiss his girl [Marie] . . . , he licks her on the face), and if we do laugh at his misconceptions about sex and money and crime (none of the gags or bits are strong enough to survive recapitulation), it's exactly like laughing at a mental defective. Released from the constraints of network TV, Mr. Martin has stuffed his own "Candide" with street language and smutty jokes: the hero gives his dog a scatological name, which is then heard through the rest of the movie, evidently in hopes of our repeating the ugly little bark of surprise that we gave it the first time. Mr. Martin plays one long scene with his pants down and trailing around his ankles; there is no reason for this in the story, but the business sums up the tone and level of this disastrous film.

Whether or not we enjoy it, Steve Martin's television persona is a complex comic achievement, which seems to divide his watchers into hopeless idolators and glumly puzzled shruggers. The "wild and crazy guy" in the white suit, with his quick and rigid bows, awkward m.c. gestures, dangling jaw, and pleading, terrified eyes, is a caricature of outward adult assurance and bottomless inner uncertainty, while his repeated and increasingly self-referential material—on something in the news, on dog droppings, on violence, on cats, on his looks, on sex, on anything—is nonsense delivered with a frantic surface knowingness and very little else: heh-heh, nothing here means *anything,* folks! It is without affect or values, and thus appeals directly to an enormous audience of young people— from their early teens to their mid-twenties, say—who know a million contemporary names and products and issues and uglinesses but as yet have few ideas or judgments to bring to bear on them and are protected only by their flimsy and perfectly unknowing sophistication. Mr. Martin's Navin Johnson,

the Jerk, is a far less subtle creation, but it strokes the same audience, and for the same reason: at least we know more than *this* dumb bastard, guys. This is a depressing direction for movie comedy to be taking, but for all I know it may be the right commercial one now. It seems just possible that **"The Jerk"** will be a big hit. (p. 168)

Roger Angell "High and Low," in The New Yorker, Vol. LV, No. 44, December 17, 1979, pp. 167-68.*

ROBERT ASAHINA

To be sure, this picaresque tale [*The Jerk*] is far from a classically constructed comedy. There are gags that might work as blackout sketches on *Saturday Night Live* that merely interrupt the story line of *The Jerk*. . . . There are narrative gaps and illogical thrusts that, I fear, were unintentional. But even some of the irrelevant material is strangely entertaining.

After Navin meets his true love, Marie . . . , he excitedly writes his mother: "Dear Mom, she looks just like you—except she's white and blonde." Later, the two lovers stroll along a moonlit beach, singing "Tonight You Belong to Me" in a pleasantly off-key duet, accompanied by ukulele and, of all things, cornet. The scene could have been nothing more than the kind of blatant lampooning of movies of the past that runs throughout [Steven Spielberg's] *1941*. Instead, it is an oddly touching romantic interlude, a pleasant contrast to the rest of the film. . . . Martin—perhaps because he works as a standup comedian—understands the role of rhythm in humor.

I must admit that I have never been a fan of either Martin or *Saturday Night Live,* where he rose to prominence. Nevertheless, in *The Jerk* he has carefully put together a persona that is a genuine comic archetype. With his eyes darting wildly, his tongue tripping clumsily in his mouth, and his arms flapping helplessly at his side, Navin is the perfect embodiment of awkwardness and insecurity. (pp. 23-4)

The Jerk, though admittedly fanciful, derives comic strength from its small moments. They ring true enough to make us squirm, and invite us to laugh not just at others but at ourselves. (p. 24)

Robert Asahina, "No Laughing Matters," in The New Leader, Vol. LXIII, No. 1, January 14, 1980, pp. 22-4.*

KEN TUCKER

Comedy Is Not Pretty! is Martin's third and most extreme collection of sweet-faced dirtiness, abrupt non sequiturs and fresh catch phrases. . . . Like most comedy albums, the new LP dulls after a few playings, and it ought to, because Martin relies so consistently on the gentle shock of his relentless meaninglessness. This *must* be going somewhere, you say about one routine after another, but they never do. He gets his laughs that way.

What *Comedy Is Not Pretty!* makes clear is the characteristic that's at once Martin's greatest fascination and biggest weakness: a complete lack of identification with his audience. . . . If his golden rule seems to be "Comedy is not pretty," its corollary is "The non sequitur is wholly subjective." For his absurdist jokes to work, Martin needs to control the atmosphere around them—which is why he doesn't do well with hecklers, why his suits are so prim and white (how can a guy *this* impeccable be *this* crazy?) and why he doesn't bother to make contact with the slavering hordes who are still wearing arrows through their heads and yelping "Ex-*cuse* me!" more than a year after Martin has gone on to something new.

Steve Martin's comedy is not only not pretty, it's also totally ironic. That's what keeps him such a daring artist and funny guy.

Ken Tucker, in a review of "Comedy Is Not Pretty!" in Rolling Stone, *Issue 311, February 21, 1980, p. 57.*

GREG LENBURG, RANDY SKRETVEDT, AND JEFF LENBURG

Much has been written about the "new wave" comedy of the late seventies. It's been defined as a backlash against the comedy of the sixties, which was preoccupied with social and political commentary. New wave comedy is not concerned with political issues. It's only concerned with silliness. In fact, Steve [Martin] has spoken proudly of deliberately weeding out anything in his act that has legitimate meaning. (p. 113)

Steve has said that comedian Jack Benny was one of his idols when he was growing up. He sees a similarity between his character and Benny's. Both characters have glaring flaws, yet they pretend to be unaware of them, even though they really know better. Benny perpetually insisted that he was thirty-nine, even when he was obviously well into his seventies; Steve maintains that he's a professional comedian while crashing into the microphone. . . .

Steve may have derived his frenetic, physical comedy style from watching another childhood idol, Jerry Lewis. He resembles Jerry in some ways; both act like incompetents and are largely physical in their approach to comedy. There is a major difference between Steve's and Lewis's viewpoints, however: Jerry does anything for a laugh, but Steve derives much of his humor by exaggerating his *concept* of doing anything for a laugh. (p. 114)

As a result of these influences [and others], Steve relates comedy not to ideas or jokes, but to personalities. A strong character, one which is original and easily identifiable, is one of the keys to success in comedy. Very few "joke-tellers" have ever become major comedians. In keeping with his personal definition of new comedy, he keeps his act totally centered upon himself rather than society. The bits and pieces may not seem logical, but they all fit into a whole; they're threaded together by the fact that they are logical expressions of Steve. This comic character is so strong, Steve doesn't really need jokes to be funny. He can just stand around and look silly (and often does). By just *being* there, he makes the audience go wild.

All of the great comedians have noticeable contrasts within their personalities. [Stan] Laurel and [Oliver] Hardy's dignity contrasted with their stupidity; W. C. Fields's delicate manner of speech and gesture was contrary to his malevolent view of humanity; [Charlie] Chaplin's lofty dreams of romance were negated by his shabby tramp's clothing. Steve's contrast could be seen as his delusions of skilled professionalism, pitted against his actual clumsiness. (pp. 115-16)

Steve's character is that of a likeable neurotic. He's an incompetent who's hungry for acceptance, so he pretends that he's a superprofessional. Like a child, he constantly rearranges the rules to his own advantage. Steve has described his comic character as a belligerent neurotic who tries to win, no matter what the consequences; he is good at heart, but he doesn't quite figure things out in a logical manner.

The character is kidding himself. He proudly announces that he's really making it. But the audience knows he's not making it. Steve knows he's not making it. What makes this delusion funny is that the audience knows that *Steve* knows he's not making it. Several of his routines are based on the distorted reasoning an anxious person will come up with in order to make a negative event acceptable, and lay the blame elsewhere. Finally, the person adjusts his thinking so that he makes excuses for everything. (pp. 116-17)

Martin's repertoire of jerks is not confined to big-headed entertainers. He is also adept at lampooning self-proclaimed intellectuals; know-it-all tourists; "sex gods" who bore people to tears while bragging about their conquests; and typical everyday-type jerks. Each of these different jerks is just as jerky as the others; everybody is parodied in equally exaggerated form, so they're all equally valid. Steve slips in and out of these various characters at random. He uses his "normal" self as the narrator of the jokes, with the characters delivering the punch lines.

Like the great comedians, Steve uses comedy as a mirror that reflects the characters' flaws to the point where we can recognize them. We can see how we have those same flaws, or at least we can see how *other* people have those flaws. Steve has said that his comedy is at its best when he presents a total human character, being vulnerable, afraid, confident, fooling himself, and lying to himself. The character he plays has so many flaws, there's bound to be at least one flaw that each person in the audience can identify with.

Steve's closing remarks about what a great time he had entertaining the audience—even though they're all going to die someday—is to him the theme of his act. He firmly believes that people respond to something deeper than the jokes and hopes his material relates to how the members of the audience feel about themselves. The meaning behind Steve's comedy is that the individual is what is important; it's all right if someone wants to do his own thing, even if that thing is being mindless for a while. Although new wave comedy purports to be apolitical, it does have a message: the power of mindlessness over matter!

This attitude is the thread that unifies all of Steve's bits. Each of the routines lasts about forty seconds, and the material is amazingly diverse. Some of his jokes are very conventional, some are odd, some have no punch lines, and some are physical or visual. This establishes a variety-show atmosphere and gives the audience the freedom to choose their own places to laugh.

Because people laugh at Steve for different reasons, it's not always easy to explain why his routines are so funny. The people bring their own ideas of humor to his comedy and decide for themselves where the funniest spots are. Steve's comedy is almost personal—like a joke shared between two friends.

The comedy seems personal because its target is not businesses or governments, but the way people think. It illustrates the humor inherent in how people's thoughts are distorted as a result of living in a world full of problems, and in how they try to survive by becoming completely crazy. (pp. 117-19)

Greg Lenburg, Randy Skretvedt, and Jeff Lenburg, in their Steve Martin: The Unauthorized Biography, *St. Martin's Press, 1980, 139 p.*

MICHAEL SRAGOW

What gives [*Dead Men Don't Wear Plaid*] some distinction is that it marks Steve Martin's most effective screen appearance yet. To put it briefly: clothes have made the comedian.

Describing how important his white suits were to his kinetic standup comedy act, Steve Martin said that they were "like leotards that define your body." With their sharp, square lines, they were a key component of the Martin comic persona: the total straight-arrow and ultimate fair-haired boy whose goofy amiability couldn't totally disguise his panic about making friends and influencing people in our post-hip era. Martin's everybody-join-in humor was the opposite of hip; his goal seemed to be finding the silliness that could bond us all.

When Martin and [Carl] Reiner first tried to transfer his humor to the screen in *The Jerk,* all they arrived at was lowest-common-denominator buffoonery. Jettisoning his wardrobe and his mock suaveness, Martin appeared to lust for the dubious mantle of Jerry Lewis. But in *Dead Men Don't Wear Plaid,* Martin gets to wear a lady-killer wardrobe. Few actors have ever looked better in long collars, padded shoulders, cuffed trousers, wide deco ties and suspenders: everything accents his rectangular body and features with an intense theatricality. Though [Martin's character] Rigby Reardon is all spruced up and ready to swing, he thinks and reacts like a nerd because his hard-boiled conscience keeps on telling him that women are poison. Riotous short circuits pop up between his élan and his etiquette. With his almost innate stylization, Martin is able to pull off gags that would merely be coarse in other comics' hands. . . .

Unfortunately, the central idea rarely transcends gimmickry: as in *Pennies from Heaven,* the moviemakers fail to transport us to that special never-never land that looms somewhere between terra firma and the silver screen. But Steve Martin is a genuine movie star. He's one comic actor who doesn't just take chances—he makes good on them.

> Michael Sragow, "Three Hapless Heroes," in Rolling Stone, *Issue 371, June 10, 1982, p. 38.**

STANLEY KAUFFMANN

The idea [to intercut a film with clips from old films] is not overwhelmingly novel, but it never wearies when well used. . . . The intercutting idea is deftly used [in *Dead Men Don't Wear Plaid*]. . . . It might have been really hilarious with a leading actor of comic talent. Steve Martin is not. In *Pennies from Heaven,* of course, he wasn't supposed to be funny, and wasn't anything else either. But I've seen some of his comedy routines on TV, and the only explanation I can find for his success is that he's inept. Martin is clumsy and insipid, and when an amateurish square comes out with an arrow "piercing" his head, talking about his wildness and craziness, it amuses people the way the branch manager of a bank might amuse his staff by putting on a paper hat at the Christmas party. The question is: how far can Martin's unsuitability for comedy take him in a comic career? (p. 24)

> Stanley Kauffmann, "Mysteries, Comic and Otherwise," in The New Republic, *Vol. 186, No. 3518, June 16, 1982, pp. 24-5.**

JACK KROLL

In a time burbling with misused and perverted intelligence, Steve Martin is a welcome apostle of pure idiocy. Not the corroded comforts of neuroticism (Woody Allen), not the subversive logic of madness and bad taste (Mel Brooks), but blessed idiocy is Martin's thing, and in director Carl Reiner he's found the perfect collaborator in creative cretinism. Well, not perfect, because as talented as Reiner is, the Martin movies he's directed and cowritten (**"The Jerk"** and **"Dead Men Don't Wear Plaid"**) are a bit scrappy; they don't have the total personality of the Allen and Brooks movies. Still, with Reiner, Martin has created an endearing hero of our time, the Jerk, an updated version of the classic Fool. And in **"The Man With Two Brains"** they have produced more laughs per quartz-vibration than in any of their previous works.

In these flicks Martin has become a kind of thinking man's Jerry Lewis. Where Lewis at his best raised regression to a creative principle, Martin converts expertise into the highest form of imbecility. . . .

[Steve Martin] has the quality of true comic mania. He's not doing shtick, he's *acting,* with a furious and funny intensity. Like Harold Lloyd, he makes you laugh because he creates a loser who somehow wins. It's this punch-drunk oscillation between triumph and defeat that's funny. . . .

> Jack Kroll, "Idiot's Delight," in Newsweek, *Vol. CI, No. 24, June 13, 1983, p. 78.*

RICHARD SCHICKEL

How sweet it is to find a movie in which the hero, having lusted after purely carnal pleasures for much of its length, finally falls in love with a woman's mind. That there is nobody attached to it, that it is, in fact, a brain kept alive in a bottle by a half-mad scientist, might strike some people as a little funny. It will strike vaster numbers of them as very funny—especially after Steve Martin pastes plastic lips on the bottle so he can kiss his beloved. . . .

[*The Man with Two Brains*] is the most assured and hilarious of the three Martin-Carl Reiner collaborations. There is something classically American about its monomaniacal pursuit of a gag every five seconds, characterization and redeeming social value be damned. The movie is rather like a Henny Youngman monologue combined with a *National Lampoon* spread. And it offers reassuring proof that the spirit of arrested adolescence lives on, at least for one more summer.

> Richard Schickel, "Head Trip," in Time, *Vol. 121, No. 25, June 20, 1983, p. B3.*

PAULINE KAEL

A comic's naked desire to make us laugh can be an embarrassment, especially if we feel that he's hanging on that laugh—that he's experiencing our reaction as a life-or-death matter. Steve Martin is naked, but he isn't desperate. (He's too anomic to be desperate.) Some performers can't work up a physical charge if the audience doesn't respond to them, but Steve Martin doesn't come out on a TV stage cold, hoping to get a rhythm going with the people in the studio. He's wired up and tingling, like a junk-food addict; he's like a man who's being electrocuted and getting a dirty thrill out of it. Steve Martin doesn't feed off the audience's energy—he instills energy in the audience. And he does it by drawing us into a conspiratorial relationship with him. . . .

When Martin comes onstage, he may do, say, just what Red Skelton used to do, but he gets us laughing at the fact that we're laughing at such dumb jokes. Martin simulates being a comedian, and so, in a way, we simulate being the comedian's audience. Martin makes old routines work by letting us know that they're old and then doing them immaculately. For him, comedy is *all* timing. He's almost a comedy robot. Onstage, he puts across the idea that he's going to do some cornball routine, and then when he does it it has quotation marks around it, and that's what makes it hilarious. He does the routine straight, yet he's totally facetious. . . .

I admired Steve Martin for the acting and the dancing he did in "Pennies from Heaven"; what he did was more than a "stretch," it was a consummation, and he may have been so startlingly right in the movie because of the doubleness behind its whole conception. Possibly there was also an attempt to achieve some sort of duality in Martin's last picture, **"Dead Men Don't Wear Plaid"**—a spoof of detective movies which spliced together footage of Martin and footage from films of the forties. Carl Reiner, who has directed all three of Martin's star vehicles . . . , worked with dedicated craftsmen and achieved a smooth composite; even the sound levels were carefully matched. Reiner and the others must have become so proud of their workmanship that they didn't register what a monotonous, droning feat they were engaged in. They smoothed out their one big chance for comic friction—the contrast between old and new.

Almost nothing of the new-generation approach is visible in the Steve Martin of slapstick package movies, such as the first burlesque he starred in, **"The Jerk,"** and his new one, **"The Man with Two Brains."** In these, he's not very different from the more frenzied and gaga of the older-generation comedians, yet he gives the impression of being fully realized. . . . When he leers in **"The Man with Two Brains,"** he leers triumphantly, like a baby grinning and dribbling milk out of its first few teeth. The performance is shameless, stupid fun. Despite the sadness in his face, the comic character we see up there has nothing in his head but a warped, infantile élan. Martin is as physical a comic as I've ever seen; the Jerk is the perfect name for him—he moves convulsively, at angles, his body shooting ahead of his thoughts.

Essentially a series of skits, **"The Man with Two Brains"** is indefensible by any known standard of comedy form—or formlessness. It's not much of anything, but it moves along enjoyably and it allows this Jerk to stay wired up for the whole picture. Sunny, grinning, lewd, he's Harpo Marx with a voice and without a harp—a Harpo whose id has chased out Art. (p. 90)

This movie has the kind of maniacal situations that are so dumb they make you laugh, and since much of what children find hilarious has this same giddiness, they'd probably like the film a lot. (p. 93)

Pauline Kael, "Silliness," in The New Yorker, *Vol. LIX, No. 19, June 27, 1983, pp. 90, 93-5.**

Walter M(ichael) Miller, Jr.

1923-

American novelist, short story writer, and scriptwriter.

Miller's *A Canticle for Leibowitz* (1960) is generally regarded as one of the outstanding achievements of speculative literature. This novel is set in the future and depicts the gradual reestablishment of civilization following nuclear catastrophe. The novel generated much popular and critical attention upon publication, and the continuing relevance of its themes has helped sustain its popularity among both young adult and adult readers.

A Canticle for Leibowitz employs a three-part structure which parallels the development of Western civilization from the Dark Ages to modern times and emphasizes the cyclical nature of history. One of the principal themes of the novel, which Miller explores through allusions to the traditions of Roman Catholicism, is the role of religion in society. In addition, Miller details the impact on society of advances in science and technology. For these reasons, critics have variously categorized *Canticle* as historical, religious, or science fiction. Many agree that the scope of *Canticle* extends beyond these areas, since Miller's blending of themes results in a wealth of interpretations. Miller's focus on the responsibility of individuals in shaping the course of society gives the novel a moral perspective as well. *Canticle* won the Hugo Award in 1961.

Miller began his literary career in the early 1950s by contributing tales to various science fiction magazines. Many of these stories were later collected in *The Science Fiction Stories of Walter M. Miller, Jr.* (1978) and *The Best of Walter M. Miller, Jr.* (1980). As a whole, Miller's short fiction has inspired relatively little critical interest. "The Darfsteller," however, won a Hugo Award in 1955 as best novelette. This story is representative of Miller's short fiction in its examination of both the constructive and destructive effects of new technology.

(See also *CLC*, Vol. 4; *Contemporary Authors*, Vols. 85-88; and *Dictionary of Literary Biography*, Vol. 8.)

Photograph by Alys M. Arceneaux

EDWIN KENNEBECK

[*A Canticle for Leibowitz,* a] very good, partly humorous historical novel, is about the role of the Church as the preserver of wisdom and spiritual life in dark ages, but its era is in the future rather than the past. (p. 632)

The telling of the story is intelligent, skillfully oblique, and often funny. Mr. Miller evidently knows a good deal about the language and protocol of the Church, and he cleverly adapts its forms—such as prayers and official pronouncements in Latin—to the pattern of his story. (pp. 633-34)

Those who have seen the motion picture "On the Beach," which I think completely avoids or cheapens the serious problems with which it pretends to deal, will find this novel an admirable contrast. Its faults in taste are at least faults brought on by the author's attempt to follow his material through. Unfortunately, Mr. Miller's various pictures do not go beyond their two-dimensional limitations: though he allows his abbots, for instance, some faults and senses of guilt, a substratum of

pietism persists. Mr. Miller has not the penetration of a Graham Greene or, for that matter, a good historian. However, even in two dimensions his story is imaginative, amusing and disturbing. (p. 634)

> Edwin Kennebeck, "The Future Church," in Commonweal, Vol. LXXI, No. 23, March 4, 1960, pp. 632-34.

EDMUND FULLER

["A Canticle for Leibowitz"] is an extraordinary novel. It is apt to arouse either enthusiasm or distaste, but little middle ground opinion. It will be a most unusual literary experience even if you don't like it—but already it has made this reviewer and many other readers enormously enthusiastic.

It is projected into the future—it has elements in common with science fiction, yet it would be quite impossible to classify it narrowly as such. It is fanciful, yet as deeply true as any book I've read. It brilliantly combines several qualities: It is prodigiously imaginative and original, richly comic, terrifyingly grim, profound both intellectually and morally, and, above all, is simply such a memorable story as to stay with a reader for years.

As a speculation on man's destiny and most horrendous possible catastrophe, its vision and scope make so good a book as "On the Beach" seem pale and childish by contrast. The humor and conviction in **"A Canticle for Leibowitz"** give it the dimension the lack of which made Aldous Huxley's "Ape and Essence" unsuccessful.

You can take your choice: Miller either is telling us our future in terms of our past, or our past in terms of our future. Civilization had been destroyed in this century, but not all of human life. In the scriptural sense, there was a remnant, after what is here called "the Flame Deluge." On that premise, we are projected six centuries ahead, and ultimately another six centuries.

As the confused traditions said: "The wise men of that age" [ours] had devised "great engines of war such as had never before been upon the Earth." . . .

[Use of these had brought] the Flame Deluge then "the Fallout, the plagues, the madness, the confusion of tongues, the rage" and then "the bloodletting of the Simplification, when remnants of mankind had torn other remnants limb from limb, killing rulers, scientists, leaders, technicians, teachers . . . for having helped to make the Earth what it had become."

Again it is the monastic orders that have kept the thread of knowledge, not even comprehending it. In the desert, the monastic community called the Albertian Order of Leibowitz has the relics of the ancient learning. The beatified, later canonized, Isaac Edward Leibowitz was one of the great scientists hidden from the wrath, and later converted, by the monastics.

The three sections of the novel, **"Fiat Homo"** [Let There Be Man], **"Fiat Lux"** [Let There Be Light], and **"Fiat Voluntas Tua"** [Thy Will Be Done], trace man thru the full recovery of science and culture to what must remain as Miller's disclosure of his destiny, when the same fearful options face him again. . . .

I urge the reading of this exciting book. It will be one of the books of the year. Whatever your response to it, you will not soon forget the experience, and you are sure to talk of it.

> *Edmund Fuller, "The Extraordinary Tale Speculating on Man's Destiny," in* Chicago Sunday Tribune Magazine of Books, *March 6, 1960, p. 1.*

ROBERT PHELPS

[*A Canticle for Leibowitz*] is a curious and original and very serious book, and it will be so satisfactory to the right reader that I think a warning is in order: though the action takes place in the future, and though a space ship takes off on the final page, this should not be confused with what is usually called science fiction. In a way, it is a cautionary tale about man's perennial inhumanity to man, and the inevitable use he will make of scientific means to that end. But even this is not Mr. Miller's gist. What he has really written is a highly imaginative, and basically joyous, celebration of human kind's instinct to keep going, and especially of those members of the race who are not so much discoverers and pathfinders, as preservers and safekeepers, whose instinct is to build and retain a tradition. . . .

In three sections, Mr. Miller . . . shows mankind up to its oldest tricks, tasting the fruits of knowledge, and killing its own brother. In AD 2600, science is dormant, asleep in the archives garnered by the Blessed Leibowitz's abbey. With no power instruments, the scale of warfare is intimate—a matter of bows and arrows and laying seige. Five hundred years later, electricity has been rediscovered, in Leibowitz's own community, and it is by the light of this new illumination that a number of agents of an ambitious prince examine the Memorabillia and make secret sketches of the abbey's fortifications, in order to capture it and exploit its buried knowledge. In the final section, AD 3700, a new scientific revolution has produced space ships, atomic fission, and thanks to Leibowitz's dedication, the Flame Deluge is re-enacted. Yet, as the bombs are falling, another generation of preserver-priests takes off with books and children for outer space.

Of course, so skeletal a reduction as this tends to make Mr. Miller's novel seem merely schematic, whereas it actually amounts to a freshly inventive cycle of stories, the century-to-century account of the dedicated but very human men who wore the Leibowitz habit and served his salvaging mission. For instance, the story of Brother Francis Gerard, who spends fifteen years making an illuminated manuscript of the blueprint for "the transistorized control system" of something called "unit six-B," is as touching a parable of faith, hope, and humility as any novel is likely to offer this year. In fact, I think it will be perfectly safe to recommend Mr. Miller's book to any reader who has ever been moved by the kind of stories found in any calendar of saints.

> *Robert Phelps, "The Year? It's A.D. 2600," in* New York Herald Tribune Book Review, *March 13, 1960, p. 4.*

MARTIN LEVIN

Mr. Miller is a fine story teller at his best—which is in the opening section of [**"A Canticle for Leibowitz"**], depicting the medieval reprise. But when his time-machine shifts gears into the neo-Renaissance, it stalls in a bog of quasi-historical novelese. These chapters are overrun with thanes and clans and polyglot hugger-mugger concerning a baronial type named Hannegan II, who operates out of the Red River country, and has designs on the states of Laredo and Denver.

A graver misdemeanor is the author's heavy-handed approach to allegory; his far too explicit moralizing dulls the luster of his imaginative format.

> *Martin Levin, "Incubator of the New Civilization," in* The New York Times Book Review, *March 27, 1960, pp. 42-3.*

THE TIMES LITERARY SUPPLEMENT

Without question *A Canticle for Leibowitz* is a most remarkable novel. The style is sharp, exact, completely individual, and above all alive. And the scale is huge—embracing life present, life past, and life future. Mr. Miller looks at life from the different angles of God and scientists and poets and priests and the Wandering Jew and—believe it or not—he makes sense out of it, and beauty too. Some critics have talked about this astonishing novel in terms of science fiction. That is an insult. Primarily and essentially it is religious and human.

> *"Seekers of the City," in* The Times Literary Supplement, *No. 3031, April 1, 1960, p. 205.*

WHITNEY BALLIETT

["A Canticle for Leibowitz"] is a work of the Imagination. . . . Miller, who is a dull, ashy writer, is forced to depend, in addition to his conjuring tricks, on heavyweight irony: A scientist founds the monastery; the monastery guards the very knowledge that leads to rediscovery and repeated annihilation; the Memorabilia are the principal baggage the monks carry when they leave the earth. But irony, after all, is only a kind of high-toned mockery. It entertains but it changes nothing. (pp. 159-60)

> *Whitney Balliett, in a review of "A Canticle for Leibowitz," in* The New Yorker, *Vol. XXXVI, No. 7, April 2, 1960, pp. 159-60,*

STANLEY J. ROWLAND, JR.

Failure to place *A Canticle for Leibowitz* . . . in its genre has caused some uncertainty and confusion in its reviews. Therefore we should first appreciate what kind of novel it is, realizing of course that all works in a given art form partake of common denominators, precluding a rigid boundary between kinds.

With this in mind we can say that *A Canticle for Leibowitz* belongs in the same category as Aldous Huxley's *Brave New World*, George Orwell's *1984*, and contemporary works such as Nevil Shute's *On the Beach* and a number of science fiction stories. These works explore the possible consequences of man's mastery of nature through technology. (p. 640)

A Canticle for Leibowitz partakes of two prime strains of American literature. One, the Gothic with its fascination with the horrible and the ominous, is rooted in medieval Christian fears of the powers of darkness and was reinforced by the influences represented in Jonathan Edwards. The other strain, that of an absolutistic moralism, not only informs Nathaniel Hawthorne's *The Scarlet Letter* and the stern judgmentalism of William Faulkner's work but is woven even into novels of manners—such as John Marquand's *Sincerely, Willis Wayde*, a work which infers a moral judgment that is absolute for its situation. This moralism, rooted in our Christian tradition, is particularly strong in American literature because of our Puritan heritage and the pietistic moralism that has flourished in our culture.

These traditional strains lie behind Mr. Miller's use of terror and his insistence on moral issues. . . . Miller weaves an atmosphere of religious certainty and human foreboding through the first section, which tells of the monks preserving some of the books and blueprints of our lost civilization.

The second section, dealing with the development of a new Renaissance and the shifting of power from the church to secular states, is the weakest, what with characters that are somewhat like Henry VIII in cowboy boots. In the third section we encounter a new age of secularism, space travel and hydrogen weapons. The author uses some monstrously deformed human beings, descendants of those whose genes were damaged in the last catastrophe, to raise the question of whether man will risk destruction again in the face of such consequences.

The book's judgment is that man will risk destruction, despite a world court, rules against warfare, and some provision for united enforcement of world order. Miller seems to find the reason partly in man's depravity and pride, and partly in a kind of catastrophic determinism: man inevitably acquires knowledge and mastery over his environment, which produces a moral order in which good is equated with the common good

and evil is equated with pain. This morality traps the power blocs in defensive postures of mutual suspicion and allows an error to trigger a holocaust.

Against this secular viewpoint the author sets an uncompromising Christian morality, made most explicit in the delineation of the abbot of the monastery. (pp. 640-41)

Miller develops the moral conflict . . . concretely in the abbot's encounter with a compassionate doctor who recommends euthanasia to hopeless sufferers dying from radioactivity. The abbot objects, saying that God does not give man something to bear without also giving him the capacity to bear it. At first the solution of legalism is tried: the euthanasia business is kept out of the monastery. But this solution is found wanting, and the author draws the issue in regard to a mother and child who have been lethally burned.

At this point Miller might have introduced some miracle or sudden experience of divine grace. But he does not, and he saves the book from being sermonic by testing the moral issues upon the hard rack of the imagination, which creates a radical situation in which Christian morality is opposed not by a chilling villain but by a compassionate and dedicated doctor who represents the best in secular humanism. He wins his case, and the mother and her child voluntarily go to the state euthanasia station with its big portable statue, vaguely reminiscent of an effeminate painting of Christ, that carries the legend "COMFORT." Finally, the abbot is made to bear the suffering that he counseled others to bear.

It is precisely its artistic integrity, its insistence on testing values in radical human terms, that allows the novel to vindicate its viewpoint of uncompromising Christian morality. In this process it undercuts not only the ethical order of secular humanism but also a respected viewpoint in modern Protestant thought: that which proceeds from a neo-orthodox analysis to pose a moral choice between "proximate solutions," and is capable of concluding that a nuclear arms race is preferable to the possible consequences of unilateral disarmament. Against this, Mr. Miller's novel implies that society is doomed when men choose to protect the secular state with nuclear armaments rather than suffer for uncompromised Christian values.

In addition to its weak midsection, *A Canticle for Leibowitz* has flaws that are apparently indigenous to its genre. Characters are not deeply developed, and the intimate relationships of individuals to each other and their environment are largely unexplored. But the relationship of society to the moral order is explored through human lives, and Mr. Miller's honest moral passion rescues his novel from the commonplace of "gloom and doom" and makes it worth reading and pondering. (p. 641)

> *Stanley J. Rowland, Jr., "With Moral Passion," in* The Christian Century, *Vol. LXXVII, No. 21, May 25, 1960, pp. 640-41.*

EDWARD DUCHARME

The greatness of Miller's accomplishment [in *A Canticle for Leibowitz*] lies not in the mere telling of his marvelous story. After all, television, the movies, and hundreds of science fiction yarns have told the story of Man's folly several times well and many times poorly. And, while *A Canticle* does have nice touches of humor and irony that the others may lack, the narrative is not significantly above the level of the rest. Rather, the achievement lies in Miller's skillful handling of thought-provoking ideas. While dealing with potentially sensational plot materials (the possible end of the world and all that sort of thing), he has placed most of his emphasis on the moral issues of Man's way—his life and survival.

Miller's narrative continually returns to the conflicts between the scientist's search for truth and the state's power. . . . It is in this area of thought-provoking concern that Miller excels. The conflict goes on, right to the very end of the novel with some men never stopping in their speculations about the implications of their acts, and with others interested only in the pursuit of abstract, scientific truths. These latter are repeatedly used by the power-seekers in the world of Miller's story. The conflict is age-old but presented in new terms. Students will have no difficulties relating these concerns to the problems they are encountering in their courses dealing with the current post-Oppenheimer period, the period during which there has been so much public consideration of the implications of science.

Nor are the characters mere puppets, playing the traditional roles in the old drama. The successive abbots of the monastery, for instance, are each an individual with a clearly defined personality. The abbots mirror their religious times to a certain degree, ranging from the very devout and religiously harsh to the apparently convivial, outgoing of the last period. Each, however, is most devoted to the preservation of the Memorabilia, the purpose of the Order. In this latter connection, the way in which the world regards the monks undergoes an interesting series of changes. Early, they are seen by society as a group of eccentrics keeping something nobody *should* want, later as keeping something nobody *does* want, finally as hoarders of something the world needs. Sound familiar? History students will find the cycles Miller describes fascinating. Some of the literal-minded will contest a few of Miller's possibilities about the future. No matter: their objections will be in the same vein as those who contest that . . . [Winston Smith] in *1984* could never be made to do the things he does. More important than these minor differences will be the fact that the novel, in one way or another, is one that involves its readers.

There are countless kinds of things that can be done with the study of the book. Students can analyze the successive presentations of the abbots' characters, attempting to account for them in terms of the story's meaning. Students can also study and attempt to explain the names of some of the characters. . . . (pp. 1043-44)

The novel would complement admirably a study of *Brave New World, 1984,* and other such well-told projections into the future. In addition to the literary study, there could be some composition work—the analysis of the differences and similarities of the works, the presentation of the characters, the relative plausibility of the events described. The novel would serve effectively in interesting science-oriented students; it would complement studies going on in other curriculum areas. It has Latin for the language student; science and mathematics for the technical; character, theme, and plot for the literary; and speculation for the humanist. Certainly, a teacher should be able to get all of his students involved in one way or another with the book.

In addition to the study of areas related to the text, there are other, more text-directed activities. Some of these include Miller's use of geography (reminiscent of Benet's "By the Waters of Babylon"), his description of the development of the nations in the ages that pass, the evolution of the monastery with suggested reasons for the growth described. These are not mere busywork studies; they are concerns vital to the understanding of a carefully-wrought work by a competent artist. Analyses of them will aid in the understanding of the book as well as in the more important area: the development of skills we care about in our readers.

Learning experiences of these types reinforce learning that is acquired in other quarters. For instance, the student's work in English and science is affected when he can read Richard Wilbur's "The Death of a Toad." His awareness of the written word is enhanced as is his understanding of evolution. *A Canticle for Leibowitz* has the same kind of reinforcement qualities with regard to much of what the student reads in magazines and newspapers as well as what he is studying in other classes. In addition, the work is one of genuine literary merit from the contemporary scene.

The novel does not, however, offer a completely easy time for the teacher. It is, first of all, a fairly difficult piece of reading. In addition, like any worthwhile book, it has an area of concern that might present some difficulty to the teacher. Much of the student's understanding of Miller's achievement will necessitate his grasping of the Catholic environment of much of the action. But, as teachers have for generations handled the similar problem in Chaucer study, so can they explain and help students understand Miller's backdrop for the story. It matters not that a large part of Miller's purpose may lie in some personal opinions about the Church; what does matter is his effective presentation of Man's dilemma so that the high school student can understand. Walter Miller's *A Canticle for Leibowitz* is a challenging contemporary novel worthy of inclusion in today's curriculum. (p. 1044)

Edward Ducharme, "A Canticle for Miller," in English Journal, *Vol. 55, No. 8, November, 1966, pp. 1042-44.*

RAYMOND A. SCHROTH

When *Canticle* first appeared, seven years ago, it was compared to *Brave New World, 1984* and *On the Beach.* But in one way *Canticle* is more satisfying: it puts its theme in theological perspective. The critics praised it, faulted it for being "too Catholic," and have generally ignored it since. Yet the paperback—with a seared monk on its cover, transfigured against the blazing wreckage of civilization—has passed from friend to friend. Now it can be read not just as a piece of brilliant science-fiction warning about the coming nuclear deluge, but as an underground sub-Scripture classic, an ethical tract. . . .

Despite all its futurism, *Canticle* seems curiously anachronistic today. This is not so much an indictment as an indication of how far our popular theology has come, even though we aren't gaining much better control of our environment. Miller's eschatology of doom is muted by our Teilhardian theology of hope.

Miller's church of the future, which will protect itself against the gates of hell by sending a spaceship full of monk-scientists, children, nuns and bishops (to preserve the apostolic succession) to another galaxy, retains, with all its learning, some of the worst aspects of the preconciliar Church. Before the ship takes off, a monk slams the door and quips: *"Sic transit mundus!"* New Rome deals with its friends and foes by concordats and interdicts, as if Old Rome had learned nothing from history. As the intercontinental missiles leave their launching pads in the war between the Atlantic and Asian states, the Pope stops praying for peace and sings the Mass in Time of War. In his conflict with the secular-humanist doctor who would put radiation victims out of their misery, the abbot can only reply with the Stoic dictum that nature imposes nothing on man that it doesn't prepare man to bear.

Yet the author of *Canticle* can hardly be expected to resolve the problem of evil. It is enough that he suggests we will never be able to replant Eden because we would never give it a chance to grow. We are like the children in [William Golding's] *Lord of the Flies:* even when we are rescued from the primitive barbarism we have created on a tropical island, we are brought into a larger context of sophisticated barbarism in war.

If *Canticle for Leibowitz* does not answer the fundamental questions, at least it asks them again at the right time: What has the Church, which was in one historical context the embodiment of culture, to offer to a modern culture that has left it behind? When man by his own genius and foolishness keeps annihilating his own creation, isn't he a fool to start all over again? Is flying the Church to a distant planet—when, on this planet, the ash from the fallout is poisoning the sea—an act of hope or a gesture of despair?

> Raymond A. Schroth, in a review of "A Canticle for Leibowitz," in America, Vol. 118, No. 3, January 20, 1968, p. 79.

HUGH RANK

A curious book, which defies narrow categories, [*A Canticle for Leibowitz*] contains elements of satire, science-fiction, fantasy, humor, sectarian religious propaganda, and an apocalyptic "utopian" vision. Although much of its meaning can be discerned by any perceptive reader, it can be better understood with a few footnotes which place it in the context of recent "Catholic" writing. (pp. 213-14)

Because characterization in satire does not present a particular person so much as it illustrates a type, the satirist must not only avoid a trite repetition of commonplace stereotypes, but must also avoid the other extreme of obscuring the type by a fuller development of character. The essential characteristics of the type must be presented in clear terms. By this criterion, *A Canticle for Leibowitz* is uneven. Many standard stereotypes of "Catholic" writing appear in the book, but some passages do develop unique presentations of types.

In the first section, for example, Brother Francis is recognizable as the naive, humble, unworldly monk; everything about him suggests the traditional, romanticized legends about Saint Francis of Assisi. Brother Fingo plays the standard role of "Brother Cook"—the happy-go-lucky bumpkin of the monastery. But, in Father Cheroki, who represents the stern absolutist and legalistic mentality, and in Abbot Arkos, who represents the pragmatic mentality, the author transcends the commonplace stereotypes. (p. 215)

The dominant character of the second section is Thon Thaddeo, the secular scholar who is the very model of the Renaissance gentleman-scientist. Although his apparent function is to serve as a foil to the arguments of the Abbot Dom Paulo, the actual development of Thon overshadows the presentation of the Abbot. Dom Paulo, as the "wise old man" and "patient sufferer," liberally dispenses his advice and heroically conceals his personal agonies. Other recognizable stereotypes form the background for the Thon-Dom arguments: Brother Kornhoer is the "humble monk" whose humble work in scientific ex-

periments outshines the publicized brilliance of the famous Thon; Brother Armbruster is the cranky conservative protesting against progress, and, as librarian, defending the carefully-preserved books from any *use*; the Poet is the effeminate parasite, the worldly fop being sheltered by the charitable monks; Marcus Apollo, the Papal Nuncio to Hannegan's court, is the suave diplomat, deeply involved in the intrigues of that court.

The characters in the final section continue the secular-religious argument started by the Thon and Dom Paulo. In the modern era, Abbot Zerchi exhibits many aspects of the American Catholic community's stereotype of the priest; although Zerchi leads a group of contemplatives, he remains the "man of action," the gruff man-of-God who has the proverbial "heart of gold and fist of iron." His opponent, Doctor Cors, heads a government medical team which aids the survivors of the nuclear attack and provides humane mercy-killing for the most hopeless of the radiation victims. Doctor Cors, like Thon Thaddeo, functions as the "village atheist" (an indispensable figure in t9e Catholic romance), acting as the intellectual foil for the dogmatic arguments of the priest. Predictably, the priest loses his temper in a moment of "just anger" and hits the doctor; the doctor, predictably, continues to admire the holy dedication of the priest. The young monk chosen as the new abbot of the interplanetary mission is a "space veteran" with technical ability and an aggressive "take charge" attitude, an image suggested by the actual influx of World War II veterans into the American Trappist monasteries.

Such a collection of characters might suggest that the book is nothing more than a piece of pious science-fiction. But the interesting aspect of the book comes from the mixture of attitudes reflecting the ambiguity within the Catholic Church in the period immediately before the Second Vatican Council. The extensive satire of religious practices, as found in the book, could not have been written a generation earlier; the extensive moralizing and firm certitude in doctrinal matters could not have been written a generation later.

Much of the humor within *Canticle* comes from the deliberate anachronisms in which known things from one era are placed in the strange context of another. The discovery of the twentieth century relics in the "medieval age" after the Flame Deluge suggests [Mark Twain's *A Connecticut Yankee in King Arthur's Court*]; in both cases, the audience is aware of the incongruities which the characters do not understand. . . . But the ingenuity [of] this humor remains secondary to the satire which playfully chides some of the past practices of the Catholic Church.

The medieval monks, for instance, live in a world of pious myths and superstitions. (pp. 215-17)

The urge to glorify the humble, an attitude common to many Christians who have erected elaborate structures in honor of the poor man of Galilee, is satirized several times in the opening chapters. When Brother Francis realizes that the Fallout Shelter contains relics of the saint, he tries "to visualize a towering basilica rising from the site. . . . If not a basilica, then a smaller church—The Church of Saint Leibowitz of the Wilderness—surrounded by a garden and a wall, with a shrine of the saint attracting rivers of pilgrims with girded loins out of the north." His desire to be a "builder" is frustrated by his assignment to the monastery copying room where he is supposed to produce exact duplicates of the ancient blueprints. But the impulse to glorify the humble does not decrease: "The stark copy was not enough: it was coldly unimaginative and did not commemorate the saintly qualities of the Beatus in any visible way." Thus, the meaningless geometric lines of the diagram become embellished with a colorful filigree of decorations added by the pious Francis.

Parodies of scholastic philosophical arguments, of the bickering quarrels among various religious orders over obscure theological points, and of the legalistic forms of liturgical practices accompany the story set in the medieval age. Minor characters (the officious bureaucrats of the Curia in New Rome, the petty tyrant in the monastery workshop) and brief topical allusions (the crusades against the savage heathens, the inquisition against Catharism in the Pacific Coast region) all contribute to the composite picture of a medieval world presented by an author with his tongue in his cheek. (pp. 217-18)

Because satire tends to accompany, rather than dominate, the story, *A Canticle for Leibowitz* is a difficult book to place into a neat category; if the satire had been sustained throughout the work, the job of the critic would be much easier. Nor can the book be described as *science-fiction* because little attention is paid to the gadgetry or the scientific technicalities which appear occasionally in the story. However, many *fantasy* elements (in addition to the basic plot situation) appear: the Wandering Jew in his timeless search for the Messiah; the Poet whose glass eye is a "conscience"; and Mrs. Grales, the two-headed woman of the final section. Mrs. Grales spends most of her time begging aid, obsequiously, for her one lifeless head. . . . (p. 218)

Basically, the book combines a satire on contemporary society and religious practices with a "reverse utopia" presenting a grim vision of a possible future. As the publisher's advertisement on the paperback edition noted, it follows "in the great tradition of *Brave New World* and *1984*." Here, in Miller's apocalyptic vision is the source of many objections by readers more accustomed to a secular-humanist nightmare vision (such as in *Brave New World* or *1984*) than to that vision of a "conservative" Catholic. The presentation of certain absolutist attitudes in the book are likely to alienate not only the non-Catholic, but also the contemporary Catholic "liberal." Had the book been postulated on the "acceptable" ideas of the secular-humanist, it might have received more note than it did; but it seems that the average reader and critic, who is quite willing to grant the ideological premises of a Dante or a Milton, is less likely to be so neutral when dealing with contemporary writers who have not been safely approved. Yet the job of the critic is to understand, to analyze, and to illuminate the work in the context of its own philosophical assumptions.

In the case of *A Canticle for Leibowitz,* the book is a song out of season, a cry of a reformer on the eve of revolution. It reflects accurately some of the confused currents of thought within the Catholic Church in the period immediately before the second Vatican Council. At this time, the "liberal" movement had progressed far enough that it was possible to satirize certain ecclesiastical practices and past history; yet at the same, the firm certitude in doctrinal matters had not been disturbed.

The full impact of the Second Vatican Council (starting in 1962) still remains unknown, but one of the most immediate and obvious results was the weakening of certitude concerning beliefs which had been accepted within the Church for ages. . . . The Second Vatican Council acted as a catalyst for reform, but in doing so it also disturbed the complacent security of many Catholics. The seemingly innocuous debate on liturgical reform soon developed into a full scale argument over traditional practices and beliefs. The subsequent controversies over birth control, priestly celibacy, and ecclesiastical authority were the

most highly publicized aspects of the new developments within the Church, but other arguments also penetrated widely and deeply into basic theological issues. This challenge of the traditional "verities" made certitude a rare commodity in the post-councilar Church.

A Canticle for Leibowitz presents a story of the future populated with priests [with] a pre-councilar mentality of certitude in their absolutist beliefs. For example, the euthanasia argument between Abbot Zerchi and Doctor Cors is a variation of the same dilemma found in scores of Catholic "ghetto" romances (c.f. the therapeutic abortion scene in Robinson's *The Cardinal*) in which the absolute law is rigidly defended. (pp. 219-20)

Other passages in the book reflect a certain defensive mentality found within pre-councilar Catholicism. The author finds need, for example, to justify the medieval Church as the preserver of culture in a barbaric world, to correct erroneous ideas about the reason for chaining Bibles, to point out the Augustinian evolutionary concepts, and to defend the Vatican's artistic treasures by emphasizing the threadbare clothes of the modern pope clad in the ancient splendor. But the major theme, the depiction of the Catholic Church as the ever-enduring institution, might prove a hurdle for the unsympathetic reader. However, one must admit the equal legitimacy of postulating a future world *with* a Church as that of presenting a churchless world; history and psychology may well be on the side of an enduring religious organization in one form or another. The actual liturgy and institutional practices as envisioned by Miller are outdated, of course, by the Second Vatican Council; but it is understandable that in 1959 such changes were totally unforeseen.

Though uneven, Miller's writing is perhaps at its best in the early section in which he truly captures the sense of the desert wilderness while carefully uncovering the basic plot situation in a series of artful revelations. In later sections, some heavy-handed apologetics in the dialogues detract from the smoothness of the writing. However, because of the genuine display of ingenuity, wit, and subtle humor, the book does survive a re-reading and is worthy of a wider audience. Neither as skillful as Powers' satire in *Morte D'Urban*, nor as savage as William Kelley's brand of churchly Black Humor in *The God Hunters*, [*A Canticle for Leibowitz*] deserves note for its own intrinsic merits and for its historical position in the relation of the modern satirist to the Catholic Church. This strange mixture of "liberal" and "conservative" attitudes reflects rather accurately the confused cross-currents of the era. If one understands the context of these ideas, the book can be enjoyed and appreciated by those who do not share the author's premises. (p. 220)

Hugh Rank, "Song Out of Season: 'A Canticle for Leibowitz'," in Renascence, *Vol. XXI, No. 4, Summer, 1969, pp. 213-21.*

MICHAEL ALAN BENNETT

Critics and reviewers have busied themselves in listing the various themes which lend substance and depth to [*A Canticle for Leibowitz*]. Stanley J. Rowland (*The Christian Century,* May 1960) [see excerpt above] has noted the thematic treatment of the issue of euthanasia and of the conflict between church (spiritual) and state (temporal) authority. Edward Ducharme (*English Journal,* November 1966) [see excerpt above] has claimed that "Miller's narrative continually returns to the conflicts between the scientist's search for truth and the state's power.'' To this list I would add that Miller also examines the occasional clash between scientific speculation and religious doctrine.

No one can deny that these are important concerns in the novel, but considerations of structure preclude that any of these issues could serve as the major theme. . . . A major theme should give unity and direction to the entire work, and none of the themes already mentioned satisfies this requirement. Their treatment is, on the whole, rather haphazard.

But one issue does receive emphasis in all three sections of the novel and is vitally connected to all the themes listed above. Miller's major theme, I believe, concerns the question of individual responsibility. He explores this theme through the various characters in the novel who either accept or reject their various responsibilities. Miller's conclusion is that if nuclear holocaust occurs, the fault will lie with each individual who did nothing to prevent it.

In **"Fiat Homo,"** the first section of the novel, Miller deals with the theme of responsibility in a totally humorous context. Brother Francis Gerard of Utah, a novice in the monastery of Blessed Leibowitz, has encountered a pilgrim while fasting in the desert. The pilgrim has directed him to an ancient fallout shelter which contains relics of the monastery's founder. Brother Francis, sure that his amazing discovery is somehow connected with his vocation to the religious life, returns to the abbey and informs the other novices of his experience.

But Francis' fellow novices improve and elaborate upon the original story until the rumor circulates that the young monk has actually met, in the guise of the pilgrim, the Blessed Leibowitz himself. Francis is immediately summoned to the office of Abbot Arkos to deny the rumors, which threaten to undermine the chances of the abbey's patron for sainthood.

From the lips of the Lord Abbot, Francis hears of the rumors for the first time. Commanded to affirm or deny the report that the Blessed Leibowitz has appeared to him, the dull-witted Francis is beset by confusion and can do neither: "I don't *think* the pilgrim was the *Beatus,*" he stammers. . . . And later still, when interviewed by the devil's advocate, whose job it is to dispute miracles, Francis remains unsure: "I always said that I *thought* he was *probably* just an old man." . . . (pp. 484-85)

The point is that once the seeds of doubt have been planted in Brother Francis' simplistic mind, his caution makes him incapable of certitude. And not being quite certain, he refuses to take upon himself the responsibility of resolving the question with which he is confronted.

Brother Francis is a comic figure, and his refusal to accept responsibility is, in itself, minor and insignificant. But the incident is important in that it prepares the reader for a more serious approach to this theme in the later sections of the novel.

With the introduction of Thon Taddeo Pfardentrott in the second section of the novel, Miller begins a serious treatment of his major theme. The Thon, a scientist from Texarkana, is the second major character in the novel who refuses to accept responsibility.

The situation of Thon Taddeo is precarious indeed. As a scientist, he is engaged in the search for truth and the betterment of mankind. But his work is made possible by the patronage of a prince who is obsessed with a desire for power. The prince is not interested in truth or human progress. Science is important to him only insofar as it can effect the achievement of his goals by perfecting superior weapons for his army. Thus, for Thon Taddeo to serve the good of humanity, he must close his eyes to the evil designs of his patron. (p. 485)

It is this moral compromise that Miller condemns. When confronted by evil, this well-meaning but hypocritical scientist merely closes his eyes. He ignores, for the sake of convenience, his clear moral duty to oppose the evil in any way that he can. . . .

Thon Taddeo is connected with the scientists who, by disclaiming their responsibility, paved the way for the destruction that has already occurred and for that which will occur in the final chapter of the novel; and all of them together are identified with Pilate, who washed his hands to symbolize that he was free of any guilt in the death of Christ. But Pilate could not rid himself of the blame for Christ's crucifixion, nor can the scientists squirm out from under the burden of responsibility for the crucifixion of mankind on a nuclear cross.

Earlier in the novel, Thon Taddeo had asked, "How can a great and wise civilization have destroyed itself so completely?" . . . The answer, Miller suggests, is that those who were in a position to know better ignored their responsibilities and failed in their moral obligations. While the world tottered on the brink of disaster, they averted their eyes. It is interesting to note that of the various alternatives open to Thon Taddeo, he chose—in Miller's view—the most regrettable. Had he approved of Hannegan's designs and supported them wholeheartedly, he would at least have accepted his responsibility and complicity. That would have been better than hollow innocence. (p. 486)

[Thon Taddeo] is not an evil man—in many ways he is quite admirable. He simply dislikes moral burdens, and therefore ignores them. In the character of Benjamin, the Wandering Jew who appears in all three sections of the novel, Miller introduces a man who chooses to shoulder a burden similar to the one Thon Taddeo has rejected. Sitting on his mountain in the desert, the old Hebrew waits for a Messiah and does "penance for Israel." . . . Dom Paulo cannot understand why Benjamin would take "the burden of a people and its past" upon himself alone. . . . Reflecting further, Paulo finds the answer: the burden is thrust upon all of us, and it is our moral duty to accept it. (p. 487)

In the final section of the novel, Miller returns again and again to the theme of responsibility and drives it home. In this chapter a second atomic age has been reached, and ambitious and foolhardy men again unleash the torrents of destruction. The question posed by Thon Taddeo ("How can a great and wise civilization have destroyed itself so completely?") haunts every page, and Miller's answer is the same. (pp. 487-88)

Miller's final statement on the theme of responsibility is also uttered by Abbot Zerchi, and it represents the culmination of the author's message. Pinned beneath a pile of rubble, the priest contemplates a dying world and, in near delirium, carries on a conversation with an imagined Doctor Cors. . . . This passage insists on the identity of all men ("Thee me Adam Man we"). His realization that "the trouble with the world is *me*" shows that Zerchi, too, has achieved the wisdom of Benjamin. He has learned that the destiny of men is the responsibility of each individual man.

Abbott Zerchi is, of course, in no way directly responsible for the holocaust that envelops the world for the second time. But

Miller considers him indirectly responsible. As a monk, isolated in his monastery from the concerns of the world, he is symbolic of all those who are unconcerned, those who drop out, those who despair. Thus, *A Canticle for Leibowitz* is a novel of and for our time. In an age when the individual man feels ever further removed from the decisions of government which affect us all, *Canticle* reaffirms an old value. Says Miller: "I am my brother's keeper!" (p. 489)

Michael Alan Bennett, "The Theme of Responsibility in Miller's 'A Canticle for Leibowitz'," in English Journal, *Vol. 59, No. 4, April, 1970, pp. 484-89.*

DAVID SAMUELSON

Up until [the publication of *A Canticle for Leibowitz*] Miller had been regarded, in Sam Moskowitz's words, as "the perennially promising author." An engineer-turned-writer, he had published some forty-odd stories in the major science fiction magazines in the Fifties; several were chosen for anthologies, sometimes of the best stories in the field, but many of his tales are rather conventional and far from distinguished. "The Darfsteller," a story about a human actor struggling quixotically to compete in an age of automated stage plays, won for him a "Hugo" in 1955 for the previous year's best novelette, but he was not able to publish a collection of stories until after the success of his novel. The first collection, *Conditionally Human* (1962), combines "The Darfsteller" with two other novelettes, demonstrates his proficiency with fiction of medium length dealing with serious intellectual and emotional themes, and shows a generally prosaic and sometimes plodding style. The second collection, *The View from the Stars* (1964), consisting of nine stories from the period 1951-1954, exhibits a considerable range of subject matter, various degrees of control over style, and a talent for compression, and makes it clear that the ability to construct effective scenes and dramatic contrasts was present early in Miller's abbreviated career. Ironically, by the time these books were published, their author was no longer writing science fiction. . . . Nevertheless "the perennially promising author" had fulfilled his promise; his last work was one of the best novels ever to emerge from the pulp science fiction field.

A novel of about 100,000 words, *A Canticle for Leibowitz* is composed of three parts, roughly equal in length, sharing the same basic setting in space but separated in time by gaps of approximately 600 years. Each part is a coherent novelette, an original variation on a conventional science fiction theme, carefully plotted and constructed for its own particular effects. Each individual story, dealing with individuals' personal struggles, brings to life the issues and ideas of the whole which, because of the interplay between the novelettes, is thus something greater than its parts. Making good use of science fictional conventions, methods, and philosophy, Miller has gone beyond them to produce a dissertation on the ambiguity of advance and the relativity of knowledge, against a background of history as an aesthetic pattern, a seamless fabric into which individuals and institutions, actual events and folklore are inextricably interwoven. Yet for all the complexity, solemnity, and high seriousness that such a description (aptly) suggests, the book is first of all an entertainment, full of fun and occasional thrills, presenting sympathetic characters in a narrative of curious and interesting situations and events. (pp. 226-29)

As an entertainment, the novel is a story, or three stories, about people, about their joys and pleasures, about their thoughts, and about their personal struggles, with their faith, with their environment, with themselves. At this level, the reader is made to *feel* such things as survival, discovery, and frustration, which bulk so large in the intellectual content of the book, even as the comic effects amuse him and predispose him to sympathy with the characters. The comedy, however, and the irony congruent with the narrator's vast perspective make it nearly impossible to identify with the characters, leading us more toward a position of relating ourselves intellectually, to their philosophical stances, and to the oblique historical parallels with our own past and present. The characters, themselves, seem to find complete commitment to an idea difficult to achieve, however strongly they may be shown as wanting to believe in it, and their relatively cerebral involvement is reinforced by the narrator's rationality and perspective.

The typically science-fictional tendency to involve the head before the heart is evident in Miller's style, too, which is entertaining in the way that cultured, intelligent conversation is. Seldom startling, his style is witty, yet relatively formal, and distinctive enough to maintain an aesthetic distance between reader and story, encouraging critical observation and appreciation. Although the directness, obviousness, and simplification of pulp style had not been blatant in the original versions of the [three sections of *A Canticle for Leibowitz* as] novelettes, Miller added dignity to his revised narrative by means of longer sentences, more sonorous rhythms, and less use of colloquial diction. Specialized words from technology and theology were already in frequent use in the earlier versions, as were words and sentences from foreign languages, from Latin of course, but also from Hebrew (in Hebrew script, the English translation of which is given), with an additional snatch of German to bring us into the industrial totalitarianism of Part Three. The net effect is a certain measure of weight and seriousness and scope, contributing to the narrator's air of omniscience but also to the dignity of the characters, whose speeches often seem somewhat elevated and self-conscious. From the perspective of the centuries, dignity may seem a bit incongruous for such puny and even comic figures, but within each story, some characters manage to stand out, as if to decree their own significance on a purely human scale of values.

The mixture of comedy and weightiness which penetrates so much of the book is visible also on the symbolic level. The allegorical identification of Miller's three eras with eras in Western civilization suggests a certain solidity which we associate with historic grandeur. The allegory also impresses upon us the idea that these are representative men and times about which we are reading. But the disparity between Miller's relatively simple men and the inflated figures of history, and between his relatively uneventful narratives and the supposedly grand movements of history is essentially comic, a sympathetic but knowing commentary on the difference between aspirations and achievements. (pp. 271-73)

Through everything, of course, as in the Poet's book, runs a kind of laughter, although it is not the same bitter, sardonic laughter as that which the Poet displays in Part Two, and which presumably causes Abbot Zerchi to dismiss the book of verse as little more than satire. Irony is a major tool of both writers, but the Poet's irony is more limited, more personal, more intent on destructive criticism, and related to a sense of outrage that the world should be as it is. The irony of Miller's narrator is to a great extent the irony of vast perspective, against which personal outrage would be rather out of place. Miller's humor involves more than irony, however; his style is witty, his characters are sympathetically treated for all their bumbling, and his approach is intellectual rather than sentimental. His people have little to be thankful for or to look forward to, but they find joy in simple tasks and meaning in greater ones, and they delight as much in contemplation as they do in playfulness. The author too appears to delight in little things, in puns and comic allusions, in episodes of slapstick, in dramatic effects of confrontation, discovery, and anticlimax.

Humor of any kind is relatively rare in science fiction, with the exception of what James Blish terms "the painful traveling-salesman banter which passes back and forth over real drawing-boards and spec sheets." Perhaps because the scientist-author or the scientist-hero sees the world rigidly in terms of weights and measures and lines of force, perhaps because he is so busy seeking immediate solutions to mundane problems that he can't see himself from the perspective of anyone else, an even rarer occasion in science fiction is the evocation of the "comic spirit." All the more to be appreciated, then, is the achievement of Walter M. Miller, Jr., for, in *A Canticle for Leibowitz,* he has written a genuine comic novel. In doing so, however, he has not written a work of "pure" science fiction; rather, he has incorporated into his novel much of what is valuable in science fiction and discarded much that is worthless for his purposes. In other words, it would be more accurate to say about *A Canticle for Leibowitz* that it uses science fiction than to say that it *is* science fiction. (pp. 277-79)

> David Samuelson, "Walter M. Miller, Jr.: 'A Canticle for Leibowitz'," in his Visions of Tomorrow: Six Journeys from Outer to Inner Space, *Arno Press, 1974, pp. 221-79.*

HAROLD L. BERGER

[*A Canticle for Leibowitz* has] a special dreadfulness: the idea that the insanity of war is chronic, that man will return to ashes what he raises up from past ashes, until he is no more. Beginning six hundred years after the "Flame Deluge," Miller's episodic narrative carries the reader through twelve centuries of recovery to the beginning of another Deluge, one which, if not the last, will teach men nothing, but will only rewind the clockwork of futility. (pp. 151-52)

No doubt Miller's novel would have seemed most illiberal in less troubled times. Not only does he despair of man (not an exceptional attitude in any age), but he displays a strongly pro-clerical feeling vis-a-vis science. . . . Yet *if* one accepts the premise about man's incorrigibility with dangerous toys, Miller's gentle static clericalism has its virtues. The clerical mentality and temperament is hardly disposed towards inventing world-blasting armaments. In all, however, Miller seems to be less assured by his faith in faith than his faith in scientific ignorance to halt the deadly cycle. Here again science fiction steps backward from the precipice, waiting for the instinct for racial survival—should that ever come—to overtake madness and the machines.

And the step backward is Miller's too. In 1952, eight years before *Canticle,* he wrote **"Dumb Waiter,"** a preachy story whose optimism now leaves one with a feeling of sadness. I read it after *Canticle*—an ironic postscript which only darkened the gloom.

Of course machines go wrong and men go wrong, but that's no reason for giving up on either: This is the message of **"Dumb Waiter."** The war was over, but bombless bombers keep "bombing" and robot cops keep giving war-withered survivors summonses for jaywalking, all the doings of Central, the computer, which no one knows how to reprogram. Miller's hero forestalls mobs of angry computer wreckers and reprograms the machine to meet the realities of peace and reconstruction. He believes that the loss of the computer will set civilization back ages. He debates with the machine haters and brands them "the machine age's spoiled children," who thoughtlessly take from the machine and crack up with the machine because, like the politicians, they haven't the will to understand the machine: . . . "If all men were given a broad technical education, there could be nothing else there, could there?"

"Technocracy—"

"No. Simply a matter of education."

"People aren't smart enough."

"You mean they don't care enough. . . . If the common man were trained in scientific reasoning methods, we'd solve our problems in a hurry."

But the author of *Canticle* no longer believed that. No longer did he see machines as servants waiting to be used wisely by knowledgeable masters. On the contrary, anything that could happen would happen. One falls down the dumb waiter shaft sooner or later. Sooner or later one drops the bomb. Sooner probably. What effect has knowledge on madness and the machines? (pp. 154-55)

> Harold L. Berger, "Catastrophe," in his Science Fiction and the New Dark Age, *Bowling Green University Popular Press, 1976, pp. 147-98.**

DAVID SAMUELSON

Although the biographical information available on Miller is sketchy, his personal experiences and the ambience of the decade in which he wrote are discernible in his fiction. His Southern origins, his wartime flying, his engineering education, his reading of history and anthropology, and his personal vision of his religion are all reflected in some of his stories. How his more private life might be involved is conjectural, but the social environment of America in the years following World War II is eminently visible. In that war, a technological elite had come to power, had defeated an evil enemy of seemingly archetypal proportions, and had emerged with a vision of unlimited energy and growth in peacetime.

Conformity, security, overpopulation, hot and Cold wars all figure in Miller's stories, though the dominant themes, an interrelated pair, are socio-technological regression and its presumed antithesis, continued technological advance. All of these he treated with respect to their social implications, particularly for the United States, but perhaps more importantly, with regard to their effect on individual behavior, including that side of behavior which can only be termed religious.

Most science fiction writers and readers would probably accede to the dictum of Leslie A. Fiedler in *Love and Death in the American Novel* (1962) that science fiction "believes God is dead, but sees no reason for getting hysterical about it." . . . The general feeling, however, is that serious science fiction and serious religion don't mix.

This assumption also seems to have distorted critical discussions of Miller's *A Canticle for Leibowitz.* Marketed simply as "a novel," it has been read as if it had little or no connection with science fiction, as if the author sprang full-blown into the literary landscape in 1960, as an apologist for, or a would be reformer of, medieval or modern Catholicism, before the winds of change which emanated from the Vatican Council convened by Pope John. Most published critiques take little note of the novel's polyphonic structure, in which other viewpoints are given almost equal time and equal weight, with a special emphasis on the viewpoint associated with science and technology. Few of them have recognized his long apprenticeship in the science fiction magazines, and the continuity between the novel and what preceded it. In [the stories collected in *The Science Fiction Stories of Walter M. Miller, Jr.*], and I think in the novel as well, Miller comes across as an unashamed technophile.

Miller's development as an artist is not as straightforwardly demonstrated as is the thematic content of his stories. The book version of *Canticle* shows decided improvements in its three parts over their magazine versions, and the story, "Conditionally Human" (1952) has been revised upward for book publication, but other changes are less obvious. Since he uses the same themes more than once, some improvement in handling can be inferred. . . . [Although] his best work is spread across the decade, the first two years have more than their share of trivia, impossible to take seriously but utterly lacking in humor. By contrast, the last five years show an increase in serious subject matter and a higher value placed on humor.

That he did not always write fast is evident in *Canticle,* which was at least five years in the making. But its richness is foreshadowed by the increasing complexity of his later stories, which were published if not written at a considerably slower rate: only four were published after the first Leibowitz short novel (1955). During these years there is evidence that Miller was learning how to illustrate a point more and to preach it less, learning how to avoid the most clichéd stereotypes and conventions, learning how to concentrate the reader's interest on a single character immersed in an action the meaning of which transcends the individual. In addition, the growth of Miller's ability to utilize humor more or less parallels the change in his writing to a more complex conception of the role of characters, and a more ambiguous and problematic approach to values, culminating in that work of utmost seriousness which is little short of a "comic" masterpiece. But this change, which I see as an improvement, is gradual and uneven, not a matter of simple chronology.

In examining Miller's concerns, and his maturing as an artist, I will rapidly survey his work under three thematic categories: technological collapse and social regression, "hard" technology and social advance, "soft" or biological technology and social or psychological ambivalence. Then, building on these summaries, I will continue with a review of the role of religion in Miller's fiction and a survey of his growth as an artist culminating in a more detailed examination of his best stories, and finally conclude with an estimate of his accomplishment.

The cyclical theme of technological progress and regress which is the foundation-stone on which *A Canticle for Leibowitz* is built is present in much of Miller's earlier writing.

Miller's best variation on this theme is his shortest, "It Takes a Thief" (1952; reprinted here as "Big Joe and the Nth Generation"). (pp. viii-x)

In none of Miller's earlier stories is there any hint that technological progress itself is to blame for the past or coming cataclysm, rather some shadowy kind of mismanagement seems to be responsible. No credible character argues against progress, and the most positive characters are always involved in rebuilding or at least preserving some semblance of technological civilization. In another dozen or so stories, technological advance is extrapolated from our present situation and, if not slavishly approved, at least favorably treated.

More of a prose poem than a story, "The Big Hunger" (1952) establishes an emotional rationale for some of Miller's other stories of man's evolution. A lyrical flight of fancy about space exploration, ostensibly narrated by the "spirit of adventure," this story alternates florid rhetoric and sentimental vignettes to take us far into the future, through several pendulum swings of expansion and contraction, as waves of explorers leave this world and others, while those who are left behind make peace with the land. A Stapledonian chronicle in miniature, it is largely successful in evoking that longing which Germans call *Fernweh* and one of the characters calls "the star-craze," a hunger which has always echoed through science fiction and which no amount of details about real space travel can ever satisfy. Echoes of this story, or of the concept it tries to dramatize, can be heard in the regression stories, in stories of human evolution, and in two elegies for the loss by certain individuals of the "freedom" of space.

In three of his best stories, Miller sides with those who are to some extent victims of technological progress, in their coming to terms with the presumed advance of civilization. "Crucifixus Etiam" (1953), his best short piece, shows us a day laborer on Mars, whose lungs are being sacrificed to the dream of making Mars air breathable for colonists within a thousand years. This story will be examined later in more detail, as will "The Darfsteller" (1955), the award-winning short novel about an ageing ham actor displaced by lifesize mannequins in a mechanized theatre of the future, and his attempt to beat the new technology at its own game. Not quite as successful is "The Lineman," Miller's last published story, a "day in the life" of a worker on the Moon. In contrast to the "tragedies" of Manue Nanti and Ryan Thornier in the stories above, Relke's experience is dark comedy, about the time a travelling whorehouse came from Earth and put the work force off schedule. Not everything is lighthearted . . . but the general tone is one of achievement, not just survival, in the midst of ever-present danger. . . . [In the course of the story Relke is taught] that "there was a God," whose creations of the universe and of human beings were on pretty equal footing.

This sense of faith is carried to extremes in two earlier stories. In "The Will" (1954), the impending death of a child is thwarted by his faith in the ability and the willingness of future time travellers to rescue and cure him after digging up his buried stamp collection. Although the premise is uncomfortably silly, the story is almost rescued by its mundane details: the parents' grief, the boy's addiction to the *Captain Chronos* television show, and the public relations use to which he is put by the program's star and producers (based presumably on Miller's own experiences with *Captain Video*).

As some of these stories show, Miller is not always sure that the fruits of technology will be as delicious as the planners contend, but the drive to progress is not to be halted, as it was in the stories of regression. In all cases, however, the technology is "hard," based primarily on the physical sciences. The Church, which has pretty much given up most claims to insert morality into physical science, has a much greater stake in the futures mankind is offered by the biological sciences. Correspondingly, questions of biological "advance" Miller treats with more circumspection; "progress" is a much more ambivalent quality in his "biological" stories. Some of these concern intelligent aliens, all dangerous to man, some of which are clearly negative symbols of possible paths of man's biological progress.

"The Triflin' Man" (1955; reprinted here as **"You Triflin' Skunk"**) is an alien father of an Earth child who is coming to claim his offspring, causing the child nightmares and severe headaches. The child's mother, however, a Southern country woman, drives away her one-time seducer with a shotgun.

If some of these stories represent natural evolution, the same is not unequivocally true in **"Blood Bank"** (1952), in which Terrans play the role of the heavy. In this *Astounding* space opera, moral indignation runs high as one puzzle: what did Commander Roki do wrong? (he ordered the destruction of an Earth ship carrying "surgibank" supplies to a disaster-stricken planet, because the ship would not stand by for inspection) gives way to another: how will Commander Roki vindicate himself, so as not to have to commit suicide as the code of his world demands of his honor? Admirably controlling suspense as Roki gradually uncovers the clues, Miller keeps us from doing the same until we have learned the particulars of this milieu and have accepted to some extent a degree of cultural relativism which most of the characters in the story do not have. Each cultural idiosyncrasy is embodied in a person and rooted in some physical, biological, or cultural peculiarity of his or her world. Although the heart of the adventure is conquest of the "Solarians," a predatory race evolved on Earth which uses standard humans as medical supplies to trade for nuclear fuel and a fascist renaissance, the story's center of interest is not in Earth, its legendary past or aborted future. Nor is it in the comic confrontation between Roki and the female pilot from a frontier world whose rickety cargo ship transports him to the Sol solar system. The primary concern is the solving of puzzles, from the technological (faster-than-light drive, reaction engine limits, ship-to-ship grapples) to the anthropological (humanity's alleged origin on Earth, the amount of space an empire can govern, how much diversity a widespread civilization can and must tolerate). These cross at the point of conflict between non-Earth humans and Solarians; not being human, the latter threaten humanity, an implicit act of war which tolerance for local customs and local biological variation cannot encompass. Common romantic and melodramatic motifs are employed for surface excitement, but the real interest is more of a cerebral nature, with the moral concern for intraspecies savagery almost a side-issue.

Although the evolution in that story may have occurred naturally, the evolved Solarians ensured their "superiority" by means of brute strength, greying the distinction between natural and forced evolution. In **"I, Dreamer"** (1953), the early training of a child to distinguish between self, semi-self, and non-self, though effective, seems grafted on. The story proper, told by the cyborg, is a ridiculous mish-mash of revolutionary politics and melodramatic seduction, with a little sadism mixed in. (pp. x-xiii)

In two other, longer tales, which will be examined in more detail later, Miller is more successful in raising hard "religious" questions about forced evolution, while telling convincing stories in an effective, symbolic manner. **"Conditionally Human"** questions man's right to play God with life and death and the fate of "lower" animals. **"Dark Benediction"** (1951), asks how humanity would respond to a fight from the

skies promising great powers, if it also demanded a physical change of the color and texture of the skin.

Both stories explicitly involve religious questions and symbolism, and feature Catholic priests in advisory, but fallible, roles. Miller's other works may not be as permeated with his religion, but its effect is apparent. (p. xiv)

Hardly an obligatory convention, like the boy-girl romances and repulsive villains Miller brings in occasionally, religion (especially the Roman Catholic version of Christianity) usually has a negative connotation in science fiction. Miller's primitive priests are conventional in that way. But the priest in **"Death of a Spaceman"** is a sympathetic figure, as are those in **"Conditionally Human"** and **"Dark Benediction,"** while the clergy in **"No Moon for Me"** and **"Crucifixus Etiam"** are neutral tones in the moral landscape. Christian doctrine does suggest a bass tone of conviction as a contrast to the uncertainty of modern man, a role it plays convincingly in *A Canticle for Leibowitz*. But the doctrine or its exponent, as in Miller's novel, may be naïve, lacking in understanding of the whole picture, or otherwise irrelevant. The exponent need not be nominally religious, either: although the psychiatrist in **"Command Performance"** cannot play this role because his advocacy of conformity is so much a part of the conventional milieu of the Fifties, the Analyst in **"The Ties that Bind"** *is* a reasonable facsimile of a priestly *raisonneur* because of the antiquity of his anthropological teaching, which predates in a sense the secular humanism of that story's Eden-like Earth.

For the technophilic Miller, unlike the technophobic C. S. Lewis, the direct opposition of science and religion won't do, at least not if it means the down-grading of science and technology. They represent for him the best that we can do today and in the foreseeable future, when it comes to knowledge and concrete achievement. As in *A Canticle for Leibowitz,* however, religion suggests a kind of wisdom, traditional, irrational, humane, which knowledge alone can not reach, but a kind of wisdom which, divorced from social and technological, and even aesthetic reality, is also inadequate as a guide for conduct. It complements the engineering question, How, with the age-old poetico-religious question, Why, even if it does not reveal *the* Answer. At the least, its presence in a Miller story indicates continuity with the present, and by implication, a universal need of mankind. At best, the religious connotation of the parable—and most of Miller's stories are parabolic in their didacticism—underlines the moral ambiguity of a situation, its need for a moral resolution. When the mass of American and British science fiction magazines were topheavy with laboratories, machines, and the "social" effects of science and technology (i.e. the effects of hypothetical inventions and discoveries on "masses" of people), Miller was one of a handful of writers concerned with effects on individuals, who stand alone, lacking the kind of certainty that only dogma can provide, and aware of both the lack and the inadequacy of the outmoded dogma.

Philosophy, or sententious content, does not by itself make a story or a writer. In his best stories, Miller managed to combine thought and action, to make ideas personal and involving, by approaching a universal ("truth") or problem by means of strong identification with an individual, who must demonstrate an important decision by means of an action, the significance of which is underscored by the fact that there is not a lot of action for action's sake cluttering up the pages. One exception is **"The Big Hunger,"** in which mankind as a whole is the protagonist, but the rule holds for the sentimental or near-sentimental **"Death of a Spaceman"** and **"The Hoofer,"** for the melodramatic **"Big Joe and the Nth Generation"** and **"Blood Bank,"** for **"The Lineman"** and **"The Ties That Bind,"** which just miss being in the first rank. And it definitely holds for those stories which are in the first rank.

"Command Performance" (reprinted here as **"Anybody Else Like Me?,"** 1952) is a very human story of suburban loneliness and conformity. . . . [Some aspects of the plot] are melodramatic, but Lisa's character and situations are real enough and realistically presented, with the kind of satire of contemporary mores (conformity and all that) for which *Galaxy* was noted.

In **"Conditionally Human,"** Terry Norris, a veterinarian, cares for animals whose intelligence has been increased to put them midway between pets and children (children are rare, because of restrictive population laws), and his occupation upsets his newlywed wife whose maternal reflexes are strong. Terry's crisis point is an order to destroy certain "units," in this case "neutroids" (apes transmuted into baby girls with tails), which exceed the allowable intelligence limits. After Terry has located one of these units, named Peony, and taken it away from its "Daddy," a petshop owner, he is visited by Father Paulson (Father Mulreany in the book version) on behalf of his bereft parishioner. The priest acts reluctantly as a moral guide for the unreligious Terry, who uses him as a sounding board, then goes to excesses not sanctioned by the church. He not only hides the illegal "deviant," but he also kills, by a carefully planned "accident," his supervisor who has come to see that the order and the "neutroid" are executed. Then he decides to take a new job with the company that produces "newts," to carry on the work of the fired employee who made the newts not only too intelligent, but also functionally, biologically human.

In a society forced by population pressures to restrict the freedom to breed, there are many malcontents. . . . Terry finds himself "adapting to an era," at first to the status quo, but then to the possible future that an artificially created race might bring about. Either choice requires a kind of moral toughness and seems to demand that he kill, if not Peony then supervisor Franklin. By contrast, the priest could never sanction murder, though he may be an indirect cause of one; he finds the creation of the neutroids an abomination but their destruction possibly even more so. . . . But Miller seems determined to stretch the Church's teachings to the limit; what if you *have* to choose between murders? Terry and Anne both make that choice— *she* threatens to kill him—on behalf of the freedom to breed or "create," but the reader, having been taken only part way down that path of argumentation, is left with a moral ambiguity. The satire cuts both ways, but seems aimed at the kind of society which makes such choices necessary.

Heavy with implications, the story is not weighty in a ponderous sense; things happen too fast for that. . . . Scenes flash by, such as Terry's conversations with the police chief, with Anne, with "Doggy" O'Reilly (Peony's "Daddy"); tension builds, Peony is shown to be adorable, and the die is cast. Though the moralizing increases, the pace never flags. The end finds the Norrises waiting it out, aware that they are pitting themselves against society. Quixotically they pursue a goal they are unlikely to achieve, recognizing that they have elected— as has the whole society, unconsciously, and in an opposite manner—to play God to a "new people."

"Dark Benediction" raises other interesting questions about man's fate, positing a biological transformation of the whole human race into a new "improved" model, a transformation which is resisted by almost everyone before it takes place. Sharing the senses of Paul Oberlin, we share his repugnance to the "dermies" whose skin has turned scaly and gray, and whose desire to touch others and spread the contagion is little short of obscene. Overtones of racial prejudice (the locale is the South), leprosy, violation of the integrity of the individual, fear of the unknown in general, and the known transition period of often fatal fever make it clear that a considerable trade-off is required. (pp. xiv-xviii)

As in all Miller's best stories, the science fictional rationalization is clear, the behavior believable, the focus not on the science fiction itself but on the situation of one troubled person. Unlike in others, however, the biological transformation in this one is a positive one, with utopian overtones. Although the repellent characteristics are given their due, the parasite which Dr. Seeves explains is responsible for them is also responsible for an increase in sensory perception and apparently, cooperative behavior. . . . The real reason why this metamorphosis is more acceptable may be its resemblance to a divine blessing. The parasite is a gift from the sky, having arrived in meteorites launched by some alien civilization; though labelled with warnings, the pods were first opened by the ignorant, unable to read the signs and driven by their "monkeylike" curiosity. As from Pandora's Box or the apple of Genesis, but perhaps in reverse, as a distribution of good, the contents spread everywhere, making it likely that everyone, eventually, will have to give in to this "dark benediction." Reception of the parasite is a passive act, moreover, requiring acceptance only of the "laying on of hands." Believing it really is beneficial, that the scientist's findings are accurate, requires, as does believing the disease is harmful, an act of faith (parasites in **"Let My People Go,"** clearly in the service of overspecialized aliens, were regarded with fear and loathing). Paul and the reader can only decide on the basis of others' behavior. . . . (pp. xix-xx)

An act of faith is also crucial in **"Crucifixus Etiam,"** Miller's best short story, but the faith is not sustained by the protagonist's Catholic religion. An elegiac, near-future projection, this story makes of technophilia a secular religious faith. . . . This is the story of a man who takes great risks to his health for the chance of high rewards; as his health begins to fail, and the rewards come to seem unobtainable, he questions the justification of his work, then comes to identify with the goal he serves but will never attain.

The man is Manue Tanti, a Peruvian laborer at work on Mars, his health endangered by implanted oxygenation equipment which encourages atrophy of the lungs. The justification is "faith in the destiny of the race of man." (p. xx)

As the work goes on and [Manue] becomes an oxygen "addict," we follow the curve of his emotions to cynicism and despair, to a controlled cursing in lieu of prayer. On the day a controlled chain reaction is started deep beneath the Martian crust, the men are finally informed of the significance of their job, laboring so that others may breathe, far in the future. . . . He finds the answer bitter—Miller calls it Manue's "Gethsemane"—but also glorious. One man asks "What man ever made his own salvation?" Another says "Some sow, some reap," and asks Manue which we would rather do. Manue himself picks up a handful of soil and thinks "Here was Mars. His planet now."

The roughly 8000 words that comprise this story are very efficiently employed. Miller uses vignettes, rather than long scenes, and avoids the sentimentality that technique seems to lead to in other short stories. Bits of action and dialogue, nothing extended, break up what is mainly narrative. The characters, bit players except for Manue, are solid individuals: the Tibetan, Gee, Manue's digging partner with whom he has nothing in common; the foreman, Vögeli, who is quick-tempered and efficient, trying to maintain his men like tools; Sam Donnell, the "troffie" (atrophied) repairman, who is a mine of misinformation; even the riot leader, Handell, and the supervisor, Kinley, though little more than roles with names, seem right in their parts. The local color and slang, brought in as if in passing, make Mars feel lived in. And the third person narration, limited to the consciousness of Manue, is particularly effective in that it restricts our senses almost claustrophobically to those of the perfect observer for this story: a Peruvian, used to thin air and small social horizons, ignorant of much but proud of his ancient heritage and comfortable in his ambition, Catholic in upbringing but able to recognize how ill-fitted his religion is to this alien world.

On a larger scale, Miller managed a similar triumph in the short novel, **"The Darfsteller."** This, too, is limited to the consciousness of one person, for whom technological advance is no unmixed blessing. Ryan Thornier, an ageing former matinee idol in the days before the stage was automated, has consistently refused to make a "tape" of his acting personality, or to work in the production or sales ends of the autodrama business. Steeped in theatrical tradition, proud of his art and even of the poverty to which his pride has brought him, Thornier is reduced to janitorial duties in an autodrama theater, his chief joy in life being the rare chance to see a third-rate live touring company play to a sparse audience. Denied that opportunity, he is given two weeks' notice before he is replaced in his job, too, by an automaton. Since this is on the eve of a mechanical stage run of a play he once starred in, the actor conceives and executes a plan to make one last performance the culmination of his career and simultaneously an act of revenge against his boss, his profession, and his world. **"The Darfsteller"** is the story of what he accomplishes, and how.

On one level this is a personal story, a near-tragedy. Learning quickly enough how the technology of the autodrama operates, Thornier sabotages the tape of an actor intended for a role he once played. Then, since there is not enough time to get a new tape before opening night, he offers himself as a replacement. Against the better judgment of everyone involved, his offer is accepted, and he puts a real bullet in the gun with which the mannequin playing his enemy is supposed to shoot him. In the actual performance, however, in which he competes against the "Maestro," the mechanical director that operates the tapes and mannequins, adjusting them to each other and to audience reactions, Thornier is reinvigorated. He dodges the bullet and catches it in his belly.

Allegorically, this is a fable of technological displacement. In case anyone misses the point, Rick, the projectionist, runs it through again in the coda. Explaining that a human specialist will inevitably lose to a specialized tool, a machine, Rick defines the function of Man as "creating new specialties." But the technology is more than a symbol; the autodrama, throughout the story, is continually vying with Thorny for center stage. To compete with it, he has to learn to understand it, which he has never tried to do before. Learning what he can from Rick, he becomes fascinated with it, to his dismay and the reader's edification. Seeing the Maestro at work, with Thornier in its system, is most instructive, and enough details

are developed to make the automation of the theater, presumably the last bastion of personalized professions, seem believable.

The creation of this illusion is assisted, moreover, by the appearance of former actors and stage people associated with the autodrama who come into town in connection with the opening. Like any technology, this one requires preparation and tending, and they have been reduced to servants of the machine in Thornier's estimation, and to some extent in their own. It is, of course, the only game in town, and it even offers a kind of "immortality" to actors in their prime, as he recognizes, comparing Mela, his one-time co-star and lover, with her unageing tapes and mannequins. The heart of the story, however, lies in Thorny's love affair with the theater, with its icons and superstitions, the image it gives him of himself (on our level of perception he is a querulous, vain popinjay), and the recaptured thrill of performance, even a mediocre performance on a stage full of mannequins and of threatening electrical equipment. As he thinks to himself, seeing the Maestro in human terms, the director with his eyes on the whole play and the reaction of the audience is always in opposition to the *Darsteller* (the true actor-artist), and prefers the mere *Schauspieler* (the crowd-pleasing entertainer). An excellent fictional creation, Ryan Thornier is always an actor, even in the role of himself with an audience of one, and the theater as microcosm is ideal for this "morality play" of man vs. machine. Though the reader may find himself in intellectual agreement with Rick, in his analysis of the situation, the rational conclusion is clearly at odds with the emotional identification with the quixotic Thornier, whose irrationality is more appealing.

The narrator in this short novel has the same distant, gently ironic detachment as in *A Canticle for Leibowitz,* with the same fondness for slapstick if not for puns as leavening in a serious tale. The construction is effective, alternating action and dialogue, narration and internal monologue, parallels and antitheses. The characters, aside from Thornier, are personalized functions, though only the theater owner, Thornier's boss, is an obvious stereotype, and even that may be excusable since he is a tormentor as seen through Thornier's eyes. And the didacticism, though clearly overt, is cleanly balanced by the felt reality of Thornier's lament. Perhaps the only thing the novel does not have, and does not need, which may be surprising in view of Miller's usual propensities, is any religious props or even a sense of religion, unless we assume that for the actor, the stage is his Church. The effect of the whole, however, is that of a minor masterpiece. (pp. xxi-xxiv)

The medium lengths, novelette, novella, short novel, were where Miller's strengths lay, where he could combine character, action, and import. Of his forty-one magazine publications, twenty-four were of middle length, including . . . the three more or less independent parts of *Canticle.* Only **"Crucifixus Etiam"** really stands out among the shorter works, followed by **"The Big Hunger," "Big Joe and the Nth Generation," "Death of a Spaceman," "The Hoofer,"** and **"Vengeance for Nikolai,"** most of which come dangerously close to sentimentality (melodrama in **"Big Joe and the Nth Generation"**) and each of which relies heavily on a gimmick, the bane of so many short stories. Whether the sustained continuity of a more conventional novel was beyond him, we can not know for certain, but it seems certain that part of the success of *Canticle* is due to its tripartite form, each third crisply etched in short novel size, with counterpoint, motifs, and allusions making up for the lack of more ordinary means of continuity.

This, too, he learned in his apprenticeship in the science fiction magazines.

Miller will no doubt continue to be remembered primarily for *A Canticle for Leibowitz,* which set a standard few science fiction stories or novel approach. In the context of his growth toward that achievement, his whole canon is of some extrinsic interest. But the stories in this collection are interesting in their own right, too, and five are minor classics in themselves. (p. xxiv)

> *David Samuelson, in an introduction to* The Science Fiction Stories of Walter M. Miller, Jr. *by Walter M. Miller, Jr., Gregg Press, 1978, pp. vii-xxv.*

Scott O'Dell

1903-

American novelist and journalist.

O'Dell's Newbery Award-winning novel *Island of the Blue Dolphins* (1960) is generally regarded as a classic of young adult literature. An exploration of the growth in confidence and sensitivity of an Indian girl who is left alone on an island for eighteen years, the novel is praised for its psychological complexity. *Island of the Blue Dolphins* and O'Dell's subsequent books for young adults are based on historical persons and events; as Barbara Wersba notes, O'Dell "uses history as the mainspring for revealing truth about human beings: their passion, their grief."

O'Dell was raised in California, and the majority of his novels are set on the West Coast or in southwestern states. Many of O'Dell's works concern the Spanish colonization of the Southwest and the conflicts between the explorers and the native peoples. His *Seven Serpents Trilogy* is praised for its intricate detailing of Mayan culture. Comprising *The Captive* (1979), *The Feathered Serpent* (1981), and *The Amethyst Ring* (1983), the trilogy portrays a young New World missionary who disapproves of his compatriots' treatment of the Mayan Indians.

O'Dell has won critical recognition for his courageous and perceptive protagonists who are often caught in conflict between their needs for both independence and social integration. Such tension is evident in Karana, the central character of *Island of the Blue Dolphins*, who is left to her own resources after enemies expel her tribe and a wild dog kills her brother. Although Karana is initially embittered, she eventually befriends both a girl from the enemy tribe and the wild dog, displaying what some critics consider a balance between self-reliance and interdependence. Like Karana, Esteban de Sandoval in *The King's Fifth* (1966), Tom Barton in *The Hawk That Dare Not Hunt by Day* (1975), Julian Escobar in *The Seven Serpents Trilogy*, and Zia in *Zia* (1976), the sequel to *Island of the Blue Dolphins*, are all protagonists whose moral and emotional strengths are tested through separation from their groups. The characters either reenter their society with a changed perspective or decide to leave permanently. Most critics agree that the strength of these first-person narrators, combined with a vivid, understated prose style, are the qualities which give O'Dell's works their impact.

(See also *Children's Literature Review*, Vol. 1; *Contemporary Authors*, Vols. 61-64; and *Something about the Author*, Vol. 12.)

ELLEN LEWIS BUELL

["**Island of the Blue Dolphins**"] is a romance only in the older sense of the word. It has no hero, no frills, none of the usual feminine props, but I think that thoughtful readers will be willing to forego these for the sake of an unusual experience.

The setting is a remote California island where, from 1835 to 1853 an Indian woman, known to history as the Lost Woman of San Nicolas lived alone. Mr. O'Dell has used the few facts known about her as the basis for a haunting story of a young

girl who is accidentally left behind when tragedy had decimated the tribe. Karana, bereft of her people, of weapons, even of cooking pots—her young brother killed by wild dogs—not only manages to exist but to wring a measure of comfort, beauty, even joy in her solitude. Mr. O'Dell never sentimentalizes her thoughts, nor ascribes to this primitive girl too much poetic feeling. His style, spare, unemotional but evocative, is beautifully fitted to his subject. (p. 40)

> *Ellen Lewis Buell, in a review of "Island of the Blue Dolphins," in* The New York Times Book Review, *March 22, 1960, pp. 40-1.*

NEW YORK HERALD TRIBUNE BOOKS

Occasionally we rejoice to find a book not written to fulfill any need or with any audience in mind, but simply because the subject has seized the author's imagination and he had to write it. These are usually books that quietly take hold of us and make our lives the richer for having read them. Such is "**Island of the Blue Dolphins.**" We will never forget the quiet courage and resourcefulness of Karana, creating a beautiful and satisfying existence for herself during eighteen solitary years on a rock island in the Pacific. Scott O'Dell, basing his story on a true incident which occurred in the early nineteenth century, wisely lets Karana tell in a simple, matter-of-fact way the details of her extraordinary experience. It is hard to imagine a young girl who would not be held spellbound by its quiet poignancy or a boy who would not be enthralled by her struggle to survive against tremendous odds—the threatening wild dogs, the scarcity of food, an earthquake and a tidal wave. . . .

There is a beautiful feeling for the passing of the seasons, and for the companionship offered by the presence around her of many animals, the massive sea elephants, the beautiful sea otters, the cormorants, the blue dolphins that leap through the waters and the pets who become her greatest solace. Above all, there is a deep sense of peace and quiet triumph as Karana achieves happiness on her wild and lonely island.

> *"Girls' Romances of Today and Yesterday," in* New York Herald Tribune Books, *May 8, 1960, p. 8.**

RUTH H. VIGUERS

[As *The King's Fifth* opens, Estéban de Sandoval is awaiting] trial for defrauding the King of Spain of his rightful share of the treasure found in the Land of Cíbola. . . . [Estéban] hopes that by writing down in careful sequence the story of the search for gold, by reliving the fighting, hardships, suffering, treachery, fears, and disappointments, he will find the answer to all that puzzles him: even he succumbed to the fever for gold. Captain Mendoza is not clearly characterized, nor should he be: the record is by "a maker of maps and not a scrivener." Estéban sees him as the leader of the *conducta* and does not censure him for thinking of nothing but gold. To the reader he is the personification of greed, and the other members of the band, with the exception of Father Francisco and Zia, are shadows of evil. . . . The recording of the trial, which periodically interrupts the adventures, does not annoy but rather gives opportunities to look back and consider the meaning of events. Mr. O'Dell must have been deeply immersed in the history and literature of the conquistadores, for Indians, villages, landscapes, lake of gold, all are vivid. As would be expected from the author of *Island of the Blue Dolphins,* the writing is subtly beautiful, often moving, and says more than may be caught in one reading. (pp. 721-22)

> *Ruth H. Viguers, in a review of "The Kings Fifth," in* The Horn Book Magazine, *Vol. XLII, No. 6, December, 1966, pp. 721-22.*

WALTER HAVIGHURST

[In *The King's Fifth*] a small party sets out to search for fortune, with a Zuni girl as their guide. In the vast country that would become Arizona they see terraced adobe cities whose people worship the sun, marvel at the huge Abyss which in time would be called the Grand Canyon, and find treasure that inflames their passions and eventually destroys them.

How the seven travelers are reduced to two—Esteban and Father Francisco—is a harsh narrative illuminated by the beauty of the enormous land and the simple integrity of the Indians.

Although the story pits white men against red men, and Spaniard against Spaniard, it is not simplified into a contest of the good against the bad. The worst men here have qualities of courage and occasional kindness, the best have lapses and limitations. Esteban de Sandoval is a wholly believable lad, vulnerable to the glitter of gold as well as to the charm of Zia, the Zuni girl, and the beauty of earth and sky. Generally the Indians are better people than the white invaders, but they are not idealized. Even the captivating Zia, with her tinkling bells and her love of Spanish horses, is a native girl rather than a heroine.

When Esteban is left alone, to bury the priest and dispose of the treasure, the story reaches a crisis of decision. His hardwon realization of false and enduring values is a part of the maturity that comes from the arduous adventure. His trial and its outcome carry him further into manhood.

There is sound history in this colorful and dramatic tale of the Conquistadors, though the shifting narrative will require close attention from younger readers, and the book is appropriately adorned with some beautiful maps and illuminations by Samuel Bryant.

> *Walter Havighurst, "Gold, Glory, and God," in* Book Week—World Journal Tribune, *December 18, 1966, p. 13.*

JOHN GILLESPIE AND DIANA LEMBO

The rare quality of [*Island of the Blue Dolphins*] lies in Mr. O'Dell's ability to depict the majesty of the heroine's lonely struggle. . . . The story is well written and the main character is vividly presented. (p. 47)

The heroine's control of her emotions and her realistic appraisal of the situation are stressed by the author. The motivations of the Indian girl are examined in greater depth than is usually accorded the fictional Indian. Young adults will admire and respect Karana's fortitude. Her transformation from her early instincts of fear and revenge to her acceptance of love for all living things is well presented. The author's knowledge of the marine life gives added interest. (p. 49)

> *John Gillespie and Diana Lembo, "Overcoming Emotional Growing Pains: 'Island of the Blue Dolphins'," in their* Juniorplots: A Book Talk Manual for Teachers and Librarians, *R. R. Bowker Company, 1967, pp. 47-50.*

PAUL HEINS

Plot and character are deftly interlinked in the story [*The Dark Canoe*] told by Nathan Clegg, sixteen, who had sailed with his brothers Jeremy and Caleb from Nantucket to find a sunken ship, the *Amy Foster,* at Magdalena Bay in Baja California. Jeremy, Nathan's idol, has mysteriously disappeared while Caleb, after the discovery of the underwater location of the *Amy Foster,* has, in a diver's outfit, been probing the wreck. . . . The skill of the author is revealed in his masterly treatment of a contrapuntal theme suggested by [Herman] Melville's *Moby Dick.* The "dark canoe" that Nathan discovers afloat is Queequeg's coffin, which had rescued Ishmael from destruction. On his sixteenth birthday Nathan receives a copy of *Moby Dick* from Caleb, who limps like Captain Ahab because of a childhood injury to one of his legs. Caleb also can quote much of the book from memory. And at the end, Nathan—who has discovered that Jeremy had been a false idol—not only learns to understand and love the once feared and hated Caleb, but saves him from destruction by quoting Starbuck's last and futile appeal to Captain Ahab. The story combines reminiscences from both sides of the American continent—elements of whaling stories, Indian and Spanish details—with suspense and mystery, highly significant events, and character revelation as well as character development. A story of tragic implications, but one in which two brothers find the right answers. (pp. 700-01)

Paul Heins, in a review of "The Dark Canoe," in The Horn Book Magazine, Vol. XLIV, No. 6, December, 1968, pp. 700-01.

THE TIMES LITERARY SUPPLEMENT

This eerie story [*The Dark Canoe*] is set on board a nineteenth-century vessel outward bound from Nantucket. At the start, the captain has apparently been murdered. He was the favourite brother of the cabinboy-narrator Nathan: golden Jeremy, in every way a contrast to lame scarred Caleb their eldest brother, who keeps to his cabin, having lost his captain's papers on Jeremy's evidence that he mishandled the ship-wrecked whaler for which they are searching. . . .

This powerful story creates splendidly the sense of suspicion after the murder, of greed and suppressed mutiny on board, and Nathan's troubled realization that his brothers are exactly the opposite of what he thought them.

"Brothers at Sea," in The Times Literary Supplement, No. 3536, December 4, 1969, p. 1390.

BETTY BAKER

If Bright Morning gave her story to an anthropologist, she would tell it the way Scott O'Dell does in [**"Sing Down the Moon"**]. In simple statements, almost devoid of emotion, the Navaho girl relates her capture by Spanish slavers, her escape and return to Canyon de Chelly just before the United States Army moves against her people. Understatement counterpoints and emphasizes the wanton destruction of crops and livestock to starve the Navahos into submission, the tribe's suffering on the Long March and during internment at Fort Sumner. . . . This shielding of the deeply personal is true Indian narrative but sacrifices the intimacy and depth one expects in a first-person viewpoint. Without fully understanding the mystic triangle of Indian, land and religion, especially strong in the Navaho, the reader can appreciate Bright Morning's strength and determination as real as that of her people and the way her story is faithful to Navaho history.

Betty Baker, in a review of "Sing Down the Moon," in The New York Times Book Review, October 18, 1970, p. 34.

JOHN ROWE TOWNSEND

The title of *Island of the Blue Dolphins*, lovely in sound and evocative in all its key words (for the 'blue' transfers itself to the ocean), sums up the attraction of the O'Dell world. But it is not a matter of settings alone; this is an admirable novel; and its successor, *The King's Fifth* (1966), is to my mind even finer, although in Britain it is not well known. The subsequent O'Dell books, up to the time of writing, have been slighter.

Island of the Blue Dolphins (1960) accepts some severe limitations. It is the story of an Indian girl who survives for many years alone on a small and desolate island. For much of its course it has only one human character; so all that large part of the more usual story which depends on dialogue and the interaction of personality is ruled out. The heroine is uneducated, has never been beyond her own tiny territory, has no wider frame of reference; so abstract thought is almost ruled

out, too, and figures of speech can only be of the simplest. There is little plot in the conventional sense; the story goes on and on with a good deal of sameness over a long period; its development is in the character of the heroine herself, and this is a theme which it is extremely difficult to make interesting for young readers.

Yet all these limitations have been converted into strengths. The fact that there is only one central character, in this remote and isolated setting, makes identification total; the reader must *be* Karana or the book is meaningless. The telling of the story has a memorable purity to which its fresh direct concreteness contributes as much as the author's excellent ear. And the long, continuous time dimension allows the story to take itself outside our clock-and-calendar system altogether, to complete the islanding of a human being's experience.

A Robinson Crusoe story has of course an appeal of its own which hardly needs to be spelled out. Survival is not an immediate problem at present for most of us in the civilized Western world, but as a theme it still touches upon our deepest inborn instincts and unconscious fears. And the details of survival, so compelling and convincing in [Daniel Defoe's] *Robinson Crusoe* itself and in all successful Robinsonnades, are absorbing here, and clearly authentic. Last, *Island of the Blue Dolphins* shows a human being in changing relationship to animal life, about which the author obviously knows a great deal. Birds, beasts and fishes are to Karana at first, and to a great extent must continue to be, either things to be hunted or competitors for the means of subsistence; but as she grows she achieves an acceptance of them as fellow-creatures. If there is a key incident in the whole book, it is the one in which she befriends her arch-enemy, the leader of the wild dogs.

It is a story with intrinsic sadness; and not only because of the early death of small brother Ramo and the later death of Karana's only close friend, the dog Rontu. It is immensely sad to lose human company throughout the years of youth. The depth of this loss is hinted at, no more, in the brief, tentative relationship with the girl who accompanies Aleutian hunters to the island; in the tiny touch of vanity over the cormorant-feather skirt; in the girl's marking her face, on being rescued after all those years, with the sign that she is still unmarried. Karana herself is no mere cipher. She has the qualities which are implied and indeed required by her situation; she is strong, sensible, intelligent, resourceful. And while she is unsentimental she can—even in the desolating absence of other human beings—love. A sad story, yes; but the sadness of *Island of the Blue Dolphins* is of a singularly inspiring kind. Among all the Newbery Medal winners there are few better books.

The King's Fifth is a more complex novel, notable among other things for its formal structure. The hero Esteban de Sandoval is in a prison cell in Spanish Mexico, awaiting trial on a charge of having deprived the King of his lawful fifth share in a treasure found far to the north in the unknown lands of New Spain. Interspersing the story of his prison life and trial is Esteban's account, written night by night in his cell, of the events that led up to it; the stories of 'now' and 'then' move forward side by side until they merge in the last chapter, when all has been told and the verdict is handed down.

The underlying story is that of a treasure hunt, in which Esteban, a cartographer, forms one of a small band led by the daring and unscrupulous adventurer Captain Mendoza. The party includes, besides Mendoza's henchmen, a young Indian girl, who is guide and interpreter, and Father Francisco, whose concern is to save souls. As an adventure story—the story of a quest followed by a trek for survival—it does very well; but it is a moral as well as a physical exploration, and there are moral as well as physical events in it.

Treasure is sinister; that is the heart of the matter. It is not merely that treasure is often both hidden and discovered in circumstances of violence and treachery. The truth is also that the hope of great unearned gain can be one of the most corrupting ever to get men in its grip. In *The King's Fifth* there are not so much good and bad characters as the innocent and the corrupted. The guide Zia, who longs to ride a horse and to help with the mapmaker's art, is innocent; so is Father Francisco; so are those Indians to whom gold is mere dirt for which they have no use. The narrator Esteban is less simple. He is led into the quest by his yearning to map what no man has mapped before, and at first devotion to his craft protects him; but the gold which is won at last from an Indian city begins to exert its baneful influence. Mendoza dies, killed by a dog he has trained in savagery; Zia goes her way, for she sees Esteban becoming another Mendoza; and Esteban finishes in the Inferno, a hot white sandy basin where his last companion, Father Francisco, dies. And only now does he grasp the enormity of the evil burden and tip the gold, enough to make many men rich, into a deep bubbling crater of foul yellow water where it will be lost for ever.

In the parallel story of the consequences—Esteban's imprisonment and trial—the seedy majesty of Spanish law and administration is seen to be similarly corrupted. No one cares for more than the outward forms of justice, but everyone hopes to recover the treasure. Esteban refuses an offer to let him escape, and is ready to serve a three-year sentence in daunting conditions, because freedom for him can now only come through expiation.

The King's Fifth is a sombre and searching book. The two that followed it were less substantial. *The Black Pearl* (1967) is the terse, masculine story of young Ramon, who seized the Pearl of Heaven from the underwater cavern of the great Devilfish; and of Ramon's father, who donated the pearl to the statue of the Madonna in the church on the coast of Lower California, mistakenly thinking to buy divine protection against wind and water; and of the tall-talking Sevillano, who sought to steal the pearl, and fought the Devilfish when it came seeking its own, and died. At last the great pearl, purified now, is placed in the hand of the Madonna-of-the-Sea as a gift of love.

The brief, spare piece of writing . . . is something between a fable and a mystery. The greed and presumption of men are punished. Who is Ramon's father to think he can buy the favours of the Almighty, who is the Sevillano to think he can defeat and steal from the mighty Devilfish? Obviously there are symbolisms involved; for while the Madonna is to be adored the dark powers represented by the Devilfish must also be reckoned with. But what are the dark powers, and are they inside or outside the minds of men? That is part of the mystery, and a mystery does not need to have a simple solution, or indeed any solution.

The way the Devilfish dominates this story makes one think of *Moby Dick*; and it is interesting but not surprising that an obsession with that book is the core of O'Dell's next novel [*The Dark Canoe* (1968)]. (pp. 154-57)

There is much in this short book: a surprising amount. It raises the difficult question whether a novel can depend upon another and still live in its own right. I am disposed to think that an author is as much entitled to draw upon a classic novel as upon myth; and *Moby Dick* as much as any novel has the size and depth of myth; the test, as I have suggested in discussing books based on myth, is whether the author has successfully absorbed his material and made it his own. By that test it must be said that *The Dark Canoe* fails. Though relevant parts of *Moby Dick* are explained, O'Dell's book does not fully live apart from Melville's; does not make full imaginative or psychological sense without it. *Sing Down the Moon* (1970) is again a short book: too short perhaps for the story it has to tell. It is concerned with the sufferings of the Navajo Indians who were driven from their homes and forced into the long, dreadful march to Fort Sumner in 1864. The story is told in the first person by a young Navajo girl, Bright Morning; and, as in *Island of the Blue Dolphins*, O'Dell shows a gift for assuming a feminine identity which is all the more remarkable in a writer whose work is generally very masculine. There is a lovely, grave simplicity in this telling; yet one feels that perhaps it has been pared down too far, that a style which was admirably suited to the lonely setting of a Pacific island is less appropriate for a story that is full of people and harsh, clashing action. With the limpid brevity of *Sing Down the Moon* goes a sense of remoteness, almost of withdrawal. (pp. 158-59)

One suspects that a quick, light step is not natural to Scott O'Dell. His is a more measured tread. And probably he is a long-distance man. His most substantial books have been his most successful, and *The King's Fifth*—a sombre, almost stately novel—is his best of all. It must be significant, too, that he has found inspiration in that most massive of classics, *Moby Dick*. His best stories grow, moreover, from roots which are planted in known experience, actual places, historical fact, books; and there is neither wit nor humour in them. His imagination is strong but it does not soar or sparkle. He is a natural heavyweight. (p. 159)

John Rowe Townsend, "Scott O'Dell," in his A Sense of Story: Essays on Contemporary Writers for Children, *J. B. Lippincott Company, 1971, pp. 154-61.*

RICHARD BRADFORD

["**Child of Fire**"] brims with violence as well as cruelty, usually involving animals. It also focuses so narrowly on a few minor and unfortunate aspects of Chicano culture that it would be an exceptionally poor introduction for young readers to that large, vivid ethnic group.

The narrator is Delaney, an Anglo (white non-Chicano) juvenile parole officer in San Diego. . . . Strangely, all of Delaney's charges have Spanish surnames.

Delaney tries to keep his "cases" from returning to jail, an apparently impossible job. Most of his charges are stereotypes: emotional, thin-skinned resentful, with an infantile sense of honor, and macho down to their stomping boots.

He takes particular interest in two of the boys, members of rival gangs (the Owls and the Conquistadores). Ernie Sierra, an Owl, seems irrevocably lost to society and, indeed, turns out to be. Manuel Castillo, however, reminds Delaney somehow of his own son, and he gets special treatment. Delaney first sees him across the border, in the Tijuana bull ring, when Castillo makes an *espontáneo*, an unauthorized leap from the seats into the ring to expose himself to the bull's horns.

The gangs haven't had a really satisfying rumble for years, due in part to Delaney's encouragement of a substitute form of rivalry between them—organized cock-fighting. This barbarous gambling "sport" is illegal on both sides of the border, but the reader is nevertheless treated to a sanguinary description of an epic chicken brawl. . . .

Castillo leaves school, finds a job on a fishing boat, leads the crew in mutiny off Ecuador, gets locked up in a Guayaquil jail, escapes and makes his way back to California. This lively experience seems to mature him. No longer interested in random violence, he finds instead a cause, a confrontation between Chicano farmworkers and a vineyard owner who is bringing in a mechanical grape-picker. There is no evidence that Castillo's agricultural background extends beyond the nurture of an occasional marijuana plant, but he quickly becomes a natural leader, a 16-year-old Cesar Chavez.

To prevent general bloodshed during the strike, Castillo pulls another, final, *espontáneo*, this time with the grape-picking machine. The novel ends with this messy self-immolation.

What is Mr. O'Dell trying to tell us? Not, certainly, that Chicano culture has become so debased that it has meaning only in hopeless, violent anger. Yet, by implication, he says little more. The only baldly stated ethnic generality occurs when Delaney tells us that "Chicanos are good mechanics," which is patent balderdash. Like Albanian baritones, some are good and some are awful.

Perhaps his message is something like this: The Spanish-speaking people of the Southwest, who were once powerful and are now relatively impotent within the Anglo-Saxon hegemony, find a certain cultural strength in symbols—the rooster, the horse, the blade—and in melodramatic gesture. That may be the message, and it may even be true, but it's a tiny part of the truth.

> *Richard Bradford, in a review of "Child of Fire,"*
> *in* The New York Times Book Review, *November*
> *3, 1974, p. 24.*

PAUL HEINS

Despite the objective quality of the narrative [in *Child of Fire*], both the story and the characters lack dimension; and even if the author is aware of the historical, psychological, and linguistic elements of the Southwest, he fails to arouse a genuine interest in his hero. There are a few bright spots in the realistic scenes of bull fighting and cock fighting; but, in general, the offhand manner of the style only adds to the banality of the story. (pp. 695-96)

> *Paul Heins, in a review of "Child of Fire," in* The
> Horn Book Magazine, *Vol. L, No. 6, December,*
> *1974, pp. 695-96.*

CAROLYN T. KINGSTON

Island of the Blue Dolphins, *The Yearling* [by Marjorie Kinnan Rawlings] and *It's Like This, Cat* [by Emily Neville] illustrate what can happen to a hero or heroine separated from normal companionship. These children use love for an animal to fill the void in their lives. . . . All three stories show that the protagonist gains strength to cope. . . . (p. 145)

These stories are among the most beautiful compositions available for children because the emotion of love described has the shimmering quality of spirituality, purified of much of the selfishness that is so great a part of what is commonly called

love. The beauty of the motivating thought is communicated through the phrasing and construction of each story to such an extent that one must sample the atmospheres created by the authors to appreciate it. Like a sunset, the experience contained in these books is dulled rather than enhanced by description. The protagonists, young as they are, find love more important than life. The welfare of another being is more essential than is their own in a rare essence of emotion. The loss of the object of such a love is carved from the tragic sense of life; the fact of its existence is the balance inherent in this love. (p. 146)

Although [*Island of the Blue Dolphins*] is based in fact, it is the author's beautiful transcription of it that makes it tragedy. Rich in metaphor, so appropriate in the Indian manner of speech, Karana's story unfolds. Scott O'Dell paints a primitive landscape and an empty horizon, seemingly always waiting for a ship to fill it, but he also paints the towering character of Karana as it progressively grows with each moment of tragedy. As the outgoing tide denudes a beach, the Indian girl's life is swept clean of companionship, not once but several times, yet her spirit does not crumple; rather, it expands under the pounding, emerging bright and polished like a rock smoothed by the sea. Her threatening universe remains the same, ready to explode with forces of destruction. It is within herself that the Indian girl finds peace. (p. 148)

> *Carolyn T. Kingston, "The Tragic Moment: Loss,"*
> *in her* The Tragic Mode in Children's Literature, *New*
> *York: Teachers College Press, 1974, pp. 124-67.**

JON C. STOTT

Each year, with the increase in number of children's books, it is often necessary to retreat from the volume of present publication to reexamine those works which have, for various reasons, endured to become classics. One such work is Scott O'Dell's *Island of the Blue Dolphins*. . . .

Although the desert island motif has been a standard fictional theme since Shakespeare's *Tempest* and Defoe's *Robinson Crusoe*, O'Dell is faced with several new problems. Because he is writing children's fiction, he must create a story in which narrative pacing is relatively fast. His specific subject matter, the lonely eighteen years spent by Karana on the Island of the Blue Dolphins, raises difficulties. . . . For a large part of her story, Karana does very little except engage in the diurnal chores of survival. How, then, has O'Dell created a story which continues to grip young readers fourteen years after its publication?

First, the story of Karana's isolation does not begin until the end of the eighth chapter, after her brother Ramu has been killed by the pack of wild dogs. By so delaying the story of her survival, O'Dell is able to create a sense of the social milieu in which she had developed, a feeling of the fear and distrust of the Aleuts, which she will harbor during her solitude, and a contrast between the activity she had known with the tribe and the desolation she faces alone. Moreover, the basic character traits she exhibits during her eighteen years of loneliness have been clearly established during the early part of the novel.

Second, O'Dell intermingles accounts of Karana's day-to-day activities with the highlights of her adventures. Thus the narrative pace is never allowed to slacken, while at the same time the reader is given a sense of her day-by-day existence. (p. 442)

[The] "how to" selections are rendered interesting not only because they are placed between narrative segments, but also because of the vividness with which O'Dell has presented them. Young readers have an interest in survival techniques, as is indicated by their own attempts to build tree houses and woods shelters. But too often this interest is catered to by such Hollywood claptrap as "Gilligan's Island." O'Dell succeeds so well because of his deep knowledge of his subject. (pp. 442-43)

But the most important aspect of the story, that which has made it the classic it is, is the portrayal of the character of Karana. Prefatory to an examination of her character, we should note two aspects. First, O'Dell very wisely chooses the first person point of view. While Karana's life is interesting, her attitude to that life is much more so. Second, as attitudes are intangible, they must be given objective correlatives in order to be fictionally realized. Thus the book is developed around a series of presentations of Karana's attitudes toward her daily survival activities, inanimate objects, animals, and other people. Each of the chapters thus contains a series of symbolic episodes which illuminate aspects of Karana's character and the changes it undergoes.

Chapters One through Eight present two main character traits which are fully explored in the remainder of the novel: Karana's sociality within her family and tribe and her fear of the Aleuts. . . . Later in the story, her desire to be reunited with her people will become the motivation behind her drive for survival, and it will create a need for a substitute animal family. Later, her hatred of the Aleuts will be seen as a character flaw she must work to overcome, as she does in her relationships with Rontu and Tutok.

In these early chapters, O'Dell introduces several incidents and motifs which foreshadow and prepare the reader for incidents and themes to be later developed. . . .

[For example], Karana is upset over the slaying of the otters, a fact which presages her growing love for animals and her adopting of Wonanee, the orphaned otter. (p. 443)

The remainder of the book, which deals with Karana's psychic and physical survival and her final departure, can be divided into three major sections, each one tracing a significant phase in her character development. . . . In each section there are a series of symbolic incidents which reveal aspects of this movement.

On first finding herself alone, Karana's hope is that she will soon be rescued by a returning ship. However, after a year, her hopes are ended and she realizes that she must take definite action herself, which she does by repairing a deserted canoe with which to paddle to a new island. When, in her attempted escape, she loses sight of the island and is forced to retreat, she refers to the island as home for the first time since her lonely stay began. In her withdrawal and return by canoe, we have the second variation on the motif of ships departing from and arriving at the island. Whereas the Aleut arrival had led to Karana's loss of family, this time, her homecoming emphasizes her growing sense of self-reliance. She faces the fact that she is completely alone and devotes her energies to the problems of survival.

In the early stages of her life on the island she has made two significant steps which have led to this position of self-reliance. First, she has turned her back on the immediate past by burning the village, knowing that painful memories cannot help her.

Second, she has understood that if she is to survive and avenge her brother's death by wild dogs, she must violate the tribal taboo which forbids women to make weapons. The task is a difficult one, and, after much trial and error making bows and arrows, she decides that to be truly secure, she must make a spear of sea-elephant tusk. As she prepares to dart an arrow at two battling sea-lions, she pauses, allowing nature to take its course. This action reveals her reluctance to kill living creatures and so foreshadows her inability to kill Rontu and her growing love of her animal friends.

Although the chief motivating force behind her actions on the island has been her desire to kill the wild yellow-eyed Aleut dog who leads the pack, she only wounds him, refusing to let fly the fatal arrow. . . . Her decision not to kill Rontu marks the second major phase of her development. She had earlier learned self-reliance, now she comes to understand that she cannot take another life in the name of vengeance. Moreover, the fact that the dog had belonged to the hated Aleut prepares us for her friendship with the girl. Her decision has been a wise one, for in befriending Rontu, her enforced loneliness has ended, and she has made the first step toward establishing an animal society to replace the human one of which she had been deprived. (pp. 444-45)

The second major phase of Karana's development ends with her friendship to Tutok. . . .

Two of Karana's activities before the arrival of the Aleuts indicate the fact that she still remains a very social being and help to explain why she becomes so close a friend to Tutok. In taming the two birds, Tainor and Larai, she is adding to her non-human family, and in making a yucca skirt and gathering cormorant feathers for a cape, she exhibits the love of fashion she had shown while living with her tribe.

When the Aleuts arrive, Karana hides, noting that "It was the girl I was afraid of." . . . But when she first sees her, Karana does not shoot. . . . Just as her mercy to Rontu indicated her forgiveness of the animal who had destroyed her brother, so her actions toward Tutok indicate a larger response, forgiveness of the representative of a group which had been her enemy. At the moment she puts her spear down, Rontu runs eagerly to the Aleut girl, apparently recognizing her. The point is clear: Rontu had been Tutok's dog, and she is the unidentified girl of the earlier Aleut visit. O'Dell has thus used the friendship between Karana and the dog as the preparation for the human friendship between the two girls. (p. 445)

[Karana's] sense of love and confidence in her new friend is so great that she can accept gifts and she can give a secret name knowing that Tutok will not betray her.

With the achievement of this relationship, a life alone can no longer be fulfilling for Karana. . . . Thus the final seven chapters of the book prepare us for her departure. (pp. 445-46)

The tidal wave and earthquake made evident the danger of future habitation of the island. . . . Immediately she sets about building a new canoe and eagerly prepares to depart when she sees a ship arriving. Although it departs before she can get ready, she spends the next two years in a state of preparedness, often thinking of the voice of her would-be rescuer calling her. When at last the ship returns, she places on her face the marking of the unmarried girl, as she had done eighteen years earlier, and, in so doing, prepares for reunion with society. . . . Boarding the ship, she has rejoined humanity, completing the process which had been interrupted eighteen years before.

We see, then, how O'Dell invests the lonely, often monotonous life of a young girl with significance. He presents details with graphic realism, arranges a series of symbolic events, and, from within the mind of his principal character, tells of the courage and love she uses to survive an inner loneliness which is greater than the outer dreariness of her life and of the maturing process in which hatred and fear have been replaced by love and sociality. (p. 446)

> Jon C. Stott, "Narrative Technique and Meaning in 'Island of the Blue Dolphins'," in Elementary English, Vol. 52, No. 4, April, 1975, pp. 442-46.

MARGARET A. DORSEY

O'Dell's [*The Hawk That Dare Not Hunt by Day*] is a fairly interesting, occasionally exciting historical novel that centers on the intrigue involved in the printing and distribution of the first English translation of the New Testament. The narrator is a 16-year-old English orphan, Tom Barton, who together with his 25-year-old Uncle Jack, is a seaman engaged in trade—and smuggling—with the Low Countries and Germany. It is the smuggler's vocation that brings Tom into contact with William Tyndale, whose ambition it is to translate the Bible into common English. Eventually Tyndale has his translation printed in Germany and Tom successfully smuggles it into England. . . . The story opens in 1524 and spans some ten years, ending with Tyndale's execution as a heretic. The religious and political turmoil of the time is presented with clarity, and in addition to Tyndale himself, King Henry VIII and printer Peter Quentel play their real-life roles. It's a well-guided journey into the past for young teens with some interest in the era; however, it lacks the vitality and the basic situational appeal of some of O'Dell's previous novels. (pp. 60-1)

> Margaret A. Dorsey, in a review of "The Hawk That Dare Not Hunt by Day," in School Library Journal, Vol. 22, No. 4, December, 1975, pp. 60-1.

JEAN FRITZ

Since good story ideas do not come along like streetcars even to master storytellers, it is a happy day when a compelling writer like Scott O'Dell meets a compelling subject like William Tyndale, the sixteenth-century martyr who first translated the Bible into English. An unlikely subject, one may think, for the author of **"Island of the Blue Dolphins," "The King's Fifth,"** and other books set on the Pacific Coast. Yet Mr. O'Dell [in **"The Hawk That Dare Not Hunt by Day"**] seems completely at home in Europe in a conniving, turbulent age, and his subject gives him scope to examine a theme that has obviously haunted him for some time. . . .

That this new story has some symbolic relation for [O'Dell] with his past books is apparent as soon as one sees that the name of Tom Barton's ship is the same as one of Scott O'Dell's earlier books—**"The Black Pearl."** Why **"The Black Pearl"**?

Before finding the answer, one must ship aboard with young Tom Barton, the narrator, and take part in the dangerous adventures that await anyone smuggling into England the new English Bible. . . . It is a race against time—for William Tyndale a race to get his Bible off European presses before his enemies, the heretic-hunters, stop him; for Tom Barton, Tyndale's friend, a race to avoid having to take on two of these very enemies as his partners.

Who wins the race? The enemies, it would appear, for William Tyndale, betrayed by one who has posed as his friend, is strangled and burned at the stake. That is the way Tom saw it, for he went, armed, to kill the traitor. Yet he does not kill because he remembers that Tyndale, who had himself (like Esteban in **"The King's Fifth"**) refused escape when given the chance, would not have condoned murder. So it becomes clear that Tom along with Tyndale and along with Ramon of the earlier book, **"The Black Pearl,"** are the real winners. Not evil but love overcomes evil.

> Jean Fritz, in a review of "The Hawk That Dare Not Hunt by Day," in The New York Times Book Review, February 22, 1976, p. 18.

JOYCE MILTON

Karana, the Indian girl left to survive alone for 18 years [in *Island of the Blue Dolphins*] was a one-in-a-million child protagonist—a loner free to work her destiny totally without interference from adults. . . .

The jacket copy of Scott O'Dell's new book, *Zia,* notes that O'Dell has received many requests to tell what happened to Karana, and one can see in this novel some of the tension between the pressure to produce a good storyteller's sequel and the author's reluctance to violate an essentially self-contained episode, based on fact, with a fictional post script.

Thus the heroine of this story is not Karana, who reappears only briefly and tragically later on, but her niece Zia. Zia and her brother Mando are apparently the only other survivors of their tribe, and they live and work under the padres of the Santa Barbara mission where they conform despite a passive, impersonal resistance to their Spanish overlords.

When we first meet Zia she has discovered a whaler's boat washed ashore and she conceives a daring plan: with her younger brother as crew she will sail to rescue the aunt she has heard about and bring her back to the mainland. From the moment Zia and Mando set out we are under the spell that O'Dell creates so effectively. The mood is portentous, and the journey is not destined to end well. . . .

Having failed in her first plan, Zia persuades the friendly Captain Nidever to go looking for Karana and Nidever takes Father Vicente, the most sympathetic of the priests, along to win Karana's confidence. But while Nidever is gone there is a revolt at the mission; the other Indians, led by a man aptly named Stone Hands, slip off in the middle of the night and Zia, who has stolen a key to help the plotters, is thrown in jail for refusing to tell where they have gone.

Zia is released from jail by Father Vicente when he returns triumphantly with Karana. Karana is at first ecstatic over her new experiences—the taste of melons, the sight of wild horses, learning to weave at the loom—but the mainland soon becomes another kind of prison. She is unable to communicate with anyone; even Zia has forgotten her native tongue and the other Indians regard her as crazy.

In the end Karana runs away to live in a cave on the beach and dies there while Zia, with nothing left to tie her to the mission, simply walks away to find her tribe's old abandoned home in the north. As much as one wants Zia to be free, her leaving has its troubling side. California is not an island, and one knows, historically that there was no escape for the Zias whose way of life was obliterated by the coming of the Spanish.

Nor does Zia's streak of detachment make for high adventure in the traditional sense. "I like you but this is not my home," Zia tells Father Malatesta calmly as she prepares to leave the mission once and for all. This kind of resigned statement is not what one expects from a child heroine. And though lots of exciting, even dangerous things happen to Zia—besides the boat trip and being thrown into jail, she is nearly caught in a brush fire set by one of Stone Hands' followers—the physical action is downplayed. O'Dell is not the arm-waving sort.

What draws one into this book, and probably accounts for the popularity of *Island of the Blue Dolphins,* as well, is O'Dell's short, loaded sentences which force the reader to participate. When Zia says, soberly, that she is scared—"I was afraid all over—in my stomach and in my head"—her emotional reactions are not spelled out to the last detail. Adults of course are so familiar with this style of writing that it hardly bears commenting upon, but young readers are rarely given this much leeway.

Once, when Zia is visiting Karana in her cave retreat, the older woman points out a fossilized "giant bird" visible in the cave wall. . . .

And for the moment O'Dell does give us the power to imagine the thing alive; just as he enables us to pin our personal hopes on Zia's gallant bid for liberty.

At times like these one decides to forgive *Zia* for not being another *Island of the Blue Dolphins.* Stood side by side the two books seem to prove that truth is not only stranger but, well, truer. Zia is not the kind of archetypal heroine who will win a devoted following, but she has a self-contained strength of her own.

Joyce Milton, "Beyond the Blue Dolphins," in Book World—The Washington Post, *May 2, 1976, p. L2.*

BARBARA WERSBA

It would be easy for the reviewer to compare ["**Zia**"] to the earlier ["**Island of the Blue Dolphins**"] and bemoan the fact that sequels are risky. But the truth is that "**Zia**" is a completely fresh creation, rich in character and action. The ending of the story, in which Karana gives her niece the courage to leave the Mission and rediscover her tribal heritage, is both surprising and correct—as it always is in good fiction. Once again Scott O'Dell has used history as the mainspring for revealing the truth about human beings: their passion, their grief.

Barbara Wersba, in a review of "Zia," in The New York Times Book Review, *May 2, 1976, p. 38.*

ETHEL L. HEINS

It is an act of bravery for an author, after so many years, to pick up and rework the threads of a story that has achieved such resounding success. But for Scott O'Dell, the return [in *Zia*] to the setting of *Island of the Blue Dolphins* means a return to his fundamental interest in early California history. Not a sequel in the strict sense, the story should be welcomed by young readers who, much more than adults, care passionately about a favorite character and long to know what happened afterwards. . . . The second book lacks the stark unity and the haunting beauty of the first, but comparison is unfair. Zia's story is not meant to duplicate Karana's; it is told with simplicity and occasional flashes of humor and has its own individuality. (pp. 291-92)

Ethel L. Heins, in a review of "Zia," in The Horn Book Magazine, *Vol. LII, No. 3, June, 1976, pp. 291-92.*

VIRGINIA HAVILAND

[In *The 290,* Scott O'Dell displays] his distinctive gifts for distilling significance from historical matter and for dealing with the sea. Jim Lynne, at sixteen an apprentice to a ship's architect for the *290* in Liverpool, immediately captures the reader's interest when in a pub on a "raving cold" November night he is approached by his ne'er-do-well, money-grubbing brother, who unsuccessfully seeks to buy information from him about the nearly finished vessel. . . . With lively conversation and with increasing tension from confrontations at sea and aboard Jim's ship, the author crisply tells the story, skillfully integrating historical elements. . . . (pp. 160-61)

Virginia Haviland, in a review of "The 290," in The Horn Book Magazine, *Vol. LIII, No. 2, April, 1977, pp. 160-61.*

JEAN FRITZ

[The title character of "**Carlota**"], trying for her father's sake to take the place of her dead brother Carlos, rides a stallion, brands cattle on their Southern California ranch, even takes part in one of the last battles of the Mexican War and, except for the battle, seems to relish her role. . . .

I am impressed with the history . . . and with many of the scenes, but at the conclusion I cease to believe in the fiction. . . . When Scott O'Dell has Carlota free her grandmother's slave and loose her father's chained eagle, I suppose he is demonstrating what he believes are feminine feelings that Carlota has repressed. But there is no indication that Carlota or anyone else in her society is sensitive to the plight of slaves or chained eagles. Mr. O'Dell is stingy with Carlota; he expects her to redefine herself but gives her too little material and not enough time.

Jean Fritz "Six by Winners," in The New York Times Book Review, *November 13, 1977, pp. 37, 63.**

MARY M. BURNS

[The Battle of San Pascal] is the climax of [*Carlota,*] an economically told story which, in its delineation of a strong-minded, independent heroine, recalls the author's memorable *Island of the Blue Dolphins.* The spare, well-honed style is artistically suited to the first person narrative. Carlota de Zubarán—a fictional counterpart of Luisa de Montero who lived in Southern California during the early nineteenth century—indicates the changing political and social climate which caused the passing of a distinctive but insular culture caught between the territorial imperatives of the warring nations. Encouraged by her father to be as self-sufficient as the son he had lost, Carlota defies the conventions of ladylike behavior valued by her matriarchal grandmother and is the only member of the immediate family able to cope with catastrophe after the Spaniards' Pyrrhic victory. She can understand the pride which motivated her father and his friends to attack the gringos; she is also capable, after her father's death, of assessing her position and protecting her assets. The principal characters are realistically portrayed as unique individuals and as universal figures in an allegorical drama. Multi-dimensional, masterfully crafted, the novel is compelling in its powerful yet restrained emotional intensity.

> *Mary M. Burns, in a review of "Carlota," in* The Horn Book Magazine, *Vol. LIII, No. 6, December, 1977, p. 670.*

GEOFF FOX

The 290 seems set fair to be a roistering yarn about a young seaman aboard a Confederate raider. The foreword gives the clue to the disappointment of the book, however: the story is based very firmly on historical fact. As a result, the novel is almost a documentary, since one episode does not precipitate another in the patterned way we expect of narrative.

The painstaking research becomes a straitjacket. A sailor is taken on board, leads a mutiny and is dismissed, never to be seen again. It does not matter to a reader that this actually happened historically—he is left wondering what the point of the incident is *in the story*. The book would be thoroughly useful background reading in a history project on the American Civil War, but is a succession of anti-climaxes as a novel.

> *Geoff Fox, "Moments of Truth," in* The Times Educational Supplement, *No. 3269, February 3, 1978, p. 36.**

KIRKUS REVIEWS

Early on [in *Kathleen, Please Come Home*] Kathleen, just 15, becomes engaged to a young wetback who warns her against the drugs friend Sybil is so free with. But Ramon is arrested and later killed in a raid, and when Kathleen realizes that it was her concerned, English-teacher mother who turned him in, she accepts Sybil's invitation to take off for Mexico . . . The two girls split when Kathleen learns that she's pregnant by Ramon, but get together again in time for an auto accident that is fatal to both Sybil and Kathleen's unborn baby. (That makes two too many convenient disasters, both of which free Kathleen from commitments.) The end sees Kathleen and Joy, another convalescent druggie, throwing away Sybil's valuable stash of heroin and heading into a straight future. O'Dell undoubtedly knows the scene better than many writers who would warn [young adults] on drugs, but still his social worker's presence can be felt at nearly every turn. Of course this sort of material has an enduring fascination for daydreaming stay-at-homes. (pp. 311-12)

> *A review of "Kathleen, Please Come Home," in* Kirkus Reviews, *Vol. XLVI, No. 6, March 15, 1978, pp. 311-12.*

MARGARETT LOKE

"Kathleen, Please Come Home" is a sympathetic portrait of a 15-year-old from a happy middle-class home who runs away. Mr. O'Dell . . . can weave a suspenseful tale, and he has done so in his latest novel, which is in large part a young woman's diary.

Romantic and impressionable, Kathleen Winters falls in love with a 17-year-old Mexican illegal alien who, at first sight, reminded her of Don Quixote. Caught with fake identification papers, Ramón is deported. When he tries to return to the United States, he is killed at the border. Who betrayed him to the authorities in the first place? Discovering that it was her mother, Kathleen heads for Tijuana with her friend Sybil.

There is a moving section in the book in which Kathleen's mother, Sara, writes down in *her* diary her reactions after she realizes that her daughter has run away. She finds it difficult to understand how her daughter could "continue to doubt that what I did was done only for her health, her happiness, all the days of her future." When Kathleen finally returns home months later, she finds her mother has sold her house and is "somewhere" in the East, following tips from the police as to the whereabouts of her daughter.

"Kathleen, Please Come Home" is unsettling in a number of ways. A fast-paced story chock-full of adventures and "colorful" characters, it seems to have all the trappings of a made-for-television movie. There are the unsavory types in San Diego (Kathleen's hometown) who prey on illegal Mexican aliens and the parents of runaways. Sybil is an inveterate drug user and would-be heroin pusher. . . . Curiously, Mr. O'Dell has chosen to present every one of the drugs as having favorable effects on Kathleen. What she got from her first taste—literally—of PCP was "a heavenly moment that seemed to last a million, million years" and a headache afterward. . . .

Mr. O'Dell's book offers few insights on the subject of runaways. Kids in flight seem merely a vehicle for a readable book.

> *Margarett Loke "Splitting Is Hard," in* The New York Times Book Review, *April 30, 1978, p. 53.**

DANIEL FLORES DURAN

O'Dell attempts a realistic portrayal of the Chicano culture in this fast-paced adventure story [*Child of Fire*]. He weaves together a fascinating tapestry of fact and fiction in this interpretation of Chicano culture: cock and bull fights, drugs, ghetto gangs, the farmworker's strikes. . . . The informed reader will find many of the elements of Chicano culture presented by O'Dell to be far off the mark, while others ring true. The teacher or librarian may wish to caution the reader against thinking that this picture of Chicano culture is complete. It is an exciting story unfortunately marred by some of the plot devices and stereotyped characterizations. (pp. 110-11)

> *Daniel Flores Duran, "Mexican American Resources: 'Child of Fire'," in* Latino Materials: A Multimedia Guide for Children and Young Adults, *edited by Daniel Flores Duran, Neal Schuman, Publishers, 1979, pp. 110-11.*

KIRKUS REVIEWS

[*The Captive* is a] brilliant first volume in a projected sequence. . . . We leave Julian, arrayed as . . . [a] god, surveying his newly acquired domain—sickened by the human sacrifices being made in his honor—but stirred moments later by visions of empire. And O'Dell leaves readers impatient for further developments. It is a measure of his seriousness and his skill that the suspense focuses not on events, which have so far been swift and stunning, inevitable and unexpected, or on the artfully foreshadowed intrigue, confrontations, and dangers that are sure to follow, but on Julian's moral choices and on what he will make of his false, exalted position.

> *A review of "The Captive," in* Kirkus Reviews, *Vol. XLVIII, No. 2, January 15, 1980, p. 71.*

JACK FORMAN

A Mayan Indian legend tells of the god Kukulcan, who, grieving over a misdeed, left earth promising to return centuries later in the body of a young man who has come from the east.

Scott O'Dell uses this legend in ["**The Captive**," the] first novel of a projected larger story called "**City of the Seven Serpents.**" "**The Captive**" is narrated by Julian Escobar, a young, idealistic Jesuit seminarian in medieval Spain who travels to New Spain with an entrepreneur to carry the Christian gospel to the Mayans. Julian is quickly disillusioned by his sponsor's mercenary interests. . . .

This is very similar to Mr. O'Dell's other matter-of-fact first-person narratives about North and South American Indian life. One can quibble here and there about plot devices (e.g., how Julian learns the Mayan language so quickly), but there's no better introduction to the rich and remote Mayan culture than through such a well-told tale. And there's more to come.

> *Jack Forman, in a review of "The Captive," in* The New York Times Book Review, *February 24, 1980, p. 33.*

LEON GARFIELD

Scott O'Dell is a much-honored author, a real general of children's literature who comes with as many medals as a prize-winning Swiss chocolate. Therefore he must be judged by the highest standards as one's expectations are keenly aroused. Alas, they are not fulfilled [with *The Captive*]. We all understand what is meant by a good bad book. It is a book that is thoroughly reprehensible and lacking in all the higher qualities of literature, such as moral values, philosophy, construction, character-drawing and general credibility, and yet contrives to be thoroughly readable. . . . Well, *The Captive* is what I can only describe as a bad good book. It is good inasmuch as it is well constructed, well researched, contains many interesting items of unfamiliar knowledge, and displays unimpeachable moral worth (Mr. O'Dell comes out very strongly aginst Slavery, Murder and Human Sacrifice; he doesn't hold with them for a moment!); but it is not very readable. It is inclined to be ponderous, and the prose style reminds one of a careful translation.

The story, told in the first person, is of Julián Escobar, a young seminarian who embarks with the conquistadors for the New World, where he witnesses the monstrous behavior of those who seek for gold. He is, naturally, horrified and repelled; and yet his own course proves to be not entirely beyond reproach. In his zeal to do good, Julian falls victim to the sin of spiritual pride and an apt parallel is drawn with Christ's Temptation in the wilderness.

It is a strong theme and might have been a gripping tale . . . but for the author's refusal to become involved in it. The very reference at the end to the Temptation in the wilderness is thought of as "the scene where Satan took Christ unto an exceeding high mountain." The *scene*. Surely no Spanish seminarian would think of Holy Writ in such theatrical terms! And so it is throughout. There is no immediacy. One gets the impression that the author is looking at a series of pictures and carefully describing them. At no time are we really with the hero. We receive no impression of his sensations. There are none of those touches that enliven the imagination. When our hero's hands are bound behind his back, there seems to be no reaction, no sense of helplessness, of indignity. . . .

It may be that I am being unjust, and that future developments will illuminate all and justify what has gone before. I hope so, for I would not like to think that so admirable an author as Scott O'Dell (*The Island of the Blue Dolphins* was a splendid book) has fallen so far from his own high standards. As it is, I can only recommend the present book to those with a passionate desire to know more about the history and culture of the Mayan Indians.

> *Leon Garfield, "Young Man among the Mayans," in* Book World—The Washington Post, *March 9, 1980, p. 7.*

JEAN FRITZ

Writers may choose their subjects, but good writers have less to say about their themes, which are apt to rise, bidden or unbidden, from the raw material of their deepest preoccupations. Never does Scott O'Dell play better music than when he introduces what seems to be his favorite motif: the pull between the individual's need for solitude and the need for society. . . .

After losing her father at the hands of the rebels and her brother at the hands of the King's men, Sarah Bishop, in fear of both parties, hides in a cave, gradually learning to take a fierce joy in her hard-won self-reliance. And when at the end of ["**Sarah Bishop**"] it is clear that Sarah will move back to town, the reader understands that Sarah is under no illusion that living with people will be easier than living alone.

Mr. O'Dell has always been a master at lighting up an era with details that seem to have been learned on the spot. . . . So this book is a vivid reflection of life in Revolutionary New York, and Scott O'Dell is obviously very much at home. First and foremost, however, this is the story of Sarah Bishop, a stout-hearted heroine who, although caught in the conflicts of her own age, might have lived anywhere at any time.

> *Jean Fritz, in a review of "Sarah Bishop," in* The New York Times Book Review, *May 4, 1980, p. 26.*

ZENA SUTHERLAND

Despite a series of highly dramatic incidents [in *Sarah Bishop*], the story line is basically sharp and clear; O'Dell's messages about the bitterness and folly of war, the dangers of superstition, and the courage of the human spirit are smoothly woven into the story, as are the telling details of period and place. To many readers, the primary appeal of the book may be the way in which Sarah, like the heroine of *Island of the Blue Dolphins*, like Robinson Crusoe, makes a comfortable life in the isolation of the wilderness.

> *Zena Sutherland, in a review of "Sarah Bishop," in* Bulletin of the Center for Children's Books, *Vol. 33, No. 10, June, 1980, p. 198.*

FRANCIS X. JORDAN

In *The Feathered Serpent,* Scott O'Dell . . . gives us the second installment of his chronicle set in old Mexico and dealing with the adventures of Julian Escobar, a young Spanish seminarian. In the sequence's first book, *The Captive,* Julian, after being cast away among the Maya, by chance assumed the role of their god, Kukulcan. *The Feathered Serpent* tells us of Julian's subsequent attempts to restore a Mayan city to its former splendor and gives us his eyewitness account of Hernán Cortés' momentous meeting with Moctezuma.

O'Dell skillfully avoids the double-barrelled problem confronting authors of multi-volumed chronicles. He manages to allude to *The Captive* in ways that will neither bore those who have read it nor alienate those who haven't. Furthermore, he concludes the present book at a natural pause in Escobar's life. When the novel ends, Julian is on the road back to his Mayan city after his near fatal encounter with Cortés.

Because the book deals with such moral ambiguities as Escobar's role in the Maya's human sacrifices . . . and because it contains scenes of violence perpetrated by both the Maya in these sacrifices and by the Spaniards in their encounters with the Indians, this fascinating book is recommended only for the more mature adolescent.

> *Francis X. Jordan, in a review of "The Feathered Serpent," in* Best Sellers, *Vol. 41, No. 10, January, 1982, p. 403.*

GEORGESS McHARGUE

The one thing a novel about the Aztec is bound to have is exotica. What with tombs lined with gold, hearts torn palpitating from sacrificial victims, feather banners, temples and palaces, it is hard to imagine an Aztec book that is dull. And Scott O'Dell's ["**The Feathered Serpent**"] is not dull.

It is the second volume in a series concerning the adventures of young Spanish seminarian Julián Escobar. . . . In ["**The Feathered Serpent**"] he is coerced by the greedy and devious dwarf Cantú, a fellow Spaniard, into accepting the role of the much-anticipated Mayan messiah, the light-skinned god Kukulcán.

Not surprisingly, the impersonation proves both hazardous and onerous. The new god incurs the hostility of the powerful priest Chalco and makes a number of ill-advised decisions. . . . Eventually, Julián and Cantú set off from their Mayan backwater to visit the capital of the Aztec overlords, arriving in time for the confrontation between Cortés and Montezuma.

As a character, Julián has more insight than many conquistadors, actual and fictional. . . . At the same time, he displays odd vacancies of personality. He seems to have little emotional life, no real curiosity about an alien society and (strangest of all) an implausible lack of awareness of the opposite sex. The result is that, while the book is not dull, neither is it deep or gripping.

> *Georgess McHargue, in a review of "The Feathered Serpent," in* The New York Times Book Review, *January 10, 1982, p. 26.*

DAVID N. PAULI

The heroine of *The Spanish Smile*, Lucinda de Cabrillo y Benvides, is the sheltered only daughter of the proud descendant of Spanish conquistadors, Don Enrique. Cloistered away in a gloomy castle, Lucinda is allowed no radio, television, newspapers or even any book written in the 20th Century. Her father pursues a deranged dream of restoring Spanish rule to California. All of the gothic machinery is in place in this story: the castle with its mysterious crypt guarded by deadly serpents, the young girl in distress and the charming young man who comes to her aid; and O'Dell's fluid style moves it along crisply.

Readers who are put off by a plethora of literary and historical references may get bogged down in a few spots. There are times also when credulity is stretched almost to the breaking point, even for a gothic. In spite of overwhelming evidence, it takes two thirds of the book for Lucinda to realize the depth of her father's madness and to begin to assert herself. Still, O'Dell has written a story that is several cuts above others in the genre.

> *David N. Pauli, in a review of "The Spanish Smile," in* School Library Journal, *Vol. 29, No. 2, October, 1982, p. 163.*

MARGARET PARENTE

Readers looking for pure escapism will find an ample portion of it in this novel about a young girl growing into adulthood [*The Spanish Smile*]. Award-winning novelist Scott O'Dell has not created an ordinary young girl as heroine of the latest of his impressive (*Island of the Blue Dolphins, Sarah Bishop*) children's books. . . .

The novel features a wide diversity of characters, some innocent and admirable, others entirely corrupted. This diversity adds interest and color to this exotic story. Although improbable and unrealistic, this book will provide enjoyable, though largely frivolous, reading.

> *Margaret Parente, in a review of "The Spanish Smile," in* Best Sellers, *Vol. 42, No. 9, December, 1982, p. 366.*

KIRKUS REVIEWS

[*The Amethyst Ring*] concludes O'Dell's dazzling drama of the temptation, fall, and redemption of Julian Escobar, the 16th-century Spanish seminarian who came in *The Captive* to rule a New World island as the Mayan god Kukulcan. Having witnessed the fall of Moctezuma in *The Feathered Serpent*, Julian returns to prepare the defense of his own island against the inevitable coming of Cortes. But Julian's dwarf companion deserts him with their ship filled with Aztec gold; the island falls to Cortes without a struggle; and Julian, escaping, becomes a solitary wanderer, wearing the amethyst ring of a captured Spanish bishop Julian had allowed his Mayan priest to kill after the bishop refused to ordain Julian. He stays in a nearby village until the gold-hungry Spanish come and kill its friendly cacique. . . . Always dodging Cortes, he ends up with Pisarro's army, sickened by their massacre of the Inca and falling hopelessly in love with the Inca king's daughter. By then Julian has come to sympathize wholly with the Indian victims against the Spanish conquerors and their priests, but he never gives up his Spanish religion. Dispirited, he returns to Spain to find the dwarf ensconced as the Marquis of Santa Cruz and the Seven Cities. . . . Julian gives up both his dream of priesthood and his share of the dwarf's gold to join a lay order, the Brothers of the Poor—a weary renunciation that could come only after the once-untried idealist had won and lost and soured on power and glory. This evolution, and the small choices Julian makes along the way, have remained the compelling focus of a trilogy crackling with intrigue, historical spectacle, and the conflict of cultures that confounds his loyalties.

> *A review of "The Amethyst Ring," in* Kirkus Reviews, *Vol. LI, No. 8, April 15, 1983, p. 462.*

PAUL HEINS

In completing the trilogy which began with *The Captive* and *The Feathered Serpent,* . . . [in *The Amethyst Ring*] the author has carried to a logical conclusion the adventures and experiences of Julián Escobar. . . . A historical novel in the sense that the splendors and the horrors of the ancient Indian cultures of America are understandingly portrayed, the narrative related by the unhappy, unheroic protagonist is not merely an account of random adventures. The author has eschewed the grand scale and the melodramatic in his telling but has been both sensitive and objectively perceptive of the memorable moments that reveal the depths of human experience. . . .

> *Paul Heins, in a review of "The Amethyst Ring," in* The Horn Book Magazine, *Vol. LIX, No. 3, June, 1983, p. 315.*

EVELYN WALKER

The Castle in the Sea is on an island off the coast of California. The time is the present. The heroine, Lucinda de Cabrillo y Benivides, has just become one of the richest young women in the world due to the horrible death of her father. However, she must deal with the legacy of madness her father left behind before she can begin to deal with her great wealth. . . . Lucinda's "novio" arrives, a young man whom she has never met yet to whom she has been promised since her childhood. Next a doctor is engaged to help Lucinda with her melancholia, then a woman is employed to be her constant companion. And last of all, her ever present guardian, Ricardo Villaverde, who seems even more mad then her dead father, watches over her. Lucinda must decide who among them is her friend and who seeks to harm her, for clearly someone is out to destroy her. O'Dell has created a romantic suspense novel that painlessly incorporates bits of Spanish history. [Young adult] fans of the genre will enjoy this one. (pp. 95-6)

> *Evelyn Walker, in a review of "The Castle in the Sea," in* School Library Journal, *Vol. 30, No. 3, November, 1983, pp. 95-6.*

Zibby Oneal

1934-

(Born Elizabeth Oneal) American novelist.

Oneal's two novels for young adults, *The Language of Goldfish* (1980) and *A Formal Feeling* (1982), are praised for their candid, unsentimental portrayals of teenagers with emotional difficulties. Struggling to preserve her childhood sensibility, the adolescent protagonist of *The Language of Goldfish* suffers so much internal tension that she attempts to commit suicide. In *A Formal Feeling* the central character contends with the conflicting emotions brought about by her mother's death and her father's remarriage. Oneal has also written three books for children.

(See also *Contemporary Authors*, Vol. 106 and *Something about the Author*, Vol. 30.)

Photograph by Julie Steedman. Courtesy of Zibby Oneal

LINDA R. SILVER

[*The Language of Goldfish*] is an intelligent, meticulously crafted book on a theme that, though fascinating to young people, has not been well handled in YA novels. Thirteen-year-old Carrie, the middle child in an affluent and happy family, is full of fears about herself and her relations with other people. More precisely, she is afraid of becoming a sexual being—although the underlying sexual basis for her mental breakdown is suggested rather than stated. . . . *Why* she is so afraid is not explained. The carefully selected, precise details of Carrie's life, including realistic and compassionate character portrayals, establish a tension between external reality and the chaos of Carrie's mind. A serious but not dismal book, enlivened by flashes of humor, this draws out readers' empathetic response and enlarges understanding. It is remarkably good writing!

> Linda R. Silver, in a review of "The Language of Goldfish," in School Library Journal, Vol. 26, No. 6, February, 1980, p. 70.

LORALEE MacPIKE

The Language of Goldfish deals with a somewhat touchy subject, the insanity of a child. Although written about and for a thirteen-year-old, it reminded me of nothing so much as Judith Guest's *Ordinary People*, and it is nearly as good, too. Carrie Stokes, good in math and art, plagued by a precocious and attractive older sister, resists the changes of growing up. Her resistance results in a gradual breakdown, including a beautifully depicted suicide attempt seen entirely from the victim's point of view, a hospitalization, and Carrie's painful return to the world of school and daily visits to a psychiatrist. The book operates on many levels; thus, her family's refusal to accept the seriousness of her illness reverberates in her friends' lack of understanding and her own unwillingness to understand why her beloved art teacher would leave her husband for another man. So too Carrie's eventual acceptance of growth and sexuality is marked by her first bra, her first dance class, her attempts at realistic drawing, her ability to accept her mother's refusal to acknowledge the reality of her breakdown. The story is believable and heartwarming. It offers reasonable hope, calm

moments of joy, and the possibility of a future, without deviating from a serious appraisal of the problems today's young people face as they try to fit themselves into worlds they don't understand.

The book's technical strengths are many. The dialogue is very good, its terseness reflecting the teenage milieu. The symbols (the island, the bra, the dancing class, Carrie's development as an artist) are there for the reader to find but are never forced. The characters are neither fiends nor angels, just real people doing their flawed best in a flawed world.

> Loralee MacPike, in a review of "The Language of Goldfish," in Best Sellers, Vol. 40, No. 1, April, 1980, p. 39.

JOYCE MILTON

At 13, Carrie [in **"The Language of Goldfish"**] is old enough to know that the "magic island" in the pond behind her house is really just a pile of moss-covered stones and that the goldfish she summons by whistling across the surface of the pond's waters don't really understand her private language. Her older sister, who once shared these fantasies, long ago dismissed them as kid stuff, but Carrie, overwhelmed by the changes going on inside her own body and by the messy world of sexuality and moral uncertainty she sees ahead, desperately hangs on to childhood.

"The Language of Goldfish," Zibby Oneal's first novel for young adults, chronicles Carrie's emotional breakdown and attempted suicide. This subject matter is bound to attract some attention for its own sake, but it would be a mistake to include this novel in the wave of pop-sociological fiction about teenage trauma. Certainly, its profile of an achieving daughter of a well-to-do family, panicked at the thought of competing socially with her more outgoing sister, would be recognizable to any clinician. And Carrie's attempts, as an art student, to translate her anxiety into studies of line and movement are entirely believable. For the most part, however, the people and events in Carrie's life are a bit flat and a bit hazy around the edges, which is entirely how she perceives them. In contrast, her inner turmoil—even during her dizzy spells when reality "slips sideways"—is conveyed in language that is poetic and precise.

No doubt many young readers will be drawn to this story because it promises to show "what it's like to go crazy." In fact, this promise is fulfilled, largely because the author has resisted the temptation to use Carrie's disordered thoughts as a vehicle for self-indulgent writing. But most readers will also see a good deal of themselves in Carrie. Her search for the magic island, which she can see in her imagination but no longer recognizes in reality, is a resonant metaphor for the lost illusions of childhood. This is a loss that sentimental people bemoan, but Mrs. Oneal reminds us that pretending is the work of childhood—and often very hard work at that. (pp. 52, 65)

> *Joyce Milton, in a review of "The Language of Goldfish," in* The New York Times Book Review, *April 27, 1980, pp. 52, 65.*

CHRISTINE McDONNELL

In [*The Language of Goldfish*], a perceptive novel which avoids clichés and exaggeration, evocative images create a sense of Carrie's inner experiences: the gaps in her consciousness, her whirling terror, and her longing for a safe place—a place like the island in the goldfish pond, a sanctuary of childhood. With strong characters, convincing scenes, and accurate, consistent dialogue, the author explores Carrie's journey and recovery and the remoteness of her affluent family. The story is not suddenly dramatic; Carrie's illness moves in an unpredictable, gradual downward spiral until the girl begins a cautious, tentative rebuilding of her life. Carefully crafted with delicacy and control, the book presents a moving portrait of a vulnerable child on the brink of young adulthood.

> *Christine McDonnell, in a review of "The Language of Goldfish," in* The Horn Book Magazine, *Vol. LVI, No. 4, August, 1980, p. 416.*

JEAN DUCAN

[In *The Language of Goldfish* readers] recognize Carrie's growing bewilderment and her muted cries for help as the pressures and tensions of suburban adolescent life threaten to overwhelm her. But the adults around her are too involved in their own concerns to respond. The themes of alienation and lack of communication are skillfully woven throughout the novel, until Carrie's attempted suicide seems inevitable.

In Carrie, the author has created a person that young readers will identify with, as she gradually learns to understand her own failures and her strengths. The novel rings true in every aspect—from the glowing imagery of Carrie's fantasies as her grasp on reality loosens to the mundane details of her long and difficult struggle to accept the harsh facts of the grown-up world.

> *Jean Ducan, in a review of "The Language of Goldfish," in* English Journal, *Vol. 70, No. 4, April, 1981, p. 77.*

PUBLISHERS WEEKLY

With the insights and literary style that mark the award-winning **"The Language of Goldfish,"** Oneal now tells the story of emotionally battered Anne Cameron, 16 [in **"A Formal Feeling"**]. Emily Dickinson's poem that starts "After great pain, a formal feeling comes" strikes Anne as an expression of her state. She adopts a formal feeling, a shell, when she goes home from boarding school for Christmas vacation. A year after her mother's death, Anne's father has remarried and she won't allow herself to come close to, or understand, her stepmother Dory. . . . The girl's worst pain, however, arises from guilt over memories of fighting with her late mother, a perfectionist who demanded the impossible and whom Anne fears she had never loved. In Oneal's uncontrived closing chapters, readers find reasons to hope that Anne's experiences are inducing her to think clearly and to break out of her armor.

> *A review of "A Formal Feeling," in* Publishers Weekly, *Vol. 222, No. 4, July 23, 1982, p. 132.*

ZENA SUTHERLAND

There is little action in this sensitive story [*A Formal Feeling*], but there is growth and change, so that when it is time for Anne to go back to boarding school after her unhappy vacation, she can accept the status quo and can weep for the person her mother really was rather than the idealized woman she had been trying to remember. A candid story, this unfolds and grows smoothly, with a perceptive meshing of personalities and relationships that are strongly drawn.

> *Zena Sutherland, in a review of "A Formal Feeling," in* Bulletin of the Center for Children's Books, *Vol. 36, No. 2, October, 1982, p. 34.*

LAURIE BOWDEN

Sixteen-year-old Anne [in *A Formal Feeling*] arrives home on a vacation from the private school her mother had chosen— her mother who has been dead just over a year. Anne avoids dealing with her life, past and present. . . . Anne's reactions are understandable: How can everyone act as if everything is all right? How could Dad marry again so soon, and to someone who is so different from Mom: Stepmother Dory's a nonintellectual who leaves dirty dishes in the sink and neglects the rose garden. Anne pursues a state of numbness, which she achieves by running, perhaps to avoid the pain of remembering the truth about her mother: that her mother's high expectations and standards were perhaps not worth living up to. A physical injury (sprained ankle) produces a catharsis through which Anne answers her questions, allowing her to let go and finally say goodbye to her mother. The sensitivity and straightforwardness in dealing with an often difficult subject makes this an outstanding book.

> *Laurie Bowden, in a review of "A Formal Feeling,"*
> *in* School Library Journal, *Vol. 29, No. 2, October,*
> *1982, p. 163.*

LINDA BARRETT OSBORNE

Anne [in *A Formal Feeling*], though reserved and difficult, is not self-pitying. She is so human and so in need of loving that she is sympathetic and engaging from the beginning, and the other characters balance her with a warmth that is genuine and free of sentimentality. *A Formal Feeling* is straightforward, absorbing, and perceptive, true to an adolescent's feelings about mothers and about grief.

> *Linda Barrett Osborne, "Learning to Live without*
> *Mother," in* Book World—The Washington Post,
> *October 10, 1982, p. 6.**

ROBERT C. SMALL

Anne Cameron's mother [in *A Formal Feeling*] was clearly an unusual and talented person, artistic, musical, and literary. Dead for a year as the book opens, she still haunts Anne, and, through her, her father, his new wife, and Anne's brother, Spencer. Although all of the family except Anne want to throw off the oppression of that memory, Anne's return from school at Christmas brings her mother's memory back into the house. Anne is frozen—the "formal feeling" of the title—by her obsession with her mother. She does not, however, seem to have loved her mother so much as been in awe of her and her many talents. . . . The book is upper class, literary, cultured, and very intellectual. It is also thoughtful and insightful. The style, dialogue, descriptions, and action are both natural and beautifully controlled. Oneal writes very well, and her flawless style raises her somewhat conventional content above itself. This is clearly one of the best young adult books of the year.

> *Robert C. Small, in a review of "A Formal Feeling,"*
> *in* The ALAN Review, *Vol. 10, No. 2, Winter, 1983,*
> *p. 23.*

PAUL HEINS

Despite the academic background [of *A Formal Feeling*], the atmosphere of the story is redolent of middle America; and although the texture of the narrative is tightly woven, the style—self-consciously descriptive and allusive—tends to be antiseptic. Centering on Anne's state of mind more than on her emotions, the novel not only lacks intensity but fails to attain the power of effective understatement. (pp. 173-74)

> *Paul Heins, in a review of "A Formal Feeling," in*
> The Horn Book Magazine, *Vol. LIX, No. 2, April,*
> *1983, pp. 173-74.*

MARION GLASTONBURY

It takes nerve in a novelist to construct a story which depends largely upon the posthumous influence of an invisible character. In [*A Formal Feeling*] . . . , the device works: we care about the outcome of retrospective disclosures because only the truth, complex and ambivalent, seems likely to set Anne free.

> *Marion Glastonbury, "Missing Persons," in* The
> Times Educational Supplement, *No. 3492, June 3,*
> *1983, p. 41.**

DOROTHY NIMMO

American children's books are admirably aware of the real world; they tend to deal directly with the problems that face adolescents, rather than obliquely through fantasy or symbol. There is something of a return to the didacticism of Victorian children's books. Out of this background of therapeutic literature on how to deal with menstruation, sexuality, colour prejudice, or alcoholism [*A Formal Feeling*] is a book dealing with bereavement but offering something more: a subtle and moving examination of how Ann, returning from boarding school to find her father remarried, comes to understand and forgive the past.

> *Dorothy Nimmo, in a review of "A Formal Feeling,"*
> *in* The School Librarian, *Vol. 31, No. 3, September,*
> *1983, p. 272.*

Katherine (Womeldorf) Paterson

1932-

American novelist, short story writer, and essayist.

Paterson is considered one of the most important contemporary authors for young adults. Much of her fiction is concerned with moral decisions and the process of self-realization in her young protagonists. Paterson has been praised for investigating topics not often treated in young adult fiction. Among the issues she examines are destructive emotional responses to difficult situations, such as the death of friends. Paterson's early work is classified as historical fiction, while her more recent novels deal with contemporary problems.

Paterson was born in China and lived there until the age of twelve, when she came to the United States. She later received a degree in theology and served as a missionary in Japan for several years. Paterson's knowledge of Japanese culture and history has provided the background for three of her novels. *The Sign of the Chrysanthemum* (1973), *Of Nightingales That Weep* (1974), and *The Master Puppeteer* (1976) share historical Japan as their setting and are highly regarded for their accurate depictions of Japanese civilization. Critics also note that these novels include well-developed characters and suspenseful plots. *The Master Puppeteer* won a National Book Award.

Beginning with *Bridge to Terabithia* (1977), Paterson shifted her setting to contemporary urban America. The novel, which won a Newbery Medal, brings together Jess and Leslie, two teenagers with different cultural backgrounds, and focuses on their friendship and Jess's reaction to Leslie's death. Paterson was praised for creating believable characters and for her sensitive treatment of death. Another novel which explores modern concerns, *The Great Gilly Hopkins* (1978), revolves around a foster child who must return to her real mother after learning to love her replacement mother. This work won a National Book Award.

Jacob Have I Loved (1980) is considered by many critics to be Paterson's best work. In this story of a teenage girl who learns to cope with the impressive accomplishments of her twin sister, Paterson examines such topics as sibling rivalry, religious beliefs, and the importance of love between family members. Although some critics were dismayed at the lack of humor in this novel, especially compared to some of her earlier works, most asserted that Paterson's characters in this work were among her most impressive creations and that her setting evoked the richness of the Chesapeake Bay area. Paterson won a second Newbery Medal for *Jacob Have I Loved*.

In her recent novel *Rebels of the Heavenly Kingdom* (1983) Paterson returns to historical fiction, this time setting her story in nineteenth-century China. Like her early work, this novel combines an exciting adventure story with extensive historical detail and believable characters.

(See also *CLC*, Vol. 12; *Children's Literature Review*, Vol. 7; *Contemporary Authors*, Vols. 21-24, rev. ed.; and *Something about the Author*, Vol. 13.)

BARBARA ELLEMAN

With dexterity, the author of *Bridge to Terabithia* . . . creates nine insightful stories [in *Angels and Other Strangers*] that stir the emotions while reflecting the joy of the Christmas season. . . . [These] tales celebrate the birth of Jesus through the loneliness, fears, hopes, and simple beliefs of men, women, and children but never lapse into sentimentality or zealous pomposity. . . . Such scope offers a broad base for family sharing where nuances of meaning can be discussed and savored.

> Barbara Elleman, in a review of "Angels and Other Strangers: Family Christmas Stories," in Booklist, Vol. 76, No. 2, September 15, 1979, p. 126.

PUBLISHERS WEEKLY

Critics and the many readers who have praised Paterson's previous books will probably mark [*Angels and Other Strangers*] A+. Each story concerns a surprising spiritual gift bestowed during the Christmas season to people who need it desperately. . . . [The] stories star entirely different characters and situations, making up a group of impressive entertainments, written with warmth and style.

> A review of "Angels and Other Strangers," in Publishers Weekly, Vol. 216, No. 13, September 24, 1979, p. 104.

KIRKUS REVIEWS

Paterson's well-tuned, sentimental Christmas stories [in *Angels and Other Strangers*] seem less well suited to a children's book than to a family magazine, especially a church magazine—and indeed the flap tells us that they were originally read in Christmas Eve church services by the author's minister husband. Of the nine, three effect epiphanies of sorts in church. . . . [Several] set up encounters between comfortable middle-class Protestants and others who are poor, black, and/or outcast; in these Paterson does well with the interplay, and she never falsifies the characters on either side or overplays her hand. This is several notches above the usual Christmas story collection, and a boon for groups concerned with the meaning of the holiday.

> *A review of "Angels and Other Strangers," in* Kirkus Reviews, *Vol. XLVII, No. 20, October 15, 1979, p. 1211.*

KAREN M. KLOCKNER

With her gifts of insight and compassion [Katherine Paterson in *Angels and Other Strangers*] weaves stories about miracles of the Christmas season—miracles that take place on a truly human level. Each story is based on the Christian message of the birth of Christ and the significance that message takes on for the characters. She writes of the poor, the desolate, and the lonely as well as of the arrogant, the complacent, and the proud. . . . The stories are deeply moving and filled with humor. They are based not on a formal, theoretical Christianity but on a faith that is rich with human understanding.

> *Karen M. Klockner, in a review of "Angels and Other Strangers: Family Christmas Stories," in* The Horn Book Magazine, *Vol. LV, No. 6, December, 1979, p. 650.*

ELLEN RUDIN

Katherine Paterson, the author of several distinguished novels for young readers, here presents a collection of nine short stories [*Angels and Other Strangers*]. . . .

Besides being entertaining, these tender stories remind us of what Christmas is all about—tolerance, forgiveness, love, patience, generosity, kindness, faith. Most seem intended for adults, although two come quite close to being genuine children's stories—**"Many Happy Reruns,"** in which a young girl runs to the statue of Jesus in a church, thinking she has killed her baby brother because she hit him in jealousy and anger; and **"Maggie's Gift,"** in which two orphans are Christmas guests of a lonely widower. This story, incidentally, is the funniest of the lot and will awaken rueful recognition in both children and adults.

This modest anthology may not win new accolades for the author, but it takes its legitimate place in her oeuvre. . . .

> *Ellen Rudin, in a review of "Angels and Other Strangers: Family Christmas Stories," in* The New York Times Book Review, *December 2, 1979, p. 40.*

BARBARA ELLEMAN

[In *Jacob Have I Loved*] Paterson weaves her background into a colorful but overly detailed canvas, sensitively picturing Louise as a strong-willed, strident, haunting character. The first-person narrative, strongest in Louise's early years, loses some of its momentum during her gradual evolution into adulthood, which happens without benefit of confrontation. More a portrait than a full-bodied novel, this nevertheless stirs the blood. (pp. 255-56)

> *Barbara Elleman, in a review of "Jacob Have I Loved," in* Booklist, *Vol. 77, No. 3, October 1, 1980, pp. 255-56.*

ZENA SUTHERLAND

". . . Jacob have I loved, but Esau have I hated," was the quotation that her senile, spiteful grandmother had pointed out to Louise [in *Jacob Have I Loved*]. . . . This theme of twin-envy is set on a small island in Chesapeake Bay, the setting made vivid and colored by local idiom. The story is told by Louise in retrospect, after she has broken away from the island and found her own career and her own family; it is brought full circle when she (now a nurse in a mountain community) delivers twins to a patient; the first is healthy, the second frail and needing attention, and Louise tells the newborn infants' grandmother to hold the first-born, "Hold him as much as you can." A strong novel, this, with depth in characterization and with vitality and freshness in the writing style. (pp. 60-1)

> *Zena Sutherland, in a review of "Jacob Have I Loved," in* Bulletin of the Center for Children's Books, *Vol. 34, No. 3, November, 1980, pp. 60-1.*

KIRKUS REVIEWS

We meet Louise Bradshaw [of *Jacob Have I Loved*] in the summer of 1941, smarting under the disproportionate attention lavished on her fragile, musically talented twin sister Caroline since their birth 13 years earlier. . . . The interesting aspect of all Louise's torment and self-sacrifice is the growing realization that it isn't being forced on her. But not until she has settled down as a nurse-midwife (the only medical help) in a small Appalachian community—marrying a man with three children to boot—does she recognize and freely accept that she was destined to fulfill herself in a life of service. Paterson has to get into these later years to make the point, and to avoid the instant realizations that substitute in too many juvenile novels. However, this tends to flatten the tone and blur the shape of the novel. Louise's earlier, intense feelings evoke recognition and sympathy, but this hasn't the resonant clarity of *Bridge to Terabitha* or *The Great Gilly Hopkins*.

> *A review of "Jacob Have I Loved," in* Kirkus Reviews, *Vol. XLVIII, No. 21, November 1, 1980, p. 1399.*

ANNE TYLER

In the years since turning from her earlier, Japan-based novels (most notably the award-winning *The Master Puppeteer*), Katherine Paterson has created a handful of engagingly rakish young Americans. The two mavericks of *Bridge to Terabithia* and the incorrigible title character of *The Great Gilly Hopkins* are spunky, independent, and sharply observed. Both books won several kinds of prizes each, but my own private prize goes to Gilly—always a foster child, never a daughter. I'd adopt her any day.

Jacob Have I Loved, Katherine Paterson's sixth novel, centers on an ugly duckling of such endurance and rough charm that readers should take to her immediately. "Wheeze" Bradshaw is a twin—a second-best twin. Her sister, Caroline, is pretty and supremely talented, while Wheeze is a gawky girl of no apparent talent at all. (p. 11)

Without even trying, Caroline acquires everything Wheeze wants. She isn't a villain, however, and this is not a stereotypic good sister/bad sister story. It's convincingly complex, ambiguous. Caroline can be a prig but she's also kindhearted. The parents do their best to be fair, although they don't always succeed. And when Caroline makes friendly overtures to Wheeze, it does not (to our relief) result in magical harmony forever after. (pp. 11, 16)

Wheeze decides to assume responsibility for her own life. She leaves the island to be educated, takes a nursing job, marries, and plays midwife to a set of twins who teach her something about her own twinship.

If the paragraph above seems abrupt—all the long, slow, growing-up period followed by slam, bang, married-and-settled—well, it's because at this point the book itself becomes abrupt. That, I think, is its one flaw: there's a change of pace that's difficult to adjust to. Leisurely details give way to summary. There's not the same deep texture that existed in the earlier scenes.

But oh, those earlier scenes! The crabbing and oyster-tonging lore are woven into the very fiber of the story; they never have that tacked-on, "educational" feeling. The atmosphere of Rass [Island] is so lovingly described—both its beauty and its discarded tin cans, the unique twists of speech, the cloistered, clannish population—that later, when it's apparent that the island is slowly sinking into the Bay, we mourn as if it were our own.

There's also a wonderful mother, an exasperating grandmother who gives us some insight into the problems of living with the aged, and a subtly handled incident in which Wheeze becomes infatuated with a much older man. . . . *Jacob Have I Loved* may lack unity, in spots, but it is a book of intense flavor and color, and it adds an endearing character to the population of Katherine Paterson's private world. (p. 16)

Anne Tyler, "Coming of Age on Rass Island," in Book World—The Washington Post, *November 9, 1980, pp. 11, 16.*

PAUL HEINS

The author of *Bridge to Terabithia* . . . has again written [in *Jacob Have I Loved*] a story that courageously sounds emotional depths. Acknowledging her great interest in life in Chesapeake Bay, she describes the activities of the watermen living on a sparsely inhabited island during World War II and shows how the ethos of its isolated, strict Methodist community affected the thoughts and feelings of a rugged but sensitive and intelligent girl. (p. 622)

In addition to evoking the atmosphere of the remote island and the stark simplicity of its life—even supplying considerable detail about the ways and means of its shellfish industry—the author has developed a story of great dramatic power; for Wheeze is always candid in recounting her emotional experiences and reactions. At the same time, the island characters come to life in skillful, terse dialogue; Wheeze's grandmother actually touches on a daemonic dimension. The everyday realism, the frequent touches of humor, and the implications of the narrative speak for themselves; the Biblical allusions add immeasurably to the

meaning of the story and illuminate the prolonged—often overwhelming—crisis in the protagonist's life. And the tension of the narrative is resolved in a final harmony best expressed by the concluding line of Milton's *Samson Agonistes:* "And calm of mind, all passion spent." (pp. 622-23)

Paul Heins, in a review of "Jacob Have I Loved," in The Horn Book Magazine, *Vol. LVI, No. 6, December, 1980, pp. 622-23.*

KATHERINE PATERSON (INTERVIEW WITH LINDA T. JONES)

[Jones]: Your first three books are set in feudal Japan. Why did you choose historical settings for your first three novels?

[Paterson]: For one thing, it's interesting. For another, if you have trouble plotting as I do, history is a great help. You have all of these wonderful events happening in history and you can weave your story in and out of them. Historical settings are fascinating and helpful. That's why I use them. (p. 192)

[Jones]: Could you give an example of where you have gotten the basic idea for one of your novels—perhaps *The Master Puppeteer* where the puppet theater is such an unusual device for a novel.

[Paterson]: I'm always interested when people say, "Where do you get your ideas for your books?" as if there were some big barrel in my basement that I went to and took an idea out of when I was in need of one. Most of my life I walk around without any ideas, wondering what on earth I'm going to do next, feeling that I'll never write another book because I'll never have another idea, which was exactly the situation I was in after I'd finished *Of Nightingales that Weep*. I didn't have an idea in the world, and so I asked my children what they'd like to have a book about, thinking that that would be a fruitful way to get an idea. They said they wanted a mystery story, which was appalling to me because I'm a great lover of mystery stories and I know how difficult they are to plot. And I said to my children who wanted the mystery story, "Do you think anyone who has been regularly beaten at chess by her six-year-old daughter has the brains to plot a mystery story?" They were too courteous to say "no," but they still wanted a mystery book. I was very sorry that I wasn't going to be able to produce a mystery story and was casting around for something else. It was at that point that I chanced upon an item that, as it turns out, was the genesis of *The Master Puppeteer*. Specifically, one morning I was reading the *Washington Post*, and there was an advertisement for the Japanese puppet theater which was going to come to the Kennedy Center. I looked at that advertisement which showed a warrior puppet head. . . . In my mind, I went right back to the puppet theater in Japan and remembered the "feel" of the theater, which was dark and somehow mysterious. The actual theater at that time was a sort of makeshift one because it had been bombed out during the war. It was filled with little ladies in black kimonos eating lunch out of wooden boxes; the smell of soy sauce and fish and pickles was in the air, and on the stage were these gorgeous, almost life-size puppets. Each Japanese puppet is manipulated by three puppeteers who are so skillful that the puppets appear to be almost alive, but not quite alive, and it occurred to me that the puppet theater would be an absolutely marvelous place to set a mystery story, if indeed one could write a mystery story, which I was still convinced at that point I could not.

The next thing that happened, which you don't have to believe, which no one is required to believe, but which is indeed the next thing that happened, is that I found myself one night in the middle of a sort of waking dream. I was seeing in my mind a boy in the upstairs of an old Japanese storehouse. He was nosing around looking for something in the storehouse. You could tell by the way he was moving that he had no business being there and also that he couldn't find whatever it was he was looking for. And as he was looking, I seemed to hear a sound of someone coming up the steps, and what he saw was the white face of a warrior puppet flashing a sword in its hand, and behind it, of course, the hooded figure of the puppeteer. And that was the end of my vision, or whatever, and when it was over, I didn't know who the boy was, what he was looking for, why he was there, or who it was that was coming up the stairs menacing him. And I had to write *The Master Puppeteer* to find out. I tell this story to children a lot, and they tend to be kind of spooked by it. But that's really what happened in the sequence of writing *The Master Puppeteer*. The amazing thing was that after telling my children that even though I could not write them a mystery story, I would try to write them an adventure story with as much suspense as possible, I wrote *The Master Puppeteer* which was in the running for the Edgar Allen Poe award and received one of the runner-up special awards given by the Mystery Writers of America. This pleased me no end, since none of us thought I had succeeded in writing a mystery story. (pp. 192-94)

[Jones]: It seems quite difficult to characterize your style of writing because it appears to be markedly different in each of your books. How do you account for this?

[Paterson]: I don't care a fig about style. I'm always amazed if anybody calls me a stylist or if anybody appreciates my style because I really don't even think about style. I think about the story. And it seems to me the story demands its own style; therefore, a story like *Of Nightingales That Weep* demands quite a different style from *The Great Gilly Hopkins*. And If I had tried to write *The Great Gilly Hopkins* in the style of *Of Nightingales That Weep*, it would have totally failed; but even *Bridge to Terabithia* and *The Great Gilly Hopkins* are different to me. These stories demanded a different style, and one of them has been unfavorably compared to the other because some people feel the style of one is better than the style of the other. Well, that seems to be a matter of personal taste, but to me that was the style in which the story had to be written. Just as the ending is an integral part of the story—it's not something I can manipulate—so is the style. And I think one of the hard things about writing a book is discovering the style of that book, the language that that story demands to be written in. In other words, discovering the proper voice, the right rhythm, and the music, if you please, of that particular book. (p. 194)

[Jones]: If you think there is one general benefit which children may gain from reading fiction, what would it be? What do you want children to get from your books?

[Paterson]: I don't separate children from adults as readers. It seems to me that all of us as we read fiction are looking for an enlargement of our lives, an enlargement of our sympathies, enlargement of our understanding, a way of learning through vicarious experience. Let me just give you an example. When we moved last year, my youngest was devastated by the move and she said, "But I've never moved before, I didn't have any practice." I think books, fiction, give us practice in life that we've never had to live through before, so when the time comes, we have in a sense been through that experience before, and the book is there in the background to comfort us and assure us that we can go through with this. Books are great

vehicles of hope for us and help and instruction in all the good ways. I don't even really mind being called a didactic writer because I think teaching is a wonderful thing. The problem comes, of course, when the story is not paramount; in fiction the story must always be paramount. Any teaching must grow naturally out of the story and not be something that you figured out in your head and are determined to get over to the kiddies. That never works. Readers of whatever age are too wise. They will smell out these kinds of faults. I hope to goodness whenever I do that, it will be sniffed out by my readers and discarded, as it's not worthy. (pp. 195-96)

Linda T. Jones, "Profile: Katherine Paterson," in Language Arts, *Vol. 58, No. 2, February, 1981, pp. 189-96.*

MARCUS CROUCH

Katherine Paterson won a second Newbery Medal with [*Jacob Have I Loved*]. I am not sure that she would have qualified for a Carnegie, but then the Americans like their emotions hot and hearts on sleeves. There is plenty of action and passion here but not a lot of stoicism.

Let me be fair. Mrs. Paterson is a woman of formidable intelligence and unshakable integrity. She shirks no issues in a story of a twin baulked at every stage of life by the effortless brilliance of her sister. Although the story is told by "Wheeze" (Louise) the reader is nevertheless able to see, despite the distorted view of the narrator, that Caroline is a gentle, kind and talented girl. It is not her fault that everything goes her way. Poor Wheeze, goaded by her half-crazy grandmother, is forced from one emotional and physical crisis to the next. She loses her career, her boy-friend, the affection (she thinks) of her parents, and the love of God. She parades her frustrations with a frankness which is familiar to American readers but which some English children may find shame-making. (pp. 161-62)

Part of the strength of the story lies in the brilliant evocation of the natural scene. There is a magnificent description of a storm which forms one of the crises of the story. Some of the character sketches are done in masterly fashion too, portraying eccentricity in a few words. But above all it is Wheeze's book. Rarely have the torments of adolescence been presented with such candour. Perhaps Mrs. Paterson does not always touch the heart. She certainly commands the intellectual respect of her readers by her surpassing honesty and her profound understanding of people and places. (p. 162)

Marcus Crouch, in a review of "Jacob Have I Loved," in The Junior Bookshelf, *Vol. 45, No. 4, August, 1981, pp. 161-62.*

ANTHEA BELL

If the American author Katherine Paterson had been writing a century ago, her evident Christian commitment would not, of course, have been anything out of the ordinary. Instead it would have been the expected norm, with a large area of common ground known to exist between the writer, her readers and her reviewers. But how does an author deal with such a commitment now, when the common assumptions are not nearly so widespread, and to express them explicitly may alienate rather than attract?. . . Looking at Katherine Paterson's novels, I think the use she makes of her beliefs in them is something of a phenomenon for the late twentieth century, and an interesting one. Perhaps the use she does *not* make of them is even more interesting.

Her Christianity is not that of the more recent born-again or charismatic movements; hers is the traditional Presbyterian variety, and has been with her from childhood. The daughter of missionaries who worked in China, she was herself a missionary in Japan for four years: hence her interest in Japanese history and culture, and the settings of her first three books.

These three are very different from the work that followed them, which represents a complete change of direction. . . . [They] are historical novels set in Japan, strong on period background and meticulous detail. *The Sign of the Chrysanthemum* and *Of Nightingales That Weep* both take place in twelfth-century Japan, against a background provided by the feuding of the powerful Heike and Genji clans, while the third, *The Master Puppeteer,* places its young hero in the world of the traditional puppet theatre in Osaka. (p. 73)

Paterson's three Japanese novels are good examples [of historical fiction]: her fascination with the background material is plain. She dwells lovingly on the mystique and technicalities of the swordsmith's art in *The Sign of the Chrysanthemum,* on courtly etiquette and historical incident in *Of Nightingales That Weep,* and in particular on the stylized conventions of the Japanese puppet theatre in *The Master Puppeteer.* She is good on Japanese conventions altogether. The reader learns a good deal about the leisurely and (to the impatient Western mind) excessive cultivation of polite small talk, in contrast to sudden moments of savagery. . . . These historical novels are all enjoyable, but whether or not Katherine Paterson's change of direction was all her own idea or prompted by a publisher's editorial suggestion, it was in turning to the twentieth century that she found her own and original voice.

Bridge to Terabithia, the book in which she made the break, is the story of a friendship. Its protagonist, Jess Aarons, is a culturally underprivileged boy: the only son in a large family, he would like to be the fastest runner in the fifth grade at Lark Creek elementary school, and has a real but undirected talent for drawing comic animals: 'Jess drew the way some people drink whiskey.' Into his life comes ten-year-old Leslie Burke. She and her trendy intellectual parents have come to this out-of-the-way country spot outside Washington because, as Leslie solemnly tells Jess, her mother and father are 'reassessing their value structure . . . they decided they were too hooked on money and success, so they bought that old farm and they're going to farm it and think about what's important.' (pp. 74-5)

The earlier and longer part of the book traces their friendship, as Jess helps Leslie to accommodate herself to Lark Creek, and she widens his horizons bewilderingly around him, introducing him to the mental furnishings of her kind of life—one where 'money is not the problem', and there is no TV but a stereo and a great many records. Most important, where there are books. Leslie suggests to Jess that they found their own imaginary kingdom, and they fix on a place beyond the dry creek bed, reaching it by swinging over on a rope. They call this imaginary country Terabithia, and Leslie lends Jess 'all her books about Narnia, so he would know how things went on in a magic kingdom.'

Some two-thirds of the way through the book, there is an episode which bears all the signs of being central to the theme, and yet which turns out otherwise. Jess's family are once-a-year churchgoers, attending by force of habit at Easter, and they take Leslie along with them. Subsequently there is a con-

versation between the children. On the one hand, Jess and his little sister May Belle unthinkingly accept the authority of the Bible. . . . On the other hand, sensitive Leslie, apparently totally unacquainted with the Christian tradition, is impressed. 'Gee, I'm really glad I came . . . the whole Jesus thing is really interesting, isn't it?. . . All those people wanting to kill him when he hadn't done anything to hurt them . . . it's really kind of a beautiful story—like Abraham Lincoln or Socrates— or Aslan.'

Now this is pushing it a bit. Merely on the level of probability, are we to suppose that an intelligent child of Leslie's literary background, conversant with the story lines of *Hamlet* and *Moby-Dick,* and owner of all the Narnia books, will not have spotted the fact that C. S. Lewis wrote religious allegory, and that Aslan *is* Jesus? And articulate as she also is, wouldn't she, if she could not work out the meaning of the allegory for herself, have inquired of her parents or teachers? A total lack of general knowledge about the Gospel stories doesn't fit in with the rest of her mental equipment.

As I said, the passage *looks* central, because it points very obviously forward. May Belle concludes the conversation. 'But Leslie . . . what if you *die*? What's going to happen to you if you *die*?' For that is just what Leslie is going to do. Stormy weather fills the creek bed with torrential water, and swinging across on her way to Terabithia, Leslie hits her head, falls in and drowns. . . . The remaining part of the book is a faithful and very moving depiction of the nature of [Jess's] grief, and its various successive stages of manifestation. Jess goes through them all: inability to take in the fact of bereavement, numbness, a certain detached satisfaction in observing that he will be the centre of interest at school as the dead girl's friend. Then, as the difficult reality forces its way into his mind, come the classic reactions of guilt, anger and blame. . . . Finally, he progresses through the small, healing ceremonies of grief to acceptance and a readiness, as he lets little May Belle into the kingdom of Terabithia, to look forward and build on his friendship with Leslie.

If one goes back again to reread the apparently central passage in which the reader is invited to smile at Jess and May Belle's shallow misapprehensions about Christianity, while appreciating that Leslie instinctively sees the point of it, one finds it does not really relate much to the book either before or after the scene. The issue of death has not been balked, or any easy religious comfort offered. It is as if, just for once, didacticism had got the better of the author, and she then realized it did not ring true. I have dwelt on this passage not from a wish to pick unfairly on what seems to me Paterson's one real lapse, but because it *is* just for once, and it *is* her one real lapse. The book stands perfectly well without it. (pp. 75-6)

The Great Gilly Hopkins is a work of true comedy. In fact it has a much more pervasive religious element than its predecessor, but the religious theme is cleverly amalgamated with the whole: the overriding impression is of the original character of the heroine. (p. 77)

Gilly cultivates toughness in a big way. Actually, of course, she is not half as tough as she makes out. Her Achilles heel is her romantic vision of a beautiful, loving mother, and she cherishes a glamorous photograph of Courtney. A professed anti-Pollyanna, it's mother-love she craves, but only from her real mother. She doesn't want anyone else softening her up, and she very soon feels threatened by the trio consisting of her warm-hearted, huge foster mother, Maime Trotter, seven-year-old William Ernest Teague, Trotter's other foster child, and blind, black old Mr Randolph, who comes over for his meals. In the proper tradition of comedy, Gilly is duly softened up despite herself. . . . (pp. 77-8)

Maime Trotter is not only the representative of human goodness—criterion and yardstick, the standard by which the behaviour of others is to be measured—but also the representative of Christianity. And Katherine Paterson neatly disarms the non-Christian reader who might find this hard to take by letting Gilly herself attack her, with some slight basis in fact. . . . For Gilly's youthful arrogance leads her into the intellectual snobbery of looking down on Maime Trotter, as well as old Miss Applegate the Sunday School teacher, and the young preacher who has trouble with his grammar. Trotter's Christianity is simple, fundamentalist; she refers frequently to the Good Book, and to taking the Lord's name in vain, but while she may not be 'smart' she is wise, warm and loving. When she boasts, 'I never met a kid I couldn't make friends with', causing unregenerate Gilly to want to throw up, she turns out to be telling only the simple truth. It takes some doing to create a genuinely good character who comes to life as successfully as Maime Trotter, and it is delightful to watch the author steer skilfully around all the possible pitfalls involved. (p. 78)

The whole novel is permeated with the ideal of Christian charity (love in the sense of *agape*), but it is never obtrusive, and to get the balance just right in a work of high comedy is remarkable: the construction of the book, that vital factor in comedy, is a joy too, and Gilly must be one of the most appealing of modern heroines. . . .

Bridge to Terabithia and *The Great Gilly Hopkins* are very different from each other (unlike the author's three Japanese novels, which are all from the same mould), and her next book, the Newbery Medal winner *Jacob Have I Loved,* is different again. A bleaker work than its immediate predecessor, it lacks that strong comic element but has strengths of its own. (p. 79)

The Rass islanders are reared in a tradition of puritanical Methodism, as exemplified by [Caroline's and Louise's] text-citing Grandma. It is Grandma's nasty Biblical crack, directed at Louise—'Jacob have I loved, but Esau have I hated'—that provides the book's title. One expects, then, knowing of the author's religious commitment from her earlier works, that there will be a pervasive Christian element here too; in fact it is less prominent than in *The Great Gilly Hopkins.* Grandma is the most overtly religious person in the book, and her fervour borders on the comic as she becomes slightly dotty with age, accusing her kind and clean-living daughter-in-law of all manner of Old Testament whoredoms. Grandma is saved from becoming too much a native of Cold Comfort Farm by Louise's realization that she still, after many decades, is 'haunted by a childish passion' for the Captain; the maturing girl's sympathy is aroused for the old lady.

As for Louise herself, however, rocked back on her heels by the discovery that the speaker in that statement of bias over Jacob and Esau is not a fallible human being—not Isaac or Rebecca—but God himself, she has turned away from religion. She loses interest in churchgoing and does not pray any more, resolving, a little like Gilly Hopkins, that she must rely on her own strength to outface a hostile world. Interestingly, that is what she more or less does. . . . It is not suggested that she regains her faith; indeed, it is indicated that she remains pretty lukewarm. Her husband is a Catholic, but 'has never suggested that I ought to turn Catholic or even religious'. I suspect that

Katherine Paterson herself would agree with another scrupulously thoughtful writer, Emily Dickinson, that 'The abdication of belief / Makes the behaviour small / Better an ignis fatuus / Than no illume at all'. But she does not impose such a view on her character.

Christianity is present in the book, not just in Grandma's rantings, but more as part of the background than as a thread in the story: I think we are to take it that the island traditions have inevitably helped to form Louise's character and give her the strength to cope with her difficulties. The learning of charity is a strong theme too, though no one specifies that it is necessarily Christian charity. The story ends, neatly and movingly, where it began, with twins: delivering the two babies, Louise finds herself in her turn paying more attention to the weaker child. By now she can understand and forgive the past, but she urges the parents to show the stronger twin affection too.

My personal preference is for the serio-comic verve of *The Great Gilly Hopkins,* but *Jacob Have I Loved* is also a very fine novel in its different way. And I do admire Katherine Paterson's ability—increasingly sure from *Bridge to Terabithia* onwards—to make her own Christian convictions evident while not letting them become obtrusive: that is an achievement to impress the least religious of serious readers. (pp. 80-1)

Anthea Bell, ''A Case of Commitment,'' in Signal, No. 38, May, 1982, pp. 73-81.

JONATHAN YARDLEY

In *Rebels of the Heavenly Kingdom,* as in much of her previous work, Katherine Paterson writes about the difficult but enlightening processes through which young people who are prematurely left to their own resources become acquainted with the compromises and obligations that are necessary to survival in the adult world. . . . [The constants in her work] are the sensitivity, humor and clarity with which Paterson considers the many nuances of her central theme.

Paterson treads a fine line between ''juvenile'' and ''adult'' fiction, and never has that line been finer than it is in *Rebels of the Heavenly Kingdom.* Indeed, she has written a more accomplished work of fiction, and certainly a deeper and more resonant one, than most of the novels written these days for an adult readership. Paterson obviously does write for a youthful audience—readers between the ages of 12 and 16, approximately—but she treats that audience as if it were grown-up: not in the manner of Judy Blume, the Jackie Susann of the acne-and-braces set, but in the manner of one mature person talking to another.

Rebels of the Heavenly Kingdom is set in mid-19th-century China, a time when the Manchu Empire was under intense internal pressure from rebellious Chinese nationalists. One insurgent group was the Taiping Tienkuo, ''the Heavenly Kingdom of Great Peace,'' which had as its inspiration a rather peculiar blend of Oriental philosophy and Christianity learned from Western missionaries. An involuntary convert to its cause is 15-year-old Wang Lee, who had been abducted from his peasant home by ''stupid and dishonorable rascals'' and then rescued from these bandits by an 18-year-old girl named Mei Lin, a passionate devotee of the Heavenly Kingdom. . . .

Wang Lee, though a mere boy, becomes an impassioned warrior of the Heavenly Kingdom who kills, wantonly and bloodily, out of an increasingly mad conviction that the cause of the kingdom is greater than any individual human life. It is a conviction in which he is abetted by Mei Lin, who herself becomes one of the most accomplished warriors in the army, a soldier of near-legendary achievements.

Wang Lee has learned to fend for himself, but in the process he has lost sight of the value and dignity of ordinary life, as expressed in the words of the Heavenly King of the Heavenly Kingdom of Great Peace: "You should not kill one innocent person or do one unrighteous act, even though it be to acquire an empire." Those words are the epigraph for Rebels of the Heavenly Kingdom, and they constitute its principal moral. But Katherine Paterson considers this moral without a trace of sermonizing or righteousness. The education to which she subjects Wang Lee—and, for that matter, Mei Lin—is a hard one, in which nothing is learned without a measure of pain. . . .

But then it is one of the many strengths of Paterson's fiction that, unlike so many who write for young readers, she always has her gaze set firmly on the realities of life. She makes Wang Lee's world actual in two ways: she gives us a wholly believable 19th-century China, and she gives us an experience that is entirely true to the way life works. In the sense that really matters, **Rebels of the Heavenly Kingdom** is a grown-up book— just as, at its conclusion, Wang Lee is himself a grown-up man.

> *Jonathan Yardley, "Boys, Bandits, Manchu Armies and Opium Wars," in Book World—The Washington Post, June 12, 1983, p. 8.*

STEPHANIE ZVIRIN

[In *Rebels of the Heavenly Kingdom*] Paterson uses 15-year-old Wang Lee's experiences over a four-year period as a device to express China's political turmoil during the mid-nineteenth century. . . . [While] Paterson bases her novel on actual history, she fails to take full advantage of the dramatic potential of her material, relying instead on some blatant contrivances to further the plot and letting the narrative bog down amidst sermonic, confusing descriptions of Heavenly philosophy. Nevertheless, Paterson is obviously a serious, polished, and evocative writer and her book holds out for special readers a meticulously fashioned view of another culture and times gone by. (pp. 1333-34)

> *Stephanie Zvirin, in a review of "Rebels of the Heavenly Kingdom," in Booklist, Vol. 79, No. 20, June 15, 1983, pp. 1333-34.*

ZENA SUTHERLAND

The historical and cultural details [in **Rebels of the Heavenly Kingdom**] are vivid, the book giving a great deal of information about [China] as well as about the Heavenly Kingdom and its warriors. It follows the lives of Wang Lee and Mei Lin as they participate (separately or together) in military marches, battles, and camp life, concluding with their union, at the close of the book, and their settlement into the ancestral hut of Wang Lee's family. This is a fascinating story, and well-told; if it does not have the emotional impact of Paterson's earlier historical fiction (*Of Nightingales That Weep, The Master Puppeteer*) it has pace and color, and it is particularly interesting in its reflection of cultural diffusion, as the militant leaders of the Taiping Rebellion fuse their interpretation of Christian doctrine with their own traditions.

> *Zena Sutherland, in a review of "Rebels of the Heavenly Kingdom," in Bulletin of the Center for Children's Books, Vol. 36, No. 11, July-August, 1983, p. 216.*

ETHEL R. TWICHELL

[In *Rebels of the Heavenly Kingdom*] Wang and Mei Lin are swept into the marches and battles of the Taiping and experience an endless parade of death and violence. Separated during the course of the war campaigns, their ultimate meeting and marriage seems almost an anticlimax after the fearful ordeals they have endured. The book portrays a sweeping panorama of human experience during a bitter period of Chinese history, but Wang and Mei Lin emerge less as real people than as pawns flung hither and thither by the tides of war. As always, the author's control over her material lends credibility to the writing and sheds light on a time which will be unfamiliar to most readers; some of them, however, may miss the involvement of heart and emotion which is so noticeable in her other work.

> *Ethel R. Twichell, in a review of "Rebels of the Heavenly Kingdom," in The Horn Book Magazine, Vol. LIX, No. 4, August, 1983, p. 456.*

RUTH M. McCONNELL

[In *Rebels of the Heavenly Kingdom* Wang Lee's] rise and fall and his recapture by the kidnappers while on a spying mission are stark and gripping; his ecstasy and growing disillusionment as the killings increase and spread to civilians in the name of peace are well conveyed. More closely bound to specific events and causes than Paterson's Japanese historic fiction, this book will have to be introduced. A "Note to the Reader" provides some background information about the events and the times, but Paterson does not adequately integrate the historical facts into the story. Often the characters are vehicles for the theme rather than individuals in their own right. However, Paterson has written a strong adventure tale whose parallels to today's cults and movements could lead to interesting discussions.

> *Ruth M. McConnell, in a review of "Rebels of the Heavenly Kingdom," in School Library Journal, Vol. 30, No. 1, September, 1983, p. 138.*

M. SARAH SMEDMAN

In her writings and conversations about her work, Katherine Paterson repeatedly raises issues which emerge as artistic challenges for her. Among these are her commitment to the young reader's right to an absorbing story and her difficulties with plotting. Herself imbued with the Christian spirit, all Paterson's stories—whether they are set in feudal Japan or World War II Chesapeake Bay—dramatize a young protagonist's encounter with the mysteries of grace and love. Her published work reveals that many of Paterson's problems with plot may derive from the challenge of discovering and sequencing a series of episodes that will present honestly and nondidactically a theme that has no sequence in it. . . . A plot, as C. S. Lewis says, "is only really a net whereby to catch something else." For Paterson in her latest novel, *Jacob Have I Loved*, that something else is the experience of swift and sudden release from hatred and vengefulness through the acceptance of and cooperation with selfless love. (p. 180)

Typically Patersonian, *Jacob Have I Loved* is a tighly woven novel; each character, each episode, each speech, each image helps to incarnate that which the author is imagining. The net which catches and binds together the whole is her adroit manipulation of several levels of story: the story which the adolescent Sarah Louise ("Wheeze") Bradshaw tells of and to herself in her attempt to comprehend the meaning of the life she is daily living; the story that the young mother and midwife Sarah Louise tells through the configuration of characters and events she selects from her memory of her tumultuous teen years rounded by the insights and incidents she adds from a maturer perspective; and the Bible stories of Jacob and Esau in the Old Testament and the birth of Christ in the New, which provides an allusive frame for the other two story levels, and which add resonance to, universalize, Louise's personal experience.

In the narrative present of most of the story, the protagonist, Wheeze Bradshaw, the elder twin by a few minutes of beautiful, fragile, talented Caroline, so envies and resents her sister's ever-present place in the limelight that she is blinded both to her own worth and to others' appreciation of that worth. The isolation of the Bradshaws' island home, Rass, and the strict Methodist ethos provide the appropriate desert setting for the nebulous guilt that presses on Louise, for the starkly simple good and evil of her family and friends, and for the human encounters which prepare her for the insights which coalesce swiftly and forcefully at the end of the novel.

Envious not only of her sister's beauty and fragility which, from the moment of Caroline's birth, have caused the family so much concern, but also of her musical talent and the sense of purpose which that talent gives her, Louise relies on fishing with Call Purnell, a reliable but prosaic boy, for friendship and to earn extra money for the family's coffers. That she, from the beginning a healthy and a good child, has not caused her family a moment's worry is of grave concern to Louise. The story she tells herself is that lack of worry symbolizes lack of love. When after years of absence Captain Wallace returns to his home at the tip of the island, Louise and Call help him to restore his house and become his friends. After a hurricane destroys his house, Louise compassionately embraces him and discovers, in an agony of bliss and shame, that she is in love with the Captain, old enough to be her grandfather. Her ensuing guilt is intensified by the bitter hurt she feels at Caroline's intrusion into the Captain's friendship. Canny, spiteful, Bible-spouting Grandmother Bradshaw discerns Louise's secret and publicly fingers the wound. When Captain Wallace, *Louise's* friend first, uses his deceased wife's legacy to send the always-favored Caroline to Baltimore to music school, Louise tries to conceal her desolation. Aware of her feelings, Grandmother Bradshaw whispers hoarsely, "Jacob have I loved, but Esau have I hated." Later, when Louise checks the reference in her Bible, she despairs. "The speaker was God. It was God who said 'Jacob have I Loved.'" . . . From the nadir of spiritual emptiness, Louise decides, "There was, then, no use struggling or even trying. It was God himself who hated me. And without cause." (pp. 181-82)

Telling herself that God had judged her before she was born and had cast her out before she took her first breath, Louise stops going to church and doesn't pray any more. . . . Louise settles into a working man's life, crabbing and oystering with her father on his boats. Almost imperceptibly, step by tiny step, she beings her ascent from her spiritual dark night through encounters with those closest to her, sacramental encounters

because they are the occasions of insights that lead her ultimately away from her rancorous obsession with herself and her sister to understanding and faith and hope.

The winter with her father on the boat is Louise's spiritual sojourn in the desert. . . . She invests every ounce of energy in work, learning from her father, who sings to the oysters, of the peace that derives from being in harmony with the rhythms of the seasons and the sea.

When Call, her only friend, returns from the army to marry Caroline, now on full scholarship at Juilliard and headed for a brilliant opera career, Louise is stunned to learn that he has never penetrated her brusque, even sardonic, shell to perceive that she cares deeply for him. . . . Had she believed in God, she would now have cursed him.

Because Grandmother Bradshaw hates the sea and refuses to cross even the narrow strip of bay to the mainland, Louise stays with her when the others go to New York for Caroline's Christmas wedding. Then it is that Grandmother shocks Louise with the story of her own unrequited love for Captain Wallace. . . . In—and for—a flash she realizes that the old woman's viciousness results from a thwarted childish passion she's carried all her life, a festering wound that has embittered her. Later that same Christmas Day, Captain Wallace leads Louise to further disquieting realizations. First, that though she wants something, she does not want to marry Call; she is not cut out to be a woman on Rass—a man perhaps, but not a woman. Second, that the Captain has always regarded her as capable of doing anything she put her mind to, but that he helped Caroline because she knew what it was she wanted to do. Finally, she realizes that to keep hiding behind the excuse that no one has given her a chance will be to continue along the stony path of self-deceit. She must decide what it is she wants to do and muster the courage to do it.

Although it would be too dramatic to say that Louise was reborn on that Christmas, certainly at this winter solstice, when light begins its annual ascension, dimensions of the girl long dormant begin to stir. She has not yet, however, relinquished the story of herself as an Esau damned by God. When her grandmother in a demon frenzy calls her mother a whore, Louise, who had been calculating such revenge for months, retaliates in Grandmother's style, hurling at her verses from Proverbs about the evils of living with a contentious woman. . . . [Paterson suggests] that Louise knows subconsciously that, like her grandmother, she carries within her the seeds of viciousness—a searing bitterness rooted in what she tells herself are undeserved favors and affection for her sister. (pp. 182-83)

Louise's smoldering anger climaxes, erupts, and thereby begins to dissipate in a conversation with her mother, a self-contained, nonobtrusive woman, who has such respect for her daughters' individuality that she will never attempt to make the girls over into images of herself. Like any idealistic youth whose illusions crash, Louise suffers shock and resentment when her mother suggests that she may be expecting too much from life, that far away places, dashing people, and exotic careers are not so romantic as they sound. At this point Louise is not able to absorb the idea that life may be satisfying, that a person may do something that makes a difference in the world, though the world does not stop to applaud publicly. What does surface in her consciousness—something she has heretofore been only vaguely aware of—is that she has never before said she wanted to leave Rass because she has been afraid to, and that her parents love her, want her to have her chance to make her own way, and will miss her when she leaves. (pp. 183-84)

The story of Louise's turbulent adolescence ends with that awareness. There are those who argue that *Jacob Have I Loved* would be a better novel if it too ended here. The subsequent and final two chapters do compress many events and much time in a very little space. However, they are essential to complete the webbing of the stories; and their swiftness and brevity are entirely in keeping with the nature of the events they record. Louise realizes the nature and power of love, which comes to her, her spirit now having been prepared as fertile soil for the good seed, instantaneously, with the concentrated force of a revelation. (p. 184)

In the last chapter the novel comes full circle. Like her mother, Louise has left home for a country at once different from and the same as that in which she grew up. She has married for love a man who, like her father, is in tune with nature, and she becomes a mother. In the last scene, she assists at the birth of twins, the second-born of whom has only the shakiest hold on life. In her effort to preserve that frail flame, Louise, having delegated the care of the stronger baby, temporarily forgets its existence. Recalling her own grandmother, she belatedly remembers that the child should be held and cuddled, not left in a cold basket. Admittedly, the episode is contrived (all art is), but, like the ending of a fairy tale, it completes the story with a balance and a harmony that are aesthetically satisfying. . . .

Paterson resolves the stories of Louise and of Jacob, ending the novel in a passage representative of her facility in drawing together disparate symbols and themes in a final, consummate image and of her exquisite use of language. The circular pattern of the novel functions symbolically on two levels. On one, it is an ironic correlative of the self-enclosed, isolated Rass and of the adolescent Louise, reenforcing the theme of entrapment. On another, it is the prophetic emblem of completion, of perfection, and reenforces the wholeness to which Louise is restored when she is able to discard her conception of herself as an Esau hated by God. (p. 185)

Louise takes the last step out of her spiritual marsh back onto a path, a wider path than that from which she fell when she had her first insight into the reasons underlying her grandmother's demonic hatred. Unlike Grandma Bradshaw, Louise chooses to put off her juvenile, if poisonous, bitterness and insecurity; to go out of herself; to leave Rass and to live with grace, love, and wonder. The irony implied by the title seems to go beyond Louise's misunderstandings to suggest to the reader, perhaps to the protagonist herself, that God, if he is all-knowing and all-loving, must himself have spoken those words ironically.

The net which catches these meanings is skilfully woven by the artist's use of the three stories. The story of the older Louise, who in her twenties has gained insights from and into her adolescent experience, extends and adds objectivity and meaning to the story of the teen-aged narrator. Setting both in the allusive frame of representative stories from the Old and New Testaments, which tell of, respectively, the mysteries of God's displeasure with and love for humankind, not only suggests the story of redemption, but connects Louise's story to the ages.

It goes without saying that the young reader need not be consciously aware of the ironies and complexities of the novel to sense and be satisfied by the rightness with which they are integrated into a whole. The power of *Jacob Have I Loved* does not depend upon the reader's discerning the third level of story. Nor is the novel's effect diminished if a reader rejects Christianity. Paterson's subtle art incorporates the third dimension inobtrusively, to be discovered and to enrich the story. For those who do not discover it, the story still works. Without violating the norms of realism, though perhaps stretching them to include a coincidence more possible than probable, it incorporates the wisdom of myth and fairy tales. . . . *Jacob Have I Loved* is a moving novel because the skillful, if not always perfect, plotting achieves one of the functions of art: within the form of the realistic novel it does capture and "present what the narrow and desperately practical perspectives of real life exclude." In so doing, "it lays a hushing spell on the imagination." (pp. 186-87)

M. Sarah Smedman, 'A Good Oyster': Story and Meaning in 'Jacob Have I Loved'," in Children's literature in education, *Vol. 14, No. 3 (Autumn), 1983, pp. 180-87.*

Ayn Rand

1905-1982

Russian-born American novelist, nonfiction writer, dramatist, scriptwriter, and editor.

Rand is chiefly remembered for her controversial novels *The Fountainhead* (1943) and *Atlas Shrugged* (1957), which promote her philosophy of "objectivism." This extreme form of individualism has been defined by Rand as "the concept of man as a heroic being, with his own happiness as the moral purpose of his life, with productive achievement as his noblest activity, and reason as his only absolute."

Rand came to the United States in 1926, having witnessed the 1917 Communist revolution in Russia. Each of her four novels is a celebration of the individual versus collective society. *We the Living* (1936) is viewed as a polemic against totalitarianism and its disregard of the individual. *Anthem* (1938) is a science fiction novelette of a future primitive society in which the word "I" is forbidden. Rand's point in this work is that the individualism which had built a complex technological civilization has been smothered by collectivism.

These first two novels are considered lesser efforts than *The Fountainhead* and *Atlas Shrugged*. In these novels, Rand dramatizes her philosophy of objectivism in lengthy works designed to glorify characters who fulfill her ideals. Howard Roark of *The Fountainhead* is an architectural genius who refuses to bend to bureaucratic pressure. John Galt, Rand's spokesperson in *Atlas Shrugged*, leads a strike of society's most effective and creative producers in an effort to collapse the collectivist social system of the present to prepare the way for a new society based on Rand's ideals. In the closing sentence of a long oration, Galt presents the credo of objectivists: "I swear—by my life and my love of it—that I will never live for the sake of another man, nor ask another man to live for mine."

Critical and reader response to Rand's work has been sharply divided, with much of the disagreement focused on her philosophy. Inherent in her concept of the ego as the moving force behind all creative human endeavors is an unwavering advocacy of self-centeredness and its concomitant opposition to the altruism so important to Christian ethics. While some critics have praised Rand for writing novels of ideas, calling her a thoughtful spokesperson for laissez-faire capitalism, many others have found her work too simplistic and didactic. The arguments about her ideas continue today, although her influence has lessened since the 1960s and earlier, when her writings had a strong cult following. After writing *Atlas Shrugged*, Rand devoted her time to lecturing about her philosophy and defending it in several collections of essays. She also edited the *Objectivist Newsletter*, later renamed *The Ayn Rand Letter*.

(See also *CLC*, Vol. 3 and *Contemporary Authors*, Vols. 13-16, rev. ed., Vol. 105 [obituary].)

HAROLD STRAUSS

["We the Living"] is slavishly warped to the dictates of propaganda. Actually Miss Rand can command a good deal of

Photograph by Phyllis Cerf Wagner

narrative skill, and her novel moves with alacrity and vigor upon occasion. It is only the blind fervor with which she has dedicated herself to the annihilation of the Soviet Union that has led her to blunder into palpable improbabilities. We refer strictly to artistic probability; we cannot here hold in question the facts upon which Miss Rand's political attitude is based.

To the unwary "We the Living" will possess the semblance of impartiality, for it is the story of a girl who was loved by two men—by Leo, an aristocrat, and by Andrei, a Communist. But the dice are heavily loaded in the favor of Leo from the beginning, for Kira, the girl, is the daughter of a formerly wealthy factory owner; aside from Leo's greater physical attractiveness, her background has imbued her whole being with a yearning for the gentility and individuality which he represents. Andrei, on the other hand, is a cog in the vast machinery of Soviet bureaucracy. . . . Kira is deeply attracted by him personally, but their political differences are too great ever to allow them peace. . . .

Miss Rand spares no detail in her descriptions of diet, shelter, and the constant G. P. U. surveillance accorded former members of the upper classes. Nevertheless it is doubtful whether Kira would ever have turned to Andrei had not Leo been stricken with tuberculosis. In order to get Leo admitted to Crimean hospitals ordinarily open only to trade union members, Kira offers Andrei her body.

Leo is saved, but only at the cost of deception and intrigue by Kira. He returns in a cynical mood and plunges into forbidden speculation in foodstuffs, which he obtains by corrupting officials of the food trust. He is detected, however, and once more the good offices of Andrei are invoked. Andrei succeeds in clearing Leo only at the cost of his own party membership and eventually his suicide. . . . His sacrifice is in vain. Leo leaves Kira for another woman (as his individualism apparently entitles him to do) and we last see Kira making an inevitably fatal attempt to escape across the Latvian border from that Russia which had denied to her everything of meaning in life.

Harold Strauss, "Soviet Triangle," in The New York
Times Book Review, April 19, 1936, p. 7.

BEN BELITT

[Ayn Rand] has written a novel ["**We the Living**"] to make it finally plain that the Soviet state, as far as she has been able to discover, is not only a farce on the face of it but is likewise fostering a race of "crippled, creeping, crawling, broken monstrosities." Miss Rand is determined that her readers shall have nothing less than the whole truth. Kira Argounova, her protagonist, speaks for her on at least one occasion: "For one insane second Kira wondered if she could tear through the crowd, rush up to that woman [a visiting English trade-union delegate] and yell to her, to England's workers, to the world, the truth that they were seeking." We are left to assume that "**We the Living**" is the answer. (p. 523)

From the very outset [Kira's] attitude toward the experiment in which she shares is one of contempt and ridicule; she "loathes their ideals but admires their methods"—which would conceivably make her a mystic. Not many chapters on, she offers herself to one Leo Kovalensky, a total stranger, a few moments after first laying eyes on him, because she "liked his face"; which, one is left to ponder, might in some way account for her "individualism." The remainder of the novel shuttles about aimlessly from bedroom to rostrum, with Kira playing the role of a patient Griselda to Leo's Don Juan. Much love-making occurs in the interim, and considerable speech-making, and one is bound to confess that the former is managed to vastly greater effect. Leo in due course of time is revealed in his true colors as a counter-revolutionary, a cad, and a gigolo; Kira dies in a snowdrift while attempting to cross the border; and, presumably, the myth of a communist state explodes to the sound of low, mocking laughter.

It is not the intention of this reviewer to quarrel with Miss Rand's politics except to point out in passing that her excessive theatricality invites suspicion. It may be, as we are asked to believe, that petty officials in Soviet Russia ride to the opera in foreign limousines while the worker goes wheatless and meatless; similarly it may be true that consumptives are denied asylum solely for the reason that they are not affiliated party members. Yet it must be said that if Miss Rand has indeed presented us with the facts, she has given us no reason to respect Kira as her spokesman. (pp. 523-24)

Ben Belitt, "The Red and the White," in The Nation,
Vol. CXLII, No. 3964, April 22, 1936, pp. 522-24.*

WILLIAM PLOMER

One often wishes that writers would yield a little more to their satirical inclinations, and that goes for Miss Ayn Rand. From internal evidence one would guess her to be a middle-class

White or Whitish Russian living in exile in America, and *We the Living* (a title of no particular significance) is so frankly counter-revolutionary that it ought to annoy readers of Red or Reddish sympathies. Writing, often graphically, of life in Leningrad in the 'twenties she seems anxious to show the corruption of those newly raised to positions of authority. . . . Miss Rand's account of the social upset following the Revolution is detailed and likely enough; she makes a certain amount of rather bitter fun of the workings of the new bureaucracy and of the lapses of the new orthodox into such unorthodoxies as private trading. But towards Kira, who stands for individualism and those little things like scent and lipsticks which Mean So Much to a woman, Miss Rand is altogether too partial. If Kira had played the game with nice Red Andrei instead of nasty White Leo . . . we might have liked her better.

William Plomer, in a review of "We the Living," in
The Spectator, Vol. 158, No. 5664, January 15, 1937,
p. 98.

LORINE PRUETTE

Ayn Rand is a writer of great power. She has a subtle and ingenious mind and the capacity of writing brilliantly, beautifully, bitterly. "**The Fountainhead**" . . . is a long but absorbing story of man's enduring battle with evil. It has drama . . . ; it has poetry, sometimes a bit too lush; and it has a challenging conception. Good novels of ideas are rare at any time. This is the only novel of ideas written by an American woman that I can recall.

The background is architecture, a field relatively new to the fiction writer, and admirably adapted to the presentation of "the creator" and "the secondhander." Howard Roark is the creator, a tough guy who works cheerfully in the quarries if he is not allowed to build in his own way. . . . Against him is the charming lad who went to school with him and won all the prizes. Peter Keating continues to win all the prizes, to use his good looks, his personality and his lack of morals to make a rapid and fraudulent success. Against him, too, is Dominque Francon, because she loves him and fears and hates the corrupting, engulfing world.

Above all, Mr. Ellsworth Toohey . . . is Roark's enemy. Ellsworth Toohey is a brilliant personification of a modern devil. Aiming at a society that shall be "an average drawn upon zeros," he knows exactly why he corrupts Peter Keating and explains his methods to the ruined and desolate young man in a passage that is a pyrotechnical display of the fascist mind at its best and its worst: the use of the ideal of altruism to destroy personal integrity, the use of humor and tolerance to destroy all standards, the use of sacrifice to enslave. (p. 7)

You will not be able to read the masterful work without . . . thinking through some of the basic concepts of our times. Miss Rand has taken her stand against collectivism, "the rule of the second-hander, the ancient monster" which has brought men "to a level of intellectual indecency never equaled on earth." She has written a hymn in praise of the individual and has said things worth saying in these days. Whether her antithesis between altruism and selfishness is logically correct or not, she has written a powerful indictment.

All her characters are amazingly literate; they all speak with her voice, expressing in dynamic fashion the counterpoint of her argument. She uses mockery, irony, savagery, to portray her second-raters. Her characters are romanticized, larger than life as representations of good and evil. But nothing she has to say is said in a second-rate fashion. (pp. 7, 18)

Lorine Pruette "Battle against Evil," in The New York Times Book Review, May 16, 1943, pp. 7, 18.

ALBERT GUERARD

["**The Fountainhead**"] tells of exciting events and colorful characters. It is daring, not offensive. Its style would satisfy the most exacting professor, yet it has the vim and snap of the best journalese. It is frankly intellectual, and fearlessly discusses life, liberty and the pursuit of happiness, but it never sinks to the highbrow. . . .

The central character is an architect, or, if you prefer, it is Architecture. But the novel is not a technical study in fictional form. . . . The real subject—a boldly general one—is The Genius, or Superman, vs. the Rabble of "Second-handers."

The characters are hard to visualize, but they talk in human words: indeed, the presentation, all the way through, displays amazing competence. The heroes move dramatically, with a swift, fantastic logic. They are strangely transparent; what we see under their skin is neither sawdust nor flesh and bone: it is an elementary formula, as in the old morality plays. Ayn Rand believes that a man, like a building, embodies one central idea, one single truth, one single purpose. Nature fails to agree with the beautiful simplicity of this conception. . . .

Ayn Rand is not to blame if her characters are not human beings. She is discussing ideas: a man of flesh and blood is no argument, because he is complex and unique. It might be better then to deal frankly with abstractions, and call the hero Art rather than Roark. But the result would be a treatise instead of a novel, and there is no market for treatises.

So the thesis is set forth in the personal relations of [the] principal characters, who ultimately realize what they represent and in the course of the action must express their motives and meaning in explicit terms. As Roark is the positive element, the others are attracted to him in spite of themselves. Paradoxically, all of them wish to destroy him. . . .

The fundamental problem is that of the individual; but it gets entangled with the totally different problem of the genius. The genius, a Messiah bringing a new revelation, refuses to submit, to conform, to co-operate. He bids for absolute power: he must rule or be broken. . . .

All this carried me back to my vanished youth. Nietzscheism was fresh and joyous in those days, with its violent denunciation of slave morality, its extolling of ruthlessness, its paeans to the superman. Ayn Rand's argument justifies [Friedrich Wilhelm] Nietzsche. Howard Roark's thought soars and swoops bewilderingly from Nietzsche through [Herbert] Spencer to Albert Jay Nock and Mr. [Herbert] Hoover. "Now, observe the results of a society built on the principle of individualism. This, our country. The noblest in the history of men. The country of greatest achievement, greatest prosperity, greatest freedom." As the whole book is a satire on American civilization, this sudden outburst of orthodox pride comes as a shock. I feel the same pride in American achievement. But I have a different explanation to offer: the Jeffersonian conception of equality. It is not because of the tyranny of a few supermen that America has become great, but through opportunity offered to all men, and the willing co-operation of all men. . . .

The book haughtily denounces the herd—and every member of the herd secretly singles himself out as a potential superman. It scorns the Profit Motive, and also praises American Prosperity. It is the acme of sophistication, and derides Greenwich village. As Brahma is the slayer and the slain, so is Ayn Rand the hare and the hounds. . . .

It is manifestly unsafe to judge an author by a single book. If "**The Fountainhead**" is a first step, something to be transcended, it is a magnificent promise. If it is a mature achievement, with which the author is fully satisfied, it is . . . marvelously clever. I am eager to give Ayn Rand the full benefit of the doubt.

Albert Guerard, "Novel on Architectural Genius," in New York Herald Tribune Weekly Book Review, May 30, 1943, p. 2.

JOHN CHAMBERLAIN

["**Atlas Shrugged**"] is a work of fiction, a piece of inspired and thoroughly exciting story-telling that drags only in some of the lengthier speeches which tend to recapitulate points already established by the action. But it is so much more than a mere novel. . . .

"**Atlas Shrugged**" will satisfy many readers on many separate planes of satisfaction. It has its Buck Rogers flavor—and pace—for those who delight in science fiction. It can be taken as a philosophical detective story. . . . It can be read as a Socratic dialogue on ethics, or as a profound political parable. Or, as Miss Rand would herself prefer, it can be accepted as a poetic celebration of man as an heroic being, "with his own happiness as the moral purpose of his life, with productive achievement as his noblest activity, and reason as his only absolute."

It is as a political parable that "**Atlas Shrugged**" has its most immediate application. . . . Miss Rand believes that whenever a government interferes with men in their voluntary pursuit of productive or creative activity it puts a drag upon the "world's motor." (The nature of that motor—the ego, the "I will it," of the individual—Miss Rand has already endeavored to explain in her best-seller of a decade ago, "**The Fountainhead**.") The drag upon the motor necessarily becomes worse with every increase in the activity of what modern political scientists have misnamed the "positive State." And the lesson, in the parable of "**Atlas Shrugged**," is that the motor must stop completely when private property relations disappear and men are bound to work under compulsion for one employer, the government.

To enforce her parable, Miss Rand divides humanity into two classes of people, the looters and the non-looters. But her looters are not the "robber barons" of old, they are the modern politicians—and those who keep them in office in order to "pressure" them into seizing and redistributing the product of such capital and labor as remain uncoerced. The fact that men can vote their own expropriation, their own chains, is immaterial: Miss Rand's point is that any coercion of producers winds up in the same place whether it is imposed by a dictator or by a vote of the majority. The world cannot survive administration by power hunters and place holders in league with the incompetent. (p. 1)

[What] would happen if the creative and productive people of the world were to go on strike? In "**Atlas Shrugged**" a far-seeing inventor, John Galt, does just that. . . . A messiah in spite of himself, John Galt undertakes a crusade to persuade all the other creative individuals of his time and country to lay down their tools—which happen to be their brains. . . . [Eventually] all of the creative individuals of the country quit and go into hiding. The "looters" and their incompetent camp followers are left with everything—and of course, the "everything" soon turns out to be nothing. (pp. 1, 9)

This is the skeleton of a vibrant and powerful novel of ideas which happens to have all the qualities of a thunderously successful melodrama. The characters are not of this world—they are intensified and purified beyond human measure for the purpose of allegory. Nevertheless, they are entirely consistent with Miss Rand's purpose, which is to combine first-rate pedagogy with first-rate entertainment. They carry conviction as [Alfred] Tennyson's Sir Galahad or Elaine the Lily Maid carried conviction, which is sufficent for the purposes of the fable.

The only place where Miss Rand's spell ceases to hold the reader is when the inventor, John Galt, offers his concept of ethics. It is wrong, he says, to "help a man who has no virtues, to help him on the ground of his suffering as such, to accept his faults, his need, as a claim." This is a pagan, not a Christian, view of charity. To the Christian, every man, no matter how lost he may seem, is potentially redeemable. The note of ethical hardness may very possibly repel the very reader who has the most need of Miss Rand's political and social message—which is that charity, whether Christian or pagan, must be voluntary if the gift is not to hurt both giver and receiver alike. To be charitable with other people's substance which is seized at the point of the politican's gun is to poison the very well-springs of goodness. Miss Rand should have left it at that without trying to rewrite the Sermon on the Mount. (p. 9)

> *John Chamberlain, "Ayn Rand's Political Parable and Thundering Melodrama," in* New York Herald Tribune Book Review, *October 6, 1957, pp. 1, 9.*

RUTH CHAPIN BLACKMAN

In a statement published as a postscript to **"Atlas Shrugged,"** Ayn Rand has defined her philosophy, "in essence," as "the concept of man as a heroic being, with his own happiness as the moral purpose of his life, with productive achievement as his noblest activity, and reason as his only absolute."

"Atlas Shrugged" is [a] . . . polemic inadequately disguised as a novel and designed to dramatize these views. The result is an astonishing mixture of anti-Communist manifesto, superman, and the lush lady novelist Ethel M. Dell—a novel that does its own purpose a disservice through caricature and oversimplification.

Miss Rand postulates an America in a time of waning strength and production. The government is being delivered into the hands of the "looters," despicable men whose plundering is rationalized by mouthing the concept that the fruits of the strong belong to the weak: from every man according to his ability, to every man according to his need. . . .

As the looters perpetrate increasingly repressive and senseless measures on the economy, chaos grows and the able men, frustrated at every turn, take to deserting their jobs and disappearing. Their establishment of a Shangri-la in the Colorado mountains is a neat but unconvincing aspect of a story that already has too little contact with reality.

For one tries in vain to project the world of **"Atlas Shrugged"** from the familiar world of contemporary America. There is no connecting link. On what grounds, for example, does Miss Rand postulate a failing economy?—the American economy today is booming. She does not say.

To be sure, her two types are familiar minorities at either end of the political scale, neither one of them as important as the great middle ground between. American political history is the history of struggle between individualism and the collective good, yet Miss Rand would, at the stroke of her wand, eliminate the whole area of working compromise, make an absolute of either extreme, and pit them against each other. It takes the heart out of her story.

Miss Rand properly condemns the whining mentality which demands handouts as its natural right. But she minimizes the philanthropy that is not a gesture of moral weakness but of strength; and she completely ignores the fact that brilliant intelligence and achievement may not always be accompanied by conscience, that the figures of the past whom she most admires have been called by others—and with reason—robber barons. . . .

Had Rearden and the other men of integrity in the book exercised their political responsibilities with the devotion which they gave to their jobs, whether industry, philosophy, or science, the looters would not have taken over. This is the drama that Miss Rand's melodramatic fabrications lack.

> *Ruth Chapin Blackman, "Controversial Books by Ayn Rand and Caitlin Thomas: 'Atlas Shrugged'," in* The Christian Science Monitor, *October 10, 1957, p. 13.*

GRANVILLE HICKS

["**Atlas Shrugged**"] comes among us as a demonstrative act rather than as a literary work. Its size seems an expression of the author's determination to crush the enemies of truth—her truth, of course—as a battering ram demolishes the walls of a hostile city. Not in any literary sense a serious novel, it is an earnest one, belligerent and unremitting in its earnestness. It howls in the reader's ear and beats him about the head in order to secure his attention, and then, when it has him subdued, harangues him for page upon page. It has only two moods, the melodramatic and the didactic, and in both it knows no bounds. (p. 4)

It would be pointless to discuss either the logic or the feasibility of the program Miss Rand so vehemently puts forth. What is important is the spirit in which the book is written. Like **"The Fountainhead," "Atlas Shrugged"** is a defense of and a tribute to the superior individual, who is, in Miss Rand's view, superior in every way—in body as well as mind and especially in his capacity for life. Its spirit, regardless of the specific doctrines it preaches, is calculated to appeal to those who feel that life could and should have more meaning than they have experienced.

Yet, loudly as Miss Rand proclaims her love of life, it seems clear that the book is written out of hate. (p. 5)

> *Granville Hicks "A Parable of Buried Talents," in* The New York Times Book Review, *October 13, 1957, pp. 4-5.*

HELEN BEAL WOODWARD

["**Atlas Shrugged**"] is the equivalent of a fifteenth-century morality play. Everyman, personified by Dagny Taggert, the strong-minded lady Operating Vice President of the Taggart Transcontinental Railroad, and by her lover, Hank Rearden, the steel tycoon, struggles against the forces of evil as represented by the bureaucrats, the scientists who sell their minds to the bureaucrats, and the craven businessmen who string along for fear of honest competition. What Hank and Dagny do not realize is that Evil seeks to destroy them precisely because they are strong and fearless. To outwit Evil the half-legendary hero John Galt cooks up an apocalyptic conspiracy, a "strike of the men of the mind." Hank and Dagny are saved, but not until by their own will they accept salvation.

The author challenges not only the concept of the welfare state but the whole Christian ethic of concern by the strong for the weak—challenges it, what's more, on the score of immorality and its tendency to sap the strong and corrode the human urge toward freedom. For readers willing to go the distance, to re-examine their own convictions, and to put up with the incidental tripe, "Atlas Shrugged" may well be worth wading through. There is no denying that it leaves a powerful, disturbing impression.

But as the shopwindow mannequin exists to display the mink stole, so the stylized vice-and-virtue characters of **"Atlas Shrugged"** serve as dummies on which to drape the author's ideas. . . .

Miss Rand also throws away her considerable gifts for writing by fixing her reader with a glittering eye and remorselessly impressing upon him her convictions. These range from a hatred of Robin Hood as "the most immoral and the most contemptible" of all human symbols to a belief in a kind of chrome-plated *laissez faire*. Much of it is persuasive. It is good to be reminded that achievement is more valuable than "adjustment"; that men have free will and rational minds; that they don't have to be ciphers or slatterns. . . . But Miss Rand is undone by her prolixity and her incontinence. She sets up one of the finest assortments of straw men ever demolished in print, and she cannot refrain from making her points over and over. . . .

The book is shot through with hatred. Miss Rand hates moralists and mystics and income taxes and the people who think that billboards deface scenery. She hates professors, "the soft, safe assassins of college classrooms," and evangelists who preach love and self-sacrifice. She hates Communism and (though she does not name it) Christianity. . . . She particularly hates altruists and bureaucrats; in fact, she envisions nothing less than the Armageddon of businessman and bureaucrat. (Interestingly enough her solution for the country's problems, pending Armageddon, is just such a solution as a nineteenth-century altruist would have doted on: a small, controlled utopia.) Altogether this is a strange, overwrought book. Take away the philosophical furbelows and what have you got? Something of a mystery, something of a thriller, but basically a great big non-stop day-dream. . . .

> Helen Beal Woodward, "Non-Stop Daydream," in The Saturday Review, New York, Vol. XL, No. 41, October 21, 1957, p. 25.

PATRICIA DONEGAN

Purporting to be a novel, *Atlas Shrugged* is a cumbersome, lumbering vehicle in which characterization, plot and reality are subordinated to the author's expression of a personal philosophy. The book is a point of view stated and restated so

often that even one who agreed with it would tire long before the book was completed.

Ayn Rand, whose last novel, **The Fountainhead,** was widely read fourteen years ago and was greeted with mixed reception from the critics, envisages a not-too-distant future in which society crumbles under the impact of the welfare state. Miss Rand, whose private obsession is private enterprise, has woven a story around this supposed disintegration. Several of her heroes, believing the society in which they live is a burden to them, systematically set out to help it destroy itself, thereby aiding the villains of the piece who by their insistence on government controls of business and welfare legislation are destroying it anyway. (pp. 155-56)

Miss Rand interrupts her story constantly to make speeches. (There is one which continues for sixty pages.) However, if one can stomach the speeches, there is a certain fascination in watching the author gleefully destroy the world. It is, to be sure, a morbid fascination, because whatever power Miss Rand has as a writer is expressed in an immense hostility, a real malevolence that takes joy in the sight of destruction.

Miss Rand's book is hardly acceptable as a novel and her premise proceeds from hate. She deplores the idea of Original Sin and considers "pity" immoral. Nowhere does she use the word "compassion." She envisages reward completely on the basis of merit, and this merit is judged only by intelligence and ability. . . . It is dispiriting to think of an outpouring of hate on this scale on any audience. (p. 156)

> Patricia Donegan, "A Point of View, in Commonweal, Vol. LXVII, No. 6, November 8, 1957, pp. 155-56.

GORE VIDAL

[*The following essay was originally published in* Esquire, *July, 1961.*]

Ayn Rand is a rhetorician who writes novels I have never been able to read. (p. 261)

This odd little woman is attempting to give a moral sanction to greed and self-interest, and to pull it off she must at times indulge in purest Orwellian newspeak of the "freedom is slavery" sort. . . . She has a great attraction for simple people who are puzzled by organized society, who object to paying taxes, who dislike the welfare state, who feel guilt at the thought of the suffering of others but who would like to harden their hearts. For them, she has an enticing prescription: altruism is the root of all evil, self-interest is the only good, and if you're dumb or incompetent that's your lookout.

She is fighting two battles. The first is against the idea of the state's being anything more than a police force and a judiciary to restrain people from stealing each other's money openly. She is in legitimate company here. But it is Miss Rand's second battle that is the moral one. She has declared war not only on [Karl] Marx but on Christ. Now, although my own enthusiasm for the various systems evolved in the names of those two figures is limited, I doubt if even the most anti-Christian free-thinker would want to deny the ethical value of Christ in the Gospels. To reject that Christ is to embark on dangerous waters indeed. For to justify and extol human greed and egotism is to my mind not only immoral but evil. For one thing, it is gratuitous to advise any human being to look out for himself. You can be sure that he will. It is far more difficult to persuade him to help his neighbor to build a dam or to defend a town or to give food he has accumulated to the victims of a famine. But since we must live together, dependent upon one another for many things and services, altruism is necessary to survival. To get people to do needed things is the perennial hard task of government, not to mention of religion and of philosophy. That it is right to help someone less fortunate is an idea which has figured in most systems of conduct since the beginning of the race. We often fail. That predatory demon "I" is difficult to contain, but until now we have all agreed that to help others is a right action. The dictionary definition of "moral" is "concerned with the distinction between right and wrong" as in "moral law, the requirements to which right action must conform." Though Miss Rand's grasp of logic is uncertain, she does realize that ot make even a modicum of sense she must change all the terms. Both Marx and Christ agree that in this life a right action is consideration for the welfare of others. In the one case it was through a state which was to wither away, in the other through the private exercise of the moral sense. Ayn Rand now tells us that what we have thought was right is really wrong. The lesson should have read: One for one and none for all. (pp. 262-64)

> Gore Vidal, *"Two Immoralists: Orville Prescott and Ayn Rand,"* in his Rocking the Boat, *Dell Publishing Co., Inc., 1963, pp. 257-64.**

NATHANIEL BRANDEN

The projection of "things as they might be and ought to be" names the essence of Ayn Rand's concept of literature. In the wave of Naturalism that has engulfed the literature of the twentieth century, her novels are an outstanding exception. They are at once a continuation of the Romantic tradition and a significant departure from the mainstream of that tradition: she is a *Romantic Realist*. "Romantic"—because her work is concerned with *values,* with the essential, the abstract, the universal in human life, and with the projection of man as a heroic being. "Realist"—because the values she selects pertain to this earth and to man's actual nature, and because the issues with which she deals are the crucial and fundamental ones of our age. Her novels do not represent a flight into mystical fantasy or the historical past or into concerns that have little if any bearing on man's actual existence. Her heroes are not knights, gladiators or adventurers in some impossible kingdom, but engineers, scientists, industrialists, men who belong on earth, men who function in modern society. As a philosopher, she has brought ethics into the context of reason, reality and man's life on earth; as a novelist, she has brought the dramatic, the exciting, the heroic, the stylized into the same context.

Just as in philosophy she rejects every version of the mystics' soul-body dichotomy: theory versus practice, thought versus action, morality versus happiness—so in literature she rejects the expression of this same dichotomy: the belief that a profound novel cannot be entertaining, and that an entertaining novel cannot be profound, that a serious, philosophical novel cannot have a dramatic plot, and that a dramatic plot-novel cannot possibly be serious or philosophical.

Atlas Shrugged—the greatest of her novels—is an action story on a grand scale, but it is a consciously philosophical action story, just as its heroes are consciously philosophical men of action. To those who subscribe to the soul-body dichotomy in literature, *Atlas Shrugged* is a mystifying anomaly that defies classification by conventional standards. It moves effortlessly

and ingeniously from economics to epistemology to morality to metaphysics to psychology to the theory of sex, on the one hand—and, on the other, it has a chapter that ends with the heroine hurtling toward the earth in an airplane with a dead motor, it has playboy crusader who blows up a multi-billion-dollar industry, a philosopher-turned-pirate who attacks government relief ships, and a climax that involves the rescue of the hero from a torture chamber. Notwithstanding the austere solemnity of its abstract theme, her novel—as a work of art—projects the laughing, extravagantly imaginative virtuosity of a mind who has never heard that "one is not supposed" to combine such elements as these in a single book. (pp. 88-9)

[Each of Rand's four novels] has a major philosophical theme. Yet they are not "propaganda novels." The primary purpose for which these books were written was not the philosophical conversion of their readers. The primary purpose was to project and make real the characters who are the books' heroes. *This* is the motive that unites the artist and the moralist. The desire to project the ideal man, led to the writing of novels. The necessity of defining the premises that make an ideal man possible, led to the formulating of the philosophical content of those novels. (p. 89)

In the novels of Ayn Rand, the sense of life projected is conscious, deliberate, explicit and philosophically implemented. It is as unique and unprecedented in literature as the premises from which it proceeds. It is a sense of life untouched by tragedy, untouched by any implication of metaphysical catastrophe or doom. Its essence is an unclouded and exaltedly benevolent view of existence, the sense of a universe in which man *belongs,* a universe in which triumph, enjoyment and fulfillment are possible—although not guaranteed—to man, and are to be achieved by the efficacy of his own effort.

No matter how terrible their struggle, no matter how difficult the obstacles they encounter, the basic sense of life of Ayn Rand's heroes—as of the novels—is indestructibly affirmative and triumphant. Whether the characters achieve victory or, as in *We the Living,* suffer defeat, they do not regard pain and disaster as the normal, as the inevitable, but always as the abnormal, the exceptional, the *unnatural.*

Ayn Rand shares with the Romantic novelists of the nineteenth century the view of man as a being of free will, a being who is moved and whose course is determined, not by fate or the gods or the irresistible power of "tragic flaws," but by the *values* he has *chosen.* (pp. 92-3)

Romanticism was a literary school whose authors discarded the role of transcriber and assumed the role of creator. For the first time in literary history, a sharp line was drawn between fiction and journalism, between artistic creation and historical reporting. The Romantic novelists did not make it their goal to record that which *had* happened, but to project that which *ought* to happen. They did not take the things man had done as the given, as the unalterable material of existence, like facts of physical nature, but undertook to project the things that men should *choose* to do. (p. 94)

Naturalism—the literary counter-revolution against Romanticism—was a regression to a pre-Romantic view of man, to a view lower than that against which the Romanticists had rebelled. It was Naturalism that reintroduced the "fate" motif into literature, and once more presented man as the helpless plaything of irresistible forces. (p. 95)

Today, the Romantic method of writing has been all but forgotten. Many commentators speak as if it were an axiom that all fiction is to be judged by the canons of Naturalism, as if no other school had ever existed. In their view—and by their sense of life—to project man as a being moved by his chosen values, and to show him at his heroic potential, is "unrealistic." Only the helpless, the passive, the sordid, the depraved are "real."

If Romanticism was defeated by the fact that its values were removed from this world, the alternative offered by Naturalism was to remove values from literature. The result today is an esthetic vacuum, left by the historical implication that men's only choice is between artistic projections of near-fantasy—or Sunday supplement exposés, gossip columns and psychological case-histories parading as novels.

It is against the background of the despair, the exhausted cynicism and the unremitting drabness that have settled over contemporary literature, that the novels of Ayn Rand have appeared.

Ayn Rand has brought values back to literature—and back *to this earth*. She has chosen to write about the most fundamental and urgent issues of our age, and to use them as the material of Romantic art. In her novels, the ruling values *are* applicable to reality, they *can* be practiced, they *can* serve as man's guide to success and happiness. As a result, her heroes predominantly *win* their battles, they *achieve* their goals, they succeed *practically* and in their own lives. ***Anthem, The Fountainhead*** and ***Atlas Shrugged*** do not end with heroic death, but with heroic victory. (p. 97)

[Ayn Rand] does not face man with the camera of a photographer as her tool, but with the chisel of a sculptor. Howard Roark, Hank Rearden, Francisco d'Anconia and John Galt are not statistical composites of men "as they are." They are projections of man as he might be and ought to be; they are projections of the human *potential*. (p. 98)

Whether she is presenting a Howard Roark or a Peter Keating, a John Galt or a Wesley Mouch, the principle of characterization is the same: to present a character by means of essentials, that is, to focus on the actions and attributes which reflect the character's basic values and premises—the values and premises that motivate him and direct his crucial choices. A successful characterization is one which makes a man distinguishable from all other men, and makes the causes of his actions intelligible. To characterize by essentials is to focus on the universal—to omit the accidental, the irrelevant, the trivial, the contingent. . . . (pp. 98-9)

To write and to characterize by means of essentials requires that one know what *is* essential and what is derivative, what is a cause and what is a consequence. It is by identifying causes that one arrives at basic principles. No such understanding is required by the Naturalist method of characterization. (p. 101)

Once, after having delivered an address to members of the publishing profession, Ayn Rand was asked: "What are the three most important elements in a novel?" She answered: "Plot—plot—and plot." The most beautifully written novel that lacks a plot, she has remarked, is like a superbly outfitted automobile that lacks a motor.

Plot . . . is central and basic to the Romantic novel; it proceeds from the concept of man as a being of free will who must choose his values and struggle to achieve them. . . . Either a man achieves his values and goals or he is defeated; in a novel,

the manner in which this issue is resolved constitutes the *climax*. Thus, plot is not, as the Naturalists have contended, an "artificial contrivance" that belies the actual facts of reality and the nature of human life. Plot is *the abstraction of man's relation to existence*. (pp. 105-06)

Purpose is the ruling principle in [Ayn Rand's] novels, in two basic respects. First, all the characters are motivated by their purposes, by the goals they are seeking to achieve, and the events of the novel dramatize the conflicts of these purposes. Second, the *author* is purposeful, that is, every event, every character and every adjective is selected by the standard of the logical requirements of the novel; nothing is accidental and nothing is included for reasons extrinsic to the needs of the plot and the theme. (p. 106)

In contradistinction to the typical philosophical novel, such as, for instance, Thomas Mann's *The Magic Mountain,* the characters in Ayn Rand's books who hold opposing views do not merely sit on verandas or on mountain tops and debate or argue their theoretical convictions, while all action is suspended. Every idea, every issue and every intellectual conflict in these novels is *dramatized*—that is, presented in terms of *action,* in terms of the practical consequences to which it leads. (p. 107)

The ingenuity and artistry of Ayn Rand as a plot-writer lie in the nature of the situations she creates, in her sense of drama and conflict, and in her matchless integration of philosophy and action.

Consider the basic plot-situation in **We the Living.** In order to obtain money to send Leo Kovalensky, the man she loves, to a tuberculosis sanitarium, Kira Argounova becomes the mistress of Andrei Taganov, an idealistic communist. Neither man knows of Kira's relationship with the other; and both men hate each other; Leo is an aristocrat—Andrei, a member of the Soviet secret police.

Now, the situation of a woman forced to sleep with a man she does not love, in order to save the life of the man she does love, is not new. . . . The originality of Ayn Rand's treatment of the subject—from the point of view of plot—is in the way she intensifies the conflict and makes it more complex. . . . [In] **We the Living,** Andrei is *not* a villain; he is profoundly in love with Kira and believes that she is in love with him; he does not know of her love for Leo. And Kira does *not* despise him; increasingly she comes to respect him. At the start of their affair, she had acted in desperation, knowing this was her only chance to save Leo and knowing that Andrei had helped to establish the system that forced such an action upon her; but as their relationship progresses, as Andrei finds the first happiness he has ever known, he begins to understand the importance of an individual life—and begins to doubt the ideals for which he has fought. And thus the conflicts involved—and the suspense about what will happen when the two men find out about each other—are brought to the highest intensity. (pp. 108-09)

In presenting the evil of dictatorship, Ayn Rand does not focus primarily on the aspect of physical brutality and horror—on the concentration camps, the executions without trial, the firing squads and the torture chambers. These elements are present in **We the Living** only in the background. Had these horrors been the *primary* focus, the impact would be less profound—because violence and bloodshed necessarily suggest a state of *emergency,* of the *temporary.* Ayn Rand achieves a far more devastating indictment of dictatorship by focusing on the "normal" *daily* conditions of existence. . . . (p. 109)

Another crucial element contributing to the power of Ayn Rand's indictment of collectivism is the fact that she presents Andrei *sympathetically;* he is not the worst representative of the system, but the best—the most idealistic and sincere. And that is why—as the events of the novel demonstrate with inexorable logic—he is as inevitably doomed to destruction as Kira and Leo. It is his *virtues* that make his survival impossible. (p. 110)

One of the most impressive examples of Ayn Rand's power as a plot-writer is the climax of *The Fountainhead.* (p. 113)

Roark's dynamiting of Cortlandt, and the events to which this leads, integrate the conflicts of the leading characters into a final focus of violent intensity, maximizing the philosophical values and issues at stake. The climax involves each of these characters intimately and, in accordance with the logic of the basic course the characters have chosen, brings each of them to victory or defeat.

Philosophically, the climax dramatizes the central theme of the book: individualism versus collectivism—the rights of the individual versus the claims of the collective. It dramatizes the role of the creator in human society and the manner in which the morality of altruism victimizes him. It dramatizes the fact that human survival is made possible by the men who think and produce, not by those who imitate and borrow—by the creators, not the second-handers—by the Roarks, not the Keatings. (p. 116)

When one reads Ayn Rand's novels in the order in which they were written, one is struck by the enormous artistic and philosophical growth from novel to novel. All the basic elements of her literary method are present from the beginning in *We the Living,* as are, implicitly, the basic elements of her philosophy. But each work is a richer and fuller expression of those elements, a more accomplished implementation, in a startlingly new and different form.

Just as, within each novel, the climax sums up and dramatizes the meaning of all the preceding events, raised to the highest peak of emotional and intellectual intensity—so, as a total work, *Atlas Shrugged* is the artistic and philosophical climax of *all* of Ayn Rand's novels, bringing the full of her dramatic, stylistic and intellectual power to its most consummate expression.

Ayn Rand has proudly referred to *Atlas Shrugged* as a "stunt novel"—proudly, because she has made the word "stunt" applicable on so high a level. By the standard of sheer originality, the idea of a novel about the minds of the world going on strike is as magnificent a plot-theme as any that could be conceived. If Ayn Rand has scorned the Naturalists who write about the people and events next door, if she has declared that the purpose of art is to project, not the usual, but the *unusual,* not the boring and the conventional, but the exciting, the dramatic, the unexpected, the rationally desirable yet the astonishingly new—then she is, pre-eminently, a writer who practices what she preaches.

Atlas Shrugged is a mystery story, "not about the murder of a man's body, but about the murder—and rebirth—of man's spirit." The reader is presented with a series of events that, in the beginning, appear incomprehensible: the world seems to be moving toward destruction, in a manner no one can identify, and for reasons no one can understand. (pp. 118-19)

There are no "red herrings" in the story, no false clues. But the mystery is to be solved by *philosophical* detection—by identifying the philosophical implications of the evidence that is presented. When the reader is finally led to the solution, the meaning and inescapable necessity of all the things he has been shown seems, in retrospect, simple and self-evident.

It is epistemologically significant that *Atlas Shrugged* is written in the form of a mystery. This is consistent with the philosophy it propounds. The reader is not given arbitrary assertions to be taken on faith; he is given the facts and the evidence; his own mind is challenged to interpret that evidence; he is placed, in effect, in the position of the people in the novel, who observe the events around them, struggle to understand their cause and meaning, and are told the full truth only when they have seen sufficient evidence to form a reasoned judgment.

The most impressive feature of *Atlas Shrugged* is its integration. The novel presents the essentials of an entire philosophical system: epistemology, metaphysics, ethics, politics (and psychology). It shows the interrelation of these subjects in business, in a man's attitude toward his work, in love, in family relationships, in the press, in the universities, in economics, in art, in foreign relations, in science, in government, in sex. It presents a unified and comprehensive view of man and of man's relationship to existence. If one were to consider the ideas alone, apart from the novel in which they appear, the integration of so complex a philosophical system would be an extraordinarily impressive achievement. But when one considers that all of these philosophical issues are dramatized through a logically connected series of events involving a whole society, the feat of integration is breathtaking.

If one were told that an author proposed to dramatize, in a novel, the importance of recognizing the ontological status of the law of identity—one could not be blamed for being skeptical. But it is of such startling dramatizations that the virtuosity of *Atlas Shrugged* is made. (pp. 119-20)

Tremendously complex in its structure, presenting the collapse of an entire society, the novel involves the lives, actions and goals of dozens of characters. . . . Yet every character, action and event has a dramatic and philosophical purpose; all are tied to the central situation and all are integrated with one another; nothing is superfluous, nothing is arbitrary and nothing is accidental; as the story moves forward, it projects, above all, the quality of the implacably, the irresistibly logical. (p. 121)

The climax of *Atlas Shrugged* is singularly typical of the spirit of the novel as a whole: the integration of the unexpected and the utterly logical—of that which starts by appearing shocking and ends by appearing self-evident. One reader has described *Atlas Shrugged* as having the quality of "cosmic humor." It is written from the perspective of a mind that has discarded the conventional categories, standards and frame of reference—and has looked at reality with a fresh glance. (p. 126)

No other climax could sum up so eloquently the thesis and the meaning of *Atlas Shrugged.* The men of ability have all gone on strike, the world is in ruins, and the government officials make a last grotesque effort to preserve their system: they torture Galt to force him to join them and save their system *somehow.* They order him to *think.* They *command* him to take control. Naked force—seeking to compel a mind to function. And then the ultimate absurdity of their position is thrown in the torturers' faces: they are using an electric machine to torture Galt, and its generator breaks down; the brute who is operating the machine does not know how to repair it; neither do the officials; Galt lifts his head and contemptuously tells them how to repair it.

The brute runs away in horror—at the realization that they need Galt's help even to torture him. The officials flee the cellar also—"the cellar where the living generator was left tied by the side of the dead one." (pp. 126-27)

There are persons to whom clarity and precision are the enemies of poetry and emotion; they equate the artistic with the fuzzy, the vague and the diffuse. Seeking in art the reflection and confirmation of their sense of life, they are psychologically and esthetically at home only with the blurred and the indeterminate: that which is sharply in focus, clashes with their own mental state. In such persons, Ayn Rand's literary style will invoke a feeling of disquietude and resentment; Ayn Rand's use of language is best characterized by a line concerning Dagny Taggart: "she had regarded language as a tool of honor, always to be used as if one were under oath—an oath of allegiance to reality and to respect for human beings." Because her writing is lucid, such persons will tell themselves that it is crude; because her writing conveys an unequivocal meaning, and does not suggest a "mobile" to be interpreted by the subjective whim of any reader, they will tell themselves that it lacks poetry; because her writing demands that they be conscious when they read it, they will tell themselves that it is not art.

But the specific trademark of her literary style is its power vividly to re-create sensory reality and inner psychological states, to induce the most intense emotions—and to accomplish this by means of the most calculated selection of words, images and events, giving to logic a poetry it had never had before, and to poetry a logic it had never had before. (p. 129)

In *Atlas Shrugged,* Ayn Rand has created more than a great novel. By any rational, objective literary standard—from the standpoint of plot-structure, suspense, drama, imaginativeness, characterization, evocative and communicative use of language, originality, scope of theme and subject, psychological profundity and philosophical richness—*Atlas Shrugged* is the climax of the novel form, carrying that form to unprecedented heights of intellectual and artistic power. (p. 140)

Just as in philosophy Ayn Rand has challenged the modern doctrines of neo-mysticism and epistemological agnosticism, so in literature she has challenged the view of man as an impotent zombie without intellect, efficacy or self-esteem. Just as she has opposed the fashionable philosophical dogmas of fatalism, determinism and man's metaphysical passivity, so she has opposed the fashionable literary projections of man as a stuporous puppet manipulated by instinct and socio-economic status. Just as she has rejected the mystics' theories of Original Sin, of man's depravity and the misery of life on earth, so she has rejected the presentations of unfocused, whim-worshipping neurotics staggering along a trail of hysterical destruction to the abyss of whimpering defeat. Just as she has rescued philosophy from the cult of the anti-mind and the anti-man, so she has rescued literature from the cult of the anti-novel and the anti-hero. As an artist, she has brought men a new sense of life. As a philosopher, she has brought them the intellectual implementation of that sense of life: she has shown what it depends upon and how it is to be earned.

When one considers the quality of enraptured idealism that dominates her work, and the affirmative view of the human potential that she projects, the most morally corrupt of the attacks leveled against her—and the most psychologically revealing—is the assertion that she is "motivated by a hatred of humanity."

It is culturally significant that writers who present dope addicts and psychopaths as their image of human nature, are *not* accused of "hatred for humanity"—but a writer who presents men of integrity and genius as her image of human nature, *is.*

In Ayn Rand's novels, the heroes, the men of outstanding moral character and intellectual ability, are exalted; the men of conscientious honesty and average ability are treated with respect and sympathy—a far more profound respect and sympathy, it is worth adding, than they have ever been accorded in any "humanitarian" novel. There is only one class of men who receive moral condemnation: the men who demand any form of the unearned, in matter or in spirit; who propose to treat other men as sacrificial animals; who claim the right to rule others by physical force. Is it her implacable sense of justice—her loyalty to those who are *not* evil—her concern for the morally innocent and her contempt for the morally guilty—that makes Ayn Rand a "hater of humanity?" If those who charge Ayn Rand with "hatred," feeling themselves to be its object, choose to identify and classify themselves with the men she condemns—doubtless they know best. But then it is not Ayn Rand—or humanity—whom they have damned. (pp. 141-42)

The most tragic victims of the man-degrading nature of contemporary literature are the young. They have watched the progression from the boredom of conventional Naturalism to the horror of nightmare Symbolism—the progression from stories about the folks next door to stories about the dipsomaniac next door, the crippled dwarf next door, the axe-murderer next door, the psychotic next door. *This,* they are now informed, is what life is *"really"* like.

In projecting the artist's view of man's metaphysical relationship to existence, art explicitly or implicitly holds up to man the value-goals of life: it shows him what is possible and what is worth striving for. It can tell him that he is doomed and that *nothing* is worth striving for—or it can show him the life of a Howard Roark or a John Galt. It is particularly when one is young, when one is still forming one's soul, that one desperately needs—as example, as inspiration, as fuel, as antidote to the sight of the world around one—the vision of life as it might and ought to be, the vision of heroes fighting for values worth achieving in a universe where achievement is possible. It is not *descriptions* of the people next door that a young person requires, but an *escape* from the people next door—to a wider view of the human potentiality. This is what the young have found in the novels of Ayn Rand—and that is the key to the enormous popularity of her novels. (pp. 143-44)

> *Nathaniel Branden, in his* Who Is Ayn Rand?: An Analysis of the Novels of Ayn Rand, *Random House, 1962, 239 p.*

BRUCE COOK

Miss Rand is a profoundly poor writer. To say that her plots are absurdly tendentious, her characters no more than wooden puppets, and her diction utterly without grace or beauty (all of which is quite true) is to give no real idea of the quality of her novels. They are *completely* bad, from conception to expression.

All her writing might quite properly be called fantastic. It is not simply that two of her four novels deal with the future, . . . but rather an atmosphere common to all which is so charged with unreality that it reminds us of nothing quite so much as the dream world of a child. . . .

[Her] opinion of contemporary fiction is so low . . . that she clearly feels herself uninfluenced by it. And quite rightly, too. Her own writing seems totally free of any realization of the terrifying complexity of the individual soul and the world in which it exists. Such realization, when truly achieved, has rendered many of our finest writers all but mute. Where others falter, more or less intimidated by what they perceive in and around them, Miss Rand forges ahead, bursting with rhetoric and brimming with assurance. To read Ayn Rand and compare her with even the better American writers is to be rather painfully reminded of [William Butler] Yeats's description of our predicament where: "The best lack of conviction while the worst / Are full of passionate intensity." (p. 122)

My point here is that the literary quality of her work can be discussed intelligently and in about the same way that we might any other writer's—but only until we open a book of hers and begin to read. . . . Apart from the obvious and dreary sameness of the language in which [she describes three of her heroes] . . . (her prose strikes as precarious balance between fake-biblical and Faith Baldwin), there is an almost identical similarity in the conception of these three. Each of them—Howard Roark of *The Fountainhead*, Leo Kovalensky of *We the Living*, and John Galt in *Atlas Shrugged*—is idealized and exalted to the point where he simply does not exist on a recognizably human level.

What she has created are fantasy men, just the sort she dreamed of as a twelve-year-old, men with qualities and abilities no real man could ever possess. Their function in the Rand cosmos is to provide suitably fantastic solutions to [the] crucial and fundamental issues of our age mentioned by Mr. Branden [see essay above]. Such simplicity and forthrightness as Miss Rand's Objectivist heroes show does, of course, have a certain appeal, but it is an appeal to the ignorant, to those who may not yet have learned, or who may be unwilling to recognize, the complexity of life.

No less a product of her childhood fantasies than the heroes she created, her philosophy seeks to remove all limits and checks which may be put upon the exceptional individual by society and government. As presented in her novels Objectivism seems to be a sort of Nietzscheism-gone-rabid. Her heroes struggle mightily against every sort of restraint—morality, public opinion, the law. Whatever impedes them in their drive toward self-realization must be swept aside. . . . They will, Miss Rand makes it clear, stop at nothing to have their way. Their motto is the oath administered by Galt to all his followers: "I swear—by my life and my love of it—that I will never live for the sake of another, nor ask another man to live for mine."

Just how *much* freedom does Ayn Rand seek for her Objectivist heroes? What may look like a moral question is just as much a political and economic one, for, as it happens, most of her heroes are businessmen of one kind or another. And the freedom she urges—or rather, *demands*—for them she tends to equate with the freedom to earn. . . . [We] see that in spite of her own contempt for religion and all things "mystical," she herself regards Objectivism as a sort of religion of finance. And this faith that she expounds with such missionary zeal, the one that has lately attracted so many converts, is really nothing more than a religion for the godless. Far from frightening adherents away, it is because of its religious quality in

particular that Objectivism has had so wide an appeal. (pp. 122-24)

Ayn Rand makes a very broad and very effective appeal. What she sets before [her followers] is a religion of self-love and self-advancement. It is mystique which may ultimately prove more attractive than that tired old Norse paganism revived by Paul Joseph Goebbels.

Ayn Rand has already been called a "New Messiah" . . . , but the role of propagandist and evangelist in which she has cast herself seems less that of Messiah than of a John the Baptist. The woman keeps howling and bleating for One to Come. God forbid that she should find her Promised One. (p. 124)

> Bruce Cook, "Ayn Rand: A Voice in the Wilderness," in Catholic World, Vol. 201, No. 1202, May, 1965, pp. 119-24.

GERALD RAFTERY

A surprising favorite among the high-school taste-makers is Ayn Rand's **"Anthem"** . . . , which is set in the far distant future and is remarkably free of its author's murky economics. Written nearly 30 years ago and published in hard cover about 10 years later, it enlarges upon ideas which are expressed in [H. G. Wells's] "The Time Machine" and implied in [Aldous Huxley's] "Brave New World"; it might almost be an extrapolation of [George Orwell's] "1984"—say, into 2084. The final scene depicts the hero, who has escaped from a deteriorated ant-like culture, vowing to restore the vanished technical civilization of our times and adopting as his motto the one word "Ego." This is somewhat more attractive than Miss Rand's current philosophy, which she expresses with the lapel emblem of a dollar sign. (p. 16)

> Gerald Raftery, "High-School Favorites," in The New York Times Book Review, Part II, February 27, 1966, pp. 14, 16.*

PHILIP GORDON

Throughout her long career as popular author and philosophizer, Ayn Rand has concentrated on her individualist-heroes to formulate from their absolute dedication to their own self-interests the model for all mankind. In contrast to those who have seen in the economic crises of the twentieth century the waste of capitalism, Rand, obsessed with the fear of collectivist association, has seen universal salvation possible only through even more intensive laissez-faire capitalism. In so far as exposing Rand's politics to a more enlightened historical awareness would be like smashing a pea with a hammer, this brief study suggests instead some intersections of Rand's fiction-tracts and popular culture in an attempt to explain the nature of her enormous appeal. While providing an ever-increasing audience with the soothing rationalization of self-primacy, all of Rand's works, but particularly *The Fountainhead* (1943) expose the sharpness of the familiar line drawn between *self* and *other;* and thus she challenges us to recognize that the society which does not encourage individualism invites a tyranny of bland mediocrity. (p. 701)

In the thirties, when American capitalism's breakdown was so conspicuous and its breakup so urgent, Rand's overwhelming fear of anything collective harmonized with the American myth of rugged individualism, and her fiction assumed a prophetic air. In her second novel, *Anthem* (1938), Rand created a science-fictional scenario of "total collectivism with all of its ultimate consequences; men have relapsed into primitive savagery and stagnation; the word *I* has vanished from the human language, there are no singular pronouns, a man refers to himself as *we* and to another man as *they*." To combat that absolute lack of individuality, Rand's new heroes operate with an absolute lack of flexibility. Crucial discoveries, of man and nature, can only be made by "a man of intransigent mind," whose theme, to be sung in Rand's subsequent novels of "rational self-interest," is typically simplistic: "Many words have been granted to me," *Anthem*'s hero proclaims, "and some are wise, and some are false, but only three are holy: 'I will it.'" Rand's sacred word is unmistakably "EGO." (pp. 701-02)

Rand has steadfastly avoided psychological terminology and formulations, offering instead the "philosophy of rational self-interest" as a prescription for the individualist in twentieth-century America. . . . Rand argues for a purely competitive world in which the best would always rise to the top. Indeed, it seems un-American to doubt the notion, "why not the best?" But, of course, under every individual capitalist's success lies the exploited working class—a state of relations which can only increase mutual hostility, even if sublimated in liberal rhetoric and rationalistic narcissim falsely promising equal opportunity. Not coincidentally, in constructing her idealized heroes, Rand has tapped the traditional justification of bourgeois individualism and, hence, of hostility toward all others: *they're out to get you.* (p. 702)

Rand's reductive, linear absolutism taps the popular mind anxious to live mythically, in black and white polarities, ignorant of the contradictions inherent in the worship of old possibilities and ahistorical directions.

In her major work, *The Fountainhead*, Rand dramatizes the struggle of an individual to maintain his integrity and not to give in to others' interests. . . . Beginning with her early works, Rand has been consistent in her commitment to the primacy of self, "that man exists for his own sake, that the pursuit of his own happiness is his highest moral purpose, that he must not sacrifice himself to others, nor others to himself." Rand makes Howard Roark, protagonist of *The Fountainhead,* an architect whose profession perfectly blends individual artistic creation with social utilization. To be constructed and used, Roark's buildings must depend on others besides himself. Although he acknowledges the importance of the ultimate occupation of his buildings, his exclusive concern is with his individual creative act and its product. . . . Roark does not mention the needs of the occupier, nor does his sense of aesthetics involve taking notice of the shape of the community. In addition to organizing the building materials, the architect organizes the inhabitants' lives within the structures, as well as organizing their perspectives on the world outside.

These are very definitely not the concerns of Rand when she isolates Roark in a shell of introverted self-expression, and provides him with a rationalization called "integrity." . . . Rand's use of "integrity" is surely based on the second definition in the *Oxford English Dictionary:* unimpaired or uncorrupted state, original perfect condition; and perhaps even the obsolete usage meaning sinlessness. No wonder the boundaries must be fenced, reinforced, and patrolled. If the behemoth's condition is threatened by the corrupt "hordes of envious mediocrities"—then Rand condones Any protective action, whatever the cost. When his own housing project is about to

be completed with some modifications he does not approve, Roark destroys his creation—better purity in others' homelessness than corruption of his aesthetics.

Violence, as *strong* action, finds ample rationalization. Never mind that a basic principle of Rand's Objectivist philosophy is the prohibition of the initial use of physical force against others: to the ideal man, any attempt to thwart his will justifies any response. (pp. 703-04)

[Rather] than conceive of reason as a historical tool, one which helps clarify the intricate relationships between individuals and society, Rand emphasizes reason as the justification and expression of the pure pursuit of individualist domination. Like many other moral systematists, Rand believes arrogantly in her own infallibility. Is it a surprise that her favorite modern novelist is Mickey Spillane, whose hero, Mike Hammer, never requiring proof beyond his own personal judgment, metes out justice immediately, lethally and illegally?

In creating her psychically stiff heroes, Rand presents nothing new with which to penetrate the legitimate and salient deliberation regarding connections of self to others. She has neither come to terms with Freud's tripartite scheme of id, ego, and super-ego (which might have helped in making a "rational" case of Roark) nor operated on the previous conflict-construct of conscious and unconscious mind. . . . Rand concedes that "man is born with certain physical and psychological needs, but he can neither discover them nor satisfy them without the use of his mind. . . . His so-called urges will not tell him what to do." (pp.707-08)

Rand proposes that we need to create a society which will foster individualists of the Howard Roark strength and type. . . . Erecting starkly simplistic frameworks highly antagonistic to her own views, Rand winds the key in her heroes' backs, and then commands them in rigid opposition. In *Anthem* the futuristic world of self-denial prevails, and in *The Fountainhead* a collectivist rat-race locks everyone's focus into conformity with each other's image of each other. In either situation, Rand's solution is an amalgamation of a new capitalism and a new intellectualism, a program she develops more fully in her later novel, *Atlas Shrugged* (1957). (pp. 708-09)

Finally, let us consider how Rand occasionally tries to humanize her heroes, for example when Roark admits how difficult it is to be so great. Unintentionally, Rand has divulged here the essential flaw of her ideal, rational man: that to consider oneself so great, to be obsessed with one's individual substance, *must* entail being against others, and thus invites the conceit that, alas, no one else can be his equal. Self means division, and division means superiority-inferiority hierarchies. This is the junction at which all of Rand's roads—the reality principle, the violent interpersonal domination, the extroflection, and the "objective rationalization"—converge and lead to exactly what her hated *collectivists* propose as their final solution, a ruling elite. Seemingly antagonistic, Toohey, *The Fountainhead*'s collectivist, and Roark, the individualist, in fact imply the same social, political, and intellectual control, just as the Soviet Union (increasingly) and the United States are both monopoly capitalistic societies, one through state collectivism and the other through private enterprise. These, among other glaring ironies, Ayn Rand does not seem to recognize. (p. 709)

Philip Gordon, "The Extroflective Hero: A Look at Ayn Rand," in Journal of Popular Culture, *Vol. X, No. 4, Spring, 1977, pp. 701-10.*

MIMI R. GLADSTEIN

[*Atlas Shrugged*] is not generally considered to be philosophically feminist. In fact, it may not be on anyone's reading list for Women's Courses, except mine. But close analysis of the book's themes and theories will prove that it should be. Much that Rand says is relevant to feminist issues. Best of all, the novel has a protagonist who is a good example of a woman who is active, assertive, successful, and still retains the love and sexual admiration of three heroic men. Though the situation is highly romantic, and science fiction to boot, how refreshing it is to find a female protagonist in American Fiction who emerges triumphant. (p. 681)

The refrain of *Atlas Shrugged* is John Galt's oath, "I swear by my life and my love of it that I will never live for the sake of another man [person] nor ask another man [person] to live for mine." (For purposes of this paper I will feminize or neuter all masculine nouns and pronouns. Though Ms. Rand refers to men and mankind, she obviously means humankind as evidenced in the rest of this study.) While the context of the oath is economic, the message is the same one advanced by feminists that no woman should live her life for or through others, as women have traditionally been encouraged to do. Typical of the studies that touch upon this issue is Edith de Rham's *The Love Fraud*. In her attack on "the staggering waste of education and talent among American Women," de Rham argues that by persuading women to concentrate their lives on men who in turn concentrate on work "Women become victims of a kind of fraud in which their love is exploited and in which they are somehow persuaded that they are involved in legitimate action." It is just this kind of exploitation that Ayn Rand deplores.

Whereas de Rham calls it *The Love Fraud*, Rand calls it self-sacrifice or altruism. Rand's attack on altruism, which is defined as an ethical principle that "holds that one must make the welfare of others one's primary moral concern and must place their interests above one's own . . . that service to others is the moral justification of one's existence, that self-sacrifice is one's foremost duty and highest virtue" is especially relevant to women because they have been the chief internalizers of this concept. This concept of self-sacrifice has encouraged women to view themselves as sacrificial animals whose desires and talents are forfeited for the good of children, family and society. This negative behavior produces looters, moochers, leeches, and parasites in Rand's vernacular. Women have been socialized to feel guilty if they fail to carry out the practice of sacrificing their careers for the advancement of others, whether it be husband, family or simply a matter of vacating a position to a more needy male. And this sacrificing of a woman's abilities and potential is not viewed with horror or outrage, but rather with acceptance, while a similar male sacrifice is seen as a great tragedy or waste. Of course, Rand rejects any sacrifice as negative because she sees it as the surrender of a greater value for the sake of a lesser one or for the sake of a nonvalue. (pp. 682-83)

Galt, Rand's spokesperson, does not believe happiness is to be achieved through the sacrifice of one's values; he believes instead that "Woman has to be woman, she has to hold her life as a value, she has to learn to sustain it, she has to discover the values it requires and practice her virtues. . . . Happiness is that state of consciousness which proceeds from the achievement of one's values." What could be more relevant to feminism?

The nature of male/female relationships is another important area of philosophical exploration for Rand. Through Dagny's associations with Francisco D'Anconia, Hank Rearden and John Galt, Rand illustrates what a relationship between two self-actualized, equal human beings can be. In such relationships, Rand denies the existence of a split between the physical and the mental, the desires of the flesh and the longings of the spirit. (pp. 683-84)

According to [Rand's] philosophy, the object of a person's desires is a reflection of one's image of self. In the novel, Dagny—our positive protagonist—uses this fact as a standard of measuring others. Since Hank Rearden is capable of wanting her, he must be worthy of her. As she puts it, "I feel that others live up to me, if they want me." . . . In this context, also, if one desires a person, one also prizes everything that person is and stands for. . . . Within this framework, the act of sexual intercourse possesses special meaning. It is a joyous affirmation of one's life, of one's beliefs, of all that one is. Dagny realizes this after her first sexual encounter with Francisco. . . . Dagny picks sexual partners who affirm her and affirm life. (p. 684)

Though Rand stresses the primacy of individual action and responsibility, she does not exclude the importance of sisterhood. It is simply that Rand sees the development of *individual* strength as primary. When Cherryl Taggart, in desperation, turns to Dagny for help, Dagny's response to Cherryl's uncertain approach is the affirmative, "We're sisters, aren't we?" . . . Dagny stresses the fact that her offer of help is not a charitable act, but a recognition of Cherryl's essential worth. She invites Cherryl to stay with her and even elicits a promise that Cherryl will return. Still, though the sisterhood is warming, it is not enough to save Cherryl, for she has not developed enough strength to cope with the horror of her situation.

The Utopia of the novel, Galt's Gulch, is inhabited by people whose behavior and ideals Ayn Rand admires. They are people who are engaged in positive and productive endeavors and the woman who chooses motherhood is deliberately included. Dagny reflects on the joyous results of such choice, two eager and friendly children.

But domestic duties are not solely the realm of women in Galt's Gulch. Various of the male inhabitants are seen cooking, cleaning, and serving. When Dagny does housework, she is paid for her contribution.

In full honesty, there are attitudes toward women and femininity in the novel that are offensive, but they are few and are heavily outweighed by the positive aspects. Most significantly, for our purposes, Dagny Taggart is an affirmative role model. She is the head of a railroad. She has sexual relationships with three men and retains their love and respect. She is not demeaned or punished for her emancipation, sexual or professional. She has no intention of giving up her railroad for the man she loves. She retains them both. She behaves according to her code of ethics and is not punished by God or society. She is that rarity in American fiction—a heroine who not only survives, but prevails. (p. 685)

Mimi R. Gladstein, "Ayn Rand and Feminism: An Unlikely Alliance," in College English, *Vol. 39, No. 6, February, 1978, pp. 680-85.*

KEVIN McGANN

The Fountainhead (1943), railed against the dragon forces of boorish "collectivisim" and conventional aesthetic standards in *this* country as concerned citizen Rand determined to save America from "dying." . . . (p. 325)

Howard Roark, an architect-genius, persists in designing great buildings without sacrificing an inch of his integrity to the inevitably compromising demands of professional peers, opinion-makers, the public taste, and his clients. . . . Throughout the book he is implicitly compared with pusillanimous Peter Keating, college roommate and then fellow architect, whose overriding desire for commercial success makes him willing to accommodate anyone who promises to further his career.

The general principle upon which the book is based—that the mass of mankind is talentless, without creativity or originality, and bitterly jealous of those few who are different—is manifested most strongly in the character of Ellsworth Toohey . . . , an architectural critic for a mammoth newspaper chain. Through his highly influential intellectual position, Toohey hypocritically manipulates public opinion in the direction of "selflessness," which, through Ayn Rand's inverted rhetoric, becomes a kind of meek mindless drift toward that ideological arch-villain, "collectivism." (pp. 325-26)

The first premise of Rand's philosophy—that everyone is ultimately selfish—is demonstrated in all three figures (Toohey, Keating, and Roark); but only one, Roark, also has "character," and the author's endorsement of his values places him far from the middling crowd, separating him from the spineless Keating and pitting him against the traitorous Toohey. The dialectic battle between a fantasy version of individualism—Roark—and a satanic version of the cooperative spirit—Toohey—culminates when Roark purposely dynamites a public-works housing project he designed because its architectural "integrity" has been compromised by the Toohey clique.

Between these forces are two other characters in *The Fountainhead* who, because they lack the courage to defend Roark's brilliant architecture before the rabble, masochistically bend their efforts to ruin it. Gail Wynand, the powerful Hearst-like publisher of Toohey's column, is an isolated cynic who at first tries to corrupt Roark to validate his own pessimism about human nature. Failing at that, and smitten finally by a glimpse of Roark's moral determination and idealistic faith . . . , Wynand throws his whole reputation into defending the young architect in his newspapers. The attempt at a personally redemptive crusade comes too late. Rand presents Wynand as a case study of the potentially enlightened capitalist-entrepreneur, but she makes him pay for his tardy patronage. Toohey subverts his organization and Wynand is stripped of his wealth [and] his wife. . . . (p. 326)

Like Wynand whom she married, Dominique Francon is a bitter example of approach-avoidance ambivalence. She is the daughter of a "successful" architect, but she despises her father's conventional mediocrity and secretly loves Roark. Her characterization is perhaps the most interesting aspect of the book. . . . She is by turns the destroyer, the seducer, the disciple, and finally an ally. The passionate relationship is in reality a struggle for dominance; when she realizes she cannot win the struggle over Roark, she is compelled to love him. (p. 327)

Although it has all the characteristics of pulp fiction, including flood-tide length and watery content, *The Fountainhead* is, of course, much more than a potboiler about the personal traumas behind the lives of busy architects. It is actually an "idea" novel, however crude or obvious, about fiercely opposing political ideologies. It is an overheard version of an internal Amer-

ican cultural debate between individualism and collectivism. . . . In articulating this struggle, Rand speaks simultaneously to the highest aspirations and the deepest suspicions of the culture, precipitating the broadly based, though mostly unspoken, acceptance of her work.

Part of *The Fountainhead*'s success is due to the way in which it includes its reader in a disenfranchised "elect." It appeals to the romantic sense of alienation and superiority, asking the reader to identify with an elite still sensitive to aesthetic "integrity" and tortured by the low-brow conventional mediocrity of a small-minded society. It has the bitterness of the "outsider" and offers a hero who is determined enough to overcome these obstacles. . . . This country, *The Fountainhead* seems to say, does not lack True Believers but rather something or someone to believe in: a Howard Roark, a moral absolutist and fervent crusader amidst the ugly spiritual malaise. Perceived by some as "radical" because its values—the emphasis on individualism, the romantic faith in the efficacy of an idea over all practical obstacles, grim moral purity—belong to an earlier, pioneer stage of economic development in a capitalist culture, it is ultimately an attack on present society from the regressive Right Wing. (pp. 328-29)

Kevin McGann, "Ayn Rand in the Stockyard of the Spirit," in The Modern American Novel and the Movies, *edited by Gerald Peary and Roger Shatzkin, Frederick Ungar Publishing Co., 1978, pp. 325-35.*

TERRY TEACHOUT

If your definition of a "modern classic" is a book which still sells briskly in both soft- and hard-cover editions a quarter-century after its publication, which deals with serious issues in a serious way, and which continues to stir up controversy as each succeeding generation discovers it, then—better brace yourself—*Atlas Shrugged* fills the bill. Sure, it's a preposterous book; sure, the reviewers demolished it; sure, virtually every reputable conservative from Russell Kirk to Frank Meyer rushed to repudiate it. Indeed, there aren't very many bad things to be said about *Atlas Shrugged* that aren't true. No novel of comparable quality has ever been so tenacious in its hold on the public, give or take *Gone with the Wind.* . . .

Rumor has it that Ayn Rand herself was, at the time of her death, hot at work on the script for a ten-hour *Atlas Shrugged* TV mini-series; and it's no rumor that she turned up on the Phil Donahue show a while back, putting down altruistic housewives right and left with a verbal sledgehammer, the very picture of her beloved "intransigence." (Ayn Rand liked intransigence like Norman Mailer likes existentialism.) And this has been going on, mind you, for *25 years.*

Surely Miss Rand and her book deserve to be commemorated on this quarter centenary, even in the pages of what Miss Rand once called "the worst and most dangerous magazine in America." For there's no graceful way to get around it: *Atlas Shrugged,* awful as it is, has left its mark on the history of American conservatism. If nothing else, its sheer ubiquity would be proof enough; but, in honor of this august occasion, let us further consider, just for fun, the possibility that the sign of the dollar, however lurid, might not be (keep it quiet, please) all bad. (p. 566)

Terry Teachout, "Farewell, Dagny Taggart," in National Review, *Vol. XXXIV, No. 9, May 14, 1982, pp. 566-67.*

DOUGLAS DEN UYL AND DOUGLAS B. RASMUSSEN

Perhaps it is fair to say that if there is one message Ayn Rand the theorist would have wanted to leave us it is, philosophy matters! The recent death of Ayn Rand provides the occasion for us to recall the importance of this message. In the heat of contemporary social and political debates we often forget to consider basic principles. The writings of Ayn Rand will always be with us as a reminder that pragmatism and expediency are ultimately self-defeating. And it is in this spirit of a concern for basic questions that we wish to briefly outline some of Rand's basic theses here.

We see three central themes in the philosophy of Ayn Rand: 1) The major metaphysical and epistemological tenets of Aristotelian realism are true—viz., reality exists and is what it is independent of our awareness of it, and yet it can be known by the human mind. 2) Self-actualization is the correct approach to ethics. There are appropriate goals for human beings to pursue, and these goals (with the appropriate means) are grounded in human nature. Values can be found in "facts" or the nature of things, thus making a doctrine of natural rights possible, and 3) The conflict between ancient and modern political philosophy over whether the state should promote freedom or virtue need not be a source of conflict. Virtue and liberty are inherently related, and laissez-faire capitalism is the only economic and political system that recognizes this intimate connection.

Rand argues for the first thesis in her *Introduction to Objectivist Epistemology*. Her basic purpose is to show that though knowledge requires that the content of our mind answer to what is actually "out there," the manner in which we come to know things (i.e., form concepts) may depend on certain cognitive processes peculiar to human nature. For example, concepts are "universals." My concept of "dog" (if correct) will apply universally to an indefinite number of dogs. Thus while only individual dogs exist in nature, the mind may hold the concept of "dog" as a universal. This view of knowledge and concepts is a version of what philosophers call the "moderate realist" tradition—a tradition initiated by Aristotle and perhaps most fully developed by Thomas Aquinas. (p. 67)

The main non-fiction work in which Rand argues for the second thesis is *The Virtue of Selfishness*. In that work, especially the essay "The Objectivist Ethics," Rand seeks to move ethics from the Kantian view in which ethics is a matter of duties to others to the Greek view of promoting well-being or self-actualization. She specifically rejects the tendency among ethicists to consider actions done for self as *a*moral. But Rand is just as insistent that self-interest is not a matter of what one feels like doing. Human nature sets the standards for what is in one's self-interest, and thus it is possible to do what one "wants" to do and still not act in one's own interest. This view of ethics places Rand squarely within the Aristotelian natural law tradition. (pp. 67-8)

But perhaps the most unique contribution Rand has made concerns showing the relationship between what we have called thesis two and thesis three. Rand argues that human excellence cannot be achieved without giving central importance to freedom of choice. . . . This is why liberty is the most important social/political value—it keeps the possibility of excellence open. Indeed Rand's theory of rights is simply a way to insure that freedom is protected. And her theory is a *natural* rights theory because the justification for these rights depends upon her naturalistic ethics. Thus moral excellence is achieved only

through political freedom, making the dichotomy between freedom and virtue a false one.

Since the free market is not paternalistic, it allows for the achievement of human excellence. This is not utopianism, since freedom cannot, by the very fact that it is freedom, guarantee that all will act to achieve their fullest potential. But the free market society does provide some incentives to this end, since the individual himself suffers most from his errors. Moreover, known and yet to be discovered possibilities for achievement are not forcibly closed off. In this connection it is vitally important to realize a point made in her essay "What is Capitalism" contained in *Capitalism: The Unknown Ideal*—the book in which much of this third thesis can be found. Rand's theory of excellence is thoroughly individualistic. Excellence should not be viewed in terms of what is excellent for some class or group, e.g., intellectuals, businessmen, artists, or whomever. The achievement of excellence must be considered in the context of an individual's own circumstances and conditions. Freedom guarantees that the possibility of excellence will be open to all as they are respectively able to understand and achieve it. (pp. 68-9)

The foregoing remarks indicate why Rand does not excessively exaggerate when she gives herself credit for understanding the moral basis for capitalism better than anyone else. Previous moral arguments were of the "necessary evil" variety. We tolerate the "selfishness" of individuals under capitalism to gain all the economic benefits that would result. Apart from the fact that this view implies that there is no moral basis for capitalism, it shows an ignorance both of human nature and the complex motives people have when they consider alternatives. . . .

In conclusion, it is worth noting that Rand is a thinker but not a professional academic. This has both advantages and disadvantages. One of the primary advantages is that she has not been held captive by many of the intellectual fashions that have swept philosophy during the twentieth century. It also means her writings are not jargonistic. One of the primary disadvantages is that she has not always bothered to work out all the details of her ideas in a way necessary to solidify her position. It is for this very reason that her thought needs professional attention. Nevertheless, Rand's philosophizing can be a source of knowledge as well as inspiration. Thus even though Rand is often rejected by professional academics and goes in and out of fashion among libertarians, it just might be that the very "stone which the builders rejected" could well be the "one to become the head of the corner." (p. 69)

> *Douglas Den Uyl and Douglas B. Rasmussen, "The Philosophical Importance of Ayn Rand," in* Modern Age, *Vol. 27, No. 1, Winter, 1983, pp. 67-9.*

TAMARA STADNYCHENKO

Ayn Rand's *Anthem* is science fiction of the "after the big one" genre. The world has undergone a cataclysmic reversal; technology and science have all but disappeared, and the accepted social structure is relentlessly communal. Individualism is not tolerated. Indeed, speaking the "unspeakable word" *I* is the only crime which merits capital punishment.

The protagonist, Equality 7-2521, is a misfit. Despite lifelong indoctrination, he defies society's laws and mores, at first with an overwhelming sense of guilt and shame, and later with an increasing certainty that he, and not the society, is rational.

He travels the epic hero's Journey of Light, descends to physical and moral depths (torture and self-betrayal), suffers a trial by fire to defend that which he considers more sacred than life itself, and finally emerges victorious. Fleeing from the city of his birth, he runs to an "uncharted forest" where he discovers remnants of the world as it was before the holocaust, finds love and freedom, and decides to establish a new world peopled with men and women who will take pride in the word *I* and who will write "the first chapter in the new history of man."

Anthem is a short novel (approximately 120 pages), but for the young reader it offers exciting action, an appealing love story, and an interesting political philosophy. Rand liberally laces her tale with symbols, irony, and mythological and Biblical themes that students are usually able to discover and interpret. . . .

Tamara Stadnychenko, "'Anthem': A Book for All Reasons," in English Journal, *Vol. 72, No. 2, February, 1983, pp. 77-8.*

Conrad (Michael) Richter

1890-1968

American novelist, short story writer, and essayist.

Richter is regarded as one of the best novelists to have written about the American frontier. Relying heavily on oral history, early newspaper accounts, letters, and diaries, Richter recreated the life and myth of the pioneers with authenticity of detail and dialect. Richter's realistic, straightforward narratives are based on his underlying philosophy that hardship strengthens character and his belief that an individual has a oneness with nature.

Richter's greatest recognition came with the publication of his Ohio trilogy: *The Trees* (1940), *The Fields* (1946), and *The Town* (1950), later reissued in one volume as *The Awakening Land* (1966). In these works, he chronicles the life of a pioneer family against the background of the changing land. The early struggle with the forest wilderness of the Ohio Valley gives way to the homesteaders' tilling of the soil and later to the establishment of a town at the beginning of the industrial age in America. The heroine of this saga, Sayward Luckett Wheeler, is one of Richter's most memorable characters; she is strong, practical, and determined to survive. Richter received the 1951 Pulitzer Prize in letters for *The Town*, but it was generally acknowledged that the award was presented for the entire trilogy.

In addition to his work dealing with the Ohio frontier, Richter also wrote fiction set in the Southwest. *The Sea of Grass* (1937), first serialized in *The Saturday Evening Post* and later made into a film, is considered the best of this work. The novel expands upon many of the short stories which had been collected in his *Early Americana* (1936). A story of the demise of the great ranges, *The Sea of Grass* depicts the conflict between the ranchers and the homesteaders in New Mexico during the late nineteenth century. Again, the virtues of self-reliance are promoted along with Richter's idea of "hardship into gain." Other novels inspired by Richter's long residence in the Southwest include *Tacey Cromwell* (1942) and *The Lady* (1957). Both these novels portray heroines determined to cope with the demands of frontier life in male-dominated societies. In accord with many of the scholars who have studied Richter's historical fiction, Edwin W. Gaston, Jr. claims that "Richter memorialized the southwestern sea of grass and the eastern sea of trees. And while other writers dealt with complex human achievement, Richter artistically promoted the worth of simple goodness."

The major accomplishments of Richter's later life are two highly praised autobiographical novels: *The Waters of Kronos* (1960), a National Book Award winner, and *A Simple Honorable Man* (1962). The first is a mystical account of a man who returns from the West to his birthplace, a Pennsylvania town that has been covered by the waters of a man-made lake. Richter allows his aging protagonist to travel back in time to his youth. The young man reaches an understanding of his relationship with his father and an acceptance of his own mortality. The companion volume, *A Simple Honorable Man*, depicts the life of the father, a minister who spent his life in the

service of others. Critics called the novel an inspiring tribute to Richter's own father.

(See also *Contemporary Authors*, Vols. 5-8, rev. ed., Vols. 25-28, rev. ed. [obituary]; *Something about the Author*, Vol. 3; and *Dictionary of Literary Biography*, Vol. 9.)

EDA LOU WALTON

"Early Americana" for [a] title names exactly the author's particular gift. All based on old tales collected from pioneers and from the children of pioneers, these stories present the poetry of early conquests. They are folklore fictionized. If they are, one and all, romantic stories, they are also true stories of quiet stern men and brave frontier women. Nor are the characters overdrawn or made to enact scenes of gun-play and violence. Violence is in the background, a kind of threat perhaps over the land, but the author is concerned chiefly with drawing character. . . .

The tales based on the authentic life stories of some of these characters and familiar to any one who has lived in the Far West—are all told in vivid, dramatic pictures that remain in the reader's mind. . . . Conrad Richter chooses often a single trait or a typical action to emphasize and by that we know his character. He paints a single scene completely and we do not forget it as the story unfolds. He chooses sometimes as the mind through which the story is told, a young girl or a child unusually sensitive to the new atmosphere of the trail or the Western town. Few of his stories, in fact, use as narrator a man accustomed to and hardened by the wilderness. This very choice of a sensitive mind as the protagonist, allows Mr. Richter to present the strange poetry of his scene or his action, to give more dramatically the sturdy bravery and stoicism of the typical Western characters observed by the narrator. . . .

Conrad Richter's short stories have authenticity, they are told in a subdued tone, usually in the tone of reminiscence, and they are finely drawn studies of character. Therefore this book will charm readers—even those readers who have known the West first hand and who will not, therefore, attend most Western "movies." Richter is a good short story writer. His prose is exact and yet poetic. Very few cliches are to be found in his descriptions and often these descriptions of country or of a person are excellent. . . . Indeed, now that his tales are collected, Mr. Richter will probably take his place among our better known writers of the true American short story.

> *Eda Lou Walton, "Pioneer Tales from the West,"*
> in New York Herald Tribune Books, *August 2, 1936,*
> *p. 6.*

STANLEY YOUNG

It may take all kinds of people to make a world, but in Conrad Richter's mind one kind stands out above all others in the winning of the American Southwest. He has centered his group of romantic stories ["**Early Americana and Other Stories**"] around pioneer men as granite-faced as the canyon walls, as tight-lipped as the desert itself, and beside them . . . he has placed the same familiar breed of pioneer woman—the stoical, stiff-spined, resolute mate. . . .

This author sets his stories in the small, outlying clusters of settlements still menaced in the last century by raiding Indians. The houses lie "like a handful of children's blocks thrown and forgotten on the immensity of the prairie," but in them are the unsung heroes of Mr. Richter's re-created West. Harte's Poker Flat and Roaring Camp and the sinks of sin which Wister's Virginian knew are outside their experience. Their eyes are big with far horizons and the starker experience of nature and the trail.

Stories with such simple, direct titles as "**New Home**," "**Smoke Over the Prairie**," "**Frontier Woman**," "**Early Marriage**" indicate at once that the author is fascinated by the times that are gone. Like Harte, he is first concerned with trying to give a realistic sense of scene. When he has made us feel how the Comanche moon looked on the roadless prairie, how the hoofs of loping horses beat on the bunch grass like a muffled drum, how the seasons come and go under the raw, hard sunlight, then he is ready, in as few words as possible, to unfold his dramatic story.

On the whole, it is quite apparent that in pattern it is too often the same story. Boy meets girl in the end with monotonous frequency. But not before Mr. Richter has demonstrated his ability to cast a glamour over everything from wagon train to buffalo jerky. . . .

All of Mr. Richter's stories give a colorful representation of the region. The suspense in the situations may rise out of nothing more complex than physical conflict versus a chance at the marriage altar, but the force and purpose of the writing

remain—that desire to represent an impression of unity in the life that is just behind us. In this Conrad Richter succeeds admirably. . . .

> *Stanley Young, "'Early Americana' and Other Recent Works of Fiction: 'Early Americana and Other Stories'," in* The New York Times Book Review, *August 2, 1936, p. 7.*

EDA LOU WALTON

[The setting for "**The Sea of Grass**"] is Old New Mexico, land of the great cattle kings and of their vast ranges then slowly being invaded by the homesteaders. . . . The resemblances between this novel and Willa Cather's "Lost Lady" are . . . so striking that one is forever remembering the earlier book as one reads the new. Although this is not the masterpiece it is a good reproduction, something more, perhaps, than a reproduction.

Conrad Richter's chief skill in story writing lies in his use of his scene. New Mexico of the early days lives in these pages. But Conrad Richter is definitely a romantic writer, never a realist. And because he is a romantic writer he casts a kind of golden glow over a scene which other authors have given us in harsh, cruel or tragic colors. Nor is he completely wrong in using this early American scene as a romanticist must. New Mexico is, indeed, a land of myth, a land of curious poetic superstitions. . . .

One wonders, indeed, about one thing only: in so consistently romantic a treatment of the Southwest as Mr. Richter's, are not the truly historical bases for the changes in this frontier country being denied? The homesteaders did finally take the land. . . . The old frontier had to go. Mr. Richter himself sees that, but for him "those were the grand old days." And today the early conquerors . . . are old men with many a yarn to tell. Mr. Richter collects their yarns.

There is just one criticism to be made of Conrad Richter, once we have acknowledged that he writes very well, that he recreates atmosphere excellently, that he is economic, impressive and dramatic in his effects: as a collector of early Americana he inclines too strongly toward the romantic only. There was more in the Old New Mexico than he gives us. A richer canvas, a bolder stroke, a certain ruthless candor would make Richter a writer of first order. He sees vividly, feels accurately, but in one range only—the poetic. He is in the grip of a continuous nostalgia (and that is the mood of this whole novel) for a dead past. And the reader of "**The Sea of Grass**" will be caught in this nostalgia for the old beauty of the grazing country ridden by powerful, proud men. He will sympathize, too, as Lutie and her son Brock did with the "nesters," the agricultural settlers. But he will feel all this only through identifying himself with one very small group of characters in their prouder and nobler moments. "**The Sea of Grass**" has not indicated that Mr. Richter's vision is greater. It has, however, indicated that he is studying his craft, through models, very carefully.

> *Eda Lou Walton, "Old Land of the Cattle Kings,"*
> in New York Herald Tribune Books, *February 7,*
> *1937, p. 2.*

ROSAMOND LEHMANN

Readers whose habit it is to turn to the last page after a glance at the first will get a misleading impression of Mr. Richter.

They will see, with dismay, these words: "That's how life was, death and birth, grub and harvest, rain and clearing, winter and summer. You had to take one with the other, for that's the way it ran." Though there is a slight element in *The Trees* of the kind of sententious platitudinising this passage suggests, there is much more to it than that. There is research, sincerity, imagination and beauty of writing. It is escape literature of a high-class sort . . . : that is, it sets the mind free and refreshes it with images and figures from an innocent, half legendary world; a world as far removed from us as if it were another planet, but real all the same, and comforting as rain in a parched land. The story is about pioneer settlers in the immense virgin forests of America after the War of Independence. . . . Mr. Richter makes skilful use of his evidently profound historical studies, and the picture of pioneer life he builds up is extraordinarily concentrated, detailed and vivid. . . . There is no exaltation of the peasant. The characters are people, not symbols or mawkish abstractions, as in so many "novels of the soil." Nor are they dumb animals, although their life is almost purely occupied with animal needs and functions. Nor are they used as Eugene O'Neill uses primitive characters—imposing an intellectual pattern on them to work out some neurosis of his own.

But the forest itself is the principal agent in this book. It takes on an overpowering life. Every activity is surrounded by and saturated in its influence, and this feeling of a gigantic elemental force is achieved without any cheap mystical effects. The story is told in a reproduction of the actual speech of early settlers, and though it rings sentimentally now and then, it is on the whole fresh, vigorous, and salted with vivid natural imagery. (p. 694)

> *Rosamond Lehmann, in a review of "The Trees,"*
> *in* The Spectator, *Vol. 164, No. 5838, May 17, 1940,*
> *pp. 693-94.*

WILLIAM Du BOIS

In his two earlier novels, **"The Sea of Grass"** and **"The Trees,"** Conrad Richter has made a solid contribution to the long shelf of Americana; in **"Tacey Cromwell"** he goes back into the Arizona Territory a half century ago, to find a protagonist in the hennaed sporting-house madam who gives the book its name. Like others of this celebrated sisterhood, Tacey yearns for a husband and social esteem. (p. 6)

Certainly there is material here for a novel of the magnetic West. Mr. Richter has packed his story into a little over 200 pages. He tells it with soundness as well as economy; and yet, for all his careful choice of character and local color, there is something unfulfilled about it, something oddly lifeless. Though the plot is honestly conceived, though it avoids most of the cruder allurements of melodrama, it emerges as a made-to-order pattern, no more moving than a pile of stereopticon slides in an old-fashioned parlor.

Perhaps Mr. Richter would have been wiser not to write in the first person, through the mind of Nugget Oldacker; certainly a boy of 9 is hardly the best reporter for the White Palace House and its painted ladies of the evening. . . .

The story moves swiftly; there are first-class vignettes of an Arizona mining town, pit-bosses brawling in the saloons, a hard-muscled drilling contest on the Fourth, a ghastly fire that all but destroys Bisbee. . . . But even here one cannot help feeling that the cleverly worked-out bits come from research rather than a remembered past.

Perhaps Mr. Richter is more at home in the wilderness than among the humans who tamed it; perhaps a deeper penetration into his subject, and more elbow-room, would have produced the novel he was trying to write. But **"Tacey Cromwell"** is an opulent canvas in a sketch-book. For all Mr. Richter's facility, he has crowded far too much into far too few pages. His story rings true in its major premise, but it does not stir the heart. (p. 7)

> *William Du Bois, "Mining Town West," in* The New
> York Times Book Review, *October 25, 1942, pp.*
> *6-7.*

HOWARD FAST

Each new book by Conrad Richter is a treat. In a time of loose writing, he works with meticulous craftsmanship and an uncanny knowledge of period. In that way, in **"The Trees,"** he performed a miracle of reconstruction; and half in prose, half in poetry, told one of the best stories of early America that exists.

Now, in **"The Free Man,"** he tells another tale of the Colonial period, a good story, but not a great one. He labors to make a point, and makes more of the point than the situation justifies. Richter comes of Pennsylvania Dutch people; worried, and justly so, about the feeling against German-Americans that came and is coming out of this war, he tells a tale of the early German settlers in Pennsylvania, and their aching desire for freedom. The point is a good one; there is lots of German blood in America, and most of it is here because it fled from a variation of what exists in Germany now. Germans love freedom; they've loved it for a long time: they've died for it, and a great many of them have died under the American flag ever since there was an American flag.

That's the theme of the story Richter tells. . . .

Where Mr. Richter worries the point is in his accent upon what the Pennsylvania Germans did in the Revolution. They didn't fight the war alone by any means—and actually they formed only a few regiments. When they fought, they fought well, as Germans usually do; and when they faced the Hessians, as they did on many occasions, they drove home their hatred of Prussianism with the point of the bayonet. In this story, it should have been left at that; they were part of a revolution that took in every minority in America, but only part of it.

This isn't the best story Conrad Richter has done, yet it has the charm and the careful technique he gives to everything he writes. It is so much better than the usual padded historical romance that it deserves to be read. I only wish that Richter had told the story with no other thought than the telling; it would have made its own point.

> *Howard Fast, "'Pennsylvania Dutch' Heroes," in*
> New York Herald Tribune Weekly Book Review,
> *August 22, 1943, p. 2.*

BRUCE SUTHERLAND

One of the greatest of . . . modern humanists is Conrad Richter, whose stories of American backgrounds have been appearing for the past ten years. (pp. 413-14)

[An] early, spontaneous, whole-hearted interest in native backgrounds and deeds of derring-do was a part of the heritage of many American boys who came to man's estate and, alas, outgrew such boyish nonsense. But not Conrad Richter. He had known his forbears as people and not as chromos on the wall; he recognized the ties between the present and the past, and as time went on, what had been a healthy boyish interest in cowboys and Indians became a mature humanism which impelled him to study the phenomenon of an American life that was rapidly vanishing.

The sources of Richter's inspiration are not hard to catalog. . . . But the most important source of all was the people who had lived through days that have now passed into history, and from them Richter garnered the little details and authenticities of early life as it was actually lived. No writer on American social history is more thoroughly at home with his material nor has anyone been more careful to preserve the spirit of times past. (p. 414)

[Richter's first widely-circulated story, **"Brothers of No Kin"**] had a remarkable reception and seemed to open the way to a brilliant writing career. E. J. O'Brien chose it as the best story of the year; it was reprinted a number of times, and magazine editors became aware of the existence of its author. Success, however, carried disillusionment with it, for the twenty-five dollar payment which Mr. Richter received only after screwing up enough courage to ask for it, was paltry. . . . This helps to explain the standardized mediocrity of the early Richter stories, with the exception of **"Brothers of No Kin."** Several of them were collected and issued as *Brothers of No Kin and Other Stories* (1924), and all that can be said for them is that they are "well-made" stories, tailored for the trade. Some have elements of nativism and local color, some have a glimmer of characterization, but for the most part they give the impression of assembly-line mass production which at best gave the author practice in the art of writing. The titular story belongs in a different category. It is a bare narrative of a man who in taking the sins of a friend upon his own head gives up the Kingdom of Heaven. . . . In this simple story of faith and self-sacrifice, the outline of Richter's later humanism is readily discernible. (p. 415)

There was nothing new or startling about the Richter stories which began to appear in the magazines early in 1934. On the surface they were Western stories of a high order, authentic, carefully conceived, and skillfully narrated. Closer scrutiny reveals how vastly different they are from the type of Western to which Americans have become accustomed. These are stories of pioneer fortitude aimed at a depression-ridden world; and the contemporary soul, battered and bewildered by life, through them is brought into closer contact with people of another age who also lived, loved, struggled, and died but whose lives form a pattern out of which emerges completeness and serenity. . . .

In the collection of short stories published as *Early Americana* (1936), Richter succeeded in relating the life of the nineteenth century Southwestern frontier to the life of the present. By depicting the people of that day during the course of the daily round of human contacts with the land, the weather, tools and equipment, enemies and friends, all against a colorful regional background, he achieved a realism that is not governed only by the outward aspects of drudgery, drabness, and despair. There were such qualities as courage and silent heroism; there was a record of solid and stubborn achievement, and Richter's insight into the spiritual side of a life that could be both drab

and terrifying is a tribute to his painstaking research and his knowledge of human nature. (p. 417)

Richter is acutely aware of what this life meant to the women; some of his finest characterizations are brought about by little flashes of insight into the souls of these women. Not all of them are frontier heroines, but stoicism, perseverance, and a grim acceptance of conditions over which they have little control are marked characteristics. Pioneer fortitude can be sickeningly overdone; extreme realism is often a false indictment of a way of life. Such pitfalls are avoided by Richter, for his interest lies neither in the legendary heroine nor in the victim of frontier neuroses. His chief concern is with ordinary women to whom the life was neither heroic nor lacklustre; it was a life that had to be lived, and, when material values failed, spiritual forces could be drawn upon for sustenance. (p. 418)

For a writer of carefully constructed, almost condensed stories the planning of a novel [such as *The Sea of Grass* (1937)] must have presented some formidable problems. There were patterns to follow, but the long, padded epic so typical of American historical fiction did not appeal to him. Faced with highly theatrical material which verged on the melodramatic, he was brief and restrained almost to the point of taciturnity in his treatment of it. The result is a completely successful short novel which meets even the most exacting literary standards.

Mr. Richter's method is objective. Against a vast background of grassland and desert faithfully, even artistically painted, the dramatic essentials unfold. A quarter of a century of change is packed into a few pages without sacrificing either perspective or proportion. . . . [*The Sea of Grass* is the story] of change which destroys and builds at the same time, of the past which succumbs to the present and of the personal tragedy which attends the tide of progress. The vastness of the theme to some extent overshadows the characters, and in less skillful hands they would be little better than stock performers in a melodrama. The stage property effects of hero, villain, and fair lady may be seen; but since life itself is not free from melodrama, certain theatricalisms could not be avoided entirely. Had they been, the truth would have suffered. The irresistible force of agrarianism meeting the immovability of established tradition and use did not result in a clear-cut victory for either, and in reconstructing one such struggle Richter had added another chapter to our social history.

By 1940, when *The Trees* was published, Richter had reached his full stature as a proponent of the American heritage. In this novel he turns to the frontier of an earlier day, to the development of the old Northwest, and in this account of the pioneering experiences of a hardy, illiterate Pennsylvania family he epitomizes the whole story of Western settlement. There is none of the glamor of historical pageantry; there are no heroics, no carefully staged dramatic situations, no great names and no great deeds. This is a story of the common man told in the homely idiom of that man; a story in which the daily and the yearly round of primitive existence is faithfully described and one which recaptures the moods and thoughts of an age that was governed almost entirely by necessity. The natural simplicity of the story is in itself a work of art. Richter's familiarity with pioneer life, the result of many years of careful study, is nowhere permitted to appear obtrusive. What he achieves is a pioneer's eye view of frontier existence and of a group of people who "never preen themselves before posterity." You would have to seek far in American fiction to find a truer picture of how our pioneer ancestors really lived, and it is safe to say that *The Trees* is one of the finest novels on this aspect of American life ever written.

The Trees is not an historical romance, nor is it an historical novel. It is a realistic narrative of the experience of the Luckett family, who migrated across the Ohio into new territory; of the trace through the endless forest, the building of a cabin, the coming of other settlers, and finally the ultimate disintegration of the family unit. Each member of the family is well and carefully characterized. . . . The death of the mother and the growing restlessness of the father throw the burden of family responsibility on [the eldest daughter] Sayward, and as a consequence "Saird" becomes the central character in the book. No romantic heroine, she is the personification of all those qualities so essential in the frontier woman. (pp. 418-20)

[Many of the book's] episodes leave a lasting impression, and all are woven together with the bits of homely lore that were a part of the lives of pioneer people. Sayward's marriage to the Bay Stater, Portius Wheeler, ends the novel and marks the passing of the frontier. Settlement had come to the land and to the people of the land.

In *Tacey Cromwell* (1942) the scene is once again the Southwest, this time a mining community in Arizona Territory toward the end of the last century. As in his other novels, Richter has been meticulous in gathering his material and has steeped himself in honky-tonk and mining-town lore of the nineties. . . . *Tacey Cromwell* is the carefully patterned story of a prostitute and a gambler who attempt to cross the great divide into the land of respectability.

Richter is an observer of human frailty but never a judge. He lets facts speak for themselves and makes no effort to tamper with the realities. . . . [It] is the character of Tacey, hard, competent, strong, and understanding, that dominates the story. Laid against a regional background of a "society" emerging from the license of a frontier mining community, this short novel depicts an important phase in the growth of American culture.

Mr. Richter's recent novel, *The Free Man* (1943), has been something of a disappointment. For the first time the short novel form proves inadequate to the theme, and failings so carefully avoided in earlier novels are noticeable. Here the author's power of expression has proved unequal to the greatness of his conception. There is a consciousness of historical things which partially blacks out the human element. It is not that Mr. Richter is not sure of his material—it is more that he has not assimilated it as carefully as in his previous works or that he has attempted to compress too much into too little space. Certainly the theme of this novel was as close to his heart as anything he has ever written—perhaps it was so close that it interfered with complete objectivity. Whatever the cause, one feels that a much greater novel should have resulted and that had circumstances been right such would have been the case. *The Free Man* is not a creative failure. It has moments of brilliance and flashes of insight into character. But the plain truth is that the novel is not up to its author's exacting standards when, considering the subject matter, it should have been one of the best books he has ever written. (pp. 420-22)

Mr. Richter's chief contribution to Americana is a restrained realism which depends greatly on brevity and understatement for its effect. This, combined with an understanding of people, a feeling for historical things which transcends mere knowledge, and the ability to think and write in terms of his characters

and their environment places him among the chosen few who have made the past of America come alive. (p. 422)

Bruce Sutherland, "Conrad Richter's Americana," in New Mexico Quarterly, *Vol. XV, No. 4, Winter, 1945, pp. 413-22.*

LOUIS BROMFIELD

I doubt that any one writing today in this country is closer in understanding and treatment of its pioneer life than Conrad Richter. He has not only given the frontier his scholarly attention and sympathetic interpretation, but he has done what is even more important; he has recreated the frontier and the early development of the nation in terms of atmosphere, character and even speech. He has that gift—the first and most important in a novelist—of creating for the reader a world as real as the one in which he lives, a world which the reader enters on reading the first page and in which he remains until the last.

"The Fields" is actually a sequel to an earlier novel, one of the best on early American life, called "The Trees." . . . The tale centered largely about the growth and development of a girl-child called Sayward.

"The Fields" continues the life of Sayward after her strange marriage to the "educated" New Englander Portius, through the raising of their family of eight children. But it is much more than that; it is also the tale of the slow battle and eventual victory over the Trees. . . .

The characters, all save perhaps the complicated husband Portius, are simple enough people, living against a background of primitive beauty. The story is told with a feeling of poetry and the picturesque turn of language which characterized the speech of the frontier. . . . The speech has not the confusing effect which dialect speech sometimes has in a novel; instead it has the strength of eighteenth-century expressions and turns of speech, possessed both of vigor and of vividness.

Sayward, the heroine, is the portrait of a simple, eternal woman dominating in an instinctive way a husband who is far more educated and subtle than herself. The children are real children, each with his own personality. . . .

"The Fields" is the kind of book which Americans of these times should read. In it they will be able to find a real sense of values, a fundamental strength. It is a down-to-earth book which is at the same time almost mystical in its appreciation of nature and of those forces from which we have derived so much of our strength in the past. Technically the book is simply but curiously constructed of a chain of incidents, each one of which illumines the characters and background and creates a satisfying unity. Nor has "The Fields" any of the disadvantages that sometimes afflict a sequel.

Louis Bromfield, "A Fine Novel of Pioneers in Ohio," in New York Herald Tribune Weekly Book Review, *March 31, 1946, p. 3.*

ORVILLE PRESCOTT

[*The Fields,* a sequel to *The Trees,*] is an equally amazing recreation of the life and speech and thought of the American frontier wilderness 140 years ago. In a series of separate episodes, each a complete unit in itself, Mr. Richter has shown through the life of one family the transformation of a hunting society into a farming one. Without needless display of his vast antiquarian background and with none of the cheap melodrama that degrades most historical fiction, he has told a wise and deeply moving story about a weak and very human man and about a woman who is almost great in her simple strength of character. Seldom in fiction has the atmosphere of another age been so completely realized. Part of the magical spell of Mr. Richter's book is cast directly by its prose, which makes loving and yet unpretentious use of the vocabulary and typical turns of phrase of its characters. A rare and haunting book is this, which on no account should be overlooked.

> Orville Prescott, in a review of "The Fields," in
> The Yale Review, *Vol. XXXV, No. 4, June, 1946,*
> p. 765.

DAYTON KOHLER

Conrad Richter has reclaimed two segments of the American past widely separated in geography and time. *Early Americana* is a collection of stories about buffalo hunters, cowpunchers, and homesteaders in the region of the Staked Plains, the Llano Estacado of Southwest border history. *The Sea of Grass* holds within its brief framework the sweep and drama of the cow country at the end of the last century, when cattlemen fought to hold their free range against the nester's fence and plow. *Tacey Cromwell* has for its background the Arizona mining town of Bisbee in its roaring boom days, a contrast between the lusty, swarming life of Brewery Gulch and the prim respectability of Quality Hill. *The Trees* and *The Fields* trace the growth of a pioneer settlement in the territory west of the Alleghenies and north of the Ohio River. In an age of period-piece fiction stuffed with names and dates, these novels have a simple human warmth and vigor because they are written in terms of their own characters and atmosphere, without reference to historical figures or events of the early eighteen hundreds, and the result is something fresh and effective in regional writing. *The Free Man,* however, links its plot with Concord and Bunker Hill; its background takes in a group of freedom-loving Pennsylvania Dutch settlers resisting British authority on the farming frontier beyond the Blue Mountains.

On one level these books belong to the eager nationalism of the depression thirties, when writers as divergent as Van Wyck Brooks and Kenneth Roberts tried to find in the certainties of a recovered past an answer to the problems of the present. (p. 221)

But to many writers the past was glorious simply because it was the past rather than a pattern of continuity with the present. This was antiquarianism, uncritical and often sentimental, the past recalled because its finished story was remote from the disorders of our time. (pp. 221-22)

In his handling of the past Conrad Richter is an artist in prose. His short, compact novels demonstrate the fact that story-telling need not be subordinated to documentation of history, for reality of the imagination can be made more compelling than the appearance of fact. To him a story is always a record of human experience, regardless of time or setting. . . .

Sometimes a writer's choice of title discloses the whole nature and scope of his work. In the case of Conrad Richter, *Early Americana* describes his interest in frontier life and his deep regional feeling. Out of the yellowing files of old newspapers, letters, land deeds, and out of tales heard at first hand from men and women who were pioneers in the early Southwest,

he has enlivened and reshaped a group of stories in the primitive tradition of much Western fiction. . . . At the same time his stories have the flavor and drama of the West with the melodrama and sentiment drained away, and their authenticity warrants closer inspection.

The qualities which set these stories apart from the two-gun epics of the pulp magazines and Hollywood horse operas are precisely those which distinguish Conrad Richter as a writer: restraint, selectiveness, a use of surface details scattered with apparent casualness, and a close narrative structure which gives these details meaning, a texture of style. *Early Americana* yields a pure pleasure. This effect comes partly from the legendary nature of the stories themselves. We feel that this is the past and that these things have happened. . . . Partly, too, this effect is the result of a style that is always clear, supple, colloquial, with an occasional tribe figure of frontier speech in its phrasing.

Richter's handling of idiom, character, and the acts of living reveal the working of a point of view. His stories are projected into a middle distance where his people act freely, away from the passions and prejudices of the present. In this middle distance the rigors and dangers of the frontier do not enlarge upon life for pictorial or dramatic effect; they are its actual substance. If the present intrudes briefly upon the past, as it does in several of the stories, it is only because the lives of these people stretch into our own time. Here we perceive the shaping of a narrative method. Some of these stories are told in reminiscence by a character who stands solidly upon the scene but somewhere on the circumference of action. The advantages of this method are twofold. The story of reminiscence takes in both past and present, and it is a form particularly suited to the literature of a late frontier like the Southwest. (pp. 222-23)

The few realistic and intelligent novels about the West have been ignored by criticism, which now takes the conventions and clichés of the Western story for granted. Writers of real talent . . . have passed almost without notice.

Something of the same indifference surrounded *The Sea of Grass* when it appeared. . . . Yet it was plain to anyone who read that the power of the novel lay in its theme . . . and that the novel as reminiscence was for Richter the best way to tell the story. . . .

The Sea of Grass is first of all a book about people. (p. 223)

These people are superior to their background. We are not reading a local colorist. The surface decoration of most Western fiction—night herding, the roundup, cowboy sprees—is lacking here. . . .

Richter's narrator is a realist. He makes no comment where none is needed.

Tacey Cromwell has the same reminiscent pattern. . . . In the hands of another writer it might have been a sentimental or moral lesson of the price a bad woman must pay. Richter gives it an air of realism and restraint because it is told by a boy innocent of the social implications of the story but shrewdly observant of the results.

In *The Trees* Conrad Richter drew for the first time upon his own resources of family legend handed down from the early Pennsylvania-Ohio frontier. To read this novel is to enter completely the world of the past, to limit all thinking and feeling to a point of view that gives no hint of time beyond the lives of its people. This is the particular triumph of Richter's art.

In one sense his novel is all detail about pioneer living, but every detail is lifelike. If Richter has his own ideas about the frontier experience, the pioneer waste, the lessons of hunger or pain, or the hardships of scratch farming in a forest clearing, we do not know what they are. Richter does not step forward to tell us what his novel is about, as another writer might do. It is enough that these things are, that they happen to the people he has assembled. Nor are they assembled so that the story may get under way. They suddenly stand before us, stepping upon the scene as the Luckett family walk out of the forest twilight and go about their business. Things happen by themselves and are understood in themselves. The story unfolds as simply and naturally as the succession of the seasons.

If the novel has a theme, it is the theme of man's seeking. (pp. 224-25)

This is the only novel I know that makes us feel what the first settlers must have felt when they faced the wilderness of trees on the American frontier, the gloom of deep woods where the sun never shone, the terror of straying from dim trails on the forest floor. These trees are not objects of natural beauty; they are a barrier that threatens man's survival. It is easy to understand the frontiersman cutting and burning to clear his fields and to destroy the woods where wild animals and raiding Indians lurked. (p. 225)

The Fields carries forward the story of *The Trees*. Here is the second stage of the conquest of the frontier. The game has almost disappeared; Indians are no longer a menace. Now is the time to farm the land and build a meeting-house and a school. Slowly a frontier settlement takes shape. . . . Outwardly very little happens in this novel, but big scenes are not needed to show the hard work and slow growth that built a frontier community.

Painstaking research underlies these books, but they illustrate the fact that the more a novelist knows about a region or a period the less his atmosphere depends on local color for its effect. Conrad Richter has a great fund of information of the precise sort that a historical novelist must have. . . . This knowledge, however, is never more than the underpinning of his story. There is no surface decoration here—merely the facts of pioneer existence springing from a background of simple necessity. The remarkable fact is that he has accomplished so much with so little reference to actual history. . . . There are no novels quite like Richter's in the whole range of historical fiction. Together they probably give us our truest picture of the everyday realities of frontier life.

The Free Man is a fable of the common man's will to freedom. It is the moving and often tragic story of early patriotism in the Pennsylvania Dutch settlements. . . . The novelette has the knowledge of place and time and the quiet narrative charm found in all Richter's books; the story is dramatic and real, the characterization full and authentic; but the final effect does not quite carry conviction. (pp. 225-26)

Conrad Richter's novels give the impression of definite achievement within a limited field. Alfred Kazin, however, has recently pointed out the importance of the minor writer in an age of crisis like our own. . . . Richter works within a recognizable and authentic folk tradition. He is an example of Kazin's minor novelist, the traditional story-teller. In *The Trees* and *The Fields* people and story are sufficient to support the structure and meaning of these novels, without need for a larger framework of topical reference. The simple and sometimes

lyric effects of Richter's work are the results of a discipline that shows itself in several ways.

Form is always appropriate to the themes and substance of his books. Perhaps it is significant that he began as a writer of short stories, for he seems to have little talent for the loose-gaited novel as it has usually been written in America. His method at best is episodic rather than chronological. Externally *The Sea of Grass* consists of only three episodes which span a generation in time. Several of the chapters in *The Trees* and *The Fields* exist as short stories complete in themselves. These books derive from the earlier *novella*, a determinable form of single effect. . . . Richter has mastered the unity of effect which the short novel demands.

In the process he has tuned a simple, colloquial style rich in elemental feeling and precise in narrative effect. It is the pioneer speech assimilated from old letters and records and regional imagery, just remote enough from our own speech to be convincing but never archaic. (pp. 226-27)

Conrad Richter's novels are regionalism as art. Although criticism cannot grow too solemn over them, they deserve attention because they have added much to our understanding of the regional scene. (p. 227)

> Dayton Kohler, *"Conrad Richter: Early Americana,"* in College English, *Vol. 8, No. 5, February, 1947, pp. 221-27.*

LOUIS BROMFIELD

For some years now we have had among us a top-flight writer working quietly on the story of one family and in a larger sense on the story of this nation's frontier. . . . Conrad Richter has been steadily piling up a record for solid and distinguished achievement. His writing is distinguished and poetic, both as to character and image. It is intensely atmospheric and backed, in the case of the historical novels, on sound research. Moreover he has the supreme gift of novelists in creating a world of utter reality in which the reader is able to lose himself completely after the first page or two.

"The Town" is a third novel devoted to the fortunes of Sayward Wheeler who as a small girl walked with her family from Pennsylvania into the vast and beautiful forest wilderness that was the Ohio territory. Her first appearance was in "The Trees"; the second in "The Fields." As the names imply, the three books are not only concerned with Sayward and her family but the growth and the astonishingly rapid development of a whole area which has played a key role in the nation's history. In the three books we live through the changes. Each book has a locale and a period of its own.

In "The Trees," it is the beautiful and sometimes terrifying forest. . . . The book is concerned with the family's battle against the overwhelming forest and the hardships of battling through to survival in a lonely cabin. The second book is concerned with the complete subduing of the terrifying forest and its conversion into one of the richest agricultural areas on earth. The third concerns the birth and rise of the town, on the very site of that first rude cabin which Sayward, as a small girl, saw raised in the wilderness out of the forest itself. . . .

Mr. Richter has reproduced the quality and the speech of these people so well that a thousand years from now, one may read his books and know exactly what these people were like and what it was like to have lived in an era when within three or four generations a frontier wilderness turned into one of the great industrial areas of the earth.

For those who know Mr. Richter's books, the characters who did not die are still there, recognizable but changed as time and experience change people, softening or embittering them. Yet "The Town" stands on its own as an entity and may be read on its own as a full, rich and comprehensive novel based upon the lives of ordinary people, brave and even heroic in their own small ways. They talk and act like real people and while here and there, one encounters a crazy one or a criminal, these exist not as specimens for a psychiatrist crowding the whole of the scene to the exclusion of all else, but as your neighbors and mine in any ordinary American community. Not one of these characters is dull, for the author has that power of good novelists which finds interest in everything, so that he is able to make even the bore an illuminating study of boredom. . . .

This is in one sense, although not the dominant one, an historical novel, but don't let that frighten you. . . . It is about people and the fundamental things of life. When you read the three books in the trilogy, you live them, and I can think of no greater tribute for a novel. That is what the top level of all fiction has always been and must always be.

> *Louis Bromfield, "Another Volume in Mr. Richter's Fine Frontier Saga," in* New York Herald Tribune Book Review, *April 23, 1950, p. 5.*

FREDERIC I. CARPENTER

The only novelist with whom Conrad Richter can well be compared is Willa Cather. . . . But Richter belongs to a later generation, which both sees the pioneers from a longer perspective and (paradoxically) enters into their lives with a greater emotional immediacy. Between the generations of Willa Cather and of Conrad Richter a myth has begun to form, and this myth has worked to deepen and (in some ways) to distort the tales of the contemporary writer. (pp. 77-8)

Richter has usually been called a simple realist, and all his tales have genuinely been characterized by a careful artistry, a classical condensation, and an emotional restraint. *The Sea of Grass* was a perfect short novel, with hardly a word wasted, and *The Trees* ran but little longer. All these pioneer novels have been packed with homely, realistic detail . . . of an earlier age. Not only external details but the very language and style of his writing have been authentically and consciously early American. By contrast, his symbols have never been explicit and his myth may perhaps be subconscious. But in his last book this myth has become increasingly dominant, and it distinguishes all his best novels from the more purely realistic pioneer tales of Willa Cather and (more recently) of A. B. Guthrie, Jr. It is this myth of the making of America which I shall emphasize, illustrating it chiefly from his recent trilogy describing the settlement of the imaginary town of "Americus," Ohio. (p. 78)

Certainly *The Sea of Grass* is the best of these western tales and may be best of all his novels. Essentially it is a swift-moving story told simply but in the words of a highly educated young man who observes its events. These spoken words retain the rich idiom and imagery of the pioneer West. . . . The inward feeling of the former days is reproduced, as well as the outward events. And the title itself becomes symbolic of all the westward pioneers whose prairie schooners sailed the sea

of grass as the old clipper ships sailed the actual ocean. The metaphor is repeated throughout the book. . . . But the narrative remains simple and direct and the symbol incidental.

Three years later, in *The Trees,* Richter changed the locale from his adopted Southwest to his native Middle West, changed the time from the early nineteenth century to the late seventeenth and, most important, changed the mood and the symbols from the open sea of grass to the shut-in world of the "woodsies," living beneath the shadow of the primeval "trees." . . . But as [the] pioneer family plunges down beneath this sea of treetops, it enters a strange "dark country" submerged under "that ocean of leaves." From the sunlit surface of the southwestern sea of grass, Richter's Ohio pioneers enter a strange, dark, green, subsurface—sometimes subconscious and sometimes almost subhuman—world of primeval, uncivilized wilderness. This strange sea change gives his trilogy of the Ohio pioneers a quality unique in American literature.

Of course, *The Trees* can be read with enjoyment merely on the level of surface realism. (p. 79)

But the surface events are not so memorable as their impact on the minds of these pioneers—and of the reader. . . .

[The] dark world beneath the shadow of the trees, with the darkness it produces in the minds of the characters, is the true theme of the novel. Moreover, it determines the plotting also. . . .

This novel, told on the level of concrete reality, thus becomes also a kind of symbolic tale of the American racial unconscious, in which the mythical pioneer reverts to savagery, both in action and in thought, in order to deal with the savagery of the wilderness. It describes the death of a part of the old civilization in this wilderness, the painful survival of another part, and the rebirth of a new, frontier civilization with the clearing-away of the trees and the settlement of the new land. On the level of myth and symbol the novel suggests the dark night of the soul which accompanied the racial experience of Americans, almost unique in the history of civilization, and the gradual "illumination" which followed.

The Fields and *The Town* continue both the realistic story and the imaginative myth. On the level of realism these novels describe the gradual growth of the family of Portius Wheeler, frontier lawyer, and of Sayward Luckett Wheeler, his wife, with their nine children, until at last the father and mother die and the youngest child reaches maturity. And they describe the gradual growth of the community in which they live from a scattered group of frontier homesteads to an incorporated town, which itself is finally incorporated into an industrial America by the arrival of the new railroad and telegraph. All the external events are narrated in realistic detail. . . . (p. 80)

The plot of these novels is realistic but complex and suggests something more than a surface realism. Briefly, Portius and Sayward Wheeler have eight children, but after the eighth the ill wife withdraws from marital relations and the husband turns to the new young school-mistress, who has a girl child named Rosa. But Sayward hastily accepts her husband back, and a last child, "Chancey" Wheeler, is born. Meanwhile the schoolteacher is married off to Portius Wheeler's disreputable old crony, Jake Tench, and Rosa grows up as one of their slovenly household. The last half of *The Town* describes poignantly the fore-fated romance of the rebellious young Chancey Wheeler with his half-sister Rosa—a romance which ends inevitably with her suicide after Chancey, who has been told the truth, breaks off the relationship. Meanwhile the other eight

Wheeler children grow up, the town grows up, and the nation of which it is a part grows up toward maturity. Against this background of history the individual characters are born, live, prosper, suffer, and die.

Ultimately, of course, the characters make the novel, and this trilogy contains characters as interesting as any others in American fiction. (pp. 80-1)

Conrad Richter not only has created a wealth of pioneer characters, and by their relationships suggested something of the patterns of early American life, but sometimes also has put into their mouths memorable affirmations of the values of that life. . . . Sometimes embodied only in character and event, sometimes suggested in symbol, rarely explicit, this "something deeper and more mysterious" [which one of the characters wonders about] always gives depth and significance to Conrad Richter's pioneer novels. Sailing the sea of grass in their prairie schooners or plunging beneath the surface of a sea of leaves into the dark wilderness of early Ohio, his pioneers live not only as actual adventurers but also as explorers of the primeval past and the racial unconscious. While they cut down the trees and plow the fields and build the new town, they also remember something of the mythical wisdom of the race—and suggest its continuing value for our times also. (p. 83)

Frederic I. Carpenter, "Conrad Richter's Pioneers: Reality and Myth," in College English, *Vol. 12, No. 2, November, 1950, pp. 77-83.*

ORVILLE PRESCOTT

[*This essay originally appeared as a series of reviews in* The New York Times *between 1942 and 1950.*]

During the eleven years 1940 through 1950 Conrad Richter wrote six novels. Of these three were slight and disappointing. The other three comprise Mr. Richter's trilogy about the pioneer settlement of Ohio from the first penetration of the forests by seminomadic hunters in the 1780s until the Civil War. *The Trees, The Fields* and *The Town* are certain to rank among the fine novels of our time. Taken together as a vast epic of the American frontier seen in terms of one family they are a majestic achievement. (pp. 137-38)

Conrad Richter's novels all seem to be efforts to convey in words vivid, accurate, emotionally suggestive impressions of important and typical phases in the development of American society. Mr. Richter is a thorough scholar steeped in the lore of the American past. With consummate artistry he writes as if he and his readers both were part of the vanished life of his stories, using the colloquial idioms and special turns of speech of his characters and never departing from their frame of reference. (p. 138)

Considering the length of the trilogy as a whole, its division into separate episodes and its loose and sprawling structure, it is amazing how emotionally powerful it is. There are wonderfully dramatic and moving stories scattered throughout all three volumes, and wonderfully perceptive full-length portraits of subtly developed characters. There is a rare quality in these glowing pages—the most finished yet unobtrusive artistry, and a profound understanding of the pioneer character as it was manifested in and affected by a way of life now vanished from the earth. These three novels are rich with the special atmosphere of the constantly changing past; and also with a special, intangible atmosphere appropriate to the characters' emotions in various circumstances. Without affectations or stylistic flour-

ishes, Conrad Richter charged his trilogy with intense emotion, an austere but pure and genuinely poetic feeling.

As the climax of *The Town* approaches it becomes apparent that this is not just a superb chronicle of a forest hamlet from the first tree cut down by Sayward's father to the bustling energy of a Civil War city, nor just Sayward's story and that of her husband and children, although it is both of these things. It is also a carefully worked-out and dramatically developed contrast between the diametrically opposed characters of Sayward and her youngest son, Chancey. (pp. 138-39)

Like Sayward in her old age, and like Sayward's feckless, forest-vagrant father, Conrad Richter seems to yearn nostalgically for the life of the wilderness, when the world was still as God made it, unspoiled by towns and factories and railroad tracks; and for the simple virtues of the pioneers—courage, loyalty, friendliness and hardihood. This rosy impression of the forest life of the frontier may be one-sided and a little sentimental; but it is an integral part of Mr. Richter's work. He has not overlooked the suffering and privation, the failures and disasters of the pioneers. But the inner core of his trilogy had to be admiring if it was to express, as I believe it does, Mr. Richter's nostalgia for the lost world of the Ohio pioneers.

So the Ohio trilogy is, in its spiritual essence, a muted and mournful lament over time and change, realistic in detail but lyrical in mood. Sayward and Mr. Richter neither deny nor defy the never-ending tide of change; but they don't like it and they are firmly convinced that it would be a good thing for the world if more people met the depressing changes of modern life with the self-reliant grit of the pioneers. (p. 140)

Orville Prescott, "The Art of Historical Fiction: Richter, Guthrie," in his In My Opinion: An Inquiry into the Contemporary Novel, *The Bobbs-Merrill Company, Inc., 1952, pp. 133-45.**

JOHN T. FLANAGAN

The impact of the two World Wars on novelists of the last several decades has perhaps minimized the role of folklore either as central or as contributory in recent American fiction. But there is one . . . novelist who has employed folklore so frequently and so richly that it is surprising that no critic has previously pointed it out. I speak of Conrad Richter, the author of a trilogy of novels about the settlement of the old Northwest Territory. . . .

Richter's fiction is not limited to this trilogy. . . . [In] his *The Sea of Grass* he achieved a memorable tale of the southwest ranching area which for sensitivity of style and subtle feeling for background rivals Willa Cather's more famous *Death Comes for the Archbishop*. In several of the short stories collected in the volume appropriately entitled *Early Americana* Richter also used various folklore themes, but such material is more apparent in the three volumes about the early Ohio Valley which so far comprise his chief artistic success, *The Trees, The Fields,* and *The Town*. (p. 6)

Many a reader accustomed to the literary conventions of historical fiction will be surprised by the speech of the Lucketts, but it is self-consistent, appropriate, and meticulously recorded. . . .

Descriptions of cabin life resuscitate archaic words until certain passages sound like a linguistic museum. (p. 8)

The Lucketts of course use the standard illiteracies, substituting "er" for the terminal "ow" in words like *window, follow,* and *borrow,* turning "yellow" into "yaller" and "sermon" into "sarment," making "afeard" out of "afraid" and "cam" out of "calm." . . .

Homely idioms recur in the Luckett conversation. . . . A woman who speaks out of turn is ironically presented: "Idy Tull had to go and say sweet as sap that has stood too long and started to work."

Chapter epigraphs in *The Town* illustrate the same interest in folk speech. . . .

The emergencies of family life far from the amenities and resources of civilization often produce odd bits of traditional lore or superstition. Particularly when immediate medical care is required do such survivals emerge from the reservoir of the past. (p. 9)

Superstitions transmitted from one generation to another sometimes affect the actions of the characters. Worth once shot an albino deer but refused to bring home the meat because he considered it tainted. . . .

Staves of old ballads and fragments of folk songs remotely derived from the border minstrelsy of another land are heard occasionally. Song makes monotonous chores less dreary or reflects the mood of the character. . . . (p. 11)

Characters who can neither sing nor recite often rely on the proverb or maxim to explain conduct at critical times or to express their own thoughts more aptly. (p. 12)

In her physical and social maturity Sayward grows farther away from the primitivism of her people. Her speech changes slightly and is less colloquial and illiterate. She has little need to rely on the cures, customs, and even domestic practices derived from tradition; outwardly she conforms more and more to the amenities of a developing civilization. Proverbial wisdom comes less frequently from her lips, the superstitions of the frontier have vanished, and much of the life of the folk has been supplanted by the conventions of the town. (pp. 12-13)

Sayward's own children, nine in number, are reared in a somewhat different environment and come to their maturity in the town of Americus rather than in the backwoods hamlet of Moonshine Church. In other words, the circumstances of life for the first generation in the forests of Ohio are quite different from the social compulsions experienced by the second. It is not only that the physical dangers of Indian attacks, of wild beasts, and of imminent starvation have disappeared, but that Sayward's children are reared in a period when personal security, a certain amount of schooling, and social respectability are established commonplaces. Sayward herself may revert occasionally to the customs or speech of her youth, but her husband Portius, except for an early period as a fugitive "woodsy," has always regarded primitive life with Back Bay contempt, and the Wheeler children quickly forget their period of cabin existence.

As a consequence, Conrad Richter employs substantially less folklore in *The Town* than in the two preceding novels. Occasionally he utilizes the homely language, especially in describing Sayward's moods or deeds, that marks the first novels. . . . Similarly, the colloquialisms of Sayward's children are the everyday abbreviations and slang of town speech rather than the older idioms of the frontier folk. Proverbs and maxims appear less frequently in the conversation. Doctors with professional training have made unnecessary the old reliance on popular cures and nostrums. Catches of old songs, vulgar riddles, country superstitions, folklore references are less a part of diurnal existence. (pp. 13-14)

But if the final novel of Conrad Richter's trilogy seems little indebted to folklore, there can be no question of the special vitality which folklore gives to *The Trees* and *The Fields*. The Luckett family and, at least in their youth, the Wheeler children live much of their lives in accordance with past conventions and traditions. Their hunting activities, the preparation of their food, their remedies in case of illness, the ceremonies of birth and marriage and death, their simple religion, their response to the supernatural, their social mores, all owe much to the dictates of the folk. Conrad Richter's fiction is the richer and the more convincing because he has seen fit to incorporate such material in his dialogue, action, and characterization. And if the portrait of Sayward Luckett Wheeler is the finest portrait ever drawn in fiction of the American frontier woman, it might be contended that her excellence rests squarely on Richter's depiction of her as a woman strongly if often unconsciously influenced by racial and folk tradition. Her cultural legacy makes her what she is and demonstrates the tremendous importance of folk survivals in the frontier period. (p. 14)

> *John T. Flanagan, "Folklore in the Novels of Conrad Richter," in* Midwest Folklore, *Vol. II, No. 1, Spring, 1952, pp. 5-14.*

JOHN T. FLANAGAN

[Although Richter's] historical trilogy is his most distinguished work to date, he is limited neither by one region nor by one fictional type. The three novels about middle western settlement are specific, documentary, and detailed, although their canvas is rather small. But his fiction about the Southwest is atmospheric, dramatic, and episodic. His four books of stories about his adopted environment are as authentic and vivid as his studies of Pennsylvania and Ohio life, yet they are different in tone and even in technique. (pp. 189-90)

New Mexico, with minor extensions into Texas and Arizona, forms the locale of Richter's southwestern fiction, and the time is generally the nineteenth century. Border raids, Indian uprisings, the arrival of settlers, and the bitter feuds of stockmen and nesters provide the plots; vaqueros, herders, half-breeds, sheriffs, outlaws, Spanish patentees, English and Yankee adventurers, and a sprinkling of lawyers and doctors are the characters; and rivalry and revenge suggest the tension of early territorial days. But Richter generally avoids sensationalism for its own sake. . . .

In 1936 Richter published his first book with a southwestern setting, *Early Americana and Other Stories*. . . . The nine stories deal mostly with the frontier period. Historical places . . . suggest the setting, and the characters in the main are ordinary figures—mountain men, soldiers, ranchers, Indians, homesteaders. Although violence enters into many of the tales, the reader is spared much of the actual brutality. Killings and mutilations are reported rather than photographed, and the rumored Apache outrages suggest a destiny which is always imminent but seldom an actuality. To insure life in such a world of savagery certain basic qualities were essential. Richter's men are quiet, tight-lipped, hawk-eyed, self-reliant, determined, proud. His women often lament the providence that brought them to the southwestern plains and criticize the men who led them there, but they remain despite their loneliness, isolation, and danger. Men and women alike possess the courage which alone can guarantee survival.

Reduced to basic events, Richter's plots are simple episodes. (p. 190)

The stories are short, succinct, uncluttered. Never interested in documentation for its own sake, Richter selects authentic details but uses them sparingly. Scenes are suggested rather than underscored. Atmosphere is more important than a specific canvas. Yet emotions are kept taut, and strong impressions of passion and danger are conveyed. Proceeding somewhat like an impressionistic painter, Richter employs bright and challenging colors but concentrates more on mood and tone than on unblurred outline.

In 1937 appeared his familiar novelette of New Mexico ranch country, *The Sea of Grass*. . . . In Conrad Richter's version of a familiar pioneer theme, the hero exults in his fight against nature and a crude environment, but the heroine is resentful, dissatisfied, and finally a fugitive. Yet neither husband nor wife perishes in the struggle, and with the occupational feud in the region settled by nature, the story ends quietly.

In his third volume about the Southwest, *Tacey Cromwell,* which appeared in 1942, Richter eschewed the grasslands for the more sophisticated and more seamy life of the small mining town. . . . Richter was less successful here than in *The Sea of Grass* in fusing atmosphere and characters. The scenes are too often the finely outlined but metallic plates of an album, accurate, colorful, but remote. If Gaye is an acceptable but conventional gambler who sincerely wishes to find a less parasitic profession, Tacey is harder to accept, the scarlet woman with the heart of gold whose reform is perhaps genuine but is not made convincing. Her life does not have the passionate justification of sin that makes Hawthorne's Hester Prynne memorable; she is cold and marmoreal. (pp. 191-92)

The Lady [is] a novelette in form which evinces all the charm and impact of a subtle artistry. Again the setting is the New Mexico of the past, the period of the open range which is fought over by ranchers and sheepmen. And again racial strands are mixed in the figures of the story. Aristocratic inheritance and opportunist cupidity symbolize the rival parties, and in the end the heritage evaporates and the avarice is cooled by death. (p. 192)

The reader of Richter's three southwestern romances cannot fail to observe a technique which suggests Willa Cather, despite a difference in scene and milieu. Avoiding an omniscient point of view and avoiding also a point of view limited to the protagonist, he has three times chosen as his narrator a young male relative of the chief family, who is occasionally in attendance, who reflects the crucial events, and who retains a warm and close interest in the action. (p. 193)

In setting as in characterization Richter . . . relies heavily on suggestion and atmosphere. No scene is ever fully developed, and there are many hiatuses in plot continuity. Yet, particularly in *The Sea of Grass* and *The Lady,* the reader is eminently conscious of a viable milieu and social order.

Like Willa Cather again, Richter is selective. Neither writer has any sympathy for the naturalistic technique, which requires complete documentation, a deliberately slow unfolding of the story, and too often a conscious choice of seamy and vicious elements. Life in the Richter romances is actually far from pretty. . . . Adultery and bribery are common practices. But the romances do not focus primarily on these things, and they are seldom exaggerated. Repetition and attenuation are not key devices here. Sensational events are suggested or reported, and they exist primarily for their effect on motivation and characterization. Even details of setting are sparse but crucial. The cool patios, the dusty plazas, the adobe buildings, the whitened sand-deep roads, the sun-baked mesas establish the scene irrevocably without need of elaboration. (p. 195)

Despite the fact that Richter has devoted four books of fiction to New Mexico and contiguous territory, he has never depicted the contemporary scene in a novel. . . . Because of this historical orientation he has been forced to derive the substance of his tales from literary sources, and when he has allowed his imagination free play he has peopled the trails and ranches of another time. One can be grateful to Conrad Richter for his accomplishment, an accomplishment which establishes him as one of the most successful and durable storytellers of our day. . . . (pp. 195-96)

> *John T. Flanagan, "Conrad Richter: Romancer of the Southwest," in* Southwest Review, *Vol. XLIII, No. 3, Summer, 1958, pp. 189-96.*

COLEMAN ROSENBERGER

"The Waters of Kronos" is an enchanted book. . . .

I have found it, too, a deeply moving book, and I believe that many readers similarly will find it speaks to them directly and affectingly with a peculiarly personal appeal.

Conrad Richter remains too little recognized for what he of a certainty is—one of the finest creative talents in American fiction. . . .

He has stood alone in his creative use of historical materials, in the working—in his own phrase—of "those slender veins of golden metal that still remain" of the American past.

In **"The Waters of Kronos"** he turns the same practiced skills to a purpose achieved with more difficulty—the mining of the world of his own youth. The reader is immersed with him in a town at the turn of the present century, "peopled with the multitudinous, imaginary forms" of his past. I know of nothing comparable to it among American novels. In the whole range of American writing of which I have any knowledge, perhaps the nearest approach in quality and theme is Thornton Wilder's play "Our Town."

In Mr. Richter's novel it is given to John Donner to re-enter the world of his youth. Out of his deep "yearning for many things vanished," he is able to return, keeping his later knowledge of the worth and sweetness of all those things which in their time he had counted but little. . . .

Shining with this heightened awareness, the re-creation of the past is marvelously evocative. . . .

But for John Donner this is a journey of discovery into greater depths than to talk on a summer evening of a time lost and gone. . . . He is driven, "back here at the source," to seek answers to questions which had become increasingly insistent to him with his years. (pp. 1, 11)

The novel closes with John Donner's sure conviction that he will meet his mother "tomorrow," and that with their meeting will come fuller knowledge and understanding. The reader can only hope that the story of John Donner's search will be carried forward into this tomorrow in a further volume. (p. 11)

Coleman Rosenberger, "Mr. Richter's Magic Touch," in New York Herald Tribune Book Review, *April 17, 1960, pp. 1, 11.*

GEORGE R. CLAY

Although the books of Conrad Richter tend to dwell on the past, there is a deceptive timeliness about much of this author's fiction, a tone of what might be called fashionable nostalgia. Each generation craves something different from the past, qualities the generation both lacks and misses. In his best work . . . Mr. Richter has afforded his readers the vicarious sense of heroism they long for without employing the pat heroics they have been schooled to suspect. His secret has been a style perfectly suited to his semi-legendary material: at once mannered and sensuous, lush yet restrained, so that inherently pompous or sentimental effects are just saved from becoming so by his instinct for severely relevant detail.

In **"The Waters of Kronos"** . . . Mr. Richter has once again attempted to infuse a highly nostalgic theme with dignity. John Donner, at the end of a long and successful life in the West, returns to Unionville, the Eastern mining town where he was born. He knows that his home valley has been inundated to make a hydro-electric station, but feels that if he can just be near what once was Unionville before he dies, he will find the answers to two haunting questions: whether he is his father's son; and whose face it was that, night after night, terrified him in the dreams of his boyhood. . . .

Donner stumbles on proof that he is, indeed, of his father's flesh and blood. And just before his actual death, when dream and reality must fuse, he looks in a mirror and realizes that the face in his childhood nightmares was not his father's, as he had suspected, but his own: the spectre of his future self, "marked with the inescapable dissolution and decay of his youth." Convinced that the "son-father-hate legend" is falsehood, he feels that he has exorcized the very root of fear and is free to die in peace. (p. 4)

Mr. Richter's device for mingling Time is successful; it is unfortunate that the revelation for which his portentous prose and insistent symbolism have prepared us seems disappointing. To challenge Freud's theories about the Oedipus complex may be a worthy objective, but it doesn't belong to the realm of fictionalized revelation. Mr. Richter's style and method are still perfectly matched, but neither one suits his message. In attempting to dramatize what he took to be a universal truth, he has made the mistake of employing fantasy to expound a private argument. (p. 5)

George R. Clay, "Mirror of the Future," in The New York Times Book Review, *May 1, 1960, pp. 4-5.*

CHAD WALSH

The actual plot of **"A Simple Honorable Man"** is so simple that it suggests a short story or vignette rather than a novel. It is the life of Harry Donner, a Pennsylvania storekeeper who—shortly before the turn of the century—feels a call to the ministry. He packs himself and his family off to college and seminary, is at last ordained, serves a succession of Lutheran churches in one mining community after another, never achieves fame, dies poor.

If the book echoes and glows in the reader's memory, it is for reasons other than bare plot. For one thing, Conrad Richter has the gift of creating real characters, whom he portrays with sympathetic understanding rather than clinical detachment. The simple, stubborn, willful, often half literate people who move through the book ring true to anyone who knew any part of the American back-country before mass communications began homogenizing it with the urban norm. Most of all, the author has succeeded in depicting a minister who is both lovable and believable, a rare feat in fiction, where Protestant parsons tend either to be impossibly holy, fatuous, or monsters of covert wickedness. (p. 4)

The sense of journeying back into a recent but forever-abandoned national past is accentuated by the way the book is written. It plays no sophisticated tricks with time; there is no breath of Freud. The characters, so to speak, are loved into convincing reality by the author. Most of all, Harry Donner, with his dark moments and occasional nights of secret groaning, is a convincing picture of a simple but not silly soul, one who finds human beings inherently worth the compassion and self-giving that come natural to him.

From a purely formal viewpoint, there are things about the novel that trouble and confuse the reader at moments. The movement of the narrative is jerky, and one coal town and church seem to fade into the next without clean transitions. But the total impact of **"A Simple Honorable Man"** is of a particular beauty. If the words were not somehow hard to utter nowadays, one would say it is the beauty of goodness. (p. 26)

Chad Walsh, "A Stubborn Seer of Latent Goodness," in The New York Times Book Review, *May 6, 1962, pp. 4, 26.*

MARVIN J. LaHOOD

When the noted historian Frederick Jackson Turner stated in an address in 1893 that the settlement of the West explained American development, he focused attention on an aspect of American culture which has received constant study and analysis ever since. . . . And perhaps the most whole-hearted exponent of [Turner's] viewpoint among contemporary American men of letters is Conrad Richter. His fiction is all but entirely a nostalgic hymn of praise for the vigor of the American pioneer. (p. 311)

Much has happened to the American dream since [President Andrew] Jackson died in 1845. Even in his lifetime those forces which would cause much of the disillusionment with that dream recorded in fiction by writers from Hamlin Garland to John Steinbeck were already in motion. Conrad Richter focuses his attention not on the corruption of the dream but on the dream itself. He belongs to that group of writers who are impressed with the strength and perseverance of the pioneer, and feel that this strength was a direct result of having dealt with the rigors of the frontier.

These writers see the West not as a symbol of man's dreams of a perfect existence but as a challenge which, if accepted, strengthens the character of man. For them the dream of the West is not one of a return to Eden, nor of a spiritual brotherhood of man. It is, rather, a vision of a land where men, if they are strong enough, can live in freedom and with a sense of accomplishment for having subdued the forces encountered in this great continent. Theirs is the literature neither of protest nor of disillusion. For them the dream was not an illusion because it was a sober dream. There were casualties, to be sure, but they accepted them as part of the price man has to pay for any adventure. And for the men and women who had the strength to survive, the rewards were substantial. (pp. 311-12)

Richter has had from his youth an attraction for the vigor of American pioneers. . . . He mourned the passing of the frontier because he felt that with its passing this quality of vigor would pass too. . . . Conrad Richter's greatest contribution to American letters is his tireless effort to put into fiction the setting and the people of an important moment in our nation's history. In the best of his novels and stories that moment lives again. (p. 312)

His first stories gave evidence that he would never write "crowded" works and that he was a good story teller, at least insofar as he wasted few words in presenting any situation. What is not clearly evident in these early stories, but what is an important aspect of all of his thinking, is his nostalgia for his ancestors and his own youth, and with this, a nostalgia for America's past. . . . Through story and research he uncovered in the American past a breed of giants that satisfied his deep desire for an image of man as hard working and persevering, as a force which triumphed over adversity. (pp. 312-13)

In the work of Conrad Richter, choosing the more difficult way always leads to success. . . .

Conrad Richter has never written a novel which does not have as one of its themes the American pioneer's struggle and resultant strength. But the place where this theme is his central and abiding concern is his trilogy. (p. 313)

On one level the trilogy is a realistic account of the settlement of the Ohio valley. Everything from household utensils to manners of speech has been conscientiously recorded by Richter. On another level the story is one more chapter in man's endless struggle with the forces of nature. (pp. 313-14)

In *The Fields* . . . Richter continues some of the techniques he used in *The Trees* to insure the faithfulness of his portrait of the early settlers. The language he writes in is the language his research revealed as spoken by these pioneers. Other elements of their lives which he includes to advantage are the prevalent folk tales, folk myths, and superstitions. As the action progresses from the primitive world of *The Trees* to the more complex world of *The Town* the language becomes more sophisticated and the superstitions begin to disappear. These details thus further help him in his effort to portray the many changes that occurred in the Ohio valley over the period covered in the trilogy.

In *The Fields* agrarian concerns are predominant. New settlers move in and the nucleus of a small community is formed. While the fierce individualism of the hunter is no longer in evidence, the people who stay and settle retain enough of their will for self-government to make the rude democracy which operates in such a community extremely vital. . . . In the course of time the dark woods are replaced by the first faint lights of spirit and intellect. (pp. 314-15)

In [*The Town*] the portrait of the great pioneer heroine Sayward is completed, but here she shares the protagonist's role with her youngest son Chancey; he is the spokesman for "modern" social thinking, she for the pioneer's views. This contrast between two ways of life, one soft and the other hard, forms the core of the novel, and it gives Richter a chance to state clearly his views on both ways—he leaves no room for doubt as to

where he stands. As the trilogy nears its end one thing becomes very clear: the pioneer's way was a hard way. Faced with the problem of survival in a hostile environment, he either met the challenge or perished. Most of our vaunted American practicality (and some of our materialism and anti-intellectualism too) was developed in this life or death contest.

Richter's trilogy is a paean of praise for the American pioneer spirit. In *The Town* the gospel of hard work is preached relentlessly. . . . The folks who didn't want to do anything on the American frontier perished. Chancey, standing at his mother's deathbed at the end of *The Town*, is just beginning to realize the sense of his mother's way of life. There is a dignity that hard work gives to a human being, no matter what the task at hand. (p. 315)

Conrad Richter's West is not the romantic, idealized West of some authors, nor is it the harsh, drought-ridden West of others. It had something of value to be won from it, and the key was hard work. (p. 316)

Marvin J. LaHood, "Richter's Early America," in University Review, *Vol. XXX, No. 4, Summer, 1964, pp. 311-16.*

THOMAS P. McDONNELL

If you live with dreadful awareness of man's perplexity in the twentieth century . . . , then you will have a very disconcerting time trying to penetrate the simplistic world of Conrad Richter's hillbilly pastoral [*The Grandfathers*]. . . .

[What] are we to make of an American short novel, so outstripped by any meaning that we can look for in American life today, that it confronts us . . . with people called Granpap, Granmam, Ant Dib, Uncle Heb, Uncle Nun, Fox, Babe, Chick, Felty, Sip, Morg, Effie, and Chariter, the Daisy Mae heroine of all this slightly amusing rural shebang? Or what are we to make of such cliché chapter-opening sentences as, "Sunday morning came to Kettle Valley mild and clear after early fog." One means, does there have to be a Kettle Valley, even without the cinematic felicities of Ma and Pa?

To carp at such bland devices would seem, no doubt, to indicate a case of chronic distemper in the overwrought urban reader. Let it be said at once, then, that *The Grandfathers* is a pleasantly bucolic tale whose reading-time may just about equal, say, three or four sessions with "The Beverly Hillbillies." Chariter, the sixteen-year-old "fatherless" daughter of Dockey Murdoch—practically every young 'un in Kettle Valley ends up fatherless—herself becomes the prime object of the spring mating season. . . .

Fill it all in—Granpap accused of arson, a property impasse between neighbors, Chariter's episode in the household of Squire Goddem, and you pretty well have the picture of Conrad Richter's vision of life in a Western Maryland mountain community. One has the slightest intimation, in reading all this, of a sometime struggle between the life-arranging insistence of the elders and the self-determination of the young. Certainly, this must be the only theme that the "grandfathers" of the novel can possibly serve. . . . [Conrad Richter has produced] a body of imaginative Americana which must sooner or later attract some critical attention. The early nannies who made clucking sounds of excess admiration for *The Sea of Grass*, for example, did not much help his cause by calling it a classic the day it was out. Following this, he was struck with one success after another . . . , before the age of [J. D.] Salinger and [John] Updike set all too solidly in. All to the good; but one is hard put to recall the vivid recreation—or even the name—of a single memorable character in this body of work. Neither has it, apparently, in any memorable or archetypal instance, recreated what must have been the traumatic experience of the American Adam reborn in the dark womb of the American continent.

In any case, with the writing of **The Grandfathers,** we are told that Richter has attempted something quite different from his other books; and one supposes that this simply means that the latest one has a slightly larger dose of country humor than the others. This granted, however, it is incredible that Richter could have attempted even this minor episode with so little awareness of what, in his own time, has already been done in the genre of American pastoral: by Jesse Stuart in *Taps for Private Tussie,* John Steinbeck in *Cannery Row,* William Faulkner in *The Reivers,* Erskine Caldwell in *God's Little Acre,* and (seriously) Al Capp in ''Li'l Abner.'' The first of these alone, and in itself a grossly underrated minor classic, is a far more engaging book than Richter's. The awakening of the young boy (Jesse Stuart?) to the wonder and fierce desire for book-learning seems much more genuine to me than Chariter's emergence from bucolic pubescence to tribal matrimony. And so on. (p. 67)

> *Thomas P. McDonnell, in a review of ''The Grand-fathers,'' in* The Critic, *Vol. 22, No. 6, June-July, 1964, pp. 67-8.*

EDWIN W. GASTON, JR.

The Free Man, Always Young and Fair, The Light in the Forest, and **The Grandfathers** seem to represent for the author a respite from the creative rigors of . . . [his] more ambitious works. Yet they are by no means—nor were they intended to be—light exercises to keep authorial techniques sharpened for bigger things. For this reason, then, the impression that the four represent interludes results more nearly from artistic lapses than from Richter's intention. . . .

[Of all] Richter's novels, **The Free Man** received possibly the sharpest critical rebuke. (p. 117)

A major reason for the novel's shortcoming is its purpose to inspire the present with lessons of the past, for Richter was writing in the midst of World War II. ''Perhaps in an understanding of the Pennsylvania Dutch, their loyalty to democracy and their love of peace,'' wrote Richter in the preface to the novel, ''may be found the secret of a peaceful Europe in the years to come.'' Such purposive tendencies, of course, were not new. American literary figures as early as Philip Freneau, of the Revolutionary War era, had similarly weakened their art in behalf of a cause. And, when Richter turned to the same Revolutionary War for examples to inspire his own age, he likewise faltered.

It must be conceded, however, that **The Free Man** was timely in recalling the occasionally neglected fact that American freedom sprang from European roots. (p. 118)

[One] of the novel's basic weaknesses [is] the improbable union of the lowly Henry Free and the aristocratic Amity Bayley. (p. 119)

And this flaw of plot underscores a more crucial failing of characterization. **The Free Man** is a vignette; as such it should provide a much clearer picture certainly of the protagonist, Henry Free, and also of his antagonist-turned-mate, Amity Bayley. In the effort to impress upon the reader Henry Free's love of freedom and his difficulty in earning it, however, Richter stresses brutality at the expense of affection that is necessary to bind the reader to the boy. . . . Moreover, the failure of Richter to depict Amity Bayley as a rounded personality results in her emerging as something more nearly resembling a china doll than a flesh-and-blood person. And it links her with a character likewise inadequately portrayed, Rudith Watrous of **Tacey Cromwell.**

Despite their flaws of characterization and their improbable mating, Henry Free and Amity Bayley in marriage do perform the service of illustrating one of the themes of the novel. Through the union of German and English, Richter . . . presents the theme of America as a melting pot of ethnic groups. It is a concept that the author had dealt with previously in ''**As It Was in the Beginning**'' and with which he would deal again in **The Light in the Forest** and in **The Lady.** The melting-pot concept is a corollary of the larger theme of historic change, which, in Richter's fiction, grows out of the processes of ''westering.'' And **The Free Man**—set earlier than any other of the author's works growing out of such processes—thus demonstrates that, virtually from the beginning of European civilization in America, ethnic lines dissolved through marriage. In turn, the themes of historic change and America as a melting pot recall Richter's essayical theory of evolutionary progress.

Henry Free's successful fight for freedom represents a second theme related to ''westering'': hardship-into-gain. And the hardship—the adversity—harkens back to Richter's theory of human-energy supply and expenditure. In his philosophical essays, the author insists that adversity enables an individual to draw on supplies of energy from his own organism and consequently to satisfy an energy hunger. In **The Free Man** he implies that man collectively is enabled to satisfy the hunger for freedom by undergoing adversity. The theme of hardship-into-gain here is a link in the chain that extends throughout Richter's fiction.

The scope of Henry Free's life further stands for the theme of man's enduring and prevailing, a concept closely related to the essayical theory of evolutionary progress. But, in the course of ''westering,'' man does not always endure. The Swiss and German settlers who die aboard the ship that brings Henry Free to America, for example, illustrate the failure. Of these, the youths who die reinforce the novel's theme of the tragedy of youthful death. Youthful death, a negative corollary, is a theme likewise employed by Richter in **Early Americana, The Sea of Grass, The Lady, The Trees, The Fields,** and **The Town.**

Shoring up these themes, with their overtones of freedom, are at least two obvious symbols in **The Free Man.** The iron collar Henry Free wears as an indentured servant represents forces that restrict man's freedom. And Queen Street, on which Amity Bayley resides in Reading, stands for aristocracy that would compel others to servitude.

As a historical service, **The Free Man** reveals important but unfamiliar aspects of American nationhood and the part played by the Pennsylvania Dutch with their ''little Declaration of Independence'' as early as April and May of 1775 and with their introduction and development of the pioneer rifle. These actual events, as well as the other themes, result in the novel's making a plea for international understanding and brotherhood. (pp. 119-21)

[In the second interlude], **Always Young and Fair,** Richter turned for the first time since his short stories of 1913-33 to the Pennsylvania of his youth. (p. 121)

In essence it is the story of a representative segment of Teddy Roosevelt's America, of the serene, bucolic life often referred to as the "age of innocence." Its final chapters, however, link the novel with Woodrow Wilson's America. And one of the strong points of the work is its successful re-creation of the spirit of the times and place.

Against this background, Richter again employs a youthful narrator to tell the story. . . . [And] like all of Richter's fictional predecessors, he is sufficiently detached to present an objective account. A portion of his detachment may be attributed here, as in nearly all of Richter's works employing a narrator, to the fact that Johnny for several years is away at college and thus unable to observe directly the events of a given moment.

As related by Johnny, Lucy Markle's story (like that of [F. Scott Fitzgerald's] Jay Gatsby) involves an attempt to stop the clock. In 1898, Private Tom Grail, aged twenty, dies in the service of Company G of the Pennsylvania National Guard in the Philippines. Supposedly he had been engaged to Lucy Markle, then aged eighteen, who, although thought by most actually to love Tom's cousin Captain Will Grail, was felt to be motivated by pity for Tom in her choice between the two.

Upon Tom's death, Lucy busies herself by caring for the dead youth's rheumatic father and in numerous other ways reflecting homage to Tom's memory. Initially she spurns the marriage offer of Will Grail, and, later, when she has consented, fails to appear for her wedding. The years speed by. . . . At a Legion hall dedication, Lucy hears a public reference to herself as a "well-preserved, gray-haired lady." Only then does she realize, in terror and with sudden resentment, that she, like all mortal flesh, has grown old and that only the memory of Tom Grail, to which she has devoted her life, has stayed forever fresh and unchanging—"always young and fair." In feverishly casting herself upon Will Grail, then, she thus prepares the way for the macabre denouement: shortly after their marriage, Will becomes an invalid for whom Lucy must care until the end of his days.

In *Always Young and Fair,* then, Richter has inadvertently veered into tragicomedy in reverse. Classical tragicomedy, of course, is a play with a plot suitable to tragedy but which ends happily like a comedy. Although doubtlessly intended as a serious vignette, *Always Young and Fair* revolves around personal actions so eccentric as to become ludicrous until the denouement, which takes a turn toward the tragic.

The character of Lucy Markle, with her vanity, her growing eccentricities, and her consuming egotism, is clearly drawn. But other aspects of characterization remain faulty. Primary among these flaws is the relationship of Lucy and Will Grail, each of whom lives unaccountably long within his own rigid reserve. That Will could be patient at first with Lucy's perversity is understandable; that he does not openly rebel earlier in a more vigorous way is not. Lucy and Will, nevertheless, become the only characters in Richter's fiction to end in tragedy because of their own willfulness, and they thus command greater attention than they might otherwise deserve. (pp. 122-23)

As an objective and realistic historical novel dealing with the relationship between the Scotch-Irish settlers of western Pennsylvania and the Tuscarawa (Delaware) Indians during 1764-65, *The Light in the Forest* has . . . [drawn praise] for its fidelity to ethnohistory. (p. 125)

Richter sets his story in 1765 in the Tuscarawa village at the forks of the Muskingum in Ohio and in western Pennsylvania. Then, using an omniscient point of view and the idiom of both the Indian and the pioneer settler, he relates the experiences of young John Cameron Butler: his captivity and rearing by Indians who name him True Son, his compulsory return by Colonel Boquet to his white parents, his inability to readjust to the white man's ways, and his unsuccessful attempt to return to his Indian foster parents. (pp. 126-27)

The title for *The Light in the Forest* Richter derives from a quotation from Wordsworth that prefaces the novel:

> Shades of the prison-house begin to close
>   Upon the growing Boy,
> But he beholds the light, and whence it flows,
>   He sees it in his joy.

And inherent in the quotation is one of the basic themes of the novel: the restrictions that civilization places on the individual. This theme actually is a corollary of the larger concept of historic change that grows out of the processes of "westering"; and historic change, in turn, is suggestive of Richter's essayical theory of evolutionary progress. As True Son, John Butler (like his adopted Indian brothers) lives as free as the open air. But returned to his white parents he experiences the constraints of civilization. . . . (pp. 127-28)

Still other corollaries of historic change, set forth in *The Light in the Forest,* are the themes of America as an ethnic melting pot (illustrated by the marriage of Little Crane and his white wife); the mixed allegiance of an individual to two opposing ethnic groups (represented mainly by John Butler); and the duality of civilization that is at once both good and evil (shown in the contrast between John's decent white father Harry, on the one hand, and his evil uncle Wilse, on the other). (p. 128)

The contrast between Indian and white, of course, is not simply that between good and evil; True Son at first thinks so but he ultimately and sadly learns better. The moment of truth, in which he discovers the Indian to be as savage as the white had insisted he was, haunts the boy. . . . Here, then, Richter introduces into his novel the theme of appearance and reality, and thereby touches also on the ambiguity of good and evil.

While objectively treating both white and Indian, the author still reflects something of a bias for the latter. His portrayal of True Son and Cuyloga reveals the author to be sympathetic with the Noble Savage concept of early Romantic literature in America. Further strengthening this impression is the fact that only two of the whites . . . are depicted as having any genuine understanding of the plight of the Indian-like white boy.

In thus sympathizing with the Indian, Richter brings to the novel the theme of brotherhood. *The Light in the Forest* thus resembles two earlier novels and a like number of earlier short stories. One of its predecessors, *Tacey Cromwell,* pleads for tolerance of human frailty, with the theme reinforced by the reaction of so-called "respectable" women to a reformed prostitute. And the two stories, **"Good Neighbors"** and **"The Laughter of Leen,"** inspired by World Wars II and I, respectively, call for understanding of a nation's wartime enemies in foreign countries. *The Free Man,* written during World War II, also makes such a plea. *The Light in the Forest* ostensibly explores still another side of the theme of brotherhood by seeking to promote harmony between two opposing ethnic groups in the same country. . . . While the short stories belong to Richter's non-"westering" fiction, the three novels grow out of processes of "westering." For this reason, the theme of brotherhood in the longer works actually serves as a corollary of the larger concept of man's enduring and prevailing—an idea related to the essayical theory of evolutionary progress. (pp. 128-30)

In the corpus of Richter's fiction, brotherhood and its larger theme of man's enduring and prevailing signify success—evolutionary progress. But in the course of "westering" man does not always succeed. To illustrate this verity, then, the author admits into *The Light in the Forest* two negative corollaries: the tragedy of youthful death and the inability of Eastern woman to adjust to frontier life. (p. 130)

On the psychologically subconscious and mystical levels, *The Light in the Forest* promotes the theme of the mystique of the wilderness by revealing the Indians in close contact with nature and by contrasting their way of free living with the white's constrictions. The mystique of the wilderness is a corollary of Richter's theme of the organic unity of man and nature, which, in turn, recalls the essayical theory that all life is governed by natural laws. (pp. 130-31)

Finally, *The Light in the Forest* . . . continues the mystical theme of the search for and reconciliation with the Spiritual Father. John Butler becomes alienated not from one, but two (his white and his Indian) earthly fathers. And since the earthly father serves as a symbol of the Spiritual, he becomes isolated inferentially from the Spiritual. Compounding his problem, John does not understand his mother, whose love could provide a key to the understanding of his earthly (and hence his Spiritual) father. . . .

[*The Grandfathers*] represents his fourth and final interlude to date. . . . [It] finds a place in the corpus of Richter's Midwestern fiction by contributing further to the panoramic view of life that the author continues to portray of his native Pennsylvania and environs. Moreover, the work is Richter's first to be devoted almost exclusively to comedy.

Although creating an initial impression that it serves as a depository for unused humorous anecdotes Richter has collected during his half-century of writing, *The Grandfathers* received favorable reviews. (p. 131)

The main story line, interlaced with tall tales and subsidiary episodes bordering on burlesque, causes *The Grandfathers* to veer dangerously close to farce. And in lesser hands than Richter's it would. One of the factors that mitigates against the work's degenerating into an installment of television's "Beverly Hillbillies" is its pastoral quality. . . . Richter, it is true, lacks the complex vision of [Robert Frost or William Faulkner], but he still is able to portray a rustic world that simplifies human conflicts and which thus evokes a response in the reader.

Further redeeming the novel from farce, Richter expertly applies liberal doses of authentic folklore. . . . In recreating a hell-fire-and-brimstone sermon, the author reveals a deft ear for folk speech. . . . (pp. 134-35)

Viewed for its contribution toward completing Richter's panoramic view of his native Pennsylvania and environs, *The Grandfathers* assumes still greater significance. . . . [Because] it is his first to deal with western Maryland, it tends even more to complement his panoramic view.

Finally, *The Grandfathers* proves meritorious in its fidelity to themes that Richter has promoted throughout his fiction. For all of its humor, the novel contains characteristic authorial

seriousness. One example is an omnisciently poignant passage in which the reader learns that Ant Dib's twins will never grow up. Less "than a week before starting school, they would take spine fever, the boy first, the girl soon after, and both die within twenty four hours of each other." This revelation, coupled with the early death of Dick Goddem, is in Richter's thematic tradition of the tragedy of youthful death. (pp. 135-36)

On the psychological-mystical level, *The Grandfathers,* harkening back to Richter's essayical theories, repeats the themes of the search for the Father and for individual identity, and of altruism. All three are embodied in the thoughts and actions of Chariter, the psychic center of the novel. . . .

These virtues notwithstanding, *The Grandfathers* is not without faults. Central among its shortcomings, the characters are derivative. (p. 136)

Another weakness occasionally appears in strained efforts for humor. . . .

Structurally *The Grandfathers* is also derivative, but the practice in this instance is not objectionable. In *Always Young and Fair,* for example, Richter had employed a story-within-a-story to foreshadow the fate of his heroine. In *The Grandfathers,* he utilizes a similar device. . . . Like virtually all of Richter's novels, *The Grandfathers* is episodic.

Although creating the impression of being interludes—respites from the creative rigors of more ambitious works—*The Free Man, Always Young and Fair, The Light in the Forest,* and *The Grandfathers* still manage to perform useful fictional functions for Conrad Richter. The two of a purely historical nature (*The Free Man* and *The Light in the Forest*) enable the author to explore topics anterior to the subjects of his Ohio trilogy and thus to fill gaps helpful to greater appreciation of the larger novels. Written during the years of two wars, they also provide outlets for messages of patriotism, reassurance, and hope for a peaceful world characterized by brotherhood and human understanding. *Always Young and Fair* provides perhaps necessary preparation for the other two autobiographical novels to follow, *The Waters of Kronos* and *A Simple Honorable Man;* for it marked Richter's first return since his earliest short stories to the use of native materials. *The Grandfathers* is notable as Richter's first full excursion into comedy and also as his initial treatment of a segment of life in western Maryland. (p. 137)

Some of [Richter's works] reveal the author to have attuned himself to the problems of contemporary life and to current literary fashions. But others (including his best efforts) show him to have avoided both; however, in turning from the present to the past for fictional materials, he has consistently focused on human qualities that he considers fundamental to man's successful adaptation to modern complexity. And, if he has defied classification either as a Naturalistic-Realistic or as a psychological writer, he has embraced characteristics of all.

Richter is one of America's most autobiographical writers. Whether he is writing of his own time or of the past, he draws largely on personal experience—either that of himself or of his family and other persons he has known. But for his historical fiction he has added to materials obtained from these oral sources those gleaned from old documents, letters, newspapers. The use of the familiar, of course, is not inherently meritorious. To the contrary, it can result (as occasionally it does for Richter) in a tendency toward sentimentality. Too, it can lead (as it does not for Richter) toward didacticism. The real significance of Richter's dependence on the familiar is that it has turned him toward an introspection that prompts his works to veer more often than generally recognized toward the mystical and mythical.

Again, the indulgence in mysticism and myth, especially for the mere sake of esotericism, fails to distinguish a writer. What does merit acclaim is the successful attempt to utilize mysticism and myth to find new forms for the novel and new concepts of man and history. But to suggest that Richter has thus succeeded would be to misrepresent his accomplishment. For the mysticism and myth with which he works are not new but conventional: the alienation from the earthly and Spiritual fathers and the subsequent search for reconciliation, and the assumption of guilt; and the myths of the making of the American racial unconscious; and time and individual identity. Hence, they do not contribute either to novelistic or to philosophical innovation. Neither, however, do the mythical and mystical elements in Richter's fiction reflect a purely esoteric purpose. They are organic parts of a whole. And the suspension thus created may be praised for the simple reason that it represents a successful attempt to elevate fiction above the level of mere popularization. In other words, Richter's mysticism and myth, while failing to reach bold new heights, at least place his fiction above that which never undertakes the task. (pp. 153-54)

Technically, Richter's artistry is perhaps first evident in concision of presentation. Most of his long fiction (which still averages less than two hundred pages) derives from the novella. In such a determinably short form of single effect, space and time are crucial. The author must forego the leisurely and chronological presentation of events to concentrate on central situations in the lives of the characters. To satisfy this requirement, Richter often has employed the middle-distance point of view, with a narrator sufficiently related to the principal characters to be aware of significant events, but detached enough to be objective. The result, in every instance except *Tacey Cromwell*, is the proper motivation of character and the adequate portrayal of event.

The deft portrayal of several characters likewise attests to Richter's artistry. Sayward Luckett Wheeler, of the Ohio historical trilogy, stands as the author's finest characterization, although Harry Donner, of *The Waters of Kronos* and of *A Simple Honorable Man,* remains in close contention. Both are portrayed as strong characters, but realistically with human failings. They epitomize elemental virtue without overly doing so. If their portrayals fail in any manner, it is because of their lack of complexity. Yet this deficiency is somewhat calculated: Sayward is essentially simple in order to form a complementary contrast with the complexity of her husband Portius and her youngest child Chancey; and Harry Donner is basically unquestioning in his religious convictions not only to underscore the troubled thoughts of his eldest son John but to reinforce the ideas of simple goodness. (pp. 154-55)

A simplicity of style, occasionally verging on the lyrical, enables Richter to create evocative settings. Punctuated with authentic and generous examples of folklore, it further permits him to re-create other "actualities" of time and place. Few writers have this quality that Robert Penn Warren calls a "true ear" for indigenous speech. Elizabeth Madox Roberts and George W. Harris before Richter had it; and Eudora Welty, Caroline Gordon, Erskine Caldwell, and William Faulkner—contemporary with Richter—have it. In this technique and among this company, Richter has no peer. And this achievement—combined with his successful presentation of plot, character, and

setting—enable his better works to maintain an admirable unity of effect. . . .

Richter's chief contribution, then, is in the field of historical fiction. Such of his works reflect an understanding of early man, a feeling for history (not per se, but the "actualities" of everyday life of the past), and the ability to think and to write in keeping with this understanding and feeling. The limitations of the genre, nevertheless, become those of its practitioner. (p. 156)

Yet his limitations do not deny Conrad Richter a position on the council of America's foremost historical novelists. . . . And if any have effectively dealt with elemental virtue, Richter has promoted with artistic restraint the worth of simple goodness. (p. 157)

> *Edwin W. Gaston, Jr., in his* Conrad Richter, *Twayne Publishers, Inc., 1965, 176 p.*

GRANVILLE HICKS

[Richter's work] is all of a piece, for his one theme has been the American past. His aim, he has said, has been "not to write historical novels but to give an authentic sensation of life in early America." This he has been remarkably successful in doing, both because he has been a careful student of the relevant documents and because he has a deep sympathy with the life of earlier times. Although his books have often been popular, he has never written down to the masses. He has gone his own way, and he has no reason to regret it.

Since he has written so often about frontier life, Richter has had occasion to show why many settlers feared and hated the Indians. But in 1953, with *The Light in the Forest,* he deliberately took the point of view of the Indians, and found an ingenious way of doing so; for this is the story of John Butler, who was stolen from his white parents as a small child and eleven years later was restored to them. John, whose Indian name is True Son, bitterly resists his repatriation, but he is influenced by his exposure to white civilization, and in the end is alienated both from the people to whom he belongs by birth and those to whom he belongs by adoption and choice. In the latter part of the book the account of True Son's flight from the whites with his cousin has a nice Huck Finn quality, but what one chiefly remembers is True Son's indictment of Anglo-Saxon culture. . . .

Richter has now written a companion volume to *The Light in the Forest—A Country of Strangers*. . . . This is the story of a girl, Mary Stanton or Stone Girl, who goes through a parallel experience. Married to an Indian, she flees with her infant son when she learns that she is to be returned to her white parents. Her flight finally takes her to Detroit, where she encounters another white girl who wishes she had been left with her Indian captors. . . .

As in all his books I have read, Richter uses a style that is simple and yet scrupulously careful. Often one declarative sentence follows another as he describes a scene or presents a character. . . . Even when his sentence structure is more complex, as of course it mostly is, Richter's writing is direct and unpretentious.

Richter is by no means unaware that these two stories have a particular relevance to our own time. (p. 27)

Richter, as demonstrated by the lists of authorities to be found in several of his novels, has learned much about the old frontier, the land west of the Alleghenies. He has a feeling for the kind of life that was led there, its faults as well as its virtues but especially its virtues. His nostalgia, however, does not lead him into sentimentality, and he is incapable of the sensationalism that spoils so much of the fiction written about the pioneers. Although I am no authority on early American history, I suspect that his fiction comes as close to historical truth as fiction can.

It is a remarkable career that he has had, always and persistently out of fashion. . . . The great changes of the past fifty years must have touched him, but they have left no mark on his fiction. Yet he has always had a respectable body of readers, and honors have been paid him. His is not a name that comes immediately to mind when one is thinking of the important novelists of recent decades, but no careful history of American fiction in the twentieth century could ignore his work. He has been fortunate enough to have a sympathetic and loyal publisher . . . and he has a loyal following too. What his career hopefully suggests is that a man of talent and integrity may, with a little luck, thumb his nose at fashion and write the kind of books he wants to write. (p. 28)

> *Granville Hicks, "Caught Between Two Ways of Life," in* Saturday Review, *Vol. XLIX, No. 20, May 14, 1966, pp. 27-8.*

WILLIAM Du BOIS

["**A Country of Strangers**"] is a companion piece to "**The Light in the Forest.**" . . . [The] earlier novel told of the return of a captive youth named True Son from the Delaware nation, of his numb misery in the home of his white parents, of his escape back to the only world he knew. Now, the author follows the same plot-pattern on the distaff side. Once again, he shows us how easily the ways of natural man, and the ways of civilization, can become mortal enemies. Once again, he makes us wonder if the gulf dividing the red man from the white is too wide to cross. . . .

In less knowing hands, some of these episodes might come close to melodrama, yet Mr. Richter never falters as he tells his story of colonial America through Stone Girl's eyes. Here, the white man is the enemy, the interloper who has already stolen the Indian's land and is beginning to destroy his reason for being. Stone Girl faces adversity without flinching.

"**A Country of Strangers,**" for all its bitter vignettes, is not a depressing book. The courage of Mr. Richter's heroine, embracing the best in both races, is poignant and memorable. His short book is historical fiction at its best.

> *William Du Bois, "Who Was the Enemy?" in* The New York Times Book Review, *July 10, 1966, p. 43.*

DAWN WILSON

While he was working on [his] philosophical essays, [Conrad Richter] was also writing short stories which illustrated his theories. Collected in a volume called *Brothers of No Kin* (1924), these stories are merely plot-ridden explanations of his ideas. At this point in his career Richter was more interested in dramatizing his esoteric philosophical notions than in re-creating meaningful life situations.

The major message of Richter's philosophy is that hard times have their own rewards; they provide the energy people need

to grow. Two stories from *Brothers of No Kin* will illustrate the type of plot manipulations Richter was willing to use to convey his message. In "**Forest Mould,**" Valentine Pierce, Jr., the son of a wealthy executive, cannot understand the need for labor of any kind. . . . [Later, after taking a job in a lumber camp,] Val finds that the arduous physical work relieves his apprehension, strengthens his body, and develops his skills so that eventually he comes to feel a satisfying sense of competence. . . . At the end of the story Val is a capable man, rightly proud of his accomplishments—accomplishments forged by adversity.

In "**Tempered Copper,**" the main character is also a rebellious youth who expects others to do his work for him. Again, using devious methods, the father in the story arranges for his son to be employed as a heavy laborer in a lumber camp. The reader is not surprised to learn that the hardship of the camp has an immediate and salutary effect on the boy. . . . Once more, Richter succeeds in conveying the hardship-into-gain message of his philosophy, but in depending on transparently contrived situations and obviously manipulated characters he fails to write an artistically effective story.

When Richter moved to New Mexico, he was not expecting to make his living from writing. (pp. 376-77)

He certainly did not expect to be so completely inspired by the Southwest—its people, their values, the land—that he could do nothing but dedicate himself to writing about his experience. . . .

Richter was so intrigued by the land and its settlers that he set out to portray in his fiction the courage and strength of the people, and the causes of the early settlers' enormous strength—causes which his own philosophy, by coincidence, so aptly explained. At last Richter had found the ideal topic for his fiction. He began writing tales of the frontier, authentic stories of danger and adventure on the early plains, which were in themselves both instances and examples of Richter's energy theories.

In the Foreword to *Early Americana* (1936), Richter explained that he sought to recreate in fiction the impact life in the early West had on its settlers. (p. 378)

[With the stories] in *Early Americana,* we notice a remarkable change in the quality of Richter's fiction. (p. 379)

Expressions of Richter's admiration for the past are found in all of his stories, but perhaps the title story in *Early Americana* includes the strongest utterance. . . . Richter wants his readers to understand, feel, and sense what it was like in earlier times. It is this attachment to the Southwest that gives his fiction a sensory quality and an immediacy missing in his earlier work. (p. 380)

Richter seems to be indicating that the rugged frontier life is meant only for those who can endure its rigors and become stronger individuals as a result of the constant perils they must face. Although Richter is once again demonstrating his theory that difficulties and problems strengthen character, he is no longer creating artificial circumstances to do so. Because frontier life was based on trials and adversities—the fiber of Richter's philosophy—he was able to focus on style and character portrayal in these stories.

Having learned how to control his material in short stories, Richter was ready to write novels. In all, he wrote three novels based on life in the early Southwest [*The Sea of Grass, Tacey Cromwell,* and *The Lady*]. . . .

Richter's main goal in his Southwestern novels was to recapture the essence of life in the past. All three Southwestern novels thus emphasize the idea that men and women of the past were of greater stature than the people of the present. Their lives were filled with a stronger sense of values—values which have been lost with the passing of years. Richter felt that the lifestyle of the pioneers and frontiersmen allowed them to experience a fuller dimension of existence. Thematically, he depicts the conflict between the old and the new in these novels, the lyrical quality of which is a result of the captivating power of the Southwestern landscape over his imagination. (p. 381)

As he was writing these tales of the Southwest, Richter was continually reminded of the past he knew even better in the East. . . . Early life in the East now seemed filled with stories begging to be told. The experience of living in the West was catalytic. Once set in motion, Richter's mind was filled with more material than he could possibly use in his lifetime. The "rich bonanza" he had found in the West enabled him to find in his former locale the richness he had overlooked before. (p. 383)

[While both *The Trees* and *The Fields*, the first two novels of the trilogy, end optimistically,] *The Town* (1950), the final novel of the trilogy, begins on a foreboding note. Richter implies that although much has been accomplished, the toil and labor of improving life will never cease. *The Town* concludes the story of the small town of Americus, a story which microcosmically presents that which Richter feels has happened to the whole of America. Civilization has advanced materially, but the sturdy race of pioneers has faded, and their message has been misinterpreted and misunderstood. The desire for ease has supplanted the doctrine of hardship. The new breed neither understand nor want to understand the lessons taught by their ancestors.

Richter uses symbolism to convey a large part of the philosophical meaning of his trilogy. The characters are pitted against their environment in their struggle to carve civilization from the wilderness. Their chief antagonists in that struggle—the trees—emerge in retrospect as disguised friends, for the trees provided the obstacles which were necessary to keep the pioneers struggling. The thematic development of the novel is managed symbolically through the characters' changing reactions to the trees—which symbolize the rugged, natural environment. Richter's philosophical message, furthermore, is implied by the role played by the trees in the development of civilization and in the creation of a sturdy breed of individuals.

In the beginning of the trilogy, the trees represent the unknown, the wilderness behind which lie forces of unpredictable power. (pp. 384-85)

This "sea of trees" influences different characters in different ways. . . . The environment offers challenges to the pioneers, challenges which test their strength and stamina.

In *The Trees*, the characters—unaware of the forces which are molding them—are pictured as primitive types reacting to the natural forces which they must tame in order to live comfortably; in *The Fields* the characters begin to shed their innocence as they become conscious of their special circumstances. . . . Obviously the trees function as the motivating force in Sayward's life—a force which she will not allow to overpower her. The third novel of the trilogy, *The Town,* opens with a

grim comparison of Sayward and the trees. Sayward realizes that she is getting older and that times have changed. . . . The town certainly offers her family many improvements, but Sayward begins to resent the ease-loving younger generation who expect to be treated generously and endowed with benefits they do not deserve. Sayward speaks out in favor of the older folks "who came here when all this ground was nothing save a howling wilderness." . . . She realizes that progress has not been entirely beneficial by any means: "The old order had changed, she told herself. The world she knew was gone. . . ." And as if unconsciously recognizing her affinity to the trees, Sayward asks to have a tree planted outside her window. She is beginning to understand what made her kinfolk stronger than the younger folks; she is beginning to realize that her supposed enemies, the trees, are actually helpful friends.

As Richter presents it, the fate of the trees parallels the fate of the entire older generation. As the older trees are cleared away, new ones are planted which, beside the old, sturdy trees, appear weak and spindly. The older trees are finally appreciated, but only a few of them remain—certainly not enough to dominate the setting. Similarly, only a few members of the older generation remain; and their influence is also waning. The new growth, the younger generation, seem to be of a different mold; they are weaker and, therefore, scornful of their strong and proud ancestors.

The trees had represented an evil force at the outset of the novels, a force which ran counter to man's "westering" spirit. But that same evil was in the long view preparatory to a state of goodness in the men and women who had learned to conquer it. The trees had strong roots, and it was hard work to clear them away for a settlement; but the labor made the people sturdy. . . . (pp. 386-87)

In *The Awakening Land,* Richter not only presented a philosophy, but also provided the reader with a means for understanding a way of life. . . . *The Awakening Land,* through the atmosphere, the dialogue, and the characters' actions, gives us a strong vicarious experience, a sense of kinship with an understanding of our ancestors which otherwise we might not have.

To understand how he was able to create this feeling, we must remember that . . . when he was writing the trilogy, Richter was living in the West; and its atmosphere—the wide spaces, the mountains, the deserts, the forests—excited his imagination. Further, the oldtimers provided him with authentic tales of early life. Thus, Richter felt that he himself was experiencing as much as he could what life in early times was like.

He found he was able to transport himself in time, and by putting himself in the place of his characters, he was able to impart to his stories his own excitement about life. He felt that not many other people would have the opportunity he had to write accurately about early life because, to do so, one had to immerse himself in his work, living alongside and sharing experiences with the original pioneers and their immediate ancestors. As he explained, "the original pioneer stock, itself, was vanishing forever, swallowed up by the totalitarianism of civilization and progress, and no one except he who intimately knew and was spiritually akin to that mind could hope to detect the real from the flood of imitation or genuinely try to reveal its secret and peculiar treasure." In *The Awakening Land,* Richter achieves his goal of imparting "to the reader a sense of having lived for a while in earlier days." (pp. 387-88)

Dawn Wilson, ''The Influence of the West on Conrad Richter's Fiction,'' in The Old Northwest, Vol. 1, No. 4, December, 1975, pp. 375-89.

MARVIN J. LaHOOD

[*Always Young and Fair* is] Richter's finest attempt at writing a psychological novel. . . . [Here] the characters in the tragedy dominate their environment, not so much as Sayward does by triumphing over it, as by being so intensely involved with each other that only the background is left for the historical setting.

Lucy Markle, the lovely young daughter of Asa Markle, a wealthy mine owner, is courted by two cousins, Tom and Will Grail, as the story begins. Tom is the less fortunate economically of the two, and when the cousins leave to fight in the Spanish-American war Lucy chooses Private Tom rather than Captain Will as her betrothed. Tom is killed in the Philippines. Lucy immediately goes into mourning and continues her devotion to her dead lover despite the pleas of her parents and the returned Will Grail. Finally she agrees to marry Will at a quiet ceremony. Instead of following her wishes her parents arrange a large wedding. When the day arrives and Lucy sees the crowd, she stubbornly locks herself in her room and refuses to join Will at the altar. Will remains faithful to her but she goes back to her devotion to Tom and the pictures of him she has placed all over the house. Finally Will goes to fight in World War I. He returns five years later a tired man desirous now only of peace and quiet. Then the Pine Mills American Legion dedicates its new post to Tom Grail. At the ceremony the main speaker's comparison of the youthful Tom of the picture that Lucy has loaned to the post for the occasion, to the aging Lucy, awakens her with a tremendous shock that she has not remained young with her lover, but has aged. She begins to despise Tom because she feels that he has caused her to deceive herself. She tries to recapture what she had with Will, but he is no longer interested. She finally gets him to agree to marry her. Coming very late to the ceremony Will gets his revenge on her for her earlier humiliation of him. They go to Maine for their honeymoon but instead of returning to Pine Mills they go to Europe and remain there for five years. When they return their delay is explained, for Lucy has aged considerably and Will is a helpless cripple. Both are bitter. Only Tom has remained young and fair. (pp. 84-5)

When reading *Always Young and Fair* it helps to realize that Lucy and Will are not new characters in Richter's fiction; only what happens to them is new. . . . They are the only major characters in Richter's fiction who end in tragedy because of their wilfulness.

Richter is very careful to show how strong-willed Lucy and Will are precisely so that their actions will [seem convincing]. (pp. 85-6)

It is apparent that time is an important factor in *Always Young and Fair*. Lucy . . . tries to stop the clock. (p. 86)

This is an unusual novel for Richter who had erected his fictional world on a substructure of nostalgia. Here we see that there can be a destructive kind of nostalgia. . . .

The book, while obviously different from Richter's other work, is in some respects very similar. In its use of a narrator who idolizes the heroine and is related to her, it is very much like the three novels of the Southwest. (p. 87)

[But] Lucy Markle is the only Richter heroine who ends so miserably. (p. 88)

Of all of Richter's works this most nearly fits into the genre of the psychological novel. It also has a curious strain of determinism in it. There is, throughout, the suggestion that Lucy and Will are ''fated'' to live the life they do. (pp. 88-9)

I call it a ''curious'' strain of determinism because there is a blending in the novel of the two causes of disaster: wilfulness and fate. This same kind of shadowy premonition of disaster also appears in the Ohio trilogy. There it assumes the character of superstition; here, occurring in a more enlightened age, it can be called fatalism.

This novel, published between *The Fields* (1946) and *The Town* (1950), shares with the latter, a sense of tragedy. Unlike *The Town* it is not didactic, nor are its tragic elements in any way relieved. It is a very short novel, and that may in some way account for its being vaguely dissatisfying. It is not a failure because . . . the characters' actions are not properly motivated. Rather, it does not attain the stature it might have because, unlike great tragedy, it is depressing; one feels no elation at the end. The two sufferers have learned only to envy and despise Tom, the fortunate third party who has escaped by real death the living death of their unhappiness. Tragedy gives a new nobility to life. *Always Young and Fair* manages only to make its protagonists envious of an early death. (p. 89)

The Grandfathers (1964) is a charming novel of rural America in the early part of this century. Chariter, the heroine, is a member of the Murdock clan of Western Maryland. The two or three years covered by the story take the Murdocks and some of their friends and neighbors through a series of episodes ranging from comic to tragic. They are drawn with Richter's undying love for people who are down to earth, vibrant, mostly honest, and true to themselves. Their speech and manners are evocative of a time and place in American life that seem attractively simple. (pp. 90-1)

This novel shares with Richter's others a careful attention to the way people spoke in the time and place depicted. The speech is authentic, the stories, customs, habits, and superstitions carefully researched and artfully woven into the fabric of the novel. *The Grandfathers* is a delightful low comic contribution to our literary record of American rural mores. . . .

The Aristocrat (1968) was Richter's last novel. Set in the Pine Grove of his birth it sketches charmingly the last few years of an aristocratic lady, Miss Alexandria Morley. Miss Morley is patterned after an actual inhabitant of Pine Grove whose integrity, candour, strength, courage, and wit Richter obviously admired. She is, in all of these traits, a memorable addition to his other heroines. (p. 92)

Clearly, the center of the book is Miss Alexandria herself, ''frail but indomitable'', in her eighties, symbolizing with the Morley mansion a time long past, a time when strong men and women dominated society rather than be dominated by it. She has the pioneer intrepidity that helped make this nation great. An index of what has befallen us is the awareness on everyone's part that this kind of individualism is an anachronism. She suffers no illusions; she knows (as does Richter) that she is the last of her breed. What a dull place Unionville (Pine Grove) will be without her.

Writing about his Pine Grove, Richter is able to evoke the memory of a rural America that is delightfully recalled and whimsically yearned for. The Morley mansion clearly dominates it, but its new apartment house, neglected park, noxious dump, busy collieries, and impressive mountains all live with the life that only first-hand experience can be transmitted into.

Although Miss Morley's last few years are sketchily drawn . . . , the book is given greater substance by forty pages of her deliverances on such topics as her parents, relations, friends, maids, and modern times. Most are delightful, a few give Richter a chance to have his say too. (pp. 92-3)

Yet she wears her wealth and her influence gracefully. Always a lady, but never afraid, always the aristocrat. (p. 93)

The first two volumes of Conrad Richter's second trilogy are a remarkable achievement. Seldom has a man written more candidly of himself and his relatives than has Richter in *The Waters of Kronos* (1960) and *A Simple Honorable Man* (1962). Richter was working on the third book, about his own life as an artist, when he died.

In this second trilogy Richter honestly attempted to portray his struggles with life's most teasing intellectual and spiritual problems: man's existence before and after this life, the tenets of organized religion, the differences in character from person to person, the father-son relationship, and the old problem of fate versus free will. He also exhibited in these two novels a great pride in various ancestors from whom he received what he considered a priceless legacy. *The Waters of Kronos* and *A Simple Honorable Man* . . . offer an invaluable insight into the mind and works of one of America's ablest authors.

The writing of *The Waters of Kronos* was a labor of love. In it the protagonist, John Donner, is very much like Richter himself, and Unionville, the scene of the novel, is Richter's beloved birthplace and long-time home, Pine Grove, Pennsylvania. The novel opens as John Donner, a noted writer, now seventy, comes back to the place of his birth to visit his ancestors' graves. The town itself is now covered by the dammed-up waters of the Kronos River. At dusk John Donner walks to the old Unionville road bordering the cemetery where an old man on a wagon pulled by three horses agrees to take him to Unionville. Incredulous, John Donner goes down the steep hill with his guide and finds the town as it was sixty years earlier. He spends the rest of the novel re-examining the scenes of his childhood and his several relatives as they were at the turn of the century. He meets everyone of importance in his childhood except his mother; at novel's end he waits for her in the house next door to hers. (pp. 107-08)

The Waters of Kronos has a much greater impact when its autobiographical implications are understood, yet few of its reviewers suggested that it might be essentially factual. Naturally they were puzzled by John Donner's journey back through time; and they are correct in feeling that what he learns doesn't seem to be important enough to justify the suspense generated throughout the novel. When the novel is read in connection with Richter's life and his other works, however, its meaning becomes clear. (p. 108)

Identifying Conrad Richter with John Donner makes it possible to examine the main problems of the novel in connection with Richter the writer, and with his works. Richter, it seems to me, intended this identification to be made. (p. 109)

Why must this successful author get back to the world of his youth? What unsolved problem of his childhood has worried him all his life? (p. 110)

The death of the body can be a terrifying thing. Richter is not as certain of immortality as his preacher-father was, and these doubts are what make death terrible. If Portius Wheeler is correct when he tells his son Chancey that there is no life after death, then death is indeed a formidable foe. But Chancey doesn't believe Portius the agnostic, and I don't think that Richter does either, finally.

What gives him hope and joy at the end of *The Waters of Kronos* is not just that he no longer identifies his fear with his father, but also that he can now draw strength from a source hitherto unavailable to him. He realizes that he is, despite his old age, "still the real and true son of his powerful, ever-living father, the participant of his parent's blood and patrimony". He realizes now that his father is "ever-living" in his son, with the immortality that breed insures. . . .

His father had known all along that he was immortal, that this earth was not his permanent home but only a place of trial. And with this realization Richter becomes aware of why his father prayed, prayers that as a boy he found painful and embarrassing. His father was fighting, with prayer, the forces of evil and death. (p. 112)

With this realization of the truth about his father and their relationship, Richter was ready to write his father's fictional biography, *A Simple Honorable Man*. . . . Although at seventy he was able to re-evaluate his relationship with his father in a more favorable light, there were still unresolved differences between them. In this beautiful tribute to his father, *A Simple Honorable Man,* the crucial remaining difference is one of faith. (pp. 112-13)

Like *The Waters of Kronos* this novel is clearly autobiographical, including many of the same persons and places as the first. Instead of using the aged narrator again, Richter tries the omniscient author technique with limited points of view. This works very well because Harry Donner's life seen variously through his own eyes, and those of his wife and their eldest son, gives the reader a balanced view otherwise difficult to obtain.

A Simple Honorable Man includes the most minute and detailed autobiographical reminiscences. Richter's nostalgia for the American past, so obvious in his carefully researched novels, brought him at seventy to an exact rendering of his relatives as he remembered them. It is an undertaking with few equals in American literature. But it is more than just a nostalgic family history, for in the two novels Richter wrestled with his own metaphysical problems. By carefully examining his father's life of faith he gained invaluable insights into his own attitudes towards his minister father and his father's God.

This is clear from a careful analysis of the ending of the novel. . . . (pp. 113-14)

Is [the] last paragraph of the novel to be taken as ironical, and the father's ministry seen as meaningful and triumphant? Or does Richter intend its almost cynical cast as his father's epitaph? The ambiguity arises from the fusion of two points of view: immediately after his father's death Richter resented the waste of such a talented and altruistic man on such humble parishes as he chose to work in. But after twenty or so years his vision had mellowed to the point where he realized that his father had followed his heart to the situations where he could do the most good, humble as they were.

The novel re-creates with fidelity the American way of life during the first third of this century in the small mining towns of Pennsylvania. Everything rings true: the names, the characters, the Christians who do not love one another, and the altruistic Harry Donner in his simple but beloved humanity. The jet set and rock-and-roll seem like science fiction beside it. Yet tragedy is not absent, nor any of the evils man is heir to. Nevertheless, it is a refreshing glimpse of a time that seems long past. (pp. 114-15)

While Conrad Richter was somewhat willing to discuss the intent and purpose of his fiction, he showed little tendency to divulge the names of those authors who influenced him and his work. . . .

Elizabeth Madox Roberts, Caroline Miller, and Willa Cather are the authors whose work Conrad Richter's is most closely related to. (p. 116)

One of the most important things Richter learned from Elizabeth Madox Roberts' work was the value of writing his Ohio trilogy in the language of the people he portrayed. Miss Roberts had great success with the idiom of the people of the land. . . . Richter was aware of the similarities in speech between her settlers of Kentucky and his own pioneers of the Ohio valley. . . .

Another aspect of Miss Roberts' work that Richter used to advantage in his trilogy was the inclusion of folk tales and folk superstitions. Besides learning something about the handling of folk speech and folk material from Miss Roberts, Richter was undoubtedly impressed with the feminine strength and positive affirmation of life of [two of her heroines] Ellen Chesser and Diony Hall. (p. 117)

The single work most closely related to the trilogy is Caroline Miller's Pulitzer Prize winning novel, *Lamb in His Bosom* (1933). There is only one major difference between Miss Miller's novel and the trilogy, and that is in the matter of religion. The God of *Lamb in His Bosom* is very much the God of the psalmist David, an Old Testament God. He is an ever present force in the lives of the characters. He answers their prayers and he punishes their sins, and is in every way immediately concerned with them. (p. 118)

The faith of Richter's characters is something quite different from this. It is no more sophisticated, but it is certainly less fervent.

The number of similarities between the Ohio trilogy and Miss Miller's novel is striking. In *Lamb in His Bosom*, the dialect, folk tales, and superstitions closely resemble the same elements in Richter's *The Trees*. . . . It was through reading Miss Roberts and Miss Miller that Richter realized that the language he was beginning to record in his notebooks was a suitable medium to use in his story about the early settlers of the Ohio valley. (pp. 118-19)

The episodic structure of [*Lamb in His Bosom*] very closely resembles the structure of the trilogy. The prose is somewhat similar too, lucid and faintly lyrical. Richter's gospel of hard work is here, as is his admiration for the closeness of family ties on the frontier. . . .

Two of the finest aspects of the trilogy, Richter's wonderful portrayal of motherhood and his belief in the cleansing action of the land, are found here too. (p. 119)

Some of the finest aspects of Conrad Richter's work are the result of his life-long admiration for Willa Cather's haunting and memorable novels. Her portrayals of Alexandra Bergson

and Antonia Shimerda served as models for Richter's greatest heroine, Sayward Luckett. . . . (p. 120)

Both writers mourned the passing of the frontier because it seemed to mark the end of the pioneer spirit too. They were both fervent admirers of the men and women of strength and character they found on the frontier. They did differ in that he never wrote a novel whose central concern was the degradation of values in the modern world. Miss Cather tried to come to grips with this new world. . . . (p. 121)

Besides differing from Richter in her willingness to try to paint the new order (an order she felt shabby when compared with the strength and quality of the pioneer spirit), Miss Cather also differed from him in her abiding interest in the artistic spirit and temperament. She felt that the true successor to the pioneer was the artist. Both face formidable obstacles, and both realize in their final triumph that they have preserved their individuality by their single-minded struggle. There is no Thea Kronborg in Richter's work. The closest he comes to seeing the artist as the true successor of the pioneer is in his own life. He undoubtedly felt that through his dedication to a career of writing he had remained faithful to the spirit of his pioneer forefathers.

Conrad Richter, as well as Miss Cather, found that living close to the land and the seasons helped to give meaningful order to life. They mourned the separation from nature that modern urban culture brought about. This separation from the order of nature is clearly one of the reasons why modern man feels vaguely alien in the world that was once his home. (pp. 121-22)

Another point at which Willa Cather's frontier novels differ from Richter's is in her choice of the immigrant as pioneer. The Lucketts of Richter's trilogy are at some remove from their immigrant forefathers. Both writers used material that they were familiar with, particularly material accumulated by observation and story in their childhood. Miss Cather's neighbors during her Nebraska girlhood were European immigrants. . . . She was fascinated by them, and they, in turn, regaled her with stories she remembered all her life. Richter, on the other hand, was two and three generations removed from his ancestors who first came to this country. Some of these ancestors he observed as a child, the others his mother and aunt told him about in story. It isn't surprising that the two writers, both of whom began their major work in their late thirties . . . , and both of whom looked on their own pasts with deep nostalgia, should have chosen for their heroes and heroines the kinds of people they knew in their youth. Their greatest pioneer heroines, Alexandra Bergson, Antonia Shimerda, and Sayward Luckett are not so far apart in nationality, geography, or time, as they are close in determination, perseverance, and indomitable strength.

Connected with this is Miss Cather's interest in the artist. It is in this regard that the European qualities of her chosen people are most important. This artistic feeling is something that Richter's pioneers do not have. In one way the European Mr. Shimerda is quite different from the "woodsy" Worth Luckett. He has brought some of the culture of the Old World to the Nebraska plain where it cannot sustain itself. Only those, like Antonia, who can adapt to the demands of the land can survive. But Worth Luckett is as much a casualty of the pioneer way of life as Mr. Shimerda. His art, hunting, although different from Mr. Shimerda's violin playing, is equally out of harmony with an agrarian society.

Miss Cather's interest in the artist leads her to an indictment of the frontier that Richter does not have to make. In this one thing, the antagonism of the pioneer community to the needs of the artist, Miss Cather finds the frontier deficient. Richter, antithetically, indicts Sayward's son Chancey's way of life (the only life in the Ohio trilogy approaching that of the artist) when he sets it against the life of his pioneer mother in *The Town*. (pp. 122-23)

[Miss Cather] does not share Richter's whole-hearted acceptance of frontier values. Her return to the frontier as her subject matter left her with two ideals which she could put together but never reconcile. The resulting tension gives her work much of its dynamism and strength. (pp. 123-24)

Richter, too, has tried to present the important aspects of the world he chose to depict, rather than tell all. A shy, retiring man, he was incapable of pouring out his art in the riot of emotion with which his contemporaries could sometimes write. Miss Cather's writing reflects the same kind of temperament.

Along with the spare "furniture" of their novels is a lucid, concise prose. In their avoidance of some of the obvious excesses of naturalism they treat sex with a never quite Puritanical reserve. Miss Cather is better at it than Richter. The love between Emil Bergson and Marie Shabata is a beautiful and memorable one. In Richter's work only the tragic romance of Chancey Wheeler and Rosa Tench in *The Town* approaches it. (p. 124)

[Miss Cather's] Alexandra, Antonia, and [Richter's] Sayward believe that through their tireless efforts to subdue the land some future generation will have advantages they didn't have. Their authors imply that this newer race will never appreciate the really valuable things in life as these three great pioneer women did. For Willa Cather and Conrad Richter the frontier experience was important precisely because it helped to develop, at least for one brief moment in our history, human beings of great substance, strength, and fortitude. (p. 126)

Among Richter's contemporaries only A. B. Guthrie, Jr. invites comparison. His two fine frontier novels, *The Big Sky* (1947) and *The Way West* (1949), are memorable portraits of two phases of the Westward movement. They are related to Richter's work in their portrayal of strong pioneer types. However, they are not concerned with the agrarian themes of *O Pioneers!*, *My Antonia*, or the Ohio trilogy, nor are they written in a similar style. Mr. Guthrie's sensibility is not so delicate as either Cather's or Richter's; he is often coarsely realistic, both in the actions he depicts, and in the language he uses. He does, however, share Richter's belief that the frontier was a developer of strong character. . . . Both authors have also tried to show that there was a time in American history when things were very difficult, and they have portrayed a breed of men and women who, by triumphing over these difficulties, rose to heroic stature. That two of their novels, *The Way West* and *The Town*, won the Pulitzer Prize in successive years is evidence that modern Americans have an abiding interest in the reality and myth of the frontier.

Conrad Richter learned many important lessons from three great American frontier novelists: Willa Cather, Caroline Miller, and Elizabeth Madox Roberts. . . . Of course, his own treatment of the American frontier is distinctly his own, for it was his personal vision of a nation young and vigorous, where men and women of great courage were tested and not found wanting. This authentic and memorable frontier is Conrad Richter's America. (p. 129)

Marvin J. LaHood, in his Conrad Richter's America, *Mouton, 1975, 145 p.*

ROBERT F. GISH

Followers of Conrad Richter and his writings about the American frontier should revel in the eight short stories in this collection—all dealing, as the titular story suggests, with **"The Rawhide Knot"** of marriage and the battle of the sexes with each other, the land, and society out West. And a changing, shifting West it is—in time, space, and idea—for Richter and for the reader.

After reading these stories, some of which first appeared in the Saturday Evening Post of the 1930s and '40s and served as practice runs for longer prize-winning fiction like his Ohio trilogy, **"The Awakening Land,"** Richter's West somehow seems at once more real and more fantastic, less ideal (and idyllic) and more alluring than, for example, the cities and "urban sprawl" now manifesting the results, the communal destiny of frontier settlement and "progress." . . .

Richter's imagined, vicarious West took him and his original Post readers back in time, as one of his stories has it, to **"The Simple Life."** He realized the irony, of course, in such nostalgia for the hard times of the good old days and incorporated it in the tone and narrative structure of his fictions (which deceptively read like history); however, for present-day readers Richter's ironic escapes into the past seem partial, serving mostly to compound the author's feeling of "If my characters, these Pioneer ancestors, could only see things now!"

All of which is to say that in the treatment of male-female relationships, especially courtship and marriage; in the treatment of white men and red men . . . , in the treatment of violence and the "Code of the West," in all the human relations of his stories, Richter's sense of irony might easily build to camp proportions for 70s readers, making situation, statement, and stereotype "funny" in ways not intended. [But] . . . Richter deserves to be read seriously. . . .

Although Richter lived much after the times he writes about, he did not imagine the myths which surface in his stories. They are indigenous to our national experience, to our literature, to the image of America as wilderness, a savage place in need of taming—reflected most saliently in Richter's stories by the civilizing force of frontier women (robust beyond belief) capturing and tying the free-spirited frontiersman. And not always in a mutually comforting way; thus the chafing connotations of a rawhide knot.

What Leslie Fiedler has classified as the Myth of the Runaway Male, the Myth of Pure Love in the Woods, the Myth of the Good Companions in the Wilderness, and the Myth of the Indian Captivity are all present in **"The Rawhide Knot and Other Stories"** in almost casebook form. In this sense, by no means a bad sense, Richter's stories are classically formulistic. And although the locale may shift from Pennsylvania to Ohio to New Mexico, from mountain man to cowboy, from massacres to floods to stampedes to shootouts, these American archetypes permeate every page with a crystalline grandeur, making Richter one of the most authentic and pure Western writers around.

Robert F. Gish, in a review of "The Rawhide Knot and Other Stories," in The Christian Science Monitor, *October 23, 1978, p. B4.*

JOHN CHAMBERLAIN

In a foreword to his posthumously published "**The Rawhide Knot and Other Stories**," Richter's daughter Harvena tells of her father's latter-day fascination with the New Mexico he moved to in middle age. Applying the same standards to stories of the early Southwest that he had used in his novels about the Eastern forests, Richter wrote five tales about the days of Bent's Fort and the Santa Fe and Chisholm Trails. They are published in "**The Rawhide Knot**" along with three stories of earlier frontiers in Appalachia and Ohio. . . .

Survivability was the test, and courage was the characteristic most prized in Conrad Richter's world. As Richter's daughter notes, violence, cruelty and harshness were necessary to the conquest of new lands. Marriage and death come paired in the Southwestern stories called "**Early Americana**" and "**The Flood**," and in the Pennsylvania tale of "**The Dower Chest**." Marriages were seldom romantic: Women and men took their mates as circumstances and availability dictated.

Pervading Richter's stories is a sense of the transient. His Frank Gant had no compunctions about defending his Southwestern range against Spaniard or Apache. Right or wrong, his squat adobe house on the San Blas plain belonged to him because he had willed it so. He dealt with territorial governors, brass-buttoned Army officers, Mexican dons and hungry Apache and Navajo chiefs like a patriarchal potentate. When the railroad came, with his daughter's heart claimed by a railroad capitalist, he had suddenly to rationalize his sense of being greatly wronged. . . .

But the railroad builders had just as much a right of pre-emption as the sheepherders and the cattlemen. Richter makes no judgment. He simply tells it as it was.

> *John Chamberlain, "Southwesterns," in* The New York Times Book Review, *December 24, 1978, p. 9.*

BARBARA MELDRUM

Conrad Richter's three novels of the Southwest provide us with provocative portraits of women on the frontier and at the same time suggest a feminine perspective on western achievement. Each novel focuses on a central female character whose story is told by a male narrator recalling the experiences of his boyhood and youth. The boy is in each instance a family relation of the man who is married to or closely associated with the leading female character. The boy thus provides a sympathetic but essentially external view of the woman: characterization is limited to what the boy knew, nuances of motivation remain mysteries, and the women emerge as essentially idealized portraits shaped by a man's nostalgia for a lost youth. Though such an approach may be frustrating for a reader interested in psychological probing of character, Richter's mode is eminently suited to portrayal of an essentially symbolic perception of Southwestern life.

The first of these novels, *Sea of Grass* (1937), is actually a double story: a tale of family relationships and a tale of the transition from open range country to an agrarian economy in New Mexico. But Richter has interwoven these two stories through the symbolic associations of the leading characters: Jim Brewton personifies the old pioneer spirit, the aggressive, conquering male who thrives in the open though harsh realities of the sea of grass; his wife Lutie is associated with the taming of that pioneer spirit by her instinctive hate for the sea of grass,

her ties with Brice Chamberlain (the eastern lawyer who champions the nesters), and her femininity. Though there is no intrinsic tie between the domestic tale and the historical theme (for what happens to the sea of grass would likely have occurred whether Lutie left her husband or not), the symbolic associations in the story are so strong that the domestic and historical themes seem to be interdependent. In this way, I believe Richter suggests a perspective on the historical theme through his handling of the Brewton family fortunes. (pp. 120-21)

[What] is it in Lutie which enables her to emerge as a flawed but still eminently admirable character, in spite of her associations with the despicable Chamberlain? It is, I believe, her essential femininity—a femininity which in men is weakness or even duplicity, but in woman is a source of strength. Lutie is both fragile and delicate, and yet strong enough to overpower even Brewton so that this towering, pagan, godlike creature, a Jove from whose eyes shoot thunderbolts, becomes a merciful God-the-Father who proclaims that Brock is his beloved son in spite of all that has happened. Here, the symbolism of characterization blends with the historical theme, for the pioneering spirit of Brewton wants and needs the civilized, humanizing influence of Lutie. . . . (pp. 122-23)

Richter's second Southwestern novel, *Tacey Cromwell* (1942), focuses on the inherent materialism of western life, for the central female character, Tacey, is both matriarchal and materialistic. Tacey is a madam in a sporting house in Socorro, New Mexico, who is living with Gaye Oldaker, half-brother of the narrator, Nugget. . . . Tacey is shown to be ambitious, eager to achieve success for Gaye and herself in spite of the stigma of her past. But when her past catches up with her, she is condemned by the community and stripped of her loved ones: though presumably in the West a person's identity can be established by merit, regardless of social class, rather than be determined by one's past, Tacey discovers that social class and prejudice overrule merit, and she is defeated. But she continues to direct the lives of her loved ones, primarily through her influence over Gaye, who is weaker than she and always yields to her direction. . . . It is a rags-to-riches story with a peculiar western twist as this one-time prostitute achieves success in a reputable career as seamstress, proves herself to be an ideal mother, and succeeds finally in joining the mainstream of respectable western society. For Tacey, western development is a material-social ideal not easily achieved and at times belied by prejudice, a double standard social morality, and an inconsistent regard for a person's individual background; but it is an ideal that can be achieved through persistence and good luck.

The materialistic-matriarchal theme of this work is developed by Richter through imagery and incident. Both Tacey and Gaye have established themselves in business. . . . [Tacey's] uncanny ability to copy the lines of fashion through observation and sewing skill leads to her success as a seamstress when the attractiveness of her product finally breaks down the barriers of prejudice; for when she can offer something the leading citizens want, they promptly forget their prejudices to the extent that they accept her product, if not herself. In her influence on Gaye's career her feminine materialism is most evident, for she urges Gaye to take a job in a real bank in lieu of his position as a faro banker. . . . Tacey is proven right in her sense of ultimate financial and social gain, for as the town becomes more "civilized," the people forego faro and follow Wall Street as stock market speculation, with bigger stakes than ever crossed the faro table, becomes the gambling pastime. . . . (pp. 123-25)

In this western tale Tacey becomes the New World Demeter, ironic though she be, as this one-time madam achieves a surrogate family, suffers as a mother, and inspires the material productivity of her loved ones.

Richter's third Southwestern novel, *The Lady* (1957), provides a more complex view of the masculine-feminine dichotomy in western experience. The lady, Ellen, is the daughter of a Mexican mother and an English father, heiress of a large sheep ranch first established by a Spanish grant. In the central plot of the novel she is involved in a power struggle with her brother-in-law Snell Beasley, a land-hungry shyster American lawyer. Thus she represents a blend of Old World and New in the clash of cultures which took place during the transition from a Spanish past to an Anglo-American dominated present.

In portraying this complex woman, Richter suggests parallels between the dualities of the racial heritage, the masculine-feminine traits Ellen embodies within herself, and the basic masculine vs. feminine conflict between Beasley and Ellen. As was true in the earlier novels, Richter focuses on the strength possible to the feminine character, a strength he seems to identify with the female principle and, in an historical sense, with an advanced stage of civilization. . . . Her complex character manifests itself in seemingly conflicting roles, for not only is she a lady who must be waited on, but she can manage the large family sheepranch; her beauty and delicacy are offset by her propensity for violence, her skill with a gun, and her expert horsemanship. The imbalance of her masculine-feminine traits provides the germ of the story, for it is her masculine reliance on violence made effectual by her marksmanship which precipitates the long train of events that eventually claim the lives of her husband and son; and it is her feminine expectation that she will be rescued from her difficulties by the men in her life which draws her loved ones into the enveloping destruction. Her salvation eventually comes when, ironically, no men remain to help her and an accident brings about the death of the villainous Beasley. Her sister then inherits Beasley's fortune, and the two sisters are reunited in love and material prosperity. (pp. 126-27)

Thus in Richter's Southwestern novels western development is portrayed in part in its more easily recognizable material forms, identified with the land and material possessions. But Richter's peculiar accomplishment is that he has internalized the achievement of western goals and has attributed both power and fulfillment to the female principle. To Richter, the real land of promise lies within the individual (though inward fulfillment may be matched by outward prosperity), and the real achievers are the women. The old myth of conquest remains, but only in the nostalgia of the narrator, whose recreation of a by-gone era is a silent recognition of the closing of the frontier and the anachronism of the myth. It is Richter's women who endure and prevail, and their femininity is the key to their success. (p. 127)

Barbara Meldrum, "Conrad Richter's Southwestern Ladies," in Women, Women Writers, and the West, *edited by L. L. Lee and Merrill Lewis, The Whitston Publishing Company, 1979, pp. 119-29.*

Carl (Edward) Sagan

1934-

American nonfiction writer, scriptwriter, and editor.

Most widely known for his television series "Cosmos," Sagan is Professor of Astronomy and Space Sciences and director of the Laboratory for Planetary Studies at Cornell University. While he has written many articles for scientific journals, Sagan is also concerned that scientific theory be accessible to the general public. Toward this end he has written books for nonscientists, contributed to popular magazines and encyclopedias, and made frequent appearances on television talk shows. Sagan's attempt at writing practical explanations is evident in *The Cosmic Connection: An Extraterrestrial Perspective* (1973), *The Dragons of Eden: A Speculative Essay on the Origin of Human Intelligence* (1977), *Broca's Brain: Reflections on the Romance of Science* (1979), and *Cosmos* (1981). In these works Sagan presents scientific theories and philosophizes about the effects of scientific inquiry on social, political, religious, and historical events. *The Dragons of Eden* was awarded the 1977 Pulitzer Prize in nonfiction. Sagan has received several other awards for his work, including two from the National Aeronautics and Space Administration.

Sagan's interests center on the origins and evolution of life on earth, the nature of the physical universe, and the possible existence of extraterrestrial life. Convinced that there is life on other planets, Sagan advocates interplanetary communication; as a consultant to NASA, he helped design the plaque bearing a message to alien life which was launched with the spaceships Pioneers 10 and 11. Using information about the atmosphere on planets in our solar system and elsewhere, Sagan suggests that amid the "billions and billions" of stars and galaxies in the universe, millions of planets may support civilizations like our own. He outlines this probability in *The Cosmic Connection, Cosmos,* and some of the essays in the collection *Broca's Brain.* In these works he also emphasizes the importance of space travel. According to Sagan, humans require exploration for their psychological well-being, and since earth has been thoroughly searched, space offers the next frontier. In addition, Sagan believes that contact with extraterrestrials will give humans a wider, less egocentric outlook, an attitude which Sagan refers to as "the cosmic perspective."

In both *The Dragons of Eden* and *Cosmos* Sagan recounts the hypothesis of the triune brain, claiming that the human brain is an evolutionary combination of reptilian, prehuman mammalian, and uniquely human aspects. According to Sagan, each of these three parts, which are referred to as the R-complex, the limbic system, and the neocortex, accounts for certain aspects of human behavior: our aversion to reptiles, our base instincts, and our rational thoughts. Sagan also attributes human intelligence to the physical evolution of the brain. From his central arguments, Sagan goes on to speculate about the goals of past civilizations and the effects on future civilizations of potential scientific advances. Many critics conclude that Sagan's underlying message throughout his works, and especially in *Cosmos,* is that in order to continue evolving intelligently, humans must utilize scientific discovery.

Much controversy surrounds Sagan's theories and his presentation of them. Some critics object to Sagan's glorification of

Dennis Brack/Black Star

rationality and to his categorical dismissal of a godlike creator. Others find his factual information about evolution and psychology faulty or oversimplified. Many commentators are dissatisfied with Sagan's lack of distinction between assumption and fact, an absence which they judge misleading. The television series "Cosmos" has been criticized for its confusing structure and its emphasis on visual effects rather than argument. Nevertheless, Sagan is praised for his attempt to unite science and philosophy and for his ability to simplify complex concepts while preserving their awesome implications. Many critics consider Sagan's arguments both inspired and logical. With a direct, factual style, a dry wit, and an enthusiasm often described as "contagious," Sagan continues to provide thought-provoking material for scientific and general discussion.

(See also *Contemporary Authors,* Vols. 25-28, rev. ed.; *Contemporary Authors New Revision Series,* Vol. 11; and *Contemporary Issues Criticism,* Vol. 2.)

EDWARD EDELSON

Carl Sagan is a scientist of quality who is also a writer of quality. He has often shown that he can write better than most science writers, and he proves it again with *The Cosmic Connection,* a book that is very nearly perfect.

If *The Cosmic Connection* has a fault, it is that it derives a good deal from Sagan's previous books. . . . This new book could be described as a carefully watered-down summary of the previous writings, arranged for a general audience.

But that description would be unfair. What Sagan has done is to leave out the mathematics, insert a good deal of philosophy and let himself roam freely. For a lesser writer, that could be a disastrous combination. But since Sagan is a man of great intelligence, wit and insight, it is a success on every level.

To illustrate this with specific quotes is difficult because of Sagan's style. He builds to his effects with care; his paragraphs, not his sentences, are the basic unit. A reviewer must paraphrase instead of quoting.

Sagan starts by describing his theme—the possibility of communicating with other intelligent civilizations in the universe. He defends the necessity of space exploration in the most convincing terms that I have encountered. . . .

[His real point is that] space exploration is psychologically important for the human race, now that the earth has become a small, well-trodden enclave.

From earth, Sagan moves on to the planets. He has played an important role in the exploration of Mars. Although he is full enough of his subject as to give Mars more room than it might deserve—and emphasizes his own theories about its history—he manages to be consistently interesting.

Then to life elsewhere. Sagan first describes, more poetically than scientifically, the process by which life arose and flourished on earth, and proposes that the same process is almost certainly going on, and has gone on for millennia, elsewhere in the galaxy and the universe. There are almost certainly millions of civilizations like ours out there, he believes, and we have not heard from any of them partly because we haven't been listening, partly because the distances are great, and perhaps because their methods of communication are far beyond our understanding.

Does this sound like heavy going? Well, consider the way Sagan argues against the possibility of UFOs as visitors from other civilizations. First he proves mathematically that there is no Santa Claus by pointing out that, given only one second per stocking, it would take Santa three years, not a single night, to fill all the stockings. Then he makes a rough estimate of the number of civilizations in the galaxy and goes on to calculate that there just is not enough metal in the galaxy to make all the spacecraft that would be needed for a true UFO visit. The demonstration is a marvelous combination of wit and science.

Writing a review that contains hardly a word of complaint is an uncomfortable and unfamiliar exercise. But aside from expressing envy that Sagan does so well as a sideline what others do with great labor as their life's work, there is nothing to say about *The Cosmic Connection*.

> Edward Edelson, "Star Struck," in Book World—
> The Washington Post, *November 25, 1973, p. 4.*

RICHARD BERENDZEN

Numerous scientists have important ideas, some even more profound than Sagan's; yet he is probably the most famous astronomer since Hoyle or even Hubble. *The Cosmic Connection* shows why: His speculations provoke and stimulate on truly arresting topics, described in fluent prose, sprinkled with wit and sarcasm. Although his syntax is straightforward, his articulation easily rivals that of Asimov or Clark. In the art of making science understandable and enjoyable for specialist and lay person alike, he is a modern James Jeans.

This book's 39 brief chapters, delivered like fireside sermonettes, center on their author's principal professional interests—exploration of the solar system and search for extraterrestrial life. Sagan weds these pursuits as well as disparate disciplines, including astronomy, biology, chemistry and anthropology. Then he wisely steps back and appraises the synthesis, thereby perceiving mankind's symbiotic relationship with the whole. How we exist because of the arduous processes of stellar, chemical, and biological evolution and, reciprocally, how we affect the universe. Voila, the cosmic connection! . . .

Sagan warns that "although I am not by training a philosopher or sociologist or historian, I have not hesitated to draw philosophical or social or historical implications of astronomy and space exploration." That he does, opening himself to potential criticism. His forceful defense of space exploration, for instance, will inform and touch almost any reader, but it probably will not convince the thoughtful skeptic.

Sagan points out that the fraction of the gross national products of the United States and the Soviet Union being spent on manned space programs is comparable to that spent by 16th century England and France on exploration by ships; but some social historians would argue that the fraction is too high, now or then. Similarly, he shows that large planetary programs cost less than the over-runs on certain military projects; but he fails to note that these same planetary programs cost far more than many space or ground-based astronomy projects and vastly more than most artistic or cultural endeavors. (p. 47)

The space program, Sagan argues, is to us what the pyramids were to Pharaonic Egypt or ziggurats were to Sumeria. But should the public pay for such monuments to pride, today or in the past?

I prefer to liken modern space research to the Renaissance, with its ennobling spirit, which left a legacy of art, music and architecture. Sagan's thesis here, however, surely must be valid: "The cost of space exploration seems very modest compared with its potential returns."

A traditional textbook this is not. Rather, *The Cosmic Connection* comprises a farrago of facts, opinions and bizarre speculations, uncritically blended. The result, nonetheless, becomes probably the most mind-expanding scientific treatise available for general readers. Here we have an engrossing tale of the moons of Barsoom (Edgar Rice Burrough's name for Mars), including a one-person baseball game on Phobos; a systems analysis of the Santa Claus hypothesis; and humorous anecdotes about reactions to the famous Pioneer 10 plaque. Sagan's droll wit permeates and enlivens. (pp. 47-8)

Even though the wit of the scientist's Russell Baker marks the book, the book's principal strengths are the grandeur of its topic and the eloquence of its prose. Generally, the ideas sparkle and the language entrances, but there are lapses into rhetorical overkill, sometimes distorting the facts.

Some serious scientists doubtlessly will fault this book for its poetic language, fanciful speculations, and imprecise detail. But readers on the non-scientific side of C. P. Snow's dichotomy will praise its simplicity, verve, and mind-boggling perspectives. As Sagan himself says, "The virtue of thinking about life elsewhere is that it forces us to stretch our imagination.''

Although I too would prefer less flamboyance, this book's importance does not depend upon its similarity to fact-laden tomes but on its synthesis and exuberance, on its reminder even to scientists that the study of nature consists of more than equations and equipment, and on its lesson that we are all one with the cosmos. (p. 48)

> Richard Berendzen, ''The Solar System and Beyond,'' in Bulletin of the Atomic Scientists: a magazine of science and public affairs, *Vol. XXXI, No. 4, April, 1975, pp. 47-8.*

PETER STOLER

Like squids, scientists protect themselves with clouds of impenetrable ink. Not Carl Sagan. His jargon-free book *The Cosmic Connection* . . . involved thousands of readers in the search for life beyond earth. Last year, during the Mars probe, he became a TV celebrity with plausible descriptions of the creatures that might be populating outer space. *The Dragons of Eden* should involve thousands more in the exploration of inner space—the human brain.

Sagan, 42, occupant of a chair in astronomy at Cornell University, is not a neuroscientist. But he writes about the brain with uncommon sense and even humor. . . .

The Dragons of Eden begins with a summary of how and when intelligence developed in various terrestrial species. In detail, Sagan describes the process of natural selection working toward the emergence of the creature Shakespeare called ''the paragon of animals.'' Sagan also explains differences in the structure of the paragon's brain and those of other animals. He offers some idiosyncratic thoughts on why man's neurological legacy makes him behave the way he does. The human brain, he points out, evolved from the brain of the reptile, one of whose species the Bible holds responsible for the Fall. According to Sagan, the reptilian brain, which forms the most primitive part of the human brain, still influences man's behavior and may help explain one of his oldest fears—the apparently inherent squeamishness about snakes. . . .

Sagan also wonders if the human fear of falling is not a memory inherited from our arboreal ancestors, who lived in trees and suffered when they forgot the effects of gravity. . . .

The author does not supply solutions. But arguing, as always, for life Out There, he believes humans must press for answers. Only by understanding our own minds, he maintains, can we hope to understand the other civilizations we are trying so hard to reach. Intelligent organisms evolving on another world may not resemble man physically or be anything like him biochemically. But they are likely to reason similarly, for whatever their worlds, they are still subject to the same laws of chemistry and physics. (p. E7)

If Sagan's speculations are sound, the prospects of using physical laws to establish contact with such a civilization are encouraging. So are the prospects of communicating with it. Many of the scientists now beaming signals into the ether might find themselves speechless if someone—or something—should answer. They can always use the author as an interpreter. Carl Sagan already knows how to communicate with laymen. Any scientist who can perform that feat should find talking to extraterrestrials as easy as π. (p. E9)

> Peter Stoler, ''Brain Matter,'' in Time, *Vol. 109, No. 21, May 23, 1977, pp. E7, E9.*

RICHARD RESTAK

A better understanding of the nature and evolution of human intelligence just possibly might help us to deal intelligently with our unknown and perilous future,'' writes Dr. Carl Sagan. . . . To help achieve this understanding Sagan begins [**''The Dragons of Eden''**] by looking at the evolution of intelligence in lower animals. Since larger brains can store more information, a critical point in evolutionary development occurred with the emergence of an organism that ''for the first time in the history of the world had more information in its brain than in its genes.'' Subsequent development led to ''the gradual (and certainly incomplete) dominance of brains over genes''; human intelligence resulted from ''a particular property of higher primate brains.'' . . .

Sagan's frame of reference in ''**The Dragons of Eden**'' is an evolutionary one. ''He who had a stone axe was more likely to win a vigorous difference of opinion. More important, he was a more successful hunter.''

Although the imagery of axes and hunters fitted in well with the exploitive sweatshop capitalism of [Charles] Darwin's time, it is certainly far less satisfying today as a total explanation for evolution. For one thing it is only a half truth. In place of competing individuals striving for biological immortality by passing on only the ''best genes,'' modern evolution stresses communities of common interest where organisms compete, cooperate, and in some cases are even altruistic. Of course, with cooperation and shared interests we have the beginnings of culture, a more potent shaper of brain structure and intelligence than Sagan suggests. . . . (p. 8)

The emphasis throughout is on intelligence as an absolute. . . . Further, as Sagan stresses repeatedly, intelligence, from the evolutionary point of view, has survival value. While this is undoubtedly true when comparing one species with another, it can only be proved in the case of contemporary human intelligence by demonstrating that intelligent people are more successful at producing offspring. Certainly contemporary demographic data do not support the view that human intelligence is correlated with fecundity.

In addition, the interdependence between brain structure and culture creates immediate problems when it comes even to defining intelligence. As we have learned from the current I.Q. controversy, intelligence is not a unitary concept capable of easy definition across cultures, or generations. For one thing, how does one prove that one generation is more intelligent than another and, as a result, happier and better off?

Sagan seems to imply that the ability to produce increasingly sophisticated technology may be one test of intelligence. Although this seems appealing at first, it does not bear close scrutiny. If atomic power really does culminate in a fiery Armageddon, would a disinterested celestial observer conclude we were *more* or *less* intelligent than our ancestors? Sagan at one point seems to admit the problem: ''Once intelligent beings achieve technology and the capacity for self destruction of their species, the selective advantage of intelligence becomes more uncertain.''

The most provocative aspect of the book is the author's capacity for colorful and sometimes bizarrely original speculations on everything from why language doesn't exist in non-human primates ("humans have systematically exterminated those other primates who displayed signs of intelligence") to differences in the sleeping habits of different animals. . . . (pp. 8, 19)

In one important area, however, the author is distinctly unspeculative. "I will not in these pages entertain any hypotheses on what used to be called the mind-body dualism, the idea that inhabiting the matter of the body is something made of quite different stuff called mind." Rather the mind is "a consequence of [the brain's] anatomy and physiology and nothing more."

With the advent of neurobiology it was perhaps inevitable that such a view would become fashionable. For one thing, as Sagan correctly points out, "there is not a shred of evidence to support" a mind-body dualism. Besides, so many of our mental experiences can now be "explained" by physiological events within the brain. To take just one, Sagan describes the experiments of neurosurgeon Wilder Penfield in which conscious patients undergoing brain surgery were made to re-experience events from many years earlier after electrical stimulation of special regions of their brain.

Given such data, it is not surprising that most of us now believe that every mental event occurs in tandem with events going on within the brain. One really *must* decide, it would seem, since to sit on the fence is often to be on the wrong side of it.

In the case of the brain-mind riddle however, sitting on the fence may be just the right situation to be in at this still early stage of research. To opt for a premature conclusion that facilely equates mind with brain is really only a labor-saving device that stunts rather than fosters further inquiry. At the root of the problem, it seems to me, is the difficulty both sides have in distinguishing a prerequisite from a cause. . . .

It is difficult to sum up a book that ranges as widely as this. While it is often insightful and challenges several scientific paradigms, it is also sometimes embarrassingly naïve and on occasion just plain fantastic. All in all, though, it is a thought provoking, maddening, generally worthwhile performance that is unlikely ever to be precisely duplicated. Perhaps Abraham Lincoln said it best in a one-line review that never quite made it to the dust jacket: "Anyone who likes this kind of book will find it just the kind of book they like." (p. 19)

> Richard Restak, "The Brain Knew More Than the Genes," in The New York Times Book Review, May 29, 1977, pp. 8, 19.

R. J. HERRNSTEIN

Like many non-specialist popularizers of psychology, Professor Sagan [in *The Dragons of Eden*] overestimates our physiological knowledge and underestimates our psychological knowledge. I'll get back to this point later. First, I must acknowledge that Professor Sagan has taken the first hard step in learning psychology. The first step in studying psychology is to convince yourself that there is something to study, above and beyond common sense and common knowledge. Professor Sagan likes the theory of the "triune brain," as formulated by a neurophysiologist named Paul MacLean in the early 1950's. Not an active theory in the technical literature these days, it nevertheless appeals to popularizers. . . . The theory depicts the human brain as combining in uneasy equilibrium our reptilian ancestry, our pre-human mammalian ancestry, and our rational, competent selves. A reptile, a mammal, and a human

reason within each skin—with these wild cards, Professor Sagan can play just about any hand he wants.

Tripartite psychologies are hardly new. . . . I have not counted, but there must be at least a dozen major psychological systems based on tripartite divisions and very few based on any number other than three. Why is this? I'm not sure I know the answer, but I'd guess that it has little to do with the facts of matter. (pp. 67-8)

The first problem with this book's tripartite psychology is . . . its inherent weakness. Another is that, as psychology as distinguished from anatomy, it is no match for [Sigmund] Freud's or Sheldon's or even Aristotle's. It appeals to brain anatomy while trying to say something about human behavior. They are not the same, although non-psychologists and beginning psychology students looking for a scientific psychology almost always gravitate to physiology and anatomy. Anatomy and physiology are tangible and technical, and biologists generally enjoy higher status in the academic pecking order than psychologists. It takes conscious effort and a certain amount of sheer study to resist the lure of physiologizing and to see that a creature's psychology not only can, but must, be studied in its own right before scientific sense can be made of it. When he physiologizes his psychological hunches, Professor Sagan is investing his hunches with specious authority from a "harder" science.

The triune brain probably appeals to Professor Sagan because it seems to jibe with his psychological intuition. It captures in an evolutionary metaphor the idea that conflicting motives, conflicting values, and conflicting forms of knowledge are the human condition. Many of the other tripartite psychologies are also metaphors expressing more or less the same idea. Without further evidence, one metaphor is about as good as another, assuming we are after science, not poetry. The evidence must, moreover, be psychological. Except for a review of language in chimpanzees, *The Dragons of Eden* lacks psychological data. Besides anatomy, there is paleontology, geology, garnishes of astronomy, chemistry, and physics, but almost no psychology.

For psychology, Professor Sagan mostly relies on intuition. His intuitions are not unreasonable; he believes we possess both logical and alogical tendencies, that we are not as rational as we think we are, that we are conscious of only a fraction of the psychic forces that move us, that some of our psychology is adaptive for a world that no longer exists, that human relationships resemble to some extent relationships among other animals. But it is a pity that Professor Sagan has ignored the evidence that refines and transcends those sensible (though hardly original) hunches of his. Even more, it is a pity that Professor Sagan has ignored the rich, growing, often surprising and occasionally sobering discipline of psychology. But then, I have yet to stumble across a popularizer who knows much psychology, let alone bothers to popularize it. (p. 68)

Professor Sagan can rest easy; his message will trouble very few (except the occasional psychologist who looks at the book). For example, Professor Sagan comments in the course of his discussion of the frontal lobes of the brain:

> Cassandric components of our nature are necessary for survival. The doctrines for regulating the future that they produced are the origins of ethics, magic, science, and legal codes. The benefit of foreseeing catastrophe is the ability to take steps to avoid it, sacrificing short-term for long-term benefits. A society that is, as a

result of such foresight, materially secure generates the leisure time necessary for social and technological innovation.

Indeed, but did we need to know the gross anatomy of the brain to say this? And what, in fact, *are* the bases of ethics, magic, science, and legal codes? How does an organism, human or otherwise, learn to sacrifice short-term for long-term benefits? What are the relevant abilities, and what are the limitations on the abilities? Would it surprise Professor Sagan to learn that there are data, real data, about the *psychology* (rather than the pseudo-physiology) of ethics, magic, and all the rest in this little passage? It would certainly surprise those of his readers who are relying on him for finding out about human psychology. (p. 69)

Though he knows how profoundly science can change our picture of the world, Professor Sagan seems not to realize that the psychological shift in outlook promises to be deeper, broader, and at times more difficult to accept than the Copernican and Darwinian ones were. Once again, people are to confront a science that challenges their egocentricity, but this time it is their very sense of themselves and their personal destinies that are to be challenged, not such relatively secondary possessions as the planet on which, or the bodies in which, they live. The intensity of their resistance is already apparent in their alarmed reactions to B. F. Skinner's conditioning procedures or A. R. Jensen's assessments of individual differences in cognitive ability. None of this surfaces in, or even ripples the surface of, Professor Sagan's book. He is asking his readers to change their minds about almost nothing, though doing so with grace, humor, and style. (p. 70)

> *R. J. Herrnstein, "Psycho-Physiology," in* Commentary, *Vol. 64, No. 2, August, 1977, pp. 66-70.*

JOHN UPDIKE

Versatile though he is, [Sagan] is simply not enough saturated in his subject [in **"The Dragons of Eden: Speculations on the Evolution of Human Intelligence"**] to speculate; what he can do is summarize and, to a limited degree, correlate the results of scattered and tentative modern research on the human brain. The research, from electroencephalograms of dreamers to endocranial casts of fossil skulls, is in progress, and Mr. Sagan, like the rest of us, must wait for sweeping conclusions. "If this result is confirmed, it would be quite an important finding," he writes in one iffy spot, and, in another, complains, "Very little work has been done in this field to date." He speaks of "many potential near-term developments in brain chemistry which hold great promise both for good and for evil," shamelessly woolgathers about how "one day we will have surgically implanted in our brains small replaceable computer modules or radio terminals which will provide us with a rapid and fluent knowledge of Basque, Urdu, Amharic, Ainu, Albanian, Nu, Hopi, !Kung, or delphinese," and, in another connection, allows, "It does not seem to me that a crisp choice among these four alternatives can be made at the present time, and I suspect that the truth will actually embrace most or all of these possibilities." Well, one begins to wonder, what *has* emerged lately in the study of human intelligence that justifies the production of this book? The dust jacket shows a pair of semi-shaggy primates sitting at ease in a ferny Eden with what appears to be a pet dimetrodon, a pre-dinosaurian reptile that vanished over a hundred million years before the first primates

appeared. The book's title also hints at a thematic center that is reptilian. (pp. 87-8)

It is difficult to discern Mr. Sagan's intellectual contribution to the exposition [of the triune brain], other than poetic chapter titles like "Tales of Dim Eden" and piquant epigraphs like— for the chapter sketching the three divisions of the brain— "When shall we three meet again . . .? (Wm. Shakespeare, 'Macbeth')." The expository pattern tends to alternate facts experimentally discovered by other scientists with personal extrapolations that seem loose, if not facetious. . . .

Mr. Sagan's speculations, where they are not cheerfully wild, seem tacked on and trivial. (p. 88)

[It] remains to say that there is much fascinating information here, amid the fluff of computer printouts, Escher lithographs, and vacuous editorializing on matters ranging from abortion law to government funding for scientific research. (p. 89)

> *John Updike, "Who Wants to Know?" in* The New Yorker, *Vol. LIII, No. 27, August 22, 1977, pp. 87-90.*

STEPHEN C. REINGOLD

In presenting [the theory of the triune brain in **The Dragons of Eden**], Sagan encourages the reader to examine human intelligence and behavior in terms of the elements they have in common with other living animals. While this is, in itself, appropriate, the association of our behavior with that of other living animals distorts the modern concept of evolution. Humans did not evolve from contemporary snakes (nor even from extinct dinosaurs). Rather, all currently living beasts had, in the unfathomable past, common ancestors who gave rise to many different evolutionary lines. Reptiles—extinct or alive— are not our evolutionary precursors. If anything, they are evolutionary siblings that have grown in a different environment. (pp. 319-20)

These points are not made clearly, if at all, by Sagan. His presentation is reminiscent of a simplistic and largely discounted 19th-century theory that stated, "ontogeny recapitulates phylogeny": in other words, in the course of embryological development, each animal goes through stages that resemble evolutionary precursors, and characteristics are sometimes maintained. So, humans would have retained the R-complex [a section of the triune brain] and reptilian behavior from the "lower" reptiles and elaborated upon them. Evolution is not that simple, and man most likely evolved from something very different from a reptile. One could as easily—and as erroneously—state that living reptiles have, in part, humanoid brains and behaviors.

To balance this criticism, I highly recommend Sagan's fifth chapter, entitled "The Abstractions of Beasts." This chapter proves quite simply that chimpanzees can "talk" to their human trainers using American Sign Language. In a clear, fascinating report of work being done at several institutions, Sagan points out that nonhuman primates are "close to the edge of language" and can communicate when taught the "language."

Sagan uses the chimpanzee-learning-language story to indicate that these primates are intelligent. But surely communication in *human* terms is not the only, or primary, sign of animal intelligence. Rather, one must look for "intelligence" in an animal by examining the way it copes with its own environment, not in the way it relates to aspects of a human environment. . . .

A concluding chapter of this entertaining and thought-provoking book considers extraterrestrial intelligence and is only a taste of the subject on which Sagan is perhaps *the* authority. (p. 320)

> *Stephen C. Reingold, in a review of "The Dragons of Eden: Speculations on the Evolution of Human Intelligence," in* America, *Vol. 137, No. 14, November 5, 1977, pp. 319-20.*

CHARLES WEINGARTNER

Subtitled "Speculations on the Evolution of Human Intelligence," [*The Dragons of Eden*] is a superlative work: erudite, facile, fascinating, and eminently readable. In it, Sagan "speculates" about what is going on inside the human head. Fundamentalists had better not get into this book; it's liable to cause a fundamentalist fit. Central to Sagan's speculations (which qualify him as a latter-day "Renaissance man," so wide is his range of references) is the *fact* of human evolution from earlier forms of life on spaceship Earth.

In order to say anything about what might be going on between our ears, Sagan has to describe the process of brain evolution. (p. 88)

Sagan devotes a good deal of attention, of course, to the neocortex [a part of the brain common to most higher primates], especially the left and right hemispheres and their distinctly differing functions. He not only restates the "basic" information now available about "hemisphericity," but dwells on the dismaying waste that results from our inability (to date) to recognize the need to nurture whole-brain functioning rather than only left-hemisphere abilities. The implications for education are impossible to overstate. (p. 93)

If you've been looking for some "hard" information to include in your rationale for supporting "open" and/or "humanistic" education, or for resisting dumb school conventions—including "accountability," "competency testing," and the ruthless and mindless standardization and constraint that these impose on both students and teachers—read Sagan's book. If nothing else, his lucid and fascinating ideas will be good for your head. They might even stir a few dormant dragons. (p. 115)

> *Charles Weingartner, "A Dragon in Your Head: Carl Sagan's 'The Dragons of Eden'," in* Media & Methods, *Vol. 15, No. 1, September, 1978, pp. 88-9, 93, 115.*

EDMUND FULLER

With the verve and accessibility which have made Dr. Sagan one of the most widely known scientists of his time [the essays in **"Broca's Brain"**] range across such topics as planetary systems (which are his speciality), the search for extraterrestrial intelligence, pseudo-science, science fiction, and religion—something for everybody who is at all interested in science.

Dr. Sagan sees us as living at a "unique transitional moment." He thinks the past 50 years have raised questions that could not even have been asked before and that the next 50 years will have answered most of them. . . . Agreeing that the next 50 years will answer a vast range of questions, probably including whether we are living in a universe that will expand

to cold emptiness or one that will collapse back upon itself, possibly to produce another Big Bang, yet still I believe, and hope, that 50 years from now an aged Dr. Sagan or his children will see the continuing proliferation of new questions arising from each answer.

[The 19th-century scientist Paul] Broca discovered "a small region in the third-convolution of the left frontal lobe of the cerebral cortex, a region now known as Broca's area." We know now what he surmised, that articulate speech "is to an important extent localized in and controlled by Broca's area." As the volume, **"Broca's Brain,"** again demonstrates, the powers peculiar to Broca's area are richly developed in Dr. Sagan. Lacking the focused thematic development of **"The Dragons of Eden,"** uneven as such a collection inevitably is, still **"Broca's Brain"** is an exciting book contributing to that scientific literacy of the layman that Dr. Sagan sees as so necessary.

> *Edmund Fuller, "Readable Contributions to Scientific Literacy," in* The Wall Street Journal, *May 29, 1979, p. 22.**

RICHARD BERENDZEN

The subtitle of [*Broca's Brain*], "Reflections on the Romance of Science," encapsulates its blend of accepted fact with personal conjecture. In Sagan's world the romance is not monogamous; it is a flirtation with virtually every branch of thought and study. Science *qua* science lies at its heart, but other relationships provide zest and perspective. In the introduction, Sagan warns that, as is his wont, he has not hesitated to interject social, political, or historical remarks. If he had, this might become his last popular book. His core topics—planetary exploration, the quest for extraterrestrial intelligence, cosmic evolution—are intrinsically fascinating, but other writers address them too. Sagan's secret lies not just in subject but in insight and perspicacious linkages.

In these *Broca's Brain* abounds, but in flow it wants badly. Its five large parts and 25 chapters connect only loosely—hardly surprising given their heterogeneous origins, many having been derived or reprinted from earlier work. Nor is the volume lavishly produced—stunning color plates can be found elsewhere; ideas dominate here.

Sagan gives us a devastating debunking of several pseudoscientific theories, a fairly technical history of American astronomy, a pithy yet synoptic commentary on cosmology, a balanced encomium to science and technology, a personal critique of science fiction. But it all begins with Paul Broca, a major 19th-century neurologist and anthropologist, who founded modern brain surgery. Today, in Paris, a hundred years after his death, his bizarre Musée de l'Homme survives, with its collections of skeletons and skulls, shrunken heads and bottled fetuses, and scores of human brains—including his own. Recounting a visit to the museum, when he held the cylindrical bottle containing Broca's brain, Sagan launches chapter 1 with a jolting free association, teaching historical anthropology and brain physiology while speculating: In some sense, is "Paul Broca still there in his formalin-filled bottle?. . . Might it be possible at some future time, when neurophysiology has advanced substantially, to reconstruct the memories or insights of someone long dead?"

And so it goes. From expression of wonderment over nature's duality of complexity and knowableness to a succinct biography of [Albert] Einstein, from an exposition of comparative planetary climatology to a comparison of science and theology, from contemplation of the origin of the Kaaba to musings over the end of the universe, the prose rushes forward. Topics outside Sagan's fields of formal education generally are treated philosophically or speculatively; in his areas of expertise, however, details abound.

Here, as in much of his earlier writing, Sagan ridicules chauvinism, broadly conceived; thus, solar system nomenclature should be "deprovincialized" to include recognition of other cultures and persons other than scientists, and even the use of robots to perform human functions is defensible. Sagan sees objections to the latter as a form of "speciesism," the "prejudice that there are no beings so fine, so capable, so reliable as human beings." Still, he himself cannot accept life centering on elements other than carbon, surviving in habitats other than planets, or evolving technologically in ways radically different from our own. Even though he has considered such possibilities more than anyone else, the world as we understand it simply does not seem to him to admit certain alternatives.

More than in his past books, Sagan here contemplates pseudoscience and religion. His trenchant, somewhat technical rebuttal to [Immanuel] Velikovksy reappears here, along with an unnecessarily detailed criticism of a modern numerologist who claims to be God. Sagan's analysis of UFO's and ancient astronaut theories will not convince true believers; but for all others his evidence should be compelling.

At first his attack on pseudoscience occupying more than a fourth of the book, seems like overkill. But this lengthy section squarely addresses seemingly mysterious topics and illogical reasoning patterns that commonly bewilder and befuddle the public. As modern astronomy, for example, has brought forth mind-boggling concepts, the esoteric yet plausible ironically has sounded increasingly like the fantastic and pseudoscientific, particularly to nonspecialists. Surely scientists have an obligation to the public that supports them to explain the differences and to share what they know of science's beauty, but too few do so. For this reason Sagan's thoughtful and articulate analysis is particularly valuable.

In contrast, Sagan's discussion of science and theology seems unsettlingly dilettantish: Either he has cut incisively through centuries of thought and reflection or he does not fully understand the issues. Many of us would agree with his piquant views, but, laconic rather than compendious in his analysis, he has trivialized a complex subject. He proceeds with tact and caution unusual for him, although it is unlikely that much of what he says will shock either scientist or theologian, especially in our post-God-is-dead era. (pp. 38-9)

Drollery distinguishes the memorable from the routine, and *Broca's Brain* contains the usual array of Saganisms. A sample:

● At an International Astronomical Union meeting, Moscow was officially ruled to be a state of mind.

● According to Jacob Bronowski, all the Easter Island monoliths resemble Benito Mussolini.

● "Both [P. T.] Barnum and H. L. Mencken are said to have made the depressing observation that no one ever lost money by underestimating the intelligence of the American public."

● Re pseudoscientists, "The fact that some geniuses were laughed at does not imply that all who are laughed at are geniuses. They laughed at Columbus, they laughed at [Robert] Fulton,

they laughed at the Wright brothers. But they also laughed at Bozo the Clown."

To the specialist, much of the information Sagan puts forth in the book will be familiar or seem conjectural. But even for such a reader there will be fresh insights. Sagan's ruminations raise a torrent of disturbing questions. . . . Sagan suggests connections—some possibly invalid—that others have not even surmised. That is one of the virtues of the book. Responsible, creative scientists occasionally should wonder aloud, even about their discipline's social dimensions, connections with other enterprises, and future prospects.

For the nonspecialist, the book will be frustrating reading, with uneven technical detail, loose connections, and an overabundance of polysyllabic jargon. But if the reader can make it through, this curious volume can answer old questions, raise new ones, open vistas, become unforgettable.

In short, Sagan has done it again. The book's title may be Broca's brain, but its subject is Sagan's. (pp. 39-40)

Richard Berendzen, "Astronomy and Other Subjects," in Science, *Vol. 205, No. 4401, July 6, 1979, pp. 38-40.*

DEWEY SCHWARTZENBURG

What can you say about a young civilization inhabiting the third planet of an ordinary G2 star found out in the sparse suburbs of the galaxy? What pictures would you show to wholly alien eyes, and what music would you play for alien ears? How would you go about packaging all this information so that it will last for millions of years?

These were the tasks facing a small group of persons with limited time and an even more limited budget when the opportunity arose to include something more than a plaque aboard the two Voyager spacecraft, bound for interstellar space via the outer planets. *Murmurs of Earth* is a beautiful and fascinating account both of the process of decision and of what was finally decided upon for inclusion in the Voyager interstellar records.

Following an introductory essay by Carl Sagan and an account of the background of the project by F. D. Drake, successive chapters (each written by a different member of the team) deal with the visual images, the verbal greetings, the sounds of Earth life, and the musical selections included in the message to any extraterrestrial intelligences who may chance to find this interstellar time capsule. Appropriately enough, most of this book is composed of the actual contents of the Voyager record, with commentary on each selection. (p. 56)

There is much to ponder in this whole affair. Our message to the galaxy is as much a social and political commentary on ourselves as it is an accurate summary of what we are all about. How, for instance, did all the members of the United States' House and Senate committees which deal with space science get their names included in the message? A moment's reflection on the dependence of NASA on the vagaries of the American political process provides the answer. But one wonders, if the record should actually be found, how many volumes of learned treatises will an alien civilization churn out in the vain attempt to decipher the meaning of these cryptic tables? And, even if they manage somehow to translate them, what will those alien beings make of the verbal greetings in 60 languages, including this one in the Chinese Amoy dialect: "Friends of space, how are you all? Have you eaten yet? Come visit us if you have time." To eat us?

The fact of the matter is that this is more a message to ourselves than a message to others, and there lies its greatest interest. As the members of the team well knew, the actual chances that either Voyager will ever be found by extraterrestrial beings is infinitesimal. As a commentary on how we see ourselves in this age, the Voyager record challenges our values. Half the musical selections, for example, come from non-Western cultures. If this is surprising, it is because, as the text points out, "The Western world finds it convenient, in this season of its predominance, to imagine that because our voices speak most loudly, nobody else has much to say." . . .

Here on Earth a phonograph record of the aural parts of the message may never be released—the Byzantine complexities of copyrights and permissions are apparently more difficult to navigate than the solar system. It is one thing to get permission to send a musical selection or a sound into interstellar space, but quite a different task to include it on a record for Earthly ears. There is an ironic parable here, where once again the story of the Voyager interstellar record reveals more about us than we intended: it seems it is a great deal easier for us humans to say "hello" to the stars than to each other. (p. 57)

> *Dewey Schwartzenburg, in a review of "Murmurs of Earth: The Voyager Interstellar Record," in As*tronomy, *Vol. 7, No. 10, October, 1979, pp. 56-7.*

JAMES H. BOOTH

Broca's Brain is the most recent production of Sagan's brain, and after justifying the title (a reference to a French neuroanatomist's celebrated cerebrum), the remainder of the book tells more of Sagan's involvement in the scientific enterprise than it does of the late Paul Broca's. . . . [The coverage] on out-of-body type thanatological experiences seems far-fetched both factually and theoretically. On points of theology, his arguments from "higher criticism" are dated, and his archeology suffers from a similarly outdated singlemindedness. Nonetheless, the volume's strengths far surpass any weaknesses, making reading it a sheer vacation.

> *James H. Booth, in a review of "Broca's Brain: Reflections on the Romance of Science," in* Science Books & Films, *Vol. XV, No. 4, March, 1980, p. 190.*

ISAAC ASIMOV

Carl has a keen sense of humor, an incisive intelligence. He's just as intelligent in his speaking as he is in his writing. . . .

I've learned a great deal from his articles. I like to think I have read just about everything he has written. Virtually everything I know about the possibility of extraterrestrial life was inspired by his writings on the subject. On that question our minds have the same set. I find it very easy to agree with Carl.

I don't agree with those who criticize him as a popularizer. I happen to think that the popularization of science is the most important thing a scientist can do, next to actually broadening science itself.

> *Isaac Asimov, "Isaac Asimov on 'Cosmos' Star," in* Horizon, *Vol. 23, No. 10, October, 1980, p. 28.*

DAVID ROBERTS

As a speculative skeptic, a lucid popularizer of science, and a belles-lettrist eager to bridge the gap between the humanities and science, Sagan stands as the latest practitioner in an illustrious tradition which, because it is fundamentally British, remains too little known among American readers. His forebears include Thomas Henry Huxley, Alfred North Whitehead, Bertrand Russell, James Jeans, Arthur Stanley Eddington, Julian Huxley, J. B. S. Haldane, and Fred Hoyle. All shared the view that science was accessible to the common man and woman, intellectually both disturbing and exciting, yet emotionally and philosophically significant. All were capable of turning a popular prose essay into, at once, a work of art and a tour de force of pedagogy.

The evolution of Sagan's own writing style is interesting. . . . As Sagan matured, his writing grew less flashy, more deeply metaphorical. Something of a poet's sensibility now infuses his musings on the significance of discovery.

The more rhapsodic moments of [the television series] **"Cosmos"** also suggest a poet, and in fact some of the lines of Sagan's narrative scan as blank verse: "We have made the ships that sail the sea of space." "I'm pleased," Sagan says, "when somebody notices that. It's true. When I try to express an emotion in prose, I find that there's a little metronome inside of me which tries to convert it—at least as far as meter goes—into poetry. It's a means of expressing feelings. I think that science has been separated artificially from feelings. One of the objectives of **"Cosmos"** is to heal that breach." (p. 30)

> *David Roberts, "Carl Sagan's 'Cosmos'," in* Horizon, *Vol. 23, No. 10, October, 1980, pp. 22-31.*

WILLIAM J. O'MALLEY, S.J.

[In *Cosmos* Carl Sagan] is an enormously gifted juggler, at one time keeping aloft a dizzying melange of balls, dishes, Indian clubs, dinosaurs, and Dopplered red shifts. His ability to explain the complex in terms of the commonplace is mesmerizing; his encyclopedic knowledge is humbling; his articulateness captivates. His staff of illustrators and technicians is skilled and inventive. On camera or in print, Dr. Sagan is artfully at ease with the arcane and his love affair with the cosmos is infectious. He is an irresistibly stimulating teacher.

And there's the rub.

Dr. Sagan and the televised **"Cosmos"** series reached a vast audience. He intrigued adults, who since college have had to leave behind pondering the ponderous and concentrate on the more pedestrian process of making a living. And he fascinated young students, especially very intelligent students, who still have the leisure and curiosity to ask what living is for. I rejoice that Dr. Sagan has opened our parochial eyes to the enormity and variety and aliveness of the universe in which we find our meaning. But I wince at the fact that, in almost every program and chapter of *Cosmos,* Dr. Sagan rejects outright (and, to me, gratuitously) any possibility of a Mind behind that universe; he carps captiously at religion; he insists on the exclusivity of accident as the cause of evolution. Amid all the glorious, mind-boggling, uplifting exposition of science, there is too often a discordant sneer. Always muted, always elegant, but nonetheless a sneer.

What was its effect on the audience, especially on the bright young audience? Well, if Dr. Sagan is intimidatingly knowledgeable and articulate, he must know about that God stuff, too, right? Trying to counterbalance Dr. Sagan's subtle assertions of atheism (with $8 million of media know-how to enhance it) is like a first-grade teacher trying to upstage "Sesame Street."...

Dr. Sagan rejects out of hand even the possibility of the transcendent in the first sentence of his book: "The Cosmos is all that is or ever was or ever will be." Later he says, "By definition, nothing we can ever know about *was* outside (the physical universe)." This seems, at least to me, somewhat arbitrary, especially from a man who pleads so eloquently for openmindedness. (p. 95)

One major argument against a Designer that Dr. Sagan makes early in his text is that the fossil record indicates that some exquisitely made species have died out. "Should not a supremely competent Designer have been able to make the intended variety from the start?" He finds that "inconsistent with an efficient Great Designer." Of course. But perhaps the reason is that efficiency is not as high on the Designer's list of priorities as it is on Carl Sagan's, just as explanations meant less to the Voice from the Whirlwind than they did to Job. Perhaps the Designer just delighted in new things and, out of all eternity, 50 billion years was not too long a time to dally with them.

In searching for a word to describe the set of rules which would dictate the unchangeables, the non-negotiables, in a reshuffling of the laws of physics, Dr. Sagan says that both the words "paraphysics" and "metaphysics" have unfortunately been "preempted by other rather different and, quite possibly, wholly irrelevant activities." (The phrase "quite possibly" is the condescending smile around the sneer.) As my contemporaries can testify, I would be the first to confess the inadequacy of much of the metaphysics I struggled through for several years in the seminary, without even Leah as a reward. But the inadequacy of the symbols does not negate the presence of the reality, any more than debunking feathery hermaphrodites negates messages from God, nor Heisenberg's discovery of indeterminacy negates the usefulness of the Bohr model of the atom. If God is really there—like the New World and neutrinos—His reality is not destroyed by the inadequacy of our maps and concepts.

As a result, Carl Sagan often becomes carping about religion, occasionally even just plain snotty. Sometimes he equates it with superstition, sometimes with thought control. Now it would be foolish to deny that the churches have too often taken their cues from Caesar rather than from Christ. They have at times been downright, bullheadedly obstructionist to new learning. But it is not quite decent to say, almost in an aside, "The suppression of uncomfortable ideas may be common in religion and politics, but it is not the path to knowledge." Conversely, he makes the scientific community sound universally and immediately tolerant, even to the subversion of ideas its members have long cherished, as though Tycho Brahe had embraced Kepler with open arms....

Twice, in almost the same words, Dr. Sagan writes that "until one day, quite by accident, a molecule arose that was able to make crude copies of itself." That was one shrewd molecule! And he dances gingerly away from that one....

Along the same line, Dr. Sagan writes: "It is only by the most extraordinary coincidence that the cosmic slot machine has this time come up with a universe consistent with us." And with no one to insert the silver dollar and pull the lever! "Extraordinary" is far too puny a word. That's a 10n chance. "If things

had been a little different, it might have been some other creature whose intelligence and manipulative ability would have led to comparable accomplishments." He seems to assume that intelligence is inevitable. Yet the marriage of accident and inevitability is, at best, an uneasy one. (p. 96)

Chapter XI of *Cosmos,* "The Persistence of Memory," deals with [Sagan's presumption that all intelligent activities are reducible to the electro-chemical activity of the brain] in painstaking detail. The brain has two lobes, one which functions inferentially, one which functions intuitively. One side uses a ruler to measure the ceiling of the Sistine Chapel; the other side envisions God's finger inches away from Adam's. But Dr. Sagan seems to restrict the function of intelligence to solving problems and creating, two activities at which he is extraordinarily gifted. Yet in the facility of his assertion several other exclusively human modes of acting get lost: all the activities less scientific folk associate with the human spirit. There is no place, as far as I can judge, for the very real difference between information and wisdom, between being interested and being moved, between shrewdness and love. Is it merely electrons traveling along his neurons that explain the almost palpable awe Dr. Sagan shows when he looks at the stars? I am left unconvinced....

Again and again, Dr. Sagan reminds us that the laws of Nature, the patterns of Nature, the laws of physics are always and everywhere the same. I have no quibble with that, but both lobes of my brain keep itching to know why. Both lobes rebel at the Sisyphean task of drawing order out of the fortuitous. Variety, yes, but not the immutable laws of physics, not the periodic table. And Dr. Sagan agrees, there is surely a design. But he balks at a Designer.

As a result, he is very often trapped into personifying the universe, evolution, Nature and many other nonintelligent forces as if they did have intelligence....

But personification and anthropomorphism are hazards to any popularizer trying to explain, through metaphor, realities his audience does not know in terms of realities they do know. The scripture writers found the same problem.

Dr. Sagan asserts, on the one hand, that to say God created the universe out of nothing is "mere temporizing." And yet he also suggests, on the other hand, that before the Big Bang, "all the matter and energy now in the universe was concentrated . . . perhaps into a mathematical point with no dimensions at all." That seems to be one micromillimeter from "nothing." Perhaps it is only words which block both Dr. Sagan and me from apprehending the same reality—just as neither "pellet" nor "wave" quite captures the reality of an electron.

A similar situation may exist in Dr. Sagan's apprehending "other universes" and my apprehending "heaven." (p. 97)

[The] analogy of black holes and time warps—available to us now through men and women of science like Carl Sagan— might be a less inadequate metaphor to understand the Ascension than is the first-century metaphor of rising up to heaven, especially since in the Einsteinian cosmos "up" has no meaning. Jesus went into another way of existing.

In Chapter X, "The Edge of Forever," Dr. Sagan has a long and ingenious explanation of how Einstein's theory of curved space gave reality a fourth dimension beyond the length, breadth and depth we are immediately in touch with. (pp. 97-8)

If he can conceive of a fourth dimension to our reality, can he not also allow the possibility of a fifth—where the laws of physics do not apply and where space and time have no meaning? It would be a dimension we are in now, thoroughly penetrated by it yet as unaware of it as we are of the neutrinos that are knifing through us every instant—as if we weren't even here. We get intimations of this fifth nonphysical dimension—in moments of ecstasy, awe, joy, prayer—when we are "taken-out of ourselves," as Paul says (again inadequately) into "the Seventh Heaven." All trustworthy receivers need not be metallic to be trustworthy. They need not be restricted even to the two lobes of the brain. The receiver of messages from the transcendent dimension is that presence within us which we have always called the human spirit. Science cannot dissect that receiver because it is not itself subject to space and time. It is the infection of God in us. . . .

Carl Sagan is, very truly, an authority. He asks me to deny the evidence of my senses (including my "common sense") and accept the fact that the desk on which I write is not oak-solid but rather aswarm with galaxies upon galaxies of moving particles. He asks me to believe him when he tells me I am being skewered at every instant by neutrinos, which pass through the whole earth without even slowing down. He offers me antimatter, electronics moving backwards in time, black holes which flush into another universe and other entities "bizarre beyond our most unconstrained fantasies." And I accept them all, gratefully, gleefully. As I said from the outset, they liberate my imagination from my skepticism and enable it to attempt capturing God in metaphors less inadequate than those to which cosmology was limited 20 centuries ago. I accept his claim because I trust Carl Sagan's experience and veracity.

But I would like him to give more than mere condescension to my experience and veracity—to say nothing of the experiences and veracity of the great giants of the last 3,000 years. . . .

Carl Sagan writes: "The incompleteness of our understanding humbles us." Not quite thoroughly enough, I believe. (p. 98)

> *William J. O'Malley, S.J., "Carl Sagan's Gospel of Scientism," in* America, *Vol. 144, No. 5, February 7, 1981, pp. 95-8.*

JEFFREY MARSH

In dispensing [*Cosmos*'s] heady intellectual mixture on TV, Sagan displays a virtuoso command of audio-visual techniques. During his comparatively straight exposition of scientific, historical, or philosophical topics, he exploits the full gamut of histrionics of the popular TV lecturer. . . . (p. 65)

Not all these techniques are successful. For his tours of remote regions of the universe, for example, Sagan takes viewers aboard his "spaceship of the imagination." This is a spare construction, windowed and arched like a cathedral designed by a Bauhaus architect, bare except for a chair and a futuristic control console over which he waves his hands mysteriously. It is an apparently pointless gimmick since for lengthy periods of time all we are treated to are reaction shots of Sagan staring appreciatively out of the window.

Another major disappointment in the visual aspect of the presentation comes from the costumed and silent mini-dramatizations of various historical periods. Ranging from 11th-century Japan to California in the 1920's, via 16th-century Germany and 17th-century Holland, these vignettes with their colorfully dressed extras and earnest heroes resemble nothing so much

as animated *Classics Comics*. In leaving out such visual distractions, the print version of *Cosmos* is more successful than the TV show.

These are comparatively minor flaws, however, to be expected in any project of this scope. More serious is Sagan's frequent failure to point out the difference between observation and reconstruction. Whereas a reader of the book can tell, from the credit accompanying each illustration, whether it is a photograph of an actual object, or a model, or a computer simulation, the TV viewer requires a considerable degree of sophistication to keep track of exactly what he is looking at. Sagan assumes that at least a significant fraction of his viewers have to be told that 10^3 means 1000, and that there are 92 naturally occurring chemical elements; one wonders whether innocent viewers—who, one must devoutly hope, are children rather than representative graduates of our unparalleled educational system—appreciate that the beautifully colored movie they are seeing of the interior workings of a cell is only a model. Do they realize that the colors shown in many of the splendid pictures are purely arbitrary, put there to make features more easily recognizable, or that the spectacular views of distant galaxies are paintings?

Most blameworthy of all in this avowedly serious attempt to explain the nature and essence of scientific thinking is Sagan's systematic blurring of the distinction between proof and assertion, and between fact and hypothesis. In principle Sagan is eager to follow the path of scientific rectitude, keeping an open mind concerning all theories and accepting or rejecting them only on grounds of objective evidence; he even makes a pious show of doing this in his discussion of the theories of Immanuel Velikovsky. When it comes to more serious matters, however, he is not so scrupulous.

A major instance of this occurs in the second program of the series, with his flat assertion that "evolution is a fact, not a theory." Since the main property of a fact is that it be directly observable, and since the concept of evolution refers to a hypothesized series of events which by definition occurred at a time when there were no intelligent observers around, the assertion is obviously false.

What Sagan should have said is that the concept of evolution is accepted by the mainstream of modern biologists. This would have been a much more accurate statement, and it would also have been consonant with his later exposition of how many biologists believe evolution took place. Unfortunately, he also fails to note that his version is by no means universally accepted.

Sagan's theory of evolution says that electrical discharges in the hydrogen-rich atmosphere of the early earth led to the emergence of self-replicating DNA molecules, which eventually led to living organisms, which by a combination of random mutations and natural selection led to man. Virtually every step of this argument is hotly contested. Experiments in hydrogen-rich atmospheres have indeed produced simpler precursors of DNA, although nothing as complicated as DNA itself, but there is significant dispute over whether the earth's atmosphere was indeed hydrogen-rich in the period assumed by Sagan. There is also no credible quantitative theory which yields a time scale compatible with that assumed by Sagan to produce the complex creatures we see now; indeed, currently fashionable theories do not posit slow cumulative change on geological time scales but rather periods of explosive development interspersed with longer periods of almost no change. None of these considerations is even hinted at by Sagan.

One might enter similar objections to his picture of the evolution of the universe since the big bang. (pp. 65-6)

Sagan makes reference to the self-correcting nature of science, and discusses some of the ways in which common sense does not prepare us for the revolutionary ideas of the universe introduced by Einstein, but the untutored viewer cannot help absorbing the message that scientific knowledge accumulates smoothly and steadily. He is told that the early scientists of Greece and Alexandria began making substantial progress once they adopted a materialist view of the world, and that science would have taken off at that time had it not been for two factors. The first . . . was the pernicious influence of mysticism, first in Pythagorean and Platonic philosophy and then in Christianity. The second was the existence of slavery, with its concomitant belief that manual labor was degrading, a belief that led to a bias toward theory over experiment. Only when these two constraints weakened, at the time of the Renaissance, could the progress of science recommence.

According to Sagan, the progress of science represents a further stage in man's evolution. In his best-seller of several years ago, *The Dragons of Eden,* Sagan expounded the notion that the human brain is a tripartite structure. The oldest part (the R complex) is shared with the reptiles, and is responsible for aggression, ritual, territoriality, and social hierarchy. Next comes the limbic system, common to all mammals, which provides us with our moods, emotions, and parental instincts. Finally comes the cerebral cortex, site of the creative and analytic functions of intelligence.

Our use of these higher functions has produced our scientific knowledge of the world, but the continuing influence of the oldest part of the brain has left the world divided according to outworn concepts of nationalism, religion, racism, and sexism and has given our aggressive instincts access to immensely destructive nuclear weapons. Should we come into contact with evidence of extraterrestrial intelligent life, we will learn a number of important lessons. The first is that we are not alone in the universe; the second is that it is possible for a technological civilization to avoid self-destruction; the third is that all life on earth, plant and animal, is related by a common ancestry and is different from any life elsewhere in the universe.

With this perspective, it is not difficult to understand why Sagan is so concerned to present his version of the universe with more certainty than it actually deserves. If one believes that mankind's future depends on the universal adoption of a scientific outlook, and that a scientific outlook must by definition be based on materialism, the possibility of a fundamental error in this overall view of the universe cannot be seriously tolerated. While there may be mistakes in minor details, and the possibility can be admitted of a revolutionary new materialistic theory, the existence of a valid *non*-materialistic explanation of the universe must be rejected.

In fact, however, there is no necessary correlation between science and the adoption of a thorough-going materialistic system of belief. Sagan himself refers to the strongly held and profoundly religious views of Kepler and Newton, the founders of modern astronomy, but regards them as quaint relics of older and dying ideologies—Kepler was also the last scientifically serious astrologer. He does not even refer to the diversity of philosophies held by scientists today, let alone attempt to reconcile them with his theories. Yet distinguished contributions

to the advancement of science have been made by Nazis and by Communists, by Orthodox rabbis and by Jesuit priests, by Hindus and Muslims, and by southern Baptists. The claim that scientific advance requires thoroughgoing materialism is absurd.

Even more absurd is Sagan's belief that the salvation of the world depends on adopting this viewpoint on a global basis. . . . We have already had over sixty years' experience with one society built according to notions of scientific materialism, where science is hailed as the foundation of a new order which will produce a new man, where scientists are given an honored position, and where history itself is regarded as a branch of evolution. Not only in this society one of the least free and most imperialistic in the history of mankind, not only is it far more unequal than societies in which the political, social, and economic institutions remain unredesigned, but it cannot even produce enough food for its own population. Clearly Carl Sagan does not regard the Soviet Union as his model of a society based on scientific ideas, but it is a measure of his intellectual irresponsibility that he has not even approached the stage of thinking seriously about who would perform the redesign of society he calls for.

It is, indeed, Sagan's self-proclaimed cosmic viewpoint that permits him to luxuriate in his irresponsibility. Purporting to observe the earth from afar, disdaining any particularistic attachment which might suggest that real differences exist among humans even though they belong to the same biological species, he concludes that an ultimate imperative for survival of the species is universal disarmament—the way to which, of course, should be led by the United States. Were he to come down to earth, he would be forced to recognize that this supposedly universalist message of surrender of national sovereignty must appear utterly bizarre to all that vast majority of mankind which does not share Sagan's own benign view of human nature and civilization. That view, a particularism masquerading as universalism, is one which is widely held only in the advanced Western nations, and which flies in the face of the bitter experience of most of the world throughout most of history. The only conceivable positive response to his call would be the unilateral disarmament of the West—and such a response would lead to the triumph not of universal good will but of universal despotism.

Sagan's unwillingness to countenance seriously any form of particularism, even on a humanity-wide scale (and even though this very unwillingness itself derives from an unacknowledged species of particularism), is seen also in his failure to come to grips with the significance of religion, which he basically regards as a malignant force, although sometimes granting it grudging legitimacy as a form of aesthetic expression. Yet while traditional religion may be beyond the pale, Sagan has no qualms about expounding, apparently in good faith, his personal messianic belief that the receipt of a radio transmission from a superior extraterrestrial intelligence (quite literally, a *deus ex machina*) will somehow transform human behavior. Thousands of years of history have shown that the widely held belief in an already received message from an even greater authority has not succeeded in making men love other men, let alone their cousins the trees, as Sagan refers to them in one of his giddier moments.

If people really come to believe, as Sagan suggests they should, that they have been brought into existence through blind chance in a vast and pointless universe which originated with a mysterious explosion and will end in oblivion, is it likely that they will also feel they owe some sort of mysterious "loyalties . . . to the species and the planet" and they have an "obligation to survive . . . to that Cosmos, ancient and vast, from which we spring"? Talk of loyalties and obligations makes sense in religious terms; to Sagan's world view the more likely response is a combination of nihilism and hedonism. (pp. 66-8)

Jeffrey Marsh, "The Universe and Dr. Sagan," in Commentary, *Vol. 71, No. 5, May, 1981, pp. 64-8.*

DAVID PAUL REBOVICH

"Cosmos" and Sagan did not disappoint viewers' desires for a serious discussion of science and astronomy from a person so qualified to offer one. Indeed, a fair criticism of "Cosmos" is that the scientific material presented—the theory of relativity, the lives of the stars, the conjecture of a fourth dimension—was too difficult for television discussion. Nonetheless, Sagan's skill as a teacher, as someone able to make the complex understandable, was always evident. It is doubtful that viewers could learn more about science in 13 hours than they did from "Cosmos." This is the triumph of the series, and Sagan's performance is far superior to the travelogue narrations of many science-nature shows. . . .

While "Cosmos" succeeds where other programs have failed or bored, Sagan's own ambitions exceed those of the conventional teacher of science, the conveyor of facts and method. Sagan seeks to make science not only understandable, but also popular. For the latter task, television is a convenient means, and cynics may see "Cosmos" as a spectacular commercial for NASA or the "thinking person's" antidote to the banalities of network programming. Indeed, political intention—Sagan laments America's paltry space budget—and a certain intellectual arrogance do underlie the series, but the pervading tone is an optimistic populism. . . .

This populism suggests a public receptivity to discussion of the wonders of the universe and the possibilities of science. But while Sagan's erudition flatters his audience—little did we know we could learn so much—the "Cosmos" series is actually predicated on a pessimistic appraisal of public understanding of the ways of nature and public commitment to modern science. . . .

More accurately, the series represents Sagan's effort to explain the perspective of the universe provided by modern science. If we have grown distant from the cosmos, it is because we have strayed from science and what it can tell us about nature and man. Sagan is concerned but undaunted. Behind public confusion about what science means and public doubt about what it promises, Sagan sees a potentially receptive audience. He realizes that overcoming public confusion and doubt requires something more than an updated account of what scientists "know" and can "do." To make science popular and an object of public commitment, Sagan sees the need to present the cosmology of science, the way science "understands" the universe and the meaning of that understanding for the human condition. (p. 91)

A substantial portion of the series ["Cosmos"] is devoted to distinguishing the methodology and findings of real science from magic, religion, and other forms of speculation. Sagan skillfully presents the mysteries of the universe and shows science's ability to explain them. But presentation of scientific insight into the workings of nature does not necessarily convey a "cosmic perspective"; and neither necessarily qualifies as a

philosophical and social justification of the scientific enterprise. But justifying modern science, which is Sagan's paramount purpose in "Cosmos," is the most efficacious means of popularizing it. The series as a whole thus possesses a purpose and grandeur greater than any one of its segments. But, to the viewer, the uniqueness of Sagan's view—his conclusion that science provides the means to transcend the human condition—and the specifics of his argument are initially difficult to ascertain.

On the surface, "Cosmos" seems to be an eclectic collection of 13 scientific and historical vignettes addressing themes and forwarding positions associated with Bronowski, Koestler, Eiseley, and Von Daniken. While extricating himself from Von Daniken's more outrageous fancies, Sagan is captivated by the possibility of extraterrestrial life and its revolutionary implications for our science and philosophy. Less romantic, if not less prosaic, than Eiseley and Koestler, Sagan speaks about the universe with their same reverence and implies that science is the key to the kingdom of true knowledge. More specific than Bronowski on science's cultural ramifications, Sagan shares his optimism for a society which vigorously pursues the scientific enterprise. Regarding contemporary society, Sagan echoes the sentiments of a host of commentators who bemoan the existence of oppression, warfare, famine, the sterility of contemporary culture, and the persistence of unenlightened opinion. But Sagan's claim that science, rather than religion, traditional philosophy, or politics, is the path to redemption seems, like those of many would-be reformers, an overly simplistic and unsubstantiated solution to the ills of the day.

Teaching the lesson that science will enable man to transcend the human condition is the primary goal of the series. From a scientist of Sagan's stature, it is not too much to expect an argument with clearly articulated assumptions and carefully justified conclusions. "Cosmos" suffers in this regard, illuminating the difficulties of making a philosophic argument in a long television series, where viewers exercise selective perception and possess varied levels of understanding. The elusiveness of specifics in Sagan's argument also reflects the structure and organization of the series itself, in particular Sagan's decision to dramatize not only how real science works but what science means for man. To confuse matters further, Sagan is not averse to resorting to simplistic negative arguments at the expense of detailing his own position. A variety of thinkers, from Plato to the medieval scholastics to contemporary theologians, are portrayed as intellectual impediments to enlightenment and progress.

Sagan's dramatizations, his use of stunning visuals ("to engage the heart as well as the mind") and historical skits, are not without substantive components. But they tend to accentuate his conclusion rather than highlight his assumptions. To the extent that the viewer gets caught up in the drama, he finds himself tempted to accept Sagan's conclusion without being precisely certain why. For example, the segments on comets and the lives of the stars reveal some of the wonders of the universe and how modern science has demystified some of the more perplexing questions about nature. These discussions are masterpieces of science education, but Sagan is not content simply to demonstrate science's considerable ability to explain natural phenomena. A subtheme, never clearly stated, is fear: man ought to fear a universe in which comets collide with planets and suns burn out. The scientific impulse emanates, Sagan hints, from man's fear of a universe which he does not totally understand or control. Man ought to pursue a science which protects him.

The tone and emphasis of the argument shift in the discussions of Mars and Venus. Here, Sagan shows that science has succeeded in repudiating the irrational, erroneous, and arrogant assertions of religion and traditional philosophy. Science offers intellectual progress; and in terms of explaining the atmosphere of Venus and the "canals" of Mars, it surely does. But Sagan seems to force the viewer into making a distinct choice between a progressive science and non-progressive philosophy or religion as ways for understanding reality. The argument to reject religion or philosophy because of their scientific shortcomings is as old as it is naive and does not enlighten us about science's meaning for man.

Sagan devotes a considerable amount of time to intellectual and biographical sketches of some of the key figures in the history of science. In these segments, we see how scientists have labored, against all odds, to advance man's knowledge of the universe. If the viewer forgets that Kepler was as much an occultist as a physicist, that Newton refused to extricate the Deity from his own cosmology, that Einstein's scientific brilliance was matched by his confusion about the technological implications of his discoveries, one does remember Sagan's more general point. Scientists have always been forward-looking intellectuals who dared conventional belief, even in the face of public derision and persecution. Historically, scientists are the "good guys" in the progress of Western civilization. But Sagan tells us less about the history of science and more about historical figures who ought to be canonized by a people committed to human excellence and progress.

This overly simple historical interpretation is carried to an embarrassing extreme when Sagan projects our future contact with advanced extraterrestrial beings. Since these beings will be superior scientists, we have nothing to fear. As long as mankind demonstrates its respect for knowledge, our contact with extraterrestrials will be marked by mutual respect and entail an interplanetary cultural vibrancy. Man's history teaches us that scientists respect intellectual change and one another. Despite Sagan's interesting discussion of different biologies and life forms, he falls victim to the anthropomorphism he otherwise critiques by assuming that extraterrestrial scientists will be like their human counterparts. This assertion is, however, quite consistent with, and reinforces, his conclusion in the last segment of the series. The answer to the question "Who Speaks for Earth?" is the scientist. The scientist is the exalted pursuer of knowledge and the witness for the paramount values and aspirations of mankind and, for that matter, any rational species. If Sagan himself cannot convince us of science's overwhelming virtue and cosmological significance, he implies that the existence of superior extraterrestrials will. He invokes Pascal's wager with a modern twist.

The dramatic, self-fulfilling quality of **"Cosmos"** does not mean that there is not a serious argument presented in the series. In fact, each segment is part of Sagan's larger, more direct analysis of the meaning of science for man. For viewers familiar with Sagan's bestselling books—***The Dragons of Eden, The Cosmic Connection, Broca's Brain***—and sympathetic to his cause, the dramatics of **"Cosmos"** appear to be a stroke of genius. For those less familiar and less convinced, **"Cosmos"** seems propagandistic, if for no other reason than that Sagan's argument is disorganized. But there is a logical argument here, more readily understood when one realizes that the 13 segments of **"Cosmos"** deal with four basic topics: the powers and mysteries of nature; man and nature; science's cultural and social benefits; and projections of man's scientific future. (pp. 93-4)

For the faithful and attentive viewer who seeks to understand Sagan's "cosmic perspective," the series is a disappointment. The viewer is required to piece together Sagan's comprehensive justification of the scientific enterprise by weeding through the visuals and dramatizations and re-arranging the essentials of Sagan's argument. This organizational problem of the series may be the result of Sagan's overambition, his desire to make science understandable and popular, interesting and entertaining, as well as justifiable in a profound philosophical sense. If this is the case, some of the confusion and disorganization of **"Cosmos"** is excusable. But **"Cosmos"** then fails at its most serious and, according to Sagan, important level. It fails because Sagan does not overcome the difficulties of interfacing an argument of the utmost seriousness with the attempt to respond and appeal to popular values, expectations, and fancies about the future. The specifics of Sagan's argument to justify the scientific enterprise compete with the other dimensions of the series—Sagan's desire to raise viewers' curiosity about nature and how science works, his own cooptation of popular themes of science fiction and speculation for his purposes, and the use of drama and dramatic generalization as a teaching device.

"Cosmos" disappoints for reasons less excusable than overambition and disorganization. Sagan's explication of the "cosmic perspective" offered by modern science sounds terribly familiar. It ought to; essentially, it is an updated version of natural Darwinism extended, as it was a century ago, to society. What saves, or ought to save, **"Cosmos"** from triviality is its updated quality. But here, too, it disappoints, because Sagan decided not to highlight and detail two of the most important elements of his argument, the concept of artificial selection and the notion of the triune brain. And, most inexcusably, Sagan neither mentions any of the traditional criticisms of science as a philosophical and social activity nor addresses his argument specifically to these criticisms.

While Sagan explains how science is progressive, based on hypotheses which may later prove to be incomplete or false, he does not discuss the ultimate philosophical status of this potentially false knowledge. Sagan puts himself in the unenviable position of making an argument from scientific authority while implying that today's science may be overturned by tomorrow's advances. He praises science's ability to control nature and offer material advance; yet he extricates science from its contributions to the debasement of nature and its encouragement, directly or indirectly, of a materialist social ethic. Science offers man the comforts of a technologically advanced society; Sagan does not care to state that technological societies are industrialized societies, organized along bureaucratic lines. Although lamenting the "bureaucratic mentality" and claiming that religion and politics reenforce this stifling, potentially destructive mind-set, Sagan admits no connection between science, technology, and bureaucracy. Science, we are told, helps man overcome the debilitations of followership. How this works in practice, for society as a whole, is apparently a yet to be explored mystery.

Above all, science enables man to adapt to his environment, and this capability is the most compelling aspect of Sagan's argument. Through science, man can practice artificial selection to transform nature and the environment to meet his needs and attain his goals. The ultimate example of artifical selection is the science of adaptation applied to the human species itself. Genetic engineering, a logical extrapolation of the scientific impulse, poses serious problems for man, admits Sagan. But he does not explain how either science or his "cosmic perspective" helps resolve moral problems other than through experience and experiment. This is particularly disturbing because Sagan suggests frequently that science is superior to any other existing philosophy or value system. However, when faced with answering the question, what ought to guide man's pursuit of science or, more properly, progressive adaptation, Sagan is silent.

This dilemma is presumably resolved if one understands the "cosmic perspective" and the substance of science. The study of the development and structure of the human brain reveals, says Sagan, the fact that science emanates from the brain's most evolutionary advanced component, the neocortex. The neocortex developed as the species dealt with the challenges of the environment to the extent that "reason" replaced biological impulse as the most efficacious means of survival. Instinct and impulse still exist in man, and irrationality marks much of human activity. This behavior, the product of the primordial parts of the brain, the R-complex and the limbic system, manifests itself in political conflicts, social strife, and psychological confusion. Science, according to Sagan, is dissociated from human foible. Moreover, if man continues to pursue an understanding of nature—to exercise his rational faculties—through space exploration, it follows that the debilitating elements of his physiology will become extraneous. The human practice of science results in an improved adaptation of the species and biological development to a more advanced life form. The problems of humanity, the tensions and conflicts in humans and between them, will be left behind. In biological terms, science is our cosmic destiny and the means to transcend the human condition.

Sagan's interpretation of the notion of the triune brain has been criticized as simplistic. Nonetheless, it is the key to Sagan's most important and probably best argument. What is disturbing is that he really does not elaborate on it in "Cosmos" and prefers to talk more about the stars and the exciting future of space exploration. One may assume that Sagan wants to avoid simply repeating his more detailed discussion of the triune brain in *The Dragons of Eden*. This is unlikely since, in substantive

terms, "Cosmos" is not much more than a summary of his popular writings. Sagan does not highlight his argument about evolution in "Cosmos," one suspects, because the viewer would thus be moved to ask, what about the meantime? How does man conduct himself today, pursuing science and technology but still under the influence of the problematic aspects of the brain?

Sagan says that he has an answer—the scientific method applied by and on society. Yet, his failure to detail what this means and inability to focus on crucial aspects of his justification for the scientific enterprise indicate an uncharacteristic uncertainty and ultimate honesty in Sagan the spokesman for science. It is reasonable to assume that Sagan knows that as a philosophical treatise on the meaning of science for the human condition, "Cosmos" is trivial. As a blueprint for a society which would vigorously pursue the scientific enterprise, "Cosmos" is embarrassingly incomplete. Sagan, then, is either frighteningly naive—indeed, "Cosmos" does resemble a piece of "social science fiction"—or guilty of duplicity—"Cosmos" does not, as Sagan claims it would, explain the cosmic perspective of science.

Such criticism may be too harsh and cynical. As a television series, "Cosmos" is refreshing, stimulating, entertaining, and educational. It is not a typical philosophic exhortation. Perhaps "Cosmos" is meant to be understood not as a treatise on science but as a parable about science, man, and the human condition. Sagan and "Cosmos" teach the lesson that, all things considered in this difficult world, science is a praiseworthy pursuit and deserves our affection and commitment. The viewer has the prerogative of examining the meaning and depth of this teaching, of joining Sagan in the quest to understand the universe and science's relevance for man. The problem with teaching through parables, however, is that most people take them at face value and do not understand, or soon forget, their meaning. This is a lesson Sagan may soon learn. (pp. 94-5)

David Paul Rebovich, "Sagan's Metaphysical Parable," in Transaction: Social Science and Modern Society, *Vol. 18, No. 5, July-August, 1981, pp. 91-5.*

Ouida Sebestyen

1924-

(Also writes under the pseudonym Igen Sebestyen) American novelist and short story writer.

Sebestyen's novels for young adults usually center on poor teenage protagonists who gain the maturity and understanding necessary to triumph emotionally over adversity. Critics often praise Sebestyen for the strength of her central characters, the poetry and realism of her diction, and for the optimistic vision of life that she presents in her work.

Sebestyen's best-known novel, *Words by Heart* (1979), is set in 1910 and is told by thirteen-year-old Lena, a black minister's daughter, who moves with her family to an all-white town. In the course of the book, Lena adopts her father's method of coping with the prejudice and violence her family encounters: "turning the other cheek." The book's title reflects Lena's journey from merely memorizing biblical verses to living by them, which is to know them "by heart." *Words by Heart* was acclaimed by many in the literary establishment and won a place on several "best books" lists. Concurrently, however, it was subject to harsh criticism from some who questioned the values which Sebestyen promoted, and she was accused of racism in portraying stereotypical black characters who are passive in the face of injustice and prejudice. Although Sebestyen's subsequent novels, *Far from Home* (1980) and *IOU's* (1982), received less critical attention than *Words by Heart*, critics were generally favorable in their assessments of these works.

(See also *Contemporary Authors*, Vol. 107.)

Courtesy of Ouida Sebestyen

KRISTIN HUNTER

[Sebestyen's *Words by Heart*], like life itself for Afro-Americans in the post-Bakke 1970s, is an anguish-provoking experience in backward time travel. Its sincerity is unquestionable, its eloquence seductive—but its message is even more regressive than the many setbacks from the gains of the '60s that blacks have suffered in this Second Reconstruction.

Appropriately, *Words by Heart* is set during the closing years of the First Reconstruction. In 1910, we travel with Lena, a 12-year-old memory whiz, and her family on a journey from hope to despair. . . .

The most puzzling and distressing aspect of Lena's character development is that she begins as a proud fighter and ends as a model of meek Christian forbearance, exactly, as Claudie observes with resignation, like her saintly father. The Bible contains, along with everything else, counsel for both modes of behavior, making Lena's transformation from sword-wielder to cross-bearer especially difficult for this reader to accept. She has learned her verses under Papa Ben's tutelage, of course, but early in the book, to his reminder that "'The Lord commanded, Thou shalt not kill,'" she responds quickly, "But Papa, in the very next chapter Moses says anybody that smited a man and killed him shall surely die."

How Lena comes to learn Papa's favorite verses and not her own "by heart," in view of all the evils that beset her family,

is unaccountable. One threat to their safety is the capricious nature of their employer, Mrs. Chism, a wealthy old dragon of a landowner who suffers unpredictable attacks of decency. She is perhaps the most complex and intriguing character in the book, but if she and people like her were consistently cruel, Lena, her family and the rest of us would be better off. Mrs. Chism is, for instance, too soft-hearted to get rid of her shiftless, dishonest poor white tenant farmers, the Haneys, who are incapable of anything but harm, until too late.

That Lena is able to feel sympathy for the Haneys at points in the novel, in spite of the threat they pose to her family; that, at the grim ending of the final and most suspenseful chapter, she decides to follow her father's dictum to "Love thy enemies and do good to them that hate you" is both appalling and incredible. One of the author's best phrases is: "Something always comes to fill the empty places . . . Something comes to take the place of what you lose." But if Sebestyen's brand of meek, turn-the-other cheek Christianity is supposed to fill the voids left by [Malcolm X] and, yes, [Martin Luther King, Jr.], then we blacks and our youngsters will be in even deeper trouble.

Kristin Hunter, "*Blurred View of Black Childhood,*" in Book World—The Washington Post, *June 10, 1979, p. E3.*

FRAN MOSHOS

What are the qualities of a moving story? Perhaps it is the recognition in our own hearts of certain human weaknesses and strengths; the truths we see in life that transcend the simple boundaries of age or time. *Words By Heart* . . . is a remarkable book about a young black girl, Lena Sills, and her family, as they journey from the still repressive South around the turn of the century to the promise of freedom in the West. . . .

Words By Heart is filled with . . . common-sense wisdom. Lena is repeatedly made to see that she can triumph over her personal misfortunes, until they no longer have the power to keep her down. It is a book filled, too, with country paths and the hot summer sun. Finally, *Words By Heart* is a story of adventure and learning and the inescapable reality of death, as Lena and her family are threatened by small-town prejudices. There is so much honesty and hope in this delicate tale that one cannot help but be moved by the prophetic words of Lena's father, words he knew by heart: "Something always comes to fill the empty places. Something comes to take the place of what you lose."

> *Fran Moshos, in a review of "Words by Heart," in The New Republic, Vol. 180, No. 25, June 23, 1979, p. 37.*

DANA G. CLINTON

The most striking fact about Ouida Sebestyen's novel **"Words By Heart"** is how instantly it calls to mind Mildred D. Taylor's 1977 Newbery Award winner, "Roll of Thunder, Hear My Cry." In both novels, a young adolescent black girl, long sheltered by loving parents in a close-knit and hard-working family, must come to terms with the reality of prejudice which exists against her people. Both Cassie (of "Roll of Thunder") and Lena (of **"Words By Heart"**) are extremely intelligent girls, the oldest children often responsible for watching over their younger siblings. Each has particularly strong ties to her father who tries both to protect her and to initiate her into an unfair social world, a world in which they can remain superior only by keeping their dignity. Family pride and the desire to be independent are motivating factors in the families' lives; in both books the family's situation is favorably compared to that of unlucky sharecroppers who will never have independence. Yet both books end on a note of mingled hope and despair and the inevitable unanswered question: why must anyone undergo such trials for the right to grow on this earth in peace with his fellow men?

In spite of these very basic similarities to an earlier novel, **"Words By Heart"** is a book of stature which should be considered a valuable addition to the developing body of novels for young readers which expose realistically the long struggle of black people to take their rightful place in the history of this country. Sebestyen moves her tale out of the South and shows that prejudice is not a regional attitude. . . .

[Lena's] final reaction of hatred after her father's murder sours in her heart as she recalls his words of love and understanding. This heroine, who realized the importance of education and secretly "borrows" books to improve her knowledge, has come a long way in a short time. She still has much growing to do, but she is now better prepared to choose the best directions. She has accepted her father's forgiving attitude but, we hope, is still susceptible to the truth of Claudie's angers and fears.

"Words By Heart" starts off a little haltingly, but the prose as well as the story quickly redeems the book from its rough beginning. Sebestyen has a keen feel for both character development and realistic speech representation, and the story gains strength by the fact that Lena does not draw all our attention, but fits snugly into a well-balanced tale. The story springs to life with the introduction of the feisty widow Chism who has "a laugh like a corn grinder" which she often "turned on and ground for a moment." Mrs. Chism provides, through her own character, a blend of humor, sadness, frailty, and determination, all the elements of the story of life portrayed in Lena's struggle. The nicest effect of **"Words By Heart"** is its ability to show us how every character in the book has arrived exactly where he is, and thereby to make us care about what might now happen to each of them.

> *Dana G. Clinton, "Black Pride in a White World," in The Christian Science Monitor, July 9, 1979, p. B6.*

CYNTHIA KING

Though early signposts point to a classic black tragedy, a female "Sounder," [**"Words By Heart"**, a] deceptively simple but strong first novel, is mostly about words—from the Bible, Walt Whitman and Ben Sills. . . .

It is 1910. Though Ben has long since given up his ambition to be a preacher, he hopes that Lena will have a chance to use her talents and not have to learn to "know her place." But in this all-white Middle Western town to which he has brought his family—Lena, his second wife Claudie, and their three small children, Ben has taken drunken Henry Haney's job at the cotton gin. Haney's son Tater seethes, spies and threatens revenge. . . .

Throughout the novel, the voice is Lena's. She listens to Ben and Claudie argue over her head; she hopes; she becomes angry; she learns to be afraid. Sometimes her voice rankles like that of an angry adolescent. Sometimes it strains, stretching credibility: "Events are blinks of time in endless time." Some of her metaphors are strained.

But sometimes, as in the beautiful contrapuntal passage during the Bible-recitation contest, in which verse and history and Lena's thoughts and memories are skillfully interwoven, Lena leaps to life, full of promise and confusion, as real as the words that astound or confound or dazzle her.

No small feat. The author—who grew up in the South and moved to West Texas, and is not black—has "aspired" bravely, reaching high with all her heart. Despite the transparent plot, and characters who state the novel's themes too bluntly, Ouida Sebestyen has written a many-layered book. She has wrapped a story with poetry, wrapped me with it, too, caught and held me, made me feel with Lena and Claudie and Ben. And then—in the last chapter, a kind of welcome coda—she shows her optimism, changing her characters from timid to heroic, vengeful to generous, pointing toward love, not cynicism, without painting black history white.

> *Cynthia King, in a review of "Words by Heart," in The New York Times Book Review, August 26, 1979, p. 34.*

PAUL HEINS

When thirteen-year-old Salty Yeager [of *Far from Home*] realized that he and Mam, his great-grandmother, who lived together on the outskirts of a Texas town, were poverty-stricken, he decided to apply for his mother's old job in a shabby boardinghouse pretentiously entitled The Buckley Arms. . . . Although Salty, who helped with a variety of chores, gradually became acquainted with a nearby family of troublesome children, most of his attention was centered on the emotional concerns of the adults living in the boardinghouse. As time went on, the boy, convinced that Tom Buckley was his father, had to learn why the man could not publicly acknowledge him. The story, set in 1929, reflects the era; the language—often humorous—frequently makes use of contemporaneous phraseology. Even though Salty's constant but frustrated attempts to communicate with his father are presented in skillfully understated terms, an excessive proportion of the narrative is focused on the marital problems of the adults living in the boardinghouse. (pp. 60-1)

> Paul Heins, in a review of "Far from Home," in The Horn Book Magazine, Vol. LVII, No. 1, February, 1980, pp. 60-1.

ZENA SUTHERLAND

Salty [hero of **Far from Home**] was thirteen. He had no idea who his father was; his mother (a mute woman) was dead, as were his grandparents; he lived alone with his great-grandmother and they were facing eviction. He took the note his mother had left, telling him to go into town to the home of Tom and Babe Buckley. . . . [It develops that] Tom is his father and that the fact must be kept from Babe, who has had many miscarriages and who is loved and protected by her husband. This is not a childlike story, but should have some of the same kind of appeal that [Harper Lee's] *To Kill a Mockingbird* has had to many adolescent and pre-adolescent readers: a vividly created microcosm of society, an abundance of sentiment without sentimentality, and a protagonist who is drawn with compassionate percipience. All of the characters are drawn in depth, in a moving story in which several of them change believably in response to the others. For some it develops that the boarding house can never be a home; for Salty, once he accepts the limitations that Tom puts on their relationship, it becomes a home. While Salty is the only child in the story, he is the focal point; in him are the passion for justice, the need for love and security, and the need to identify and belong that all children feel. A fine novel.

> Zena Sutherland, in a review of "Far from Home," in Bulletin of the Center for Children's Books, Vol. 34, No. 1, September, 1980, p. 21.

RUDINE SIMS

Words By Heart is the latest book honored by the literary establishment even though it perpetuates negative images and stereotypes. . . . [It] has been honored for the excellence of the author's craft, but it is flawed because it presents an outsider's perspective on Black lives and fails to recognize the political, racial and social realities that shape the Black Experience in this country. And . . . it features the death of a "noble" Black man, that very expendable literary creation.

Based on a short story published in 1968, **Words by Heart** shares with other late sixties children's fiction about Blacks the implied purpose of raising the consciousness of white readers to racial injustice. *The Horn Book* suggests that "it dramatizes the Black people's long struggle for equal opportunity and freedom," but the dramatization fails because the statements the book makes about the human condition are fallacious. Unlike books written from a Black perspective—Mildred Taylor's *Roll of Thunder, Hear My Cry,* for example—**Words By Heart,** for all its literary artistry, fails to do more than evoke pity and compassion through heart-rending sentimentality. (p. 12)

On the surface this is a well-written, poignant story, offering such time honored themes as "Love thy neighbor" and "Overcome evil with good." . . . The Sills family is portrayed as warm, close and strong. The father is in many ways, admirable—wanting a better life for his family and placing a high value on education. However, the portrait of this Black family, supposedly seen from its center (Lena's point of view), is out of focus. The viewpoint remains that of an ethnocentric outsider. In its totality, the book perpetuates some negative images, some tired stereotypes and some implicit themes that are, from a Black perspective, questionable at the very least. There are both major and minor problems.

One problem, indicative of the book's perspective, is the tendency to associate things black with things negative. . . . There are uninviting descriptions of the Black characters. Ben Sills' hands are "perched on his knees like spiders ready to jump." Lena sees in her reflection "spiky plaits and a rascal face." . . . The rest of the audience is "an orchard of pink-cheeked peaches," and the standard of beauty that is invoked reflects their ethnocentric perspective.

The main problem with Scattercreek, too, seems to have been that it was all Black. While the move west represented potential freedom from the oppression prevalent in the South of that era, the book suggests that Scattercreek also provided refuge, but was inferior because it was an all-Black town. . . . [The] implication is that [Lena's father, Ben Sills] chose an all-white town because there was something shameful about living in an all-Black one. This attitude contrasts to positive descriptions, like those given by Zora Neale Hurston of the richness of life in Eatonville, Florida, the "pure Negro" town in which she was born.

It is through Sills' talks with Lena that the most insidious messages about the nature of racism occur. Sills stubbornly refuses to acknowledge racism as the motivation for the hatred the Haneys—and others—express. There are threats and name-calling, the mysterious death of the Sills' dog, a knife thrust through a fresh loaf of bread the night Lena wins the contest. Yet Sills insists: "This is a good town we've come to . . . they took us in." He attributes whites' behavior to their fear of change or to their hopelessness and frustrations with being poor sharecroppers, rather than to racism. He proposes that the white people's actions be met with understanding. . . . Although Ben does recognize that, even in Bethel Springs, some cannot accept them, for the most part Claudie's fears are made to seem almost unreasonable in this "good town." (pp. 12-13)

When discussing the family's history and the Black Experience in general, Sills refuses to place the blame where it belongs: "They reconstructed us—one little loss at a time. . . . Somehow we got put in our place again." The anonymous, unspecified forces at work are never labeled, never named. The violence that Black people experienced in the post-Civil War period is only touched on in one brief paragraph and, in fact, some of the historical information given is not correct. (p. 13)

The most overtly racist behavior comes from unsympathetic characters whose behavior can be "explained away" in large part by their situation or personality traits. The Haneys are stereotypes of poor-white Southerners—lazy, hard-drinking, irresponsible, gun-toting males, dirty children and women kept barefoot, pregnant and silent. Another prejudiced person in the story is Mrs. Chism, the woman for whom both Sills and Haney work and from whom Ben Sills rents his home. She is an eccentric elderly woman—lonely, unhappy, seemingly oblivious to the effects of placing Sills and Haney in competition with each other and indifferent to the effects of her sharp-tongued barbs on other people. Neither her own children nor her neighbors like her, and only one person attends what was meant to be her large and elaborate dinner party. . . . In any case, the portrayal of the "bad guys" as mostly atypical or unlikeable people projects a picture of a utopian town where racism is an aberration.

Moreover, the cumulative picture of Ben Sills is the prototype of the "good Negro"—hard-working, Bible-quoting, understanding, passive, loving and forgiving towards whites, and willing to "wait on the Lord" until whites are ready to accept his family. . . . This stereotypic portrait of passivity does not advance the art of writing about the Black Experience, and in the late 1970's it need not have been perpetuated.

The characterization of Sills will be justified by the fact that he had wanted to be a minister, but it is false to equate godliness with passivity. (pp. 13-14)

The most disturbing aspect of this book is its ending. Given the characterization of Ben Sills, it is entirely consistent for him to crawl, though fatally wounded, a considerable distance to help [Haney's son] Tater, his attacker. (Sills doesn't even try to leave to get help for himself; that option "never occurred to him.") Given the described relationship between Lena and her father, it is also consistent for her to help Tater—for her father's sake and for the sake of her own humanity. But only if one can equate justice with vengeance can the message implicit in Lena's decision to lie about her knowledge of her father's murder be seen as consistent behavior—or acceptable. The message is that if a white boy, as part of his rite of passage into male adulthood, even goes so far as to kill a Black person, the proper Christian response is to "let God handle it." (Can you imagine literary prizes bestowed on a book in which a rotten Black boy murders an angelic white man and is forgiven by the white man's daughter?) That message remains untempered despite the intimation that Tater may eventually be healed both physically and morally, and despite the closing scene in which Tater's father silently picks the cotton of the family his son has made fatherless. He knows that the cotton crop represents money the Sills family will need to survive, but the question of whether his helping is motivated by remorse, guilt or a desire to buy Lena's continued silence is left unanswered. Given the characterization of Haney as hate-filled and lacking in hope, Lena's hope that he has acquired a new sense of morality is totally unfounded. (p. 15)

The idea that hard work and submission and gradualism will overcome is untenable. Hard work is no threat to people on whom one depends for one's livelihood. Hard work was never a defense against oppression; it is not today. This is an irresponsible message to give to any young readers. . . .

"Love thy neighbor" and "overcome evil with good" are worthwhile themes. In an ideal world, where racial differences don't count, it wouldn't matter which characters exemplify those themes. However, in a book set in the real world, where racial differences *do* count, when the responsibility for loving,

forgiving and overcoming evil with good lies solely with the book's Black characters, the action takes on racist overtones. The implication is that white people should be understood and forgiven, even for violent racist acts. . . .

In these troubled times, when the [Ku Klux Klan] still operates on the assumption that they can threaten and kill with relative impunity, it is important to recognize that *Words by Heart* invokes a third Judeo-Christian tenet—"Thou shalt not kill." A prize-winning book that plays "overcome evil with good" against "thou shalt not kill" has a responsibility to see that the latter receives equal time. (p. 17)

> *Rudine Sims, " 'Words by Heart': A Black Perspective," in* Interracial Books for Children Bulletin, *Vol. 11, No. 7, 1980, pp. 12-15, 17.*

FAY WILSON-BEACH AND GLYGER G. BEACH

Ouida Sebestyen's novel *Words by Heart* will strike a responsive chord in the hearts of anyone who has ever believed that mobility is achieved not by skin color but by hard work (the Puritan work ethic), God's favor (Full Gospel Businessmen's Association) or intelligence. All three elements are embodied in this tale of a young Black girl growing up in the all-white town of Bethel Springs. . . .

By the end of the novel it is evident that Lena's "magic mind" has not won her any significant number of friends or increased her stature in the neighborhood or school. Ben's hard work and dependability earn him the hatred of his neighbors and eventually his murder. And what we are left with is God's favor, which according to this book is worse than nothing at all.

We see the author extolling the virtue of forgiveness but not that of justice. Instead of calling for justice, the author calls for passivity in the face of injustice. The quest for justice is ignored, as is an authentic use of the scriptures. . . .

In addition, the author gives Ben Sills a theology that is closer to that of a plantation master than to those families he left behind in Scattercreek. It is objectionable therefore, to see the words of Bible-wielding oppressors put in the mouth of a Black man whom the author could have developed as a free-thinking, freedom-seeking Black man. From the time he "explains away" the first sign of violence—the stabbing of a loaf of bread with a butcher knife—Ben Sills speaks of forgiveness, patience, love and understanding for those who would harm him and his family. Ben speaks of the love expounded by Christ in the New Testament—"love your enemies, do good to those who hate you." He has no understanding of the radicality of Christ's strategy. Christ's intent was to stir the people in order to bring order and justice to the community.

Words by Heart does not use scripture to encourage change. The book quotes scripture that would have people give control of their lives to a benign God; it blatantly ignores scriptural admonitions that would support people taking responsible actions in their own affairs as well as those of their neighbors, and yes, those of their country. (p. 16)

Good theology leads one to ask questions and probe the quality of human life. Good theology does not serve the vested interests of a few, but of the whole. Good Christian theology does not allow death without resurrection, as this book does. Ben Sills' death does not stir this community to any redemptive acts. After Ben's murder, the white characters indulge in post mortem trivia; there is no move to see justice done. There is no place in the book where the white characters are held responsible or accountable for Ben's death, either individually or collectively. The book only hints at the possibility that Mr. Haney, father of Ben's murderer, may be picking the Sills' cotton because he's sorry for the trouble his family has caused the Sills family. (He might just be stealing it.) There is no renewal of life and no justice in this story. Mr. Haney is not saved, Tater is not saved, no one is saved. Why does the death of the only Black man in the story end in tragedy and insignificance? (And even if the Haneys had been saved—or experienced some kind of renewal—nothing would redeem the racist injustice and brutality of Ben Sills' murder.)

It must be stated that *Words by Heart* is not a book for Black children but for white racists. The author wrote a book extolling outdated, oppressive theologies at a time when the world is crying for liberation and models to point the way.

The author wrote a book about love, a passive love, that in no way resembles the love that civil rights leader Martin Luther King, Jr. got from his forebears. King preached a non-violent love that would propel men and women to agitate and confront an unjust society. The author advocates and portrays a love so distorted by her own perspective that it is inactive and unresponsive, narrow and restricted. (pp. 16-17)

The cry of liberation has been lifted up by Black, feminist, Latin American and other theologies. This book is an insult to all these efforts to achieve human liberation.

We do not need a repetition of history's ugliness. Rather, we need to know how resistance, confrontation and negotiation can change attitudes and laws and, hence, behavior. We need books that expound a theology of liberation and not oppression. We need to see the plantation theology condemned, not lifted up. Lena, in refusing to tell her stepmother who killed Ben, contends that she was holding to the first law, "forgive your enemies." We must always choose God's law over man's law only if we properly interpret or understand God's law. Lena obviously did not. The scripture also says: "let justice run down like rivers of water" and "thou shalt not kill." (p. 17)

> *Fay Wilson-Beach and Glyger G. Beach, "'Words by Heart': An Analysis of Its Theology," in* Interracial Books for Children Bulletin, *Vol. 11, No. 7, 1980, pp. 16-17.*

PATRICIA LEE GAUCH

It is risky for an author to tackle stock characters and stock situations in a novel. Take **"Far From Home."** Down-and-out orphan of deaf-and-dumb mother begs mother's former employer (and maybe lover) for room at failing boarding house only to meet aging prankster, pregnant bootlegger's wife and nosey neighborhood kid. Not only could this have ended up a stock story, it could have ended up a melodrama.

It didn't, largely because of an honest character named Salty. . . .

At times the activity around Buckley Arms, a kind of 1920's Noah's ark, flips by like a penny movie. The prankster Hardy is forever clowning, Jo has her baby in Salty's room, Mam runs away, and a Fourth of July parade almost steals the ending. But while Salty goes along with it all, he is never taken over by it. Author Sebestyen sees to that with moments like Salty's first lonely night at the Arms, when he gets lost in the yard stumbling over tin cans and "grabbing at moon shadows."

Amid the parades and fireworks Ouida Sebestyen lets her character touch the others honestly "with a little bluster of hope" and produces an aching irony, for it is July 1929, the end of an era. One only wonders if she needed the nonstop action and a cast that size when she had a year like '29, a character like Salty and a notably sensitive style.

> *Patricia Lee Gauch, in a review of "Far from Home," in* The New York Times Book Review, *January 18, 1981, p. 31.*

DENISE M. WILMS

Thirteen-year-old Stowe Garrett [of *IOU's*] shares a close relationship with his mother. It's been the two of them since his father left long ago, and they've forged a peaceful, independent life-style that seems worth their meager day-to-day existence. Annie Garrett has taught her son to be responsible and to think for himself, so when he gets a sudden phone call from relatives informing him that his seriously ill grandfather, who had cut Annie out of his life in grief and anger years ago, wants to see him, he keeps the news to himself. . . . Stowe eventually decides against visiting his grandfather, but Annie learns of the call and determines to go in hopes of reconciliation. The meeting never happens because Lee Earl Albright dies before they get there, but Stowe realizes that family bonds are stronger than he thinks and that he must seek out and forgive his own father lest a destructive pattern repeat itself. Sebestyen's mother-son portrait is a pleasure to watch, and Stowe's sensitivity to the feelings of others springs directly from it. This is a delicate revelation of matters of the heart, and speaks strongly of the powers of love.

> *Denise M. Wilms, in a review of "IOU's," in* Booklist, *Vol. 78, No. 15, April 1, 1982, p. 1023.*

KIRKUS REVIEWS

Parent-child relationships appear to be a Sebestyen preoccupation, . . . [*IOU's*] is about nothing but the particularly close relationship between Stowe, 13, and his brave, wise, loving, financially-strapped mother. . . . More like a couple than a mother and child, the two discuss their relationship, quarrel maturely, express their mutual trust and affection, do a jaunty little softshoe step together on a dusty road, and, on a seesaw with "their weight balancing finally after years of being unequal," daydream playfully about their imagined future house in the country. He does decide to keep from her his dying grandfather's wish, relayed through a cousin's phone call, to see Stowe: As Annie wasn't mentioned, he won't go either. Finally, though, Annie decides on her own to make the journey, and when she and Stowe arrive too late she regrets not having reached out earlier. And Stowe, as always, comes to see the loss her way. Besides prompting Stowe to consider getting in touch with his own father and to speculate in passing about his own future status as a father, a grandfather, and a funeral subject, the major outcome of the experience is to strengthen the bond between Stowe and Annie, after only a token challenge in the form of a concerned old aunt who questions Annie's exclusive emotional investment in Stowe. But it's hard not to share the aunt's concern, and hard not to find Annie and Stowe a little cloying and idealized in a slightly sickly way—though Sebestyen unquestionably writes with sensitivity and shading and seems to get down into Stowe's feelings and the pair's interactions.

A review of "IOU's," in Kirkus Reviews, *Vol. L, No. 8, April 15, 1982, p. 496.*

MARY M. BURNS

Reflecting on the summer of his thirteenth year, Stowe Garrett [the hero of *IOU's,*] concludes that it has been a time of good-byes. . . . But goodbyes also mean the chance to explore possibilities as yet barely apprehensible—the hopeful note on which the book concludes. Written from the adolescent's perspective, the story explores with sensitivity and insight the relationship between two remarkable individuals—Stowe and his unconventional mother Annie. Separated from her husband, disinherited by her father, Annie has struggled to keep their fragile household afloat, specializing in tasks which permit her to work at home. The work is hard, and the return small; yet the bond between mother and son is strong. And it is from these three elements that the central conflict emerges. Angered because husband and father both failed her, Stowe dreams of someday supporting them himself. His ambitions, however, are frequently sabotaged by adolescent ambivalence and stubbornness. . . . The resolution is neither glib nor simple but rather reflective of reality where large losses are sometimes followed by small advances. What is most important is that Stowe and his mother emerge from adversity not necessarily unscathed but undaunted. With feeling, but not without humor, the novel works on many levels. The characters, developed in action and dialogue, are remarkably well rounded, and the theme, as in *Words by Heart* . . . is a substantial one.

Mary M. Burns, in a review of "IOU's," in The Horn Book Magazine, *Vol. LVIII, No. 4, August, 1982, p. 418.*

HAZEL ROCHMAN

Thirteen-year-old Stowe [the hero of **"IOU's"**] and his mother, Annie, like each other. Deserted by her husband and estranged from her father, Annie has enjoyed bringing up Stowe on her own in spite of the economic hardship. Their teasing, affectionate relationship is questioned by Stowe's friend Brownie, who can only see parents in terms of adversarial authority and who taunts Stowe about his need for his mother's approval. . . .

Stowe's ambivalence is wonderfully captured. He has moments of sudden recklessness, exhilarated at having risked pursuing his way even if his mother might be right. But he also nurses a secret prayer: "Let me be better to her than they were. . . . I want to make it up to my mother."

The crisis of his grandfather's dying helps release Stowe's dammed-up feelings. He lets go of his hatred and exposes himself to the terror of loss. With Annie's love he feels able to travel "the scariness of new country" and to begin the search for his own father, breaking the pattern of what happened with hers.

Although Ouida Sebestyen allows her characters to talk too explicitly about these themes, making connections for the reader that would be better left tentative, this is a powerful story. As in Miss Sebestyen's award-winning **"Words by Heart,"** the young protagonist, strengthened by the love and integrity of a parent, takes on moral responsibility in a harsh world.

Hazel Rochman, in a review of "IOU's," in The New York Times Book Review, *September 19, 1982, p. 41.*

JOSEPH O. MILNER

In abstract, Ouida Sebestyen's **Words by Heart** seems a religious *Charlotte's Web*. It recounts the growth of Lena from bright, ambitious girlhood to a maturity equal to that of her too-good black Papa who, at the cost of his own life, teaches her to love her white enemies. . . . Unpleasantries are foreshadowed and then explode with a poor white sharecropper's family whom Lena and her father have replaced as "hands" for a wealthy and paranoid woman. Finally, Lena makes a long trek into the wastelands to help her wounded Papa, only to be asked by him to help his assailant (the white sharecropper's son), who is himself near death. The bright and aspiring Lena, her father's unforgetting, less optimistic second wife, Claudie, the lonely, unlovely, rich Mrs. Chism, the ignorant and defeated sharecropper family, and the less fully developed white townfolk are all appealingly and convincingly portrayed. Papa, however, is so much a modern Jesus that readers might find it difficult to suspend their disbelief; his perfection is overwhelming. (pp. 171-72)

[Papa] is finally committed to a life of service and love: "That's what we're here for, to serve each other. . . . The greatest people who ever lived served others." [Lena] tries to emulate her father on the playground but can't speak up for the taunted Haney boy; she does better in going to see Mrs. Chism after she gets word that her fine party was a flop, but she is misunderstood; and finally, with great misgiving, she does the ultimate good by taking the torn Tater Haney back home and by never telling Claudie who shot Papa. She is not Papa, but she has trodden close to his steps of pure service. The ideals of obedience and sacrifice win Lena's ultimate allegiance. (p. 172)

Joseph O. Milner, "The Emergence of Awe in Recent Children's Literature," in Children's Literature: Annual of the Modern Language Association Group on Children's Literature and The Children's Literature Association, *Vol. 10, edited by Francelia Butler, Yale University Press, 1982, pp. 169-77.**

BEVERLY HALEY

Everything has its price. To gain something, you must lose something. And the dearer the prize, the greater the cost. [In *Words by Heart*] Lena wins the Bible recitation contest, but she pays with her personal pride. And later, to gain her father's respect, she must force herself to bring those memorized words to life. "A price must be paid" recurs as a major theme in Ouida Sebestyen's novels—*Words by Heart, Far From Home,* and *IOU's.* . . . She tries, she says, to create a "sense of miraculous heroes, a sense of individual worth and potential." She wants her stories to show how things have been, how they ought to be, how they can be.

Sebestyen's characters provide the vehicle for dramatizing the themes. Family plays a central role in all three novels, but not family in the traditional sense. (p. 3)

Reminiscent of [John] Steinbeck's worlds, Sebestyen's protagonists suffer the effects of poverty, of being misfits, and of doing battle against the world in general and themselves in particular. Despite their lack of material wealth, Sebestyen's heroes gleam with a sense of nobility and purpose that the glimpses of those characters wealthy in possessions fail generally to reveal.

Their situations demand of each protagonist—Lena, Salty, Stowe—that they grow up prematurely. All experience a death in the family that forces additional maturity on them. This early maturing imposes pain, but it also endows them with a largeness of purpose and of character that most teenagers do not acquire in such breadth and depth. But they lack experience to help them fulfill the demands on them, so they sometimes falter in their attempts. Lena steals books from Mrs. Chism. . . . Salty [in *Far From Home*] resents the burden that Mam is. . . . Stowe, in *IOU's,* resents having to think about things instead of just doing them as his friend Brownie is free to do. . . . (p. 4)

Just as Sebestyen dramatizes the irony that the materially rich may be poor in common sense and decency while the materially poor possess riches of other kinds, so too do the teenagers rise to become the adult when that role is demanded. Tom Buckley in *Far From Home* can love only one person. When Salty dresses in Tom's old military uniform for the home entertainment night, Tom explodes. . . . Salty, the teenager, must grow taller than Tom, the adult who can't love his own son. Salty is left alone, Sebestyen explains, "to find his place in a complex world, a safe, loving center."

In *Words,* Lena must be a bigger person than Mrs. Chism in that rich woman's irrational demands; bigger than Mr. Starnes, who forbids his son Winslow to associate with the black girl (Later in the novel, Winslow becomes the adult when he calmly stands up for his friend Lena); and bigger than the Haneys, the poor white trash competing for Mrs. Chism's favors. When Lena's father dies, the preacher admits his inability to be the adult comforter of the child. . . . (pp. 4, 6)

Sebestyen's protagonists are spirited, independent teenagers bent on being better than they are now and better than others. They are honest, loyal, proud, and loving. Yet they could not be accused of being goody-goody. They flame orange-red in their passion to possess the best in life; they push; they lie; they use their power to hurt; they have their moments of despair. They are human beings trembling on the edge of adulthood who grow up through the events in their lives. They grow stronger as a result of adversity and the fact that they are misfits in society because of age, social class, race, or sex. And for those minor characters who are in most ways flabby and weak of will, there come small deeds or words to surprise the protagonist and the reader with redeeming traits.

Violence erupts—the knife driven through the loaf of bread on the Sillses' kitchen table, the mysterious death of the pet dog, the violation of human dignity because of racial prejudice in *Words*; jeers from neighbors, rejection by his own father, the loneliness of Jo in her birth-giving, the quarreling between Hardy and Rose Ann in *Home;* and in *IOU's* the humiliations of having to return part of the groceries at the checkout stand because Annie doesn't have enough money, the embarrassment of Brownie and Stowe making fools of themselves in their anger over Karla's growing up before they do and leaving them behind and out of her life, getting lost in the cave on the mountain campout. These and other violences are set in relief against the tenderness between people who love deeply and who fight for that love.

Sebestyen lightens the opposing tones of violence and of tenderness with a third tone—that of playfulness and an enduring sense of hope. The protagonists are, after all, children. One not merely hopes but believes they will never lose the child within that makes them laugh and be bold and believe in a happy ending somewhere, that takes delight in the joy of now. (p. 6)

The author's diction captures the flavor of a time, a place, and particular people. Its poetic, musical simplicity elevates the people who are poor materially to match their richness of character. Wealthy Mrs. Chism, on the other hand, reveals her baseness of character through her "back-of-the-barn" language. Thus diction and style add texture to the writer's use of force/counterforce in characters, themes, and events.

Sebestyen's aim beyond telling a story is, she says, to nourish and enlarge young minds. Those of any age who read her words risk catching the fire of life. . . . (p. 13)

Beverly Haley, "Words by Ouida Sebestyen," in The ALAN Review, *Vol. 10, No. 3, Spring, 1983, pp. 3-4, 6, 13.*

(Edward) Rod(man) Serling

1924-1975

American scriptwriter, short story writer, dramatist, and producer.

Serling was one of television's most respected writers. He has been recognized for bringing the maturity and quality of stage drama to television during its early years and for offering provocative entertainment throughout his career. Serling's diverse works address a wide range of controversial issues, including prejudice and political corruption. Critics contend that Serling's iconoclastic attitude, which compelled him to tackle social topics neglected by his peers and to create memorable stories around them, helped move him to the forefront among writers of television's Golden Age.

Serling began selling scripts to radio as a college undergraduate. Like many other radio dramatists, he began to write for television during the early 1950s. In 1955 alone, twenty of his plays were produced on such acclaimed live television drama series as "Playhouse 90," "Studio One," and "Kraft Television Theater." It was on the last-named program that Serling's drama *Patterns* was first aired. A story of the inhumanity and ruthlessness involved in big business, it made Serling an instant success and won an Emmy Award. It was also the first drama to be repeated by a network in response to popular demand. Serling's best-known teleplay, *Requiem for a Heavyweight*, was broadcast on "Playhouse 90" in 1956. An account of the descent of a physically and spiritually defeated prize fighter, this drama was awarded an Emmy and, like *Patterns*, was later adapted for film. Serling won a Peabody Award for outstanding service in broadcasting for *Requiem for a Heavyweight*, the first time this award was given to a television writer. He won a total of six Emmys during his career, as well as several other awards for outstanding television writing.

Throughout the mid-1950s and 1960s, Serling impressed most critics with the consistently high quality of his work. He was less popular, however, with network managers and sponsors, whom he publicly criticized for their censorship of television scripts and writers. Serling believed that in order for television to function as an art form as well as entertainment, writers had to have the freedom to explore attitudes and draw conclusions regardless of whether the entire audience shared these views. Serling became known as television's "angry young man" for his zealous dedication to his beliefs, gaining the admiration of many of his contemporaries and helping set the tone for future television drama.

When the demand for live drama died at the end of the 1950s, Serling was among the few writers who successfully adapted to television's new demands. His series "The Twilight Zone," which aired from 1959 to 1964, exemplifies Serling's imagination and versatility. Combining elements of science fiction, fantasy, suspense, and horror, "The Twilight Zone" was the first show of its kind to adapt individual dramas to a series format. It was also unique in its significant concentration on the quality of the writing, rather than on the acting or the production aspects, although these too were highly praised. Narrated by Serling himself, the show was generally hailed for its innovations. A later, similar program, "Rod Serling's

Night Gallery," which was broadcast from 1970 to 1973, shared "The Twilight Zone"'s eerie tone, but critics contend that it lacked the high quality of its predecessor. Both programs, however, were popular with their audiences, and especially with young people, who continue to appreciate the shows through reruns. Serling's popularity was further enhanced with his screenplays for the films *Seven Days in May* (1964) and *Planet of the Apes* (1968), which he wrote with Michael Wilson. *Twilight Zone—The Movie* (1982) is an adaptation of four favorite "Twilight Zone" scripts, including Serling's classic "It's a Good Life."

Some of Serling's detractors have charged that his works were too slick and overly didactic, concentrating more on their messages than on plot and characterization. It is also noted, however, that Serling brought a strong moral sense to his art and that his creativity and craftsmanship helped shape television during its formative years.

(See also *Contemporary Authors*, Vols. 65-68, Vols. 57-60 [obituary] and *Dictionary of Literary Biography*, Vol. 26.)

ROBERT LEWIS SHAYON

Murder was brilliantly done on the (NBC) Kraft Television Theatre in January and repeated "by popular demand" early in February. The unplanned second performance of an original television drama ["**Patterns**"] so soon after its first showing is an unusual video event. The notability is doubly compounded when the play pyramids its prestige almost exclusively by word of mouth. Of even sharper interest to this viewer is the fact that the "murder" which climaxes the drama is unwittingly (I hope not deliberately) condoned by the author and producer in subtle yet painful violation of commonly honored and deeply cherished moral principles. . . .

In the years I have been viewing television I do not recall being so engaged by a drama, nor so stimulated to challenge the haunting conclusions of an hour's entertainment.

"**Patterns**" is the story of murder in the executive echelon of a typical big-business corporation. I call it murder; in the story the victim [Andy] dies suddenly of a heart attack, but the fatality comes stunningly on the heels of an executive conference in which the company's president [Ramsey] plunges an invisible dagger, tipped with the poison of fear, hate, and resentment, into the life-urge of an unwanted member of his high command. . . .

"**Patterns**" is the kind of a script that strikes a match to production talents. Director, cast, even stagehands suddenly become aware they're touching a piece of uranium in the TV desert. You're inching open a curtain on truth. . . . Rod Serling's lines are spare, measured out with intensity, precision. (p. 23)

How wonderful that rich, young, bedeviled TV can come up with so meaningful a theme, so honest and revealing a treatment! It *can* happen here. . . . Then Fred Staples returns from the hospital where Andy has died (the two men were really fond of each other—no rivalry between them but Ramsey's). Righteously indignant, Staples walks into Ramsey's office to tell him off and to quit—but moments later he walks out—still on the job. How has Ramsey persuaded him? The tyrant has admitted his lack of humanity, but he has waved aloft the banner of impersonal achievement. "It is no one's business! It belongs only to the best! To those who can control it. Keep it growing, producing—keep it alive! It belongs to us right now! In the future, to whoever can give it more . . . I don't ask to be liked—fight me, take over if you can. And watch the business grow . . ."

Young Staples then stands revealed in his true hollowness. . . . He had admitted wanting the job, had left it to Andy to take the lead in the showdown. His big ethical explosion is a naked rationalization. He is Ramsey's man. They are all Ramsey's—Staples's wife, the other executives who conform—even Ramsey himself, who hasn't the courage to fire Andy but must kill him by cowardly indirection. All except Marge, Andy's secretary, who takes her potted plant and quits when she gets the news from the hospital.

I repeat. The author and producer may not have wanted to imply a favorable judgment on the play's ending; but that's how the final armed truce between Ramsey and Staples comes out. Poor old Andy is dead and swept under the carpet. Ahead lie fulfilment and peak achievement for the living—on terms of competitive struggle alone. Rising sales curve is God and Ramsey is his prophet. Inefficiency is heresy and crime is compassion. It is a fine thing to have struck so firm and brilliant a note as "**Patterns**." It is shocking to think that the moral climate of our time is so committed or befogged that a drama of such seriousness and merit should fail to penetrate into the utter issue raised by the situation and to stand up and be counted on the side of decency. (pp. 23-4)

> *Robert Lewis Shayon, "The Efficient Murderer," in* The Saturday Review, *New York, Vol. XXXVIII, No. 9, February 26, 1955, pp. 23-4.*

J. P. SHANLEY

Rod Serling, whose compactly constructed television drama, "**Patterns**," was acclaimed three months ago, turned to a different kind of theme in "**The Rack**." . . .

In "**Patterns**" Serling dealt with high pressure business tactics and their effects on a group of executives. In "**The Rack**" he borrowed from contemporary history and told the story of an Army captain charged with collaborating with the enemy in North Korea. . . .

["**The Rack**"] was not written with the expert conciseness that distinguished "**Patterns**," nor was it so flawlessly presented. There were some uneven moments in "**The Rack**," but its principal theme was controversial and compelling.

It posed a question that has been asked recently in similar nonfictional situations: Shall a repatriated prisoner of war be punished for acts he has committed under duress while in captivity? . . .

"**The Rack**" was particularly effective when its author, probing beyond normal codes and standards of conduct, considered the complex human factors that operate when the minds and bodies of men are subjected to cruel and relentless pressures. Serling was not willing to settle for superficial melodrama. His play was intelligent and provocative.

> *J. P. Shanley, "Trial for Treason," in* The New York Times, *Section 2, April 17, 1955, p. 15.*

J. P. SHANLEY

Since Mr. Serling also wrote "**Patterns**" and "**The Rack**," two of the outstanding television plays of this year, there was reason to look forward with some anticipation to his latest script.

But "**Strength of Steel**" was a dreary potboiler. . . . No word has been received about just when Mr. Serling wrote it. It may long have antedated his better creative efforts. It seems hard to believe that the same writer had been responsible for them.

"**Strength of Steel**" is the story of a young Air Force wife. Her husband packs off for Alaska, leaving her to wait for him in Pittsburgh. They say good-by stickily and then the undaunted bride moves in with her father-in-law.

The old gent . . . is a nasty type who wants no part of his son's wife. He treats her shabbily, even after they learn that his son is overdue from a patrol flight.

Dad blames the girl for the whole thing. He tells her unequivocally: "You married him so you could get yourself out of the gutter."

The wife takes understandable umbrage at this kind of talk, but she stays around until she learns that her husband has died.

Mr. Serling resorts to a tired device to end his drama. The widow lets the old gent know that he soon will be a grandfather. Then she tells him off and that does it. They fall into each other's arms blubbering heavily as a camera dollies in for the climactic scene.

J. P. Shanley, "TV: 'Strength of Steel'," in The New York Times, *June 17, 1955, p. 47.*

TOD RAPER

Don't look for any green-headed monsters or rattling skeletons, or Shirley Temple fairy tale atmosphere [in **"The Twilight Zone"**]. Each episode is set up in the context of the plot to be shocking, unexpected, but at the same time, in retrospect, valid and honest. . . .

We watched the pilot film, **"Where Is Everybody?"** this morning and in the half-hour felt the hair on our neck rise, the skin on our back cringe, and our heart flop at the finish with a feeling of relief. Here is presented the situation of a man walking into town in a state of amnesia, and nobody is in town. A cigar butt in the chief of police's office is smoking; the coffee is perking in a cafe. But nobody is there. Serling puts over a sense of loneliness that is hair-raising, and then in three minutes lifts the whole thing. It's magic. . . .

"The Twilight Zone" is . . . about the hottest show that CBS-TV has coming up, and the most interesting. It's a collection of stories of imagination that reach out and touch the stars. There's fantasy, stories of the unusual, the bizarre, the different, the novel. They are stories of the unreal told in terms of reality. They dramatize events that have never happened but conceivably might happen. . . .

Best of all, [Rod Serling] has a new idea for television. We think you'll like **"The Twilight Zone."**

Tod Raper, "'Twilight Zone' Is Hottest CBS Series," in Columbus Dispatch, *August 23, 1959, p. 3A.*

HELM.

Rod Serling has fashioned a stark drama of an imaginative nightmare [*Where Is Everybody?*] that puts [*Twilight Zone*] in orbit with an auspicious takeoff. It may well turn out to be one of CBS-TV's strongest entries, generic in its appeal and with the arresting quality of skirting the current cycles. It gives tv a new and much-needed dimension, far off the beaten path of westerns and private eyes. If the word hadn't been abused, it could be honestly labelled adult drama.

Serling has stood for qualitative writing and here, in his own venture, he is inspired to heights corresponding with the moon phase of the story. If the title is mystical, all the more in its favor, it is not a detached contrivance. It refers to the fifth dimension, that of imagination, in which a human guinea pig takes a journey into the shadows. . . .

Compelling drama that never released its taut grip, the writing and narration of Serling . . . gave it an epic dimension of greatness in an early season of mediocrity.

Helm., in a review of "Where Is Everybody?" in Variety, *October 5, 1959.*

BRENDAN GILL

"Requiem for a Heavyweight" is a *real* movie, dominated by a camera that, like our own eyes, picks its way through a profusion of helter-skelter objects to see clearly, as if without effort, precisely what it needs to see. It's a picture so nearly perfect of its kind that my temptation is to dwell on the "perfect" and forget the question of kind, but I mustn't lose my head; what we have here is a prizefighters-and-gangsters melodrama of exceptional humanity and finesse. . . . The script, by Rod Serling, is a sentimental pastiche, as the soft-hard title indicates. No matter—the sources from which it borrows being first-rate, the end product is a distillation of the first-rate. . . . (p. 216)

Brendan Gill, "Ways and Means," in The New Yorker, *Vol. XXXVIII, No. 35, October 20, 1962, pp. 215-17.**

STANLEY KAUFFMANN

[*Requiem for a Heavyweight*] combines sportswriter's sentimentality with "common-man" portentousness (the heroic concealed in what you and I are silly enough to think is small-scale or vapid). The plot is incredible: a top-rank boxer is desperate for a job a week after he quits boxing, and a mousy State Employment Agency woman changes character and chases him after one meeting. When Serling's dialogue is not trying for dumb-brute poetry, it slips into scriptwriter's hand-me-downs. ("I love that guy like a brother." "Now you listen and listen good.") (p. 27)

Stanley Kauffmann, "The Rise of Jane Fonda," in The New Republic, *Vol. 147, No. 21, November 24, 1962, pp. 26-7.**

PHILIP T. HARTUNG

You don't have to believe **"Seven Days in May,"** but, except for the confusing opening scenes showing riots in front of the White House and then introducing far too many characters in a hurry, it proves to be one of the most exciting films in years. . . . **"Seven Days"** succeeds in giving its far-fetched story an it-could-happen-here tone. Rod Serling's well-written script . . . is mainly concerned with a Pentagon plot, under the leadership of Gen. James Scott, Chairman of the Joint Chiefs of Staff, to kidnap the President of the United States and take over the government. The plotters are particularly unhappy now (the time is set in the not-too-distant future) because the cold war has ended with President Lyman's plan for universal nuclear disarmament—a plan agreed to by Russia and ratified by the U.S. Senate. Since Lyman's popularity is at a low point, General Scott decides now is the time to pull the coup.

What happens from then on is thrilling, not only because of the action during the intrigues and counter-intrigues, but also because of the people involved and their behavior. . . . The script softens the general-as-villain theme a bit when the Georgia Senator explains that the real enemy is a nuclear age that has thrown today's people into despair, "people who look for a leader like Senator McCarthy or General Walker." There's nothing soft about the film itself, however, and it's guaranteed to keep audiences on their chairs right to the rousing finale. (p. 632)

Philip T. Hartung, "What Five-Sided Building?" in Commonweal, *Vol. LXXIX, No. 21, February 21, 1964, pp. 632-33.**

BRENDAN GILL

"'Seven Days in May' is an almost perfect thriller"—such was the opinion I was about to set down when my conscience intervened; the wary cravenness of that "almost" struck me as patently unjust, for, in fact, there wasn't a single moment of this high-flown melodrama that I didn't enjoy, or a single aspect of it that I would have liked to see changed, and gratitude alone should suffice to make one generously incautious. With a sense, therefore, of having provided no handy trapdoor of qualification through which to escape, let me paint myself into the tight corner of total praise: **"Seven Days in May"** is a perfect specimen of its kind. . . .

[The] plot of the picture, . . . like that of any good thriller, is far easier to admire than to describe, mounting in ever more dangerous spirals of intrigue to a climax that had me not only on the edge of my chair but ready to leave the country if things didn't reach a fortunate conclusion. . . .

[I] give away no important secrets when I mention that the setting is Washington, the time a few years hence, and the crucial action a right-wing conspiracy on the part of high Pentagon brass to kidnap the President of the United States and take over the federal government. That such a conspiracy might occur and then come within a hairbreadth of success is apt to appear, at first glance, preposterous, and it is the art of thrillers to make sure that, at second glance, we see not the hokum within but a surface of unimpeachable plausibility. Here, for example, in the model opening scene of **"Seven Days in May,"** is the veritable White House, serenely familiar above its sweep of lawn, and here are two opposing lines of pickets, marching back and forth in front of the high White House fence as we have often watched them do in newsreels. Suddenly, the pickets are rioting, and the camera itself is caught up in the melee, rocking madly this way and that, while police sirens are heard screaming up Constitution Avenue; we cut to the President's office, where the President is being given a medical checkup, and from that moment on we are helpless not to believe what [director John] Frankenheimer and his ingenious colleagues wish us to believe. I walked out of the theatre more than half convinced that the President of the United States is a troubled, virtuous man named Jordan Lyman. . . . (p. 112)

> *Brendan Gill, "A + ," in* The New Yorker, *Vol. XL, No. 1, February 22, 1964, pp. 112, 114, 116.**

JACK BEHAR

In *Requiem for a Heavyweight* Serling's gross intention is to write a television play in something of a celebratory mode: to represent a good if witless man—submerged in the stereotype of the prize fighter and treated as an object—who becomes the victim of the prize-fighting racket and the soft-hard mindedness of those who run it, especially Maish and the mob behind him. (p. 36)

In *Requiem for a Heavyweight* . . . the question is: Can Mountain be saved from the stereotype that already has all but consumed him? Or: Can Mountain be saved from Maish, the father-figure who has all but unsexed him? The answer the television play gives is somewhat evasive, since although Mountain cannot quite be saved from Maish, the hope is that he might come to save himself by administering something of his sheer animal goodness to deprived children.

The major virtue of the television play (one wholly absent from the movie adaptation) is that it forces on us the sheer presence of Maish, Army, and Mountain in an overwhelmingly physical way. Speaking face to face, crowding out almost everything Serling brings into the film adaptation, they fill the screen, they command our attention, and they are held to their mythic types. This is not the case with the movie; things spread dangerously thin, so that most of the anxiety-filled moments of the television play are wholly lost. . . . The television play is uncluttered by Serling's later unhappy inventions, so that the "requiem" for Mountain has a chance to sound out cleanly and intensely within the limits set by a modestly small initiating idea, but one with the force behind it of our obsessive interest in the fight game and the mythical life of the exhausted pug. The quite incredible scenes in the movie adaptation—inserted to pep things up, no doubt—in which Ma, the threatening lesbian mobster, appears, are more than enough to strain to the breaking point any attempt to approximate "literal reality." In the television play we never see Mr. Henson, the gangster patriarch who threatens Maish's life—only his lackeys. It is enough that one of the lackeys appears to make credible the force his boss commands: he nails Maish's hand down to the floor with his shoe and grinds the lesson in, so to speak. In the movie, on the other hand, Ma appears in the odd disguise of a reject do-it-yourself Gestapo officer, ready to oversee the sadomasochistic carnage, her lesbian pulchritude concealed beneath the heavy sexless leer. Her (his) presence appears to be a bad joke, as one might conclude charitably; nonetheless, the utterly phony scenes in which Ma figures undercut the relevant drama of the movie (thin to begin with), shifting the emphasis to the visible lesbian, sadomasochistic world behind it. (pp. 36-8)

The obvious contrivances in the film version are to be interpreted not only as Serling's attempt to "fill out" the television scenario, but also as an effort to toughen it. The rather sentimental ending of the television play that has Mountain going home to Tennessee hopefully to be reborn, his dignity still intact, is replaced by the scenes which give us his final degradation; he enters the ring, burdened by his knowledge of what he must do, and finally yields up the ghost in whooping like a good Indian—a dead Indian. This conclusion is made almost inevitable by a sequence of action, the ineptness of which I find quite inexplicable, a breakdown in Hollywood professionalism. I am referring to the strange sequence that shatters whatever rightness of design the dramatic action might conceivably have had: Maish's getting Mountain drunk at Jack Dempsey's . . . , the pathetic failure of Mountain's effort to find a new life, and Maish's final meeting with Grace [Mountain's girlfriend]. The whole sequence, of course, is designed to bring Mountain into the ring as a whooping Indian wrestler, and this is more transparent than it has any right to be. What should appear to be a struggle for Mountain's soul becomes instead merely an excuse to impose what Serling apparently considers to be a tragic conclusion. Maish confronts Grace, telling her in a display of deadly honesty, that she should leave Mountain to the end that Maish (and, as it were, the fates) has engineered for him. Strangely enough, Maish's plea that Grace stop feeding Mountain illusions about the future silences her immediately, although all that Grace has been doing is trying to secure Mountain a modest sort of job in a boys' camp. Presumably the point is that Maish, in his confused and unacknowledged love for Mountain, must impose the final humiliation because he knows that Mountain can never live in the humdrum world Grace would have him enter. Of course Maish needs Mountain if he is to save his own life, so that it is not easy to make sense of his final act of honesty. If we are to take the honesty seriously, then he should not seem to be playing God so as to save himself from the mob; whereas he appears to be doing precisely this. After the meeting with Maish, Grace disappears, and Mountain is left to negotiate as best he can with Maish.

On the whole, what is merely hokum in the movie—Ma and her gang, Mountain's getting drunk, the one violent brawl we have at the end—tends to overshadow what is modestly decent in it, the middle section that is concerned with the small romance between Mountain and Grace. The conclusion is very dubiously contrived; after Mountain is confronted with Maish's imminent end, there is little he can do except get his manager out of hock to the underworld. We are apt to think that what becomes Mountain's fate is shaped merely by necessities which Serling had to satisfy: the need to fill out a television script that wanted toughening, toughening easily provided by a dose or two of violence, a tease of straight lesbianism, and at least the possibility visually registered of Maish's getting stomped on by the gangland gestapo.

Beneath the obvious failures of the movie version exist attitudes which, unexamined and self-perpetuating, seem dangerously shallow and complacent. The clue, I believe, is in some words Serling writes in the preface to the "reading version" of the film script as a dedication to a lost world he once knew:

> To the Mountain Riveras—to the punchies, the cauliflowered wrecks, the mumbling ghosts of Eighth Avenue's bars, the dancing masters of another time who now walk on rubber legs. To the has-beens, the never-weres, the also-rans— this book is dedicated with affection and respect.

These are not unimpressive clichés, although, on the other hand, it is not unimaginable that a Walter Winchell could have done as well by the "Mountain Riveras." The carefully processed New Yorkese makes "affection and respect" hard to come by. There exists in the language the sign of an easily spent emotional identification, self-serving, hardly self-effacing, in fact merely a form of attitudinizing. And the attitudinizing exhibited here, furthermore, compromises the realism that Serling would be faithful to, which becomes, in effect, a veneer under which is concealed lazily nostalgic feeling and a thin curiosity. Serling probably felt pity for Mountain Rivera, but all the respect he can show him is to impose upon him the burden of being a sacrificial hero, which is after all small tribute to one's respect, particularly so when what we need so badly is the man himself. We get, therefore, only another form of distortion and idealization; the warm feelings toward the "cauliflowered wrecks" end, predictably, in abstraction.

Presumably the intent of both the television play and the movie version is to rescue "the mumbling ghosts," to bring them back alive from the lower depths of Broadway, not only to enact their "requiem." That is to say, to restore them, not to bury them in abstraction and hokum and ritual sacrifice—certainly not to make the sacrifice the measure of their dignity. The problem Serling faces but cannot solve, apparently, is what to do with Mountain after he has brought him back to life in the scenes with Grace. In the television play, Serling has finally to send him back to Tennessee; in the movie version, he makes him into a victim, but a victim who is somehow a hero, a sadly sentimental paradox. It is to be identified, I think, with the tough-guy sentimentality of Broadway, the notion that underneath a hard surface crust everyone is a man of good feeling, or could be if only he did not always have to be on his guard lest the world cave in on him. Maish is the exemplar here, a man of essentially good feeling who finds himself hopelessly caught as he desperately tries to stay alive in a mean world.

What saves the movie version from being a total failure as an attempt to save the man from the stereotype, to restore him to *our* world, is that it succeeds in telling us what Mountain's world has been like: not merely impoverished by Mountain's incapacity for words and the usual *ersatz* masculine camaraderie, but loveless, sexless, empty beyond the emptiness of those who use Mountain. . . . The point the movie makes is that personal communication and the concomitant awakening of the spirit, even at this rudimentary level, have no chance against the world in which men bide their time in old Broadway hotels. The scene between Mountain and Grace is well conceived, touching and serious beneath the confused play of words; but its excellence is soon swamped by the crudeness and artificiality of what follows. Ma comes back to life, and we move finally to Mountain's disgraceful yelping and the pseudo-sacrificial end. (pp. 38-41)

What we needed in the television play was a fuller exploration of [Mountain's] needs, not simply the standard, needlessly timid recognition that they exist. The television play, that is to say, lacked sex, repressing therefore the main issue, which in the film adaptation Serling makes some effort to represent in the scene between Mountain and Grace at the end of the movie. All that comes of it, however, is in the good-girl lines which Grace speaks to Maish: "I just think the next thing he wanted he should have gotten—I wish to God it were something I could have given to him." Thus is prepared the necessary fadeout, and so fades out too a belated effort to focus the small disabling human fear and repression next to which the contrived sacrificial end is of literally no importance. This opportunity missed, all that we can get is a none too interesting exercise in the analysis of a corrupt and corrupting ritual dramatically generalized. What we hope to have explored openly is the relation between the ordinary enough pathos of disgraced manhood, the loss of meaning, the victimization of Mountain's primitive loyalty, and—beneath these—the sexless, all-too-masculine, all-too-repressive world in which Mountain has lived his life. If Mountain is not to be seen as a good simple sort who goes willingly to the slaughter, his loyalty to Maish simply the product of his mindlessness, Serling must rise to an honorable treatment of sex. But he does not. He feeds Mountain to the slaughter.

Between the faces and bodies that register wildly and beautifully for a moment in the television play and the astonishing ineptness of so much in the movie adaptation, it is not hard to choose. The television camera keeps the world small, claustrophobic, intensely inane, as it were, while the big screen merely invites the hokum that, in retrospect, seemed rather predictable. On the one hand, there is the dark, exaggerated largeness of things in the television play, the product of a style that can descend of course into a familiar kind of artiness; and on the other, a hopeless, depressing stiffness. . . . In the end, then, we have a realized aliveness, spontaneity, a sense of real bodies, some closeness of design, in the television play, and only dourness, easy evil, stiffness, mock brutality, in the movie adaptation. The television play triumphs precisely because it is necessarily obedient to the relatively narrow frame of things imposed by the television camera, and hence it remains uncorrupted by the pseudo-realistic excess and unwitting parody. . . . The movie adaptation, in contrast, extends but does not intensify—indeed, thins and flattens out—what we have in the television play, and except perhaps for the initial sequence which we get from the point of view of the defeated Mountain, it is visually uninteresting, more dead than alive. (pp. 42-3)

Jack Behar, "On Rod Serling, James Agee, and Popular Culture," in TV As Art: Some Essays in Criticism, edited by Patrick D. Hazard, National Council of Teachers of English, 1966, pp. 35-64.*

PHILIP T. HARTUNG

[There is a lot of action in **"Planet of the Apes"**], but more vital are the arguments between apes and man, and, as presented in the screenplay . . . , they are fascinating. Man does not always come out best. Surprisingly enough, the film has some good humor, thanks, among other things, to the script's putting clichés into the mouths of those apes who think they're so damn smart. The finale of **"Planet of the Apes"** will make your blood run cold. I can't remember when a science-fiction film like this socked you in the face at the end with a warning to mankind. (p. 625)

Philip T. Hartung, "The Naked Human," in Commonweal, Vol. LXXXVII, No. 20, February 23, 1968, pp. 624-25.*

ROBERT LEWIS SHAYON

The new Rod Serling teleplay, **Certain Honorable Men,** . . . presented no acts of physical violence. But an uglier form of violence—the suppression of the truth—haunted its ninety-five minutes of plot dealing with the mask and the reality of Congressional ethics, much as Banquo's ghost cried out in the empty chair at Macbeth's table. . . .

Viewers had no difficulty relating the author's fiction to the real life material of the 1967 Senate censure of Senator Thomas J. Dodd for "conduct which is contrary to accepted morals, derogates from the public trust . . . and tends to bring the Senate into dishonor and disrepute." Some viewers, however, did have difficulty—reconciling Mr. Serling's necessarily selective choice of dramatic essentials, among the complex elements offered by the true case, with the always troubling problem of how gatekeepers in the media use truth for their private, particular purposes.

The Champ Donahue case, as shaped by the author, searched out the simplest form of violations of traditional ethics—the acceptance of money bribes and corrupt favors. The Dodd case involved more sophisticated, significant, and insidious human failures that have impact on the effectiveness and justice of government service. These are failures in courage, energy, and detachment, where Congressmen take or withhold action, not for financial reasons but for fear of displeasing industry groups or political superiors; where duty is shirked by doing as little as possible; and where powers are used not for the public good but for a bloc with which a power holder identifies himself. From such a perspective, Congress appears as the chief ethical violator in the Dodd case. (p. 55)

It could be argued that a dramatist has every right to fashion an entertainment as he pleases, and to use only that which his artistic judgment tells him is manageable esthetically and relevant to his purpose. He must be judged on his work and not on what others think he might have done. It is a torturous question; and every talent that works in TV, which is the most public and portentous of all the agenda-setters in our society, must search his conscience to draw the shadowy line that separates freedom of choice from public responsibility. But it is also fair game to speculate, as a viewer, what might have happened had the author chosen to deal with the more subtle and inchoate substance of the Dodd story. Aside from Mr. Serling, what other gatekeepers sat at decision points in the communications channels that led from a playwright's private vision of dramatic truth to his national audience? (pp. 55, 86)

It may reasonably be concluded that **Certain Honorable Men** would never have completed its long journey to its TV audience had it, in any way, touched the deeper, more sensitive, and far more significant ethical issues. (p. 86)

Robert Lewis Shayon, "An Uglier Violence," in Saturday Review, Vol. LI, No. 41, October 12, 1968, pp. 55, 86.

CLEVELAND AMORY

We've learned through short experience to beware of any show which is titled Somebody's Something. It's inclined not to be anybody's anything. And **Rod Serling's Night Gallery** is no exception. Mr. Serling was one of the giants of "The Golden Age of Television." Now he is more of an endangered species. . . .

Most episodes contain three separate stories, so if you don't like the first, you can always look forward to the next two. On the other hand, if you don't like either the first or the second, you can always look forward to the third. By the same token, if you don't like the first or the second or the third—well, look at it this way, it's over. They are the kind of thing that [Alfred] Hitchcock did so well, and still does in reruns. And it really is infuriating, 50 years after Hitchcock, to have something not anywhere near as good. . . .

Opening in a museum with paintings, with Mr. Serling as host, the series each week offers such maggots—or do we mean nuggets?—as a baby sitter who discovers her strange-looking employer is Count Dracula, a vampire returning from the dead to have a fancy funeral in the Eternal Rest Room, and an 11-year-old girl befriending a monster known as The Thing. Curiously enough, such drivel attracts a wide variety of name stars. . . .

Two shows stand out in our mind particularly—perhaps because they were written by Mr. Serling himself, and reasonably well. One was a story in which a man of the future sends his deformed son to another planet in accordance with The Federal Conformity Act of 1993. It could have been touching, but, being in this show, it wasn't. Another was a story in which a widow . . . who had a green thumb refused to sell her little cottage to a mean industrial developer. Again, it had its points—aside from the fact that, like so many stories here, it didn't really have an end. Someone should tell Mr. Serling and [executive producer Jack] Laird that in stories like this, it's very important to have an end. We admit that it's basically good news that they *are* ending, but somehow that's not enough. An ending should be either logical or very illogical, either funny or a twist or *something*. Otherwise you feel cheated—and, believe us, what you've got here is highway robbery.

Cleveland Amory, "Rod Serling's 'Night Gallery'," in TV GUIDE® Magazine, Vol. 20, No. 6, February 5, 1972, p. 40.

MARK OLSHAKER

The voice was unmistakable. The stories were "weird" and "spooky," the twist endings intriguing. But there was an added element that happened to be a rare commodity in television entertainment—a moral point of view. Rod Serling . . . was always trying to get a point across.

The format was pop science fiction, but the themes were the basic operatives of the human mind. The characters either rose to their situations or were destroyed by them. While other shows portrayed World War II as an epic of brave men in combat, *Twilight Zone* gave us **"Death's Head Revisited,"** the story of a Nazi commandant returning to Dachau and there confronted by the ghosts of the inmates he slaughtered. And Serling's humanity always showed through, as in a Christmas episode, **"Night of the Meek":** A drunken loser whose only joy is playing a department store Santa each year, finds the real Kris Kringle's bag of miracles and helps his fellow losers inherit the earth—at least for one night.

Serling's career embodied the entire course of American television. He was the brightest of the Golden Age's "bright young men" and the only one to adapt when live drama died. He became known as TV's angry young man during the 1950s, when he demanded of himself scripts that not only entertained but made a comment. Serling's teleplays confronted the major social and personal issues of the day—the Red Scare, POW collaboration in Korea, the unrelieved tension between black and white—at a time when few others would touch them.

And he confronted these issues head-on, decrying the spineless and chilling fear that caused network execs to quake each time a Serling script suggested there were still problems to be solved. . . .

[Serling's tone was] high-minded, idealistic, if sometimes overly formal and didactic, believing that mass drama could do something. And he did do something: With a staggering artistic stamina during those early days Serling turned out over 100 quality scripts. He sprang upon the public consciousness in 1955 with **"Patterns"** on *Kraft Television Theater*—a story of the emotional destruction wreaked by corporate inhumanity that won Serling his first Emmy. A year later he topped himself with his most famous work, **"Requiem for a Heavyweight,"** on *Playhouse 90*.

When his market dried up, Serling conceived of *Twilight Zone,* which he produced, hosted and did much of the writing for. With the series, Serling and his magic voice became a part of mass culture and modern folklore. But it also made him a "media person," much in demand for talk shows and commercials. For the rest of his life Serling continued to wrestle with the conflict of the serious artist vs. the public personality. . . .

It is unclear what directions Serling would have moved in had he lived the additional years he had a right to expect. It is doubtful he would have wanted much more to do with television. At the time of his death *Twilight Zone* was more than ten years old. And the video era he embodied was essentially over—the medium that was half his age had grown old far faster than he had.

Mark Olshaker, "Requiem for a Heavyweight: Final Tribute," in New Times, *Vol. 5, No. 2, July 25, 1975, p. 68.*

LAWRENCE VENUTI

Near the end of his life Serling was little more than a background voice in the mass media, yet during the fifties and early sixties he was one of the loudest and most outspoken critics of American society and the television industry. His stark, realistic screenplays, produced on such live dramatic programs as *Playhouse 90* and *Kraft Television Theater,* subjected American institutions and values to close scrutiny, confronting controversial issues like the fierce competition in corporations, corruption in labor unions, police violence, and racial prejudice. Not surprisingly, he soon incurred the wrath of the television censors. (p. 354)

Yet when Serling developed *The Twilight Zone* in 1959, he was in fact criticized for "pandering his work," for evading his avowed moral responsibility as a writer. What was so difficult for his critics to accept was his sudden and bewildering shift from realistic drama, in which social commentary and moral issues were the writer's main concern, to fantasy, which seemed pure escapist entertainment devoid of serious import. The fact is that *The Twilight Zone* was Serling's calculated response to the growing oppressiveness of television censorship, and in many of his screenplays for this series he continued his critical examination of American society—but in an oblique and perhaps more inventive way. Instead of relying on realism to convey his message, Serling embodied it in fantasy and managed not only to avoid the censorship which had plagued his earlier writing, but also to maintain his integrity as a socially concerned writer. Indeed, *The Twilight Zone* may be Serling's greatest achievement: its combination of sophisticated dramatic techniques with social criticism has rarely been equalled in the history of television. (p. 355)

In theme and style *Patterns* is typical of Serling's television scripts during the fifties. Like his other critiques of American institutions, it powerfully dramatizes his oft-quoted observation that "our society is a man-eat-man thing on every possible level." In accordance with the extremity of this view, Serling's pursuit of his quarry is usually relentless and uncompromising. *Patterns* focuses sharply on the suspect values in American business, exposing the dishonesty inherent in the corporate drive for profit as well as the unethical compromises an ambitious executive must make in order to remain in that bitterly competitive world. The stylistic qualities of the screenplay are appropriate for Serling's forceful exposures: the language is direct and colloquial, with a tendency toward overstatement; the characterizations approach stereotypes and are sufficiently but not minutely drawn . . . ; the structure of the play is quite spare, uncomplicated by an elaborate plot development, and the action moves quickly to a climactic conclusion. Most importantly, *Patterns* reflects Serling's conviction that realism is the most effective means of social commentary. . . . Here he asserts that "drama—be it fiction or motion picture or stage play—has traditionally been a vehicle of social criticism. That function would be altogether timely, particularly during this day and age. There is much to criticize: diverse and demanding collections of human anguish that literally scream out for a comment; injustices that so diminish the human condition that one wonders where in the name of God *is* that school of literary protest that might move and sway public opinion—as [Henrik] Ibsen did, as Harriet Beecher Stowe did, as Clifford Odets did, and as Arthur Miller did." For Serling, writing should be "a weapon of truth, an act of conscience, an article of faith." (p. 356)

The fantastic worlds Serling created in many of his screenplays for [*The Twilight Zone*] were a far cry from the realism he had employed during the fifties, and he was quickly accused of conforming with the network commercialism that he had fought for the first ten years of his career. In his writing for *The Twilight Zone,* however, Serling did not shrink from the social criticism which had characterized his previous work in television; he rather embodied his examination of American society in fantasy. Of course, his messages were not entirely explicit, and less sophisticated viewers, enthralled by the fantastic plot, might not always perceive its significance, yet his narrations before and after each episode often made his themes more obvious or at least pointed to the intention behind the fantastic surface. Serling, moreover, was quite capable of conveying his themes in an oblique way: he had acquired much experience with this sort of indirection from his numerous confrontations with the censors who often forced him to 'cover the tracks' of his social commentary. Even though television censorship moved Serling to give up his commitment to critical realism, *The Twilight Zone* shows that he did not surrender his conception of the responsible writer's function in society. (pp. 361-62)

["The Twilight Zone"] is "the dimension of the imagination," and in their exploration of the imagination the screenplays ranged widely through many varieties of fantasy, including science fiction, horror, and the occult. Within this broad framework, however, the area Serling had charted for his more engaging work was primarily psychological, and the fantastic plots of many episodes hinge on some aspect of human psychology. In the Twilight Zone, dreams and hallucinations tend to be prophetic of real events; traumatic experiences which have been repressed for years abruptly resurface and literally come alive; characters who yearn for a more pleasant past, for their childhood or adolescence, sometimes find their wishes fulfilled. Interestingly, this psychological fantasy enabled Serling to deepen his social criticism, and in several screenplays he continued his investigation of the business world and prejudice with greater attention to his characters' personalities. (p. 362)

Serling entered television as a realistic playwright who had dedicated his writing to social commentary, but he was compelled by the oppressive television censors to give up his commitment to realism. Nonetheless, when he developed *The Twilight Zone,* he was able to adapt his talents and interests to a new genre, fantasy, and he continued his examination of American society in an oblique but effective way. With his fantasy series, Serling could avoid the commercial censorship that had forced many writers out of television and that played a large part in making it the cultural wasteland we consider it today. . . . [It] remains true that the most influential mass medium, the one which carries the greatest authority with a major portion of the American population and which easily molds viewers' opinions, is essentially controlled by a group that is concerned merely with attracting more consumers. Unfortunately, there are currently very few writers in television who can meet the challenge posed by the sponsors with Serling's dedication and inventiveness. (p. 366)

Lawrence Venuti, "Rod Serling, Television Censorship, 'The Twilight Zone'," in Western Humanities Review, *Vol. XXXV, No. 4, Winter, 1981, pp. 354-66.*

Zoa (Morin) Sherburne

1912-

American novelist, short story writer, and poet.

Sherburne is best known for her novels which realistically explore problems often faced by today's young adults. Her teenagers typically struggle to come to terms with such traumatic family situations as divorce, remarriage, death, and mentally ill or physically handicapped parents. Sherburne's protagonists encounter such difficulties as unwanted pregnancy, involvement with drugs, unrequited first love, and unpopularity. *Too Bad about the Haines Girl* (1967), one of the first young adult books to confront the problem of teenage pregnancy, is perhaps her best-known work.

In addition to her realistic novels, Sherburne has also written science fiction and Gothic novels. *The Girl Who Knew Tomorrow* (1970) is the story of Angie, a girl with extrasensory perception who must learn to use her gift without abusing it. *Why Have the Birds Stopped Singing?* (1974) is a Gothic tale in which the protagonist travels back in time, assuming the identity of one of her ancestors. Both the protagonist and her ancestor are epileptic; Sherburne's sympathetic treatment of this affliction is generally considered the strongest asset of the book.

Sherburne has also published over 300 short stories and verses in various magazines. Her work is often praised for its vivid characterizations and well-developed plots.

(See also *Contemporary Authors*, Vols. 1-4, rev. ed.; *Contemporary Authors New Revision Series*, Vol. 3; and *Something about the Author*, Vol. 3.)

ALBERTA EISEMAN

When Karen Hale [protagonist of **"Almost April"**] went to Oregon to live with her father and his new wife, Jan, she was all set to dislike them both. She had not seen her father for years, and her mother's recent death had left her bitter and unhappy. The Hales' love and understanding, and Jan's obvious desire to make her happy, won Karen over. Then her friendship with Nels Carlson reopened the rift with her father. . . .

This is a fast-reading story of a difficult year in a young girl's life, for the many adjustments always present during the teens are complicated, in Karen's case, by her unhappy background. The windswept coast of the Pacific makes an exciting background for the stormy romance between Karen and Nels.

> Alberta Eiseman, "A Crucial Year," in The New York Times Book Review, *February 5, 1956, p. 24.*

LOUISE S. BECHTEL

The cards are stacked against the Karen of [**"Almost April"**] in ways that should make many unadjusted girls feel they are lucky: parents divorced, mother dies, Karen lives with difficult grandmother; grandmother ill. . . . For us, Karen is an unpleasant sort of girl, even when she begins to see the light and reform her ways, so that all ends happily. It is a story with rather more adult implications than most junior novels; it is well written and expert at describing teen-age emotions.

Louise S. Bechtel, in a review of "Almost April," in New York Herald Tribune Book Review, *March 11, 1956, p. 7.*

ALBERTA EISEMAN

A summer job in Mountcastle, the most exclusive section of town, was the fulfillment of a dream for Leeann Storm [protagonist of **"The High White Wall"**]. Ever since she could remember, the ivied wall surrounding this residential area had symbolized for her a secure, enviable way of life, and she had gladly escaped from her own overcrowded home. . . . Though she missed her family, Leeann had no trouble adjusting to the Kingsley's beautiful house, and enjoyed taking care of their two little girls and doing secretarial work for their older son Dirk. . . . She found that she was able to help Dirk make some difficult decisions, and that a lot of her own thinking needed to be rearranged, too.

An ambitious 18-year-old, anxious to get away from her own environment, does not always make a likable heroine, yet Mrs. Sherburne has penciled in her backgrounds skillfully, and has made the reader entirely sympathetic with Leeann's motives. All of which—unfortunately—made it doubly difficult for this reviewer to accept the sudden change in Leeann's values as she finds herself falling in love with Dirk.

Alberta Eiseman, "Escape," in The New York Times Book Review, *February 3, 1957, p. 32.*

JENNIE D. LINDQUIST

Younger teen-agers will enjoy [the experiences of Leeann, protagonist of **The High White Wall**]. There is nothing particularly original about them but the book is well written and the characterization exceptionally good. Leeann, her family, the children behind the high wall, their parents, and the two young men who bring romance into the story are all real people. The part about the death of Leeann's little sister is very well done. (p. 141)

Jennie D. Lindquist, in a review of "The High White Wall," in The Horn Book Magazine, *Vol. XXXIII, No. 2, April, 1957, pp. 140-41.*

JANE COBB

The more one considers the before and after of the Misses, Queens and Princesses . . . the more interesting the situation becomes. These are not just pretty, costumed girls beaming out of the newspaper —the Miss or Princess career has a beginning and an end. In **"Princess in Denim"** Zoa Sherburne presents such a career in interesting detail.

The heroine is Eden, a nice girl who keeps house for her father and likes to ride horseback. Her friend Steve enters her picture in the contest for Tulip Princess. . . .

[She] became Tulip Princess, and she had a wonderful time. Then the wheels of commerce began to grind; she was entered in the Miss Washington contest and it wasn't fun. It was vicious and exhausting. The entire experience was tough on Eden, but she learned a lot about herself and life, as will the reader.

Jane Cobb, "Contest Winner," in The New York Times Book Review, *March 23, 1958, p. 36.*

ALBERTA EISEMAN

Zoa Sherburne, in ["**Jennifer**"], the latest of her perceptive, well written books, tackles the subject of alcoholism, or, to be more precise, the effect of a mother's alcoholism on a 16-year-old girl.

Jennifer Martin and her parents have moved to the state of Washington in an attempt to make a new life for themselves after the death of Jennifer's twin sister and Mrs. Martin's subsequent breakdown. Jenny would like to make friends with the high school crowd, but her own feelings of inadequacy and her constant fear of a relapse on her mother's part make her withdrawn and unsociable. . . .

Though dealing with a potentially morbid subject, the author never forgets the audience for whom she is writing. She tells a lively story with plenty of dances, dresses and conflicting romances. Her heroine is unusually appealing and "best friend" Patsy a delightful, humorous creation. And there is a touching relationship, remarkably, skillfully developed, between Jennifer and her parents, joined so closely by their heartbreaking problem, yet painfully unable to discuss it.

Alberta Eiseman, "Family Problem," in The New York Times Book Review, *March 8, 1959, p. 40.*

POLLY GOODWIN

Zoa Sherburne has chosen an unusual and difficult theme for

["**Jennifer**," a] realistic teen-age novel and, handling it with discernment and taste, comes thru with flying colors. . . . [Primarily] it is the story of Jennifer's own problem—her fears that her mother may not have won her battle [with alcoholism], her reluctance to make friends and invite them to her home.

How Jennifer wins her own victory—surprisingly with her mother's help—and the family draws closer together in love and understanding is a moving story told with warmth and wisdom.

Polly Goodwin, in a review of "Jennifer," in Chicago Sunday Tribune Magazine of Books, *April 5, 1959, p. 14.*

VIRGINIA KIRKUS' SERVICE

[In **Evening Star,** sixteen-year-old] Nancy, a native of an island just off the state of Washington, lives a split existence. Sometimes she is merely Nancy, the pretty daughter of a hotel owner. At other times she is Evening Star, the descendant of an American Indian. Ashamed of her heritage at one moment, proud the next, Nancy fears that she will not find social acceptance. A summer guest and a tentative romance teach Nancy that it is her exotic background which gives her an added dimension of charm and distinction. A romantic story which handles its theme with discretion and sympathy.

A review of "Evening Star," in Virginia Kirkus' Service, *Vol. XXVII, No. 23, December 1, 1959, p. 881.*

RUTH HILL VIGUERS

There is a freshness about [**Evening Star**] which may be due in part to its setting among the San Juan Islands of Puget Sound, pictured in all their evergreen beauty. The characters are drawn with both warmth and a light touch and are such good company it is a pleasure to know them.

Ruth Hill Viguers, in a review of "Evening Star," in The Horn Book Magazine, *Vol. XXXVI, No. 2, April, 1960, p. 137.*

GRACE M. ZAHN

Following her sister's wedding, 16-year-old Elizabeth [protagonist of **River at Her Feet**] expected a dramatic change in her own life. When a 23-year-old celebrity visited a neighbor, Elizabeth interpreted his casual friendship as love. The familiar plot, contrived setting, and breezy style make Elizabeth's ensuing anguish unconvincing. (pp. 83-4)

Grace M. Zahn, in a review of "River at Her Feet," in School Library Journal, *an appendix to* Library Journal, *Vol. 11, No. 8, April, 1965, pp. 83-4.*

CHRISTINE MYERS

Simple, yet meaningful and real, [**River at Her Feet**] treats the growing pains of sixteen-year-old Elizabeth. . . . [One] summer brings some self-knowledge, partial independence, romance, and adventure. With sensitivity and liveliness, Zoa Sherburne catches the anxieties, thoughts, and actions of her attractive heroine.

Christine Myers, in a review of "River at Her Feet," in English Journal, *Vol. 54, No. 5, May, 1965, p. 461.*

DEIRDRE WULF

Girl in the Mirror is the account of how awkward, overweight Ruth Ann copes with the remarriage of her widowed father. It goes almost without saying that the new stepmother, Tracy, is tall, slim, elegant, gracious, as well as a very paragon of patience in her handling of the nasty child. When Ruth Ann's father is killed in a car crash, the two women are thrown together to make a new life for themselves. The events, however, unfold in a vacuum, for we are given no feeling of who these people are, where and how they live. The setting is suburban, colorless, hermetic, as stifling perhaps as the life of an unhappy young girl obsessed with her own physical ugliness. The details of dieting and of meals, their anticipation, preparation, and consumption are insistent and tedious, though appropriately so in this context, but the dullness of the book is due more to a lack-lustre quality in its characters than to any deficiency in plot or development.

> Deirdre Wulf, "Young Ladies in Distress," in Book Week—World Journal Tribune, October 23, 1966, p. 12.*

JOAN LEAR SHER

Ruth Ann's father has always been "the only important person in her world." [In **"Girl in the Mirror"**], for the first time since her mother died, her closeness to him is strained. Her father's interest in a slim, graceful young nurse drives Ruth Ann into fits of depression—and fits of eating. . . . Eventually, her father's remarriage and the tragic events that follow force Ruth to take an active interest in life, and to realize that her future is in her own hands. Zoa Sherburne's poignant picture of a girl who has retreated from reality is well drawn, although Ruth Ann sometimes tends to be a parlor analyst, and at other times is incredibly naive.

> Joan Lear Sher, in a review of "Girl in the Mirror," in The New York Times Book Review, November 6, 1966, p. 20.

NANCY E. PAIGE

[*Too Bad About the Haines Girl*], about a popular, intelligent, "nice" high school girl who becomes pregnant, is well written, peopled by believable, appropriate characters, but it goes no farther than to tell us that an unmarried, pregnant high school girl is a miserable person whose future is in very serious jeopardy. . . . Whether [Melinda] and her boyfriend will forsake their educational plans to marry and raise an unwanted child, or whether Melinda will, instead, bear the illegitimate child and give it up for adoption, and how both young people will deal with the social, emotional, and other pressures attendant on either decision are matters beyond the scope of the book. . . . In short, though a competent writer, Miss Sherburne side-steps all the difficult and significant issues inherent in the problem she presumes to deal with. The result is an unimportant book.

> Nancy E. Paige, in a review of "Too Bad about the Haines Girl," in School Library Journal, an appendix to Library Journal, Vol. 13, No. 8, April, 1967, p. 91.

PHYLLIS COHEN

Mrs. Sherburne's junior romances have often dealt with complex problems—alcoholism in the family, mental illness, a death in the family, etc. [In *Too Bad about the Haines Girl*] she tackles the increasingly common problem of the teen-age unwed mother, and it is by far her best book. There have been so many teen-age stories on this theme lately, that it's almost become a cliche rather than the daring subject it was only fifteen years ago. Of all that I've read, though, *Too Bad about the Haines Girl* comes closest to an honest discussion of the whole problem . . . .

The whole book treats of Lindy's growing panic, acceptance of the situation, and her inability to tell her parents. The story ends with her parents learning about it. But nothing is solved, nothing is settled. There are too many factors involved for a simple solution. Although Jeff and Lindy have planned marriage, marriage now would be terrible for both. . . . And giving the baby up for adoption is just too final and terrible to think about. . . . No doubt the problem will be solved, but the story is a sad one. Saddest of all is Lindy's loss of her youth. She is pretty, talented, and has just been chosen the school Valentine Queen. None of the dances, parties, contests, fun of the last year of high school is for her, and all the plans she made for college are finished. The last paragraph of the book shows what a long way Lindy has come. "It was the familiar tune that she and Jeff had dubbed their song—the same recording that they had danced to so many times last year, when they were young."

This book is not a sermon. The author does not discuss the moral aspects at all. She has presented a common situation and one normal, healthy girl's reactions. . . . The author is not trying to teach anything. Lindy and Jeff are two good kids who messed up their lives, but they are not horrid examples. Their story will not prevent a single girl from messing up her life, but it will give her some hours of reading entertainment and an understanding of how this happens to the nicest, happiest kids.

> Phyllis Cohen, in a review of "Too Bad about the Haines Girl," in Young Readers Review, Vol. III, No. 9, May, 1967, p. 14.

THE BOOKLIST

After her father's voluntary disappearance when she is nine years old Angie Scofield uses her ability to see into the future and read the past to support the family, and exploited by both her mother and her manager she forfeits a natural life to make television and personal appearances. . . . Although the treatment of extrasensory perception is somewhat simplistic, [*The Girl Who Knew Tomorrow*] is an appealing story with well-done characterizations. . . .

> A review of "The Girl Who Knew Tomorrow," in The Booklist, Vol. 66, No. 20, June 15, 1970, p. 1274.

MARIANNE HOUGH

This modern-day girls' story [*The Girl Who Knew Tomorrow*] achieves nothing and goes nowhere. . . . Angie's father deserts his wife and two daughters, leaving conflict between Mother and Grandmother (the one who most selflessly cares for sensitive, bewildered Angie). When the girl's special gift becomes known, her lonely mother is influenced by the attentions of a man who persuades the family to exploit her. . . . Finally, her beloved Grandmother dies, but not before Angie has been transferred mentally for a deathbed conversation in the old woman's room thousands of miles away. The final message to Angie is, of course, to give it all up until her gift can be used only for helping others. If readers could, first of all, accept the easily-come-by use of second sight, they would still find the predictable ending a letdown. Touching on much, exploring little in depth, this novel is scarcely above women's pulp-magazine level.

> *Marianne Hough, in a review of "The Girl Who Knew Tomorrow," in* School Library Journal, *an appendix to* Library Journal, *Vol. 17, No. 4, December, 1970, p. 66.*

KIRKUS REVIEWS

[Zoa Sherburne, with her novel **Leslie**,] turns to the problem of drugs and the result is a real pot boiler. Leslie's very first joint involves her as an accessory to a fatal hit-and-run accident and eventually lands her in the hospital when the car's driver Chip . . . slips LSD in her coffee to keep her from going to the police. Though Leslie's mom is a cardboard model of the well-meaning, ineffectual parent, the grownups' superior wisdom is never in doubt—Tom, mother's new boyfriend, arrives on the scene just in time to provide the guidance of a benevolent father and the kindly juvenile court judge lets Leslie off with a warning—after all, she's basically a good girl. Worse than the heavy dose of moralizing warnings (including a verbatim account of a policeman's speech to a school assembly) is the total lack of feeling for youthful lifestyles. . . . Sherburne fails to demonstrate even minimal empathy with the age group she is writing about, and as a result, Leslie's decision to come clean has less impact than a Sunday school sermon.

> *A review of "Leslie," in* Kirkus Reviews, *Vol. XL, No. 19, October 1, 1972, p. 1154.*

JOHN W. CONNER

Adolescent novels about the drug culture are very popular at the moment. I predict that when the drug culture stimulus loses momentum, **Leslie** will continue to be read. Here, at last, is a novel about the drug scene which embraces the average adolescent with an average adolescent's concerns for family and friends and fair play and virtue. . . .

Leslie is a so-so looking young lady who is pleasantly surprised by the attentions of Chip Carter, a handsome young man who has never noticed Leslie before. Chip's attention does not sweep Leslie off her feet, because his real nature comes to the surface on their first date. Chip sideswipes a pedestrian on their way home and runs from the scene of the accident. When she discovers the pedestrian has died, Leslie is beside herself. Then her friends tell her that Chip is the biggest supplier of drugs for other students in school. Confronted with the facts Leslie is frantic, not knowing what to do. . . .

Zoa Sherburne develops this conflict with a masterful sense of timing. . . . With her usual good dramatic sense for character the author develops Leslie's mother from a carping, emotionally-soured divorcee to a warm, concerned mother for Leslie. Zoa Sherburne's sensible grasp of mother-daughter relationships makes **Leslie** a very believable tale, terrifying in that the dangers of involvement in the drug culture are so imminent.

> *John W. Conner, in a review of "Leslie," in* English Journal, *Vol. 62, No. 3, March, 1973, p. 480.*

THE BOOKLIST

[**Why Have the Birds Stopped Singing?** is an] entertaining time-travel adventure with its share of suspense and romance. Sixteen-year-old Katie, on a tour with schoolmates, unknowingly stops at the Washington State birthplace of her great-great-great grandmother. Katie is epileptic, and when she forgets her medicine and falls, she wakes in her look-alike namesake ancestor's shoes. Although we are told that epilepsy is not inherited, Katie's mid-nineteenth-century double has it; and this unfortunate link, however weak, keeps the plot going through modern Katie's attempts to be understood by ancestor Kathryn's uncle, who keeps her locked up. . . . [Readers] may sense nagging structural gaps in the tale. However, the well-drawn historical setting and an unbroken line of tension will hold readers.

> *A review of "Why Have the Birds Stopped Singing?" in* The Booklist, *Vol. 70, No. 21, July 1, 1974, p. 1202.*

BARBARA H. BASKIN AND KAREN H. HARRIS

The news that her mother is coming home after years in a psychiatric hospital is upsetting to Kathleen Frazier [in **Stranger in the House**]. She, her younger brother Wimpy, her father, and their housekeeper have developed a comfortable living pattern that has excluded Mrs. Frazier. The housekeeper promises to stay if she is needed, but Kathleen remains uneasy, remembering the trauma of her mother's previous visits. Hoping to keep her free from stress, all but Wimpy treat her as an invalid. By excluding the mother from involvement in daily problems, they inadvertently but effectively exclude her from family membership. . . . [One day an] incident vividly dramatizes to the family that overprotection is basically a rejecting behavior and manifestly deleterious to growth. Kathleen realizes that she had been selfish and punitive in the deliberate exclusion of her mother from participation in or knowledge of her school and social life. Kathleen begins to share confidences with her mother, who reciprocates. The improved relationship augurs well for Mrs. Frazier's ultimate adjustment.

The hurtful aspect of local gossip is well presented, and difficulties attendant upon return to normal living after extended institutionalization are simply but effectively portrayed. Although both problems and solutions are unbelievably uncomplicated, the story is effective in introducing some ramifications of such situations and developing empathy for them. (p. 294)

[**Why Have the Birds Stopped Singing?**] presents an accurate if incomplete picture of the symptoms, ramifications, and means of control of epilepsy. The acceptance and accommodations made to the disorder by [Katie's] contemporary family and friends provide a commendable model. The author's denial that the condition is inheritable while using it as a device to link different generations of family members is self-contradictory. Pacing is good, and the setting and characterizations are standard for this genre. (p. 295)

> *Barbara H. Baskin and Karen H. Harris, "An Annotated Guide to Juvenile Fiction Portraying the Handicapped, 1940-1975: 'Stranger in the House' and 'Why Have the Birds Stopped Singing?'," in their* Notes from a Different Drummer: A Guide to Juvenile Fiction Portraying the Handicapped, *R. R. Bowker Company, 1977, pp. 294-95.*

Nevil Shute (Norway)

1899-1960

English novelist.

Shute was a popular novelist of the 1940s and 1950s who is best known for his futuristic novel *On the Beach* (1957). An aeronautical engineer and aviator, Shute served in both world wars, and the majority of his novels are based on his experiences and reflect his lifelong passion for aviation. Many are set in Australia, where Shute eventually settled. Primarily a storyteller, Shute peopled his works with ordinary characters, but related extraordinary circumstances. Several of his novels—*On the Beach, No Highway, Pied Piper,* and *A Town Like Alice*—were made into films.

One of the most interesting aspects of Shute's career was his penchant for predicting the future. In *What Happened to the Corbetts* (1939), he related the story of an English family terrorized by the bombing of their town. Shortly thereafter, the English faced a similar situation. *No Highway* (1948) depicts the crash of a jet due to metal fatigue; within a few years a similar crash occurred. Shute was fascinated with predicting such events. In his postscript to *In the Wet* (1953), he wrote: "No man can see into the future, but unless somebody makes a guess from time to time and publishes it to stimulate discussion it seems to me that we are drifting in the dark, not knowing where we want to go or how to get there."

On the Beach is one of the first novels to probe the possibility of nuclear annihilation. It tells the story of the last survivors of a nuclear war, who await death by radiation. Although some critics contended that the novel lacked drama because Shute avoided the depiction of suffering, others praised its terrifying sense of despair. *On the Beach* has gained relevance in view of current concern about nuclear warfare.

Several of Shute's other works also treat subjects of interest to young adults. In *An Old Captivity* (1940) and *Vinland the Good* (1946), Shute recounts Viking adventures and explorations. In *Pied Piper* (1942), an elderly gentleman escorts a group of children through German-occupied France. In *A Town Like Alice* (1950), the Japanese force a group of women and children to wander from town to town and survive by their own means. In his works, Shute favors strong-willed, able young people who face adversity with the strength of moral conviction.

(See also *Contemporary Authors*, Vol. 102.)

THE TIMES LITERARY SUPPLEMENT

What happened to the Corbetts? Well, one evening, like everybody else in Southampton and in all the important cities of England, they were subjected to intense aerial bombardment. War had started before anybody was prepared. . . . Corbett was fortunate enough to own a yacht out at Hamble, whither he took his wife and three small children. That is the first half and by far the most original part of [*What Happened to the Corbetts* (published in the United States as *Ordeal*)]. The second half of the book tells how the Corbetts managed to sail their boat to France, where Joan Corbett and the little children are packed off to Canada, while Peter returns to join the Navy.

Courtesy of William Heinemann Ltd.

The first half of the book is the more interesting. Mr. Shute not only possesses a very clear idea of what may be the things to come, but a style of first-class competence to convey his ideas to us. He writes quite objectively about the occurrences and the behaviour of his characters, and there is throughout a resemblance to Mr. [H. G.] Wells's earlier scientific novels. Mr. Shute, moreover, has interesting theories about the technique of aerial bombardment and the possibilities of defence. The account of the sailing of a small yacht across the channel, the crew consisting of Mr. and Mrs. Corbett, is well told. This novel is both exciting and provocative.

A review of "What Happened to the Corbetts," in The Times Literary Supplement, *No. 1993, February 18, 1939, p. 103.*

BEN RAY REDMAN

"Ordeal" is the story of the Corbett family during the first weeks of a war that was the more terrible for being so mysterious. Peter and those like him had no idea of what was really happening or going to happen. Official information was disturbingly meager. No army movements were reported and nothing was heard of the Fleet. All that the man in the street knew was that he and his were being mercilessly bombed on every cloudy night, and that the Air Force was supposedly carrying out satisfactory "reprisals." . . .

Mr. Shute traces the hesitant and baffled steps towards safety in a matter-of-fact, entirely convincing style that stems from the school of Defoe. . . .

Granted his subject, it would have been easy for Mr. Shute to write a highly exciting and affecting story. He has chosen instead to write one that is simply credible and absorbing. He has held his imagination on a short rein and eschewed dramatic effects no less than horror. While avoiding sensationalism, he has also avoided many sensations that would seem proper to his narrative. He has never raised his voice above the level of the calm, factual reporter (the outbreak of cholera is announced in a tone that would serve to inform us of a case of mumps next door) and he has felt no need of "developing" his characters. Dr. Gordon's death moves us no more than would the sight of an unknown name in an obituary column, and Collins's crash has no personal meaning for us. We hear the bombs but are not terrified. . . .

In view of all this, it would be easy to conclude that Mr. Shute's determined "under-writing" had kept him from realizing the potentialities of his theme. But this would be to condemn him for not doing something that he has not attempted. He has chosen to make us think rather than feel, and to that end he has written his story as economically as possible, in the commonest terms that would serve his purpose. It is because Peter and Joan are no more than a nice young couple that they can stand for all nice young couples similarly fated. They are significant not as individuals, not as a novelist's contrived characters, but as symbols. In **"Ordeal,"** Mr. Shute has written the story of all Joans and Peters; written it with complete success, according to the pattern of his intention. Readers who ask for more power and more passion, for the shrill scream of horror and the ache of tragedy, will be asking for something he did not mean to give.

> Ben Ray Redman, "War and the Average Man," in The Saturday Review of Literature, *Vol. XIX, No. 22, March 25, 1939, p. 5.*

HASSOLDT DAVIS

["**Ordeal**"] is an astonishing performance for the author of last year's best-seller, **"Kindling."** If that random tale was escape from reality, this is an incursion upon it, the grim reality of the possible war in England which has concerned us for a considerable time. It is not alarmist; it is sane fiction laconically suggesting the dilemma of the average man in the event of England being attacked from the air. Mr. Shute states at the end of his book, "If a writer has any quality of value to the community it is that of using his imagination to foresee what lies ahead of us," and though that assertion may not be universally applicable it is peculiarly so in his own case, for not only has he the novelist's skill to present his forecast dramatically, but his long experience as an aeronautical engineer lends authority to the book. . . .

["**Ordeal**"] is a grisly record by implication, for there are few visible horrors in it. The reader is made poignantly aware of the monstrous suffering entailed by the war, but no corpses are flung into his lap. There is one casualty per bomb, one death per three—the usual average—but in this view of mass destruction the perspective is such that the gory details are not apparent. The death of old Mrs. Littlejohn by a flying shaft of glass is sufficient to indicate the total tragedy. There are no

hysterical histrionics anywhere in the writing of the novel, though Corbett's anguish to decide whether his duty is first to the family or to the State could be more dramatically shown, and the children, perhaps, could scream a little louder without spoiling Mr. Shute's fine detachment from the scene; his story is told, you would say, through clenched teeth to keep his emotions in.

> Hassoldt Davis, "If War Should Come to England," in The New York Times Book Review, *March 26, 1939, p. 4.*

FRED T. MARSH

["**An Old Captivity**"] is a strangely ordered tale. For the most part it holds the interest skillfully, keeps you pegging away page after page, unwilling to put the book down. Mr. Shute can spin a yarn in cracking good prose, and since through three-quarters of the novel he knows expertly what he's talking about . . . , you enjoy and feel confidence in the accumulation of data and details through which the story moves and has its being.

For this is a fictional record of an airplane flight from Scotland to Greenland, via Iceland, thence to Cape Cod, the Vineland of the Norse Vikings. . . .

Mr. Shute is a practical man about airplanes and pilots qua pilots. But there's a broad streak of romantic mysticism underneath, and this flowers forth in the last quarter of this novel in a way to put to shame even James Hilton in his "Lost Horizon" or [Rudyard] Kipling's "Brushwood Boy." But to this reader it came as a shock and disappointment. It did not seem to him apt or well done, even of its kind, with its Eskimo curse and its transmigration hocus-pocus and its mystic conundrumry—was it a vision or a waking dream? And that brings us back to the opening pages in this oddly put together yarn.

For no apparent reason, so far as the story is concerned, a psychiatrist named Morgan and a Senior Master of Imperial Airways named Donald Ross meet on a train in France. The train is held up overnight and the two enter into conversation. "Do you do dreams and all that?" asks the airman. On being assured he does, the pilot mentions a strange, incomprehensible dream he had some five years ago: "You don't think I'd be likely to go crackers as I get older?" he asks. "I said gently, 'We've got a long evening before us. Would you like to tell me about it?'"

That's all. We never hear of the psychiatrist again, what he thinks of the tale, whether he ever gets to Italy. We hear nothing of the future of the airman either. The story of five years ago is not told in the first person or by the psychiatrist in the third person. It's a straightaway novel by the omnipotent novelist who has dangled a hanging introduction further to confuse us as we think over the tale after finishing it. It's a trick and a poor one.

But from page 9 to page 246 this is a first-rate and adult story of an imaginary expedition by plane to Greenland. Donald Ross had been a pilot on a Canadian airline for some years until the company he worked for folded up. Now he is back in England out of a job. A friend gives him a tip to the effect that a Professor Lockwood, an Oxford archaeologist, is planning an expedition to Greenland and is looking for an experienced pilot. Ross gets the job. The professor, with little realization of the danger, expense and time involved in such an undertaking, thinking only of his plans for proving to the world that Celts from Scotland or Ireland had preceded the Norse Vikings to

Greenland, places the whole burden of preparation on the aviator. His daughter, Alix, a dowdy bluestocking and a snob, opposes the expedition. But when she finds she can't prevent it, she determines to go along, too. Between her and young Ross there is cordial dislike at first sight. . . .

[The pilot] is a weary man when, after numerous adventures, they arrive on the Greenland plain where the real work is to begin. By the time that is finished he has cracked up and an overdose of the sleeping tablets, which had stopped working in small quantities, sends him off into a thirty-six-hour coma. During that time he has the dream of a thousand years ago when he was Haki and Alix was Hekja, Celts from the Scottish Highlands, boy and girl together scampering over the Greenland wastes until the Norsemen come under Leif Ericson and made the Scots their slaves. This dream is a North Country idyl of rather feeble proportions, or so it seems to me. But when the details of the dream are verified by later discoveries and strange markings set on stone, this reader lost all interest. There is no law forbidding the novelist to touch on ancient mysteries or deal with matters in heaven and earth of which our philosophy little dreams of. Explorers and adventure writers seem often to develop a mystical side. But Mr. Shute here lacks the touch.

Fred T. Marsh, "The Story of a Strange Flight," in The New York Times Book Review, February 25, 1940, p. 6.

THE CHRISTIAN SCIENCE MONITOR

[The] combination of straightforward adventure with the shadow of a dream is one which has often been tried in literature, with varying degrees of success. "Lost Horizon" is one of the most notable of the recent books of this type; **"An Old Captivity"** is less impressive, but is still an excellent example of what an imaginative author can do to satisfy some readers' predilection for swift-paced action, while he appeals at the same time to an audience fond of a more subtle and provocative narrative.

The one who likes adventure will perhaps be the better rewarded. Seldom has a story of an airplane flight been more vividly and expertly delineated. From the moment of the take-off from Southampton, the vicissitudes of the strangely assorted crew provide a narrative of increasing suspense. . . .

The coincident theme, dealing with the pilot's psychological adventure, so to speak, is a blend of fantasy, legend, and Celtic mysticism. It centers on a dream which Ross experiences shortly after their arrival at the site of Brattalid, where the survey is to take place. Apparently reluctant to follow such an obvious course as to let Ross's Celtic ancestry be the tacit cause of the dream, Mr. Shute brings in other items which might be supposed to have some contributing influence, such as the sense of fatigue which Ross allows to envelop him, and his unthinking use of some pernicious sleeping tablets, foisted upon him by a none-too-scrupulous chemist. Psychological analysis of Ross's "dream," plus a touch of Eskimo superstition, also enter the story at this point.

For some readers, fantasy thus transmuted by emphasis on explanation and on seeming casual influences loses much of its charm; but Mr. Shute endeavors to satisfy this audience by leaving inexplicable much of Ross's extraordinary excursion into a bygone century.

Nevertheless, although Mr. Shute's handling of fantasy and mystery may provide subject for argument, his gift for presenting graphic narration is unquestioned; especially so, when

he concerns himself with men who "take the wings of the morning and dwell in the uttermost parts of the sea."

M.W.S., "Adventure Combined with the Shadow of a Dream," in The Christian Science Monitor, May 4, 1940, p. 11.

KATHERINE WOODS

["Pied Piper"] is] a novel which piles up dramatic force with quiet realism, glows as quietly with valiant tenderness, and points a significant theme without over-emphasis. John Sidney Howard did not know what was happening to France when he consented to take Ronnie and Sheila back to England, after the invasion of the Low Countries; and when he learned that no more express trains were running, that was not worth worrying about. But at Dijon, where 5-year-old Sheila was ill, ominous tidings came on the heels of equally ominous confusion. By the time he left that once delightful town a little French girl— aged 8, like Ronnie—had been added to their company; and the dreadful German drive was no secret any more. The invaders' concentration camp would mean death for an old man with a weak heart, but it was not himself Howard was thinking of as he looked about and tried to look ahead; "Children in France, if she were beaten down, would have a terrible time." He must get these children out, quick. . . .

That **"Pied Piper"** is the work of a master story-teller need scarcely be pointed out; and not many readers will seriously object that the last link in the chain of events is forged almost too deftly, or that one or two of the characters may occasionally speak from the author's mind rather than their own. The 70-year-old hero is wholly lovable.

In its deft simplicity of realism **"Pied Piper"** becomes a novel for more than one reading, as scenes, characters, incidents, encounters take their place in a crescendo progress, and vignettes are sharp against the fog of historic tragedy.

Katherine Woods, "Journey in France," in The New York Times Book Review, January 4, 1942, p. 7.

CLIFTON FADIMAN

["Pied Piper"] is] shrewdly contrived and, I suppose, sort of sentimental, but a great many sentimental things happen in a war and somehow Mr. Shute gives not the slightest impression of forcing the pathetic note.

The narrative has to do with John Howard, a seventy-year-old Englishman who is peacefully fishing in a Jura mountain village as France begins to fall. On his homeward journey, through a series of circumstances too complicated to detail, he is compelled to attach to him six children of various nationalities and backgrounds, all of whom he must bring safely to England. The adventures on the way, horrible, whimsical, and touching, make a first-rate yarn. The children themselves are not too real . . . but the quietly heroic old Howard comes out quite in the round, and the subordinate figures, especially a French girl who had been the mistress of Howard's dead son, are clearly sketched.

The total effect of the book, despite its grim background, is one of entertainment. (p. 58)

Clifton Fadiman, "The Thirties," in The New Yorker, Vol. XVII, No. 48, January 10, 1942, pp. 57-8.*

GEORGE DANGERFIELD

If you have an adventure story to tell, you must never let your scenery get out of hand. The more unusual your characters and their doings, the more recognizable must be the world through which they move. The soul may be strange, the motives unlikely, but the clothes and the furniture must conform to daily living. . . . [Robert Louis] Stevenson, John Buchan, Francis Iles—in short, writers of great or good adventure or detective fiction—have in almost all their books obeyed [this rule]. Let it be said for Mr. Shute that he obeys it too.

"Pied Piper" is a most improbable tale, in a quite probable setting. An old Englishman, Mr. Howard, is trapped in France by the German invasion of 1940. He agrees to escort two little English children back to England, their parents having decided to stay in Geneva. . . .

It is an old and honorable tradition that, in stories dealing with fugitives, the fugitives should be captured at the last moment. Mr. Howard, in the hands of the Gestapo, is rescued by means which, while ingenious and unlikely as fact, are most agreeable as theory. The author finds a weak spot in Nazi barbarism; he exploits it for all he is worth; the reader is delighted.

When compared with other literature upon the collapse of France, **"Pied Piper"** is merely a tenuous idyll. It is not, however, attenuated. It never stagnates, it has plenty of suspense, it is not implausible. It is, to be sure, the sort of book which you can take or leave alone. But, if taken, it will certainly please.

> George Dangerfield, "Shute . . ." in The Saturday Review of Literature, *Vol. XXV, No. 2, January 10, 1942, p. 9.*

VIRGINIA KIRKUS' BOOKSHOP SERVICE

On Shute's name [*Vinland the Good*] will secure attention. But in substance, in manner, it will prove again how impossible it is to pigeonhole that writer. For the first time he has turned the clock back—but used an effectively modern medium for telling an ancient story. Here is the opening chapter of the drama of America's story—the story of Eric the Red and Leif the Lucky—real discoverers of America, but to most school children little known figures. . . . Shute has chosen a screen continuity technique—with dialogue and vignetted backgrounds as his medium, and done it effectively. . . . The story itself is a good one—as Eric gets in hot water first in Norway, then in Iceland, and finally goes to Greenland to start a new world. And then his son retraces his steps—and expands beyond his father's horizon to yet more new worlds. An interesting experiment, skillfully done.

> A review of "Vinland the Good," in Virginia Kirkus' Bookshop Service, *Vol. XIV, No. 15, August 1, 1946, p. 352.*

JOHN H. BERTHEL

[*Vinland the Good*] retells the story of Leif Ericson's discovery of North America. In its short compass and in film script style it gives full rein to Nevil Shute's gentle satire and his sense of timelessness. Leif and his friends are used to show that the seemingly unconscious striving of Everyman, and not the carefully laid plans of the great, make history. This charming work can stand as a tale of high adventure, but it carries also a quiet criticism of outmoded teaching practices in the field of history.

> John H. Berthel, in a review of "Vinland the Good," in Library Journal, *Vol. 71, No. 17, October 1, 1946, p. 1331.*

BOSLEY CROWTHER

With so many present-day authors cutting flirtatious eyes, not to mention the patterns of their stories, at the market of Hollywood, it might be discreetly suspected that Nevil Shute was shooting straight for that mart in retelling the saga of Leif Ericson in movie-scenario form. That, at least, could be one explanation for the structure of his **"Vinland the Good."** But, in due and considerate fairness, it must be presumed that Mr. Shute would have written his "script" with more regard for formula if he had been angling directly for a "buy." He would, for instance, have paid more attention to the aspects of boy-meets-girl; he would have tossed in a great deal more business of freebooting, feasting and fights. It stands pretty much to reason that the author chose the movie-script form because he felt that it was eminently appropriate for drawing popular interest to a bleak, obscure romance. . . .

His version of the old and flinty legend of Leif, the man of the North, who led an exploring expedition to these shores in 1003 and was, as a consequence of his visit, the true discoverer of the "new world," is not told in the stiff, tongue-twisting rhetoric of the Norse sagas from which it is taken, nor is it winded in such poetic stanzas as Mr. [Henry Wadsworth] Longfellow used to spin the tale. It is a straight camera-conscious visualization of a robust adventurer's career as it might be scanned by an English schoolmaster trying to hold a group of restless boys. . . .

Beneath and behind the sheer mechanics of the author's scenario there is rich and lusty vitality, color and imagery. Mr. Shute, a heroic romancer, has told the story of Leif in vivid style. And because his neo-ballad is in a mid-twentieth-century form, it should be understandable and stimulating to young, cinema-cultivated minds.

> Bosley Crowther, "Saga of Leif the Lucky," in The New York Times Book Review, *November 3, 1946, p. 22.*

JOHN WOODBURN

I had a feeling that Mr. Shute was at some disadvantage where I was concerned, inasmuch as I had learned from the jacket [of **"No Highway"**] that, beside being a successful author, he was also an aeronautical engineer, a subject of which I am deeply ignorant and hence, perhaps, defensively critical. I quickly discovered that Nevil Shute can write lucidly and dramatically about the study of aeronautics. Indeed, for me this material turned out to be the most pleasurable part of the book.

"No Highway" has as its part-time narrator a likable young Englishman named Scott, who is in charge of the Structural Department of the Royal Aircraft Establishment at Farnborough, where highly-trained, assorted physicists, some of them nuclear, are engaged in subjecting aircraft to all imaginable stresses and strains. Among his staff was Theodore Honey, a shabby, unworldly, absent-minded, meek, stubborn prototype of all the bemused professors of page, stage, or silver screen. Mr. Honey had set up the tailplane of a B.O.A.C. Reindeer and was simulating difficult flying stresses to see how much it would take. His calculations led him to believe that 1,440 hours of such flying conditions would cause that and similar Reindeer tailplanes to disintegrate.

Most of his colleagues had respect for Mr. Honey, but his side interests in pyramidology, automatic writing, and ouija boards made them uneasy and embarrassed. When a Reindeer crashed inexplicably in Canada with a total mortality of personnel, including a Russian diplomat, Scott decided to send Mr. Honey to inspect the wreckage. Enroute to the landing field at Gander Mr. Honey made the disquieting discovery that the Reindeer in which he was flying would pass the danger point of 1,440 hours before they got to Gander. . . .

["No Highway"] has a kind of suave tailoring which I suppose accounts for the popularity of [Mr. Shute's] other novels, and which inevitably extends to the characters. They seemed to me to have their faces cut out, to leave spaces for Hollywood to fill in. . . . As entertainment goes, and it certainly does, **"No Highway"** is a well-cooked, deftly-served blue-plate special, and a lot of people are going to be faithful to it, after their fashion, while I cry for madder music and stronger wine.

> *John Woodburn, "Ouija Saves the Day," in* The Saturday Review of Literature, *Vol. XXXI, No. 36, September 4, 1948, p. 10.*

JAMES HILTON

One of Max Beerbohm's short stories deals with the predicament of a man who, by means of palmistry, suddenly becomes aware of imminent disaster threatening the public conveyance in which he is traveling—in his case a train. Mr. Nevil Shute, in his new novel, **"No Highway,"** makes it a trans-Atlantic air liner, while his machinery of doom involves such scientific stuff as the fatigue point of metals after calculated stresses. The result is just as exciting and rather more plausible. . . .

One thing more certain than fatigue in metals is the absence of fatigue in reading Mr. Shute's novels. He has the knack of leading the reader quietly yet breathlessly from one suspense to another. The plot of **"No Highway"** is ingenious, even for its author, who has invented many such in his time; it builds absorbing as well as literate entertainment, and probably no author now writing can make better fictional use of scientific technology. To which is added a somewhat synthetic love story which no one need believe in who doesn't want to, and an American female movie star whom no one should believe in at all. She illustrates Mr. Shute's strength by exploring his weakness—that combined with a superb gift of narrative he has an imagination that probes situations more easily than emotions. For this reason he portrays with effortless verisimilitude the surface-values of English character—notably that gift of understatement which is no mere verbal trick, but a code of manners for the mind, imposing its own pattern of predictable behavior on some millions of Englishmen. That a people so blessed (or afflicted) should breed lovable eccentrics like Mr. Honey is no more remarkable than that, at a time of crisis, they should find voice in a Winston Churchill.

"No Highway" is first rate yarning, and Mr. Honey is Mr. Shute's most endearing character to date. Although in his extracurricular activities he is sentimentalized, as a scientist he keeps his integrity, and his involvement in practical matters affecting life, death and national policy generates a play of whimsy around the central drama.

> *James Hilton, "Taking Hold of the Wings of Morning," in* New York Herald Tribune Weekly Book Review, *September 5, 1948, p. 3.*

R. D. CHARQUES

[I read **A Town Like Alice** (published in the United States as **The Legacy**)] with simple, doubtless too simple, pleasure. It is the quintessence, or very nearly, of readableness. Lively, fluent, inventive, spirited, a story-teller with a swift and sympathetic eye for character and the surest instinct for avoiding the heights and depths of story-telling, Mr. Shute deserves, I think, every bit of the popularity which *A Town Like Alice* will earn. It is the story of a young woman who took charge of a British party of captive women and children in Malaya and then went to look for an Australian sergeant, a "ringer," in the Queensland "outback." The Malayan scenes are wonderfully good in their acutely simple way; the Australian scenes carry just a hint of too idyllic sentiment. But it is all very, very readable. Is it "literature"? Why ever not?

> *R. D. Charques, in a review of "A Town Like Alice," in* The Spectator, *Vol. 184, No. 6364, June 16, 1950, p. 836.*

THE TIMES LITERARY SUPPLEMENT

The heroine of [*A Town Like Alice*] is Jean Paget, an English typist who is captured, together with some 40 other women and children, by the Japanese in Malaya. They are forced to march aimlessly, month after month, from one place to another. Many of them die. At last, under Jean's leadership, they settle at a Malay village and work in the ricefields. . . . The second half of the book is about Jean's experiences in Australia, where she goes in search of Joe Harmon, the lorry-driver who helped her and the women on the march and was—literally—crucified by the Japanese for doing so. She finds that Joe has gone to England in search of her; while waiting for him to return, she plans various schemes for improving the amenities of the dreary Queensland back-blocks township, all of which, by means of a legacy, she is able to put triumphantly into practice.

Mr. Shute, with his high moral purpose and happy ending, is perhaps reminiscent of the nineteenth-century didactic novelist, or the contemporary Soviet Russian writer whose aim is to "improve" reality rather than merely to reflect it. The simple, robust, expanding Australian scene is particularly suitable to such treatment. His method, however, is that of a highly skilled entertainer. He tells his story in a smooth, straightforward colloquial style, using a favourite device of Mr. Somerset Maugham's: an impersonal, detached narrator who is Jean's London solicitor.

> *"Danger Abroad," in* The Times Literary Supplement, *No. 2524, June 16, 1950, p. 369.**

KATHLEEN SPROUL

The most thrilling stories of human magnificence are often those enforced on quiet protagonists who never intended to be heroes. That Nevil Shute should encounter such a tale in Sumatra promised well. His former books have marked him a direct-line descendant from those elite among the ancient wandering minstrels who could, from a first quiet sentence, implant irresistible urge to hear a tale.

In its beginning **"The Legacy"** carries this authority; unfortunately, before the end tale-spinning magic is not enough. For here has been attempted a hybrid creation and the two elements fall apart from an unseemly mid-point divide. The inspiring episode, transplanted from Sumatra to Malaya, is a truly great story, to which by slow, unaccented documentation, Mr. Shute has contributed almost unbearable poignancy and tension. But his own undiluted invention taking over later seems in contrast painfully contrived. . . .

The story is told by the elderly solicitor who handles the legacy Jean receives after her return to England. Even with that point-of-view device stretched far too thin, the merciless odyssey is gripping. But Jean herself moves only within the terrible urgency of the tale. She is never really alive on her own because we gain only an unrevealing minimum of her thinking and feeling. (p. 21)

[In the second half of **"The Legacy"**] the step-by-step detailing of her determined sentimental journey, including ice-cream sodas, loses all resemblance to the other breathless trek and becomes tedious travelogue. According to the jacket blurb, here is "the stirring appeal of men and women who dare to build while others are accepting defeat." But, sadly, Mr. Shute's own appeal seems quite unstirringly fabricated. With Jean's lack of dimension increasingly apparent, and an alarming coyness added, her easy achievements are merely items ticked off to delay the curtain a conventional interval.

It is hard to understand why Mr. Shute threw away, in favor of contrived romance, his chance to expand into further magnificence that epic march of the women and children. Possibly here is a clue to what separates the storyteller, no matter how skilled, from the novelist. There were two kinds of minstrels: Mr. Shute's ancestors may have been the ballad-singers, who could, it is true, hold their audiences spellbound for a time. But the spell of the epic-singers has lasted much longer, because they had a further skill: they left us to resolve for ourselves some of the puzzles they proposed concerning the relationship of gods and heroes to men. (p. 26)

> Kathleen Sproul, "Malayan Death March," in The Saturday Review of Literature, Vol. XXXIII, No. 24, June 17, 1950, pp. 21, 26.

VIRGINIA KIRKUS' SERVICE

In 1939 Nevil Shute wrote a horrifyingly prophetic book, **Ordeal**, which made the life of the average citizen under bombardment only too real, as time proved. . . . And now comes Shute again [in **On the Beach**] with a portrait of the last stand of mankind against an enemy over which there was no control—radiation, gradually encompassing and destroying the world. There has been a brief atomic war, launched by two nations and resulting in mutual destruction within a brief month. But then the real catastrophe comes, as the death dealing effects encompass the living world. In Australia, where only the upper fringes so far lie within the circle, the people of the community of which he writes have exact scientific knowledge of when their doom will descend. To some it brings cessation from all activities; to others, indulgence in excesses of one kind or another; to still others, refusal to face the inevitability of the end, and a grim determination to go on as if next Spring would find the blooming of bulbs planted in the Fall—and they there to see it. . . . The people of the story are very real; their tragic awareness becomes the possession of the reader. One hopes—to the end—for a miracle. But there is no miracle. It is an obsessive, nightmarish book, the more so because it is written on almost a deadpan level of narration, deliberately shorn of histrionics.

> A review of "On the Beach," in Virginia Kirkus' Service, Vol. XXV, No. 13, July 1, 1957, p. 449.

JOHN T. WINTERICH

[The main premise of **"On the Beach"**] was made to order for Nevil Shute, who never tells the same story twice and who tells any story surpassingly well. The Shute formula is simple: Given such and such circumstances, what would people beset by those circumstances be most likely to do? That should be every novelist's formula, but a less assured practitioner frequently bends it to suit his own convenience. Not Nevil Shute. He holds to his design all the way, with relentless logic and a glowing sense of story supported by a mass of convincing detail (gas pumps as hitching posts, for instance) that establishes superb verisimilitude.

This quality dominates **"On the Beach"** even more than is usual in a Nevil Shute novel. For this could be the blueprint for all of us. His handful of Australians plan for the future (next year's farm crop, even next year's flower garden) in the certainty that their planning, like themselves, must come to nothing. No man or woman anywhere in the world can read this book without asking: "If and when this happens to me, shall I do as well?" **"On the Beach"** is a terrible tract for the times, presented with vigor and conviction, and absorbingly readable.

> John T. Winterich, "Doomed People," in The Saturday Review, New York, Vol. XL, No. 30, July 27, 1957, p. 12.

GEORGE HARRISON

Though we are reading of the last days of humanity on an earth made uninhabitable by radioactivity, no one in [**"On the Beach"**] gets very excited about it. Mr. Shute quotes T. S. Eliot's dictum that the world will end not with a bang but a whimper, but the last people on earth do not even whimper as they await the approaching radioactive pall. Calmly, they face the inevitable, knowing with certainty that death is only three or six months away, yet planting daffodils to bloom next spring, and studying shorthand for possible future jobs. Even the young American submarine commander stays faithful to his wife at home, emotionally unable to admit his rational awareness that she and their children are dead.

I believe **"On the Beach"** should be read by every thinking person. Nevil Shute has done an unusually able and imaginative job in depicting how people might act if there were a radioactive holocaust such as he envisages. The story is so well told that it caught my interest from the start, and held my attention to the end. All sorts of treatments of this problem are possible and Mr. Shute has treated the one he selected with extreme skill both from the scientific and the literary point of view. But I do wish those Australians hadn't taken it all quite so calmly, for there were a good many things they could have done to give humanity another chance. (pp. 1, 9)

> George Harrison, "A Novelist's Warning to Man," in New York Herald Tribune Book Review, July 28, 1957, pp. 1, 9.

GERALD SYKES

If [**"On the Beach"**] . . . is ever televised, there may be a wilder stampede than Orson Welles wrought two decades ago with his Martians. The time is 1963, a final war has been fought, some 4,000 cobalt bombs have been dropped, and the end of humanity has come in all but the extremities of the

Southern Hemisphere. In Australia, the residents of Melbourne know that winds are inexorably bringing radiation sickness and death in a few months. At the last moment the Government will issue suicide pills.

Cars and planes lie about unused—no gasoline. An old man in his club drinks more port than before—too much of it. A young woman who once dreamed of seeing Paris and of having children now resigns herself to as many brandies as she can put away. (p. 4)

The humdrumness of the characters is no doubt intentional, since it makes their story more convincing. This is the orderly, unimaginative way most people would probably behave at the last trump. . . . [**"On the Beach"**], after all, is a disguised sermon, shrewdly designed to drive home what the aftermath of atomic war would mean and merits the widest possible reading.

Unlike his predecessors in the British novel of dismal prophecy (Aldous Huxley in "Brave New World" and George Orwell in "1984"), the more middlebrow Nevil Shute . . . makes no attempt to appeal to the moral imagination. Philosophic passion is inconceivable in this cast of drab conformists, who permit life to be taken away from them without any assertion of its meaning or dignity. . . .

If humanity ever does surrender as supinely as Mr. Shute's dramatis personae (I for one don't believe it could)—it will only deserve what it gets. (p. 14)

> *Gerald Sykes, "Supine Surrender," in* The New York Times Book Review, *July 28, 1957, pp. 4, 14.*

WILLIAM DUNLEA

Nevil Shute is a journeyman fabulist; fantasy simulating reality is his preserve. A more gifted writer wouldn't be so successful visualizing men and women of a residual humanity, with no future and nothing to think about it. [*On the Beach*] is not prophesy but fictional essayism; it is not eschatology, it is Univac. The prophet concerns himself with the future while it is still present; Mr. Shute hires fate as his co-author and has a wry old time knocking down his props. We are not harrowed that they become extinct, and it isn't even disturbing that the author alone has survived.

Mr. Shute is too seldom inclined to let the obvious or the twice-told alone. When the dialogue is not straight banality it makes too cheap sport of the habits of life that make life a habit. . . .

Suspense would seem as irrelevant as characterization; in the transmitter sequence it comes naturally; otherwise the chills are rather spineless. As respects dramatic possibilities, Mr. Shute rubbed off the wrong half of the globe first. Had the other been so full of phlegmatic sangfroid it could hardly have blown up. Or is this what may prove most lethal in the end?

> *William Dunlea, "Fable of the Terminal Year 1963,"* in Commonweal, *Vol. LXVI, No. 21, August 23, 1957, p. 524.*

EDITH FOWKE

The theme of Nevil Shute's [*On the Beach*] is dramatic and awe-inspiring: it is nothing less than the end of the world. Nor is his plot impossible, or even unlikely: the headlines of our daily papers proclaim it all too probable. . . .

Despite its powerful theme, Nevil Shute's book is a very bad novel. The people in it are dull and unimaginative, and the ending is anti-climactic rather than apocalyptic. In fact, his characters are so flat and unappealing that you may well feel their final death from the inevitable radioactive sickness is no great loss.

In his earlier novels Mr. Shute showed himself skilful in handling melodrama and suspense, but here his limitations are so obvious as to be painful. It may be said that the effect is partly deliberate, as indicated by his quoting Eliot's famous lines about the world ending not in a bang but in a whimper. But Eliot makes you feel the tragedy of such an ending, while Shute renders it merely distasteful.

He may be right in assuming that people under sentence of death would continue living much as they do now when the death sentence is a matter of years rather than months, but he completely fails to add the tragic perspective which could have made this life-as-usual significant and moving. In *Our Town* Thornton Wilder managed to convey the tragic overtones implicit in trivial incidents; in *On the Beach* the trivial incidents remain trivial.

> *Edith Fowke, in a review of "On the Beach," in* The Canadian Forum, *Vol. XXXVII, No. 441, October, 1957, p. 166.*

DAVID DEMPSEY

There is always a temptation when an author dies to pay him greater homage in retrospect than was ever given during his lifetime. It is both unnecessary and inappropriate in the case of Nevil Shute . . . to perform extensive ceremonial rites. A simple memorial service will do, and even this may be more than he would have wanted, or expected. . . . He was not an important writer, although in terms of influence he wrote, with **"On the Beach,"** at least one important book. You approached him, as The Times Literary Supplement once remarked, by simply posing the question: Is his new story as good as the last? With him, "story" was almost everything.

I was continually coming across his novels—there are twenty-one all told—in what might be called the likely places: out-of-the-way summer cottages, Adirondacks cabins and similar vacation spots where others had preceded me. To put it bluntly, his were books that, once finished, you left behind.

Yet he *was* read, which is more than can be said of some authors who are not left behind; and his popular success, considering much of what he wrote, was both baffling and reassuring. How could a man who approached his subjects with such decency succeed in a fiction market that is dominated today by the cynically realistic school of writing?

One answer is that he restores a sort of old-fashioned goodness to the world. There are almost no villains in Shute's novels, and although in the hands of a man of less conscience the results might have been treacle, in his they were merely pleasantly naïve. . . .

[There is an] afterglow of human warmth and kindness that has become the trade-mark of this author's career. In a world of evil, goodness endures. On this note, Mr. Shute, may we say farewell?

> *David Dempsey, "Amid Evil, Good Endures," in* The New York Times Book Review, *April 3, 1960, p. 4.*

DAVID MARTIN

On the Beach was the first book of Nevil Shute's I ever read and I confess that it influenced my outlook on the problem of nuclear war and human survival. Until then I secretly believed that such a world catastrophe could never happen. Mankind was too rational to destroy itself. Like many others, this did not prevent me from being active against war, but always with a certain emotional reservation, founded mainly on historical and political optimism. Nevil Shute's book, while not demolishing the optimism, qualified it greatly and made me begin to see that Bertrand Russell might be right and that the chances of human survival were not quite so good. Undoubtedly, *On the Beach* had a similar effect on other readers. It may have caused some to grow disheartened, but some would have drawn from it a new sense of urgency and of the terrible reality of the threat. (pp. 193-94)

On the Beach is one of the rare novels that are absolutely honest. It is not the book of a highly speculative man, and the reactions of the people in the story to their impending annihilation is curiously uncomplicated and uniform. An intellectual novelist, such as [Albert] Camus, would first of all have striven for sharper and finer differentiations; Commander Towers and Lieutenant-Commander Holmes would be anti-types. Some characters would rebel against their fate, some would face death with dignity and some without; some would welcome the last capsule as the consummation of their own death-wish; some would find God, some the Devil, and others themselves.

This would have produced a work more interesting than *On the Beach,* but probably much less effective with the great public; weaker as a social document and as propaganda, less memorable in the long run. A difficult question is raised. If it is axiomatic that first-class novels should place their protagonists before harrowing choices, how did Shute manage to eliminate conflicts to such a degree, to simplify them so much and yet to create the impression that the book is 'true' and that things could happen just in the way he describes?

I think the answer is that he has instinctively grasped the new element that confronts us all: the qualitative change in the situation, from which subtler but less courageous (or more desperate) minds run away. The death that awaits the people of *On the Beach,* the certainty of which robs the plot of tension, dwarfs personal dramas. It brings to the surface not individual complexities but the human archetype. And because Nevil Shute was a humane man—which all his books prove—and because he was fond of people, he succeeded in writing a pessimistic novel on a dreadful theme which affirms love and dignity. It is this which has made it so difficult (and in fact so pointless that few have seriously attempted it) to criticise him on the score that *On the Beach* inculcates defeatism. (p. 194)

Shute's style has some surprising oddities. His characterisation is always rather simple. Love is a comparatively uncomplicated business, with now and then the dropping of a chaste garment. But his characters are almost always 'real'. He may not have had a good ear for dialogue . . . , but he did know what makes people tick and he understood their hopes and feelings. . . . He must have known a great deal more about the inner life of ordinary people than many of his more critically appreciated fellow writers. It has been said of Vance Palmer that he was an old-fashioned novelist. Shute, the one-time engineer and designer of dirigibles, the one-eyed hater of civil servants, was even more old-fashioned. This did not stop him from writing the most effective story about the decisive problem of our time.

It actually helped him. It helped him because it made him accept the unchangeable—or in any case the unchanged—nature of the human animal without taking refuge in despair or false certainties. Millions of mid-twentieth century readers could recognize themselves more easily in the characters he created than in the characters of, say, [William] Faulkner or [Louis] Aragon. If we are serious about the typical, we must recognize that here we have it, however 'limited'.

It means that, as writers, we can learn much from Shute, whatever our views are. It may also mean that the mass of readers still respond more directly to the naturalistic approach, when it is a genuine product, than to any other. This is only a different way of saying that the truly popular writer is the one best equipped to tackle the great themes, because his readers can identify themselves in his work. When we do find such writers with enough conscience and skill to address themselves to the kind of problem tackled in *On the Beach,* we ought to be grateful. (p. 195)

To me, his women are more convincing than his men—especially in *On the Beach,* where the heart rather than the mind is brought into action. I find it a little strange that Towers, in charge of the last submarine, keeps up the spiritualised half-illusion that his family is somehow still waiting for him. But when gentle Mary Holmes reacts to her husband's suicide instruction with an hysterical and illogical outburst, I am moved by the paradoxical and eternal unreason of it all. She knows that they both must die in the same week, but there is a part of her that stubbornly clings to a conviction that it is impossible. Right to the very end, while consciously facing the inevitable, the people in *On the Beach* not only go on behaving as if they are *immortal* but somehow believing it! Surely it is this which gives the book its power and the author his stature? It is so easy to be high-flown, but I think we might say that *On the Beach* is a popular novel about immortality. The mind behind it is a religious mind but—and this would amuse Shute could he read it—less Christian than Buddhist. It accepts the causal law without fuss. Their common *karma* has caught up with the people of Melbourne, whose guilt is their nonresistance to power. (pp. 195-96)

Mary plants her garden, Peter brings home a garden seat on his last journey up the Frankston line, a young technician stakes all on a motor race, a girl in love goes trout fishing with the man whom convention and instinct still forbid her to seduce. They act as they always did.

They act too much as they always did, it's true. Nevil Shute, in his anxiety to remain unforced, leant over backward and produced a strained unforcedness. As in all his other books, his characters are too uniformly good. This is partly responsible for his popularity, because people are tired of introverting into psychopaths . . . not only tired but unable. He could not create refined shadings, and there are no villains. If he pits the personal good of individuals against an evil force it is a vague, impersonal evil; folly rather than evil. Collossal stupidity is the cause of his war, whose civilian victims perish with resignation. His approach to people often touches the naïve, but he gets away with it—first because he makes up for his relative poverty of motivation by concentrating boldly on the universal domestic motif; second by exploiting to the utmost his technical knowledge of ships, planes and racing cars to project a complexly realistic background for his uncomplicated psychology; and third by what can only be called sheer narrative grip. The last quality, these days, seems to become ever more exclusively the prerogative of the popular writer. But on top of this there is in Shute's novels a quality of seriousness. Graham Greene, who is incomparably more skilful and barely less popular, in novels like *The Quiet American* or *Our Man in Havana,* leaves one feeling that life is grim but that it doesn't matter. Shute, totally incapable of satire, makes one feel that life does matter.

If he will be remembered for any book it will be for *On the Beach,* with its Jules Verne-like prophetic detail. Most of his earlier work is good when it relies on documentation. . . . Through all his books (those I have read) runs the theme of organization: the organizing of enterprises and the coördinating of people. His experiences with the building and flying of the airships R.100 and R.101, discussed in [his autobiography] *Slide Rule,* seem to have been decisive for him in this, as in other, respects.

People love to read about the unfolding of a big undertaking, whether it has to do with the running of an R.A.F. aerodrome in wartime, the founding of a township in the Gulf country—never mind about the way the ringers are supposed to talk and sit—or the fitting out of a nuclear submarine for an exploration of America under the death cloud. And Nevil Shute, who enjoyed this sort of thing in real life, which was the modern part of the man, never put a foot wrong when writing about it. He needed a firm frame and knew how to use it. (pp. 195-96)

In many ways he must have been a man out of his time, and what is weak in his work could be explained by this; but also what is strong, in as much as millions of good people are out of their time since Munich and Hiroshima. He wrote for them, and perhaps he wrote too much for them. It is a tenable criticism; but it is quite as much a criticism of us who do not want 'to swallow the pill' and who do not believe that suicide must be the final answer to death. If we are better moderns and more soundly based optimists than Nevil Shute was, why have we failed to write novels on the dangers threatening human existence—novels that can speak to people as intimately as did *On the Beach*? There is an easy answer to the question, but the less easy one will be more useful. . . .

Success may have come to him because he did not take it too seriously; for many years fiction writing was merely his hobby and it remained something of a hobby, and never a passion, to the end of his life. His insight into individuals stayed always at the same level. What became more serious were his themes, and the turning point was the second World War. (p. 198)

In this, his most genuinely creative period, death was a frequent motif. One senses that it became the subconscious propellant of *On the Beach.* It is the culmination of the agnostic melancholy which underlies much of Shute's writing and which gives poignancy even to such a happy novel as *Pastoral.* Nowhere was Shute explicit about his own philosophy, but I see him as an unacknowledged disciple of Epicurus, who taught that death is not to be feared and that those who live well die well, with no question of any cosmic purpose arising. No heaven seems to await even the believers in *On the Beach,* notwithstanding that some of them perish in hopes of rejoining their loved ones. Peter and Mary Holmes and Commander Towers are churchgoers. But their goodness is independent of religion; they would be good in any case. The young scientist who wins the last Grand Prix motor race never goes near a church and is just as good and just as stoic. It would be wrong to equate Shute with those who hold that the world's end does not matter because it may be part of a divine, inscrutable purpose. In *On the Beach*

death has no purpose; it is merely a consequence. Unless, of course, the novel is mainly meant as a warning.

When all is said, good deeds draw their moral significance from the fact that they live after us to cause good—at least in the general opinion of ordinary people who are not theologians and to whom, Christian or not, this is the most and probably only valid eternity. But nothing, bad or good, lives after Commander Towers, that well-meaning descendent of Captain Nemo, has sunk his submarine in Bass Strait. There can hardly be heaven 'above' or hell 'below' if there is no world in the middle. . . . (p. 199)

In a very clever age, Shute appealed to competence rather than to cleverness, and he never accused scientists and technicians but the men who employed them. He wanted peace and disliked building war planes, but he was not wise enough to stop his machines being shipped to Franco's Spain. There were many things he did not know or understand. He did not analyze social problems, but he could see that something was wrong and warned against the results of certain actions: there's no point in blaming him for not being a social or political thinker and for not indicating a way out. His morality was sound, and so at bottom were his instincts. The people in *On the Beach* are not bewildered, simply because they—mankind—have left it too late. The popular novelist is concerned with averages. . . .

Behind that significant book lies an appalling thought, going beyond even its text—the thought that human endeavour *can* end, and that this would reduce to nothingness Shakespeare as well as Shute, depriving not only the present of a future but the past of meaning. 'For from this instant there's nothing serious in mortality'.

Nevil Shute Norway advises us to be sincere. Unhappily, he is not here to tell us how he wants us to understand *On the Beach*—as a judgment, a prophecy, or a challenge? Did he, who was no fool, and who knew his readers so well, believe the catastrophe would come to pass? Could the man of action see a meaning in this final, heroic and anti-heroic, resignation? His readers can see something, but it is elusive. Whatever it is, it reflects a truth greater writers have missed and which is in the souls of multitudes. For all that, it may have to be resisted. (p. 200)

> *David Martin, "The Mind That Conceived 'On the Beach'," in* Meanjin, *Vol. XIX, No. 2, June, 1960, pp. 193-200.*

CARLTON W. BERENDA

[In *On the Beach*] Shute portrays the end of all men upon earth. Not on a planetary or cosmic scale, but through the eyes and hearts of utterly convincing persons, Shute carries the reader to the radioactive death of man, after a third world war. The story and its motion picture are by now well known to many of us. And we have all shared in the pain-filled pages of the novel.

It is what lies beyond or beneath the obviously depressing portrayal that makes this work something more than a story well told. When men are driven to the very brink, when they are stripped of all hope of life continuing in this world, what will men do? And might we not learn something about the essential nature of man when he faces the final moment?

Shute, at first glance, seems to use the most trivial of compulsive behavior patterns to describe man under the ultimate duress. While waiting for the lethal cloud of radioactive dust to move down from the war-torn mortuary of the northern hemisphere, the people of Melbourne, Australia, simply go about their daily business. Knowing full well that within less than a year the deadly dust shall have reached them, these people continue to make their plans for years ahead—building their gardens, fixing fence posts, purchasing seed to be planted for another summer that they will never see.

The United States naval officer, Dwight Towers, who has placed his crew and atomic powered submarine under direction and control of the Australian navy, knows quite well that his wife and children in the United States are no longer among the living; but though he is obviously attracted to the Australian woman, Moira Davidson, he not only remains loyally in love with his wife—he also purchases some exquisite jewelry for her, for "when he returns." And even though there is no longer a U.S. government, he refuses to break U.S. naval regulations. . . . How trivially compulsive and self-deluding can men be? In the time when Commander Towers decides to take his submarine out beyond the territorial waters of Australia so that in his dying moments his boat can be patriotically sunk outside a foreign nation, he refuses to allow his Moira to come aboard to die with him: U.S. navy regulations forbid women aboard its sea-going ships!

There is here a tragicomic note that reverberates and penetrates into the depths of man—the "absurd" man of the late Albert Camus who found his tragic death eight days before Shute. From any cosmic point of view, man has always been absurd in his natural state—devoted to trivial activities as meaningless as the rolling of the stone of Sisyphus. And the triumph of man lies in his complete realization that whatever he does is ultimately without meaning and that he finds his real significance in his devotion to mythic symbols. He creatively gives meaning to his trivial world by his dedication to such symbols. How significant such symbols can be, Nevil Shute quietly reveals in the transformation of Moira from a near-alcoholic to a mature and balanced woman. In her growing love of Dwight, and under the vital symbol of his dedication to his own symbols, Moira finds her own meaning in life shortly before her own moment of death.

Whether we all die together "on the beach," or die separately one by one, whatever we do before that death remains trivial in itself—the absurd nonsense of symbols "full of sound and fury, signifying nothing" but their idiotic terminus in our deaths. And whatever meaning remains is given through the conscious and willful commitment of man to what is forever without meaning in itself. Man is the only creature who must live by myth and who, in full consciousness, must *know* this! In such knowing and in such living lie his courage and his triumph. (pp. 232-33)

Carlton W. Berenda, "The Meaning of Man in Nevil Shute's 'On the Beach'," in Books Abroad, *Vol. 34, No. 3, Summer, 1960, pp. 232-33.*

JULIAN SMITH

The basic idea for what would become **On the Beach** grew out of the wishful thinking then current in Australia: that radiation from a nuclear war in the northern hemisphere would be held above the equator by the trade winds. Shute's first intention seems to have been to write a kind of modern Swiss Family Robinson about the continuation of civilization in Australia. . . .

The idea for the book "started as a joke," Shute told a friend. "Now that I was living in Australia I kidded my friends in the northern hemisphere, telling them that if they weren't careful with atomic explosions they'd destroy themselves and we Australians would inherit the world." "The idea stayed in my mind in that form for about a year, in a slightly cynical and humorous form," he wrote an interviewer; but, when his research showed him that Australia would not escape nuclear doom, "it became an attractive speculation—what would ordinary people in my part of the world do with that year? . . ." (p. 124)

On the Beach envisions a world destroyed by gadgets, but this world still loves the gadgets which have destroyed and will outlast their makers. The best example is the cataclysmic auto race that comes late in the novel. . . . Round and round the track goes mankind, it is concerned only with proving that one machine is faster than another; therefore, it is concerned more with the efficiency of the machines than with the safety of the men who use them.

But Shute is not mocking man; he is only explaining how things are. In fact, he bought a brand new Jaguar XK 140 when he started writing **On the Beach** and raced it himself in order to write about racing in the novel—or that was his excuse. And the character with whom he most obviously identifies, his physicist-spokesman John Osborne, devotes his last weeks to winning the world racing championship; he then puts his Ferrari on blocks, carefully preparing it for eternal storage, before taking a suicide pill in the driver's seat. As radiation poisoning becomes general at the novel's end, an American submarine captain takes his submarine out to sea and sinks it, crew and all, in international waters rather than leave it behind unprotected. Meanwhile, back on the beach, a young woman watches the submarine until it is lost to sight; then, in the novel's last sentence, she "put the tablets in her mouth and swallowed them down with a mouthful of brandy, sitting behind the wheel of the big car." Drug, drink, car—these things are the best the world has to offer. Shute is not criticizing; he is only saying that man seems unable to reject the creations of his machine culture. (pp. 127-28)

In whittling the subject of the end of the human race down to size, Shute had decided to center his story on people who live in a small suburban sea-side town like his own. He started his novel, therefore, with the young family man Peter Holmes (an avatar of 1939's Peter Corbett) and found a way to have him discover a dying world. For that reason, the novel opens with a dramatization of the basic attitude of all the characters through Lieutenant Commander Holmes who awakens with a sense of happiness that puzzles him until he remembers this is the day he gets a new duty assignment. He has been "on the beach," and he wants to do nothing more than to work—like all the other characters, he plans to keep busy until the end.

Not until the third page do we even know that there has been a war, and even then not what kind or of what degree. Instead, we are simply told there had been a short war and that it had ended a year previously. As Peter Holmes gets dressed, we learn the war lasted for thirty-seven days in 1962 and that no history of the conflict and little record outside of seismographic readings exist. That there can be a war without a history, a war measured only on seismographs, is such a chilling understatement that no more information is needed.

Shute quietly demolishes the optimist's prime argument against the possibility of total nuclear war: that man is too rational to destroy himself. Speaking of man collectively, Shute admits such a belief might be true; but his view is that nuclear weapons increase the power of the minority of irrational men. Thus, the novel has someone, no one knows exactly who or why, drop a hydrogen bomb on Tel Aviv. When the British and the Americans make a demonstration flight over Cairo, the Egyptians retaliate by bombing Washington and London in Russian-made bombers with Russian markings. With the nations' statesmen dead, the British and American military unleash their bombers on Russia before the Egyptian ploy is discovered. The horror of this scenario is that the responses to the first provocation were rational to the extent that they were based upon the accepted military reasoning of the time. Once the bombs started falling, they fell until they were all used; in Shute's eyes, the great folly is not in using the bombs but in having had them in the first place.

Careful not to criticize anyone, Shute makes Commander Towers a sympathetic and reasonable figure; and he has him state that, had he been in control of the bombs and missiles, he would have used them down to the last one once the war had started. To Shute, order, obedience, and organization are the foundations of civilization and the prerequisites of ideal existence; rational men like Dwight Towers should not be asked or expected to violate that order simply because to destroy mankind is immoral. Instead, the novel cautions that civilized men should not place themselves or their leaders in the position of having to make an either/or choice between disobedience and destruction. (pp. 129-30)

On the Beach's message, if any, is that human society was a nice try; unfortunately, it worked too well, trundling down the path until it found a way to destroy itself. It is not the novel of an angry, or even an anxious, man; it is that of a man who has seen the possibilities and accepted them. Mankind endures in obedience only, making its appointed rounds, going about its business as usual. If a thousand rockets have been launched, why not launch the rest? Dwight Towers floods and sinks his submarine with all the crew aboard when the men begin to show signs of radiation sickness—after all, if they die ashore with the boat in dock, no one would be left to safeguard that piece of highly classified military property. That no one would be left, anyway, makes no difference to Towers. (p. 130)

Many reviewers were made uncomfortable by the way Dwight Towers keeps talking of his wife and children in Connecticut as though they are alive, and of the presents he buys to give them when he returns home. But Towers' fidelity and sense of homecoming is logical in so far as the condition of mankind has undergone a massive change. Except for a relative handful, those who were living are now dead—and the land of the dead has become the real world, the permanent world. Only the world of the living is transitory; for all the farmers harrowing their fields, all the housewives planning their gardens, and all the doctors operating on patients to give them a few more years of useful life know, intellectually, that they will be dead in a matter of months or weeks. But the man in our without-end real world who plants a tree knows he will not live to see it mature. How soon death will come is completely relative. Besides, as Jack Turner says in *The Chequer Board*, "'All be the same in a hundred years.'"

The story of Jack Turner is worth remembering: Turner's stoicism and his discovery on the verge of death that all men are

basically the same marked the beginning of Shute's long road to *On the Beach*. Moreover, Shute's idea of sending a dying man around the world to discover his own meaning prefigures the two long voyages of Commander Towers' submarine. The voyages of U.S.S. *Scorpion* . . . keep the otherwise static story moving physically to Queensland and then to the West Coast of the United States. Voyages of discovery, they show that man's universal fate is death. Shute sends his characters "travelling hopefully" again: "'Even if we don't discover anything that's good,'" says Towers of an impending voyage, "'it's still discovering things. I don't think we *shall* discover anything that's good, or very hopeful. But even so, it's fun just finding out. . . . Some games are fun even when you lose. Even when you know you're going to lose before you start. It's fun just playing them.'" . . . (pp. 131-32)

On the Beach may well be the first important fictional study of ecological disaster. When Moira asks if scientists can do anything to stop the radioactive dust that is drifting down to the southern hemisphere, Towers answers, "'Not a thing.'" "'It's just too big for mankind to tackle. We've just got to take it.'" Moira rejects her fate as unfair, for "'No one in the Southern Hemisphere ever dropped a bomb. . . . We had nothing to do with it. Why should we have to die because other countries nine or ten thousand miles away from us wanted to have a war?'" . . . Shute had discovered Spaceship Earth for himself, and probably did more than any other writer or thinker of the 1950s to make a large audience understand that men must suffer equally the results of what they do at home or allow to happen far away. Moreover, the novel's stylistic stoicism and objectivity make for an absolute sincerity that left the burden of responsibility on the reader, and made it clear to him that the novelist did not care one way or another how he reacted. After all, "'It's not the end of the world,'" says Shute's alter ego, the auto-racing scientist. "'It's only the end of us. The world will go on just the same, only we shan't be in it. I dare say it will get along all right without us.'" . . . (pp. 133-34)

[Philip Wylie] suggested that *On the Beach* "ought to be compulsory reading at the Pentagon, West Point, Annapolis. Ike [Eisenhower] should set aside his western and puzzle his way through it." But Shute was not writing for presidents and generals who already knew about the possibilities of nuclear war. When I came across a letter from then Senator John Kennedy that thanked Shute's American publishers for sending him a copy of the novel, I wondered for a minute whether or not he would have dared the Cuban Missile Crisis had he read *On the Beach*. However, I returned to reality when I thought that presidents do not need novelists to tell them what can happen—they already know, or are supposed to. Moreover, Shute was talking to the ordinary reader, to the man charged with the extraordinary responsibility of telling his politicians what to do.

And when I read John Kennedy's letter, I suddenly remembered that 1962, the year Shute chose for Armageddon, was also the year of the Cuban Missile Crisis. And if the contemporary reader quivers a bit when he remembers that Shute's nuclear war grew out of the Arab-Israeli conflict, he also recognizes that Shute has once more seen the future. (p. 134)

Julian Smith, in his Nevil Shute (Nevil Shute Norway), *Twayne Publishers, 1976, 166 p.*

Stephen (Joshua) Sondheim

1930-

American composer, lyricist, and scriptwriter.

Sondheim is generally acknowledged to be the best composer-lyricist currently working on Broadway. In collaboration with producer-director Harold Prince, he created a series of innovative and ambitious musicals which have earned enthusiastic acclaim from critics, although most have been only moderately successful at the box office. His work has won numerous Tony Awards, the most recent being for *Sweeney Todd* (1979).

Sondheim's mentor was the renowned lyricist Oscar Hammerstein II, who was a neighbor and family friend. It was Hammerstein who urged him to accept the job of lyricist for *West Side Story* (1957), although his training had been in musical composition and he was reluctant to accept a job which did not allow him to write both music and lyrics. Although Sondheim received little mention in reviews of this musical, the show itself was very popular and led to his being asked to write the lyrics for *Gypsy* (1959). Following these two early successes, Sondheim began to write both music and lyrics for all of his shows, beginning with *A Funny Thing Happened on the Way to the Forum* (1962). A spoof of traditional musical comedy and based on the plays of Plautus, a classical Roman dramatist, *Forum* is Sondheim's most purely comedic work to date and also his most financially successful. His next two works, *Anyone Can Whistle* (1964) and *Do I Hear a Waltz?* (1965), were not well received either by critics or by the public, although the earlier work has since engaged a cult following.

Sondheim entered into a long and fruitful period of collaboration with Harold Prince beginning with *Company* in 1970. The musicals that Sondheim and Prince created are considered outstanding for their stylistic and thematic sophistication. They tend to be less optimistic than the typical Broadway musical, and critics use words such as desolation, despair, and disillusion in describing the tone of their productions. Termed "concept musicals" by various critics, some of these shows rely on theme rather than plot for unity. For instance, *Company* explores, in an episodic plot, the benefits and disappointments of marriage in contemporary urban America. Although the lyrics are entertaining and the ending affirms the institution of marriage, Sondheim's songs for this show display a vision of love which is unromantic and unsentimental. Critics enjoyed both *Company* and its successor, *Follies* (1971), but thought that they did not provide the cheerful escapism which Broadway's musical theater audiences were seeking.

This was not the case with *A Little Night Music* (1973). Critics agreed that in this show Prince and Sondheim had conceived a musical which was in line with public taste while maintaining their usual high standards of sophistication and innovation. *Night Music* is a romantic operetta based on the Ingmar Bergman film *Smiles of a Summer Night*. Set in a Swedish forest, the musical dramatizes and sometimes satirizes love and flirtation among people of various ages, and all of the music is written in variations of triple time. The score includes romantic love songs, demonstrating that Sondheim can successfully depart from the irreverent songs which are usually regarded as his forte. One of them, "Send in the Clowns," is

the only Sondheim song which has achieved fame and popularity outside of the theater.

Pacific Overtures (1976) and *Sweeney Todd: The Demon Barber of Fleet Street* (1979) are also Prince-Sondheim collaborations. The former deals with the Westernization and exploitation of Japan by the United States. Such Japanese art-forms as Kabuki theater and haiku poetry are effectively utilized. *Sweeney Todd* originated in a nineteenth-century tale about a barber who murders his clients; Sondheim based his version on a 1973 play by Christopher Bond which added elements of class struggle and oppression to the legend and invited comparison with the works of German dramatist Bertolt Brecht. The political nature of these two musicals is further evidence of the daring of their creators, who risked blending politics and entertainment on Broadway. *Pacific Overtures* impressed critics but was largely ignored by the theater-going public; however, *Sweeney Todd* had a long Broadway run despite its political content and gruesomeness. Sondheim has continued to take advantage of unconventional sources in his recent collaborative effort with James Lapine, *Sunday in the Park with George* (1984). Inspired by a Georges Seurat painting, this musical is a fanciful exploration of the famous painter and his grandson.

Critic Peter Reilly has described Sondheim's career as "parallel to without being a part of the mainstream of the American musical theater.'' Although some of his work is complex and not readily accessible, Sondheim has set a high standard for Broadway musicals. His songs express ideas which directly relate to the themes and action of the plays; therefore, they often work only when sung by the character for whom they were written. For this reason, his songs usually do not translate well off the stage, but critics feel that this is a significant improvement over musicals which are little more than showcases for various disparate songs. Although many critics have pointed to a lack of warmth and an emotional detachment in his songs, they agree that Sondheim has greatly raised the artistic level of American musical theater.

(See also *Contemporary Authors*, Vol. 103.)

ROBERT COLEMAN

"West Side Story" is a timely re-telling of the Romeo and Juliet legend against the raw violence of youthful gang wars. It has earthy humor and simple beauty. And, best of all, it has tremendous drive. It moves with the speed of a switchblade knife thrust.

The Arthur Laurents book is lean and wiry. It never uses two words where one will do. It is an excellent framework for an extraordinary score by Leonard Bernstein, biting and tender lyrics by Stephen Sondheim, and magnificent staging by Jerome Robbins. It is a felicitous blending of all facets of theatre. . . .

Laurents, Bernstein and Sondheim made no compromises with popular taste. They have shunned the happy ending of the average Broadway song-and-dancer. Laurents, as a sort of offstage Mercutio, says in effect, "A plague on both your houses." He has no sympathy for juvenile delinquents. He lashes out at their jungle code, their defiance of society. . . .

"West Side Story" is a superlative musical. A chiller, a thriller, as up-to-the-minute as tomorrow's headlines.

> Robert Coleman, "'West Side Story' a Sensational Hit!" in Daily Mirror, *September 27, 1957. Reprinted in* New York Theatre Critics' Reviews, *Vol. XVIII, No. 15, September 30-October 6, 1957, p. 254.*

JOHN CHAPMAN

["**West Side Story**"] is a bold new kind of musical theatre— a juke-box Manhattan opera. It is, to me, extraordinarily exciting. In it, the various fine skills of show business are put to new tests, and as a result a different kind of musical has emerged.

The story is, roughly, Shakespeare's recounting of the love and deaths of Romeo and Juliet. But the setting is today's Manhattan, and the manner of telling the story is a provocative and artful blend of music, dance and plot—and the music and the dancing are superb.

In this present-day version of the theatre's greatest romance, the Montagues and Capulets become young New York gangs, one native, the other Puerto Rican. . . .

The music of **"West Side Story"** is by Leonard Bernstein, and it is superb. . . .

The story, about the fundamentally innocent hoodlums of our town, is by Arthur Laurents, and it is a lovely and moving one. But Laurents is not alone in telling this story, for his collaborator is Jerome Robbins, the choreographer. Robbins and his superb young dancers carry the plot as much as the spoken words and lyrics do.

The lyrics, by Stephen Sondheim, have simple grace, and there is a lovely tribute by the sidewalk Romeo to his dusky girl, Maria. There is a really beautiful scene in which the boy and the girl go through a make-believe wedding in a shop for bridal clothing. And there is an uproariously funny one in which a so-called juvenile delinquent gets a going-over by all the authorities whose problem he is—the cop, the judge, the social worker and the psychiatrist. This young hoodlum manages to make his elders look pretty silly.

> John Chapman, "'West Side Story' a Splendid and Super-Modern Musical Drama," in Daily News, *New York, September 27, 1957. Reprinted in* New York Theatre Critics' Reviews, *Vol. XVIII, No. 15, September 30-October 6, 1957, p. 252.*

JOHN McCLAIN

["**West Side Story**"] is a story with music, but I do not call it a musical because it strikes me as an entirely new form. There are arias, duets, choral numbers; there is ballet and jive, and there is an appealing libretto. It is the most exciting thing that has come to town since "My Fair Lady."

Here is one of the rare blends of talent that obviously struck no snags. The idea, a rather loose modernization of the Romeo and Juliet theme, was conceived by Jerome Robbins. It was transmitted by him to Leonard Bernstein, Arthur Laurents and a young man named Stephen Sondheim, and together they devised book, music, lyrics and choreography which should remain for many seasons as the most fortunate union in the history of money.

Taking it from the top I would say that Mr. Bernstein is responsible for the true importance of the piece, for the music is always magnificent. . . .

The story by Mr. Laurents is only wonderful. He has captured the talk of the juveniles, or a reasonable facsimile, and woven it into a magic fabric.

Young Mr. Sondheim has gone all the way with the mood in his lyrics. His ballads are the lament of the sincere, and he can come up with the most hilarious travesty of our times in, **"Gee, Officer Krupke"**—a plaint which should settle the problem of juvenile delinquency forever.

Then there is Jerome Robbins, the old master, who directed and did the dances. This should be his monument, for there has never been a happier integration, a more sensitive blending of story, song and movement.

> John McClain, "Music Magnificent in Overwhelming Hit," in Journal American, *September 27, 1957. Reprinted in* New York Theatre Critics' Reviews, *Vol. XVIII, No. 15, September 30-October 6, 1957, p. 254.*

BROOKS ATKINSON

Since Ethel Merman is the head woman in **"Gypsy,"** which opened at the Broadway last evening, nothing can go wrong. She would not permit **"Gypsy"** to be anything less than the most satisfying musical of the season. . . .

In the book Arthur Laurents has written for her (based on the memoirs of Gypsy Rose Lee) she is the female juggernaut who drives her two daughters into show business and keeps their noses to the grindstone until one of them is a star.

"**Gypsy**" is a musical tour of the hotel rooms and backstages of the seamy side of show business thirty years ago when vaudeville was surrendering to the strip-tease. Jo Mielziner has designed a savory production. Jule Styne has supplied a genuine show-business score, and Stephen Sondheim has set amusing lyrics to it.

> Brooks Atkinson, "Theatre: Good Show!" in The New York Times, *May 22, 1959, p. 31.*

KENNETH TYNAN

[*The following essay was first published in* The New Yorker, *May 30, 1959.*]

Quite apart from considerations of subject matter, perfection of style can be profoundly moving in its own right. If anyone doubts that, he had better rush and buy a ticket for *Gypsy*, the first half of which brings together in effortless coalition all the arts of the American musical stage at their highest point of development. So smooth is the blending of skills, so precise the interlocking of song, speech, and dance, that the sheer contemplation of technique becomes a thrilling emotional experience. . . . I have heard of mathematicians who broke down and wept at the sight of certain immaculately poised equations, and I have actually seen a motoring fanatic overcome with feeling when confronted by a vintage Rolls-Royce engine. *Gypsy*, Act I, confers the same intense pleasure, translated into terms of theatre. Nothing about it is superfluous; there is no display of energy for energy's sake. No effort is spared, yet none is wasted. Book, lyrics, music, décor, choreography, and cast seem not—as so often occurs—to have been conscripted into uneasy and unconvinced alliance but to have come together by irresistible mutual attraction, as if each could not live without the rest. . . . Since the task is worth while, the result is art.

As everyone must surely be aware, the show is based on the memoirs of Gypsy Rose Lee. . . . (pp. 319-20)

[A] lot of people are equally responsible for the wonder of . . . [the] first act. Jule Styne, the most persistently underrated of popular composers, has contributed to it nine songs, all of which are both exciting in themselves and relevant to the action—from the opening chorus, "**May We Entertain You?**", a splendid pastiche of ragtime vapidity, to "**Everything's Coming Up Roses,**" in which Rose, whistling in the dark, tries to persuade herself that life without June is going to be just peachy. In addition, we have "**Small World,**" an elastically swaying tune used by Rose to seduce Herbie, the agent who becomes her lover; "**Little Lamb,**" sung by Gypsy to one of her mother's menagerie of pets; "**You'll Never Get Away from Me,**" Rose's jovial assertion of her man's dependence; "**If Momma was Married,**" in which the daughters complain about their enslavement; and "**All I Need Is a Girl,**" a song-and-dance number in the [Fred] Astaire manner. . . . The credit for . . . the whole physical gesture of the evening, belongs to Jerome Robbins, who, as director and choreographer, has poured into *Gypsy* the same abundance of invention with which he galvanized *West Side Story*. From the latter show he has borrowed a lyricist, Stephen Sondheim, and a librettist, Arthur Laurents, both of whom have brought to their new jobs an exemplary

mixture of gaiety, warmth, and critical intelligence. (pp. 320-21)

The second half, which is briefer, is also less effective. There are several reasons for this. One has to do with plot; having seen the grooming of Baby June, we now watch the grooming of Gypsy, and this makes for redundancy. Another is that Act II contains only three new songs; the rest are reprises. . . . But I don't see how anyone could deny that the show tapers off from perfection in the first act to mere brilliance in the second. (pp. 321-22)

> Kenneth Tynan, "The American Theatre: 'Gypsy'," *in his* Curtains: Selections from the Drama Criticism and Related Writings, *Atheneum Publishers, 1961, pp. 319-22.*

BROOKS ATKINSON

[It] is the impeccable taste of the music, the lyrics and the story that seems so astonishing in "**West Side Story.**" Given two lots of hoodlums somewhere on the gritty pavements of New York, how could the authors of the show endow them with so much common humanity, and raise their hopes and troubles to the level of literature?

But that is what "**West Side Story**" manages to do. The world of the Jets and the Sharks is full of violence and danger. The amenities of civilization seem unmanly and bogus to these tense youths, who are seething with fear and hatred. Nothing could be uglier than the rumble that leaves two victims dead in the shadows of a summer night.

Somehow Mr. Bernstein, Stephen Sondheim, the lyricist, and Arthur Laurents, author of the book, have suggested another dimension. The beauty is graceless, but it is there, somewhere in the background. What these youths get in life is barbaric, but they are not unaware of things that are unattainable—happiness that belongs to other people, an ideal world that can be read about but never entered. Tragedy is too big a word to describe the plight they find themselves in. But they are not vicious people. . . .

Without being sentimental, Mr. Robbins and his associates are compassionate. . . .

No wonder the audience was full of enthusiasm. "**West Side Story**" is a wonderful piece of work.

> Brooks Atkinson, "Theatre: Musical Is Back," in The New York Times, *April 28, 1960, p. 31.*

WILLIAM K. ZINSSER

There is an engaging song in *West Side Story* in which the young heroine, Maria, blurts out the joy of being in love:

> I feel pretty, oh, so pretty,
> That the city should give me its key.
> A committee
> Should be organized to honor me. . . .

Besides being pleasant, the lyric is a model of craftsmanship. It states a simple emotion, clearly and with precision, and yet it is not dry. It has a girlish lilt, a touch of humor, and, as all good lyrics should, an element of surprise—in this case a triple, mainly internal rhyme.

Nevertheless the man who wrote it, Stephen Sondheim, wanted to remove the song from *West Side Story* during its tryout. He felt that the lyric, though technically expert, was wrong for Maria: she would not use a three-syllable word or express herself in such a complex pattern. Sondheim was overruled by his three collaborators, composer Leonard Bernstein, writer Arthur Laurents, and director-choreographer Jerome Robbins; but he still broods over the fact that the song gives the show a false moment.

Sondheim's reaction illustrates the particular nature of his talent—a talent of first magnitude, for at thirty-one he has already written the lyrics to two of the most robust and admired hits of the contemporary musical theater, the other being *Gypsy* (1959). If he were merely a brilliant technician, the two shows would not have made such an impact. It is because his lyrics so surely fit not only the moment but the total mood and character of the story that *West Side Story* and *Gypsy* have an extra unity, maturity, and dramatic strength. Thus when, early in *Gypsy*, Rose announces in an acrid song that it's all right for "some people" to go on "living life in a living room," but not for *her*, the audience knows that cold ambition is to be the goad for all that follows; and every lyric that she sings thereafter reveals some facet of the same hard personality. "Those are the lyrics," Sondheim says, "that come easiest—ones that deal with bitter, driving, hostile, and ambitious people." (p. 98)

> *William K. Zinsser, "On Stage: Stephen Sondheim," in* Horizon, *Vol. III, No. 6, July, 1961, pp. 98-9.*

HOBE MORRISON

The title of **"A Funny Thing Happened on the Way to the Forum"** is misleading. The musical . . . isn't funny—it's uproarious. Moreover, the show isn't about any single thing that happens, but includes just about every preposterous incident imaginable. Also, while there are several mentions of the forum, nobody goes there, so the reference serves merely to establish a sort of franchise.

Although the new show is billed as a musical comedy, it's really a wildly antic knockabout farce with songs and practically continuous laughs. . . . [Instead] of even a nominal story line, it's an incredible collection of uninhibited buffoonery, frequently in the old fashioned vaudeville and burlesque style. . . .

[The show] is, in essence, a gigantic spoof of traditional musical comedy. . . . The gags are packed into the dialog, bits of visual business and song lyrics and even the tone of some of the numbers is good for laughs. For example, a ballad titled **"Lovely"** is a travesty of romantic tunes in general and the **"West Side Story"** song hit [**"I Feel Pretty"**], in particular. By no coincidence, Stephen Sondheim wrote the lyrics for **"West Side Story"** and both words and music for **"A Funny Thing."** . . .

Sondheim's songs are amusing, with frequently laughable lyrics involving outrageous puns and tongue-twister word combinations, but there don't seem to be any numbers that disk jockey repetition will turn into psychological warfare on the public. For stage production purposes, the best seem to be **"Comedy Tonight," "Love I Hear," "Lovely," "Everybody Ought to Have a Maid," "Impossible," "Bring Me My Bride," "That Dirty Old Man,"** and **"That'll Show Him."**

> *Hobe Morrison, in a review of "A Funny Thing Happened on the Way to the Forum," in* Variety, *May 16, 1962, p. 65.*

JOHN CHAPMAN

["**Anyone Can Whistle**"] is an unusual, far-out musical with a briskly syncopated score, educated lyrics, original and frisky dances, waltzing scenery and an imaginative story which the cast and I had to cope with rather strenuously.

This book and the lack of a melody I could whistle impeded my enjoyment of the last two acts, which didn't quite fulfill the high promise of the joyously daffy first act.

Arthur Laurents, the librettist (and director), has imagined a depressed town ruled by a lady mayor. But this is no ordinary depression; the town has manufactured something that won't wear out—so when everybody has one the big factory closes and only a miracle can help.

So a big fake miracle happens when a big rock in the square spurts water, thanks to a secretly rigged pump. Cures loom, even for the inmates of the Cookie Jar, which is the municipal euphemism for the asylum. A joyful chorus sings, "Hear ye the beautiful bells, build ye the new motels."

From here on events become desperately complicated, but the main idea is that the world is mad and we all are crazy so we might as well enjoy it. In the course of the evening Laurents and the songwriter Stephen Sondheim throw darts or take wallops at venal politics and psychiatry and subjects between. . . .

Sondheim's witty chorus songs are generally more appealing than his romantic solos.

> *John Chapman, " 'Anyone Can Whistle' Original," in* Daily News, *New York, April 6, 1964. Reprinted in* New York Theatre Critics' Reviews, *Vol. XXV, No. 11, April 20-26, 1964, p. 303.*

RICHARD WATTS, JR.

High aim is always commendable in the theater, and there can be no doubt of the lofty and praiseworthy ambition of **"Anyone Can Whistle."** But some actual fulfillment must accompany the dream, and it seemed to me that the new musical comedy by Arthur Laurents and Stephen Sondheim . . . was so ponderously heavy-handed and clumsily vague in its presentation of a somewhat obscure thesis that it could bring the entire idea of good intentions under suspicion. . . .

Mr. Laurents, who wrote the book and staged the production, seems to have had in mind a serious moral parable in terms of comic fantasy. . . .

As a story, it is meandering, devious and not very enlivening in its humor. But this is presumably beyond the point, since it is all apparently meant to be an allegory. Mr. Laurents tells us that the mentally ill can't be distinguished from the gullible pilgrims to the shrine, that those who expose a fraudulent miracle are sure to be denounced as lacking in faith and piety, and that the courageous nonconformist in a conforming world is in danger of being considered mad and the dedicated idealist is bound to be dismissed as a victim of frustration.

These ideas, provided I am right in thinking they are what the author was driving at, may not be startling, but they could have freshness for a musical comedy. The unfortunate thing is that **"Anyone Can Whistle"** is neither bright and invigorating as sheer entertainment nor pointed and witty as satirical parable. And I thought Mr. Sondheim's score suffered from the composer's determination to escape any accusation of giving the audience a good, lively tune.

Richard Watts, Jr., "Musical Play Turns Allegorical," in New York Post, *April 6, 1964. Reprinted in* New York Theatre Critics' Reviews, *Vol. XXV, No. 11, April 20-26, 1964, pp. 301-02.*

HOWARD TAUBMAN

There is no law against saying something in a musical, but it's unconstitutional to omit imagination and wit. In an attempt to be meaningful, **"Anyone Can Whistle"** forgets to offer much entertainment.

Arthur Laurents and Stephen Sondheim, the authors, . . . have aimed for originality, and for that one respects them. Their trouble is that they have taken an idea with possibilities and have pounded it into a pulp.

Mr. Laurents's book lacks the fantasy that would make the idea work, and his staging has not improved matters. Mr. Sondheim has written several pleasing songs but not enough of them to give the musical wings.

Howard Taubman, "The Theater: 'Anyone Can Whistle'," in The New York Times, *April 6, 1964, p. 36.*

HOBE MORRISON

Whatever it's supposed to be getting at, **"Anyone Can Whistle"** should have the distinction of not leaving audiences apathetic. If it isn't entertaining, it's at least apt to be irritating. . . .

[**"Anyone Can Whistle"**] has a book by Arthur Laurents, with music and lyrics by Stephen Sondheim, in what's evidently meant to be a sort of song and dance theatre of the absurd. . . .

The book is a kind of surrealist fable about a corrupt Never-Neverland town in which the supposedly crazy people are sane. The point seems to be something or other about the stultifying effect of that pathetically riddled target, conformity. . . .

Maybe it's supposed to be Brechtian, or something, and obviously it's meant to be symbolic, profound, sophisticated and clever as all get out. By normal entertainment standards, however, it's an enigma—a large, pretentious, numbing shambles. There's not a genuinely memorable song in the show, although the title number, **"A Parade in Town," "Everybody Says Don't"** and **"So Little to Be Sure Of"** are briefly, mildly listenable. . . .

In a season already notable for musical mishaps, **"Anyone Can Whistle"** is an outstanding clinker.

Hobe Morrison, in a review of "Anyone Can Whistle," in Variety, *April 8, 1964, p. 80.*

WALTER KERR

"Do I Hear a Waltz?" is an entirely serious and very dry musical about an American tourist who goes to Venice and doesn't have any fun. What more can I tell you? . . .

From his earlier play, **"The Time of the Cuckoo,"** and without doing much more than thinning it out, Arthur Laurents has devised a small diary in which the loneliness, and then the stubbornness, and then the rueful awakening of starchy Leona Samish can be recorded for sound. Leona is single, and likely to be. She has come abroad looking for a "wonderful, mystical, magical miracle," but is not finding it.

By the sixth song of the evening, she is still sitting alone over evening coffee singing "Here we are together, me and I." There is a man hovering in the background, to be sure—a shopkeeper, married, rather blunt about these relationships for a girl like Leona. . . . Eventually, though briefly, she surrenders. . . .

And there we have it, a straight play, played at straight-play pace, virtually unrelieved by either dancing or comedy, soberly acted, economically directed, and depending for its life upon Richard Rodgers' thoughtful songs. I call them thoughtful because they, too, cling close—firmly, with some dignity—to the plainness in Leona's life. **"Take the Moment,"** the storekeeper urges. **"Do I Hear a Waltz?"** sings Leona wistfully, then a bit more warmly. **"Stay,"** pleads the storekeeper in fine white high notes. **"Thank You Very Much"** whisper both, as they realize the moment is over.

With lyricist Stephen Sondheim's assistance, Mr. Rodgers has taken pains to step away from the plaintive and into the cozy-lively on a few—though not too many—occasions. . . .

Mr. Sondheim seems a perfectly agreeable rhyming companion for Mr. Rodgers to be doing his work with, and if the excursions into animation never quite lift the roof off it is no doubt because they, like the narrative, are at heart mild complaints. The most effective music comes, significantly, when the corners of a bright tune are turned down. There is a chorus of **"We're Gonna Be All Right"** in which . . . [the two] young-marrieds who have been having a spot of trouble, hush their voices and rein in their spirits to suggest that it may *never* be all right. The contrast has an edge to it and for a moment the overcast crackles. And a ballad for three women, **"Moon in My Window,"** is rich with the bittersweet of broken promises and unexpectedly assuaged hearts. . . .

But there is—as the play is saying—an emotional drought in Venice, and while musical-comedy asceticism is a rare and perhaps admirable thing it cannot, and does not, do much for the evening's pulse. . . . In all of her travels, and for all of her wistfulness, Leona Samish hears a waltz only once.

Walter Kerr, "Kerr Reviews 'Do I Hear a Waltz?'" in New York Herald Tribune, *March 19, 1965, p. 14.*

RICHARD WATTS, JR.

The Venice of the American tourist provides a colorful background of which Richard Rodgers takes expert advantage in **"Do I Hear a Waltz?"** His new musical play . . . is so winning in its score, lyrics, setting, cast, production, spirit and general atmosphere that it offers an evening of charming and tasteful entertainment despite certain strong reservations I have concerning the libretto by Arthur Laurents.

In a Richard Rodgers show, the music deserves first attention, and his latest score, while perhaps not one of his most spectacular, is tuneful and thoroughly appealing. The lyrics contributed by Stephen Sondheim are deft and intelligent, and the attractive numbers are delightfully sung. . . .

Since the story plays a large part in **"Do I Hear a Waltz?,"** its frailties are important, but they should blind no one to its blessings. The score is filled with pleasures including the haunting title song, the charming **"Moon in My Window"** and the brightly sardonic **"Perfectly Lovely Couple."** There is also an entertaining number called **"No Understand,"** which centers around the problem of speaking English for an Italian. . . .

> *Richard Watts, Jr., ''American in a Musical Venice,'' in* New York Post, *March 19, 1965. Reprinted in* New York Theatre Critics' Reviews, *Vol. XXVI, No. 5, April 5-11, 1965, p. 360.*

DOUGLAS WATT

Let's hear it for **"Company,"** the newest and slickest thing in town. As smooth as the steel-and-glass buildings of midtown Manhattan and as jumpy as an alley cat, it is Broadway's first musical treatment of nerve ends.

[Robert] is a bachelor whose closest friends include three girls and five married couples. At the beginning and end, he is being given a surprise party by the pairs on his 35th birthday. In between, he remembers troublesome scenes with all of them and at the finish decides that marriage is—well, go see for yourself.

Brilliance is all in this show. George Furth's book is diamond-sharp, funny and chilling both. But Stephen Sondheim's songs, while equally scintillating, shine through time and again with a welcome and essential warmth. They make the evening. And interestingly, though Sondheim obviously has been listening to the sounds of today, he wisely favors his own which apply perfectly to the 30-ish crowd onstage.

> *Douglas Watt, '' 'Company' Has Brilliant Fun with Couples in Manhattan,'' in* Daily News, New York, *April 27, 1970. Reprinted in* New York Theatre Critics' Reviews, *Vol. XXXI, No. 13, May 11-16, 1970, p. 260.*

CLIVE BARNES

Creatively Mr. Sondheim's lyrics are way above the rest of [**"Company"**]; they have a lyric suppleness, sparse, elegant wit, and range from the virtuosity of a patter song to a kind of sweetly laconic cynicism in a modern love song. The music is academically very interesting. Mr. Sondheim must be one of the most sophisticated composers ever to write Broadway musicals, yet the result is slick, clever and eclectic rather than exciting. It is the kind of music that makes me say: ''Oh, yeah?'' rather than ''Gee whiz!'' but I readily concede that many people will consider its sheer musical literacy as off setting all other considerations. (p. 262)

> *Clive Barnes, '' 'Company' Offers a Guide to New York's Marital Jungle,'' in* The New York Times, *April 27, 1970, p. 40.*

MARTIN GOTTFRIED

"Company" is quite simply in a league by itself. Artistry, excitement, intelligence and professionalism have been so long gone from Broadway that it's almost easy to forget when the musical theatre held the promise of greatness, and yet that was only as long ago as the last work of Leonard Bernstein (**"West Side Story"**), Jerome Robbins (''Fiddler On The Roof'') and Stephen Sondheim (**"Anyone Can Whistle"**). Sondheim's new musical . . . is a tremendous piece of work, thrilling and chilling, glittering bright, really funny (and not so funny), exceed-

ingly adult, gorgeous to look at and filled with brilliant music. . . .

The theme of **"Company"** is bachelorhood in the New York of clever, successful, alcoholic, partying, sexually promiscuous, divorce-ridden people in their mid-30s—the New York of Fire Island and the Hamptons, of discotheques and beautiful clothes and money. The central character—Robert—is given a surprise 35th birthday party by the five couples who are his friends. George Furth's book then flashes back and forward to each of these couples. . . . They all have unattractive marriages but insist that the marriages may be wrong but not marriage itself. Robert feels pressure to get married and they all want to marry him off though, to him, marriage seems to be just to ward off loneliness (just for company) and makes one dull, cranky, bored (and boring), old and fat. In the end, he concludes that friends (company) are no substitute for love. . . .

"Company" is brutally unsentimental and sometimes unemotional, mostly because it is so grown-up and frightfully honest. . . .

The general excitement, though, grows from Sondheim's music. It is at once intricate and simple, serious and theatrical. Sondheim has been influenced by Bernstein, who was influenced by [Aaron] Copland, who was influenced by [Igor] Stravinsky, which isn't a genealogy to sneeze at, but he can hardly be called unoriginal (though one song is definitely in the [George] Gershwin mode). He is the most exciting, stimulating, theatre-minded composer at work today. His freedom from standard forms, his meters, harmonies, modulations, long-lined constructions (which braid in and out of the action), dissonances and plain music are so superior to what we hear in the theatre that comparisons are absurd.

The lyrics he wrote for himself combine absolute craft with a content that matches the show's and, in patter songs, they are in a class with W. S. Gilbert himself.

> *Martin Gottfried, in a review of ''Company,'' in* Women's Wear Daily, *April 27, 1970.*

WALTER KERR

[The hero in **"Company,"** Bobby,] wants no part of marriage or, as a song says, of **"The Little Things You Do Together,"** (''Neighbors you annoy together, children you destroy together''), but he's willing to listen to—he cannot escape—the finger-wagging advice, in buzzing overlapping rhythms, of his matchmaking friends. Only trouble is, when he asks how any of them feels about being married, he gets an at best ambiguous and at worst despairing answer. ''You're always sorry, you're always grateful,'' a trio of furrowed-brow husbands carols to him (in quite a nice little lazy-beat song), ending with a dying ''you're always alone.''

The mood is misanthropic, the view from the peephole jaundiced, the attitude middle-aged mean. That, of course, is a highly original stance for a Broadway musical to be taking. . . .

Stephen Sondheim has never written a more sophisticated, more pertinent, or—this is the surprising thing in the circumstances—more melodious score; and the lyrics are every bit as good (''You'll always be what you were / Which has nothing to do with—all to do with—her''). . . .

All of this is exemplary. Now ask me if I liked the show. I didn't like the show. I admired it, or admired vast portions of it, but that is another matter. Admiration stirs in the head; liking sends out its signals somewhere lower in the anatomy, the pit of the stomach maybe, and gradually lets you know that you are happy to have been born, or to have been lucky enough to have come tonight. I left **"Company"** feeling rather cool and queasy, whatever splendors my head may have been reminding me of, and there is a plain reason for that. At root, I didn't take to [Bobby's] . . . married friends any more than he did. I agreed with him.

"One is lonely and two is boring" is, in short, [Bobby's] . . . summary of his own experience, and the evening occupies itself with justifying his conviction. That doesn't make the evening boring: It makes it, between musical shots in the arm, over-insistent and lemony. Perhaps the whole thing is just too single-minded, like Alceste. In any event, its aura as well as its aftertaste is a middling one, somewhere between arid and energetic, dyspeptic and dynamic, farewell and hail. Personally, I'm sorry-grateful. (p. 264)

> *Walter Kerr, "'Company': Original and Uncompromising," in* The Sunday Times, *London, May 3, 1970. Reprinted in* New York Theatre Critics' Reviews, *Vol. XXXI, No. 13, May 11-17, 1970, p. 263.*

MARTIN GOTTFRIED

"Follies" is in a class of its own. It is safe to say that no Broadway musical has ever attempted its grandeur of vision, the size of its presence. This being so, it cannot be compared in any "good, better, best" sense with any musical in the past. So, if it does not always work, and it doesn't always, one is nonetheless aware that this is happening in a new-found dimension. Like a girl you love but do not always like, **"Follies"** is very great though it is not always good.

It is about age and an age, the glory of the past and the follies in letting nostalgia make that past seem more glorious (memory's compromise with reality), the truth of growing old and the acceptance of that truth. This is the general—philosophical—point of the show and it is often too sentimental. . . .

Ghosts are the theme of **"Follies"** and they stalk the show. Nearly every character is played by two people, the aging one of reality and the memory. It is this idea, and the awesomeness of its execution that give the show its monumental feeling—a breath away from the living.

The show hangs on the story of four of the partygoers, two girls who loved the man one of them married and the guy the losing girl did marry. The winner's husband has grown very successful but he is bored with her. The loser's husband is a cheater. During the party, the courtships are recalled and acted out, along with one last stab at changing the past, which, unlike marriage, cannot adapt with time but can only crumble.

James Goldman wrote this story and he was given short shrift by Prince and Sondheim, who were obviously more interested in the concept. This is their show and they are a remarkable, new kind of team—a producer-director and a composer-lyricist. Prince has made the show into a constant ballet—it is the most complete dance theatre since "Fiddler on the Roof"—and he has solved the problem of integrating choreography into his work by making Michael Bennett both choreographer and co-director. . . .

The Prince-Bennett musical sequences are magnificent. From solo turns to production numbers and finally into a mini-version of a full-fledged follies show (turned expressionist), they have recreated the past with dazzling success. Nor is it ever camp, not ever, and that is important because the show is the antithesis of camp. **"Follies"** does not mock the past, nor does it glamorize it with supercilious condescension. In fact, while celebrating the past, it (if sympathetically) shakes its heads over those who would live there. The body cannot grow younger.

Sondheim's work is stunning, though in choosing this show's theme he has willed himself into his most dangerous area as a composer. His score is a recreation of every song writer of the 20s and 30s, an attempt to outdo, in their own styles, Kern, Gershwin, Rodgers, Arlen, Ruby and so on (and by "and so on" I mean there are replicas of theatre composers probably nobody but Sondheim would recognize). It is a brilliant trick, consummately pulled off—in the stunning lyrics as well as in the music—but it is a trick nevertheless and, anyhow, Sondheim has just got to stop his compulsive satirizing. He is much too good a composer for it, which this score proves anyway. For all the mimicry of old show music, he has refreshed it with his own melodic invention, harmonic ingenuity, metric surprises and structural explorations.

> *Martin Gottfried, "'Follies': '. . . Monumental'," in* Women's Wear Daily, *April 5, 1971.*

T. E. KALEM

The frontier of the American musical theater is wherever Harold Prince and Stephen Sondheim are. Last season, the producer-director and composer-lyricist collaborated on *Company,* which focused a diamond-cutting laser beam on marriage, Manhattan-style. With *Follies,* Prince and Sondheim, together with Choreographer and Co-Director Michael Bennett, have audaciously staked out some unknown territory. They have put together the first Proustian musical. . . .

Compacted of memory, dreams and desire, the illusions and disillusions of love, the shifting structure of the self, *Follies* fuses all into one of the great haunting themes of the Western mind: Time. *Follies* is a triple-edged title. It means the *Ziegfeld Follies,* the follies of people in love, and the follies one commits by not fully knowing who one is or what one wants. . . .

The replica of a *Follies* show highlights the evening. The recreation is titled *Loveland,* and there is a shivery moment as the tall, lovely girls descend the traditional staircase. Beauty dapples the stage like a cascade of roses. Each of the four principals does a song or dance number denoting his or her folly: Buddy's is self-hatred; Sally's, being in love with love; Phyllis', a blurred identity; Ben's, self-proving quests, no satisfying goals.

Rarely have such searching, unsentimental questions and answers been put to a Broadway audience with such elegance and expertise. Sally's number **Losing My Mind** is the torch-singing peak of the show, but Sondheim's entire score is an incredible display of musical virtuosity. It is a one-man course in the theatrical modes of the '20s, '30s, and '40s musicals, done not as parody or mimicry, but as a passionately informed tribute.

> *T. E. Kalem, "Seascape with Frieze of Girls," in* Time, *Vol. 97, No. 15, April 12, 1971, p. 78.*

HENRY HEWES

The most important musical of the Broadway season is *Follies,* concocted by some of the collaborators who made *Company* the best musical of the last two seasons. The new work uses song and dance to suggest our evolution from the Twenties, Thirties, and Forties, when we counteracted our comparatively simple problems with childishly glamorized entertainments. But it resolutely resists the audience's wish to find these eras nostalgic and charming. Instead, it presents the ghosts of the past as painful exhumations.

Indeed, the theater itself has been turned into the gutted shell of a former Broadway pleasure palace. . . .

Into this special environment march the living remains of some of the old show girls and their husbands, who are meeting for a last reunion before their theater is totally demolished. . . . They are all bona fide members of the "Whatever Became of —?" Club.

Soon there is more applause for a run-down beauty parade of the no-longer-blooming old girls, accompanied by an aged tenor over-resonating **"These Beautiful Girls."** This song, which could easily become as popular a beauty contest perennial as "A Pretty Girl Is Like a Melody," carries in its lyrics a subtle sense of mock. As in the rest of his score, Stephen Sondheim has found a precise viewpoint between parody and facsimile.

Now James Goldman's less sure-handed plot is introduced. Two former show girls, Sally and Phyllis, arrive followed by their husbands, Buddy and Ben. Sally, we discover, has never relinquished her romantic longing for the more handsome Ben, and the main event of the evening is to be the exorcism of her psychological obsession. The others have troubles, too, which they will reveal in snatches of song and in vague dialogue.

Because the plot is weak and spreads its focus wide on four characters, *Follies* is forced to rely more heavily on song and dance and production effects than did *Company.* Fortunately, this is what the audience wants, a triumph of energy and skill over the depressingly real environment. . . .

We vaguely comprehend that the courtship of two "Follies" girls by two young stage-door Johnnies was superficial and accidental, and that their ensuing marriages could not count on memories or continuing illusions to make them work. The character who sees this most clearly and who, as a result, dominates the show is Phyllis. The most moving moment in *Follies* comes at the end of her song **"Could I Leave You?"** when, after expressing all of the dissatisfactions of her life with Ben, she sings, "Could *I* leave *you*? Yes. . . . Will I leave you? Guess!"

Ambitiously, *Follies* attempts to resolve the intramarital/extramarital mess with a series of "follies" performed in old extravaganza style. It is a brilliant theatrical effect when, after almost two uninterrupted hours of shabby environment, bright lacy scenery appears along with show girls in technicolor. Moreover, all of these "follies" expertly capture the flavor of the old musical comedies. Yet, their statement about what is wrong with each of the foursome is virtually impossible to grasp. . . . At the end, as a gray New York City dawn is seen through a hole in the theater's back wall, the couples appear helplessly reunited, determined to face a no-longer-romanticized tomorrow as a realistic today. It is an arbitrary denouement and no more convincing than the old happy endings.

If we are disappointed that *Follies* is tackling a larger task than it can achieve, we are also aware of the magnitude of the

enterprise. Michael Bennett's choreography is surgically precise and maintains a high level of style and vitality. Stephen Sondheim's lyrics are sophisticatedly penetrating, and his music has the flavor of each remembered prototype. And Harold Prince has produced the show without stint and has directed it with care. (p. 16)

Henry Hewes, "Folly in Folliesland," in Saturday Review, *Vol. LIV, No. 18, May 1, 1971, pp. 16, 65.*

ARLENE CROCE

Stephen Sondheim's lyrics for the show *Follies* reach their acme of wit in the very first song, in which he rhymes "celestial" with "the best ya'll (agree)." The song, *Beautiful Girls,* is sung by an aging, flabby tenor . . . as a line of women, former Follies girls attending a reunion in the crumbling shell of their old and soon-to-be-demolished theater, goes tottering down a staircase in a creaky reprise of the famous Follies showgirl parade.

The women are all either approaching menopause or are well beyond it, some are overweight, the party clothes they have worn for the occasion are for the most part in striking bad taste, and Sondheim's rhyme, with its play on "bestial," makes the dowdy spectacle of their exhibition seem not only ironic and sad but actively disgusting. In the finale, when the tenor holds a howling top note on "bee-*yow*-tee-ful" as the "girls" straggle into a tableau, there isn't even a trace of irony left, and the disgust we feel turns to indignation: at least the old Follies never exploited human beings as harshly as they are exploited here.

There probably never has been such a scene in an American musical before, but its offensiveness does not end with this one outburst. The whole show is permeated by a retching fear and hatred of growing old, as staged, it continually juxtaposes past and present in such a way as to make the decrepitude of the present a rebuke to the romanticism of the past and a form of revenge upon it, as if the dream of success and happiness and eternal love must be turned into its hideous opposite— cynicism and failure and ugliness and nightmarish relations between the sexes—as the price of maturity. And since the intellectual resources of James Goldman's book are not what one would call major, the show leaves us feeling that we have been fed these damaging romantic illusions about life by means of the simplest things imaginable—in popular songs and bright colors and the sight of pretty girls going up and down staircases. It suggests that we *believed* the songs we sang and accepted the frivolous extravaganzas as a metaphor for reality, and that now it's time to wake up and die. Later on in the show there's another ensemble number . . . called *Who's That Woman?,* which paints a kind of Dorian Gray-like picture of hell in the House of Revlon. As the old girls belt it out ("Lord, Lord, Lord, that woman is me!"), they are joined in a fast tap by ghosts of their former Follies selves, succulent young girls in their physical prime who can have no idea, poor things, that they're doomed to go the way of all flesh.

This number, which is the best ensemble number in the show— the only one in which anyone seems to be having any fun— happens to be the worst number in the original-cast album. . . . I don't know why it should be so cacophonous. . . . I mention it only because, like several other numbers on the record, it conveys hardly anything of the show's grosser intentions to the listener. In that sense, *Follies* sounds better than it plays. Anyone who hasn't seen it staged might think *Beautiful Girls* a fairly amusing parody of Nacio Herb Brown and nothing more. . . . In context, however, it's destructive and cruel.

Follies belongs to that line of musicals in which the songs are constantly being invaded by the plot and *vice versa*. The portion of Sondheim's score that is not Tin Pan Alley parody is concerned with Sally and Buddy and Phyllis and Ben, four middle-aged neurotics who come to the party and cry extensively into their beer about the days when they were four young neurotics together. . . .

It is strange to hear *Follies* praised, not only for its "adult" (read "sour") outlook but for its music and its dramatic continuity; the general impression is that it's a new type of musical like *Company,* the other Sondheim hit which was also produced and directed by Harold Prince. As a composer Sondheim may one day develop his own style, but here he still sounds like Leonard Bernstein's kid brother (let's not go into whose kid brother Bernstein sounds like), and models for many of the numbers in *Follies* existed as long ago as Kurt Weill's *Street Scene* and *Lady in the Dark,* two shows I'd just as soon not flash back to. The moralizing and factitiousness of those shows (which were also supposedly about real people) were dreary *then;* so was the semi-operatic form, which is preserved in *Follies* like a secret soft-drink formula. . . . To his credit, Sondheim seems to have offered his pastiches in a genial spirit, like a host showing us his collection of old movies; but to some critics this is enough to make him the king of a new genre. (p. 110)

Musicals about foundation men who are cracking up and women who are haunted by their youth are probably going to be around for a while, if *Follies* is any indication of a trend. The prospect is bitterly ironical. *Follies* is supposed to be an anti-"escape" musical, a show about real life, but because its version of life is a simple reversal of a banal theme, putting darkness in place of light, despair in place of hope, it offers us nothing but escape by another route. The proferred refuge is guilt, wonderful, all-absorbing universal guilt, the banality of the Seventies. We don't believe in Prince Charming any more; why should we believe in the toad the witch turned him into? (p. 111)

> *Arlene Croce, "Stephen Sondheim's 'Follies': A Pretty Girl Is Like a Malady, Etc.," in* Stereo Review, *Vol. 27, No. 1, July, 1971, pp. 110-11.*

MARTIN GOTTFRIED

["**A Funny Thing Happened on the Way to the Forum**"] has a book that is not only marvelous but without period in respect to its style. The Burt Shevelove-Larry Gelbart script is tremendously funny—it is literary, consistent and impeccably structured. It may well be the best book in all our musical theatre. . . .

The final contribution that makes for [its successful revival] . . . is Stephen Sondheim's score, which went unappreciated even when the show was winning its various prizes. Since this music cannot be separated from the book, you almost forget it is there—the composer suffers because of his very success. It is easier to notice Sondheim's lyrics—they are so clever they are a dazzling exercise on their own. But his music is superb: Technically fresh, filled with melody, accurate in satire and, most of all, theatrically conceived.

> *Martin Gottfried, in a review of "A Funny Thing Happened on the Way to the Forum," in* Women's Wear Daily, *April 3, 1972.*

DOUGLAS WATT

Exquisiteness is so much the concern of "**A Little Night Music,**" a beautifully designed and staged operetta of intimate proportions . . . that there is little room for the breath of life.

Derived from an Ingmar Bergman movie, "Smiles of a Summer Night," it takes place at the turn of the century in Sweden, where a handful of people—including a married lawyer and an actress—are caught up in the vagaries of love. Light mockery and occasional laughter float on the sweetly-scented night air, but the atmosphere is sterile. Though much of the talk and activity are given over to sex, there seems to be little of it around.

Stephen Sondheim's carefully wrought score, which never opens itself to an actual love song, is entirely in waltz time or variations on it. It is delicate in nature and creates, with its excellently shaped lyrics, something of the effect of [Maurice] Ravel's "Valses Nobles et Sentimentales" equipped with superior Broadway rhymes. The effect of Hugh Wheeler's book, on the other hand, is that of a cross between Shakespeare and [Anton] Chekhov humors with strong overtones of Broadway brashness. . . .

Everywhere, in fact, "**A Little Night Music**" reveals the work of superior theatrical craftsmanship. But stunning as it is to gaze upon and as clever as its score is, with its use of trio and ensemble singing, it remains too literary and precious a work to stir the emotions.

> *Douglas Watt, "'A Little Night Music', Operetta That's Exquisite but Fragile," in* Daily News, *New York, February 26, 1973. Reprinted in* New York Theatre Critics' Reviews, *Vol. XXXIV, No. 5, March 5-11, 1973, p. 348.*

MARTIN GOTTFRIED

"**A Little Night Music**" is exquisite to look at; it has a wonderful score; its lyrics are a model of the craft; I saw it twice, liked it better the second time, and find that what it is trying to do is more interesting than what it did, for the show has little life, little musical theatricality and little reason for its own existence. Coming as it does after their adventurous and inspired "**Company**" and "**Follies,**" the new Stephen Sondheim-Harold Prince musical . . . is a deep disappointment for me. This enormously talented team, composer-lyricist and producer-director, has been solitarily evolving the Broadway musical theater. Though a show of theirs that does not work is still beyond the talent and imagination of most everyone else who does musicals, it is depressing to find them stepping backwards and the main problem, I think, was a conceit.

The conceit was to create a musical of classical elegance, beginning with a title that represents sheer chutzpah drawn, as it is, from no less than Mozart ("Eine Kleine Nachtmusik"). The story they chose was Ingmar Bergman's charming stylish movie of sexual-romantic revolving doors, "Smiles of a Summer Night." . . .

Nevertheless, Mr. Sondheim's score is enchanting, without question his finest yet, a true progress and development for him as a composer. His melodies are strong and lyrical; his harmonies, as usual, are disarmingly grateful to Ravel; his dissonances are refreshing and effective; his varied applications of three-four time keep the songs interesting and different; the structures are nearly all of inventive length and style; his music is always singable and theatrical, doubtless due to a familiarity with the operas of Janacek. . . .

Sondheim is also the only lyricist, probably, who could have done such a score justice, and though one could quibble with a word choice here or a syllable accent there, it would be ridiculous in the face of his formidable craftsmanship, invention and poetry.

Martin Gottfried, in a review of "A Little Night Music," in Women's Wear Daily, *February 26, 1973.*

T. E. KALEM

[*A Little Night Music*] is a jeweled music box of a show: lovely to look at, delightful to listen to, and perhaps too exquisite, fragile and muted ever to be quite humanly affecting. It is a victory of technique over texture, and one leaves it in the odd mental state of unbridled admiration and untouched feelings. . . .

Nothing lends the show quite so much strength as Stephen Sondheim's score. It is a beauty, his best yet in an exceedingly distinguished career. The prevailing waltz meter is more suggestive of *fin de siècle* Vienna than the Scandinavian north, but why carp? In a show almost without choreography, Sondheim's lyrics are nimble-witted dances. Literate, ironic, playful, enviably clever, altogether professional, Stephen Sondheim is a quicksilver wordsmith in the grand tradition of Cole Porter, Noël Coward and Lorenz Hart. There are three standout numbers. One is *Liaisons* . . . , a lament that courtesans are not the elegantly larcenous creatures they used to be. Equally arresting are *Send In the Clowns* . . . , a rueful gaze into the cracked mirror of the middle years, and *The Miller's Son* . . . , a gather-ye-rosebuds-while-ye-may paean to the flesh.

T. E. Kalem, "Valse Triste," in Time, *Vol. 101, No. 11, March 12, 1973, pp. 86, 89.*

CHARLES MICHENER

Broadway is notoriously unappreciative of chance takers, but in recent years, at least, it has come to honor Sondheim's work with a regularity bordering on inevitability. . . . This year was no different: **"A Little Night Music,"** his third show in three years, was named best musical, and Sondheim walked off with the Tony for best words and music.

Which is as it should be—and shouldn't. For the embarrassment of Tonys on Sondheim's mantelpiece also points up the embarrassing state into which the Broadway musical—America's great original contribution to the theater—has fallen. Once upon a time, the musical show was Broadway's brightest beacon to the world, sweeping from Catfish Row to Siam with passionate assurance, finding ballet in floating crap games and love in the garment industry. Once, it nurtured much of the best musical talent in the country, whether it belonged to a Russian Jewish immigrant named Irving Berlin, a Yale blue blood named Cole Porter or a symphonic conductor/composer named Bernstein.

Today, the fact that the beacon is flickering at all is due mainly to the work of Sondheim and his kinetic producer-director, Harold Prince. At a time when "old" means the high camp of "No, No, Nanette" and "Irene," Sondheim is virtually alone in trying to preserve the great tradition of dramatic songwriting that Jerome Kern and Oscar Hammerstein II began more than 40 years ago with "Showboat." In an age when

"new" means the puerility of rock musicals, he is trying to update the tradition for the '70s by writing songs that are complex, sophisticated and genuinely contemporary. . . . Sondheim and Prince still believe in extravagant music dramas that try to be serious as well as spectacular, pertinent as well as diverting.

It is a precarious situation—as anyone knows who has witnessed the recent raggle-taggle parade of musical flops on Broadway. (p. 54)

Thank heaven, then, for **"A Little Night Music."** . . . **"Night Music"** examines the basic musical-comedy subject—love—in all its foolish, febrile aspects: post-adolescent love—as felt by a giddy, repressed child-bride and her gloomy, repressed stepson; middle-aged love—as felt by an actress too long wedded to the stage and a lawyer too late wedded to a young girl; badly married love—as felt by a predatory, desperate countess and her prowling, Don Juan count; carnal love—as felt by a lusty chambermaid and a lusty footman.

Hugh Wheeler's graceful book, which is faithful to most of Bergman's characters, is brought to glittering life by Prince's immaculate staging and by a skillful company of authentic singing actors. **"Night Music"** has the fine detail, the density of shadings, usually found only in good productions of Chekhov—or in a Hal Prince musical. And unlike the mordant **"Company"** and **"Follies,"** this Prince-Sondheim music drama ends unambiguously and cheerfully: each lover gets his true love, the repressed get unrepressed, the unsatisfied satisfied, the desperate undesperate.

But the warm, beating heart of this tender, witty musical for lovers and other grownups is Steve Sondheim's music and words. His music fits **"Night Music"** as perfectly as the lace-over-chiffon bodices and long skirts fit its leading ladies. In keeping with an age of grand, stylized gestures, his score is something of a tour de force: all the songs are written in a variation of triple time. To go with the show's *fin de siècle* sense of emotional unease, their chromatic melodies, sudden key shifts and haunting dissonances evoke [Richard] Strauss's "Der Rosenkavalier" and [Maurice] Ravel's "Valses Nobles et Sentimentales." Is it operatic, as some critics have suggested? A bit, perhaps, but **"Night Music"**'s music also retains a rhythmic pulse and tunefulness that keep it firmly planted in the Broadway tradition.

Sondheim has sometimes been criticized for writing "unhummable" melodies—but at least two Act II solos give the lie to this charge: **"The Miller's Son,"** a gorgeous half-ballad, half-patter song . . . , and **"Send In the Clowns,"** a moving bittersweet song, which . . . [is delivered] in the classic *diseuse* tradition of Mabel Mercer and Edith Piaf. Still, solos are the exception in **"Night Music"**—and rightly so. For how better to convey the multitracked, missed connections between lovers and rivals than to have them singing simultaneously in Sondheim's dazzling array of contrapuntal duets and trios, a quartet and even a double quintet?

Employing every lyric device at his command . . . , Sondheim stitches his words and music together like needlepoint. The effect is to dare you not to gasp at the cleverness of it. But the intention is deeper. "Steve," says playwright Arthur Laurents, who wrote the books for three previous Sondheim shows, "is the only lyricist who almost always writes songs that can only be sung by the particular character they are written for." Like their counterparts in **"Company"** and **"Follies,"** the lovers in **"Night Music"** exist, as the "chorus" describes them, in a state of "perpetual anticipation . . . Playing a role / Aching to start / Keeping control / While falling apart."

It's a lyric that Alexander Pope would have been pleased to write. But Sondheim's sense of enlightenment is 1973 Freudian, not eighteenth-century rationalist. "At least half of my songs deal with ambivalence, feeling two things at once," he says. "I like neurotic people. I like troubled people. Not that I don't like squared-away people, but I *prefer* neurotic people. I like to hear rumblings beneath the surface." Sondheim's genius transforms these rumblings into songs as bright and cutting as a lightning bolt over the New York skyline—songs like **"The Ladies Who Lunch,"** from **"Company,"** which turned the clink of Scotch-washed ice cubes into an elegy for the city's pampered but desperate women, or **"Waiting for the Girls Upstairs,"** from **"Follies,"** a moving, ironic anthem for the stage-door Johnny in all males. (pp. 54-5)

Sondheim wrote the lyrics to Bernstein's music for the epochal **"West Side Story."** He had finally arrived where he wanted to be.

Or rather half of him had. For though he considered himself "a composer first," Broadway typed him as a lyricist, and on his next show he had to settle for doing the marvelous words to Jule Styne's music for **"Gypsy,"** and hearing them sung by the great Ethel Merman. . . . Three years later, Sondheim wrote both the rollicking words and music for his third straight hit, **"A Funny Thing Happened on the Way to the Forum,"** whose co-author, Burt Shevelove, became another great mentor in his life. . . .

But after **"Forum,"** . . . Sondheim ran temporarily aground. Despite its brilliantly original score and lyrics, a 1964 show, **"Anyone Can Whistle,"** closed after nine performances, and a year later his collaboration with Richard Rodgers on **"Do I Hear a Waltz?"** proved not only financially but artistically disappointing. . . . Five years later, he came back with **"Company"**—having found the perfect collaborator in producer-director Hal Prince. (p. 61)

[It] was not until **"Company"** that they merged into what has become Broadway's most creative partnership. **"Company"** hit Broadway the way Rodgers and Hart's "Pal Joey" had done 30 years earlier—like a wake-up drink with an extra dash of Tabasco. For a musical, it charted fresh territory—the minefields of love among the urban upper-middle class. Its thrust was as knowing and penetrating as [Edward] Albee's or [Harold] Pinter's. Best of all, it accomplished what serious musical theater had been aiming at for decades: the total integration of book, music and movement into a seamless form that did not have to sacrifice either high intelligence or high entertainment. Sondheim and Prince had given the Broadway musical comedy a new lease on life. (pp. 61, 64)

Shortly after the opening of **"A Little Night Music,"** a gala benefit was held at the Shubert Theatre called **"Sondheim: A Musical Tribute."** After a glittering succession of performers had sung and danced their way through more than 40 Sondheim songs, Broadway's reigning music man sat down at the piano and, with tears streaming down his face, sang the title number from **"Anyone Can Whistle"**: "Maybe you could show me how to let go, lower my guard, learn to be free / Maybe if you whistle, whistle for me." Whereupon he was suddenly surrounded by a stageful of stars singing, from **"Company"**: "What would we do without you? How would we ever get through?" What would America's embattled musical stage do without Steve Sondheim? More than anyone else he is provid-

ing the night music that has always been the heartbeat of Broadway, and because of him the beat goes on. (p. 64)

Charles Michener, "Words and Music—by Sondheim," in Newsweek, *Vol. LXXXI, No. 17, April 23, 1973, pp. 54-6, 61, 64.*

REX REED

Authentic genius is never recognized until the genius is dead, so the saying goes, but Stephen Sondheim is proving it a lie. At forty-three he has composed the music and/or lyrics for only (!) eight Broadway shows and one television special, yet practically everybody who knows or cares anything about the subject regards him as already the most important force in American theater music since Cole Porter. His songs are witty, sardonic, intelligent, brilliantly structured, and, above all, courageous. If there's a tired old rule to be broken, he breaks it. If there's a bright new idea kicking around, he has it. And since the whole rollicking history of Broadway musicals is seemingly at his talented fingertips, when a new chord must be struck, he strikes it. All of which explains why the opening of a new show by Stephen Sondheim automatically becomes an Event.

The event at hand, the composer's latest contribution to the great tradition, is a dazzling tour de force called *A Little Night Music*. It is his most ambitiously conceived and richly creative work to date. . . . (p. 94)

Like the arcane games and puzzles Sondheim reportedly collects as a hobby, his songs are not made up of mere surfaces, their inner workings as exposed as the contents of an open-faced sandwich. They are rather like fine watches, and just as functional. They often literally take the place of dramatic scenes, with the dialogue being sung instead of spoken. And, to serve the needs of drama, they need to take many forms. The score of *Night Music*, for example, contains patter songs, contra-puntal duets and trios, a quartet, and even a dramatic double quintet to puzzle through. . . . Even when the music is least hummable—hummability isn't everything—your attention is held, waiting to pounce on the clue that will lead you into the meaning of the next song. My own favorite is *Send In the Clowns*, a ripely over-the-hill sigh . . . that throbs with worldly wisdom. And I have never heard a better set of lyrics than those for *Liaisons*, a lament croaked with sad regret by . . . an old duenna who longs for the dear dead days when people had taste and style. "Where," [she asks] . . . ruefully, "is style? Where is skill? Where is forethought? Where's discretion of the heart, or passion in the art, where's craft?" Stephen Sondheim is of course answering all these questions before we've even had a chance to let them soak in. His is the style that is happening today in theater music; he is where the craft is. His work renews my faith that whatever temporarily ails that "fabulous invalid" called Broadway, it is not terminal, and the patient will move on not only to recovery, but to better health than ever. As a matter of fact, I feel a lot better myself. Sondheim has taken the musical and dramatic values of such great predecessors as [Harold Arlen, Irving Berlin, and Cole Porter] and catapulted them into the turbulent Seventies. His music has enriched my life, and it's a tonic I fully endorse for anybody who is as fed up as I am with the clutter and clatter that is passing itself off as music these days. (pp. 94-5)

Rex Reed, "There's Hope for Broadway in a Little Sondheim," in Stereo Review, *Vol. 31, No. 1, July, 1973, pp. 94-5.*

STEPHEN SONDHEIM

It's hard to talk about lyrics independently of music, but I will try. Obviously, all the principles of writing apply to lyrics: grace, affinity for words, a feeling for the weight of words, resonances, tone, all of that. But there are two basic differences between lyric writing and all other forms, and they dictate what you have to do as a lyric writer. They are not even rules, they are just principles. First, lyrics exist in time—as opposed to poetry, for example. You can read a poem at your own speed. I find most poetry very difficult, and there are a few poets I like very much. Wallace Stevens is one, but it takes me a good 20 minutes to get through a medium-length Wallace Stevens poem, and even then I don't understand a lot of it, yet I enjoy it and can read it at my own speed. That's the point. On the stage, the lyrics come at you and you hear them once. If there's a reprise you hear them twice, if there are two reprises you hear them three times, but that's all. Quite often you've had the experience, or you've heard friends say, "Gee, I didn't get the lyric until I heard the record." Well that's the problem, you only get it once. The music is a relentless engine and keeps the lyrics going.

This leads to the second principle. Lyrics go with music, and music is very rich, in my opinion the richest form of art. It's also abstract and does very strange things to your emotions. So not only do you have that going, but you also have lights, costumes, scenery, characters, performers. There's a great deal to hear and get. Lyrics therefore have to be underwritten. They have to be very simple in essence. That doesn't mean you can't do convoluted lyrics, but essentially the thought is what counts and you have to stretch the thought out enough so that the listener has a fair chance to get it. Many lyrics suffer from being much too packed. (p. 64)

I have a book of Hammerstein's lyrics and one of Cole Porter's. Hammerstein's you fall asleep reading, while Porter's is an absolute delight, like reading light verse. "Oh, what a beautiful mornin' " is not anywhere near as much fun to read as to hear. An imitation Hammerstein lyric that I did is **"Maria"** in *West Side Story,* a lyric I am not terribly fond of except for one good line: "Maria, I've just kissed a girl named Maria." I remember when I wrote that I thought, "I can't do anything that bland and banal but I'll fix it later." Of course when it went with the music it just soared, it was perfect. The fancier part of the lyric "Say it loud and there's music playing / Say it soft . . ." etc. etc. (I'm too embarrassed to quote it) is a very fruity lyric, too much, overripe. (p. 65)

On one level, I suppose, lyric writing is an elegant form of puzzle, and I am a great puzzle fan. There's a great deal of joy for me in the sweat involved in the working out of lyrics, but it can lead to bloodlessness, and I've often been capable of writing bloodless lyrics (there are a number of them in *West Side Story*).

Anyway, all the principles extend from this one, which is lyrics existing in time. They also help shape the music, just as the music shapes them. The rigidity of lyric writing is like sonnets, and creating this rigidity makes creating characters difficult, because characters, if they are to be alive, don't tend to talk in well-rounded phrases. But on the other hand, the power that is packed into the rigid form can give it enormous punch and make the characters splat out at you. An example from my own work is **"The Ladies Who Lunch"** in *Company* which is so packed that it gives out a ferocity, mainly because I chose a fairly rigid form, full of inner rhymes and with the lines in

the music almost square—not that it's sung square, I mean the lines are very formed. (p. 66)

The major thing I got from Arthur [Laurents] was the notion of sub-text. Now, this is a word that I had heard tossed around by Actors Studio types for a long time and really rather sneered at; but what it means simply is, give the actor something to act. I think this is a real secret; if I had to sell secrets about lyric writing I would sell this secret about sub-text. Watch how even some Broadway lyrics that you admire just sit there, with nothing for the actor to play. They just play the next logical step. A playwright when he writes a scene always gives some sub-text, or it's a very shallow scene. Well, that happens with lyrics. They may be very good, but if they're just on the surface, if there's no pull, there's a kind of deadness on the stage.

This concerns dramatic lyric writing, of course, I'm not talking about the Cole Porter kind of lyric writing which I'll get to later. I'm talking about the texture of a play where you are really dealing with character. There's a song in *Follies* called **"The Road You Didn't Take"** which on the surface is a man saying, "Oh, I never look back on the past, I mean, my goodness, it just wouldn't be worth it." He's doing it to con himself as well as the lady he is with; in point of fact, he is ripped to shreds internally. Now, the actor has the ripped-to-shreds that he can play. There's also a stabbing dissonance in the music, a note in the music that tells you, the audience, that something is not quite Kosher about what this guy is saying. But more important, it gives the actor something to play. (p. 71)

I go about starting a song first with the collaborators, sometimes just with the book writer, sometimes with the director. We have long discussions and I take notes, just general notes, and then we decide what the song should be about, and I try to make a title. If I am writing the music as well as the lyric I sometimes try to get a vamp first, a musical atmosphere, an accompaniment, a pulse, a melodic idea, but usually the tone comes from the accompaniment figure, and I find that the more specific the task, the easier. If somebody says write a song about a lady in a red dress crying at the end of a bar, that's a lot easier than somebody saying write a song about a fellow who's sorry. . . . So what you want is something specific, but not too specific.

Then I usually make a list of useful rhymes related to the song's topic, sometimes useful phrases, a list of ideas that pop into my head. Then I try to make a prose statement to the point, so that it won't get lost. . . . I find it useful to write at the top of the page a couple of sentences of what the song is to be about, no matter how flimsy. (p. 72)

You should stage your numbers when you are writing them. Never just write a love song and give it to the director and the choreographer, expecting them to invent. That's not their job. That's their job *after* you've invented. When you've invented the staging they can do anything they want with it, completely change it, but they have to have at least a blueprint, some idea of the theatrical use of the song. (p. 73)

In the genesis of a song, another important principle that I've always believed in is: content dictates form. There's a song in *Company* called **"Getting Married Today."** In content, it is about this hysterical girl who doesn't want to get married except that she's forced to in her own head, so it suggested the counterpoint and the contrast between a serene choir and a hysterical lady, between the slow and the fast and the serene and the hysterical. (p. 74)

Words have to sit on music in order to become clear to the audience. I am talking about clarity, remember, and clarity has to do with that thing I talked about, time. You don't get a chance to hear the lyric twice or to read it, and if the lyric doesn't sit and bounce when the music bounces and rise when the music rises, it isn't just a question of mis-accents, which are bad enough, but if it is too crowded and doesn't rise and fall with the music, the audience becomes confused. There's a song in *West Side Story* called **"America"** and thank God it's a spectacular dance because it wouldn't get a hand otherwise. It has 27 words to the square inch. (p. 76)

You try to make your rhyming seem fresh but inevitable (I guess it's what you try for in all kinds of writing), you try for surprise but not so wrenching that the listener loses the sense of the line. (p. 83)

Another function of rhyme is that it implies education. One of the most embarrassing moments of my life as a lyric writer was after a runthrough of *West Side Story* when some of my friends including Sheldon Harnick were out front. I asked Sheldon after the show, "What do you think?" knowing he was going to fall to his knees and lick the sidewalk. But he didn't, and I asked him to tell me what was wrong. "There's that lyric **'I Feel Pretty'**" he said. Now, I thought **"I Feel Pretty"** was just terrific, I had spent the previous year of my life rhyming "day" and "way" and "me" and "be," and with **"I Feel Pretty"** I wanted to show that I could do inner rhymes too. So I had this uneducated Puerto Rican girl singing, "It's alarming how charming I feel." You know, she would not have been unwelcome in Noel Coward's living room. Sheldon was very gentle, but oh! did it hurt. I immediately went back to the drawing board and wrote a simplified version of the lyric which nobody connected with the show would accept; so there it is, embarrassing me every time it's sung, because it's full of mistakes like that. Well, when rhyme goes against character, out it should go, and rhyme always implies education and mind working, and the more rhymes the sharper the mind. (pp. 84-5)

It's always better to be funny than clever, and a lot harder. . . . In *West Side Story* there's the section in **"Gee Officer Krupke"** which uses a favorite technique of mine, parallel lines where you just make a list. . . . [**"Gee Officer Krupke"** is] not exceptionally funny on its own, but it brought down the house every night because the form helps make it funny. It was a genuine piece of humor because it depended not on cleverness but on the kids' attitudes, and that is what humor is about: character, not cleverness. (pp. 86-7)

Stephen Sondheim, "On Theater Lyrics: Theater Lyrics," in Playwrights, Lyricists, Composers on Theater, *edited by Otis L. Guernsey, Jr., Dodd, Mead & Company, 1974, pp. 61-97.*

DOUGLAS WATT

Although Sondheim's dazzling accomplishments as a rhymester appear to be uncontested, it is sometimes said that his composing doesn't measure up to his lyric writing. . . . For my part, I find Sondheim as resourceful a composer as he is a lyricist. As a writer of sophisticated show tunes, he was schooled in a theatrical tradition that reached a peak with [Richard Rodgers and Oscar Hammerstein], and he has sought to advance that tradition in the face of its seeming decline. In **"Company,"** he experimented with the genre in many provocative ways; in **"Follies,"** he openly imitated earlier song-

writers; in **"A Little Night Music"** (which contains his most successful song, **"Send in the Clowns"**), he attempted to impose stylistic unity on the score by using only three-quarter time and several of its variants. We have in Sondheim the classic figure of the innovative musician working within familiar forms, but he is all the freer to experiment because the commercial value of the songs is not the factor it would have been, say, fifteen or twenty years ago, when the sophisticated show tune—"On the Street Where You Live" and "I Could Have Danced All Night" come to mind—represented the pinnacle of popular songwriting. Such songs possess a quality—seductiveness—almost altogether absent in contemporary pop. But in Sondheim's songs—and this may contribute to the alienation some listeners feel from them—a causticity frequently undercuts the gaiety in the more bubbly numbers, while his sentimental exercises can become pretentious, as in the long-winded **"Follies"** duet **"Too Many Mornings,"** which, with its ever-shifting key and time signatures, I find self-conscious. (p. 74)

"Sondheim: A Musical Tribute" is a two-record set perpetuating a Sunday evening at the Shubert Theatre a couple of years back which celebrated Sondheim's achievements. . . . [The] recording is only intermittently enlivening, since it contains a plethora of unfamiliar pieces—songs dropped from shows, songs from a television musical, and one from an early, unproduced musical called **"Saturday Night"**—that are not especially striking in themselves, and that in the case of the television show, which was called "Evening Primrose," are simply cloying. The nadir is reached with Sondheim himself singing, to his own piano accompaniment, the unmemorable title song from **"Anyone Can Whistle,"** a flop musical of 1964. Angela Lansbury, who starred in it, offers two other numbers from it: **"A Parade in Town,"** an attractive march that was unfortunately eclipsed by a couple of other "parade" show tunes of the same period, . . . and **"Me and My Town."** Partly as a result of such indulgence, some of the more telling selections in the album are songs for which Sondheim furnished only the words—**"Do I Hear a Waltz?"** and **"We're Gonna Be All Right,"** both from **"Do I Hear a Waltz?,"** for which Richard Rodgers composed the music; **"America,"** from **"West Side Story,"** with its Leonard Bernstein score; and **"If Mama Was Married,"** from **"Gypsy,"** whose tunes were provided by Jule Styne. There are fine things from **"Company"** (the delightful female trio **"You Could Drive a Person Crazy,"** to name just one) and from **"Follies"** (. . . **"I'm Still Here"**). . . . (p. 75)

However one responds to his songs, [Sondheim] is the most arresting Broadway songwriter practicing today. (p. 77)

Douglas Watt, "Popular Records," in The New Yorker, *Vol. LI, No. 25, August 11, 1975, pp. 74-6.**

LOUIS SNYDER

Whether or not it becomes a Broadway smash with its offbeat oriental setting and treatment, **"Pacific Overtures"** may move to be a step forward in American musical theatre creativity. . . .

The show has the ingenuity, intelligence and taste of . . . previous Prince-Sondheim collaborations . . . without adhering to a traditional style or format. . . .

In one of his most intriguing and inventive scores to date, Sondheim has made use of Japanese instruments, tonal colors and rhythms to produce viable, native authenticity, without alienating the hungry show-tune ear. Although none of the nine musical numbers promise to be a hit out of context, all of the set pieces mesh into the quasi-episodic progress of the story.

"Someone in a Tree," sung by four eavesdroppers to the U.S.-Japanese peace negotiations, is a theatrically visual inspiration. **"Please Hello,"** which depicts the me-too arrival of British, Dutch, Russian, and French admirals through the newly opened Japanese door, is a cleverly contrived ensemble, tinged with musical satire. Sets of numbers called **"Poems"** and **"Prayers,"** though practically unknown in the lexicon of musical comedy, are equally moving and revelatory. . . .

To some, **"Overtures"** may seem like a bittersweet Bicentennial pill. The persistence of Presidents Fillmore and Pierce, via Commodore Perry, to reopen trade with Japan had its poignant and tragic repercussions, as the searing, all-dancing, all-Westernized finale **"Next"** emphasizes.

> *Louis Snyder, in a review of "Pacific Overtures,"*
> *in* Variety, *November 19, 1975, pp. 64-5.*

MARTIN GOTTFRIED

Stephen Sondheim's music [for **"Pacific Overtures"**], . . . is simply formidable—a huge amount of it built into sung sequences so extensive and cubic they rise from and engulf the show. Sondheim didn't pretend to write Oriental music, but instead grasped its texture and, much more importantly, the show's purposes. This is true theater music, much more melodic than one hearing suggests, and tremendously varied. The score places him at the very pinnacle of American stage composers and entirely apart from conventional theater songwriters.

His lyrics assume a great responsibility, telling as much of the story as the John Weidman-Hugh Wheeler book. They are not merely impeccable in terms of lyric writing technique, though. They seem the work of a lover of Japanese poetry and never phoney about that. I only wish they might have been as open hearted as some of the music.

> *Martin Gottfried, " 'Overtures'—A Remarkable Work of Theater Art," in* New York Post, *January 12, 1976. Reprinted in* New York Theatre Critics' Reviews, *Vol. XXXVII, No. 1, January 12-18, 1976, pp. 389-90.*

CLIVE BARNES

The translation of a culture—and a translation of a translation at that—this is only the beginning of the beguiling and sometimes bewildering complexities of the new musical **"Pacific Overtures."** . . . It is a very serious, almost inordinately ambitious musical, and as such is deserving of equally serious attention.

It is the story of what happened when "four black ships" came to "a land of changeless order." It is all about the Westernization of Japan, and, obliquely and finally, why Seiko watches are today the third largest-selling watch in Switzerland. It is about a change of scene, a change of heart—but stylistically it is also about a type of theater. . . .

[The] musical is to tell the story of Japan's Westernization as if it were a Kabuki drama—but, of course, it soon becomes much more complicated than that. Mr. Sondheim's music is in a style that might be called Japonaiserie (Leonard Bernstein

quite often seems to be trysting with Madame Butterfly in the orchestra pit) but also uses some authentic Japanese instruments.

The lyrics are totally Western and as is the custom with Mr. Sondheim—devilish, wittily and delightfully clever. Musically there is a disparity between Mr. Sondheim's operettalike elegance and ethnic overlay, but even this succeeds with all its carefully applied patina of pastiche—that on demand can embrace [Sir Arthur] Sullivan or [Jacques] Offenbach. Mr. Sondheim is the most remarkable man in the Broadway musical today—and here he shows it victoriously.

But it could be a pyrrhic victory. The form of the musical itself is perhaps not up to the seriousness of the material and the sensitivity and sensibility with which it is presented. Moreover, Mr. Weidman's book, while strikingly original, does not always rest happily within the conceptual format of the show—at times it seems as though we are well and truly in the world of Suzie Wong. . . .

There are generic and stylistic discrepancies in the musical that are not easily overlooked—but the attempt is so bold and the achievement so fascinating, that its obvious faults demand to be overlooked. It tries to soar—sometimes it only floats, sometimes it actually sinks—but it tries to soar. And the music and lyrics are as pretty and as well-formed as a bonsai tree. **"Pacific Overtures"** is very, very different.

> *Clive Barnes, "Theater: 'Pacific Overtures', Musical About Japan," in* The New York Times, *January 12, 1976, p. 39.*

JACK KROLL

"Pacific Overtures" is an audacious attempt to create a musical play by mixing American sensibility and technique with those of Japan—specifically the ancient Kabuki theater. When 28-year-old John Weidman showed Prince a play he'd written about the opening of Japan to the West in 1853 by Commodore Matthew Perry, the producer got the idea of turning it into the fourth musical of his fruitful collaboration with composer-lyricist Stephen Sondheim. The result is the most original—though not the best—product of Prince's brilliant atelier. . . .

No other team in the American theater could have achieved this show's integration of elements, its harmony of form, color, sound and movement. Sondheim's feeling for the weight and wit of measured language allows him to deftly absorb Japanese poetic forms such as haiku into his lyrics. And his parallel gift for the histrionic shapes and gestures of music lets him slip with sneaky grace between Western and Eastern modes. . . .

It was one thing for the well-matched sensibilities of Prince and Sondheim to explore the anxieties and fantasies of the urban upper-middlebrow world in **"Company"** and **"Follies."** It's quite another for them to dramatize the crucial moment of metamorphosis in an alien culture—and through the eyes of that culture. The first act is an almost total success as Prince and Sondheim blend Zen and zap to show the impact of Perry's visit on a Japan that has cut itself off from the world for more than 200 years. . . .

But in the second act a fuzzy seriousness starts to erode this synthesis of wit and warmth. And the finale is a high-kicking lecture on the evils of Westernized Japan with its transistorized culture and polluted air. Ah, poor little Nippon, you might still be floating happily among the pearls and prawns of the Pacific if we corrupt Western finks hadn't gunboated you into the modern world. This didactic bathos brings **"Pacific Overtures"** to a stumbling close, exposing a streak of cultural sentimentality that's been kept in abeyance for most of the evening by sheer theatrical creativity.

But that creativity can't be gainsaid. It produces as brilliant a first act as you'll see in any musical and a show that voluptuates with invention and sheer beauty.

> Jack Kroll, *"Zen and Zap,"* in Newsweek, *Vol. LXXXVII, No. 4, January 26, 1976, p. 59.*

PETER REILLY

[The album] **"Side by Side by Sondheim"** is a tribute, bouquet, what-have-you to the work of Stephen Sondheim, probably the most gifted and productive creative force now at work in the American lyric theater. It is a collection of songs from an astonishing career that began—at the top—with *West Side Story* (he was then only twenty-five years old) and has continued on to the recent *Pacific Overtures*.

The release ["**Side by Side**"] is a recorded version of the "musical entertainment" first presented at London's Mermaid Theatre last year by three young English performers. In the recent past we've also had original-cast recordings, from that same stage, of evenings devoted to the works of Noël Coward and Cole Porter. If this last go with Sondheim is the least successful of the three, it is so for reasons that have little to do with the quality of his work or with Ned Sherrin's direction of his three talented performers. It has to do, oddly enough, with the problem of translation. . . . Sondheim's work is so characteristic a dissection of the overexposed nerve endings and quirky responses of the genus "New Yorker" that any transplantation, either geographical or simply out of the context of such strong "books" as *Gypsy, West Side Story,* or *A Little Night Music,* is likely to disorient the audience from a necessary frame of reference. . . .

Sondheim, . . . coldly brilliant, rigidly committed to intelligence-above-all, and with the eye and ear (and heart) of a night-desk detective sergeant laying out the evidence in a crime of passion, is hardly a lighthearted boulevardier. He is New York. He is also—dare one say it?—more than a little provincial in being trapped in the very small, very select, very social reaches of New York's upper Bohemia. So much of his work reflects the attitudes of that milieu: at once clever and mistrustful, intelligent yet oddly disdainful, crisp and chic but still wildly, unpredictably (and only temporarily) sentimental. . . . [Detachment] comes through in his songs for such characters as Rose in *Gypsy,* Leona in *Do I Hear a Waltz?,* and in practically every song he wrote for every character in both *Follies* and *Company!* There is much understanding—no, *comprehension*—but little pity, gentleness, or compassion in Sondheim's work. . . .

If you really listen to Sondheim's lyrics—and you *have* to listen, they are that good—then you know that his is a very dark talent indeed, that it needs a very specific kind of instinctive, indigenous, *New York* performance to put it across. . . .

Sondheim is still, if for no more than his mastery of lyric techniques (and there *is* a great deal more), one of the contemporary greats. But what he does is quite special, traveling a course that is parallel to without being a part of the mainstream of the American musical theater. This is not, in other

words, the kind of place you want to show up at without a firm invitation.

> Peter Reilly, in a review of *"Side by Side by Sondheim,"* in Stereo Review, *Vol. 38, No. 1, January, 1977, p. 102.*

MARTIN GOTTFRIED

It's difficult to see the sense in an all-Stephen Sondheim revue being done in a Broadway theater by an all-British cast, and it was even more difficult after seeing **"Side by Side by Sondheim."** . . .

Sondheim is, of course, the most important composer and lyricist working in the American musical theater today. By "important" I mean that his contributions have gone beyond the creation of fine songs. He has added to the very structure of our musical theater, developing approaches and techniques that have expanded its possibilities.

In the process he has helped to make several landmark musicals and all of this is in addition to truly brilliant musical scores.

But true as that is, he has still written but six shows as a composer-lyricist and three as just a lyricist. That is not enough to establish him as a legendary figure as I'm sure he would be the first to insist.

Moreover, sophisticated and theatrical as his music may be, it has still not won the heart of the American people to the extent of putting him in a class with Kern or Gershwin or Berlin or Porter or Rodgers. So it is presumptuous for an all-Sondheim song revue to be presented theatrically.

It is also odd for one to be done by a strictly English company and not only because Sondheim's work is so American. The English are notoriously uncomfortable with musicals, especially our musicals. They just don't seem to be able to grasp the style, the flair, the spirit, as the **"Side by Side by Sondheim"** company is demonstrating. . . .

The songs themselves cover the Sondheim catalogue well enough. There is not a great deal of variety in tone because so much of his work takes the same attitude, but the interspersing of songs for which he wrote just lyrics helps create some variety. . . .

Several omissions were glaring: **"Rose's Turn"** from **"Gypsy"** may be the best number ever written for the American stage. **"Something's Coming"** was surely Sondheim's best lyric for **"West Side Story."** **"Every Day a Little Death"** from **"A Little Night Music,"** could well be the most serious and honest song he ever wrote for a musical. **"I'm Here"** from his TV musical, **"Evening Primrose,"** is the kind of exciting number this show needed. I don't know why none of these were done.

> Martin Gottfried, *"Foggy 'Sondheim' by British Cast,"* in New York Post, *April 19, 1977. Reprinted in* New York Theatre Critics' Reviews, *Vol. XXXVIII, No. 10, May 9-15, 1977, pp. 269-70.*

THOMAS P. ADLER

In 1974 Stephen Sondheim and Burt Shevelove collaborated on a musical adaptation of [Aristophanes's] *The Frogs.* . . . In lyrics to a song entitled **"The Sound of Poets"** that might well express their writer's own artistic credo, the Chorus [in *The Frogs*] charges the poet to

> Bring a sense of purpose,
> Bring the taste of words,
> Bring the sound of wit,
> Bring the feel of passion,
> Bring the glow of thought
> To the darkening earth. . . .

These are all things that Sondheim, the single most important force in the American musical theatre during the 1960s and 1970s, has achieved since that night twenty years ago when New York audiences first heard his lyrics in the revolutionary dance musical *West Side Story*. And if the myopic critics did not even mention his name the next morning in their notices, they have had numerous occasions since then to remedy their oversight in reviewing the nine other shows that Sondheim has been creatively involved in either as lyricist or as lyricist/composer. . . . In this paper I will test out a number of critical approaches—generic, formalist, thematic—in an attempt to assess Sondheim's contribution to the musical as a form, focusing particularly on those shows (usually done in collaboration with producer/director Hal Prince) that depart most markedly from the integrated book musical epitomized by Rodgers and Hammerstein's *Oklahoma!* and *South Pacific*. I would argue, ultimately, that Sondheim is distinct among writers for the American musical stage, in that he has a philosophy, an ideology that he continually expresses and deepens throughout his musicals and that raises them above the realm of popular entertainment—though they are, happily, still that—and places them among those works for the American stage that can be said to have not only artistic merit but a literary value as well. (p. 513)

The integrated book musical which, in theory anyway, ideally permits only those songs that either advance the plot or reveal character, is an extension or outgrowth of the representational, illusion-of-reality drama that dominated the American stage at least until the beginning of World War II (and is still a potent force today). Yet when we acknowledge that no matter how "realistic" a play is in its trappings we, as audience, are still tacitly aware that we are in a theatre watching only an "imitation of reality," pretending that we are *not* pretending, then it becomes clear that the *total* illusion-of-reality is, strictly speaking, an artificial goal—though its very artificiality opens up the possibility of its becoming art. How much more true this must necessarily be of the musical, where the suspension of disbelief must be even more complete, since most people do not go singing and dancing through life.

The aesthetic principle governing the occurrence of song in the organic book musical is analogous to that governing the use of poetry in drama. Just as poetry, according to T. S. Eliot, is appropriate in the drama only when prose is no longer capable of containing and conveying the emotion, so, too, one can justifiably break into song only when dialogue can no longer adequately express feeling or, in Sondheim's own words, "'the climaxes of emotion and action erupt into music because they can't go further without it.'" This is perhaps nowhere better evident in the musicals Sondheim has been associated with than at the end of *Gypsy*. . . . In "Rose's Turn," the boundary between the sung and the said becomes virtually indistinguishable as Mama Rose, while admitting that she pushed her daughters into show business so that they could achieve in reality what she had dreamed of accomplishing for herself, desperately pleads for her own belated chance at stardom. Her knowledge that the talent and the drive and the ego essential for success

supported and nurtured by daughter Gypsy Rose, in what Sondheim views as an imperative reversal of roles. . . . (pp. 514-15)

Developments in the non-musical drama in the 1940s and 50s in the direction of non-representational, non-illusionistic staging helped alter audience expectations about the musical theatre as well, and their demand for the integrated book musical began to wane, opening the way for acceptance of freer forms. . . . [Some of the new plays turned] a seeming liability into a definite asset, deliberately emphasizing that we are in a theatre, glorying in the theatrical form *as* form. Readily accepting non-realistic devices of staging and structure in even our serious drama, we now no longer demand that every song lyric develop the plot line or enhance character motivation. Song can become commentative (or editorial, if you like), illustrative, connective, a punctuation device or be used for exposition, or contrapuntally, or even—and this would ordinarily be anathema in the dramatic form—serve as a breather. In short, when song can once again exist for itself and still, instead of detracting from the aesthetic design and integrity of the whole, complement it, the uses of song within the musical drama become almost boundless. Martin Gottfried and others have termed this new type of musical the "concept musical." We might also, despite Sondheim's disparagement of the too exclusively didactic [Bertolt] Brecht as "'humorless . . . his points so obvious in the text itself that the songs have no surprise or wit'" . . . , call this new freer kind of musical the *"epic musical,"* if by "epic" we understand what Brecht did: a play which narrates or "relates" rather than exclusively dramatizes or "incarnates" the events. Some critics, including Emanuel Azanberg who finds shows like *Company* and *Follies* "soulless," would go so far as to attribute a dose of Brechtian alienation or estrangement to Sondheim's musicals; it seems to me, however, that Sondheim avoids this precisely because his music is, by its very nature, emotional in its appeal, and also because there almost always is, with the exception of *Pacific Overtures*—which the scenic designer Boris Aronson says flatly is "'about issues and not about people and moods'"— a central figure(s) with whom we empathize (as there often is, too, in Brecht, his theory notwithstanding).

Pacific Overtures . . . is the most unconventional of Sondheim's musical plays and, because it is political in its thrust, also the most overtly Brechtian. . . . Stylistically, it owes several debts to the Kabuki theatre: first, for its Reciter, who is alternately observer, narrator, storyteller, ironic and/or moral commentator and bridge between action and audience; second, for its black-clad stagehands who shift scenery; and finally, in its use of a *hanamichi* or runway. . . . In general, scenes without music alternate with those with music; some of them, such as the **"Day of the Rat,"** are entirely sung scenes. There are even times when we have lyric-as-poem, as in **"Your Turn,"** with its haiku-like and tanka-like forms, or the enchanting **"Someone in a Tree,"** which, built on the Berkeleyan notion that nothing exists but that it's seen or observed, stresses the importance of the least individual, or of the lesser phenomenon over the larger. . . . (pp. 515-17)

Except for a minor thread, *Pacific Overtures* lacks what most musicals consider indispensable, a love interest—which may partially account for its limited popularity. (Indeed, even when there is a love plot in his shows, Sondheim tends to eschew the love duet that has become a staple of the musical comedy form.) But the real reason for its failure with audiences—and

Weidman's book is more at fault here—quite likely resides in the inability to keep interest from waning in Act II, which is essentially no more than a series of separate scenes illustrating the thesis that capitalism and industrialization bring dehumanization in their wake, that the hallowed idea of progress has its sour notes as a culture and its beauty are destroyed, that the distorted values which we introduced to Japan have ironically come back to haunt us: for the pupil learned the master's lesson only too well and now beats the West at its own game. At the end, time is telescoped and we are suddenly thrust into the present when, in the song **"Next,"** we see the influence, particularly in things economic, that Japan today exerts over the rest of the world.

Sondheim employs song in almost as radical a fashion in *Company* . . . , which is not just his most contemporary but his most sophisticated score as well, having something of the unity and integrality, the repetition and reverberation of motifs, that we ordinarily expect only in a symphonic composition. Here, song is sometimes used for ironic comment, as in the brittle and cynically brilliant **"Ladies Who Lunch,"** that hymn to suburban matrons who fill up their empty days in empty ways, "Keeping house but clutching a copy of *Life* / Just to keep in touch"; sometimes to illustrate a scene, as in **"The Little Things You Do Together"**; sometimes to be illustrated *by* (or parallel) a scene, as is the case with **"Another Hundred People,"** a song that encapsulates the play's emphasis on the "lonely crowd syndrome," what Sondheim regards as "'the increasing difficulty of making one-to-one relationships in an increasingly dehumanized society'." . . . At other times, the song might exist outside of or divorced from the scene, perhaps for the purpose of character comment as in **"You Could Drive a Person Crazy"**—an affectionate parody of the Andrews Sisters; or it might be, all by itself, a short, self-contained playlet, a structure which Hammerstein taught Sondheim to strive after as an ideal. . . .

From what has been said thus far, one should not conclude, however, that Sondheim only rarely uses song for its traditional function of revealing character, since he displays an especial affection for what he terms the "inner monologue song," as is particularly evident in both *Follies* (1971) and *A Little Night Music* (1973). (pp. 517-18)

The triptych of songs that begins [*A Little Night Music*], all essentially soliloquies complete with subtext or "subline," demonstrates the validity of Laurents' assertion that Sondheim "'is the only lyricist who almost always writes songs that can only be sung by the particular character they are written for'." Each of these songs, like the play itself, concerns the nature of time: In **"Now,"** we see the rational mind of the middle-aged lawyer Fredrik at work, weighing each side of every question in a lyric structured on the processes of logical reasoning and the literary allusions to be expected from an educated man; in **"Later,"** the lyric is frenzied and the sound harsh, as befits his morose son Henrik, a life-denying, guilt-ridden ministerial student straining to break free of the self-control and repression that have brought him close to the edge of madness; and in **"Soon,"** the sound is lilting and melodious and the sentiments dreamy and romantic, as is Fredrik's coquettish teenage bride Anne who sings it. Even the rhyming words are tailored to the individual, with Fredrik, for instance, characteristically rhyming "imbecilities" and "possibilities" with "facilities," and "arouse her" with "trouser," "penchant" with "trenchant," and "risque" with "'A'." . . . (p. 518)

Sondheim has a great affinity for and facility with words, as is indicated by the string of rhymes, the product of a controlling and shaping intelligence, that one finds in his lyrics. The number of rhymes within the lyrics to a single song often impresses just in itself. . . . Yet quality of rhyme takes precedence over mere quantity, for by Sondheim's own criterion, "'You try to make your rhyming seem fresh but inevitable, and you try for surprise but not so wrenchingly that the listener loses the sense of the line. . . . The true function of the rhyme is to point up the word that rhymes. . . . Also, rhyme helps shape the music, it helps the listener hear what the shape of the music is. Inner rhymes, which are fun to work out if you have a puzzle mind, have one function, which is to speed the line along." . . . Here, for instance, are four extraordinarily apt and ingenious sequences of rhymes, again all from one song in *Pacific Overtures:* "Victoria," "Gloria," "euphoria," and "emporia"; "tentative," "representative," "argumentative," and "preventative"; "Czar," "caviar," and "ajar"; and "immorality," "neutrality," "extraterritoriality," and "nationality." . . .

Although in general Sondheim feels "suspicious" of alliteration and distrusts it for being too facile, he does recognize that if used "'subtly, it can be terrific. . . .'" (p. 519)

Like Cole Porter (the only other American composer/lyricist who can begin to touch Sondheim in artistry and ingenuity), Sondheim displays a fondness for allusions to real personages in his lyrics. . . . Yet Sondheim normally succeeds even better than Porter ever did in suiting the lyric line to the character singing it, which may account in large measure for why relatively few of his songs have become popular hits when divorced from the musical drama they were written for.

This is clearly evident in *Follies* . . . which centers on four major, well-developed characters and so, again, depends strongly on the interior monologue song. Its title carries both literal and metaphoric meanings, referring in the first place to a lavish stage spectacle a la Ziegfeld—so that there is always an excuse for stopping the narrative line abruptly and breaking very naturally into a musical showcase number, as in the lavish Felliniesque **"Loveland"** sequence. Yet the title refers also to the folly of love, as well as to the folly of thinking we can recapture the past and somehow live our youth over again, either as an individual person or as a nation, which Sondheim himself points to as the central theme: "'the collapse of the (American) dream'" and "'all your hopes tarnish and . . . if you live on regret and despair you might as well pack up, for to live in the past is foolish'." . . . *Follies,* like *Night Music,* becomes a Proustian investigation about the nature of time: about the decay of material things like the theatre building on the point of demolition, or of our aging physical bodies; about the changes in theatrical fashions; about the persistence of memory, and the way memory nostalgically embroiders fact, turning it into illusion and delusion. The past is palpably present on the stage, both to the ear and to the eye: to the ear in Sondheim's music, a pastiche of the show music of the past, with the composer/lyricist commenting on the various styles at the same time that he imitates them; to the eye in the presence of the ghostly showgirls, larger than life, as well as in the presence of the earlier, younger selves of the main (and even of some minor) characters, dimmer than life, who recall what the older people dreamed of becoming but did not. (pp. 519-20)

The play's central thematic statement, expressed through Ben's song **"The Road You Didn't Take,"** concerns the relationship between the passage of time and the possibility for human choice to alter the future. As one grows older, one's options grow progressively fewer, so life becomes a matter of ever-diminishing possibilities. . . . This notion of choice as determinism, what I like to call "the road not taken syndrome" after Robert Frost's famous poem—and which Sondheim evidently also had in mind—recurs frequently as a motif peculiar to American drama. . . .

Related to Sondheim's notion that it finally becomes "too late" for effective human choice must be its obverse: the implication that at some point(s) in his or her life the character can make the existential choice to appreciably alter the course of his destiny. And it is this pattern and conflict that recurs most frequently in Sondheim's musical dramas, and is usually expressed most pointedly in the penultimate song. Typically, the Sondheim musical focuses on unresponsive, vulnerable characters psychologically afraid of participating fully in life, of committing themselves to actively developing their full potential as *feeling* human beings. (p. 521)

Anyone Can Whistle (1964—again with book by Laurents) is subtitled "A Musical Fable" and is built around two premises that Shakespeare reworked again and again: first, as the lyrics to one of the songs say, that "No one's always what they seem to be"; and, second, that reason is not necessarily the highest good—that which appears to be sanity is often lunacy in disguise, and that the lunatics, the seeming fools, might turn out to be the saviors of the world. Nurse Fay Apple has charge over the Cookies, the residents of the Cookie Jar for the Socially Pressured, the local loony bin. These inmates (who bear the surnames of such famous artists and philosophers as Brecht, Chaplin, Engels, Freud, Gandhi, Ibsen, Kierkegaard and Mozart) have been committed because "they . . . made other people nervous by leading individual lives." . . . Eventually, they are proved to be as sane or saner than those running free on the streets—or those sitting in the audience when, in a Pirandelloesque sleight-of-hand accomplished through lighting effects at the end of Act One, the actors become the audience and the audience become the characters in the play. Sondheim, himself an inveterate game player, uses lyric word puzzles or nonsense syllogisms to illustrate the premise that the reasonable is often unreasonable: "The opposite of Left is right, / The opposite of right is wrong, / So anyone who's Left is wrong, right?" . . .

Fay, a firm believer in science, reason, control, cannot let go of her inhibitions and live, and so desperately needs a miracle to show her the way. She pleads with Dr. Hapgood—actually a loony in disguise who knows that "Either you die slowly or have the strength to go crazy." . . . Under his guidance, Fay learns that the nonconformists are the strength of the world, that we must change the world to accommodate people and not vice versa; and for herself she learns to dance, to commit herself to Hapgood, and finally even to whistle, as a real, miraculous rainbow of water gushes from the rock to underscore her change. Although *Whistle* was neither a popular nor total artistic success, it has developed a cult following over the years; if its concept is overly complex and in need of simplification, if its music is overly derivative of Bernstein, and if perhaps it is ultimately the victim (if such a thing is possible) of an excess of imagination, it was, nevertheless, undoubtedly a pivotal experiment in Sondheim's development as an artist.

In *Company,* every bit as much a landmark musical as *Oklahoma!*, the thirty-fiveish bachelor Robert is psychologically afraid of committing himself to marriage; instead, he defensively chooses to be a visitor, an appendage, in the lives of his married friends. . . . He [finally] opts for marriage in a bril-

liantly dramatic soliloquy song called **"Being Alive,"** in which he works to a new position intellectually and emotionally, from shying away from "Someone you have to let in, / Someone whose feelings you spare," to desperately pleading that "Somebody crowd me with love, / Somebody force me to care," since "alone is alone, not alive." . . . He does not reach his affirmation easily or facilely because he possesses the maturity to see the darker side of committing oneself totally to another person: the risks of being "used" selfishly or of being "hurt," of being encroached upon, or of being emotionally naked. (The show's unromantic and unsentimental treatment of marriage would, by itself, make it stand out from most other musicals.)

Company, which might be seen as a modern psychomachia, ends as it began, with the other characters wishing Robert a "Happy Birthday" as the new light comes up at dawn. It is a *birth*-day for Robert; he has "put on the new man," become morefully human. As Joanne, the chief catalyst, says, "you'll (n)ever be a kid again, kiddo." . . . Perhaps, in light of *Company,* we can even see how *Pacific Overtures* relates to Sondheim's more personal musicals: To move from isolation always implies the risk of compromise, of some loss of integrity and individuality; yet it also includes possibilities for development that never existed before, and the opportunity for real growth outweighs the risks.

Finally, in *Night Music,* a minor character, Petra the maid, rather than a major figure, expresses the recurrent thematic motif through the song, **"I Shall Marry the Miller's Son."** In it she reveals that she will eventually submit herself to the rhythms of life and, through the ritual of marriage, assume her proper place in the social and cosmic orders. But "in the meanwhile," she will "celebrate what passes by," so that when she dies she will at least have lived. . . . This emphasis on celebrating everything in life, no matter how small or seemingly trivial . . . should be seen as more than simply a hedonistic, *carpe diem* attitude; it—and the similar ideas in *Waltz*—really stand closer to the Shakespearean notion of things brought to completion in the fullness of time. For the awareness of death as the fitting culmination of Nature's unending process of birth, life and love hangs over the end of *Night Music,* since Madame Armfeldt dies in the third smile of the summer's night, accepting death as the final thread in life's fabric, secure in the knowledge that she has passed some of her store of wisdom on to her young granddaughter Frederika. She also knows that the foolish lovers are now wiser, too, as they waltz across the stage "at last with their proper partners" . . . , in a ritualized dance symbolic of regeneration. Nature's pattern, seen even in the temporarily unsettling condition of perpetual sunlight, becomes, therefore, the real hero of the play.

The taste of words, wit, passion, especially that very rare ingredient in a musical, the glow of thought—Sondheim displays all these gifts in abundance throughout his dramas. So the American musical theatre has him to thank today for "being alive," and what is more, for being *adult.* (pp. 522-24)

Thomas P. Adler, "The Musical Dramas of Stephen Sondheim: Some Critical Approaches," in Journal of Popular Culture, *Vol. XII, No. 3, Winter, 1978, pp. 513-25.*

HOWARD KISSEL

What distinguishes **"Sweeney Todd"** from simple Victorian dramaturgy is its deliberate theatricality, its desire not just to scare us, but to invest the horror with irony. Nineteenth-century realism assumed its audience was naive and innocent; post-Brechtian theater presumes its audience is theatrically knowing and socially guilty. . . .

Sondheim's score reinforces this complex emotional (or anti-emotional) structure. In some ways it is his most melodic, richest work—yet, even at its lushest moments, the context never lets the music seem merely "beautiful." The tenderest moment, musically, for example, is a love song the vengeful barber sings to his razor. Another lovely song, **"Pretty Ladies,"** is one Todd sings to distract the "customer" whose throat he most wants to slit. As one would expect, the score is full of wit and sardonic humor—the first act closes brilliantly with a duet in which Todd and his neighbor discuss how the professions of their victims might affect the flavor of the meat pies.

The score overflows with ensemble numbers, many of which create haunting effects with harmonies in falsetto voices. The choral writing is particularly stunning, building as it often does from somber, monochromatic lines into glorious chords that, as my companion noted, have a "Dies Irae" quality, Sondheim's work will doubtless be described as "operatic," a term I find confusing—for me, opera, at its best, is simply the highest form of theater, a way of capturing all the energy, all the emotional rhythms of the drama, in music. If that is what "operatic" means, **"Sweeney Todd"** is marvelously operatic. . . .

"Sweeney Todd" is not just a musical—it is total theater, a brilliant conception and a shattering experience.

> *Howard Kissel, in a review of "Sweeney Todd," in* Women's Wear Daily, *March 2, 1979.*

RICHARD EDER

The musical and dramatic achievements of Stephen Sondheim's black and bloody **"Sweeney Todd"** are so numerous and so clamorous that they trample and jam each other in that invisible but finite doorway that connects a stage and its audience; doing themselves some harm in the process.

That is a serious reservation, and I will get back to it. But it is necessary to give the dimensions of the event. There is more of artistic energy, creative personality and plain excitement in **"Sweeney Todd"** . . . than in a dozen average musicals.

It is in many ways closer to opera than to most musicals; and in particular, and sometimes too much for its own good, to the Brecht-Weill "Threepenny Opera." Mr. Sondheim has composed an endlessly inventive, highly expressive score that works indivisibly from his brilliant and abrasive lyrics.

It is a powerful, coruscating instrument, this muscular partnership of words and music. Mr. Sondheim has applied it to making a Grand Guignol opera with social undertones. He has used a legend commemorated in broadsheets, and made into a half-dozen 19th-century play versions; and most recently into a modern version written by Christopher Bond and shown in London in the early 70's.

It is the story of a barber, unjustly convicted and transported to Australia by a wicked judge who coveted his wife. Upon his return the barber takes the name Sweeney Todd, and takes his general and particular revenge by slitting the throats of his clients, who are then turned into meat pies by his industrious associate, Mrs. Lovett.

Mr. Sondheim and his director, Harold Prince, have taken this set of rattletrap fireworks and made it into a glittering, dangerous weapon. With the help of Hugh Wheeler, who adapted the book from Mr. Bond's play, they amplify every grotesque and exaggerated detail and step up its horsepower. . . .

In stylized attitudes, and gutter costumes, a whole London underworld appears, serving, in the manner of the Threepenny Opera, as populace and as sardonic chorus. In cut-off, laconic phrases they sing verses of the Sweeney Todd ballad; a work whose musical strength is deliberately bitten off until it swells out in the bloody finale. . . .

Mr. Sondheim's lyrics can be endlessly inventive. There is a hugely amusing recitation of the attributes given by the different professions—priest, lawyer, and so on—to the pies they contribute to. At other times the lyrics have a black, piercing poetry to them.

His score is extraordinary. From the pounding Sweeney Todd Ballad, to a lovely discovery theme given to Todd's young friend, Anthony, in various appearances, to the most beautiful Green Finch and Linnet Bird sung by Joanna, Todd's daughter, and through many others, Mr. Sondheim gives us all manner of musical strength. . . .

There is very little in **"Sweeney Todd"** that is not, in one way or other a display of extraordinary talent. What keeps all its brilliance from coming together as a major work of art is a kind of confusion of purpose.

For one thing, Mr. Sondheim's and Mr. Prince's artistic force makes the Grand Guignol subject matter work excessively well. That is, what needs a certain disbelief to be tolerable—we have to be able to laugh at the crudity of the characters and their actions—is given too much artistic power. The music, beautiful as it is, succeeds, in a sense, in making an intensity that is unacceptable.

Furthermore, the effort to fuse this Grand Guignol with a Brechtian style of sardonic social commentary doesn't work. There is, in fact, no serious social message in Sweeney; and at the end, when the cast lines up on the stage and points to us, singing that there are Sweeneys all about; the point is unproven.

These are defects; vital ones; but they are the failures of an extraordinary, fascinating, and often ravishingly lovely effort.

> *Richard Eder, "Stage: Introducing 'Sweeney Todd',"*
> *in* The New York Times, *March 2, 1979, p. C3.*

EDWIN WILSON

No matter how divided audiences are on the new musical **"Sweeney Todd"**—and they are likely to be sharply divided—few will be able to deny its enormous impact. It comes across as forcefully as any musical in recent memory.

The division will be largely over the musical's subject matter. . . .

"Sweeney Todd" incorporates all the contrasting cliches of 19th Century melodrama: the corrupt rich (the judge) versus the downtrodden; the evil versus the innocent (Sweeney's daughter Johanna, in a straw bonnet and long blond curls, is the essence of Victorian purity); a sordid daily existence versus dreams of escape. Two of the most effective, as well as most melodic, songs in **"Sweeney Todd"** deal with fantasies of a better life. In one, Mrs. Lovett describes to Sweeney what a beautiful life they could lead at a resort **"By the Sea."** In another, a young assistant to Mrs. Lovett, not knowing of her complicity with Sweeney, paints a picture of happiness for the two of them together. No harm will come to her, he sings, **"Not While I'm Around."**

A major part of the evening is sung, and that which is not is often accompanied by music. Mr. Sondheim's score—in its range, in its depth, in its rightness—is probably his best so far. . . .

There are times, especially at the climax, when the audience's emotions are flooded by sights and sounds so powerful that the effect is one usually achieved only in opera.

Whether for the controversy of its subject matter or the artistry of its presentation, **"Sweeney Todd"** will be talked about for a long time to come.

> *Edwin Wilson, "Sondheim Writes a Musical to Talk About," in* The Wall Street Journal, *March 6, 1979, p. 22.*

JOHN BEAUFORT

British Grand Guignol meets Broadway spectacular in **"Sweeney Todd, the Demon Barber of Fleet Street."** But the "musical thriller" based on British playwright Christopher Bond's 1973 adaptation attempts to do more than shock and horrify the spectator. The sophisticated team of director Harold Prince, composer-lyricist Stephen Sondheim, and librettist Hugh Wheeler has attempted to translate the lurid theatricalism of Grand Guignol into a form approaching grand opera. The result is a horror-comic epic employing song for much of its unfoldment. . . .

Besides retelling the gruesome tale of the demon barber, **"Sweeney Todd"** seeks to set forth a parable about the squalid horrors of an England where grinding poverty pays the price of prosperity and where the law distinguishes between rich and poor. For those unfamiliar with the Victorian "penny dreadful," Sweeney . . . disposes of his victims with the help of a Mrs. Lovett . . . , who grinds up the remains as filling for her meat pies. . . .

The Sondheim score is a dazzling achievement of variety and invention. Along with its minor-key dissonances, it includes tenderly romantic solos and duets for the hero and heroine as well as rich choral passages. For macabre humor, nothing equals the duet in which Sweeney and Mrs. Lovett appraise the lady's pies. . . .

The lurid make-believe of **"Sweeney Todd"** is certainly not for all playgoers. And some may complain that this musical version overreaches itself. Yet by any Broadway standard, this is a triumph of audacious theatricalism.

> *John Beaufort, "Grand Guignol to Music," in* The Christian Science Monitor, *March 7, 1979, p. 16.*

JACK KROLL

In sheer ambition and size, there's never been a bigger musical on Broadway than **"Sweeney Todd,"** the latest in the astonishing series of collaborations between composer-lyricist Stephen Sondheim and director Harold Prince. As for achievement, well, it has to be said again—these men and their collaborators must be judged by the standards they themselves have set, the highest standards in the American professional theater. Judged thereby, **"Sweeney Todd"** is brilliant, even

sensationally so, but its effect is very much a barrage of brilliancies, like flares fired aloft that dazzle and fade into something cold and dark. This "musical thriller" about a homicidal barber, a tonsorial Jack the Ripper in Dickensian London, slashes at the jugular instead of touching the heart. . . .

Sondheim has been inching closer and closer to pure opera, and **"Sweeney Todd"** is the closest he's come yet. The show's texture is almost entirely musical, flowing from song to song over a glittering orchestral fabric woven of Sondheim's eloquent melodies. . . . Sondheim ranges wide, from the stark, dark **"Ballad of Sweeney Todd"** to the yearning love song **"Johanna"** to the apocalyptic **"City on Fire,"** when London erupts in a spurt of lunacy and gore.

The central mood is a sardonic nihilism, most effective when the homicidal barber sings lovingly to his "friend," the gleaming razor, and when Todd and Mrs. Lovett sing a show stopping catalog of the people of many different professions—a priest, poet, lawyer, squire and royal marine—who will end up as filling for their meat pies.

The problem is one of concept and unity: **"Sweeney Todd"** wants to make the same fusion of popular and high culture that Brecht and Weill made in "The Threepenny Opera." But the fusion is never really made. There's Broadway in the fun and games of the meat-pie song, in which Mrs. Lovett asks Todd if he prefers to eat a general "with or without his privates." And there's Brecht in another song, which proclaims: "The history of the world, my sweet / Is who gets eaten and who gets to eat."

There's something emotionally and intellectually equivocal about the show's swing from a dubious pessimism at the start, when Sondheim characterizes London as "a hole in the world like a great black pit / And it's filled with people who are filled with shit," to the easy moralizing at the end, like a taming of Oscar Wilde: "To kill for love is such a thrill / You don't even notice you lose what you kill." This equivocating gets most uncomfortable in the figure of Johanna, who is treated both tenderly as the endangered innocent and satirically as the Victorian virgin, her head positively infested with Shirley Temple curls.

Nevertheless, as an exhibition of sheer theatrical talent, **"Sweeney Todd"** must be seen by anyone who cares about the gifts and risks of Broadway at its best. (p. 101)

> *Jack Kroll, "The Blood Runs Cold," in* Newsweek, *Vol. XCIII, No. 11, March 12, 1979, pp. 101, 103.*

JOHN LAHR

Much of the hope for the musical's survival resides in the acerbic intelligence of Stephen Sondheim, whose tenth musical, *Sweeney Todd,* opened in New York [in the winter of 1979]. In collaboration with his director/producer, Hal Prince, Sondheim has given a sense of occasion back to the musical and moved it away from the Shubert Alley formula of "no girls, no gags, no chance." . . . Sondheim has become the American musical: a king on a field of corpses.

Traditional musicals dramatize the triumph of hope over experience. Characteristic of their flirtation with modernism, Sondheim's shows make a cult of blasted joys and jubilant despairs. He admits that joy escapes him. "If I consciously sat down and said I wanted to write something that would send people out of the theater *really* happy, I wouldn't know how to do it.'' His mature musicals sing about a new American excellence: desolation. . . .

Sondheim's early lyrics mined the familiar mainstream vein of hope and attainment, and gave the musical eloquent expressions of its bourgeois dream. The sense of anticipation—that peculiarly American expectation of a magical insulation from life (true love, fame, money)—was superbly defined in **"Something's Coming"** from Sondheim's first Broadway show, *West Side Story* [1957]. . . .

In 1959 *Gypsy* gave voice to the mythology of pluck and luck that show business acts out. With the hyperbole of [John F.] Kennedy's New Frontier racing the heart of the nation, skepticism was as ''un-American'' in the theater as it was in the society. Whatever small irony the songs gave to the characterization of Rose and her girls in their uphill battle to show-biz fame and fortune, their message was clear: **"Everything's Coming Up Roses."** (p. 72)

After *Gypsy,* Sondheim's next three musicals, although experimental in lyric technique, were still very much part of the Broadway mainstream. *A Funny Thing Happened on the Way to the Forum* (1962), a smash hit, used songs as respites from hilarious action; *Anyone Can Whistle* (1964) was a legendary mess that tried to make songs comment on the action; and *Do I Hear a Waltz?* (1965), his uninspired collaboration with the granddaddy of the traditional musical, Richard Rodgers, left Sondheim wondering why such musicals needed to be mounted. . . . (p. 73)

[*Company* (1970) was] a musical in tune with the new, winded, post-protest times. Sondheim had come of age: his own diminished sense of life and guarded emotions were now shared by a nation obsessed with its despair. Sondheim's glib toughness echoed the mood of the unromantic era. He became a phenomenon new to the Broadway musical: a laureate of disillusion.

A society that feels itself irredeemably lost requires a legend of defeat. And Sondheim's shows are at the vanguard of this atmosphere of collapse. He shares both the culture's sense of impotence and its new habit of wrenching vitality from madness. He is a connoisseur of chaos. (*Sweeney Todd* revels in murder.) Sondheim's musicals do not abandon the notion of abundance, only adapt it. They show Americans a world still big, but in death-dealing, not well-being.

Sondheim's mature scores mythologize desolation. *Company* chronicles the deadening isolation of city life. *Follies* (1971) records in pastiche the death of the musical and dramatizes the folly of aspiration by staging the theatrical ''ghosts'' of the past. *A Little Night Music* (1973)—more attenuated and bitter than Ingmar Bergman's *Smiles of a Summer Night,* on which it is based—depicts love among the ruins of a decadent and rootless Swedish aristocracy. And *Pacific Overtures* (1975) shows the destruction of Japanese culture through the encroachment of the West. (pp. 73-4)

Most of Sondheim's characters are numbed survivors whose songs examine fear, loss, betrayal, and anger. At the finale of *Company,* the central figure realizes he needs to make a human connection. . . .

It is a passive climax. The spirit doesn't soar, it surrenders. Life is no longer dramatized as an adventure but as a capitulation. Impotence reigns, and all that is left to man's abused freedom is to justify its debasement. Laceration replaces longing as the popular delirium, and, typically, **"Being Alive"** lets

the public applaud its emptiness: "Somebody force me to care, / Somebody let me come through."

The theme of the dead heart trying to resuscitate itself dominates much of Sondhiem's work. . . . The heart is so well defended from hurt that little can penetrate it. Instead of celebrating the ease and spontaneity of emotion that was the stock-in-trade of the traditional musical responding to a world it insisted was benign, Sondheim's songs report the difficulty of feeling in a world where, as his song says, there's ''so little to be sure of.'' . . .

As Sondheim dramatizes again and again, commitment is something in which he has no faith. He is at a loss for compelling words about love. He has publicly denounced **"I Feel Pretty"** from *West Side Story* [see excerpt above]: ''Somebody doesn't have something to say.'' Sondheim's judgment of his song could be leveled at the emotional impoverishment of a great deal of his work. In his large and impressive catalogue, most of the love songs are written in collaboration with other composers . . . whose music has a melodic grace Sondheim's music lacks. Sondheim can be brilliant in his diagnosis of the failure of relationships, but never quite believable about their success. Romance, once the bread and butter of the musical, is now only stale crumbs on Sondheim's table.

While words for passion fail him, those for rage come easily. In the loveless and faithless worlds he writes about, anger is the surest test of feeling. Sondheim's scores bristle with the bitchy irony of deep-dish journalism. (Both make profit in exploiting pain.) Sondheim uses wit to sell his anger. In a superb song like **"The Ladies Who Lunch,"** from *Company,* Sondheim lets mockery have a field day. With her checklist of the various bourgeois pastimes, the sozzled singer uses anger to stir things up and create the illusion of movement in a stalled life. . . .

Mockery is disillusion in action; but by the time Sondheim brought it to Broadway it had been accepted in American life. . . . The youth culture made mockery a ''life-style.'' . . . Their satire identified the social cancer. But Sondheim never lets his maliciousness go beyond the wisecrack. The jeers at marriage in **"The Little Things You Do Together"** (from *Company*) are as facile as they are smug. By making delightful his disgust with family, Sondheim sells the sickness while others before him sold the antidote. . . . (p. 74)

The metaphor for *Company,* Sondheim wrote recently in *The Dramatists Guild Quarterly,* was New York City: ''We were making a comparison between a contemporary marriage and the island of Manhattan.'' The traditional musical made the city into a the playground, from which the characters emerged undaunted and invigorated by New York's obstacles. Manhattan, *Company* suggests, is a lethal, suffocating battlefield where survival hardens the heart and infects all contact with desperation. Now, the battle is shown as hardly worth the prize. Sondheim put it brilliantly in **"Another Hundred People."** . . . (pp. 74, 76)

This song captures New York as the contemporary middle-class audience experiences it. The answering service, the television, the intercom, the beeper—all the devices that keep urban dwellers ''in touch'' also help them hide. They magnify the citizens' terrifying isolation. As Sondheim's song says, New York is ''a city of strangers,'' its frantic pace at once a distraction and a destiny. If there is no peace here, at least there is exhaustion—a state of collapse where neither the dead heart nor a death-dealing society matters. *Company* exalts fatigue; *Follies* exploits its cultural manifestation: nostalgia. . . .

[*Follies*] sets the musical dreams of the past against the brutal actualities of the performers' present lives. It is an extravaganza of irony. In its delectation of decay, *Follies* puts older stars . . . back on the boards. This crude juxtaposition trades on nostalgia to make a point about it, and them. But *Follies'* appetite for carrion is at once breathtaking and sinister. . . . In making death the subject of story and song, *Follies* also makes it spectacular. The audience is asked not only to watch decay, but to *love* it. Sondheim's **"I'm Still Here,"** . . . turns devastation into delight. . . .

Follies' disenchantment isn't convincing because it hungers for traditional success. ("In America today," said *Follies'* co-director and choreographer, Michael Bennett, a few years after the show, "either you're a star or you're nobody.") The show's numbers take their energy not from what they ironically reveal about their characters, but from their vision of the old mythic forms dusted off and lovingly put before an audience. "It's a schizophrenic piece," Sondheim says. "And it's supposed to be." But the split in the show's consciousness is deeper than he realizes. *Follies* is paralyzed by the nostalgia it wants to expose. "Hope doesn't grow on trees," a character says at the end. "You make your own." That's what the musical has always believed. *Follies* wants to detach itself from the form and content of the traditional musical, but manages only to return to the *status quo ante*.

Before it was art, the musical was fun. In trying to push the musical toward greater artiness, Sondheim's shows have lost much of their fun. As a lyricist, Sondheim disdains the enchanters. . . . But in their technical expertness, Sondheim's songs often lose in resonance what they try to gain in statement. "The danger of argument in verse," [W. H.] Auden warns in *The Dyer's Hand,* "is that verse makes ideas too clear and distinct." Sondheim polishes every idea; the result is lucid and cold. . . . (p. 76)

"Anybody can rhyme 'excelsior' and 'Chelsea or'," Sondheim has said. "I'd rather have an ear-catching rhyme." This is more clever than clear. Sondheim speaks proudly of how his songs define and advance the characters in his musicals. But what distinguishes the characters in most of his later work is that they have no character. As he himself has pointed out, "In *Company* we were up against one of the oldest dramatic problems in the world: how do you write about a cipher without making him a cipher? In *Follies* we deliberately decided not to create characters with warts and all. Everybody would be, not a type, but an essence. . . . *Pacific Overtures* was an attempt to tell a story that has no characters at all." Sondheim makes an asset out of a liability and calls it a breakthrough. (pp. 76, 78)

Of all Sondheim's shows, *Company* is the most substantial. The limitations in Sondheim's music—its cold technique, its nervousness about emotion, its stylish defensiveness—match the brittle world *Company* describes. It is not the absence of hits—**"Send in the Clowns"** is one of his few—but the lack of heart in Sondheim's music that has been his real nemesis. His music never risks embarrassment. Instead, he hides his deepest feelings behind style, which keeps both his music and his musicals from as yet reaching their fullness. . . .

To many people, including Bernstein, **"Send in the Clowns"** augured a breakthrough, the emergence of a personal language at once passionate and penetrating. But this now seems unlikely. *Pacific Overtures* followed *A Little Night Music,* another "smart" idea that allowed Sondheim to dodge deep personal feelings in a virtuoso display of technique. *Sweeney Todd* updates his boulevard nihilism. It makes an opera of cannibalism and gore, but without a shudder. . . . Death is now resolutely Sondheim's dominion; but even his appetite for blood is bloodless. Death, what Henry James called "that distinguished thing," is turned into shallow camp in a world where evil holds no odium and life no significance.

From My Lai to Guyana, the American public has become casual about absorbing catastrophe. And Sondheim has turned this numbed anguish into a mass product. Too chic to register disapproval, Sondheim is an entrepreneur of modern anxieties. His musicals claim victory for themselves as new departures, but they are the end of the musical's glorious tradition of trivialization. Sondheim's cold elegance matches the spiritual pall that has settled over American life. His musicals are chronicles in song of the society's growing decrepitude. They foreshadow the newest barbarism—a nation that has no faith in the peace it seeks or the pleasure it finds. (p. 78)

> John Lahr, "Sondheim's Little Deaths," in Harper's,
> Vol. 258, No. 1547, April, 1979, pp. 71-4, 76, 78.

ALAN RICH

Sweeney Todd, the demon barber of Fleet Street, has suffered the wrongs of a corrupt society and, with his trusty razor, dispatches an impressive number of Londoners in his one-man war of vengeance. Yet, in the musical masterpiece [*Sweeney Todd*] . . . , there is yet another victim: Stephen Sondheim, who has had the audacity to be brilliant in an artistic medium where mediocrity is highly prized, and unclassifiable in a world divided by journalists into neat categories.

This is Sondheim's second brilliant, unclassifiable show in a row, and *Sweeney Todd* repeats almost every error that consigned *Pacific Overtures* to the dustbin after its pathetically short run three seasons ago. . . . [Once] again Sondheim has created an abrasive and complex musical score, with tunes that refuse to fall into easy-to-remember patterns and lyrics that demand the exercise of attention and memory. What is it with Sondheim & Company, one may justifiably ask: a death wish? . . .

[Whether or not *Sweeney Todd* is an opera] is a question that richly deserves to be begged—or, better yet, banned. For years Broadway's journeyman journalists have flung "opera" as an awestruck compliment at any score that cannot be whistled on first hearing (including, ironically, Sondheim's own *Anyone Can Whistle*). And, for just that many years, Broadway's ticket-buying public has taken the reviewers' "opera" as a synonym for "plague."

Call his work by whatever name you wish, it is Sondheim's level of creativity—beginning, actually, with the vastly underrated *Anyone Can Whistle* in 1964—that has sustained the hope of many serious critics that perhaps something like a free and innovative musical drama might someday eventuate in commercial theater. Lord knows there hasn't been much outside of Sondheim to sustain that hope. And from a serious critical standpoint, Sondheim *as composer/lyricist*—apart, that is, from the somewhat variable quality of the books—has steadily risen in stature, in variety of technique mastered, in subtlety and genuine depth of style from *Anyone Can Whistle* to *Sweeney Todd.* (p. 80)

Whistle was astounding for its vitality and, specifically, for its many extended scenes in which music and action moved continuously from one set of materials to another, as against the customary song-dialogue-song format, Yet, how much more freely Sondheim was later to manage this matter of musical continuity—the **"Girls Upstairs"** scene from *Follies,* **"Weekend in the Country"** from *A Little Night Music,* the gorgeously conceived **"Chrysanthemum Tea"** and **"Something in a Tree"** scenes from *Pacific Overtures,* and now virtually all of *Sweeney Todd.*

It is this continuity above all—and you're perfectly welcome to think of it as operatic if it makes you any happier—that give his latest show its almost breathless momentum.

In a sense, the entire score is a musical unit, given its shape by the **"Ballad of Sweeney Todd"** that introduces the show, closes it off, and recurs at key moments along the way. The device is that of the *"Morität"* in the Brecht-Weill *Dreigroschenoper,* but Sondheim's musical style owes nothing to this earlier model. His ballad is, in fact, a set of marvelously spooky choral variations on a theme unmistakably derived from the Gregorian Dies Irae, each variation a brilliantly devised change both of music and of character.

The scope of *Sweeney Todd* is broader than anything he has yet dealt with. The setting—Dickensian London, its milling crowds, its folk tunes and street cries, the Victorian blandnesses of its young peoples' love songs—gives him the chance to create an uncommonly full background of genre pieces to set off the bitter ironies of the story up front. Some of the music for the juveniles has an ingenuousness, an almost childlike quality, that was first tried out, I would guess, in the **"Pretty Lady"** in *Pacific Overtures;* I don't recall anything like it in earlier scores. Toward the end there is a neat parody of your basic "row dow diddle dow day" parlor ballad, here used with devastating effect to offset a moment of high dramatic conflict.

But the great music in *Sweeney Todd* is the stupendous, iridescent suite of numbers for the principals: Len Cariou as Sweeney, invested by his music, if not always by the book, as a figure of genuine lyric, tragic stature; Angela Lansbury in the role of her life as the piemaker who cooks up a method of disposing of the barber's victims. They are cleverly introduced in successive songs: Sweeney's apostrophe to London, "a hole in the world like a great black pit," hard by Mrs. Lovett's wrenching lament about her "worst pies in London." From this initial mismating of sentiments the movement—musical, dramatic, lyrical, however it may be taken—of these two characters toward a mingling of purpose, culminating in the sweeping waltz ("A little priest . . .") that brings down the first curtain, seems almost like an unbroken line, and the effect is dazzling. That waltz, by the way, is a wonder; its lyrics a paean to the joys of cannibalism; its icy, slithering music a panoply of creative heat. (pp. 80-1)

> Alan Rich, *"Sweeney Todd Triumphs on Disc,"* in *High Fidelity, Vol. 29, No. 8, August, 1979, pp. 80-1.*

WILLIAM ANDERSON

Sondheim based his musical version [of *Sweeney Todd*] on a recent London stage play, and it is a positive feast (!) for English majors. There are traces of Jonathan Swift (his icily ironic *Modest Proposal*), of the *Beggar's Opera* (the Brecht version, not the life-celebrating John Gay original), of Charles

Dickens' pestilential nineteenth-century London, of [William] Hogarth's prints, France's Grand Guignol theater of horror, and even *I Remember Mama* (the culinary secret of her meatballs). . . . The relentless misanthropy ("The history of the world . . . is who gets eaten and who gets to eat"), the lewdness, the venality, and the scatological language of the play are relieved only by the blackest of comedy. . . .

Wild horses couldn't drag me to see this depressing spectacle again, and I mightily resisted listening to the original-cast album. . . .

But what is the message? Why, simply what Utopian pastoralists from William ("dark Satanic mills") Blake to the latest anti-nuke Luddites have tried to tell us for years: the Industrial Revolution Was a Big Mistake, for it has brutalized all mankind. They may very well be right, but it is a considerable irony that this message is addressed to and (if understood) endorsed by (*eight* Tonys, remember) an urban audience that wouldn't know the difference between a manure spreader and a butter churn and that would rather die or pay $5 a gallon (whichever comes first) than empty their three-car garages. *There's* a Zeitgeist for you!

> William Anderson, *"Sweeney and the 'Zeitgeist',"* in Stereo Review, *Vol. 43, No. 2, August, 1979, p. 7.*

PAUL WITTKE

Sondheim's lyric ancestors are Oscar Hammerstein, Cole Porter, Noël Coward, and W. S. Gilbert. He may lack Porter's and Coward's nonchalant gaiety, irreverent fun, and rueful melancholy, and Hammerstein's compassion and rugged simplicity, but he is more than their equal (and Gilbert's) in verbal felicity. Sondheim's wit is mordant, intellectual, edgy rather than funny, the hard-hitting repartee of contemporary New York. (p. 309)

Sondheim incorporates disparate styles [of other composers] . . . into a style purely his own. Furthermore, he shapes each score to an individual sound that belongs to that show alone.

In *Company,* Sondheim forged a style of pop influenced by rock that captured the staccato beat of Manhattan; the pastiche music of *Follies* is a valentine to his great Broadway predecessors; and *A Little Night Music* is a wormwood operetta, entirely composed of variants of the Viennese waltz.

Pacific Overtures, a turning point in Sondheim's career, discarded plot and embodied only an idea—corruption disguised as a political process. It was all gesture within the self-defined framework of Kabuki theater. The score carried the entire weight; while the lyrics advanced the dramatic movement, the music commented on the interior drama of the characters, saying what they dared not, telling what was really happening behind its placid façade. In this respect, it foreshadowed the technique of *Sweeney Todd.*

The creators of this version of an 1842 Victorian melodrama call it a musical thriller, an apt description. It is all clean, nasty fun. But behind its rambunctious action—murder, rape, cannibalism, and trapdoor derring-do—there is a Brechtian cautionary tale. And while we are often repelled, the insidious onrush of the music and the paradoxical way in which Sweeney is presented force us to have an ambivalent feeling of both pity and distaste for him. Sondheim's talent elevates a grotesque melodrama centered on a blood-thirsty psychopath to an almost tragic level. (pp. 309-10)

Sweeney is encased in **"The Ballad of Sweeney Todd,"** first heard after a short, dull organ prelude. It seems such an authentic folk ballad—sounding like an Irish jig, simultaneously sad, jaunty, and spooky—that we almost forget Sondheim composed it himself. A scurrying low accompanying figure reflects the sinister, disturbed, tortured mind of Todd. As in all Sondheim musicals the opening number tells us what the show is about. But here he goes further. The first word, "*Attend* (the tale of Sweeney Todd), is meant in all phases of its meaning: pay attention to, be present at, etc. (pp. 310-11)

Sondheim uses image technique, throughout; for example, the word "London" in Sweeney's **"There's No Place Like London,"** and Mrs. Lovett's **"The Worst Pies in London."** Though related, dramatically and psychologically, their music is entirely different. Todd's "London" when first heard is expansive and lyrical; a few measures later, it sounds ominous, an abrupt change of mood that exactly characterizes him. Mrs. Lovett's romantic-sounding "London" is really flippant and amoral and tells us that she is capable of conceiving her revolting pie business. In **"Johanna"** Anthony sings "I am in the dark beside you. Buried sweetly in your yellow hair." In Act II, Anthony, before rescuing her from an asylum, is taught by Todd how to make wigs, "There's tawny and there's golden saffron." The image has been planted long before. Even the simple ding dong of a banal parlor song sung by Lovett (nervously) and the beadle (innocently) is echoed eerily by Tobias in the bakehouse.

The myriad uses of the Beggar Woman's motive is adroit. Her semitone (Alms! . . . Alms! . . . For a miserable woman / On a miserable chilly morning") later becomes the basis of her crazed **"City on Fire."** And her gyrating "beadle dee dee" figure is mixed up with "deedle deedle dumpling," a musical reminiscence of the **"Pie Song."** The double play of her plea is typical Sondheim. She is a pathetic creature seeking both alms and arms. (pp. 311-12)

Sondheim has surely read T. S. Eliot's *Sweeney Agonistes.* Eliot's antihero does not have the same source as Sondheim's, but there is a subliminal connection. Eliot knew that Victorian mothers used Todd's name to frighten disobedient children into good behavior. In *Fragment of an Agon,* he wrote "I'll be the cannibal./I'll convert you!/Into a stew." Eliot's and Sondheim's Sweeneys are blood brothers in subject, mood, and music-hall style (p. 312)

"Try a Little Priest" ends Act I and is a knockout. It begins with a five-note motive of the song, "Seems a downright shame . . . Seems an awful waste . . ." and is followed by Mrs. Lovett's theme "When you get it, / If you get it—" Todd joins in contrapuntally; the music becomes more animated as they begin to be enveloped in their insane world. . . . The lyrics are a masterpiece of gallows humor. They, like the show, may not be to everyone's taste, but there is no denying their linguistic and musical intelligence.

But the real triumphs of *Sweeney* are Todd's **"Epiphany"** and the Judge's **"Mea culpa."** In this vein Sondheim has no equal. Unwillingly in these infernal scenes characters on the verge of dementia compel us to enter into their world. And it is scary. **"Epiphany"** is the pivotal situation of the work. Here Todd goes off the deep end and never returns. *Sweeney,* in spite of its gayer moments, becomes grimmer and grimmer. Ironically, this and the Judge's scene destroy the validity of much of the

piece. The comic element is subordinated and we are watching a Peter Grimes tragedy. The basic characters of Lovett and Todd clash; they no longer mesh as a team. She retains her fairy-tale slightly unbelievable witchlike role; he evokes in us a dichotomy of response, disgust and sympathy at the same time. He becomes larger than life, she diminishes. How does Sondheim mean us to take this? We are never sure, but the scene is magnificent. A rhythmic figure flutters through the orchestra while Todd rages, "I had him." Mrs. Lovett's quiet "Easy, now Hush, my love" is sung above steady dissonant chords accompanied by a pounding rhythm. Todd's philosophy, "There's a hole in the world / Like a great big pit," at first fragmented, comes into full focus as the orchestra reflects his violence. At **"I'll never see Johanna"** Todd is calmer; we hear the falling semitone of the Beggar Woman. Then his mind is flooded again and the scene careens to the final gruesome "I'm alive at last and full of joy." We are chilled to the bone; this is tremendous theater. (pp. 312-13)

Act I of *Sweeney Todd* is psychologically motivated. Act II is all action; it unravels at a frantic pace; characters and themes dart back and forth like a movie that has been speeded up. The opening "God, that's good" intermingles with the merriment (chorus) of the pie customers (are we all unconscious cannibals?). As Sweeney impatiently awaits the arrival of his barber chair, Mrs. Lovett plays a double role as patroness and mollifier. This contrapuntal scene is proof of Sondheim's musical maturity, as are all the multilayered scenes that follow. . . . The Beggar Woman's **"City on fire"** sets the scene for the final unfoldment. Its short, nervous phrases and obsessive rhythm mirror her madness and the excitement of the chase. Mrs. Lovett's search for the key, the Beggar Woman's ratlike scampering, Johanna and Anthony's dream of escape, the duet of the Judge and Todd (ironically repeating **"Pretty Woman"**), the murder of the Judge, the revelation that the Beggar Woman is Todd's wife Lucy, the escape of the young lovers, the incineration of Mrs. Lovett, the murder of Todd by the innocent fool Tobias—all this, a montage of excitement, is handled with consummate musical and dramatic skill. The curtain comes down as the final stanzas of the Ballad are heard.

Unfortunately, a didactic ending is tacked on. Must we be told that: "No one can help, nothing can hide you / Isn't that Sweeney there beside you?"

But *Sweeney Todd,* with few exceptions, is all of a piece. There is no doubt that it is Sondheim's show. The music and lyrics are too deeply embedded in this musical thriller to be otherwise. (pp. 313-14)

> *Paul Wittke, in a review of "Sweeney Todd," in* The Musical Quarterly, *Vol. LXVI, No. 2, April, 1980, pp. 309-14.*

EDITH OLIVER

[In **"Marry Me a Little"**], a single young woman and a single young man, each living alone in an apartment in New York . . . , sing seventeen songs by Stephen Sondheim that were pulled from his shows during rehearsal. . . . [Their] unawareness of each other as they move about the apartment, even when they share the same bed at the end, is the running joke of this mini-musical. None of the songs struck me as exactly vintage Sondheim, although **"Saturday Night," "The Girls of Summer," "Pour le Sport,"** and the title song come close, but an evening of non-vintage Sondheim is richer than most evenings, certainly Off Broadway.

Edith Oliver, "Off Broadway," in The New Yorker, *Vol. LVII, No. 5, March 23, 1981, pp. 124, 126-27.**

EDWIN WILSON

Two things set ["**Merrily We Roll Along**"] apart right away. It is a Hal Prince-Stephen Sondheim collaboration and it tells its story backward. . . . The notion of moving backward comes from the 1930s play by Kaufman and Hart from which the musical is derived.

Unfortunately, this pedigree does not help. Neither the impressive talents of its creative team, nor the device of reversing the chronology can camouflage the commonplace nature of the story. . . .

The story of success corrupting a young idealist is all to familiar and the creators have been able to do very little to make it seem new or to make us care about the characters involved.

Edwin Wilson, "Broadway Rolls Along, Not Always Merrily," in The Wall Street Journal, *November 19, 1981, p. 26.**

BRENDAN GILL

"**Merrily We Roll Along**," which closed after sixteen performances . . . , was a blunder, all the more mysterious because it was carried out by some of the least blunder-prone people on Broadway—Hal Prince, who produced and directed it; Stephen Sondheim, who wrote the music and lyrics; and George Furth, who wrote the book. What on earth could have drawn them to this old play by George S. Kaufman and Moss Hart? It is a work remarkable only for the fact that its plot unfolds by starting in the present and going back and back through time. . . . Mr. Furth breathed little life into a book bristling with clichés of attitude and language, and for once Mr. Sondheim was unable to turn into memorable song those feelings of alienation and abortive affection he has so often given melodious utterance to. . . . The mercy of memory is its selectivity; this "**Merrily**" has already joined its predecessor in those dim recesses of my mind that I reserve for the failed efforts of people I admire.

Brendan Gill, "Strivers," in The New Yorker, *Vol. LVII, No. 42, December 7, 1981, p. 110.**

WALTER KERR

I suppose the question most frequently asked around town these days is why Harold Prince and Stephen Sondheim should have risked trying to fashion a musical out of "**Merrily We Roll Along**". . . . In effect, Prince and Sondheim were starting out with a known quantity: a weak book. (p. D3)

I think they picked "**Merrily We Roll Along**" because it was precisely what *they* wanted to do, precisely what they had been doing for most of their distinguished, if not always rewarding, collaboration. "**Merrily**" offered them the one thing they seem determined to sell: disenchantment.

"**Company**" was a technically fascinating musical devoted to exploring total disenchantment in marriage, climaxed by the hero's now utterly inexplicable decision to marry. "**Follies**," heralded by a poster displaying a disastrous crack in the facade of a theater, examined the death of enchantment in marriage and in the theater both. "**Pacific Overtures**" is harder to ca-

tegorize: I think we can say, however, that the Japanese were duly disenchanted with their American guests. And we know about "**Sweeney Todd**," with its imposed Brechtian schema, "Man Eats Man." The worm in the apple, the blight on the rose, the fingernail in the tasty meat pie.

And here, in "**Merrily**," were the worm and the blight and the fingernail ready-made. (pp. D3, D6)

Compromise, the sellout, loss of integrity—these are not so much fighting words to Prince and Sondheim as they are creative words, words that help them choose their materials, words that drive them to work. There is nothing wrong with the choice. The subject matter is valid because it is rooted in truth. . . . It's not our business to tell creative men what to create so long as it's got a whiff of life deep inside it.

But there is, increasingly to my mind, something wrong with the work. The insistence on a single theme, a single attitude, is becoming monotonous. In the case of the already vanished "**Merrily**," it also tended to make the composer and director seem smug: They were castigating a hero who wouldn't stand up for his right to do musicals *his* way, whereas they were plainly doing this one *theirs*. And there may be a more serious problem. The pair may have been at this particular kind of iconoclastic work for so long that they have begun to take their theme for granted. Taking it for granted, they are neglecting to dramatize it. . . .

Mr. Sondheim's lyrics, trying to help unscramble the confusion, fell victim to yet another expository overload ("How can you get so far off the track? / Why don't you turn around and go back?"). . . .

Well, no need to go back to the sweet continental melancholia of "**A Little Night Music**." Just a need, I suspect, for the frequent collaborators to stop parroting themselves and take fresh stock of their imaginative energies. They are much too innovative to allow themselves to become so predictable. (p. D6)

Walter Kerr, "A Libretto Has to Face the Music," in The New York Times, *December 13, 1981, pp. D3, D6.*

PETER REILLY

The story of *Merrily We Roll Along* reaches backward in time to retrace the lives of several people attending a class reunion, and Sondheim's score is typically inventive and complex. Perhaps the clearest explanation is Sondheim's own, as he presents it in the album booklet: "Since *Merrily We Roll Along* is about friendship, the score concentrates on the friendship of Mary, Frank, and Charlie by having all their songs interconnected through chunks of melody, rhythm, and accompaniment. And since the story moves backwards in time, it presented an opportunity to invent verbal and musical motifs which could be modified over the course of the years, extended and developed, reprised, fragmented, and then presented to the audience in reverse. . . ."

Aside from all this technical experimentation, Sondheim's music and lyrics again demonstrate his cool detachment from his characters, his generally dark and sorrowful view of the unsatisfying messes people can make of their lives. But, as in other Sondheim shows, the detachment is broken and the darkness is lit up by sudden shafts of sentiment like that of the lovely *Not a Day Goes By,* as fine a song as he has written.

It's pointless to speculate about why **Merrily** wasn't a success with theater-goers. What's important to say now is that this beautifully produced and engineered album is a must for anyone interested in the finest of American musical creativity.

> *Peter Reilly, " 'Merrily We Roll Along': The Broad-way-Cast Album of Sondheim's Latest Music-Theater Experiment," in* Stereo Review, *Vol. 47, No. 10, October, 1982, p. 81.*

KARL LEVETT

Stephen Sondheim is the present genius-in-resident of the American musical. Over the last 20 years, he has singlehand-edly staked out new territory for the musical theatre. This past summer he chose for the first time to create for Off-Broadway, a Work-in-Progress entitled **Sunday in the Park with George**. Only the first act was on view and this not open for critical review. The musical's inspiration is Georges Seurat's painting "Un Dimanche à la Grande Jatte" and the show contrives to reveal Seurat's relationship to the characters in the painting. This is fragile and subtle stuff for a musical. As yet James Lapine's book is convoluted and cloudy, while Sondheim, who lyrically can never be dull, seems hesitant to commit himself melodically to any straightforward song or emotional thrust. This arrangement, however, that allows Sondheim to work in freedom without Broadway pressure, is a significant move. (p. 31)

> *Karl Levett, "New York," in* Drama, *No. 150, Winter, 1983, pp. 30-1.**

FRANK RICH

Mr. Sondheim has always functioned as a theater man first, a songwriter second. Unlike all but a few of his theatrical con-temporaries, he has never aspired to write songs that have a pop life of their own; all of his songs reflect the dramatic situations and characters of the musicals they were written to serve. What is more remarkable is how well Mr. Sondheim fulfills this mission. Yank one of his songs out of its original context, and you're often left with a self-contained play.

One example on the new record ["**A Stephen Sondheim Eve-ning**"] is an eight-minute masterpiece: "**Someone in a Tree**" from "**Pacific Overtures.**" Its subject, of all things, is the treaty by which the United States "opened up" Japan in 1853. Be-cause there is no Japanese account of what went on in the treaty house where Commodore Perry negotiated with his hosts, Mr. Sondheim imagines how four Japanese might speculate, many years later, about what happened at that fateful session. Among the characters singing are both the older and younger selves of a boy who overlooked the treaty house . . . from a tree on that historic day.

With its ever-shifting perspectives on a single event, "**Someone in a Tree**" is, literally speaking, a mini-"Rashomon," but it is also a metaphysical statement about memory and history and existence. "I'm a fragment of the day," sings the boy about his role as witness to the treaty-signing, then adding: 'If I weren't, who's to say / Things would happen here the way / That they happened here?'' The music further dramatizes the song's themes by playing its own Eastern tricks with time—both extending and compressing a crucial moment in the life of the characters and their civilization.

It's amazing that the man who can write a piece as sophisticated and difficult as "**Someone in a Tree**" can also, when he wants to, concoct effortless low humor. . . .

As a humorist, Mr. Sondheim is perhaps best known for his pastiche numbers. The Whitney concert [recording] includes one of the cleverest from "**Follies**" (1971)—"**You're Gonna Love Tomorrow/Love Will See Us Through.**" To some, Mr. Sondheim's skill at imitation and parody is a form of self-indulgence—but, here again, one finds that he is serving the dramatic needs of a show, not playing games. The two songs that make up this piece, sung by a pair of couples, are packed with references to Kern and Porter; the contrapuntal climax is pure Berlin. But, in "**Follies,**" this number was part of a surreal, Fellini-esque flashback sequence in which some con-temporary middle-aged characters look back ironically at the false innocence purveyed by the Ziegfeld Follies: The number really isn't a replica of an old-fashioned Broadway song but a jaundiced rememberance of such a song. Accordingly, the sunny lyrics contain sporadic, anachronistic references to Hara Kiri, an "ego" needing "bolstering" and "ennui." As in "**Someone in a Tree,**" Mr. Sondheim has refracted the past through the present to serve his thematic purposes.

What is not to be found very often in the Whitney concert are those detached, world-weary refrains about life's disenchant-ments that are also frequently used to pigeonhole Mr. Sond-heim—songs like "**You Must Meet My Wife**" or "**Every Day a Little Death**" or "**I'm Still Here**" or "**The Ladies Who Lunch.**" Intentionally or not, this concert goes out of its way to forsake such songs for those others which demonstrate the often overlooked openheartedness—and melodiousness—of the Sondheim canon.

Even in the lushest, most Ravel-like of these songs, there is an adult skepticism about the permanence of romantic liaisons. But they are love songs, nonetheless. Their dramatic setting is frequently the end of a couple's affair or a character's yearning for a partner who is out of reach. And so the lonely bachelor of "**Company**" begs to find "somebody" who will hold him "too close" in "**Being Alive**"; the sailor of "**Sweeney Todd**" hopes someday to find and free the imprisoned maiden, "**Jo-hanna,**" the parting lovers of "**Anyone Can Whistle**" cherish their brief, "marvelous moment" together in the discordant "**With So Little to Be Sure Of,**" a wife in "**Merrily**" sings that "**Not a Day Goes By**" when she still won't love, however painfully, the husband whom she's suing for divorce.

But if these songs reveal Mr. Sondheim at his most moving, they, too, are not the end of his emotional spectrum. He is also capable of writing a more sprightly and sexier, even in-nocent, song about men and women—one in which we hear inexperienced young characters dream of romance without end. These songs have the feeling of the early Sondheim lyrics for "**Something's Coming**" in "**West Side Story**" and "**All I Need is the Girl**" in "**Gypsy.**" . . .

But one can dip into any Sondheim score and find . . . delights. This writer's talent hasn't let up in the 30 years that separate "**Saturday Night**" and "**Sunday in the Park with George**"— it's just grown too fast for Broadway to keep up with him. (p. 4)

> *Frank Rich, "Sondheim Says Goodbye to Broad-way—For Now," in* The New York Times, *Section 2, July 24, 1983, pp. 1, 4.*

JOHN ROCKWELL

Sondheim's verbal felicity has remained with him throughout his career. He has that gift for clever rhymes that has distinguished lyricists since W. S. Gilbert ("beauty celestial the best you'll / agree" from *Follies,* for instance). Better still, he has the ability to link musical construction with verbal cadence, to let the rhythm of the words shape the structure of a phrase. To take yet another of many possible examples, the song **"Broadway Baby,"** again from *Follies,* includes a stanza that begins "At / my tiny flat . . ." This is an unexpected rhyme, to start with. And it helps define the melodic structure of the song itself.

That sense of melody, shape and overall formal design only really came into its own after 1970, with *Company* (*Forum,* for all its cleverness and charm, was not much more than a revue). (p. 214)

Company formed a trilogy with *Follies* (1971) and *A Little Night Music* (1973), mirroring and exalting a certain early-seventies sensibility. The basic Broadway audience was and is a conservative one. But New York has a brittle, more sophisticated side, too, shared by the people who create and perform the productions. The Prince-Sondheim shows, with their alternating, overlapping irony and sentimentality, effected a marriage between what has been called the suburban "bridge-and-tunnel crowd" and the witty, nostalgic, sometimes homosexual element of contemporary New York. The lyrics and the dramatic situations were close enough to most people's lives to seem comforting. But they were also peppered with a sophistication and even a kinkiness that could titillate. These shows were celebrations of marriage and love, yet their seeming normalcy was undercut and contrasted with wit and camp (especially in *Follies,* with its parade of veteran female performers). The Sondheim-Prince shows avoided cliché, as so many Broadway productions these days fail to do. They evoked nostalgia without being fettered by the past. And they each had their conceptually bold sides, as well. *Company,* a celebration of marriage, was riven with acerbic asides about modern mores. *Follies,* a tale of two marriages set at a reunion of Ziegfeld-type showgirls, offered a feast for Broadway nostalgists in a clever, contemporarily complex package. And *A Little Night Music* . . . was a waltz-musical that conveyed much of what Ravel attempted in *La Valse,* without the Old World ennui.

Sondheim's melodies are shaped differently from those of Broadway's past in part because his way of working is different. What makes his best songs so fine is their synchronism of words and music, the music supporting the text and the text defining the music, with both the sense and the sound of the words playing their parts. **"Send in the Clowns"** from *A Little Night Music* is Sondheim's best-known song. It lacks his characteristic wit and naughty patter, but otherwise it can stand as representative of his method. . . . The lyrics are full of a sweet suggestiveness, intimations of acrobats soaring and falling as a metaphor for love, and the allusion to clowns evokes both lovers and love itself. (pp. 214-16)

Sondheim's sensitivity to the marriage of words and music, and his ability to reflect the realities of his own time, can also be heard in his wittier, wickeder songs. **"Poor Baby"** from *Company,* for instance, is a study in cattiness, a sequence of women casting doubt on a male friend's current companion— a litany of bitchiness that builds into a complex ensemble texture. Sondheim's songs often build that way, from simple (or not so simple) melody and accompaniment to complicated set pieces. (p. 216)

Company and *A Little Night Music* were hits; *Follies,* although it ran for a year, lost its entire investment. *Pacific Overtures* of 1976 and *Sweeney Todd* of 1979 were conceptually bolder but only marginally successful at the box office, while *Merrily We Roll Along,* full of fine, cleverly interlocking songs but crippled by its awkward book, closed precipitously. *Pacific Overtures* is about yet another kind of marriage—an audacious attempt to recount the story of Japan's Westernization through a mixture of Western musical comedy and Kabuki drama. The resultant fresco was hard for audiences to identify with—all that foreignness in the musical and dramatic idioms, the lack of a single romantic hero or heroine, the distance from contemporary life. Yet some of the music was quite remarkable in its marriage of Japanese and Western sounds and effects. And the lyrics were as charming as ever ("If the tea the Shogun drank will / Serve to keep the Shogun tranquil").

Sweeney Todd . . . is the most operatically ambitious Sondheim-Prince collaboration yet. So grandiose are its ambitions, in fact, that controversy has arisen as to whether it actually is an opera. . . . *Sweeney Todd*'s operatic aspirations lurk everywhere in the score. The story itself is a wonderful one, mixing Dickensian atmosphere, Grand Guignol humor, lyricism and terror in a way that seems perfectly suited to its creators' sensibilities. . . . With its mosaic construction, rapidly shifting moods, recurrent leitmotifs and complex ensembles, *Sweeney Todd* belongs on the operatic stage far more deservedly than most of the new operas that jostle for position there.

Sondheim has not attained his status as America's finest living composer of musicals without doubts being voiced. Classical critics fault him for not doing his own orchestrations. Others complain of his supposed inability—a reflection of his own guarded personality, Leonard Bernstein has suggested—to express simple, direct, intense emotion, and of his tuneless tunes. They have accused him and Prince of mixing up genres that should be kept separate, and of being more devoted to campy exploitation than genuine emotion. (pp. 216-18)

Even Sondheim's champions must admit to a disturbing undercurrent in his work, without necessarily sharing Croce's lurid vehemence [see excerpt above]. There is a sometimes cynically vulgar, manipulative side to Broadway, and it has infected the conception and execution of Sondheim's work. . . . (p. 218)

Many of the more moderate complaints against Sondheim seem to be about "flaws" perceived by his admirers as virtues. As a man of today, Sondheim refuses to accept the pat, sweet directness that once defined our national character, at least as that character was projected in musicals and musical films. Although he echoes elegant interwar artifice, he is inevitably different from the great masters of the American popular song— more fragmented emotionally and musically, drier, more ironic, more ambivalent. And he would only deny himself were he to attempt to be anything different than he is. . . . On the other hand, his songs are not all *that* tuneless. And what they lack in directness, they gain in subtlety and complexity. If his work approaches opera, that hardly means other composers cannot write old-fashioned, simple-minded musicals. Indeed they do, season after season. Sondheim's major contribution may even be a conservative one, sustaining the conventions and the intellectual respectability of the old-fashioned Broadway musical. Perhaps the creative moment for formulaic simplicity has passed, at least if it is to be achieved with genius.

Or perhaps not. The obvious source for the renewal of the traditional musical lies in rock. The two worlds, once so seemingly antithetical, have already begun to merge. (pp. 218-19)

Sondheim stands for a different sensibility, which was responsible for the revival of cabaret life in New York in the early seventies. The composers and performers who led this revival were part of the same spirit that infused Broadway and blended so compatibly with suburban conservatism. Like Sondheim, they sought a more overtly dramatic expression through music. (pp. 219-20)

What lends Sondheim's work its fascination is its very tension between art and entertainment, a tension mirrored in his creative relationship with Prince. He may be torn, and his conflicts may inhibit his art. But the very essence of his art *is* conflict, so that to wish away the tension would be to wish away the art. (p. 220)

> *John Rockwell, "Urban Popular Song, the Broadway Musical, the Cabaret Revival & the Birth Pangs of American Opera: Stephen Sondheim," in his* All American Music: Composition in the Late Twentieth Century, *Alfred A. Knopf, 1983, pp. 209-20.*

SAMUEL G. FREEDMAN

In his 13 shows—he wrote only lyrics for three, music and lyrics for the rest—Sondheim has staked out a turf as big as the emotional landscape of post-World War II America. Even when the shows have been set abroad or in the past, their themes have addressed contemporary topics—or universal ones, Sondheim might aver—by way of metaphor. This is particularly true of the Sondheim shows since 1970. He has treated the travails of modern marriage in **"Company,"** the corrosion of American optimism in **"Follies,"** injustice and revenge in **"Sweeney Todd,"** idealism and compromise in **"Merrily We Roll Along"** and Western imperialism in **"Pacific Overtures."** As Sondheim once put it, "I love to write in dark colors about gut feelings." (p. 25)

Sondheim has come to subsume all his influences so thoroughly that they cannot be readily identified in his work. He also has resisted any concession to trend—so much so that he sometimes wonders if he is passé without knowing it. . . . And in his lyrics, he tries to avoid slang since it can become dated, even inventing curses for his characters in **"West Side Story."**

But Sondheim's voice is not a static thing; it does not exist in a vacuum. His voice is largely defined by the projects he has selected. Beyond the emotional terrain he has tackled, he has made musicals out of seemingly unlikely sources—Plautus (**"Forum"**), Aristophanes (**"The Frogs"**), a Bergman film (**"Night Music"**), Grand Guignol (**"Sweeney Todd"**), Kabuki (**"Pacific Overtures"**) and now, with **"Sunday in the Park With George,"** Seurat's divisionist art. (pp. 26, 28)

At the level of individual characters, Sondheim has said, "I like neurotic people. I like troubled people. Not that I don't like squared-away people, but I prefer neurotic people." He elaborates on the notion: "What 'neurotic people' means to me is people with conflicts. And that's like saying I like to write about character. I don't like to write about oversimplified people unless it's for something like farce, like **'Forum.'** Songs can't develop uncomplicated characters or unconflicted people. You can't just tell the sunny side and have a story with any richness to it. Good drama is the study of human passions." (p. 28)

Early in his career, Sondheim learned the importance of writing in character, the skill that is perhaps his greatest. He still cringes at one line he wrote in the lyrics to **"West Side Story"** [see excerpt above]. . . . "There always comes a time," Sondheim says, "when you have to face the cast. And if an actress says to you, 'Excuse me, but if I'm from the streets how do you want me to read this alarming-charming deal? Am I imitating something I heard on TV?' You have to be prepared for it. It's not just so you can show your fellow songwriters, 'See how in-character I wrote.' It's because there's an actress who has to sing that. And eventually it's naked and it's got to be right. Context is everything."

At the same time, Sondheim's lyrics are notable for their sophistication. . . . In his lyrics, one hears words like "acquiesce" and "ameliorate," references to Proust and Pound. In **"The Little Things You Do Together"** in **"Company,"** Sondheim built a rhyme on *pursue, accrue* and *misconstrue.* He has invoked multiple and virtually simultaneous narrators in such songs as **"Now/Later/Soon"** in **"A Little Night Music"** and **"Someone in a Tree"** in **"Pacific Overtures."** (pp. 28, 30)

> *Samuel G. Freedman, "The Words and Music of Stephen Sondheim," in* The New York Times, *April 1, 1984, pp. 22-60.*

FRANK RICH

In his paintings of a century ago, Georges Seurat demanded that the world look at art in a shocking new way. In **"Sunday in the Park With George,"** their new show about Seurat, the songwriter Stephen Sondheim and the playwright-director James Lapine demand that an audience radically change its whole way of looking at the Broadway musical. Seurat, the authors remind us, never sold a painting; it's anyone's guess whether the public will be shocked or delighted by **"Sunday in the Park."** What I do know is that Mr. Sondheim and Mr. Lapine have created an audacious, haunting and, in its own intensely personal way, touching work. Even when it fails—as it does on occasion—**"Sunday in the Park"** is setting the stage for even more sustained theatrical innovations yet to come.

If anything, the show . . . owes more to the Off Broadway avant-garde than it does to past groundbreaking musicals, Mr. Sondheim's included. **"Sunday"** is not a bridge to opera, like **"Sweeney Todd"**; nor is it in the tradition of the dance musicals of Jerome Robbins and Michael Bennett. There is, in fact, no dancing in **"Sunday,"** and while there's a book, there's little story. In creating a work about a pioneer of modernist art, Mr. Lapine and Mr. Sondheim have made a contemplative modernist musical that, true to form, is as much about itself and its creators as it is about the universe beyond.

The show's inspiration is Seurat's most famous canvas, "A Sunday Afternoon on the Island of La Grande Jatte." That huge painting shows a crowd of bourgeois 19th-century Parisians relaxing in a park on their day off. But "La Grande Jatte" was also a manifesto by an artist in revolt against Impressionism. . . .

[Seurat] could well be a stand-in for Mr. Sondheim, who brings the same fierce, methodical intellectual precision to musical and verbal composition that the artist brought to his pictorial realm. In one number in **"Sunday,"** Seurat's work is dismissed by contemporaries as having "no passion, no life"—a critique frequently leveled at Mr. Sondheim. But unlike the last Sondheim show, **"Merrily We Roll Along,"** this one is usually not a whiny complaint about how hard it is to be a misunderstood, underappreciated genius. Instead of a showbiz figure's self-martyrdom we get an artist's self-revelation.

As is often the case in Sondheim musicals, we don't care about the characters—and here, more than ever, it's clear we're not meant to care. To Seurat, these people are just models for a meditative composition that's not intended to tell any story: In his painting, the figures are silent and expressionless, and even Dot is but fodder for dots. Mr. Lapine and Mr. Sondheim tease us with their characters' various private lives—which are rife with betrayals—only to sever those stories abruptly the moment Seurat's painting has found its final shape. It's the authors' way of saying that they, too, regard their "characters" only as forms to be manipulated into a theatrical composition whose content is more visual and musical than dramatic.

As a result, when Seurat finishes "La Grande Jatte" at the end of Act I, we're moved not because a plot has been resolved but because a harmonic work of art has been born.

[In Act II, the] show jumps a full century to focus on a present-day American artist also named George. . . . This protagonist is possibly a double, for Mr. Sondheim at his most self-doubting. George makes large, multimedia conceptual sculptures that, like Broadway musicals, require collaborators, large budgets and compromises. . . .

The fanciful time-travel conceits that link this George to Seurat are charming. Rather less successful is the authors' reversion to a compressed, conventional story about how the modern George overcomes his crisis of confidence to regenerate himself as a man and artist. When George finally learns how to "connect" with other people and rekindles his esthetic vision, his breakthrough is ordained by two pretty songs, **"Children and Art"** and **"Move On,"** which seem as inorganic as the equivalent inspirational number (**"Being Alive"**) that redeems the born-again protagonist in Mr. Sondheim's **"Company."**

The show's most moving song is **"Finishing the Hat"**—which, like many of Mr. Sondheim's best, is about being disconnected. Explaining his emotional aloofness to Dot, Seurat sings how he watches "the rest of the world from a window" while he's obsessively making art. And if the maintenance of that solitary emotional distance means that Seurat's art (and, by implication, Mr. Sondheim's) is "cold," even arrogant, so be it. **"Sunday"** argues that the esthetic passion in the cerebrally ordered classicism of modern artists is easily as potent as the sentimental passion of romantic paintings or conventional musicals. . . .

[The] lyrics can be brilliantly funny. Mr. Sondheim exploits the homonyms "kneads" and "needs" to draw a razor-sharp boundary between sex and love; a song in which Seurat's painted figures break their immortal poses to complain about "sweating in a picture that was painted by a genius" is a tour de force. But there's often wisdom beneath the cleverness. . . .

Both at the show's beginning and end, the hero is embracing not a woman, but the empty white canvas that he really loves—for its "many possibilities." Look closely at that canvas—or at **"Sunday in the Park"** itself—and you'll get lost in a sea of floating dots. Stand back and you'll see that this evening's two theater artists, Mr. Sondheim and Mr. Lapine, have woven all those imaginative possibilities into a finished picture with a startling new glow.

Frank Rich, "'Sunday in the Park with George': New Musical by Sondheim and Lapine," in The New York Times, *May 3, 1984, p. C21.*

ROBERT BRUSTEIN

In the halcyon days of Gershwin, Porter, and Rodgers and Hart, Broadway musicals used to be about music. Beginning with *Oklahoma,* and culminating with *My Fair Lady,* Broadway musicals usually featured the book. **Sunday in the Park with George,** a new work by James Lapine (book and direction) and Stephen Sondheim (music and lyrics), is the first Broadway musical that is mainly about the set.

This show has a very good set—indeed, a brilliant one—by Tony Straiges—and since the design is primarily intended as a stage canvas for the reproduction (substituting costumed actors for the original figures) of the large pointillist painting "A Sunday Afternoon on the Island of the Grande Jatte" by Georges Seurat, one could sit and look at it for hours. This, in fact, is precisely what the audience finds itself doing at the Booth Theater. A popular joke about heavyweight musicals was that you came out of the theater humming the costumes. Stephen Sondheim's score is designed to send you out of the theater singing the set.

And it would were the music just a little more tuneful. Sondheim, once again frowning on melody, is here composing in a minimalist, vaguely serial style which functions primarily as a setting for his surprising, often witty lyrics. This disdain for melody, coupled with a certain emotional coldness and remoteness, explains, I think, why so many Sondheim musicals have a large following but not a large audience. **Sunday in the Park with George,** I suspect, will share that fate. The idea is original—to bring the advanced techniques of such works as the Wilson-Glass *Einstein on the Beach* into the commercial mainstream—but although the evening is packed with succulent ocular feasts and crammed with vibrant theatrical images, the show is ultimately wearisome, even a little silly. (p. 25)

[The image of Seurat's painting] is the essence of the work; the rest is landfill. Having developed an exquisite idea, and possessed with the theatrical resources to realize it, they somehow lacked the ultimate resolve to let it find a natural shape, molding it instead to routine conventional forms—a case of the imagination trying to do the work of the will. Without the second act, and without the modest but foolish plot, *Sunday in the Park with George* might have been a genuine breakthrough in American musical theater. At the moment, it seems more like an effort to adapt the insights of serious art to the entertainment needs of popular audiences. . . .

Forced to a judgment, I would like to find some way to express my admiration for this effort, so unique in a musical theater dominated by the noisy displays of *Dreamgirls, Cats,* and *La Cage aux Folles,* along with my disappointment over how the achievement of such talented people is sometimes compromised by a certain facileness and slickness. I suspect that if **Sunday in the Park with George** had been a short musical piece exclusively concerned with the execution of a painting on stage, it would have been a masterpiece. In its present inflated form, it is merely a handsome, pleasing, if occasionally meretricious entertainment. (p. 26)

Robert Brustein, *"Monday on the Stage with Steve,"* in The New Republic, *Vol. 190, No. 24, June 18, 1984, pp. 25-6.*

Scott Spencer

1945-

American novelist.

Spencer is best known for *Endless Love* (1979), the story of sixteen-year-old David Axelrod's obsessive love for Jade Butterfield. Although young adults may be attracted to the book because of its adolescent protagonist, it is not a "teen romance." Spencer focuses on David's possessive, destructive love and portrays it with an unrelenting intensity that some critics found overwhelming. Others thought that Spencer's powerful writing was instrumental in making his story believable and found it a welcome contrast to what Larry Swindell called "the emotional timidity of most American fiction." Most critics consider *Endless Love* a serious work of fiction and were generally impressed with Spencer's talent. The book was made into a motion picture.

Spencer's earlier novels, *Last Night at the Brain Thieves Ball* (1973) and *Preservation Hall* (1978), also deal with characters whose uncontrollable desires place them at odds with the rest of the world.

PUBLISHERS WEEKLY

For much of the way ["**Last Night at the Brain Thieves Ball**"] is a clever and witty satire on the kind of electronic snooping and secret manipulation of people's lives that lies behind Watergate. A rather prim and prissy professor of experimental psychology finds himself forcibly recruited into a secret outfit called NESTER (New England Sensory Testing and Engineering Research). . . . The madhouse atmosphere inside NESTER and the professor's growing rebellion are conveyed so expertly that when Mr. Spencer comes up with a final far-fetched solution to the whole thing, and an explanation that falls pretty flat, the reader is all the more disappointed. (pp. 61-2)

> *A review of "Last Night at the Brain Thieves Ball," in* Publishers Weekly, *Vol. 204, No. 4, July 23, 1973, pp. 61-2.*

MARTIN LEVIN

What if there were a clandestine organization that extended market analysis to its ultimate possibilities? Like using real people as guinea pigs? . . . Scott Spencer fancies that such a scientific purgatory might resemble New England Sensory and Testing Research—NESTOR. . . . To NESTOR comes a malcontent experimental psychologist, agreeable to living beyond freedom and dignity. Through his reactions to the techniques of what he finally decides is "a claque of satans," the author develops a light-fingered satire of technology. "**Last Night at the Brain Thieves Ball**" belongs in the same league with Shepherd Mead's "The Big Ball of Wax."

> *Martin Levin, in a review of "Last Night at the Brain Thieves Ball," in* The New York Times Book Review, *September 16, 1973, p. 32.*

PSYCHOLOGY TODAY

An experimental psychologist answers a two-sentence classified ad in "a weekly magazine of refined opinion." The result is *Last Night at the Brain Thieves Ball*. . . . This clever, comic story . . . is that kind of insightful science fiction that publishers hope won't get pigeonholed and critics pretend is not part of the genre. The obvious comparison for Spencer is Kurt Vonnegut; although their styles differ both writers deftly mix comedy, social comment and science fiction. But read Spencer for himself; within a few years we may be comparing other writers to him.

> *A review of "Last Night at the Brain Thieves Ball," in* Psychology Today, *Vol. 7, No. 6, November, 1973, p. 140.*

PUBLISHERS WEEKLY

"**Preservation Hall**," with its deeply personal passion and anguish, is in fact in the province of a first novel, yet it's written with such expert control that one is glad the author waited to tackle its larger theme. Set in New York and in the Maine wilderness, subjecting its characters to the isolating cataclysm of a storm, the novel stings at our age-old fears and makes the pain seem fresh and revelatory. Virgil and Tracy Morgan, successful, likable New Yorkers, have gone to their country property for a winter holiday. . . . But not until a crisis is visited on the younger Morgans that holiday week through an invasion by another couple . . . will a catharsis be forced. No longer immune, Virgil will mourn his past insufficiency of feeling and attempt a retribution that will shatter his comfortable life.

A review of "Preservation Hall," in Publishers Weekly, *Vol. 210, No. 4, July 26, 1976, p. 68.*

KATHA POLLITT

Readable and swiftly paced, **"Preservation Hall"** surmounts some potentially major weaknesses. The obvious plot, for instance: one sees . . . disaster coming for at least 100 pages, and Virgil and Tracy are so smug and so cute (they name their pond Veronica Lake) that at least one reader could hardly wait. But the strengths of the book are what stay in the mind, and they center around Earl. He emerges as a complex, original figure—a difficult, aloof and oddly formal man whose misfortune is to possess the energy of genius without its gifts. He is that rare person who wants from life at 50 exactly what he wanted at 25, and his persistence lends something heroic even to his monstrous self-pity.

It's a mark of Spencer's skill that although we hear the whole story from Virgil's point of view, ultimately Earl's resentment of his son's success seems less mean-spirited than Virgil's shame at his father's failure. Since the first-person voice in fiction nowadays is all too often the voice of sheer self-justification on the part of the author-as-hero, Spencer deserves a good deal of praise for having the imagination to know more about his characters than they do themselves.

Katha Pollitt, in a review of "Preservation Hall," in The New York Times, *January 2, 1977, p. 12.*

ANNE TYLER

At first glance, **Endless Love** seems likely to be a chore for the reader. Its central character is yet another adolescent boy, more or less out of tune with his parents. When we meet him, he's setting fire to his girlfriend's house. In short order he confesses to his crime and enters a posh psychiatric clinic. . . .

But it's soon apparent that David is no ordinary adolescent. He isn't merely passing through a phase; his age is incidental. In fact, he's a full-blown tragic hero. He is obsessed by such a consuming passion for Jade Butterfield, his girlfriend, that it colors and reshapes his life—even destroys it. That so grand an emotion should strike someone too young to handle it does complicate events, of course; but it seems probable that at any age, at any point when David's intensity happened to combine with the flamboyance and disarray of Jade Butterfield's family, he would have met with disaster. He makes errors that are irreversible, a grownup's errors; they cannot be patched over (like Holden Caulfield's) with a little psychiatric counseling or a few more birthdays.

What is required from the reader is that he view David's love affair seriously. This takes some time. There is nothing unforgettable about Jade Butterfield, and her family is downright irritating—one of those self-consciously modern families in which the parents have only younger friends, experiment with LSD, obtain Enovid for their daughters, and invade their children's worlds with a kind of acquisitiveness and greed. We could dismiss them all, if it weren't for David.

He is single-minded, unnaturally focused, somehow triumphantly sane even when he seems more withdrawn than any sane man is supposed to be. Emerging as he does from a narrow, airless world (rather faded, ex-communist parents, a grim apartment in a declining Chicago neighborhood), he conveys a sense of stark sobriety that rivets the reader's gaze upon him. We may smile, at first, at his earnestness; so did the Butterfields smile. But then we fall under his spell. We begin to believe, as surely as David himself, that some people may be joined together in webs and tangles from which there is no escape. By the end of the book his love affair is to us, too, tragic and permanent and deeply, surprisingly moving.

While it's very much an original, **Endless Love** has something in common with Iris Murdoch's *A Word Child* and Robertson Davies's *Fifth Business*—two other novels that give a full measure of respect to the linkages of fate. In all three books, certain people either willingly or unwillingly serve as catalysts in certain other people's lives—or sometimes, more actively, as monkey wrenches. David Axelrod is never entirely innocent (his determined hunt for various Butterfields makes the book as absorbing as a detective story), but he is, in many ways, a victim. He is done in by the bizarre openness of the Butterfields, by his pinched background that makes that openness so appealing, and by his own charm and obvious good intentions, which cause some of the Butterfields, guiltily, secretively, to sustain the threads that bind him to them. (p. 35)

There are other Butterfields, however, who will have nothing to do with David, who hate and fear him. This adds an important element; for as well plotted as **Endless Love** is—masterfully plotted, so it's difficult not to cheat and flip to the final page—the true genius of the book is its characterization of David. Really, the more hostile Butterfields remind us, who is David Axelrod but one of those rejected lovers you can find on the back page of any newspaper? You see them shadowing ex-sweethearts, receiving injunctions from the local courts—untrustworthy, fragile people, nuisances at best, eternal losers, or at worst outright maniacs, likely to leap in any direction at the slightest provocation. In the course of this novel, David not only burns up a house but breaks parole, causes a fatal traffic accident, and manhandles his mother. But he's never merely a villain, and if we feel any fear in this book it is *for* him, not *of* him. This is largely because Scott Spencer places us so squarely in David's world. The "upper-class ping" of the Butterfields' voices, the grinding desperation of David's sexual contacts with Jade, the bleakness and moral uprightness of the objects in his parents' bureau drawers—all combine to give us a sense of a genuine, believable life. (pp. 35-6)

[David] is unerringly perceptive, sympathetic even to those he harms in the course of his obsession. As the novel winds down—as we draw back and see David from outside (28 years old now, unemployed and poorly educated, failed, beaten down, probably someone we'd pass hurriedly on a sidewalk)—we have an immense sense of loss and waste. Something *happens* in this book; both its hero and its readers have been changed by the time it ends. Scott Spencer is a magnificent writer, and **Endless Love** is his finest novel. (p. 36)

Anne Tyler, in a review of "Endless Love," in The New Republic, *Vol. 181, No. 11, September 15, 1979, pp. 35-6.*

BRIGITTE WEEKS

[*Endless Love*] is like quicksand. Beneath the surface it seethes, inhales and sucks the reader down. Fictional life with Scott Spencer is no relaxation, no refuge from the city or the suburbs. His is an all-encompassing, near-suffocating world that forces involvement and is unwilling to relinquish us to mere daily life. (p. 1)

The boundaries between sanity and madness are blurred in *Endless Love*. . . . We do not know if David is insane. His intricate self-analysis lays out every layer of his obsession with Jade. She herself is almost a cypher and seems too matter-of-fact to inspire such devotion. We are not really concerned with her. It is as if we were looking through the lens of a high-powered microscope into David's very being. A startling scene meets the eye: luxuriant, full of astonishing detail, but verging on the grotesque, a little ominous.

Scott Spencer has chosen to write of worlds slightly off-balance, with colors too bright and characters contorted by their affections or twists of fate. His first novel, *Last Night at the Brain Thieves Ball,* was a warming-up exercise for the imagination. . . . The warping factor in *Preservation Hall* was less visionary: the fanaticism of a political cadre. There is something comic about its bungling operation, but nonetheless, its influence turns a romantic retreat in Maine into a nightmare. In that book another complex and optimistic relationship bends and buckles under unnatural stress. Spencer succeeds in making us care more for David Axelrod, but he too is condemned. His love for Jade is heroic. He will sacrifice anything—family, future, his very sanity—to his love for Jade, and yet this passion engenders only moments of glory and a lifetime of emptiness and death-in-life. Spencer's heroes carry a heavy curse.

The women, on the other hand, seem in a strange reversal to survive the ravages of love that have traditionally been fatal to them. David's mother Rose, unhappy in marriage, bereft of her son, widowed, still struggles on, survives to take David back. Ann, Jade's mother, and a crucial protagonist in their saga, also loses her husband, first to divorce and then to death, but she continues on and visits David in prison while touring as the author of a successful book. Jade herself is given tangible life after love. But for David's father Arthur there is a heart attack, for Hugh death in the path of a speeding taxi, and for David himself only life without a mainspring.

Spencer has enormous power as a writer. He takes no easy options. He details the endless nuances of human feeling with infinite care. His writing is fearless and at times overwhelming as he piles phrase on phrase. . . . At other times his prose is spare and splendid: "Our bodies were fluttering. Birds caught in a cold chimney." This gift for the sudden, inescapable image keeps the continuing soul-searching from drifting into hopeless abstraction. The emotional is intertwined with the physical, tears with anguish. David cries wrenchingly and often.

Is this novel enjoyable? Successful? The answer to the latter must be equivocal. Scott Spencer is becoming a writer of astonishing depth and power. Yet the canvas is too crowded, there is no room to breathe, no space between the reader and the protagonist. The reader cannot be force-fed like the paté-de-fois goose. He needs more time and space to appreciate the riches offered. "Enjoyable?" Too soft a word for Scott Spencer. The sensations aroused by reading this novel are more akin to the legendary thrill of riding some fearsome, swooping, sickening rollercoaster—"What the hell am I doing here?" one moment, and the next a short walk to join the line for another ride. The speed, the fear, the anticipation sharpen the pleasure of walking quietly on solid ground. And that is the joy of *Endless Love*. (p. 4)

Brigitte Weeks, "Burned for Life," in Book World— The Washington Post, September 16, 1979, pp. 1, 4.

EDWARD ROTHSTEIN

[Scott Spencer] has achieved something quite remarkable in ["Endless Love," an] unabashedly romantic and often harrowing novel. He has created an adolescent love that is believably endless; in fact, we believe that there is no end to which the lover will not go to reach his beloved. . . .

Mr. Spencer carries us along by giving David, who tells the story, a powerful voice—violent, erotic, overwrought, naïve. . . . David feasts on . . . reckless passion and on pain: sobs crack like falling trees; lovers, covered with menstrual blood, look like victims of a savage crime. On occasion he lapses into romantic clichés—his love is "more real than time, more real than death, more real, even, than she and I"—but his language is usually compelling, subtly rhythmic, finely tuned.

Mr. Spencer has an acute grasp of character and situation. He gives us details that make these often tormented people uncommonly convincing. There are the erotic ties within the Butterfield family that are threatened by David's intrusion; the absence of such ties in his own parents; his mother's confused pain at his obsession; his father's active interest in it. But unfortunately Jade herself seems hardly there; in fact, she is little more than "affection's symbolic locus," like the mechanical heart she and David visit in the Museum of Science. (p. 13)

Although this is a love story, it may be something else as well: much of the drama lies not in David's love for Jade, but in his confrontations with the world from which his passions have exiled him. Mr. Spencer's earlier and less successful novels explored similar themes. In his first, "Last Night at the Brain Thieves Ball" (1973)—a tepid and cliché-ridden sci-fi yarn—an experimental psychologist leaves the ordinary world to join a totalitarian think-tank that seeks control over the brains of its subjects; the psychologist is eventually punished for inadequate control over his own desires. Mr. Spencer's often impressive second novel, "Preservation Hall" (1976), isolates two couples in a Maine blizzard. The narrator's tenuous control over his irrational fears and passions is tested by the pressure of other lives; he too is threatened with punishment.

David is similarly isolated. He carries his dream of endless love "beyond all reasonable limits . . . stepping outside of the law." His love cuts him off from society, family, and even from Jade herself; the worship of his feelings, he says, is his only spiritual life. Dangerous and narcissistic, petulantly adolescent, his love becomes a threat to the social and moral order, a "war with all the world." He kindles adolescent dreams in Jade's parents, who divorce and search for other loves, and he ignites forgotten needs in his own father and mother.

At times Mr. Spencer seems to suggest parallels between David's love and the political and cultural passions of the older generation—his parents' devotion to the Communist Party, Jade's parents' countercultural sympathies. All the characters are destructively innocent in their comprehension of "eros and civilization''; and the Butterfields' curious ''openness'' unleashes possibilities that neither David nor Jade can control.

But this is not what makes the novel so compelling. We want David to succeed in his love. In his heroic insistence, he becomes a figure from the countercultural myths of the 1960's: the rebel whose heightened sensitivity makes him a victim of society's brutal laws and institutions. His adolescent endless love becomes a sign of authenticity in a world of compromise. This tends to undercut the moral and social subtleties that Mr. Spencer has created; it betrays his confusion about his themes. Nevertheless, this confusion expresses both our attraction to the isolating force of sexual desire and our nostalgia for adolescent love.

Mr. Spencer's considerable talents prevent such confusion from destroying what is an exceptionally powerful novel. He has great sympathy for his characters, and the skill to arouse our feelings for them. Such care and sympathy may not be the endless love of the title, but it is something we could certainly use more of, and not only in our fiction. (pp. 13, 26)

> Edward Rothstein, ''A Dangerous Affair,'' in The New York Times Book Review, *September 23, 1979, pp. 13, 26.*

LARRY SWINDELL

There'll be excitement [over *Endless Love*]. This testament of eloquent anguish—served ironically by a title Barbara Cartland might have discarded—cannot fail to cause a stir among people who take fiction seriously. It may also dazzle its way to commercial success, for its readability and gamier appointments. The important news, though, is that *Endless Love* is not an oracle of promise, but Spencer's very fulfillment. He has shown just what he can do. . . .

Endless Love is much more courageous [than Spencer's previous novels]. In contrast to the emotional timidity of most American fiction, it is demonstrative past all embarrassment. Indeed, the book's design demands excessiveness—of a kind that would be scorned as ''overwriting'' in tamer stuff, but is here the root of seductive power. . . .

Spencer's technique is certainly provocative. Shunning the convention of the flashback, he orchestrates past and present as a fugue, achieving rather ingeniously a unified narrative in which bygone events become active elements in the continuity and the reader finds himself in the thrall of suspense over things already committed to history—or, in this case, memory. . . .

Endless Love is triumphantly a novel of character and action. David's own development is an exceptional literary accomplishment. An often exasperating youth, he is involuntarily cruel to his ineffectual parents, who cannot comprehend his obsession. (The Axelrods, and particularly David's father, are vividly drawn. Spencer has an extraordinary faculty for depicting parents and children who cannot articulate their love for each other.) Ann Butterfield, for whose late emergence as a writer David is the ironic catalyst, is thoroughly dissected. The only apparent exception to Spencer's command for fully fleshed characterization is Jade, but surely this is intentional. Jade must remain a kind of abstraction, for it is the idea of Jade as much as it is Jade herself with whom David is so infatuated. The sex in *Endless Love*—there are several passages of combustible, pulsating activity—is both quite marvelous and essential, as powerful proof of David's trance.

A novel delivered with such conviction easily implies an autobiographical tissue, but Spencer may confound us. His books are all highly individual, and not strait-jacketed by any one background. (David Axelrod shares with Virgil Morgan, the focal character of *Preservation Hall,* the narrative voice that is unmistakably the author's, yet they are an alluring contrast. Virgil is clearly stamped as one of life's winners, yet his well-ordered existence finally becomes unraveled. David seems a loser from the word go . . . but is he, really?) Though given to richness, *Endless Love* is forcefully direct. There are nuances suggestive of [John] Updike, and observations that ring of [John] Cheever; yet Spencer is more old-fashioned and eschews neither coincidence nor contrivance to serve his need. There has lately been some quiet speculation that Spencer may be ''the next'' John Irving, that *Endless Love* may capture the core of the *Garp* audience. Perhaps. Irving and Spencer are quite different in both style and technique; yet they are both enormously sympathetic.

Endless Love is remarkable for being an urgently compassionate novel that never becomes a sentimental one. Sentimentality is a net for emotional trapeze artists in prose. Spencer soars with no net below, and catches the bar every time.

> Larry Swindell, ''Hearts on Fire,'' in The Village Voice, *Vol. XXIV, No. 39, September 24, 1979, p. 47.*

THOMAS R. EDWARDS

In spite of [Samuel] Richardson, Emily Brontë, or [D. H.] Lawrence, you would hardly know from reading most Anglo-American fiction that it's love that makes the world go round. For the Protestant imagination, passionate sexual desire needs to be satirized, sentimentalized, or domesticated, as if it were some severe but exotic disease which, properly isolated, needn't interfere with *important* concerns like money, politics, manly adventure, or social education. Now, even in a more lenient moral climate, we get lots of sexual performance but not much love. Most of the great love stories are still imports.

Scott Spencer's *Endless Love,* a serious novel of wholehearted desire, thus seems odd and intriguing. . . .

Spencer plays it straight. David is neither a teenage monster nor a victim of an absurd social system, he's just an intelligent and sensitive boy in love.

His extreme passion does of course have a background. His own parents are earnest Jewish ex-communists who give their emotions to important public causes but aren't very good at private love. He is drawn to Jade Butterfield (a name, as I'm sure Spencer knows, that seems to have leaped out of a Harlequin Romance) because her family so clearly represents liberated feeling. . . .

But Spencer knows the difference between conditions and causes. David doesn't love Jade because he's an adolescent or feels unloved at home or finds her ''lifestyle'' seductive; nor is it the fault of the age or the culture he has to grow up in. He loves her, Spencer seems to say, simply because he has a mysterious gift for loving which most people lack. And that gift makes of him a kind of figure usually relegated to ''popular'' fiction and song, films and soap-operas—the lover as, in essence, criminal and maniac. His kind of love is what young people are told they will outgrow and almost always do, if only because they've been told they will; it's what some adults talk to priests and psychiatrists about, what keeps the sensational press and the police courts so busy. I admire the book for being able to play so close to the muddy stuff of mass entertainment without quite getting its hands dirty. . . .

"Madness" is not the question; to call David mad, or pitiful, or ridiculous, is only to avoid feeling something of what intensity of desire is like. He says it better by describing himself as an operatic actor—playing his role intensely, perhaps even overplaying it, since, even though the performance and the audience may be "illusions," only in the role is there a chance of living up to his own best possibilities. This odd, scrupulous, rather exhausting novel succeeds in making one think again about a kind of feeling one may not usually be prepared to take seriously. (p. 43)

> *Thomas R. Edwards, "It's Love!" in* The New York Review of Books, *Vol. XXVII, No. 3, March 6, 1980, pp. 43-5.*

SIMON BLOW

'Style,' Thornton Wilder once wrote, 'is but the faintly contemptible vessel in which the bitter liquid is recommended to the world.' Wilder's paradox, however, has not been heeded by Scott Spencer while writing his saga, *Endless Love*.

Scott Spencer's writing in this novel is as self-indulgent as his belief that the traumatic teenage love affair described can affect us as pure and untainted. Repeated sexual imagery palls faster than any other and is rarely evocative of selfless tenderness. Of sex, yes. But that, apparently, is not what the novel is about.

> *Simon Blow, "Quick Eye," in* New Statesman, *Vol. 99, No. 2560, April 11, 1980, p. 558.*

Joan (Carol) D(ennison) Vinge

1948-

American short story writer and novelist.

Vinge is the recipient of Hugo Awards for her novelette "Eyes of Amber" (1977) and her novel *The Snow Queen* (1980). She writes both adult and young adult fiction and has adapted as a children's book the popular "Star Wars" movie, *Return of the Jedi* (1983). Her characters are usually outcasts from society. Like her adult works, Vinge's first young adult novel, *Psion* (1982), places as much emphasis on the psychological turmoil of the protagonist as on the suspense generated by external action. Cat, the protagonist of *Psion*, is a teenage loner whose telepathic powers alienate him from his planet Ardattee. Caught in a power struggle between two interplanetary civilizations, Cat must battle with his own isolation and loneliness as well as with enemy forces.

The redeeming virtue of love and communication is a recurrent theme in Vinge's work. Carl Yoke observes that the alienation of her characters is not an end in itself, but rather a necessary step in their movement toward transcendence. Through love and communication, Vinge's characters overcome their estrangement and may achieve the power to change society. Yoke further comments: "Their common enemy is often the values of the society in which they find themselves. From the exertion of their mutual struggle, they forge new value systems and come to a more complete realization of their own potentials." Thus, Vinge's long fantasy *The Snow Queen* (1980) is both a traditional science fiction battle of evil against good and a story of the love between two individuals alienated from society. Eventually, the force of their love results in the successful overthrow of the corrupt Winter Queen.

Vinge's stories are characteristically set in a fully realized, minutely detailed world. Critics often praise the skill with which Vinge creates the believable and complex social structures of her futuristic world. *The Outcasts of Heaven Belt* (1978) exemplifies Vinge's close attention to societal values. This novel concerns the war between a fallen democracy and a socialist military society, both of which are contrasted to the protagonist's idealized society founded on complex kinship and marriage ties. Although some critics feel that the multiple levels in Vinge's stories are not always successful, most find her work thematically rich, tightly constructed, and psychologically and sociologically complex.

(See also *Contemporary Authors*, Vols. 93-96.)

Photograph by Jay Kay Klein

A review of "Fireship," in Publishers Weekly, *Vol. 214, No. 19, November 6, 1978, pp. 75-6.*

PUBLISHERS WEEKLY

This impressive debut volume ["**Fireship**"] is composed of two novelettes. . . . [The title story is] a tightly constructed adventure story, told with a deft, light touch. "**Mother and Child**," the second story, traces the maturation of a young woman, a priestess, in a medieval type of world where humans are manipulated "for their own good" by benevolent aliens. This story works on a number of levels and is a rich reading experience. The two tales are absolutely dissimilar, and they are both absolutely marvelous. (pp. 75-6)

ROBIN G. ADAMS

Fireship actually houses two distinct mini-novels, *Fireship* and *Mother and Child*. Both are evidence of Vinge's rightful place as one of s-f's luminaries. They are both well written, highly enjoyable works, and demonstrate the variety of style found in science fiction.

Fireship is a light-hearted adventure story. . . . *Mother and Child* is a more thoughtful work. A post-holocaust tribal priestess, born with hearing and perfect vision into a deaf and nearly-blind world, bears a child that could bridge the gap between her tribe and its warring neighbor, and restore to them all the knowledge of their ancestors. It is a sensitive portrayal, skillfully handled from the viewpoints of several characters. Together the two works are an excellent choice for any s-f collection, or a good place to start one.

Robin G. Adams, in a review of "Fireship," in Kliatt Young Adult Paperback Book Guide, *Vol. XIII, No. 3, April, 1979, p. 20.*

PUBLISHERS WEEKLY

[With **"Eyes of Amber and Other Stories"**] Joan Vinge has put together a rewarding collection of six carefully crafted, emotionally rich stories. Included are her first, the bittersweet **"Tin Soldier,"** in which a cyborg (a man with artificial parts) falls in love with a spacefaring woman; and her latest, **"Mediaman,"** an action/love story set in the universe of Vinge's first novel. . . . Most moving of all, however, are **"View from a Height,"** . . . which concerns a woman who volunteers for a one-way trip out into the universe; and **"The Crystal Ship,"** in which a young woman's life is redeemed by an alien who is an outcast from his own people.

A review of "Eyes of Amber and Other Stories," in Publishers Weekly, *Vol. 216, No. 6, August 6, 1979, p. 90.*

ANTHONY R. LEWIS

[The title novella in *Fireship*] is a competent adventure story. The protagonist, whom we do not meet until late in the story, has by his existence called into being an antagonist. This antagonist would normally be considered the hero. He is a human/computer symbiosis, not a cyborg. The computer personality is more appealing than the human in most aspects. The "hero" gets involved in interplanetary intrigue, fights assorted villains, wins in the end, and gets to bed a female. But the culmination is not that of the typical super-agent story. Victory is achieved by the (not-quite Hegelian) synthesis of the protagonist (villain) and the antagonist (our hero) which suggests a higher order of human/computer symbiosis is possible. . . . [By itself, this story] would not justify the book.

The second novella, *Mother and Child,* more than justifies the existence of this book. . . . The story is this: an alien planet, with two cultures. One is agricultural worshipping the Mother Goddess (the Kotaane), the other is urban and patriarchal (the Neaane). The Kotaane have an additional sense, which is either absent in the Neaane or is suppressed by deliberate mutilation. These cultures are coming into conflict. Mixing into this is a second group of aliens, the Colonial Service. A Kotaane priestess, pregnant by her smith husband, is stolen by Neaane forces and becomes concubine to their king. Her subsequent life, childbirth, exile, and recovery form the story. It is a good story. As for the plot; you may have read something similar called the *Iliad* (by Homer's time all the major plots were known).

This story has aliens; two types of aliens. They don't act alien; they seem to be human beings. This is not a failure of imagination on the writer's part. It is, rather, a recognition of the existence of certain universals necessary to build a culture. These are needed if you are discoid, amorphous, felinoid, or even humanoid. Could this story have been about Earth humans at different technological levels? Yes. Why then is it SF? . . . The story is about love and loyalty and integrity and courage. Perhaps it is the inclusion of these characteristics that makes it SF; these qualities are rarely found in the current mainstream novels. There are villains but they are not completely evil; their good is a different and conflicting good from that of the protagonists. Be it understood, there is evil in the Neaane culture; the evil of suppressing abilities and human qualities, of persecuting people for what they are, rather than what they do. If you keep working at it, good wins in the end because evil is intrinsically weak. Again, maybe that's why this got labelled

SF instead of mainstream. The story is worth reading. (pp. 165-66)

Anthony R. Lewis, in a review of "Fireship," in Analog Science Fiction/Science Fact, *Vol. XCIX, No. 10, October, 1979, pp. 165-66.*

PUBLISHERS WEEKLY

There are memorable characters [in **"The Snow Queen"**] and a complex, suspensefully orchestrated plot that builds with steady inevitability from a slow start to a symphonic finale. A few may be put off by Vinge's unabashedly romantic approach—which does lead to scattered spots of overwriting—but many more will be captivated. That, plus an expert use of familiar SF concepts, could take the book past its certain popularity with the genre audience to success in the larger market beyond. . . . **"The Snow Queen"** is a triumph for a fine writer who is still growing and will someday surpass her achievement here.

A review of "The Snow Queen," in Publishers Weekly, *Vol. 217, No. 5, February 8, 1980, p. 69.*

JAMES GUNN

[**The Snow Queen**] has a complicated plot, whose complications—unfortunately for the success of the novel—unfold so deliberately that its final shape is clear only in retrospect. Moon Dawntreader, the protagonist, is a young woman born to fisherfolk of the Summer people. She is in love with her cousin, Sparks. Both were conceived at the last Festival in Carbuncle. Moon, though she does not know it, is the clone of Arienrhod, the Snow Queen of the title, who rules the Winter stage of Tiamat and has prolonged her life through the slaughter of the gentle, immortal Mers and now hopes to prolong her reign, even after her death in the ritual that marks the coming of summer, by making her clone the Summer Queen. . . . The novel aims at the inevitability of myth, but the author . . . does not seem to appreciate that the myth must be established early so that the reader can follow its working out.

The long (536 pages) novel is rich with character, color and invention . . . , but the book is not as good as the sum of its parts. It's as if the author knows the words but not the tune. This reader, at least, felt unmoved by the characters and their fates; I didn't care what happened to any of them. The source of that indifference, I believe, lies in the manner in which events simply happen to the characters: they don't purpose anything, with the exception of Arienrhod, whose plans are frustrated, in the end, with surprising suddenness and ease.

James Gunn, in a review of "The Snow Queen," in Book World—The Washington Post, *May 25, 1980, p. 8.*

LINDSY VAN GELDER

This delicious book [**The Snow Queen**] is a futuristic translation of the girl-rescues-boy fairy tale by Hans Christian Andersen: the love story of Moon and Sparks. . . .

This complicated, lyrical, anti-colonialist novel works as first-rate adventure, but its greatest achievement is the creation of a literal world of characters: human, robot, amphibian, male and female; from castes, tribes, and political systems across a galaxy. Not since I read the Oz books 25 years ago have I been so drawn into a writer's total reality.

*Lindsy Van Gelder, in a review of "The Snow Queen,"
in* Ms., *Vol. IX, No. 1, July, 1980, p. 29.*

JACK SULLIVAN

["**The Snow Queen**"] gets nicely off the ground several times only to be dragged down again and again by banality. The best passages occur in the exposition itself, as Miss Vinge establishes the sociological and cosmic rules of the planet Tiamat, with its unstable twin suns, its Winter and Summer Queens, its Black Gates to other worlds, its outer region "where space was twisted like a string, tied into knots so that far became near and time was caught up in the loop."

Unfortunately, Miss Vinge's human and alien characters speak such awful gibberish that it's difficult to keep one's attention on the world they inhabit. . . . The worst offender is the heroine, Moon Dawntreader, the Queen's clone, who apparently sees herself as a font of profundity and poetry. . . .

These people are a bad influence on Miss Vinge. Whenever one of them makes a speech, her own prose becomes insufferable: "The Sea rested, sublime in Her Indifference, an imperturbable mirror for the face of universal truth. *Today never ends in Carbuncle . . . will tomorrow really ever come?*" Miss Vinge must think this is really terrific, or she wouldn't use capital letters and italics; that's much more fantastic than anything in this novel. (p. 29)

Jack Sullivan, "Ordinarily Fantastic," in The New York Times Book Review, *August 3, 1980, pp. 12, 29.**

RICHARD LUBBOCK

Science, religion, magic, moral philosophy, anthropology, and indeed almost all the arts and sciences intermingle most deliciously in Joan D. Vinge's *The Snow Queen*. . . .

The author describes herself as "an anthropologist of the future," by which she means alternate universes, and her work certainly contains strong echoes of Margaret Mead, Sir James Fraser and innumerable other strains of scientific, social and literary thought.

The Snow Queen is a fantastical elaboration of Hans Christian Andersen's folk tale of the same name. It records events on Tiamat, a world which exists in two states of being, Summer and Winter, alternating every century and a half. The Change is governed by a nearby revolving black hole, which provides a relativistically time-offset Stargate to the seven worlds of The Hegemony—the remote, political empire to which Tiamat is affiliated. The Stargate is closing. Summer approaches and the 150-year reign of Arienrhod, the Snow Queen, is drawing to a close. Her youth and beauty have been sustained by regular injections of "the water of life", a silvery serum extract of the blood of an intelligent sea-creature, the mer, which is slaughtered for the purpose. Now Arienrhod's extended life must end, but she seeks to outlast Summer and rule other Winters by reproducing her exact body and mind in clones grown from her own cells.

Vinge spins her intricate story in sensuous pleasure-giving prose that restores to the child in the reader all the delights of Faerie even while posing problems of adult concern. In her carefully crafted world of Festivals and Sybils, aristocrats and fisher folk, she lodges such moral questions as the propriety of one mind-form preying physically upon another, and the bitter probability that sharper than a serpent's tooth it is to have a thankless clone.

Like all fairy stories, *The Snow Queen* is irreproachable in terms of plausibility. Perhaps the properties of "real" black holes aren't quite right for this story. Perhaps human nature does not in fact work the way anthropologist Vinge proposes. Never mind. Somewhere . . . in superspace, Arienrhod *must* rule over Tiamat, and Moon and Sparks and Starbuck must fight and play.

The growing interest in science-fiction suggests that, like *The Snow Queen*'s world of Tiamat, our world is also confronted by a profound transformation. Our Change marks the end of the three-centuries-old Winter ruled over by the King of Pessimism, Sir Isaac Newton, and the advent of the lab-tested magical world of alternate quantum realities. This is the *peripeteia* that heralds the downfall of realism and the restoration of science fiction to its proper, central throne in literature.

Richard Lubbock, "Long Live the New Queen of Faerie," in Books in Canada, *Vol. 10, No. 1, January, 1981, p. 8.*

CHRISTOPHER PRIEST

[With *The Snow Queen* we] are in the presence . . . of a successor to [Frank Herbert's] *Dune* and [Ursula Le Guin's] *The Left Hand of Darkness*.

However, comparisons are odious. . . . Because perhaps it ought to be said . . . that *The Snow Queen* is the quintessence of a certain kind of science fiction, a journey as far into the heartlands of the genre as it is possible to go without starting to come back. The publishers call this "worldcraft," and it is a form of novel that more and more sf writers are essaying these days: "worldcraft" is the depiction of an entire planet or world, described politically, culturally, geographically, sociologically, scientifically and sometimes cartographically. . . . We glimpse this world through visits to highlife and lowlife, in long journeys across the world's surface or away from it into space, through witnessing the power struggles and conniving of the characters, by fearing for innocents at risk, by seeing the final triumph of a certain kind of moral rectitude, by thrilling to hints and clues to darker powers and supernormal talents, and in ogling the spectacular scenery that unfolds before the reader's eye in cascades of descriptive prose. Whatever, you can be assured that there is a lot of this sort of thing in *The Snow Queen*: 536 pages in all, competently handled.

Yes, the book is competent but not inspired. (pp. 51-2)

It is . . . reasonably well told, because it is planned and narrated with unassuming craft, but it is also moderately badly written. It is by no means a poor book, but it is an ordinary one, an overlong one.

At fault is Vinge's vocabulary, the choices she made in three crucial areas. In words, in people and in idiom. (p. 52)

Consider her use of the English language. In spite of the fact that *The Snow Queen* occasionally reads like an Anne McCaffrey novel with long words, Vinge seems to prefer the plainest, least evocative words. There is no merit in linguistic exotica for its own sake, but after a few hundred pages the reader starts hungering for apparitions that are not "strange," for hatred that is not "ill-concealed," for dreamers who are not "headstrong," and so on. I searched in vain for the odd or appealing word (not counting sf nonce-words), for the newly turned phrase, the surprising simile. Caution is the hallmark of Vinge's prose, to the detriment of her images.

Then there is the vocabulary of her characters' responses. Again, Vinge is scrupulously tasteful in her approach to character, but in her anxiety not to go wrong, she underplays her hand. In a novel as long as this there is plenty of time for character development, and part of the pleasure of a lengthy read is in watching the people grow . . . but (1) the book is too long anyway, (2) the sloth of the characters' development is part of the reason the book is so long, and (3) the plot actually moves much faster than our recognition of the characters. It is often difficult to remember who is who; particularly, her characters cannot exist without constantly looking at each other or touching each other. Fingers tremble, hands briefly touch, arms are gripped, eyes avert themselves; once noticed, this kind of thing can be extremely distracting. The vocabulary she selects from is limited. And when not body-languaging to each other the characters are given to flashing italicized thoughts at the reader, in the tedious tradition of the *Dune* books. This is a stylistic mannerism not often found outside science fiction; it is passed along from one generation of writer to the next, as if it were actually useful and not intrusive. Page 277: "And now? *Yes . . . now!*" Who on earth thinks like that? I'm sure Vinge herself doesn't. It's stuff and nonsense, and merely adds more words to passages that are already overlong. On page 27 a character called Starbuck looks in a mirror and helpfully asks himself, "Who is Starbuck?", which is good timing as it leads the author into a long account of who Starbuck is. The author has picked up lazy habits from other science fiction writers, and she is much the worse for it.

But it is in the vocabulary of her chosen idiom that Vinge is, surprisingly, weakest. No one can write this sort of novel without running into a major creative difficulty. In a described world of a remote future, or of a remote part of the universe, the author will be imaginatively isolated from the very forces which made him or her into a writer: language, nation, culture, art, myth, slang, scenery, history, folklore, etc. This is a problem that can sometimes be solved by simply ignoring it (eg. in the *Star Wars* movies), but Vinge is an intelligent and conscientious writer and has I think appreciated the difficulty. The people of another world, when described as a coherent part of that world, would possess such an intangible underlay of assumptions, recognitions and cultural shorthand that any attempt at capturing it must be doomed. (And never mind the insuperable problem of having to write the book in English.) The twin traps for the author are banality and incomprehensibility, and the most demanding imaginative task inherent in writing this kind of novel is finding a safe line between them. In some ways the very size, and importance, of this problem might make the "worldcraft" type of novel congenitally unwritable, at least by serious novelists. Yet, Le Guin has almost pulled it off a couple of times, which underlines the degree of the challenge. Vinge has made an honorable attempt, but she is too often banal in her choice of metaphors, too often given to placing long introspective plot catch-ups in her characters' minds.

I recognized in the *The Snow Queen* a sincere attempt to write a good story, and I was only sorry I could not enjoy it more. (pp. 52-4)

Christopher Priest, in a review of "The Snow Queen," in The Magazine of Fantasy and Science Fiction, *Vol. 60, No. 5, May, 1981, pp. 50-4.*

SALLY ESTES

When 16-year-old Cat, [protagonist of *Psion*] . . . , gets a chance to "volunteer" for a psi research project, he embarks on a tumultuous series of experiences leading not only to the awakening of his telepathic powers and the discovery that he can care for others but also to his brutal enslavement and near death. Finally accepting his dual human-alien heritage, Cat experiences an incredible heightening of his extraordinary psionic power when he faces a potent, power-hungry psion in a deadly confrontation that not only destroys Cat's enemy but also Cat's psionic power. In her first novel for young people, . . . [Joan D. Vinge] pulls no punches in fleshing out a viable, grim, multi-planetary civilization as the setting for a complex, borderline-adult story that combines the excitement and adventure of space opera with more psychological depth in character development than is usual in teenage science fiction. Vinge demonstrates her mastery of sustained suspense carried in part by Cat's emotional stream of consciousness and in part by the intensity of the action.

Sally Estes, in a review of "Psion," in Booklist, *Vol. 79, No. 1, September 1, 1982, p. 37.*

CARL YOKE

> But she wore the nomad's tunic she had brought back with her from Persiponë's, the only clothing she owned, its gaudy color as alien as she suddenly felt herself, among the people who should have been her own.

These lines from the "footrace" scene in Joan Vinge's *The Snow Queen* clearly express the psychological alienation of Dawn Moontreader Summer, the novel's heroine. Though she stands in a crowd of people from her own clan, she feels that she is an outsider, that she is somehow divorced from the very culture in which she was raised. This is the fundamental experience of a person alienated, estranged, or disenfranchised. (p. 103)

Moon's portrayal as an alienated being is no accident. She is but one of several such characters in *The Snow Queen*. Equally estranged are Sparks, Moon's cousin and lover; Jerusha, a highly capable but emotionally tortured police inspector; BZ Gundhalinu, Jerusha's pride-ridden and rigidly structured aide; and Arienrhod, the beautiful but power-crazed Winter Queen. Moreover, these characters reflect a pattern that predominates in Vinge's writing. Most of her major works contain at least one alienated character, usually the protagonist. . . .

To find alienation the major theme of Vinge's writing is no surprise, for as critic Blanche Gelfant has indicated, it "is the inextricable theme of modern American fiction." (p. 105)

While being alienated certainly implies being neurotic, it does not inevitably spell psychological disaster. Some individuals do struggle and fail in their attempts to cope with their cultures. Others succeed. . . . Inevitably, success is impelled by love, for it is characters who love themselves, another, and the world who do transcend. . . . The belief that man can transcend his alienation is held by several philosophers and psychologists, who have been termed "utopian existentialists." While accepting that estrangement is a condition of present-day society, they believe that it can be overcome by future sociological and psychological developments.

Among this group, psychologist Erich Fromm, in particular, believes that transcendence is possible. He sees alienation as evolutionary. "Human nature drives toward unity with the 'all,' with nature; but unity on the highest level requires a temporary separation, and consequent loneliness. One goes out in order to return enriched. Separation, though painful, is a progressive step." . . .

Though there is no evidence that Vinge has consciously based her characters in Fromm's psychology, the fact is that they closely parallel his thinking. They exhibit the qualities of alienated individuals. Then, by virtue of their experiences, they form new value systems and manage to transcend their estrangement. They do this by learning to love, and they learn to love by learning to communicate. In maturing, some of them even develop the potential to change their cultures. (p. 107)

Perhaps the purest and most direct example of a character at odds with the norms of her society, lonely, tense, and frustrated occurs in Amanda Montoya of **"Phoenix in the Ashes."** Like Moon Shadow she too has been ostracized. She chose love over a marriage arranged by her father, but when the sailor she promised to wait for fails to return, she is forced from her father's home and her dowry is distributed between her two sisters. Now she lives in an adobe cottage on her father's land but far from the main house, and gleans his fields for food. Though he refuses to acknowledge her existence, he has not so completely forgotten her that he would force her to become a beggar or a whore, the only occupations left to a woman of San Pedro who has lost her family sponsorship. In this rigid, male-dominated society, women are regarded as valuable property. From birth they are impressed with the need for obedience and chastity; their role is to serve their husbands and fathers blindly. They weave and cook but do not read.

Amanda's rebellion costs her dearly. Even though other pockets of civilization remain in this postbomb world, San Pedro maintains only limited trading relationships. Because of religious stringency, leaving the society is nearly impossible. So, eight years after her rebellion, Amanda survives at a minimum level. She is bitter, she is lonely, and she finds that "the staid ritual life in San Pedro [is] suffocating her, and her dreams [are] dying." (pp. 110-11)

If Vinge's characters are not at odds with their own societies, they are at odds within the societies they find themselves and are alienated from them. This displacement occurs, for example, to Etaa, the Kotaane priestess of the powerful novelette **"Mother and Child."** While she never loses faith with her own native Nature cult, Etaa is twice removed from it physically. First, she is kidnapped by Meron, King of Tramaine. Then, she is kidnapped from Tramaine by Wic'owoyake, one of the silicon-based life forms believed to be gods by Meron and his people. (p. 111)

[It] is clear that alienation is a major component of Vinge's characterization. It does produce withdrawal from one's own kind, rebellion against a society's values, loneliness (the affective corollary of alienation), tension, anxiety, frustration, even physical illness, but it is not an irreversible condition like Sören Kierkegaard's "sickness unto death." Rather, it is evolutionary. It is a stage a personality must pass through on its way to transcendence. From this point of view, it parallels

Erich Fromm's position and is much like what an adolescent passes through in his search for identity.

For Vinge alienation is the result of the compelling drive of her characters toward the realization of their potentials. Completing their quests for fulfillment brings them into conflict with the values of the societies in which they find themselves because the societies themselves are neurotic and unrealized. Yet, Vinge's characters escape their alienation with both dignity and integrity because they persevere in their attempts to grasp reality, both inside and outside themselves. They continue to strive to understand themselves, to align themselves with nature, and to communicate with all things, especially in emotional terms. Moon realizes this as she tries to make friends with Blodwed's caged pets in *The Snow Queen*. "She lost track of time or any purpose beyond the need to communicate even to the smallest degree with every creature, and earn for herself the reward of its embryonic trust. . . ." Like Moon, Vinge's other characters also succeed in achieving something like Fromm's "productive orientation characterized by the ability to love and create." For Vinge, communication and love are psychologically opposed to alienation and loneliness.

Because love is the ultimate communication, and communication, in the broadest and deepest sense of the word, is the means for breaking down alienation, Vinge frequently focuses her stories on love relationships. In particular, she brings together an alienated man and an alienated woman and lets them work at communicating. Bound together by their loneliness and prompted by the events of the story that continuously force them together, they eventually break down the barriers between them and achieve a love relationship based upon mutual trust. Their common enemy is often the values of the society in which they find themselves. From the exertion of their mutual struggle, they forge new value systems and come to a more complete realization of their own potentials. Battling to survive at both the physical and psychological levels, they do produce or promise to produce changes in the value system of the society itself.

Such is the case in **"Legacy."** Mythili and Chaim are both alienated. When he is chosen as media man and she as pilot of Sabu Siamang's rescue mission to Planet Two, a sequence of events forces them not only to communicate with but to trust one another. When Siamang kills Sekka-Olefin, the prospector he is supposed to be rescuing, for the computer software he controls and subsequently tries to cover up the crime, both Mythili and Chaim are forced to recognize the fact that the values of their society are not only undesirable but psychologically unhealthy. Mythili's refusal to cover up the crime forces Siamang to try to kill her. The incident makes Chaim aware of the limits of his own integrity and forces him to make a realistic choice in order to save them both: he convinces Siamang to abandon Mythili on the planet's surface rather than "spacing" her on the way home. He argues that she will either freeze or suffocate if they jam the oxygen valve on her suit. Either way, her death will look like an accident. But Dartagnan knows something that neither Mythili nor the drug-crazed Siamang knows—the air of Planet Two is breathable, at least for a short time. Olefin told him that when Siamang was out of the shelter. Chaim's choice is difficult but realistic. He also knows that Mythili can make it back to Olefin's shelter and fix his landing module, if she does not panic. Under the existing conditions, it is the best possible decision. When they finally land on Mecca, their home asteroid, Dartagnan publicly charges Siamang with the murder, knowing full well that he may also be charged with Mythili's death if she fails to escape. She does escape, however, and he ruins his career as a media man, but he has learned something valuable about himself and his world. So has she. Subsequent situations force greater understanding, eventually permitting them to build new, more healthy value systems and to fall in love. (pp. 115-17)

The Snow Queen presents [a] . . . more complicated variation on the pattern. It is similar to **"Mother and Child"** in that it moves cyclically, from innocent love through alienation to mature love, and it involves more than one other alienated individual. As the novel begins, Moon and Sparks are naively happy, but when they both seek acceptance as sibyls and Sparks is rejected, he leaves his warm, southern homeland for Carbuncle, the capital, in the north. As Moon's selection for training overtly marks the beginning of her alienation (she is unaware that the very nature of her birth has already marked her), Sparks's rejection marks his alienation. Instead of being forced together to learn to understand each other, themselves, nature, God, and their people, they are torn apart. Reality is thrust upon them through their experiences and relationships with the outside world. Into the mix, Vinge inserts Arienrhod, the Winter Queen. She is Moon's mother, by cloning, though the two do not know one another, and she is Moon's mirror image: evil, insensitive, power mad, and accomplished in the ways of the world.

As events unfold, Arienrhod permits Starbuck, her right hand and lover, to be ousted by Sparks and then takes him as lover. The relationship is logical. Arienrhod possesses the secret of longevity, so age is not a factor, and as Moon's genetic equivalent, she bears the physical and mental characteristics that attracted Sparks to Moon in the first place. But her power over Sparks is so complete that she corrupts him, and as he becomes more dependent upon her, his alienation deepens.

The relationship among Moon, Sparks, and Arienrhod is broadly defined by Hans Christian Andersen's fairy tale, also entitled "The Snow Queen" and one of the novel's sources. In Andersen's story, Kay, a young boy, is struck in the eye and the heart by slivers from a magic mirror invented by a wicked hobgoblin and then shattered. The mirror's power is to distort all that is beautiful and to turn the heart cold. Kay wanders off to live with the Snow Queen, oblivious to the cares and concerns of Gerda, a young girl who loves him. She is persistent, and she learns what is wrong with him, finds him, and heals him with a kiss whose power is drawn from her innocence.

Moon's psychological journey, however, is not that simple. While Sparks is writhing uncomfortably in the clutches of Arienrhod, she must first solve the problem of her own alienation. Her destiny is not her own; she is manipulated by the Old Empire computer, which places her inevitably into conflict with the values of both the Winters and the Summers. While she is trying to realize her personality, she is also gaining experience that broadens her perception of reality. Though she bears the same genetic program as Arienrhod, environment has shaped her differently.

In the other stories, communication between the alienated female and the alienated male mutually brought them to a better understanding of reality and fostered new value systems that brought love, but in *The Snow Queen* it is Moon who must force the personality transcendences. Not until she finally locates Sparks and sleeps with him is he even aware that he is under some kind of "spell." Only then, and after his father

has acknowledged his parentage, is Sparks's alienation resolved. (pp. 119-20)

While the pattern of an alienated woman forced through a series of experiences with an alienated man expresses Vinge's concern for communication, the enlarged perception of reality that each character acquires also brings a benefit with it. It is that each transcended protagonist finds herself with the ability to change the values of her society or the promise to do so. As the Summer Queen, for example, Moon will integrate the values of the Winter and Summer peoples and through the power of the sibyl computer, will begin to recreate the Old Empire civilization on Tiamat. Where Arienrhod has failed because of her insensitivity and alienation, Moon will succeed because of her ability to love in a psychologically healthy way. (p. 120)

In order to frame the fight her characters must wage against the values of the various societies in which they find themselves, Vinge usually sets her stories in worlds that are either very primitive or have been destroyed by some disaster. This permits her to create societies that have values that are obviously unhealthy and that suffer from Fromm's socially patterned defect. The distopic worlds, where created by technology, also suggest the dangers of human folly.

"Legacy" and *The Outcasts of Heaven Belt*, for example, are set in an asteroid system whose civilizations have been virtually destroyed by a civil war that killed a hundred million people. What remains are fragile societies slowly disintegrating into chaos. Natural resources are scarce. . . . Cooperation has been replaced by division. It is a society that is psychologically unhealthy and one that easily breeds estrangement. (p. 121)

Vinge's distopic worlds also serve another purpose. They represent and support the winter season in the death and revival of vegetation archetype that she uses as a broad metaphor to symbolize the psychological development of her characters. Simply stated, the winter period, or death phase of vegetation, is equivalent to the alienation of the characters. The revival of vegetation in the spring is equivalent to the personality transcendence of the characters. The distopic worlds are the "waste land" or "wounded land" of the Grail Quest myths. In those myths, the "wounded land" (it is either suffering from drought or infertility, though it may indeed be wounded in other ways) is connected with the illness of the Fisher King, and the task of the hero is to cure both the land and the King. This is not to suggest that Vinge is writing Grail Quest stories. It is simply to point out a device that she uses to emphasize the psychological condition of her characters, who, since they are suffering from alienation and loneliness, are ill and must be cured.

While it occurs in a number of variations, the death and revival of vegetation story occurs in many of the world's mythologies. It is a personification of the fate of most vegetation during the changing seasons. (p. 123)

While the archetype is clearly present in all the stories being considered here, it is most obvious in *The Snow Queen*. In that novel, Vinge stresses that "the Change" is coming, that time when the Summers will ascend the throne of Tiamat after ritualistically destroying the Winter Queen and her consort. Quite imaginatively, after she is destroyed, the Vegetation Queen returns in the person of Moon, Arienrhod's clone, and with her comes the promise of revived vegetation. In the novel, Moon's presence promises the return of the reproductive energies of Nature as well as the revival of Old Empire culture and technology.

While several other symbols, devices, and motifs support this archetype, among the most important of them is Vinge's use of what Robert Graves has identified in his book of the same name as "The White Goddess." She is a goddess of the moon, most often portrayed as having three aspects: the New Moon, who is the white goddess of birth and growth; the Full Moon, who is the red goddess of love and battle; and the Old Moon, who is the black goddess of divination and death. As such, she goes through a cyclical process each month that results in renewal. It must be remembered, as Graves points out, that this Triple Goddess is the personification of primitive woman— "the creatress and destructress. As the New Moon or Spring, she was girl; as the Full Moon or Summer, she was woman; as the Old Moon or Winter, she was hag."

For each aspect of the White Goddess, Graves traces variations through many cultures. Most often, the three aspects are represented by the three mythical goddesses: Arianrhod, Blodeuwedd, and Cerridwen. Arianrhod is a Welsh goddess, who in the *Romance of Math the Son of Mathonwy* gives birth to a divine child. She then transforms into Blodeuwedd, a treacherous love goddess who destroys the divine child and then transforms again into a death goddess, known as the Old-Sow-Who-Eats-Her-Farrow, that is, her litter of pigs. In other words, she feeds on the flesh of the dead child. Not coincidentally, Arienrhod of *The Snow Queen* feeds symbolically off of Sparks. Like the divine child, Sparks is restored to life. Arianrhod, the Welsh goddess, was an orgiastic goddess whose worship included male sacrifices.

In Celtic legend, the third aspect (the Old Moon of death and divination) is Morgan le Fay, King Arthur's sister, a death goddess who often assumes the form of the raven. Morgan in Irish is "the Morrigan," meaning "Great Queen," and "le Faye" means "the fate." She was not the gentle figure depicted in *Morte d'Arthur* but rather she was more like "black, screaming hag, Cerridwen." From this analysis, of course, Vinge has constructed Fate Ravenglass, the gentle sibyl of the novel who chooses Moon to be queen. Moreover, she has also adopted and adapted other aspects of the "White Goddess." Arianrhod is loosely transformed into Arienrhod, Blodeuwedd becomes Blodwed, and Moon, who appears in the novel only as a young girl, obviously represents the New Moon, or the birth and regeneration, phase of the goddess. But even though Vinge has adopted their names, she has not necessarily paralleled her characters with the meanings attributed to them by myth. Arienrhod becomes both love goddess and death goddess in the novel, but she portrays love only in its most negative aspects. Blodwed, an illiterate and crude girl who tortures her pets in order to get them to obey her, performs only one important function in the book: she releases Moon in time for her to participate in the footrace that will determine the candidates for Summer Queen. While this is significant, her role hardly qualifies her for the reputation of her treacherous namesake.

There is one other characteristic of the "White Goddess" that is important to the novel. Cerridwen, the Old Moon aspect, is also known as the goddess of "Life-in-Death and Death-in-Life." She is the woman dicing with Death in Coleridge's *Ancient Mariner*. To be under her spell is to be in a "purgatory awaiting resurrection," and as Graves determines, that purgatory is in a "calm silver-circled castle at the back of the North Wind." All of Vinge's alienated characters are figuratively in a purgatory awaiting resurrection, and thus they are in a state of "Death-in-Life." Tarawassie, for example, exists in such a state because of her chitta addiction, and Sparks is literally locked into such a state by the Winter Queen.

By its cyclical nature, its emphasis on growth and rebirth, and its reflection of the "Life-in-Death" state, the "White Goddess" motif clearly supports the death and revival of vegetation archetype.

Another supportive device is the fertility theme. It has obvious connections to the archetype because the death and subsequent revival of vegetation implies infertility and fertility, respectively. Except for **"Eyes of Amber,"** where no particular emphasis is given to it other than the fact that Titan is just entering its spring season, all the stories place a premium on fertility. (pp. 124-26)

In addition to the fertility theme, Vinge also uses a cluster of images suggesting coldness to support the dying and reviving vegetation archetype. Snow is the most prominent image, but also included in the cluster are ice and winter and adjectives like frozen and white, which suggest coldness. As a symbol, the cold cluster signifies the winter season, that season when the Earth is devoid of most vegetation. Psychologically, it signifies that period when the character is alienated and lonely. But, like winter it holds the promise of rebirth, renewal, and regeneration. (p. 127)

While the dying and revivifying vegetation archetype is not as obvious in her other stories, it is clearly present in some form. . . . It is more easily identified if one remembers that the vegetation archetype is itself a more specific statement of the life principle. It must also be remembered that while the archetype is a major device in Vinge's work, it is merely supportive of a psychological point of view that dominates her stories. Simply stated, all of us must pass through a period of alienation in order to achieve maturity and productivity that can be considered psychologically healthy. We transcend our alienation by communicating fully with one another. Because it is the most fundamental means of communicating, love is the most frequent instigator of this evolution of personality. And because love is achieved, so too is integrity, indentity, independence, pride of self, creativity, productivity, and happiness.

For Vinge then, alienation is a normal developmental process, a position with which many psychologists and psychiatrists agree. David Oken writes, for instance, that turbulence and alienation are essential features of the identity crisis that characterizes alienation and further that "a placid, unruffled adolescence is a danger sign, indicating that the struggle was felt to be so fearsome that it was given up before it could be started." In this opinion, he confirms Erich Fromm's view that alienation is evolutionary. Inevitably, Vinge's major characters suffer this "trial by fire" and pass through their hellish alienation to achieve a rebirth. (pp. 129-30)

Carl Yoke, "From Alienation to Personal Triumph: The Science Fiction of Joan D. Vinge," in The Feminine Eye: Science Fiction and the Women Who Write It, *edited by Tom Staicar, Frederick Ungar Publishing Co., 1982, pp. 103-30.*

CAROLYN CAYWOOD

[**Return of the Jedi—The Storybook Based on the Movie**] simplifies the plot but covers the main action and reveals the crucial secrets. . . . It is an adequate vehicle for those who want to recall the pleasure of the movie, but those who have not seen the film will find the book disappointing. The excitement, suspense and sense of wonder have not made the transition to print. Though Jabba the Hutt is still repulsive, the Emperor is incongruously lacking in menace and even the Ewoks lose some of their appeal.

Carolyn Caywood, in a review of "Return of the Jedi: The Storybook Based on the Movie," in School Library Journal, *Vol. 30, No. 1, September, 1983, p. 129.*

RICHARD LAW

[Joan D. Vinge is a] science fiction writer attuned to Existentialism, but her isolated or beleaguered characters survive what William Barrett calls the modern "encounter with Nothingness." A representative character is Emmylou Stewart in the homiletic story, **"View from a Height."** Lacking natural immunities essential for life on Earth, Emmylou volunteered for permanent duty as an explorer isolated in an observatory in space. Being "trapped in the arc of blackness . . . meaningless, so insignificant," she falls into depression but recovers and expresses valiant acquiescence: "We're all on a one-way trip into infinity. If we're lucky we're given some life's work we care about, or some person. Or both, if we're very lucky."

Optimistic fatalism is the prevailing attitude in the work of Vinge. Her strength is the romance, a genre older than the novel—"a fact which has developed," in Northrop Frye's words, "the historical illusion that it is something to be outgrown, a juvenile and undeveloped form." Without denying the existence of evil or the data of suffering, this tender-minded author highlights innocence and beauty, which belong to human experience as surely as do their opposites. She recalls treasured impressions—allusions to fairy tales and childhood memories are frequent—and commends the endearing or admirable traits in men, women, and children. Underlying her sentimental science fiction fables is a steadfast belief in the power of the human spirit to endure pain, promote decency, and preserve love.

Whether it is a reflective piece, a long exotic fantasy like *The Snow Queen*, or a juvenile space adventure, nearly every work by Joan Vinge is a love story, sentimental and idealized, but not to be confused with silly television and film servings. Most of her characters who love are not glamorous or handsome; some are permanently disabled, some are deformed, some are freaks. They have been losers and might never be much better

than survivors; and their love, no matter how poetic, will not dissolve the hard conditions of existence. Love is not a panacea, not perpetual ecstasy, and not a magic charm in Vinge's fiction. It is emotional interdependence, mutual commitment, caring and sacrifice shared. *The Outcasts of Heaven Belt* (1978) is a light space-adventure entertainment. It also is designed to address its epigraph from *Ecclesiastes:* "Two are better than one, because they have a good reward for their labours. For if they fall, the one will lift up his fellow: but woe to him that is alone when he falleth; for he hath not another to help him up." The ideal of unity in adversity is sensitively exhibited by two fugitives, Shadow Jack, a certified defective, and Bird Alyn, rejected as an ugly, ungainly cripple. Mutual empathy upholds them: "She had comforted him, out of compassion and her own need; his need had bound him to her, and made them friends." They and other couples in Joan Vinge's works illustrate the concept that "the unifying element, the common bond of need that join(s) every human being, could be used as a force against disintegration and decay." (pp. 16-17)

The Outcasts of Heaven Belt is a marriage and family fairy tale. It is true that for sentimental style of expression, the poetic allusions, soothing reflections, the regard for innocence and domesticity, for children and gentle animals, nearly all of Vinge's science fiction has a fairy tale ambience. But the need for faith and hope and the benefits of human interdependence reflected in her works are true-to-life. Joan Vinge speaks to the imagination in a transitional age that psychotherapist Rollo May diagnoses as suffering "bankruptcy of inner values." For lack of love and will, the contemporary world is schizoid. Those attributes are necessary for people who yearn to exercise "the conjunctive emotions and processes." The source of love and will is care, concern, compassion. . . .

The tough-minded science fiction writers [such as Joanna Russ and Alice Sheldon] expose the thoughtless assumptions and philosophical rationalizations supporting the age-old sexist order. The tender-minded imagine models of love in a better order—at least a retreat—wherein harmony between the sexes is cultivated. (p. 18)

Richard Law, "Science Fiction Women: Victims, Rebels, Heroes," in Patterns of the Fantastic, *edited by Donald M. Hassler, Starmont House, 1983, pp. 11-20.**

Cynthia Voigt

1942-

American novelist.

Voigt's novels for young adults are noted for their realistic plots and well-developed, individualized characters. The role of the family figures prominently throughout Voigt's work. Her first novel, *Homecoming* (1981), introduces Dicey Tillerman, who is also the protagonist of Voigt's Newbery Prize-winning *Dicey's Song* (1982). In *Homecoming*, twelve-year-old Dicey must take charge of her three younger siblings after their mother, who is on the brink of a mental breakdown, deserts them. This novel recounts the hardships faced by the children during their search for a home and the warmth and love that binds them together. Although some critics found the work overly detailed and lacking in credibility, most gave the book favorable reviews. *Dicey's Song*, which many critics consider more tightly constructed than *Homecoming*, follows the lives of the Tillerman children after they move in with their grandmother. Critics commend the depth with which Voigt portrays the children's psychological growth as they struggle to adapt.

Voigt's recent *A Solitary Blue* (1983) chronicles the painful adolescence of Jeff Green, a boy introduced as a secondary character in *Dicey's Song*. This work also revolves around family issues: Jeff's mother has deserted him, leaving him in the charge of his distant and reserved father. Together the father and son learn to trust each other and to enjoy the love developing between them. *Tell Me If the Lovers Are Losers* (1982) explores the friendship between four individuals with strikingly different backgrounds and attitudes toward life. *The Callender Papers* (1983) differs from Voigt's other novels, for it is a mystery set in the past. However, like the other novels, its plot is realistic and carefully paced and its thematic foundation is based on the family.

(See also *Contemporary Authors*, Vol. 106 and *Something about the Author*, Vol. 33.)

Photograph by Walter Voigt

MARILYN KAYE

The characterizations of the children [deserted by their mother in *Homecoming*] are original and intriguing, and there are a number of interesting minor characters encountered in their travels. While the scope and extent of their journey has an element of unbelievability about it, the abundance of descriptions that detail their efforts to survive and keep going help achieve a semblance of reality. The only real problem with the story is that it's just too long, and despite the built-in suspense of the plot, the ongoing tension suffers in the multitude of crises.

> Marilyn Kaye, in a review of "Homecoming," in
> School Library Journal, *Vol. 27, No. 8, April, 1981,
> p. 144.*

ZENA SUTHERLAND

[In *Homecoming* the father of four children] had walked out long ago, and now Momma had left them in a parking lot and

disappeared; en route to the Connecticut home of a great-aunt, the four children decided to walk there. Dicey, thirteen, takes charge of the younger three. . . . The writing style is good, the children strongly characterized if a bit precocious, and many of the incidents on the various stages of their journeys have drama (the six-year-old steals food when they are all hungry; a mercenary farmer tries to capture them, claiming they're his foster children; they are rescued by a circus owner and stay with the circus for a time) but the book is too long, too detailed, too uneven in pace to have real impact.

> Zena Sutherland, in a review of "Homecoming," in
> Bulletin of the Center for Children's Books, *Vol. 34,
> No. 9, May, 1981, p. 183.*

KATHLEEN LEVERICH

Despite flaws, the alarmingly hostile characterization of most adults, an overly long ending, [*Homecoming*] is a glowing book. Its disturbing undercurrent of hostility and cynicism is counter-balanced by the [children's] obvious love and loyalty to one another, and by the capability, cleverness and determination that characterize all the survival episodes on the road and the homemaking scenes in Maryland.

The bleak fundamentals of the children's situation may be strong stuff for many young readers, but for those who have the resilience to take it, the accomplishments of this feisty band of complex and, in contrast to the adults, sympathetically conceived kids makes for an enthralling journey to a gratifying end.

> *Kathleen Leverich, in a review of "Homecoming,"* in The New York Times Book Review, *May 10, 1981, p. 38.*

KAREN M. KLOCKNER

The children [in *Homecoming*] . . . are carefully individualized, and the author reveals with subtlety and perceptiveness the psychological stress on each of them. She has a good command of language and moves easily between descriptive passages and dialogue. Throughout the book the children try to understand why they have been left in [their] . . . situation and what they should do about it. Although the outcome is not wholly convincing, the account of the events leading up to it is imaginative, thought-provoking, and worked out to the finest detail. (p. 439)

> *Karen M. Klockner, in a review of "Homecoming,"* in The Horn Book Magazine, *Vol. LVII, No. 4, August, 1981, pp. 438-39.*

BOOKLIST

An eastern college for women of high ability is the setting for [*Tell Me If the Lovers Are Losers*], an unusual teenage novel about three disparate freshmen who come together as roommates in 1961. . . . Volleyball becomes their common ground as Hildy, who has an almost mystical impact on her teammates, coaches and leads the freshmen toward the championship. Vivid imagery vies with effectively subtle understatement in a thoughtful multiple-character study written in the third person but filled with introspection, primarily from Ann's perspective. Characterizations—not only major but supporting ones—are consistently and distinctively individualized while interactions and mutual influences are developed naturally, making this both provocative and rewarding. . . .

> *A review of "Tell Me If the Lovers Are Losers," in* Booklist, *Vol. 78, No. 14, March 15, 1982, p. 950.*

SCHOOL LIBRARY JOURNAL

[*Tell Me If the Lovers Are Losers*] is heavy going. . . . After a sluggish start, during which the girls get acquainted (eventually they develop a strong bond of friendship and respect), there is lots of volleyball action as that sport becomes the center of the girls' lives their first semester. The story offers a good look at adjusting, coping, and competing to win. But it is thick with philosophy as each girl presents her background and view of life. The girls talk like very intelligent college students. The author also gives midwestern Hildy a prim, precise and stilted voice that does not register as true or representative of the region. Nothing special is done with the time period. One can come to know these roommates, but there is much to go through to get there.

> *A review of "Tell Me If the Lovers Are Losers," in* School Library Journal, *Vol. 28, No. 9, May, 1982, p. 88.*

KATHLEEN LEVERICH

The forging of the [volleyball] team is the real story [in **"Tell Me If the Lovers Are Losers"**], and it's a compelling, immensely satisfying one. A collection of six disparate and, in many respects, disagreeable young women grows through stress and self-discipline from anarchy and infighting, past tolerance and mutual respect, to devotion and loyalty.

As with Mrs. Voigt's previous novel, **"Homecoming,"** the theme of this book is bonding. No problem in that, but **"Tell Me If the Lovers Are Losers"** suffers (and to an even greater extent) from the same excesses that marred the earlier work: exaggeration of character and the sacrifice of the theme to improbable theatrics. No literary or thematic purpose is served by the melodramatic ending; on the contrary, the book is considerably diminished. And readers would be more inclined to accept the characters if their personalities were drawn in subtle shadings instead of in caricatures.

Mrs. Voigt is a wonderful writer with powerfully moving things to say. Her books, however, overcompensate for what she apparently feels are excessively subtle conflicts and an atmosphere that is too rarified for the general reader. When she dispenses with contrivances and sensationalism, her characters and scenes come alive in their own unique and exciting way.

> *Kathleen Leverich, in a review of "Tell Me If the Lovers Are Losers," in* The New York Times Book Review, *May 16, 1982, p. 28.*

DENISE M. WILMS

[*Dicey's Song*] details Dicey's settlement into adolescence and a new life with Gram. . . . The story is a perceptive exposition of two strong personalities, Dicey and Gram, neither of whom is perfect but both of whom learn powerful lessons in reaching out and accepting love. . . . The vividness of Dicey is striking; Voigt has plumbed and probed her character inside out to fashion a memorable protagonist. Unlike most sequels, this outdoes [*Homecoming*] by being more fully realized and consequently more resonant. (p. 50)

> *Denise M. Wilms, in a review of "Dicey's Song,"* in Booklist, *Vol. 79, No. 1, September 1, 1982, pp. 49-50.*

ZENA SUTHERLAND

The strong characterization of *Homecoming* . . . to which [*Dicey's Song* is a sequel] is one of the most trenchant facets again, in this story of the four children who live with their grandmother on the Eastern Shore of Maryland. . . . [*Dicey's Song*] is much more cohesive than *Homecoming,* in part because the physical scope is narrower, in part because the author has so skillfully integrated the problems of the individual children in a story that is smoothly written. Dicey learns how to make friends, how to accept the fact that she is maturing physically, how to give and forgive, how to adjust—in a touching final episode—to the death of the mother whose recovery she had longed for. A rich and perceptive book.

> *Zena Sutherland, in a review of "Dicey's Song," in* Bulletin of the Center for Children's Books, *Vol. 36, No. 2, October, 1982, p. 38.*

ALICE DIGILIO

[With *Dicey's Song,* Cynthia Voigt] proves that heroines of young adult fiction *can* be mature, considerate, even exemplary, and still seem quite real. Dicey Tillerman, the heroine of *Dicey's Song,* is not just good, she is strong, like a birch sapling, and it is Voigt's skill in convincing us of that strength that makes her seem so real. (p. 8)

Of course the journey [that began in *Homecoming*] isn't over once Gram's house has been reached. Dicey still must play the leader, making accommodation with a proud and independent grandmother (who reluctantly has to go on welfare to support them all), trying to help Sammy, Maybeth and James navigate successfully through a new world.

Dicey is a fulcrum for the characters balanced about her: zany Sammy who, at 8, is trying to be good, for a change; Maybeth, a musical prodigy who still can't quite read; James, bookish and serious, but struggling to make friends; Gram, hard-nosed and intensely private, shielding herself from further pain. Dicey seems to know how to exploit one's strength to compensate for another's weakness. And she and Gram somehow keep everything and everyone in equilibrium.

In spite of its carefully circumscribed rural setting, *Dicey's Song,* is rich with themes and harmonies, even verities. Loyalty and love, "reaching out" as Gram says, are the qualities Voigt writes about here with grace and wit. (pp. 8-9)

> *Alice Digilio, in a review of "Dicey's Song," in* Book World—The Washington Post, *February 13, 1983, pp. 8-9.*

MARILYN KAYE

Mrs. Voigt has a nice way with language, blunt, taut and precise. She uses small but powerful images that rise above the ordinary yet still remain within the grasp of a juvenile audience. She keeps her distance and sustains an objectivity that prevents the story from falling into melodrama.

"Dicey's Song" . . . is a series of movements and contrasts. But under it all there's a goal of harmony that's eventually realized as Dicey learns what to reach out for and what to give up.

> *Marilyn Kaye, in a review of "Dicey's Song," in* The New York Times Book Review, *March 6, 1983, p. 30.*

MICHELE SLUNG

Spunky heroines: I've lived my life since girlhood wanting to be one and to this day they remain my preferred characters in fiction. But, in reading these two new novels, *Them That Glitter and Them That Don't* [by Bette Greene] and *The Callender Papers* [by Cynthia Voigt], I missed that familiar frisson of identification with the protagonists of either book. This isn't, I hasten to add, simply because I'm from the wrong age-group, or I don't think it is; certainly, I continue to *become* Alice or Dorothy over and over again, when I reread their adventures. . . .

This magical process of "identification" can't be achieved by formula; rather, it's like what they say about love: it's chemical. . . . [There] wasn't a single moment in either book that I had that connection with, and I want to explain why.

Both Bette Greene and Cynthia Voigt have chosen to write about worlds which they are viewing from the outside. . . . [Voigt] places hers in the later 19th century and has given us a gothic plot ("eine kleine Gothik"), the conventions of which she takes on earnestly and with a funless air of being duty-bound to provide the necessaries. In *The Callender Papers* the self-contained and resolute but unconvincingly juvenile heroine is a mere 12-year-old, an orphan, sent to a mysterious manse to help an old acquaintance of her guardian sift through and arrange some family papers. . . .

Though the authors are strangers to the situations they're portraying, both novels are narrated in the first person by the heroines. A set-up like this is hardly an invitation to failure—witness a large portion of our literary classics—but neither Greene nor Voigt is up to the job. Though it's hard to tell, Jean Wainwright of *The Callender Papers* is still a teenager, though some years have gone by, as she recounts her story. But the sensibility she conveys is a rather middle-aged one and her gothicky discoveries are predictable (beyond my affection and tolerance for such predictability). But, mostly, one hears Voigt's own voice mouthing the words. . . .

Neither *Them That Glitter and Them That Don't* nor *The Callender Papers* are actually bad books, but for me, they're the kind of novels one might settle for and shouldn't. One doesn't have to identify with a protagonist in order to love a book, but one's senses should be engaged, or one's intellect, if not one's central emotions. Both of these spunky heroines seem too artificial to be affecting. And they seem older than their years; however, it isn't their circumstances that have made them that way. No, one doesn't have to look any further than their authors to understand the reason for their unnatural maturity. But it shouldn't be so.

> *Michele Slung, "Adolescent Heroines," in* Book World—The Washington Post, *May 8, 1983, p. 14.**

KIRKUS REVIEWS

Less ambitious than Voigt's other novels, [*The Callender Papers*] conforms to an established juvenile-fiction genre, but it is a superior example of its type. Written in the first person with a touch of period primness, it's the story of Jean Wainwright's 13th summer in 1894, which she spends away from Aunt Constance, the admirable girls'-school headmistress who raised her, in the employ of wintery Mr. Thiel, the widower of Aunt Constance's girlhood friend Irene Callender. Mr. Thiel has summoned Jean to sort and dispose of several cartons of Callender family papers, a dull and bewildering task. But the Callender family mystery proves more intriguing: Why is Mr. Thiel not on speaking terms with Enoch Callender, Irene's younger brother, who lives nearby? Was Irene murdered, and if so by whom? And what happened to her child, who disappeared soon after its mother's death? As the summer and her task proceed, Jean becomes better acquainted with both Enoch and Mr. Thiel, and with Mac, the local doctor's son, who becomes her partner in tracking down the family secrets. . . . [Through] it all she exhibits a direct good sense and alert intelligence that win regard from all parties, and from readers as well. Readers may suspect all along what Jean discovers only at the end—that she herself is the Callender heir, Mr. Thiel is her father, and Enoch, spoiled and discontented, is responsible for his doting sister's death. But knowing that doesn't lessen the suspense or the satisfaction to be found in this engaging, aptly plotted, character-centered identity-mystery.

A review of "The Callender Papers," in Kirkus Reviews, Vol. LI, No. 6, March 15, 1983, p. 308.

ETHEL L. HEINS

Fluent but never terse, the author compounds the mystery [that is the center of **The Callender Papers**] with a multitude of details and digressions, some of which border on melodrama. And Jean, so young in years, may strain the reader's credulity with her mature, self-possessed first-person account, which occasionally dips into fairly complex moral, and even philosophical, discussions.

Ethel L. Heins, in a review of "The Callender Papers," in The Horn Book Magazine, Vol. 59, No. 4, August, 1983, p. 458.

MIRIAM BERKLEY

Uncovering what the past has hidden, Jean [in **"The Callender Papers"**] finds the present menacing. Thinking carefully, as she has been taught to do, doesn't protect her from the evil she meets in life for the first time. She learns that what lies beneath the surface in people is not always what one imagines as she slowly pieces together what is really going on. . . .

As in her Dicey Tillerman books, Cynthia Voigt gives us a spunky young heroine forced into precocious independence and resourcefulness, as well as adults who'll victimize kids if allowed. Although this genre novel is entertaining, interesting and well-written, it does not, and does not pretend to, offer the sensitively drawn, richly memorable real-life characters and situations that made its predecessors so rewarding.

Miriam Berkley, in a review of "The Callender Papers," in The New York Times Book Review, August 14, 1983, p. 29.

GLORIA P. ROHMANN

Written in a purposefully detached style, early sections of [**A Solitary Blue**] read like a journalistic case-study of child neglect. The confrontation with [Jeff's mother], Melody, which would seem to be the climax, comes quite early in the book, and further chapters, while necessary to show Jeff's ultimate resolution of his relationship with his parents, are choppy, episodic and disconnected. The last section, in which he meets Dicey Tillerman and her family [from Voigt's earlier books] . . . is unnecessary and dull. While well-written (the character of the father is outstanding), the book ultimately disappoints: Melody is a monster, and Jeff's feelings are never clearly portrayed. The theme of a child abandoned by his mother will be interesting to some, but many will lose interest in later chapters. (p. 140)

Gloria P. Rohmann, in a review of "A Solitary Blue," in School Library Journal, Vol. 30, No. 1, September, 1983, pp. 139-40.

KIRKUS REVIEWS

[**A Solitary Blue**] is the story of Jeff Greene, the guitar-playing high school boy Dicey Tillerman meets in **Dicey's Song** (1982)—but the connection isn't made until near the end. The story begins, matter-of-factly but with **Kramer vs. Kramer** pathos,

when Jeff at seven finds his mother Melody's note explaining that she loves him but had to leave him to help the world's less fortunate and "make things better." Jeff is left with his stiff, expressionless father. . . . The summer Jeff turns 12, his mother invites him to stay with her at her grandmother's house in Charleston; and though he doesn't see much of her he is overcome with love—cherishing her memory through the year, writing monthly unanswered letters, and buying a cheap used guitar because she had played one. . . . The next summer Jeff returns to Charleston, but sees even less of his mother—she is off on long trips with her dreadful boyfriend—and goes home dangerously withdrawn. The healing process begins several months later with a move from Baltimore to a Chesapeake Bay cabin he and his father choose together. Jeff does well at his new school, makes some friends, meets Dicey, and hangs out with the Tillermans—and he and his father, still reserved, become closer and easier with each other. . . . Later Jeff resolves his mixed heritage by deciding to go into ecology: "No, not saving the world or getting back to the good old prehistoric days, not that," he tells his father. "But responsible management of it, somehow . . . with computers too. . . .'" This doubly simplistic resolution is disappointing, and Voigt's lack of sympathy for Melody's postulated type is a problem from the start. However, Jeff's own feelings at every stage are compellingly real and affecting; the growing closeness between him and his father is moving and subtly developed; and his own emotional development and growing character (that old-fashioned term is the only word for it) brings out Voigt at her best, as well. (pp. J178-J179)

A review of "A Solitary Blue," in Kirkus Reviews, Vol. LI, Nos. 13-17, September 1, 1983, pp. J178-J179.

JANE LANGTON

In "Bleak House," Charles Dickens gave us Mrs. Jellyby, who took such a charitable interest in far-away Borrioboola-Gha that she failed to notice when her own wretched children were falling down the stairs.

Cynthia Voigt [in **"A Solitary Blue"**] has created a contemporary version of Mrs. Jellyby, an equally appalling mother-philanthropist. . . . (p. 34)

The reader guesses from the beginning of this beautifully written story that the mother is a washout—guesses too that the father's still waters run deep. The book has a natural suspense. One wants to see the boy discover the truth about his parents for himself. There is an "I could have told you so" satisfaction in seeing him betrayed once again by his mother, pleasure in watching the development of his new friendship with his responsible father. Professor Greene's repressions and inhibitions begin to seem like virtues compared with Melody's treacherous "I love you's".

"A Solitary Blue" takes its name from the great blue heron Jeff sees in a South Carolina marsh while he is visiting his mother. Its solitude matches his own.

The story is slightly damaged by the appearance of a flock of new characters at the end, but nothing can undo the artistic thoroughness of this study of a boy in pain. (pp. 34-5)

Jane Langton, in a review of "A Solitary Blue," in The New York Times Book Review, November 27, 1983, pp. 34-5.

Erich von Däniken

1935-

(Also transliterated as Daeniken) Swiss nonfiction writer.

Von Däniken is known for his controversial *Erinnerungen an die Zukunft* (1968; *Chariots of the Gods? Unsolved Mysteries of the Past*) and its companion volumes in which he concludes that extraterrestrial beings visited Earth in ancient times. Von Däniken speculates that these beings were worshipped as gods and that they may have advanced the evolution of human beings by mating with them. Although von Däniken's unconventional theories are dismissed by religious and scientific authorities, his work has attracted wide interest among the general public and was the basis for several television documentaries.

As a student in a Catholic boys' school in Switzerland, von Däniken began to doubt his religious teachings. While reading the Old Testament, he found references which suggested a multitude of gods rather than one. In his studies of other religions and cultures, he also found evidence of multiple deities. Von Däniken's worldwide travels to ancient ruins and to such archaeological enigmas as the stone monoliths on Easter Island helped confirm his hypothesis that visitors from outer space may have been the gods of past civilizations.

In reviews of *Chariots of the Gods?* and his other writings, critics have contended that von Däniken's research methods are unscientific and that his theories are based on misleading documentation. His technique of presenting evidence by asking rhetorical questions has been called deceptive and his premise racist. His work has been described as fantasy and as "science fiction in reverse." However, von Däniken comments that scientists "are doing yesterday's thinking. I try to see with tomorrow's eyes."

(See also *Contemporary Authors*, Vols. 37-40, rev. ed.)

ERICH VON DÄNIKEN

[*The following excerpt was originally published in German as an introduction to* Erinnerungen an die Zukunft *in 1968.*]

It took courage to write [*Chariots of the Gods?*] and it will take courage to read it. Because its theories and proofs do not fit into the mosaic of traditional archaeology, constructed so laboriously and firmly cemented down, scholars will call it nonsense and put it on the Index of those books which are better left unmentioned. Laymen will withdraw into the snail shell of their familiar world when faced with the probability that finding out about our past will be even more mysterious and adventurous than finding out about the future.

Nevertheless, one thing is certain. There is something inconsistent about our past, that past which lies thousands and millions of years behind us. The past teemed with unknown gods who visited the primeval earth in manned spaceships. Incredible technical achievements existed in the past. (p. vii)

But how did these early men acquire the ability to create them?

There is something inconsistent about our religion. A feature common to every religion is that it promises help and salvation

© Nancy Crampton

to mankind. The primitive gods gave such promises, too. Why didn't they keep them? Why did they use ultra-modern weapons on primitive peoples? And why did they plan to destroy them?

Let us get used to the idea that the world of ideas which has grown up over the millennia is going to collapse. (pp. vi-viii)

Modern laboratories must take over the work of archaeological research. Archaeologists must visit the devastated sites of the past with ultrasensitive measuring apparatus. Priests who seek the truth must again begin to doubt everything that is established.

The gods of the dim past have left countless traces which we can read and decipher today for the first time because the problem of space travel, so topical today, was not a problem, but a reality, to the men of thousands of years ago. I claim that our forefathers received visits from the universe in the remote past, even though I do not yet know who these extraterrestrial intelligences were or from which planet they came. I nevertheless proclaim that these "strangers" annihilated part of mankind existing at the time and produced a new, perhaps the first, *homo sapiens*.

This assertion is revolutionary. It shatters the base on which a mental edifice that seemed to be so perfect was constructed. It is my aim to try to provide proof of this assertion.

Erich von Däniken, in an introduction to his Chariots
of the Gods? Unsolved Mysteries of the Past, translated by Michael Heron, Bantam Books, 1971, pp.
vii-ix.

WILHELM ROGGERSDORF

*[The following excerpt was originally published as an introduction
to the German edition of von Däniken's* Gods from Outer Space
in 1968.]

Erich von Däniken is not a scholar. He is an autodidact, which
the dictionary defines as a man who is self-taught. Probably
this helps explain the success his first book [*Chariots of the
Gods?*] met with all over the world. Completely free from all
prejudices, he had to demonstrate personally that his theses
and theories were not unfounded and hundreds of thousands
of readers were able to follow him along the adventurous road
he took—a road that led into regions that were surrounded and
protected by taboos.

Besides, his fearless questioning of all the previous explanations of the origin of the human race seems to have been long
overdue. Erich von Däniken was not the first man who dared
to challenge them, but his questions were more impartial, more
direct and more audacious. In addition, he was able to say
exactly what he wanted to say, unlike a professor, for example,
who would have felt bound to take the opinions of his colleagues or the representatives of similar academic disciplines
into consideration. What is more, he came up with some startling answers.

Men who bluntly ask bold questions that cast doubt on time-
honored, accepted explanations have always been a nuisance
and people have never been overfussy about how they silenced
them. In the past their books were banished to secret libraries
or put on the index; today people try to hush them up or make
them look ridiculous. Yet none of these methods has ever
succeeded in disposing of questions which concern the reason
for our very existence. (pp. vii-viii)

> *Wilhelm Roggersdorf, "About Erich von Däniken,"*
> in Gods from Outer Space: Return to the Stars or
> Evidence for the Impossible *by Erich von Däniken,*
> *translated by Michael Heron, Bantam Books, 1972,*
> *pp. vii-viii.*

SR. M. MARGUERITE, RSM

[*Chariots of the Gods?*] raises a bewildering amount of questions—most of them unanswered. It challenges future research
in the light of the far-distant past. It widens the imagination
as to the number of planets that possibly support life, possibly
not under conditions laid down by scientists for supporting life
on this earth; but who knows if there are other conditions and
other kinds of life?. . .

According to von Däniken's thesis and/or theory there were
long ago godlike men who descended, jet propelled, to the
planet earth. The illustrations of them in the thousands-of-
years-old rock formations, whether in South America, Alaska,
Easter Island, Africa or Asia all show headgear that on first
inspection seems awkward, but in later years can be likened
to the headgear of the astronauts; and what was at first supposed
to be horns are really antennae.

These being—gods, if the primitive natives on earth thought
them so—taught the inhabitants such facts as are recorded in
the inscriptions at Palenque, Mexico, or in Assyria, or in Honduras—or wherever—impregnated some of their women, and
returned to their own habitat. The convincing fact to the author
is that the pictures and inscriptions, though so far apart geographically, are all similar in content and theme. His hypothesis
is that there were cartographers who were able to fly far above
the earth and make maps similar now to maps so made. (p. 421)

Von Däniken speaks at length of the Sumerians, their fantastic
span of life, their representations of the gods always as star
symbols. One of their achievements seems to be scientifically-
ground lenses.

Perhaps it is appropriate for a non-scientist to review this book.
She comes to it wide eyed and wide open to suggestions, one
of the most practical of which is to read the book in connection
with Genesis (especially the destruction of Sodom and Gomorrah—atom bomb?), Ezekiel (helicopters?) and Isaiah for
secrets of the far past to be revealed. There are many scientific
suppositions explaining some of the events of the Old Testament; for instance, in the transfer of the Ark of the Covenant,
Uzzah (sic) fell dead when he gripped the Ark to steady it: it
may have been electrically charged! Also—the communication
between God and Moses: Moses, with Egyptian know-how,
may have equipped the Ark with electronic devices!

I could go on and on. It is really a book for scientists, physicists,
archaeologists, metallurgists, and geologists. But to the layman, accustomed to the science-fiction of Jules Verne and
Aldous Huxley, much of which has materialized into actual
fact, the book is also of practical interest. (pp. 421, 423)

But in case a reader's faith in the old, old traditions might
waver, there is the reassurance. Says von Däniken, "I am quite
convinced that when the last questions about our past have
been given a genuine and convincing answer, SOMETHING,
which I call GOD for want of a better name, will remain for
eternity."

So if God taught electricity, atomic bombs, transistors, and
other such items to a people whose history is long destroyed
(probably by the flood or by an atomic bomb) who are we to
question? At any rate, we are glad to hear that He is not dead,
and we can deepen our faith that "a thousand years in His
sight are but as one day". (p. 423)

> *Sr. M. Marguerite, RSM, in a review of "Chariots
> of the Gods?" in* Best Sellers, *Vol. 29, No. 21,
> February 1, 1970, pp. 421, 423.*

JACK W. WEIGEL

[In *Chariots of the Gods?* Von Däniken] pursues two lines of
argument: first, many reputable scientists believe there are
probably a number of different sites in the unvierse where
intelligent life has arisen; second, shreds of quotations from
ancient texts and modern archaeology prove human development took a sudden leap forward several millennia before Christ.
He shrugs off the more mundane interpretations of the data
which are favored by archaeologists as being obviouly ridiculous. His "proofs" are essentially circular; he cites many
remarkable achievements of ancient civilization, but insists
they only serve to confirm his theory, since they couldn't possibly have been accomplished by mere ancient humans. . . .

Unless a . . . furor should arise over Von Däniken's book, there is little reason for any library to invest in it.

Jack W. Weigel, in a review of "Chariots of the Gods? Unsolved Mysteries of the Past," in Library Journal, *Vol. 95, No. 3, February 1, 1970, pp. 492-93.*

POUL ANDERSON

Here we go again.

It would be interesting and perhaps important to know why men have such a perennial fascination with the idea of wildly spectacular events and civilizations in the distant past. . . .

The pattern is always the same: an omnium-gatherum of what myths, legends and historical records will fit the author's thesis, they being trimmed to fit if necessary while those that can't be so treated are ignored; a snowstorm of data either irrelevant or erroneous; page after page of rhetoric; and a repeated reminder that the dogmatic Establishment also persecuted Galileo. The trouble with refuting any of these books is not that it's hard—rather, it's unsportingly easy—but that to go down the line, point by point, takes more time and print than is worth anybody's while. . . .

In justice, I should say that [von Däniken] seems quite sincere, and concerned with raising questions rather than erecting new orthodoxies. . . . His glorious culture of the past was not terrestrial at all; it belonged to visitors from space who, guiding and interbreeding with primitive man, gave rise to the religions, technologies and societies of early historical times.

Now it *is* orthodox these days to believe that probably many inhabited planets exist in the universe. The feasibility of interstellar travel is debatable, but equally good men are ranged on both sides of the argument. As reputable a scientist as Carl Sagan has wondered whether the nonhuman benefactors of man in Sumerian chronicles may actually have been visitors from another star. The point is that Sagan admits this is sheer speculation with no strong evidence to back it, while von Däniken claims he can demonstrate that something of the kind did in fact happen.

We can dismiss at once his notion that the Outsiders brought man into existence by contributing their superior chromosomes to pre-man. First, everything we know about genetics and biopoesis indicates that our genus could more readily be crossed with moose or tobacco plants than with any extraterrestrials. Second, Homo Sapiens does not suddenly appear in the fossil record; on the contrary, several early types like Neanderthal man have lately had to be put in the same species.

But might not the Outsiders have been remembered in stories about gods, fiery chariots, heavenly realms, rains of fire and the rest? Might they not have given the elements of civilization to our ancestors, who drew pictures of them for us to see today? For instance, how can the Piri Reis map show Earth on an accurate Cairo-centered equidistant projection, if it weren't copied from a photograph taken from orbit? Well, the Piri Reis map is interesting and admittedly somewhat puzzling, but it isn't that accurate. Besides, if you look down on Cairo, you don't see the the whole planet in equidistant projection. Try it with a globe.

The other "proofs" are even feebler. Thus, it is asserted that various works of art, ranging from paleolithic European to late Aztec, show nonhuman beings in unmistakable spacesuits or spacecraft. To my eye, they show nothing of the sort; I see shamans in costume, gods surrounded by emblems, that kind of thing. The Sumerians used huge numbers and wrote down vivid descriptions of the world as observed from a great height. So what? Their minds and imaginations were as good as yours or mine. The astronomical analog computer from 82 B.C., discovered off Antikythera, does not prove that the makers had a heliocentric concept, it merely proves they were ingenious mechanics. . . .

The claim that Ezekiel's vision of "wheels within wheels" describes a spaceship and its crew is typical of the use of myth in this whole genre. We find never a word about Ezekiel's other visions, which were of quite different things. Likewise, the Ark of the Covenant simply cannot have acted as a condenser and electrocuted Uzzah (2 Samuel 6:7). Ask your radio repairman—though if you show him the book, he's likely to ask you what the hell is meant by "an electric conductor of several hundred volts." (p. 211)

The corrections could go on and on. . . .

Nonetheless the publisher says [*Chariots of the Gods?*] is an international bestseller. I am afraid we will always have with us that personality type which [science-fiction writer L. Sprague] de Camp has named the credophile. (p. 212)

Poul Anderson, "The Past That Never Was," in National Review, *Vol. XXII, No. 7, February 24, 1970, pp. 211-12.*

PUBLISHERS WEEKLY

As in his **"Chariots of the Gods"** . . . , Däniken once more strains scientific credulity [in **"Gods From Outer Space"**], but intrigues and fascinates with his bold theories and speculations about mysterious "visitors" from outer space in ancient and prehistoric times. . . . His interpretations of the old myths and writings are less provocative and exciting than certain of the tangible evidences he discusses, such as possible ancient "airports" in Peru and Chile and artifacts found around the world which science has never explained. Däniken may be a "Sunday archaeologist" but such open-ended possibilities as he proposes make for absorbing reading and appeal to the eternally curious amateur in each of us.

A review of "Gods from Outer Space: Evidences for the Impossible," in Publishers Weekly, *Vol. 199, No. 10, March 8, 1971, p. 67.*

RAYMOND L. HOUGH

[*Gods from Outer Space*] reads like a transcript of dictation; the author leaps suddenly from one topic to another. This fault is somewhat redeemed by the content—much of his archaeological evidence is unknown outside professional circles. Von Däniken gives us his answers to questions for which there will probably never be enough evidence to find the truth. His book may be interesting reading for some, but one must have faith to believe.

Raymond L. Hough, in a review of "Gods from Outer Space: Return to the Stars or Evidence for the Impossible," in Library Journal, *Vol. 96, No. 14, August, 1971, p. 2503.*

S. K. OBERBECK

OK, Bible scholars, fasten your seat belts and hear this: Moses used a laser gun on the Israelites' enemies. The Ark of the Covenant was really a two-way radio transmitter by which Moses kept contact with what came to be called "God." Those "wheels within wheels" Ezekiel spied in the heavens were a spacecraft, or space station, from which superior interstellar visitors looked down on the crude ways of men. Thus, the avenging "angels" who rained fire and brimstone on Sodom and Gomorrah were actually spacemen who zapped the wicked cities with atomic holocaust.

Readers inclined to take this gospel with a grain of salt as large as Lot's wife will fly in the face of some 14 million other readers who have harkened to the intriguing theories of . . . Erich von Däniken. Von Däniken's books have been translated into 32 languages since he challenged the orthodoxy of Creation in 1968 with the German-published **"Chariots of the Gods?"** . . .

Von Däniken, whose style and method combine elements of Carlos Castaneda, Ripley's "Believe It or Not" and "Star Trek," followed up with **"Gods From Outer Space"** and is ringing up more sales on another mind-boggling book, **"The Gold of the Gods."** . . . In this one, von Däniken claims to have seen a vast "Zoo," a subterranean storehouse of gold animal statues, and an astonishing "Metal Library," containing thousands of embossed gold-leaf "documents," in caves 800 feet beneath Peru and Ecuador. These caves prove, he contends, visits by our astral ancestors. As in his other books, he questions—the rhetorical question is his favorite device—mysteries such as the building of pyramids and Mayan temples (probably landing platforms for spaceships), and ancient figures, such as a four-toed Inca "Star God" (representations of space creatures).

Juan Moricz, a Hungarian-born Argentine adventurer who claims to have discovered the Ecuadorian caves, says von Däniken was never actually inside them. No matter, "Dänikenitis" continues to rampage. . . . Lecture audiences lap up the von Däniken gospel, while orthodox critics argue that his theories are as full of holes as his native Swiss cheese. (p. 104)

The millions of people all over the world (including China) who are obviously eager to accept his theories make up one of the amazing phenomena of a world that seems to be looking for new gods to worship. "The great geographical religions—Hinduism, Christianity, Islam—may well be passé," says von Däniken. "I expect that a new religion will arise, a religion of the unknown, indescribable, indefinable something we cannot understand." Von Däniken is due to appear on U.S. TV and the college lecture circuit this month. "My next book is top secret," he says. "But I can tell you that this time I have the facts to come at the problem from another angle entirely." Whatever the facts, von Däniken has certainly found gold. (p. 106)

> S. K. Oberbeck, "Deus ex Machina," in Newsweek, Vol. LXXXII, No. 15, October 8, 1973, pp. 104, 106.

ROBERT MOLYNEUX

The irrepressible von Däniken is back with more evidence of ancient astronauts. He's a curious writer: others have treated the subject better and more intelligently, many before him; his books aren't even particularly well written. But von Däniken does have a disarming ability to ask penetrating questions, and most of the current popular interest in this area can be traced to him. [*The Gold of the Gods*] is in many ways his weakest, though he does present some information which may prove (or disprove) what he has been saying all along. He discusses a huge South American tunnel system which he claims was used by the "gods" when they first arrived here—von Däniken even tells us how to find the tunnels. There are also a number of photos of gold artifacts purportedly made by the "gods" or their successors. If all this is investigated—as it should be—we'll know how credible his theories really are.

> Robert Molyneux, in a review of "The Gold of the Gods," in Library Journal, Vol. 99, No. 2, January 15, 1974, p. 144.

TED PETERS

How has von Däniken managed to get such a grip on the curiosity of Europeans and Americans? I submit that his views are received so avidly because they appear to wed scientific method with religious doctrine. A decade ago, as Theodore Roszak and others have pointed out, our young people repudiated the West's scientific mind-set. But today's college students have turned away from the counterculture of the '60s and, like the older generation, profess to value science. At the same time, both groups are in quest of new religious foundations. Unfortunately, most of these people are not sophisticated enough in either science or religion to be able to discriminate between good and bad science and between true and false religion. That is why a book like *Chariots of the Gods?* has been so eagerly received. It seems to blend science and religion in an exciting and respectable way. In fact, however, it does nothing of the sort. Consider von Däniken's "science" first.

In his delightful *Fads and Fallacies in the Name of Science* . . . [1957], Martin Gardner describes the characteristics which distinguish the pseudo-scientist, or crank, from the orthodox scientist. For one thing, the pseudo-scientist works in almost total isolation; i.e., he holds no fruitful dialogue with fellow researchers. Of course he insists that his isolation is not his fault but that of the established scientific community and its prejudice against new ideas. He never tires of citing the numerous novel scientific theories which were initially condemned but later proved true.

Second, the pseudo-scientist is likely to be paranoiac. Gardner lists five ways in which these paranoid tendencies manifest themselves: (1) the pseudo-scientist considers himself a genius and (2) regards his colleagues as ignorant blockheads; (3) he believes himself unjustly persecuted and discriminated against; (4) he focuses his attacks on the greatest scientists and the best-established theories; and (5) he often employs a complex jargon and in many cases coins words and phrases (neologisms) of his own. Do any of these characteristics fit Erich von Däniken? Except for the fifth, I suggest that they do.

Von Däniken's thesis is this: the postulate that the earth was once visited by spacemen from another world serves better to account for ancient artifacts than do the scientific theories now accepted. . . . Why then has the scientific community either refused to consider von Däniken's position or rejected it out of hand? For several reasons. First, scientific investigation as now carried on is out of date, because the investigations do not ask of the past questions based on our knowledge of space travel; i.e., they presuppose that ancient man could not fly, consequently they cannot accurately assess evidence that he did when they find it. . . . Yet the only conclusions available to research are those which are arrived at in response to the questions asked. If you do not ask the right questions, the right answers will never appear. To put it another way, von Däniken claims that if archaeology does not question its data on the basis of what we now know about space travel, it cannot possibly set up an explanatory theory that takes account of space travel. In principle, there is nothing wrong with this claim; it is sound hermeneutics.

But the second reason von Däniken advances to explain orthodox science's prejudiced condemnation of his postulate sounds a bit more "pseudo." He argues that today's scientists stubbornly persist in refusing to admit that they need to change their methods and theories. . . Since they assume that ours is the most advanced civilization in the history of this planet, they are blind to any evidence that civilizations higher than our own once existed. . . . For example, present archaeological theory explains artifacts in terms of "primitive" religion and refuses to entertain other possibilities. . . . Thus the orthodox scientific community has shut itself off from the truth beforehand. Here is a clear symptom of the pseudo-scientist: the established scientists are blockheads who cannot see past their noses.

Von Däniken's third reason is an extension of the second. He claims that modern science will not consider any theoretical explanations which tend to cast doubt on the accuracy of the Jewish and Christian Bibles. . . . It is amazing that, after all we have been through with Galileo, Darwin, Freud and fundamentalism, von Däniken should still speak of a scientific-religious conspiracy to defend the literal authority of the Bible. In projecting a conspiracy against himself, the pseudo-scientist reveals one of the most serious symptoms of paranoia. Certainly von Däniken's ego seems to be of grandiose dimensions, for what greater establishment could a theorist seek to triumph over than a unified Judeo-Christian-scientific conspiracy?

Von Däniken's fourth argument for the credibility of his claim is that the orthodox scientific community has frequently erred in the past. . . . Here surely is the pseudo-scientist harping on an obvious theme to his own advantage.

An examination of von Däniken's argument from literary and archaeological evidence indicts him beyond appeal. Invariably he employs a four-step formula: (1) he reports an interesting archaeological discovery or cites a passage from ancient literature; (2) he describes it as only partly explained or even baffling; (3) he raises a hypothetical question regarding its origin, sometimes suggesting intervention from outer space; and (4) he goes on to another subject.

Thus von Däniken speaks about Easter Island and the hundreds of gigantic stone statues that have been standing there since time immemorial. . . . [Von Däniken] dangles questions before the reader: ". . . who did the work? And how did they manage it?" . . . This surely is an egregious case of the *argumentum ad ignorantiam;* it proceeds by way of an unanswerable challenge to disprove rather than by way of a serious attempt to prove. We are supposed to conclude that highly skilled technicians from space were responsible. Von Däniken then turns to another topic.

But let me cite a few facts about Easter Island that will reveal the "pseudo" quality of von Däniken's scientific investigation.

The Norwegian explorer Thor Heyerdahl seems to have resolved the mystery in his book *Aku-Aku: The Secret of Easter Island.* . . . He persuaded some of the natives of the island to demonstrate [a] procedure for carving and erecting the statues. . . . Von Däniken quotes Heyerdahl in *Chariots of the Gods?*—but very selectively.

Von Däniken also plays the numbers game. He asks, for example, ". . . is it really a coincidence that the height of the pyramid of Cheops [in Egypt] multiplied by a thousand million—98 million miles—corresponds approximately to the distance between the earth and the sun?. . . But in *Fads and Fallacies* Gardner analyzes the baffling numbers technique. If you set about measuring a complicated structure like the pyramid of Cheops, he says, you will soon have dozens of measurements to play with; and if you have the patience to juggle them about in various ways, you are bound to come out with many figures that coincide with important historical dates or with scientific calculations. (pp. 560-62)

Bible readers will be interested in another of von Däniken's arguments. He writes: ". . . *without actually consulting Exodus,* I seem to remember that the Ark was often surrounded by flashing sparks. . . . Undoubtedly the Ark was electrically charged." . . . He goes on to insist that God was really a spaceman with whom Moses communicated via an electrical transmitter whenever he needed help or advice. Well, I *have* consulted Exodus and could not locate the flashing sparks. I am not flatly saying that von Däniken's thesis is wrong. But I say that if scholarly integrity is part of what defines genuine science, Erich von Däniken definitely belongs on the pseudo-science side of the ledger. (p. 562)

What such theories make clear, it seems to me, is that their authors are driven by a strong desire to reexplain the more mysterious dimensions of our spiritual existence in naturalistic categories. Theorists like von Däniken . . . believe that all reality is just a finite number of natural laws, all of which can in principle be known—and then perhaps manipulated—by the human mind. Obviously the mood or mind-set of naturalistic scientific thinking has a grip on these authors and their followers. But they are scientific only in mood, because in their haste to supply the ultimate explanation they have flouted the rules basic to scientific method: tedious experimentation and cautious hypothesizing.

It must be said, however, that the urge to reexplain religious mysteries is not unique to UFO theologians; it has been pervasive among religious intellectuals for the past two centuries. How often have we been told that the ecstatic prophets and demon-possessed characters of the Bible were merely victims of what we now know as epilepsy? Or that the fire and brimstone which the Lord sent down on Sodom and Gomorrah were really the result of an explosion of the sulphur beds underlying those cities? No, the naturalistic perspective is as much a part of our religious consciousness today as is the Bible itself. In this sense, von Däniken is simply doing what other theologians are doing. What is at issue is whether he does it well or not. In my opinion he does not do it well at all. (p. 563)

Ted Peters, "Chariots, UFOs, and the Mystery of God: The Science and Religion of Erich von Däniken," in The Christian Century, Vol. XCI, No. 20, May 22, 1974, pp. 560-63.

ROBERT MOLYNEUX

Von Däniken can be readily criticized on several counts, but he is at least entertaining. Here [in **"In Search of Ancient**

Gods''] he returns with more nagging questions and sometimes outlandish statements, all delivered in a machine-gun pace which can leave his readers and critics breathless and outdistanced. His latest rehashes much of what he has already written. . . .

> Robert Molyneux, in a review of "In Search of Ancient Gods: My Pictorial Evidence for the Impossible," in Library Journal, Vol. 99, No. 19, November 1, 1974, p. 2858.

CHOICE

[*In Search of Ancient Gods*] is another rehash of [von Däniken's] theme with plenty of pictures. The photographs do present genuine archaeological mysteries, but what this amateur makes of them is incredible. Unfettered by the logical constraints imposed upon a scientific theory, von Däniken freely mixes *non-sequiturs* and circular arguments in a transparent appeal for sympathy, asking the lay reader to have faith in one whom the scientists scorn. The rambling, choppily written text is a string of sentences with no chapters, table of contents, or index. The bibliography is a pretentious token of scholarship. Perhaps as romance this stuff is good escape literature, but once is enough.

> A review of "In Search of Ancient Gods: My Pictorial Evidence for the Impossible," in Choice, Vol. 11, No. 12, February, 1975, p. 1792.

JOHN J. BEGLEY, S.J.

I cannot take [*Miracles of the Gods*] seriously. I say this not because of the author's thesis concerning the origin of what constitutes a peripheral concern to both theologians and believers alike, visions and miracles; but because the author treats with contempt much that believers take very seriously: the Church, the New Testament, and theology. The Church is condemned for its arrogance and dictatorial behavior in withholding its approval from all reported visions and miracles. The New Testament is rejected for its alleged inconsistencies, misrepresentations, and basic untruthfulness. Theologians and pastors are castigated for their duplicity in withholding from the faithful the truth about the New Testament in order to protect their own livelihood.

In support of his thesis regarding the untruthfulness of the New Testament, the author refers to a number of scripture scholars. References are consistently incomplete. Page numbers are never cited. . . . So much for scholarship.

Visions and miracles are real according to von Däniken and can be accounted for in the following way. Extraterrestrial beings visited this and other solar systems and left behind descendants. . . .

Von Däniken advances his rejection of Christian faith with the expectation that "a sound thrashing by Christian specialists" awaits him. I suspect that specialists will give this book as much attention as it deserves.

> John J. Begley, S.J. in a review of "Miracles of the Gods," in Best Sellers, Vol. 36, No. 2, May, 1976, p. 56.

THE BOOKLIST

Certain adherents of the Christian religion and readers who demand that a book develop a single, consistent thesis will be turned off by von Däniken's sprawling effort [*Miracles of the Gods*]. His declared subject is "visions," yet in building a case for the autogenesis of healing miracles and visions, von Däniken dismisses much that he observed at Lourdes as manipulative hoax, then reverses himself to say that visions emanate either from the conscious residual energies of the dead or from extraterrestrial beings. No doubt the popularity of his *Chariots of the Gods?* will generate sufficient interest in this production. (pp. 1219-20)

> A review of "Miracles of the Gods: A New Look at the Supernatural," in The Booklist, Vol. 72, No. 17, May 1, 1976, pp. 1219-20.

KENNETH L. FEDER

It is about as difficult for an archaeologist in 1979 to avoid the theories of Erich von Däniken as it was for a sixteenth-century European peasant to avoid the Black Plague. This analogy can certainly be extended to the dread experienced when faced with these representative phenomena. (p. 20)

[*Chariots of the Gods?*] was impossible to read in one sitting. It was easy reading in that the average syllable content per word approached unity. However, because so much of the information was erroneous in terms of misleading statements and out-of-context references, characterized by verbal sleight-of-hand or out-and-out untruths, a lot of time was wasted in teeth gnashing and walking around the room searching for the book after repeatedly throwing it against the wall.

I could differentiate at least three basic arguments presented in *Chariots*: (1) Human biological evolution was engineered by intermating with spacemen. . . . (2) There exist ancient prehistoric artifacts and structures that directly and empirically record the presence of aliens among us. (3) There exist ancient prehistoric artifacts and structures whose complexity and technological sophistication indicate "help from above" in the form of some sort of extraterrestrial Peace or Urban Job Corps. While the first two of these arguments possessed a charm unto themselves, I was repelled by the third construct.

Of the first two arguments, the first was just silly. The second appealed to those interested in inkblots (if you look hard enough at anything for long enough it begins to look like lots of things). It was the third argument that bothered me most. The basis of the third theory is simply that ancient, so-called "primitive" peoples were stupid and could never, by themselves, have accomplished the great feats of engineering, astronomy, and so forth, which are apparent in the archaeological record. It troubled me greatly, not so much that von Däniken could write a book like *Chariots of the Gods?*, but that millions of people would buy the *argument* as well as the book.

I initially regarded this third von Däniken argument as the ultimate extension of the hyperdiffusionist ideology. The diffusionist model was quite popular in historical and anthropological circles in the United States and Europe during the first three decades of this century. Ultimately, the diffusionist perspective was predicated on the assumption that people are essentially dull and unimaginative. From this, it was inferred that while cultures in various parts of the world had evolved along very complex lines, it was highly unlikely that these complexities had occurred independently. That is, it was assumed that there were a very limited number of cultural "hearths" and that all innovations (agriculture, writing, urban civilization) were developed at these hearths and spread out, or diffused from these places. (pp. 20-1)

Archaeology has shown the diffusionist model to be inconsistent with the data. Intensive archaeological analysis in the last several decades has shown that in most cases the complex developments seen in the Near East, Far East, and New World were the result of long, internal, cultural evolutionary processes. In fact, evidence of the wholesale *movement* of complex cultural traits does not exist until well after an area was well on the road to complex development. (p. 21)

Very much as did the extreme diffusionists, von Däniken posited a cultural hearth, a source of all development and innovation—except that the hearth was not on this planet. Instead, we must hypothesize a happy band of extraterrestrials proselytizing science and technology, returning again and again until Peking or Java or Heidelberg or Neanderthal Man (or Woman) could get it right. However, on a closer inspection of the evidence the wily von Däniken uses to buttress his extraterrestrial theory, I came to the conclusion that this explanation was in fact insufficient.

The implications of von Däniken's work and the reasons for its acceptance are undoubtedly far more invidious than some commonly held belief that ancient people were dumb. It was very curious, I thought, that von Däniken was ever ready to provide examples of "proof" of his third hypothesis—that the archaeological record contained developments that the local people could not be credited with—from sites in Asia, Africa, and the Americas, while his European data were sorely deficient. After all, if Earth's peoples are essentially dull and uninventive, the ancient astronauts would have, out of necessity, taught everyone the skills they had brought. There could be no playing favorites or unfair advantages given to any one group.

It became quite clear to me, at least impressionistically, what was going on. Von Däniken's hypothesis that extraterrestrials must have aided humanity on the road to civilization was not based on the assumption that *all* people were dumb and uninventive—just some. . . . In fact, all groups save one, Europeans, must have been helped by the ancient astronauts. Von Däniken and his followers could accept that ancient Greeks developed complex architecture and the concept of the atom. They could believe that the ancient Romans built the Coliseum and sophisticated aqueduct systems. But the ancient Egyptians build the pyramids? The Africans Zimbabwe? American Indians develop a sophisticated calendar? Impossible! It became abundantly clear to me that the essence of von Däniken's argument was beyond mere diffusionism; it was based on racism. (pp. 21-2)

Von Däniken and his readers have little trouble accepting the imagination, creativity, and abilities of ancient Europeans. They do, however, have a great deal of trouble when it comes to other—that is, nonwhite—people. *Chariots of the Gods?* should be seen then as one in a long line of pseudoscientific works based on or intended to prove the superiority of one race / people / culture. In this light, von Däniken's *Chariots of the Gods?* is not simply a silly little book; it is a dangerous little book.

This and subsequent works are a long way from proving that human biology and culture are products of interaction with extraterrestrials. Nor do they prove that the archaeological record bears evidence of technological sophistication beyond the capacity of the ancients, European, African, Asian, or otherwise. In fact, they are just stories about what might have been—science fiction in reverse.

The phenomenon of Erich von Däniken's success does prove one thing: the credulity of a large number of people. His success rests on a contradiction faced by those who believe that non-Europeans are somehow not as intellectually developed or as culturally capable as Europeans: the archaeology of many of these supposedly inferior non-European groups attests to great technological sophistication in the past. Erich von Däniken's work can be used to neatly solve this paradox. Those great civilizations were not produced by dark-skinned folks, folks! Those benevolent astronauts from galaxies we know not where found just the spots on this tiny planet that needed enlightenment, but kept themselves carefully hidden from all those smart Europeans, busy with their monument and civilization building. (p. 23)

> Kenneth L. Feder, "Foolsgold of the Gods," in The Humanist, Vol. 40, No. 1, January-February, 1980, pp. 20-3.

MARY ANNE BONNEY AND SUSAN JEFFREYS

[*Signs of the Gods*] gives us a number of novel theories—the Ark of the Covenant was, obviously, a portable nuclear reactor (you will be immediately won over to this view by a photograph of a model and a drawing of a photograph of the same model); ancient religious sites can be joined up to form a pattern of pentagons (a map with all the sites unnamed and the majority at the bottom of the sea bears out this theory). Von Däniken is good at coming up with bold and imaginative theories but sloppy over his evidence; he doesn't argue his case—just shoves in a few screamers and an inadequate diagram and moves on to the next theory. With a bit more work and a bit less hysteria he could have produced a book that at the very least was thought provoking.

> Mary Anne Bonney and Susan Jeffreys, "Psychic Shortlist," in Punch, Vol. 279, No. 7288, July 9, 1980, p. 71.*

JULIA M. EHRESMANN

With as much speciosity as ever, the original popularizer of the theory of prehistoric extraterrestrial visitors brings forward [in *Signs of the Gods?*] more "unexplained" phenomena to repeat his "gods-astronaut" proposal. . . . Along with typographical errors, there are quotes from encyclopedias, names of esteemed professors, and plenty of von Däniken's exclamation-pointed epigrams.

> Julia M. Ehresmann, in a review of "Signs of the Gods?" in Booklist, Vol. 77, No. 7, December 1, 1980, p. 488.

STEPHANIE ZVIRIN

Von Däniken's continuing search for traces of ancient astronauts takes him to the South Pacific's Kiribati Islands, where he examines giant footprints and monoliths as still further evidence of intergalactic visitations. . . . Whether considered as a piece of radical reinterpretation of world history or as a bit of unconvincing comparative hucksterism, von Däniken's [*Pathways to the Gods*] still reads like a daring and exotic adventure story.

> *Stephanie Zvirin, in a review of "Pathways to the Gods: The Stones of Kiribati," in* Booklist, *Vol. 79, No. 6, November 15, 1982, p. 410.*

JO-ANN D. SULEIMAN

[Von Däniken's usual arguments are presented in *Pathways to the Gods*], but valuable space and reader attention is taken up by a polemic against detractors and by name dropping. These qualities, and the sloppy organization of the book, detract from the precision and objectivity required of such an argument.

> *Jo-Ann D. Suleiman, in a review of "Pathways to the Gods: The Stones of Kiribati," in* Library Journal, *Vol. 108, No. 2, January 15, 1983, pp. 128-29.*

Barbara Wersba

1932-

American novelist, poet, and dramatist.

Although she began as a children's author, Wersba has been writing mainly for young adults since the publication of her novel, *The Dream Watcher* (1968). This story of a teenager named Albert, who learns to accept his eccentricities despite alienation from his peer group and family, is thematically representative of Wersba's later works. Like Albert, Steve in *The Country of the Heart* (1975), J. F. in *Tunes for a Small Harmonica* (1976), and Harvey in *The Carnival in My Mind* (1982) are all misfit adolescents who gain confidence in their individuality.

In order to become more independent, Wersba's protagonists often reject their parents' values. For example, in *Run Softly, Go Fast* (1970), Davy leaves home to pursue his idealistic goals. However, like most of Wersba's teenage characters, Davy discovers that even those values which seem outdated, such as the importance of familial relationships, have significance in his life. Because most of her protagonists resolve their identity crises and are better able to understand the point of view of their parents and role models, Wersba has been characterized as an optimistic fiction writer.

Critics are mixed in their response to Wersba's novels. Some find her characters too stereotyped; others consider them well-rounded and believable in their responses to problems that arise in their lives. It has been suggested that her characters' development is strengthened by their struggle with ethical decisions in morally ambiguous situations. Many reviewers argue that her topics of interest to young adults, which include sex, drugs, and counterculture lifestyles, are included only for their sensationalism and add little to the advancement of plot. Critics generally agree, however, that Wersba's dark humor and her accurate portrayals of upper-class lifestyles add much to her fiction.

Wersba has also written *Twenty-six Starlings Will Fly Through Your Mind* (1980), a poetic ABC reader which has been commended for its sophisticated and melodic verse.

(See also *Children's Literature Review*, Vol. 3; *Contemporary Authors*, Vols. 29-32, rev. ed.; and *Something about the Author*, Vol. 1.)

SUSAN A. ROTH

Anti-hero [Albert] Scully [in *The Dream Watcher*] broods unhappily and self-consciously about not fitting into the ready-made social forms espoused by his hyper-tense mother, but most of all about not actually *living* anything. . . . Scully's a young Thoreau without self-trust until 80-year-old Orpha Woodfin enters early in the story. . . . When, at her death, Albert finds that she's been lying about her glamorous past, all he knows is that she made sense. Most young readers will take nicely to Scully, and many boys will delight at seeing sensitivities usually reserved for the other sex encompassed in one who, very much his own man, represents the more contemplative segment of the Now generation.

Photograph by Charles Caron. Courtesy of McIntosh & Otis, Inc.

Susan A. Roth, in a review of "The Dream Watcher," in School Library Journal, *an appendix to* Library Journal, *Vol. 15, No. 1, September, 1968, p. 160.*

KIRKUS SERVICE

[Albert Scully's situation in *The Dream Watcher* is] the All-American Nightmare . . . and he's the Perfect Failure ("my trouble was simply being a total failure")—lousy in school, no friends, odd tastes, odd interests. Well, what happens (the only thing that happens) is that he meets this little old lady who lives in a dilapidated house smack in the middle of the development and they talk and they talk and she tells him about her fame as an actress in Europe and her brother who became a Zen Buddhist monk and her poet husband who died of consumption . . . and then she dies—destitute and divested of her legend. It might be the ultimate betrayal but he still has "what was good and beautiful" and all the quotes from Thoreau and Shaw and Rilke and the rest of Bartlett's. . . . The whole Scene, from the East Village to a pregnant schoolgirl to the Vietnam War in a long semi-literate soliloquy with no real maturity and no new message.

A review of "The Dream Watcher," in Kirkus Service, *Vol. XXXVI, No. 17, September 1, 1968, p. 988.*

THE BOOKLIST

[In *The Dream Watcher* Albert] is losing a lonely battle with society's materialistic criteria for success, of which his mother is number-one advocate, until friendship with an eighty-year-old self-designated actress gives him the courage to be himself. The author crowds so much social criticism into the narrative that Albert sometimes becomes a representative of protest; but his story, told in first person, is real enough to be moving.

> *A review of "The Dream Watcher," in* The Booklist and Subscription Books Bulletin, *Vol. 65, No. 5, November 1, 1968, p. 304.*

POLLY GOODWIN

[In *The Dream Watcher*] the author, with skill and compassion, has created a good, honest human being, an individualist who needs his dreams and will have the strength, you feel sure, to be himself. She has written an unusual and very fine book about an extraordinary friendship, a book that is thoughtful, often funny and with a hero to remember.

> *Polly Goodwin, in a review of "The Dream Watcher," in* Book World—The Washington Post, *November 3, 1968, p. 18.*

LAURA POLLA SCANLON

Rarely does an author manage to capture the suburban scene with the painful fidelity achieved [in *The Dream Watcher*]. . . . [Albert Scully] is constantly being urged to "get with it." "It" is the Pepsi generation life in his development, "Blitherwood, New Jersey." . . . Readers will be reminded of *The Catcher in the Rye.* The theme is similar and the same bitter-sweet humor runs through it. But this is no imitation. It's an eloquent restatement of the old plea for the individual. (pp. 288-89)

> *Laura Polla Scanlon, in a review of "The Dream Watchers," in* Commonweal, *Vol. LXXXIX, No. 8, November 22, 1968, pp. 288-89.*

JOHN ROWE TOWNSEND

The basic story of Barbara Wersba's ["**Run Softly, Go Fast**"] is good—and at times moving. It is about a destructive, loving-and-hating relationship between a young man [Davy] and his father [Leo]. . . . After a series of rows, Davy takes wing to the East Village. Two years later Leo dies in a hospital. There has been no reconciliation. Davy can't feel anything—or so he says. The story is recounted by him in a narrative written after the funeral; and having put it all on paper he begins at last to understand and forgive.

Yet the book does have failures which come from a consciousness that it was being written "for" young adults. It has chapters on hippie life, drugs, sex and the rest that give the impression all the currently fashionable ingredients have been duly pitched into the mixture. There's something determinedly positive about the ending (the air of "coming to terms" in the last chapter) that doesn't quite ring true. And the sophistication of Miss Wersba's technique doesn't fully conceal the occasional use of hackneyed situations, machine-made characters.

There is a second, partly overlapping theme. The book can also be read as a pilgrim's progress through the teens, during which Davy moves from his suffocating home—with a detour among the hippies—to the arms of a nice girl called Maggie and early success as a painter. This last set-up appears to represent the author's chosen compromise between hip and square. . . .

Technically, **"Run Softly, Go Fast"** is highly accomplished. It works mainly through flashback, but with forward jumps, sudden flights of dialogue and verbatim "repeats" of key passages. Maybe the technique gets in the way. I do not doubt the book's underlying sincerity, but to me at least it fails to speak clearly, and only occasionally strikes a responding chord.

> *John Rowe Townsend, in a review of "Run Softly, Go Fast," in* The New York Times Book Review, *November 22, 1970, p. 38.*

SHERYL B. ANDREWS

Books about alienated youth, the drug scene, and Middle Class America seem to abound these days. And at first glance, it might appear that [*Run Softly, Go Fast*] should be classified as a fluently readable story but one that dwells on what are becoming trite conventions in books for older teen-agers. Such an assumption would be a mistake. . . . There are no sympathetic characters in the book, with the possible exception of Maggie, the girl Davy is living with in The Village. But there are many convincing ones. And the strength of the book is that it rings true. In spite of its preoccupation with the Establishment, hippies, drugs, and sex, the book succeeds in clearly and forcefully conveying basic human weakness and blindness as well as the universal need for love and understanding, which must begin in the individual himself. A vendetta that ends in a benediction.

> *Sheryl B. Andrews, in a review of "Run Softly, Go Fast," in* The Horn Book Magazine, *Vol. XLVI, No. 6, December, 1970, p. 624.*

JEAN C. THOMPSON

[In *Run Softly, Go Fast*] Davy, 19, begins writing to analyze why he hardly seems to care about his father's untimely death. In a disjointed style appropriate to his youth and confusion about his reaction to the loss, Davy chronicles his struggle with his father, Leo. . . . On reading his ruminations at the end of the book, Davy discovers what most young readers would have sensed earlier: he'd left things out, the story had two sides! The introspective style is more irritating here than entertaining. The emphasis is on feeling over action and the result is often tepid. This is participatory literature over-obviously designed to make youngsters see to the other side of the generation gap. The author's scheme is to create a narration flawed by the subjectivity of the narrator, and she does it successfully. The result, however, is critical ambivalence and doubtful tolerance from the intended audience.

> *Jean C. Thompson, in a review of "Run Softly, Go Fast," in* School Library Journal, *an appendix to* Library Journal, *Vol. 17, No. 6, February, 1971, p. 70.*

JOHN W. CONNER

[*Run Softly, Go Fast*] is overwritten. Barbara Wersba's descriptions of events tend to slow the ultimate action of the narrative. David Marks is a kaleidoscope of artistic intentions rather than a flesh and blood boy. . . . David's mother becomes the only real character in the novel when she enters her son's East Village pad and challenges him to try to make amends with his dying father. The other characters, Maggie who shares David's East Village pad, and Rick who shared David's love for art, are really only supporting players who reflect David's current feelings.

Despite these flaws, I believe this will be a very successful book for older adolescents. The fact that the author has created types rather than characters allows a concerned adolescent reader to enter in without being totally usurped by a character. . . . Barbara Wersba has skillfully revealed the elements of conflict between David and his father. (pp. 530-31)

Barbara Wersba understands the agony of establishing personal values. *Run Softly, Go Fast,* is an excellent study of personal values. Long after the individual conflicts portrayed in the novel cannot be remembered, an adolescent reader will recall David's chagrin when his adult heroes revealed themselves as limited men. This is a fine book for a value-conscious older adolescent. (p. 531)

> *John W. Conner, in a review of "Run Softly, Go Fast," in* English Journal, *Vol. 60, No. 4, April, 1971, pp. 530-31.*

PUBLISHERS WEEKLY

[Barbara Wersba] has written a memorable story of a sensitive young boy who discovers a miniature circus in his backyard. . . . **"Let Me Fall Before I Fly"** generates a mystical, dreamlike quality that will enchant readers.

> *A review of "Let Me Fall Before I Fly," in* Publishers Weekly, *Vol. 200, No. 10, September 6, 1971, p. 51.*

DORIS ORGEL

[In *Let Me Fall Before I Fly* a boy watches a make-believe circus] for hours on end in the grass, until he knows each feature of every performer by heart. And the more he grows to love the circus, the farther he drifts from his own, the real, world.

Then comes a storm. The circus disappears. Now both the child and the book are in terrible trouble. For the child has "lost the desire to live." And the book is up against the single subject which, to my mind, cannot be dealt with in children's literature—namely, total, unrelieved despair.

At this point the child's parents and a doctor intervene. They restore the child to normality, unconvincingly so. Meantime some highly questionable speculations have been made concerning the link between genius and alienation. Finally a resolution is attempted in the form of a dream in which the child, no longer passive spectator, takes part himself in his beloved circus. But the symbolism fails. If the circus is supposed to be the work of art, then to describe it as "both image and reality, fact and dream, fiction and longing," only adds to the confusion. And the child, who is supposed to be the artist, is still as faceless as he has been nameless all along. Functioning neither as individual nor as symbol, he remains, in the author's own words, "distant, peculiar, vague" throughout. So does the book.

> *Doris Orgel, in a review of "Let Me Fall Before I Fly," in* The New York Times Book Review, *October 17, 1971, p. 8.*

DIANE GERSONI-STAVN

Can a boy in a boy's book have a mother who isn't vapid? Yes, but usually only if she's cruelly domineering or lax in her maternal obligations. In Barbara Wersba's **The Dream Watcher,** for example, there are two important women. One is a poor, alcoholic spinster on welfare whose poetic allusions and fantasized stories of her glorious past on the stage inspire the terribly normal, average Albert Scully to appreciate his own capabilities and potential. . . . But, what about young Albert's mom, the really significant woman in his life? She is a castrator who constantly puts down her unsuccessful hard-drinking insurance man of a husband . . . while Wersba treats Mr. Scully sympathetically (he had always wanted to be a pilot but his wife steered him toward business), she has little patience with the wife's own frustrations. Why does Mrs. Scully daydream about being a celebrity? If she's emasculated her husband, as it's implied, what in her own background limited *her* ability to relate to people and led her to cope by restructuring her reality? These questions never even come to the fore in this book; boys see only the father as immediate victim, the son as probable, long-range victim, and the mother as vulture. (pp. 263-64)

> *Diane Gersoni-Stavn, "The Skirts in Fiction about Boys: A Maxi Mess," in* Sexism and Youth, *edited by Diane Gersoni-Stavn, R. R. Bowker Company, 1974, pp. 260-71.**

PUBLISHERS WEEKLY

[In *The Country of the Heart*] Hadley is a famous poet, aged 40, angry and dying. Steven is in college, an aspiring poet full of pat answers and puppy-like devotion to his "idol," Hadley, who has miraculously rented a house in his hometown. Predictably, she repulses his advances, mocks him mercilessly but softens, at first, grudgingly. As their relationship grows, Hadley and Steven . . . become lovers—finally, briefly. The author's insights are admirably original and comprehensive. A story that could have been insufferably maudlin is rescued deftly and elevated—to excellence.

> *A review of "The Country of the Heart," in* Publishers Weekly, *Vol. 208, No. 2, July 14, 1975, p. 60.*

KAREN HARRIS

[*The Country of the Heart* is an] extended cliché about an 18-year-old would-be poet who falls in love with a middle-aged successful woman poet. . . . The novel, which takes the form of a statement by the aspiring poet addressed to his now dead love, is written in the pretentious and overblown style common to daytime soaps.

> *Karen Harris, in a review of "The Country of the Heart," in* School Library Journal, *Vol. 22, No. 1, September, 1975, p. 128.*

GEORGESS McHARGUE

It is hard for a writer to write about writers. In respect of that, at least, Barbara Wersba's *The Country of the Heart* . . . is something of a tour de force. Here we have two writers: a famous, caustic, self-absorbed woman poet of 40 and an un-formed, vulnerable, aspiring young man of 18. . . . (The two literary types are not new, either to fiction or to history.)

Steven makes all the mistakes. He blunders wide-eyed into the life of a woman who wants only to work and be alone, blathers about the sublimity of art, tremblingly proffers his poems, and is crushed when, having initiated him into sexual love and given him excellent, if disillusioned, professional advice, Hadley deliberately antagonizes him and turns him out. Only much later does he learn that from the beginning she knew she was dying.

The story itself is perhaps a bit of a hype. (Why do fictional young writers always turn out talented, never give up and settle for the real estate business?) Yet since we must accept the characters as the author dated them, it must be said that Wersba's deft control of tone is remarkably convincing. The voice of the narrator and the character of Steven are unmistakably one, alternately naive, self-conscious, pretentious, and, yes, talented. This is not really a book about death (we feel the affair must have ended in any case). It is a perceptive look at "growing up literary."

> *Georgess McHargue, "For Young Readers: Love and Death," in* The New York Times Book Review, *January 4, 1976, p. 8.*

PUBLISHERS WEEKLY

A honey of a story, laced with humor and tender feelings, [*Tunes for a Small Harmonica*] boasts characters made truly human by the author's expertise. J. F. (Jacqueline) is a rich 16-year-old, the despair of her soignée mother and a worry to her best friend, Marylou. J. F. dresses like Steve McQueen and chain smokes. Her mother sends her to a shrink and Mary-lou buys her a harmonica to help her cut down on cigarettes. To her surprise, J. F. becomes expert on the harmonica and falls in love with her poetry teacher, Harold Murth. . . . The complications which follow are many, merry and a constant string of surprises to say nothing of delight.

> *A review of "Tunes for a Small Harmonica," in* Publishers Weekly, *Vol. 210, No. 2, July 12, 1976, p. 72.*

DIANE HAAS

Occasional stylistic weaknesses [in *Tunes for a Small Harmonica*] fail to mar this entertaining tale of a tomboy's first crush. . . . J. F.'s parents are a bit stereotypical, but the action is fast paced and J. F. is winning and believable, even as she matches wits with a quack psychologist.

> *Diane Haas, in a review of "Tunes for a Small Harmonica," in* School Library Journal, *Vol. 23, No. 1, September, 1976, p. 127.*

HUMAN—AND ANTI-HUMAN—VALUES IN CHILDREN'S BOOKS: A CONTENT RATING INSTRUMENT FOR EDUCATORS AND CONCERNED PARENTS

[*The Country of the Heart*'s] strongest asset is Ms. Wersba's realistic depiction of the hard work involved in writing, which destroys the myth that artists lead glamorous lives of leisure. However, the book is seriously flawed overall.

In a style that is flowery to the point of pretentiousness, readers are fed the concept of the "driven artist." States Hadly: "Art-ists can't have both life and art." By failing to question the validity of this elitist view of the artist, the book reinforces the notion that art and social commitment are necessarily op-posed. The extreme individualism implicit in this view is fur-ther supported by Hadley's martyr-like desire to suffer her painful dying in isolation.

Steve's desire to find life's meaning through Hadley, to have their love endure forever, to retreat from the world to the bedroom, reflects attitudes towards love that are escapist and sexist. Steve's love is also possessive, implying that jealousy is a natural component of "True Love." Rather than preparing young people to enter into mature, give-and-take relationships, these old romantic notions encourage unreal expectations.

The male pronoun is used for both sexes. Not until the end of the story, when Hadley is dying, is the age factor dealt with—and then not effectively. Because its good features do not compensate for its extreme reinforcement of negative values in human relationships, this book should be avoided. (p. 179)

> *"The Analyses: 'The Country of the Heart','" in* Hu-man—And Anti-Human—Values in Children's Books: A Content Rating Instrument for Educators and Con-cerned Parents, *edited by the Council on Interracial Books for Children, Inc., Racism and Sexism Re-source Center for Educators, 1976, pp. 178-79.*

ZENA SUTHERLAND

Funny, frank, and sophisticated, [*Tunes for a Small Harmon-ica*] has—despite such exaggeration as the inept, neurotic psy-chiatrist—memorable characters, brisk dialogue, and a yeasty style. It is consistent and believable as a first-person account, and it faces many broad concerns of all adolescents.

> *Zena Sutherland, in a review of "Tunes for a Small Harmonica," in* Bulletin of the Center for Children's Books, *Vol. 30, No. 6, February, 1977, p. 99.*

BARBARA H. BASKIN AND KAREN H. HARRIS

It is never really clear [in *Let Me Fall Before I Fly*] whether the boy's imaginary world should be considered fantasy or hallucination, but as a fantasy, the story is unsatisfactory be-cause of the presence of the psychiatrist and the child's death wish. The author contrasts the boy's generosity and selflessness while hallucinating with his selfish, belligerent, and dishonest behavior needed to accommodate reality, leaving the reader to wonder if the author is suggesting that a world of irrationality is preferable to the real one. The format suggests a child's book, but the confusing and quasi-surrealistic style renders it an unlikely choice for that audience. (p. 338)

> *Barbara H. Baskin and Karen H. Harris, "An An-notated Guide to Juvenile Fiction Portraying the Handicapped, 1970-1975: 'Let Me Fall Before I Fly'," in their* Notes from a Different Drummer: A Guide

to Juvenile Fiction Portraying the Handicapped, *R. R. Bowker Company, 1977, pp. 337-38.*

MARGARET PARISH

[In *Tunes for a Small Harmonica,* a] sixteen-year-old tomboy, J. F., struggles to define who she is against a backdrop of adults who mostly succeed in giving her remarkably little help and encouragement.

Readers who wonder what became of intrepid heroines of juvenile fiction like Pippi Longstocking, Harriet the Spy and Queenie Peavy might find their reincarnations in J. F., five years older, a lot wealthier, and perhaps a little wiser. (p. 89)

> *Margaret Parish "Of Love and Sex and Death and Becoming and Other Journeys," in* English Journal, *Vol. 67, No. 5, May, 1978, pp. 88-90.**

LANCE SALWAY

[*Tunes for a Small Harmonica*] is laced with eccentric characters and a slick narrative style that made me laugh out loud. It's a good, amusing read but I felt that Ms. Wersba's central character was somewhat strangled by the author's sophisticated humour: I cared about what J. F. said and did, and not about the character herself. And the book's ending seemed too neat and contrived to be altogether convincing. Still . . . , this is splendid entertainment.

> *Lance Salway, in a review of "Tunes for a Small Harmonica," in* Signal, *No. 29, May, 1979, p. 111.*

MAGGIE PARISH

Positively-portrayed mothers—the kind whose parenting readers might someday want to emulate, seem to be in the minority in . . . works of contemporary realistic fiction. . . . (p. 101)

What of the mothers in contemporary realistic fiction for young adults who are shown to be mostly destructive influences on their sons and daughters? *The Dreamwatcher . . .* is one good example of this phenomenon. The mother in *The Dreamwatcher* seems to have no redeeming features. A compulsive consumer, obsessed with her house's appearance and her own, she literally seems to drive her husband to drink and her son to the brink of despair. Then the protagonist meets an old woman dressed in shabby velvet, who quotes Thoreau and Shakespeare and treats her new friend with admiration and respect. The mother in this book is stereotyped, but the book works as literature anyway; the protagonist's redemption is an absorbing theme, and while we never see the positive attributes that his mother might have, we do see, and the protagonist must confront and accept, the negative attributes of his "fairy godmother," who is a whole person with strengths and weaknesses, after all. (Another strongly negative portrayal of a mother figure in a book by Barbara Wersba occurs in *Tunes for a Small Harmonica*). . . . (p. 103)

> *Maggie Parish, "The Mother As Witch, Fairy Godmother, Survivor or Victim in Contemporary Realistic Fiction for Young Adults," in* English Journal, *Vol. 68, No. 7, October, 1979, pp. 101-03.**

PUBLISHERS WEEKLY

Inseparable as they fly far beyond the imagination, Wersba's lyrics and Palladini's pictures [in *Twenty-Six Starlings Will Fly Through Your Mind*] seem like the creation of one astonishingly gifted person. . . . The paintings and powerful drawings mesh perfectly with the poetry to describe characteristics inherent in the *shape* of each letter, not just words they embrace; to combine letters in harmonies and dissonances; and to use nouns and verbs and adjectives that stretch the mind, never the predictable or simple term. The book is a revelation, a treasure for adults too.

> *A review of "Twenty-Six Starlings Will Fly through Your Mind," in* Publishers Weekly, *Vol. 218, No. 6, August 8, 1980, p. 83.*

PATRICIA DOOLEY

[*Twenty-Six Starlings Will Fly Through Your Mind*] is an idiosyncratic, surrealistic paean to the alphabet rather than an alphabet book. Each letter is arbitrarily characterized ("A, secret and determined. . . . B, glancing shyly"); but readers inevitably begin to wonder why "H" is "the uncle of I," or why "I" is "pale and discouraged." . . . Why is S "the good letter . . . bringing silver and silence" rather than a bad one bringing sadism and sin? The dauntless anthropomorphism and imperious tone raise the expectation of logic when there is none. Readers who like either sense or nonsense may be baffled by a book that falls in between. Another question arises over the potential audience. This "alphabet" could be read neither to nor by "Emily, who is learning to read," and who is exhorted and addressed several times in the text: among the words dropped (rather than used, or given any context) are "quadratics," "fandango," "palladium," "vacuous," and "whimsey." . . . It's not enough to say that the splendor of the illustrations justifies the book, since they are so closely tied to the text that they can't be enjoyed alone. This looks like another coffee-table book for tripping teens. (pp. 159-60)

> *Patricia Dooley, in a review of "Twenty-Six Starlings Will Fly through Your Mind," in* School Library Journal, *Vol. 27, No. 2, October, 1980, pp. 159-60.*

JANICE M. BOGSTAD

[As] much as I like [*Twenty-Six Starlings Will Fly Through Your Mind*], I have to make some criticisms of its content. There is far too much reinforcement of passive-female imagery, especially in the illustrations, but in the text as well. "A, the secret and determined guide," is pictured as a man with moustache and feathered hat, while "C, the moon's cousin," is female where the text indicates no gender distinctions. "G is an old-fashioned girl" while "I is pale and discouraged," and also female, as is "V, pointed and shy," in opposition to "W," who is male and who "wanders the woodlands." In roughly half the cases, gender is not assigned to the letters by illustration or text even when activity is associated with them. I find these passages eminently more acceptable than the others.

A second reservation which comes to mind is the audience for which this book is intended. The vocabulary is quite unusual, to the extent that one would not expect a child who needs to learn the alphabet to comprehend the book even if it were read to her or him. Hence if fails, perhaps not to its detriment, as a piece of didactic poetry. On the other hand, it succeeds in creating an imaginative and interesting approach to the mysteries and positive qualities of reading as a potentially private and liberating activity. (p. 91)

> Janice M. Bogstad, "Is There Poetry in Children's Poetry?" in The Lion and the Unicorn, *Vol. 4, No. 2, Winter, 1980-81, pp. 83-92.*

NICHOLAS TUCKER

[A] rare but . . . frank mention of what now seems to have become a forbidden topic occurs in Barbara Wersba's quite delightful *Tunes for a Small Harmonica.* Here, the 16-year-old heroine J. F. asks her best friend Marylou if they could try kissing "in the name of science" to establish whether J. F. was properly gay or not. But although the kiss is passionate, J. F. feels nothing, and concentrates instead on her new love for her weedy English teacher, Harold Murth. When all her efforts fail in this direction too, she again decides that "Only sex could make us forget that we were teacher and pupil, adolescent and adult. In my mind's eye, I saw us lying in bed smoking cigarets and talking about our lives, sharing confidences. The only trouble was that my mind's eye could not get our clothes off. We lay in bed completely dressed." The attempted seduction is yet another flop, described once more in that bantering, witty style that American writers can always seem to pull off so much more deftly than their counterparts in Britain. . . . (p. 77)

> Nicholas Tucker, "School Stories, 1970-80," in Children's literature in education, *Vol. 13, No. 2 (Summer), 1982, pp. 73-9 [the excerpt of Barbara Wersba's material used here was originally published in her* Tunes for a Small Harmonica, Harper & Row, 1976, The Bodley Head, 1979].*

KIRKUS REVIEWS

Unsuccessfully bittersweet but sometimes funny, [*The Carnival in my Mind*] tells of 14-year-old prepschool misfit Harvey Beaumont's brief, smitten interlude with Chandler Brown, 20, a shabby-elegant would-be actress who seems cast from a worn-out Sally Bowles-Holly Golightly mold. Harvey, who feels unlovable because he's short—and because his mother is devoted to her Irish setters, but barely acknowledges his existence—is delighted to be taken seriously by the rakishly glamorous Chan (or so he sees her); and when the dogs that crowd his mother's Fifth Avenue apartment get too much for him, he moves into Chan's apartment. . . . Harvey and Chan get along well, enjoy their domestic routine despite her heavy sherry drinking, sleep together chastely, and basically live on his allowance—though every now and then she turns up with a mysterious wad to spend at Cartier's, Saks, or the Plaza. Harvey is crushed to learn from a vindictive third party how Chan earns the money, but he sticks with her until, crushed herself after a terrible performance off-off-Broadway, she decides to return to Grosse Pointe, Michigan. . . . Chan is a tawdry, one-dimensional character, but the novel is entertaining when it takes itself less seriously. Holmes [the manservant], with a smaller role, is a more effective type character; [and] Harvey's mother's preoccupation with the dogs makes for an amusing caricature. . . . [This] is the sort of glamour fantasy that makes for easy, undisturbing escape. (pp. 874-75)

> A review of "The Carnival in My Mind," in Kirkus Reviews, *Vol. L, No. 15, August 1, 1982, pp. 874-75.*

ALICE DIGILIO

Humor in the young adult novel is often overdone, applied in great dollops suited to the taste of 10-year-olds. Not so [in *The Carnival in My Mind*]. Barbara Wersba's new comic novel is the literary equivalent of a *New Yorker* cartoon. . . .

Wersba, also a playwright, has a knack for setting her scenes, and delivering the punch lines in a manner worthy of Woody Allen. . . .

Beneath the comedy—the antics of the setters, Harvey's efforts to stretch his tiny frame, the formality of Holmes the butler amidst the craziness and chaos of the Beaumont apartment— is a poignant strain. Harvey feels unloved. . . . Clearly, his attraction to Chandler grows out of this need for a bit of mothering (as well as the glamor attached to taking tall beauties to tea at the St. Regis at his tender age). And Chandler, on her part, is a frustrated mother. The illegitimate daughter she once bore has been taken from her and lives with her family in Michigan.

All the relationships in the novel, eccentric as they are, make sense. Something grows out of them, and most important, Harvey grows up—begins to understand his mother, his remote father, Chandler, and himself. All of which makes a very satisfying novel for the reader of any age.

> Alice Digilio, in a review of "The Carnival in My Mind," in Book World—The Washington Post, *August 8, 1982, p. 6.*

JACK FORMAN

Wersba realistically paints New York life and writes as usual with verve and skill [in *The Carnival in My Mind*] but it is difficult to believe in Harvey who is conversant with [George Bernard Shaw, composer Gustav Mahler, and Franz Kafka] and in the other exaggeratedly drawn characters in this message-laden story.

> Jack Forman, in a review of "The Carnival in My Mind," in School Library Journal, *Vol. 29, No. 1, September, 1982, p. 145.*

GEORGESS McHARGUE

I believe the butler, the dogs, the tragicomic trials of being young, male and short [in *The Carnival in My Mind*]. But can I believe a mother who literally doesn't notice when her kid moves out for a period of months? And can I believe a physically normal adolescent boy who daily shares a bed with a beautiful female without once having "anything happen"? Similarly skeptical readers will wish Harvey's carnival were one in which the games weren't rigged. (p. 63)

> Georgess McHargue, "Coming of Age," in The New York Times Book Review, *November 14, 1982, pp. 48, 63.*

PAUL HEINS

In a fluent, literate style with effectively economical dialogue and with a considerable amount of sympathetic humor, the author has created a gallery of unconventional characters [in *The Carnival in My Mind*]. At the same time, she has been unabashedly frank, avoiding the sordid and evoking the surprising emotional experiences which endowed a hitherto despondent adolescent with *joie de vivre*. (pp. 662-63)

> *Paul Heins, in a review of "The Carnival in My Mind," in* The Horn Book Magazine, *Vol. LVIII, No. 6, December, 1982, pp. 662-63.*

GERRY McBROOM

[*The Carnival in My Mind*] is a disappointment for this Wersba fan. Despite interesting characterization, it reads like a formula novel; teenage boy who has problems finds an older female friend who also has problems. They help each other overcome these and live happily ever after. I do not recommend this one.

> *Gerry McBroom, in a review of "The Carnival in My Mind," in* The ALAN Review, *Vol. 10, No. 3, Spring, 1983, p. 21.*

T(erence) H(anbury) White

1906-1964

(Also wrote under the pseudonym James Aston) Indian-born English novelist, short story writer, poet, and nonfiction writer.

White's fame rests on his tetralogy *The Once and Future King* (1958). In this series of novels, based on Sir Thomas Malory's *Le morte d'Arthur,* White reworked the legend of King Arthur by weaving modern issues into a medieval fantasy world. Despite the fantastic nature of much of the work, Arthur and his knights are developed as believable human beings. Critics agree that his Arthurian epic reveals White's finest literary qualities: the universality of the issues with which his characters deal, the extensive knowledge he conveys in such diverse areas as animal behavior, outdoor sports, and history, and his excellent prose style. The works are further enlivened by irreverent humor, for he hoped not only to inform but to entertain. *The Once and Future King* is appreciated by readers of all ages.

White's early novels, diaries, and volumes of poetry inspired little critical or popular interest. With *The Sword in the Stone* (1938), the first book of his tetralogy, White won much acclaim and a wide readership. This book, along with *The Witch in the Wood* (1939; retitled *The Queen of Air and Darkness*) and *The Ill-Made Knight* (1940), were later revised and combined with the previously unpublished *The Candle in the Wind* to form *The Once and Future King.* White's tetralogy is infused with what he considered the moral perspective of his own time. As an avowed pacifist, White challenged the concept that "might makes right." *The Sword in the Stone* portrays Arthur as a young boy who comes under the tutelage of the wizard Merlyn in order to learn the ways of the world. Critics particularly admire Merlyn's teaching methods: he transforms Arthur into a number of different animals so that his pupil might learn the sundry possibilities of life. Critics also praised White's blending of history and fantasy through a deliberately anachronistic time frame.

White also wrote other works appreciated by readers of all ages. *Mistress Masham's Repose* (1946), which delighted critics, focuses on a girl who chances upon a colony of Lilliputians—a race of little people originally conceived by Jonathan Swift in his book *Gulliver's Travels. The Goshawk* (1951) is a diary that recounts White's attempts to train a goshawk for the sport of falconry. White's relating of the rapport that he gradually developed with the bird is considered especially affecting. *The Master: An Adventure Story* (1957) centers on two youngsters who stumble upon the abode of an evil genius. This work has been favorably compared with the adventure stories of Robert Louis Stevenson. In all of these works, White was praised for his sensitive depiction of people who attempt to live in harmony with nature, beasts, and their fellow human beings.

In 1977, another volume of White's Arthurian epic was published as *The Book of Merlyn.* Continuing where *The Candle in the Wind* concluded, *The Book of Merlyn* is set on the eve of the battle in which King Arthur meets his death. Critics were generally disappointed in this book, finding excessively didactic the long passages in which White vented his anger at

the brutalities of twentieth-century war. However, White's epic is regarded by some critics as the finest reworking of the legends of Camelot to be published in the twentieth century. He is credited with making the legends more accessible and pertinent to modern readers. *The Sword in the Stone* was adapted into a popular animated film, and *The Once and Future King* was the basis for the successful theater production and film *Camelot.*

(See also *Contemporary Authors,* Vols. 73-76 and *Something about the Author,* Vol. 12.)

DAVID GARNETT

T. H. White has made . . . the same assumption which [Leo] Tolstoy made in writing *War and Peace*: that there are no essential differences between historical characters and people living to-day. For that reason *The Sword in the Stone* is not just a boy's book about monsters, or a funny book about knights in armour, nor a purely whimsical book like Kenneth Graeme's *Wind in the Willows.* It has something in common with all these, but has the life and solidity that they lack. The best bits of it indeed are the direct descriptions of nature, of country life, of the behaviour and appearance of bird, beast, and fish. Like Tolstoy, still more like Rostov [of *War and Peace*], or

Levin [of *Anna Karenina*], White has a passion for all country sports and crafts. He can describe haymaking because he has obviously worked in the hayfield, or an owl eating a mouse, because he has fed owls on mice. Thus he enters into the soul of a hawk, of a grass-snake, of a badger, of a fish, because he has kept them, tamed them, spent months of his life learning to know them. It is not idle whimsicality which leads him to translate their characters into terms which all his readers may understand, but poetic insight. He has thus without magic equipped himself to describe Arthur's training as though he himself had been Merlin's pupil. It will be remembered that Arthur was turned into a fish, a bird, etc. These chapters in *The Sword in the Stone* show, in my opinion, real poetic imagination which is all the more moving because they are broken up by passages of great comic buffoonery. . . .

Predictions are rash: but *The Sword in the Stone* should be enormously popular and become one of those curious classics of English literature which are as much part of the lives of grownup people as of their children. I do not wish to give the impression that I think it perfect. It is frequently commonplace and there are two quite bad chapters: the ruthless extermination of the anthropophagi by Robin Hood's men who cannot (even with the help of Lord Lilford) be got into the same continent as the poor Sciopods and pigmies. And there is a visit to the Fascist giant's castle who beats his prisoners with rubber truncheons—but yet fails to be a convincing giant. Perhaps the reason is that T. H. White has kept goshawks and merlins and badgers and grass snakes, and looked into their souls and loved them, but has never been in a concentration camp or known a torturer. On the other hand, his boar hunt is good and exactly corresponds to my memories of the hunts to which I was taken by a French postman—yet I strongly suspect that Mr. White hasn't hunted wild boars. In any case his description of tilting sounds as though he had spent years training for it and had given it up in disgust. . . .

The Sword in the Stone is, in short, the most delightful book for old and young.

> *David Garnett, in a review of "The Sword in the Stone," in* The New Statesman & Nation, *Vol. XVI, No. 393, September 3, 1938, p. 349.*

WILLIAM SOSKIN

Many of us who have found a lack of magic in our lives during the last few years will welcome T. H. White's phantasy, **"The Sword in the Stone."** . . .

Mr. White's book contains the very best brand of magic. He tells us of the childhood of Wart, the youngster who was to become King Arthur, mentor and patriarch of the Knights of the Round Table, and so depends on none other than Merlin for the wizardry and prestidigitation that hurl his little hero into many universes, seat him on the lap of Athene, project him forward in time and space to the shining vacuity of our own World Fair days, give him Robin Hood and the Maid Marian to play with, and turn him into all sorts of animals so that he may know many ways of thought and life. . . .

Ordinarily a phantasy that encompasses past, present and future and the supernatural as well as the component substances of the world—earth, water and fire—becomes rather a bore because of its tendency of swallowing universes without digesting them properly. In the case of **"The Sword in the Stone"** the method is diametrically opposed to such pretentiousness, for

Mr. White's leisurely and charming accounts of ordinary, normal life on the great medieval manor, of the hunt, of falconry, of the English countryside and the English weather in a day when weather behaved itself and snow lay evenly everywhere three feet deep, constitute the basic substance of his story. He has given it such excellent solidity that its excursions into the fantastic are made quite comfortably and with no violation of the modern reader's sense of reality.

What is more, not only the people but the birds and the beasts of his story have extraordinarily well developed characters, and we are never made to strain our imaginations to encompass their natures. The snake who teaches Wart, in his snake incarnation, the historical past that reaches back to primeval life, is an extraordinarily sensitive creature who merely desires to give Wart substance upon which to dream so that his long months of hibernation may not be bleak and thoughtless. . . .

[The] verse which Mr. White has included in his book, always for good jovial reasons, is one of the most entertaining of its features. Sometimes, as in the case of the anthem sung in the great hall on Christmas day, it is fine spoofing:

> God save King Pendragon,
> May his reign long drag on.
> God save the king.

Sometimes, when it is translated to a modern scene, such as the ice-cream, chocolate and pastry room of Queen Morgan's castle, with its chronium bar and streams of whipped cream and fruit juice, the verse becomes almost vaudeville:

> Way down inside the large intestine,
> Far, far away.
> That's where the ice cream cones are resting.
> That's where the éclairs stay.

The people of this medieval pageant are no less affecting than the birds and beasts. Merlin, with white moustaches and beard and a professorial, fussbudget manner, is directly and lovingly related to the philosophers of "The Crock of Gold." He is the symbol of true, humane wisdom, a fellow who lives by gentleness and who knows that learning and education are essentially an understanding of all levels and conditions of life. That is why he contrives to identify his charge, Wart, with Nature, to make him understand and feel the functioning of the fish, the badger and the bird. Writing of these animals, Mr. White negotiates a remarkable feat in that he can express the most gory or plundering instincts they have, the impulses and desires far removed from men's milky, nervous habits, and do it with natural relationship to a central flow of life—the life of men and trees and animals—with very little distortion.

We have come to know, to our grief these days, that medievalism is not so far removed from our collective lives as we thought. But in this book about medieval people Merlin expresses the most modern and most exalted of scientific creeds in his curriculum of education for Wart. The best thing for disturbances of the spirit, he says, "is to learn. That is the only thing that never fails. . . . Learn why the world wags, and what wags it. That is the only thing which the poor mind can never exhaust, never alienate, never be tortured by, never fear or distrust, and never dream of regretting."

Yes, Mr. White is related to James Stephens, of the "Crock of Gold." And many readers will roar at the antics of his knights and warriors clanking about dizzily under the burden of their armor, jousting and duelling like medieval Marx Brothers, and there will be critics who find resemblances to "Alice in Wonderland'' in the book. Mr. White is mercifully less droll than the author of ''Alice.'' The story also will recall Davy and the Goblin, and ''Back of the North Wind'' and ''The Wind in the Willows.'' It is blessed company, indeed, and ''**The Sword in the Stone**'' belongs there rightfully and proudly.

William Soskin, ''A Book That Is Kin to 'Alice in Wonderland','' in New York Herald Tribune Books, *January 1, 1939, p. 3.*

CLIFTON FADIMAN

[''**The Sword in the Stone**''] is] a crazy cross between, or among, ''Stalky & Co.,'' ''Alice in Wonderland,'' ''The Wind in the Willows,'' ''A Connecticut Yankee in King Arthur's Court,'' and the creations of Walt Disney. Hearing no voices to the contrary, I assume I make myself perfectly clear.

''**The Sword in the Stone**'' is about medieval England, a young boy called the Wart, his slightly older playmate Kay, his eccentric tutor Merlin; and an odd collection of other characters. . . . The Wart (really the boy Arthur, you know) goes through a variety of experiences, chivalric or magical, the result of which is to make him fit to assume the kingship. (You remember from your Malory the beautiful legend of the sword that only the innocent and unwitting young Arthur could dislodge.)

The best parts of the book deal with such matters as falconry— about which Mr. White knows everything—and jousting and how fish feel. When Mr. White is being, as he thinks, funny in the Mark Twain tradition, he is pretty dreadful, and you may as well hop over the designedly humorous parts. In general, this isn't everybody's cup of tea, and a lot of perfectly intelligent people will think it rather silly. It *is* silly if it's taken seriously as a tract on education or as a picture of medieval manners, but then Mr. White doesn't insist that you take it in any special way at all. I think he wrote the book just for a lark, and a very nice lark it turned out to be, too.

Clifton Fadiman, ''Three Novels to Open,'' in The New Yorker, *Vol. XIV, No. 47, January 7, 1939, pp. 45-6.**

VIDA D. SCUDDER

[*The Sword in the Stone*] is riotously funny. Breathlessly, joyously, not at all in the leisurely tempo of old romance, it proceeds with unwearied gusto and endless variety of invention. And we grow increasingly sure that [Sir Thomas] Malory would like it as well as we do. For here his robust English temper has full right of way. Never did the continuity of English life, unchanged down the centuries, shine out more clearly than in this absurd jumble of old and new. Confusions do not matter; do we not move in the Timeless, since Merlin is master of ceremonies—and to Merlin past and future are all a muddle. A magnificent Merlin!

What a tutor for Arthur! Merlin can initiate his pupil into all that modern science can offer, giving him the one capacity most needed by a king, or anybody else, to identify himself with alien forms of life. Becoming a fish, Arthur learns from the great pike, 'Mr. M.,' in a thrilling and quite awful scene the secret of Power—not to mention the relativity of our vision of things. As a bird, a Merlin, he meets superbly the challenge to courage. Science becomes the handmaid of romance as the tender-hearted snake instructs him on world history—inciden-

tally giving a startlingly fresh account of Saint George and the Dragon. The delightful owl Archimedes leads him into the presence of Athene, where he perceives this mysterious universe moving from chaos toward harmony, gaining what may be to the author the equivalent of the Vision of the Holy Grail. It is the Badger at the last, however, that tells him how Man is the only creature to have guessed the Divine Riddle, and to receive the full blessing of the multiple God.

So comes the end. Deep insights have flashed on us, absurd anticlimaxes have rejoiced us. As Arthur prepares to draw the sword from the stone, we revert almost to the very language of Malory; indeed, all along Kay and Ector come straight from him, even if the fourteenth-century Sir Ector would never have taken an interest in haying. Atmosphere grows mystical in that courtyard as the fate of England waits on the issue, while the unseen presences of all the forces in nature recall the boy's lessons and nerve his arm. The education is finished, the King can reign. It is a splendid scene. And we leave Merlin appropriately and completely mixed up.

If you are a boy, you can find here the best battles and enchantments going. If you are a serious-minded adult, you will savor the suggestions of advanced educational theory. If you are just an ordinary person, it would be a pity for you to miss King Pellinore, blood-brother to the White Knight, and his household pet, the Blatant Beast; or Friar Tuck, turned into a pink china Cupid on Morgan le Fay's mantelpiece; or the living room of Madame Mim, B.A. Whoever you may be, don't miss this book. (pp. 3, 5)

Vida D. Scudder, in a review of ''The Sword in the Stone,'' in The Atlantic Monthly, *Vol. 163, No. 2, February, 1939, pp. 3, 5.*

OTIS FERGUSON

[*The Sword in the Stone* is] a wise book and learned in many ways, and at times boldly absurd or disrespectful; but the best of it is that it creates enough illusion and makes its lore fascinating enough so that young people will actually learn more about medieval England from it than they will from twenty schoolbooks—and, incidentally, so will the rest of us, including the authors of the books, who never lived in the thirteenth century at all. For in matters of hunting, speech, fighting, castle economy, polite society and especially the care and use of animals, Mr. White is widely and accurately informed. Not only is he to be trusted, but his humorous liberties chase the dull solemnity of history out the window (Merlin, for example, can cast terrific spells but often crosses them up or gets tangled in his beard). And its deliberate anachronisms should not be so confusing as they are helpful in suggesting the link between past and present and in keeping the reader's wits sharp. . . . It is longish perhaps and gets weary through the middle, but it is fascinating for over a hundred pages, illuminating everywhere and quite fine at the end.

Otis Ferguson, ''Good Prince Arthur,'' in The New Republic, *Vol. LXXXXVIII, No. 1263, February 15, 1939, p. 55.*

CLIFTON FADIMAN

T.H. White, whose odd Arthurian grotesque, ''**The Sword in the Stone,**'' you may remember, has done himself a sequel, which he calls ''**The Witch in the Wood.**'' Sorry, but it isn't quite as good, the novelty of his special brand of humor, that of anachronism, being pretty well exhausted by the first book. There are some funny oddments in it—the paynim Palomides, who talks babu, and particularly our old friends Sir Grummore and King Pellinore. There are also some fine unicorn hunting and a good many comic medieval villagers. The story has to do with Queen Morgause (the Witch in the Wood), her four sons (who grew up to be Gawaine, Agravaine, Gaheris, and Gareth), and the manner in which she came to collaborate with her half-brother, King Arthur, in the production of Mordred. As I've suggested, there's nothing here as funny as the best things in **"The Sword in the Stone"** or as moving as the nocturnal description of the hawks, but those who savored the first book may want to try the sequel. It's not unamusing. (pp. 68-9)

Clifton Fadiman, "A Novel from Belgium," in The New Yorker, *Vol. XV, No. 38, November 4, 1939, pp. 68-9.**

IRIS BARRY

The moonstruck madness and learned gayety which so appealed to readers of Mr. White's **"The Sword in the Stone"** comes bubbling along just as merrily in [**"The Witch in the Wood"**]. What with the presence of old Merlyn, who remembers the future as well as the past, and the author's own habit of making time perfectly elastic, the adventures of Queen Morgause set down here assume a peculiarly sprightly air. Alone in her northern fortress, she takes a complicated beauty-bath and plans details of the role in which she will next dramatize herself. Shall it be the brave devoted little mother? Her ministrations to her children always confuse and sometimes terrify them. Or shall she decide to vamp a visiting knight? Whatever she elects, one may be sure that she alone will have a wonderful time, but hardly any one else will escape trouble. It is with considerable pleasure that we later see this feather-headed lady falling negligently through a hole in the ice or alarming her swains to the point of flight.

These are once more the days of King Arthur who is, however, only just beginning to see the reasons for having a Round Table. Lancelot is still a child. King Lot is about to do battle with Arthur, which is why he leaves Queen Morgause alone and so sets a lot of serious events in motion. Things generally are getting a little out of hand, there are too many stupid large knights careering round mischievously in armor, slashing at folks. The poorer people of England are in wretched plight. And yet, the author manages to convey fun and amusement are not lacking; human nature hasn't changed much. Obviously Mr. White knows a great deal about human nature and makes cunning use of his knowledge.

Mr. White writes particularly well, with a special lightness of touch, about children and animals and simple people—his picture of the children in bed with their dogs is brilliant. By far the best thing in the whole book, however, is the heart-breaking tale of the children and the unicorn which they catch. One really hates the Queen for neither knowing nor caring what has happened: the whole episode is uncannily horrible.

This author plays some curious if deliberate tricks. Even the title perplexes, for though one might properly call Morgause a witch she does not live in a wood. Then the whole action culminates in Morgause's meeting with King Arthur, but they have barely laid eyes on one another before the book closes abruptly. No doubt there is to be a sequel, but one cannot help wishing for more details. And there is little promise, even so,

that we shall meet King Pellinore again, which is a pity, for he is a most engaging fellow and his conversations with Grummore and with the tutor are truly funny. Last of all, it is easy to see why a defiant minority refuses to succumb to Mr. White's entertaining but often outrageous volumes. The mixture of seriousness and levity, the occasional archness and buffoonery that follow beautiful and grave passages, even the ease of the writing all combine into a highly individual dish. Its flavor cannot well be described but may be imagined roughly as an odd mixture of [William Branch] Cabell and William Morris with more than a dash of Tiffany Thayer.

Iris Barry, "More Moonstruck Madness," in New York Herald Tribune Books, *November 5, 1939, p. 6.*

BEATRICE SHERMAN

T.H. White has an outstanding capacity for writing about medieval times as merry and lively days, with their own share of the problems of living and loving, war and peace, but with more than their fair share of fun. His **"Sword in the Stone"** of last year will be remembered widely and happily for its enchantingly rowdy picture of the boyhood of King Arthur, known as the Wart. [**"The Witch in the Wood"**] is a sort of sequel in the same rambunctious vein, at once learned and lusty and comic. The story carries on with Arthur's battles against the kings who refused to recognize his right to the title of King of England even after he had drawn Excalibur from the stone. But the greater part of the book deals with the doings in the castle and village of Lothian when King Lot and all his knights and foot soldiers had gone off to bear their part in the battle against Arthur. . . .

In the course of his rambling story Mr. White has a fine time lampooning wars, chivalry, mother love, teachers, festivals, drinking bouts and what not. He gives the rich flavor of Arthurian times, based on much sound erudition, but does not scruple to introduce howling anachronisms such as quotations from [Rudyard] Kipling twisted to his purpose, odd bits of American slang, modern military terms, a ballad about Bonnie Prince Charlie. And some of his funning has hard common sense at the bottom of it.

Though **"The Witch in the Wood"** is not exactly an out-and-out sequel to **"The Sword in the Stone,"** it shares the disadvantages inherent in most sequels. It is a gay and buoyant book, but the author's gusty style doesn't hit the reader with the full force of the first volume's fresh impact. And one regrets that there isn't more about our old friend the Wart. The four Lothian lads are a good substitute for Arthur and his boyhood companions, but inevitably they seem like second-string players. The Pip-Pip and Ta-Ta style of British humor—flourishing on misunderstanding—which is indulged in continually by Pellinore, Grummore and Palomides, is worked pretty strenuously. But after all, this is quibbling. Why not go the whole hog: totus porcus, as King Lot's old tutor used to say, and call **"The Witch in the Wood"** a most enjoyable book, gay and giddy enough to make any reader long for the good old days in the land of Lothian and Orkney, or lacking that, for more of T.H. White's version of them.

Beatrice Sherman, "More Rowdy Doings at King Arthur's Court," in The New York Times Book Review, *November 5, 1939, p. 6.*

WILLIAM J. GRACE

If "**The Witch in the Wood**" is not a spurious book, I shall eat my hat or seek the Questing Beast therein mentioned. That thousands may read Mr. White's new book, as they did his previous "**The Sword in the Stone**" is possible. Many things are possible.

The book is definitely meant to be funny. It spares no efforts in that direction. It has a toodle-oo type of humor sometimes to be found in the Englishman who has been intellectually arrested on the threshold of the sixth form. Such a person is apt to be bashful in the presence of great literature and may think it best to treat such an uncomfortable matter lightly. So he cracks a tribal joke about the masterpiece, fingers his school-tie and fails completely to understand what is before him. Mr. White in revising the Arthurian material for popular consumption succeeds admirably in completely failing to understand either its spiritual significance or its aristocratic wit. He too-dles-oo through material that inspired Tennyson (remember him?) and reaches a very high degree of banality. (pp. 121-22)

The jacket of the book states quite frankly that "like its predecessor, it is really indescribable." I would not add to that comment. (p. 122)

> *William J. Grace, in a review of "The Witch in the Wood," in* Commonweal, *Vol. XXXI, No. 5, November 24, 1939, pp. 121-22.*

BEATRICE SHERMAN

That scholarly, witty and enthusiastic medievalist, Mr. T.H. White, has produced a third fine book devoted to the Arthurian legends. Sir Lancelot of the Lake, the "Chevalier Mal Fet," is the central figure; and the darkly mystic, thwarted character which Mr. White finds him to be dominates the book. Hence "**The Ill-Made Knight**" is a more thoughtful, adult and sub-dued piece of writing than "**The Sword in the Stone**" or "**The Witch in the Wood.**" It has its fits of farce and comedy—its irreverent poking of fun at some of the solemnities of the days of chivalry—but not the out-and-out joyful boisterousness of the earlier volumes. It does a fine inside job of its study of Lancelot and of the cycle of the Round Table's history, viewing them from the vantage of modern standards. "**The Ill-Made Knight**" is a better book than "**The Witch in the Wood.**" It ranks with "**The Sword in the Stone,**" but is a different sort of book, more mystical than magical, more a novel than a prime fairy story.

The tone here has something of the spirit of debunking. Mr. White (who has an intimate acquaintance with Malory) shows what he considers the true Lancelot, Arthur, Guenever and the others, without the romantic trappings of [Lord Tennyson's] heroes. . . .

Lancelot, Arthur and Guenever, who all loved one another, are pictured in an eternal triangle that would baffle the efforts of a 1940 psychoanalyst. But the author doesn't handle it so. He tells in simple language of the aspirations, loves and loyalties of fallible yet decent people. He makes these well-known figures seem real human beings facing stupendous problems.

They are not, however, stewing in their own juices all the time. Comic adventure raises its merry head frequently. Lancelot met the young Elaine when he rescued her, pink and naked, from a cruel and ridiculous enchantment which had held her

captive for years in a bath of boiling water. . . . And the blistering comments on the sanctified Galahad by his comrades in arms supply an ironic picture of how the completely holy must ever appear to the less saintly.

On the other hand, there is a good deal of random killing, with some uncomfortably realistic details of the bludgeoning and butchering that went on in tournaments. Lancelot himself was so frequently hacked up that this reader was surprised he survived the last page.

The most moving and beautifully told episode in the book is the account of how Lancelot achieved his heart's desire when he was prepared for the ultimate humiliation.

A great part of the story's charm, as in its predecessors, is the rich background of medieval lore—odd bits of information, long lists of heraldic terms, a lovely collection of items in one course of a meal—rhythmic and resounding words that impart their medieval color even though the reader doesn't know exactly what they all mean. Details of weight and construction of armor—or of Guenever's bathroom in the castle—are illuminating and interesting.

For one reason or another you are bound to find this new story of an old hero an absorbing and inspiriting tale. More power to the White Knight.

> *Beatrice Sherman, "T.H. White's New Spoof on the Arthurian Legend," in* The New York Times Book Review, *November 10, 1940, p. 6.*

FLORENCE HAXTON BULLOCK

"**The Ill-Made Knight**" (who is none other, of course, than Sir Lancelot, "best knight in all the world"—and how he worked to earn that title!) is drawn in chunks from Malory, from [John] Milton's "History of England," from one Thomas Bulfinch perhaps (though Mr. White who claims falconry as his favorite sport and medievalism as his specialty is obviously a student of sources) and, whether he likes it or not, from [Lord Tennyson's "Idylls of the King"]. Mr. White most shows his awareness of the inextricability of the sentimental Victorian from the Arthurian cycle when he scoffs at this or that poetic legend and re-creates it in a broader tone.

"**The Ill-Made Knight**" (which was preceded by two other novels of medieval England, "**The Sword in the Stone**" and "**The Witch in the Wood**") is devoted to the prolonged chivalric love affair of Guinever, herein called Jenny and sometimes Gwen, with the scrupulous but gettable young French Knight of the Round Table, Sir Lancelot, he of the ugly face and the noble nature. King Arthur is here, of course—a pleasant, Babbitt-like fellow, who had the quite original idea of gathering all the likely young men of the kingdom at his Round Table and diverting their cock-fighting instincts to the rescuing of damsels in distress, the quest of the Holy Grail, et cetera. . . .

The focus of Mr. White's story is on Lancelot, whom we follow onward from the picture of him as a small boy looking at his ugly face in the polished surface of a kettle-hat, through his unwitting and decidedly unwilling amour with Elaine (young Lance was convinced that his strength as a fighter was closely bound up with his virginity). But he did at last succumb to Guinever. . . .

The narrative, slow-moving and, of course, without great novelty save in the approach, abounds with the amusing paraphernalia of chivalry: "slightly magic" apple trees, ladies upon white palfreys, mysterious and beautiful, the elaborate gear of the knights, the palace cuisine, all handled extravagently and humorously. . . . And so it goes—a tale whose telling is enhanced by a liberal use of the broadest satire and absurd anachronisms, but which serves in toto both to debunk and to build up again on a more likely, human basis, the life of a period which has been fairly glamorized out of existence. **"The Ill-Made Knight"** is an excellent fellow worker in the field which Mr. Ford Madox Ford's "Ladies Whose Bright Eyes" tackled so brilliantly and in which our own John Erskine has done his creditable bit.

> Florence Haxton Bullock, "Meet Lancelot and His Lady," in New York Herald Tribune Books, November 17, 1940, p. 6.

OLIVE B. WHITE

When a novelist enchanted by one of the world's great matters reaches his third volume, as Mr. White does in his successor to **"The Sword in the Stone"** and **"The Witch in the Wood,"** he has committed himself to a quest that will not let him go. [**"The Ill-Made Knight"**] matches the others in virtuosity and wit, and it outdoes them in wisdom, swift, scalpel-sharp, of a kind infrequently consorting with cleverness. . . .

As he should be in any treatment of the Round Table, Lancelot is the hero. Straightway the reader needs one warning: here is no nineteenth-century sentimentalizing, no languishing, soft condonement of sin in the guise of "fated passion" and "great love." The men and the morals follow more ancient models. Even as a boy, Lancelot is ugly, soul-tormented, ferocious with himself, powerful, and pitiable, self-named "the Chevalier Mal-Fet—the Ill-Made Knight." Beyond his beloved Malory, Mr. White knows surely the poets of the deep Middle Ages, Chrétien de Troyes and others who judged their material in the light of a critical moral realism. . . . His Lancelot dreams and prays, struggles toward God, falls, strives to live in and by his conscience, goes mad in his own decision that he is but a swindle, and, in the end, is "forced to have it out with his spiritual doom." His is the human dignity and agony of self-knowledge. The violence of our day is recapturing one honesty at least for literature: as in Homer and Virgil, Dante and Shakespeare, a strong man may weep and be the more honorable and manly for his tears.

> Olive B. White, in a review of "The Ill-Made Knight," in Commonweal, Vol. XXXIII, No. 9, December 20, 1940, p. 235.

TIME

The men & women of Lilliput stood a good six inches in their stocking feet. Mounted on speedy rats and armored in the wing cases of beetles, they hunted mice and moles, and caught fish with horsehair. . . . They spoke English fluently, but after the manner (somewhat corrupted) of their 18th Century creator, Jonathan Swift. They would say: "He fell Victim to intoxication, and dismounted from his Nag to seek the Safety of the *Terra Firma*."

These descendants of the original (*Gulliver's Travels*) Lilliputians are the discovery of British Author T.H. White. . . . He has put them to good use in a book that is freakish fantasy from start to finish. Supposedly a children's book, [*Mistress Masham's Repose*] will entertain most adults. . . .

Author White's colony of Lilliputians is located on a tiny lake-island in a vast English estate. . . . The present-day heiress to the tumbledown estate is ten-year-old Maria, "one of those tough and friendly people who do things first and think about them afterward." The plot of *Mistress Masham's Repose* revolves around the efforts of Maria's fiendish guardians to abduct the Lilliputians and sell them to Hollywood.

The book's charm lies in Author White's nostalgic evocation of 18th Century life, his knowledge of animal and country lore (in private life he is an ardent naturalist), and his ability to make genuinely dramatic such absurdities as the thrilling rescue of Maria by the Lilliputian rat-cavalry. The best things in *Mistress Masham's Repose* are the mischievous parodies of human clichés-of-thought. . . . (p. 108)

> "In Lilliput Land," in Time, Vol. XLVIII, No. 16, October 14, 1946, pp. 108-09.

WILLIAM J. GRACE

If **"The Witch in the Wood'** is not a spurious book, I shall eat my hat or seek the Questing Beast therein mentioned. That thousands may read Mr. White's new book, as they did his previous **"The Sword in the Stone"** is possible. Many things are possible.

The book is definitely meant to be funny. It spares no efforts in that direction. it has a toodle-oo type of humor sometimes to be found in the Englishman who has been intellectually arrested on the threshold of the sixth form. Such a person is apt to be bashful in the presence of great literature and may think it best to treat such an uncomfortable matter lightly. so he cracks a tribal joke about the masterpiece, fingers his school-tie and fails completely to understand what is before him. Mr. White in revising the Arthurian material for popular consumption succeeds admirably in completely failing to understand either its spiritual significance or its aristocratic wit. He toodles-oo through material that inspired Tennyson (remember him?) and reaches a very high degree of banality. (pp. 121-22)

The jacket of the book states quite frankly that "like its predecessor, it is really indescribable." I would not add to that comment. (p. 122)

> William J. Grace, in a review of "The Witch in the Wood," in Commonweal, Vol. XXXI, No. 5, November 24, 1939, pp. 121-22.

FRANCIS X. CONNOLLY

It is difficult not to do this extraordinary book a disservice by praising it with extravagant enthusiasm. In a world which is overgenerous with its superlatives, the use of such terms as great and good may well be questioned. They should not be questioned in this case. **"Mistress Masham's Repose"** is a masterpiece of narration, literary ingenuity, humor and satire and Mr. White, on the basis of this book, deserves to be mentioned in the company of Evelyn Waugh, C. S. Lewis and George Orwell as one of the few fortunate possessors of a splendid prose style.

The story itself concerns Maria, a ten-year-old orphan who lives at Malplaquet, an enormous ruin four times as large as Buckingham Palace, attended only by a fierce Governess, Miss Brown ("She was cruel in a complicated way"), a repulsive guardian, the Rev. Mr. Hater, and a kind old cook, Mrs.

Noakes. . . . Exploring an islet in one of the lakes of Malpla-quet, Maria stumbles on a colony of five hundred Lilliputians, descendants of Captain John Biddel's captives mentioned in "Gulliver's Travels." The book is charged with its own creative power of the imagination, but once it associates its private magic with the powerful illusion of Dean Swift, it moves with an additional energy. The world of Lilliput is alive again.

Maria's delight in her miniscule friends is shortlived. Miss Brown and Mr. Hater discover the secret, and plot to seize and sell the little people to Hollywood. Maria is imprisoned in the dungeon and threatened with death. How she escapes their clutches with the aid of the Lilliputian Army and the old professor, how the estate is restored and the two villains punished, and how it all ends in a most satisfactory Christmas celebration, is the substance of the narrative. It is enough to say here that there are few more exciting tales than this account of the battle between the creatures of wonder and wisdom and the twin giants of avarice and pride.

Mr. White's fantasy differs from the usual fairy story in several important respects. Without spoiling the illusion of the novel, he has succeeded in realizing universal types in his characterizations. The old professor is a priceless portrait of the antiquarian, the Lord Lieutenant a vivid caricature of the eccentric fox-hunting country aristocrat, and the Lilliputian schoolmaster the epitome of rugged honesty, respectability and discretion. The book abounds in humor both of situation and language. Much of its charm for the sophisticated reader consists in a rich and scholarly knowledge, artfully concealed, of eighteenth-century literature, history and architecture. The lovely mustiness of old books and marvelously useless learning lends fragrance and charm to a plot lively enough to make your pulses jump. There are no sermons in the book, but one must be an irretrievable adult not to pick up some wisdom from this delightful story. . . .

Perhaps Mr. White is saying, in a very oblique way, that the world always needs a reminder that innocence, honesty and trust—and impractical learning—will win their way to a happy ending. If he doesn't say it in so many words, he is showing how it can be done for the duration of his novel and for as long after as the memory of it persists. May it be read for the century to come.

> *Francis X. Connolly, in a review of "Mistress Masham's Repose," in* Commonweal, *Vol. XLV, No. 5, November 15, 1946, p. 125.*

CHARLES LEE

["**The Elephant and the Kangaroo**"] is a satirical fantasy set in Ireland. . . .

The apparatus required for this latest demonstration of White magic includes one "practical" Englishman, who looks like the author and bears his name, thinks like an encyclopedia, does oil paintings adorned with glass eyes stuck to the canvas with putty, and lives on an Irish farm; his landlord, Mikey O'Callaghan, an Irish Jeeter Lester; his landlord's wife, whose resistance to reason is a shield on which whole legions of logic are daily shattered; his dog Brownie, who feeds on glue and enjoys a game in which his master plays the role of flea. Then there are neighborhood associates, made up of a varied assortment of leftover Neanderthals—plus the Archangel Michael, who drops in one day via the chimney to advise the building of an ark against the coming of a second flood; a

Dutch barn which can be converted into said ark. Finally there is a flood. . . .

[It] is not entirely clear what "**The Elephant and the Kangaroo**" is all about. If the story is simply whimsey, it is a failure. If it is more, what is it? A satire on the "practical" Englishman, a savage assault on the Irish or on the human race in general, a kind of dully droll poem on "the cruelty of Time and Life," a comment of some sort or another on religion and reason?

Whatever it is, it does not come off.

> *Charles Lee, "Ould Sod, Trampled," in* The New York Times Book Review, *April 13, 1947, p. 18.*

THOMAS SUGRUE

Were there a group libel law in force, it could be invoked by the Irish to put Mr. T. H. White in jail for several thousand years. In "**The Elephant and the Kangaroo**," Mr. White's new novel, there is enough fun poked at Eire and her inhabitants to fill an indictment longer than the St. Patrick's day parade on a mild March 17. Nothing is spared, not even Irish whiskey, not even Irish piety. Coming from an Englishman it is the sign and seal of social success. . . .

[This is] a story which, for all the author's usual wit and skill at narrative, is pointless and rather dull. A dreamy second-rate English writer floating out of Ireland on a Dutch barn is perhaps a symbol of England herself, forced from the island after 400 years by a flood of history. The aroused Irish, hurling anathema and artillery at him, are no doubt those rebels who tried so futilely to accomplish the expulsion in generation after generation. The long, pseudo-Rabelaisian catalogues of Irish foolishness and stupidity probably represent the final benediction of a retiring conqueror. They speak well for the trouble the Irish have given their landlords.

It is natural to wonder why Mr. White felt impelled to indulge in his aimless, broad burlesque. It lacks his fine touch of fancy and his hitherto faultless taste. Its humor is slapstick, farcical, at times unkind and often without focus. His "aborigines" of Kildare are neither amusing nor purposeful. For such a fine and facile talent as Mr. White possesses there are surely more efficacious themes; even Mikey O'Callaghan could do no worse than the plot of "**The Elephant and the Kangaroo**." Mr. White lost this one in the first inning.

> *Thomas Sugrue, "A Second Noah's Ark," in* New York Herald Tribune Weekly Book Review, *April 20, 1947, p. 23.*

THE TIMES LITERARY SUPPLEMENT

Mr. White's theme [in *The Goshawk*] is as old as Babylon but his allusiveness is of the twentieth century. He has the gift of words, which calls for as much effort to control as he who has it not expends in striving after expression. The book is about the training of a hawk, a very ancient art: there is still a freemasonry of falconers—austringers—scattered about the world. Yet, on putting the book down one feels that the goshawk, though central to it, has been secondary to one's enjoyment—that the tension that has held throughout the 200 pages is, one may almost say, the moral aura of this difficultly achieved *rapport* between civilized man and slaying bird. That Mr. White should devote himself completely to a hawk, going sleepless, losing count of time, exacting his ultimate of patience, would seem freakish in a world of other tensions were he not able to hold the reader to a belief that this is something nearer to the heart of reality. One rubs one's eyes at last and says, "All this for a bird," and tries to shake things back into their proper proportions; but they refuse to be shaken back; things are not quite as they were: somewhere beyond the welfare state a hawk stoops to his kill, and a man has by infinite pains entered the realm of the bird and shared the vision of that blazing eye. Here, perhaps, in a world of tourism, is the one realm that is left for adventure.

Mr. White can turn on himself suddenly, waiting on the bird, and reflect on an education costing up to £3,000 leading to a gamekeeper's cottage and a hawk. The clue is his love of learning: "I had learned always, insatiably, looking for something which I wanted to know." A love of creation and mastery has kept his personal life stripped to essentials. "To divest oneself of unnecessary possessions: that was the business of life." At moments he seems a sort of western Omar, with a handful of philosophy and a headful of words. . . .

He recited Shakespeare through the night watches. Certainly to understand falconry enriches the text of the plays. A people who had flown the hawk must have felt the force of the metaphors in their marrow which we feel only in our heads. Mr. White could recapture something physical thus through his £3,000 education and the hawk. The means to it were a monastic seclusion and self-government, its attendant virtue was a purgation of civilized sentiment: maggots at their work on a dead sheep are seen as "clean, vital, symbolical of an essential life-force perfectly persisting." And "Gos" the hawk, whose heart and breathing are faster than the human, is the heightened vibration at the centre. Mr. White communicates this also to the countryside of the bird's range, meadows at dawn or under the moon. The sun, the rain, the harvest faces, all seem to share the quickened heartbeat of the hawk. Actually Mr. White is pitting "the hurly-burly of present-day lunacy" against "the savage decency of ages long overpowered." That is why *The Goshawk* is a Morality.

"A Modern Morality," in The Times Literary Supplement, *No. 2581, July 20, 1951, p. 455.*

JOSEPH WOOD KRUTCH

["**The Goshawk**"], widely hailed in England with such phrases as "a masterpiece," "unforgettably interesting," and "an ornithological 'Moby Dick,'" is certainly nature writing with a difference. Ostensibly it describes how the author undertook to train a hawk for the intricate sport of falconry. Actually it is the story of a sick soul which took this unusual method of relieving its frustrations.

Mr. White never tells us what reasons other than the prevalent ones he may have had for hating the modern world, but he is almost hysterically angry from almost the first sentence and he was obviously far beyond the point where the healing presences of any Wordsworthian primroses could do him any good.

Beginning as he does in medias res, Mr. White never tells us even what first suggested falconry as an occupation but it is soon evident that falconry became for him an escape, a ritual and a vicarious participation in the cruelty of the universe. Because it has been practiced by aristocrats since before the dawn of history it represents the antithesis of the modern and the democratic. Because the hawk is fierce and bloody he represents a protest against everything which is sentimental and namby-pamby. Finally, because to train a hawk by the

old-fashioned methods Mr. White used requires from the trainer sleepless nights and all sorts of exasperating hardships the trainer punishes himself at the same time that he is punishing others.

Whether or not either the experiences themselves or the writing of a book about them purged the author's soul is not clear, but at least the account is characterized everywhere by a sort of D. H. Lawrence fury in the writing and a tendency to turn aside frequently from the many technical details of falconry in order to work in obiter dicta about the loathsome depravity of our times and bloody vignettes of a rabbit's split skull or a badger torn to pieces by dogs. . . .

That this book is written with sincerity and force nearly everyone will admit. Not everybody, on the other hand, is going to find it pleasant reading and there is bound to be considerable difference of opinion concerning its mood and intention. By its admirers it will be called strong, manly, unsentimental. Here is the story of a man who rejects modern civilization and who returns to the ancient, the primitive, and the violent, thus seeking health by contact with the ruthlessness of nature. Others will object that the cult of violence is, in its own way just as sentimental as its opposite and will suspect in Mr. White's glorification of violence something uncomfortably close to the kind of romanticism which inspired recent unsuccessful political experiments in certain parts of Europe.

Joseph Wood Krutch, "The Violent Taming of a Violent Hawk," in New York Herald Tribune Book Review, *March 23, 1952, p. 4.*

HENRY MORTON ROBINSON

At first glance "**The Goshawk**" . . . appears to be a day-to-day account of a curiously personal conflict between a full-grown man and a fledgling hawk. It should be stated at once, however, that this is no mere handbook; although we are introduced to the terminology and furniture of falconry, the information is rather sketchy and incidental. Nor, according to my poor lights, is T. H. White the ideal hawk-master. He quivers excessively; try though he may, he is unable to conceal an inner tumult that must have been disturbingly apparent to so sensitive a creature as "Gos."

At times we wonder why Mr. White went through the physical and emotional ordeal of training his bird. Is he courageously attempting to revive popular enthusiasm in a medieval sport closely allied to his known Arthurian interests? Or is "**The Goshawk**" merely a pretext for some excellent, if rather broody, writing about the English countryside? Either motive is legitimate; one suspects, however, that the really important action of the book takes place on a deeper level.

Perceptive readers may feel that basic loves and antagonisms were loosed—and at least partly resolved—during Mr. White's struggle to dominate his hawk. It is this unstated, yet always-hovering motivation that gives the book its peculiar charm. Lacking such motivation, "**The Goshawk**" might justly be indicted on charges of preciousness and affectation. . . .

As the struggle unfolds, Mr. White makes us increasingly aware that in matching himself with Gos—overmatching himself, as the tragic event shows—he is grappling with a mysterious, ruthless power, embodied in a bird that never voluntarily stoops (unless killing be its mood) to the level of earth-treading man.

Henry Morton Robinson, "Dominating the Hawk," in The New York Times, *March 23, 1952, p. 6.*

JOHN BAYLEY

What goes on inside Rockall? A fascinating hypothesis is supplied this week by T. H. White, in [*The Master*], which he himself describes as 'a simple adventure story with a suppressed moral.' I don't think most readers will want to bother very much about the moral, which is supposedly the fashionable modern one of megalomania, brainwashing and the thirst for absolute power, etc. Nor, oddly enough, does one take the adventure part of the book very breathlessly either. . . . The real gratification, as in T. H. White's former novels, comes from the author's personality and his mode of conveying it, a mode that seems particularly English in its assumption and corresponding avoidance of certain things—bravery, loyalty, sex and so forth—and its appearance—despite these limitations—of absolute intellectual freedom, which comes from its unself-conscious abruptness and its inconsequential poetic drift around arresting topics, like the expression of a puffin's eye or the fact that one shouts a warning to *oneself* if one is pushed over a cliff. As also in the writing of Richard Hughes and Arthur Ransome there is an added twist of pleasurable fraudulence in the spectacle of someone so obviously intelligent keeping up so determinedly English a *persona*! I recommend *The Master* wholeheartedly, not least because Mr. White and his two brisk and practical child heroes maintain this brave and refreshing pretence of not knowing why hollowed-out islands and caverns under-sea have such fascination for us. There are many critics today to tell them, but fortunately they are still too busy on *The Tempest* and *Kubla Khan* to get around to the adventure story. (p. 290)

> *John Bayley, in a review of "The Master," in* The Spectator, *No. 6714, March 1, 1957, pp. 290-91.*

MAURICE RICHARDSON

The Master is an ingenious extravaganza on the borders of science fiction, satire and straight adventure. It has affinities with the *Hibbert Journal* and the *Boy's Own Paper*. It reminds me of *The Tempest*, *20,000 Leagues Under The Sea*, and *Lost Horizon* with perhaps a breadth of *High Wind in Jamaica*. Nicky and Judy, children of a duke, land from a yacht on the island of Rockall with their dog and are first pushed into the sea, then shot at, then rescued by the Master's agents. The Master is a physicist of genius aged 157 with singular telepathic powers, and a brain so extraordinary that he has to paralyse his higher critical centres with whisky before he can get down to mundane matters as opposed to the global and cosmic problems which are his preoccupation. His agents include a stock philosophical Chinaman, a Welsh doctor, an ex-R.A.F. pilot, and a Negro whose tongue has been cut out. His grand design is the compulsory reform of the human race by means of rays.

It sounds, put baldly like that, too pubescent a fantasy altogether. But though I do not myself think that Mr. White has quite brought it off—it remains too much of a mish-mash of ideas and wheezes—it is remarkable how readable he has made it. The children are alive and distinct. Their reactions, varying from the emotional to the matter of fact, are just right. The descriptions of their physical experiences of the island, the sea and the sun are very nicely done. Some of the agents, the latter-day Calibans, have character and the Master himself smacks far more of Prospero than of that insipid old thing, the Lama of Shangri La. His downfall incidentally is neatly brought about, after all human attempts have failed, by the dog. You can take him or leave him, but he is less of a bore than you expect.

> *Maurice Richardson, in a review of "The Master," in* The New Statesman & Nation, *Vol. LIII, No. 1356, March 9, 1957, p. 316.*

DONALD BARR

"The Master," subtitled "An Adventure Story," concerns two well-born English children held captive in a hollow rock in mid-Atlantic, where amid the sough of water and air and the whir of a helicopter a murderous antique of a scientist and his grotesque staff have devised a means to rule the world. It is one of the most beguiling and yet one of the most straightforward of Mr. White's tales; and while in some respects it is a new departure for him, it resumes firmly a career that had seemed to sink into confused dabbling.

Mr. White was born in 1906 in India of English parents, was at Cheltenham and Cambridge, was a schoolmaster at Stowe; then threw over teaching and the more solidly worked novels of his teaching years, rewrote the Arthurian legends in a new style—fashioned of conscious anachronisms, faint twitches of bawdry and gusts of lyricism—and made his fame. Then growing malice, and some delicately tendentious fantasy; then a series of books, satires and works on falconry and eighteenth-century gossip, each more dismally received than the last. Then "The Master." Never has Mr. White's taste been surer, or his style more easily directed to all ages and sorts of readers at once, than in this. (p. 4)

"The Master" is a splendid adventure. Like most adventures that obliterate the reader's age, it recalls Robert Louis Stevenson. That magical sense that the real and palpable world is infested with waifs and strays from eternity is Stevenson's. The secret war that rattles through the unconscious city and is fought out in gentlemen's clubs and seedy *pensions* is one myth: it comes to [Joseph] Conrad and [John] Buchan and the early Graham Greene from Stevenson's "New Arabian Nights." And the other myth, the myth of "The Master," of the cave or isle or enchanted castle which is like a solid model of Man's peril and destiny—though its scenario is as old as [Shakespeare's] "The Tempest," as old as [Homer's] "The Odyssey," as old as childhood itself—comes to us through [Stevenson's] "Treasure Island." For it was surely Stevenson who taught Mr. White the sinister effect of charming eccentricities—the sinister Chinese gentleman named Mr. Blenkinsop, the huge tongueless Negro called Pinkie who is a professed follower of Gandhi, the ex-doctor Totty McTurk who has a different dialect every day.

Where once Mr. White based his fantasy on anachronisms, which are the comic way of suggesting eternal things, now he makes clever use of this myth wherein the familiar gesture and the homely phrase suddenly take on a mad ceremoniousness, like rituals through which philosophy is speaking; and this is the beautiful melodramatic way of hinting at eternal things. (pp. 4, 24)

> *Donald Barr, "In the Real World of Fantasy," in* The New York Times Book Review, *March 24, 1957, pp. 4, 24.*

THE TIMES LITERARY SUPPLEMENT

Mr. White has now brought to a conclusion the great work which began in 1938 with the publication of *The Sword in the Stone*. In 1940 *The Witch in the Wood* and in 1941 *The Ill-Made Knight*, carried on the tangled story; at last *The Candle in the Wind* completes a crowded architectural design. *The Candle in the Wind* is published as the fourth book in an omnibus volume, *The Once and Future King,* which contains revised versions of the three previous works. The whole 300,000 words make a unity, whose tone appears now as something much deeper and more serious than a casual reading of the earlier volumes would lead the reader to suppose.

The subject of the long book is the complete Matter of Britain, the cycle of King Arthur from his mysterious birth to the mystery surrounding the close of his reign. As the author points out in a note on the jacket (which should surely be printed more permanently within the text) the Matter of Britain is a solemn theme. Malory, weaving together many strands of legend, fills his pages with exciting tales of adventure, awful tales of enchantment, and heartrending tales of forbidden love. . . .

Malory called his work *The Morte d'Arthur.* Arthur's death is what matters; for it teaches the lesson that God is not mocked, and that retribution will overtake the sinner even in this world.

The sin Arthur had committed was, of course, incest. Of course, because incest is the natural foundation of tragedy. It is a sin, or at any rate an occurence, which stirs feelings of revulsion in even the most free-thinking pagan; it can be committed by inadvertence, and once committed cannot be undone. The story may be unfamiliar, since it is unsuitable for treatment in the books for boys from which most of us derive our knowledge of the Round Table. But it is the essential skeleton of the full legend.

Arthur was the only son of King Uther Pendragon, and illegitimate. He was brought up in secret, far from the court, so that only Merlin knew the identity of his mother. Presently Arthur himself committed adultery, and the fruit of that illicit intercourse was Mordred. Arthur did not know, could not know (because Merlin had forgotten to inform him) that Queen Morgause was his half-sister. But he knew that adultery is mortal sin; from that sin came the ruin of the Round Table and the downfall of the rule of righteousness on earth.

The tragedy is implicit in the very beginning of the Matter of Britain; in the words of Mr. White ''it is the tragedy, the Aristotelian and comprehensive tragedy, of sin coming home to roost.'' Yet, although Arthur failed in the end, he enjoyed a happy and glorious youth; his happiness and glory make up the atmosphere of the first book in the tetralogy. That opening book has been largely rewritten, for in 1938 the world was a pleasanter and more innocent place than it is to-day. As originally published *The Sword in the Stone* had two themes, the wonder and beauty of the world of nature, and the slightly comic conventions of the chivalrous life. . . .

All this is reproduced in the revised version; but reproduced in a grimmer form, suitable to our Age of Iron. . . .

In general, the new version of *The Sword in the Stone* has lost the flippancy of the original. At the close, when young Arthur has drawn the magic sword and unexpectedly finds himself rightful King of Britain, chivalry intrudes, and duty, and a reminder that the task of ruling is a heavy burden. As a whole, the tale has been refashioned by a writer who remembers the gas-chambers of Belsen; we cannot recapture nowadays the innocent optimism of the League of Nations.

The second book, *The Witch in the Wood,* was as originally written the weakest part of the composite structure. . . . This section, now named *The Queen of Air and Darkness,* has been wholly rewritten and greatly improved. There is deeper horror at the wicked magic of Queen Morgause, and less tittering at her promiscuity. It is a loss that we see so little of Sir Palomides, the heathen knight who talks Babu English; but he still appears, as do King Pellinore and his quarry, the Blatant Beast. The book ends with a description of the wedding of King Pellinore and his Flemish princess, a description which epitomizes, in its mingled love and mockery, Mr. White's attitude to the Middle Ages. . . .

In this second book Mr. White introduces his sole personal contribution to the legendary Matter of Britain; though, as he points out, he has added nothing that cannot be deduced from Malory. He suggests that King Arthur stands for the centralizing power of the Anglo-Norman monarchs, and that his enemies represent Gaelic hostility to the Saxon. Perhaps it is a mistake thus to rationalize the feuds of a fairy story; but the Matter of Britain, as handled by Mr. White, is strong enough to carry this additional superstructure. The third book, *The Ill-Made Knight,* is little altered. This is the core of Arthurian romance as most of us remember it: the Round Table, the Grail, and the love of Lancelot for Guinevere. Mr. White expounds the complicated subject of courteous love very fairly. At a time when most marriages were arranged, and bride and bridegroom might meet as strangers on their wedding day, nobody expected a passionate devotion between husband and wife. It may very well happen that a man falls in love with the wife of his friend, and he cannot be blamed for such a happening. But he must not allow his love to issue in physical adultery; partly because that is sinful, still more because it is dishonourable.

Arthur, of course, knew that Lancelot was in love with his Queen, and that she returned his love. But he took it for granted that two people of such scrupulous honour would never cuckold him. That is why on a careless reading of the story he appears as a complaisant husband. Lancelot himself truly loved and admired King Arthur, which made his remorse all the stronger when he knew himself to be false to the ideal of courtly chivalry.

The Grail, on the other hand, which some see as the mainspring of the Matter of Britain, is here deliberately played down. In Mr. White's version the quest for it came about more or less by accident. . . . To some readers this may seem a fault of emphasis, for the Grail is a subject far above the matter of most romances; yet, considered in cold blood, the Grail has very little to do with King Arthur. The disadvantage of this quest, as an element in any story, is that its achievement is the crown and end of life. Those who attain it have nothing left to accomplish on earth, and can only go on to their eternal reward in Heaven.

So we come to the new book, the end of this great work. *The Candle in the Wind* deals with the plotting of Mordred and his kinsmen of the house of Orkney, and with their undying enmity to King Arthur. We have now reached the autumnal decay of the Middle Ages, and Mordred in his person and in his dress deliberately foreshadows Shakespeare's King Richard III. He foreshadows also a greater villain of a more recent epoch; Sir Agravaine, his half-brother, suggests casually that he can stir up discontent by playing on the racial enmity between Saxon and Gael, and their common enmity to the Jews; the Eylfot, the cross with crooked limbs, might make a handy badge for the new movement. This is surely a mistake of tact. Such a neat double meaning will tempt any author, but any author ought to resist it; the thoroughgoing parable sends the reader searching for more parables on every page, and when he cannot discover them he grows restless. . . .

The story is familiar. The characters are not, for all that Mr. White claims to have taken them directly from Malory. Moralists have noted with regret that wickedness is in general more interesting than virtue. It is the author's achievement to have drawn good men, Lancelot, Arthur, and the misguided Gawaine, and to have made their goodness as exciting as any evil. They are brave, they keep their promises, they accept with their eyes open the consequences of their actions: compared to the characters in contemporary popular fiction they are strangely adult. Even Guinevere is a good woman, though not quite good enough. As a study of intelligent people, living in the light of a code which they cannot always obey, this is a tale for grown-up readers.

But Mr. White is much more than a spinner of good plots; his prose gives as much pleasure as his matter. There are witty and learned asides on every subject under the sun, from the correct method of bending the long bow to the misadventures of medieval flying machines. Perhaps it is a mistake to mingle genuine history with myth; occasionally the author gets himself into a tangle when he seeks to reinforce some detail of his background with an example from recorded history. The world of Malory is a universe complete in itself; we do not need to be reminded that the "legendary" King William Rufus swore by the Holy Face of Lucca, or that the Holy Shroud lurked unrecognized until the late fourteenth century. When we are told, as an example of the medieval career open to talent, that the father of Pope Adrian IV was a serf, we cannot help recalling that the serfs of the Abbey of St. Alban never owed obedience to the dynasty of Pendragon. But that is the only false note in the book which lives continuously in the same atmosphere, an atmosphere devised by its author. To sustain one ambience through such a long work is evidence of astonishing technical skill.

In three fields particularly the author excels. He can draw living people; he can describe a landscape; and he can enter into the inmost minds of birds and beasts. Whether it is a hedgehog disputing with a badger, or a white-fronted goose flying across the North Sea, we see with their eyes and feel with their limbs. This ambitious work, so long in the building, now stands complete. It will long remain a memorial to an author who is at once civilized, learned, witty and humane.

"Arthurian Achievement," in The Times Literary Supplement, *No. 2930, April 25, 1958, p. 224.*

RICHARD WINSTON

In a sense Time is the hero and chief victim of T. H. White's version of the Arthurian legends—Time with his scythe bent out of shape, his beard knotted and his hoary locks adorned by a dunce-cap. If in this guise he resembles old Merlin spinning round as he disappears, or scratching his head while trying to discover whether something has already happened or is about to happen—why, that is precisely how Mr. White means it to be. . . .

In twisting the forelock of Time T. H. White is only following in the footsteps of Sir Thomas Malory, who clothed Arthur's sixth-century Welshmen in Norman armor. Taking the same liberties consciously, Mr. White introduces with malice afterthought the contemporary problems of communism, fascism, militarism and pacifism—to name only the biggest—into medieval England. He is within his rights. In their totality, after all, the Arthurian legends constitute "the Matter of Britain," in which these same problems in various forms have been

repeatedly thrown up throughout history. Like all myth, the legends of Arthur are timeless, and Mr. White contrives not only to say this but to get the maximum of fun out of demonstrating it. The difficulty, if there is one, lies with the changing character of his audience as the "Matter" develops toward its tragic end. "I have tried," he tells us, "to look at it through the innocent eyes of young people"—but by the end of this volume the young can surely no longer be so innocent, for they have been asked to reflect upon the tragedies of Arthur's incest with his half-sister and Lancelot's adultery with Guinevere. But Mr. White's instincts are right; in practice, if not in theory, he knows that the young are no longer so innocent, and he does not try to be as saintly and priggish as his Galahad.

"The Once and Future King"—the title is a whimsical but perfectly accurate translation of *Rex quondam, Rexque futurus*—is an omnibus volume containing the whole of the Arthur story. . . . Mr. White has trimmed and coordinated so that the work may stand as a tetralogy.

His revisions will be greeted with cries of anguish by some devoted followers, with approval by others. Madame Mim, for example, has vanished completely from **"The Sword in the Stone,"** and her evaporation is much regretted by this reader. On the other hand, the giant Galapas will not be missed. The Wart's singular education now includes a transformation into the world of the ants where "everything that is not forbidden is compulsory." As satire on communism this chapter seems rather forced, although in itself a *tour de force* of psychological insight into the insect world. We can only regret that it replaces the humanitarian lesson on evolution imparted by the sleepy snake in the original version. . . .

"The Witch in the Wood" has been radically reduced. Retitled **"The Queen of Air and Darkness,"** it now contains only fourteen chapters and centers upon the childhood of the Orkneys and the "lack of security" (the phrase becomes irresistibly funny as Mr. White uses it) that drives the sons of Morgause to cruelty. The unpleasant scenes with Queen Morgause are balanced by the uproarious adventures of King Pellinore and of that grandest animal character in modern literature, the Questing Beast. To those who know Mr. White it is enough to say that both Beast and King fall in love.

"The Ill-Made Knight" appears to be substantially unaltered. But in the larger context the interpretation of Lancelot has a depth, coherence and subtlety that make it perhaps the most impressive section of the tetralogy. The seriousness that predominates in the latter chapters of this book continues on into **"The Candle in the Wind,"** which concludes the story along the lines of Malory. But the relationship between Arthur and Mordred is far more guilt-ridden than anything to be found in the pages of the medieval romance.

Here, then, is a whole stout volume of T. H. White's unique wit, vast and curious learning and brooding wisdom, a volume of levity and gravity for young and old. His faithful readers will rejoice; it is to be hoped that thousands of new ones will meet Uncle Dap and the Beast Glatisant, Sir Grummore and Sir Ector and Sir Palomides, Piggy and Sir Meliagrance—to mention only a few of the marvelous minor characters who lurch around the heroic triangle of Arthur, Guinevere and Lancelot.

Richard Winston, "T. H. White's Arthurian Omnibus Rolls to a Triumphant Conclusion," in New York Herald Tribune Book Review, *August 24, 1958, p. 3.*

ERWIN D. CANHAM

Since 1939 a great many readers, this reviewer and his family included, have been earnest, indeed passionate, devotees of T. H. White's *"The Sword in the Stone."* That unique and utterly captivating book deals with the youth of King Arthur and the remarkable pedagogy of the magician Merlin. . . .

Now [with *The Once and Future King*] Mr. White, after over two decades of work, has extended his tale into the entire Arthurian epic. . . .

Thus England's noblest tale, the composite memories of its golden age, have been put together by an expert medievalist who is also a brilliant storyteller, a wit, a master of romance and invention. T. H. White does nothing better than his superb descriptions of nature and men trying to feel like animals. Young Arthur, Wart as he was nicknamed, in the form of a fish swimming in the castle moat is a masterpiece of delicious metamorphosis.

But it is all delightful. And it has been acclaimed in Britain as few books have ever been. . . . And with reason. For out of these pages emerges an incredibly rich, living, breathing tapestry. It is the Middle Ages told in terms we can understand—can feel and taste and smell. It is exquisite and whimsical and sometimes monstrous. And it is timeless, too, in its epic of the struggles of good and evil.

This great tetralogy can be read on several levels. It is a gripping and integrated story, even—in the first volume—a story children savor and understand. Its characters are lovingly and humorously drawn. Many of them, like King Pellinore and Sir Grummore Grummorsum, are captivatingly pawky. They are all as real as can be. Even on the most superficial level, especially in the evocation of nature and animals and the techniques of medievalism, it is a masterpiece.

But at a deeper level, it is what Mr. White calls the Matter of Britain. That is, the very heart and essence of Britain's emergence, politically and perhaps spiritually, from the mists of the Middle Ages into the modern world. It is Britain's traditional saga, much more than myth; its racial memory, its riddle, its meaning. So thought Tennyson. Mr. White makes the Round Table, with its quest for justice and order, more important than the Grail, which to him is almost an invention or a pretext. He has his fun with ecclesiasticism.

And at a still deeper level, it is the struggle of human living for good and against sin, with the temporary triumph of tragedy but the eternal invincibility of good. Arthur is also "the Future King." His meaning, along the pathway of human seeking, promises that man's birthright is never destroyed.

All this, and infinitely more, is woven together with literary genius, archaelogical authority, and a freshness which is as bright as the dawn of history and the memories we associate with a golden age. It is hard to say at which level White's greatness is most special. All of us, certainly, will feel vividly such passages as those in which we are put into the bodies of geese and flown across the North Sea, or into the prickly lump of a hedgehog fighting a badger, or, alas, into an ant in the Orwellian totalitarianism of the slave community.

> Erwin D. Canham, "'A Yankee's Odyssey'—Far Frontiers—'The Once and Future King': Arthur and the 'Matter of Britain'," in The Christian Science Monitor, August 28, 1958, p. 11.

J. R. CAMERON

The recent death of the British novelist Terence Hanbury White probably passed unnoticed among the majority of readers, yet White is the major interpreter of the Arthurian legend in the twentieth century, and his book *The Once and Future King* possibly will endure as one of the great works of romantic fiction in English literature. It is unjust that the novel has been given so little critical acclaim, and it seems appropriate at this time to evaluate its uniqueness and significance in the evolution of the Arthurian story.

White's treatment of the Matter of Britain is a further demonstration that practically every age has found in the legend something of its own problems and conflicts. In his *Morte Darthur* Malory selected and condensed certain episodes from early French romances to remind his contemporaries of the necessity for more loyalty and leadership in fifteenth-century society. . . .

After four centuries of neglect, even ridicule, the legend found a champion in Tennyson, whose *Idylls of the King* saw the tragedy of Camelot as a failure of men to aspire to spiritual excellence. A traditionalist who disapproved of the growing materialism of the nineteenth century, Tennyson used the legend to remind his generation that strength of soul was vital to moral evolution. The inability of Arthur's subjects to rise to the king's high moral and ethical level symbolizes the failure of sensual men in every age to work towards perfection.

Between Tennyson and White, the only author to undertake a major treatment of the Arthuriad was the American poet Edwin Arlington Robinson, who wrote three long poems dealing with the subject: *Merlin* (1917), *Lancelot* (1920), and *Tristram* (1927). (p. 45)

There is a temptation for a student of the Arthurian legend to lapse into superlatives when discussing White's *The Once and Future King*. Anyone acquainted with the history of the legend is bound to be even more impressed and delighted than the general reader with this book about (as one reviewer of Robinson's poems called them) "that over-worked and much over-poeticized Camelot crowd." White's book is an extraordinary achievement in that he has told the familiar story with almost complete fidelity to the main plot and characters of Malory, and yet has made the well-worn Matter of Britain more exciting, and the tragedy more apparent, than they have ever been before. His success is due to a happy blend of imagination, scholarly research, psychological insight and humor.

Unlike most authors who have taken up Arthurian materials, White does not rely solely on literary sources—mainly Malory—for his subject matter. He is qualified not only as an artist, but also as a scholar who is intimately acquainted with medieval life. His imagination has enabled him to invent background which more fully explains the motives of the characters, but which at the same time is entirely faithful to the spirit of the early legend. His academic interest in the minutiae of medieval civilization has kept his story rooted in realism.

White is further aware that if the principal characters of the legend are to be acceptable to a twentieth-century reader, they must reveal normal emotional and intellectual reactions. Malory made no attempt to analyze the characters or to explain the inconsistencies of his idealized chivalric heroes; Tennyson robbed his characters of most of their reality by making them semi-allegorical; Robinson indulged in profound introspection of character, but his Camelot was too somber and coldly rational to be really human. White has not adopted the stereotyped Middle Ages of most fiction; his characters are simple, but not quaint, nor are they impossibly noble or impossibly evil. This "Camelot crowd" gossips, changes fashions, serves on juries, suffocates in cumbersome armor, pays feudal dues to the king, and builds great cathedrals as tributes to an intensely personal God. The men grow old, and the women plump.

This realism of action is balanced by truth of psychological insight. White succeeds with his characters because he has not attempted to fashion them in his own image. They do not judge life through the eyes of a medieval figure of romance, of a nineteenth century moralist, or of a twentieth century intellectual. Although White's work reveals the influence of his age in other respects—including its naturalism of speech, its leaning to Freudian psychology, and its concern with the problem of war—his characters are universalized insofar as they consider their problems and relationships with a simplicity of emotion common to average human beings in every age. As a result, the reader can share their joys and woes because he identifies himself with them on a basis of common humanity.

It would be grossly unjust to call White a mere humorist. On the other hand, in spite of the serious intent and essentially tragic implications of the novel, one of the chief impressions left with the reader is that this is the work of a man with a puckish, sometimes broad and farcical, often satiric humor. Judging by the general run of Arthurian material over the past seven centuries, one would think that nothing funny ever happened in the Middle Ages. Malory, Tennyson and Robinson treated the story with intense seriousness. But laughter is a characteristic of life anywhere, and no society lacking it is truly credible. White's wise and successful evocation of laughter in Camelot, including his playful use of anachronism, is a distinguished contribution to Arthurian literature.

Finally, White has heightened the realism by avoiding archaisms of speech except for humor. His characters speak in simple, even colloquial terms. They do not, furthermore, exhibit that turn for subtle intellectual analysis which, in some of Robinson's passages, suggests a remoteness from real life. After all, there never were any very profound intellects in Arthurian romance.

In an age that has managed to survive two world wars, and is preparing for a third, White attempts to find in the Arthurian legend some answer to the puzzle of how mankind can achieve a stable, progressive society. Malory said that men must be chivalrous; Tennyson said that men must subdue their animal instincts and behavor like Christians—which is virtually what Malory meant by chivalry. Robinson suggested that man must follow the beckonings of some higher life, of the Light, but he failed to make his meaning clear. White's message is that force never solves anything, and that might is not the means to the end of a peaceful civilization characterized by liberty, equality, and a well-formulated code of Christian law. (pp. 46-7)

White is careful to avoid taxing the adultery of Lancelot and Guinevere with responsibility for the failure of Arthur and the fall of Camelot. He blames the tragedy on the greed and selfishness and violence in the heart of man. Perhaps men are basically good, and can be shown how to live in peace and brotherhood, but the process requires much more time than the reign of one king. King Arthur overestimates the goodness and perfectibility of men. He dies wondering if the energies of men

can ever be channelled into constructive rather than destructive action. It is a problem that bewilders many modern statesmen.

The central mystery of the Arthuriad, after all, has always been the failure of Arthur's kingdom to endure. Arthur is a great leader; the kingdom he establishes is characterized by peace, justice, prosperity, and freedom from oppression. What more do men want? Why should the love of Lancelot and Guinevere have the power to corrupt the other knights, to turn them against their king? Why should Mordred be able to gain the support of many members of the Round Table, and of a significant portion of the population? Malory said that the people were "new fangle," but what new political or social philosophy could improve on an established Arthur ideal of honor, justice, and truth? If men are not satisfied with these things, what do they desire?

Tennyson assumed that man was capable of perfection. After two world wars, White is not so sure. Perhaps visionaries such as King Arthur are too optimistic about the human race. If man can never reconcile his nature and his ideals, then no real progress is possible, and hopes for peace and goodwill in the world are chimerical. (p. 48)

> J. R. Cameron, "T. H. White in Camelot: The Matter of Britain Revitalized," in The Humanities Association Bulletin, Vol. XVI, No. 1, Spring, 1965, pp. 45-8.

JOHN K. CRANE

As a man, but not as a writer, T. H. White may be best compared to Ernest Hemingway. They were more than contemporaries and look-alikes; they were also remarkably close in psychological orientation. Both were big, handsome men, each extremely vital in his approach to life. Yet each was haunted by the very talent he possessed—frightened of not only sudden death but the failure of his powers through the onslaught of age. Both were fatalists, not at all sure that the masses of humanity weren't tacitly trying to destroy each other and that God wasn't in on it all behind the scenes. Both were afraid of war, though both (White not as much as Hemingway) felt they had to participate to demonstrate their ability to deal with reality despite its horrifying definition. As substitutes for the conflict and challenges of war and life, both substituted the conflict and challenge of sport—each felt that sport was a miniature battleground in which man had a chance to test himself for the bigger fight ahead. Each had consistent need to prove himself the better of the opposition and the fear that life seemed to mount against him, and each was furious when he failed to meet the test. Each failed to meet the test much more obviously with the coming of his forties and fifties, and both died premature deaths couched in unshakeable despair. (p. 17)

White could not exactly be called misanthropic, but his love and his respect for mankind were closely guarded. This self-protection was due mainly to the constant threat or actuality of war during the second half of his life. He one day discovered that only men and ants make war upon one another, and he was shocked at the way men of the 1930's, 1940's, and 1950's followed blindly into battle because leaders, haranguing on national patriotism, baited them to it. White's masterpiece, *The Once and Future King,* is, ultimately, an examination of mankind's addiction to warfare and of his moral and physical destruction by it. (p. 18)

He was a firm believer in the statement he has Merlyn make in *The Sword in the Stone* that the best thing for being sad was learning something. So White learned things which were huge and diverse. In the "Pleasures of Learning" lecture that he gave many times in America in 1963, he liked to catalogue the things he had attempted in order to relieve the sadness and fear which dominated his life. Shooting a bow and arrow, flying airplanes, plowing with horses, riding show jumpers, training falcons, deep-sea diving, sailing, swimming, shooting, fishing, racing cars, throwing darts, painting, carpentering, knitting, translating, and writing are just a few. Almost all of these, of course, appear in his writings at one point or another. (p. 19)

White cannot be classified as a modern British writer in terms of his total literary production. The few early novels that he attempted—*They Winter Abroad, First Lesson, Earth Stopped,* and *Gone to Ground* were in the style and substance of modern British literature but were duds and flops. He was better when reverting to the style and the material of an earlier day; therefore, his best work grounds itself in the medieval era (*The Once and Future King, The Book of Beasts*), the eighteenth century (*Mistress Masham's Repose, The Age of Scandal, The Scandalmonger*), the nineteenth century (*Farewell Victoria*), or the timeless history of Irish Mythology (*The Elephant and the Kangaroo, The Godstone and the Blackymor*). In each of these ages, his imagination manages to "improve" and extend what he felt contemporary authors had left undone. White's poetry (*Loved Helen and Other Poems, The Green Bay Tree*) also smacks of an earlier day, but it is imitation rather than an extension or improvement.

Not White's greatest works but certainly his most distinctive and in some ways his most memorable are the diaries he published in book form from time to time. These provide the best picture of the author himself and the peculiar blend of enthusiasm for and fear of existence so especially characteristic of him. *England Have My Bones, The Goshawk, The Godstone and the Blackymor,* and *America at Last* are perhaps White's most flawless and realistic books. (pp. 20-1)

In every White book we find some distinct element which makes it unmistakably his, but that element is elusive when we must ultimately define it. The best estimation of his approach to life seems to me to have been presented in his own words in the sadness-learning statement by Merlyn and in the portrait of Lord Camelford [in *The Scandalmonger*]. White was a homosexual who was determined not to foist his problem upon others; thus, he became a semirecluse who tried to manufacture for himself entertaining diversions, but every diversion was permeated by the loneliness and fatalism which continually tried to gain control of his existence.

For this reason, a White book—be it prose, fiction, poetry, or whatever—usually possesses a dualism between surface and sub-surface. A work at first appears to be lilting and fabulistic, but this characteristic is invariably a masque for the sombre and reflective countenance which always lurks behind. And this masque, as Sylvia Warner has stated [in *T. H. White: A Biography*], always has painted on it a pair of raised-eyebrows, for White's tone is continually that of a man who is not surprised by what he sees in life but is rather insistently critical of it. The criticism is generally delivered lightly, with a pointed finger rather than with an upraised switch. If his eyebrows are raised, his voice accompanies them with a "tsk-tsk" of forced indignation. (p. 186)

White was a very versatile original writer at his best—and very stodgy and imitative at his worst. Never a great creator of realistic characters, his finest work is that in which he sets characterization aside in favor of humor, satire, fantasy, and amateur philosophizing. Beyond fiction, his own life was interesting and dynamic to a degree that even one of his daybooks makes good reading. But when White tried to write poetry, Gerard Manley Hopkins seemed to be a model he could neither duplicate nor avoid. Likewise, in his early fiction, the influence of Conan Doyle, Aldous Huxley, Evelyn Waugh and others is much too obvious.

White, in fact, never was able to steer clear of another author's work in creating his own. In his early years, he imitated and failed; in his later ones, he extended and spoofed and, consequently, succeeded. Malory, Swift, Horace Walpole, and Stevenson all retire far into the background when White is delving into their respective milieus. As a scholar, White is interesting and entertaining but probably not lasting, for he could never dispel a sense of dabbling and dilettantism for himself or his readers.

So T. H. White is important to English Literature mainly as a novelist and a diarist. *Farewell Victoria, The Once and Future King, Mistress Masham's Repose, The Elephant and the Kangaroo* are certainly the finest examples of the White style; for they contain the most compelling combination of fantasy, satire, humor, and philosophical reflection. They are the books in which the eyebrows are raised the highest and in which the determination to make life worthwhile, despite the odds against doing so, is the strongest. None of these works could be called "modern" British fiction, but all of them are important and memorable contributions by a fine British writer.

As a diarist, White's own dominating personality, his fear of the unknown, his determination to overcome that fear, the endeavors through which he does so, and the musings upon the actual course of life as he knows it magnetize these themes together and universalize them. *England Have My Bones, The Goshawk, The Godstone and the Blackymor,* and *America At Last* are unique in the canon of English Literature. They are the type of book written about deceased authors by intimate acquaintances, but these works possess the intimacy of the man himself as he lived them and realized them. In this particular genre, whatever one chooses to call it, White probably has no equal. Hemingway's *A Moveable Feast* and [Norman] Mailer's *Armies of the Night* are the only books which seem to me to be even close to White's.

T. H. White was a man who despised life as it was made for him by his mother, his homosexuality, organized religion, and world politics. Yet, by receding within himself and speaking to the world from this hideaway, he was—like Mundy, Merlyn, the Professor at Malplaquet, Mr. White of Burkestown, and Tim White of the journals—able to fashion his life into a meaningful existence in which his own standards and personal morality replaced those which would otherwise have been imposed upon him by the modern world's manufactured machinery, manufactured war, manufactured god, and manufactured Hell. (pp. 186-88)

> *John K. Crane, in his* T. H. White, *Twayne Publishers, Inc., 1974, 202 p.*

JOHN MULLIN

[*The Book of Merlyn*] was intended by the author to conclude his narrative series on King Arthur, the four books eventually brought together in *The Once and Future King*. It was never published. Written after the outbreak of World War II, its pacifist intention, together with the more mundane concerns of paper shortage, destroyed its chances of being printed. Texas Press discovered the manuscript in the archives of the Humanities Research Center at the University of Texas in 1975, and so, over 35 years later, White is able, posthumously, to end his Arthurian tale as he wished, with the King, discouraged by the end of his Round Table ideal, returning to the tutelage of his childhood mentor, Merlyn, and the company of Archimedes the owl, the badger, the hedgehog and the rest of the seer's teaching assistants, for a final lesson about war, human society, the wonders of the natural world and the reasons for hope.

Ultimately, it is a moving tale. Partly because the setting and purpose of much of the book evoke another era and a species of writer now, I suppose, entirely gone. Merlyn spirits a weary Arthur away from his tent on the eve of his final battle with Mordred at Salisbury and conveys him to the badger's sett under the hill where they find the committee of animals, many dusty tomes, stamped leather chairs and madeira. . . .

There is also present, however, a *saeva indignatio,* a fury at the persistently cruel and pompous human race, which White expresses through argument and satire rather than romance. . . . Surprising statistics are provided and much evidence of White's own researches on the subject. These passages, although filled with sincere outrage, can be shrill and not always convincing. More interesting is Arthur's experience of the ant and geese communities. . . .

If the recurring contempt for humanity is distorting and disturbing, at least White produces a number of provocative insights about man's relationship with his fellow creatures and with his own kind, several passages of compelling prose, including the descriptions of the English countryside, the freedom of flight and the various fates of Guinevere, Lancelot and Arthur.

> John Mullin, in a review of "The Book of Merlyn," in America, Vol. 137, No. 10, October 8, 1977, p. 224.

JOSEPH McLELLAN

A basic charm of *The Once and Future King* is the way the author threw himself into the story he borrowed from Malory. If you are looking for simple adventure, for knights and ladies in the slightly stiff poses of medieval tapestry or Gothic sculpture, you do not read White; you go to *Le Morte d'Arthur,* a more direct though still tertiary source. White's reworking is valuable for the myriad, living and deep reflections of the author's complex personality—in Merlyn the genial misanthrope, in Arthur the harrassed idealist who groans under the task of being an ordinary man with an extraordinary assignment, even in Guinevere and perhaps most of all in Lancelot, the good man who does grave wrong.

White's tendency to project his own concerns into the Arthurian matter is evident throughout *The Once and Future King,* but nowhere so much as in [*The Book of Merlyn*], where the narrative thread is almost completely dropped. Driven by the conflict between his English loyalties and his pacifism, White plunges into a curious Platonic dialogue on the nature of man, the ideal society, and the causes and prevention of war. . . .

In terms of the book's artistic quality, the fortunes of war undoubtedly did White a favor. With this material at its end,

The Once and Future King (already a book with more than its share of odd bumps and ridges) would have been hopelessly lopsided and it would not have attracted the wide readership that wanted a modern look at King Arthur. But it is also fortunate that this curious appendix has now surfaced. It will be read not for its contribution to the story of Arthur but for its rhetoric—and being by White, the rhetoric is superb.

> Joseph McLellan, "Last Words from a Genial Misanthrope," in Book World—The Washington Post, October 16, 1977, p. E8.

HAROLD C. SCHONBERG

[Those] of us who love **"The Once and Future King"** are intemperate in their adoration of the book. We read it again and again, amazed at its sweep, moved by the compassion that White brought to the human condition, marveling at the grace with which he carried his scholarship, humbled at the sheer poetry of the conception. . . .

Thus **"The Book of Merlyn"** was eagerly awaited. But as one reads these pages it is easy to see why White dropped most of it and ended **"The Once and Future King"** the way he did. His instinct was right. **"The Book of Merlyn"** is didactic, while **"The Once and Future King"** is not. Even worse; it is often immature in its reasoning, lacking the wisdom that permeates White's magnum opus. (p. 15)

In **"The Sword in the Stone,"** it will be remembered, Merlyn changes Arthur into a bird, a fish, a badger and so on. White was going to complete the circle by having Arthur, on the eve of his last battle, brought back to the badger's "sett," or warren, where the problems of mankind are discussed. Paramount among those is the problem of war. White intended the ending to be an antiwar parable (much as **"The Once and Future King"** is a parable against the use of force). But he got carried away. . . . **"Merlyn"** starts out well enough, with the magician coming back to Arthur and trying to comfort him. . . . (pp. 15, 46)

Arthur cannot be comforted. Merlyn takes him to the badger's sett, where he meets his old friends—the hedgehog, the goat, the pike, the snake, Archimedes the owl. There is a long and rather confused discussion of man's place in the universe. Only man is vile—"man, the little atrocity." White goes into a bitter, even hysterical, diatribe. The animals decide that Arthur still has something to learn from the beasts. He had done so as a boy. But two species had been overlooked—the ant and the goose.

So Arthur is changed into an ant. The ant stands for Fascism and Communism, conformity, regimentation, denial of individual rights. The wild goose, as Arthur learns when he is changed into one, is quite different. Indeed, it represents everything that mankind aspires to be. The geese live in peace, have their own laws that are never transgressed, look on the entire world as their home, are free to do what they want. To be a wild goose, indeed, is to enjoy complete freedom. There are no boundaries. "How can you have boundaries if you fly?" White, himself something of an anarchist, could only hope that mankind could find an equivalent social structure.

These two episodes are by far the best part of **"Merlyn,"** and White must have known so. He inserted both into Book I of **"The Once and Future King."** In the case of the ant episode, it is almost verbatim. He did drop the very last part of the goose parable; otherwise that too is nearly a word-for-word transfer.

The rest of **"Merlyn"** goes downhill. Arthur and his friends discuss war. There is very little that White finds good about man, the complete predator. Nor can he find any real solutions. He does offer some vague, idealistic ideas: abolish boundaries, tariff barriers, passport and immigration laws; convert mankind into a federation of individuals; abolish nations and states; allow no unit larger than a family. All of which has as much application to the problems of the modern world as a cup of chamomile tea to a cure for cancer.

Then is anything worth the effort? White does offer some hope at the end. At least there is Truth. Man might be stupid, ferocious, unpolitical, almost hopeless. "But here and there, oh so seldom, oh so rare, oh so glorious, there were those all the same who would face the rack, the executioner, and even utter extinction, in the cause of something greater than themselves." Here White rises to the great pages of **"The Once and Future King."**

Unfortunately, there are not too many of those pages in **"The Book of Merlyn."** Yet it is safe to say that all White loyalists will rush to read it, if only to savor the way their hero's mind works. And there are a few brilliant passages, especially at the very end, that Warner so justly admires and that do have the poetry and panorama of **"The Once and Future King"** at its best. If **"The Book of Merlyn"** is a failure (and, after all, it was never intended to be read, for White had discarded it in favor of a better ending to his great book), it nevertheless is the failure of a wonderful writer and of a man who so desperately wanted the world to live up to his dream: a dream in which the state never exceeds the individual, and in which the future lies with the personal soul. (p. 46)

> *Harold C. Schonberg, "Unhappy Ending," in* The New York Times Book Review, *November 27, 1977, pp. 15, 46.*

SYLVIA TOWNSEND WARNER

The Book of Merlyn was written with the improvidence of an impulse. It holds much that is acute, disturbing, arresting, much that is brilliant, much that is moving, besides a quantity of information. But Merlyn, the main speaker, is made a mouthpiece for spleen, and the spleen is White's. His fear of the human race, which he seemed to have got the better of, had recurred, and was intensified into fury, fury against the human race, who make war and glorify it.

No jet of spleen falls on the figure of Arthur. Whenever he emerges from the torrent of instruction, he is a good character: slow to anger, willing to learn, and no fool. He is as recuperable as grass, and enjoys listening to so much good talk. When Merlyn tells him that to continue his education he must become an ant, he is ready and willing. Magicked into an ant, he enters the ants' nest which Merlyn keeps for scientific purposes. What he sees there is White's evocation of the totalitarian state. Compelled by his outward form to function as a working ant, he is so outraged by the slavish belligerence and futility of his fellow workers that he opposes an ant army in full march, and has to be snatched away by Merlyn. (p. xviii)

[In Chapter 13] the intention to convince drives out the creative intention to state, and with but one intermission—when the hedgehog leads Arthur to a hill in the west-country, where he sits looking at his sleeping kingdom under the moon and is reconciled to the bad because of the good—the book clatters on like a factory with analysis, proof and counterproof, exhortation, demonstration, explanation, historical examples, parables from nature—even the hedgehog talks too much.

Yet the theme was good, and timely, and heartfelt, and White preserves an awareness of persons and aerates the dialectics with traits of character and colloquial asides. It is clear from the typescript that he recognized the need for this, for many of these mitigations were added by hand. Whenever he can escape from his purpose—no less aesthetically fell for being laudable—into his rightful kingdom of narrative, *The Book of Merlyn* shows him still master of his peculiar powers. It is as though the book were written by two people: the storyteller and the clever man with the notebook who shouts him down.

Perhaps he went astray in that stony desert of words and opinions because he lacked his former guide. In the final chapter, Malory has returned. Under his tutelage White tells how, after Arthur's death in battle, Guenever and Lancelot, stately abbess and humble hermit, came to their quiet ends. These few pages are among the finest that White ever wrote. Cleverness and contention and animus are dismissed: there is no place for them in the completed world of legend, where White and Malory stand farewelling at the end of the long journey. . . . (pp. xix-xx)

> *Sylvia Townsend Warner, "The Story of the Book," in* The Book of Merlyn: The Unpublished Conclusion to "The Once and Future King" *by T. H. White, University of Texas Press, 1977, pp. ix-xx.*

PUBLISHERS WEEKLY

[*The Maharajah and Other Stories*] is a uniquely charming miscellany of the supernatural, the grotesque and the beautiful. White is preeminent among that distinguished little band of English writers for whom rural pursuits, the English countryside and children are a never-diminishing lode of curiosity and fantasy. This is seen to chilling effect in **"The Spanish Earl,"** a captivating piece of grotesquerie about a noble boy in the reign of Charles II, who lived as a well-kept dog. . . . Although an inevitable sameness is to be found in the collection, White's superb storytelling is an invitation to join him at the fireside for some old-fashioned but satisfying storytelling.

> *A review of "The Maharajah and Other Stories," in* Publishers Weekly, *Vol. 220, No. 5, July 31, 1981, p. 47.*

FRANK KELLY

White's principal subjects [in *The Maharajah and Other Stories*] are deformity and aberration—both physical and psychological—and the everpresent tension between the rational world with its prescribed forms and the world of elemental passions. The dilemma of a physician who is caught in this tension is skillfully portrayed in **"The Maharajah."** **"A Sharp Attack of Something or Other"** recalls the best tales of Saki in its wit and in its faintly sinister atmosphere. **"Soft Voices at Passenham"** is a delicately drawn but nonetheless affecting ghost story.

But at least half of the stories are not up to his standard, principally because of a failure of technique. Often White sets up an elaborate structure with no pay-off and his textures sometimes overwhelm the narrative. In **"The Man"** White writes of an adolescent boy, "Nearly all the things which he felt seemed to be wrong, according to the people who surrounded him," but there is no follow-through on this perception. **"The Black Rabbit"** sets up a mysterious tutorial relationship between a boy and a gamekeeper, but the boy's questions about animals' pain are deflected in a singularly unsatisfactory way. **"The Troll"** promises delightful horrors, but the quite literal *deus ex machina* which White resorts to at the end is typical of the wrenching reversals which too frequently destroy his otherwise solid narratives.

There are a few gems in this collection, but most of the stories prove only how far White had progressed by the time he wrote *The Once and Future King*. . . . (p. 293)

> *Frank Kelly, in a review of "The Maharajah and Other Stories," in* Best Sellers, *Vol. 41, No. 8, November, 1981, pp. 292-93.*

Tennessee Williams

1911-1983

(Pseudonym of Thomas Lanier Williams) American dramatist, novelist, short story writer, poet, and scriptwriter.

Along with Arthur Miller, Williams is universally acknowledged as one of the two greatest American dramatists of the post-World War II era. His stature is based almost entirely upon works he completed during the first half of his career. He earned Pulitzer Prizes for *A Streetcar Named Desire* (1947) and *Cat on a Hot Tin Roof* (1955) and New York Drama Critics Circle Awards for *The Glass Menagerie* (1945), *Streetcar, Cat,* and *The Night of the Iguana* (1961). His later plays are considered by critics to be derivative of and less successful than his earlier works. Williams's lyrical style and his thematic concerns are distinctive in American theater; his material came almost exclusively from his inner life and was little influenced by other dramatists or by contemporary events. One critic noted, "Williams has remained aloof from trends in American drama, continuing to create plays out of the same basic neurotic conflicts in his own personality."

Recurrent in Williams's work is the conflict between reality and illusion, which Williams sometimes equates with a conflict between truth and beauty. A whole range of thematic concerns center around human sexuality: sex as life-affirming, contrasted with death and decay; sex as redemptive, contrasted with sex as sin; sex as an escape from the world, and sex as a way of being at one with the world. Williams followed D. H. Lawrence in attaching a cosmic significance to sex, and audiences and critics initially saw his "preoccupation" with sex and violence as perversion. Williams's protagonists are usually lonely, vulnerable dreamers and misfits who confront stronger, more worldly characters. Williams shows the attractive and unattractive qualities of both types of people, but critics agree that he identifies more with the "lost souls," exemplified by Blanche DuBois of *Streetcar*. While the vision of human nature and the world usually presented in Williams's plays ranges from bleak to sordid, in some he offers comfort in the form of a transitory moment of human communication—the type which Blanche ironically refers to in *Streetcar* as "the kindness of strangers."

Williams once told an interviewer, "My work is *emotionally* autobiographical. It has no relationship to the actual events of my life, but it reflects the emotional currents of my life." Critics and biographers have made much use of Williams's family background as a means of analyzing his plays. Williams's father, Cornelius, was a coarse businessman from a prominent Tennessee family who traveled constantly and moved his family several times during the first decade of Williams's life. Biographers say that Cornelius called his son "Miss Nancy" because the child preferred books to sports. His mother, Edwina, was a southern belle and the daughter of a clergyman; Williams portrays her in his plays as domineering and possessive. Williams was very close to his older sister, Rose, who was institutionalized for schizophrenia for much of her life. His insight into lonely, outcast characters, as well as the warring inclinations towards Puritanism and liberality demonstrated in his plays, is often traced to his family life.

© *Thomas Victor 1984*

Williams's most explicit dramatic portrayal of his family occurs in *The Glass Menagerie*. The play is set in St. Louis, where the Williams family lived after 1918. Tom, the narrator of the play, dreams of being a writer and represents Williams. Tom's sister, Laura, is crippled both physically and socially. His mother, Amanda, is a fading southern belle who lives in the past. The action of the play concerns Amanda persuading Tom to bring to the house a "gentleman caller," whom they hope will marry Laura and provide for her future. Tom brings a man who is already engaged, upsetting his mother and causing Laura to retreat more deeply into her fantasy world of records and her glass animal collection. Tom then leaves his family, following in his father's footsteps. The simplicity of *Menagerie*'s plot is counterbalanced by lyrical language and profuse symbolism, which some critics consider overwhelming. However, this emotionally compelling play was extremely popular, and Williams followed its formula in his later work. Laura is a typical Williams heroine in that she is too fragile to live in the real world. Laura's and Amanda's escapes from the world through fantasy and living in the past, respectively, foreshadow later plays where the characters escape through alcohol and sex.

Williams established an international reputation with his next play, *A Streetcar Named Desire,* which many critics consider his best work. The play begins with the arrival of Blanche at the home of her sister, Stella, and her brother-in-law, Stanley, a lusty, crude, working-class man. Blanche has presided over the decay and loss of her family's estate and has witnessed the suicide of her young husband. She comes to Stella and Stanley seeking comfort and security, but clashes with Stanley. While Stella is in the hospital giving birth, Stanley rapes Blanche, causing her to lose what little is left of her sanity. At the end, Blanche is committed to a sanitarium. In *Streetcar*, Williams uses Blanche and Stanley to illustrate dichotomies and conflicts, several of which recur in his plays: illusion vs. truth, weakness vs. strength, and the power of sexuality to both destroy and redeem. But he does not allow either character to become one-dimensional or to dominate the audience's sympathies. Stanley's brutishness is balanced by his love for Stella, his dislike of hypocrisy, and his justifiable anger at Blanche's mockery of him and her intrusion on his home. Blanche's hypocrisy—her pretentious refinement despite her promiscuity—is balanced by the audience's knowledge of the ordeals she has endured and by her gentleness and capacity for love. Williams's skillful balancing of Stanley and Blanche and the qualities each represents, both in *Streetcar*'s dialogue and plot and on a symbolic level, has provided subject matter for many scholarly essays and has earned the admiration of critics. Some find that Williams's portrayal of strengths and weaknesses in both characters is ambiguous and detracts from the play, but most contend that his thorough character development heightens dramatic interest in the conflicts they represent.

Although none of Williams's later plays attained the universal critical and popular acclaim of the first two, several works from the 1940s and 1950s are considered significant achievements in American drama. In *Summer and Smoke* (1948), Williams continues his exploration of the tension between the spirit and the flesh begun in *Streetcar*, and in *The Rose Tattoo* (1951), one of his most lighthearted plays, he celebrates the life-affirming power of sexuality. *Cat on a Hot Tin Roof* is mainly concerned with questions of truth, lies, and self-deception, and contains some of Williams's most memorable characters: Brick, a weak man who drinks to forget guilt; Maggie, his strong wife who is determined to save them both; and Big Daddy, whom critics see as a dramatization of Williams's own father. *The Night of the Iguana*, which Williams said is about "how to get beyond despair and still live," was his last play to win a major prize and heralded the end of Williams's period of critical and popular favor.

Later in his career the "emotional currents" of Williams's life were at a low ebb. Such plays as *Suddenly Last Summer* (1958) and *Sweet Bird of Youth* (1959), which are filled with violence, grotesquerie, and black comedy, reflected Williams's traumatic emotional state. In his *Memoirs* (1975), Williams referred to the 1960s as his "Stoned Age," and he explained in an interview that "after 1955, specifically after *Cat on a Hot Tin Roof* . . . I needed [drugs, caffeine, and alcohol] to give me the physical energy to work. . . . But I am a compulsive writer. I have tried to stop working and I am bored to death." Williams continued to produce plays until his death, but critical reception became increasingly negative. Much of Williams's later work consisted of rewriting his earlier plays and stories, and his new material showed little artistic development, according to critics. Gore Vidal said in 1976, "Tennessee is the sort of writer who does not develop; he simply continues. By the time he was an adolescent he had his themes. . . . I am not aware that any new information (or feeling?) has got through to him in the [past] twenty-eight years." It was not only a lack of new themes which caused

critics to denounce Williams's late work, but the absence of freshness and dramatic soundness in his treatment of these themes. Gerald Weales, a noted Williams scholar, voiced the critical consensus when he said, "Audiences have withdrawn from Williams—I suspect, not because his style has changed or his concerns altered, but because in his desperate need to cry out he has turned away from the sturdy dramatic containers which once gave the cry resonance and has settled for pale imitations of familiar stage images . . . and has substituted lyric argument for dramatic language."

Williams was subject to much negative and even hostile criticism for a writer of his stature. Many of the qualities for which he is faulted in his less successful works are directly related to those for which he is praised in his earlier successes. His lyricism and use of symbols are hallmarks of such plays as *Streetcar*, but in other plays critics accuse him of being overly sentimental or heavy-handed when he allows symbols to take the place of characterization through dialogue. Williams is lauded for his compassionate understanding of the spiritually downtrodden, but he has sometimes been accused of crossing the line between sympathetic interest and perverse sensationalism in his portrayal of these characters. Although critics are nearly unanimous in expressing their disappointment and sadness that the mastery of Williams's early work was not continued in his later plays, they were quick to point out upon Williams's death that his contributions to American theater had been remarkable. This opinion was expressed in an editorial in *The Nation*: "The plays for which Williams will be remembered . . . are not the 'first act' of some mysteriously unfinished life in art—they *are* that life. They transformed the American stage, they purified our language, they changed the way we see ourselves. None of his later plays, however erratic they may have been, diminish that accomplishment by so much as a hair."

(See also *CLC*, Vols. 1, 2, 5, 7, 8, 11, 15, 19; *Contemporary Authors*, Vols. 5-8, rev. ed., Vol. 108 [obituary]; *Dictionary of Literary Biography*, Vol. 7; and *Dictionary of Literary Biography Documentary Series*, Vol. 4.)

In this volume commentary on Tennessee Williams is focused on his play *A Streetcar Named Desire.*

HOWARD BARNES

Tennessee Williams has written a savagely arresting tragedy in "A Streetcar Named Desire." His dramatization of a woman's crack-up . . . is a work of rare discernment and craftsmanship. Although it is almost explosively theatrical at times, it is crowded with the understanding, tenderness and humor of an artist achieving maturity. . . .

Instead of leaning heavily on symbolism, as the title might have led one to expect, Williams has to do with very human beings in completely recognizable circumstances. The fact that there actually is, or was, a streetcar called Desire clanging through New Orleans, has merely set a fine imagination to work. The result is a somber and sometimes shocking account of gradual degradation, cruelty, kindness and sheer animal living. Blanche Du Bois might very well have existed in another city and another time. The documentation of her tragic destiny is so unerring that **"A Streetcar Named Desire"** becomes one of the finest plays of many seasons.

On two counts, it is somewhat disappointing. The talented author might well have foreshortened some of his scenes in a chiaroscuro of death and desire, humiliation and insanity. And he might have crowded the final stanzas of the work with a bit more sympathy. They are curiously touching, but they lack some of the nobility that defines high tragedy. These are minor defects. As a whole **"A Streetcar Named Desire"** has tremendous dramatic excitement, honesty and impetus, leaving a spectator properly limp at the ending. The pathetic attempts of Blanche to deceive her nice sister and brutal brother-in-law; her failure to find surcease in marriage to a nice friend of the family and her ultimate madness are superb chapters in a notable play.

Howard Barnes, "A Long-Run Trolley," in New York Herald Tribune, *December 4, 1947. Reprinted in* New York Theatre Critics' Reviews, *Vol. VIII, No. 21, December 8-12, 1947, p. 252.*

RICHARD WATTS, JR.

[The essay from which this excerpt is taken originally appeared in The New York Post, *December 4, 1947.]*

[A Streetcar Named Desire] is a feverish, squalid, tumultuous, painful, steadily arresting and oddly touching study of feminine decay along the lower Mississippi. . . . Mr. Williams is an oncoming playwright of power, imagination and almost desperately morbid turn of mind and emotion. In his latest work to reach Broadway, the dramatist is telling the story of a doomed Southern girl who seems startlingly like what the foolish old mother of his previous drama, **"The Glass Menagerie,"** might well have been at a similar age. Hers, to put it mildly, is not a pleasant life story. Essentially a romantic and dreamy young woman, it is her fate to represent in her frail spirit the decline and fall of a long line of decadent Southern aristocrats, and, for all her sentimental imagination, she ends as a simpering, witless prostitute.

Two characteristic traits of Mr. Williams' morbid imagination are distinguishable in his new play. I should say that one was admirable and the other less praiseworthy. Despite the blackness of fate which he depicts, there is a frequent quality of lyric originality in his pessimism that gives it an inescapable vitality. Things may look depressing to him, but there is always the rich tumult of life to make up for it. On the other hand, his doomed heroines are so helplessly enmeshed in their fate they cannot put up a properly dramatic battle against it.

There is something a little embarrassing about watching the torment of as helpless a victim of a playwright's brooding imagination as the heroine of **"A Streetcar Named Desire,"** particularly when her downfall is studied with almost loving detail. The result is that the play has a painful, rather pitiful quality about it. Yet its characters are so knowingly and understandably presented, the vividness of its life is so compelling, and the theatrical skill of its portrait of spiritual and moral decay so impressive that it never ceases to be effective and powerful. (pp. 30-1)

Richard Watts, Jr., "'Streetcar Named Desire' Is Striking Drama," in Twentieth Century Interpretations of "A Streetcar Named Desire": A Collection of Critical Essays, edited by Jordan Y. Miller, Prentice-Hall, Inc., 1971, pp. 30-1.

LOUIS KRONENBERGER

A Streetcar Named Desire is by all odds the most creative new play of the season—the one that reveals the most talent, the one that attempts the most truth. It carries us into the only part of the theater that really counts—not the most obviously successful part, but the part where, though people frequently blunder they seldom compromise; where imagination is seated higher than photography; and where the playwright seems to have a certain genuine interest in pleasing himself. . . .

That is the most important thing about *A Streetcar Named Desire;* a more important thing, it seems to me, than that *A Streetcar* is by no means always a good play. It falls down in places; it goes wrong in places. But what is right about it is also, in today's theater, rare. There is something really investigative, something often impassioned, about Mr. Williams' feeling for his material. There is something—in the play's best scenes— that reveals deeper intimations, as well as sharper talent, than most of Mr. Williams' fellow-playwrights can boast. And there is a willingness to be adventurous in the pursuit of truth. . . .

In Blanche, Mr. Williams hasn't quite contrived a real, progressive study in disintegration; except toward the end, his method is too static, with Blanche often a kind of fascinating exhibit—but an exhibit none the less. What both she and the play need is less repetition and more variety; there were times, toward the middle of the play, when I found myself fairly bored. In the last and best third, however, there is a genuine release of emotional excitement; and the conflict between Blanche and her brother-in-law—which may not be Mr. Williams' theme, but is certainly his story—is always good theater, and quite often good drama. And just because it doesn't much induce us to take sides, it comes to move us, in the end, as part of the malignity and messiness of life itself. It brings a certain dry pity, along with a certain new power, into Mr. Williams' work; *A Streetcar* is an enormous advance over that minor-key and too wet-eyed work, *The Glass Menagerie.*

Louis Kronenberger, "A Sharp Southern Drama by Tennessee Williams," in PM Daily, *December 5, 1947, p. 18.*

WOLCOTT GIBBS

Mr. Williams has written a strong, wholly believable play that, starting in a low key, mounts slowly and inexorably to its shocking climax. I think [A Streetcar Named Desire] is an imperfect play, . . . but it is certainly the most impressive one that has turned up this season, and I wouldn't be surprised if it was a sounder and more mature work than **"The Glass Menagerie,"** the author's previous compliment to Southern womanhood. (p. 50)

The reservations I have may easily be captious. Principally, it seems to me that in the emotional surge of writing his play Mr. Williams has been guilty of establishing a too facile and romantic connection between Belle Rêve [the mansion where Stella and Blanche were brought up] and the Vieux Carré [the part of New Orleans where the play is set]. Not knowing much about the South, old or new, it was hard for me to visualize the girls' ancestral home, except as something vaguely resembling the House of Usher, but Stella is written and played as a pretty, reasonably cultivated girl, in no sense unbalanced, and her abrupt and cheerful descent into the lower depths of New Orleans seems rather incredible. Mr. Williams attempts, though the evidence on the stage is against him, to portray [Stanley] as a man of enormous sexual attraction, so that the very sight of him causes her to see colored pinwheels, but even that is scarcely enough. It is the same, to some extent, with Blanche; whatever the forces working against her may have been, her degradation is much too rapid and complete, her fall from whatever position she may have occupied in a top level of society to the bottom of the last level a good deal more picturesque than probable. As I say, it is conceivable that these transitions do occur in the South, but it is my suspicion that Mr. Williams has adjusted life fairly drastically to fit his special theme. The only other thing I might complain about (Blanche's arrival from Laurel, where apparently she had just been tossed out of a cheap hotel, with a trunkful of pretty expensive-looking jewelry and clothes perplexed me *some*, but I'm willing to let it go) is the somewhat strained and literary analogy that keeps turning up between the streetcars named for passion and death and the tragic conflict in the heroine's mind. Mr. Williams seems to me much too good a playwright now to bother his head with these ladies'-club mystifications. **"A Streetcar Named Desire"** is a brilliant, implacable play about the disintegration of a woman, or, if you like, of a society; it has no possible need for the kind of pseudo-poetic decoration that more vacant authors so often employ to disguise their fundamental lack of thought. (pp. 52, 54-5)

> *Wolcott Gibbs, "Lower Depths, Southern Style," in* The New Yorker, *Vol. XXIII, No. 43, December 13, 1947, pp. 50, 52, 54-5.*

KAPPO PHELAN

As was surely obvious in his earlier **"Glass Menagerie,"** [Williams] again proves his dramatic imagination [in **"A Streetcar Named Desire"**]. I think it is safe to say that every telling gesture and effect was securely wrought into the script before ever rehearsals started. You must envision a scene whose transparent wall allows both the heat-laden street as well as this burning room to come into focus. And the sounds are important: from upstairs, outside, all over. As the protagonist topplingly progresses among horrors, one hears her private mockeries: bells, a gunshot, voices. It is extraordinarily interesting to watch the stage being so precisely controlled. And further, the language is as sure. A kind of interior syntax is set up with complex, often lovely, period sentences (speeches) dealt to the heroine and opposed to the current, inarticulate slipshod of the others. Gertrude Stein was not wrong in tracking emotion as well as history through grammar.

In view of all this excellence, it will seem graceless to admit to some puzzles. The first of these has to do with theme. At first glance, it seems that Mr. Williams has conjured nothing more (nor less) than a melodrama, an especial Freudian case-history with all on stage only more or less diseased, the conflict being one of degree. And yet somehow the remembered lines do seem to indicate a further dimension as though the lying nobility projected by the heroine were not only dying, but rather mistaken, though nevertheless a strength. (p. 254)

On the esthetic level, the two most important streams in modern theater will spring, I think, from the work of [Federico García] Lorca and [Bertolt] Brecht. Mr. Williams is a Lorca man. That he has some of the poetry of his original is apparent, and that he has all of what I can only call the sad Freudian absorption

has been twice proved. But whether he has the human charity I can only suspect. In a sense, here must be his next play: yes or no. (p. 255)

> *Kappo Phelan, in a review of "A Streetcar Named Desire," in* Commonweal, *Vol. XLVII, No. 10, December 19, 1947, pp. 254-55.*

JOSEPH WOOD KRUTCH

[*The article from which this excerpt was drawn was originally published in* The Nation, *December 20, 1947.*]

Two years ago when Tennessee Williams was being hailed as the best new playwright to appear in a decade I was among those who were inclined to wait and see, but **"A Streetcar Named Desire"** . . . is amply sufficient to confound us doubters. In mood and manner it is, to be sure, strikingly like **"The Glass Menagerie."** Indeed, the theme and even the story might be said to be the same, since both dramas are concerned with the desperate, unsuccessful effort of a female character to hang on to some kind of shabby gentility. But the new work is sure and sustained where the former was uncertain and intermittent. Gone are all the distracting bits of ineffectual preciosity, all the pseudo-poetic phrases, and all those occasions when the author seemed about to lose his grip upon the very story itself. From the moment the curtain goes up until it descends after the last act everything is perfectly in key and completely effective. The extent of Mr. Williams's range is still to be demonstrated. He may or he may not have much to say, and it is quite possible that sickness and failure are the only themes he can treat. But there is no longer any doubt of his originality, or of his power within the limits of what he has undertaken. Since 1930 only three new talents which seemed to promise much have appread in our theater, and of Mr. Williams one must say what one said of [Clifford] Odets and [William] Saroyan. Only time can tell just how far a young man who begins like this may possibly go. (pp. 38-9)

That the play is not merely the ugly, distressing, and possibly unnecessary thing which any outline must suggest is due, I suppose, in part to its sincerity, even more to the fact that the whole seems to be contemplated with genuine compassion and not, as is the case with so much modern writing about the lower depths, merely with relish. It remains, as there is no point in trying to deny, morbid enough. The mood and the atmosphere are what really count, and both are almost unrelievedly morbid, even, or perhaps especially, in those moments when a kind of grotesque comedy emerges. Yet despite the sensational quality of the story neither the atmosphere nor the mood is ever merely sensational. The author's perceptions remain subtle and delicate, and he is amazingly aware of nuances even in situations where nuance might seem to be inevitably obliterated by violence. The final impression left is, surprisingly enough, not of sensationalism but of subtlety.

Comparing, as one inevitably does, this play with its predecessor, the difference in merit between the two seems to be almost entirely the result of the author's vastly increased mastery of a method which is neither that of simple realism nor of frank fantasy. Obviously Mr. Williams is a highly subjective playwright. His stories are not told primarily either for their own sakes or in order to propound a merely rational thesis, but chiefly because they enable him to communicate emotions which have a special, personal significance. Already one begins to take it for granted that his plays will be immediately recognizable by their familiar themes and a sensibility as unique as that of a lyric poet. Yet he never quite abandons dramatic objectivity as a method. To go one step farther in the direction of subjectivity would inevitably be to reach "expressionism" or some other form of nonrepresentational art. But though there is in the plays as written a certain haunting dream-like or rather nightmarish quality, the break with reality is never quite made, and nothing happens which might not be an actual event. Even the almost dadaist suggestion of the title is given—and more meaningfully than in the case of **"The Glass Menagerie"**—a rational explanation. (pp. 39-40)

> *Joseph Wood Krutch, in a review of "Streetcar Named Desire," in* Twentieth Century Interpretations of "A Streetcar Named Desire": A Collection of Critical Essays, *edited by Jordan Y. Miller, Prentice-Hall, Inc., 1971, pp. 38-40.*

JOHN MASON BROWN

[The article from which this excerpt is taken was originally published in The Saturday Review of Literature, *December 27, 1947.]*

A Streetcar Named Desire is bound to raise [a mirage of familiarity] in the minds of those who saw *The Glass Menagerie*. Tennessee Williams' new play *is* new. No one can question that. In story, setting, incident, and some of the details of its characterizations, it is a work quite different from its predecessor. It is better, deeper, richer than was that earlier drama. . . . Yet new as it is, it is scarcely novel. Even the surprises, many and startling, which it holds resemble more closely misfortunes engulfing old friends than misadventures overtaking new people.

The reasons for this are obvious. The mood of *Streetcar* is the same as that of *The Glass Menagerie*—only more so. Once again Mr. Williams is writing of the decay of Southern gentility. Once again he is a dramatist of despair, though this time frustration has been replaced by disintegration. Once again the world into which he leads us is full of shadows. It is a place of gauzes and transparencies in which the reality is suggested rather than reproduced. Although now set in New Orleans' French Quarter instead of in one of St. Louis's poor districts, the scene continues to be a slum. Its physical grubbiness remains a match for the emotional dilapidation of some of the characters it houses.

Mr. Williams' recurrent concern is with the misfits and the broken; with poor, self-deluded mortals who, in Emerson's phrase, are pendants to events, "only half attached, and that awkwardly," to the world they live in. They are victims of the same negation as the characters in *The Glass Menagerie,* and sustain themselves by identical illusions. If they lie to others, their major lie is to themselves. In this way only can they hope to make their intolerable lives tolerable. Such beauty as they know exists in their dreams. The surroundings in which they find themselves are once again as sordid as is their own living.

Blanche Du Bois, the central figure in Mr. Williams' new play, is a schoolteacher turned whore, whose mind ultimately collapses. Though younger and far more relentlessly explored as a character, she is a kissing-cousin of the dowdy Amanda who, in *The Glass Menagerie,* sustained herself by her unreliable prattle of a white-columned past. The man who falls in love with Blanche is the same Gentleman Caller with whom, in Mr. Williams' earlier script, Amanda's crippled daughter fell in love. His ingenuousness is unchanged; the childlike quality in

a hulking male is no less constant. He is as surely a victim of his mother as Amanda's sailor son, in Mr. Williams' previous work, was the victim of Amanda.

Yet, in spite of these seeming duplications, *A Streetcar Named Desire* is no replica of *The Glass Menagerie*. If it repeats certain patterns, it does so only to extend them. It is a maturer play; in fact, in some respects the most probing script to have been written by an American since Clifford Odets wrote *Awake and Sing!* (pp. 89-91)

In general, Mr. Williams has more in common with William Saroyan, another good Chekhovian, than with Mr. Odets. He has something of the same enchantment, of the same lyricism, of the same reliance upon music, and of the same ability to evoke mood and transcend realism. But Mr. Saroyan's innocence; his glistening, youthful belief in man's goodness; his flagrant, unashamed sentimentality; the bluebird's song he keeps singing in the presence of pain or in the midst of misery; and his eruptive, though dangerous, talent for what amounts to written improvisation are characteristics conspicuous by their absence in Mr. Williams.

Mr. Williams is a more meticulous craftsman. His is a manifestly slower, less impromptu manner of writing. His attitude toward his people is as merciless as Mr. Saryoan's is naïve. He is without illusions. His men and women are not large-spirited and noble, nor basically good. They are small and mean; above all, frustrated. He sees them as he believes they are, not as they would like to be or as he would like to have them. They have no secrets from him or from us when he is through with them. They may have little sweetness, but they are all lighted.

Mr. Williams' approach to them is as tough-minded as James M. Cain's would be. This is the more surprising, considering how Chekhovian or Saroyanesque are his moods. Indeed, there are scenes in *A Streetcar Named Desire* which suggest the most unlikely of collaborations. They sound as if Mr. Cain and Mr. Saroyan had written them jointly. For the magic that one associates with Mr. Saroyan at his best is there. It is there in spite of the brutality of the action, the spiritual squalor of the heroine, the utter negation of the mood, and the sordidness of the episodes. Mr. Williams' new-old play is at once absorbing and appalling; poignant and amoral; drab and magical. Although a smear in a biological laboratory rather than "a slice of life," it has its haunting, moonlit aspects.

I doubt if any woman in any American play has been drawn more unsparingly than is Blanche Du Bois, the schoolteacher whose gradual descent into madness is followed in *A Streetcar Named Desire*. [August] Strindberg could not have been more ruthless in dealing with her selfishness. He, however, would have hated her, where Mr. Williams, without pleading for her, understands—and would have us understand—what has brought about her decline. He passes no moral judgment. He does not condemn her. He allows her to destroy herself and invites us to watch her in the process.

Mr. Williams names an outside cause for the first unhinging of her mind—the fact that Blanche's husband, whom she loved dearly, had turned out to be a homosexual. Upon her discovery of his secret he had blown out his brains. Although this outward tragedy may have damaged her reason, Mr. Williams presents it as being by no means the only tragedy of Blanche Du Bois's life. Her abiding tragedy comes neither from her family's dwindling fortunes nor from her widow's grief. It is sprung from her own nature. From her uncontrollable duplicity. From her pathetic pretensions to gentility, even when she is known as a prostitute in the little town in which she was brought up. From her love of the refined when her life is devoted to coarseness. From the fastidiousness of her tastes and the wantonness of her desires. From her incapacity to live up to her dreams. Most particularly, from her selfishness and her vanity, which are insatiable. (pp. 91-2)

> John Mason Brown, "Southern Discomfort: Tennessee Williams' 'Streetcar'," in his Dramatis Personae: A Retrospective Show, *The Viking Press, 1963, pp. 89-94.*

ROSAMOND GILDER

Surely playwriting is the most difficult of the arts and its successful achievement is among the world's miracles. It does not matter how hard the tidy mind of man applies itself to the formulation of rules for the making of a 'good play', the kernel of truth eludes definition. What makes both Shakespeare's *Antony and Cleopatra* and Tennessee Williams' *A Streetcar Named Desire* good theatre? Is it because they both convey a heightened sense of reality—a poet's projection of the core of experience in terms of the spoken word, the human presence? Tennessee Williams' lost souls in a sordid basement flat in New Orleans are as palpitatingly alive as Shakespeare's royal lovers whose downfall shook the world. In both cases—so widely divergent, so utterly unlike—the artists' profound understanding illuminates as by lightning flashes the dark regions of the human heart.

A Streetcar Named Desire, as its title suggests, is concerned, like Shakespeare's epic tragedy, with love—with its devastations, with its triumphs. In it we see once again, as in *The Glass Menagerie,* the break-up of a social order and its effect on the women, bearers of life, who survive. Stella and Blanche du Bois are the last of a lost civilization. Stella has found salvation in the arms of a man who is at the beginning, not the end, of a cycle. Her husband Stan is passionate, violent, primitive, a second-generation Pole who is battling his way up from the bottom. Her older sister Blanche is the victim of the collapse of the old order. It is she who stayed at home on the family estate, nursed the old people, lived with death and decay, suffered the anguish of seeing her world of refinement and elegance fall to pieces around her. . . . At the last her nerves give way, her mind cracks and she—like the world her forbears once lived in—is brutally cast aside by the upsurging, ruthless new life personified by Stan. (p. 10)

The first part of the play is particularly effective. In this section gigantic, tragic forces are implied, not stated: the furies hover in the wings and have not yet gained admittance. The audience is caught up into the dark, menacing mood with its flashes of raucous humor and exuberant high spirits without knowing or caring about the conduct of a plot. In this play, as in *The Glass Menagerie,* Mr. Williams makes use of stage magic as well as word magic: lighting, music, unusual stage effects—such as the backdrop which becomes transparent and shows the street beyond the house wall—street cries, church bells, the thousand sounds of activity which heighten the sense of palpitating urban life, of brutal intimacies and close-packed, crowded living. An interminable poker game forms an important part of this atmosphere and explodes in a free-for-all fight at the climax of the first act.

It is followed immediately by a sort of coda—a scene of masterly theatric imagination—when Stella's husband, standing at the foot of the circular iron stairway that leads to the neighbor's flat, calls his wife back to him after their violent quarrel. She comes slowly down the steps, bathed in an intense white light, her head bent, her nightrobe trailing behind her—drained of will, drawn by a primordial force beyond her understanding into the arms of the man who waits for her at the foot of the stairs.

In the second part of the play the tension slackens though the action becomes more melodramatic. By presenting insanity as the solution of his problem Mr. Williams brings up an arguable point. But whatever exception one may take to the confusion of motives that this theme introduces there is no doubt at all that Mr. Williams has written a play which redeems the current scene from banality and by the very arguments and questions it arouses broadens the scope of the theatre and gives it renewed stature. (pp. 10-11)

> Rosamond Gilder, "The Playwright Takes Over," in Theatre Arts, *Vol. XXXII, No. 1, January, 1948, pp. 10-13.**

HARRY TAYLOR

[*Taylor's article, from which the following excerpt was taken, originally appeared in* Masses and Mainstream, *April, 1948.*]

[If], as in Williams' case, there was never more than a small patch of happy boyhood in a youth-time dominated by a developing family tragedy, by poverty and hard work and many menial jobs, his static stare will always give him back the same gloomy landscape in which even the small Eden seems a lying mirage and the relationship of forces remains fixed in an endless and cannibalistic assault of the insensitively powerful upon the pathetic and defenseless. The more he stares at the incidents of his life, the more they are the same. He grows older, he knocks about on his own, he writes plays, he is welcomed and acclaimed; yet, curiously, he is still the traumatized youngster inexorably re-creating the pattern of his trauma, unable to break through to adult reality. That is why the characters he hates or fears or despises always win; while those to whom his sympathy is drawn invariably go down. In such a context there can be no conflict, no human dignity which is at the same time strong and healthy, and no future except for evil. And, indeed, for all their beauty of dialogue, atmosphere and characterization, this is a just description of Williams' plays. (pp. 97-8)

Some will say: Why bother Williams with the outer world or the enlargement of his view and of reality? Surely a man who can write *A Streetcar Named Desire* may be forgiven pessimism and the repetition, itself an effect of pessimism, that comes from always seeing the same things the same way. But that is precisely the reason for this appraisal. For it is my contention that Williams has been robbing himself as well as his audience of the full possibilities of his dramatic intelligence and, as we shall see, even of perfection of craft. (p. 98)

Unquestionably, [*Streetcar* is the play] toward which . . . all Williams' work has been heading. On the way he has picked up speed and power and definition, and the story now stands at what is probably dead end. And still, for all its enhanced movement and characterization and the rest of the eloquent testimony to his deepened mastery of theatre, Williams, as a direct consequence of his socio-philosophical position, has been unable to achieve conflict. Confrontations, yes, and savage, almost animal. . . . But there can be no conflict in a man's methodically beating a child to death. The prisoner of a view in which the dominant reality is monstrously destructive and implacable, Williams has once more opposed it with a poor, hazy-minded being already broken in the toils and armed only with obstinate illusions rather than with reasonable will.

Streetcar is an absorbing and beautifully written play . . . , but it is not a great play as most of our critics would have us believe. Great drama cannot emerge out of flight and hysteria, but arises from genuine conflict, an element that can only be generated by the writer's conviction that the battle is vital and that the means to wage it exist. Williams will write greatly only if he can re-examine reality and emotionally recognize what his intellect may already have grasped: that the forces of good in this world are adult and possess both the will and the power to change our environment. . . .

This is no special plea for social plays. But surely the absence of the socio-historic periphery in the author's mind weakens his attack even on personal drama, depriving it of the aura of larger reality and of moral conviction.

Williams once wrote: "The one dominant theme in most of my writings, the most magnificent thing in all nature, is valor— and endurance." However he may believe this to be so, it is not true of his work. Only the passionate conviction of the value of human valor, endurance and dignity, and an understanding of the historic forces that embody these qualities can springboard his next greatest leap forward of craft and artistic stature. But first of all, of simple craft: the knowledge that great drama cannot be evoked from the opposition of will with non-will but only by the firmly engaged conflict of powerful wills. (p. 99)

> Harry Taylor, "The Dilemma of Tennessee Williams," in Two Modern American Tragedies: Reviews and Criticism of Death of a Salesman / A Streetcar Named Desire, *edited by John D. Hurrell, Charles Scribner's Sons, 1961, pp. 97-9.*

HAROLD CLURMAN

[The essay from which this excerpt is taken was originally published in 1948.]

Some of the reviewers [of *A Streetcar Named Desire*] thought Blanche Du Bois a "boozy prostitute," and others believed her a nymphomaniac. Such designations are not only inaccurate but reveal a total failure to understand the author's intention and the theme of the play. Tennessee Williams is a poet of frustration, and what his play says is that aspiration, sensitivity, departure from the norm are battered, bruised, and disgraced in our world today.

It would be far truer to think of Blanche Du Bois as the potential artist in all of us than as a deteriorated Southern belle. Her amatory adventures, which her brother-in-law (like some of the critics) regards as the mark of her inferiority, are the unwholesome means she uses to maintain her connection with life, to fight the sense of death which her whole background has created in her. The play's story shows us Blanche's seeking haven in a simple, healthy man and that in this, too, she is defeated because everything in her environment conspires to degrade the meaning of her tragic situation. . . . Her lies are part of her will-to-beauty; her wretched romanticism is a futile reaching toward a fullness of life. She is not a drunkard, and she is not insane when she is committed to the asylum. She is an almost willing victim of a world that has trapped her and

in which she can find "peace" only by accepting the verdict of her unfitness for "normal" life.

The play is not specifically written as a symbolic drama or as a tract. What I have said is implicit in all of the play's details. The reason for the play's success even with audiences who fail to understand it is that the characters and the scenes are written with a firm grasp on their naturalistic truth. Yet we shall waste the play and the author's talent if we praise the play's effects and disregard its core. Like most works of art the play's significance cannot be isolated in a single passage. It is clear to the attentive and will elude the hasty. (p. 74)

One of the greatest parts ever written for a woman in the American theatre, [Blanche] demands the fullness and variety of an orchestra. . . . The part represents the essence of womanly feeling and wounded human sensibility. Blanche lies and pretends, but through it all the actress must make us perceive her truth. She is an aristocrat (regardless of the threadbare myth of Southern gentility); she is an aristocrat in the subtlety and depth of her feeling. She is a poet, even if we are dubious about her understanding of the writers she names; she is superior by the sheer intensity and realization of her experience, even if much of what she does is abject.

If she is not these things, she is too much of a fraud to be worthy of the author's concern for her. If the latter is true, then the play would be saying something rather surprising— namely, that frank brutaility and naked power are more admirable than the yearning for tenderness and the desire to reach beyond one's personal appetites. . . . It is essential to the play that we believe and are touched by what she says, that her emotion convinces us of the soundness of her values. All through the play, indeed, we must be captured by the music of the girl's martyred soul. Without this there is either a play whose viewpoint we reject or no play at all—only a series of "good scenes," a highly seasoned theatrical dish. (p. 77)

[What] is Stanley Kowalski? He is the embodiment of animal force, of brute life unconcerned and even consciously scornful of every value that does not come within the scope of such life. He resents being called a Polack, and he quotes Huey Long, who assured him that "every man is a king." He screams that he is a hundred per cent American, and breaks dishes and mistreats his women to prove it. He is all muscle, lumpish sensuality, and crude energy, given support by a society that hardly demands more of him. He is the unwitting antichrist of our time, the little man who will break the back of every effort to create a more comprehensive world in which thought and conscience, a broader humanity are expected to evolve from the old Adam. His mentality provides the soil for fascism, viewed not as a political movement but as a state of being.

Because the author does not preach about him but draws him without hate or ideological animus, the audience takes him at his face value. . . . For almost more than two-thirds of the play, . . . the audience identifies itself with Stanley Kowalski. His low jeering is seconded by the audience's laughter, which seems to mock the feeble and hysterical decorativeness of [Blanche's] behavior. The play becomes the triumph of Stanley Kowalski with the collusion of the audience, which is no longer on the side of the angels. (p. 78)

As creative spectators, we cannot satisfy ourselves at a play like *A Streetcar Named Desire* with the knowledge that it is a wonderful show, a smash hit, a prize winner (it is and will be all of these). It is a play that ought to arouse in us as much feeling, thought, and even controversy as plays on semipolitical themes; for it is a play that speaks of a poet's reaction to life in our country (not just the South), and what he has to say about it is much more far-reaching than what might be enunciated through any slogan.

I have heard it said, for example, that Tennessee Williams portrays "ordinary" people without much sense of their promise, and reserves most of his affection for more special people—that minority which Thomas Mann once described as life's delicate children. I find this view false and misleading, but I would rather hear it expressed than to let the play go by as the best play of the season, something you must see, "great theatre."

If the play is great theatre—as I believe—it is precisely because it is instinct with life, a life we share in not alone on the stage, but in our very homes by night and day. (p. 80)

> Harold Clurman, "The American Playwrights: Tennessee Williams," in his Lies Like Truth: Theatre Reviews and Essays, *The Macmillan Company, 1958, pp. 72-80.*

GEORGE JEAN NATHAN

[*A Streetcar Named Desire*], which might well have been titled *The Glans Menagerie,* has been criticized in some quarters as an unpleasant [play]. The criticism is pointed. But the fact that a play is unpleasant, needless to say, is not necessarily a reflection on its quality. . . . There is a considerable difference between the unpleasant and the disgusting, which is the designation Mr. Williams' critics probably have in mind, and his play is not disgusting. . . . Williams has managed to keep his play wholly in hand. But there is, too, a much more positive borderline between the unpleasant and the enlightening, and he has tripped over it, badly, While he has succeeded in making realistically dramatic such elements as sexual abnormality, harlotry, perversion, venality, rape, and lunacy, he has scarcely contrived to distil from them any elevation and purge. His play as a consequence remains largely a theatrical shocker which, while it may shock the emotions of its audience, does not in the slightest shock them into any spiritual education. (pp. 163-64)

[Williams has an] apparent conviction that theatrical sensationalism and dramatic substantiality are much the same thing and that, as in the present case, one can handily pass the former off for the latter, and for something pretty artistic into the bargain, by gilding it with occasional literary flourishes accompanied by off-stage vibra-harps, flutes, and music boxes. . . . To fashion any such festering materials into important drama it is essential that they be lifted out of life into a pattern larger than life, as, among others, [August] Strindberg and his contemporary disciple, [Eugene] O'Neill, have appreciated. Williams in considerable part leaves them where he found them and deludes himself into a belief that he has made of the gutter a broad sea by now and then sailing in it little papier-mâché poesy boats, propelled by doughty exhalations.

Impressionistically, the play suggests a wayward bus occupied by John Steinbeck, William Faulkner and James Cain, all tipsy and all telling stories simultaneously, and with Williams, cocking his ear to assimilate the goings-on, as the conductor. Critically, it suggests that he is a little deaf and has not been able to disentangle what may be valid from the bedlam and assimilate it to possibly meritorious ends. Theatrically and popularly,

however, the result will surely impress a lot of people. . . . (pp. 164-65)

Like a number of his contemporaries, Williams seems to labor under the misapprehension that strong emotions are best to be expressed strongly only through what may delicately be termed strong language. . . . [Justified] or not in certain cases, it seems to me that in this specific instance he has at times used it not because it is vitally necessary but for purposes of startle and because his dramatic gifts do not yet include the ability to achieve the desired effect without easy recourse to such terminology. His writing—to fall back on a description I have used before—sometimes sounds altogether too much like a little boy proudly making a muscle. (p. 165)

That [Blanche's story] holds one's interest is not to be denied. But it holds it much as it is perversely held by a recognizably fixed prize-fight or a circus performer projected out of what appears to be a booming cannon by a mechanical spring device. It is, in other words, highly successful theatre and highly successful showmanship, but considerably less than that as critically secure drama.

In this general view of the play, I hope that no one will suspect that I am subscribing to such definitions as [Saint] Jerome's "Ugliness is but skin-deep; the business of Art is to reveal the beauty underlying all things." Such sweet sentiments, though generally accepted as true, are much too broad and sometimes faulty. The revelation of fundamental ugliness and depravity has been known to be not only the business of art but even occasionally its triumph. The form and style and manner of the revelation may be beautiful, but the revelation itself is not. A better definition might be that the business of art is to reveal whatever is basically true, whether beautiful or ugly, in terms of the highest aesthetic competence. The ugliness in Williams' play may in the definition of the Jeromes be only skin-deep, but the ability to prick deeper into it and draw from it the blood drops of common humanity, and in them a true count of dramatic art, is absent. (pp. 165-66)

> George Jean Nathan, "The Year's Productions: 'A Streetcar Named Desire'," in his The Theatre Book of the Year, 1947-1948: A Record and an Interpretation, *Alfred A. Knopf, 1948, pp. 163-66.*

W. DAVID SIEVERS

[*Originally a dissertation presented at the University of Southern California in 1951, the essay from which the following excerpt is taken was first published in 1955 in Sievers's book* Freud on Broadway: A History of Psychoanalysis and the American Drama.]

In *A Streetcar Named Desire,* Williams has depicted profoundly the origins and growth of schizophrenia. He has shown Blanche struggling to master her conflicting drives of sex and *superego,* to live up to an inner image of a belle of the old South while living in circumstances in which it is an anachronism. At first she is in rebellion against her own nature but in touch with reality. As the various doors of escape are closed to her and she finds Stanley across her one remaining path, her mind is unable to cope with this impossible conflict. She closes the door to reality and escapes to a psychotic world where gallant gentlmen will give her shelter.

There were some critics who considered Blance as fit only for a hospital but not the tragic stage. Edward Chodorov, for example, questioned in his letter to the present author whether *Streetcar* met the requirements of tragedy. The director of the

Broadway production, Elia Kazan, takes issue with Chodorov's position and in an astute analysis calls the play a poetic tragedy:

> We are shown the final dissolution of a person of worth, who once had great potential, and who, even as she goes down, has worth exceeding that of the 'healthy', coarse-grained figures who kill her.

It is not merely an academic issue to test a play such as *Streetcar* by the classic, Aristotelian standards, for with it much of the modern drama may stand or fall. As Kazan points out, Blanche is a character of some dignity who strives to rise above her circumstances. In the love scene with Mitch she lifts the play to universality, and Williams achieved the tragic irony of Sophocles in the discrepancy between reality and Blanche's distorted impression of it. Aristotelians balk, however, at the fact that Blanche achieves no insight, and to the contrary regresses until her final exit is made with no sublime tragic awareness of the forces that determined her destiny. But there is an escape from the dilemma—modern psychoanalytic psychology suggests a reinterpretation of Aristotle that restores *Streetcar* to the rank of tragic drama and at the same time confirms the universal insight of the observant Stagirite. It is simply that although Blanche closes her mind to any awareness as she escapes to psychosis, the insight happens *to the audience*. Williams is able to depict with his raw power the growth of psychosis out of simple defense mechanism, to show the conflict in a sensitive spirit between ugly reality and the quest for beauty. Blanche's tragedy is that of the individual unable to integrate the sex drive, to reconcile the physical hunger with tender and spiritual yearnings. Because of her sheltered background she cannot find security by other means than sexual ones. Thus she has as little free will to choose her destiny as had Oedipus. By illuminating Blanche's sickness, by dramatizing the dark unconscious forces with which Blanche grapples and by which she is defeated, the dramatist, like the psychoanalyst, makes it possible for others to be purged of guilt and fear, to say "There, but for the grace of whatever mental health I have been able to achieve, go I." To understand and participate in Blanche's fate is to escape it. Williams must be credited with a psychological masterpiece; *Streetcar* is powerful naturalism but also infinitely more—it affords a clear perception into the pressures that degrade, both the social forces which make for an environment of brutality and the individual's unconscious forces which make him a psychic cripple helpless to deal with his environment. Blanche is no less a tragic figure than Antigone or Medea—whether she is literally destroyed or whether it is only her mind seems but a technicality. It is a tragic experience in the theatre to participate in the disintegration of a personality. (pp. 92-3)

> *W. David Sievers, "Most Famous of Streetcars," in* Twentieth Century Interpretations of "A Streetcar Named Desire": A Collection of Critical Essays, *edited by Jordan Y. Miller, Prentice-Hall, Inc., 1971, pp. 90-3.*

ERIC BENTLEY

[*The essay "Boredom in New York" was originally published in 1948; "Better than Europe" was originally published in 1949.*]

[In the dialogue of *A Streetcar Named Desire* there is] a liveliness that the American theater has heard from only two or three native playwrights. It is a dialogue caught from actual life and then submitted to only the gentlest treatment at the

playwright's hands. In such a dialogue—as Odets showed us ten years ago—some approach to American life is possible. Life is no longer encased in wisecracks. Its subtle and changing contours are suggested by the melody and rhythm and passion of active speech.

A Streetcar Named Desire seems to me on the borderline of really good drama. If it is never safely across the border, it is because here too the sentimental patterns are at work which cramp most honest effort in the theater today. Perhaps we are not sure how limited, how small, Williams's play is until the last scene. But in realistic and psychological work the last scene is a test case. We look there to find the answer to the question: how deep does the play go? The episode of the black-coated couple from the madhouse compels the answer: not very.

Streetcar is a greater occasion in the theater than you would think from reading the script. Williams writes plays that our actors can perform and that our directors can direct. That's the advantage of being conventional. (pp. 33-4)

But there is a deeper incoherence in *Streetcar,* one that recalls Arthur Miller as well as *Glass Menagerie.* Williams can write very well when he writes realistically, when, for example, he writes dialogue based on observation of character; in fact, all his dramatic talent lies in that direction. But he seems to imagine that his talent is lyrical; read his poems (in *Five Young American Poets 1944*) and you will see that it is not. The love of lyricism seems to affect Williams's work in the same way that vagueness of purpose affects Miller's. The outlines are blurred. (p. 89)

> *Eric Bentley, "Boredom in New York" and "Better than Europe," in his* In Search of Theater, *Alfred A. Knopf, 1953, pp. 23-37, 80-90.*

JOSEPH WOOD KRUTCH

Tennessee Williams grew up in the South. Like so many other Southern writers, the existence of a decayed aristocracy was one of the inescapable facts of the society with which he was most familiar. That representatives of such a decayed aristocracy should appear in his plays may mean no more than that they were part of his experience. Nevertheless it seems to be obvious that his persistent concern with them does have a greater significance. These helpless survivors from the past, feeble and pathetic clingers to a dead tradition, take on the importance of symbols. They are not accidental facts; they mean something.

Upon the answer to the question "What do they mean? Of what are they symbols?" depends the whole meaning of the plays so far as our own special theme is concerned. Let us consider it in connection with *A Streetcar Named Desire*. (pp. 126-27)

Blanche, the nymphomaniac, is horrified by what some would call her sister's "normality." She makes a feeble and ridiculous attempt to instruct both the sister and the husband in the genteel tradition, and she is violently repelled by their contented animality. But because she can neither lead their life nor the genteel life of which she dreams, her last defenses crumble and she is led away to an asylum, certifiably insane.

Everything depends upon, as the phrase goes, which side the author is on. It appears that to many members of the audience this question presents no difficulty. They are, and they assume that the author is, on the side of the sister. She is "healthy," "adjusted," "normal." She lives in the present; she accepts things as they are; and she will never be confined to a mad-house. Her husband is crude, even somewhat brutal, but he is also virile; he is the natural man and one of literature's many kinsmen of Lady Chatterley's lover. Virility, even orgiastic virility, is the proper answer to decadence. Stella, the repre-sentative of a decayed aristocracy, is rejuvenated by a union with a representative of "the people." (pp. 127-28)

[While] one section of the audience takes the side of Stella almost as a matter of course another section understands and shares Blanche's revulsion. Her instincts are right. She is on the side of civilization and refinement. But the age has placed her in a tragic dilemma. She looks about for a tradition ac-cording to which she may live and a civilization to which she can be loyal. She finds none. Ours is a society which has lost its shape.

Behind her lies a past which, at least in retrospect, seems to have been civilized. The culture of the Old South is dead, and she has good reason to know that it is. It is, however, the only culture about which she knows anything. The world of Stella and of her husband is a barbarism,—perhaps, as its admirers would say, a vigorous barbarism—but a barbarism nonetheless. Blanche chooses the dead past and becomes the victim of that impossible choice. But she does choose it rather than the "ad-justment" of her sister. At least she has not succumbed to barbarism. (pp. 128-29)

[One's] choice of sides will depend largely upon one's attitude toward Stella's "virile" husband. The real question is whether he is villain or hero. If we knew which he is to his creator, we should know whether Williams should be classified among that group of "moderns" who see in a return to the primitive the possible rejuvenation of mankind or whether he belongs rather with traditionalists, such as the esoteric T. S. Eliot on the one hand or the popular Maxwell Anderson on the other, who maintain that from the past itself we shall still have to learn if we are ever to learn at all what civilization means.

I cannot tell you what Williams thinks or says. I can, after due warning, report a very significant thing which he is said to have said. At third hand I have it that when queried in con-versation about the meaning of *A Streetcar Named Desire*, or rather about the significance of its chief male character, he replied: "It means that if you do not watch out the apes will take over."

If this report is accurate, and I repeat that I have it only at third hand, the question is answered. Williams, despite all the violence of his plays, despite what sometimes looks very much like nihilism, is really on the side of what modernists would call the Past rather than the Future—which means, of course, on the side of those who believe that the future, if there is to be any civilized future, will be less new than most modern dramatists from [Henrik] Ibsen on have professed to believe. (p. 129)

> *Joseph Wood Krutch, "How Modern Is the Modern American Drama?" in his* "Modernism" in Modern Drama: A Definition and an Estimate, *Cornell Uni-versity Press, 1953, pp. 104-34.**

KENNETH TYNAN

[*The article from which this excerpt was taken was originally published as "American Blues: The Plays of Arthur Miller and Tennessee Williams," in Encounter, May, 1954.*]

If Willy Loman [of Arthur Miller's *Death of a Salesman*] is the desperate average man, Blanche DuBois is the desperate exceptional woman. Willy's collapse began when his son walked into a hotel apartment and found him with a whore; Blanche's when she entered "a room that I thought was empty," and found her young husband embracing an older man. In each instance the play builds up to a climax involving guilt and concomitant disgust. Blanche, nervously boastful, lives in the leisured past; her defence against actuality is a sort of aristo-cratic *Bovarysme*, at which her brutish brother-in-law Stanley repeatedly sneers. Characteristically, Williams keeps his de-tachment, and does not take sides: he never denies that Stan-ley's wife, in spite of her sexual enslavement, is happy and well-adjusted, nor does he exaggerate the cruelty with which Stanley reveals to Blanche's new suitor the secrets of her nym-phomaniac past. The play's weakness lies in the fact that the leading role lends itself to grandiose over-playing by unintel-ligent actresses, who forget that when Blanche complains to her sister about Stanley's animalism, she is expressing, how-ever faintly, an ideal. . . . (p. 128)

When, finally, she is removed to the mental home, we should feel that a part of civilisation is going with her. Where ancient drama teaches us to reach nobility by contemplation of what is noble, modern American drama conjures us to contemplate what might have been noble, but is now humiliated, ignoble in the sight of all but the compassionate. (p. 129)

> *Kenneth Tynan, "American Blues . . . ," in* Two Modern American Tragedies: Reviews and Criticism of Death of a Salesman / A Streetcar Named Desire, *edited by John D. Hurrell, Charles Scribner's Sons, 1961, pp. 124-30.**

JOHN GASSNER

Among the new plays of the 1947-48 season *A Streetcar Named Desire* was not only the best but the most indicative of the flexibility of realism. Strongly rooted in the reality of character and environment, and replete with stinging naturalistic detail, this tragedy of a fallen member of the Southern landed aris-tocracy, nevertheless, abounds in poetic overtones. These are justified, in part, by Blanche's refinement of language. She is well bred and she has had sufficient education to have taught school for a while. Her consuming need, moreover, is to make herself and others constantly aware of her refinement. She is concealing her tawdry past of alcoholism, incontinence, and common prostitution. She is compensating for her fallen estate. Her memories being as unbearable as her present circum-stances, she must transform both by building a dream-world for herself. Obviously, this world contains a large measure of self-delusion, as well as a good deal of pretentious public behavior. She makes "poetry," which her cultural background enables her to "activize" in the form of "manners" and to articulate in dialogue. Her drama becomes "poetic drama." Not realistic drama with poetic varnish, but realistic drama naturally and necessitously poetic. How necessitously, we can realize from the fact that her very refinement betrays her by becoming excessive—hysterically fastidious rather than natu-ral. Her manners become mannerisms, and her speech verges on preciosity. As if in atonement, she crucifies herself on a cross of culture. In *Streetcar*, poetic drama becomes psycho-logical reality. (p. 355)

[There] is an ambiguity in Blanche's situation—or, rather, we have here a series of ambiguities. Placed in opposition to Stan-ley Kowalski at the beginning of the play, she is the aristocrat who condescends to the plebeian when she is not actually scorning him. This is compulsive conduct on her part, because she must feel superior to her sister's husband if she is not to feel inferior in view of her helplessness. But her behavior does not commend her to us. She is also an element of disease threatening the healthiness of her sister's relations with Stan. We can be grateful at first when Stan, disconcerted by Blanche, tries to take Blanche down a peg. Yet there is a certain splendor in Blanche's personality—a tragic splendor until the clinical aspects of her character dim it. Her sister avoided shipwreck by compromise—by marrying Stan and by satiating herself at the trough of commonplace gratifications in marriage. Stella is fortunate in this respect, as ordinary people, who have an aptitude for "the blisses of the commonplace," are fortunate. Blanche, on the contrary, cannot renounce her view of herself as a rare individual. Like other tragic characters, she *longs* for "the blisses of the commonplace" but is as incapable of accepting them as she is incapable of courting them efficiently. Tragic characters are "efficient" only in courting, suffering and encompassing their own destruction. Antigone, Oedipus, Hamlet, and Lear are tremendously efficient in this respect. Therein lies their *arête*, their specialness and stature, even when it is wrapped in folly, as in the case of Lear's dotage. Therein lies also their ultimate *hamartia*, or tragic flaw, which is, above all, their inability to recognize, in the words of Keats, that life has its impossibilities.

Thus far the ambiguities are dramatically, indeed tragically, fruitful. Reality is encountered meaningfully when it becomes plain that Blanche comes to a haven to which she will be unable to *decline* and therefore "adjust." She must turn safety into hell, given the necessities of her character. Also, those who can provide the haven must either eject her from it or turn it into hell for her. Overabundant in animal health and devoid of tender-mindedness, Stan must try to eject her; and, failing to eject her, to quarantine her psychologically (by proving her to have been a harlot), because she has brought unease, if not indeed disease, into his home. And her sister Stella must eject her as an insane accuser of Stan, after the latter has violated Blanche. Otherwise Stella could not remain with Stan, to whom she is bound by sexuality, love, and economic convenience, especially now that she has borne a child. Stan must also turn the haven into hell for Blanche as a necessity of his brutish inclinations, which have been inflamed by the sex-duel that has arisen between them—not without necessitous, if perhaps only half-conscious, initiative on her part. And these ambiguities, too, produce "poetry"—as dialogue, character insight, and atmosphere.

Williams, however, not only enriched but muddled his play with his ambiguities; they are at times only *melodramatically* fruitful. He reduced potential tragedy to psychopathology. Blanche's psychological situation, indeed, is already so untenable when she enters the home of Stan and Stella that she should be receiving psychiatric care. Williams, moreover, muddled the social basis for Blanche's drama, which he himself underscored with references to her Southern plantation. The aristocratic family's fortunes declined, it is true, and left her economically insecure; but she could have supported herself honorably as a teacher had she not become a victim of neurosis. Her plight is attributed to the bizarre—and to me specious—circumstance that her husband killed himself after realizing that he was a hopeless homosexual. As the daughter of a Southern "Cherry Orchard" family, she might have become quite credibly ill adjusted to reality by over-refinement and pride. But Williams, unsatisfied with normal motivations, adds the

causative factor of marriage to a homosexual which has not been established as inevitable. Nor is it convincing that the young husband's death should have led her to seduce schoolchildren and take up with soldiers in a neighboring camp. [Anton Chekhov's play] *The Cherry Orchard* is pyramided upon normal motivation. Therefore the characters, their failure, and their social reality, or their symbolic value as representatives of a dying aristocracy, are equally believable. In *Streetcar,* in so far as Blanche's role is concerned, only her illness is believable—and even that is suspect, in so far as its inevitability is questionable.

It is also curious how Stan's role changes from that of an opponent who has reason to guard his marriage against Blanche to the role of a brute who in violating Blanche also violates his marriage. And if it is argued that the point of the play is precisely that Blanche, who needs every consideration, is thrust into a brute world that gives her no consideration, then, I say, Williams has destroyed the tragic possibilities of *Streetcar* in another way: He has settled for pathos whereas the ambience of his characterization of Blanche suggests a play possessed of a sharper, more equitable, and harder insight—namely, that of tragedy. I would argue, indeed, that having missed that insight—which is surely a defect or insufficiency in the author's thinking—Williams *had* to turn Stan into a brute. Stan was not a mere brute at the beginning of the play; and, later, he could claim the right to warn his wartime-buddy Mitch against marriage with Blanche because she had been a harlot. But Stan became a brute unmistakably in the rape scene toward the end of the play.

Williams, indeed, seems to have succumbed to a generally jaundiced view of normality by giving the impression that the common world is brutish, as if life in a poor neighborhood and Stan and Stella's sexually gratifying marriage were brutish. That is hardly the case, of course, and Williams himself contradicts this view, here and there, in his picture of the New Orleans Latin Quarter and of some aspects of the sister's life with Stan. But *Streetcar* exhibits a good deal of ambivalence on the author's part. The realist and the esthete are at odds with each other in this play. Enough variation in emphasis is possible, given the individual actor and the individual director, to make different stage productions yield different impressions, if not indeed somewhat different themes. But *Streetcar,* for all its dramatic momentum and surge, is a divided work. Ambiguities split the emphasis between realistic and decadent drama, between normal causation and accident, between tragedy and melodrama. Although *Streetcar* crackles with dramatic fire, it lacks a steady flame. Its illumination flickers. (pp. 356-58)

John Gassner, "'A Streetcar Named Desire': A Study in Ambiguity," in his The Theatre in Our Times: A Survey of the Men, Materials and Movements in the Modern Theatre, Crown Publishers, Inc., 1954, pp. 355-63.

C. N. STAVROU

Are [Gustave Flaubert's novel] *Madame Bovary* (1857) and *A Streetcar Named Desire* (1947) pleas against "man's inhumanity to man," or dry admonitions against the folly of

"Charm'd magic casements, opening on the foam
Of perilous seas, in faery lands forlorn"?

Critiques of Flaubert's novel . . . and Williams's drama . . . cautiously eschew a positive answer to this question. They seem inclined to support the interpretation that Flaubert and

Williams are on the side of cynicism and realism. Despite the ambiguity in this respect, which they concede inheres in the French novel and the American play alike, they favor the view that both works castigate "romanticism" and "escapism." Such an interpretation, however, not only unaccountably ignores the avowed intentions of both artists, but gratuitously obfuscates the import of two works whose pretensions to greatness reside in simplicity and economy rather than in complexity and exhaustiveness. (p. 10)

In contrasting the affluent daydreams and subsequent dysphoria of their heroines, Flaubert and Williams leave room for pity and tears as well as ironic amusement and solecistic laughter. There is never any question, however, that, of all the characters in both works, only Emma and Blanche are endowed with a sensibility comparable to that of their creators.

Emma and Blanche reflect their authors' double perspective— the disturbing recognition that man's illusions incapacitate him for reality which is unbearable to him without these illusions. Both women refuse to accept a normal life among people who appear to them insensitive, unperceptive, and unrefined. Each cherishes an ideal of gentility, a code of gallantry according to which she imagines her ancestors lived and loved but which, alas, is neither acknowledged nor understood by any of her contemporaries. Little wonder they find existence vapid if not sordid, and habitually revert in fancy to the proverbial past. Disillusioned in marriage . . . they rush impetuously into a series of unsatisfying liaisons. Invariably, their fitful snatches of amatory bliss are succeeded by periods of despondency. Repeated disappointments, however, serve only to impel them to more reckless escapades and, ultimately, to virtual nymphomania. For Eros—the negation of Thanatos, the final and absolute reality, from which they recoil in horror—becomes, as it always is in the characteristic [Ernest] Hemingway protagonist, an indispensable drug to them. Symbolism is employed in both works to underscore this: Flaubert personifies Death as a loathsome, disfigured, blind beggar; Williams personifies Death as an old, blind, Mexican woman vending funeral flowers. In both works, the imminence of the heroine's tragedy is betokened by the introduction of the character who personifies Death.

Unable to come to terms with the present, and neither able nor willing to abandon the substitute world of their inner lives, Emma and Blanche are rebuffed and mauled by the Anti-romantic. At its hands, their yearnings for love meet with ruthless exploitation, and their frivolous enthusiasms with malicious ridicule. The Anti-romantic in *Madame Bovary* is represented principally by Rodolphe, the cynical squire and coarse adulterer. His counterpart in *A Streetcar Named Desire* is the gaudy seed-bearer, Kowalski. Rodolphe and Kowalski share many traits in common: a crassness born of insensitivity to human decencies; a hypocritical sense of propriety; an animal greed where women and money are concerned. (pp. 11-12)

Emma and Blanche are consigned to defeat, but in their very defeat there is implicit an indictment, an indictment of the cruelty, greed, and boorishness in human beings. In Williams, this becomes patently clear by a reading (or viewing) of his other plays. . . .

The endings of *Madame Bovary* and *A Streetcar Named Desire* are depressing but neither defeatist nor pessimistic. Escapism receives a qualified rebuke. Nevertheless, Flaubert and Williams recognize, and sympathize with, the need of those whom the implacable fires of human desperation drive to suicide and insanity. The defeats of Emma and Blanche are not dictated by the jaundice or nihilism of their creators; Lear-like, both are wracked on the wheel of fire to demonstrate the thesis that the tragic gap between inner dream and external actuality can never be bridged so long as the human race is mired in paranoiac acquisitiveness and besotted with pharisaical morality. (p. 13)

C. N. Stavrou, "Blanche Du Bois & Emma Bovary," in Four Quarters, Vol. VII, No. 3, March, 1958, pp. 10-13.*

WINIFRED L. DUSENBURY

In Blanche DuBois, the leading character of *A Streetcar Named Desire,* Tennessee Williams is accused of having created a sexual pervert, who is insane by the end of the play, and whose portrayal is so particular as to have little relevance to life, or meaning to the American theatre. Williams, however, makes the point that it is the isolation resulting from social and hereditary factors which makes Blanche abnormal. Doubtless the accusation that Williams is strongly influenced by D. H. Lawrence is also true, but the playwright has made purposeful use of the sexual instinct by dramatizing its contrasting effect in two sisters and cannot be charged with mere sensationalism. The theme of the play, like that of Paul Green's *The House of Connelly,* indicates that members of the Southern plantation-owning class cannot exist in isolation. Stella is able to adapt herself to a new mode of living through her intense physical love for the Polish Stanley Kowalski, whereas Blanche cannot relate herself to any mode of life open to her in the modern age, and so perishes. Since, as Erich Fromm points out, "Complete isolation is unbearable and incompatible with sanity," it is obvious that her end is the only possible logical conclusion to the drama. (pp. 140-41)

[As in] *The Glass Menagerie,* the fact of the unbearable physical closeness of human beings to each other and their psychic separateness is dramatized with clarity in *A Streetcar Named Desire.* The isolating effect of crowded conditions is perhaps made even more explicit than in the other [play], . . . and the irony of the fact that the bathroom, associated with Stanley's vulgarity, is also Blanche's only place of retreat and relaxation is symbolic of the theme of the two sisters—one of whom belongs through the most physical of means, the other of whom cuts herself off from the life of the household. . . . The blows which [Blanche] suffers . . . are enough to vanquish the spirit of a woman better equipped than Blanche to meet the loneliness of poverty and the alienation from all loved ones. . . . It is no wonder that she, like Tom in *The Glass Menagerie,* speaks of her life in the apartment as "a trap." She has run like a mouse to a far corner and cannot escape. Reality is unbearable. Tom gets away by joining the Merchant Marine; but with every possible tie to life broken, Blanche can escape only into insanity. (pp. 141-42)

The character can be justified on the literal level as the dramatization of the progress of a woman into complete isolation. In the beginning Blanche admits to Stella:

> I'm not going to put up at a hotel. I want to be *near* you, got to be *with* somebody, I *can't* be *alone!* Because—as you must have noticed—I'm—*not* very well. (Scene I)

The fact that she has come to the Quarter in the finery she is wearing indicates at first glance that Blanche is very much out of place, and her frightened words indicate that she is appealing to Stella as a last hope. The next time she explains her lone-liness is to Mitch. To his sympathetic ear she tells how she loved when she was young, how she accused her husband of homosexuality, how he shot himself, and how ever since, the searchlight which had been on the world has been turned off with only candles to take its place. "I understand what it is to be lonely," she tells him. It is almost impossible not to compare Williams' two plays in their treatment of the near-belonging of Laura and of Blanche. In each case the kiss of a man who seems to be sincere brings the girl to a sudden joyful sense of being one with a lover. After Mitch indicates his sympathy and kisses her, saying, "You need somebody. And I need somebody too. Could it be—you and me, Blanche?" She breathes with long, grateful sobs, "Sometimes—there's God—so quickly!" She is saved for the moment. But as in the case of Laura, this scene only makes her final isolation more devas-tating. Step by step she reaches the point of immutable lone-liness until memory of the past and dreams of the future flood over her, mercifully to blot out the present. (pp. 142-43)

> *Winifred L. Dusenbury, "Socioeconomic Forces,"
> in her* The Theme of Loneliness in Modern American
> Drama, *University of Florida Press, 1960, pp. 113-
> 54.**

MARION MAGID

[*Magid's essay, from which the following excerpt was taken, was
originally published in* Commentary, *January, 1963.*]

The total effect of Williams' work has been to plunge ordinary conceptions of the male-female relation into such disorder that the services of a Harry Stack Sullivan seem needed to straighten them out again. The first of these grand subversions was the figure of Stanley Kowalski, which appeared before the Amer-ican public and before the world in the person of Marlon Brando. Though numerous actors have since played the part, Brando remains forever etched in memory as the embodiment of Amer-ican malehood, and Kowalski is probably the most famous male figure in modern drama. Doubtless at this moment Bran-do's Korean counterpart is playing the role in whatever passes at the Seoul Repertory Company for a torn t-shirt. (p. 77)

Leaving Brando's performance out of it and taking Kowalski at face value, as written by Williams—what are we to make of him? Even forgetting temporarily certain cultural data—that members of the lower middle class are rather more inclined toward the sham genteel in their sexual mores than toward the nobly savage and that it is primarily college graduates who are as conscientious about their sex life as though it were some humanist obligation—one still wonders how Stella and Stanley ever got together. How did Stella ever get over those initial hurdles—Stanley's table manners, Stanley's preferences in dress, Stanley's recreational interests, Stanley's friends, Stanley's stupidity? If we accept Stanley as ape, the character of Stella ceases to be interesting except clinically. Williams claims al-legiance with Lawrence in his philosophy of sex, yet in the creation of Kowalski he forgets utterly Lawrence's basic les-son—that profound sexual experience civilizes, humanizes, lends grace and delicacy. Lady Chatterley is attracted specifically by the natural aristocracy of the gamekeeper which his skill and power as a lover only confirm. Despite his presence on the stage in satin pajamas and his continued invocation of the "colored lights" we do not really believe in the instinctive animal beautiy (purity?) of Stanley in bed because out of it he behaves with such benighted crudity. Did Stanley rape Stella,

too, just by way of a how-do-you-do? Do all women burn to be raped? Is this the locker-room fantasy that is Williams' version of animal purity?

"They come together with low, animal moans," the stage directions say. Earlier Stella launches into the first of those hushed sexual confidences which run through all of Williams' plays and ring such an astonishingly false note. "I can hardly stand it when he's away for a night," says Stella. "When he's away for a week I nearly go wild. . . . And when he comes back I cry on his lap like a baby. . . . " It is hard to know what is more unpleasant in this image, the overt sentimentality it expresses, or the latent brutality it masks: a fascination with the image of the helpless creature under the physical domi-nation of another, accepting his favors with tears of gratitude. That the emotion of gratitude is not the predominant one that women feel for their lovers seems to have escaped Williams, fixated as he seems to be upon the delights his heroes must be capable of affording. (pp. 77-8)

> *Marion Magid, "The Innocence of Tennessee Wil-
> liams," in* Twentieth Century Interpretations of "A
> Streetcar Named Desire": A Collection of Critical
> Essays, *edited by Jordan Y. Miller, Prentice-Hall,
> Inc., 1971, pp. 73-9.*

ROBERT B. HEILMAN

Since Tennessee Williams has had a persistent interest in the idea of tragedy, there is good reason for looking at his serious plays in the light of a theory of tragedy. In this essay the term *tragedy* is used for a drama that is centrally concerned with a split personality, not a pathological split, such as Williams sometimes dramatizes, but a representative division between the different imperatives and impulses that human beings feel. A tragic character is strong enough so that an impulse that drives him can be destructive rather than simply annoying, and so that some kind of reordering is imaginable for him. Since reordering implies consciousness of what one is and has done, a tragic character needs the kind of intelligence that will make him more than a blind automaton in action and feeling. (p. 770)

In his earlier plays Williams tends to focus his attention on characters who don't come through, who because of some weakness or disability stay out of the world or opt out of it. Laura Wingfield in **The Glass Menagerie** (1944) cannot face the ordinary problems of life; Blanche Dubois in **Streetcar Named Desire** (1947) lacks stamina to bear up under the stresses that experience brings. Laura stays at home for good; Blanche ends up in a sanatorium. Williams' early predilection for the structure of melodrama appears in another way in his male protagonists, who face the world vigorously and in their own ways seem headed for triumph; Tom Wingfield escapes from financial constraint and family burdens to travel and write, and Stanley Kowalski, endowed with sexual virility and a keen sense of how the world goes, is ready to charge over all ob-stacles. So we have the familiar dualism of victors and victims. But **Streetcar** has other convolutions that come out of a richer imagination. There is the paradoxical attraction, for a moment at least, of opposites: Stanley, carrying the no-longer-resistant Blanche into the bedroom, tells her, "We've had this date with each other from the beginning!" . . . The sexual common ground points up a world of imperfect choices: in Blanche, sexuality is allied with indiscriminateness, sentimentality, a decayed but yet not wholly unattractive gentility, in a word, the end of a line, the collapse of a tradition; in Stanley, with a coarse new order, vigorous but rude and boorish. Stella,

Stanley's wife and Blanche's sister, has to make a choice: she cries in bitter grief for the sister, but chooses Stanley, whose "maleness," as Williams' master Lawrence might call it, is evidently meant to compensate for conspicuous narrowness, gaucherie, and arrogance (though the arrogance is modified in turn by his dependence on Stella). What is notable here is Williams' improvement on the basic Lawrence melodrama, which, as in *Lady Chatterley* and *St. Mawr,* puts sexuality and all the other virtues on one side, and nonsexuality and the vices on the other.

With Blanche, Williams goes a step further away from the univocal record of disaster. In her view, as well as in Stella's, a crucial trauma in her life was the discovery that her young husband . . . was homosexual, and the shock of his consequent suicide. This might be, of course, simply something that happened to her. But Williams is feeling his way into personality rather than stopping at bad luck. He makes Blanche say, of her husband's suicide, "It was because, on the dance floor—unable to stop myself—I'd suddenly said—'I know! I saw! you disgust me!'" . . . Here is a flash of something new: Williams transcends the story of the victim and finds complicity, or tragic guilt, in the heroine. It is quite evident that Williams wants to give this episode major importance, for he has the "Varsouviana"—the music for the dance from which Blanche's husband broke away to shoot himself—played at key moments throughout the drama. And here several problems arise. If we grant that the music attaches to her sense of guilt rather than simply to the whole shocking experience, still the effect is lyric rather than dramatic: it creates an indefinite feeling rather than establishes a definite development of consciousness. Blanche speaks virtually no additional words on this central experience; it remains a wound, the center of a morally static situation, in which it is not clear whether a sense of guilt persists as strongly as a sense of shock and privation. At any rate, infinite regret, plus an infusion of self-pity, provides Blanche with no way of coming to terms with the disaster that borders on tragedy; when there is no reordering, shock becomes illness, and illness eventually triumphs. By the end *Streetcar* has drifted back to the history of the victim, with its seductive appeal to the strange human capacity for sinking luxuriously into illness as an aesthetic experience. Yet, as we have seen, it makes a sufficiently diverse claim on the feelings to avoid a purely monopathic structure. (pp. 771-73)

> *Robert B. Heilman, "Tennessee Williams: Approaches to Tragedy," in* The Southern Review, *Vol. I, No. 4, October, 1965, pp. 770-90.*

R. H. GARDNER

The emotional quality of all Mr. Williams' serious work is essentially the same, and in theme, subject matter, and philosophy *A Streetcar Named Desire* is the classic Williams play. (p. 112)

Early in the proceedings Mr. Williams provides a clue to his intentions in his choice of names. He has a wonderful feeling for words and, like any poet, puts them to symbolic use. Belle Reve (beautiful dream), Elysian Fields (paradise), desire, cemetery, Blanche DuBois (white wood)—all combine to produce a double image of, on the one hand, a sublime purity too perfect to be real and, on the other, a reality (earthly passion, death) too harsh to tolerate that purity. The devastating impact of the latter upon the former is indeed the central theme that runs through most of Mr. Williams' work.

Stella is a standard sort of girl, healthy in both the animal passion she feels for her husband and pride in the baby she carries within her. Blanche, however, is a strangely delicate and defenseless creature. "You didn't know Blanche as a girl," Stella tells Stanley during one of their arguments on the subject. "Nobody, nobody, was tender and trusting as she was. But people like you abused her and forced her to change." As Blanche herself puts it, "I never was hard or self-sufficient enough. When people are soft—soft people have to shimmer and glow—they've got to put on soft colors, the colors of butterfly wings. . . . " And it is true that, though Blanche does not radiate the glow of physical health her sister does, she glows in a way that Stella doesn't. Behind all her transparent pretensions exists a genuine appreciation of beauty that Stella, being a normal, healthy girl, has never experienced.

Here we encounter another one of Mr. Williams' pet themes—the superiority of difference. "You know—you're—well—very different!" exclaims the gentleman caller to the crippled sister in *The Glass Menagerie.* "Surprisingly different from anyone else I know. . . . The different people are not like other people, but being different is nothing to be ashamed of. Because other people are not such wonderful people." There also appears to be something special about sick people. . . . [Maggie remarks] in *Cat on a Hot Tin Roof* about the charm of the sick and the defeated. Blanche, too, we now discover, thinks highly of the infirm. They have, she tells Mitch (the man she hopes to marry), "such deep, sincere attachments."

Mr. Williams' preoccupation with illness, disease, and death assumes at times the proportions of an obsession. . . . There is not a major Williams play in which the illness theme is not introduced in one way or another. No passage, however, can quite match Blanche's account of her last days at Belle Reve, before foreclosure set into motion the train of disastrous events culminating in her arrival in New Orleans.

> I, I, *I* took the blows in my face and my body! All of those deaths! The long parade to the graveyard! . . . You just came home in time for the funerals, Stella. And funerals are pretty compared to deaths. . . . You didn't dream, but I saw! *Saw! Saw!* And now you sit there telling me with your eyes that I let the place go! How in hell do you think all that sickness and dying was paid for? Death is expensive, Miss Stella! And old cousin Jessie's right after Margaret's, hers! Why the Grim Reaper had put up his tent on our doorstep! . . . Stella, Belle Reve was his headquarters!

We must bear in mind that Blanche herself is sick, afflicted with a psychic illness growing out of her inability—soft, glowing, beauty-haunted creature that she is—to face the harshness of human existence. The same is true, to a greater or less degree, of Brick in *Cat,* Alma in *Summer and Smoke,* Valentine in *Orpheus Descending,* Chance in *Sweet Bird of Youth,* and the Reverend Shannon in *The Night of the Iguana.* Their sickness is a symbol, a badge, a veritable *proof* of their vulnerability, their sensitivity, and, by extension of the same reasoning, their goodness. Good people cannot, in Williams' world, help but be sick, since goodness provides no defense against the brutal forces that cause sickness.

What, then, do we have in *Streetcar?* A central character whose gentleness and innate fineness of spirit do not equip her for a life in which brutality and death hold sway. Unable to bear the pressure, she has retreated to a world of fantasy and nightmare. But that is not all we have. There is another element, without which no Tennessee Williams play would be worthy of the name: sexual depravity. As a diversion from the grim life at Belle Reve, Blanche has taken up promiscuity on a grand scale. . . . She has chosen this road of sensuality, she explains, because of her feeling that the opposite of death (as suggested by the symbolism of the two streetcars) is desire.

Stella's husband, Stanley, loathes Blanche, not only because her pretensions to Old Southern refinement and strait-laced morality offend his earthy, Polish soul, but also because he recognizes in her genuine revulsion to his natural bestiality a threat to his relationship—founded upon that bestiality—with his wife. But there is another reason, too. Blanche, the embodiment of spiritual aspiration, is the exact antithesis of Stanley, the pure animal. Sensing this, he sets about deliberately to destroy her. The means by which he accomplishes his purpose are as systematic as they are heartless. First, he smashes the illusion of youthful innocence she has tried to create about herself. He does this by investigating her past and reporting it in flamboyant detail to Stella and Mitch, the latter of whom represents her last chance to escape into some semblance of domestic stability. Then, having deprived her of both mental (her illusions) and physical (Mitch) sanctuary, Stanley corners Blanche one night while his wife is in the hospital and rapes her. From this final horror, there is for her but one sanctuary—madness.

The play owes its distinctive power to the methodical, calculated manner in which Stanley goes about his task. Arousing revulsion in the spectator through the deliberate destruction of a helpless, suffering, or essentially innocent creature by a vicious force is Mr. Williams' specialty. In one way or another, he does it in most of his plays. (pp. 113-15)

And what is the fate of those unfortunate enough to have been born gentle and pure, with a hunger for beauty and an aching need for love? They naturally are the ones whose destiny it is to be eaten, to provide sport and sustenance for the vicious and greedy. But, before being devoured, they must first undergo a weakening ordeal, so that when the time comes they will be too helpless to put up a fight. This weakening process occurs through corruption—which, in the way it serves to debase the person in his own eyes, is somewhat Chekhovian. The difference is that, whereas Chekhov saw waste as the corrupting agent, for Williams it is sex.

It is indeed difficult to avoid the conclusion that Williams regards sex (because of its suggestion of use of one person by another) as a corrosive element of evil. It destroys, among other things, the purity of human relationships. (p. 118)

This unavoidably corrupting influence is the thing that seems to bother Mr. Williams the most—for, once corrupted, the pure do not simply join the ranks of the impure. They become, like the principals in *Sweet Bird of Youth*, something monstrous. Longing for their lost purity and loathing themselves for having lost it, they achieve satisfaction only by twisting the knife in the wound, weakening themselves through greater and greater excesses, seeking even more revolting forms of debauchery with which to punish themselves—until, drained of all goodness and flopping helplessly upon the exposed sands of the ultimate degradation, they are pounced upon by the brutal forces of nature and devoured.

It is this portrayal of purity in terms of its opposite—moral putrescence—that gives Williams' work its unique flavor. De-

pravity alone would be intolerable; but, by contrasting depravity with the purity out of which it has sprung, he manages to give his characters the illusion of tragic stature—a trick comparable to, but not identical with, Shakespeare's projection of Antony's past strength into the play to contrast his present weakness. Williams' unerring ability to find a dramatic excuse for depicting degeneracy may, in view of the public's curiosity concerning such matters, be one of the reasons for his success at the boxoffice. (pp. 118-19)

[Shakespearean tragedy] arises from a contest in which two powerful adversaries fight to a climactic conclusion. Significance surrounds the struggle because of the hero's greatness and the fact that he has transgressed the natural, "good" order of the universe. His destruction at the end thus creates in us a sense of "rightness" at the same time that it saddens us with its example of waste. In any event, so great has the hero seemed—so huge in stature, so strong in character—that, when finally he is overcome, it is as if some immense edifice were toppling, shaking the earth with the force of its fall.

Williams' plays produce exactly the opposite impression. For, having equated goodness with weakness, strength with viciousness and universl order with evil, they convey no sense of "rightness" at the end. The destruction of the hero represents less a fall than an extermination. For one thing, there is no place for him to fall *to*. He has already sunk to the very bottom of the human barrel, where he lies, arms outflung, soft underbelly exposed, waiting for the heel of violence to squash him like a bug.

Rather than elevating, this experience is simply morbid—comparable in some respects to what the Romans must have felt while watching a decrepit Christian being eaten by a lion. The impact lies not in the power of the conflict but in the death shrieks of the victim. Much of Williams' dialogue, excellent thought it may be, is but a prolonged cry of agony.

The morbid impact of this experience is deepened as a result of Williams' willingness on occasion to exchange his role as a serious playwright creating a work of art for that of a small boy scribbling words on an outhouse wall. . . . Williams' smuttiness seems deliberate and, since it degrades the use of a fine talent, constitutes his most objectionable trait as a dramatist. A more crucial fault, of course, is his inability, despite his insistence upon their erstwhile goodness, to excite mature sympathy for his characters.

The closest we come to sympathy in a typical Williams play is the sickening kind of pity we might feel for a dumb animal caught in a trap and slowly tortured to death by forces beyond its comprehension; but this is overshadowed by our feeling of horror at the sheer brutality of the act. Thus, while eroticism, hate and low-grade pity are all involved, horror is the dominant emotion evoked by *Streetcar* and most Williams plays. And, since he offers no universal justification for the circumstances responsible for the horror, we perceive in them no larger meaning, no significant form, and, consequently, we experience no release at the end. Our spirits, instead of soaring, sag—oppressed by an insupportable weight of . . . horror.

We are thus forced to the conclusion that, though Tennessee Williams has a big talent, he does not write big drama. He is, in fact, the dramatic counterpart of Edgar Allan Poe—a dealer in horror. As such, he is, of course, magnificent. . . . Still, one cannot help regretting that his morbid outlook and fascination for the gutter prevent his putting his fertile imagination, poetic vision and superb sense of theater to better use. (pp. 120-21)

R. H. Gardner, "Streetcar to the Cemetery," in his The Splintered Stage: The Decline of the American Theater, The Macmillan Company, 1965, pp. 111-21.

LEONARD BERKMAN

Though the extent to which *A Streetcar Named Desire* exemplifies traditional tragedy may command increasing attention as this paper progresses, a demonstration of that idea is not the central aim at hand. It is, rather, one fragment of the question of tragic stature that most concerns us here: the terms according to which "victory" may be considered within the heroine's grasp, the course of her struggle toward victory, and the pivotal moment in which the struggle turns to defeat. (p. 249)

[If] an argument is to be put forth that Blanche does *not* begin and proceed and end at the same low point, that argument must hinge on a value that . . . remains to Williams and to his tragedy. Decidedly there is such a value, one that American dramatists of the late 1940s and '50s cling to desperately (Miller, the most important exception.) This is *the belief in intimate relationships* (the establishing of the complex network of human love at least on a one-to-one basis) *as paramount among life's pursuits*. Not only is Blanche's struggle to achieve intimacy central to the tensions of the play, but the very difficult, clasically noble means which she must exert to achieve it— the admitting of humiliating truths, the giving of compassion in the face of shock, the learning to moderate her life so that her continued individuality is compatible with the individuality of others—stand in testament to a by no means peculiarly midtwentieth century view of heroism. Conventionally phrased, can he who strives for order in his society succeed if he cannot bring order to his own house? (pp. 251-52)

How, in accordance with this focus upon intimacy, do we chart the course of Blanche's life on stage? First, in attending to the state of her struggle for intimacy at the outset of *Streetcar*'s action, it is necessary to note the extent of her experience with intimacy up to the time of her arrival in New Orleans. Of Blanche's relationship with her family while her parents were alive, Williams has Blanche and Stella make scarcely a comment. . . . Implicit in Blanche's on-stage relationship with her younger sister, however, is a family mutually giving of intermittent and sudden affection to one another while being mutually reluctant, apart from Blanche's quickness to express hostile emotion, to be truthful to one another. (p. 252)

Blanche's youthful marriage to Allan Grey matches in a crucial respect the limits to intimacy that held sway in Blanche's family: Whatever the goodness of Blanche and Allan's exchanges of affection and shared poetic sensibilities, a solidification of their intimacy through the telling of certain truths never succeeded in coming about. It is not the existence of Allan's homosexuality that signals the failure of Blanche's marriage; it is, rather, that Blanche must uncover this information by accident, that Blanche is incapable of responding compassionately to this information, that in short there *never* existed a marriage between them in which Allan could come to her in full trust and explicit need. Though Blanche does turn wholly to that kind of fleeting "intimate" affair with strangers in which no deeply personal demands can be placed upon her, the point *Streetcar* makes is not that Blanche's fall has as its source the collapse of her marriage, but instead that, immersed

in dishonesty even before that collapse and nearly having yielded to it utterly, Blanche is beginning (as shown in the action of the play) to force the truth to break through. Blanche's most fundamental regret, as we see her in New Orleans, is not that she happened to marry a homosexual. . . . Blanche's concern is more directly that, when made aware of her husband's homosexuality, she brought on the boy's suicide by her unqualified expression of disgust. In Blanche's refusal to shirk a responsibility that the conventional society of her time and place would have eagerly excused, she is doing more when she talks of her past to Mitch than simply telling him her life's story. Hoping for intimacy with Mitch, she is rising to the height that intimacy demands.

From Blanche's entrance on stage to the moment of her confession of guilt to Mitch all of the difficulties of her achieving any sort of intimate relationship come into play. To an extent Stan and Stella have what Blanche wants. Their intimacy involves a degree of humility, spirited affection, and overt need, certainly, as well as the working out of a pattern of living generally suitable to them both. However unsuitable such a pattern might be for Blanche, she is confronted constantly with evidence of the intimacy she desires and, simultaneously, with demonstrations of how exclusive even of her partial participation such intimacy is. Blanche's behavior vis-à-vis her own sister underscores *their* incompatibility for intimacy; Stella, despite her genuine feeling for Blanche, must condescend to Blanche and must flatter her or lie to her in order to be able to get along with her, just as Blanche herself feels she must "put on airs" in order to bring herself to tolerate the situation in which she now finds herself. Although Blanche's desire to be truthful and spontaneous toward Stan and Stella provokes sporadic moments of risk, as when she admits flirting with Stan and when she impulsively kisses Stella's hand, intimacy remains beyond her reach. It is with Mitch that prospects soar. (pp. 252-54)

Tellingly, Mitch's kisses are by no means fended off by Blanche when they come, in rapid succession, in response to Blanche's story of her marriage. It is specifically the intermingling of sex with compassion that Blanche longs for; sex without compassion, that she cannot accept. Crucially, Mitch's embrace is what provokes Blanche's exclamation about God. Sex (or what passed for sex in Blanche's hotel room) has not been God, or even sufficient opiate, for her; it is, in contrast, only the kind of intimacy Mitch is, temporarily at least, capable of sharing with Blanche that can restore Blanche to grace.

Blanche maintains with Mitch the height she has reached, for in her next important scene with him she tells him of the promiscuous affairs she has had. . . . Blanche has a positive impetus for revealing her past to Mitch completely, since her difficult admissions can bind the two of them all the more deeply together.

With the second confession, however, elements of tragic irony come into ascendance. There is an assertion of T. S. Eliot's to which Williams firmly and sorrowfully assents: "Human kind cannot bear very much reality." The painful implication in this statement for Williams is that reality—in this context, intimacy—is nevertheless what human kind finds most glorious and must always pursue. There is tragic irony, in short, in that Mitch's response to Blanche's initial tackling of truth encourages Blanche to make further truthful admissions that will only, in Mitch's eyes, condemn her. Mitch, after Blanche's second confession, of course does not embrace her tenderly again; he calls her dirty and demands his sexual due. (pp. 254-55)

That is the point of Blanche's downfall: the finding herself turned by her impulses toward truth in intimacy back into the whore-image from which, through truth, she struggles to escape. Stan's capability for the rape Mitch only verbally indicates is the physical incarnation of Blanche's defeat. For again, as in her time of hotels, she *is* no longer being excluded from "intimacy" in the ordinary usage of the word; but, just as she feared, it is the act of sex itself which denies intimacy to her thereafter. (p. 255)

Blanche cannot at all be accurately seen as the weak hypocrite John Mason Brown portrays her as being [see excerpt above]; the morality she persists in avowing is not her lie. The conscious drive toward propriety and refinement that her upbringing and environment have confirmed within her are not less profoundly respected by her than the sexual and emotional longing which she had to forego propriety to satisfy. Ultimately it is neither drive that Blanche would want to yield.

In this light, is it the pathetic helplessness of insanity that Blanche demonstrates as she allows herself to be led into exile "as if she were blind" (and with no attempt at violence once the doctor has become personalized)? It is likelier that although her hopes for her own future have been crushed, and although she is moving through a siege of terror, she remains free, up through her last moment on stage, to affirm that ideal toward which she has always striven. Confronted by the presence of the doctor, she can drop the pretense that Shep Huntleigh has at last come for her; but she is affirmative in maintaining the image of herself that mocks the cardplayers for the courtesy they would never think of showing to her, and she is affirmative in fighting the medical imprisonment being forced upon her until she has gained from the doctor the perceptive gallantry and kindness she has always settled for when a mutually intimate relationship was precluded. Blanche could well have persisted in accusing Stan of raping her, and she could as well have retracted her accusation so as to try to avoid being taken away. It is a tribute to her recognition of the wider meaning of her situation that she did neither.

Blanche's approval of the doctor, her equating him with the men she has fleetingly known and to the ship doctor of her death fantasy, her asking of him no more than the "kindness of strangers," is her way of proclaiming what she now knows: Doomed by the life she has led, her struggle for intimacy has come to its end. The future she sees has only strangers, at best kind strangers, in it. Blanche's tragic power lies in her ultimate acceptance of that very future she has fought so painfully, and almost successfully with Mitch, to resist. Blanche attains this acceptance with tragic dignity, forsaking her anguish but not forsaking, as the reverberations of her final statement tell us, her vision of the intimacy, her God, in whose arms she could not remain. (pp. 256-57)

> Leonard Berkman, "The Tragic Downfall of Blanche duBois," in Modern Drama, Vol. 10, No. 2, December, 1967, pp. 249-57.

MARTIN GOTTFRIED

[*A Streetcar Named Desired* followed *The Glass Menagerie*] in its concern with the quality of human love, but I do not mean to suggest that it had a literary content as such. There are intellectual points represented in the play, and a conscious interplay of ideas—the pitting of Kowalski's animal life force against Blanche's fragile poetry is the central one. But the play, in true left-wing style, represents the introduction of a new kind of meaning and a new way of stating it into the American theater. *Streetcar* is about *abstract* ideas—ways of living. The closest it ever gets to actually *stating* a point is in saying that "desire is the opposite of death."

That is its guiding point. The breakdown of Blanche DuBois is the breakdown, or death, of a way of life. Beauty and sensitivity are qualities too fragile for their new, hard, healthy but pitiless replacements. The Old South that Blanche and her lost plantation represent had to collapse and Williams does not flinch from that necessity. But he weeps for the betrayal of the lovely and the refusal of the new world to allow Blanche "a cleft in the rock of the world that I could hide in."

The dramatic intensity, the beauty of language and the expertise in construction of this play came as no accident. In writing *Streetcar,* Williams called upon his deepest resources as a master playwright in the dazzle of inspiration. A battery of accessory awarenesses contribute to the play's substance. For example, he uses a sense of painting and color to establish contextual as well as theatrical points. In setting the "Poker Night" scene he writes, "There is a picture of Van Gogh's of a billiard parlor at night. The kitchen now suggests that sort of lurid nocturnal brilliance, the raw colors of childhood's spectrum. Over the yellow linoleum of the kitchen table hangs an electric bulb with a vivid green glass shade. The poker players . . . wear colored shirts, solid blues, a purple, red-and-white check, a light green, and they are men at the peak of their physical manhood, as coarse and direct and powerful as the primary colors. There are vivid slices of watermelon on the table, whiskey bottles and glasses."

Playwrights seldom have fully developed senses of painting, but they will on occasion set a scene with some knowledge of visual values. I have never come across any stage direction that approached this description of Williams's for depth of understanding in matters of composition, color, symbolism, shape, effect and dramatic value (even its *writing* is poetic).

Williams also used an unusual knowledge of and sensitivity to music in constructing *Streetcar*. A blues piano motif is repeatedly employed to represent the easygoing sensuality of New Orleans's French Quarter. It counterplays against the polka that Blanche heard the night her young husband shot himself. Williams also requests the changing of keys from major to minor and suggests specific dramatic usage of music (for example, "Blanche is singing in the bathroom a saccharine popular ballad which is used contrapuntally with Stanley's speech").

But for all such knowledgeable construction, it is the play's central concept—its story, its mood and its lavish characters—that makes it so magnificent a work.

Stanley Kowalski and Blanche DuBois are two of the finest character creations in all the American dramatic literature, perhaps matched only by O'Neill's Hickey in *The Iceman Cometh.* It is almost incredible that a single man could have created two people so entirely opposite and managed a full appreciation of both. Kowalski is extraordinary. He is brutal and stupid, operating almost entirely on animal reflex, but his vitality is the energy of life and his love for Stella is absolute and *real.* He is also enormously funny and serves as a channel for a free outpouring of the Williams sense of humor. Blanche is usually listed prominently in the Williams Collection of Great Female Characters. There is no denying it—the playwright has an enormous feeling for fragile women, strung with webs from more romantic times. His sympathy is always with the lost, the obsolete, the faded, and when they are women it blossoms with a beating sadness. Of all these women, from Amanda of *The Glass Menagerie* through Serafina delle Rose of *The Rose Tattoo* and all the way to the Gnädiges Fräulein in *Slapstick Tragedy,* none is more pitied, none more loved, than Blanche DuBois.

Blanche is the absolute romantic, still believing in purity, honor and gallantry even while her own life has become sordid and soiled. But she *does believe,* and the lies she tells, whether about her past or about her surroundings, are dreams of beauty. . . . She is quick and clever, neurotic and melodramatic, too crystalline, too brittle, too delicate for the new, shoulder-to-shoulder brawling of modern life.

But it would be a mistake to take her for just a symbol of the doomed Old South. While Blanche represents the grand gentility of that way of life (whether it ever existed or not), she is terribly personal and must not be robbed of that personality. Williams writes plays about people and they are his first love.

By mixing such opposites as Blanche and Kowalski, Williams creates an electric situation through character, as opposed to plotting. Given these two characters, and the ways of life they represent, one must be eliminated for the other to exist; pure romance and pure sensuality cannot survive side by side, although they do contain elements of each other (Stanley and Stella, the blood-mated married couple, have a real romance in their animal relationship, while Blanche is almost a nymphomaniac, although only because of her early, traumatic marriage to a homosexual). Blanche devoutly believes that "deliberate cruelty is not forgivable" and Kowalski is congenitally cruel. Blanche lives by the paper moon in the cardboard sky and Kowalski by basics—beer, bowling and bed. Blanche would be religious and Kowalski atheistic, she is the dream and he the earth. In their collision she *must* be destroyed, but all beauty, all poetry, all pity are with her. She—as the play—is written with breathtaking delicacy. (pp. 250-53)

> *Martin Gottfried, "A Word on Plays—I," in his* A Theater Divided: The Postwar American Stage, *Little, Brown and Company, 1967, pp. 237-79.**

HAROLD CLURMAN

A Streetcar Named Desire is still a beautiful play, the most fully achieved of Tennessee Williams' writings. . . . Its beauties are of several kinds. It is admirably constructed, its language is fluent, euphonious, delicate and sinewy. It possesses oblique humor and a romantic glow which occasionally verges on a sentimentality I do not find in the least objectionable. It is imbued with a theatrical atmosphere, a kind of magic spell which makes certain plays endure beyond our interest in their ideas, novelty or topical relevance.

It is just these qualities, plus the opportunity the play offers for fine acting and vivid staging, which may obscure its essential meaning. Its value in this regard was generally overlooked when it was first produced in 1948 and, judging by comments I have heard and read, it is still missed. The play is appreciated as a sort of superior sob story, but it is more significantly an American parable.

It is not, as one reviewer has hastily summarized it, a conflict between the realist and the romantic but a dramatization of sensibility crushed by a brutishness so common among us that many people take Stanley Kowalski to be the play's "hero." For them, Kowalski is the ordinary down-to-earth guy, virile, hard-working, a devoted husband, only occasionally guilty of bouts of drinking and sudden aggressiveness without special malice, whose pastimes of poker or bowling are certainly harmlessly convival. If he is coarse in speech and uncouth in manner, well, aren't we all today a little like that? Kowalski at least is without pretensions.

His sister-in-law, a high school English teacher, prates about [Edgar Allan] Poe, [Nathaniel] Hawthorne and other of our literary masters; she affects highflown speech and lofty ideals, while in fact she is part of a Southern psuedo-aristocracy gone to seed. She lies, she drinks, she has been sexually incontinent. Seeing the situation in this light, a good part of the audience laughs at Blanche and "sides" with Kowalski, whose idol is Huey Long and who is "100 per cent American, born and raised in the greatest country on earth and proud as hell of it." When Blanche speaks of trying to progress beyond our animal condition many are inclined to laugh at her, and indeed she *is* slightly absurd. . . .

Blanche's intellectual background, like so much of our own, is shallow; the roots of her cultivation and idealism are weak and they are easily eroded, but she has true instincts and feelings; she does aspire to a fullness of life, a recognition of something more than our gross needs for simple survival. Kowalski resents the accusation implied by Blanche's very presence; he is therefore bent on destroying her. He stands for the norm, the "compact majority," the mass scornful of that dimension of affectivity and thought outside the area of vulgar use and creature comfort. Such as he are always suspicious and finally virulently embattled against the "highbrow," the "eggheads," the poets, the spiritually hungry. The latter in our society are rarely strong or immovably self-assured. They are not prepared or armed to withstand the weight of the adversary's oppression. For the Kowalskis, people like Blanche are "troublemakers" disturbing the pace of their slothful habit. They must be gotten rid of as Stanley Kowalski, after raping her, gets rid of Blanche, who has "always depended on the kindness of strangers." (p. 635)

> *Harold Clurman, in a review of "A Streetcar Named Desire," in* The Nation, *Vol. 216, No. 20, May 14, 1973, pp. 635-36.*

LEONARD QUIRINO

So much has been written about *A Streetcar Named Desire* in terms of its theatrical presentation as interpreted by a specific director and set of actors and so much concern has been lavished on the social attitudes and psychological constitution of its characters that the author's primary intention as revealed in his use of mythic symbolism and archetypal imagery to create a dialectic between soul and body to depict universally significant problems such as the conflict and mutual attraction between desire and death has been generally obscured or denigrated as pretentious. My own intention in this essay is to consider the play neither as interpreted in any specific production nor as it may embody a study of satyriasis, nymphomania, or reconstruction in the South, but, rather, as it constitutes what an examination of its symbolism reveals to be Tennessee Williams' intention: a tragic parable dramatizing existence, the fact of incarnation, itself. Far from wishing to dissolve Williams' carefully constructed characters and theatrical effects into illustrations of archetypal figures or myths devoid of the author's particular "signature," I shall try to suggest how Williams' special use of two very ordinary symbols—the cards of destiny and the voyage of experience—aesthetically patterns the mosaic of his literary and theatrical imagery in *Streetcar,* investing the play with an artistry and meaning that transcend the mere theatricality and sensationalism with which it has so often been credited and discredited.

"Catch!" . . . says Stanley Kowalski throwing a bloodstained package of meat to his wife, Stella, at the opening of the first scene of *A Streetcar Named Desire.* Laughing breathlessly, she manages to catch it. "This game is seven-card stud," reads the last line of the play. In between, much of the verbal and theatrical imagery that constitutes the drama is drawn from games, chance and luck. Williams had called the short play from which *Streetcar* evolved *The Poker Night,* and in the final version two of the most crucial scenes are presented within the framework of poker games played onstage. Indeed, the tactics and ceremonial of games in general, and poker in particular, may be seen as constituting the informing structural principle of the play as a whole. Pitting Stanley Kowalski, the powerful master of Elysian Fields against Blanche DuBois, the ineffectual ex-mistress of Belle Reve, Williams makes the former the inevitable winner of the game whose stakes are survival in the kind of world the play posits. For the first four of the eleven scenes of *Streetcar,* Blanche, by reason of her affectation of gentility and respectability, manages to bluff a good hand in her game with Stanley; thus, in the third scene Stanley is continually losing, principally to Mitch the potential ally of Blanche, in the poker game played onstage. However, generally suspicious of Blanche's behavior and her past, and made aware at the end of the fourth scene that she considers him an ape and a brute, Stanley pursues an investigation of the real identity of *her* cards. As, little by little, he finds proof of what he considers her own apishness and brutality, he continually discredits her gambits until, in the penultimate scene, he caps his winnings by raping her. In the last scene of the play, Stanley is not only winning every card game being played onstage, but he has also won the game he played with Blanche. Depending as it does on the skillful manipulation of the hands that chance deals out, the card game is used by Williams throughout *Streetcar* as a symbol of fate and of the skillful player's ability to make its decrees perform in his own favor at the expense of his opponent's misfortune, incompetence, and horror of the game itself.

Equally as important as the symbol of the card game in *Streetcar* is the imagery connected with the mythic archetype of the voyage which Williams portrays both as quest for an imagined ideal and as flight from disillusioning actuality. "They told me," says Blanche in her first speech, "to take a streetcar named Desire, and then to transfer to one called Cemeteries and ride six blocks and get off at—Elysian Fields." Putting together the allegorical names of these streetcars and their destination at Elysian Fields with Williams' portrayal of Blanche as resembling a moth, traditionally a symbol of the soul, we find in her journey a not too deeply submerged metaphor for the soul's disastrous voyage through life. . . . [We] can understand the implications of Blanche's statement late in the play, "The opposite [of death] is desire," to be more than merely sexual. Shuttling between yearning and frustration defines the basic rhythm of life itself for Blanche. Opening with her arrival in the land of life in death, the play chronicles the human soul's past and present excursions in the only vehicle that fate provides her, the rattle-trap streetcar of the body; the play closes with the soul's departure for incarceration in another asylum, another kind of living death. (pp. 77-9)

Blanche's first speech provides the introduction to Williams' treatment of her journey in the universal terms of life (desire) and death (cemeteries). In depicting her destination, Elysian Fields, which proves unwelcome and unwelcoming to Blanche, Williams continues to fuse and juxtapose images of life and death. (p. 80)

He depicts Stella . . . as one of the happy dead: after a night in bed with Stanley, "Her eyes and lips have that almost narcotized tranquility that is in the faces of Eastern idols." . . . While Stella can bridge the two worlds of Belle Reve and Elysian Fields, Blanche is unwelcome in both.

This distinction is important to note because too many critics have made oversimplified, sociologically oriented interpretations of the conflict in *Streetcar* as a representation of Williams' nostalgia for vanished, decadent southern aristocracy and his horror of vital industrial proletarianism. Other critics, noticing that Williams *compares* as well as contrasts Belle Reve with Elysian Fields, claim that his presentation of social conditions is ambivalent and confusing. But Williams, usually little interested in sociology beyond its reflection of the human predicament of survival, does not use Blanche's pretentious cultural standards—which he exposes as pitiful—to measure Belle Reve against Elysian Fields; rather, he emphasizes the uninhabitability of both for his supremely romantic heroine to the extent that she symbolizes the soul. The vitality and "raffish charm" of Elysian Fields is outweighed by its brutality; the fabled graciousness of Belle Reve by its debauchery. The former world with its brawling, bowling cocks-of-the-walk is male-dominated; the latter as its grammatically incorrect name (feminine adjective modifying masculine noun) suggests is a female-oriented, effeminate world whose scions, as symbolized by Blanche's young husband, are apt to be disinclined to propagate. Blanche's remark to Stella about Stanley early in the play, "But maybe he's what we need to mix with our blood now that we've lost Belle Reve . . . " proves, in the light of his (and even Mitch's) rought treatment of her, ironic. There can be no copulation or reconciliation between the world of the "beautiful dream" and the world of death in life actuality that will be mutually and ideally satisfactory. Stella's erotic will to life at any cost, her ability to shut one eye to the claims of the ideal and the other to the horrors of the actual, Williams portrays not as an easy truce between the two worlds but as a "narcotized," quasifatalistic commitment to survival that resolves none of the existential problems it poses.

Elysian Fields, the world that has replaced Belle Reve, will do, Williams seems to be saying, for the insensitive Stanley and the pragmatic Stella . . . ; but it can only further the process of destroying Blanche which Belle Reve had begun. Its amusement-park thrills, its desperately gay and feverish music provide sufficient fulfilment only for the undemanding. The spirit of the whole place is characterized by the name of one of its nightspots, the "Four Deuces"—the poorest of the best hands in poker. (pp. 81-2)

When Blanche says of Desire "It brought me here" we may take her to mean not only the streetcar that bore her to Elysian Fields, the land of the living dead, but human desire which brought her into existence. Incarnation is what she is ashamed of, and the flesh is what she has abused in her self-punishment for submitting to its importunate demands. . . . Blanche has been conditioned to believe that the anarchy of the flesh must, whenever possible, be transcended in the interests of family and culture; Williams, however, dramatizes the futility of attempts to transcend the limitations of the human animal.

At the end of [the] fourth scene, imploring Stella to leave Stanley, Blanche delivers a harangue which in its cadence and hysterical rhetoric betrays her desperation and vulnerability. . . . Williams frames this speech, just before it begins and immediately after it ends, with the sound of two trains running like the old rattle-trap of Desire: at the same time, he has Stanley enter, unheard because of the noise of the trains, and remain to listen unobserved to Blanche's speech. Her two destroyers, desire and Stanley Kowalski, are thus made to hover like fateful accomplices over Blanche as she implores Stella to join with her in battle against them. That Stanley is placed in the strategically superior position of the unobserved viewer of the scene forecasts his eventual triumph over Blanche. To emphasize the inefficacy of Blanche's appeal and struggle against her fate, Williams ends the scene with Stella's embracing Stanley "fiercely"—joining the "brutes"—as Stanley grins at Blanche in victory. From that point on, Stanley begins to gain the upper hand in the struggle with Blanche. (pp. 84-5)

The predominating conflict of flesh and spirit modifies and includes all the other conflicts—sociological, psychological, moral, cultural—which *A Streetcar Named Desire* presents. It would be an oversimplification, as I have stated above, to see Belle Reve and Elysian Fields merely as opposites when Williams has subtly pointed out their similarity and the shortcomings they share in fulfilling the claims of the ideal. And it would be simpleminded to call Williams' presentation of both the attractiveness and failure of these two ways of life as ambivalence and to claim that it mars the play. By pitting the sterility of Belle Reve against the fertility of Elysian Fields, the weakness of Blanche against the insensitive stolidity of Stanley, her cultural pretensions against his penis-status, her sorority-girl vision of courtship and good times against his "colored-lights" orgasms, the simulated pearls of her lies against the swinish truth of his facts, her uncontrollable epic fornications against Stanley's own, less hysterical mastery in this area of experience, Williams attempts to dramatize the inevitable succumbing of the former to the greater power of the latter. If he seems to favor Blanche, it is because she is the weaker and because, at one time, as Stella attests, she showed great potential for tenderness and trust, the qualities of a typical victim. Only her stifled potential and her futile aspirations to transcend or mitigate the harshness of actuality—to cover the naked light bulb with a paper lantern—seem to qualify her, in Williams' eyes, as a symbol of the trapped soul. Not even her moral code, "Deliberate cruelty . . . is the one unforgivable thing . . . the one thing of which I have never, never been guilty," admirable as far as it goes, qualifies her as a symbol of transcendence so much as her pitiful attempts to combat actuality do. And, ironically and tragically enough, it is her very preference for soulful illusion and for magic over actuality which paves the way for her voyage to the madhouse. (pp. 86-7)

While Williams dramatizes the plight of the incarnated, incarcerated soul primarily in terms of her futile voyage in quest of fulfilment—or, failing that, of peace and rest—he portrays the roles that fate and luck play in existence primarily in images of gaming. And the master of games in *Streetcar* is Stanley Kowalski. By reason of his amoral fitness for survival in a world which, in Williams' Darwinian view, is geared to the physically strongest at the expense of the meekly vulnerable, Stanley has an "in" with the fates. Though the intrusion of Blanche into his world rattles Stanley and threatens to undermine the self-confidence that sustains his power, he systematically allays his own fears at the expense of aggravating Blanche's. Though he loses at the poker games played in scene three, he wins at those played in the last scene of the play.

Introducing fate into his play by way of luck at games, Williams pits Stanley's chances of survival against Blanche's. When Williams summed up the moral of the play as, "If we don't watch out, the apes will take over" . . . he expressed the same view of existence that he delegated to Blanche in her speech denouncing the poker players as "a party of apes." That the tone and strategy of the play reveal it not merely as a cautionary drama but as a tragedy of the futility of attempting to flee the apes, I have stressed above. What the play really demonstrates is that, willy-nilly, the apes *must* take over since apishness is presented throughout as the natural, unavoidable condition not only of survival but of existence itself. (p. 88)

Throughout the play, images drawn from gaming, chance and luck compete in number with those suggesting water and voyage. The sixth scene, for example, renders Mitch's marriage proposal to Blanche within the framework of imagery suggesting the game of chance which Blanche is desperately playing with him and with survival. . . . The presence of the Pleiades in the sky seems to comfort Blanche; her reference to them as bridge ladies not only aligns them with the imagery of existence as a game of chance, but the familiarity with which Blanche treats the seven nymphs who, even as stars, must constantly flee the mighty, devastating hunter, Orion, suggests mythically and cosmically, a parallel to her own danger, pursued as she is by Stanley's vital lust for domination and destruction. The scene ends with Blanche's pathetic belief that Mitch's proposal is a sign that the gods have furnished her with an eartly protector. "Sometimes—," she says, "there's God—so quickly!" (p. 90)

Generally, the two major image patterns concerned with voyage (particularly as escape from fate by means of water) and with games (as the framework of human chance and destiny) are only very casually suggested; occasionally they are even joined in a single speech as when Blanche, for example, explains to Mitch why she has come to Elysian Fields: "There was nowhere else I could go. I was *played out*. You know what played out is? My youth was suddenly gone up the *water-spout*, and— I met you . . . " (my italics . . .). In the last scene of the play, Williams more forcefully calls attention to his two most important image patterns in a superbly executed finale that boldly juxtaposes them. (p. 91)

After introducing the theme of the fatal card game as an analogue of earthly existence, the last scene of *Streetcar* shifts to focus on Eunice and Stella as they prepare Blanche for another journey. Speaking from the bathroom which has been her refuge throughout the play, Blanche asks, "Is the coast clear?" . . . In having Blanche ask for a bunch of artificial violets to be pinned with a seahorse on the lapel of her jacket, Williams portrays her insignia: the violet which traditionally symbolizes innocence in flower language together with the creature whose natural habitat would be water—not land. (p. 92)

Throughout *A Streetcar Named Desire*, Williams used every device of theatrical rhetoric to portray and orchestrate existence as a study game. From the desperate gaiety of the tinny "Blue Piano" which Williams says in his first stage direction "expresses the spirit of the life which goes on here" to the brawling of the Kowalskis and their neighbors, from the cries of the street vendors ("Red hot!" and "Flores para los muertos") to what Elia Kazan called the "ballet" of the passerby in quest of money or sex, Williams created in *Streetcar* a frenetic dramatization of spiritual frustration and physical satiation alike, of life fraught with death (Blanche) and of death burning with life (Elysian Fields). Though not without its quieter moments and lyrical interludes, the play might best be characterized as a syncopated rendition of what Williams views as the basic rhythm of physical existence: tumescence and detumescence, desire and death. (p. 94)

To point out the symbolic, mythic and tragic implications of the literary and theatrical imagery in *Streetcar* is not to deny that the play is often as jazzy and comic as the vision of existence it depicts (though close inspection reveals that the jazz is usually desperate and the comedy often very cruel). Elements of melodrama, frequently present in tragedy, are also evident in its structure—to such an extent that they have sometimes blinded viewers to its other qualities. Even the usually perspicacious Susan Sontag wrote in her controversial essay of 1964, "Against Interpretation," that *Streetcar* should be enjoyed merely as "a forceful psychological melodrama . . . about a handsome brute named Stanley Kowalski and a faded mangy belle named Blanche DuBois . . . " and that any *other* interpretation of the play would be unwarranted.

What I have tried to do in this essay, however, is to avoid rehashing the most blatantly realistic aspects of the play and to view it, instead, in terms of Williams' persistent concern with creating universal and "timeless" worlds in his plays. In play after play, Williams has consistently (albeit with varying degrees of success) employed symbolism and the mythic mode to universalize the significance of the realistic action he posits, not only, apparently, because he thinks of symbolism and universality as essentials of art, but also because these qualities seem to be characteristic of his personal reactions to life in general. (p. 95)

Read in the light of Williams' personal and aesthetic predilections, all the images, symbols and allusions, even what appear to be only the most casual or realistic of details in *Streetcar,* combine to reveal a tragic parable of the pitiable and terrible fate of the human soul. Incarnated in treacherous, decaying matter, the soul, it appears, has been destined to voyage continually from one broken world to another, the only kinds of environment open to it in a flawed universe. . . . As Tennessee Williams dramatizes his vision of existence in *A Streetcar Named Desire,* we see that "from the beginning" the cards of destiny have indicated a seemingly endless voyage for the human soul through progressively disastrous worlds, and the name of the game is tragedy. (pp. 95-6)

> Leonard Quirino, *"The Cards Indicate a Voyage on 'A Streetcar Named Desire',"* in Tennessee Williams: A Tribute, *edited by Jac Tharpe, University Press of Mississippi, 1977, pp. 77-96.*

NORMAND BERLIN

Each new production of *A Streetcar Named Desire* seems to offer the excitement of witnessing a new interpretation. A great play has within it the potentiality for differing interpretations; indeed, this may be the test of greatness. The different interpretations of *Streetcar* by directors invariably stem from different attitudes toward the two main characters, Blanche DuBois and Stanley Kowalski. Some directors tip the audience toward Blanche, others toward Stanley—and this tipping controls the nature of the tragedy and its effect. The director chooses sides, and the audience, of necessity, must play the director's game.

My aim in this essay is to explore the possibility that Tennessee Williams wishes to keep the sides balanced, that, in fact, complementarity informs the play's art and meaning. (p. 97)

At the outset we must recognize that different interpretations can be caused by fuzziness of writing, blurring of effects, lack of coherence. . . . One of our finest critics, Eric Bentley, believes that in *Streetcar* "Williams does not write with complete coherence." . . . Bentley's view is an echo of and has been echoed by others. But another view is possible: that Tennessee Williams, after O'Neill America's finest playwright, knows exactly what he is doing in *Streetcar,* offering a play with balanced sides built in, dramatizing an attitude toward life based on duality and complementarity. This balancing is achieved in every aspect of the drama—in the treatment of theme and character, in the symbolism, in the movement, in the specific stage actions. Balances are always precarious, in art as in life. Williams maintains his, I wish to demonstrate, and the critics and directors have lost theirs at times. (pp. 97-8)

The genteel Blanche and the raw Stanley ride the same streetcar, but for different reasons. Blanche goes to her sexual affairs to relieve the broken quality of her life, looking for closeness, perhaps kindness, in that physical way. She cannot see herself as a whore because sexual activity was for her a temporary means for needed affection, the only refuge for her lonely soul. Stanley rides the streetcar because that is the necessary physical function of his life, natural, never compensating for emotional agony because his soul is never lost, what Blanche calls "brutal desire—just—Desire!" Desire is the common ground on which Stan and Blanche meet, a streetcar on which both are passengers, the scales on which both are measured. On one side of the scale a fading, fragile woman for whom sexual activity is a temporary release from loneliness; on the other side a crude, physical man for whom sexual activity is a normal function of life. The needs of both are clearly presented by Williams and should be clearly understood by the audience, which must neither wholly condemn Blanche for her whorishness nor Stanley for his brutishness. The scales are balanced so finely that when Stanley condemns Blanche for her sexual looseness and Blanche condemns Stanley for his apishness, each seems *both* right and wrong, right in the light of truth, wrong in the light of understanding.

Desire or sexual impulse, therefore, is common to both Blanche and Stanley and provides one measure of their similarity and difference. (pp. 98-9)

Complementarity provides the pressure of the play's movement, beginning with the audience's first encounter with Stanley and Blanche. When the curtain rises, the audience witnesses Stanley's sure command of the stage—vigorous, shouting, deftly throwing a package of meat at Stella. Blanche's entrance reveals a delicate creature, frazzled, uncertain, burdened with a suitcase, lost. Within the play's first minute the audience is forced to absorb the dialectic that will give the play its dynamic tension. Within each scene the dialectic continues, becoming more persistent as the play progresses. A brief look at scene three will reveal Williams' method.

Scene three presents the poker night. . . . In each segment of the scene Williams plays with the audience's sympathies, forcing us to side with Stanley when Blanche is teasing and artificially genteel, forcing us to condemn Stanley when he breaks the radio and hits Stella, and forcing us to pity the repentant Stanley who wishes to have his baby back. Balances in our attitude toward character; changes in our emotional responses. And important changes in movement. Stella goes *up* the stairs to escape a raging Stanley, only to come *down* to the baying Stanley. Stanley falls down on his knees to show his repentance, only to rise and lift Stella to show his victory. Stanley's victory is Blanche's defeat. A confused Blanche ends the scene by talking about the confusion in the world and reasserting her need for kindness. She will give powerful voice to her confusion in the next scene, wondering how her sister could return to the brutal Stanley, calling him "common," "bestial," a "survivor of the Stone Age," and imploring her sister not to *"hang back with the brutes!"* Blanche's "superior attitude," as Stella calls it, will alienate the audience because of the speech's *tone,* but the *content* of her speech offers ideas about civilization and progress that the audience must consider true. And again we have complementarity and balance.

Williams does not even allow the rape, which could be considered the supreme brutalization of Blanche by Stanley, to upset the balance he presents throughout. For Williams betrays a respect for Stanley's "animal joy," for men at the peak of their manhood, for the natural desires of the Stanley Kowalskis, who were born to have women, *and* Williams invests the play with a sense of the inevitability of that violent encounter between executioner and victim, who had that date from the beginning.

What I am suggesting . . . is that the ambiguity and confusion often felt in specific productions and readings of *Streetcar* are prodded by Williams' delicate art but are not his intent. He aims for complementarity, duality, balance, a difficult challenge for a dramatist, but a necessary one for Williams in this play because it holds the key to the play's meaning and tragic effect. The tensions are present throughout and are basic to the

tragedy. We end with pity and terror, themselves balance emotions, the natural result of all that came before. As Blanche DuBois leaves the stage, we, like Stella, are allowing her to go because we have sided at times with Stanley, we have been annoyed by her falsity and superiority, we have wondered at her cruelty to her now dead homosexual husband, we have considered her a disturbing interruption in her sister's seemingly idyllic life in Elysium. But we feel compassion for this fragile creature who has been living with death, who is trying to hold on to vanishing values, and who needs what we all need, kindness. We feel the terror of her departure to death within the walls of an asylum not only because we pity Blanche, but because we are forced to ask the frightening question: Is the world so possessed by the apes that there is no place for a Blanche DuBois? Both better and worse than those around her—the balance again—Blanche commands our attention as we witness her disintegration. She passes through, and the curtain comes down to block out the light over *that* poker game as we return to *this* one, . . . but all, I suspect, affected by Williams' superb dramatization of a basic human dialectic reflecting what our deepest experience tells us is the reality of things, presenting a complementary vision more complex than a one-sided interpretation allows. (pp. 100-03)

Normand Berlin, "Complementarity in 'A Streetcar Named Desire'," in Tennessee Williams: A Tribute, *edited by Jac Tharpe, University Press of Mississippi, 1977, pp. 97-103.*

Appendix

The following is a listing of all sources used in Volume 30 of *Contemporary Literary Criticism*. Included in this list are all copyright and reprint rights and acknowledgements for those essays for which permission was obtained. Every effort has been made to trace copyright, but if omissions have been made, please let us know.

THE EXCERPTS IN CLC, VOLUME 30, WERE REPRINTED FROM THE FOLLOWING PERIODICALS:

The ALAN Review, v. 7, Spring, 1980; v. 8, Fall, 1980; v. 8, Spring, 1981; v. 9, Spring, 1982; v. 10, Winter, 1983; v. 10, Spring, 1983; v. 11, Fall, 1983. All reprinted by permission.

America, v. 144, February 7, 1981 for "Carl Sagan's Gospel of Scientism" by William J. O'Malley. © 1981. All rights reserved. Reprinted with permission of America Press, Inc. and the author./ v. 118, January 20, 1968; v. 127, September 16, 1972; v. 135, July 10, 1976; v. 135, December 11, 1976; v. 137, October 8, 1977; v. 137, November 5, 1977. © 1968, 1972, 1976, 1977. All rights reserved. All reprinted with permission of America Press, Inc.

Analog Science Fiction/Science Fact, v. XCVII, March, 1977 for a review of "The Sword of Aldones" by Lester del Rey; v. XCVII, November, 1977 for a review of "The Forbidden Tower" by Lester del Rey; v. XCVIII, August, 1978 for a review of "Stormqueen" by Lester del Rey; v. XCIX, October, 1979 for a review of "Fireship" by Anthony R. Lewis. Copyright © 1977, 1978, 1979 by The Condé Nast Publications, Inc. All reprinted by permission of the respective authors.

The Antioch Review, v. XXV, Fall, 1965. Copyright © 1965 by the Antioch Review Inc. Reprinted by permission of the Editors.

Arizona Quarterly, v. 33, Summer, 1977 for "Scrambling the Unscrambleable: 'The Nick Adams Stories'" by Stuart L. Burns. Copyright © 1977 by Arizona Board of Regents. Reprinted by permission of the publisher and the author.

Astronomy, v. 7, October, 1979. Copyright © 1979 AstroMedia Corp. All rights reserved. Reprinted by permission.

The Atlantic Monthly, v. 163, February, 1939 for a review of "The Sword in the Stone" by Vida D. Scudder. Copyright © 1939, renewed 1967, by Vida D. Scudder. Reprinted with permission./ v. 221, June, 1968 for "Black Anger" by Robert Coles. Copyright © 1968, by Robert Coles. Reprinted with permission of the author./ v. 180, September, 1947. Copyright © 1947, renewed 1975, by the Atlantic Monthly Company, Boston, MA. Reprinted with permission.

Best Sellers, v. 22, March 1, 1963; v. 24, November 1, 1964; v. 29, February 1, 1970; v. 30, November 15, 1970; v. 30, March 1, 1971; v. 31, December 1, 1971; v. 32, January 15, 1973; v. 33, May 15, 1973; v. 33, November 15, 1973; v. 36, April, 1976; v. 36, May, 1976; v. 36, September, 1976; v. 37, July, 1977; v. 38, December, 1978; v. 38, February, 1979; v. 39, July, 1979; v. 40, April, 1980; v. 40, September, 1980; v. 41, November, 1981; v. 41, January, 1982; v. 42, September, 1982; v. 42, December, 1982; v. 43, April, 1983. Copyright © 1963, 1964, 1970, 1971, 1973, 1976, 1977, 1978, 1979, 1980, 1981, 1982, 1983 Helen Dwight Reid Educational Foundation. All reprinted by permission.

Billboard, v. 88, July 4, 1976; v. 89, February 19, 1977; v. 92, December 20, 1980. © copyright 1976, 1977, 1980 by Billboard Publications, Inc. All reprinted by permission.

Book Week—The Sunday Herald Tribune, August 22, 1965; August 29, 1965. © 1965, *The Washington Post.* Both reprinted by permission.

Book Week—The Washington Post, August 8, 1965. © 1965, *The Washington Post.* Reprinted by permission.

Book Week—World Journal Tribune, October 23, 1966; December 18, 1966. © 1966, *The Washington Post.* Both reprinted by permission.

Book World—The Washington Post, March 19, 1972 for "The Need to Communicate" by Joyce Carol Oates. © 1972 Postrib Corp. Reprinted by permission of *The Washington Post* and the author./ November 3, 1968. © 1968 Postrib Corp. Reprinted by permission of *Chicago Tribune* and *The Washington Post.*/ November 25, 1973; January 12, 1975; April 11, 1976; May 2, 1976; July 31, 1977; October 16, 1977; May 13, 1979; June 10, 1979; September 16, 1979; March 2, 1980; March 9, 1980; May 25, 1980; October 19, 1980; November 9, 1980; January 11, 1981; April 5, 1981; September 13, 1981; August 8, 1982; September 22, 1982; October 10, 1982; February 13, 1983; May 8, 1983; June 12, 1983; October 2, 1983. © 1973, 1975, 1976, 1977, 1979, 1980, 1981, 1982, 1983, *The Washington Post.* All reprinted by permission.

Booklist, v. 73, September 1, 1976; v. 76, September 15, 1979; v. 76, December 15, 1979; v. 76, May 15, 1980; v. 77, October 1, 1980; v. 77, December 1, 1980; v. 78, December 1, 1981; v. 78, March 15, 1982; v. 78, April 1, 1982; v. 78, April 15, 1982; v. 78, June 15, 1982; v. 79, September 1, 1982; v. 79, October 15, 1982; v. 79, November 15, 1982; v. 79, February 15, 1983; v. 79, June 15, 1983; v. 79, August, 1983; v. 80, September 1, 1983; v. 80, October 1, 1983; v. 80, October 15, 1983. Copyright © 1976, 1979, 1980, 1981, 1982, 1983 by the American Library Association. All reprinted by permission of the American Library Association.

The Booklist, v. 66, June 15, 1970; v. 70, July 1, 1974; v. 70, July 15, 1974; v. 72, May 1, 1976. Copyright © 1970, 1974, 1976 by the American Library Association. All reprinted by permission of the American Library Association.

The Booklist and Subscription Books Bulletin, v. 65, November 1, 1968. Copyright © 1968 by the American Library Association. Reprinted by permission of the American Library Association.

Bookworld, Chicago Tribune, February 27, 1972 for "Brooks, Bums, Dodgers, Men" by Heywood Hale Broun. Reprinted by permission of the author and Bill Cooper Associates Agency, Inc.

Books, May 13, 1962. © 1962 I.H.T. Corporation. Reprinted by permission.

Books Abroad, v. 34, Summer, 1960. Copyright 1960 by the University of Oklahoma Press. Reprinted by permission.

Books and Bookmen, n. 326, November, 1982 for "Espionage and Kidnapping" by Reginald Hill. © copyright Reginald Hill 1982. Reprinted by permission of the author.

Books in Canada, v. 10, January, 1981 for "Long Live the New Queen of Faerie" by Richard Lubbock. Reprinted by permission of the author.

British Book News, January, 1981; July, 1981; February, 1983. © *British Book News,* 1981, 1983. All courtesy of *British Book News.*

Bulletin of the Atomic Scientists: a magazine of science and public affairs, v. XXXI, April, 1975. Copyright © 1975 by the Educational Foundation for Nuclear Science, Chicago, IL 60637. Reprinted by permission of *The Bulletin of Atomic Scientists: a magazine of science and public affairs.*

Bulletin of the Center for Children's Books, v. 21, February, 1968; v. 30, December, 1976; v. 30, February, 1977; v. 32, February, 1979; v. 32, March, 1979; v. 33, June, 1980; v. 34, September, 1980; v. 34, November, 1980; v. 34, December, 1980; v. 34, May, 1981; v. 35, October, 1981; v. 36, October, 1982; v. 36, July-August, 1983; v. 37, September, 1983. © 1968, 1976, 1977, 1979, 1980, 1981, 1982, 1983 by The University of Chicago. All reprinted by permission of the University of Chicago Press.

The Canadian Forum, v. XXXVII, October, 1957. Reprinted by permission.

Catholic Library World, v. 45, March, 1974. Reprinted by permission.

Catholic World, v. 201, May, 1965. Copyright 1965 by The Missionary Society of St. Paul the Apostle in the State of New York. Used by permission.

The Chicago Sun-Times, October 5, 1959. Reprinted with permission of *The Chicago Sun-Times.*

Chicago Sunday Tribune Magazine of Books, March 6, 1960 for "The Extraordinary Tale Speculating on Man's Destiny" by Edmund Fuller. Reprinted by permission of the author./ April 5, 1959. Reprinted by permission of *Chicago Tribune.*

Children's Book News, v. 5, November-December, 1970. Copyright © 1970 by Baker Book Services Ltd. Reprinted by permission.

Children's Book Review Service, v. 9, November, 1980. Copyright © 1980 Children's Book Review Service Inc. Reprinted by permission.

Children's literature in education, v. 12, Summer, 1981; v. 13, Summer, 1982; v. 14, Autumn, 1983. © 1981, 1982, 1983, Agathon Press, Inc. All reprinted by permission of the publisher.

Choice, Vol. 11, February, 1975. Copyright © 1975 by American Library Association. Reprinted by permission of the American Library Association.

The Christian Century, v. LVI, December 6, 1939./ v. LXXVII, May 25, 1960; v. XCI, May 22, 1974. Copyright 1960, 1974 Christian Century Foundation. Reprinted by permission from the May 25, 1960, May 22, 1974 issues of *The Christian Century.*

The Christian Science Monitor, March 7, 1979 for ''Grand Guignol to Music'' by John Beaufort; June 27, 1979 for ''Digging Around in Old Plots'' by Thomas Bedell; July 9, 1979 for ''Black Pride in a White World'' by Dana G. Clinton; July 18, 1979 for ''Tradition Under Judgement'' by Michael J. Bandler; October 14, 1981 for ''An Escape from Slavery'' by Stephen Krensky; November 6, 1982 for ''Fine Novel of Ordinary Lives'' by Judith Chettle. © 1979, 1981, 1982 The Christian Science Publishing Society. All rights reserved. All reprinted by permission of the respective authors./ May 4, 1940; September 29, 1955; October 10, 1957; August 28, 1958; January 25, 1962; April 25, 1963; September 26, 1963; August 9, 1972; October 23, 1978. © 1940, 1955, 1957, 1958, 1962, 1963, 1972, 1978 The Christian Science Publishing Society. All rights reserved. All reprinted by permission from *The Christian Science Monitor.*

College English, v. 12, November, 1950./ v. 8, February, 1947 for ''Conrad Richter: Early Americana'' by Dayton Kohler; v. 39, February, 1978 for ''Ayn Rand and Feminism: An Unlikely Alliance'' by Mimi R. Gladstein. Copyright © 1947, 1978 by the National Council of Teachers of English. Both reprinted by permission of the publisher and the respective authors.

College Literature, v. VII, Fall, 1980. Copyright © 1980 by West Chester State College. Reprinted by permission.

Columbus Dispatch, August 23, 1959. Reprinted by permission.

Commentary, v. 35, January, 1963 for ''The Innocence of Tennessee Williams'' by Marion Magid. Copyright © 1963 by the American Jewish Committee. All rights reserved. Reprinted by permission of the publisher and the author./ v. 41, January, 1966 for ''Cooling It'' by George Dennison. Copyright © 1966 by George Dennison. All rights reserved. Reprinted by permission of the publisher and the author./ v. 64, August, 1977 for ''Psycho Physiology'' by R. J. Herrnstein; v. 59, March, 1980 for ''Judy Blume's Children'' by Naomi Munson; v. 71, May, 1981 for ''The Universe and Dr. Sagan'' by Jeffrey Marsh; v. 72, July, 1981 for ''Hemingway's Private War'' by Kenneth S. Lynn; v. 73, May, 1982 for 'Rediscovering Judaism'' by Ruth R. Wisse. All rights reserved. All reprinted by permission of the publisher and the respective authors.

Commonweal, v. XXI, November 24, 1939; v. XXXIII, December 20, 1940./ v. LXVI, August 23, 1957; v. LXVII, November 8, 1957; v. LXXI, March 4, 1960; v. LXXIX, February 21, 1964; v. LXXXII, September 24, 1965; v. LXXXVII, February 23, 1968; v. LXXXIX, November 22, 1968; v. XCVI, July 14, 1972. Copyright © 1957, 1960, 1964, 1965, 1968, 1972 by Commonweal Publishing Co., Inc. All reprinted by permission of Commonweal Foundation./ v. XLII, October 5, 1945; v. XLV, November 15, 1946; v. XLVII, December 19, 1947; v. LI, November 25, 1949; v. LV, November 30, 1951. Copyright © 1945, renewed 1973; copyright © 1946, renewed 1974; copyright © 1947, renewed 1975; copyright © 1949, renewed 1977; copyright © 1951, renewed 1979 by Commonweal Publishing Co., Inc. All reprinted by permission of Commonweal Foundation.

Crawdaddy, December, 1977 for ''Evil Minds, Dirty Habits'' by Bruce Malamut. Copyright © 1977 by Crawdaddy Publishing Co., Inc. All rights reserved. Reprinted by permission of the publisher and the author.

Creem, v. 8, October, 1976; v. 10, March, 1979. © copyright 1976, 1979 by Creem Magazine, Inc. Both reprinted by permission.

The Critic, v. 22, June-July, 1964; v. 27, June-July, 1969; v. 28, November-December, 1969. © *The Critic* 1964, 1969. All reprinted with the permission of the Thomas More Association, Chicago, Illinois.

Critique: Studies in Modern Fiction, v. XXI, n. 1, 1979 for ''The Uses of Myth in Pat Conroy's 'The Great Santini''' by Robert E. Burkholder. Reprinted by permission of the author.

Daily Mirror, September 27, 1957. Reprinted by permission.

Daily News, New York, September 27, 1957; April 6, 1964; April 27, 1970; February 26, 1973. © 1957, 1964, 1970, 1973, New York News, Inc. All reprinted by permission.

down beat, v. 47, May, 1980. Copyright 1980. Reprinted with permission of *down beat.*

Drama, n. 150, Winter, 1983. Reprinted by permission of the British Theatre Association.

Elementary English, v. 52, April, 1975 for ''Narrative Technique and Meaning in 'Island of the Blue Dolphins''' by Jon C. Stott. Reprinted by permission of the publisher and the author.

Encounter, v. II, May, 1954. © 1954 by Encounter Ltd. Reprinted by permission of the publisher.

English Journal, v. 54, May, 1965 for a review of ''River at Her Feet'' by Christine Myers; v. 55, November, 1966 for ''A Canticle for Miller'' by Edward Ducharme; v. 58, March, 1969 for ''Two Books with Soul: For Defiant Ones'' by Ann Allen Shockley; v. 59, April, 1970 for ''The Theme of Responsibility in Miller's 'A Canticle for Leibowitz''' by Michael Alan Bennett; v. 60, April, 1971 for a review of ''Run Softly, Go Fast'' by John W. Conner; v. 62, March, 1974 for a review of ''Leslie'' by John W. Conner; v. 65, May, 1976 for

1981; v. L, April 15, 1982; v. L, August 1, 1982; v. L, August 15, 1982; v. LI, February 1, 1983; v. LI, March 15, 1983; v. LI, April 15, 1983; v. LI, September 1, 1983. Copyright © 1972, 1975, 1976, 1978, 1979, 1980, 1981, 1982, 1983 The Kirkus Service, Inc. All reprinted by permission.

Kirkus Service, v. XXXVI, September 1, 1968. Copyright © 1968 The Kirkus Service, Inc. Reprinted by permission.

Kliatt Young Adult Paperback Book Guide, v. XII, Winter, 1978; v. XIII, April, 1979; v. XVII, November, 1983; v. XLIII, January, 1984. Copyright © by Kliatt Paperback Book Guide. All reprinted by permission.

Language Arts, v. 55, March, 1978 for "Profile: James and Christopher Collier—More Than Just a Good Read" by Hughes Moir; v. 58, February, 1981 for "Profile: Katherine Paterson" by Linda T. Jones. Copyright © 1978, 1981 by the National Council of Teachers of English. Both reprinted by permission of the publisher and the respective authors.

Library Journal, v. 71, October 1, 1946./ v. 95, February 1, 1970; v. 96, August, 1971; v. 99, January 15, 1974; v. 99, November 1, 1974; v. 103, November 15, 1978; v. 104, October 15, 1979; v. 107, January 15, 1982; v. 107, June 1, 1982; v. 107, July, 1982; v. 108, January 15, 1983; v. 108, September 15, 1983. Copyright © 1970, 1971, 1974, 1978, 1979, 1982, 1983 by Xerox Corporation. Reprinted from *Library Journal,* published by R. R. Bowker Co. (a Xerox Company), by permission.

The Lion and the Unicorn, v. 3, Winter, 1979-80; v. 4, Winter, 1980-81. Copyright © 1980, 1981 *The Lion and the Unicorn.* Both reprinted by permission.

The Listener, v. 93, March 20, 1975 for "Deaths for the Idle" by Marghanita Laski; v. 97, February 3, 1977 for "Sentimental Americans" by Paddy Kitchen; v. 97, April 7, 1977 for "Fresh Spring Crimes" by Marghanita Laski. © British Broadcasting Corp. 1975, 1977. Reprinted by permission of the respective authors.

The Magazine of Fantasy and Science Fiction, v. 60, May, 1981 for a review of "The Snow Queen" by Christopher Priest. © 1981 by Mercury Press, Inc. Reprinted by permission of *The Magazine of Fantasy and Science Fiction* and the author.

Masses and Mainstream, v. 1, April, 1948.

Meanjin, v. XIX, June, 1960 for "The Mind That Conceived 'On the Beach'" by David Martin. Reprinted by permission of the author.

Media & Methods, v. 6, September, 1969; v. 15, September, 1978. Copyright © 1969, 1978. All rights reserved. Both reprinted by permission.

Melody Maker, February 27, 1971; October 21, 1972; March 19, 1977; September 1, 1979; November 29, 1980; December 13, 1980; May 15, 1982. © IPC Business Press Ltd. All reprinted by permission.

Midwest Folklore, v. II, Spring, 1952.

Modern Age, v. 27, Winter, 1983. Copyright © 1983 by the Intercollegiate Studies Institute, Inc. Reprinted by permission.

Modern Drama, v. 10, December, 1967. Copyright *Modern Drama,* University of Toronto. Reprinted by permission.

Modern Fiction Studies, v. XIV, Autumn, 1968. Copyright 1968 by Purdue Research Foundation, West Lafayette, IN 47907, U.S.A. Reprinted with permission.

Ms., v. II, January, 1974 for "A Singular Parent" by Lucy Rosenthal; v. IX, July, 1980 for a review of "The Snow Queen" by Lindsy Van Gelder. © 1974, 1980 Ms. Magazine Corp. Both reprinted by permission of the respective authors.

The Musical Quarterly, v. LXVI, April, 1980. Copyright © 1980 by G. Schirmer, Inc. Reprinted by permission.

The Nation, v. CXLII, April 22, 1936; v. 165, December 20, 1947./ v. 186, June 21, 1958; v. 206, May 13, 1968; v. 216, May 14, 1973; v. 233, November 21, 1981; v. 236, June 11, 1983. Copyright 1958, 1968, 1973, 1981, 1983 *The Nation* magazine, The Nation Associates, Inc. All reprinted by permission.

National Review, v. XVII, September 7, 1965; v. XXII, February 24, 1970; v. XXXIV, May 14, 1982; v. XXXIV, July 23, 1982; v. XXXIV, October 15, 1982. © National Review, Inc., 1965, 1970, 1982; 150 East 35th St., New York, NY 10016. All reprinted by permission.

The New Leader, v. LI, March 25, 1968; v. LXIII, January 14, 1980. © 1968, 1980 by The American Labor Conference on International Affairs, Inc. Both reprinted by permission.

THE EXCERPTS IN CLC, VOLUME 30, WERE REPRINTED FROM THE FOLLOWING BOOKS:

Amis, Kingsley. From *The James Bond Dossier*. J. Cape, 1965. Copyright © 1965 by Kingsley Amis. All rights reserved. Reprinted by permission.

Baker, Carlos. From *Hemingway: The Writer As Artist*. Fourth edition. Princeton University Press, 1972. Copyright © 1952, 1956, 1963, 1972, by Carlos Baker. All rights reserved. Excerpts reprinted by permission of Princeton University Press.

Baskin, Barbara H. and Karen H. Harris. From *Notes from a Different Drummer: A Guide to Juvenile Fiction Portraying the Handicapped*. Bowker, 1977. Copyright © 1977 by Barbara H. Baskin and Karen H. Harris. All rights reserved. Reprinted with permission of the R. R. Bowker Company.

Behar, Jack. From "On Rod Serling, James Agee, and Popular Culture," in *TV As Art: Some Essays in Criticism*. Edited by Patrick D. Hazard. National Council of Teachers of English, 1966. Copyright 1966 National Council of Teachers of English, 508 South Sixth Street, Champaign, Illinois 61820. Reprinted by permission of the publisher and the author.

Bentley, Eric. From "Boredom in New York" and "Better than Europe," in *In Search of Theatre,* Knopf, 1953. Atheneum, 1975. Copyright 1948, 1949, 1950, 1951, 1952, 1953, renewed 1981 by Eric Bentley. All rights reserved. Reprinted by permission of Atheneum Publishers.

Berger, Harold L. From *Science Fiction and the New Dark Age*. Bowling Green University Popular Press, 1976. Copyright © 1976 by The Popular Press. Reprinted by permission.

Berlin, Normand. From "Complementarity in 'A Streetcar Named Desire'," in *Tennessee Williams: A Tribute*. Edited by Jac Tharpe. University Press of Mississippi, 1977. Copyright © 1977 by the University Press of Mississippi. Reprinted by permission.

Boas, Franz. From a foreword to *Mules and Men*. By Zora Neale Hurston. J. B. Lippincott Company, 1935. Copyright, 1935, by Zora Neale Hurston. And renewed 1963 by John C. Hurston and Joel Hurston. Reprinted by permission of the Literary Estate of Franz Boas.

From "Book Bait: 'The Silent World'," in *Book Bait: Detailed Notes on Adult Books Popular with Young People*. Edited by Elinor Walker. Third edition. American Library Association, 1979. Copyright © 1979 by the American Library Association. All rights reserved. Reprinted by permission.

Boyd, Ann S. From *The Devil with James Bond*. John Knox Press, 1967. © 1967 by M. E. Bratcher. Used with permission of John Knox Press.

Branden, Nathaniel. From *Who Is Ayn Rand?: An Analysis of the Novels of Ayn Rand*. Random House, 1962. Copyright © 1962 by Nathaniel Branden. All rights reserved. Reprinted by permission of the author.

Brooks, Cleanth, Jr. and Robert Penn Warren. From "'The Killers', Ernest Hemingway: Interpretation," in *Understanding Fiction*. Edited by Cleanth Brooks, Jr. and Robert Penn Warren. Appleton-Century-Crofts, Inc., 1959. © 1959. Reprinted by permission of Prentice-Hall, Inc., Englewood Cliffs, NJ 07632.

Brown, Sterling. From *The Negro in American Fiction*. The Associates in Negro Folk Education, 1937.

Clurman, Harold. From "The American Playwrights: Tennessee Williams," in *Lies Like Truth: Theatre Reviews and Essays*. Macmillan, 1958. Copyright 1948, and renewed 1976, by Harold Clurman. © Harold Clurman 1958. All rights reserved. Reprinted with permission of Macmillan Publishing Company.

Crane, John K. From *T. H. White*. Twayne, 1974. Copyright © 1974 by Twayne Publishers. All rights reserved. Reprinted with the permission of Twayne Publishers, a Division of G. K. Hall & Co., Boston.

Däniken, Erich Von. From an introduction to *Chariots of the Gods?: Unsolved Mysteries of the Past*. By Erich Von Däniken, translated by Michael Heron. G. P. Putnam's Sons, 1969, Souvenir Press, 1969. Copyright © 1968 by Econ-Verlag GMBH. English translation copyright © 1969 by Michael Heron and Souvenir Press. Reprinted by permission of The Putnam Publishing Group. In Canada by Souvenir Press Ltd.

DeFalco, Joseph. From *The Hero in Hemingway's Short Stories*. University of Pittsburgh Press, 1963. © 1963 by University of Pittsburgh Press. Reprinted by permission of the University of Pittsburgh Press.

Duran, Daniel Flores. From "Mexican American Resources: 'Child of Fire'," in *Latino Materials: A Multimedia Guide for Children and Young Adults*. Edited by Daniel Flores Duran. Neal Schuman, Publishers, 1979. Copyright © 1979 by Daniel Flores Duran. All rights reserved. Reprinted by permission.

Smith, Julian. From *Nevil Shute (Nevil Shute Norway)*. Twayne, 1976. Copyright © 1976 by Twayne Publishers. Reprinted with the permission of Twayne Publishers, a Division of G. K. Hall & Co., Boston.

Snelling, O. F. From *Double O Seven James Bond: A Report*. Neville Spearman—Holland Press, 1964. © O. F. Snelling, London 1964. Reprinted by permission.

Sondheim, Stephen. From ''Theater Lyrics,'' in *Playwrights, Lyricists, Composers on Theater*. Edited by Otis L. Guernsey, Jr. Dodd, Mead, 1974. Copyright © 1964 The Authors League of America, Inc. Copyright © 1964, 1965, 1966, 1967, 1968, 1969, 1970, 1971, 1972, 1973, 1974 by The Dramatists Guild, Inc. All rights reserved. Reprinted by permission of Dodd, Mead & Company, Inc.

Taylor, Angus. From *Philip K. Dick & the Umbrella of Light*. T-K Graphics, 1975. Copyright 1975 by Angus Taylor. Reprinted by permission of the author.

Townsend, John Rowe. From *A Sense of Story: Essays on Contemporary Writers for Children*. Lippincott, 1971. Copyright © 1971 by John Rowe Townsend. All rights reserved. Reprinted by permission of Harper & Row, Publishers, Inc.

Townsend, John Rowe. From *Written for Children: An Outline of English-Language Children's Literature*. Revised edition. J. B. Lippincott, Publishers, 1974. Copyright © 1965, 1974 by John Rowe Townsend. Reprinted by permission of Harper & Row, Publishers, Inc. In Canada by Penguin Books Ltd.

Turner, Darwin T. From *In a Minor Chord: Three Afro-American Writers and Their Search for Identity*. Southern Illinois University Press, 1971. Copyright © 1971 by Southern Illinois University Press. All rights reserved. Reprinted by permission of Southern Illinois University Press.

Turner, George. From ''Philip K. Dick Saying It All Over Again,'' in *Philip K. Dick: Electric Shepherd*. Edited by Bruce Gillespie. Norstrilia Press, 1975. © Norstrilia Press and the Contributors 1975. Reprinted by permission of George Turner.

Tynan, Kenneth. From *Curtains: Selections from the Drama Criticism and Related Writings*. Atheneum Publishers, 1961. Copyright © 1961 by Kenneth Tynan. All rights reserved. Reprinted with the permission of Paradise Films SA.

Vaidyanathan, T. G. From '''The Nick Adams Stories' and the Myth of Initiation,'' in *Indian Studies in American Fiction*. M. K. Naik, S. K. Desai, S. Mokashi-Punekar, eds. Macmillan, India, 1974. © Karnatak University, Dharwar, 1974. Reprinted by permission.

Walker, Alice. From ''Dedication: 'On Refusing to Be Humbled by Second Place in a Contest You Did Not Design: A Tradition by Now','' in *I Love Myself When I Am Laughing . . . And Then Again When I Am Looking Mean and Impressive*. By Zora Neale Hurston, edited by Alice Walker. The Feminist Press, 1979. Copyright © 1979 by Alice Walker. All rights reserved under international and Pan-American Copyright conventions. Reprinted with permission of The Feminist Press, Box 334, Old Westbury, NY 11568.

Wall, Cheryl A. From ''Zora Neale Hurston: Changing Her Own Words,'' in *American Novelists Revisited: Essays in Feminist Criticism*. Edited by Fritz Fleischmann. G. K. Hall & Co., 1982. Copyright © 1982 by Fritz Fleischmann. Reprinted by permission.

Warner, Sylvia Townsend. From ''The Story of the Book,'' in *The Book of Merlyn: The Unpublished Conclusion to ''The Once and Future King''*. By T. H. White. University of Texas Press, 1977. Copyright © 1977 by Shaftesbury Publishing Company. All rights reserved. Reprinted by permission.

Warrick, Patricia S. From ''The Labyrinthian Process of Artificial: Philip K. Dick's Androids and Mechanical Constructs,'' in *Philip K. Dick*. Edited by Joseph D. Olander and Martin Harry Greenberg. Taplinger, 1983. Copyright © 1983 by Martin Harry Greenberg and Joseph D. Olander. Published by Taplinger Publishing Co., Inc., New York. All rights reserved. Reprinted by permission.

Williams, Sherley Anne. From a foreword to *Their Eyes Were Watching God: A Novel*. By Zora Neale Hurston. University of Illinois Press, 1978. Foreword copyright © 1978 by the Board of Trustees of the University of Illinois Press. Reprinted by permission of the University of Illinois Press.

Wilson, Edmund. From *The Wound and the Bow: Seven Studies in Literature*. Houghton Mifflin Company, 1941, Farrar, Straus and Giroux, 1978. Copyright 1929, 1932, 1938, 1939, 1940, 1941, by Edmund Wilson; copyright renewed © 1966, 1968, 1970 by Edmund Wilson. All rights reserved. Reprinted by permission of Farrar, Straus and Giroux, Inc.

Yoke, Carl. From ''From Alienation to Personal Triumph: The Science Fiction of Joan D. Vinge,'' in *The Feminine Eye: Science Fiction and the Women Who Write It*. Edited by Tom Staicar. Ungar, 1982. Copyright © 1982 by Frederick Ungar Publishing Co., Inc. Reprinted by permission.

Young, Philip. From a preface to *The Nick Adams Stories*. By Ernest Hemingway. Charles Scribner's Sons, 1972. Copyright © 1972 The Ernest Hemingway Foundation. Preface by Philip Young. Copyright © 1972 Charles Scribner's Sons. All rights reserved. Reprinted with the permission of Charles Scribner's Sons.

Zelazny, Roger. From an introduction to *Philip K. Dick: Electric Shepherd*. Edited by Bruce Gillespie. Norstrilia Press, 1975. © Norstrilia Press and the Contributors 1975. Reprinted by permission of Roger Zelazny.

Cumulative Index to Authors

This index lists all author entries in the Gale Literary Criticism Series and includes cross-references to other Gale sources. References in the index are identified as follows:

Author Index

Author Index

Author Index

Author Index

Author Index

Author Index

Author Index

Cumulative Index to Critics

Critic Index

Critic Index

Critic Index

Critic Index

Critic Index

Critic Index

Critic Index

Critic Index

Critic Index

Critic Index

Critic Index

Critic Index

Critic Index

Critic Index

Critic Index

Critic Index

Critic Index

Critic Index

Critic Index

Critic Index

Critic Index

Critic Index

Critic Index

Critic Index

Critic Index

Critic Index

Critic Index

Critic Index

Critic Index

Critic Index

Critic Index

Critic Index

Critic Index

Critic Index

Critic Index

Critic Index

Critic Index

Critic Index

Critic Index

Critic Index

Critic Index